LONGMAN

Modern

LEARNER'S

DICTIONARY

D1504381

LONGMAN

Handy

LEARNER'S
DICTIONARY

Longman

Handy

LEARNER'S
DICTIONARY

Longman

Pearson Education Limited
Edinburgh Gate, Harlow, Essex CM20 2JE, England
and Associated Companies throughout the world

Visit our website: http://www.longman-elt.com/dictionaries

© Pearson Education Limited 1999
All rights reserved; no part of this publication may be reproduced,
stored in a retrieval system, or transmitted in any form or by any
means, electronic, mechanical, photocopying, recording or otherwise,
without the prior permission of the Publishers.

First published 1988
This edition published 1999
Fourth impression 2000

British Library Cataloguing in Publications Data

A catalogue record for this book
is available from the British Library.
ISBN 0 582 36471 X

Set in 5.5/7pt Nimrod

Printed in China
NPCC/04

Acknowledgements

Director
Della Summers

Editorial Director
Adam Gadsby

Publisher
Laurence Delacroix

Lexicographic Revisions
Jenny Watson

Production Editor
Peter Braaksma

Pronunciation Editor
Dinah Jackson

Cover
Andrea Hoyle

Production
Clive McKeough

Contents

Guide to the dictionary

Spelling

different spelling

> **age·is·m** , agism /'eɪdʒɪzəm/ n [U] the making of unfair differences between people because of their age, esp. treating young people more favourably than old people **ageist** adj, n

British spelling
American spelling

> **an·aes·thet·ic** ‖ also **anes-** AmE /ˌænɪs'θetɪk/ n [C;U] substance that stops one from feeling pain, either in a part of the body (**a local anaesthetic**) or in the whole body, making one unconscious (**a general anaesthetic**)

irregular plurals

> **a·pex** /'eɪpeks/ n **-es** or **apices** /'eɪpɒsiːz/ highest point: the apex of a triangle

irregular verbs

> **a·rise** /ə'raɪz/ vi **arose** /ə'rəʊz ‖ ə'roʊz/, **arisen** /ə'rɪzən/ happen; appear

Pronunciation/Stress

pronunciations are shown using symbols from the International Phonetic Alphabet - see inside front cover

> **ba·by** /'beɪbi/ n **1** very young child: (fig.) the baby of the class (= the youngest) **2** very young animal or bird: a baby monkey **3** AmE infml person, esp. a girl or woman **4** infml one's special responsibility **~ish** adj like a baby

stress syllables are clearly marked

> **bal·loon** /bə'luːn/ n **1** bag filled with gas or air so that it can float **2** small rubber bag that can be blown up and used as a toy

British and American pronunciations are separated by a double bar (‖)

> **bath** /bɑːθ ‖ bæθ/ n **baths** /bɑːðz, bɑːθs ‖ bæðz, bæθs/ **1** container in which one sits to wash the whole body **2** act of washing one's whole body at one time

Meaning

clear and simple explanations using a defining vocabulary of 2000 words

> **beam¹** /biːm/ n long heavy piece of wood, esp. used to support a building

words with the same spelling but different use or meaning

> **an·tique** /æn'tiːk/ adj old and therefore valuable ♦ n valuable old object

more than one meaning	**be·come** /bɪˈkʌm/ *v* **became, become** **1** begin to be: *become king* | *become warmer* **2** *vt* be suitable for: *Such behaviour hardly becomes someone in your position.*
Words that you may not know are written like THIS. You can find all these words in the dictionary.	**be·drag·gled** /bɪˈdrægəld/ *adj* wet, LIMP, and muddy
common idioms and phrases are shown in heavy type	**bee** /biː/ *n* **1** stinging insect that makes honey **2** **a bee in one's bonnet** fixed idea; OBSESSION **3** **the bee's knees** *infml* the best person or thing
phrasal verbs (= verbs which have a special meaning when they are used with a particular adverb or preposition)	**boil**[1] /bɔɪl/ *vi/t* **1** bring or come to the temperature at which a liquid changes to gas: *100°C is the boiling point of water.* **2** cook at this temperature: *to boil eggs* **3** **boil dry** boil till no water remains ♦ *n* [S]: *Bring the soup to the boil.*
	boil away *phr vi* disappear by boiling
examples showing how to use the word or phrase	**boil down to** *phr vt* be no more than: *It all boils down to a question of money.*
	boil over *phr vi* **1** (of a boiling liquid) flow over the sides of the container **2** get out of control (and develop into): *The conflict boiled over into war.*
labels showing style, region, etc.	**bol·shy** /ˈbɒlʃi | ˈbəʊl-/ *adj infml* (of a person or their behaviour) showing an unwillingness to help in a common aim

Grammar

parts of speech	**bone-dry** /ˌ· ˈ·◂/ *adj* perfectly dry
	bon·fire /ˈbɒnfaɪə | ˈbɑːnfaɪər/ *n* large outdoor fire
words which are part of the same word family and which have different parts of speech are shown like this	**boy** /bɔɪ/ *n* young male person **~hood** *n* time of being a boy **~ish** *adj* like a boy
countable and uncountable nouns	**choco·late** /ˈtʃɒklɪt | ˈtʃɑːkələt, ˈtʃɑːk-/ *n* **1** [U] solid brown substance eaten as a sweet **2** [C] small sweet covered with this **3** [U] hot drink made from this ♦ *adj* dark brown
intransitive and transitive verbs	**co·in·cide** /ˌkəʊɪnˈsaɪd | ˌkoʊ-/ *vi* **1** happen at the same time **2** (of opinions, etc.) agree
	com·pli·ment[2] /ˈkɒmplɪment | ˈkɑːm-/ *vt* express admiration of

Grammar codes

[C] countable: a noun that can be counted and has a plural form: *This is a **dictionary***. | *There are many **dictionaries** in the library.*

[U] uncountable: a noun that cannot be counted, and that has no plural form: *We drink **milk** with our dinner.* | *There isn't much **milk** left.* | *The book contained some interesting **information** about the town.*

[P] plural: a noun that is used only with a plural verb or pronoun, and that has no singular form: *These **trousers** are too tight.*

[S] singular: a noun that is used only in the singular, and that has no plural form: *There was a **babble** of voices.* | *Let me have a **think** about it.*

[the] a noun that is the name of an actual place, organization, etc., and that is always used with the definite article: *the **White House*** | *This land belongs to the **Crown**.*

vt a transitive verb: a verb that is followed by a direct object, which can be either a noun phrase or a clause: *She **rides** a bicycle to school.* | *He **made up** a good excuse.* | *We **decided** to leave.* | *I've **given up** eating meat.*

vi an intransitive verb: a verb that has no direct object: *They all **came** yesterday.* | *We **set off** at 7 o'clock.*

Symbols used with words in the same family

Words which are related to the headword are often given at the end of an entry. Sometimes they have a definition. Sometimes, if their meaning is clear, there is no definition. Sometimes a word is exactly the same as the headword, and so it is not written again. Sometimes a word has a different ending from the headword, and so the new ending is shown.

The following symbols are used to show exactly how these related words are formed:

♦ shows that a related word is exactly the same as the headword

~ shows that a related word is formed by adding an ending directly to the headword

— shows that the form of the headword changes slightly before the new ending can be added

an·ger /'æŋgə‖ -ər/ *n* [U] fierce displeasure and annoyance ♦ *vt* make angry

an·nounce /ə'naʊns/ *vt* state loudly or publicly: *He announced the winner of the competition.* ~**ment** *n* public statement

a·nom·a·ly /ə'nɒməli‖ə'nɑ:-/ *n fml* something different from the usual type: *A cat with no tail is an anomaly.* —**lous** *adj*

ap·pro·pri·ate² /ə'prəʊprieɪt‖ ə'proʊ-/ *vt* 1 set aside for a purpose 2 take for oneself —**ation** /ə,prəʊpri'eɪʃən‖ ə,proʊ-/ *n* [C;U]

A

A, a /eɪ/ the 1st letter of the English alphabet

a /ə; *strong* eɪ/ also (*before a vowel sound*) **an** — *indefinite article, determiner* **1** one: *a pencil* | *a doctor* | *a thousand pounds* **2** (before some words of quantity): *a few weeks* | *a little water* **3** for each: *6 times a day* | *£2 a dozen*

a·back /əˈbæk/ *adv* **be taken aback** be suddenly shocked

ab·a·cus /ˈæbəkəs/ *n* frame with sliding balls on wires, used for counting

a·ban·don /əˈbændən/ *vt* **1** leave completely **2** give up: *to abandon our search* **3** give (oneself) up completely to a feeling: *He abandoned himself to grief.* ~**ment** *n* [U]

a·base /əˈbeɪs/ *vt fml* make (esp. oneself) lose self-respect

a·bashed /əˈbæʃt/ *adj* uncomfortable and ashamed

a·bate /əˈbeɪt/ *vi fml* (of wind, pain, etc.) become less fierce ~**ment** *n* [U]

ab·at·toir /ˈæbətwɑː ‖ -ɑːr/ *n BrE for* SLAUGHTERHOUSE

abbess /ˈæbɪs, ˈæbes/ *n* woman who is the head of a CONVENT

ab·bey /ˈæbi/ *n* house of religious men or women; MONASTERY *or* CONVENT

ab·bot /ˈæbət/ *n* man who is the head of a MONASTERY

ab·bre·vi·ate /əˈbriːvieɪt/ *vt* make shorter –**ation** /ə,briːviˈeɪʃən/ *n* short form of a word

ab·di·cate /ˈæbdɪkeɪt/ *vi/t* give up (a position or right) officially –**cation** /,æbdɪˈkeɪʃən/ *n* [U]

ab·do·men /ˈæbdəmən, æbˈdəʊ- ‖ -ˈdoʊ-/ *n* part of the body containing the stomach **abdominal** /æbˈdɒmɪnəl ‖ -ˈdɑː-/ *adj*

ab·duct /əbˈdʌkt, æb-/ *vt* take (a person) away illegally; KIDNAP ~**ion** /-ˈdʌkʃən/ *n* [U]

ab·er·ra·tion /,æbəˈreɪʃən/ *n* [C;U] change away from one's usual behaviour

a·bet /əˈbet/ *vt* **-tt-** **aid and abet** *law* give help to (a crime or criminal) ~**tor** *n*

a·bey·ance /əˈbeɪəns/ *n* [U] *fml* **fall into abeyance** stop being done or used

ab·hor /əbˈhɔː ‖ əbˈhɔːr,æb-/ *vt fml* hate very much ~**rent** /əbˈhɒrənt ‖ -ˈhɔːr-/ *adj* deeply disliked ~**rence** *n* [U]

a·bide /əˈbaɪd/ *vt* **abided** *or* **abode** /əˈbəʊd ‖ əˈboʊd/, **abode** bear; TOLERATE: *I can't abide rudeness.*

abide by *phr vt* obey (laws, etc.)

a·bid·ing /əˈbaɪdɪŋ/ *adj* without end: *an abiding love*

a·bil·i·ty /əˈbɪləti/ *n* [C;U] power; skill

ab·ject /ˈæbdʒekt/ *adj fml* **1** deserving great pity: *abject poverty* **2** without self-respect; HUMBLE: *an abject apology* ~**ly** *adv*

a·blaze /əˈbleɪz/ *adj* **1** on fire; burning **2** shining brightly

a·ble /ˈeɪbəl/ *adj* **1** having the power, time, etc. to do something: *Will you be able to come?* **2** clever; skilled

a·blu·tions /əˈbluːʃənz/ *n* [P] *fml* washing oneself

a·bly /ˈeɪbli/ *adv* skilfully

ab·norm·al /æbˈnɔːməl ‖ -ˈnɔːr-/ *adj* not ordinary; unusual ~**ly** *adv* ~**ity** /,æbnɔːˈmæləti ‖ -nər-/ *n* [C;U]

a·board /əˈbɔːd ‖ əˈbɔːrd/ *adv, prep* on or onto (a ship, plane, etc.)

a·bode¹ /əˈbəʊd ‖ əˈboʊd/ *n law* **of/with no fixed abode** having no place as a regular home

abode² *v past t. and p. of* ABIDE

a·bol·ish /əˈbɒlɪʃ ‖ əˈbɑː-/ *vt* bring to an end by law –**ition** /,æbəˈlɪʃən/ *n* [U]

a·bom·i·na·ble /əˈbɒmɪnəbəl, -mənə- ‖ əˈbɑː-/ *adj* hateful; very bad –**bly** *adv*

ab·o·rig·i·nal /,æbəˈrɪdʒənəl◂/ *adj* (of people and living things) having lived in a place from the earliest times **aboriginal** *n*

ab·o·rig·i·ne /,æbəˈrɪdʒəni/ *n* an aboriginal, esp. in Australia

a·bort /əˈbɔːt ‖ əˈbɔːrt/ *v* **1** *vt* cause (a child) to be born too soon for it to live **2** *vi/t* end before the expected time: *abort the space flight* ~**ive** *adj* unsuccessful; coming to nothing ~**ion** /əˈbɔːʃən ‖ əˈbɔːr-/ *n* [C;U] medical operation to abort a child

a·bound /əˈbaʊnd/ *vi* [(in, with)] exist or have in large numbers or great quantity

a·bout¹ /əˈbaʊt/ *prep* **1** on the subject of: *a book about cats* **2** in; through: *walking about the streets* **3** concerning: *She told us all about the stars.* **4** busy or concerned with: *While you're about it, make me a cup of tea too.* **5** **what/how about:** a (making a suggestion): *How about a drink?* **b** what news or plans have you got concerning: *What about Jack?*

about² *adv* **1** in all directions or places; around: *papers lying about on the floor* **2** somewhere near: *Is there anyone about?* **3** a little more or less than: *about 5 miles* **4** so as to face the other way **5 be about to** be going to: *We're about to leave.*

about-turn /·,· '·, ·'· ·/ *n esp. BrE* change to the opposite position or opinion

a·bove¹ /ə'bʌv/ *prep* **1** higher than; over: *fly above the clouds* **2** more than **3** too good, honest, etc. for: *He's not above stealing.* **4 above all** most important of all

above² *adv* **1** higher: *the clouds above* **2** more: *aged 20 and above* **3** earlier in a book: *the facts mentioned above* | the **above-mentioned** *facts*

a·bove-board /ə,bʌv'bɔːd◄, ə'bʌvbɔːd ‖ ə'bʌvbɔːrd/ *adj* without any trick or attempt to deceive

a·bra·sive /ə'breɪsɪv/ *adj* **1** causing the rubbing away of a surface **2** rough and annoying: *an abrasive personality*

a·breast /ə'brest/ *adv* **1** side by side **2 keep/be abreast of** know the most recent facts about

a·bridge /ə'brɪdʒ/ *vt* make (a book, etc.) shorter

a·bridg·ment /ə'brɪdʒmənt/ *n* something abridged: *an abridgment of the play for radio*

a·broad /ə'brɔːd ‖ ə'brɔːd/ *adv* to or in another country

a·brupt /ə'brʌpt/ *adj* **1** sudden and unexpected: *an abrupt stop* **2** (of behaviour, etc.) rough and impolite **~ly** *adv* **~ness** *n* [U]

ab·scess /'æbses/ *n* swelling on or in the body, containing pus

ab·scond /əb'skɒnd, æb- ‖ æb'skɑːnd/ *vi fml* go away suddenly because one has done something wrong

ab·seil /'æbseɪl/ *vi* go down a cliff by sliding down a rope

ab·sence /'æbsəns/ *n* **1** [C;U] (period of) being away: *absence from work* **2** [U] non-existence: *the absence of information about the crime*

ab·sent¹ /'æbsənt/ *adj* **1** not present **2** showing lack of attention: *an absent look on his face*

ab·sent /əb'sent, æb- ‖ æb-/ *vt* keep

(oneself) away

ab·sen·tee /,æbsən'tiː◄/ *n* person who is absent from a place

absent-mind·ed /,·· '··◄/ *adj* so concerned with one's thoughts as not to notice what is happening, what one is doing, etc.

ab·so·lute /'æbsəluːt/ *adj* **1** complete; undoubted: *absolute nonsense* **2** having unlimited power: *an absolute ruler* **3** not measured by comparison with other things; not RELATIVE **~ly** /,æbsə'luːtliː◄/ *adv* **1** completely **2** certainly: *'Do you think so?' 'Absolutely.'*

ab·solve /əb'zɒlv ‖ -ɑːlv/ *vt* free (someone) from fulfilling a promise, or from punishment

ab·sorb /əb'sɔːb, əb'zɔːb ‖ -ɔːrb/ *vt* **1** take in (liquids, heat, etc.) **2** fill the attention of: *I was absorbed in a book.* | *an absorbing task* **~ent** able to ABSORB (1) **absorption** /-ɔːpʃən ‖ -ɔːrp-/ *n* [U]

ab·stain /əb'steɪn/ *vi* keep oneself from drinking, voting, etc. **~er** *n*

ab·sten·tion /əb'stenʃən/ *n* [C;U] act of abstaining, esp. from voting

ab·sti·nence /'æbstɪnəns/ *n* [U] abstaining, esp. from alcoholic drink

ab·stract /'æbstrækt/ *adj* **1** existing as a quality or CONCEPT rather than as something real or solid: *Beauty is abstract but a house is not.* | *The word 'hunger' is an* **abstract noun.** **2** general rather than particular: *an abstract discussion of crime, without reference to actual cases* **3** (in art) not showing things as a camera would see them ♦ *n* **1** abstract work of art **2** short form of a statement, speech, etc.

ab·struse /əb'struːs, æb-/ *adj fml* difficult to understand

ab·surd /əb'sɜːd ‖ -ɜːrd/ *adj* unreasonable; (funny because) false or foolish **~ly** *adv* **~ity** /əb'sɜːdəti, -'zɜː- ‖ -ɜːr-/ *n* [C;U]

a·bun·dant /ə'bʌndənt/ *adj* more than enough **~ly** *adv* **–dance** *n* [S;U]

a·buse¹ /ə'bjuːz/ *vt* **1** treat cruelly or violently **2** use badly: *abuse one's power* **3** say bad things to or about

a·buse² /ə'bjuːs/ *n* **1** cruel or violent treatment of someone: *reports of* **child abuse 2** [C;U] wrong use: *the abuse of drugs* **3** [U] cruel or rude words **abusive** *adj*

a·bys·mal /ə'bɪzməl/ adj very bad

a·byss /ə'bɪs/ n great hole that seems bottomless: (fig.) *the abyss of nuclear war*

ac·a·dem·ic /ˌækə'demɪk◂/ adj 1 about schools and education 2 not related to practical situations; THEORETICAL: *a purely academic question* ◆ n 1 university teacher 2 someone who values skills of the mind more than practical ones ~**ally** adv

a·cad·e·my /ə'kædəmi/ n 1 society of people interested in the advancement of art, science, or literature 2 school for training in a special skill: *a military academy*

ac·cede /ək'siːd, æk-/ vi fml 1 agree to a demand, etc. 2 come to a high position

ac·cel·e·rate /ək'seləreɪt/ vi/t (cause to) move faster –**ration** /ək,selə'reɪʃən/ n [U]

ac·cel·e·ra·tor /ək'seləreɪtə‖-ər/ n instrument in a car, etc., that is used to increase its speed

ac·cent¹ /'æksənt‖'æksent/ n 1 particular way of speaking, usu. connected with a place or a social class 2 mark written over or under a letter, such as that on the 'e' of 'café' 3 importance given to a word or part of a word by saying it with more force

ac·cent² /ək'sent‖'æksent/ vt pronounce with added force

ac·cen·tu·ate /ək'sentʃueɪt/ vt direct attention to; give importance to

ac·cept /ək'sept/ v 1 vi/t receive (something offered), esp. willingly 2 vt believe or agree to: *Did she accept your reasons for being late?* ~**able** adj good enough; worth accepting: *an acceptable gift* ~**ance** n [C;U]

ac·cess¹ /'ækses/ n [U] 1 way in; entrance 2 means of using or getting something: *Students need access to books.* ~**ible** /ək'sesɪbəl/ adj easy to get or get to ~**ibility** /ək,sesɪ'bɪləti/ n [U]

access² vt obtain (stored information) from a computer's memory

ac·ces·sion /ək'seʃən/ n coming to a high position: *the Queen's accession to the throne*

ac·ces·so·ry /ək'sesəri/ n 1 thing that is added but is not a necessary part: *car accessories such as a radio* | *a black dress with matching accessories* (=handbag, shoes, etc.) 2 also **accessary** –*law* person who is not present at a crime but who helps in doing it

ac·ci·dent /'æksɪdənt/ n something, usu. unpleasant, that happens unexpectedly: *serious accidents on the motorway* | *I met her by accident.* ~**al** /ˌæksɪ'dentl◂/ adj ~**ally** adv

ac·claim /ə'kleɪm/ vt greet with public approval **acclaim** n [U]

ac·cli·ma·tize also **-ise** BrE /ə'klaɪmətaɪz/ vi/t make or get used to the weather in a new place –**tization** /ə,klaɪmətaɪ'zeɪʃən‖-tə-/ n [U]

ac·co·lade /'ækəleɪd/ n strong praise

ac·com·mo·date /ə'kɒmədeɪt‖ə'kɑː-/ vt fml 1 provide with a place to live in 2 help by making changes: *to accommodate your wishes* –**dating** adj helpful –**dation** /ə,kɒmə'deɪʃən‖ə,kɑː-/ n [U] place to live; room, house, etc.

ac·com·pa·ni·ment /ə'kʌmpənimənt/ n 1 something which is used or provided with something else 2 music played at the same time as singing or another instrument

ac·com·pa·nist /ə'kʌmpənəst/ n player of a musical accompaniment

ac·com·pa·ny /ə'kʌmpəni/ vt 1 go with, as on a journey 2 happen at the same time as: *Lightning usually accompanies thunder.* 3 play a musical accompaniment to

ac·com·plice /ə'kʌmpləs‖ə'kɑːm-, ə'kʌm-/ n person who helps someone to do wrong

ac·com·plish /ə'kʌmplɪʃ‖ə'kɑːm-, ə'kʌm-/ vt succeed in doing ~**ed** adj skilled ~**ment** n 1 [C] something one is skilled at 2 [U] act of accomplishing something

ac·cord /ə'kɔːd‖ə'kɔːrd/ vi agree: *That does not accord with your previous statement.* ◆ n [U] 1 **in accord (with)** in agreement (with) 2 **of one's own accord** without being asked; willingly

ac·cord·ance /ə'kɔːdəns‖-ɔːr-/ n **in accordance with** in a way that agrees with

ac·cord·ing·ly /ə'kɔːdɪŋli‖-ɔːr-/ adv because of what has happened; therefore

according to /·'··· ·/ prep 1 from what is said or written: *According to my watch, it's 4 o'clock.* 2 in a way that agrees with: *paid according to the amount of work done*

ac·cor·di·on /ə'kɔːdiən‖-ɔːr-/ n musical instrument played by pressing the middle part together to force air through holes controlled by KEYS¹ (3) worked by the fingers

ac·cost /əˈkɒst ‖ əˈkɔːst, əˈkɑːst/ vt go up and speak to (esp. a stranger), often threateningly

ac·count¹ /əˈkaʊnt/ n 1 report; description: *give an account of what happened* | **By all accounts**, (=according to what everyone says) *she's a good player.* 2 record of money received and paid out 3 money kept in a bank or BUILDING SOCIETY 4 arrangement that lets one buy goods and pay for them later 5 advantage; profit: *He turned his knowledge to good account.* 6 **bring/call someone to account** cause (someone) to give an explanation 7 **of great/no account** of great/no importance 8 **on account of** because of 9 **on no account/not on any account** not for any reason 10 **take into account/take account of** give thought to; consider

account² v **account for** phr vt 1 give or be an explanation for 2 give a statement showing how money has been spent

ac·coun·ta·ble /əˈkaʊntəbəl/ adj responsible **-bility** /əˌkaʊntəˈbɪləti/ n [U]

ac·coun·tan·cy /əˈkaʊntənsi/ work of an accountant

ac·coun·tant /əˈkaʊntənt/ n person who controls and examines money accounts

ac·cred·it·ed /əˈkredɪtɪd/ adj 1 officially representing one's government in a foreign country 2 having the power to act for an organization 3 officially recognized as reaching a certain standard or quality

ac·crue /əˈkruː/ vi fml come as an increase or advantage

ac·cu·mu·late /əˈkjuːmjʊleɪt/ vi/t make or become greater; collect into a mass **-lation** /əˌkjuːmjʊˈleɪʃən/ n [C;U]

ac·cu·ra·cy /ˈækjʊrəsi/ n [U] being accurate; exactness

ac·cu·rate /ˈækjʊrət/ adj exactly correct **~ly** adv

ac·cu·sa·tion /ˌækjʊˈzeɪʃən/ n [C;U] (statement) accusing someone of something

ac·cuse /əˈkjuːz/ vt charge (someone) with doing wrong: *He was accused of murder.* | *The accused (men) were found guilty.* **accuser** n **accusingly** adv

ac·cus·tom /əˈkʌstəm/ vt be accustomed to be in the habit of; be used to

ace /eɪs/ n 1 playing card with one mark or spot on it 2 person of the highest skill 3 (in

tennis) very fast and strong SERVE that the opponent cannot hit back ♦ adj infml very good or very skilled

a·cer·bic /əˈsɜːbɪk ‖ -ɜːr-/ adj (of a person or manner) clever in a rather cruel way

ache /eɪk/ vi have a continuous dull pain: *My head aches.* | (fig.) *I'm aching to go to the party.* **ache** n: *a headache*

a·chieve /əˈtʃiːv/ vt succeed in doing or obtaining: *achieve results* **~ment** n 1 [U] successful achieving of something 2 [C] something achieved

a·chiev·er /əˈtʃiːvə-vər / 1 successful person 2 **low achiever** student etc. who is not successful

A·chil·les' heel /əˌkɪliːz ˈhiːl/ n small but important weakness

ac·id /ˈæsɪd/ adj sour; bitter **acid** n 1 [C;U] chemical substance containing HYDROGEN 2 [U] sl the drug LSD

acid rain /ˌ· ˈ·/ n [U] rain containing harmful quantities of acid as a result of industrial POLLUTION

acid test /ˌ· ˈ·/ n test of the value of something

ac·knowl·edge /əkˈnɒlɪdʒ ‖ -ˈnɑː-/ vt 1 admit; recognize as a fact: *to acknowledge defeat* | *an acknowledged expert* 2 show one is grateful for 3 state that one has received: *acknowledge a letter* 4 show that one recognizes (someone) as by smiling, etc. **-edgment, -edgement** n [C;U]

ac·ne /ˈækni/ n [U] skin disorder common among young people, in which spots appear on the face and neck

a·corn /ˈeɪkɔːn ‖ -ɔːrn, -ərn/ n nut of the OAK tree

a·cous·tics /əˈkuːstɪks/ n 1 [U] scientific study of sound 2 [P] qualities that make a place good or bad for hearing in **acoustic** adj

ac·quaint /əˈkweɪnt/ vt fml 1 **acquaint someone with** tell; make known to 2 **be acquainted (with)** have met socially; know **~ance** n 1 [C] person whom one knows slightly 2 [S;U (with)] knowledge gained through experience

ac·qui·esce /ˌækwiˈes/ vi agree, often unwillingly **-escent** adj

ac·quire /əˈkwaɪə ‖ -ər/ vt gain; come to possess

ac·qui·si·tion /ˌækwɪˈzɪʃən/ n 1 [U] act

of acquiring **2** [C] something acquired
-tive /ə'kwɪzɪtɪv/ adj in the habit of
acquiring things

ac·quit /ə'kwɪt/ vt -tt- **1** decide that
(someone) is not guilty: *The jury acquitted
him (of murder).* **2** cause (oneself) to act in
the stated way: *He acquitted himself rather
badly.* ~**tal** n [C;U]

a·cre /'eɪkə‖-ər/ n a measure of land
equal to 4,840 square yards

a·cre·age /'eɪkərɪdʒ/ n [S;U] area
measured in acres

ac·rid /'ækrɪd/ adj (of taste or smell)
bitter; stinging

ac·ri·mo·ny /'ækrɪməni‖-moʊni/ n [U]
bitterness of manner or language **–nious**
/ˌækrɪ'məʊniəs◀‖-'moʊ-/ adj

ac·ro·bat /'ækrəbæt/ n person skilled in
walking on ropes, etc., esp. in a CIRCUS ~**ic**
/ˌækrə'bætɪk◀/ adj **-ics** n [P;U]

ac·ro·nym /'ækrənɪm/ n word made from
the first letters of a name, such as NATO

a·cross /ə'krɒs‖ə'krɔːs/ adv, prep from
one side to the other; on or to the other side
(of): *a bridge across the river* | *Can you
swim across?*

a·cross-the-board /·,··'·/ adj influencing
or having effects on people or things of all
types or at every level **across-the-board**
adv

a·cryl·ic /ə'krɪlɪk/ n, adj (cloth) made
from a chemical substance

act¹ /ækt/ v **1** vi do something: *She acted
on my suggestion.* | *The doctor acted
correctly.* **2** vi/t perform in a play or film
3 vi produce an effect: *Does the drug take
long to act?*

    act up phr vi behave badly

act² n **1** something that one has done; an
action of a particular kind: *an act of
terrorism* | *a kind act* **2** law made by
parliament, etc. **3** main division of a stage
play **4** short event in a stage or CIRCUS
performance **5** example of insincere
behaviour used for effect: *She was just
putting on an act.*

act·ing /'æktɪŋ/ adj appointed to do the
duties of a position for a short time

ac·tion /'ækʃən/ n **1** [U] process of doing
something: *We must take action quickly.*
2 [C] something done; ACT: *Her prompt
action saved his life.* **3** [C;U] way something
works **4** [U] effect: *the action of light on*

photographic film **5** [C;U] military fighting
or a fight **6** [U] main events in a book, play,
etc.: *The action takes place in Italy.* **7** [C;U]
law legal charge of guilt: *bring an action
against him* **8 in/into action** in/into
operation **9 out of action** not working
10 take action begin to act —see also
INDUSTRIAL ACTION

ac·tiv·ate /'æktɪveɪt/ vt make active
-ation /ˌæktɪ'veɪʃən/ n [U]

ac·tive /'æktɪv/ adj doing things; able to
take action ~**ly** adv

ac·tiv·ist /'æktɪvɪst/ n person taking an
active part in politics

ac·tiv·i·ty /æk'tɪvɪti/ n **1** [U] movement
or action: *political activity* **2** [C] something
done, esp. for interest or pleasure: *leisure
activities*

ac·tor /'æktə‖-ər/ **actress** /'æktrɪs/
fem. — n person who acts in a play, film, etc.

ac·tu·al /'æktʃuəl/ adj existing as a fact;
real ~**ly** /'æktʃuəli, -tʃəli/ adv **1** in fact;
really **2** (showing surprise): *He actually
offered me a drink!*

ac·u·men /'ækjʊmən, ə'kjuːmən/ n [U]
fml ability to judge quickly

ac·u·punc·ture /'ækjʊˌpʌŋktʃə‖-ər/ n
[U] method of curing diseases by putting
special needles into certain parts of the
body

a·cute /ə'kjuːt/ adj **1** severe; very great:
acute shortage of water **2** (of the mind or
senses) working very well **3** (of an angle)
less than 90° **4** (of a mark) put above a letter,
e.g. 'é', to show pronunciation ~**ly** adv
~**ness** n [U]

ad /æd/ n infml advertisement

AD /ˌeɪ 'diː/ (in the year) since the birth of
Christ: *in 1066 AD*

ad·age /'ædɪdʒ/ n old wise phrase;
PROVERB

ad·a·mant /'ædəmənt/ adj fml refusing
to change one's mind

Adam's ap·ple /'ædəmz 'æpəl‖ 'ædəmz
ˌæpəl/ n lump at the front of the throat that
moves when one talks or swallows

a·dapt /ə'dæpt/ vt make suitable for new
conditions ~**able** adj able to change
~**ability** /əˌdæptə'bɪlɪti/ n [U] ~**ation**
/ˌædæp'teɪʃən/ n [C;U] act of adapting: *an
adaptation of the play for radio*

a·dapt·er, -or /ə'dæptə‖-tər/ n **1** person
who adapts **2** electrical PLUG allowing more

than one piece of equipment to run from the same SOCKET

add /æd/ v **1** vt put with something else: *add a name to the list* **2** vi/t join (numbers) together **3** vt say also

  add to phr vt increase: *His absence added to our difficulties.*

  add up phr vi make sense; seem likely: *The facts just don't add up.*

ad·der /'ædə‖-ər/ n small poisonous snake

ad·dict /'ædɪkt/ n person who cannot stop a harmful habit **~ion** /ə'dɪkʃən/ n [C;U] **~ive** /ə'dɪktɪv/ adj habit forming

ad·dic·ted /ə'dɪktɪd/ adj dependent on something, esp. a drug

ad·di·tion /ə'dɪʃən/ n **1** [U] act of adding **2** [C] something added **3 in addition (to)** as well (as) **~al** adj as well; added **~ally** adv also

ad·di·tive /'ædɪtɪv/ n substance, esp. a chemical one, added to something else

ad·dled /'ædld/ adj infml (of someone's brain) having become confused

add-on /'··/ n piece of equipment that can be connected to a computer that increases its usefulness

ad·dress /ə'dres‖ə'dres, 'ædres/ n **1** number, town, etc. where someone lives **2** speech made to a group of people ♦ vt **1** write a name and ADDRESS (1) on **2** direct a speech to: *She addressed the crowd.*

ad·ept /'ædept, ə'dept‖ə'dept/ adj highly skilled **adept** /'ædept/ n person who is adept at something

ad·e·quate /'ædɪkwət/ adj enough; good enough **~ly** adv **-quacy** n [U]

ad·here /əd'hɪə‖-'hɪr/ vi stick firmly, as with glue **adherence** n [U] **adherent** n loyal supporter of something

  adhere to phr vt remain loyal to (an idea, plan, etc.)

ad·he·sive /əd'hi:sɪv/ n, adj (a substance such as glue) that can stick **-sion** /əd'hi:ʒən/ n [U]

ad hoc /ˌæd 'hɒk‖-'hɑːk, -'hoʊk/ adj made for a particular purpose

ad·ja·cent /ə'dʒeɪsənt/ adj fml very close; (almost) touching

ad·jec·tive /'ædʒɪktɪv/ n word which describes a noun, such as *black* in *a black hat* **-tival** /ˌædʒɪk'taɪvəl◄/ adj

ad·join /ə'dʒɔɪn/ vi/t fml be next to (one

another)

ad·journ /ə'dʒɜːn‖-ɜːrn/ vi/t stop (a meeting, etc.) for a while **~ment** n [C;U]

ad·ju·di·cate /ə'dʒuːdɪkeɪt/ vi/t fml act as a judge; decide about **–cator** n **–cation** /ə,dʒuːdɪ'keɪʃən/ n [U]

ad·junct /'ædʒʌŋkt/ n something added without being a necessary part

ad·just /ə'dʒʌst/ vi/t change slightly so as to make right **~able** adj **~ment** n [C;U]

ad lib /ˌæd 'lɪb/ adv spoken, played, performed, etc. without preparation **ad-lib** vi **-bb-** invent and say without preparation **ad-lib** adj

ad·min·is·ter /əd'mɪnɪstə‖-tər/ vt fml **1** manage (business affairs, etc.) **2** (to) give: *administer medicine/punishment*

ad·min·is·tra·tion /əd,mɪnɪ'streɪʃən/ n **1** [U] management or direction of the affairs of a business, government, etc. **2** [C] esp. AmE national government: *the Clinton Administration* **3** [U] act of administering **–trative** /əd'mɪnɪstrətɪv‖-streɪtɪv/ adj **-trator** /-streɪtə‖-tər/ n

ad·mi·ra·ble /'ædmərəbəl/ adj very good **–bly** adv

ad·mi·ral /'ædmərəl/ n naval officer of high rank

ad·mire /əd'maɪə‖-'maɪr/ vt regard with pleasure; have a good opinion of **admiring** adj **admirer** n **admiration** /ˌædmə'reɪʃən/ n [U] feeling of pleasure and respect

ad·mis·si·ble /əd'mɪsɪbəl/ adj that can be accepted or considered

ad·mis·sion /əd'mɪʃən/ n **1** [U] being allowed to enter a building, join a club, etc. **2** [U] cost of entrance: *admission charges* **3** [C] statement admitting something; CONFESSION

ad·mit /əd'mɪt/ vt **-tt-** **1** allow to enter; let in **2** agree to the truth of (something bad) **~tance** n [U] right to enter **~tedly** adv it must be agreed that

ad·mon·ish /əd'mɒnɪʃ‖-'mɑː-/ vt fml scold gently; warn **-ition** /ˌædmə'nɪʃən/ n [C;U]

ad nau·se·am /ˌæd 'nɔːziæm‖-'nɒ:-/ adv repeatedly and to an annoying degree

a·do /ə'duː/ n without more ado with no further delay

ad·o·les·cent /ˌædə'lesənt◄/ adj, n (of) a boy or girl who is growing up **–cence** n [S;U]

a·dopt /ə'dɒpt‖ə'dɑːpt/ vt **1** take

(someone else's child) into one's family for ever **2** take and use (a method, suggestion, etc.) **-ive** *adj* having adopted a child **~ion** /ə'dɒpʃən ‖ ə'dɑːp-/ *n* [C;U]

a·dore /ə'dɔː ‖ ə'dɔːr/ *vt* **1** love and respect deeply; worship **2** like very much **adorable** very lovable **adoring** *adj* loving **adoration** /,ædə'reɪʃən/ *n* [U]

a·dorn /ə'dɔːn ‖ ə'dɔːrn/ *vt* add beauty to; decorate **~ment** *n* [U]

a·dren·a·lin /ə'drenəl-ɪn/ *n* [U] chemical made by the body during anger, etc., causing quick or violent action

a·drift /ə'drɪft/ *adv, adj* (of boats) floating loose; not fastened

a·droit /ə'drɔɪt/ *adj* quick and skilful **~ly** *adv*

ad·u·la·tion /,ædʒ'leɪʃən/ *n* [U] *fml* praise or admiration that is more than is necessary or deserved

ad·ult /'ædʌlt, ə'dʌlt/ *n* (of) a fully grown person or animal ♦ *adj* **1** relating to or typical of adults **2** *euph* (of films, books, etc.) containing a lot of sex

a·dul·ter·ate /ə'dʌltəreɪt/ *vt* make impure by adding something of lower quality

a·dul·ter·y /ə'dʌltəri/ *n* [U] sexual relations between a married person and someone outside the marriage **adulterer, adulteress** /-trɪs/ *fem.* — *n* **-terous** *adj*

ad·vance¹ /əd'vɑːns ‖ əd'væns/ *vi/t* go or bring forward in position, development, etc. **advanced** *adj* **1** far on in development **2** modern

advance² *n* **1** forward movement or development **2** money provided before the proper time **3** **in advance** before in time ♦ *adj* coming before the usual time

ad·vanc·es /əd'vɑːnsɪz ‖ əd'væn-/ *n* [P] efforts to become friends with someone

ad·van·tage /əd'vɑːntɪdʒ ‖ əd'væn-/ *n* **1** [C] something that may help one to be successful **2** [U] profit; gain **3** **take advantage of: a** make use of somebody, as by deceiving them **b** make use of; profit from **~ous** /,ædvən'teɪdʒəs◄, ,ædvæn-/ *adj*

ad·vent /'ædvent/ *n* **the advent of** the coming of (an important event, etc.)

ad·ven·ture /əd'ventʃə ‖ -ər/ *n* **1** [C] exciting and perhaps dangerous experience **2** [U] excitement; risk **-turer** *n* **1** person who has or looks for adventures **2** person

who hopes to make a profit by taking risks with his/her money **-turous** *adj* **1** also **adventuresome** /əd'ventʃəsəm ‖ -tʃər-/ *AmE* — fond of adventure **2** exciting

ad·verb /'ædvɜːb ‖ -ɜːrb/ *n* word which adds to the meaning of a verb, an adjective, another adverb, or a sentence, for example *slowly, tomorrow,* and *here* **~ial** /əd'vɜːbiəl ‖ -ɜːr-/ *n, adj*

ad·ver·sa·ry /'ædvəsəri ‖ 'ædvərseri/ *n fml* opponent; enemy **-sarial** /,ædvə'seəriəl◄ -vɜːr'ser-/ *adj*

ad·verse /'ædvɜːs ‖ -ɜːrs/ *adj fml* unfavourable: *adverse comments* **~ly** *adv* **-sity** /əd'vɜːsɪti ‖ -ɜːr-/ *n* [C;U] bad luck; trouble

ad·vert /'ædvɜːt ‖ -ɜːrt/ *n BrE infml* advertisement

ad·ver·tise /'ædvətaɪz ‖ -ər-/ *vi/t* make (something for sale) known to people, e.g. in a newspaper **-tiser** *n* **-tising** *n* [U] business of doing this **~ment** /əd'vɜːtɪsmənt ‖ ,ædvər'taɪz-/ *n* notice of something for sale

ad·vice /əd'vaɪs/ *n* [U] opinion given to someone about what to do

ad·vise /əd'vaɪz/ *vt* **1** give advice to **2** [(of)] *fml* inform: *Please advise me of the cost.* **3** **well-advised/ill-advised** wise/unwise **advisory** giving advice **adviser** also **advisor** *AmE* — *n* **advisable** *adj* sensible; wise

ad·vo·cate /'ædvəkət, -keɪt/ *n* person who speaks in defence of another person or of an idea; supporter **advocate** /-keɪt/ *vt*

ae·gis /'iːdʒɪs/ *n* **under the aegis of** with the protection or support of

aer·i·al¹ /'eəriəl ‖ 'er-/ *n* wire, rod, etc. that receives radio or television signals

aerial² *adj* in or from the air: *aerial photography*

aer·o·bat·ics /,eərə'bætɪks, ,eərəu- ‖ ,erə-, ,erou-/ *n* [U] ACROBATIC tricks done in an aircraft **aerobatic** *adj*

aer·o·bics /eə'rəubɪks ‖ e'rou-/ *n* [U] active physical exercise done to strengthen the heart and lungs **aerobic** *adj*

aer·o·drome /'eərədrəum ‖ 'erədroum/ *n esp. BrE* small airport

aer·o·dy·nam·ics /,eərəudaɪ'næmɪks ‖ ,erou-/ *n* [U] science of movement through the air **aerodynamic** *adj* **1** concerning aerodynamics **2** using the principles of aerodynamics

aer·o·nau·tics /ˌeərəˈnɔːtɪks ǁ ˌerəˈnɔː-/ n [U] science of the flight of aircraft

aer·o·plane /ˈeərəpleɪn ǁ ˈer-/ n BrE ǁ airplane AmE — n flying vehicle with wings and one or more engines

aer·o·sol /ˈeərəsɒl ǁ ˈerəsɔːl/ n container from which liquid is forced out in a fine mist

aer·o·space /ˈeərəspeɪs, ˈeərəʊ- ǁ ˈerə-, ˈeroʊ-/ n [U] the air around the Earth and space beyond it

aes·thet·ics ǁ also **es-** AmE /iːsˈθetɪks, es-ǁ es-/ n [U] science of beauty, esp. in art
aesthetic adj **–ically** /-kli/ adv

a·far /əˈfɑː ǁ əˈfɑːr/ adv **from afar** lit from a long distance

af·fa·ble /ˈæfəbəl/ adj friendly and pleasant **–bly** adv

af·fair /əˈfeə ǁ əˈfer/ n **1** event; set of events **2** something to be done; business **3** sexual relationship outside marriage —see also FOREIGN AFFAIRS

af·fect /əˈfekt/ vt cause a change in; influence: Smoking affects your health. **~ed** adj not natural; pretended **~ation** /ˌæfekˈteɪʃən/ n [U] unnatural behaviour

af·fec·tion /əˈfekʃən/ n [U] gentle, lasting fondness **~ate** adj **~ately** adv

af·fi·da·vit /ˌæfəˈdeɪvɪt/ n law written statement for use as proof

af·fil·i·ate /əˈfɪliᵊt/ vi/t (esp. of a group) join to a larger group **–ation** /əˌfɪliˈeɪʃən/ n [C;U]

af·fin·i·ty /əˈfɪnəti/ n [C;U] close connection or liking

af·firm /əˈfɜːm ǁ əˈfɜːrm/ vt fml declare; state **~ation** n, and (statement) meaning 'yes' **~ation** /ˌæfəˈmeɪʃən ǁ ˌæfər-/ n [C;U]

af·firm·a·tive ac·tion /əˌfɜːmətɪv ˈækʃən ǁ -ɜːr-/ n [U] POSITIVE DISCRIMINATION

af·fix[1] /əˈfɪks/ vt fml fix; fasten

af·fix[2] /ˈæfɪks/ n SUFFIX OR PREFIX

af·flict /əˈflɪkt/ vt cause to suffer; trouble **~ion** /əˈflɪkʃən/ n [C;U] fml

af·flu·ent /ˈæfluənt/ adj wealthy; rich **-ence** n [U]

af·ford /əˈfɔːd ǁ əˈfɔːrd/ vt **1** be able to pay for **2** be able to risk: I can't afford to neglect my health.

af·front /əˈfrʌnt/ vt be rude to; offend **affront** n

a·fi·cio·na·do /əˌfɪʃəˈnɑːdəʊ ǁ -doʊ/ n **-dos** someone who is keenly interested in a particular activity or subject

a·field /əˈfiːld/ adv **far afield** far away

AFL-CIO /ˌeɪ ef ˌel ˌsiː aɪ ˈəʊ ǁ -ˈoʊ/ n [the] American Federation of Labor and Congress of Industrial Organizations; an association of American trade unions

a·float /əˈfləʊt ǁ əˈfloʊt/ adv, adj **1** floating **2** on a ship **3** out of debt

a·foot /əˈfʊt/ adv, adj being prepared; happening

a·fore·said /əˈfɔːsed ǁ əˈfɔːr-/ adj said or named before

a·fraid /əˈfreɪd/ adj **1** frightened: afraid of the dark **2** sorry for something that has happened or is likely to happen: 'Are we late?' 'I'm afraid so.'

a·fresh /əˈfreʃ/ adv fml again

af·ter /ˈɑːftə ǁ ˈæftər/ prep, conj **1** later than: after breakfast | after you leave **2** following: Your name comes after mine in the list. | It rained day after day. **3** because of: After I packed it so carefully, the clock arrived broken. **4** in spite of: After I packed it so carefully, the clock arrived broken. **5** looking for: The police are after him. **6** fml in the style of: a painting after Rembrandt **7** **after all** in spite of everything ♦ adv later; afterwards

af·ter-ef·fect /ˈɑːftərɪfekt ǁ ˈæf-/ n effect (usu. unpleasant) that follows some time after the cause

af·ter·math /ˈɑːftəmæθ ǁ ˈæftər-/ n period following a bad event: the aftermath of the war

af·ter·noon /ˌɑːftəˈnuːn◂ ǁ ˌæftər-/ n [C;U] time between midday and sunset

af·ter·shave /ˈɑːftəʃeɪv ǁ ˈæftər-/ n [C;U] pleasant smelling liquid put on the face after shaving (SHAVE)

af·ter·thought /ˈɑːftəθɔːt ǁ ˈæftərθɔːt/ n idea that comes later; something added later

af·ter·wards /ˈɑːftəwədz ǁ ˈæftərwərdz/ adv later; after that

a·gain /əˈgen, əˈgeɪn ǁ əˈgen/ adv **1** once more; another time: Say it again. **2** back to the original place or condition: He's home again now. **3** besides; further: I could eat as much (=the same amount) again. **4** **again and again** very often

a·gainst /əˈgenst, əˈgeɪnst ǁ əˈgenst/ prep **1** in the direction of and meeting or touching: The rain beat against the windows. **2** in opposition to: Stealing is

against the law. 3 as a protection from: *They were vaccinated against cholera.* **4** having as a background: *The picture looks good against that red wall.*

age /eɪdʒ/ *n* **1** [C;U] length of time someone has lived or something has existed: *What are the children's ages?* **2** [U] one of the periods of human life: *to look after her in her old age* **3** [C] period of history: *This is the nuclear age.* **4** [C] long time: *We haven't met for ages.* **5 of age** old enough (usu. at 18 or 21) to be responsible in law for one's own actions **6 under/over age** too young/too old to be legally allowed to do something ♦ *vi/t* make or become old

aged *adj* **1** /eɪdʒd/ of the stated number of years: *a boy aged 10* **2** /'eɪdʒɪd/ very old: *an aged man*

age·is·m, agism /'eɪdʒɪzəm/ *n* [U] the making of unfair distinctions between people because of their age, esp. treating young people more favourably than old people **ageist** *adj, n*

a·gen·cy /'eɪdʒənsi/ *n* work or business of an agent: *an employment agency*

a·gen·da /ə'dʒendə/ *n* **-das** list of things to be talked about at a meeting

a·gent /'eɪdʒənt/ *n* **1** person who does business for other people: *An estate agent sells houses.* **2** person or thing that produces a result: *Soap is a cleansing agent.*

ag·gra·vate /'ægrəveɪt/ *vt* **1** make worse **2** annoy: *an aggravating delay* **-vation** /ˌægrə'veɪʃən/ *n* [C;U]

ag·gre·gate /'ægrɪgɪt/ *n* [C;U] total

ag·gres·sion /ə'greʃən/ *n* [U] starting a quarrel or war without just cause **-sor** /ə'gresə ‖ -ər/ *n* person or country that does this

ag·gres·sive /ə'gresɪv/ *adj* **1** always ready to attack **2** brave and determined

ag·grieved /ə'griːvd/ *adj fml* showing hurt feelings

a·ghast /ə'gɑːst ‖ ə'gæst/ *adj* surprised and shocked

ag·ile /'ædʒaɪl ‖ 'ædʒəl/ *adj* able to move quickly **agility** /ə'dʒɪlɪti/ *n* [U]

ag·i·tate /'ædʒɪteɪt/ *v* **1** *vt* shake (a liquid) **2** *vt* make anxious; worry **3** *vi* [(for)] argue strongly in public **-tator** *n* person who agitates for political or social change **-tation** /ˌædʒɪ'teɪʃən/ *n* [U]

a·glow /ə'gləʊ ‖ ə'gloʊ/ *adj* bright with colour or excitement

AGM /ˌeɪ dʒiː 'em/ *n* annual general meeting of a club, organization, etc., held once a year to elect officials, report on the year's business, etc.

ag·nos·tic /æg'nɒstɪk, əg- ‖ -'nɑː-/ *n, adj* (person) believing that nothing can be known about God **~ism** /-tɪsɪzəm/ *n* [U]

a·go /ə'gəʊ ‖ ə'goʊ/ *adj, adv* back in time from now: *a week ago*

a·gog /ə'gɒg ‖ ə'gɑːg/ *adj* excited and eager

ag·o·nize also **-ise** *BrE* /'ægənaɪz/ *vi infml* make a long and anxious effort when trying to make a decision, etc. **-nized** *adj* expressing great pain **-nizing** *adj* causing great pain

ag·o·ny /'ægəni/ *n* [C;U] great suffering

agony aunt /'··· ,·/ *n BrE* woman who gives advice in a part of a newspaper or magazine that contains letters from readers about their personal problems (an **agony column**)

ag·o·ra·pho·bi·a /ˌægərə'fəʊbiə ‖ -'foʊ-/ *n* [U] fear of open spaces

a·grar·i·an /ə'greəriən ‖ ə'grer-/ *adj* of land, esp. farmland

a·gree /ə'griː/ *v* **1** *vi/t* share the same opinion; say 'yes': *I agree with you.* | *We agreed to go home.* | *They met at the agreed place.* **2** *vi* (of statements, etc.) be the same; match **~able** *adj* pleasant **~ably** *adv* **~ment** *n* **1** [U] state of agreeing: *The two sides cannot reach agreement.* **2** [C] arrangement between people or groups; CONTRACT: *to break an agreement*

agree with *phr vt* **1** suit the health of **2** be in accordance with

ag·ri·cul·ture /'ægrɪˌkʌltʃə ‖ -ər/ *n* [U] growing crops; farming **-tural** /ˌægrɪ'kʌltʃərəl◂/ *adj*

ag·ron·o·my /ə'grɒnəmi ‖ ə'grɑː-/ *n* [U] science of managing soil and growing crops

a·ground /ə'graʊnd/ *adv, adj* (of a ship) on or onto the shore or bottom of a sea, lake, etc.

a·head /ə'hed/ *adv, adj* **1** in front **2** into the future: *to plan ahead* **3** [(of)] in advance; succeeding better: *to get ahead of our rivals*

AI /ˌeɪ 'aɪ/ *n* ARTIFICIAL INTELLIGENCE

aid /eɪd/ *n* **1** [U] help *She came to my aid at once.* | *to collect £1,000* **in aid of** *medical research* **2** [C] person or thing that helps: *an* aid in learning a language **3 What is something in aid of?** BrE infml What is something for?: *What's that handle in aid of?* —see also FIRST AID ♦ vt fml help

aide || also **aid** AmE /eɪd/ n person who helps someone in a more important position, esp. a politician

AIDS, **Aids** /eɪdz/ n [U] Acquired Immune Deficiency Syndrome; very serious disease caused by a VIRUS which breaks down the body's natural defences against infection

ail /eɪl/ vi be ill: *an ailing child* ~**ment** n illness

aim /eɪm/ v **1** vi/t point (a weapon, etc.) towards **2** vi direct one's efforts; intend: *I aim to be a writer.* ♦ n **1** act of directing a shot **2** desired result; purpose: *What is your aim in life?* ~**less** adj without purpose

ain't /eɪnt/ infml short for: am not, is not, are not, has not, or have not

air[1] /eə ǁ er/ n **1** [U] mixture of gases that we breathe **2** [U] space above the ground: *travel by air* **3** [C] general character of a person or place: *an air of excitement at the meeting* **4 clear the air** get rid of misunderstanding, etc., by stating the facts clearly **5 in the air: a** (of stories, talk, etc.) being passed on from one person to another **b** uncertain **6 on/off the air** broadcasting/not broadcasting —see also HOT AIR, THIN AIR **airs** n [P] unnatural behaviour to make one seem important

air[2] v **1** vi/t dry (clothes, etc.) in a warm place **2** vi/t make or become fresh by letting in air: *to air the room* **3** vt let people know: *He's always airing his opinions.* **4** vt broadcast **airing** n [C;U]

air·bag /'eəbæg ǁ 'er-/ n bag in a car, that fills with air to protect people in an accident

air·borne /'eəbɔːn ǁ 'erbɔːrn/ adj **1** carried by the air **2** (of aircraft) flying

air·bus /'eəbʌs ǁ 'er-/ n tdmk aircraft carrying many passengers on short flights

air-con·di·tion·ing /'·· ‚··,··/ n [U] system using machines (air-conditioners) to control the indoor air temperature –**tioned** adj

air·craft /'eəkrɑːft ǁ 'erkræft/ n -**craft** flying machine

aircraft car·ri·er /'·· ‚···/ n warship that carries aircraft

air·field /'eəfiːld ǁ 'er-/ n place where

aircraft can land

air·force /'eəfɔːs ǁ 'erfɔːrs/ n branch of a country's military forces that fights in the air

air-host·ess /'eə‚həʊstɪs ǁ 'er‚hoʊ-/ n woman who looks after passengers in an aircraft

air·i·ly /'eərɪli ǁ er-/ adv in a light AIRY (2,3) manner

air·lift /'eə‚lɪft ǁ 'er-/ n carrying of large numbers of people or amounts of supplies by aircraft, esp. to or from a place that is difficult to get to **airlift** vt

air·line /'eəlaɪn ǁ 'er-/ n business that carries passengers and goods by air

air·lin·er /'eə‚laɪnə ǁ 'er‚laɪnər/ n large passenger aircraft

air·lock /'eəlɒk ǁ 'erlɑːk/ n **1** BUBBLE in a tube, etc., that prevents the flow of liquid **2** enclosed space or room into which or from which air cannot accidentally pass

air·mail /'eəmeɪl ǁ 'er-/ n [U] system of sending letters, etc. by air

air·plane /'eəpleɪn ǁ 'er-/ n AmE for AEROPLANE

air pock·et /'· ‚··/ n downward air current causing a plane to drop suddenly

air·port /'eəpɔːt ǁ 'erpɔːrt/ n place where aircraft regularly land, with buildings for waiting passengers, etc.

air·ship /'eə‚ʃɪp ǁ 'er-/ n lighter-than-air aircraft with an engine but no wings

air·space /'eəspeɪs ǁ 'er-/ n [U] sky above a country, regarded as that country's property

air strike /'· ·/ n attack by military aircraft

air·strip /'eə‚strɪp ǁ 'er-/ n piece of ground where aircraft can land if necessary

air·tight /'eətaɪt ǁ 'er-/ adj not letting air in or out

air time /'eətaɪm ǁ 'er-/ n [U] time spent broadcasting a song, speech, advertisement, etc.

air-to-air /‚· · '·◄/ adj to be fired from one aircraft to another

air·wor·thy /'eə‚wɜːði ǁ 'er‚wɜːrði/ adj (of an aircraft) in safe working condition –**thiness** n [U]

air·y /'eəri ǁ 'eri/ adj **1** open to the fresh air **2** not practical: *airy notions* **3** cheerful and careless

aisle /aɪl/ n passage between seats in a church, theatre, etc.

a·jar /ə'dʒɑː ‖ ə'dʒɑːr/ *adv, adj* (of a door) slightly open

aka /'ækə, ˌeɪ keɪ 'eɪ/ *abbrev. for:* also known as

a·kim·bo /ə'kɪmbəʊ ‖ -boʊ/ *adj, adv* (of the arms) bent at the elbows and with the hands on the HIPS

a·kin /ə'kɪn/ *adj* [(to)] like; similar

a·lac·ri·ty /ə'lækrəti/ *n* [U] *fml* quick and willing readiness

a·larm /ə'lɑːm ‖ ə'lɑːrm/ *n* 1 [C] warning of danger 2 [U] sudden fear 3 [C] apparatus that gives a warning: *a burglar alarm* 4 [C] clock that can be set to make a noise at any time to wake people: *set the alarm (clock) for 6.30* ♦ *vt* frighten: *alarming news* ~**ist** *n* person who always expects danger, often without good reason, and says so to others ~**ist** *adj*

a·las /ə'læs/ *interj* (cry expressing sorrow)

al·be·it /ɔːl'biːət ‖ ɒːl-/ *conj fml* even though: *an important, albeit small, mistake*

al·bi·no /æl'biːnəʊ ‖ æl'baɪnoʊ/ *n* person or animal with white skin, very light hair, and pink eyes

al·bum /'ælbəm/ *n* 1 book for sticking photographs, etc. into 2 long-playing record

al·che·my /'ælkəmi/ *n* [U] former science concerned with turning metals into gold –**mist** *n*

al·co·hol /'ælkəhɒl ‖ -hɒːl/ *n* [U] (drinks containing) the liquid that makes one drunk ~**ism** *n* [U] diseased condition caused by the continued drinking of too much alcohol ~**ic** /ˌælkə'hɒlɪk◄ ‖ -'hɒː-/ *adj, n* person unable to stop drinking alcohol

al·cove /'ælkəʊv ‖ -koʊv/ *n* small partly enclosed space in a room for a bed, etc.

ale /eɪl/ *n* [U] kind of beer

al·eck /'ælɪk/ *n* —see SMART ALECK

a·lert /ə'lɜːt ‖ ə'lɜːrt/ *adj* quick to see and ask; watchful ♦ *n* 1 warning of danger 2 **on the alert** ready to deal with danger ♦ *vt* warn

al·fres·co /æl'freskəʊ ‖ -koʊ/ *adj, adv* in the open air

al·gae /'ældʒiː/ *n* [P] very small plants that live in or near water

al·ge·bra /'ældʒɪbrə/ *n* [U] branch of MATHEMATICS using letters to represent values

a·li·as /'eɪliəs/ *n* -**ases** false name used esp. by a criminal ♦ *adv* also called:

Edward Ball, alias John Smith

al·i·bi /'ælɪbaɪ/ *n* proof that a person charged with a crime was somewhere else when it happened

a·li·en /'eɪliən/ *n* 1 foreigner who has not become a citizen of the country where he lives 2 (in films and stories) a creature from another world ♦ *adj* 1 foreign 2 different and strange

a·li·en·ate /'eɪliəneɪt/ *vt* make unfriendly –**ation** /ˌeɪliə'neɪʃən/ *n* [U]

a·light¹ /ə'laɪt/ *vi* alighted *or* alit /ə'lɪt/ *fml* get down; come down: *to alight from a train*

alight² *adj* on fire; burning

a·lign /ə'laɪn/ *vi/t* come or put into a line 2 **align oneself with** come into agreement with: *They aligned themselves with the army.* ~**ment** *n* [C;U]

a·like /ə'laɪk/ *adj, adv* like one another; the same

al·i·men·ta·ry /ˌælə'mentəri◄/ *adj* concerning food and the way it is treated: *the alimentary canal* (=tubelike passage leading from the mouth to the stomach)

al·i·mo·ny /'æləməni ‖ -moʊni/ *n* [U] money that one must pay regularly to a former wife or husband

a·live /ə'laɪv/ *adj* 1 living; in existence: (fig.) *The argument was kept alive by the politicians.* 2 full of life; active 3 **alive to** AWARE of 4 **alive with** covered with (insects, etc.)

al·ka·li /'ælkəlaɪ/ *n* -**lis** *or* -**lies** [C;U] substance that forms a chemical salt when combined with an acid –**line** *adj*

all¹ /ɔːl ‖ ɒːl/ *determiner* the whole of; every one of: *all the bread* ǀ *all these questions* ǀ *He ate it all.*

all² *adv* 1 completely: *It's all dirty.* ǀ *He's all alone.* 2 for each side: *The score was 3 all.* 3 **all along** from the beginning 4 **all at once** suddenly 5 **all in:** a very tired b with everything included: *It cost £2000 all in.* 6 **all out** using all possible strength and effort 7 **all over** everywhere 8 **all right: a** safe or satisfactory **b** I agree; yes 9 **all the** by so much: *If you help, we'll finish all the sooner* 10 **all there** having a good quick mind 11 **all the same** even so; in any case 12 **all the same to** make no difference to: *It's all the same to me what you do.* 13 **all told** all together 14 **all up** at an end; ruined

15 not all that *infml* not very

all³ *pron* **1** everyone or everything: *This is all I have.* | *I brought all of them.* **2 all in all** considering everything **3 (not) at all** (not) in any way: *I don't agree at all.* **4 in all** counting everyone or everything **5 once and for all** for the last time

Al·lah /'ælə/ *n* (the Muslim name for) God

al·lay /ə'leɪ/ *vt fml* make (fear, etc.) less

all clear /,· '·/ *n* [*the*+S] **1** signal that danger is past **2** GO-AHEAD

al·lege /ə'ledʒ/ *vt fml* declare without proof: *an alleged thief* **allegedly** /ə'ledʒɪdli/ *adv* **allegation** /,ælɪ'geɪʃən/ *n fml* unproved statement

al·le·giance /ə'liːdʒəns/ *n* [U] loyalty to a leader, country, etc.

al·le·go·ry /'ælɪɡəri ‖ -ɡɔːri/ *n* [C;U] (style of) story, poem, etc. in which the characters represent ideas and qualities

al·ler·gy /'æləʤi ‖ -ər-/ *n* condition of being made ill by a particular food, drug, etc. –**gic** /ə'lɜːdʒɪk ‖ -ɜːr-/ *adj*

al·le·vi·ate /ə'liːvieɪt/ *vt* make (pain, etc.) less –**ation** /ə,liːvi'eɪʃən/ *n* [U]

al·ley /'æli/ *n* **1** narrow street or path **2** track along which balls are rolled in BOWLING or SKITTLES

al·li·ance /ə'laɪəns/ *n* **1** [C] close agreement or connection made between countries, etc. for a shared purpose **2** [U] act of forming an alliance or state of being in an alliance

al·li·ga·tor /'ælɪɡeɪtə ‖ -ər/ *n* animal like a CROCODILE

al·lo·cate /'æləkeɪt/ *vt* give as a share –**cation** /,ælə'keɪʃən/ *n* [C;U]

al·lot /ə'lɒt ‖ ə'lɑːt/ *vt* **-tt-** allocate

al·lot·ment /ə'lɒtmənt ‖ ə'lɑːt-/ *n* **1** [C;U] allocation **2** [C] (in Britain) small piece of land rented to grow vegetables on

al·low /ə'laʊ/ *vt* let (someone) do something without opposing them; let (something) be done; permit: *They allowed him to come.* **2** provide (esp. money or time) ~**able** *adj* ~**ance** *n* **1** money provided regularly **2 make allowances** take something into consideration

allow for *phr vt* take into consideration: *We must allow for the train being late.*

al·loy /'æloɪ ‖ 'ælɔɪ, ə'lɔɪ/ *n* mixture of metals

all right /,· '·/ *adj, adv* **1** safe, unharmed,

or healthy **2** acceptable **3** I/we agree **4** *infml* beyond doubt **5 That's/It's all right** (used as a reply when someone thanks you or says they are sorry for something they have done)

all-round /'· ·/ *adj* having ability in many things, esp. in various sports ~**er** /,· '·/ *n*

all-singing all-dancing /,· '·· ,· '·/ *adj infml* (of a machine, etc.) having all possible features; DELUXE

al·lude /ə'luːd/ *v* **allude to** *phr vt fml* speak about indirectly **allusion** /ə'luːʒən/ *n* [C;U]

al·lure /ə'ljʊə ‖ ə'lʊr/ *vt* attract or charm by the offer of something pleasant: *an alluring smile*

al·ly /'ælaɪ ‖ 'ælaɪ, ə'laɪ/ *n* person, country, etc. that helps one or agrees to help ♦ /ə'laɪ ‖ ə'laɪ, 'ælaɪ/ *vt* **1** unite by agreement, marriage, etc. **2 allied (to)** related or connected (to)

al·ma ma·ter /,ælmə 'meɪtə, -'mɑː- ‖ -'mɑːtər/ *n* school, college, etc. which one attended

al·ma·nac /'ɔːlmənæk ‖ 'ɒːl-, æl-/ *n* book giving information about the sun, moon, sea, etc.

al·might·y /ɔːl'maɪti ‖ ɒːl-/ *adj* very great

al·mond /'ɑːmənd ‖ 'ɑː-, 'æ-, æl-/ *n* kind of nut

al·most /'ɔːlməʊst ‖ 'ɒːlmoʊst, ɒːl'moʊst/ *adv* very nearly: *almost everyone* | *almost finished*

alms /ɑːmz ‖ ɑːmz, ɑːlmz/ *n* [P] money, food, clothes, etc. given to poor people

a·loft /ə'lɒft ‖ ə'lɔːft/ *adv fml* high up

a·lone /ə'ləʊn ‖ ə'loʊn/ *adv, adj* **1** without others: *He lives alone.* **2** only: *You alone can do it.* **3 leave/let alone: a** leave untouched or unchanged **b** allow to be by oneself

a·long /ə'lɒŋ ‖ ə'lɔːŋ/ *adv* **1** forward; on: *Come along!* **2** with others: *Bring your sister along (with you).* ♦ *prep* **1** from end to end of: *walk along the road* **2** somewhere along the length of

a·long·side /ə,lɒŋ'saɪd ‖ ə,lɔːŋ-/ *adv, prep* close to the side (of)

a·loof /ə'luːf/ *adj, adv* distant in feeling; not friendly ~**ness** *n* [U]

a·loud /ə'laʊd/ *adv* in a voice that can be heard: *to read aloud*

al·pha·bet /'ælfəbet/ *n* letters used in writing ~**ical** /,ælfə'betɪkəl◄/ *adj* in the order of the alphabet

al·pine /'ælpaɪn/ *adj* of or relating to the Alps or other high mountains

al·read·y /ɔːl'redi ‖ ɒːl-/ *adv* 1 by or before an expected time: *Are you leaving already?* 2 before now: *I've seen the film twice already.*

al·right /ɔːl'raɪt ‖ ɒːl-/ *adj, adv* ALL RIGHT

Al·sa·tian /æl'seɪʃən/ *n* large WOLF-like dog

al·so /'ɔːlsəʊ ‖ 'ɒːlsoʊ/ *adv* 1 as well; besides 2 **not only... but also...** both... and ...

also-ran /'·· ·/ *n* person who has failed to win at a sport or in an election

al·tar /'ɔːltə ‖ 'ɒːltər/ *n* table used in a religious ceremony

al·ter /'ɔːltə ‖ 'ɒːltər/ *vi/t* make or become different **~ation** /ˌɔːltəˈreɪʃən ‖ ˌɒːl-/ *n* [C;U]

al·ter·ca·tion /ˌɔːltəˈkeɪʃən ‖ ˌɒːltər-/ *n* [C;U] noisy argument or quarrel

alter ego /ˌæltər 'iːgəʊ, ˌɔːl- ‖ ˌæl tər 'iːgoʊ, ˌɒːl-/ *n* **alter egos** very close and trusted friend

al·ter·nate¹ /ɔːl'tɜːnᵻt ‖ 'ɒːltɜːr-, ˌæl-/ *adj* (of two things) happening by turns; first one and then the other: *He works on alternate days.* **~ly** *adv*

al·ter·nate² /'ɔːltəneɪt ‖ 'ɒːltər-/ *vi/t* happen or follow by turns **~nation** /ˌɔːltəˈneɪʃən ‖ ˌɒːltər-/ *n* [C;U]

al·ter·na·tive /ɔːl'tɜːnətɪv ‖ ɒːl'tɜːr-, æl-/ *adj* 1 to be done or used instead; other 2 different from what is usual or TRADITIONAL: *alternative medicine* 3 not based on or not accepting the established standards of ordinary society: *alternative theatre* ♦ *n* [(to)] something that can be done or used instead **~ly** *adv*

al·though /ɔːl'ðəʊ ‖ ɒːl'ðoʊ/ *conj* though

al·ti·tude /'æltᵻtjuːd ‖ -tuːd/ *n* height above sea level

al·to /'æltəʊ ‖ -toʊ/ *n* **-tos** (person with) a singing voice between SOPRANO and TENOR

al·to·geth·er /ˌɔːltəˈgeðə ‖ ˌɒːltəˈgeðər/ *adv* 1 completely: *altogether different* 2 considering everything together: *Altogether, it was a good trip.*

al·tru·is·m /'æltruː-ɪzəm/ *n* [U] unselfishness **-ist** *n* **-istic** /ˌæltruːˈɪstɪk/ *adj*

al·u·min·i·um /ˌæljuˈmɪniəm, ˌælə-/ *BrE* ‖ **aluminum** /əˈluːmᵻnəm/ *AmE* — *n* [U] light silver-white metal

al·ways /'ɔːlwᵻz, -weɪz ‖ 'ɒːl-/ *adv* 1 at all times: *The sun always rises in the east.* 2 for ever: *I'll always love you.* 3 very often and annoyingly: *He's always complaining.*

am /m, əm; *strong* æm/ *v* 1st person sing. present tense of BE

am, AM /ˌeɪ 'em/ *abbrev. for:* ante meridiem (*Latin*) = before midday (used after numbers expressing time)

a·mal·gam /əˈmælgəm/ *n* mixture or combination

a·mal·gam·ate /əˈmælgəmeɪt/ *vi/t* (of businesses, etc.) unite; combine **-ation** /əˌmælgəˈmeɪʃən/ *n* [C;U]

a·mass /əˈmæs/ *vt* gather or collect in great amounts

am·a·teur /'æmətə, -tʃʊə, -tʃə, ˌæmæˈtɜː ‖ 'æmətʃʊr, -tər/ *n* person who does something for enjoyment and without being paid: *amateur actors* | *amateur sport* **~ish** *adj* lacking skill

a·maze /əˈmeɪz/ *vt* fill with great surprise: *I was amazed to hear the news.* | *an amazing film* **~ment** *n* [U] **amazingly** *adv*

am·a·zon /'æməzən ‖ -zɑːn, -zən/ *n* tall, strong woman

am·bas·sa·dor /æmˈbæsədə ‖ -ər/ *n* minister of high rank representing his/her own country in another country

am·ber /'æmbə ‖ -ər/ *n* [U] (yellow colour of) a hard substance used for jewels

am·bi·dex·trous /ˌæmbɪˈdekstrəs◄/ *adj* able to use both hands equally well

am·bi·ence /'æmbiəns/ *n* feeling of a place; ATMOSPHERE (3)

am·big·u·ous /æmˈbɪgjuəs/ *adj* having more than one meaning; not clear **-uity** /ˌæmbᵻˈgjuːᵻti/ *n* [C;U]

am·bi·tion /æmˈbɪʃən/ *n* 1 [U] strong desire for success 2 [C] whatever is desired in this way: *to achieve one's ambitions* **-tious** *adj* **-tiously** *adv*

am·biv·a·lent /æmˈbɪvələnt/ *adj* having opposing feelings about something **-lence** *n* [U]

am·ble /'æmbəl/ *vi* walk at an easy gentle rate

am·bu·lance /'æmbjᵻləns/ *n* motor vehicle for carrying sick people

am·bush /'æmbʊʃ/ *n* [C;U] surprise attack from a place of hiding **ambush** *vt*

a·me·ba /əˈmiːbə/ *n AmE for* AMOEBA

a·me·li·o·rate /əˈmiːliəreit/ vt fml improve –**ration** /əˌmiːliəˈreiʃən/ n [U]

a·men /ɑːˈmen, eɪ-/ interj (at the end of a prayer) may this be true

a·me·na·ble /əˈmiːnəbəl/ adj willing to be influenced

a·mend /əˈmend/ vt change and improve ~**ment** n [C;U]

a·mends /əˈmendz/ n [P] **make amends** pay for harm or damage done

a·me·ni·ty /əˈmiːnɪti ‖ əˈme-/ n something (e.g. a park or swimming pool) that makes life pleasant

A·mer·i·can foot·ball /əˌmerɪkən ˈfotbɔːl ‖ -bɒːl/ n [U] BrE game played between two teams of 11 players using an OVAL ball that can be handled or kicked

am·e·thyst /ˈæmɪθɪst/ n [C;U] (purple colour of) a stone used in jewellery

a·mi·a·ble /ˈeɪmiəbəl/ adj good tempered; friendly –**bly** adv

am·i·ca·ble /ˈæmɪkəbəl/ adj done in a friendly way: reach an amicable agreement –**bly** adv

a·mid /əˈmɪd/ also **amidst** /əˈmɪdst/ prep fml among

a·miss /əˈmɪs/ adj, adv fml 1 wrong(ly) or imperfect(ly) 2 **take something amiss** be offended

am·i·ty /ˈæmɪti/ n [U] fml friendship

am·mo·ni·a /əˈməʊniə ‖ əˈmoʊ-/ n [U] gas with a strong smell, used in explosives and chemicals

am·mu·ni·tion /ˌæmjʊˈnɪʃən/ n [U] bullets, bombs, etc.

am·ne·si·a /æmˈniːziə ‖ -ʒə/ n [U] loss of memory

am·nes·ty /ˈæmnəsti/ n general act of forgiveness, esp. by a state to people guilty of political offences

a·moe·ba ‖ also **ameba** AmE /əˈmiːbə/ n -bas or -bae /-biː/ living creature that consists of only one cell –**bic** adj

a·mok /əˈmɒk ‖ əˈmɑːk/ also **amuck** — adv run amok run wildly about trying to kill people

a·mong /əˈmʌŋ/ also **amongst** /əˈmʌŋst/ — prep 1 in the middle of: a house among the trees 2 in the group of; one of: He's among the best of our students. | They talked about it among themselves. (=together) 3 to each of (more than 2): Divide it among the five of you.

a·mor·al /eɪˈmɒrəl, æ- ‖ eɪˈmɔː-, -ˈmɑː-/ adj having no understanding of right or wrong

am·o·rous /ˈæmərəs/ adj feeling or expressing love, esp. sexual love ~**ly** adv

a·mor·phous /əˈmɔːfəs ‖ -ɔːr-/ adj having no fixed form or shape

a·mount¹ /əˈmaʊnt/ n quantity; total: large amounts of money

amount² v **amount to** phr vt be equal to

amp /æmp/ also **ampere** /ˈæmpeə ‖ ˈæmpɪr/ — n standard measure of the quantity of electricity

am·phet·a·mine /æmˈfetəmiːn, -mɪn/ n [C;U] drug used, esp. illegally, by people wanting excitement

am·phib·i·an /æmˈfɪbiən/ n animal, such as a FROG, that can live both on land and in water –**bious** adj

am·phi·thea·tre BrE ‖ -**ter** AmE /ˈæmfɪˌθɪətə ‖ -tər/ n open building with rows of seats round a central space

am·ple /ˈæmpəl/ adj enough; plenty amply adv

am·pli·fy /ˈæmplɪfaɪ/ vi/t fml 1 explain in more detail 2 make (esp. sound) stronger –**fier** n instrument for making sound louder –**fication** /ˌæmplɪfɪˈkeɪʃən/ n [U]

am·pu·tate /ˈæmpjʊteɪt/ vi/t cut off (part of the body) for medical reasons –**tation** /ˌæmpjʊˈteɪʃən/ n [C;U]

a·muck /əˈmʌk/ adv AMOK

am·u·let /ˈæmjʊlɪt, -let ‖ ˈæmjʊlət/ n object worn to protect one against evil, bad luck, etc.

a·muse /əˈmjuːz/ vt 1 cause to laugh: an amusing story 2 cause to spend time pleasantly ~**ment** n 1 [U] state of being amused 2 [C] something that passes the time pleasantly **amusement arcade** place where people play games on machines by putting coins in them **amusement park** park with big machines that people ride on

an /ən; strong æn/ indefinite article, determiner (used before a vowel sound) a: an elephant

a·nach·ro·nis·m /əˈnækrənɪzəm/ n person, thing, or custom in the wrong period of time: To say 'Julius Caesar looked at his watch' is an anachronism. –**nistic** /əˌnækrəˈnɪstɪk◂/ adj

an·a·con·da /ˌænəˈkɒndə ‖ -ˈkɑːn-/ n large S American snake

a·nae·mi·a ‖ also **anemia** *AmE* /ə'ni:miə/ *n* [U] lack of enough red blood cells –mic *adj*

an·aes·the·si·a ‖ also **anes-** *AmE* /,ænɪs'θi:ziə ‖ -ʒə/ *n* [U] state of being unable to feel pain, etc.

an·aes·thet·ic ‖ also **anes-** *AmE* /,ænɪs'θetɪk/ *n* [C;U] substance that stops one from feeling pain, either in a part of the body (**a local anaesthetic**) or in the whole body, making one unconscious (**a general anaesthetic**) –**thetist** /ə'ni:sθətɪst ‖ ə'nes-/ *n* –**thetize** *vt*

an·a·gram /'ænəgræm/ *n* word made by changing the order of the letters in another word: *'Silent' is an anagram of 'listen'*

a·nal /'eɪnəl/ *adj* of, concerning the ANUS

an·al·ge·sic /,ænəl'dʒi:zɪk/ *n, adj* (substance) which makes one unable to feel pain

a·nal·o·gy /ə'nælədʒi/ *n* 1 [C] degree of likeness 2 [U] explaining one thing by comparing it with something else –**gous** /-gəs/ *adj* like or alike in some ways

an·a·lyse ‖ also **-lyze** *AmE* /'ænəl-aɪz/ *vt* examine carefully, often by dividing something into parts

a·nal·y·sis /ə'næləsɪs/ *n* 1 [C;U] examination of something; analysing 2 [U] PSYCHOANALYSIS **analyst** /'ænələst/ *n* analytic /,ænə'lɪtɪk◄/ *adj*

an·ar·chy /'ænəki ‖ -ər-/ *n* [U] 1 absence of government 2 social disorder –**chism** *n* [U] –**chist** *n* person who wishes for this –**chic** /æ'nɑːkɪk ‖ -ɑːr-/ *adj*

a·nath·e·ma /ə'næθəmə/ *n* something hated

a·nat·o·my /ə'nætəmi/ *n* 1 [U] scientific study of living bodies 2 [C] way a living thing works: (fig.) *the anatomy of modern society* –**mical** /,ænə'tɒmɪkəl◄ ‖ -'tɑ:-/ *adj*

an·ces·tor /'ænsəstə, -ses- ‖ -ses-/ *n* person from whom one is descended –**tral** /æn'sestrəl/ *adj*

an·ces·try /'ænsəstri, -ses- ‖ -ses-/ *n* [C;U] all one's ancestors

an·chor /'æŋkə ‖ -ər/ *n* 1 piece of heavy metal for lowering into the water to stop a ship from moving 2 something that makes one feel safe ♦ *v* 1 *vi* lower the anchor 2 *vt* fix firmly in position ~**age** *n* place where ships may anchor

an·chor·per·son /'æŋkə,pɜːsən ‖ 'æŋ-

kər,pɜːrsən/ also **-man** /-,mæn/ *masc.* **-woman** /-,wʊmən/ *fem.* — *n esp. AmE* broadcaster usu. on television, in charge of a news broadcast, to connect one part of the broadcast with the next

an·cho·vy /'æntʃəvi ‖ 'æntʃoʊvi/ *n* -vies *or* -vy small strong-tasting fish

an·cient /'eɪnʃənt/ *adj* 1 of times long ago: *ancient Rome* 2 very old

an·cil·la·ry /æn'sɪləri ‖ 'ænsəleri/ *adj* providing additional help

and /ənd, ən; *strong* ænd/ *conj* 1 (joining two things) as well as: *John and Sally* ‖ *We're cold and hungry.* 2 then; therefore: *Water the seeds and they will grow.* 3 (showing that something continues without stopping): *We ran and ran.* 4 (used instead of **to** after **come, go, try**): *Try and open it.*

an·droid /'ændrɔɪd/ *n* (in stories) ROBOT in human form

an·ec·dote /'ænɪkdəʊt ‖ -doʊt/ *n* short interesting story that is true –**dotal** /,ænɪk'dəʊtl◄ ‖ -'doʊtl◄/ *adj* containing or telling anecdotes

a·ne·mi·a /ə'ni:miə/ *n* [U] *AmE for* ANAEMIA

an·es·the·si·a /,ænɪs'θi:ziə ‖ -ʒə/ *n* [U] *AmE for* ANAESTHESIA

a·new /ə'nju: ‖ ə'nu:/ *adv* again

an·gel /'eɪndʒəl/ *n* 1 messenger of God 2 very kind and beautiful person ~**ic** /æn'dʒelɪk/ *adj*

an·ger /'æŋgə ‖ -ər/ *n* [U] fierce displeasure and annoyance ♦ *vt* make angry

an·gle¹ /'æŋgəl/ *n* 1 space between two lines that meet, measured in degrees 2 corner 3 point of view 4 **at an angle** not upright or straight ♦ *vt* 1 turn or move at an angle 2 represent (something) from a particular point of view

angle² *vi* catch fish with a hook and line **angler** *n*

angle for *phr vt* try to get, by tricks or indirect questions: *to angle for an invitation*

An·gli·can /'æŋglɪkən/ *n, adj* (member) of the Church of England

an·gli·cize also **-ise** *BrE* /'æŋglɪsaɪz/ *vt* make English

an·gry /'æŋgri/ *adj* 1 full of anger 2 (of the sky or clouds) stormy **angrily** *adv*

angst /æŋst/ *n* [U] anxiety and anguish

caused esp. by considering the sad state of the world

an·guish /'æŋgwɪʃ/ n [U] great suffering, esp. of the mind ~**ed** adj

an·gu·lar /'æŋgjɵlə‖-ər/ adj 1 having sharp corners 2 (of a person) thin

an·i·mal /'ænɵməl/ n 1 living creature that is not a plant 2 all these except human beings 3 MAMMAL 4 person considered as lacking a mind and behaving like a wild non-human creature ♦ adj 1 of animals 2 of the body

an·i·mate¹ /'ænɵmɵt/ adj alive

an·i·mate² /'ænɵmeɪt/ vt give life or excitement to –**mated** adj cheerful and excited: an animated discussion –**mation** /,ænɵ'meɪʃən/ n [U] 1 cheerful excitement 2 process of making CARTOONS

an·i·mis·m /'ænɵmɪzəm/ n [U] religion according to which animals, plants, etc. are believed to have souls

an·i·mos·i·ty /,ænɵ'mɒsɵti‖-'mɑː-/ n [C;U] powerful hatred

an·kle /'æŋkəl/ n thin part of the leg, above the foot

an·nals /'ænlz/ n [P] history or record of events, etc., produced every year: It will go down in the annals (=history) of modern science.

an·nex /ə'neks‖ə'neks, 'æneks/ vt take control of (land, etc.) ~**ation** /,ænek'seɪʃən/ n [C;U]

an·nexe /'æneks/ n building added to a larger one

an·ni·hi·late /ə'naɪəleɪt/ vt destroy completely –**lation** /ə,naɪə'leɪʃən/ n [U]

an·ni·ver·sa·ry /,ænɵ'vɜːsəri‖-ɜːr-/ n day that is an exact number of years after something happened

an·no·tate /'ænəteɪt/ vt fml add notes to (a book) –**tation** /,ænə'teɪʃən/ n

an·nounce /ə'naʊns/ vt state loudly or publicly: He announced the winner of the competition. ~**ment** n public statement

an·nounc·er /ə'naʊnsə‖-ər/ n person who gives information, introduces people, etc. on radio or television

an·noy /ə'nɔɪ/ vt make a little angry; cause trouble to: an annoying delay ~**ance** n [C;U]

an·nu·al¹ /'ænjuəl/ adj 1 happening once every year 2 for one year; my annual salary ~**ly** adv

an·nual² n 1 plant that lives for one year 2 book produced each year with the same name but new contents

an·nu·i·ty /ə'njuːɵti‖ə'nuː-/ n fixed sum of money paid each year to someone

an·nul /ə'nʌl/ vt -ll- cause (a marriage, etc.) to stop existing ~**ment** n [C;U]

an·ode /'ænəʊd‖'ænoʊd/ n part of an electrical instrument which collects ELECTRONS

an·o·dyne /'ænədaɪn/ adj unlikely to offend or annoy anyone

a·noint /ə'nɔɪnt/ vt put oil on, esp. in a ceremony

a·nom·a·ly /ə'nɒməli‖ə'nɑː-/ n fml something different from the usual type: A cat with no tail is an anomaly. –**lous** adj

a·non¹ /ə'nɒn‖ə'nɑːn/ adv lit soon

anon² abbrev. for ANONYMOUS

a·non·y·mous /ə'nɒnɵməs‖ə'nɑː-/ adj without a name; not giving the name: an anonymous letter –**mity** /,ænə'nɪmɵti/ n [U]

an·o·rak /'ænəræk/ n 1 short coat with a HOOD 2 infml person whose very strong interest in a subject makes him/her seem strange

an·o·rex·i·a /,ænə'reksiə/ n [U] dangerous condition in which there is a loss of desire to eat –**ic** adj

an·oth·er /ə'nʌðə‖-ər/ determiner, pron 1 one more: Have another drink. 2 a different one: I'll do it another time. 3 more; in addition: It'll cost you another $20. 4 **one another** each other

an·swer¹ /'ɑːnsə‖'ænsər/ n 1 what is said or written when someone asks a question or sends a letter; reply 2 something discovered by thinking: I'm getting fat — the answer is to eat less.

answer² v 1 vi/t give an answer (to): She answered with a smile. 2 vi/t attend or act in reply to (the telephone ringing, a knock at the door, etc.): Answer the phone, will you! | The dog answers to the name of Fred. 3 vi/t be as described in: He answers to the description you gave. 4 vt be satisfactory for ~**able** adj 1 able to be answered 2 responsible: The school is answerable to your parents for your safety.

    answer back phr vi/t reply rudely (to)

    answer for phr vt 1 be responsible for 2 pay or suffer for

an·swer·ing ma·chine /'ɑːnsərɪŋ

mə.ˌʃiːn‖/ˈæn-/ also **an·swer·phone** /ˈɑːnsəfəʊn‖ˈænsərfoʊn/ BrE — n machine that records telephone messages

ant /ænt/ n insect living on the ground and famous for hard work

an·tag·o·nize also **-nise** BrE /ænˈtægənaɪz/ vt make into an enemy **-nism** n [U] hatred; opposition **-nist** n opponent

Ant·arc·tic /ænˈtɑːktɪk‖-ɑːr-/ adj, n (of or concerning) the very cold most southern part of the world

an·te·ced·ents /ˌæntɪˈsiːdənts/ n [P] fml past family or past history

an·te·cham·ber /ˈæntɪˌtʃeɪmbə‖-ər/ also **anteroom** — n small room leading to a larger one

an·te·di·lu·vian /ˌæntɪdɪˈluːviən/ adj very old-fashioned

an·te·lope /ˈæntɪləʊp‖ˈæntəloʊp/ n **-lopes** or **-lope** graceful animal like a deer

an·te·na·tal /ˌæntɪˈneɪtl◀/ adj existing or happening before birth: an antenatal clinic

an·ten·na /ænˈtenə/ n 1 (pl. **-nae** /-niː/), insect's FEELER 2 AERIAL¹

an·them /ˈænθəm/ n religious song of praise

an·thol·o·gy /ænˈθɒlədʒi‖ænˈθɑː-/ n collection of poems or other writings

an·thro·poid /ˈænθrəpɔɪd/ adj like a person

an·thro·pol·o·gy /ˌænθrəˈpɒlədʒi‖-ˈpɑː-/ n scientific study of the human race **-gist** n

an·thro·po·mor·phic /ˌænθrəpəˈmɔːfɪk‖-ɔːr-/ adj regarding a god, animal, etc, as having human qualities

an·ti·bi·ot·ic /ˌæntɪbaɪˈɒtɪk◀‖-ˈɑː-/ n medical substance, such as PENICILLIN, that can kill harmful bacteria in the body

an·ti·bod·y /ˈæntɪˌbɒdi‖-ˌbɑː-/ n substance produced in the body which fights disease

an·tic·i·pate /ænˈtɪsəpeɪt/ vt 1 expect: We anticipate trouble. 2 do something before (someone else) 3 guess (what will happen) and act as necessary **-pation** /ænˌtɪsˈpeɪʃən/ n [U]

an·ti·cli·max /ˌæntɪˈklaɪmæks/ n unexciting end to something exciting

an·ti·clock·wise /ˌæntɪˈklɒkwaɪz‖-ˈklɑːk-/ adv in the opposite direction to the movement of a clock

an·tics /ˈæntɪks/ n [P] strange, amusing movements or behaviour

an·ti·cy·clone /ˌæntɪˈsaɪkləʊn‖-kloʊn/ n area of high air pressure, causing settled weather

an·ti·dote /ˈæntɪdəʊt‖-doʊt/ n something that prevents the effects of a poison or disease

an·ti·freeze /ˈæntɪfriːz/ n [U] chemical put in water to stop it freezing, esp. in car engines

an·tip·a·thy /ænˈtɪpəθi/ n [C;U] fixed strong dislike; hatred

an·ti·quat·ed /ˈæntɪkweɪtɪd/ adj old-fashioned

an·tique /ænˈtiːk/ adj old and therefore valuable ♦ n valuable old object

an·tiq·ui·ty /ænˈtɪkwəti/ n 1 [U] great age 2 [U] ancient times 3 [C] something remaining from ancient times

an·ti·Sem·i·tis·m /ˌæntɪ ˈsemətɪzəm/ n hatred of Jews **-Semitic** /-sɪˈmɪtɪk/ adj

an·ti·sep·tic /ˌæntɪˈseptɪk◀/ n, adj (chemical substance) preventing disease by killing bacteria

an·ti·so·cial /ˌæntɪˈsəʊʃəl◀‖-ˈsoʊ-/ adj 1 harmful to society 2 not liking to mix with people

an·tith·e·sis /ænˈtɪθəsɪs/ n **-ses** /-siːz/ fml direct opposite

ant·ler /ˈæntlə‖-ər/ n horn of a deer

an·to·nym /ˈæntənɪm/ n word opposite in meaning to another word

a·nus /ˈeɪnəs/ n hole through which solid waste leaves the bowels

an·vil /ˈænvɪl/ n iron block on which metals are hammered to the shape wanted

anx·i·e·ty /æŋˈzaɪəti/ n 1 [C;U] fear and worry 2 [U] strong wish: anxiety to please him

anx·ious /ˈæŋkʃəs/ adj 1 worried and frightened 2 causing worry 3 wishing strongly: anxious to please them **-ly** adv

an·y /ˈeni/ determiner, pron 1 no matter which: Take any you like. 2 some; even the smallest number or amount: Are there any letters for me? 3 **in any case** also **at any rate** — **a** whatever may happen **b** besides ♦ adv at all: I can't stay any longer.

an·y·bod·y /ˈeniˌbɒdi, ˈenibədi‖-ˌbɑː-/ pron anyone

an·y·how /ˈenihaʊ/ adv 1 carelessly 2 in spite of everything

an·y·one /ˈeniwʌn/ pron 1 all people; no matter who: Anyone can cook. 2 even one person: *Is anyone listening?*

an·y·place /'eniplers/ *adv AmE for*
ANYWHERE

an·y·thing /'eniθɪŋ/ *pron* 1 any object,
act, event, etc.; no matter what: *He'll do
anything for a quiet life.* 2 even one thing:
Can you see anything? 3 **anything but** not
at all 4 **anything like** at all like 5 **as easy
as anything** very easy

an·y·way /'eniweɪ/ *adv* in spite of
everything; anyhow

an·y·where /'eniweə‖-wer/ *adv* 1 at or
to any place 2 **anywhere near** at all near
or nearly

a·or·ta /eɪ'ɔːtə‖-'ɔːr-/ *n* largest ARTERY in
the body

a·pace /ə'peɪs/ *adv* quickly

a·part /ə'pɑːt‖ə'pɑːrt/ *adv* 1 distant;
separated: *villages three miles apart* 2 into
parts: *to take a clock apart* 3 **apart from**: a
except for **b** as well as 4 **tell/know apart**
be able to see the difference between

a·part·heid /ə'pɑːtheɪt, -teɪt, -taɪt,
-taɪd‖-ɑːr-/ *n* [U] (in South Africa) the
system formerly established by government
of keeping different races separate

a·part·ment /ə'pɑːtmənt‖-ɑːr-/ *n* 1 room
2 *AmE for* FLAT[1] (5)

ap·a·thy /'æpəθi/ *n* [U] lack of interest in
things **–thetic** /ˌæpə'θetɪk◂/ *adj*

ape /eɪp/ *n* large monkey with no tail ♦ *vt*
copy (behaviour) stupidly

a·per·i·tif /ə,perɪ'tiːf/ *n* alcoholic drink
before a meal

ap·er·ture /'æpətʃə‖'æpərtʃʊr/ *n* hole;
opening

a·pex /'eɪpeks/ *n* -es *or* apices /'eɪpɪsiːz/
highest point: *the apex of a triangle*

aph·o·rism /'æfərɪzəm/ *n* short wise
saying

aph·ro·dis·i·ac /ˌæfrə'dɪziæk/ *n, adj*
(drug, etc.) causing sexual excitement

a·piece /ə'piːs/ *adv* each: *They cost 10p
apiece.*

a·plomb /ə'plɒm‖ə'plɑːm/ *n* [U] calm
self-control

a·poc·a·lypse /ə'pɒkəlɪps‖ə'pɑː-/ *n* [U]
(writing about) the end of the world **–lyptic**
/ə,pɒkə'lɪptɪk◂‖ ə,pɑː-/ *adj* telling of great
future misfortunes

a·poc·ry·phal /ə'pɒkrəfəl‖ə'pɑː-/ *adj*
(of a story) probably untrue

a·pol·o·get·ic /ə,pɒlə'dʒetɪk◂‖ə,pɑː-/

adj making an apology **~ally** /-kli/ *adv*

a·pol·o·gist /ə'pɒlədʒɪst‖ə'pɑː-/ *n*
person who strongly supports a particular
belief and can give arguments in defence of it

a·pol·o·gize also **-ise** *BrE* /ə'pɒlədʒaɪz‖
ə'pɑː-/ *vi* say one is sorry for a fault **–gy** *n*
1 statement of sorrow for a fault, for
causing trouble, etc. 2 **an apology for** a
very poor example of (something)

ap·o·plex·y /'æpəpleksi/ *n* [U] sudden
loss of ability to move, feel, think etc.;
STROKE[1] (5) **–plectic** /ˌæpə'plektɪk◂/ *adj*
1 of or concerning apoplexy 2 violently
excited and angry

a·pos·tle /ə'pɒsəl‖ə'pɑː-/ *n* 1 one of the
12 first followers of Christ 2 leader of a new
faith

a·pos·tro·phe /ə'pɒstrəfi‖ə'pɑː-/ *n* the
sign ('), as in *I'm*

a·poth·e·o·sis /ə,pɒθi'əʊsɪs‖ə,pɑːθi'oʊ-,
ˌæpə'θiːəsɪs/ *n* **-ses** /-siːz/ 1 highest
possible honour and glory 2 perfect
example

ap·pal *BrE‖* **appall** *AmE* /ə'pɔːl‖ə'pɔːl/
vt **-ll-** shock deeply: *We were appalled to
hear the news.* **~ling** *BrE‖* **~ing** *AmE adj*
1 shocking 2 of very bad quality **~lingly**
adv: *an appallingly bad driver*

ap·pa·ra·tus /ˌæpə'reɪtəs‖ -'ræ-/ *n* [C;U]
set of instruments, tools, etc. needed for a
purpose

ap·par·el /ə'pærəl/ *n* [U] *fml* clothes

ap·par·ent /ə'pærənt/ *adj* 1 easily seen:
The reason became apparent. 2 not
necessarily real; seeming: *her apparent lack
of concern* **~ly** *adv* it seems that

ap·pa·ri·tion /ˌæpə'rɪʃən/ *n* GHOST

ap·peal /ə'piːl/ *n* 1 [C;U] strong request
for something: *an appeal for forgiveness*
2 [U] attraction; interest: *He hasn't much
sex appeal.* 3 [C;U] formal request (in law,
sport) for a new decision ♦ *vi* 1 make a
strong request: *to appeal for money* 2 please;
attract: *Does the job appeal to you?* 3 ask for
a new decision **~ing** *adj* attractive

ap·pear /ə'pɪə‖ə'pɪr/ *vi* 1 come into
sight: *Spots appeared on my skin.* | *They
finally appeared* (=arrived) *at 9.00.* 2 come
in view of the public: *Her new book appears
next month.* | *He's appearing* (=performing)
at the Theatre Royal. 4 seem: *He appears to
be angry.* 5 be present officially, as in a
court of law **~ance** *n* [C;U] 1 (an example

of) the act of appearing **2** way a person or thing looks: *He changed his appearance by growing a beard.* **3** **put in/make an appearance (at)** attend (a meeting, party, etc.), esp. for a short time only

ap·pease /ə'piːz/ *vt* satisfy, esp. by agreeing to demands ~**ment** *n* [C;U]

ap·pend /ə'pend/ *vt fml* add (esp. something written onto the end of a letter) ~**age** *n* something added to, or hanging from, something else

ap·pen·di·ci·tis /ə,pendɪ'saɪtɪs/ *n* [U] disease of the appendix

ap·pen·dix /ə'pendɪks/ *n* -dixes *or* -dices /-dɪsiːz/ **1** small organ leading off the bowel **2** something added at the end of a book

ap·per·tain /,æpə'teɪn ‖ -ər-/ *v* **appertain to** *phr vt fml* belong to

ap·pe·tite /'æpɪtaɪt/ *n* [C;U] desire, esp. for food

ap·pe·tiz·er *also* **-iser** *BrE* /'æpɪtaɪzə ‖ -ər/ *n* something eaten to increase the appetite **-tizing** *adj* causing appetite: *appetizing smells*

ap·plaud /ə'plɔːd ‖ ə'plɒːd/ *vi/t* **1** praise by striking one's hands together; CLAP **2** approve strongly **applause** /ə'plɔːz ‖ ə'plɒːz/ *n* [U] loud praise

ap·ple /'æpəl/ *n* kind of hard round juicy fruit —see also ADAM'S APPLE

ap·pli·ance /ə'plaɪəns/ *n* apparatus; machine

ap·plic·a·ble /ə'plɪkəbəl, 'æplɪkəbəl/ *adj* having an effect; related: *The rule is applicable only to UK citizens.*

ap·pli·cant /'æplɪkənt/ *n* person who applies for a job, etc.

ap·pli·ca·tion /,æplɪ'keɪʃən/ *n* **1** [C;U] request: *to write applications for jobs* **2** [U] act of putting something to use **3** [C] particular practical use: *the industrial applications of this discovery* **4** [C] putting something on a surface **5** [U] careful effort

ap·ply /ə'plaɪ/ *v* **1** *vt* request officially: *apply for a job* **2** *vt* use for a purpose: *apply the brakes* **3** *vt* put onto a surface: *apply ointment to your skin* **4** *vi/t* give or have an effect: *Does the rule apply to me?* **5** *vt* cause to work hard: *apply oneself to the task* **applied** *adj* practical: *applied physics*

ap·point /ə'pɔɪnt/ *vt* **1** choose for a job

2 *fml* fix; decide: *the appointed time* ~**ment** *n* **1** [C;U] arrangement for a meeting **2** [C] job: *a teaching appointment*

ap·por·tion /ə'pɔːʃən ‖ -ɔːr-/ *vt* divide and share out

ap·po·site /'æpəzɪt/ *adj fml* exactly suitable

ap·praise /ə'preɪz/ *vt fml* judge the value of **appraisal** *n*

ap·pre·cia·ble /ə'priːʃəbəl/ *adj* noticeable: *an appreciable difference* **-bly** *adv*

ap·pre·ci·ate /ə'priːʃieɪt/ *v* **1** *vt* be thankful for **2** *vt* understand and enjoy the good qualities of: *She appreciates good wine.* **3** *vt* understand fully: *I appreciate your difficulties.* **4** *vi* (of property) increase in value **-ciative** /-ʃətɪv/ *adj*: *an appreciative audience* **-ciation** /ə,priːʃi'eɪʃən/ *n* [C;U]

ap·pre·hend /,æprɪ'hend/ *vt fml* ARREST

ap·pre·hen·sion /,æprɪ'henʃən/ *n* [U] anxiety; fear **-sive** /-sɪv/ *adj* worried

ap·pren·tice /ə'prentɪs/ *n* person learning a skilled trade ♦ *vt* send as an apprentice: *apprenticed to an electrician* ~**ship** *n* [C;U]

ap·proach[1] /ə'prəʊtʃ ‖ ə'proʊtʃ/ *v* **1** *vi/t* come near **2** *vt* make an offer or request to: *approach him about borrowing the money* **3** *vt* begin to consider or deal with

approach[2] *n* **1** act of approaching: *the approach of winter* **2** way of getting in **3** method of doing something **4** speaking to someone for the first time ~**able** *adj* easy to speak to or deal with

ap·pro·pri·ate[1] /ə'prəʊpri-ɪt ‖ ə'proʊ-/ *adj* correct; suitable **-ly** *adv*

ap·pro·pri·ate[2] /ə'prəʊprieɪt ‖ ə'proʊ-/ *vt* **1** set aside for a purpose **2** take for oneself **-ation** /ə,prəʊpri'eɪʃən ‖ ə,proʊ-/ *n* [C;U]

ap·prov·al /ə'pruːvəl/ *n* [U] **1** favourable opinion **2** official permission **3** **on approval** (of goods from a shop) to be returned without payment if unsatisfactory

ap·prove /ə'pruːv/ *v* **1** *vi* **((of))** have a favourable opinion: *I don't approve of smoking.* **2** *vt* agree officially to **approvingly** *adv*

ap·prox·i·mate /ə'prɒksɪmɪt ‖ ə'prɒː-/ *adj* nearly correct but not exact **-ly** *adv*: *approximately 300* ♦ /-meɪt/ *vi* come near **-mation** /ə,prɒksɪ'meɪʃən ‖ ə,prɒː-/ *n*

[C;U]

a·pri·cot /'eɪprɪkɒt ‖ 'æprɪkɑːt/ n 1 [C] round orange or yellow fruit with a stone 2 [U] colour of this fruit

A·pril /'eɪprəl/ n 1 the 4th month of the year 2 **April fool** /,·· '·/ n (person who has been deceived or made fun of by) a trick played on the morning of April 1st

a·pron /'eɪprən/ n garment worn to protect the front of one's clothes

apt /æpt/ adj 1 likely: apt to slip 2 exactly suitable: an apt remark 3 quick to learn ~**ly** adv ~**ness** n [U]

ap·ti·tude /'æptɪtjuːd ‖ -tuːd/ n [C;U] natural ability

aq·ua·lung /'ækwəlʌŋ/ n apparatus for breathing under water

aq·ua·ma·rine /,ækwəmə'riːn◄/ n 1 [C] glass-like stone used for jewellery 2 [U] its blue-green colour

a·quar·i·um /ə'kweəriəm ‖ ə'kwer-/ n -iums or -ia /-iə/ glass container for live fish

a·quat·ic /ə'kwætɪk, ə'kwɒ- ‖ ə'kwæ-, ə'kwɑː/ adj living or happening in water

aq·ue·duct /'ækwɪdʌkt/ n bridge that carries water across a valley

Ar·a·bic /'ærəbɪk/ n main language of North Africa and the Middle East ♦ adj: The signs 1, 2, 3, etc. are Arabic numerals.

ar·a·ble /'ærəbəl/ adj (of land) used for growing crops

ar·bi·ter /'ɑːbɪtə ‖ 'ɑːrbɪtər/ n someone who is in a position to make influential judgments or to settle an argument

ar·bi·trage /'ɑːbɪtrɑːʒ ‖ 'ɑːr-/ n [U] process of buying something (esp. a CURRENCY or COMMODITY) in one place and selling it at another place at the same time in order to profit from differences in price between the two places

ar·bi·tra·ry /'ɑːbɪtrəri ‖ 'ɑːrbɪtreri/ adj 1 based on chance rather than reason 2 typical of uncontrolled power –**rily** adv –**riness** n [U]

ar·bi·trate /'ɑːbɪtreɪt ‖ 'ɑːr-/ vi/t act as judge in an argument –**trator** n –**tration** /,ɑːbɪ'treɪʃən ‖ ,ɑːr-/ n [U] settlement of an argument by the decision of a person or group chosen by both sides: go to arbitration

arc /ɑːk ‖ ɑːrk/ n part of the curve of a circle

ar·cade /ɑː'keɪd ‖ ɑːr-/ n covered passage with shops

ar·cane /ɑː'keɪn ‖ ɑːr-/ adj mysterious and secret

arch /ɑːtʃ ‖ ɑːrtʃ/ n curved part over a doorway or under a bridge ♦ vi/t make an arch: The cat arched her back.

ar·chae·ol·o·gy /,ɑːki'ɒlədʒi ‖ ,ɑːrki'ɑː-/ n [U] study of ancient remains –**gist** n –**gical** /,ɑːkiə'lɒdʒɪk əl ‖ ,ɑːrkiə'lɑː-/ adj

ar·cha·ic /ɑː'keɪ-ɪk ‖ ɑːr-/ adj no longer used; old

arch·bish·op /,ɑːtʃ'bɪʃəp◄ ‖ ,ɑːrtʃ-/ n chief BISHOP

ar·cher /'ɑːtʃə ‖ 'ɑːrtʃər/ n person who shoots with a BOW² (1) ~**y** n [U]

ar·che·type /'ɑːkɪtaɪp ‖ 'ɑːr-/ n 1 original of which others are copies 2 perfect example –**typal** /,ɑːkɪ'taɪpəl◄ ‖ ,ɑːr-/, -**typical** /,ɑːkɪ'tɪpɪkəl◄ ‖ ,ɑːr-/ adj

ar·chi·pel·a·go /,ɑːkɪ'peləgəʊ ‖ ,ɑːrkɪ'peləgoʊ/ n area with many small islands

ar·chi·tect /'ɑːkɪtekt ‖ 'ɑːr-/ n person who plans buildings ~**ure** /-,tektʃə ‖ -ər/ n [U] art of building; way of building

ar·chives /'ɑːkaɪvz ‖ 'ɑːr-/ n [P] 1 historical records 2 place where these are kept

Arc·tic /'ɑːktɪk ‖ 'ɑːr-/ n, adj 1 (cap.) (of or concerning) the very cold most northern part of the world 2 very cold

ar·dent /'ɑːdənt ‖ 'ɑːr-/ adj very eager ~**ly** adv

ar·dour BrE ‖ **ardor** AmE /'ɑːdə ‖ 'ɑːrdər/ n [C;U] fml strong excitement

ar·du·ous /'ɑːdjuəs ‖ 'ɑːrdʒuəs/ adj fml needing effort; difficult ~**ly** adv

are /ə; strong ɑː ‖ ər; strong ɑːr/ v present tense pl. of BE

ar·e·a /'eəriə ‖ 'eriə/ n 1 [C;U] size of a surface 2 [C] part of the world's surface: a parking area behind the cinema 3 [C] subject of activity: the area of language teaching

a·re·na /ə'riːnə/ n 1 enclosed space used for sports 2 place of competition: the political arena

aren't /ɑːnt ‖ 'ɑːrənt/ v short for: 1 are not 2 (in questions) am not

ar·got /'ɑːgəʊ ‖ 'ɑːrgɑt/ n [C;U] speech spoken and understood by only a small group of people

ar·gue /'ɑːgjuː‖'ɑːr-/ v 1 vi express disagreement; quarrel 2 vi/t give reasons for or against something **arguable** adj perhaps true, but not certain **arguably** adv: Arguably, the criminal is a necessary member of society

ar·gu·ment /'ɑːgjꭚmənt‖'ɑːr-/ n 1 [C] quarrel 2 [C;U] reason given for or against; use of reason ~**ative** /,ɑːgjꭚ'mentətɪv◀‖ ,ɑːr-/ adj quarrelsome

ar·id /'ærɪd/ adj 1 (of land) very dry 2 uninteresting; dull

a·rise /ə'raɪz/ vi arose /ə'rəuz‖ə'rouz/, arisen /ə'rɪzən/ happen; appear

ar·is·toc·ra·cy /,ærə'stɒkrəsi‖-'stɑː-/ n highest social class –**rat** /'ærꭢstəkræt, ə'rɪ-‖ə'rɪ-/ n member of this class –**ratic** /,ærꭢstə'krætɪk◀, ə,rɪ-‖ə,rɪ-/ adj

a·rith·me·tic /ə'rɪθmətɪk/ n calculation by numbers ~**al** /,ærɪθ'metɪkəl◀/ adj

ark /ɑːk‖ɑːrk/ n (in the Bible) large ship, used by Noah in the flood **out of the ark** extremely old

arm[1] /ɑːm‖ɑːrm/ n 1 upper limb 2 something shaped like this: the arm of a chair 3 part of a garment that covers the arm 4 part or division of the armed forces 5 **arm in arm** (of two people) with arms joined 6 **keep someone at arm's length** avoid being friendly with someone 7 **with open arms** gladly and eagerly —see also ARMS

arm[2] vi/t supply with weapons: the armed forces

ar·ma·da /ɑː'mɑːdə‖ɑːr-/ n collection of armed ships

Ar·ma·ged·don /,ɑːmə'gedn‖,ɑːr-/ n (esp. in the Bible) great battle or war causing terrible destruction and bringing the end of the world

ar·ma·ment /'ɑːməmənt‖'ɑːr-/ n 1 **armaments** [P] weapons and military equipment 2 [U] act of preparing for war

arm·chair /'ɑːmtʃeə, ,ɑːm'tʃeə‖ 'ɑːrmtʃer, ,ɑːrm'tʃer/ n chair with supports for the arms ♦ adj ready to give advice or pass judgment, but not taking an active part

ar·mi·stice /'ɑːmꭢstꭢs‖'ɑːrm-/ n agreement to stop fighting for a time

ar·mour BrE‖ armor AmE /'ɑːmə‖ 'ɑːrmər/ n [U] 1 protective covering for the body in battle 2 protective metal covering

on military vehicles: an **armoured car** ~**y** n place where weapons are stored

arm·pit /'ɑːm,pɪt‖'ɑːrm-/ n hollow place under one's arm

arms /ɑːmz‖ɑːrmz/ n [P] 1 weapons 2 **lay down one's arms** stop fighting and yield 3 **take up arms** get ready to fight with weapons 4 **up in arms** very angry and ready to argue: They're up in arms over/about the low pay. —see also SMALL ARMS

ar·my /'ɑːmi‖'ɑːr-/ n 1 military forces that fight on land 2 large group: an army of ants

a·ro·ma /ə'rəumə‖ə'roumə/ n pleasant smell ~**tic** /,ærə'mætɪk◀/ adj

a·ro·ma·ther·a·py /ə,rəumə'θerəpi‖ ə,rou-/ n [U] use of pleasant smelling plant oils to make one feel healthy and relaxed –**pist** n

a·rose /ə'rəuz‖ə'rouz/ past t. of ARISE

a·round /ə'raund/ adv, prep 1 **a** in various places; round: I'll show you around (the house). **b** somewhere near: Is there anyone around? 2 a little more or less than; about: around 10 o'clock 3 **a** moving in a circle; measured in a circle: turn around and around | 3 metres around **b** on all sides: The children gathered around.

a·rouse /ə'rauz/ vt 1 fml cause to wake 2 make active; excite: arouse suspicion

ar·range /ə'reɪndʒ/ v 1 vt put in order: arrange flowers 2 vi/t plan: arrange to meet her 3 vt set out (music) for different instruments, etc. ~**ment** n 1 [C;U] (act of making) an agreement or plan: make arrangements for the wedding | I have an arrangement with the bank. 2 [C] something that has been put in order: a beautiful flower arrangement 3 [C] (example of) the setting out of a piece of music in a certain way

ar·ray /ə'reɪ/ n fine show, collection, or ordered group

ar·rears /ə'rɪəz‖ə'rɪrz/ n [P] 1 money owed from the past: He was two weeks in arrears with the rent. (=he owed rent for two weeks) 2 work waiting to be done

ar·rest /ə'rest/ vt 1 seize by the power of the law 2 stop (a process) 3 attract (attention) ♦ n [C;U] act of arresting

ar·riv·al /ə'raɪvəl/ n 1 [U] act of arriving 2 [C] person or thing that has arrived: to *welcome the new arrivals*

ar·rive /ə'raɪv/ *vi* 1 reach a place: *arrive home* 2 happen; come: *The day arrived.* 3 win success

arrive at *phr vt* reach; come to: *arrive at a decision*

ar·ro·gant /'ærəgənt/ *adj* proud in a rude way –**ly** *adv* –**gance** *n* [U]

ar·row /'ærəʊ ‖ 'ærəʊ/ *n* 1 pointed stick to be shot from a BOW² (1) 2 sign (→) used to show direction

arse¹ /ɑːs ‖ ɑːrs/ *n BrE taboo sl* 1 also **ass** *AmE* — BOTTOM (2) 2 also **arsehole** ‖ **asshole** *AmE* /'ɑːshəʊl, ‖ 'ɑːrshoʊl/ — a the ANUS b stupid annoying person

arse² *v* **arse about/around** *phr vi BrE taboo sl* waste time

ar·se·nal /'ɑːsənəl ‖ 'ɑːr-/ *n* place where weapons are stored

ar·se·nic /'ɑːsənɪk ‖ 'ɑːr-/ *n* [U] very poisonous substance

ar·son /'ɑːsən ‖ 'ɑːr-/ *n* [U] crime of setting fire to property –**ist** *n*

art /ɑːt ‖ ɑːrt/ *n* 1 [U] the making or expression of what is beautiful, e.g. in music, literature, or esp. painting 2 [U] things produced by art, esp. paintings: *an art gallery* 3 [C;U] skill in doing anything: *the art of conversation* **arts** *n* [P] subjects of study that are not part of science —see also FINE ARTS

ar·te·fact /'ɑːtɪfækt ‖ 'ɑːr-/ *n* ARTIFACT

ar·te·ry /'ɑːtəri ‖ 'ɑːr-/ *n* 1 tube that carries blood from the heart 2 main road, railway, etc.

art·ful /'ɑːtfəl ‖ 'ɑːrt-/ *adj* 1 cleverly deceitful 2 skilfully put together –**ly** *adv*

ar·thri·tis /ɑː'θraɪtɨs ‖ ɑːr-/ *n* [U] painful disease of the joints –**tic** /ɑː'θrɪtɪk ‖ ɑːr-/ *adj*

ar·ti·choke /'ɑːtɨtʃəʊk ‖ 'ɑːrtɨtʃoʊk/ *n* [C;U] 1 also **globe artichoke** — plant whose leafy flower is eaten 2 also **Jerusalem artichoke** — plant whose potato-like root is eaten

ar·ti·cle /'ɑːtɪkəl ‖ 'ɑːr-/ *n* 1 thing; object: *an article of clothing* 2 piece of writing in a newspaper 3 complete or separate part in a written law agreement 4 word used with nouns, such as *a*, *an*, and *the* in English

ar·tic·u·late¹ /ɑː'tɪkjɨlɨt ‖ ɑːr-/ *adj* 1 (of people) able to express thoughts and feelings clearly in words 2 (of speech) having clear separate sounds and words –**ly** *adv*

ar·tic·u·late² /ɑː'tɪkjɨleɪt ‖ ɑːr-/ *v* 1 *vi/t* speak or say clearly 2 *vt* unite by joints: *an articulated lorry* –**lation** /ɑː,tɪkjɨ'leɪʃən ‖ ɑːr-/ *n* [U]

ar·ti·fact, arte- /'ɑːtɨfækt ‖ 'ɑːr-/ *n* something made by people

ar·ti·fice /'ɑːtɨfɨs ‖ 'ɑːr-/ *n* 1 [C] clever trick 2 [U] CUNNING

ar·ti·fi·cial /,ɑːtɨ'fɪʃəl◀ ‖ ,ɑːr-/ *adj* 1 made by people; not natural 2 not sincere –**ly** *adv* –**ity** /,ɑːtɨfɪʃi'ælɨti ‖ ,ɑːr-/ *n* [C;U]

artificial in·tel·li·gence /,···· ·'·· / *n* [U] branch of computer science which aims to produce machines that can understand, make judgments, etc., in the way humans do

artificial res·pi·ra·tion /,···· ··'··/ *n* [U] making someone breathe again by pressing the chest, blowing into the mouth, etc.

ar·til·le·ry /ɑː'tɪləri ‖ ɑːr-/ *n* [U] (part of the army that uses) large guns

ar·ti·san /,ɑːtɨ'zæn ‖ 'ɑːrtɨzən/ *n* CRAFTS-MAN

art·ist /'ɑːtɨst ‖ 'ɑːr-/ *n* 1 person who works in one of the arts, esp. painting 2 inventive and skilled worker 3 also **artiste** /ɑː'tiːst ‖ ɑːr-/ — professional singer, dancer, etc. who performs in a show –**ry** *n* [U] inventive imagination and ability –**ic** /ɑː'tɪstɪk ‖ ɑːr-/ *adj* 1 of art or artists 2 showing skill in art –**ically** /-kli/ *adv*

art·less /'ɑːtləs ‖ 'ɑːrt-/ *adj* simple and natural; almost foolish –**ly** *adv*

as¹ /əz; *strong* æz/ *adv, prep* 1 (used in comparisons and examples) equally; like: *He's as old as me.* | *small animals such as cats and dogs* | *She escaped dressed as a man.* 2 when considered as being: *As a writer, she's wonderful.*

as² *conj* 1 (used in comparisons): *He's as old as I am.* 2 in the way that: *Do as I say!* | *Leave it as it is.* 3 because: *As I have no car, I can't go.* 4 when; while: *He saw her as she was getting off the bus.* 5 though: *Tired as I was, I tried to help.* 6 **as for** when we speak of; concerning 7 **as if/though** in a way that seems 8 **as it is** in reality 9 **as it were** as one might say 10 **as of/from** starting from (a time) 11 **as yet** *fml* up until now

asap /,eɪ es eɪ 'piː, 'eɪsæp/ *abbrev. for:* as soon as possible

as·bes·tos /æs'bestəs, æz-/ n [U] soft grey material that protects against fire or heat

as·cend /ə'send/ vi/t fml 1 go up 2 **ascend the throne** become king or queen ~**ancy**, ~**ency** n [U] controlling influence; power ~**ant**, ~**ent** n **in the ascendant** having or nearly having a controlling power or influence

as·cent /ə'sent/ n 1 [C;U] act or process of 2 [C] ascending; way up

as·cer·tain /ˌæsə'teɪn ‖ ˌæsər-/ vt fml discover; make certain ~**able** adj

as·cet·ic /ə'setɪk/ n, adj (a person) avoiding physical pleasures and comforts, esp. for religious reasons ~**ism**/ə'setə'sɪzəm/ n [U]

as·cribe /ə'skraɪb/ v **ascribe to** phr vt believe to be the work of: He ascribes his success to luck.

a·sep·tic /eɪ'septɪk, ə-/ adj without bacteria; clean

a·sex·u·al /eɪ'sekʃuəl/ adj 1 without sex 2 not interested in sex

ash /æʃ/ n [U] also **ashes** pl. — powder left when something has been burnt ~**en** adj pale grey **ashes** [P] remains of a dead body after burning

a·shamed /ə'ʃeɪmd/ adj feeling shame

a·shore /ə'ʃɔː ‖ ə'ʃɔːr/ adv on or to the shore

ash·tray /'æʃtreɪ/ n dish for tobacco ash

a·side /ə'saɪd/ adv to the side: She stepped aside to let them pass. ♦ n remark not intended to be heard by everyone present

ask /ɑːsk ‖ æsk/ v 1 vi/t say a question: 'Where is it?' she asked. | Ask him where to go. 2 vi/t make a request for: She asked him to wake her at 6.00. 3 vt invite: Ask them to tea. 4 **ask for trouble/it** behave so as to cause (something bad): If you park there, you're really asking for trouble!

ask after phr vt ask for news of

a·skance /ə'skæns, ə'skɑːns ‖ ə'skæns/ adv **look askance** without liking or pleasure

a·skew /ə'skjuː/ adv not properly straight

a·sleep /ə'sliːp/ adj 1 sleeping 2 (of an arm or leg) unable to feel

asp /æsp/ n small poisonous snake

as·par·a·gus /ə'spærəgəs/ n [U] plant whose stems are eaten as a vegetable

as·pect /'æspekt/ n 1 particular side of a plan, problem, etc. 2 direction in which a room, building, etc. faces

as·per·sion /ə'spɜːʃən, -ʒən ‖ -ɜːr-/ n fml unkind or harmful remark: They cast aspersions on my new book.

as·phalt /'æsfælt ‖ 'æsfɔːlt/ n [U] black material used for road surfaces

as·phyx·i·ate /əs'fɪksieɪt, ə-/ vt kill by lack of air **-ation** /æs,fɪksi'eɪʃən, əs-/ n [U]

as·pire /ə'spaɪə ‖ ə'spaɪr/ vi direct one's hopes and efforts **aspiration** /ˌæspə'reɪʃən/ n [C;U] strong desire

as·pi·rin /'æsprən/ n **-rin** or **-rins** [C;U] (TABLET of) medicine that lessens pain and fever

ass /æs/ n 1 DONKEY 2 foolish person 3 AmE for ARSE[1] (1)

as·sail /ə'seɪl/ vt fml attack ~**ant** n fml attacker

as·sas·sin /ə'sæsən/ n person who assassinates

as·sas·sin·ate /ə'sæsəneɪt ‖ -sən eɪt/ vt murder a ruler, politician, etc. **-ation** /ə,sæsə'neɪʃən ‖ -sən'eɪ-/ n [C;U]

as·sault /ə'sɔːlt ‖ ə'sɒːlt/ n [C;U] sudden violent attack **assault** vt

assault course /·'· ˌ·/ n area of land on which soldiers train by climbing or jumping over objects, etc., in order to develop their fitness and courage

as·sem·ble /ə'sembəl/ vi/t gather or put together: to assemble radios | A crowd assembled.

as·sem·bly /ə'sembli/ n 1 [C] group of people gathered together for a purpose 2 [U] assembling of machine parts

assembly line /·'·· ˌ·/ n arrangement of workers and machines in which each person has a particular job, the work being passed from one worker to the next until the product is complete

as·sent /ə'sent/ vi fml agree ♦ n agreement

as·sert /ə'sɜːt ‖ ə'sɜːrt/ vt 1 declare forcefully 2 make a strong claim to: He asserted his authority. 3 **assert oneself** act in a way that shows one's power ~**ive** adj forceful; showing CONFIDENCE ~**ion** /ə'sɜːʃən ‖ -ɜːr-/ n forceful statement or claim

as·sess /ə'ses/ vt judge the value or

amount of ~**ment** n [C;U] ~**or** n

as·set /'æset/ n 1 property that has value and may be sold 2 valuable quality or skill

asset-strip·ping /'·· ,·/ n practice of buying a company cheaply, selling all its assets to make a profit, and closing it down

ass·hole /'æshəʊl ‖ -hoʊl/ n AmE for ARSE[1] (2)

as·sid·u·ous /ə'sɪdjuəs ‖ -dʒuəs/ adj with careful attention ~**ly** adv

as·sign /ə'saɪn/ vt 1 give as a share or duty 2 decide on; name: assign a day for the meeting ~**ment** n [C] duty or piece of work 2 [U] act of assigning

as·sig·na·tion /,æsɪg'neɪʃən/ n (secret) meeting

as·sim·i·late /ə'sɪmɪ̱leɪt/ vi/t take in and accept (food, ideas, foreign people) –**ation** /ə,sɪmɪ̱'leɪʃən/ n [U]

as·sist /ə'sɪst/ vi/t fml help ~**ance** n fml ~**ant** n person who helps

as·so·ci·ate /ə'səʊʃieɪt, -'səʊsi-‖ ə'soʊ-/ v 1 vi/t join as friends or partners 2 vt connect in the mind **associate** /ə'səʊʃɪ̱t, -ʃɪ̱t ‖ ə'soʊ-/ n: He's a business associate.

as·so·ci·a·tion /ə,səʊsi'eɪʃ ən, ə,səʊʃi-‖ ə,soʊ-/ n 1 [C] society of people joined together 2 [U] act of joining together 3 [C;U] connecting things in the mind

as·sort·ed /ə'sɔːtɪ̱d ‖ -ɔːr-/ adj of various types; mixed

as·sort·ment /ə'sɔːtmənt ‖ -ɔːr-/ n mixture

as·suage /ə'sweɪdʒ/ vt fml reduce (suffering)

as·sume /ə'sjuːm ‖ ə'suːm/ vt 1 believe without proof: Let's assume he isn't coming. 2 begin to use or perform: to assume control 3 pretend to have: to adopt an assumed name

as·sump·tion /ə'sʌmpʃən/ n 1 [C] something believed without proof 2 [U] act of assuming

as·sure /ə'ʃʊə ‖ ə'ʃʊr/ vt 1 tell firmly; promise 2 make (oneself) sure or certain 3 BrE insure, esp. against death **assurance** n 1 [U] belief in one's own powers 2 [C] firm promise 3 [U] BrE insurance **assured** adj certain, esp. of one's own powers

as·te·risk /'æstərɪsk/ n star-like mark (*)

a·stern /ə'stɜːn ‖ -ɜːrn/ adv in or at the back part of a ship

as·te·roid /'æstərɔɪd/ n very small PLANET

asth·ma /'æsmə ‖ 'æzmə/ n [U] disease that causes difficulty in breathing ~**tic** /æs'mætɪk ‖ æz-/ adj

as·ton·ish /ə'stɒnɪʃ ‖ ə'stɑː-/ vt surprise greatly: astonishing cold ~**ment** n [U]

as·tound /ə'staʊnd/ vt shock with surprise

as·tral /'æstrəl/ adj of, from, or concerning stars

a·stray /ə'streɪ/ adj, adv off the right path

a·stride /ə'straɪd/ adv, prep with a leg on each side (of)

as·trin·gent /ə'strɪndʒənt/ adj 1 able to tighten the skin and stop bleeding 2 bitter; severe

as·trol·o·gy /ə'strɒlədʒi ‖ ə'strɑː-/ n study of the supposed influence of the stars on events and character –**ger** n –**gical** /,æstrə'lɒdʒɪkəl◄ ‖ -'lɑː-/ adj

as·tro·naut /'æstrənɔːt ‖ -nɒt, -nɑːt/ n traveller in a spacecraft

as·tron·o·my /ə'strɒnəmi ‖ ə'strɑː-/ n [U] scientific study of the sun, stars, etc. –**mer** n –**mical** /,æstrə'nɒmɪkəl◄ ‖ -'nɑː-/ adj 1 of astronomy 2 very large: astronomical sums of money

as·tro·phys·ics /,æstrəʊ'fɪzɪks, ,æstrə-‖ ,æstroʊ-, ,æstrə-/ n [U] science of the nature of the stars and the forces that influence them –**ical** adj

as·tute /ə'stjuːt ‖ ə'stuːt/ adj able to see quickly something that is to one's advantage ~**ly** adv ~**ness** n [U]

a·sy·lum /ə'saɪləm/ n 1 [U] protection and shelter 2 [C] becoming rare MENTAL HOSPITAL

a·sym·met·ric /,eɪsɪ'metrɪk◄, ,æ-/ also –**rical** /-trɪkəl◄/ adj having sides that are not alike

at /ət; strong æt/ prep 1 (showing where): at the airport 2 (showing when): at Christmas 3 towards: Look at me. 4 by: surprised at the news 5 (showing how someone does something): good at games 6 (showing a state or continued activity): at school ı at war 7 (showing price, level, age, etc.): sold at 10 cents each ı to stop work at 60 8 **at a/an** in only one: He went upstairs two at a time.

ate /et, eɪt ‖ eɪt/ past t. of EAT

a·the·is·m /'eɪθi-ɪzəm/ n [U] belief that

there is no God –**ist** *n*

ath·lete /'æθli:t/ *n* person who practises athletics

ath·let·ics /æθ'letɪks, əθ-/ *n* [U] physical exercises such as running and jumping

athletic *adj* 1 of athletics 2 physically strong and active

at·las /'ætləs/ *n* book of maps

ATM /,eɪ ti: 'em/ *n esp. AmE* Automated Teller Machine; CASHPOINT

at·mo·sphere /'ætməsfɪə‖-fɪr/ *n* 1 gases surrounding a heavenly body, esp. the Earth 2 air 3 general feeling of a place –**spheric** /,ætməs'ferɪk◂/ *adj* 1 of or concerning the Earth's atmosphere 2 mysteriously beautiful and strange: *atmospheric music*

at·oll /'ætɒl‖'ætɔːl, 'ætɒl, 'ætoʊl/ *n* ring-shaped CORAL island

at·om /'ætəm/ *n* smallest unit of an ELEMENT /ɪc /ə'tɒmɪk‖ə'tɑː-/ *adj* 1 of atoms 2 using the power that comes from splitting atoms

atom bomb /'·· ·/ also **atomic bomb** /·,·· '·/ — *n* bomb that uses the explosive power of NUCLEAR energy

a·tone /ə'təʊn‖ə'toʊn/ *vi* make repayment (for a crime, etc.) ~**ment** *n* [U]

a·tro·cious /ə'trəʊʃəs‖ə'troʊ-/ *adj* very cruel or bad ~**ly** *adv*

a·troc·i·ty /ə'trɒsɪti‖ə'trɑː-/ *n* 1 very cruel act 2 something very ugly

at·tach /ə'tætʃ/ *vt* 1 fasten 2 cause to join: *He attached himself to another group of tourists.* 3 regard as having (special meaning or importance) 4 **be attached to** be fond of ~**ment** *n* [C;U]

at·tach·é /ə'tæʃeɪ‖,ætə'ʃeɪ/ *n* person who helps an AMBASSADOR

at·tack /ə'tæk/ *n* 1 [C;U] (act of) violence 2 [C] words intended to hurt 3 [C] sudden illness ♦ *vt* 1 make an attack 2 begin (something) with eagerness and interest ~**er** *n*

at·tain /ə'teɪn/ *vt fml* succeed in; reach ~**able** *adj* ~**ment** *n* 1 [U] act of attaining 2 [C] a skill

at·tempt /ə'tempt/ *vt* try: *I attempted to leave.* ♦ *n* 1 effort made to do something 2 **attempt on someone's life** effort to murder someone

at·tend /ə'tend/ *v* 1 *vt* be present at: *attend the meeting* 2 *vi* give attention 3 *vi*

look after ~**ance** *n* 1 [C;U] act of being present 2 [C] number of people present: *a large attendance* ~**ant** *n* person who looks after a place or people

at·ten·tion /ə'tenʃən/ *n* [U] 1 careful thought: *pay attention to the teacher* 2 particular care or consideration: *Old cars need lots of attention.* 3 **at/to attention** (of a soldier) standing straight and still

at·ten·tive /ə'tentɪv/ *adj* 1 listening carefully 2 politely helpful ~**ly** *adv* ~**ness** *n* [U]

at·ten·u·ate /ə'tenjueɪt/ *vi/t* (cause to) become thin, weak, less valuable, etc.

at·test /ə'test/ *vt fml* 1 declare to be true 2 be proof of: *His success attests (to) his ability.*

at·tic /'ætɪk/ *n* room below the roof of a house

at·tire /ə'taɪə‖ə'taɪr/ *n fml* clothes ♦ *vt* put on clothes

at·ti·tude /'ætɪtjuːd‖-tuːd/ *n* 1 way of feeling and behaving 2 *fml* position of the body

at·tor·ney /ə'tɜːni‖-ɜːr-/ *n AmE for* LAWYER

at·tract /ə'trækt/ *vt* 1 excite the admiration or interest of: *He was attracted by her smile.* 2 draw towards: *Flowers attract bees.* ~**ive** *adj* interesting, pleasing ~**ively** *adv* ~**iveness** *n* [U] state of being attractive ~**ion** /ə'trækʃən/ *n* 1 [U] power of attracting 2 [C] something attractive

at·tri·bute[1] /'ætrɪbjuːt/ *n* 1 quality that belongs to a person or thing 2 something regarded as a sign of a person or position

at·tri·bute[2] /ə'trɪbjuːt‖-bjət/ *v* **attribute to** *phr vt* 1 believe to be the result of: *He attributes his success to hard work.* 2 ASCRIBE to.

at·tri·tion /ə'trɪʃən/ *n* [U] process of tiring, weakening, or destroying by continual worry, hardship, or repeated attacks: *a war of attrition*

at·tune /ə'tjuːn‖ə'tuːn/ *v* **attune to** *phr vt* make used to or ready for

a·typ·i·cal /eɪ'tɪpɪkəl/ *adj* not typical ~**ly** /-kli/ *adv*

au·ber·gine /'əʊbəʒiːn‖'oʊbər-/ *n* [C;U] *esp. BrE* EGGPLANT

au·burn /'ɔːbən‖'ɔːbərn/ *adj, n* [U] (esp. of hair) reddish brown

auc·tion /'ɔːkʃən‖'ɒːk-/ *n* public

meeting to sell goods to whoever offers the most money ♦ *vt* sell by auction

auc·tio·neer /ˌɔːkʃə'nɪə ‖ ˌɒːkʃə'nɪr/ *n* person in charge of an auction, who calls out the prices

au·da·cious /ɔː'deɪʃəs ‖ ɒː-/ *adj* 1 (foolishly) daring 2 disrespectful ~ly *adv* –city /ɔː'dæsɪti ‖ ɒː-/ *n* [U]

au·di·ble /'ɔːdəbəl ‖ 'ɒː-/ *adj* able to be heard –bly *adv*

au·di·ence /'ɔːdiəns ‖ 'ɒː-, 'ɑː-/ *n* 1 people listening to or watching a performance 2 formal meeting with someone important: *have an audience with the Pope*

au·di·o /'ɔːdi-əʊ ‖ 'ɒːdioʊ/ *adj* of sound radio signals

audio-vis·u·al /ˌ⋯ '⋯◂/ *adj* of both sight and hearing

au·dit /'ɔːdət ‖ 'ɒː-/ *vt* examine (business accounts) officially audit *n* ~or *n*

au·di·tion /ɔː'dɪʃən ‖ ɒː-/ *n* test performance given by a singer, actor, etc. audition *vi*

au·di·to·ri·um /ˌɔːdə'tɔːriəm ‖ ˌɒː-/ *n* space where an AUDIENCE (1) sits

aug·ment /ɔːg'ment ‖ ɒːg-/ *vi/t fml* increase

au·gur /'ɔːgə ‖ 'ɒːgər/ *vi* augur well/ill (for) be a sign of good/bad things in the future (for): *This rain augurs well for farmers.*

au·gust /ɔː'gʌst ‖ ɒː-/ *adj* noble and grand

Au·gust /'ɔːgəst ‖ 'ɒː-/ *the* 8th month of the year

aunt /ɑːnt ‖ ænt/ *n* sister of one's father or mother, or wife of one's uncle

au pair /ˌəʊ 'peə ‖ oʊ 'per/ *n* young foreigner who lives with a family and helps with housework

au·ra /'ɔːrə/ *n* effect or feeling produced by a person or place

au·ral /'ɔːrəl/ *adj* of or related to the sense of hearing

aus·pic·es /'ɔːspəsɪz ‖ 'ɒː-/ *n* [P] *fml* under the auspices of helped by

aus·pi·cious /ɔː'spɪʃəs ‖ ɒː-/ *adj fml* showing signs of future success ~ly *adv*

aus·tere /ɔː'stɪə, ɒ- ‖ ɒː'stɪr/ *adj* 1 without comfort; hard: *an austere life* 2 without decoration; plain ~ly *adv* –terity /ɔː'sterəti, ɒ- ‖ ɒː-/ *n* [C;U]

au·then·tic /ɔː'θentɪk ‖ ɒː-/ *adj* known to be real; GENUINE ~ally /-kli/ *adv* ~ate *vt* prove to be authentic ~ation /ɔːˌθenti 'keɪʃən ‖ ɒː-/ *n* [U] ~ity /ˌɔːθen'tɪsəti ‖ ˌɒː-/ *n* [U] quality of being authentic

au·thor /'ɔːθə ‖ 'ɒːθər/ authoress /'ɔːθərəs ‖ 'ɒː-/ *fem.* — *n* 1 writer 2 person who thinks of an idea or plan ~ship *n* [U]

au·thor·i·tar·i·an /ɔːˌθɒrə'teəriən ‖ ɒːˌθɑːrə'ter-, əˌθɒ:-/ *n, adj* (person) demanding total obedience to rules ~ism *n* [U]

au·thor·i·ta·tive /ɔː'θɒrətətɪv, ə- ‖ ɒː'θɑːrəteɪtɪv, əˈθɒː-/ *adj* deserving respect; able to be trusted ~ly *adv*

au·thor·i·ty /ɔː'θɒrəti, ə- ‖ ɒː'θɑː-, ə'θɒː-/ *n* 1 [U] power to command: *Who is in authority here?* 2 [C] person or group with this power 3 [C] authoritative person, book, etc.: *He's an authority on plants.*

au·thor·ize also *-ise BrE* /'ɔːθəraɪz ‖ 'ɒː-/ *vt* give formal permission for –ization /ˌɔːθəraɪ'zeɪʃən ‖ ˌɒːθərə-/ *n* [C;U]

au·tis·m /'ɔːtɪzəm ‖ 'ɒː-/ *n* [U] mental illness preventing a person from communicating with others autistic /'ɔːtɪstɪk ‖ ɒː-/ *adj*

au·to·bi·og·ra·phy /ˌɔːtəbaɪ'ɒgrəfi ‖ ˌɒːtəbaɪ'ɑː-/ *n* written account of one's own life –phical /ˌɔːtəbaɪə'græfɪkəl ‖ ˌɒː-/ *adj*

au·to·crat /'ɔːtəkræt ‖ 'ɒː-/ *n* 1 ruler with unlimited power 2 person who behaves like that ~ic /ˌɔːtə'krætɪk◂ ‖ ˌɒː-/ *adj*

au·to·graph /'ɔːtəgrɑːf ‖ 'ɒːtəgræf/ *n* SIGNATURE of someone famous ♦ *vt* sign one's name on

au·to·mate /'ɔːtəmeɪt ‖ 'ɒː-/ *vt* change (a process, etc.) to automation

auto·mat·ic /ˌɔːtə'mætɪk◂ ‖ ˌɒː-/ *adj* 1 (esp. of a machine) able to work by itself 2 done without thought 3 certain to happen ♦ *n* (automatic) gun ~ally /-kli/ *adv*

au·to·ma·tion /ˌɔːtə'meɪʃən ‖ ˌɒː-/ *n* [U] use of machines that need no human control

au·tom·a·ton /ɔː'tɒmətən ‖ ɒː'tɑː-/ *n* -ta /-tə/ *or* -tons 1 thing or machine that works by itself 2 person who acts without thought or feeling

au·to·mo·bile /'ɔːtəməbiːl ‖ 'ɒːtəmoʊ-/ *n AmE fml for* car

au·ton·o·mous /ɔːˈtɒnəməs ‖ ɒːˈtɑː-/ *adj* governing itself

au·ton·o·my /ɔːˈtɒnəmi ‖ ɒːˈtɑː-/ *n* [U] self-government

au·top·sy /ˈɔːtɒpsi ‖ ˈɒːtɑːp-/ *n* POSTMORTEM

au·tumn /ˈɔːtəm ‖ ˈɒː-/ *n* [C;U] season between summer and winter ~**al** /ɔːˈtʌmnəl ‖ ˈɒː-/ *adj*

aux·il·i·a·ry /ɔːgˈzɪliəri, ɔːk- ‖ ɒːgˈzɪljəri, -ˈzɪləri/ *adj* helping; adding support **auxiliary** *n* 1 helper 2 foreign soldier in the service of a country at war

a·vail /əˈveɪl/ *vi* avail oneself of *fml* make use of ♦ *n* [U] **of/to no avail** of no use; without success

a·vail·a·ble /əˈveɪləbəl/ *adj* able to be got, used, etc.: *Those shoes are not available in your size.* **-bility** /əˌveɪləˈbɪləti/ *n* [U]

av·a·lanche /ˈævəlɑːnʃ ‖ -læntʃ/ *n* mass of snow crashing down a mountain: (fig.) *an avalanche of letters*

av·ant-garde /ˌævɒŋ ˈgɑːd◄ ‖ ˌævɑːŋ ˈgɑːrd◄/ *adj, n* [U] (of) people who produce the newest ideas, esp. in the arts

av·a·rice /ˈævərɪs◄/ *n* GREED for wealth **avaricious** /ˌævəˈrɪʃəs◄/ *adj*

a·venge /əˈvendʒ/ *vt* punish for harm done; REVENGE: *to avenge his death*

av·e·nue /ˈævɪnjuː ‖ -nuː/ *n* 1 road between two rows of trees 2 way to a result

a·ver /əˈvɜː ‖ əˈvɜːr/ *vt* -rr- state forcefully

av·e·rage /ˈævərɪdʒ/ *n* 1 [C] amount found by adding quantities together and then dividing by the number of quantities 2 [C;U] level regarded as usual ♦ *adj: the average rainfall | girls of average intelligence* ♦ *vt* 1 calculate the average of 2 be or do as an average: *I average 8 hours' work a day.*

a·verse /əˈvɜːs ‖ əˈvɜːrs/ *adj* not liking

a·ver·sion /əˈvɜːʃən ‖ əˈvɜːrʒən/ *n* 1 [S;U] strong dislike 2 [C] hated person or thing

a·vert /əˈvɜːt ‖ əˈvɜːrt/ *vt* 1 prevent from happening: *avert accidents* 2 *fml* turn away (one's eyes)

a·vi·a·ry /ˈeɪviəri ‖ ˈeɪvieri/ *n* large cage for keeping birds in

a·vi·a·tion /ˌeɪviˈeɪʃən ‖ ˌeɪ-, ˌæ-/ *n* [U] flying in aircraft **-tor** /ˈeɪvieɪtə ‖ ˈeɪvieɪtər, æ-/ *n*

av·id /ˈævɪd/ *adj* extremely keen ~**ly** *adv*

av·o·ca·do /ˌævəˈkɑːdəʊ◄ ‖ -doʊ◄/ *n* -dos *or* -does green tropical fruit

a·void /əˈvɔɪd/ *vt* keep away from, esp. on purpose ~**able** *adj* ~**ance** *n* [U]

a·vowed /əˈvaʊd/ *adj* openly admitted: *his avowed supporters*

a·vun·cu·lar /əˈvʌŋkjʊlə ‖ -ər/ *adj* of or like an uncle

a·wait /əˈweɪt/ *vt fml* wait for

a·wake[1] /əˈweɪk/ *adj* not asleep

a·wake[2] *also* **awaken** /əˈweɪkən/ *vi/t* **awoke** /əˈwəʊk ‖ əˈwoʊk/ *or* **awakened**, **awoken** /əˈwəʊkən ‖ əˈwoʊ-/ *or* **awaked** wake: (fig.) *People must be awakened to the dangers of nuclear weapons.*

a·wak·en·ing /əˈweɪkənɪŋ/ *n* 1 act of waking from sleep: (fig.) *her awakening to social injustice* 2 **rude awakening** sudden consciousness of an unpleasant state of affairs

a·ward /əˈwɔːd ‖ əˈwɔːrd/ *vt* give officially: *award prizes* ♦ *n* something awarded

a·ware /əˈweə ‖ əˈwer/ *adj* having knowledge or understanding: *politically aware* ~**ness** *n* [U]

a·wash /əˈwɒʃ ‖ əˈwɒːʃ, əˈwɑː/ *adj* 1 covered with water: *The streets were awash.* 2 **awash with** having too much of

a·way[1] /əˈweɪ/ *adv* 1 to or at another place: *Go away! | She lives 3 miles away.* 2 so as to be gone: *The sounds died away.* 3 continuously: *He's hammering away.*

away[2] *adj* (of a sports match) played at the place, sports field, etc. of one's opponent

awe /ɔː ‖ ɒː/ *n* [U] respect mixed with fear

awe-in·spir·ing /ˈ· ·ˌ· / *adj* causing feelings of awe

awe·some /ˈɔːsəm ‖ ˈɒː-/ *adj* causing feelings of awe

aw·ful /ˈɔːfəl ‖ ˈɒː-/ *adj* 1 very bad: *awful weather* 2 very great: *an awful lot of work* ~**ly** *adv* very

awk·ward /ˈɔːkwəd ‖ ˈɒːkwərd/ *adj* 1 not moving skilfully; CLUMSY 2 difficult to handle 3 inconvenient: *They came at an awkward time.* 4 EMBARRASSING: *an awkward silence* ~**ness** *n* [U]

aw·ning /ˈɔːnɪŋ ‖ ˈɒː-/ *n* movable cloth roof put up as a protection against sun or rain

a·woke /əˈwəʊk ‖ əˈwoʊk/ *past t. of* AWAKE

a·wok·en /əˈwəʊkən‖əˈwoʊ-/ *past p. of*
AWAKE

a·wry /əˈraɪ/ *adj, adv* **1** not in the planned
way **2** twisted or bent

axe /æks/ *n* **1** tool for cutting down trees
2 **have an axe to grind** have a selfish
reason for one's actions ♦ *vt* put a sudden
end to (jobs, plans, etc.)

ax·i·om /ˈæksɪəm/ *n* principle accepted as
true **~atic** /ˌæksɪəˈmætɪk◄/ *adj* not needing
proof

ax·is /ˈæksɪs/ *n* **axes** /ˈæksiːz/ **1** line
round which something spins: *the Earth's
axis* **2** fixed line against which positions are
measured on a GRAPH

ax·le /ˈæksəl/ *n* bar on which a wheel
turns

a·ya·tol·lah /ˌaɪəˈtɒlə‖-ˈtɑː-/ *n* Shiite
Muslim religious leader

aye /aɪ/ *n, adv* (person who votes) yes

az·ure /ˈæʒə, ˈæʒjʊə, ˈæzjʊə‖ˈæʒər/
adj, n [U] bright blue

B

B, b /biː/ the 2nd letter of the English
alphabet

b *abbrev. for:* born

baa /bɑː/ *vi, n* (make) the sound a sheep
makes

bab·ble /ˈbæbəl/ *vi/t* talk quickly and
foolishly **babble** *n* [S]

babe /beɪb/ *n lit* baby

ba·boon /bəˈbuːn‖bæ-/ *n* kind of large
monkey

ba·by /ˈbeɪbi/ *n* **1** very young child: (fig.)
the baby of the class (=the youngest) **2** very
young animal or bird: *a baby monkey*
3 *AmE infml* person, esp. a girl or woman
4 *infml* one's special responsibility **~ish** *adj*
like a baby

baby-sit·ter /ˈ‥ ‥ ‚‥/ *n* person who looks
after children while their parents are out
baby-sit *vi* **-sat/-sæt/‥ *pres. p.* -sitting

bach·e·lor /ˈbætʃələ‖-lər/ *n* **1** unmarried
man **2** person with a first university degree

back¹ /bæk/ *n* **1** the part of one's body
opposite the chest, from the neck to the
bottom of the SPINE (1) **2** the part furthest
from the direction that something moves in
or faces: *the back of the aircraft/of the
house | the back wheel of a bicycle* **3** the less
important side of something **4** the part of a
chair that one leans against **5** the end of a
book or newspaper **6** **back to back** with the
backs facing each other **7** **back to front**
with the back part in front **8** **be glad to see
the back of someone** be glad when
someone goes away **9** **behind someone's
back** without their knowledge **10** **break
the back of** do most or the worst part of
(something) **11** **get off someone's back**
stop annoying someone **12** **have/with
one's back to the wall** (be) in the greatest
difficulties **13** **put one's back into** work
very hard at **14** **put someone's back up**
annoy someone **15** **turn one's back on
someone** leave someone (esp. when one
should stay) **~less** *adj: a backless dress*

back² *adv* **1** in or into an earlier place: *Put
the book back on the shelf.* **2** towards the
back: *Lean well back.* **3** away from the
speaker: *Stand back!* **4** in reply: *Phone me
back.* **5** in an earlier time: *back in 1983*

back³ *v* **1** *vi/t* more backwards: *back the
car down the road* **2** *vt* support and
encourage **3** *vt* bet money on (a horse, etc.)
4 *vt* be or make the back of: *curtains backed
with satin* **~er** *n* **1** someone who supports a
plan with money **2** someone who bets on a
horse

back down *phr vi* give up an argument

back onto *phr vt* (of a place) have at
the back: *a house backing onto the river*

back out *phr vi* not fulfil a promise

back up *phr vt* support in an argument,
etc.

back·ache /ˈbækeɪk/ *n* [C;U] pain in the
back

back·bench /ˌbækˈbentʃ◄/ *n* any of the
seats in the British parliament on which
members who do not hold an official
position in the government or opposition
may sit **backbencher** *n*

back·bit·ing /ˈbækbaɪtɪŋ/ *n* [U] unkind
talk about someone who is absent

back·bone /ˈbækbəʊn‖-boʊn/ *n* **1** [C]

spine (1): (fig.) *She's the backbone* (=main support) *of the local party.* 2 [U] strength of character

back·break·ing /ˈbækbreɪkɪŋ/ *adj* (of work) very hard

back·date /ˌbækˈdeɪt/ *vt* make effective from an earlier date

back·drop /ˈbækdrɒp ‖ -drɑːp/ *n* background

back·fire /ˌbækˈfaɪə ‖ ˈbækfaɪr/ *vi* 1 (of a car, etc.) make a noise because the gas explodes too soon 2 have the opposite effect to that intended

back·ground /ˈbækgraʊnd/ *n* 1 scenery behind the main object 2 (information about) conditions existing when something happens or happened 3 person's family, experience, education, etc.

back·hand /ˈbækhænd/ *n* stroke (in tennis, etc.) with the back of the hand turned in the direction of movement ~ed /ˌbækˈhændɪd◀/ *adj* 1 using or made with a backhand 2 (of a remark) indirect, esp. sarcastic ~er /ˈbækhændə ‖ -ər/ *n* 1 backhand 2 bribe

back·ing /ˈbækɪŋ/ *n* 1 help; support 2 something that makes the back of an object

back·lash /ˈbæklæʃ/ *n* sudden violent movement, esp. against a political or social movement

back·log /ˈbæklɒg ‖ -lɔːg, -lɑːg/ *n* things (esp. work) remaining to be done

back num·ber /ˌ· ˈ··/ *n* newspaper, etc. earlier than the most recent one

back of be·yond /ˌ· · ·ˈ··/ *n* [the+S] *infml* a very distant place, difficult to get to

back·pack /ˈbækpæk/ *n esp. AmE* rucksack ~er *n* ~ing *n* [U]: *to go backpacking in the mountains*

back·ped·al /ˌbækˈpedl ‖ ˈbækˌpedl/ *vi* -ll- *BrE* ‖ -l- *AmE* 1 pedal backwards 2 take back a statement; change an earlier opinion

back seat /ˌ· ˈ·/ *n* 1 [C] seat at the back of a car 2 [S] less important position

back·side /ˈbæksaɪd/ *n* one's bottom¹ (2)

back·slap·ping /ˈbækslæpɪŋ/ *adj* (of behaviour) too friendly and noisy

back·slide /ˈbækslaɪd/ *vi* go back to a worse condition -**slider** *n*

back·stage /ˌbækˈsteɪdʒ/ *adv, adj* 1 behind a theatre stage 2 in private

back·street /ˈ·· ·/ *n* street away from the main streets, esp. in a poor area of town

back·stroke /ˈbækstrəʊk ‖ -stroʊk/ *n* way of swimming on one's back

back·track /ˈbæktræk/ *vi* 1 go back over the same path 2 backpedal (2)

back·up /ˈbækʌp/ *n* [C;U] thing or person ready to be used in place of or to help another

back·ward /ˈbækwəd ‖ -ərd/ *adj* 1 towards the back 2 late in development: *a backward child* ~**ness** *n* [U]

back·wards /ˈbækwədz ‖ -ərdz/ *adv* 1 towards the back, the beginning, or the past: *say the alphabet backwards* 2 with the back part in front: *put one's hat on backwards* 3 **know something backwards** know something perfectly

back·wa·ter /ˈbækwɔːtə ‖ -wɒtər, -wɑː-/ *n* 1 part of a river outside the current 2 place not influenced by outside events

back·yard /ˌbækˈjɑːd◀ ‖ -ˈjɑːrd◀/ *n* 1 yard behind a house 2 area under one's personal control

ba·con /ˈbeɪkən/ *n* [U] salted or smoked pig meat

bac·te·ri·a /bækˈtɪəriə ‖ -ˈtɪr-/ *n sing.* -**rium** /-riəm/ [P] very small living creatures that may cause disease

bad /bæd/ *adj* **worse** /wɜːs ‖ wɜːrs/, **worst** /wɜːst ‖ wɜːrst/ 1 unpleasant: *bad news* 2 morally wrong 3 unhealthy: *Smoking is bad for you.* 4 not of acceptable quality 5 severe: *a bad cold* 6 rotten: *The apples went bad.* 7 disobedient: *a bad boy* 8 **feel bad about** be sorry or ashamed about 9 **have/get a bad name** lose or have lost people's respect 10 **in a bad way** very ill or in trouble 11 **not bad/not so bad** really rather good ~**ly** *adv* 1 in a bad way: *We played badly.* 2 seriously: *We were badly beaten.* 3 a great deal: *He needs help badly.*

bad debt /ˌ· ˈ·/ *n* debt that is unlikely to be paid

bad·dy /ˈbædi/ *n infml* bad person

bade /bæd, beɪd/ *past t. and p. of* bid²

badge /bædʒ/ *n* something worn to show one's rank, membership, etc.

bad·ger¹ /ˈbædʒə ‖ -ər/ *n* black and white night animal that lives in holes in the ground

badger² *vt* ask again and again

badly-off /ˌ··ˈ·/ *adj* 1 poor 2 lacking

bad·min·ton /ˈbædmɪntən/ *n* [U] game

similar to tennis, played with a SHUTTLECOCK over a high net

bad-mouth /'· ·/ vt sl esp. AmE speak badly of

baf·fle /'bæfəl/ vt be too difficult for (someone): a baffling question

bag¹ /bæg/ n 1 soft container that opens at the top: a shopping bag 2 bags of esp. BrE plenty of 3 **in the bag** certain to be won, gained, etc.

bag² v -gg- 1 vt put into a bag 2 vt kill (animals or birds) 3 vt take possession of 4 vi be baggy

bag·gage /'bægɪdʒ/ n [U] LUGGAGE

bag·gy /'bægi/ adj hanging in loose folds: baggy jeans

bag·pipes /'bægpaɪps/ n [P] musical instrument with pipes and a bag of air

bail¹ /beɪl/ n [U] 1 money paid so that a prisoner may be set free until tried (TRY¹ (3)) 2 **go/stand bail** pay this money

bail² v bail out phr v 1 vt pay bail for someone 2 vt help someone with money 3 vi/t remove water from a boat 4 AmE BALE out (1)

bail³ n piece of wood laid on top of STUMPS¹ in cricket

bai·liff /'beɪlɪf/ n BrE 1 law official who takes possession of goods when money is owed 2 farm manager

bait /beɪt/ n [S;U] food used to attract fish, etc., to be caught ♦ vt 1 put bait on (a hook, etc.) 2 make (an animal or a person) angry intentionally

bake /beɪk/ 1 vi/t (cause to) cook in an OVEN 2 vi/t (cause to) become hard by heating 3 vi become hot: I'm baking! **baker** n person who bakes bread for sale **bakery** place where bread is baked (and sold)

baked beans /,· '·/ n [P] beans cooked in TOMATO sauce, sold in tins

bak·ing pow·der /'·· ,··/ n [U] powder used to make bread and cakes light

bal·ance¹ /'bæləns/ n 1 [S;U] state in which weight is evenly spread: It was difficult to keep my balance on the icy path. 2 [C] instrument for weighing 3 [C] amount remaining somewhere: my bank balance 4 **in the balance** uncertain(ly) 5 **on balance** considering everything

balance² v 1 vi/t keep steady 2 vi (of two things, e.g. debts) be equal 3 vt compare (two things): balance the advantages against the disadvantages

balance of pay·ments /,·· '··/ n [(the) S] the difference between the amount of money coming into a country and the amount going out, including trade in insurance, banking, etc.

balance of pow·er /,·· '··/ n [(the) S] the way that power is divided between the members of a group, organization, etc.

balance of trade /,·· · '·/ n [(the) S] the difference in value between a country's IMPORTS and EXPORTS

bal·co·ny /'bælkəni/ n 1 piece of floor that sticks out from an upstairs wall 2 upstairs seats in a theatre

bald /bɔːld ‖ bɒːld/ adj 1 with no hair on the head 2 plain: a bald statement **~ing** adj becoming bald **~ness** n [U]

bale¹ /beɪl/ n large tightly tied mass of esp. soft material: a bale of cotton

bale² v bale out phr v 1 vi BrE escape from an aircraft 2 vi/t remove water from a boat

balk /bɔːk, bɔːlk ‖ bɔːk, bɔːlk/ vi be unwilling to agree: I balked at the price.

ball¹ /bɔːl ‖ bɒːl/ n 1 round object used in games 2 round mass: a ball of string/clay 3 round part of the body: eyeballs 4 **on the ball** showing up-to-date knowledge and readiness to act 5 **play ball** COOPERATE 6 **start/keep the ball rolling** begin/continue something **balls** [P] taboo sl 1 TESTICLES 2 nonsense

ball² n 1 formal occasion for dancing 2 **have a ball** have a very good time

bal·lad /'bæləd/ n 1 poem that tells a story 2 popular love song

bal·last /'bæləst/ n [U] heavy material carried to keep a ship steady, or to be thrown from a BALLOON (1) to make it rise higher ♦ vt fill or supply with ballast

ball·cock /'bɔːlkɒk ‖ 'bɒːlkɑːk/ n hollow floating ball that opens and closes a hole through which water flows

bal·le·ri·na /,bælə'riːnə/ n female ballet dancer

bal·let /'bæleɪ ‖ bæ'leɪ, 'bæleɪ/ n 1 [C] dance with music in which a story is told 2 [C] music for such a dance 3 [S;U] art of doing such a dance 4 [C] group of ballet dancers

ball game /'· ·/ n infml state of affairs

bal·lis·tic mis·sile /bə,lɪstɪk 'mɪsaɪl ‖

-'mɪsəl/ n MISSILE that is guided as it rises into the air but then falls freely

bal·lis·tics /bə'lɪstɪks/ n [U] science of the movement of objects, such as bullets fired from a gun **ballistic** adj **go ballistic** infml suddenly become very angry

bal·loon /bə'luːn/ n 1 bag filled with gas or air so that it can float 2 small rubber bag that can be blown up and used as a toy 3 **when the balloon goes up** when the action starts or the moment of danger arrives ♦ vi swell up like a balloon

bal·lot /'bælət/ n 1 [S;U] (paper used in a) secret vote 2 [C] number of votes recorded ♦ 1 vi vote or decide by secret ballot 2 vt find out the views (of a group) by holding a vote

ballot box /'·· ·/ n box in which voters put their BALLOTS (1)

ball park /'· ·/ n [S] infml range of numbers, prices, etc. within which the correct figure is likely to be

ball·point /'bɔːlpɔɪnt ‖ 'bɔːl-/ n pen with a ball at the end that rolls thick ink onto the paper

ball·room /'bɔːlrʊm, -ruːm ‖ 'bɔːl-/ n large room suitable for a BALL² (1)

balls /bɔːlz ‖ bɒːlz/ v **balls-up** phr vt BrE taboo sl spoil **balls up** /'··/ n

balm /bɑːm ‖ bɑːm, bɑːlm/ n [C;U] oily liquid used to lessen pain

balm·y /'bɑːmi ‖ 'bɑːmi, 'bɑːlmi/ adj (of air) soft and warm

bal·sa /'bɔːlsə ‖ 'bɔː-/ n [C;U] (light wood of) a tropical tree

bal·us·trade /ˌbælə'streɪd ‖ 'bæləstreɪd/ n upright posts with a bar along the top, guarding an edge where people might fall

bam·boo /ˌbæm'buː◂/ n -boos [C;U] (hollow jointed stems of) a tropical plant of the grass family

ban /bæn/ vt -nn- forbid ♦ n order forbidding something

ba·nal /bə'nɑːl, bə'næl/ adj uninteresting because ordinary ~**ity** /bə'næləti/ n [C;U]

ba·na·na /bə'nɑːnə ‖ -'næ-/ n long yellow tropical fruit

banana skin /·'·· ˌ·/ n BrE infml event or situation likely to cause difficulty or make one look foolish

band¹ /bænd/ n 1 narrow piece of material for fastening, or putting round something: a rubber band 2 STRIPE (1) 3 area

between measurable limits: the £10,000—£30,000 income band

band² n group of people, esp. musicians playing popular music —see also ONE-MAN BAND; STEEL BAND

band³ v **band together** phr vi unite for a purpose

band·age /'bændɪdʒ/ n narrow piece of cloth for tying round a wound ♦ vt tie up with a bandage

b and b /ˌbiː ən 'biː/ abbrev. for: (small hotel providing) bed and breakfast

ban·dit /'bændɪt/ n armed robber —see also ONE-ARMED BANDIT

band·stand /'bændstænd/ n raised open-air place for a band to play

band·wag·on /'bænd,wægən/ n **jump on a bandwagon** join something that is popular, for personal gain

ban·dy¹ /'bændi/ vt **bandy words** quarrel

bandy² adj (of legs) curved outwards at the knees

bane /beɪn/ n cause of trouble ~**ful** adj harmful

bang¹ /bæŋ/ vi/t hit violently and noisily: I banged my head against the ceiling. **bang** n

bang² adv exactly: bang in the middle

bang·er /'bæŋə ‖ -ər/ n BrE 1 SAUSAGE 2 old car 3 noisy FIREWORK

ban·gle /'bæŋgəl/ n band worn as decoration

ban·ish /'bænɪʃ/ vt 1 send away as a punishment 2 stop thinking about ~**ment** n [U]

ban·is·ter /'bænəstə ‖ -ər/ n also **banisters** — upright posts with a bar along the top, beside a staircase

ban·jo /'bændʒəʊ ‖ -dʒoʊ/ n -jos or -joes stringed instrument used esp. to play popular music

bank¹ /bæŋk/ n 1 land beside a river or lake 2 raised heap of earth, etc. 3 mass of snow, clouds, etc. 4 set of things arranged in a row: a bank of oars

bank² n 1 place where money is kept and paid out on demand 2 place where something is kept for use: a blood bank ~**er** n person who owns, works in, or controls a BANK² (1)

bank³ vi/t keep (money) in a bank
bank on phr vt depend on

bank⁴ vi (of an aircraft, etc.) raise one side

while turning

bank hol·i·day /ˌ· ˈ···/ n BrE official public holiday on a weekday

bank·ing /ˈbæŋkɪŋ/ n [U] business of a BANK² (1)

bank note /ˈ· ·/ n piece of paper money

bank rate /ˈ· ·/ n [the+S] the rate of interest fixed by a central bank

bank·roll /ˈbæŋkrəʊl ‖ -roʊl/ n AmE supply of money ♦ vt infml supply money for or pay the cost of (a business, plan, etc.)

bank·rupt /ˈbæŋkrʌpt/ adj unable to pay one's debts: (fig.) morally bankrupt (=completely without morals) ♦ n person who is bankrupt ♦ vt make bankrupt or very poor ~cy n [C;U] state of being bankrupt

ban·ner /ˈbænə ‖ -ər/ n 1 lit flag 2 piece of cloth with a political message on it, carried by marchers

banns /bænz/ n [P] public declaration of an intended marriage

ban·quet /ˈbæŋkwɪt/ n formal dinner banquet vi

ban·ter /ˈbæntə ‖ -ər/ n [U] light joking talk banter vi

bap·tis·m /ˈbæptɪzəm/ n 1 [C;U] Christian religious ceremony of touching or covering a person with water 2 **baptism of fire**: a soldier's first experience of war b any unpleasant first experience –tize also -ise BrE /bæpˈtaɪz/ vt perform baptism on

bar /bɑː ‖ bɑːr/ n 1 long narrow piece of solid material: a bar of chocolate | (fig.) bars of sunlight 2 length of wood or metal across a window, etc. 3 group of musical notes 4 place where drinks, etc. are served 5 bank of sand or stones under water 6 BARRIER 7 (cap.) the legal profession, esp. BARRISTERS: She was called to the Bar. (=became a barrister) 8 **behind bars** in prison 9 **prisoner at the bar** person being tried in a court of law ♦ vt -rr- 1 close with a bar: They barred themselves in. | (fig.) to bar the way to success 2 forbid; prevent: He was barred from playing football. ♦ prep 1 except 2 **bar none** with no exception

barb /bɑːb ‖ bɑːrb/ n sharp point of a fish hook, etc. with a curved shape ~ed adj 1 with short sharp points: **barbed wire** 2 (of speech) sharply unkind

bar·bar·i·an /bɑːˈbeəriən ‖ bɑːrˈber-/ n wild uncivilized person

bar·bar·ic /bɑːˈbærɪk ‖ bɑːr-/ adj 1 very cruel 2 like a barbarian –**barism** /ˈbɑːbərɪzəm ‖ bɑːr-/ n [U] condition of being a barbarian –**barous** adj –ity /bɑːˈbærəti ‖ bɑːr-/n [C;U] great cruelty

bar·be·cue /ˈbɑːbɪkjuː ‖ ˈbɑːr-/ n 1 metal frame for cooking meat outdoors 2 party where this is done ♦ vt cook on a barbecue

bar·ber /ˈbɑːbə ‖ ˈbɑːrbər/ n person who cuts men's hair

bar·bi·tu·rate /bɑːˈbɪtʃərɪt ‖ bɑːrˈbɪtʃərɪt, -rɪt/ [C;U] drug that makes people sleep

bar code /ˈ· ·/ n black lines printed on goods for sale, able to be read by a computer

bard /bɑːd ‖ bɑːrd/ n 1 poet 2 **the Bard** Shakespeare

bare /beə ‖ ber/ adj 1 without clothes or covering 2 with nothing added: the bare facts 3 empty: a room bare of furniture ♦ vt bring to view; EXPOSE ~**ly** adv hardly

bare·back /ˈbeəbæk ‖ ˈber-/ adj, adv riding, esp. a horse, without a SADDLE (1)

bare bones /ˌ· ˈ·/ n [P] simplest but most important parts or facts

bare·faced /ˌbeəˈfeɪst◄ ‖ ˈberfeɪst/ adj shameless

bare·foot /ˈbeəfʊt ‖ ˈber-/ adv without shoes

bar·gain¹ /ˈbɑːgɪn ‖ ˈbɑːr-/ n 1 agreement to do something in return for something else 2 something sold cheap 3 **into the bargain** besides everything else

bargain² vi talk about the conditions of a sale, etc.

bargain for/on phr vt take into account; expect

barge¹ /bɑːdʒ ‖ bɑːrdʒ/ n flat-bottomed boat

barge² vi move heavily and rudely

barge in phr vi rush in rudely; interrupt

bar·i·tone /ˈbærɪtəʊn ‖ -toʊn/ n (man with) a singing voice between TENOR and BASS¹

bark¹ /bɑːk ‖ bɑːrk/ v 1 vi make the noise dogs make 2 vt say in a fierce voice 3 **bark up the wrong tree** infml have a mistaken idea **bark** n 1 sharp loud noise made by a dog 2 **his bark is worse than his bite** infml he is not as bad-tempered, unfriendly, etc. as he appears

bark² *n* [U] outer covering of a tree

bar·ley /ˈbɑːli ‖ ˈbɑːrli/ *n* [U] grasslike grain plant grown as a food crop

bar·man /ˈbɑːmən ‖ ˈbɑːr-/ **barmaid** /ˈbɑːmeɪd ‖ ˈbɑːr-/ *fem.* — *n* -**men** /-mən/ person who serves drinks in a BAR (4)

barm·y /ˈbɑːmi ‖ ˈbɑːrmi/ *adj sl* foolish; mad

barn /bɑːn ‖ bɑːrn/ *n* farm building for storing things in

bar·na·cle /ˈbɑːnəkəl ‖ ˈbɑːr-/ *n* small SHELLFISH that collects on rocks, ships, etc.

ba·rom·e·ter /bəˈrɒmɪtə ‖ -ˈrɑːmətər/ *n* instrument for measuring air pressure so as to judge what weather is coming: (fig.) *a barometer of public opinion*

bar·on /ˈbærən/ *n* **1** baroness /ˈbærənɪs/ *fem.* — British noble of the lowest rank **2** powerful businessman

bar·on·et /ˈbærənɪt, -net/ *n* British KNIGHT, below a baron in rank

ba·roque /bəˈrɒk, bəˈrəʊk ‖ bəˈrouk, -ˈrɑːk/ *adj* **1** in a decorated style fashionable in 17th-century Europe **2** (too) greatly ornamented

bar·rack /ˈbærək/ *vi/t BrE* interrupt by shouting

bar·racks /ˈbærəks/ *n* building where soldiers live

bar·rage¹ /ˈbærɑːʒ ‖ bəˈrɑːʒ/ *n* heavy gunfire: (fig.) *a barrage of questions*

bar·rage² /ˈbærɑːʒ ‖ ˈbɑːrɪdʒ/ *n* **2** bank of earth, etc. built across a river

bar·rel /ˈbærəl/ *n* **1** round wooden container: *a beer barrel* **2** long tube-shaped part of a gun, etc. **3** **over a barrel** in a difficult position

bar·ren /ˈbærən/ *adj* **1** unable to produce children, fruit, crops, etc. **2** useless; empty: *a barren discussion* ~**ness** *n* [U]

bar·ri·cade /ˈbærɪkeɪd, ˌbærɪˈkeɪd/ *n* something quickly built to block a street, etc. ♦ *vt* close or defend with a barricade

bar·ri·er /ˈbæriə ‖ -ər/ *n* something placed in the way to prevent movement: (fig.) *a barrier to success | the sound barrier*

bar·ring /ˈbɑːrɪŋ/ *prep* except for

bar·ris·ter /ˈbærɪstə ‖ -ər/ *n* (esp. in England) lawyer who has the right to speak in the highest courts

bar·row /ˈbærəʊ ‖ -roʊ/ *n* **1** small cart to be pushed **2** WHEELBARROW

bar·tend·er /ˈbɑːˌtendə ‖ ˈbɑːrtendər/ *n* *AmE for* BARMAN

bar·ter /ˈbɑːtə ‖ ˈbɑːrtər/ *vi/t* exchange goods for other goods **barter** *n* [U]

base¹ /beɪs/ *n* **1** part of a thing on which a thing stands **2** origin from which something develops or is made **3** centre from which something is controlled, plans made, etc. **4** centre for military operations, stores, etc. **5** main part or substance of a mixture: *a vegetable base* **6** point which a player must touch in BASEBALL to make a run **7** **not get to first base** (with) not even begin to succeed (with) ♦ *vt* provide with a centre: *a company based in Paris* ~**less** *adj* without good reason

base on/upon *phr vt* form by using something else as a starting point: *a film based on a novel*

base² *adj* **1** *esp. lit* (of people or behaviour) dishonourable **2** (of metal) not regarded as precious ~**ly** *adv* ~**ness** *n* [U]

base·ball /ˈbeɪsbɔːl ‖ -bɔːl/ *n* **1** [U] American national team game **2** [C] ball used in this game

base·ment /ˈbeɪsmənt/ *n* room in a house below street level

base rate /ˈ· ·/ *n* standard rate of interest on which a bank bases its charges for lending and interest on borrowing

bas·es /ˈbeɪsiːz/ *n pl. of* BASIS

bash /bæʃ/ *vt* hit hard ♦ *n* **1** hard blow **2** **have a bash** *infml* make an attempt

bash·ful /ˈbæʃfəl/ *adj* SHY ~**ly** *adv*

ba·sic /ˈbeɪsɪk/ *adj* most necessary; FUNDAMENTAL: *basic principles* ~**ally** /-kli/ *adv* in spite of surface behaviour or details; in reality **basics** *n* [P] basic parts or principles

ba·sil /ˈbæzəl/ *n* [U] sweet HERB used in cooking

ba·sin /ˈbeɪsən/ *n* **1** round container for liquids; bowl **2** WASHBASIN **3** hollow place where water collects **4** large valley

ba·sis /ˈbeɪsɪs/ *n* bases /ˈbeɪsiːz/ **1** the facts, principles, etc. from which something is formed, started, or developed: *the basis of an opinion* **2** the stated way of carrying out an action, process, etc.: *working on a part-time basis*

bask /bɑːsk ‖ bæsk/ *vi* lie in enjoyable warmth: (fig.) *She basked in* (=enjoyed) *her employer's approval.*

bas·ket /ˈbɑːskɪt ‖ ˈbæ-/ *n* light woven

container: *a shopping basket*
bas·ket·ball /'bɑːskɪtbɔːl ‖ 'bæskɪtbɒːl/ *n* **1** [U] indoor game in which players try to throw a ball into a basket **2** [C] large ball used in this game

bass¹ /beɪs/ *n* **1** (man with) the lowest human singing voice **2** instrument with the same range of notes as this: *a bass guitar* **3** DOUBLE BASS

bass² /bæs/ *n* kind of fish that can be eaten

bas·soon /bə'suːn/ *n* large WOODWIND musical instrument

bas·tard /'bæstəd, 'bɑː- ‖ 'bæstərd/ *n* **1** child of unmarried parents **2** *sl* unpleasant person **3** *sl* man of the stated kind: *You lucky bastard!*

baste /beɪst/ *vt* **1** pour fat over (meat) during cooking **2** fasten with TACKS (3)

bas·ti·on /'bæstiən ‖ -tʃən/ *n* **1** part of a castle wall that sticks out **2** place where a principle is defended: *a bastion of freedom*

bat¹ /bæt/ *n* **1** stick for hitting the ball in cricket, BASEBALL, etc. **2** off one's own bat without being told to do something

bat² *vi/t* **1** strike or hit (as if) with a bat **2** *vt* not bat an eyelid show no sign of shock

bat³ *n* **1** mouselike animal that flies at night **2** as blind as a bat not able to see well

batch /bætʃ/ *n* group; set

bat·ed /'beɪtɪd/ *adj* with bated breath too frightened or excited to breathe

bath /bɑːθ ‖ bæθ/ *n* baths /bɑːðz, bɑːθs ‖ bæðz, bæθs/ **1** container in which one sits to wash the whole body **2** act of washing one's whole body at one time **3** liquid in a container used for some special purpose: *an eyebath* **4** place with a swimming pool or baths for public use ♦ *v* **1** *vi* have a BATH (2) **2** *vt* give a bath to (a baby, etc.)

bathe /beɪð/ *v* **1** *vi esp. BrE* swim in the sea, etc. **2** *vi AmE* have a BATH (2) **3** *vt* put in liquid: *bathe your eyes* ♦ *n* a swim **bather** *n* swimmer

ba·thos /'beɪθɒs ‖ -θɑːs/ *n* [U] sudden change from beautiful ideas to ordinary foolish ones

bath·robe /'bɑːθrəʊb ‖ 'bæθroʊb/ *n esp. AmE* DRESSING GOWN worn before or after bathing

bath·room /'bɑːθrʊm, -ruːm ‖ 'bæθ-/ *n*

1 room with a bath **2** *AmE for* TOILET (1)

bath·tub /'bɑːθtʌb ‖ 'bæθ-/ *n esp. AmE for* BATH (1)

bat·on /'bætɒn ‖ bæ'tɑːn, bə-/ *n* short stick used by the leader of an ORCHESTRA, or as a weapon by a policeman, etc.

bats·man /'bætsmən/ *n* -men /-mən/ player in cricket who tries to hit the ball with a BAT¹ (1)

bat·tal·ion /bə'tæljən/ *n* army unit of 500–1,000 soldiers

bat·ten /'bætn/ *v* batten down *phr vt* fasten with boards

bat·ter¹ /'bætə ‖ -ər/ *vi/t* **1** beat hard and repeatedly **2** cause to lose shape by continual use

batter² *n* [U] mixture of flour, eggs, and milk for making PANCAKES, etc.

bat·ter·ing ram /'··· ·/ *n* (in former times) heavy log used for breaking down castle doors

bat·ter·y /'bætəri/ *n* **1** apparatus for producing electricity **2** army unit of big guns **3** line of boxes in which hens are kept **4** set of things used together: *a battery of tests*

bat·tle /'bætl/ *n* short fight between enemies or opposing groups ♦ *vi* fight; struggle

bat·tle·axe *BrE* **-ax** *AmE* /'bætl-æks/ *n* **1** heavy axe for fighting **2** fierce woman

bat·tle·field /'bætlfiːld/ *n* place where a battle is fought

bat·tle·ments /'bætlmənts/ *n* [P] wall round a castle roof, with spaces to shoot through

bat·tle·ship /'bætl.ʃɪp/ *n* large warship with big guns

bat·ty /'bæti/ *adj sl* slightly mad

bau·ble /'bɔːbəl ‖ 'bɒː-/ *n* cheap jewel

baulk /bɔːk, bɔːlk ‖ bɒːk, bɒːlk/ *v BrE for* BALK

bawd·y /'bɔːdi ‖ 'bɒː-/ *adj* about sex in a rude, funny way **-ily** *adv* **-iness** *n* [U]

bawl /bɔːl ‖ bɒːl/ *vi/t* shout loudly

bay¹ /beɪ/ *n* **1** wide opening along a coast **2** division of a large room or building, separated by shelves, etc.

bay² *vi* make the deep cry of a large hunting dog

bay³ *n* hold/keep at bay keep (an enemy, etc.) away

bay·o·net /'beɪənɪt, -net/ *n* knife on the

end of a RIFLE ♦ *vt* drive a bayonet into

bay win·dow /ˌ· ˈ·/ *n* 3-sided window sticking out from a wall

ba·zaar /bəˈzɑː ‖ -ˈzɑːr/ *n* **1** sale to get money for some good purpose **2** market in an Eastern town

ba·zoo·ka /bəˈzuːkə/ *n* long gun that rests on the shoulder and fires ROCKETS

BC /ˌbiː ˈsiː/ *abbrev. for:* before (the birth of) Christ

be[1] /bi; *strong* biː/ *v aux pres. t. sing.* I **am**, you **are**, he/she/it **is**; *pres. t. pl.* we/you/they **are**; *past t. sing.* I **was**, you **were**, he/she/it **was**; *past t. pl.* we/you/they **were**; *past p.* **been**; *pres. p.* **being 1** (forms continuous tenses with **-ing**): *I am/was reading.* **2** (forms passives with **-ed**): *We are/were invited.* **3** (used with **to**) **a** must: *You are not to smoke.* **b** (shows future plans): *They are to be married soon.*

be[2] *v* **1** (shows that something is the same as the subject): *Today is Tuesday.* **2** (shows where or when): *He's upstairs.* **3** (shows a group or quality): *She's a doctor.* | *I'm cold.* | *Be careful!* **4** (shows that something exists): *There's a hole in your sock.*

beach /biːtʃ/ *n* sandy or stony shore ♦ *vt* move (a boat) onto a beach

beach ball /ˈ· ·/ *n* large light ball to play with on the beach

beach bug·gy /ˈ· ˌ··/ *n* motor vehicle for use on sandy beaches

beach·comb·er /ˈbiːtʃˌkəʊmə ‖ -ˌkoʊmər/ *n* person who searches a beach for useful things to sell

beach·head /ˈbiːtʃhed/ *n* area on an enemy's shore that has been captured

beach·wear /ˈbiːtʃweə ‖ -wer/ *n* [U] clothing for the BEACH

bea·con /ˈbiːkən/ *n* fire or flashing light that gives warning

bead /biːd/ *n* **1** small ball with a hole through it, for threading on string **2** drop of liquid: *beads of sweat* **~ed** *adj*

bead·y /ˈbiːdi/ *adj* (of eyes) small and bright

bea·gle /ˈbiːgəl/ *n* short-legged hunting dog

beak /biːk/ *n* bird's hard horny mouth

bea·ker /ˈbiːkə ‖ -ər/ *n* **1** drinking cup **2** glass cup used in chemistry

beam[1] /biːm/ *n* long heavy piece of wood, esp. used to support a building

beam[2] *n* **1** line of light from some bright object **2** radio waves sent out to guide aircraft, etc. **3** bright look or smile ♦ *v* **1** *vi* (of the sun, etc.) send out light (and heat) **2** *vt* send out (esp. radio or television signals) in a certain direction **3** *vi* smile brightly

bean /biːn/ *n* **1** seed or POD of any of various plants, esp. used as food: *baked beans* | *coffee beans* **2** full of beans full of life and eagerness **3** not have a bean have no money at all **4** spill the beans tell a secret

bear[1] /beə ‖ ber/ *n* large, heavy furry animal that eats meat, fruit, and insects

bear[2] *v* bore /bɔː ‖ bɔːr/, borne /bɔːn ‖ bɔːrn/ **1** *vt* carry **2** *vt* support (a weight) **3** *vt* have; show: *The letter bore no signature.* | *to bear a famous name* **4** *vt* suffer or accept (something unpleasant) without complaining **5** *vt fml* give birth to **6** *vi/t* produce (a crop or fruit) **7** *vi* move in the stated direction: *Cross the field, bear left, and you'll see the house.* **8** *vt* be suitable for: *His words don't bear repeating.* **9** *vt fml* keep (a feeling toward someone) in one's mind: *I don't bear him a grudge.* **10 bear in mind** remember to consider **11 bring something to bear (on)** direct something, e.g. force or persuasion (on); EXERT **~able** *adj* TOLERABLE **~ably** *adv*

bear down *phr v* **1** *vt fml* defeat **2** *vi* use all one's strength and effort

bear down on/upon *phr vt* come towards forcefully and threateningly, esp. at high speed

bear on/upon *phr vt* relate to

bear out *phr vt* support the truth of

bear up *phr vi* show courage or strength in spite of difficulties

bear with *phr vt* show patience towards

beard /bɪəd ‖ bɪrd/ *n* hair on the face below the mouth **~ed** *adj*

bear·er /ˈbeərə ‖ ˈberər/ *n* **1** person who brings or carries something, e.g. the body at a funeral **2** person to whom a cheque is to be paid

bear·ing /ˈbeərɪŋ ‖ ˈber-/ *n* **1** [S;U] way of behaving **2** [S;U] connection; RELEVANCE: *This has no bearing on the subject.* **3** [C] direction shown by a compass **4** understanding of one's position: *get/lose* *one's bearings*

bear·skin /'beə,skɪn || 'ber-/ *n* tall black fur cap worn by certain British soldiers

beast /biːst/ *n* 1 4-footed animal 2 person or thing one does not like ~**ly** *adj* bad; nasty

beat¹ /biːt/ *v* **beat, beaten** /'biːtn/ *or* **beat** 1 *vt* hit again and again, esp. with a stick: *beat a drum* | *the rain beating against the windows* 2 *vt* mix with a fork, etc.: *Beat the eggs.* 3 *vi* move regularly: *I could hear his heart beating.* 4 *vt* defeat: *I beat him at tennis.* 5 **beat about the bush** talk indirectly about something 6 **Beat it!** *infml* Go away! 7 **beat time** make regular movements to measure the speed of music ~**er** *n* tool for beating things ~**ing** *n* 1 act of giving repeated blows, usu. as punishment 2 defeat

beat² *n* 1 single stroke or blow: *the beat of the drum* 2 regular STRESS (4) in music or poetry 3 usual path followed by someone on duty

be·a·tif·ic /ˌbiːə'tɪfɪk◄/ *adj* showing joy and peace: *a beatific smile*

beau·ti·cian /bjuː'tɪʃən/ *n* person who gives beauty treatments

beau·ti·ful /'bjuːtɪfəl/ *adj* giving pleasure to the mind or senses ~**ly** *adv* -**tify** /-tɪfaɪ/ *vt* make beautiful

beau·ty /'bjuːtɪ/ *n* 1 [U] quality of being beautiful 2 [C] someone or something beautiful

bea·ver /'biːvə || -ər/ *n* animal like a big rat that builds dams across streams ♦ *vi* work hard

be·calmed /bɪ'kɑːmd || bɪ'kɑːmd, -'kɑːlmd/ *adj* (of a sailing ship) unable to move because there is no wind

be·came /bɪ'keɪm/ *past t. of* BECOME

be·cause /bɪ'kɒz, bɪ'kəz || bɪ'kɒz, bɪ'kəz/ *conj* 1 for the reason that: *I do it because I like it.* 2 **because of** as a result of: *I came back because of the rain.*

beck /bek/ *n* **at one's beck and call** always ready to do what one asks

beck·on /'bekən/ *vi/t* call with a movement of the finger

be·come /bɪ'kʌm/ *v* **became** /bɪ'keɪm/, **become** 1 begin to be: *become king* | *become warmer* 2 *vt* be suitable for: *Such behaviour hardly becomes someone in your position.*

becoming *adj* 1 attractive 2 suitable

bed¹ /bed/ *n* 1 [C] piece of furniture to sleep on 2 bottom or base: *bed of a river* 3 [C] piece of ground for plants 4 [U] love-making; sex

bed² *vt* -**dd**- 1 put in or on a bed: *a machine bedded in cement* 2 plant 3 have sex with

bed down *phr v* 1 *vt* make (a person or animal) comfortable for the night 2 *vi* make oneself comfortable for the night

bed·clothes /'bedkləʊðz, -kləʊz || -kloʊðz, -kloʊz/ *n* [P] sheets, etc. on a bed

bed·ding /'bedɪŋ/ *n* [U] materials for a person or animal to sleep on

be·dev·il /bɪ'devəl/ *vt* -**ll**- *BrE* || -**l**- *AmE* cause continual trouble for

bed·fel·low /'bed,feləʊ || -loʊ/ *n* 1 person who shares a bed 2 close companion; partner

bed·lam /'bedləm/ *n* [S;U] place of wild noisy activity

bed of roses /ˌ· ·'··/ *n* [S] happy comfortable state

bed·pan /'bedpæn/ *n* container for a sick person's body waste

be·drag·gled /bɪ'drægəld/ *adj* wet, LIMP, and muddy

bed·rid·den /'bed,rɪdn/ *adj* too ill or old to get out of bed

bed·room /'bedrʊm, -ruːm/ *n* room for sleeping in

bed·side /'bedsaɪd/ *n* 1 side of a bed: *bedside lamp* 2 **bedside manner** way in which a doctor behaves when visiting a sick person

bed·sit·ter /ˌ· '··/ *also* **bed·sit** /'bedsɪt/ *n BrE* room for both living and sleeping in

bed·sore /'bedsɔː || -sɔːr/ *n* sore place on the skin, caused by lying too long in bed

bed·spread /'bedspred/ *n* decorative cover for a bed

bed·stead /'bedsted/ *n* main framework of a bed

bed·time /'bedtaɪm/ *n* time for going to bed

bee /biː/ *n* 1 stinging insect that makes honey 2 **a bee in one's bonnet** fixed idea; OBSESSION 3 **the bee's knees** *infml* the best person or thing

beech /biːtʃ/ *n* large forest tree with green or copper-brown leaves

beef /biːf/ *n* [U] meat of farm cattle ♦ *vi* complain ~**y** *adj* (of a person) big and strong

bee·hive /'biːhaɪv/ *n* HIVE

bee·line /'biːlaɪn/ n make a beeline for go straight towards

been /biːn, bɪn ‖ bɪn/ n 1 past participle of BE 2 gone and come back: Have you ever been to India?

beer /bɪə ‖ bɪr/ n [U] alcoholic drink made from MALT —see also SMALL BEER ~y adj: beery breath

beet /biːt/ n 1 root from which sugar is made 2 BEETROOT

bee·tle /'biːtl/ n insect with hard wing coverings

beet·root /'biːtruːt/ n -roots or -root [C;U] BrE large red root vegetable

be·fall /bɪ'fɔːl ‖ -'fɔːl/ vi/t befall /-'fel/, befallen /-'fɔːlən ‖ -'fɔː-/ fml happen (to)

be·fit /bɪ'fɪt/ vt -tt- fml be suitable for: befitting behaviour

be·fore /bɪ'fɔː ‖ -'fɔːr/ prep 1 earlier than 2 ahead of; in front of ♦ adv already; formerly: I've seen you before. ♦ conj 1 before the time when 2 rather than

be·fore·hand /bɪ'fɔːhænd ‖ -'fɔːr-/ adv before something else happens

be·friend /bɪ'frend/ vt fml be a friend to

beg /beg/ v -gg- 1 vi/t ask for (food, money, etc) 2 vt fml request politely: I beg to differ. 3 **beg the question** to take as true something that is not yet proved 4 **going begging** not wanted by anyone

beg·gar /'begə ‖ -ər/ n person who lives by begging ~ly adj much too little

be·gin /bɪ'gɪn/ vi/t began /bɪ'gæn/, begun /bɪ'gʌn/ 1 start; take the first step 2 **to begin with** as the first reason ~ner n person starting to learn ~ning n [C;U] starting point

be·grudge /bɪ'grʌdʒ/ vt to GRUDGE

be·guile /bɪ'gaɪl/ vt fml 1 charm 2 deceive; cheat

be·half /bɪ'hɑːf ‖ bɪ'hæf/ n **on behalf of** for; in the interests of: I'm speaking on John's behalf.

be·have /bɪ'heɪv/ vi 1 (of people or things) act in a particular way 2 show good manners

be·hav·iour BrE ‖ -ior AmE /bɪ'heɪvjə ‖ -ər/ n [U] way of behaving

be·head /bɪ'hed/ vt cut off the head of

be·hest /bɪ'hest/ n fml **at someone's behest** by someone's command

be·hind /bɪ'haɪnd/ prep 1 at or to the back of: hide behind the door 2 less good than:

He's behind the others in mathematics. 3 in support of ♦ adv 1 behind something 2 where something was before: I've left the key behind! 3 late; slow: We're behind with the rent. ♦ n infml BUTTOCKS

be·hold /bɪ'həʊld ‖ -'hoʊld/ vt beheld /bɪ'held/ lit see

be·hold·en /bɪ'həʊldən ‖ -'hoʊl-/ adj be beholden to have to feel grateful to

beige /beɪʒ/ adj, n pale brown

be·ing[1] /'biːɪŋ/ n 1 [U] existence: When did the club come into being? 2 [C] living thing, esp. a person

being[2] v present participle of BE

be·lat·ed /bɪ'leɪtɪd/ adj delayed; too late ~ly adv

belch /beltʃ/ v 1 vi pass gas up from the stomach 2 vt send out (large amounts of smoke, etc.) **belch** n

be·lea·guered /bɪ'liːgəd ‖ -ərd/ adj 1 having a lot of problems 2 surrounded by enemies

bel·fry /'belfri/ n tower for bells

be·lie /bɪ'laɪ/ vt fml give a false idea of

be·lief /bə'liːf/ n 1 [S;U] feeling that something is true, or can be trusted 2 [C] idea that is believed: religious beliefs

be·lieve /bə'liːv/ v 1 vt consider to be true 2 vi have religious faith **believable** adj that can be believed **believer** n

believe in phr vt 1 think that (something exists): believe in fairies 2 feel sure of the value of: believe in lots of exercise

be·lit·tle /bɪ'lɪtl/ vt fml cause to seem unimportant: Don't belittle your efforts.

bell /bel/ n 1 metal object that makes a ringing sound: church bells | a bicycle bell 2 cup-shaped object: the bell of a flower 3 **ring a bell** remind one of something

bel·lig·er·ent /bə'lɪdʒərənt/ n, adj 1 (country that is) at war 2 (person who is) ready to fight

bel·low /'beləʊ ‖ -loʊ/ vi/t shout in a deep voice

bel·lows /'beləʊz ‖ -loʊz/ n -lows instrument for blowing air into a fire, etc.

bel·ly /'beli/ n 1 infml the part of the human body between the chest and legs 2 curved surface like this: the belly of a plane ~ful /-ful/ n infml too much

bel·ly·ache /'beli-eɪk/ vi complain repeatedly

belly but·ton /'·· ,·'·/ *n infml* NAVEL

be·long /bɪ'lɒŋ ‖ bɪ'lɔːŋ/ *vi* be in the right place: *This chair belongs upstairs.* ~**ings** *n* [P] one's property

belong to *phr vt* **1** be the property of **2** be a member of

be·lov·ed /bɪ'lʌvd/ *n, adj* (person who is) dearly loved

be·low /bɪ'ləʊ ‖ -'loʊ/ *adv, prep* in a lower place (than); under: *He saw the valley below.* | *below the knee* | *See page 85 below.*

belt[1] /belt/ *n* **1** band worn round the waist **2** circular piece of material that drives a machine **3** area with a particular quality, crop, etc. **4 below the belt** *infml* unfair or unfairly —see also BLACK BELT, GREEN BELT

belt[2] *v* **1** *vt* fasten with a belt **2** *vt infml* hit hard **3** *vi sl, esp. BrE* travel fast

belt out *phr vt infml* sing loudly

belt up *phr vi sl* be quiet

belt·way /'beltweɪ/ *n AmE for* RING ROAD

be·moan /bɪ'məʊn ‖ -'moʊn/ *vt fml* express sorrow for

be·mused /bɪ'mjuːzd/ *adj* unable to think clearly

bench /bentʃ/ *n* **1** [C] long seat **2** [C] long worktable: *a carpenter's bench* **3 a** [*the+S*] place where a judge sits in court **b** judges as a group —see also FRONT BENCH

bend /bend/ *vi/t* **bent** /bent/ (cause to) move into a curve or move away from an upright position: *bend the wire* | *bend down to kiss the child* ♦ *n* **1** curve: *a bend in the road* **2 round the bend** *infml* mad **bends** [P] pain suffered by divers who come to the surface too quickly

be·neath /bɪ'niːθ/ *adv, prep fml* **1** below; under **2** not worthy of: *beneath contempt*

ben·e·dic·tion /ˌbenɪ'dɪkʃən/ *n* religious blessing

ben·e·fac·tor /'benɪˌfæktə -ər/ **bene-factress** /-trɪs/ *fem.* — *n* person who gives money, etc. —**tion** /ˌbenɪ'fækʃən/ *n* **1** [U] giving of money **2** [C] money given

ben·e·fi·cial /ˌbenɪ'fɪʃəl◀/ *adj* (of things) helpful; useful

ben·e·fi·cia·ry /ˌbenɪ'fɪʃəri ‖ -'fɪʃieri/ *n* receiver of a benefit

ben·e·fit /'benɪfɪt/ *n* **1** [U] advantage; profit: *She's had the benefit of a very good education.* **2** [C;U] money paid by the government to people who need it because of sickness, etc: *unemployment benefit* [C]

event to raise money for some person or special purpose **4 the benefit of the doubt** favourable consideration given because there is no proof of guilt or wrongness ♦ *v* **1** *vt* be helpful to **2** *vi* gain advantage

be·nev·o·lent /bɪ'nevələnt/ *adj* wishing to do good; kind –**lence** *n* [U]

be·nign /bɪ'naɪn/ *adj* kind and harmless

bent[1] /bent/ *v* **1** *past t. and p. of* BEND **2 bent on** determined on: *She's bent on winning.*

bent[2] *n* special natural skill: *a natural bent for languages*

bent[3] *adj BrE sl* **1** dishonest **2** HOMOSEXUAL

be·queath /bɪ'kwiːð, bɪ'kwiːθ/ *vt fml* give to others after death

be·quest /bɪ'kwest/ *n fml* something bequeathed

be·rate /bɪ'reɪt/ *vt fml* speak angrily to

be·reaved /bɪ'riːvd/ *adj fml* having lost someone by death: *a bereaved mother* **bereavement** *n* [C;U]

be·reft /bɪ'reft/ *adj* completely without: *bereft of hope*

be·ret /'bereɪ ‖ bə'reɪ/ *n* round soft flat cap

ber·ry /'beri/ *n* small soft fruit with seeds

ber·serk /bɜː'sɜːk, bə- ‖ bɜːr'sɜːrk, 'bɜːrsɜːrk/ *adj* violently angry

berth /bɜːθ ‖ bɜːrθ/ *n* **1** sleeping place in a ship or train **2** place where a ship can be tied up in harbour **3 give someone a wide berth** avoid someone ♦ *vi/t* tie up (a ship)

be·seech /bɪ'siːtʃ/ *vt* **besought** /bɪ'sɔːt ‖ -'sɒːt/ *or* beseeched *fml* ask eagerly

be·set /bɪ'set/ *vt* beset, *present participle* besetting attack continuously: *beset by doubts*

be·side /bɪ'saɪd/ *prep* **1** at the side of **2** in comparison with **3 beside oneself** almost mad (with joy, etc.) **4 beside the point** having nothing to do with the main question

be·sides /bɪ'saɪdz/ *adv* also ♦ *prep* in addition to

be·siege /bɪ'siːdʒ/ *vt* **1** surround (a place) with armed forces: (fig.) *They besieged her with questions.*

be·sot·ted /bɪ'sɒtɪd ‖ bɪ'sɑː-/ *adj* made foolish or unable to behave sensibly

be·spoke /bɪ'spəʊk ‖ -'spoʊk/ *adj* (of clothes) made to someone's measurements

best[1] /best/ *adj* (*superlative of* GOOD) **1** the

highest in quality or skill: *the best tennis player in America* **2 the best part of** most of —see also SECOND BEST

best² /bɪst/ *adv* (superlative of WELL) **1** in the best way: *She did best.* **2** to the greatest degree; most: *He thinks he knows best.* **3 as best one can** as well as one can

best³ *n* [S] **1** the greatest degree of good: *She wants the best for her children.* **2** one's best effort: *I did my best.* **3 All the best!** (used when saying goodbye) I wish you success! **4 at its/one's best** in as good a state as possible **5 at (the) best** if the best happens **6 make the best of** do as well as one can with (something unsatisfactory)

bes·ti·al /'bestiəl‖'bestʃəl/ *adj* (of human behaviour) very cruel ~ity /ˌbestiˈælɪti‖ˌbestʃiˈ-/ *n* [U]

best man /ˌ· '·/ *n* man attending the BRIDEGROOM at a wedding

be·stow /bɪ'stəʊ‖-'stoʊ/ *vt fml* give

best·sel·ler /best'selə‖-ər/ *n* book, etc. that sells in very large numbers

bet /bet/ *n* **1** agreement to risk money on a future event **2** sum of money risked in this way ♦ *vi/t* bet *or* betted; *pres. p.* betting **1** risk (money) on a race, etc. **2** be sure: *I bet he's angry!*

be·tide /bɪ'taɪd/ *vt lit* woe betide you, him, etc. you, he, etc. will be in trouble

be·tray /bɪ'treɪ/ *vt* **1** be unfaithful to **2** make known (a secret): (fig.) *Her face betrayed* (=showed) *her nervousness.* ~er *n* ~al *n* [C;U]

be·trothed /bɪ'trəʊðd‖-'troʊðd/ *adj lit* having promised to marry

bet·ter /'betə‖-ər/ *adj* **1** higher in quality; more good: *a better way to do it* **2** well again after illness ♦ *adv* **1** in a better way: *It works better now.* **2 go one better (than)** do better (than) **3 had better** ought to; should: *I'd better not tell him.* **4 know better (than)** be sensible enough not to ♦ *n* **get the better of** defeat ♦ *vi/t* **1** improve **2 better oneself: a** earn more **b** educate oneself ~ment improvement betters *n* [P] people better then oneself

be·tween /bɪ'twiːn/ *prep* **1** in the space or time that separates: *Stand between Sue and Brian.* | *Don't eat between meals.* **2** (shows connection): *an air service between London and Paris* **3** (shows division or sharing): *The difference between spaghetti and noodles.* | *Between us, we collected £17.* ♦ *adv* **1** in the space or time between things **2 few and far between** very rare

bev·el /'bevəl/ *vt* -ll- *BrE* ‖ -l- *AmE* make a sloping edge on bevel *n*

bev·er·age /'bevərɪdʒ/ *n fml* liquid for drinking, esp. one that is not water or medicine

bev·y /'bevi/ *n* large group

be·wail /bɪ'weɪl/ *vt fml* express sorrow for

be·ware /bɪ'weə‖-'wer/ *vi/t* (used in giving orders) Be careful!: *Beware of the dog.*

be·wil·der /bɪ'wɪldə‖-ər/ *vt* confuse: *a bewildering mass of detail*

be·witch /bɪ'wɪtʃ/ *vt* **1** use magic on **2** charm: *a bewitching smile*

be·yond /bɪ'jɒnd‖bɪ'jɑːnd/ *prep* **1** on the further side of: *beyond the mountains* **2** outside the limits of; more than: *beyond belief* **3 beyond me** too hard for me to understand ♦ *adv* further: *fly to Cairo and beyond* —see also BACK OF BEYOND

bi·as /'baɪəs/ *n* [C;U] fixed unfair opinion; PREJUDICE ♦ *vt* -s- *or* -ss- cause to form fixed opinions: *a biased judgment*

bib /bɪb/ *n* **1** piece of cloth or plastic tied under a child's chin **2** top part of an APRON

Bi·ble /'baɪbəl/ *n* holy book of the Christians and Jews: (fig.) *This dictionary is my bible.* biblical /'bɪblɪkəl/ *adj*

bib·li·og·ra·phy /ˌbɪbliˈɒɡrəfi‖-ˈɑːɡ-/ *n* list of writings on a subject –pher person who writes such a list

bi·car·bon·ate /baɪˈkɑːbənɪt, -neɪt‖-ˈkɑːr-/ *n* [U] chemical used in baking and as a medicine

bi·cen·te·na·ry /ˌbaɪsenˈtiːnəri‖-ˈtenəri, -ˈsentəneri/ *esp. BrE* ‖ bicentennial /ˌbaɪsenˈteniəl/ *esp. AmE* — *n* 200th ANNIVERSARY bicentenary *adj*

bi·ceps /'baɪseps/ *n* biceps muscle of the upper arm

bick·er /'bɪkə‖-ər/ *vi* quarrel about small matters

bi·cy·cle /'baɪsɪkəl/ *n* 2-wheeled vehicle ridden by pushing its PEDALs bicycle *vi*

bid¹ /bɪd/ *vi/t* bid **1** offer (a price) at a sale **2** (in card games) declare what one intends to win ♦ *n* **1** amount that is bid **2** attempt: *a rescue bid* ~der *n*

bid² *vt* bade /bæd, beɪd/ *or* bid, bidden /'bɪdn/ *or* bid; *pres. p.* bidding *lit* order: *She*

bide

bade him come. ~**ding** *n* [U]

bide /baɪd/ *vt* **bide one's time** wait till the right moment

bi·en·ni·al /baɪˈeniəl/ *adj* happening once every two years

bier /bɪə/ *n* movable table for a COFFIN

bi·fo·cals /baɪˈfəʊkəlz ‖ ˈbaɪfoʊ-/ *n* [P] glasses made in two parts, suitable both for looking at distant objects and for reading **bifocal** *adj*

big /bɪg/ *adj* **-gg-** **1** of more than average size, importance, etc.: *big ears* | *a big decision* **2** generous: *big hearted* **3** *infml* very popular

big·a·my /ˈbɪgəmi/ *n* [U] being married to two people at the same time –**mist** *n* –**mous** *adj*

big·head /ˈbɪghed/ *n infml* CONCEITED person

big·ot /ˈbɪgət/ *n* person who will not change an unreasonable opinion ~**ry** [U] behaviour typical of a bigot

big shot /ˌ· ˈ·/ also **big noise** — *n* person of great importance or influence

big·wig /ˈbɪgwɪg/ *n infml* important person

bi·jou /ˈbiːʒuː/ *adj* (esp. of a building) small and pretty

bike /baɪk/ *n*, *vi* BICYCLE

bi·ki·ni /bɪˈkiːni/ *n* woman's small two-piece swimming costume

bi·lat·er·al /baɪˈlætərəl/ *adj* with two sides or two groups: *a bilateral agreement*

bile /baɪl/ *n* [U] **1** liquid formed in the LIVER **2** bad temper

bilge /bɪldʒ/ *n* [U] **1** ship's bottom, with dirty water in it **2** *infml* foolish talk

bi·lin·gual /baɪˈlɪŋgwəl/ *adj* using two languages

bil·i·ous /ˈbɪliəs/ *adj* sick because food is not DIGESTed properly

bill¹ /bɪl/ *n* **1** list of things that must be paid for **2** plan for a future law **3** *AmE* piece of paper money **4** printed notice **5 fill the bill** be suitable for the job **6 foot the bill** pay and take responsibility (for) ♦ *vt* **1** send a bill to **2** advertise in printed notices **3 bill and coo** (of lovers) kiss and speak softly to each other

bill² *n* bird's beak

bil·let /ˈbɪlɪt/ *n* private home where soldiers are put to live ♦ *vt* put in billets

bill·fold /ˈbɪlfəʊld ‖ -foʊld/ *n AmE for*
WALLET

bil·liards /ˈbɪljədz ‖ -ərdz/ *n* [U] game played on a table, with balls and long sticks

bil·lion /ˈbɪljən/ *determiner*, *n* **billion** *or* **billions** **1** one thousand million **2** *BrE* one million million ~**th** *determiner*, *n*, *adv*

bil·low /ˈbɪləʊ ‖ -loʊ/ *n* rolling mass of smoke, etc. like a large wave **billow** *vi*

bin /bɪn/ *n* large container for storing things, or for waste

bi·na·ry /ˈbaɪnəri/ *adj* **1** double **2** using only 0 and 1 as a base: *the binary scale*

bind /baɪnd/ *v* **1** *vt* tie up: *bind the prisoner's arms* | *bind up a wound* | (fig.) *bound together by friendship* **2** *vt* fasten (a book) into its cover **3** *vi/t* (cause to) stick together in a mass **4** *vt* cause to obey, esp. by a law or a promise: *a binding agreement* | *He felt bound to tell her.* ~**er** **1** person or thing that binds books **2** removable cover for holding sheets of papers, etc. ~**ing** *n* book cover

binge¹ /bɪndʒ/ *n* short period of drinking or eating too much

binge² *vi* eat a lot in a very short time

bin·go /ˈbɪŋgəʊ ‖ -goʊ/ *n* [U] game played for money, by covering numbered squares on a card

bi·noc·u·lars /bɪˈnɒkjŭləz, baɪ- ‖ -ˈnɑːkjŭlɑrz/ *n* [P] pair of glasses like short TELESCOPEs for both eyes

bi·o·chem·is·try /ˌbaɪəʊˈkemɪstri ‖ ˌbaɪoʊ-/ *n* [U] chemistry of living things

bi·o·da·ta /ˈbaɪəʊˌdeɪtə ‖ ˌbaɪoʊ-/ *n AmE for* CURRICULUM VITAE

bi·o·de·gra·da·ble /ˌbaɪəʊdɪˈgreɪdəb əl ‖ ˌbaɪoʊ-/ *adj* able to be made harmless by the chemical action of bacteria, etc.

bi·og·ra·phy /baɪˈɒgrəfi ‖ -ˈɑːg-/ *n* written account of someone's life –**pher** *a* person who writes this –**phical** /ˌbaɪəˈgræfɪkəl◄/ *adj*

bi·ol·o·gy /baɪˈɒlədʒi ‖ -ˈɑːl-/ *n* [U] scientific study of living things –**gist** *n* –**gical** /ˌbaɪəˈlɒdʒɪkəl◄ ‖ -ˈlɑː-/ *adj*

bi·on·ic /baɪˈɒnɪk ‖ -ˈɑːn-/ *adj* having more than human strength, speed, etc.

bi·o·pic /ˈbaɪəʊˌpɪk ‖ ˈbaɪoʊ-/ *n* biographical film

bi·op·sy /ˈbaɪɒpsi ‖ -ɑːp-/ *n* removal of material from a living body to test it for possible disease

bi·o·tech·nol·o·gy /ˌbaɪəʊtekˈnɒlədʒi ‖

‚baıɒʊtek'nɒ:-/ n [U] use of living cells, bacteria, etc. in industry

bi·ped /'baıped/ n two-footed creature

bi·plane /'baıpleın/ n aircraft with two pairs of wings

birch /bɜːtʃ‖bɜːrtʃ/ n 1 tree with smooth wood and thin branches 2 rod made from this wood, formerly used for punishing

bird /bɜːd‖bɜːrd/ n 1 [C] creature with wings and feathers that can fly 2 [C] sl woman 3 [the+S] rude noise made as sign of disapproval 4 [U] BrE sl period of time spent in prison 5 **birds of a feather** people of the same kind —see also EARLY BIRD

bird's-eye view /ˌ· ·ˈ·/ n view seen from above, like a map

bi·ro /'baıərəʊ‖'baırəʊ/ n biros tdmk for BALLPOINT

birth /bɜːθ‖bɜːrθ/ n 1 [C;U] act, time, or process of being born: She gave birth to a fine baby. 2 [U] family origin: French by birth

birth con·trol /'· ·ˌ·/ n [U] CONTRACEPTION

birth·day /'bɜːdeı‖'bɜːrθ-/ n ANNIVERSARY of the day one was born

birth·mark /'bɜːθmɑːk‖'bɜːrθmɑːrk/ n mark on the skin at birth

birth·rate /'bɜːθreıt‖'bɜːrθ-/ n number of births during a particular time

birth·right /'bɜːθraıt‖'bɜːrθ-/ n something that belongs to someone because of the family or nation they were born into

bis·cuit /'bıskɪt/ n 1 flat thin dry cake 2 AmE for SCONE 3 **take the biscuit** be very surprising

bi·sect /baı'sekt‖'baısekt/ vt divide into two

bi·sex·u·al /baı'sekʃʊəl/ n, adj (person) sexually attracted to people of both sexes

bish·op /'bɪʃəp/ n 1 Christian priest of high rank 2 piece in CHESS ~**ric** /'bɪʃəprɪk/ n DIOCESE

bi·son /'baısən/ n bisons or bison large wild hairy cowlike animal

bis·tro /'biːstrəʊ‖-trəʊ/ n small BAR or restaurant

bit¹ /bıt/ v past t. of BITE

bit² /bıt/ n 1 small piece: bits of paper/of news for a short time: We walked around for a bit. 3 **a bit** rather: I'm a bit tired. 4 **bit by bit** gradually 5 **do one's bit** do one's share of work 6 **every bit as** quite as; no less: She's every bit as good as you are. 7 **not a bit of it**

not at all

bit³ n single unit of computer information

bit⁴ n part of a BRIDLE that goes inside the horse's mouth

bitch /bıtʃ/ n 1 female dog 2 derog unpleasant woman ♦ vi sl 1 complain continually 2 make nasty or hurtful remarks about others ~**y** adj making nasty remarks about people

bite /baıt/ v bit /bıt/, bitten /'bıtn/ 1 vi/t cut with the teeth 2 vi/t (of snakes and insects) sting 3 vi (of fish) accept food on a hook 4 vi take firm hold: The wheels won't bite on the ice. 5 have or show an effect: The new taxes are beginning to bite. 6 **bite off more than one can chew** attempt too much 7 **bite the bullet** suffer bravely **bite the dust** infml be killed or defeated ♦ n 1 [C] piece removed by biting 2 [C;U] wound made by biting 3 [S] something to eat 4 [U;S] sharpness; bitterness **biting** adj painful: biting wind/remarks

bit·ter /'bıtə‖-ər/ adj 1 not sweet; tasting like beer or black coffee 2 very cold: a bitter wind 3 causing grief: bitter disappointment 4 full of hate: bitter enemies 5 **to the bitter end** to the end in spite of all unpleasant difficulties ♦ n [U] BrE bitter beer ~**ly** adv ~**ness** n [U]

bit·ter·sweet /ˌbıtə'swiːt◂‖-tər-/ adj pleasant, but mixed with sadness

bi·tu·men /'bıtʃʊmɪn‖bə'tuː-/ n [U] sticky black substance used esp. in road-making

biv·ou·ac /'bıvu-æk/ n camp without tents ♦ vi -**ck**- spend the night in a bivouac

bi·zarre /bə'zɑː‖-'zɑːr/ adj very strange ~**ly** adv

blab /blæb/ vi -**bb**- sl tell a secret

black¹ /blæk/ adj 1 of the colour of night: (fig.) Your hands are black. (=very dirty) 2 of a dark-skinned race 3 (of coffee) without milk 4 very bad; hopeless 5 very angry: a black look 6 (of humour) funny about unpleasant or dangerous people or events: black humour ♦ n 1 [U] black colour 2 [C] black person ♦ vt 1 make black 2 (of a British trade union) refuse to work with: Black their cargo. ~**ly** adv 1 angrily 2 sadly ~**ness** n [U]

black belt /ˌ· 'ˌ/ n (person who holds) a high rank in JUDO, KARATE, etc.

black·ber·ry /'blækbəri‖-beri/ n black

berry from a prickly wild bush

black·board /'blækbɔːd ‖ -bɔːrd/ *n* board used in schools for writing on

black box /ˌ· '·/ *n* apparatus fitted to an aircraft to record information about an accident

black·cur·rant /ˌblæk'kʌrənt ‖ -'kɜːr-/ *n* garden bush with small blue-black berries, often made into drinks

black e·con·o·my /ˌ· ·'···/ *n* [*the*+S] business activity carried on unofficially, esp. to avoid taxation

black·en /'blækən/ *vi/t* make or become black: (fig.) *They blackened his character by spreading lies.*

black eye /ˌ· '·/ *n* dark skin round the eye, from being hit

black·head /'blækhed/ *n* spot on the skin with a black top

black hole /ˌ· '·/ *n* area in outer space into which everything is pulled, even light itself

black ice /ˌ· '·/ *n* [U] ice that cannot be seen, on a road

black·leg /'blækleg/ *n BrE* person who works when others are on STRIKE[2] (1)

black·list /'blæk,lɪst/ *n* list of people to be avoided or punished **blacklist** *vt*

black mag·ic /ˌ· '··/ *n* magic used for evil purposes

black·mail /'blækmeɪl/ *n* [U] 1 getting money from someone by threatening to make known unpleasant facts 2 influencing of someone's actions by threats, causing anxiety, etc.: *He accused his mother of using emotional blackmail to stop him leaving home.* ♦ **blackmail** *vt* ~**er** *n*

black mar·ket /ˌ· '··◂/ *n* [S] unlawful buying and selling of goods, etc.: *We bought our dollars on the black market.* ~**eer** /ˌ· ·'·/ *n*

black·out /'blækaʊt/ *n* 1 darkness, ordered by the government during wartime or caused by electrical failure 2 short loss of consciousness 3 intentional prevention of reporting: *a news blackout* **black out** *vi/t*

black sheep /ˌ· '·/ *n* family member who brings shame on it

black·smith /'blæk,smɪθ/ *n* metalworker who makes iron things

black spot /'· ·/ *n* part of a road where many accidents have happened

blad·der /'blædə ‖ -ər/ *n* 1 skin bag inside the body, where waste liquid collects 2 any bag that can be filled with air or liquid

blade /bleɪd/ *n* 1 sharp cutting part of a knife, etc. 2 flat part of an OAR, PROPELLER, or BAT[1] (1) 3 long narrow leaf: *blades of grass*

blame /bleɪm/ *vt* 1 consider responsible for something bad 2 **be to blame** be guilty ♦ *n* [U] responsibility for something bad ~**less** *adj* free from guilt ~**worthy** *adj* guilty

blanch /blɑːntʃ ‖ blæntʃ/ *vi/t* make or become white

bland /blænd/ *adj* 1 (of food) without much taste 2 (of people or their behaviour) showing no strong feelings or opinions, esp. so as to avoid giving offence ~**ly** *adv* ~**ness** *n* [U]

blank[1] /blæŋk/ *adj* 1 without writing 2 empty or expressionless: *My mind went blank.* ~**ly** *adv*: *He looked at me blankly.* ~**ness** *n* [U]

blank[2] *n* 1 empty space 2 CARTRIDGE with no bullet in it 3 **draw a blank** be unsuccessful

blank cheque *BrE* ‖ **blank check** *AmE* /ˌ· '·/ *n* 1 cheque that is signed, but with the amount left blank 2 complete freedom to do what one wants

blan·ket /'blæŋkɪt/ *n* thick bed covering: (fig.) *A blanket of snow covered the hills* —see also WET BLANKET ♦ *vt* cover as if with a blanket ♦ *adj* including all cases: *a blanket rule*

blank verse /ˌ· '·/ *n* [U] poetry that does not rhyme

blare /bleə ‖ bler/ *vi/t* make the loud noise of a horn blowing

bla·sé /'blɑːzeɪ ‖ blɑː'zeɪ/ *adj* seeming not to be concerned or excited about something, or about many things in general

blas·phe·my /'blæsfəmi/ *n* [C;U] bad language about God and holy things –**mous** *adj* blaspheme /blæs'fiːm/ *vi*

blast[1] /blɑːst ‖ blæst/ *n* 1 strong air movement 2 rush of air from an explosion 3 sound of a brass wind instrument 4 **at full blast** as hard as possible

blast[2] *v* 1 *vi/t* break up (rock, etc.) with explosives 2 *vt* DAMN

blast off *phr vi* (of a spacecraft) leave the ground **blast-off** /'· ·/ *n* [U]

bla·tant /'bleɪtənt/ *adj* too noticeable; shameless **~ly** *adv* **–tancy** *n* [U]

blaze /bleɪz/ *n* 1 [S] bright flame: (fig.) *a sudden blaze of anger* 2 [C] big dangerous fire 3 [C] white mark ♦ *vi* 1 burn or shine brightly 2 spread news about: *The news was blazed across the front page.* 3 **blaze a trail** lead the way

blaz·er /'bleɪzə ‖ -ər/ *n* loose-fitting JACKET, with the sign of a school, etc. on it

bleach /bliːtʃ/ *vi/t* make or become white or pale ♦ *n* [U] chemical used for bleaching cloth

bleach·ers /'bliːtʃəz ‖ -ərz/ *n* [*the*+P] *AmE* cheap unroofed seats for watching a BASEBALL game

bleak /bliːk/ *adj* cold and cheerless: *bleak weather* | (fig.) *bleak prospects* **~ly** *adv* **~ness** *n* [U]

blear·y /'blɪəri ‖ 'blɪri/ *adj* (of eyes) red and tired **–ily** *adv* **–iness** *n* [U]

bleat /bliːt/ *vi, n* (make) the sound of a sheep or goat

bleed /bliːd/ *v* **bled** /bled/ 1 *vi* lose blood 2 *vt* draw blood from, as doctors once did 3 *vt* draw off liquid or air from 4 **bleed someone dry/white** take all someone's money, esp. gradually

bleep /bliːp/ *n* repeated high sound made by a machine (a **bleeper**) to attract attention ♦ *vi/t* make, or call someone with, this sound

blem·ish /'blemɪʃ/ *n* mark, etc. that spoils perfection **blemish** *vt*

blend /blend/ *vi/t* mix together ♦ *n* mixture **~er** kitchen mixing machine

blend in *phr vi* go together well

bless /bles/ *vt* **blessed** *or* **blest** /blest/ 1 ask God's favour for 2 make holy 3 **be blessed with** be lucky enough to have **~ed** /'blesɪd/ *adj* 1 holy 2 desirable 3 *infml* (used to give force to expressions of annoyance)

bless·ing /'blesɪŋ/ *n* 1 [C] God's favour 2 [C] something one is glad of 3 [U] approval

blew /bluː/ *past t. of* BLOW[1]

blight /blaɪt/ *n* 1 [U] disease of plants 2 [C] something that spoils 3 [U] condition of ugliness, disorder, and decay **blight** *vt*: (fig.) *blighted hopes*

blind /blaɪnd/ *adj* 1 unable to see 2 unwilling to recognize: *blind to her faults* 3 without reason or purpose: *blind panic*

4 slightest: *He didn't take a blind bit of notice.* 5 **turn a blind eye (to)** pretend not to see or notice (something, esp. something illegal) ♦ *vt* 1 make unable to see or understand 2 **blind with science** confuse or fill with admiration by a show of detailed or specialist knowledge **~ly** *adv* **~ness** *n* [U]

blind al·ley /ˌ· '··/ *n* narrow street with no way out

blind drunk /ˌ· '·/ *adj* extremely drunk

blind·ers /'blaɪndəz ‖ -ərz/ *n* [P] *AmE for* BLINKERS

blind·fold /'blaɪndfəʊld ‖ -foʊld/ *vt* cover (the eyes) with a piece of cloth ♦ *n* piece of material to cover the eyes ♦ *adv* with the eyes covered: *I could do it blindfold.*

blind spot /'· ·/ 1 part of an area that cannot easily be seen 2 something one is never able to understand

blink /blɪŋk/ *vi/t* shut and open (the eyes) quickly: (fig.) *The lights blinked in the distance.* **blink** *n* 1 act of blinking 2 **on the blink** not working properly

blink·ers /'blɪŋkəz ‖ -ərz/ *n* [P] 1 leather pieces fixed to prevent a horse from seeing sideways 2 inability to see or understand **blinkered** *adj*

bliss /blɪs/ *n* [U] complete happiness **~ful** *adj* **~fully** *adv*

blis·ter /'blɪstə ‖ -ər/ *n* 1 watery swelling under the skin 2 swelling like this on a rubber tyre, painted wood, etc. ♦ *vi/t* form blisters **~ing** *adj* 1 very hot 2 very angry and intended to hurt: *a blistering attack*

blithe /blaɪð ‖ blaɪð, blaɪθ/ *adj* free from care **~ly** *adv*

blitz /blɪts/ *n* 1 sudden violent attack, esp. from the air 2 period of great activity for some special purpose: *an advertising blitz*

bliz·zard /'blɪzəd ‖ -ərd/ *n* severe snowstorm

bloat·ed /'bləʊtɪd ‖ 'bloʊ-/ *adj* unpleasantly swollen

blob /blɒb ‖ blɑːb/ *n* drop of liquid or small round mass

bloc /blɒk ‖ blɑːk/ *n* group of people, nations, etc. acting as a unit —see also EN BLOC

block /blɒk ‖ blɑːk/ *n* 1 solid piece of material: *a block of wood/ice* 2 large building divided into parts: *an office block* 3 distance between one street and the next:

The shop is 4 blocks away. **4** group of things considered together: *a block of theatre seats* **5** blockage ♦ *vt* **1** prevent movement through **2** shut off from view **3** prevent the success of: *to block legislation*

block·ade /blɒˈkeɪd ‖ blɑ:-/ *n* surrounding of a place, by ships or soldiers, to stop people or goods from going in or out: *to raise /lift* (=end) *a blockade* ♦ *vt* surround in this way

block·age /ˈblɒkɪdʒ ‖ ˈblɑ:-/ *n* something that stops movement; OBSTRUCTION: *a blockage in the pipe*

block·bust·er /ˈblɒkˌbʌstə ‖ ˈblɑ:k ˌbʌstər/ *n* something very big, effective, or successful

block cap·i·tals /ˌ· ˈ···/ also **block letters** /ˌ·ˈ··/ *n* [P] CAPITALS (3)

block vote /ˌ· ˈ·/ *n* single vote made by a representative of a large group, e.g. a trade union, and regarded as representing all the group members

bloke /bləʊk ‖ bloʊk/ *n BrE infml* man

blond /blɒnd ‖ blɑ:nd/ *adj* **1** (of hair) light-coloured; yellow **2** also **blonde** *fem.* — having blond hair **blonde** /blɒnd ‖ blɑ:nd/ *n* blonde woman

blood /blʌd/ *n* **1** [U] red liquid that flows through the body: *blood donors* **2** [U] family relationship: *people of noble blood* **3** [C] fashionable young man **4 in cold blood** cruelly and on purpose **5 make someone's blood boil** make someone very angry **6 make someone's blood run cold** frighten someone ~**less** *adj* without fighting ~**y** *adj* **1** bleeding **2** (used for giving force to a remark): *You bloody fool!* ~**ily** *adv*

blood·bath /ˈblʌdbɑ:θ ‖ -bæθ/ *n* merciless killing; MASSACRE

blood·cur·dling /ˈblʌdˌkɜ:dlɪŋ ‖ -ɜ:r-/ *adj* very frightening

blood group /ˈ· ·/ *n* class of human blood

blood·hound /ˈblʌdhaʊnd/ *n* large dog that tracks people and animals

blood poi·son·ing /ˈ· ˌ···/ *n* [U] condition in which an infection spreads from a part of the body through the BLOODSTREAM

blood pres·sure /ˈ· ˌ··/ *n* [C;U] measurable force with which blood flows through the BLOODSTREAM

blood·shed /ˈblʌdʃed/ *n* [U] killing, usu. in fighting

blood·shot /ˈblʌdʃɒt ‖ -ʃɑ:t/ *adj* (of the eyes) red

blood sport /ˈ· ·/ *n* killing of birds and animals for pleasure

blood·stain /ˈblʌdsteɪn/ *n* spot of blood ~**ed** *adj*

blood·stream /ˈblʌdstri:m/ *n* flow of blood round the body

blood·suck·er /ˈblʌdˌsʌkə ‖ -ər/ *n* **1** creature that bites and then sucks blood from the wound **2** person who tries to get as much money as possible from other people

blood·thirst·y /ˈblʌdˌθɜ:sti ‖ -ɜ:r-/ *adj* eager to kill; too interested in violence

bloody-mind·ed /ˌ· ˈ··◂/ *adj* unhelpful; unreasonable ~**ness** *n* [U]

bloom /blu:m/ *n* **1** flower **2 in the bloom of** at the best time of/for ♦ *vi* **1** produce flowers **2** show as healthy colour **3** BLOSSOM (2)

blos·som /ˈblɒsəm ‖ ˈblɑ:-/ *n* **1** flower of a tree or bush **2 in blossom** bearing flowers ♦ *vi* **1** produce blossoms **2** develop favourably

blot¹ /blɒt ‖ blɑ:t/ *n* **1** spot, esp. of ink **2** shameful fault: *a blot on her character* **3** something ugly: *a blot on the landscape*

blot² *vt* -**tt**- **1** make blots on **2** dry up (ink) **3 blot one's copybook** spoil one's good record

blot out *phr vt* cover; hide: *Clouds blotted out the sun.*

blotch /blɒtʃ ‖ blɑ:tʃ/ *n* large spot or mark ~**y** *adj*

blouse /blaʊz ‖ blaʊs/ *n* woman's shirt

blow¹ /bləʊ ‖ bloʊ/ *v* blew /blu:/, blown /bləʊn ‖ bloʊn/ **1** *vi/t* send out air; move by the force of air: *The wind blew the tree down.* | *He blew the candle out.* **2** *vi/t* sound made by blowing: *to blow a trumpet* **3** *vt* clean (one's nose) by blowing through it **4** *vi/t* melt (an electrical FUSE) **5** *vt sl* lose (a favourable chance) as the result of foolishness **6** *vt infml* spend (money) freely **7** *vi sl* leave quickly **8** *vt infml* DAMN: *Well, I'm blowed!* **9 blow hot and cold (about)** be favourable (to) at one moment and unfavourable (to) at the next **10 blow one's own trumpet/horn** *infml* praise oneself **11 blow one's top/stack** *sl* explode with anger **12 blow someone a kiss** kiss one's hand, then wave or blow over it towards someone **13 blow someone's brains out** *infml* kill someone by a shot through the head 14 **blow someone's mind** *sl* fill someone with wonder 15 **blow the whistle on** *sl* cause something undesirable to stop, by bringing it to the attention of esp. the public

blow over *phr vi* (of a storm) stop blowing: (fig.) *The scandal will soon blow over.*

blow up *phr v* 1 *vi/t* explode 2 *vt* fill with air: *blow up the tyres* 3 enlarge (a photograph): (fig.) *The affair was blown up by the newspapers.* 4 (of bad weather) start blowing: *There's a storm blowing up.*

blow^2 *n* act of blowing: *Give your nose a good blow.*

blow^3 *n* 1 hard stroke with the hand or a weapon 2 sudden misfortune 3 **come to blows** start to fight —see also BODY BLOW

blow-by-blow /ˌ · · ˈ·◂/ *adj* with full details, given in the order in which they happened

blow·lamp /ˈbləʊlæmp‖ˈbloʊ-/ *n* also **blow·torch** /-tɔːtʃ‖ -tɔːrtʃ/ — lamp that blows a flame (e.g. for burning off paint)

blown /bləʊn‖bloʊn/ *past p. of* BLOW¹

blow·out /ˈbləʊaʊt‖ˈbloʊ-/ *n* 1 very big meal 2 bursting of a container (esp. a tyre)

blub·ber^1 /ˈblʌbə‖-ər/ *n* [U] fat of sea creatures, esp. WHALES

blubber^2 *vi* weep noisily

blud·geon /ˈblʌdʒən/ *vt* 1 hit with something heavy 2 force to do something, by threats

blue /bluː/ *adj* 1 of the colour of the clear sky 2 sad; DEPRESSED 3 concerned with sex; improper: *blue films* ♦ *n* [U] 1 blue colour 2 **out of the blue** unexpectedly **blues** *n* 1 [S;U] slow sad song or music from the southern US 2 [U] sadness

blue-blood·ed /ˌ· ˈ·◂/ *adj* of noble birth

blue-bot·tle /ˈbluːˌbɒtl‖ -ˌbɑːtl/ *n* large blue-green fly

blue chip /ˌ· ˈ·/ *n, adj* (an industrial share) that is expensive and in which people have confidence

blue-col·lar /ˌ· ˈ·◂/ *adj* of or concerning workers who do hard or dirty work with their hands

blue-eyed boy /ˌ· · ˈ·/ *n infml, esp. BrE* someone's favourite (male) person

blue moon /ˌ· ˈ·/ *n* [S] **once in a blue moon** *infml* almost never

blue mur·der /ˌ· ˈ··/ *n* scream/shout **blue murder** *infml* complain very loudly

blue·print /ˈbluːˌprɪnt/ *n* copy of a plan for making or building something: (fig.) *a blueprint for the reforms*

blue-sky /ˌ· ˈ·◂/ *adj AmE* done in order to test ideas, rather than for any particular practical purpose

blue·stock·ing /ˈbluːˌstɒkɪŋ‖-ˌstɑː-/ *n* woman thought to be too highly educated

bluff^1 /blʌf/ *vi* deceive someone by pretending to be stronger or cleverer than one is: *They say they'll blow up the place, but they're only bluffing.* 2 **bluff it out** escape trouble by continuing a deception **bluff** *n* [S;U] 1 action of bluffing 2 **call someone's bluff** tell someone to do what they threaten to do

bluff^2 *adj* (of a person) rough and cheerful

blun·der /ˈblʌndə‖-ər/ *n* stupid mistake ♦ *vi* 1 make a blunder 2 move awkwardly ~**er** *n*

blunt /blʌnt/ *adj* 1 not sharp: *a blunt pencil* 2 not trying to be polite ♦ *vt* make less sharp ~**ly** *adv* roughly and plainly ~**ness** *n* [U]

blur /blɜː‖blɜːr/ *n* [S] something whose shape is not clearly seen ♦ *vt* **-rr-** make hard to see: (fig.) *to blur a distinction*

blurb /blɜːb‖blɜːrb/ *n* short description of the contents of a book

blurt /blɜːt‖blɜːrt/ *v* **blurt out** *phr vt* say suddenly without thinking

blush /blʌʃ/ *vi* become red in the face, from shame **blush** *n* —see also **spare someone's blushes** (SPARE) ~**ingly** *adv*

blus·ter /ˈblʌstə‖-ər/ *vi* 1 speak roughly and noisily 2 (of wind) blow roughly **bluster** *n* [U] ~**y** *adj* windy

B-movie /ˈbiː ˌmuːvi/ *n* cheaply made cinema film not considered to be of very good quality

board /bɔːd‖bɔːrd/ *n* 1 [C] flat piece of wood, etc.: *floorboards* | *a notice board* | *a chessboard* 2 BLACKBOARD 3 (cost of) meals: *board and lodging* 4 committee of people controlling something 5 **above board** completely open and honest 6 **across the board** including all groups or members, as in an industry: *a wage increase of £10 a week across the board* 7 **go by the board** (of plans) come to no result 8 **on board** on a ship or public vehicle 9 **sweep the board** win nearly everything ♦ *v* 1 *vt* cover with boards 2 *vt* go on board a ship, etc. 3 *vi* get meals and lodging for payment: *to board with a friend* **-er** *n* person who pays to live and receive meals somewhere

boarding card /'·· ·/ *n* official card to be given up when one enters an aircraft

board·ing·house /'bɔːdɪŋhaus ‖ 'bɔːr-/ *n* private lodging house that supplies meals

boarding school /'·· ·/ *n* [C;U] school at which children live instead of going there daily from home

boast /bəust ‖ boust/ *v* 1 *vi* talk too proudly 2 *vt* have (a cause for pride): *This computer boasts many ingenious features.* ♦ *n* 1 act of boasting 2 cause for pride **~ful** *adj* full of self-praise

boat /bəut ‖ bout/ *n* 1 water vehicle, esp. smaller than a ship —see also in the same boat (SAME¹) ♦ *vi* go in a boat, esp. for pleasure

boat·er /'bəutə ‖ 'boutər/ *n* stiff hat made of STRAW

boat·swain /'bəusən ‖ 'bou-/ *n* chief seaman on a ship

boat·train /'·· ·/ *n* train that takes people to or from ships in port

bob¹ /bɒb ‖ bɑːb/ *vi* **-bb-** move quickly up and down: *a boat bobbing on the water*

bob² *vt* cut (a woman's hair) to shoulder-length or shorter ♦ *n* a bobbed haircut

bob·bin /'bɒbɪn ‖ 'bɑː-/ *n* small roller for thread

bob·ble /'bɒbəl ‖ 'bɑː-/ *n* ball of wool, etc. used for decoration

bob·by /'bɒbi ‖ 'bɑːbi/ *n* BrE *infml* policeman

bobby socks, bobby sox /'·· ,·/ *n* [P] AmE girl's socks reaching above the ankle

bob·sleigh /'bɒbsleɪ ‖ 'bɑːb-/ — also **bob·sled** /-sled/ — *vi, n* (ride in) a small vehicle that runs on metal blades, used for sliding down snowy slopes

bode /bəud ‖ boud/ *vi* **bode well/ill** be a good/bad sign for the future

bod·ice /'bɒdɪs ‖ 'bɑː-/ *n* top part of a woman's dress

bod·i·ly /'bɒdɪli ‖ 'bɑː-/ *adj* of the human body; PHYSICAL ♦ *adv* taking hold of the whole body

bod·y /'bɒdi ‖ 'bɑːdi/ *n* 1 person or animal's whole physical structure, alive or dead 2 this without the head or limbs 3 main part of something: *The important news comes in the body of the letter.* 4 group

of people: *an elected body* 5 object; piece of matter: *The sun is a heavenly body.* 6 large amount: *a body of water such as a lake* 7 **keep body and soul together** remain alive (by getting money for food)

body blow /'·· ·/ *n* 1 (in boxing BOX²) blow that falls below the breast and above the waist 2 a serious SETBACK

bod·y·guard /'bɒdigaːd ‖ 'bɑːdigaːrd/ *n* man or group of men guarding someone important

bod·y·work /'bɒdiwɜːk ‖ 'bɑːdiwɜːrk/ *n* [U] outside parts of a motor vehicle

bog¹ /bɒg ‖ bɑːg, bɔːg/ *n* [C;U] 1 area of soft wet ground 2 BrE *sl* LAVATORY **~gy** *adj*

bog² *v* **bog down** *phr vi/t* sink into a bog: (fig.) *to get bogged down in one's work*

bo·gey·man /'bəugimæn ‖ 'bou-/ *n* imaginary evil spirit

bog·gle /'bɒgəl ‖ 'bɑː-/ *v* **the mind boggles** (used to say that something is difficult to imagine or believe)

bo·gus /'bəugəs ‖ 'bou-/ *adj* pretended; false

bo·he·mi·an /bəu'hiːmiən, bə- ‖ bou-, bə-/ *adj* not following accepted social customs

boil¹ /bɔɪl/ *vi/t* 1 bring or come to the temperature at which a liquid changes to gas: *100 °C is the boiling point of water.* 2 cook at this temperature: *to boil eggs* 3 **boil dry** boil till no water remains **~ing** *adj* extremely hot ♦ *n* [S]: *Bring the soup to the boil.*

boil away *phr vi* disappear by boiling

boil down *phr vt* be no more than: *It all boils down to a question of money.*

boil over *phr vi* 1 (of a boiling liquid) flow over the sides of the container 2 get out of control (and develop into): *The conflict boiled over into war.*

boil up *phr v* 1 *vt* make hot and cook 2 *vi* reach a dangerous level

boil² *n* painful infected swelling under the skin

boil·er /'bɔɪlə ‖ -ər/ *n* large container for boiling water, e.g. to provide heating in a house

boiler suit /'·· ·/ *n* OVERALLS

bois·ter·ous /'bɔɪstərəs/ *adj* noisily cheerful **~ly** *adv*

bold /bəuld ‖ bould/ *adj* 1 daring; courageous 2 without respect or shame

3 clearly marked: *a bold drawing* **~ly** *adv*
~ness *n* [U]

bol·lard /'bɒlɑd ‖ 'bɑːlərd/ *n* short thick
post, in the street or for tying boats to

bol·shy /'bɒlʃi ‖ 'boul-/ *adj infml* (of a
person or their behaviour) showing an
unwillingness to help in a common aim

bol·ster¹ /'bəʊlstə ‖ 'boulstər/ *n* long
PILLOW

bolster² *v* bolster up *phr vt* encourage;
support

bolt¹ /bəʊlt ‖ boult/ *n* 1 bar that fastens a
door or window 2 screw used with a NUT (2)
to hold things together 3 THUNDERBOLT 4 **a
bolt from the blue** something unexpected
and unpleasant —see also NUTS AND BOLTS

bolt² *v* 1 *vt* fasten with a BOLT¹ (1) 2 *vi* run
away suddenly 3 *vt* swallow (food) hastily ♦
n [S] 1 act of running away 2 **make a bolt
for it** run away ♦ *adv* **bolt upright**
straight and stiff

bolt·hole /'bəʊlthəʊl ‖ 'boulthoul/ *n*
place one can escape to

bomb /bɒm ‖ bɑːm/ *n* 1 [C] container
filled with explosive 2 [the+S] the NUCLEAR
bomb 3 **(go) like a bomb** (go) very well
4 **spend/cost a bomb** spend/cost a lot of
money ♦ 1 *vt* attack with bombs 2 *vi infml*
move quickly 3 *vi AmE infml* fail **~er** *n*
1 aircraft that drops bombs 2 person who
throws bombs

bom·bard /bɒm'bɑːd ‖ bɑːm'bɑːrd/ *vt*
attack heavily with gunfire: (fig.) *He was
bombarded with questions.* **~ment** *n* [C;U]

bom·bas·tic /bɒm'bæstɪk ‖ bɑːm-/ *adj*
using high-sounding meaningless words
~ically *-kli/ adj*

bomb·shell /'bɒmʃel ‖ 'bɑːm-/ *n* great
shock

bo·na fi·de /ˌbəʊnə 'faɪdi◄ ‖ 'bounə
faɪd/ *adj* real

bo·nan·za /bə'nænzə, bəʊ- ‖ bə-, bou-/
n something very profitable

bond /bɒnd ‖ bɑːnd/ *n* 1 something that
unites: *a bond of friendship* 2 official
document promising to pay back money,
usu. with interest 3 state of being stuck
together ♦ *vt* unite; stick **bonds** *n* [P]
chains or ropes for tying someone up

bond·age /'bɒndɪdʒ ‖ 'bɑːn-/ *n* [U] *lit*
slavery

bone /bəʊn ‖ boun/ *n* [C;U] 1 any of the
various hard parts of the body which are

surrounded by flesh and skin 2 **cut to the
bone** reduce as much as possible 3 **feel in
one's bones** believe strongly though
without proof 4 **have a bone to pick with
someone** have something to complain
about 5 **make no bones about** feel no
doubt or shame about —see also BARE BONES,
FUNNY BONE ♦ *vt* take bones out of (fish,
etc.) **~less** *adj* **bony** *adj* 1 very thin,
showing the bones 2 (of food) full of bones

bone-dry /ˌ· '·◄/ *adj* perfectly dry

bone-i·dle /ˌ· '·◄/ *adj* very lazy

bon·fire /'bɒnfaɪə ‖ 'bɑːnfaɪr/ *n* large
outdoor fire

bonk /bɒŋk ‖ bɑːŋk/ *v* 1 *infml* hit,
usu. not very hard 2 *vi/t sl* have sex (with)
♦ *n* 1 *infml* hit 2 *sl* act of having sex

bon·net /'bɒnɪt ‖ 'bɑː-/ *n* 1 round hat tied
under the chin 2 *BrE* lid over the front of a
car

bon·ny /'bɒni ‖ 'bɑːni/ *adj* pretty and
healthy

bo·nus /'bəʊnəs ‖ 'bou-/ *n* 1 additional
payment beyond what is usual 2 anything
pleasant in addition to what is expected

boo /buː/ *interj, n* **boos** shout of
disapproval ♦ *vi/t* shout 'boo'

booby prize /'·· ·/ *n* prize given for the
worst performance in a competition

booby trap /'·· ·/ *n* harmless-looking
thing used for surprising people
unpleasantly, such as a hidden bomb ♦
booby-trap *vt* **-pp-**

book¹ /bʊk/ *n* 1 set of sheets of paper
fastened together, to be read or written in:
books on travel | *a bookseller* | *bookshelves* |
a bookshop 2 collection of matches, tickets,
etc. fastened like a book 3 main division of
the Bible or of a long poem 4 **a closed book**
subject about which one knows very little
5 **by the book** according to the rules 6 **in
someone's good/bad books** in favour/
disfavour with someone 7 **throw the book
at** (esp. of the police) make all possible
charges against **books** *n* [P] business
accounts

book² *v* 1 *vi/t* order (tickets, etc.) in
advance: *to book a seat/a band* 2 *vt* write
down a legal charge against: *booked for
speeding* **~able** *adj*

book up *phr vt* keep (a place or time)
for people who have made arrangements in
advance

book·case /'bʊk-keɪs/ n piece of furniture to hold books

book club /'· ·/ club that offers books cheaply to its members

book·end /'bʊkend/ n support for a row of books

book·ing /'bʊkɪŋ/ n a case or act of BOOKing² (1): *Buy a ticket at the* **booking** *office.*

book·keep·ing /'bʊk,kiːpɪŋ/ n [U] keeping business accounts –**er** n

book·let /'bʊklət/ small thin book

book·mak·er /'bʊk,meɪkə‖-ər/ also **bookie** /'bʊki/ *infml* — person who takes BETS (2) on races

book·mark /'bʊkmaːk‖-maːrk/ n something put in a book to keep one's place

book·stall /'bʊkstɔːl‖-stɔːl/ n table or open hut where books and magazines are sold

book·worm /'bʊkwɜːm‖-wɜːrm/ n person who loves reading

boom¹ /buːm/ vi **1** make a deep hollow sound **2** grow rapidly: *Business is booming.* **boom** n: *a boom in exports*

boom² n **1** long pole to which a sail is attached **2** heavy chain across a river to stop logs floating down or to prevent ships sailing up **3** long pole on the end of which a camera or MICROPHONE can be moved about

boo·mer·ang /'buːməræŋ/ n curved stick which makes a circle and comes back when thrown ♦ vi have the opposite effect to that intended

boon /buːn/ n *fml* comfort; help

boon·docks /'buːndɒks‖-daːks/ n [the+P] *AmE infml* rough country area where few people live

boor /bʊə‖bʊr/ n rude person ~**ish** *adj* ~**ishly** *adv*

boost /buːst/ vt raise; increase **boost** n ~**er** something that boosts **2** additional amount of a drug

boot¹ /buːt/ n **1** heavy shoe that comes up over the ankle **2** *BrE* space at the back of a car for boxes, etc. **3** give/get the boot *infml* dismiss/be dismissed from a job **4** put the boot in *sl* kick someone **5** too big for one's boots too proud

boot² v **1** vt *infml* kick **2** vi/t also **boot up** *phr vi/t* make (a computer) ready for use by putting in instructions

 boot out *phr vt infml* send away rudely

and sometimes with force

boot³ n to boot in addition

booth /buːð‖buːθ/ n **1** tent, hut, etc. where goods are sold **2** small enclosed space: *a telephone/voting booth*

boot·leg /'buːtleg/ vi/t -**gg**- make, carry, or sell illegally ♦ *adj*: *bootleg cassette tapes* ~**ger** n

booze /buːz/ vi *sl* drink alcohol ♦ n [U] *sl* alcoholic drink **boozer** *sl* **1** person who boozes **2** *BrE for* PUB **boozy** *adj sl* showing signs of heavy drinking

booze-up /'· ·/ n *BrE sl* party with a lot of drinking

bop /bɒp‖baːp/ vi dance as in a DISCOTHEQUE ♦ n

bor·der¹ /'bɔːdə‖'bɔːrdər/ n **1** edge **2** line between two countries

border² vt put or be a border to

 border on *phr vt* be very much like: *Your remarks border on rudeness!*

bor·der·line /'bɔːdəlaɪn‖'bɔːrdər-/ *adj* that may or may not be something: *Anne will pass the exam, but Sue is a borderline case.* (=may pass or fail) ♦ n (line marking) a border

bore¹ /bɔː‖bɔːr/ v *past t. of* BEAR²

bore² n dull person or activity ♦ vt make (someone) tired or uninterested: *a boring job* ~**dom** n [U] state of being bored

bore³ vi/t make a round hole (in) ♦ n **1** hole made by boring **2** measurement of the hole inside a gun, pipe, etc.

born /bɔːn‖bɔːrn/ *adj* **1** be born come into existence by birth **2** being something by nature: *a born leader* **3** born and bred having grown up from birth in the stated place **4** born of owing existence to

born-a·gain /'· ··/ *adj* having accepted a particular religion, esp. EVANGELICAL Christianity, esp. through a deep spiritual experience: *a born-again Christian* | (fig.) *a born-again jogger*

borne /bɔːn‖bɔːrn/ v *past p. of* BEAR²

bo·rough /'bʌrə‖-roʊ/ n town, or division of a large town

bor·row /'bɒrəʊ‖'baːroʊ, 'bɔː-/ v **1** vi/t receive something that is lent, and will be returned **2** vt copy (ideas, words, etc.) ~**er** n

bor·stal /'bɔːstl‖'bɔːr-/ n *BrE* former prison school for young offenders

bos·om /'bʊzəm/ n *lit* **1** the front of the human chest, esp. the female breasts

2 place where one feels love, sorrow, etc.
3 **a bosom friend** a very close friend 4 **in the bosom of** in a close relationship with
boss /bɒs ‖ bɔːs/ *n infml* person who controls others; employer, etc. ♦ *vt* give orders to or tell others to do something

bot·a·ny /'bɒtəni ‖ 'bɑː-/ *n* [U] scientific study of plants –**nist** *n* –**nical** /bə'tænɪkəl/ *adj*

botch /bɒtʃ ‖ bɑːtʃ/ *vt* repair (something) badly ♦ *n* bad piece of work

both /bəʊθ ‖ boʊθ/ *determiner, pron* this one and that one: *both of us* ‖ *both New York and London*

both·er /'bɒðə ‖ 'bɑːðər/ *v* 1 *vt* cause inconvenience to; annoy in little ways: *Does the noise bother you?* 2 *vi* trouble oneself: *Don't bother to lock the door.* ♦ *n* [C;U] trouble; inconvenience ~**some** *adj* causing bother

bot·tle /'bɒtl ‖ 'bɑːtl/ *n* 1 narrow-necked container for liquids 2 container for holding a baby's milk 3 *BrE sl* courage 4 **the bottle** alcoholic drink, esp. when drunk too much: *He's on/hitting the bottle again.* ♦ *vt* put into bottles

  bottle out *phr vi BrE sl* lose one's courage

  bottle up *phr vt* control (feelings) unhealthily

bottle green /ˌ·· '·◂/ *n, adj* [U] very dark green

bot·tle·neck /'bɒtlnek ‖ 'bɑː-/ *n* narrow part of a road which slows down traffic: (fig.) *a bottleneck in production*

bot·tom¹ /'bɒtəm ‖ 'bɑː-/ *n* 1 [C] base; lowest part or level: *the bottom of the stairs* ‖ *He came bottom of the class.* 2 [C] part of the body that one sits on 3 [S] ground under the sea, a lake, etc. 4 [S] far end: *the bottom of the garden* 5 [S] cause: *get to the bottom of the trouble* 6 **at bottom** really 7 **from the bottom of one's heart** truly 8 **knock the bottom out of** take away the necessary support on which something rests ~**less** *adj* very deep

bottom² *v* **bottom out** *phr vi* reach the lowest point before rising again

bottom line /ˌ·· '·/ *n* [*the*+S] 1 the amount of money shown (as profit or loss) at the bottom of a set of accounts 2 the most important result in the end, esp. with regard to money

bot·u·lis·m /'bɒtʃʰəlɪzəm ‖ 'bɑː-/ *n* [U] form of food poisoning

bou·doir /'buːdwɑː ‖ -ɑːr/ *n lit* woman's private room

bough /baʊ/ *n* large branch of a tree

bought /bɔːt ‖ bɒːt/ *v past t. and p. of* BUY

boul·der /'bəʊldə ‖ 'boʊldər/ *n* large rock

bounce /baʊns/ *v* 1 *vi* (of a ball) spring back again: *The ball bounced against the wall.* 2 *vi/t* move up and down quickly: *She bounced into the room.* 3 *vi* (of a cheque) be returned by the bank as worthless ♦ *n* 1 [C;U] act of bouncing 2 [U] behaviour which is full of life **bouncer** *n* strong person employed (esp. at a club) to throw out unwelcome visitors **bouncing** *adj* (esp. of babies) strong and healthy

bound¹ /baʊnd/ *v past t. and p. of* BIND

bound² **bound to** sure to: *It's bound to rain* 2 **bound up in** busy with

bound³ *vi* jump; LEAP **bound** *n* —see also BOUNDS

bound⁴ *adj* going to (a place): *bound for home*

bound·a·ry /'baʊndəri/ *n* outer limit; border

bound·less /'baʊndləs/ *adj* unlimited

bounds /baʊndz/ *n* [P] 1 furthest limits 2 **out of bounds** forbidden to be visited

boun·ty /'baʊnti/ *n* 1 [C] something given out of kindness, or offered as a reward 2 [U] *fml* generosity -**tiful** *adj fml* generous

bou·quet /bəʊ'keɪ, buː- ‖ boʊ-, buː-/ *n* 1 bunch of flowers 2 smell of a wine

bour·geois /'bʊəʒwɑː ‖ ˌbʊr'ʒwɑː/ *n, adj* 1 (person) of the MIDDLE CLASS 2 (person) too interested in material possessions ~**ie** /ˌbʊəʒwɑː'ziː ‖ ˌbʊər-/ *n* [U] the MIDDLE CLASS

bout /baʊt/ *n* short period of activity or illness

bou·tique /buː'tiːk/ *n* small fashionable shop, esp. for clothes

bo·vine /'bəʊvaɪn ‖ 'boʊ-/ *adj tech* relating to cows

bow¹ /baʊ/ *vi/t* bend forward, to show respect **bow** *n*

  bow out *phr vi* give up a position or stop taking part in something

  bow to *phr vt* obey; accept: *I bow to your judgment.*

bow² /bəʊ ‖ boʊ/ *n* 1 piece of curved wood with a string, for shooting arrows 2 similar piece of wood for playing stringed musical instruments **3** knot formed by doubling a string into two curved pieces ♦ *vi/t* **1** bend; curve **2** play (music) with a bow

bow³ /baʊ/ *n* front of a ship

bowd·ler·ize also **-ise** *BrE* /'baʊdləraɪz/ *vt* remove unacceptable parts from (a book)

bow·els /'baʊəlz/ *n* [P] **1** tube that carries waste matter from the stomach **2** inside part: *the bowels of the earth*

bowl¹ /bəʊl ‖ boʊl/ *n* **1** deep round container for liquids, etc. **2** anything in the shape of a bowl

bowl² *v* **1** *vi/t* throw or roll (a ball) in a sport **2** *vt* (in cricket) force a player out of the game by doing this **3** *vi* play BOWLS or BOWLING ~**er** *n* person who bowls

bowl over *phr vt* **1** knock down **2** surprise greatly

bow-legged /'bəʊ,legd, -,legɪd‖'boʊ-/ *adj* having legs curving outwards at the knees

bowler hat /,bəʊlə 'hæt ‖ ,boʊlər-/ *n BrE* man's round hard hat

bowl·ing /'bəʊlɪŋ ‖ 'boʊ-/ *n* [U] indoor game in which a big ball is rolled along a track (a **bowling alley**)

bowls /bəʊlz ‖ boʊlz/ *n* [U] outdoor game in which a big ball (a **bowl**) is rolled on grass (a **bowling green**)

bow tie /,bəʊ 'taɪ ‖ ,boʊ-/ *n* TIE¹ (1) fastened at the front with a BOW² (3)

bow win·dow /,bəʊ 'wɪndəʊ ‖ ,boʊ 'wɪndoʊ/ *n* curved window

box¹ /bɒks ‖ bɑːks/ *n* **1** [C] stiff container for solids: *a box of chocolates* **2** [C] small enclosed space: *a telephone box* | *a box at the theatre* **3** [S] *BrE sl* television: *What's on the box?* —see also BLACK BOX, PANDORA'S BOX ♦ *vt* put in boxes

box in *phr vt* enclose in a small space

box² *vi/t* fight with the FISTS, for sport: *a boxing match* ~**er** *n* ~**ing** *n* [U]

Boxing Day /'·· ·/ *n* British public holiday on the first weekday after Christmas

box num·ber /'· ,··/ *n* number used as a mailing address, esp. in replying to newspaper advertisements

box of·fice /'· ,··/ *n* place where tickets are sold in a cinema, etc.: *The show was a box-office success.* (=made a large profit)

boy /bɔɪ/ *n* young male person ~**hood** *n* time of being a boy ~**ish** *adj* like a boy

boy·cott /'bɔɪkɒt ‖ -kɑːt/ *vt* refuse to trade with or take part in **boycott** *n*

boy·friend /'bɔɪfrend/ *n* woman's male companion

bra /brɑː/ *n* woman's undergarment supporting the breasts

brace¹ /breɪs/ *n* **1** something that stiffens or supports **2** wire worn to straighten the teeth **braces** *n* [P] bands over the shoulders to keep trousers up

brace² *vt* **1** support **2** prepare (oneself) **bracing** *adj* health-giving

brace·let /'breɪslɪt/ *n* decoration for the wrist

brack·en /'brækən/ *n* [U] FERN which grows in forests

brack·et /'brækɪt/ *n* **1** support for a shelf, etc. **2** either of various pairs of signs used for enclosing a piece of information, for example ( ) or [ ] **3** group of people: *the 16–25 age bracket* ♦ *vt* **1** put in brackets **2** put together

brack·ish /'brækɪʃ/ *adj* (of water) not pure; a little salty ~**ness** *n* [U]

brag /bræg/ *vi* **-gg-** talk too proudly; BOAST

braid /breɪd/ *n* **1** *n, vt AmE for* PLAIT **2** *n* [U] threads of silk, gold, etc. twisted together to make edging for material: *gold braid*

braille /breɪl/ *n* [U] type of raised printing that blind people can read

brain /breɪn/ *n* **1** the organ in the head that controls thought **2** mind; INTELLIGENCE **3** *infml* clever person **4 have something on the brain** think about something continually, or too much ♦ *vt infml* hit on the head ~**less** *adj* stupid ~**y** *adj* clever **brains** *n* [U] **1** material of which the brain consists **2** ability to think

brain·child /'breɪntʃaɪld/ *n* [S] someone's successful idea

brain drain /'· ·/ *n* movement of skilled people to other countries

brain·pow·er /'breɪn,paʊə ‖ -,paʊr/ *n* [U] ability to reason

brain·storm /'breɪnstɔːm ‖ -stɔːrm/ *n* **1** *BrE* sudden short madness **2** *AmE for* BRAINWAVE ~**ing** *n* [U] rapid exchange of ideas among a group to find answers to problems

brain·wash /'breɪnwɒʃ ‖ -wɒːʃ, -wɑːʃ/ *vt* force someone to change their beliefs ~**ing** *n* [U]

brain·wave /'breɪnweɪv/ *n BrE* sudden

clever idea

braise /breɪz/ vt cook (meat or vegetables) slowly in a covered dish

brake /breɪk/ n apparatus for slowing or stopping a vehicle **brake** vi/t

bram·ble /'bræmbəl/ n common wild prickly bush

bran /bræn/ n [U] crushed skin of grain

branch¹ /brɑːntʃ‖bræntʃ/ n **1** stem growing from the trunk of a tree **2** division; part: *branch of a railway/of a family*

branch² vi form branches

branch out phr vi add to one's range

brand /brænd/ **1** product of a particular producer: *my favourite brand of soup* ‖ (fig.) *his own brand (=special kind) of humour* **2** mark made, esp. by burning, to show ownership ♦ vt **1** give a lasting bad name to: *He was branded as a liar.* **2** mark with a BRAND (2): (fig.) *The experience branded her for life.*

bran·dish /'brændɪʃ/ vt wave (e.g. a weapon) about

brand-new /ˌ·'·◁/ adj completely unused

bran·dy /'brændi/ n [C;U] strong alcoholic drink made from wine

brash /bræʃ/ adj bold and disrespectful ~ly adv ~ness n [U]

brass /brɑːs‖bræs/ n [U] **1** bright yellow metal **2** musical instruments made of this: *a brass band* **3** BrE sl money —see also TOP BRASS

brat /bræt/ n derog child, esp. a bad-mannered one

bra·va·do /brə'vɑːdəʊ‖-doʊ/ n [U] unnecessary show of boldness

brave /breɪv/ adj ready to meet pain or danger; fearless ♦ vt meet (danger, etc.) without showing fear ~ly adv ~ry /'breɪvəri/ n [U]

bra·vo /'brɑːvəʊ, brɑː'vəʊ‖-voʊ/ interj, n -vos (shout of) well done!

brawl /brɔːl‖brɒːl/ n noisy quarrel **brawl** vi

brawn /brɔːn‖brɒːn/ n [U] **1** human muscle **2** meat from the head of a pig ~y adj strong

bray /breɪ/ vi make the sound a DONKEY makes **bray** n

bra·zen /'breɪzən/ adj without shame

bra·zi·er /'breɪziə‖-ʒər/ n container for burning coals

breach /briːtʃ/ n **1** [C;U] act of breaking a law, promise, etc.: *breach of contract* **2** [C] hole (in a wall, etc.) **3** **breach of the peace** law fighting in public ♦ vt break through

bread /bred/ n [U] **1** food made of baked flour **2** food as a means of staying alive: *earn one's daily bread* **3** sl money **4** **bread and butter** one's way of earning money to live on **5** **know which side one's bread is buttered** know who or what will be of most gain to oneself

bread·crumb /'bredkrʌm/ n very small bit of bread

bread·line /'bredlaɪn/ n **on the breadline** very poor

breadth /bredθ, bretθ/ n [U] **1** width **2** broad range; SCOPE

bread·win·ner /'bred,wɪnə‖-ər/ n person whose wages support a family

break¹ /breɪk/ v **broke** /brəʊk‖broʊk/, **broken** /'brəʊkən‖'broʊ-/ **1** vi/t separate suddenly into parts: *to break a window* ‖ *The rope broke.* **2** vi/t make or become by breaking: *The box broke open.* **3** vi/t make or become useless due to damage: *a broken watch* **4** vt disobey; not keep: *break a promise/an appointment* **5** vi/t interrupt; stop: *break one's journey/the silence* **6** vi/t (cause to) fail or be destroyed: *The scandal could break him politically.* **7** vi/t bring or come into notice: *The news broke.* **8** vt do better than (a record) **9** vi (of a voice) change suddenly **10** vt discover the secret of (a CODE) **11** **break new/fresh ground** do something new and different **12** **break one's back** make every possible effort **13** **break the back of** finish the main or worst part of **14** **break the ice** begin to be friendly with people one did not know before **15** **break wind** let out gases from the bowels

break away phr vi escape: (fig.) *break away from old traditions*

break down phr v **1** vi/t destroy; to be reduced to pieces: (fig.) *They broke down her resistance.* **2** vi (of machinery) stop working **3** vi fail: *The peace talks have broken down.* **4** vi (of a person) lose control of one's feelings **5** vi/t separate into kinds; divide: *break the figures down into several lists*

break even phr vi make neither a loss nor a profit

break in phr v **1** vi enter a building by

force 2 *vi* interrupt 3 *vt* make (a person or animal) accustomed to something new

break into *phr vt* 1 enter by force 2 begin suddenly: *to break into song* 3 interrupt 4 use part of, esp. unwillingly: *We'll have to break into our savings.*

break of *phr vt* cure (someone) of (a bad habit)

break off *phr vi/t* 1 stop; end 2 separate from the main part: *A branch broke off.*

break out *phr vi* 1 (of something bad) start suddenly: *War broke out.* 2 show or express something suddenly: *He broke out in a rash.* 3 escape

break through *phr vi/t* 1 force a way through 2 make a new advance

break up *phr v* 1 *vi/t* divide into small pieces; separate 2 *vi/t* bring or come to an end: *Their marriage broke up.* 3 *vi/t* (cause to) suffer greatly 4 *vi* (of a crowd) cease to be together 5 *vi BrE* begin the school holidays 6 *AmE* amuse greatly

break with *phr vt* end one's connection with

break² *n* 1 act of breaking or a condition produced (as if) by breaking: *a break in the clouds* 2 pause for rest: *a coffee break* 3 change from the usual pattern or custom: *a break from the past | a break in the weather* 4 *infml* chance (esp. to make things better); piece of good luck 5 **break of day** DAWN 6 **make a break for it** try to escape

break·a·ble /ˈbreɪkəbəl/ *n, adj* (something) easily broken

break·age /ˈbreɪkɪdʒ/ *n* [C;U] 1 example of breaking 2 something broken

break·a·way /ˈbreɪkəweɪ/ *n* person or thing that escapes: *a breakaway group*

break·down /ˈbreɪkdaʊn/ *n* 1 sudden failure in operation: *a breakdown in the peace talks* 2 sudden weakness or loss of power in body or mind: *a nervous breakdown* 3 division into kinds; detailed explanation (of figures, etc.) —see also NERVOUS BREAKDOWN

break·er /ˈbreɪkə‖-ər/ *n* 1 large wave rolling onto the shore 2 person or thing that breaks something: *an ice-breaker*

break·fast /ˈbrekfəst/ *n* [C;U] first meal of the day

break-in /ˈ· ·/ *n* entering of a building illegally and by force

break·neck /ˈbreɪknek/ *adj* at **breakneck speed** dangerously fast

break·out /ˈbreɪkaʊt/ *n* violent or forceful escape from an enclosed space or a difficult situation, esp. an escape from prison

break·through /ˈbreɪkθruː/ *n* important advance or discovery

break·up /ˈbreɪkʌp/ *n* 1 coming to an end 2 division into parts

break·wat·er /ˈbreɪk,wɔːtə‖-,wɔːtər, -,wɑː-/ *n* strong wall built into the sea to reduce the force of the waves

breast /brest/ *n* 1 milk-producing part of a woman's body: *a breast-fed baby* 2 upper front part of the body: *his breast pocket | a bird with a red breast* 3 **make a clean breast of** tell the whole truth about ♦ *vt* push aside with one's chest: (fig.) *The ship breasted the waves.*

breath /breθ/ *n* 1 [U] air taken into and breathed out of the lungs 2 [C] single act of breathing air in and out once 3 sign or slight movement (of something): *There's a breath of spring in the air. | There wasn't a breath of wind.* 4 moment: *In one breath he said he loved me, in the next that he didn't.* 5 **get one's breath (back)** also **catch one's breath** — return to one's usual rate of breathing 6 **hold one's breath** stop breathing for a time 7 **out of breath** breathing very fast, as after running 8 **take one's breath away** surprise one greatly 9 **under one's breath** in a whisper 10 **waste one's breath** talk uselessly ~**less** *adj* ~**lessly** *adv*

breath·a·lyse /ˈbreθəlaɪz/ *vt* measure the alcohol drunk by a driver using special apparatus (=a **breathalyser**)

breathe /briːð/ *v* 1 *vi/t* take (air, etc.) into the lungs and send it out again 2 *vt* say softly; whisper 3 *vt* send out (a smell, feeling, etc.) 4 **breathe again** feel calm after feeling anxious 5 **breathe down someone's neck** *infml* keep too close a watch on someone 6 **breathe one's last** *fml* die ~**er** *n* short rest **breathing space** *n* short time between periods of worry, work, etc.

breath·tak·ing /ˈbreθ,teɪkɪŋ/ *adj* very exciting or unusual

breech·es /ˈbrɪtʃɪz/ *n* [P] short trousers fastened at or below the knee

breed /briːd/ v **bred** /bred/ 1 vi (of animals) produce young 2 vt keep (animals, etc.) for the purpose of producing young ones 3 vt produce; cause: *Flies breed disease.* ♦ n kind of animal or plant: *a new breed of rose* ~**er** n person who breeds animals or plants ~**ing** n [U] 1 business of breeding animals, etc. 2 polite manners

breeding-ground /'·· ·/ n 1 place where the young, esp. of wild creatures, are produced 2 place or point of origin: *a breeding-ground of crime*

breeze /briːz/ n 1 light gentle wind 2 sl, esp. AmE something easily done ♦ vi come and go quickly and unceremoniously **breezy** adj 1 rather windy 2 cheerful in manner

breth·ren /'breðrən/ n [P] (used in church, etc.) brothers

brev·i·ty /'brevɨti/ n [U] shortness

brew /bruː/ vi/t prepare (beer, tea, coffee): (fig.) *Trouble is brewing.* ♦ n result of brewing: *a strong brew* ~**er** n person who makes beer ~**ery** n place where beer is made

bribe /braɪb/ vt influence unfairly by gifts ♦ n something offered in this way: *judges who take bribes* ~**ry** /'braɪbəri/ n [U] giving or taking bribes

bric-a-brac /'brɪk ə ˌbræk/ n [U] small decorations in a house

brick /brɪk/ n 1 [C;U] (piece of) baked clay for building: *brick walls* 2 something shaped like a brick 3 **bang/beat one's head against a brick wall** waste one's efforts by trying to do something impossible 4 **drop a brick** do or say something foolish and socially uncomfortable ♦ n **brick in/up** phr vt fill or enclose with bricks

brick·lay·er /'brɪkˌleɪə ‖ -ər/ n workman who puts bricks in place –**ing** n [U]

brid·al /'braɪdl/ adj of a bride or wedding

bride /braɪd/ n woman about to be married, or just married

bride·groom /'braɪdgruːm, -grʊm/ n man about to be married, or just married

brides·maid /'braɪdzmeɪd/ n girl attending the bride at a wedding

bridge¹ /brɪdʒ/ n 1 structure carrying a road or railway over a river, etc. 2 raised part of a ship where the captain and officers stand 3 upper part of the nose

4 part of a musical instrument over which the strings are stretched 5 piece of metal that keeps false teeth in place ♦ vt build a bridge across

bridge² n [U] card game for four players

bridge·head /'brɪdʒhed/ n position far forward in enemy land

bri·dle /'braɪdl/ n leather bands round a horse's head to control its movements ♦ v 1 vt put a bridle on 2 vi show displeasure

brief¹ /briːf/ adj 1 short: *a brief visit* 2 in brief in as few words as possible ~**ly** adv

brief² n 1 short statement of facts or instructions 2 BrE set of instructions setting limits to someone's powers or duties —see also BRIEFS ♦ vt give necessary instructions or information

brief·case /'briːfkeɪs/ n flat leather case for papers

briefs /briːfs/ n [P] short UNDERPANTS

bri·gade /brɪˈɡeɪd/ n 1 army unit of about 5,000 soldiers 2 organization with certain duties: *the Fire Brigade*

brig·a·dier /ˌbrɪɡəˈdɪə ‖ -ˈdɪr/ n officer commanding a brigade

bright /braɪt/ adj 1 giving out light; shining 2 (of a colour) strong: *bright red* 3 cheerful; happy 4 clever 5 showing hope or signs of future success: *a bright future* ~**en** vi/t make or become bright ~**ly** adv ~**ness** n [U]

bright spark /ˌ· '·/ n BrE infml clever or cheerful person

bril·liant /'brɪljənt/ adj 1 very bright: *brilliant blue* 2 very clever: *a brilliant idea* 3 very hopeful; successful: *a brilliant career* ~**ly** adv –**liance**, –**liancy** n [U]

brim /brɪm/ n 1 edge of a cup, etc. 2 bottom part of a hat ♦ vi -**mm**- be full of liquid

brine /braɪn/ n [U] salty water

bring /brɪŋ/ vt **brought** /brɔːt‖ brɔːt/ 1 carry or lead towards someone: *Bring him to the party.* 2 cause to come: *His letter brought many offers of help.* 3 be sold for 4 law make (a charge) officially

bring about phr vt cause

bring around/over/round phr vt persuade into a change of opinion

bring back phr vt 1 return or cause to return: *That song brings back memories.* 2 obtain and return with

bring down phr vt 1 cause to fall or

come down: *bring down prices* **2** reduce or lower: *to bring someone down to your own level*

bring down on *phr vt* cause (something bad) to happen: *bring trouble down on the family*

bring forward *phr vt* **1** introduce; suggest: *bring forward a plan* **2** bring something in the future nearer to the present

bring in *phr vt* **1** cause to come; introduce **2** produce as profit; earn

bring off *phr vt* succeed in doing

bring on *phr vt* **1** cause to happen: *bring on a fever* **2** help to develop; improve

bring out *phr vt* **1** produce; cause to appear: *Responsibility brings out the best in her.* **2** cause (workers) to STRIKE¹ (6) **3** encourage, esp. to talk

bring round/to *phr vt* cause to regain consciousness

bring through *phr vt* cause to come successfully through (illness, etc.)

bring together *phr vt* cause (esp. a man and a woman) to meet

bring up *phr vt* **1** educate and care for (children) **2** mention a subject **3** *esp. BrE* VOMIT (food)

brink /brɪŋk/ *n* edge; VERGE: *on the brink of disaster*

brink·man·ship /'brɪŋkmənʃɪp/ *n* [U] *infml* art of trying to gain an advantage by going to the limit of safety, esp. in international politics, before stopping

brisk /brɪsk/ *adj* quick and active: *a brisk walk* ~**ly** *adv* ~**ness** *n* [U]

bris·tle /'brɪsəl/ *n* [C;U] short stiff hair on a brush, etc. ◆ *vi* (of hair) stand up stiffly: (fig.) *bristling with anger* ~**tly** /'brɪsli/ *adj*

bristle with *phr vt* have plenty of: *streets bristling with armed guards*

brit·tle /'brɪtl/ *adj* **1** hard but easily broken **2** lacking WARMTH or depth of feeling

broach /brəʊtʃ ‖ brəʊtʃ/ *vt* introduce (a subject) for conversation

broad /brɔːd ‖ brɒːd/ *adj* **1** large when measured from side to side; wide **2** not limited; respecting the ideas of others: *broad opinions* | *a broadminded person* **3** not detailed: *in broad outline* **4** full; clear: *in broad daylight* **5** (of speech) showing clearly where the speaker comes from: *a*

broad Scots accent **6** not acceptable in polite society: *broad humour* ~**en** *vi/t* make or become broader: *Travel broadens the mind.* ~**ly** *adv* more or less; mostly ~**ness** *n* [U]

broad·cast /'brɔːdkɑːst ‖ 'brɔːdkæst/ *n* radio or television presentation ◆ *v* **broadcast 1** *vi/t* send out (broadcasts) **2** *vt* make widely known: *He broadcast the news to his friends.* ~**er** *n* ~**ing** *n* [U]

broad·side /'brɔːdsaɪd ‖ 'brɔːd-/ *n* **1** forceful spoken or written attack **2** firing of all the guns on one side of a ship

bro·cade /brə'keɪd ‖ brəʊ-/ *n* [U] decorative cloth with a raised pattern

broc·co·li /'brɒkəli ‖ 'brɑː-/ *n* vegetable similar to a CAULIFLOWER

bro·chure /'brəʊʃə, -ʃʊə ‖ brəʊ'ʃʊr/ *n* small book of instructions, or giving details of a service offered

brogue¹ /brəʊg ‖ brəʊg/ *n* strong thick shoe

brogue² *n* Irish ACCENT (1)

broil /brɔɪl/ *vi/t AmE for* GRILL: (fig.) *broiling hot weather*

broke¹ /brəʊk ‖ brəʊk/ *v past t. of* BREAK¹

broke² *adj* completely without money

bro·ken¹ /'brəʊkən ‖ 'brəʊ-/ *v past p. of* BREAK¹

broken² *adj* **1** violently separated; damaged: *a broken window* | (fig.) *broken dreams* | (fig.) *a broken man* **2** not kept to; destroyed: *a broken promise* | *a broken home* (=where a child's parents do not live together) **3** imperfectly spoken or written: *broken English*

broken·heart·ed /ˌbrəʊkən 'hɑːtɪd◀ ˌbrəʊkən 'hɑːr-/ *adj* filled with grief

bro·ker¹ /'brəʊkə ‖ 'brəʊkər/ *n* person who buys and sells shares, etc. for others

broker² *vt* arrange details of a plan, so that people can agree to it: *an agreement brokered by the UN*

bro·ker·age /'brəʊkərɪdʒ ‖ 'brəʊ-/ *n* [U] **1** (place of) business of a broker **2** fee charged by a broker

brol·ly /'brɒli ‖ 'brɑːli/ *n BrE infml* UMBRELLA (1)

bron·chi·al /'brɒŋkiəl ‖ 'brɑːŋ-/ *adj* of the tubes of the WINDPIPE

bron·chi·tis /brɒŋ'kaɪtɪs ‖ brɑːŋ-/ *n* [U] illness of the bronchial tubes

bronze /brɒnz ‖ brɑːnz/ *n* [U] **1** (the reddish-brown colour of) a metal that is a

buck

mixture of copper and tin 2 MEDAL made of bronze ♦ *vt* give this colour to: *bronzed by the sun*

brooch /brəʊtʃ‖broʊtʃ/ *n* decoration pinned to a dress

brood /bru:d/ *n* family of birds, etc. ~**y** *adj* 1 (of a hen) wanting to sit on eggs 2 sad and silent ~**ily** *adv* ~**iness** *n* [U] ♦ *vi* think long and sadly about something

brook¹ /brʊk/ *n* small stream

brook² *vt fml* allow or accept without complaining

broom /bru:m, brʊm/ *n* sweeping brush with a long handle —see also NEW BROOM

broth /brɒθ‖brɔ:θ/ *n* [U] thin soup

broth·el /'brɒθəl‖'brɑ:-, 'brɔ:-/ *n* house of PROSTITUTES

broth·er /'brʌðə‖-ər/ *n* 1 male relative with the same parents 2 male member of the same profession, religious group, etc. ~**hood** *n* 1 [U] condition or feeling of friendliness and companionship 2 [C] all the people in a profession, etc. ~**ly** *adj* 1 like a brother 2 friendly

broth·er-in-law /'··· ·, ·/ *n* brothers-in-law brother of one's husband or wife; one's sister's husband

brought /brɔ:t‖brɔ:t/ *v* past t. and p. of BRING

brow /braʊ/ *n* 1 EYEBROW 2 FOREHEAD 3 top of a hill

brow·beat /'braʊbi:t/ *vt* -**beat**, -**beaten** /-bi:tn/ frighten into doing something

brown /braʊn/ *adj, n* (of) the colour of earth or coffee ♦ *vi/t* make or become brown

brown·ie /'braʊni/ *n* member of an association similar to the Guides (GUIDES), for younger girls

Brown·ie point /'·· ·/ *n* [usu. pl.] mark of notice and approval for something good that one has done

browse /braʊz/ *vi* 1 read without clear purpose 2 feed on young plants, grass, etc. **browse** *n* [S]

bruise /bru:z/ *n* discoloured place where the skin has been hurt ♦ *v* 1 *vt* cause a bruise on 2 *vi* show a bruise

brunch /brʌntʃ/ *n* [C;U] late breakfast or early LUNCH

bru·nette also **brunet** *AmE* /bru:'net/ *n* woman of a fair-skinned race with dark hair

brunt /brʌnt/ *n* **bear the brunt of** suffer the heaviest part of (an attack)

brush¹ /brʌʃ/ *n* 1 [C] instrument for sweeping, painting, etc., made of hair, nylon, etc: *a toothbrush | a clothes brush* 2 [C] act of brushing 3 [C] short unpleasant meeting: *a brush with the police* 4 [U] (land covered by) small rough trees and bushes 5 [C] tail of a fox

brush² *v* 1 *vt* clean with a brush 2 *vi/t* touch or move lightly

brush aside/away *phr vt* refuse to pay attention to

brush off *phr vt* refuse to listen to or have a relationship with (someone) **brush-off** /'· ·/ *n* [*the*+S] clear refusal to be friendly: *She gave me the brush-off.*

brush up *phr vt* improve one's knowledge of (something known but partly forgotten) by study: *I must brush up my French.*

brusque /bru:sk, brʊsk‖brʌsk/ *adj* quick and rather impolite ~**ly** *adv* ~**ness** *n* [U]

brus·sels sprout /ˌbrʌsəlz 'spraʊt/ *n* vegetable like a very small CABBAGE

bru·tal /'bru:tl/ *adj* without tender feeling; cruel ~**ly** *adv* ~**ity** /bru:'tælti/ *n* [C;U] ~**ize** also -**ise** *BrE* /'bru:təl-aɪz/ *vt* 1 cause to become brutal: *the brutalizing effects of war* 2 treat brutally

brute /bru:t/ *n* 1 rough cruel person 2 animal ♦ *like* (that of) an animal in being cruel or very strong: *brute force* **brutish** *adj* like animals rather than people

BSE /ˌbi: es 'i:/ *n* [U] bovine spongiform encephalopathy; disease that kills cattle by destroying the brain and nervous system

bub·ble /'bʌbəl/ *n* hollow ball of liquid containing air or gas ♦ *vi* 1 form, produce, or rise as bubbles: *She was bubbling (over) with happiness.* 2 make the sound of bubbles rising in liquid **bubbly** *adj* 1 full of bubbles 2 showing happy feelings freely 3 *n* [U] *BrE infml* champagne

buck¹ /bʌk/ *n* 1 [C] male of certain animals, esp. the deer, cat, and rabbit 2 [C] *sl, esp. AmE* American dollar 3 [*the*+S] responsibility: *to pass the buck*

buck² *v* 1 *vi* (of a horse) jump up with all four feet off the ground 2 *vt* throw off (a rider) by doing this

buck up *phr vt* 1 try to improve 2 make

happier

buck·et /'bʌkɪt/ n 1 (contents of) an open container with a handle, for liquids 2 large quantity: *The rain came down in buckets.* ♦ *BrE infml* rain very hard ~**ful** /-fʊl/ n contents of a bucket

bucket shop /'·· ·/ n *infml, esp. BrE* business that obtains large quantities of tickets for air travel and sells them to the public at a low price

buck·le¹ /'bʌkəl/ n metal fastener for a belt, etc.

buckle² *vi/t* 1 fasten with a buckle 2 bend; twist: *a buckled wheel* 3 begin to yield: *Her knees buckled.*

buckle down *phr vi* begin to work seriously

bud /bʌd/ n 1 flower or leaf before it opens 2 **nip something in the bud** do harm to (something), esp. so as to keep from succeeding —see also TASTE BUD ♦ *vi* **-dd-** produce buds ~**ding** adj beginning to develop

Bud·dhis·m /'bʊdɪzəm‖'buː-, 'bʊ-/ n [U] eastern religion taught by Buddha **Buddhist** n, adj

bud·dy /'bʌdi/ n 1 *infml* companion; friend 2 *AmE sl* (used as a form of address to a man)

budge /bʌdʒ/ *vi/t* move a little

bud·ger·i·gar /'bʌdʒərɪɡɑː‖-ɡɑːr/ also **bud·gie** /'bʌdʒi/ *infml* —n small brightly coloured Australian bird

bud·get /'bʌdʒɪt/ n 1 plan of how to spend money, esp. public money taken in by taxation 2 amount of money stated in this ♦ *vi* plan one's spending ♦ adj cheap: *budget prices*

buff¹ /bʌf/ n, adj [U] (of) a faded yellow colour

buff² *vt* polish (metal) with something soft

buff³ n person interested in a subject: *a film buff*

buf·fa·lo /'bʌfələʊ‖-loʊ/ -os, -oes, or -o 1 cowlike African or Asian animal with curved horns 2 BISON

buff·er /'bʌfə‖-ər/ n spring on a railway vehicle that takes the shock when it hits anything

buffer zone /'·· ·/ n NEUTRAL area separating opposing forces or groups

buf·fet¹ /'bʊfeɪ‖bə'feɪ/ n table, etc. where one can get food to be eaten near by

buf·fet² /'bʌfɪt/ *vt* hit sharply: *buffeted by the wind*

buf·foon /bə'fuːn/ n noisy fool

bug /bʌg/ n 1 *AmE* any insect 2 GERM 3 apparatus for secret listening 4 eager interest in something: *the travel bug* 5 fault in a computer program ♦ *vt* **-gg-** 1 fit with a BUG (3) 2 trouble (someone) continually

bug·bear /'bʌgbeə‖-ber/ n something that worries or annoys people

bug·ger /'bʌgə‖-ər/ n *sl, esp. BrE* 1 unpleasant person or thing 2 person of the stated kind: *You lucky bugger!* ♦ *interj* (used for adding force to expressions of displeasure) ~**y** n [U] SODOMY

bug·gy /'bʌgi/ n PUSHCHAIR

bu·gle /'bjuːgəl/ n brass musical instrument **bugler** n

build¹ /bɪld/ *vi/t* built /bɪlt/ make by putting pieces together: *build houses/ships* | (fig.) *Hard work builds character.* ~**er** n ~**ing** n 1 thing with a roof and walls; house, etc. 2 work of a builder

build on *phr vt* 1 base on 2 depend on

build up *phr v* 1 *vt* increase; develop: *build up a business* 2 *vi* praise (something or someone) so as to influence the opinion of others

build² n shape and size of one's body

building so·ci·e·ty /'·· ·,···/ n *BrE* business organization into which people pay money in order to save it and gain interest, and which lends money to people who want to buy houses

bulb /bʌlb/ n 1 round root of certain plants 2 glass part of an electric lamp ~**ous** adj fat and round

bulge /bʌldʒ/ n 1 swelling on a surface 2 sudden increase ♦ *vi* swell

bu·lim·i·a /bʊ'lɪmɪə/ n [U] dangerous condition in which one frequently eats too much and then VOMITS, because of fear of getting fat **bulimic** /buː'lɪmɪk/ adj

bulk¹ /bʌlk/ n 1 [U] great size or quantity 2 **in bulk** in large quantities 3 **the bulk of** most of ~**y** adj large and fat

bulk² *v* **bulk large** play an important part

bulk·head /'bʌlkhed/ n wall which divides a ship, etc. into several parts

bull /bʊl/ n 1 male of cattle and some other large animals 2 **bull in a china shop** person who is rough where care is needed 3 **take the bull by the horns** face difficulties with courage

bull·doze /'buldəʊz‖-doʊz/ vt move (earth, etc.) with a powerful machine (a **bulldozer**): (fig.) bulldoze a plan through Parliament

bul·let /'bulət/ n piece of shot fired from a small gun: a **bullet-proof** car —see also **bite the bullet** (BITE)

bul·le·tin /'bulətɪn/ n short official report

bulletin board /'··· ,·/ n 1 place in a computer system for leaving/reading messages 2 AmE for NOTICEBOARD

bul·lion /'buljən/ n [U] bars of gold or silver

bul·lish /'bulɪʃ/ adj marked by, tending to cause, or hopeful of rising prices (as in a STOCK EXCHANGE)

bul·lock /'bulək/ n BULL that cannot breed

bull's-eye /'·· ·/ n centre of a TARGET

bull·shit /'bul,ʃɪt/ n [U] sl nonsense ♦ vi/t -tt- sl talk nonsense, esp. confidently in order to deceive, persuade, or get admiration

bul·ly /'buli/ n person who hurts weaker people ♦ vt hurt in this way

bul·rush /'bulrʌʃ/ n tall grasslike waterside plant

bul·wark /'bulwək‖-wərk/ n wall built for defence

bum[1] /bʌm/ n BrE sl BUTTOCKS

bum[2] n AmE sl TRAMP (1) or lazy person ♦ vt -mm- sl ask for; beg

bump /bʌmp/ v 1 vi/t knock violently 2 vi move along in an uneven way ♦ n 1 (sound of) a sudden blow 2 swelling ~y adj uneven
  bump into phr vt meet by chance
  bump off phr vt infml kill
  bump up phr vt increase

bump·er /'bʌmpə‖-ər/ n protective bar on the front or back of a car ♦ adj very large: a bumper harvest

bun /bʌn/ n 1 small round sweet cake 2 hair twisted into a tight shape

bunch /bʌntʃ/ n 1 number of small things fastened together: 2 group: a bunch of girls ♦ vi/t form into a bunch

bun·dle /'bʌndl/ n 1 number of articles fastened together: a bundle of sticks/laundry 2 a mass: a bundle of nerves/laughs ♦ v 1 vi/t hurry roughly 2 vt make into a bundle

bung[1] /bʌŋ/ n round piece of material to close the hole in a container

bung[2] vt BrE infml throw roughly
  bung up phr vt block up (a hole)

bun·ga·low /'bʌŋgələʊ‖-loʊ/ n house all on one level

bun·gee jump·ing /'bʌndʒi ,dʒʌmpɪŋ/ n [U] sport of jumping from a high place, held by a stretchy rope

bun·gle /'bʌŋgəl/ vt do (work) badly ~**gler** n

bunk[1] /bʌŋk/ n bed fixed to a wall, often above or below another

bunk[2] n do a bunk BrE sl run away

bun·ker /'bʌŋkə‖-ər/ n 1 place to store coal 2 shelter for soldiers 3 (IN GOLF) sandy place from which it is difficult to hit the ball

bun·ny /'bʌni/ n (child's word for) a rabbit

buoy /bɔɪ‖'buːi, bɔɪ/ n floating object fastened to the bed of the sea to show a danger, rocks, etc.

buoy[2] v **buoy up** phr vt 1 keep floating 2 keep high

buoy·an·cy /'bɔɪənsi‖'bɔɪənsi, 'buːjənsi/ n [U] 1 tendency to float 2 cheerfulness 3 ability, e.g. of prices or business activity, to remain or return quickly to a high level after a period of difficulty ~**ant** adj showing buoyancy

bur·den /'bɜːdn‖'bɜːr-/ n fml heavy load or duty ♦ vt fml load; trouble

bur·den·some /'bɜːdnsəm‖'bɜːr-/ adj being a burden: a burdensome task

bu·reau /'bjʊərəʊ‖'bjʊroʊ/ n bureaus or bureaux /'bjʊərəʊz‖'bjʊroʊz/ 1 BrE writing desk with a lid 2 AmE for CHEST OF DRAWERS 3 government department 4 business office

bu·reauc·ra·cy /bjʊ'rɒkrəsi, ‖-'rɑː-/ n 1 [U] group of government officials who are appointed, not elected 2 [C;U] government by such a group, usually supposed to be ineffective and full of unnecessary rules ~**rat** /'bjʊərəkræt‖'bjʊr-/ n appointed official ~**ratic** /,bjʊərə'krætɪk◂‖,bjʊr-/ adj ~**ratically** /-kli/ adv

bur·geon /'bɜːdʒən‖'bɜːr-/ vi fml grow; develop

bur·ger /'bɜːgə‖'bɜːrgər/ n HAMBURGER

bur·glar /'bɜːglə‖'bɜːrglər/ n thief who breaks into buildings ~**gle** also ~**glarize** /'bɜːgləraɪz‖'bɜːr-/ AmE — vt break into (a building) to steal ~**y** n [C;U] (example of) the crime of being a burglar

bur·i·al /'beriəl/ n [C;U] (ceremony of)

burying

bur·ly /'bɜːli ‖ 'bɜːrli/ *adj* (of a person) strong and heavy

burn¹ /bɜːn ‖ bɜːrn/ *v* burnt /bɜːnt ‖ bɜːrnt/ *or* burned 1 *vi* be on fire: *a burning match/house* 2 *vt* damage or destroy by fire or acid: *burn old letters* 3 *vt* use for heating or lighting: *a wood-burning stove* 4 *vi* be very hot: *burning sands* 5 *vi* feel or wish very strongly: *She's burning to tell you.* 6 **burn one's boats/bridges** destroy all means of going back, so that one must go forward 7 **burn one's fingers** also **get one's fingers burnt** *infml* — suffer the unpleasant results of a foolish action 8 **burn the candle at both ends** *infml* work or be active from very early until very late; use up all one's strength by doing too many different things ~**er** *n* part of a cooker, etc. that produces flames ~**ing** *adj* 1 on fire 2 very strong and urgent

burn away *phr vi* disappear by burning

burn down *phr vi* destroy (a building) by fire

burn out *phr v* 1 *vt* make (a building) hollow by fire 2 *vi* stop burning because there is nothing left to burn 3 *vi/t* stop working through damage caused by heat: (fig.) *He was burned out* (=no longer active) *at 38.*

burn up *phr vt* destroy completely by fire or great heat

burn² *n* mark made by burning

bur·nish /'bɜːnɪʃ ‖ 'bɜːr-/ *vt* polish by rubbing

burn·out /'bɜːnaut ‖ 'bɜːr-/ *n* [C;U] moment when the engine of a ROCKET or JET uses up all its fuel and stops operating

burp /bɜːp ‖ bɜːrp/ *v, n* BELCH

bur·row /'bʌrəu ‖ 'bɜːrou/ *n* hole where a rabbit, etc. lives ♦ *vi/t* make a hole; dig

bur·sar /'bɜːsə ‖ 'bɜːrsər/ *n* person in a college who has charge of money, buildings, etc.

bur·sa·ry /'bɜːsəri ‖ 'bɜːr-/ *n* SCHOLARSHIP (1)

burst¹ /bɜːst ‖ bɜːrst/ *vi/t* burst 1 break suddenly by pressure from inside: *a burst tyre* 2 (cause) to come into the stated condition suddenly, often with force: *They burst open the door.* 3 be filled to breaking point (with a substance or usu. pleasant

feeling): *I'm bursting* (=very eager) *to tell someone the news.* | *The river burst its banks.*

burst in on/upon *phr vt* interrupt noisily

burst into *phr vt* 1 enter hurriedly 2 BREAK **into** (2)

burst out *phr v* 1 *vi* begin suddenly (to use the voice without speaking): *They burst out laughing/crying.* 2 say suddenly

burst² *n* sudden outbreak or effort: *a burst of speed*

bur·y /'beri/ *vt* 1 put into a grave 2 hide away: *buried treasure* | (fig.) *She buried her head in her hands.*

bus /bʌs/ *n* large passenger-carrying motor vehicle ♦ *vt* -ss-, -s- take by bus

bush /buʃ/ *n* 1 [C] low woody plant: *rose bush* 2 [U] wild land in Australia 3 **beat about the bush** avoid coming to the main point ~**y** *adj* (of hair) growing thickly

busi·ness /'bɪznɪs/ *n* 1 [U] trade; the getting of money 2 [C] money-earning activity; shop, etc. 3 [C;U] one's employment; duty: *A teacher's business is to teach.* 4 [S] affair; matter 5 **have no business to** have no right to 6 **like nobody's business** very fast or well 7 **Mind your own business!** Don't ask about things that don't concern you. ~**like** *adj* doing things calmly and effectively

busi·ness·man /'bɪznɪsmən/, **-woman** /-ˌwumən/ *fem.* — *n* **-men** /-mən/ person in a business firm

busk /bʌsk/ *vi BrE* play music in the street, etc., to earn money ~**er** *n*

bus stop /'· ·/ *n* place where buses stop for passengers

bust¹ /bʌst/ *vt* busted *or* bust *infml* 1 break, esp. with force 2 *sl* (of the police) take to a police station 3 *sl* (of the police) enter without warning to look for something illegal 4 **-buster** *n infml* person who destroys or breaks up the stated thing: *a crimebuster* ♦ *adj infml* 1 broken 2 **go bust** (of a business) fail

bust² *n* 1 human head and shoulders as shown in a SCULPTURE 2 woman's breasts

bus·tle /'bʌsəl/ *vi* be busy, often noisily **bustle** *n* [S]

bust-up /'· ·/ *n sl* 1 noisy quarrel 2 a coming to an end of a relationship or partnership

bus·y /'bɪzi/ adj 1 working; not free 2 full of work: *a busy morning* 3 esp. AmE (of telephones) in use ♦ vt keep (oneself) busy
busily adv

but /bət; strong bʌt/ conj 1 rather; instead: *not one, but two* 2 yet at the same time; however: *I want to go, but I can't.* 3 (shows disagreement or surprise): *But I don't want to!* | *But that's wonderful!* ♦ prep 1 except: *nobody but me* 2 **but for** except for; without ♦ adv lit 1 only: *You can but try.* 2 **all but** almost ♦ n unwanted argument: *No buts! You're going!*

butch·er /'bʊtʃə‖-ər/ n 1 person who kills animals for food, or sells meat 2 cruel killer ♦ vt kill and prepare for food 3 kill bloodily ~y n [U] cruel needless killing

but·ler /'bʌtlə‖-ər/ n chief male servant

butt¹ /bʌt/ vi/t push with the head or horns
butt in phr vi interrupt

butt² n 1 person that people make fun of 2 end of something: *cigarette butt* 3 BOTTOM¹ (2) 4 large barrel

but·ter /'bʌtə‖-ər/ n [U] yellow fat made from cream ♦ vt spread butter on
butter up phr vt sl praise too much; FLATTER

but·ter·cup /'bʌtəkʌp‖-ər-/ n yellow wild flower

but·ter·fin·gers /'bʌtə,fɪŋgəz‖'bʌtər ,fɪŋgərz/ n person likely to drop things

but·ter·fly /'bʌtəflaɪ‖-ər-/ n 1 insect with large coloured wings 2 person who spends all his/her time running after pleasure: *a social butterfly* 3 **have butterflies in one's stomach** feel very nervous before doing something

but·ter·scotch /'bʌtəskɒtʃ‖-ərskɑːtʃ/ n sweet food made from sugar and butter boiled together

but·tock /'bʌtək/ n either of the two fleshy parts on which a person sits

but·ton /'bʌtn/ n 1 small round object passed through a hole to fasten a garment, etc. 2 button-like object pressed to start a machine ♦ vi/t fasten with a button

but·ton·hole /'bʌtnhəʊl‖-hoʊl/ n 1 hole for a button 2 BrE flower to wear on one's coat or dress ♦ vt stop and force to listen

but·tress /'bʌtrəs/ n support for a wall ♦ vt support; strengthen

bux·om /'bʌksəm/ adj (of a woman) fat and healthy, esp. having large breasts

buy /baɪ/ vi/t bought /bɔːt‖ bɔːt/ 1 obtain by paying money 2 accept; believe ♦ n something bought ~**er** n person who buys, esp. professionally for a firm

buy·out /'baɪaʊt/ n situation in which a person or group gains control of a company by buying all or most of its shares

buzz /bʌz/ v 1 vi make the noise that bees make: (fig.) *The room buzzed with excitement.* 2 vi/t call someone with an electrical signalling apparatus (a **buzzer**) 3 fly low and fast over: *Planes buzzed the crowd.* ♦ n 1 [C] noise of buzzing 2 infml telephone call: *Give me a buzz.* 3 sl pleasant feeling as if from a drug
buzz off phr vi infml go away

buzz·word /'bʌzwɜːd‖-wɜːrd/ n word or phrase, esp. related to a specialized subject, which is thought to express something important but is often hard to understand

by /baɪ/ prep, adv 1 beside; near: *Sit by me.* 2 through; using: *enter by the door* | *travel by car* | *earn money by writing* 3 past: *He walked by (me) without speaking.* 4 before: *Do it by tomorrow.* 5 (shows who or what does something): *a play by Shakespeare* | *struck by lightning* 6 (shows amounts and measurements): *They overcharged me by £3.* | *a room 5 metres by 4* | *pay by the hour* 7 (shows how or with what): *hold it by the handle* 8 (in promises, etc.): *By God, he's done it!* 9 (shows the size of groups following each other): *The animals went in two by two.* 10 during: *to sleep by day* 11 **by and by** before long 12 **by and large** on the whole; usually

bye /baɪ/ also **bye-bye** /ˌ· '·‖'·· ⁄ — interj infml goodbye

by-e·lec·tion, **bye-election** /'· ·,·/ n election held between regular elections, in only one place

by·gone /'baɪgɒn‖-gɔːn/ adj past: *in bygone days* ♦ n [P] **let bygones be bygones** forgive past quarrels

by·law /'baɪlɔː‖-lɔː/ n law made by a local council, a railway, etc.

by·pass /'baɪpɑːs‖-pæs/ n road that goes round a busy town, etc. ♦ vt avoid by going round

by·play /'baɪpleɪ/ n [U] action of less importance going on at the same time as the main action

by·prod·uct /'· ‚·/ n something produced while making or doing something else

by·stand·er /'baɪ‚stændə‖-ər/ n person who watches without taking part

byte /baɪt/ n unit of computer information equal to eight BITS[3]

by·way /'baɪweɪ/ n smaller road or path which is not much used or known

by·word /'baɪwɜːd‖-wɜːrd/ n (name of a) person, place, or thing thought to represent some (usu. bad) quality: *a byword for cruelty*

by·zan·tine /baɪ'zæntaɪn, tiːn, bɪ-‖ 'bɪz əntiːn, -taɪn/ adj secret, indirect, and difficult to understand

C

C, c /siː/ the 3rd letter of the English alphabet

c written abbrev. for: **1** cent(s) **2** CIRCA **3** CUBIC **4** centimetre(s) **5** COPYRIGHT

C abbrev. for: **1** CELSIUS **2** century

cab /kæb/ n **1** taxi **2** the part of a bus, train, etc. where the driver sits

cab·a·ret /'kæbəreɪ‖‚kæbə'reɪ/ n [C;U] performance of music and dancing in a restaurant, etc.

cab·bage /'kæbɪdʒ/ n **1** [C;U] round vegetable with thick green leaves **2** [C] *infml* **a** inactive person who takes no interest in anything **b** someone who has lost the ability to think, move, etc. as a result of illness, etc.

cab·in /'kæbɪn/ n **1** small room on a ship **2** small roughly built house

cab·i·net /'kæbɪnɪt/ n **1** piece of furniture with shelves and drawers **2** chief ministers of a government

ca·ble /'keɪbəl/ n **1** [C;U] thick heavy rope used on ships etc.: *a cable railway* **2** [C] wire carrying electricity, telephone messages, etc. **3** [U] system of broadcasting television

signals through cables under the ground: **cable TV 4** [C] TELEGRAM ♦ vi/t send or tell by TELEGRAM

cable car /'·· ·/ n car supported in the air by a cable, for crossing valleys, etc.

cache /kæʃ/ n secret store of things

cack-hand·ed /‚kæk 'hændɪd◁/ adj BrE unskilful; CLUMSY

cack·le /'kækəl/ vi **1** make the noise a hen makes **2** laugh unpleasantly **cackle** n

ca·coph·o·ny /kə'kɒfəni‖kə'kɑː-/ n [C;U] unpleasant mixture of loud noises **-nous** adj

cac·tus /'kæktəs/ n **-tuses** or **-ti** /-taɪ/ fleshy desert plant with PRICKLES

ca·det /kə'det/ n young person training in the armed forces or police

cadge /kædʒ/ vi/t derog get or try to get by asking; borrow

ca·dre /'kɑːdə, -drə 'keɪdə‖ 'kædri, 'kɑːdrə/ n (member of) an inner group of trained people

cae·sar·e·an /sɪ'zeəriən‖-'zer-/ n operation to take a baby out by cutting, instead of by ordinary birth

caf·e also **café** /'kæfeɪ‖kæ'feɪ, kə-/ n small restaurant serving light meals and drinks

caf·e·te·ri·a /‚kæfə'tɪəriə‖-'tɪr-/ n restaurant where people collect their own food, often in a factory, college, etc.

caf·feine /'kæfiːn‖kæ'fiːn/ n [U] chemical in coffee, tea, etc., that makes one feel more active

cage /keɪdʒ/ n container with bars, for keeping birds or animals in ♦ vt put in a cage

cag·ey /'keɪdʒi/ adj secretive

Cain /keɪn/ see **raise Cain** (RAISE)

ca·jole /kə'dʒəʊl‖-'dʒoʊl/ vt persuade by praise or false promises

cake /keɪk/ n **1** [C;U] soft sweet food baked with flour, etc.: *a birthday cake* **2** [C] flat piece of something: *a cake of soap* **3** (**sell**) **like hot cakes** very quickly **4** **have one's cake and eat it too** have the advantages of something without the disadvantages that go with it —see also PIECE OF CAKE ♦ vt cover thickly: *shoes caked with mud*

CAL /kæl/ abbrev. for: computer-assisted learning

ca·lam·i·ty /kə'læmɪti/ n terrible misfortune **-tous** adj

cal·ci·um /ˈkælsɪəm/ n [U] metal substance found in bones and chalk

cal·cu·late /ˈkælkj⸳leɪt/ vt 1 find out by using numbers: *calculate the cost* 2 plan, intend: *take a calculated risk* –**lable** adj able to be measured –**lator** n small machine that calculates –**lation** /ˌkælkj⸳ˈleɪʃən/ n [C;U]

cal·cu·lat·ing /ˈkælkj⸳leɪtɪŋ/ adj coldly SHREWD

cal·en·dar /ˈkæl⸳ndə ‖ -ər/ n 1 list of the days and months of the year 2 system of naming and dividing the months, etc.

calf¹ /kɑːf ‖ kæf/ n calves /kɑːvz ‖ kævz/ 1 [C] young of cattle and some other large animals 2 [U] its leather: *calfskin boots*

calf² n calves back of the human leg, between knee and ankle

cal·i·bre also -ber AmE /ˈkæl⸳bə ‖ -ər/ n 1 [S;U] quality: *work of (a) high calibre* 2 inside size of a tube or gun; bullet size

call¹ /kɔːl ‖ kɒːl/ v 1 vi/t speak or say loudly 2 vt name: *We'll call the baby Jean.* 3 vt tell to come: *Call a doctor!* 4 vi a make a short visit: *Let's call at Bob's.* b make regular visits: *The milkman calls every day.* 5 vi/t telephone 6 vt say publicly that something is to happen: *call a meeting/an election/a strike* 7 vt consider to be: *She called me a coward.* 8 vt waken: *Please call me at 7.*

call back phr v 1 vt cause (someone) to return 2 vi/t return a telephone call

call by phr vi visit when passing

call for phr vt 1 demand 2 need; deserve 3 collect

call in phr vt ask to come: *call the doctor in*

call off phr vt 1 decide not to have (a planned event) 2 tell to keep away

call on/upon phr vt 1 visit 2 fml ask to do something

call out phr vt 1 order officially to help: *Call out the army!* 2 order to STRIKE

call up phr vt 1 telephone 2 BrE order to join the armed forces

call² n 1 shout; cry 2 telephone conversation 3 short visit 4 demand; need: *There's no call for rudeness.* 5 command to meet, come, or do something 6 **on call** ready to work if needed

call box /ˈ· ·/ n hut with a public telephone

call·er /ˈkɔːlə ‖ ˈkɒːlər/ n person who visits or makes a telephone call

call girl /ˈ· ·/ n woman PROSTITUTE who makes her arrangements by telephone

cal·lig·ra·phy /kəˈlɪgrəfi/ n [U] (art of) beautiful handwriting

call·ing /ˈkɔːlɪŋ ‖ ˈkɒː-/ n fml profession; trade

cal·li·pers /ˈkæl⸳pəz ‖ -ərz/ n [P] 1 instrument for measuring distance between surfaces 2 leg supports to help someone to walk

cal·lous /ˈkæləs/ adj unkind; without sympathy ~**ness** n [U]

cal·low /ˈkæləu ‖ -lou/ adj young and inexperienced

call-up /ˈ· ·/ n order to serve in the armed forces

cal·lus /ˈkæləs/ n an area of hard skin

calm /kɑːm ‖ kɑːm, kɑːlm/ adj 1 not excited; quiet 2 (of weather) not windy 3 (of the sea) smooth **calm** n [S;U] **calm** vi/t make or become calm: *We tried to calm him down.* ~**ly** adv ~**ness** n [U]

cal·o·rie /ˈkæləri/ n unit of heat, or of ENERGY produced by a food

calve /kɑːv ‖ kæv/ vi give birth to a CALF

calves /kɑːvz ‖ kævz/ n pl. of CALF

ca·lyp·so /kəˈlɪpsəu ‖ -sou/ n kind of West Indian song

cam·ber /ˈkæmbə ‖ -ər/ n upward curve in the middle of a road surface

cam·cord·er /ˈkæmkɔːdə ‖ -kɔːrdər/ n small VIDEO camera that can be carried around

came /keɪm/ v past t. of COME

cam·el /ˈkæməl/ n large long-necked animal with one or two large HUMPS on its back

cam·e·o /ˈkæmi-əu ‖ -ou/ n -os 1 piece of jewellery consisting of a raised shape on a darker background 2 small part in a film, etc. acted by a famous person 3 short piece of fine writing or acting which shows the character of a person, place, or event

cam·e·ra /ˈkæmərə/ n 1 apparatus for taking photographs or moving pictures 2 **in camera** in secret

cam·ou·flage /ˈkæməflɑːʒ/ n [C;U] use of colour, shape, etc. to hide an object **camouflage** vt

camp¹ /kæmp/ n 1 [C;U] place where people live in tents or huts for a short time 2 [C] group of people with the same esp. political ideas 3 **break/strike camp** take up and put away tents ♦ *vi* set up or live in a camp: *We go camping every summer.* **~er** *n* person who camps

camp² *adj infml* **1** (of a man) behaving or looking like a woman, esp. intentionally **2** so unreal, unnatural, etc. as to be amusing

cam·paign /kæm'peɪn/ *n* connected set of military, political, or business actions intended to obtain a particular result ♦ *vi* lead, take part in or go on a campaign

cam·pus /'kæmpəs/ *n* [C;U] grounds of a university, college or school: *campus* (=university) *life*

can¹ /kən; *strong* kæn/ *v aux* **1** be able to: *Can you swim?* | *I can't hear you.* **2** be allowed to; may: *You can go home now.* **3** (shows what is possible): *He can be very annoying.* | *It can't be true.*

can² /kæn/ *n* **1** metal container for foods or liquids: *a can of beans* | *a petrol can* **2** carry the can *esp. BrE* take the blame ♦ *vt* **-nn-** preserve (food) in a can

ca·nal /kə'næl/ *n* watercourse dug for boats to travel along or to bring water

ca·nar·y /kə'neəri/ *n* small yellow songbird

can·cel /'kænsəl/ *vt* **-ll-** *BrE* ‖ **-l-** *AmE* **1** decide not to have (a planned event): *cancel a trip* **2** destroy the value of (a cheque, etc.) by drawing a line through it **~lation** /ˌkænsə'leɪʃən/ *n* [C;U]

  cancel out *phr vi/t* balance; equal: *The two debts cancel each other out.*

can·cer /'kænsə‖-ər/ *n* [C;U] diseased growth in the body **~ous** *adj*

can·did /'kændɪd/ *adj* honest; sincere **~ly** *adv*

can·di·date /'kændɪdət‖ -deɪt, -dət/ *n* **1** person to be chosen or elected for a position **2** person taking an examination **-dature** *n* [U] being a candidate

can·died /'kændid/ *adj* covered with shiny sugar

can·dle /'kændl/ *n* wax stick with string inside, which gives light when it burns: *We ate by candlelight.*

can·dle·stick /'kændl̩stɪk/ *n* holder for a candle

can·dour *BrE* ‖ **-dor** *AmE* /'kændə‖ -ər/ *n* [U] being CANDID

can·dy /'kændi/ *n* [C;U] *esp. AmE* sweets, chocolate, etc.

cane /keɪn/ *n* **1** stem of certain tall plants, used for making furniture, for punishing children, etc. **2 the cane** punishment with this ♦ *vt* hit with a cane

ca·nine /'keɪnaɪn, 'kæ-‖ 'keɪ-/ *adj, n* (of, for, typical of) a dog

can·is·ter /'kænɪstə‖ -ər/ *n* metal box for holding a dry substance or a gas

can·ker /'kæŋkə‖ -ər/ *n* [C;U] disease of trees, and of animal and human flesh

can·na·bis /'kænəbɪs/ *n* [U] drug produced from HEMP, smoked in cigarettes

canned /kænd/ *adj* (of music, laughter, etc.) recorded in advance and broadcast in an unnatural or annoying way

can·ni·bal /'kænɪbəl/ *n* **1** person who eats human flesh **2** animal that eats its own kind **~ism** *n* [U]

can·ni·bal·ize also **-ise** *BrE* /'kænɪbəlaɪz/ *vt* use parts (of a broken machine) to repair another machine of the same kind **-istic** /ˌkænɪbə'lɪstɪk◄/ *adj*

can·non¹ /'kænən/ *n* **cannons** or **cannon** big gun, fixed to a carriage or used on military aircraft

cannon² *vi* hit or knock forcefully, esp. by accident

cannon fod·der /'·· ˌ·-/ *n* [U] ordinary soldiers thought of as nothing but military material without regard for their lives

can·not /'kænət, -nɒt‖ -nɑːt/ *v* can not: *We cannot accept.*

can·ny /'kæni/ *adj* clever; not easily deceived

ca·noe /kə'nuː/ *n* light boat moved by a PADDLE

can·on /'kænən/ *n* **1** religious law **2** accepted standard of behaviour or thought **3** kind of Christian priest **~ize** also **-ise** *BrE vt* declare to be a SAINT **~ical** /kə'nɒnɪkəl‖ kə'nɑː-/ *adj* according to religious law

can·o·py /'kænəpi/ *n* **1** cloth roof over a bed, etc.: (fig.) *a canopy of leaves* **2** cover over the front of a plane

cant /kænt/ *n* [U] insincere talk

can't /kɑːnt‖ kænt/ *v short for:* can not: *I can't come tonight*

can·tan·ker·ous /kæn'tæŋkərəs/ *adj* quarrelsome

can·teen /kæn'tiːn/ *n* **1** place in a factory, office, etc. where food is served **2** *BrE* set of knives, forks, and spoons

can·ter /'kæntə‖-ər/ n [S] horse's movement, slower than a GALLOP ♦ vi/t

can·ti·le·ver /'kæntɪ‚liːvə‖-ər/ n armlike beam sticking out from an upright support, esp. for a bridge

can·vas /'kænvəs/ n 1 [U] strong cloth used for tents, etc. 2 [C] oil painting done on this

can·vass /'kænvəs/ vi/t go through (a place) or to (people) to ask for votes or find out opinions ~er n

can·yon /'kænjən/ n deep narrow valley

cap /kæp/ n 1 soft flat head-covering with no BRIM 2 protective top of a bottle, tube, etc. ♦ vt -pp- 1 cover the top of 2 do or say better than: He capped my joke with a funnier one. 3 give a cap to (someone) as a sign of honour, esp. for playing in a national team

ca·pa·ble /'keɪpəbəl/ adj 1 clever: a very capable doctor. 2 able to do or be: That remark is capable of being misunderstood. -bly adv -bility /‚keɪpə'bɪləti/ n 1 [C;U] having skills and apparatus necessary for the stated type of war: nuclear capability 2 [P] undeveloped qualities and abilities

ca·pac·i·ty /kə'pæsəti/ n 1 [S;U] amount that something can hold: The seating capacity of this theatre is 500. 2 [C;U] ability; power 3 [C] position: speaking in my capacity as minister 4 **filled to capacity** completely full

cape[1] /keɪp/ n loose outer garment without SLEEVEs

cape[2] n piece of land sticking out into the sea

ca·pil·la·ry /kə'pɪləri‖'kæpəleri/ n very thin tube, esp. a BLOOD VESSEL

cap·i·tal /'kæpɪtl/ n 1 [C] town where the centre of government is 2 [S;U] wealth, esp. when used to produce more wealth or start a business 3 [C] letter in its large form; A, B, C, etc.: write in capitals/in capital letters 4 **make capital of** use to one's advantage ♦ adj punishable by death: a capital offence

cap·i·tal·is·m /'kæpɪtl‚ɪzəm/ n [U] system based on the private ownership of wealth -ist n person who owns capital

cap·i·tal·ize also -ise BrE /'kæpɪtl‚aɪz/ vt 1 write with a capital letter 2 supply money to (a firm)

    capitalize on phr vt use to one's advantage

capital pun·ish·ment /‚··· '···/ n [U] punishment by death according to law

ca·pit·u·late /kə'pɪtʃʊleɪt/ vi accept defeat; stop opposing -lation /kə‚pɪtʃʊ'leɪʃən/ n [C;U]

cap·puc·ci·no /‚kæpʊ'tʃiːnəʊ‖-noʊ/ n [C;U] coffee made with hot FROTHY milk

ca·price /kə'priːs/ n [C;U] sudden foolish change of behaviour -cious /kə'prɪʃəs/ adj changing; untrustworthy

cap·size /kæp'saɪz‖'kæpsaɪz/ vi/t (cause a boat to) turn over

cap·sule /'kæpsjuːl‖-səl/ n 1 tiny container of medicine to be swallowed whole 2 part of a spacecraft where the pilots live

cap·tain /'kæptɪn/ n 1 leader of a team 2 person in command of a ship or aircraft 3 officer of middle rank in the armed forces ♦ vt be the captain of

cap·tion /'kæpʃən/ n words written above or below a picture

cap·ti·vate /'kæptɪveɪt/ vt charm; attract: her captivating beauty

cap·tive /'kæptɪv/ n prisoner, esp. taken in war ♦ adj: (fig.) a captive audience (=group not able or not allowed to stop watching or listening) -tivity /kæp'tɪvəti/ n [U] state or condition of being a captive

cap·tor /'kæptə‖-ər/ n person who captures someone

cap·ture /'kæptʃə‖-ər/ vt 1 make a prisoner of; take control of by force 2 preserve on film, in words, etc. ♦ n 1 [U] capturing; being captured 2 [C] person or thing captured

car /kɑː‖kɑːr/ n 1 vehicle with wheels and a motor, used for carrying people 2 railway carriage: restaurant car

ca·rafe /kə'ræf, -'rɑːf/ n glass bottle with a wide top, used for serving wine, etc. at meals

car·a·mel /'kærəməl, -mel/ n 1 [U] burnt sugar 2 [C] sweet made of boiled sugar

car·at /'kærət/ n unit expressing the purity of gold, or the weight of a jewel

car·a·van /'kærəvæn/ n 1 BrE small home to be pulled by a car 2 BrE covered cart for living in 3 group of people with vehicles or animals crossing a desert, etc.

car·bo·hy·drate /‚kɑːbəʊ'haɪdreɪt, -drət‖‚kɑːrboʊ-/ n [C;U] food such as sugar which provides heat and ENERGY, and may make one fat

car·bon /'kɑːbən ‖ 'kɑːr-/ n [U] substance found in diamonds, coal, etc.

car·bon·a·ted /'kɑːbəneɪtɪd ‖ 'kɑːr-/ adj (of drinks) containing BUBBLES because CARBON DIOXIDE has been added

carbon cop·y /ˌ· '·· '·/ n 1 very similar person or thing 2 copy of a page made using special coated paper

carbon di·ox·ide /ˌkɑːbən daɪ'ɒksaɪd ‖ ˌkɑːrbən daɪ'ɑːk-/ n [U] gas produced by breathing out, burning CARBON, etc.

carbon mon·ox·ide /ˌkɑːbən mə'nɒksaɪd ‖ ˌkɑːrbən mə'nɑːk-/ n [U] poisonous gas with no smell, produced by burning CARBON in very little air: *carbon monoxide poisoning*

car boot sale /ˌ· '· ·/ also **car boot** /ˌ· '·/ n sale where people sell things from the back of their cars

car·bun·cle /'kɑːbʌŋkəl ‖ 'kɑːr-/ n large painful swelling

car·bu·ret·tor BrE ‖ **-retor** AmE /ˌkɑːbjʊ'retə, -bə- ‖ 'kɑːrbəreɪtər/ n apparatus that mixes the air and petrol in a car engine

car·cass /'kɑːkəs ‖ 'kɑːr-/ n dead body, esp. of an animal

car·cin·o·gen·ic /ˌkɑːsɪnə'dʒenɪk◀ ‖ ˌkɑːr-/ adj causing CANCER **~gen** /kɑːˈsɪnə'dʒən ‖ ˌkɑːr-/ n

card /kɑːd ‖ kɑːrd/ n 1 a [C] one of 52 bits of stiff paper used for various games **b** [P] games played with these 2 [C] bit of stiff paper with various uses: *a membership card* | *a birthday card* | *a postcard* 3 [U] cardboard 4 **get one's cards** BrE be dismissed from one's job 5 **lay/put one's cards on the table** say what one intends to do 6 **on the cards** probable: *They say war's on the cards.* 7 **play one's cards right** act in the most effective manner to get what one wants

card·board /'kɑːdbɔːd ‖ 'kɑːrdbɔːrd/ n [U] thick stiff paper: *a cardboard box*

car·di·ac /'kɑːdiæk ‖ 'kɑːr-/ adj of the heart

car·di·gan /'kɑːdɪɡən ‖ 'kɑːr-/ n short knitted (KNIT) coat with SLEEVEs, usu. fastened at the front

car·di·nal /'kɑːdənəl ‖ 'kɑːr-/ n 1 priest of the highest rank in the Roman Catholic Church ♦ adj fml most important; main

cardinal num·ber /ˌ··· '·· ·/ n 1, 2, 3, etc.

care¹ /keə ‖ ker/ n 1 [C;U] worry; anxiety: *free from care* | *her many cares* 2 [U] protection; charge: *under a nurse's care* 3 [U] serious attention: *Take care not to drop it.* 4 **care of** also **in care of** AmE — (used when addressing letters to mean) at the address of 5 **take care of** be responsible for 6 **take into care** put (esp. a child) into a home controlled by the state to make sure of proper treatment **~ful** adj attentive; CAUTIOUS **~fully** adv **~less** adj 1 not taking care; inattentive 2 free from care; not worried **~lessly** adv **~lessness** n [U]

care² vi 1 be worried; mind: *I don't care where we go.* 2 **care to** like to; want: *Would you care to sit down?* **-ing** adj kind

care for phr vt 1 look after; nurse 2 like to have: *Would you care for a drink?*

ca·reer /kə'rɪə ‖ -'rɪr/ n 1 profession 2 general course of a person's life ♦ vi rush wildly: *career down the hill*

care·free /'keəfriː ‖ 'ker-/ adj free from anxiety

car·er /'keərə ‖ 'kerər/ n [C] someone who takes care of a child, old person, etc.

ca·ress /kə'res/ n light loving touch ♦ vt give a caress to

care·tak·er /'keəˌteɪkə ‖ 'kerˌteɪkər/ n person employed to look after a building

car·go /'kɑːɡəʊ ‖ 'kɑːrɡoʊ/ n **-goes** or **-gos** [C;U] goods carried by a ship, plane, or vehicle

car·i·ca·ture /'kærɪkətʃʊə ‖ -tʃʊr/ n funny drawing (or written description) of someone to make them seem silly ♦ vt make a caricature of

car·nage /'kɑːnɪdʒ ‖ 'kɑːr-/ n [U] killing of many people

car·nal /'kɑːnl ‖ 'kɑːrnl/ adj physical, of the flesh, or esp. sexual: *carnal desires*

car·na·tion /kɑː'neɪʃən ‖ kɑːr-/ n sweet-smelling white, pink, or red flower

car·ni·val /'kɑːnɪvəl ‖ 'kɑːr-/ n [C;U] period of public rejoicing

car·ni·vore /'kɑːnɪvɔː ‖ 'kɑːrnɪvɔːr/ n flesh-eating animal **-vorous** /kɑː'nɪvərəs ‖ kɑːr-/ adj

car·ol /'kærəl/ n religious song of joy, esp. sung at Christmas

carp¹ /kɑːp ‖ kɑːrp/ n **carp** or **carps** large FRESHWATER fish

carp² vi complain unnecessarily

car park /ˈ· ·/ n open or enclosed place where cars and other vehicles may be left

car·pen·ter /ˈkɑːpəntə ‖ ˈkɑːrpəntər/ n person who makes wooden objects –**try** n [U] work of a carpenter

car·pet /ˈkɑːpət ‖ ˈkɑːr-/ n [C;U] cloth for covering floors —see also RED CARPET ♦ vt cover (as if) with a carpet

car pool /ˈ· ·/ n 1 agreement made by people to take turns driving each other to work, etc. 2 BrE number of cars owned by a company for the use of its members

car·riage /ˈkærɪdʒ/ n 1 [C] vehicle, esp. horse-drawn 2 [C] BrE railway passenger vehicle 3 [U] (cost of) moving goods 4 [C] movable part of a machine: the carriage of a typewriter 5 [S;U] fml way of walking

car·riage·way /ˈkærɪdʒweɪ/ n BrE division of a road on which traffic goes: the northbound carriageway

car·ri·er /ˈkæriə ‖ -ər/ n 1 person or business that carries goods 2 person or animal that passes diseases to others without catching them 3 military vehicle or ship that carries soldiers, etc.: aircraft carrier

carrier bag /ˈ··· ·/ n esp. BrE paper or plastic bag, esp. with handles

car·ri·on /ˈkæriən/ n [U] dead or decaying flesh

car·rot /ˈkærət/ n long orange root vegetable

car·ry /ˈkæri/ v 1 vt move while supporting; have with one: carry a gun | carry a child on one's back 2 vt take from one place to another: Pipes carry oil across the desert. | Flies carry disease. 3 vt bear the weight of: This beam carries the whole roof. 4 vt have as a usual or necessary result: Such a crime carries a serious punishment. 5 vt contain; have: All the newspapers carried the story. 6 vt win by voting: The motion was carried. 7 vi reach a distance: Her voice doesn't carry very far. 8 **be carried away** get excited

carry off phr vt perform successfully

carry on phr vi 1 continue: carry on talking 2 behave in a foolish excited manner **carry-on** /ˈ·· ·/ n piece of foolish behaviour

carry on with phr vt 1 have a love affair with (someone) 2 **to carry/be carrying on with** for the present time

carry out phr vt fulfil; complete

carry through phr vt 1 help to continue: Her courage carried her through. 2 fulfil; complete: carry a plan through

cart /kɑːt ‖ kɑːrt/ n 1 wheeled vehicle pulled by an animal, or pulled or pushed by hand 2 **put the cart before the horse** do things in the wrong order ♦ vt carry; take: carting these books around

carte blanche /ˌkɑːt ˈblɑːnʃ ‖ ˌkɑːrt-/ n [U] full freedom

car·tel /kɑːˈtel ‖ kɑːr-/ n combination of independent firms, to limit competition

cart·horse /ˈkɑːt.hɔːs ‖ ˈkɑːrt.hɔːrs/ n heavy powerful horse, used for heavy work

car·ti·lage /ˈkɑːtəlɪdʒ ‖ ˈkɑːr-/ n [C;U] elastic substance found round the joints in animals

car·ton /ˈkɑːtn ‖ ˈkɑːrtn/ n CARDBOARD or plastic box

car·toon /kɑːˈtuːn ‖ kɑːr-/ n 1 humorous drawing of something interesting in the news 2 film made by photographing a set of drawings –**ist** n

car·tridge /ˈkɑːtrɪdʒ ‖ ˈkɑːr-/ n 1 tube containing explosive and a bullet for a gun 2 part of a record player that holds the needle 3 container of MAGNETIC TAPE

cart·wheel /ˈkɑːt-wiːl ‖ ˈkɑːrt-/ n circular movement in which a person turns over by putting their hands on the ground and moving their legs sideways in the air

carve /kɑːv ‖ kɑːrv/ v 1 vt make by cutting wood, stone, etc.: carve one's name on a tree: (fig.) She carved herself (out) a good position in business. 2 vi/t cut (cooked meat) into pieces **carver** n 1 person who carves 2 knife for carving meat **carving** n something carved from wood, etc.

cas·cade /kæˈskeɪd/ n waterfall ♦ vi pour like a waterfall

case¹ /keɪs/ n 1 [C] example; situation: I'll make an exception in your case. | several cases of fever | police investigating a case of robbery 2 [C] legal question to be decided; arguments supporting one side of a question: to judge this case | the case for the defence 3 [C;U] gram form of word showing the part it plays in a sentence 4 [C] person having medical treatment 5 **in any case** whatever happens 6 **in case of: a** because of anxiety about: insure the house in case of fire **b** if (something) happens: In case of fire, *ring the bell.* **7 (just) in case** so as to be safe (if): *Take your coat in case it rains.*

case² /ˈkeɪs/ n large box or container: *a packing case* | a **suitcase**

case·ment /ˈkeɪsmənt/ n window that opens like a door

cash /kæʃ/ n [U] **1** money in coins or notes **2** money in any form ♦ vt exchange (a cheque, etc.) for cash

   cash in on *phr vt* take advantage from

cash card /ˈ· ·/ n plastic card used for obtaining one's money from a machine outside a bank, at any time of day

cash crop /ˈ· ·/ n crop grown for sale

ca·shew /ˈkæʃuː, kəˈʃuː/ n (tropical American tree with) a small curved nut

cash·ier¹ /kæˈʃɪə ‖ -ˈʃɪr/ n person who receives and pays out money in a bank, shop, etc.

cash·ier² /kæˈʃɪə, kə- ‖ -ˈʃɪr/ vt dismiss with dishonour from service in the armed forces

cash·mere /ˈkæʃmɪə ‖ ˈkæʒmɪr, ˈkæʃ-/ n [U] fine soft wool

cash·point /ˈkæʃpɔɪnt/ n BrE machine from which one can get money

cash reg·is·ter /ˈ· ·,··/ n machine for recording the amount of sales

cas·ing /ˈkeɪsɪŋ/ n protective covering, as on a tyre

ca·si·no /kəˈsiːnəʊ ‖ -noʊ/ n -nos building where people play cards or other games for money

cask /kɑːsk ‖ kæsk/ n barrel for liquids

cas·ket /ˈkɑːskɪt ‖ ˈkæs-/ n **1** box for jewels, letters, etc. **2** AmE for COFFIN

cas·se·role /ˈkæsərəʊl ‖ -roʊl/ n deep dish for cooking and serving meat; food cooked in this

cas·sette /kəˈset/ n container of MAGNETIC TAPE, or of photographic film

cas·sock /ˈkæsək/ n priest's long garment

cast¹ /kɑːst ‖ kæst/ vt cast **1** fml throw: *cast a net* | *a snake casting off its skin* | *The sun casts long shadows.* **2** give (a vote) **3** make by pouring hot metal: *cast a statue* **4** choose as an actor; choose actors for (a play) *~ing* n thing made by pouring metal

   cast aside *phr vt* get rid of

   cast away *phr vt* leave (someone) somewhere as the result of a shipwreck

   cast down *phr vt* make sad; UPSET

   cast off *phr vi/t* unloose (a boat)

cast² n **1** actors in a play, film, etc. **2** act of throwing a fishing line, etc. **3** hard covering to protect a broken bone **4** object made by casting metal **5** general shape or quality: *an inquiring cast of mind* **6** slight SQUINT (1)

cas·ta·nets /ˌkæstəˈnets/ n [P] musical instrument made of two hollow shells to be knocked together

cast·a·way /ˈkɑːstəweɪ ‖ ˈkæst-/ n shipwrecked person

caste /kɑːst ‖ kæst/ n [C;U] Hindu social class

cast·er /ˈkɑːstə ‖ ˈkæstər/ n **1** small wheel on a chair, etc. **2** container with holes for salt or sugar

cas·ti·gate /ˈkæstɪɡeɪt/ vt fml punish severely; CRITICIZE

casting vote /ˌ· ·ˈ·/ n deciding vote when both sides have an equal number of votes

cast i·ron /ˌ· ˈ·/ n hard but easily breakable type of iron **cast-iron** /ˌ· ˈ·◄/ adj **1** made of cast iron **2** very strong; un- breakable: *a cast-iron stomach* | *a cast-iron excuse*

cas·tle /ˈkɑːsəl ‖ ˈkæ-/ n **1** large building that can be defended against attack **2** one of the powerful pieces in the game of CHESS

cast-off /ˈ· ·/ n, adj (piece of clothing) thrown away by the original owner

cas·trate /kæˈstreɪt ‖ ˈkæstreɪt/ vt remove the sex organs of (a male) **–tration** /kæˈstreɪʃən/ n [C;U]

cas·u·al /ˈkæʒuəl/ adj **1** informal: *casual clothes* **2** resulting from chance: *casual meeting* **3** employed for a short time: *casual labour* **4** not serious or thorough: *the casual reader* ~**ly** adv

cas·u·al·ty /ˈkæʒuəlti/ n person killed or hurt in an accident or battle

cat /kæt/ n **1** small furry animal often kept as a pet **2** animal related to this; lion, tiger, etc. **3 let the cat out of the bag** tell a secret (usu. unintentionally) **4 rain cats and dogs** rain very heavily

cat·a·clys·m /ˈkætəklɪzəm/ n fml violent event, such as an EARTHQUAKE ~**ic** /ˌkætəˈklɪzmɪk/ adj

cat·a·comb /ˈkætəkuːm ‖ -koʊm/ n underground burial place with many rooms

cat·a·logue also **-log** AmE /ˈkætəlɒɡ ‖ -lɔːɡ, -lɑːɡ/ n **1** [C] list of places, goods for sale, etc., in order **2 a catalogue of**

disasters/errors many disasters/errors one after the other ♦ *vt* make a list of

cat·a·lyst /'kætl-ɪ̣st/ *n* something that quickens activity without itself changing

cat·a·pult /'kætəpʌlt/ *n BrE* Y-shaped stick with a rubber band, for shooting small stones ♦ *vt* fire (as if) from a catapult: (fig.) *He was catapulted to fame.*

cat·a·ract /'kætərækt/ *n* 1 large waterfall 2 eye disease causing blindness

ca·tarrh /kə'tɑː ‖ -'tɑːr/ *n* [S;U] disease of the nose and throat, causing a flow of liquid

ca·tas·tro·phe /kə'tæstrəfi/ *n* sudden terrible misfortune –**phic** /ˌkætə'strɒfɪk◀ -'strɒ:-/ *adj*

cat·call /'kætkɔːl ‖ -kɒːl/ *v, n* (make) a loud whistle or cry expressing disapproval

catch[1] /kætʃ/ *v* **caught** /kɔːt ‖ -kɒːt/ 1 *vt* get hold of (a moving object) and stop it: *catch a ball* 2 *vt* make a prisoner; trap: *catch a fish/a thief* 3 *vt* discover some something: *I caught him reading my diary.* 4 *vt* be in time for: *catch a train* 5 *vt* get (an illness) 6 *vt/t* get hooked or stuck: *My skirt caught in the door.* 7 *vt* hear; understand 8 *vt* to hit (a person or animal) 9 **catch fire** start to burn 10 **catch it** *infml* be in trouble for doing something wrong 11 **catch one's breath a** stop breathing for a moment because of surprise or shock **b** rest for a short while after hard work 12 **catch sight of** see for a moment 13 **catch someone's eye** attract someone's attention by looking at them ~**ing** *adj* infectious

    catch on *phr vi* 1 become popular 2 understand

    catch out *phr vt* discover doing something wrong

    catch up *phr vi/t* 1 come up from behind; draw level 2 **caught up in** completely interested in or involved

catch[2] *n* 1 getting and holding a ball 2 (amount of) something caught: *big catch of fish* 3 hook, etc. for fastening something 4 hidden difficulty; SNAG

catch-22 /ˌ· ··'·/ *n* [U] situation from which one is prevented from escaping by something that is part of the situation itself: *I can't get a job unless I belong to the union, and I can't join the union until I've got a job — it's a catch-22 situation*

catch·ment ar·e·a /'kætʃmənt ˌeəriə ‖ -ˌeriə/ *n* area from which a school gets its

pupils, a hospital gets its patients, etc.

catch·phrase /'kætʃˌfreɪz/ *n* fashionable phrase that everyone uses

catch·y /'kætʃi/ *adj* (of a tune, etc.) easy to remember

cat·e·gor·i·cal /ˌkætə"gɒrɪk əl ‖ -'gɒː-, -'gɑː-/ *adj* (of a statement) unconditional; made without doubt ~**ly** /-kli/ *adv*

cat·e·go·ry /'kætɪˌgɒri ‖ -gɒːri/ *n* division in a system; class –**gorize** also -**ise** *BrE* /-gəraɪz/ *vt* put in a category

ca·ter /'keɪtə ‖ -ər/ *vi* provide food and drinks at a party ~**er** *n*

    cater for *phr vt BrE* provide what is necessary: *magazines catering for all opinions*

cat·er·pil·lar /'kætəˌpɪlə ‖ -tərˌpɪlər/ *n* 1 wormlike creature that eats leaves 2 endless chain of plates on the wheels of a TRACTOR, etc.

ca·thar·sis /kə'θɑːsɪ̣s, kæ- ‖ kə'θɑːr-/ *n* -**ses** /-siːz/ [C;U] getting rid of bad feelings by expressing them through art or by reliving them **cathartic** *adj*

ca·the·dral /kə'θiːdrəl/ *n* chief church of a DIOCESE

cath·ode /'kæθəʊd ‖ -oʊd/ *n* part of an electrical instrument from which ELECTRONS leave

cath·o·lic /'kæθəlɪk/ *adj* 1 *fml* general; broad: *catholic tastes* 2 (*cap.*) ROMAN CATHOLIC ♦ *n* (*cap.*) a ROMAN CATHOLIC

Cath·o·li·cism /kə'θɒlɪ̣sɪzəm ‖ kə'θɑː-/ *n* [U] teachings of the ROMAN CATHOLIC Church

cat's eyes /'. ./ *n* [P] small objects in the middle of a road that shine when lit by car lights

cat·tle /'kætl/ *n* [P] cows and BULLS

cat·ty /'kæti/ *adj* indirectly SPITEFUL

cat·walk /'kætwɔːk ‖ -wɒːk/ *n* narrow raised PLATFORM (2)

cau·cus /'kɔːkəs ‖ 'kɒː-/ *n* political meeting to decide future plans

caught /kɔːt ‖ kɒːt/ *v past t. and p. of* CATCH

caul·dron /'kɔːldrən ‖ 'kɒːl-/ *n lit* large pot for boiling things

cau·li·flow·er /'kɒlɪˌflaʊə ‖ 'kɒːlɪˌflaʊr, 'kɑː-/ *n* [C;U] green vegetable with a large white head of flowers

cause /kɔːz ‖ kɒːz/ *n* 1 [C;U] thing that produces a result: *the cause of the accident*

2 [U] reason: *no cause for complaint* 3 [C] purpose strongly supported: *good causes such as famine relief* ♦ *vt* be the cause of: *to cause trouble*

cause·way /'kɔːzweɪ ‖ 'kɔːz-/ n raised road across water, etc.

caus·tic /'kɔːstɪk ‖ 'kɒː-/ adj 1 able to burn by chemical action 2 (of remarks) bitter; nasty

cau·tion /'kɔːʃən ‖ 'kɒː-/ n 1 [U] great care 2 [C] spoken warning by a policeman, etc. —see also **throw caution to the wind** (THROW) ♦ *vt* warn **~ary** adj giving a warning

cau·tious /'kɔːʃəs ‖ 'kɒː-/ adj with caution; careful **~ly** adv

cav·al·cade /ˌkævəl'keɪd, 'kævəlkeɪd/ n procession of riders, vehicles, etc.

cav·a·lier /ˌkævə'lɪə◄ ‖ -'lɪr◄/ adj thoughtless; OFFHAND

cav·al·ry /'kævəlri/ n [U] soldiers on horseback, or (now) with armoured vehicles

cave[1] /keɪv/ n underground hollow place

cave[2] v cave in *phr vi* (of a roof) fall down 2 give up opposition; YIELD

ca·ve·at /'keɪviæt, 'kæv-/ n *law* warning

cav·ern /'kævən ‖ -ərn/ n large cave **~ous** adj (of a hole) very large

cav·i·ar /'kæviɑː ‖ -ɑːr/ n [U] salted eggs (ROE) of a large fish

cav·il /'kævəl/ vi -ll- *BrE* ‖ -l- *AmE* find fault unnecessarily

cav·i·ty /'kævəti/ n *fml* hole in a solid mass, such as a tooth

ca·vort /kə'vɔːt ‖ -ɔːrt/ vi *infml* (esp. of a person) jump or dance about noisily

cc abbrev. for: CUBIC centimetre

CD /ˌsiː 'diː◄/ n abbrev. for: compact disc; small round piece of plastic on which sound, information, etc. is stored

CD-ROM /ˌsiː diː 'rɒm ‖ -'rɑːm/ n compact disc on which very large quantities of information can be stored for use by a computer

cease /siːs/ vi/t *fml* stop (an activity) **~less** adj unending; continuous **~lessly** adv

cease-fire /'· ·/ n agreement to stop fighting; TRUCE

ce·dar /'siːdə ‖ -ər/ n [C;U] (wood of) a tall EVERGREEN tree

cede /siːd/ vt *fml* give (esp. land, after losing a war)

cei·ling /'siːlɪŋ/ n 1 upper surface of a room 2 official upper limit on prices, etc.

cel·e·brate /'seləbreɪt/ v 1 vt/i mark (an event) by enjoying oneself 2 vt praise; honour **–brated** adj famous **–bration** /ˌselə'breɪʃən/ n [C;U]

ce·leb·ri·ty /sə'lebrəti/ n 1 [C] famous person 2 [U] fame

cel·e·ry /'seləri/ n [U] plant whose greenish-white stems are eaten as a vegetable

ce·les·ti·al /sə'lestiəl ‖ -tʃəl/ adj *fml* of the sky or heaven

cel·i·bate /'seləbət/ n, adj (person who is) unmarried and not sexually active, esp. for religious reasons **–bacy** n [U]

cell /sel/ n small room: *prison cell* 2 small unit of living matter 3 apparatus for making electricity chemically 4 single group of people in a secret organization: *Communist cells*

cel·lar /'selə ‖ -ər/ n underground room for storing things: *wine cellar*

cel·lo /'tʃeləu ‖ -lou/ n -los kind of large VIOLIN held between the knees **cellist** n person who plays a cello

cel·lo·phane /'seləfeɪn/ n [U] *tdmk* CLING FILM

cel·lu·lar /'seljələ ‖ -ər/ adj 1 having many holes; POROUS 2 consisting of CELLS (2)

cellular phone /ˌ··· '·/ also **cell phone** /'·. ·/ n telephone that can be carried around and used anywhere

cel·lu·loid /'seljəlɔɪd/ n [U] *tdmk* 1 strong plastic formerly used for making photographic film 2 **on celluloid** on cinema film

cel·lu·lite /'seljəlaɪt/ n [U] fat just below the skin, causing an unpleasant uneven surface

Cel·si·us /'selsiəs/ adj, n (in) the temperature scale in which water freezes at 0° and boils at 100°

Cel·tic /'keltɪk, 'seltɪk/ adj of the Celts, a European people who include the Irish, Scots, Welsh, and Bretons

ce·ment /sɪ'ment/ n [U] 1 grey powder that becomes hard like stone when mixed with water, and is used in building 2 any thick sticky glue used for filling holes or joining things ♦ vt join with cement: (fig.) *to cement our friendship*

cem·e·tery /'semɪtri‖-teri/ n piece of ground used for burials

cen·o·taph /'senətɑːf‖-tæf/ n MONUMENT in memory of people killed in war

cen·sor /'sensə‖-ər/ n official who examines books, films, etc. to remove anything offensive ♦ vt examine as a censor ~**ship** n [U] work of a censor; censoring

cen·so·ri·ous /sen'sɔːriəs/ adj fml always looking for mistakes or faults; severely CRITICAL

cen·sure /'senʃə‖-ər/ n [U] fml blame; disapproval ♦ vt express disapproval of

cen·sus /'sensəs/ n official counting, esp. of a country's population

cent /sent/ n (coin equal to) 0.01 of certain units of money, e.g. the dollar

cen·taur /'sentɔː‖-ɔːr/ n imaginary creature, half man and half horse

cen·te·na·ry /sen'tiːnəri‖-'te-, 'sentəneri/ n 100th ANNIVERSARY

cen·ten·ni·al /sen'teniəl/ n AmE for centenary

cen·ter /'sentə‖-ər/ n, v AmE for CENTRE

cen·ti·grade /'sentɪɡreɪd/ adj, n CELSIUS

cen·ti·me·tre BrE ‖ **-ter** AmE /'sentɪˌmiːtə‖-ər/ n (unit of length equal to) 1/100 of a metre

cen·ti·pede /'sentɪpiːd/ n wormlike creature with many legs

cen·tral /'sentrəl/ adj 1 at the centre 2 most important; main ~**ly** adv ~**ise**, **-ize** BrE vt bring under central control ~**ization** n [U] /ˌsentrəlaɪ'zeɪʃən‖-trələ-/

central heat·ing /ˌ··'··/ n [U] heating buildings by pipes from a single point

central pro·ces·sing u·nit /ˌ·· '···,·-/ n the most important controlling part of a computer system

cen·tre BrE ‖ **-ter** AmE /'sentə‖-ər/ n 1 [C] middle point 2 [C] place for a particular activity: a shopping centre 3 [the+S] a middle position, in politics, not supporting EXTREME (2) ideas ♦ vi/t gather to a centre: His interests are centred on/round his family.

cen·tre·piece /'sentəpiːs‖-ər-/ n thing in the centre or most important position

cen·tri·fu·gal /ˌsentrɪ'fjuːɡəl◄, sen'trɪfjʊɡəl‖sen'trɪfjʊɡəl/ adj tending to move out from the centre

cen·trist /'sentrɪst/ n, adj (of) a person who supports the CENTRE (3)

cen·tu·ry /'sentʃəri/ n 1 100 years 2 100-year period counted forwards or backwards from Christ's birth 3 (in cricket) 100 runs made by one player

ce·ram·ics /sɪ'ræmɪks/ n [U;P] (making of) pots, bricks, etc. **-ic** adj

ce·re·al /'sɪəriəl‖'sɪr-/ n 1 [C] food grain 2 [C;U] breakfast food such as CORNFLAKES

ce·re·bral /'serɪbrəl‖sə'riː-, 'serə-/ adj 1 of or connected with the brain 2 showing too much serious thinking

cerebral pal·sy /ˌserɪbrəl 'pɔːlzi‖sə,riːbrəl 'pɒːlzi, ˌserəbrəl-/ n [U] illness caused by brain damage during or before birth, resulting in difficulty in speech and movement

cer·e·mo·ni·al /ˌserɪ'məʊniəl◄‖-'moʊ-/ adj for a ceremony: ceremonial banquet ♦ n [C;U] ceremony

cer·e·mo·ni·ous /ˌserɪ'məʊniəs‖-'moʊ-/ adj formally polite

cer·e·mo·ny /'serɪməni‖-moʊni/ n 1 [C] set of solemn actions to mark an important event: a wedding ceremony 2 [U] formal behaviour

cer·tain[1] /'sɜːtn‖'sɜːrtn/ adj 1 sure; without doubt: I'm certain he saw me. | It's certain to rain. 2 sure to happen: facing certain death 3 **make certain** do something to be sure: Make certain he knows. ~**ly** adv of course

cer·tain[2] determiner, pron 1 some, not named: There are certain reasons against it. 2 some, not a lot: a certain amount of profit.

cer·tain·ty /'sɜːtnti‖'sɜːr-/ n 1 [C] established fact 2 [U] freedom from doubt

cer·tif·i·cate /sə'tɪfɪkət‖sər-/ n official paper stating facts: marriage certificate

cer·ti·fy /'sɜːtɪfaɪ‖'sɜːr-/ vt declare officially that something is true: to certify the prisoner insane **-fiable** adj BrE infml mad

cer·ti·tude /'sɜːtɪtjuːd‖'sɜːrtətuːd/ n [U] fml state of being or feeling certain

cer·vi·cal /'sɜːvɪkəl‖'sɜːr-/ adj of the narrow opening (**cervix**) of the WOMB

ce·sar·e·an /sɪ'zeəriən‖-'zer-/ n CAESAREAN

ces·sa·tion /se'seɪʃən/ n [C;U] fml short pause or stop

cess·pit /'ses,pɪt/ n underground hole where a house's SEWAGE is gathered

cf *written abbrev. for:* compare

CFC /ˌsiː ef ˈsiː/ *n abbrev. for:* chlorofluorocarbon; gas used in REFRIGE-RATORS, AEROSOLS, etc., which causes damage to the Earth's OZONE LAYER

ch *written abbrev. for:* CHAPTER (1)

chafe /tʃeɪf/ *v* 1 *vt* rub; make sore by rubbing 2 *vi* become impatient: *chafe at the delay*

chaff /tʃɑːf ‖ tʃæf/ *n* [U] outer parts of seeds, separated from the grain

cha·grin /ˈʃægrɪn ‖ ʃəˈgrɪn/ *n* [U] *fml* annoyance and disappointment

chain /tʃeɪn/ *n* 1 length of metal rings joined together 2 set of connected things: *chain of mountains/of events* ♦ *vt* fasten with a chain: *prisoners chained to the wall*

chain re·ac·tion /ˌ··ˈ··/ *n* set of events so related that each causes the next

chain-smoke /ˈ··/ *vi/t* smoke (cigarettes) continually **–smoker** *n*

chain store /ˈ··/ *n* group of shops under one ownership

chair /tʃeə ‖ tʃer/ *n* 1 movable seat for one person 2 position of a chairperson 3 position of a PROFESSOR ♦ *vt* be chair-person of

chair·man /ˈtʃeəmən ‖ ˈtʃer-/ **–woman** /-ˌwʊmən/ *fem.* — *n* — **-men** /-mən/ person in charge of a meeting, or directing the work of a group

chair·per·son /ˈtʃeəˌpɜːsən ‖ ˈtʃerˌpɜːr-sən/ *n* chairman or chairwoman

chal·et /ˈʃæleɪ ‖ ʃæˈleɪ/ *n* 1 Swiss wooden house 2 small house or hut for holidays

chalk[1] /tʃɔːk ‖ tʃɔːk/ *n* 1 [U] kind of soft white rock 2 [C;U] this material used for writing or drawing 3 **not by a long chalk** not at all *–y adj*

chalk[2] *vt* write with chalk

chalk up *phr vt* succeed in getting

chalk·board /ˈtʃɔːkbɔːd ‖ ˈtʃɔːkbɔːrd/ *n AmE for* BLACKBOARD

chal·lenge /ˈtʃælɪndʒ/ *vt* 1 invite to a fight, match, etc. 2 question the loyalty or rightness of ♦ *n* 1 invitation to compete 2 something exciting that needs a lot of effort **–lenging** *adj* difficult but exciting **–lenger** *n*

cham·ber /ˈtʃeɪmbə ‖ -ər/ *n* 1 *lit* bedroom 2 a law-making body **b** room where it meets 3 enclosed space: *the four chambers of the heart*

cham·ber·maid /ˈtʃeɪmbəmeɪd ‖ -ər-/ *n* woman who cleans hotel bedrooms

chamber mu·sic /ˈ·· ˌ··/ *n* [U] music for a small group of musicians or players (a **chamber orchestra**)

cha·me·le·on /kəˈmiːliən/ *n* small LIZARD that changes colour to match its surroundings

champ[1] /tʃæmp/ *vi* 1 (of a horse) bite noisily 2 be impatient 3 **champ at the bit** be restless and difficult to control because of being impatient to do something

champ[2] *n infml for* CHAMPION (1)

cham·pagne /ʃæmˈpeɪn/ *n* [U] expensive white wine with BUBBLES

cham·pi·on /ˈtʃæmpiən/ *n* 1 person or animal that wins a competition 2 person who defends a principle or another person ♦ *vt* defend; support **~ship** *n* 1 competition to find the champion 2 position of being the champion 3 act of championing

chance /tʃɑːns ‖ tʃæns/ *n* 1 [U] good or bad luck 2 [C;U] likelihood: *no chance of winning | The chances are* (=it is likely) *he already knows.* 3 [C] favourable occasion; OPPORTUNITY: *a chance to travel* 4 [C;U] risk 5 **by chance** by accident 6 **on the (off) chance** in view of the (unlikely) possibility —see also MAIN CHANCE ♦ *v* 1 *vt* take a risk 2 *vi fml* happen accidentally: *We chanced to meet.* ♦ *adj* accidental *~y adj* risky

chan·cel /ˈtʃɑːnsəl ‖ ˈtʃæn-/ *n* eastern part of a church

chan·cel·lor /ˈtʃɑːnsələ ‖ ˈtʃænsələr/ *n* (*often cap.*) state or legal official of high rank

chan·de·lier /ˌʃændəˈlɪə ‖ -ˈlɪr/ *n* branched hanging holder for lights

change /tʃeɪndʒ/ *v* 1 *vi/t* make or become different: *change the subject | water changed into ice* 2 *vt* give and receive in return: *change a library book | change pounds into dollars* 3 *vi/t* put different clothes on 4 *vi/t* leave and enter (different vehicles) 5 **change one's mind** form a new opinion ♦ *n* 1 changing; something new: *a change of clothes | Let's have fish for a change.* 2 **a** money returned when something bought costs less than the amount paid **b** low-value coins or notes —see also SEA CHANGE *~able adj* often changing

change of life /ˌ· · ˈ·/ *n* MENOPAUSE

chan·nel¹ /'tʃænl/ n 1 narrow sea passage 2 passage for liquids 3 television station 4 **channel hop/surf** change from one TV channel to another again and again 5 way along which information passes: *go through the official channels* vt -ll- *BrE* -l- *AmE* send through channels; direct: *channel my abilities into something useful*

chant /tʃɑːnt ‖ tʃænt/ vi/t sing (words) on one note **chant** n

cha·os /'keɪ-ɒs ‖ -ɑːs/ n [S;U] complete confusion **-otic** /keɪ'ɒtɪk ‖ -'ɑːtɪk/ adj

chap¹ /tʃæp/ n esp. *BrE* man

chap² vi/t -pp- (cause to) become sore, rough and cracked: *chapped lips*

chap·el /'tʃæpəl/ n small church

chap·er·on, -one /'ʃæpərəʊn ‖ -roʊn/ n older person who goes with a younger person and is responsible for their behaviour **chaperon, -one** vt

chap·lain /'tʃæplɪn/ n priest in the armed forces, a hospital, etc.

chap·ter /'tʃæptə ‖ -ər/ n 1 main division of a book, usu. numbered 2 special period of history

char /tʃɑː ‖ tʃɑːr/ vi/t -rr- blacken by burning **charred** adj

char·ac·ter /'kærəktə ‖ -ər/ n 1 [C;U] qualities that make a person or thing different from others: *a man of good character* | *the character of the town* 2 [U] moral strength, honesty, etc. 3 [C] person in a book, etc. 4 [C] person, esp. an odd one 5 [C] written letter or sign: *Chinese characters* **~less** adj ordinary; dull

char·ac·ter·is·tic /ˌkærəktə'rɪstɪk◄/ adj typical ♦ n special quality **~ally** /-kli/ adv

char·ac·ter·ize also **-ise** *BrE* /'kærəktəraɪz/ vt 1 be typical of 2 describe the character of

cha·rade /ʃə'rɑːd ‖ ʃə'reɪd/ n 1 foolish unnecessary action 2 [P] game in which words are acted by players until guessed by other players

char·coal /'tʃɑːkəʊl ‖ 'tʃɑːrkoʊl/ n burnt wood, used for drawing with, etc.

charge /tʃɑːdʒ ‖ tʃɑːrdʒ/ n 1 vt/i ask in payment 2 vt record (something) to someone's debt 3 vi/t rush as if to attack 4 vt ACCUSE of a crime: *charged with stealing* 5 vt *fml* command; give as a duty 6 vt/i (cause to) take in electricity: *charge a battery* | (fig.) *a highly charged political*

question (=causing strong feelings or much argument) ♦ n 1 [C] price asked or paid 2 [U] control; responsibility: *I'll take charge of the money.* 3 [C] statement blaming a person for wrongdoing: *a charge of murder* 4 [C] rushing attack by soldiers, animals, etc. 5 [C;U] electricity put into a BATTERY 6 **in charge (of)** responsible (for)

charge card /'· ·/ n plastic card which allows one to obtain goods at a particular shop and pay later

char·gé d'af·faires /ˌʃaːʒeɪ dæ'feə ‖ ˌʃɑːrʒeɪ dæ'fer/ n official who represents his/her government where there is no AMBASSADOR

char·i·ot /'tʃærɪət/ n ancient two-wheeled horse-drawn vehicle

cha·ris·ma /kə'rɪzmə/ n [U] *fml* great charm; power to win public admiration **~tic** /ˌkærɪz'mætɪk◄/ adj: *charismatic leader*

char·i·ty /'tʃærɪti/ n 1 [U] generosity and help to the poor, etc. 2 [U] kindness shown in judging others 3 [C] organization for helping people **–table** adj **–tably** adv

char·la·tan /'ʃɑːlətən ‖ 'ʃɑːr-/ n person who falsely claims a special skill

charm /tʃɑːm ‖ tʃɑːrm/ n 1 [C;U] power to delight people 2 [C] magic words; SPELL 3 [C] object worn to bring good luck 4 **work like a charm** happen or take place with complete success ♦ vt 1 please; delight: *charming manners* 2 control by magic **~er** n person who charms **~ing** adj very pleasing

chart /tʃɑːt ‖ tʃɑːrt/ n 1 information in the form of a picture or GRAPH: *a sales chart* 2 map, esp. of the sea ♦ vt 1 record (information) over a period of time 2 make a chart of

char·ter /'tʃɑːtə ‖ 'tʃɑːrtər/ n 1 [C] official statement of rights and freedoms 2 [U] hiring of buses, planes, etc.: *charter flights* ♦ vt hire (a bus, etc.) **~ed** adj officially allowed to practise a profession: *a chartered accountant*

chase /tʃeɪs/ vi/t follow rapidly, in order to catch or drive away ♦ n 1 chasing something or someone 2 **give chase** chase someone

chas·m /'kæzəm/ n very deep crack in the earth

chas·sis /'ʃæsi/ n **chassis** /'ʃæsiz/ frame on which a vehicle is built

chaste /tʃeɪst/ *adj* avoiding wrong sexual activity **chastity** /'tʃæstɪti/ *n* [U]

chas·ten /'tʃeɪsən/ *vt* improve by punishment or suffering

chas·tise /tʃæ'staɪz/ *vt fml* punish severely

chat /tʃæt/ *vt* -tt- talk informally **chat** *n* ~ty *adj* 1 fond of chatting 2 having the style of informal talk: *chatty letter*

chat up *phr vt BrE infml* talk to someone (esp. of the opposite sex) in a friendly way, esp. in order to begin a relationship

chât·eau /'ʃæʊ∥'ʃæ'toʊ/ *n* -teaus or -teaux /'ʃæʊz∥'ʃæ'toʊz/ *French castle*

chat·ter /'tʃætə∥-ər/ *vi* 1 talk rapidly about small things 2 (of the teeth) knock together from cold or fear ♦ *n* [U] 1 chattering talk 2 rapid speechlike sounds ~**er** *n*

chat·ter·box /'tʃætəbɒks∥-tərbɑːks/ *n* person who chatters

chauf·feur /'ʃəʊfə, ʃəʊ'fɜː∥'ʃoʊfər, ʃoʊ'fɜːr/ **chauffeuse** /ʃəʊ'fɜːz∥-'fɜːrz/ *fem.* — *n* paid driver of a private car **chauffeur** *vi/t*

chau·vin·is·m /'ʃəʊvɪnɪzəm∥'ʃoʊ-/ *n* proud belief that one's own country, or one's own sex, is the best **-ist** *n, adj* —see also MALE CHAUVINIST

cheap /tʃiːp/ *adj* 1 low in price 2 **a** of poor quality **b** low or offensively unpleasant 3 without serious feeling: *cheap emotions* 4 needing little effort: *a cheap victory* 5 *AmE infml* STINGY 6 **feel cheap** feel ashamed ♦ *adv* at a low price ~**en** *vi/t* make or become cheaper ~**ly** *adv* ~**ness** *n* [U]

cheat /tʃiːt/ *vi/t* 1 act dishonestly; treat someone deceitfully: *cheating at cards* | *cheat her out of her money* 2 avoid or escape as if by deception: *to cheat death* ♦ *n* person who cheats

check /tʃek/ *n* 1 [C] examination to make sure something is correct 2 [S;U] stop; control: *keep the disease in check* 3 [C;U] pattern of squares 4 [C] *AmE* restaurant bill 5 [C] *AmE for* CHEQUE 6 [C] *AmE for* TICK[1] (2) 7 [U] (in CHESS) position of the king when under direct attack ♦ *v* 1 *vi/t* examine; make sure: *check a letter for spelling mistakes* 2 *vt* hold back; control: *check the increase in crime* 3 *vt AmE* put

somewhere to be looked after: *check one's coat at the theatre* 4 *vt AmE* TICK[2] (2)

check in *phr vi* report one's arrival at an airport, etc. **check-in** /'· ·/ *n* [C;U]

check out *phr vi* 1 leave a hotel after paying the bill 2 **a** find out if something is true by making inquiries **b** be found to be true after inquiries have been made

check up on *phr vt* inquire thoroughly about

check·ered /'tʃekəd∥-ərd/ *adj AmE* CHEQUERED

check·list /'tʃek,lɪst/ *n* complete list; INVENTORY

check·mate /'tʃekmeɪt/ *n* [C;U] 1 (in CHESS) position of a king when under direct attack so that escape is impossible 2 (a) complete defeat ♦ *vt* 1 (in CHESS) win the game with a checkmate 2 stop; completely defeat

check·out /'tʃek-aʊt/ *n* pay desk in a self-service shop

check·point /'tʃekpɔɪnt/ *n* place where a CHECK (1) is made on people, traffic, etc.

check·up /'tʃek-ʌp/ *n* general medical examination

ched·dar /'tʃedə∥-ər/ *n* [U] firm yellow or orange cheese

cheek /tʃiːk/ *n* 1 [C] either side of the face below the eye 2 [U] rude behaviour ♦ *vt esp. BrE* speak rudely to ~**y** *adj* rude

cheer /tʃɪə∥tʃɪr/ *n* 1 [C] shout of praise or joy 2 [U] happiness; good spirits ♦ *vi/t* 1 make or become happy: *cheering news* | *Cheer up!* 2 shout in approval; encourage by shouting ~**ful** *adj* happy ~**fully** *adv* ~**less** *adj* saddening ~**y** *adj* merry

cheer·i·o /,tʃɪəri'əʊ∥,tʃɪri'oʊ/ *interj BrE* goodbye

cheese /tʃiːz/ *n* [C;U] solid food made from milk

cheese·cake /'tʃiːzkeɪk/ *n* [U] cake made with soft white cheese

chee·tah /'tʃiːtə/ *n* spotted African animal of the cat family, able to run very fast

chef /ʃef/ *n* chief cook in a restaurant, etc.

chem·i·cal /'kemɪkəl/ *adj* of chemistry ♦ *n* chemical substance

chem·ist /'kemɪst/ *n* 1 scientist specializing in chemistry 2 *BrE* person who sells medicines, soap, etc.

chem·is·try /'kemɪstri/ *n* [U] science of

natural substances and how they combine and behave

chem·o·ther·a·py /ˌkiːməʊˈθerəpi, ˌke-‖-moʊ-/ n [U] use of chemical substances to treat and control diseases

cheque BrE ‖ **check** AmE /tʃek/ n written order to a bank to pay money —see also BLANK CHEQUE, TRAVELLER'S CHEQUE

cheque card /'·· ·/ n BrE card given to people by a bank, promising to pay out the money written on their cheques up to a certain amount

chequ·ered /'tʃekəd ‖-ərd/ adj BrE partly bad and partly good: his chequered career

cher·ish /'tʃeriʃ/ vt fml 1 care for; love 2 keep (hope, etc.) in one's mind: cherish a memory

cher·ry /'tʃeri/ n small round fruit with a stone

cher·ub /'tʃerəb/ n 1 pretty child, esp. one with wings in a painting 2 (pl. **-ubim** /-əbɪm/ kind of ANGEL ~**ic** /tʃəˈruːbɪk/ adj

chess /tʃes/ n [U] board game for two players

chest /tʃest/ n 1 upper front part of the body 2 large strong box 3 **get (something) off one's chest** bring (a worry) into the open by talking

chest·nut /'tʃesnʌt/ n 1 kind of smooth reddish-brown nut 2 joke or story so old and well-known that it is no longer funny or interesting ♦ adj reddish-brown

chest of drawers /ˌ· · '·/ n piece of furniture with drawers

chew /tʃuː/ vi/t 1 crush (food, etc.) with the teeth 2 **bite off more than one can chew** attempt more than one can deal with or succeed in finishing

    chew over phr vt infml think about (a question, problem, etc.)

chewing gum /'·· ·/ n sweet sticky substance to be chewed but not swallowed

chic /ʃiːk/ adj, n [U] (with) good style

chick /tʃɪk/ n baby bird

chick·en¹ /'tʃɪkən/ n 1 [C] common farmyard bird, esp. a young one 2 [U] its meat 3 **count one's chickens before they're hatched** make plans depending on something which has not yet happened ♦ adj sl cowardly

chicken² v **chicken out** phr vi sl decide not to do something because one is frightened

chicken pox /'·· ·/ n [U] infectious disease that causes spots

chic·o·ry /'tʃɪkəri/ n [U] 1 plant whose leaves are eaten as a vegetable 2 powder made from its roots, added to coffee

chide /tʃaɪd/ vi/t chided or chid /tʃɪd/, chid or chidden /'tʃɪdn/ fml or lit speak to (someone) angrily; REBUKE

chief /tʃiːf/ n leader; head of something: the chief of police ♦ adj 1 highest in rank 2 main 3 **-in-chief** of the highest rank: commander-in-chief ~**ly** adv mainly; specially

chief·tain /'tʃiːftən/ n leader of a tribe, etc.

child /tʃaɪld/ n children /'tʃɪldrən/ 1 young human being 2 son or daughter 3 someone who behaves like a child ~**hood** n [C;U] time of being a child ~**ish** adj unsuitable for a grown person ~**less** adj having no children ~**like** adj simple; lovable

child·min·der /'tʃaɪldˌmaɪndə ‖-ər/ n esp. BrE someone who looks after other people's children, esp. when the parents are at work

chill /tʃɪl/ v 1 vi/t make or become cold 2 vi/t (cause to) have a feeling of cold as from fear: a chilling murder story 3 vi about **chill out** relax ♦ n 1 [C] illness with coldness and shaking 2 [S] unpleasant coldness ~**y** adj 1 rather cold 2 unfriendly

chil·li /'tʃɪli/ n [C;U] (powder made from) the hot-tasting red seed case of a kind of pepper

chime /tʃaɪm/ n sound of a set of bells ♦ vi/t 1 make this sound 2 infml be in agreement

chim·ney /'tʃɪmni/ n hollow passage to let out smoke from a fire

chim·ney·pot /'tʃɪmnipɒt ‖-pɑːt/ n pipe fixed on top of a chimney

chim·ney·stack /'tʃɪmnistæk/ n 1 tall chimney of a building such as a factory 2 BrE group of small chimneys

chim·ney·sweep /'tʃɪmniswiːp/ n person who cleans the insides of chimneys

chim·pan·zee /ˌtʃɪmpænˈziː, -pən-/ also **chimp** /tʃɪmp/ — n kind of African APE

chin /tʃɪn/ n the part of the face below the mouth

chi·na /'tʃaɪnə/ n [U] 1 baked clay

2 plates, cups, etc. made from this

chink[1] /tʃɪŋk/ n narrow crack

chink[2] n, v CLINK

chi·nos /'tʃiːnəʊz ‖ -noʊz/ n [P] loose cotton trousers

chip[1] /tʃɪp/ n 1 small piece broken off 2 place from which this was broken 3 thin piece of potato cooked in fat: *fish and chips* 4 small piece of material on which an INTEGRATED CIRCUIT is formed 5 flat plastic object used for representing money in certain games 6 **a chip off the old block** a person very like their father in character 7 **have a chip on one's shoulder** be quarrelsome or easily offended, as a result of feeling badly treated 8 **when the chips are down** when a very important point is reached —see also BLUE CHIP

chip[2] vi/t -pp- (cause to) lose a small piece from the edge

   chip in phr v infml 1 vi interrupt a conversation 2 vi/t add (one's share of money)

chi·rop·o·dist /kə'rɒpədɪst, ʃə- ‖ -'rɑː-/ n person who treats the human foot -dy n [U]

chirp /tʃɜːp ‖ tʃɜːrp/ vi make the short sharp sound of small birds **chirp** n ~y adj (of people) cheerful

chis·el /'tʃɪzəl/ n metal tool for shaping wood or stone ♦ vt/i -ll- BrE ‖ -l- AmE cut with a chisel

chit /tʃɪt/ n signed note showing sum of money owed (for drinks, etc.)

chiv·al·ry /'ʃɪvəlri/ n [U] 1 beliefs and practices of KNIGHTS in the MIDDLE AGES 2 good manners shown by a man towards women -rous adj

chlo·rine /'klɔːriːn/ n [U] greenish yellow, strong-smelling substance used to DISINFECT places, esp. swimming baths

chlor·o·form /'klɒrəfɔːm, 'klɔː- ‖ 'klɔːrəfɔːrm/ n [U] chemical used as an ANAESTHETIC

chock-a-block /,tʃɒk ə 'blɒk◀ ‖ 'tʃɑːk ə ,blɑːk/ adj infml very crowded

choco·late /'tʃɒklɪt ‖ 'tʃɑːkələt, 'tʃɔːk-/ n 1 [U] solid brown substance eaten as a sweet 2 [C] small sweet covered with this 3 [U] hot drink made from this ♦ adj dark brown

choice /tʃɔɪs/ n 1 [C] act of choosing 2 [U] power of choosing: *have no choice but to*

obey 3 [C] variety to choose from: *a big choice of shops* ♦ adj 1 of high quality 2 well chosen

choir /kwaɪə ‖ kwaɪr/ n 1 group of singers 2 part of a church where they sit

choke /tʃəʊk ‖ tʃoʊk/ v 1 vt/i stop breathing because the breathing passage is blocked 2 vt fill (a passage) completely: *roads choked with traffic* ♦ n apparatus that controls air going into a petrol engine

   choke back phr vt control (esp. violent or sad feelings) as if by holding in the throat: *He choked back his tears.*

chol·e·ra /'kɒlərə ‖ 'kɑː-/ n [U] serious tropical disease of the stomach and bowels

cho·les·te·rol /kə'lestərɒl ‖ -roʊl/ n [U] substance found in all cells of the body, which helps to carry fats

choose /tʃuːz/ vi/t chose /tʃəʊz ‖ tʃoʊz/, chosen /'tʃəʊzən ‖ 'tʃoʊ-/ 1 pick out from many: *choose a cake* 2 decide: *choose where to go*

chop[1] /tʃɒp ‖ tʃɑːp/ vt -pp- cut with a heavy tool: *chop wood/onions*

chop[2] n 1 quick cutting blow 2 piece of lamb or PORK with a bone in it

chop·per /'tʃɒpə ‖ 'tʃɑːpər/ n 1 heavy tool for chopping 2 sl HELICOPTER

chop·py /'tʃɒpi ‖ 'tʃɑː-/ adj (of water) with short rough waves

chop·sticks /'tʃɒpstɪks ‖ 'tʃɑːp-/ n [P] pair of thin sticks used in East Asia for lifting food to the mouth

cho·ral /'kɔːrəl/ adj of a CHOIR

chord /kɔːd ‖ kɔːrd/ n 1 2 musical notes sounded together 2 straight line joining two points on a curve —see also **strike a chord** (STRIKE[1])

chore /tʃɔː ‖ tʃɔːr/ n bit of regular or dull work

chor·e·og·ra·phy /,kɒri'ɒgrəfi, ,kɔː- ‖ ,kɔːri'ɑːg-/ n arranging dances for the stage –pher n **choreograph** /'kɒriəgrɑːf, 'kɔː- ‖ 'kɔːriəgræf/ vt

chor·is·ter /'kɒrɪstə ‖ 'kɔːrɪstər, 'kɑːr-/ n singer in a CHOIR

chor·tle /'tʃɔːtl ‖ 'tʃɔːrtl/ vi give several laughs of pleasure and satisfaction **chortle** n

cho·rus /'kɔːrəs/ n 1 [C] group of singers 2 [C] part of a song repeated after each VERSE 3 [S] something said by many people together: *a chorus of groans* ♦ vt sing or say together

chose /tʃəʊz‖tʃoʊz/ v past t. of CHOOSE

cho·sen /'tʃəʊzən‖'tʃoʊ-/ v past p. of CHOOSE

Christ /kraɪst/ n man on whose teaching Christianity is based; Jesus

chris·ten /'krɪsən/ vt 1 make into a member of the Christian church by BAPTISM name giving of a name 2 name (esp. a ship) at an official ceremony 3 use for the first time ~ing n ceremony of BAPTISM

Chris·tian /'krɪstʃən, -tiən/ n person who believes in the teachings of Christ ♦ adj 1 of Christianity 2 having qualities such as kindness, generosity, etc.

Chris·ti·an·i·ty /ˌkrɪsti'ænəti/ n [U] the religion based on the life and teachings of Christ

Christian name /'·· ·/ n (esp. in Christian countries) a person's FIRST NAME

Christ·mas /'krɪsməs/ n 1 also Christmas Day /ˌ·· '·/ — holy day in honour of Christ's birth; December 25th 2 period before and after this

chrome /krəʊm‖kroʊm/ n [U] hard metal used esp. as a shiny covering on car parts, etc.

chro·mo·some /'krəʊməsəʊm‖ 'kroʊməsoʊm/ n tiny thread in every living cell that controls the nature of human beings, animals or plants

chron·ic /'krɒnɪk‖'krɑː-/ adj 1 (of a disease) lasting a long time 2 infml very bad: His work is really chronic.

chron·i·cle /'krɒnɪkəl‖'krɑː-/ n record of historical events ♦ vt make a chronicle of

chro·nol·o·gy /krə'nɒlədʒi‖-'nɑː-/ n 1 [U] science that gives dates to events 2 [C] list of events in order –ogical /ˌkrɒnə 'lɒdʒɪkəl◁‖ˌkrɑːnə'lɑː-/ adj arranged in order of time

chro·nom·e·ter /krə'nɒmətə‖- 'nɑːmətər/ n very exact clock

chrys·a·lis /'krɪsəlɪs/ n shell-like form of an insect that will become a MOTH or BUTTERFLY

chry·san·the·mum /krɪ'sænθəməm/ n garden plant with large brightly coloured flowers

chub·by /'tʃʌbi/ adj pleasantly fat

chuck /tʃʌk/ vt 1 throw 2 sl give up; leave: chuck (in) his job

chuck·le /'tʃʌkəl/ vi laugh quietly chuckle n

chum /tʃʌm/ n friend ~my adj friendly

chunk /tʃʌŋk/ n thick lump ~y adj thick: chunky sweater

church /tʃɜːtʃ‖tʃɜːrtʃ/ n 1 [C] building for public Christian worship: a regular churchgoer 2 [S] profession of priests and ministers: enter the church 3 [C] (usu. cap.) branch of Christianity: the Catholic Church

church·yard /'tʃɜːtʃjɑːd‖'tʃɜːrtʃjɑːrd/ n church burial ground

churl·ish /'tʃɜːlɪʃ‖-ɜːr-/ adj bad-tempered; rude ~ly adv

churn¹ /'tʃɜːn‖'tʃɜːrn/ n container in which cream is shaken to make butter

churn² vi/t shake about violently

churn out phr vt produce a large quantity of

chute /ʃuːt/ n sloped passage for something to slide down

chut·ney /'tʃʌtni/ n [U] hot-tasting mixture of fruits

CIA /ˌsiː aɪ 'eɪ/ n Central Intelligence Agency; US government department that collects information, esp. secretly

CID /ˌsiː aɪ 'diː/ n Criminal Investigation Department; branch of the UK police force made up of DETECTIVES

ci·der /'saɪdə‖-ər/ n [U] alcoholic drink made from apples

ci·gar /sɪ'gɑː‖-'gɑːr/ n roll of tobacco leaves for smoking

cig·a·rette /ˌsɪgə'ret‖ˌsɪgə'ret, 'sɪgə ˌret/ n paper tube of cut tobacco for smoking

cin·der /'sɪndə‖-ər/ n bit of burnt coal, etc.

cin·e·ma /'sɪnəmə/ n 1 [C] theatre where films are shown 2 [S] films as an art or industry

cin·na·mon /'sɪnəmən/ n [U] yellowish-brown SPICE used in cooking

ci·pher /'saɪfə‖-ər/ n 1 system of secret writing 2 unimportant person

cir·ca /'sɜːkə‖'sɜːr-/ prep fml (used with dates) about: circa 1000 AD

cir·cle /'sɜːkəl‖'sɜːr-/ n 1 curved line on which every point is equally distant from the centre 2 ring 3 group of people 4 upper floor in a theatre ♦ vi/t 1 move round in a circle 2 draw a circle round

cir·cuit /'sɜːkɪt‖'sɜːr-/ n 1 circular

journey round an area **2** circular path of an electric current ~**ous** /sɜːˈkjuːɪtəs ‖ sɜːr-/ adj going a long way round: *a circuitous route*

cir·cu·lar /ˈsɜːkjɜlə ‖ ˈsɜːrkjɜlər/ adj **1** shaped like a circle **2** moving in a circle **3** not direct ♦ n printed notice given to many people

cir·cu·late /ˈsɜːkjɜᵇleɪt ‖ ˈsɜːr-/ vi/t **1** move along a closed path **2** spread widely: *circulate rumours* **3** move about freely –**tion** /ˌsɜːkjɜᵇleɪʃən ‖ ˌsɜːr-/ n **1** [U] flow round a closed system: *the circulation of the blood* **2** [U] passing of money among people: *the number of £5 notes in circulation* **3** [S] number of copies of a newspaper sold

cir·cum·cise /ˈsɜːkəmsaɪz ‖ ˈsɜːr-/ vt cut off the skin at the end of the male sex organ or part of the sex organ (CLITORIS) of a woman –**cision** /ˌsɜːkəmˈsɪʒən ‖ ˌsɜːr-/ n [C;U]

cir·cum·fer·ence /səˈkʌmfərəns ‖ sər-/ n distance round: *the Earth's circumference*

cir·cum·nav·i·gate /ˌsɜːkəmˈnævɪɡeɪt ‖ ˌsɜːr-/ vt fml sail right round

cir·cum·scribe /ˈsɜːkəmskraɪb ‖ ˈsɜːr-/ vt fml limit

cir·cum·spect /ˈsɜːkəmspekt ‖ ˈsɜːr-/ adj fml careful

cir·cum·stance /ˈsɜːkəmstæns, -stəns ‖ ˈsɜːr-/ n **1** (*usu. pl.*) conditions that influence a person or event **2 in/under no circumstances** never **3 in/under the circumstances** because of the conditions

cir·cum·stan·tial /ˌsɜːkəmˈstænʃəl◂ ‖ ˌsɜːr-/ adj fml **1** (of a description) detailed **2 circumstantial evidence** information worth knowing but not directly important

cir·cum·vent /ˌsɜːkəmˈvent ‖ ˌsɜːr-/ vt avoid by cleverness: *circumvent the tax laws*

cir·cus /ˈsɜːkəs ‖ ˈsɜːr-/ n **1** performance of skill and daring by a group of people and animals **2** *BrE* place where several streets join **3** noisy badly behaved meeting or other such activity: *the media circus travelling with the President*

cir·rho·sis /sɪˈrəʊsəs ‖ -ˈrəʊ- n [U] serious LIVER disease

cis·sy /ˈsɪsi/ n, adj *BrE for* SISSY

cis·tern /ˈsɪstən ‖ -ərn/ n container for storing water, esp. for a TOILET

cite /saɪt/ vt **1** fml mention as an example **2** law call to appear in court

cit·i·zen /ˈsɪtɪzən/ n **1** person living in a city or town **2** person with full membership of a country ~**ship** n [U]: *apply for French citizenship*

cit·ric ac·id /ˌsɪtrɪk ˈæsɪd/ n [U] weak acid from fruit juice

cit·rus /ˈsɪtrəs/ adj (of fruit) of the orange family

cit·y /ˈsɪti/ n **1** [C] large important town **2** [C] its citizens **3** [S] (*cap.*) the centre for money matters in London —see also INNER CITY

civ·ic /ˈsɪvɪk/ adj of a city or its citizens

civ·il /ˈsɪvəl/ adj **1** not military or religious **2** polite –**ly** adv politely ~**ity** /sɪˈvɪləti/ n [C;U] politeness

civil en·gi·neer·ing /ˌ·· ··ˈ··/ n [U] building of public roads, bridges, etc.

ci·vil·ian /sɪˈvɪljən/ n, adj (person) not of the armed forces

civ·i·li·za·tion also **-sation** *BrE* /ˌsɪvəlaɪˈzeɪʃən ‖ -vələ-/ n **1** [U] high level of human development and social organization **2** [C] particular civilized society: *ancient civilizations*

civ·i·lize also **-ise** *BrE* /ˈsɪvəl-aɪz/ vt **1** bring to civilization: *civilized nations* **2** improve in manners

civil rights /ˌ·· ˈ·/ n [P] a citizen's rights to freedom and equality

civil ser·vant /ˌ·· ˈ··/ n person employed in the civil service

civil ser·vice /ˌ·· ˈ··/ n [the+S] **1** government departments, except the armed forces and law courts **2** people employed in this

civil war /ˌ·· ˈ·/ n war between people from the same country

CJD /ˌsiː dʒeɪ ˈdiː/ n [U] Creutzfeldt Jakob Disease; fatal disease that destroys the brain and nervous system, thought to be related to BSE

clad /klæd/ adj lit clothed; covered

claim /kleɪm/ v **1** vt/i demand (something) as one's right: *claim on the insurance* **2** vt declare to be true: *He claims to be rich.* ♦ n **1** demand for something as one's right; right to something **2** something claimed, esp. money under an insurance agreement **3** statement; declaration

clai·mant /ˈkleɪmənt/ n fml person who claims something

clair·voy·ant /kleəˈvɔɪənt ‖ kler-/ adj, n

(of a) person who can see what will happen in the future –**ance** *n* [U]

clam[1] /klæm/ *n* large shellfish

clam[2] *v* **clam up** *phr vi* become silent

clam·ber /'klæmbə‖-ər/ *vi* climb with effort

clam·my /'klæmi/ *adj* unpleasantly wet and sticky

clam·our *BrE* ‖ **-mor** *AmE* /'klæmə‖-ər/ *n* [S;U] loud confused noise, esp. of complaint ♦ *vi* demand noisily: *a baby clamouring to be fed*

clamp[1] /klæmp/ *n* apparatus with a screw, for fastening things together

clamp[2] *vt* fasten with a clamp

clamp down on *phr vt* limit; prevent: *clamp down on drunken driving* **clampdown** /'klæmpdaυn/ *n*

clan /klæn/ *n* Scottish family group

clan·des·tine /klæn'destɪn/ *adj* secret –**ly** *adv*

clang /klæŋ/ *vi/t* make a loud ringing sound **clang** *n* [S]

clank /klæŋk/ *vi/t* make a sound like a heavy metal chain **clank** *n* [S]

clap /klæp/ *v* **-pp-** 1 *vi/t* strike (one's hands) together: *The audience clapped loudly.* 2 *vi* strike lightly with the open hand: *clap him on the back* 3 *vt infml* put quickly: *clapped her in jail* 4 **clap eyes on** *infml* see (someone or something) ♦ *n* 1 [C] loud explosive noise, esp. of thunder 2 [S] clapping: *Give him a clap!* 3 [S] *sl* GONORRHEA

clapped-out /,· '·◄/ *adj esp. BrE* 1 (of a person) tired 2 (of a thing) old and worn out

clap·trap /'klæptræp/ *n* [U] nonsense

clar·et /'klærət/ *n* [U] red wine from Bordeaux ♦ *adj* deep red

clar·i·fy /'klærɪfaɪ/ *vt fml* make more easily understood –**fication** /,klærɪfɪ'keɪʃən/ *n* [C;U]

clar·i·net /,klærɪ'net/ *n* kind of WOODWIND musical instrument ~**tist** *n* person who plays the clarinet

clar·i·ty /'klærɪti/ *n* [U] clearness

clash /klæʃ/ *v* 1 *vi* come into opposition 2 *vi* (of colours) look wrong together 3 *vi* (of events) be planned for the same time 4 *vi/t* make a loud metallic noise ♦ *n* 1 [C] disagreement 2 [S] metallic noise

clasp /klɑːsp‖klæsp/ *n* 1 metal fastener 2 firm hold ♦ *vt* 1 seize firmly 2 fasten

with a clasp

class /klɑːs‖klæs/ *n* 1 [C] social group of a particular rank: *the ruling class* 2 [U] system of dividing society into such groups 3 **a** [C] group of students taught together **b** [C;U] period of time they are taught for 4 [C] division; level: *a first-class carriage* 5 [U] high quality; ELEGANCE —see also FIRST CLASS ♦ *vt* put into a class; consider –**y** *adj* fashionable and of high class

clas·sic /'klæsɪk/ *adj* 1 of the highest rank 2 typical: *classic example* 3 having a long history; TRADITIONAL ♦ *n* piece of literature or art, a writer or artist of lasting importance **classics** *n* [P] ancient Greek and Roman literature

clas·si·cal /'klæsɪkəl/ *adj* 1 following ancient Greek or Roman models 2 (of music) with serious artistic intentions 3 TRADITIONAL

clas·si·fy /'klæsɪfaɪ/ *vt* arrange into classes –**fied** *adj* 1 divided into classes 2 officially secret –**fication** /,klæsɪfɪ'keɪʃən/ *n* [C;U]

class·room /'klɑːsrυm, -ruːm‖'klæs-/ *n* room in a school, etc. in which a class meets for a lesson

clat·ter /'klætə‖-ər/ *n* [S;U] noise of hard objects hitting each other: *a clatter of dishes* ♦ *vi/t* make a clatter

clause /klɔːz‖klɔːz/ *n* 1 *gram* group of words containing a subject and verb 2 *law* separate division of a piece of legal writing

claus·tro·pho·bi·a /,klɔːstrə'fəυbiə‖ ,klɔːstrə'foυ-/ *n* [U] fear of being shut in

claw[1] /klɔː‖klɔː/ *n* 1 sharp nail on an animal's or bird's toe 2 limb of a CRAB, etc. 3 curved end of some tools

claw[2] *vi/t* tear or pull with claws

claw back *phr vt* take back by taxation **clawback** *n*

clay /kleɪ/ *n* [U] earth from which bricks, pots, etc. are made

clean[1] /kliːn/ *adj* 1 not dirty 2 not yet used: *clean piece of paper* 3 morally pure: *clean joke* 4 smooth; regular: *clean cut* 5 **come clean** tell the unpleasant truth ♦ *n* [S] act of cleaning ♦ *adv* completely: *I clean forgot.* | *They got clean away.* –**liness** /'klenlɪnɪs/ *n* [U] being clean (1) ~**ly** /'kliːnli/ *adv* quickly; with one movement: *The knife cut cleanly through the cake.*

clean[2] *vt* make clean ~**er** *n* person or

thing that cleans **~er's** *n* **1** shop where clothes, etc. are cleaned with chemicals **2 take someone to the cleaner's** cause someone to lose all their money, etc.

clean out *phr vt* **1** make (the inside of a room, drawer, etc.) clean and tidy **2** take all someone's money

clean up *phr vi/t* **1** clean thoroughly **2** *sl* gain money as profit

clean-cut /ˌ· '·◄/ *adj* **1** well-shaped **2** neat and clean in appearance

cleanse /klenz/ *vt* make pure **cleanser** *n* chemical, etc. used for cleaning

clean-shav·en /ˌ· '·◄/ *adj* with no beard

clean sweep /ˌ· '·/ *n* **1** complete change **2** complete victory

clear¹ /klɪə ‖ klɪr/ *adj* **1** easy to see through: *clear glass* **2** without marks, etc.: *clear skin* | (*fig.*) *a clear conscience* **3** easy to hear or understand **4** certain: *I'm not clear where she lives.* | *a clear case of murder* **5** open; empty: *The road's clear of snow.* **6** free; no longer touching: *We're clear of danger now.* | *He swung clear of the wall.* **7** (of wages or profit) remaining after all taxes, etc. have been paid ♦ *n* [U] **in the clear** free from guilt, debt, etc. ♦ *adv* **1** in a clear way: *shout loud and clear* **2** completely: *The prisoner got clear away.* **3** out of the way: *jump clear of the train* **~ly** *adv* **1** in a clear way: *speak clearly* **2** undoubtedly: *clearly wrong*

clear² *v* **1** *vi/t* become clear; remove something unwanted: *The sky cleared.* | *clear snow from the road* **2** *vt* get past without touching: *clear a fence* **3** *vt* give official approval to **4** *vt* free from blame **5** *vt* earn as CLEAR (7) profit or wages: *She clears £10,000 a year*

clear away *phr vt* make an area tidy by removing

clear off *phr vi* go away

clear out *phr v* **1** *vi* go away **2** *vt* empty

clear up *phr v* **1** *vt* explain: *clear up the mystery* **2** *vi* tidy

clear·ance /ˈklɪərəns ‖ ˈklɪr-/ *n* **1** [U] official approval **2** [C;U] distance between objects **3** [U] also **security clearance** — official acceptance that one is in no way an enemy of one's country **4** [C] also **clearance sale** /'·· ·/ — time when a shop sells goods cheaply so as to get rid of as many as possible

clear-cut /ˌ· '·◄/ *adj* clear in meaning

clear·ing /ˈklɪərɪŋ ‖ ˈklɪr-/ *n* area cleared of trees

cleav·age /ˈkliːvɪdʒ/ *n* **1** division caused by splitting **2** space between a woman's breasts as seen when she is wearing a dress

cleave /kliːv/ *vt* **cleaved** *or* **cleft** /kleft/ *or* **clove** /kləʊv ‖ kloʊv/, **cleaved** *or* **cleft** *or* **cloven** /ˈkləʊvən ‖ ˈkloʊ-/ divide or make by a cutting blow

cleave to *phr vt lit* remain loyal to

clef /klef/ *n* sign at the beginning of a line of written music to show the PITCH¹ (of) notes

cleft /kleft/ *v past t. of* CLEAVE

cleft stick /ˌ· '·/ *n* **(caught) in a cleft stick** (caught) in a very awkward position

clem·en·cy /ˈklemənsi/ *n* [U] *fml* mercy **-ent** *adj* (of weather) not severe

clem·en·tine /ˈkleməntiːn, -taɪn/ *n* type of small orange

clench /klentʃ/ *vt* close tightly: *clench one's fists*

cler·gy /ˈklɜːdʒi ‖ -ɜːr-/ *n* [P] priests

cler·gy·man /ˈklɜːdʒimən ‖ -ɜːr-/ *n* **-men** /-mən/ Christian priest

cler·ic /ˈklerɪk/ *n* clergyman **~al** *adj* **1** of priests **2** of clerks

clerk /klɑːk ‖ klɜːrk/ *n* **1** office worker **2** official in charge of court records, etc.

clev·er /ˈklevə ‖ -ər/ *adj* **1** quick at learning **2** showing skill: *clever idea* **~ly** *adv* **~ness** *n* [U]

cli·ché /ˈkliːʃeɪ ‖ kliːˈʃeɪ/ *n* expression or idea used so often it has lost much of its force

click /klɪk/ *n* slight short sound, as of a camera ♦ *v* **1** *vi/t* make a click **2** *vi* fall into place; understand **3** *vi* be a success **4** *vi/t* press a button on a computer MOUSE (3)

cli·ent /ˈklaɪənt/ *n* **1** person who pays for advice from a professional person **2** customer

cli·en·tele /ˌkliːɒnˈtel ‖ ˌklaɪənˈtel, ˌkliː-/ *n* clients; customers

cliff /klɪf/ *n* steep rock face, esp. on a coast

cliff·hang·er /ˈklɪfˌhæŋə ‖ -ər/ *n* **1** competition, etc. whose result is in doubt until the very end **2** story told in parts, each of which ends at a moment of exciting uncertainty

cli·mac·tic /klaɪˈmæktɪk/ *adj* forming a climax

cli·mate /'klaɪmɪt/ n 1 average weather conditions 2 condition of opinions: *political climate* –**matic** /klaɪ'mætɪk/ adj

cli·max /'klaɪmæks/ n 1 most powerful part of a story, usu. near the end 2 ORGASM ♦ vi/t bring or come to a climax

climb /klaɪm/ v 1 vi/t move, esp. using hands and feet: *climb a ladder | go climbing in the Alps 2 vi rise: The road climbs steeply.* 3 vi (of a plant) grow upwards ♦ n 1 journey by climbing 2 place to climb ~**er** n person or thing that climbs

climb down phr vi infml admit that one has been wrong **climb-down** /'· ·/ n

clinch[1] /klɪntʃ/ vt settle (an agreement) firmly

clinch[2] n EMBRACE

cling /klɪŋ/ vi clung /klʌŋ/ hold tightly ~**ing**, also ~**y** adj 1 (of clothes) tight-fitting 2 (of a person) too dependent

cling film /'· ,·/ n [U] BrE tdmk very thin plastic for wrapping food

clin·ic /'klɪnɪk/ n place for specialized medical treatment ~**al** adj 1 of clinics or hospitals 2 coldly scientific

clink /klɪŋk/ vi/t (cause to) make a sound like pieces of glass knocking together **clink** n [S]

clip[1] /klɪp/ n small esp. metal object for holding things together: *paper clip* **clip** vt -**pp**-

clip[2] vt -**pp**- 1 cut with scissors, etc. 2 sl hit ♦ n 1 cutting 2 sl quick blow: *a clip round the ear* ~**pers** n [P] scissor-like tool ~**ping** n 1 piece cut off 2 CUTTING (2)

clip·board /'klɪpbɔːd ‖ -bɔːrd/ n board with a CLIP for holding papers

clique /kliːk/ n derog closely united group of people

clit·o·ris /'klɪtərɪs/ n small front part of the female sex organ

Cllr BrE written abbrev. for: COUNCILLOR

cloak /kləʊk ‖ kloʊk/ n loose outer garment without SLEEVES ♦ vt keep secret

cloak-and-dag·ger /ˌ· · '··/ adj mysterious; secret

cloak·room /'kləʊkrʊm, -ruːm ‖ 'kloʊk-/ n room where coats, etc. may be left

clob·ber[1] /'klɒbə ‖ 'klɑːbər/ vt sl 1 attack severely 2 defeat completely

clobber[2] n sl BrE one's belongings

clock /klɒk ‖ klɑːk/ n 1 instrument for measuring time 2 **around/round the**

clock all day and all night 3 **put the clock back** return to old-fashioned ideas 4 **watch the clock** think continually of how soon work will end 5 **work against the clock** work very quickly in order to finish a job before a certain time ♦ vt record (time, speed, distance, etc.)

clock in/out phr vi record the time of arriving at/leaving work

clock up phr vt infml 1 record (a distance travelled, a speed reached, etc.) 2 succeed in getting

clock·wise /'klɒkwaɪz ‖ 'klɑːk-/ adv in the direction of the movement of a clock

clock·work /'klɒkwɜːk ‖ 'klɑːk-wɜːrk/ n [U] 1 machinery wound up with a key 2 **like clockwork** without trouble

clod /klɒd ‖ klɑːd/ n lump or mass of clay or earth

clog[1] /klɒg ‖ klɑːg/ n wooden shoe

clog[2] vi/t -**gg**- (cause to) become blocked or filled

clois·ter /'klɔɪstə ‖ -ər/ n covered passage usu. forming part of a college, MONASTERY, etc. ~**ed** adj sheltered from the world

clone /kləʊn ‖ kloʊn/ n 1 exact GENETIC copy of a plant or animal, produced from one of its cells 2 very similar person or thing ♦ vt produce as a clone (1)

close[1] /kləʊz ‖ kloʊz/ v 1 vi/t shut: *close one's eyes | When does the shop close?* 2 vt bring to an end: *close a bank account* 3 **close a deal (with)** settle a business agreement ♦ n [S] fml end of a period of time: *at the close of play*

close down phr vi/t (of a factory, etc.) stop operating **closedown** /'kləʊzdaʊn ‖ 'kloʊz-/ n

close in phr vi surround gradually

close[2] /kləʊs ‖ kloʊs/ adj 1 near: *close to the shops | a close friend* 2 thorough: *close inspection* 3 without fresh air; too warm 4 decided by a small difference: *a close finish to the race* ♦ adv 1 near: *close behind/together* 2 **close on** almost 3 **close to home** near the (usu. unpleasant) truth 4 **(sail) close to the wind** (to be) near to dishonesty or improper behaviour ♦ n 1 courtyard 2 BLIND ALLEY ~**ly** adv ~**ness** n [U]

closed cir·cuit tel·e·vi·sion /ˌ· ,·· '····/ also **CCTV** BrE /ˌsiː siː tiː 'viː/ n [U] television cameras which film in a public place to prevent crime

closed shop /ˌ· ˈ·◁/ n place of work where one must belong to a particular TRADE UNION

close-knit /ˌkləʊs ˈnɪt◁ǁ ˌkloʊs-/ also **closely-knit** /ˌ·· ˈ·◁/ — adj tightly bound together by social, political, etc. beliefs and activities

close-set /ˌkləʊs ˈset◁ǁ ˌkloʊs-/ adj set close together: close-set eyes

close shave /ˌkləʊs ˈʃeɪv ǁ ˌkloʊs-/ n infml situation in which something dangerous or very unpleasant is only just avoided

clos·et /ˈklɒzɪt ǁ ˈklɑː-, ˈklɔː-/ n esp. AmE built-in cupboard —see also WATER CLOSET ♦ adj not publicly admitted; secret ♦ vt enclose (esp. oneself) in a private room

close-up /ˈkləʊs ʌp ǁ ˈkloʊs-/ n photograph taken from very near

clo·sure /ˈkləʊʒə ǁ ˈkloʊʒər/ n [C;U] closing: hospital closures

clot /klɒt ǁ klɑːt/ n lump formed from liquid: blood clot ♦ v/t -tt-

cloth /klɒθ ǁ klɔːθ/ n [C;U] (piece of) material made by weaving

clothe /kləʊð ǁ kloʊð/ vt provide clothes for

clothes /kləʊðz, kləʊz ǁ kloʊðz, kloʊz/ n [P] things to cover the body; garments

cloth·ing /ˈkləʊðɪŋ ǁ ˈkloʊ-/ n [U] clothes

cloud /klaʊd/ n 1 [C;U] white or grey mass floating in the sky which is formed from very small drops of water 2 [C] similar floating mass: clouds of smoke/mosquitoes 3 [C] something threatening: the clouds of war 4 **have one's head in the clouds** be impractical 5 **under a cloud** out of favour ♦ v 1 vt/i cover with clouds 2 vt confuse: cloud the issue ~y adj 1 full of clouds 2 not clear

clout /klaʊt/ n 1 [C] blow with the hand 2 [U] influence, esp. political ♦ vt strike, esp. with the hand

clove¹ /kləʊv ǁ kloʊv/ v past t. of CLEAVE

clove² n dried flower of a tropical tree used in cooking

clove³ n any of the smallest pieces into which the root of the GARLIC plant can be divided

clo·ven /ˈkləʊvən ǁ / v past p. of CLEAVE

clo·ver /ˈkləʊvə ǁ ˈkloʊvər/ n [C;U] 1 three-leafed plant often grown as food for

cattle 2 **in clover** living in comfort

clown /klaʊn/ n 1 performer in a CIRCUS who makes people laugh 2 person acting like this ♦ vi behave foolishly

cloy /klɔɪ/ vi/t (of food) become unpleasant because too sweet: (fig.) cloying sentimentality

club¹ /klʌb/ n 1 society of people who meet for amusement; building where they meet: tennis club 2 NIGHTCLUB 3 heavy stick used as a weapon 4 stick for striking the ball in GOLF 5 playing card with one or more black three-leafed figures on it —see also BOOK CLUB ♦ vt -bb- hit with a heavy stick

club² v club together phr vi share the cost of something with others

club·bing /ˈklʌbɪŋ/ n [U] (practice of) going to NIGHTCLUBS

cluck /klʌk/ vi make the noise a hen makes **cluck** n

clue /kluː/ n 1 something that helps to find the answer to a problem 2 **not have a clue** know nothing; be unable to understand ~less adj stupid

clued up /ˌkluːd ˈʌp◁/ adj infml very well-informed

clump¹ /klʌmp/ n group of trees, etc.

clump² vi walk heavily

clum·sy /ˈklʌmzi/ adj 1 awkward in movement 2 TACTLESS –sily adv –siness n [U]

clung /klʌŋ/ v past t. and p. of CLING

clus·ter /ˈklʌstə ǁ -ər/ n group of things close together ♦ vi form a close group

clutch¹ /klʌtʃ/ v 1 vt hold tightly 2 vi try to seize: He clutched at a branch. ♦ n 1 act of clutching 2 apparatus connecting and disconnecting the working parts of a car engine **clutches** n [P] control: in the clutches of the enemy

clutch² n (chickens born from) a number of eggs laid by one bird: (fig.) a clutch of new trainees

clut·ter /ˈklʌtə ǁ -ər/ vt make untidy ♦ n [U] scattered disorderly things

cm written abbrev. for: centimetre(s)

Co. /kəʊ ǁ koʊ/ abbrev. for: COMPANY (1)

C.O. /ˌsiː ˈəʊ◁ ǁ -ˈoʊ◁/ n Commanding Officer; person in the armed forces in charge of others

coach /kəʊtʃ ǁ koʊtʃ/ n 1 BrE long-distance bus 2 railway carriage 3 large horse-drawn carriage 4 person who trains

coach·work /'kəʊtʃwɜːk ‖ 'kəʊtʃwɜːrk/ n outside body of a car

co·ag·u·late /kəʊˈægjʊleɪt ‖ koʊ-/ vi/t change from a liquid to a solid

coal /kəʊl ‖ koʊl/ n [C;U] (piece of) black mineral that can be burnt: *a coalmine*

co·a·lesce /ˌkəʊəˈles ‖ ˌkoʊ-/ vi fml grow together; unite

coal·face /'kəʊlfeɪs ‖ 'koʊl-/ n surface where coal is cut in a mine

coal·field /'kəʊlfiːld ‖ 'koʊl-/ n area where there is coal under the ground

co·a·li·tion /ˌkəʊəˈlɪʃən ‖ ˌkoʊ-/ n union of political parties for a special purpose

coarse /kɔːs ‖ kɔːrs/ adj 1 not fine; lumpy 2 rough in manner; insensitive ~ly adv ~ness n [U] coarsen vi/t

coast /kəʊst ‖ koʊst/ n 1 seashore 2 the coast is clear all danger has gone ♦ vi 1 go downhill on a bicycle, etc. without effort or power 2 achieve without effort or difficulty ~al adj

coast·guard /'kəʊstgɑːd ‖ 'koʊstgɑːrd/ n 1 police organization responsible for the coast and nearby sea 2 member of the coastguard

coast·line /'kəʊstlaɪn ‖ 'koʊst-/ n shape of a coast

coat /kəʊt ‖ koʊt/ n 1 outer garment with SLEEVES, fastened at the front 2 animal's fur, etc. 3 covering on a surface: *coat of paint* ♦ vt cover (a surface) ~ing n thin covering

coat hang·er /'· ¸·/ n HANGER

coat of arms /¸· · '·/ n coats of arms patterns or pictures, usu. on a shield, used by a noble family, town, etc. as their special sign

coax /kəʊks ‖ koʊks/ vt 1 persuade gently 2 obtain (something) by gently persuading

cob /kɒb ‖ kɑːb/ n 1 long hard central part of an ear of corn 2 strong short-legged horse 3 male SWAN

cob·ble¹ /'kɒb əl ‖ 'kɑː-/ also **cob·ble·stone** /'kɒbəlstəʊn ‖ 'kɑːbəlstoʊn/ n rounded stone used for road surfaces –bled adj covered with cobbles

cobble² vt put together quickly and roughly

cob·bler /'kɒblə ‖ 'kɑːblər/ n shoe repairer

co·bra /'kɒbrə, 'kəʊ- ‖ 'koʊ-/ n kind of poisonous snake

cob·web /'kɒbweb ‖ 'kɑːb-/ n a SPIDER's net of spun threads

co·caine /kəʊˈkeɪn ‖ koʊ-/ n [U] drug used against pain, or for pleasure

cock /kɒk ‖ kɑːk/ n 1 fully-grown male bird, esp. a chicken 2 hammer of a gun 3 a TAP for controlling the flow of liquid in a pipe 4 sl PENIS ♦ 1 vt/i raise up: *The horse cocked its ears.* 2 vt set (the hammer of a gun) in the correct position for firing 3 cock a snook (at) BrE infml show open disrespect (for)

cock·a·too /ˌkɒkəˈtuː ‖ 'kɑːkətuː/ n -toos Australian bird with a large CREST (1) on its head

cock·e·rel /'kɒkərəl ‖ 'kɑː-/ n young cock

cock·eyed /ˌkɒkˈaɪd◀ ‖ ˌkɑːk-/ adj 1 stupid 2 CROOKED (1)

cock·le /'kɒkəl ‖ 'kɑː-/ n small shellfish used for food

Cock·ney /'kɒkni ‖ 'kɑːkni/ n 1 [C] person from the industrial parts of London 2 [U] the way Cockneys talk

cock·pit /'kɒkˌpɪt ‖ 'kɑːk-/ n part of a plane where the pilot sits

cock·roach /'kɒk-rəʊtʃ ‖ 'kɑːk-roʊtʃ/ n large black insect which lives esp. in dirty or old houses

cock·sure /ˌkɒkˈʃʊə◀ ‖ ˌkɑːkˈʃʊr◀/ adj too self-confident

cock·tail /'kɒkteɪl ‖ 'kɑːk-/ n 1 mixed alcoholic drink 2 (bad) combination: *a lethal cocktail of drugs and alcohol* 3 (used in the name of some dishes:) **fruit/prawn cocktail**

cock-up /'· ·/ n BrE sl confused state of affairs

cock·y /'kɒki ‖ 'kɑːki/ adj sl too sure of oneself

co·coa /'kəʊkəʊ ‖ 'koʊkoʊ/ n [U] 1 brown powder tasting of chocolate 2 hot drink made from this

co·co·nut /'kəʊkənʌt ‖ 'koʊ-/ n [C;U] (flesh of) a very large tropical nut

co·coon /kəˈkuːn/ n silky covering that protects some insects in their inactive stage ♦ vt protect from hardship

cod /kɒd ‖ kɑːd/ n cod or cods large sea fish

code /kəʊd ‖ koʊd/ n 1 system of signs, or of secret writing: *computer code* 2 collection of laws or social customs ♦ *vt* translate into a code

co·ed·u·ca·tion /ˌkəʊedjʊˈkeɪʃən ‖ ˌkoʊedʒə-/ *n* [U] education of boys and girls together ~**al** *adj*

co·erce /kəʊˈɜːs ‖ koʊˈɜːrs/ *vt fml* force to do something –**cive** *adj* –**cion** /kəʊˈɜːʃ ən ‖ koʊˈɜːrʒən/ *n* [U]

co·ex·ist /ˌkəʊɪɡˈzɪst ‖ ˌkoʊ-/ *vi* exist at the same time ~**ence** *n* [U] (esp. of countries) existing together peacefully

cof·fee /ˈkɒfi ‖ ˈkɔːfi, ˈkɑːfi/ *n* [C;U] (drink made by pouring boiling water onto) the (crushed) berries of a tropical tree

coffee ta·ble /ˈ·· ˌ·/ *n* low table

cof·fers /ˈkɒfəz ‖ ˈkɔːfərz, ˈkɑː-/ *n* [P] money that an organization, etc. has

cof·fin /ˈkɒfɪn ‖ ˈkɔː-/ *n* box in which a dead person is buried

cog /kɒɡ ‖ kɑːɡ/ *n* 1 tooth on the edge of a wheel that moves another wheel **2 cog in the machine** unimportant person in a very large organization

co·gent /ˈkəʊdʒənt ‖ ˈkoʊ-/ *adj fml* forceful; CONVINCING: *cogent arguments* **cogency** *n* [U]

cog·i·tate /ˈkɒdʒəteɪt ‖ ˈkɑː-/ *vi fml* think carefully

cog·nac /ˈkɒnjæk ‖ ˈkoʊ-, ˈkɑː-/ *n* [U] kind of BRANDY

cog·nate /ˈkɒɡneɪt ‖ ˈkɑːɡ-/ *adj fml* related: *cognate languages*

co·hab·it /kəʊˈhæbɪt ‖ koʊ-/ *vi fml* live together as though married ~**ation** /kəʊˌhæbəˈteɪʃən ‖ koʊ-/ *n* [U]

co·her·ent /kəʊˈhɪərənt ‖ koʊˈhɪr-/ *adj* (of speech, ideas, etc.) reasonably connected; clear –**ence** *n* [U] ~**ly** *adv*

co·he·sive /kəʊˈhiːsɪv ‖ koʊ-/ *adj* sticking together –**sion** /-ˈhiːʒən/ *n* [U]

coil /kɔɪl/ *vi/t* twist into a circle ♦ *n* **1** connected set of twists: *coil of rope* **2** twisted wire that carries an electric current **3** coil of metal or plastic which is fitted inside the UTERUS to prevent a woman from having children

coin /kɔɪn/ *n* piece of metal money ♦ *vt* **1** make (coins) **2** invent (new words) **3 coin (the) money (in)** also **coin it (in)** make or earn a lot of money very quickly

co·in·cide /ˌkəʊɪnˈsaɪd ‖ ˌkoʊ-/ *vi* **1** happen at the same time **2** (of opinions, etc.) agree

co·in·ci·dence /kəʊˈɪnsɪdəns ‖ koʊ-/ *n* [C;U] accidental and surprising combination of events: *By sheer coincidence, we have the same birthday.* –**dental** /kəʊˌɪnsɪˈdentl ‖ koʊ-/ *adj*

coke /kəʊk ‖ koʊk/ *n* [U] **1** substance left after gas has been removed from coal **2** COCAINE

col·an·der /ˈkʌləndər, ˈkɒ- ‖ ˈkʌləndər, ˈkɑː-/ *n* bowl with holes, for separating liquid from food

cold¹ /kəʊld ‖ koʊld/ *adj* **1** low in temperature: *cold wind* **2** unfriendly: *a cold stare* **3** (of cooked food) allowed to get cool **4** unconscious: *I knocked him out cold.* **5 get/have cold feet** lose courage **6 give/get the cold shoulder** treat/be treated unsympathetically ~**ly** *adv* ~**ness** *n* [U]

cold² *n* **1** [U] low temperature **2** [C;U] illness of the nose and throat **3 (out) in the cold** not noticed; unwanted

cold-blood·ed /ˌ· ˈ··◄/ *adj* **1** (of snakes, etc.) having a body temperature that varies with the surroundings **2** cruel; without feeling: *cold-blooded murder*

cold-heart·ed /ˌ· ˈ··◄/ *adj* unkind

cold tur·key /ˌ· ˈ··/ *n* [U] *sl* (the unpleasant sick feeling caused by) the sudden stopping of the use of a drug by an ADDICT

cold war /ˌ· ˈ·◄/ *n* severe political struggle without actual fighting

col·ic /ˈkɒlɪk ‖ ˈkɑː-/ *n* [U] severe pain in the bowels

col·lab·o·rate /kəˈlæbəreɪt/ *vi* **1** work together **2** help the enemy –**rator** *n* –**ration** /kəˌlæbəˈreɪʃən/ *n* [U]

col·lage /ˈkɒlɑːʒ ‖ kəˈlɑːʒ/ *n* picture made by gluing various materials or objects onto a surface

col·lapse /kəˈlæps/ *v* **1** *vi* fall down suddenly; *The bridge collapsed under the weight of the train.* **2** *vi* fall helpless **3** *vi/t* fold flat ♦ *n* [C;U] collapsing: (fig.) *the collapse of the peace talks* –**lapsible** *adj* that can be folded for packing, etc.

col·lar /ˈkɒlə ‖ ˈkɑːlər/ *n* **1** part of a garment that fits round the neck **2** band put round an animal's neck ♦ *vt* seize and hold

col·lar·bone /ˈkɒləbəʊn ‖ ˈkɑːlərboʊn/ *n* bone joining the RIBS to the shoulders

col·late /kəˈleɪt/ *vt fml* **1** compare (copies

of books, etc.) to find the differences
2 arrange (the sheets) of (esp. a book) in the proper order

col·lat·er·al /kəˈlætərəl/ n [S;U] property promised as SECURITY for a debt

col·league /ˈkɒliːg ‖ ˈkɑː-/ n fellow worker

col·lect /kəˈlekt/ v **1** vt/i gather together: *collect taxes | A crowd collected in the street.* **2** vt save (stamps, etc.) as a HOBBY **3** vt fetch: *collect one's skirt from the cleaners* **4** vt regain control of (oneself, one's thoughts, etc.) **~ed** adj controlled; calm **~ive** adj shared by many people: *collective ownership* **~ive** n business owned and controlled by the people who work in it **~ively** adv: *collectively responsible* **~or** n person who collects something: *ticket collector* **~ion** /kəˈlekʃən/ n **1** [U] collecting **2** [C] set of things, sum of money, etc. collected

collect² adj, adv AmE to be paid for by the receiver: *Call me collect.*

collective bar·gain·ing /·,·· ˈ···/ n [U] talks between unions and employers about working conditions, etc.

col·lege /ˈkɒlɪdʒ ‖ ˈkɑː-/ n **1** school for higher education; part of a university **2** group of people with a common profession or purpose: *the Royal College of Nursing*

col·lide /kəˈlaɪd/ vi **1** crash violently **2** be opposed: *The government collided with the unions.*

col·lie·ry /ˈkɒljəri ‖ ˈkɑː-/ n coal mine

col·li·sion /kəˈlɪʒən/ n [C;U] colliding

col·lo·qui·al /kəˈləʊkwiəl ‖ -ˈloʊ-/ adj (of words, style, etc.) suitable for informal conversation **~ly** adv **~ism** n colloquial expression

col·lude /kəˈluːd/ vi fml act in collusion

col·lu·sion /kəˈluːʒən/ n fml secret agreement to deceive

co·lon¹ /ˈkəʊlən ‖ ˈkoʊ-/ n lower part of the bowels

colon² n the mark (:)

colo·nel /ˈkɜːnl ‖ ˈkɜːr-/ n army or airforce officer of middle rank

co·lo·ni·al /kəˈləʊniəl ‖ -ˈloʊ-/ adj of or about colonies (COLONY (1)) ♦ n person living or having lived in a COLONY (1) **~ism** n [U] principle of having colonies

col·o·nize also **~ise** BrE /ˈkɒlənaɪz ‖ ˈkɑː-/ vt make into a colony: *colonize*

Australia **~nist** n person living in a new COLONY (1) **~nization** /ˌkɒlənaɪˈzeɪʃən ‖ ˌkɑːlənə-/ n [U]

col·on·nade /ˌkɒləˈneɪd ‖ ˌkɑː-/ n row of PILLARS

col·o·ny /ˈkɒləni ‖ ˈkɑː-/ n **1** place lived in and controlled by people from a distant country **2** group of people of the same kind, living together

col·or /ˈkʌlə ‖ -ər/ n AmE COLOUR

co·los·sal /kəˈlɒsəl ‖ kəˈlɑː-/ adj extremely large

co·los·sus /kəˈlɒsəs ‖ kəˈlɑː-/ n **-suses** or **-si** /-saɪ/ very large person or thing

col·our BrE ‖ **color** AmE /ˈkʌlə ‖ -ər/ n **1** [C;U] red, blue, green, etc. **2** [C;U] paint or DYE **3** [U] appearance of the skin **4** [U] interesting details of a place, thing, or person —see also OFF COLOUR **5 off colour** in bad health ♦ v **1** vt give colour to **2** vi BLUSH **3** vt change; influence **~ed** adj **1** having colours; not just white, or black and white **2** (of people) black or brown **~ful** adj **1** brightly coloured **2** exciting **~ing** n [C;U] **1** substance giving colour **2** skin colour, showing health **~less** adj **1** without colour **2** dull **colours** n [P] **1** official flag **2** something worn as the sign of a club, team, etc. **3 show one's true colours** show one's real nature or character —see also FLYING COLOURS

colour-blind /ˈ·· ·/ adj unable to see the difference between colours

colour sup·ple·ment /ˈ·· ,···/ n magazine printed in colour and given free with a weekend newspaper

colt /kəʊlt ‖ koʊlt/ n young male horse

col·umn /ˈkɒləm ‖ ˈkɑː-/ n **1** PILLAR **2** something like this shape: *a column of figures | a marching column of soldiers* **3** a division of a page **4** newspaper article —see also FIFTH COLUMN **~ist** /ˈkɒləmɪst, -ləmnɪst ‖ ˈkɑː-/ n writer of a newspaper column

co·ma /ˈkəʊmə ‖ ˈkoʊ-/ n unnatural deep sleep

co·ma·tose /ˈkəʊmətəʊs ‖ ˈkoʊmətoʊs/ adj **1** in a coma **2** inactive and sleepy

comb /kəʊm ‖ koʊm/ n **1** [C] toothed piece of plastic, etc. for tidying the hair or as an ornament **2** [S] act of combing **3** HONEYCOMB ♦ vt **1** tidy (hair) with a comb **2** search (a place) thoroughly

com·bat /'kɒmbæt ‖ 'kɑːm-/ n [C;U] struggle; fight **combat** vt/i -tt- BrE ‖ -t- or -tt- AmE: to combat inflation ~**ant** /'kɒmbətənt ‖ kəm'bætənt/ n person who fights ~**ive** adj fond of fighting

com·bi·na·tion /ˌkɒmbəˈneɪʃən ‖ ˌkɑːm-/ n 1 [U] combining: We worked well in combination. 2 [C] people or things combined 3 [C] numbers needed to open a special lock: combination lock

com·bine¹ /kəmˈbaɪn/ vi/t join together; unite

com·bine² /'kɒmbaɪn ‖ 'kɑːm-/ n 1 group of people, businesses, etc. acting together 2 also **combine harvester** /ˌ·· '···/ machine that cuts and THRESHES grain

com·bus·ti·ble /kəmˈbʌstɪbəl/ adj burning easily

com·bus·tion /kəmˈbʌstʃən/ n [U] process of burning

come /kʌm/ vi came /keɪm/, come 1 move towards the speaker; arrive 2 reach a particular point: The water came up to my neck. | We came to an agreement. | The bill comes to £18.50. 3 have a particular position: Monday comes after Sunday. 4 happen: How did you come to be invited? 5 begin: I came to realize the truth. 6 become: come apart | come undone | My dream came true. 7 be offered, produced, etc.: Shoes come in different sizes. | Milk comes from cows. 8 sl have an ORGASM 9 **come and go** pass or disappear quickly 10 **how come?** how did it happen (that)? 11 **to come** in the future **comer** n 1 esp. AmE person who appears likely to be successful in their job 2 **all comers** everyone who comes and tries **coming** n [S] arrival **coming** adj future: the coming winter

come about phr vi happen

come across/upon phr vt find by chance

come across phr vi be effective and well received

come along phr vi 1 improve; advance 2 arrive by chance 3 **Come along!** Hurry up!

come apart phr vi break into pieces without the need of force

come at phr vt advance towards in a threatening manner

come away phr vi become disconnected without being forced

come back phr vi return

come between phr vt cause trouble between

come by phr vt obtain; receive

cown down phr vi 1 fall 2 **come down in the world** fall to a lower standard of living 3 **come down in favour of/on the side of** decide to support

come down on phr vt punish

come down to phr vt be no more than: It all comes down to a question of money.

come down with phr vt catch (an infectious illness)

come forward phr vi offer oneself to do something, help someone, etc.

come from phr vt have a (place) as one's home

come in phr vi 1 become fashionable 2 **come in handy/useful** be useful

come in for phr vt receive (esp. blame)

come in on phr vt take part in

come into phr vt 1 INHERIT 2 begin to be in (a state or activity)

come of phr vt result from: No good will come of it.

come off phr v 1 vi happen as planned 2 vt **come off it!** stop lying or pretending

come on phr vi 1 improve; advance 2 (of weather, illness, etc.) begin 3 **Come on!** Hurry up!

come out phr vi 1 appear 2 become known 3 (of colour, etc.) be removed 4 STRIKE 5 (of a photograph) be successful 6 declare oneself to be HOMOSEXUAL

come out against phr vt declare one's opposition to

come out in phr vt be partly covered by (marks caused by an illness)

come out with phr vt say, esp. suddenly

come over phr v 1 vt (of feelings, etc.) influence suddenly: What's come over you? 2 vi make a short informal visit

come round phr vi 1 also **come to —** regain consciousness 2 change one's opinions 3 happen as usual

come through phr v 1 vi (of news, etc.) become known 2 vi/t SURVIVE

come to phr vt 1 enter the mind of: The idea came to me suddenly. 2 concern: He's ignorant when it comes to politics. 4 COME round

come under phr vt 1 be in (a

particular class): *Rabbits come under the heading of pets.* **2** be governed or controlled by

come up *phr vi* **1** happen **2** come near

come up against *phr vt* meet (difficulties)

come up with *phr vt* think of (a plan, reply, etc.); produce

come·back /'kʌmbæk/ *n* return to strength or fame

co·me·di·an /kə'miːdiən/ *n* **1** comedienne /kə,miːdi'en/ *fem.* — actor who makes people laugh **2** amusing person

come·down /'kʌmdaʊn/ *n* fall in importance

com·e·dy /'kɒmɪdi ‖ 'kɑː-/ *n* **1** [C;U] (type of) funny play, film, etc. **2** [U] amusing quality of something —see also BLACK COMEDY

com·et /'kɒmɪt ‖ 'kɑː-/ *n* bright heavenly body with a tail

come-up·pance /,kʌm 'ʌpəns/ *n* well-deserved punishment or misfortune

com·fort /'kʌmfət ‖ -ərt/ *n* **1** [U] lack of pain or anxiety; physical satisfaction **2** [C] something that satisfies physical needs **3** [C;U] (person or thing that brings) help for an unhappy person ♦ *vt* make less unhappy

com·for·ta·ble /'kʌmftəbəl, 'kʌmfət- ‖ 'kʌmfərt-, 'kʌmft-/ *adj* **1** giving comfort: *a comfortable chair* **2** feeling comfort; not suffering or anxious —**bly** *adv*

comfortably off /,··· '·/ *adj* fairly rich

com·fy /'kʌmfi/ *adj infml* comfortable

com·ic /'kɒmɪk ‖ 'kɑː-/ *adj* **1** funny **2** of COMEDY ♦ *n* **1** children's magazine with sets of funny drawings **2** COMEDIAN —**al** *adj* funny **comics** *n* [P] *AmE* part of a newspaper with funny drawings

comic strip /'·· ·/ *n* set of drawings telling a short funny story

com·ma /'kɒmə ‖ 'kɑːmə/ *n* the sign (,)

com·mand /kə'mɑːnd ‖ kə'mænd/ *v* **1** *vt/i* order; direct: *command them to attack | your commanding officer* **2** *vt* deserve and get: *command respect* **3** *vt* control (a place) from above ♦ *n* **1** [C] order, instruction **2** [U] control: *take command of the army* **3** [C] division of an army, air force, etc. **4** [S;U] ability to use something: *a good command of spoken English* ~**er** *n* **1** naval officer of middle rank **2** any officer in

command

com·man·dant /,kɒmən'dænt ‖ 'kɑːmən-dænt/ *n* officer in charge of a military organization

com·man·deer /,kɒmən'dɪə ‖ ,kɑːmən-'dɪr/ *vt* seize (property) for public use

com·mand·ment /kə'mɑːndmənt ‖ kə'mænd-/ *n* law given by God

com·man·do /kə'mɑːndəʊ ‖ kə'mæn-doʊ/ *n* -**dos** *or* -**does** (member of) a fighting force trained to make quick RAIDS

com·mem·o·rate /kə'meməreɪt/ *vt* honour the memory of —**rative**/-mərətɪv/ *adj*: *commemorative stamps* —**ration** /kə,memə'reɪʃən/ *n* [U]

com·mence /kə'mens/ *vi/t fml* begin; start ~**ment** *n* [U]

com·mend /kə'mend/ *vt fml* **1** praise **2** put into someone's care ~**able** *adj* worthy of praise ~**ation** /,kɒmən'deɪʃən ‖ ,kɑː-/ *n* **1** [U] praise **2** [C] official prize

com·men·su·rate /kə'menʃərət/ *adj fml* equal; suitable: *a job commensurate with his abilities*

com·ment /'kɒment ‖ 'kɑː-/ *n* [C;U] written or spoken opinion ♦ *vi/t* make a comment

com·men·ta·ry /'kɒməntəri ‖ 'kɑːmən-teri/ *n* **1** [C] collection of opinions on a book, etc. **2** [C;U] description broadcast during an event: *football commentary*

com·men·tate /'kɒmənteɪt ‖ 'kɑː-/ *vi* broadcast a description —**tator** *n*

com·merce /'kɒmɜːs ‖ 'kɑːmɜːrs/ *n* [U] buying and selling; trade

com·mer·cial /kə'mɜːʃəl ‖ kə'mɜːr-/ *adj* **1** of or used in commerce: *commercial law/vehicles* **2** producing profit **3** (of television or radio) paid for by charges made for advertisements ♦ *n* television or radio advertisement ~**ly** *adv* ~**ize** also -**ise** *BrE* — *vt* make into a matter of profit rather than religion, art, etc.

com·mis·e·rate /kə'mɪzəreɪt/ *v* commiserate **with** *phr vt* express sympathy for —**ration** /kə,mɪzə'reɪʃən/ *n* [C;U]

com·mis·sion /kə'mɪʃən/ *n* **1** [C;U] payment for selling goods, made to the salesman **2** [C] job or duty given to someone **3** [C] group officially appointed to find out and report on facts **4** [C] paper appointing an officer in the armed forces **5** out of

commission (of a ship) not ready for active service ♦ *vt* 1 give a COMMISSION (2, 4) to 2 place an order for: *commission a portrait*
~er *n* 1 member of a COMMISSION (3) 2 government representative in certain countries —see also HIGH COMMISSIONER

com·mis·sion·aire /kə,mɪʃə'neə ‖ -'ner/ *n esp. BrE* uniformed attendant at the entrance to a cinema, hotel, etc.

com·mit /kə'mɪt/ *vt* **-tt-** 1 do (something wrong) 2 send (someone) to prison or a MENTAL hospital 3 **commit oneself**: **a** make oneself responsible **b** give a firm opinion
~ment *n* responsibility to do something
~tal *n* [C;U] committing someone to prison, etc.

com·mit·tee /kə'mɪti/ *n* group chosen to do special business

com·mod·i·ty /kə'mɒdɪti ‖ kə'mɑː-/ *n* article of trade; product

com·mo·dore /'kɒmədɔː ‖ 'kɑːmədɔːr/ *n* 1 high-ranking naval officer 2 president of a sailing club

com·mon¹ /'kɒmən ‖ 'kɑː-/ *adj* 1 ordinary; usual: *common salt* | *the common cold* 2 shared in a group: *common knowledge* 3 rough in manner; VULGAR **~ly** *adv*

common² *n* 1 area of grassland with no fences which all people are free to use 2 **in common** in shared possession

common de·nom·i·na·tor /ˌ·· ·'····/ *n* quality or belief shared by all the members of a group

com·mon·er /'kɒmənə ‖ 'kɑːmənər/ *n* person who is not a member of a noble family

common law /ˌ·· '·/ *n* [U] unwritten law based on custom and court decisions rather than on laws made by Parliament ♦ **common-law** /'·· ·/ *adj*

common-or-gar·den /ˌ·· '··◄/ *adj BrE infml* ordinary

com·mon·place /'kɒmənpleɪs ‖ 'kɑː-/ *adj* ordinary; dull

Com·mons /'kɒmənz ‖ 'kɑː-/ *n* [*the*+S] the HOUSE OF COMMONS

common sense /ˌ·· '·◄/ *n* [U] practical good sense gained from experience

Com·mon·wealth /'kɒmənwelθ ‖ 'kɑː-/ *n* 1 association of independent states that used to be parts of the British Empire 2 official title of certain countries, such as Australia

com·mo·tion /kə'məʊʃən ‖ -'moʊ-/ *n* [S;U] noisy confusion

com·mu·nal /'kɒmjʊnəl, kə'mjuːnl/ *adj* shared by a group

com·mune¹ /'kɒmjuːn ‖ 'kɑː-, kə'mjuːn/ *n* 1 group who live and work together and share their possessions 2 local government division in France, etc.

com·mune² /kə'mjuːn/ *vi* exchange thoughts, ideas, or feelings: *commune with nature*

com·mu·ni·ca·ble /kə'mjuːnɪkəbəl/ *adj fml* (esp. of ideas, thoughts, illnesses, etc.) that can be (easily) passed from one person to another

com·mu·ni·cate /kə'mjuːnɪkeɪt/ *v* 1 *vi/t* make (opinions, etc.) known 2 *vt* pass on (a disease) 3 *vi* (of rooms) be connected
–cator *n* person who communicates
–cation /kə,mjuːnɪ'keɪʃən/ *n* 1 [U] communicating 2 [C] *fml* message, letter, etc. **–cations** *n* [P] ways of travelling or sending messages

com·mu·ni·ca·tive /kə'mjuːnɪkətɪv/ *adj* willing to give information

com·mu·nion /kə'mjuːnjən/ *n* [U] 1 *fml* sharing of beliefs, feelings, etc. 2 (*cap.*) Christian ceremony of sharing bread and wine

com·mu·ni·qué /kə'mjuːnɪkeɪ ‖ kə-ˌmjuːnɪ'keɪ/ *n* official report

com·mu·nis·m /'kɒmjʊnɪzəm ‖ 'kɑː-/ *n* [U] 1 social and political system by which the state owns the means of production 2 (*cap.*) one-party system of government on this principle **–nist** *n, adj*

com·mu·ni·ty /kə'mjuːnɪti/ *n* 1 [C] group of people with shared interests 2 [S] people in general; the public 3 [U] shared possession

com·mute /kə'mjuːt/ *v* 1 *vi* travel regularly between home and work 2 *vt* make (a punishment) less severe **–muter** *n* person who commutes to work

com·pact¹ /kəm'pækt/ *adj* neatly packed into a small space

com·pact² /'kɒmpækt ‖ 'kɑːm-/ *n* 1 container for face powder 2 *AmE* small car

compact disc /ˌ·· '·, ·ˌ· '·/ *n* CD

com·pan·ion /kəm'pænjən/ *n* 1 person who spends time with another 2 HANDBOOK

~**able** *adj* friendly ~**ship** *n* [U] friendly company

com·pa·ny /ˈkʌmpəni/ *n* 1 [C] business firm; people working together: *a bus/theatre company* 2 [C] group of about 120 soldiers 3 [U] **a** presence of companions: *I was grateful for her company.* **b** companions, esp. guests 4 **be good/bad company** be a good/bad person to be with 5 **part company (with/from)** finish a relationship

com·pa·ra·ble /ˈkɒmpərəbəl ‖ ˈkɑːm-/ *adj* similar

com·par·a·tive /kəmˈpærətɪv/ *adj* 1 *gram* expressing an increase in quality or quantity: *'Worse' is the comparative form of 'bad'.* 2 measured or judged by a comparison that is not stated: *She's a comparative newcomer to television.* (=has not been on television often) 3 making a comparison: *a comparative study of European languages* ♦ *n gram* comparative form of an adjective or adverb ~**ly** *adv*

com·pare /kəmˈpeə ‖ -ˈper/ *v* 1 *vt* judge (one thing) against another thing, to show likeness or difference 2 *vt* show the likeness between (two things) 3 *vi* be worthy of comparison

com·pa·ri·son /kəmˈpærɪsən/ *n* 1 [C;U] (statement of) comparing: *Paris is small in comparison with London.* 2 [U] likeness: *There's no comparison between them.*

com·part·ment /kəmˈpɑːtmənt ‖ -ɑːr-/ *n* separate division of a space; small room in a railway carriage, etc.

com·pass /ˈkʌmpəs/ *n* 1 instrument for showing direction, with a needle that points to the north 2 *fml* range; limit: *outside the compass of this department* **compasses** *n* [P] instrument for drawing circles

com·pas·sion /kəmˈpæʃən/ *n* [U] sympathy; pity ~**ate** *adj* ~**ately** *adv*

com·pat·i·ble /kəmˈpætɪbəl/ *adj* able to exist or work together ~**bly** *adv* ~**bility** /kəmˌpætɪˈbɪlɪti/ *n* [U]

com·pat·ri·ot /kəmˈpætriət ‖ -ˈpeɪt-/ *n* person of the same nationality as another

com·pel /kəmˈpel/ *vt* -ll- force to do something ~**ling** *adj* important; urgent: *compelling reasons*

com·pen·sate /ˈkɒmpənseɪt ‖ ˈkɑːm-/ *vt/i* pay, or give something, to balance a loss ~**sation** /ˌkɒmpənˈseɪʃən ‖ ˌkɑːm-/ *n* [S;U]

something given to compensate ~**satory** /ˌkɒmpənˈseɪtəri ‖ kəmˈpensətɔːri/ *adj*

com·pere /ˈkɒmpeə ‖ ˈkɑːmper/ *n BrE* person who introduces a radio or television show **compere** *vi/t*

com·pete /kəmˈpiːt/ *vi* try to win in a competition

com·pe·tence /ˈkɒmpətəns ‖ ˈkɑːm-/ *n* [U] ability to do what is needed ~**tent** *adj* ~**tently** *adv*

com·pe·ti·tion /ˌkɒmpəˈtɪʃən ‖ ˌkɑːm-/ *n* 1 [C] test of strength, skill, etc. 2 [U] trying to win: *keen competition between them* 3 [U] person or people against whom one competes

com·pe·ti·tive /kəmˈpetɪtɪv/ *adj* 1 decided by competition 2 liking to compete

com·pe·ti·tor /kəmˈpetɪtə ‖ -ər/ *n* person, firm, etc. that competes

com·pile /kəmˈpaɪl/ *vt* make (a book, etc.) from collected facts ~**piler** *n* ~**pilation** /ˌkɒmpɪˈleɪʃən ‖ ˌkɑːm-/ *n* 1 [U] act of compiling 2 [C] something compiled

com·pla·cen·cy /kəmˈpleɪsənsi/ *n* [U] unreasonable feeling of satisfaction ~**cent** *adj* ~**cently** *adv*

com·plain /kəmˈpleɪn/ *vi/t* say that one is unhappy: *to complain that the room is too hot*

com·plaint /kəmˈpleɪnt/ *n* 1 [C;U] (statement of) complaining 2 [C] illness: *a liver complaint*

com·ple·ment /ˈkɒmpləmənt ‖ ˈkɑːm-/ *n* 1 something that makes another thing seem good 2 full number needed 3 *gram* noun or adjective after a verb such as 'be' or 'become' ♦ /-ment/ *vt* make (another thing) seem good ~**ary** /ˌkɒmpləˈmentəri◂ ‖ ˌkɑːm-/ *adj* 1 making a good combination 2 ALTERNATIVE (2): *complementary medicine*

com·plete /kəmˈpliːt/ *adj* 1 having all necessary parts; whole 2 finished; ended 3 total; thorough: *complete silence* ♦ *vt* 1 make whole 2 finish ~**ly** *adv* in every way ~**pletion** /-ˈpliːʃən/ *n* [U]

com·plex¹ /ˈkɒmpleks ‖ ˌkɑːmˈpleks◂/ *adj* 1 difficult to understand 2 made of many connected parts ~**ity** /kəmˈpleksɪti/ *n* [C;U]

com·plex² /ˈkɒmpleks ‖ ˈkɑːm-/ *n* 1 one or more buildings for a particular purpose: *a new sports complex* 2 emotional problem relating to a particular subject: *an inferiority complex*

com·plex·ion /kəm'plekʃən/ *n* **1** natural appearance of the skin: *good/dark complexion* **2** general character of a situation

com·pli·ance /kəm'plaɪəns/ *n* [U] *fml* complying (COMPLY) **-ant** *adj*

com·pli·cate /'kɒmplɪkeɪt ‖ 'kɑːm-/ *vt* make difficult to deal with **-cated** *adj* COMPLEX **-cation** /ˌkɒmplɪ'keɪʃən ‖ ˌkɑːm-/ *n* added difficulty

com·plic·i·ty /kəm'plɪsɪti/ *n* [U] *fml* taking part with someone else in a crime

com·pli·ment¹ /'kɒmplɪmənt ‖ 'kɑːm-/ *n* expression of praise **compliments** *n* [P] good wishes

com·pli·ment² /'kɒmplɪment ‖ 'kɑːm-/ *vt* express admiration of **~ary** /ˌkɒmplɪ'mentəri◄ ‖ ˌkɑːm-/ *adj* **1** expressing admiration **2** given free: *complimentary tickets*

com·ply /kəm'plaɪ/ *vi fml* agree to do something; obey

com·po·nent /kəm'pəʊnənt ‖ -'poʊ-/ *n* any part of a whole machine or system

com·pose /kəm'pəʊz ‖ -'poʊz/ *v* **1** *vi/t* write (music, poetry, etc.) **2** *vt* get (oneself) under control **3 be composed of** consist of **-posed** *adj* calm **-poser** *n* writer of music

com·pos·ite /'kɒmpəzɪt ‖ kɑːm'pɑː-/ *adj, n* (something) made up of different parts

com·po·si·tion /ˌkɒmpə'zɪʃən ‖ ˌkɑːm-/ *n* **1** [U] act of writing music, poetry, etc. **2** [C] something written **3** [U] mixture or arrangement of parts

com·post /'kɒmpɒst ‖ 'kɑːmpoʊst/ *n* [U] decayed plant matter, used to improve the soil

com·po·sure /kəm'pəʊʒə ‖ -'poʊʒər/ *n* [U] calmness

com·pound¹ /'kɒmpaʊnd ‖ 'kɑːm-/ *adj* consisting of two or more parts ♦ *n*: *chemical compounds*

com·pound² /kəm'paʊnd/ *vt* **1** make by combining parts **2** make worse: *compound an error*

com·pound³ /'kɒmpaʊnd ‖ 'kɑːm-/ *n* enclosed area containing buildings

com·pre·hend /ˌkɒmprɪ'hend ‖ ˌkɑːm-/ *vt fml* **1** understand **2** include

com·pre·hen·sion /ˌkɒmprɪ'henʃən ‖ ˌkɑːm-/ *n* [U] *fml* power of understanding **-sible** /-sɪbəl/ *adj* understandable **-sibly** *adv*

com·pre·hen·sive /ˌkɒmprɪ'hensɪv◄ ‖ ˌkɑːm-/ *adj* **1** thorough; including a lot **2** *BrE* teaching pupils of all abilities together ♦ *n* a COMPREHENSIVE (2) school

com·press /kəm'pres/ *vt* **1** force into less space **2** put (ideas, etc.) into fewer words **~ion** /-'preʃən/ *n* [U]

com·prise /kəm'praɪz/ *v* consist of; have as parts

com·pro·mise /'kɒmprəmaɪz ‖ 'kɑːm-/ *n* [C;U] agreement reached by each side agreeing to some of the other side's demands ♦ *v* **1** *vi* make a compromise **2** *vt* put into a dishonourable position

com·pul·sion /kəm'pʌlʃən/ *n* **1** [U] force that makes a person do something **2** [C] strong desire **-sive** /-sɪv/ *adj* caused by a compulsion: *compulsive drinking*

com·pul·so·ry /kəm'pʌlsəri/ *adj* that must be done by law, etc. **-rily** *adv*

com·punc·tion /kəm'pʌŋkʃən/ *n* [U] feeling of guilt

com·pute /kəm'pjuːt/ *vt* calculate

com·put·er /kəm'pjuːtə ‖ -ər/ *n* ELECTRONIC machine that stores, recalls, and deals with information **~ize** also **-ise** *BrE* — *vt* use or begin to use a computer to control (an operation) **~ization** /kəmˌpjuːtəraɪ'zeɪʃən ‖ -tərə-/ *n* [U]

com·pu·ting /kəm'pjuːtɪŋ/ *n* [U] use of computers

com·rade /'kɒmrɪd, -reɪd ‖ 'kɑːmræd/ *n* **1** *fml* close companion **2** fellow member of a union or political party **~ship** *n* [U]

con /kɒn ‖ kɑːn/ *vt* **-nn-** trick (a trusting person) ♦ *n infml for* CONFIDENCE TRICK

Con *written abbrev. for:* CONSERVATIVE PARTY

con·cave /ˌkɒn'keɪv◄, kən- ‖ ˌkɑːn'keɪv◄, kən-/ *adj* curved inwards

con·ceal /kən'siːl/ *vt* hide **~ment** *n* [U]

con·cede /kən'siːd/ *vt* **1** admit as true **2** give as a right **3** end a game or match by admitting defeat

con·ceit /kən'siːt/ *n* [U] too high an opinion of oneself **~ed** *adj*

con·ceive /kən'siːv/ *v* **1** *vt* think of; imagine **2** *vi/t* become PREGNANT **-ceivable** *adj* imaginable; possible **-ceivably** *adv*

con·cen·trate /'kɒnsəntreɪt ‖ 'kɑːn-/ *v*

1 *vi* direct all one's attention: *concentrate on the problem* **2** *vt/i* bring or come together in one place **3** *vt* make (a liquid) stronger ♦ *n* [C;U] concentrated liquid

con·cen·tra·tion /ˌkɒnsənˈtreɪʃən ‖ ˌkɑːn-/ *n* **1** [U] close attention **2** [C] close gathering

concentration camp /ˌ·'·· ·/ *n* large prison where many prisoners are kept in poor conditions, esp. during a war

con·cen·tric /kənˈsentrɪk/ *adj* (of circles) having the same centre

con·cept /ˈkɒnsept ‖ ˈkɑːn-/ *n* general idea; NOTION; ~**ual** /kənˈseptʃuəl/ *adj* of or based on the formation of CONCEPTS ~**ualize** also -**ualise** *BrE* — *vi/t* form a concept (of)

con·cep·tion /kənˈsepʃən/ *n* **1** [C;U] understanding **2** [U] forming of an idea **3** [C;U] *fml* starting of a new life by the union of a male and female sex cell

con·cern /kənˈsɜːn ‖ -ɜːrn/ *vt* **1** be about (a subject) **2** be of importance to: *problems which concern all of us* **3** worry: *I'm concerned about her.* ♦ *n* **1** [C] something that matters to someone **2** [U] worry: *no cause for concern* **3** [C] business; firm: *a going concern* ~**ing** *prep* about

con·cert /ˈkɒnsət ‖ ˈkɑːnsərt/ *n* **1** musical performance **2** **in concert: a** working together **b** playing at a concert

con·cert·ed /kənˈsɜːtɪd ‖ -ɜːr-/ *adj* done together by agreement: *a concerted effort*

con·cer·ti·na /ˌkɒnsəˈtiːnə ‖ ˌkɑːnsər-/ *n* small ACCORDION ♦ *vi* (of a vehicle) become pressed together as the result of a crash

con·cer·to /kənˈtʃɜːtəʊ ‖ -ˈtʃertoʊ/ *n* -**tos** piece of music for one instrument supported by an orchestra

con·ces·sion /kənˈseʃən/ *n* **1** something CONCEDEd after a disagreement **2** official permission to do something: *oil concessions in the North Sea* ~**aire** /kənˌseʃəˈneə ‖ -ˈner/ *n* holder of a CONCESSION (2)

con·cil·i·ate /kənˈsɪlieɪt/ *vt* remove the anger of ~**ation** /kənˌsɪliˈeɪʃən/ *n* [U] ~**atory** /kənˈsɪliətəri ‖ -tɔːri/ *adj* trying to conciliate

con·cise /kənˈsaɪs/ *adj* expressing a lot in a few words ~**ly** *adv* ~**ness** *n* [U]

con·clude /kənˈkluːd/ *v fml* **1** *vt/i* bring

or come to an end **2** *vt* come to believe **3** *vt* settle: *conclude an agreement*

con·clu·sion /kənˈkluːʒən/ *n* **1** decision; settlement **2** end –**sive** /-sɪv/ *adj* ending all doubt: *conclusive proof*

con·coct /kənˈkɒkt ‖ -ˈkɑːkt/ *vt* **1** make by mixing parts **2** invent (something false) ~**ion** /-ˈkɒkʃən ‖ -ˈkɑːk-/ *n* mixture

con·cord /ˈkɒŋkɔːd ‖ ˈkɑːŋkɔːrd/ *n* [U] friendly agreement

con·course /ˈkɒŋkɔːs ‖ ˈkɑːŋkɔːrs/ *n* place where crowds can gather

con·crete¹ /ˈkɒŋkriːt ‖ ˈkɑːŋkriːt/ *adj* **1** real or solid; not ABSTRACT: *A car is a concrete object.*

con·crete² /ˈkɒŋkriːt ‖ ˈkɑːŋkriːt/ clear; particular: *concrete proposals n* [U] building material made of sand, cement, etc. ♦ *vt* cover (a path, wall, etc.) with concrete

con·cu·bine /ˈkɒŋkjʊbaɪn ‖ ˈkɑːŋ-/ *n* woman who has sex with, but is not married to, an Eastern ruler

con·cur /kənˈkɜː ‖ -ˈkɜːr/ *vi* -**rr**- *fml* **1** agree **2** happen at the same time ~**rence** /kənˈkʌrəns ‖ -ˈkɜːr-/ *n* [C;U] ~**rent** *adj* ~**rently** *adv*

con·cuss /kənˈkʌs/ *vt* damage (the brain) by a heavy blow ~**ion** /-ˈkʌʃən/ *n* [U]

con·demn /kənˈdem/ *vt* **1** express disapproval of **2** state the punishment for: *condemn him to death* | (fig.) *She was condemned to life in a wheelchair.* **3** declare (a building, etc.) unfit for use ~**ation** /ˌkɒndəmˈneɪʃən, -dem- ‖ ˌkɑːn-/ *n* [C;U]

con·dense /kənˈdens/ *vt/i* **1** make (a gas) liquid **2** make (a liquid) thicker **3** put into fewer words –**denser** *n* –**densation** /ˌkɒndenˈseɪʃən, -dən- ‖ ˌkɑːn-/ *n* [U] **1** act of condensing **2** drops of water formed when steam condenses

con·de·scend /ˌkɒndɪˈsend ‖ ˌkɑːn-/ *vi* **1** do something unsuited to one's social or professional position **2** *derog* behave as though one is grander than others ~**ing** *adj* –**scension** /-ˈsenʃən/ *n* [U]

con·di·ment /ˈkɒndəmənt ‖ ˈkɑːn-/ *n fml* something used for giving taste to food

con·di·tion¹ /kənˈdɪʃən/ *n* **1** [U] state; way of being: *a car in poor condition* **2** [C] something necessary for something else: *I'll come on condition that John comes too.* **3** [C] illness **4** **in/out of condition** thoroughly fit/not fit **5** **on no condition**

never **conditions** n [P] surrounding facts: *better working conditions* –**tional** adj depending on conditions –**tionally** adv

condition² vt 1 train to behave in a certain way 2 put special liquid on (skin, hair, etc.) to improve the condition of ~**ing** n [U]

c·on·di·tion·er /kənˈdɪʃənə ‖ -ər/ n liquid used to improve the condition of hair or clothing: **fabric conditioner**

con·do·lence /kənˈdəʊləns ‖ -ˈdoʊ-/ n [C;U] expression of sympathy

con·dom /ˈkɒndəm ‖ ˈkɑːn-, ˈkʌn-/ n usu. rubber covering worn over the male sex organ during SEXUAL INTERCOURSE, as a means of birth control and as a protection against disease

con·do·min·i·um /ˌkɒndəˈmɪniəm ‖ ˌkɑːn-/ also **con·do** /ˈkɒndəʊ ‖ ˈkɑːndoʊ/ infml — n AmE block of flats which are each owned by the people living in them

con·done /kənˈdəʊn ‖ -ˈdoʊn/ vt forgive (wrong behaviour)

con·du·cive /kənˈdjuːsɪv ‖ -ˈduː-/ adj fml likely to produce: *conducive to health*

con·duct¹ /kənˈdʌkt/ v 1 vt direct; lead 2 vt/i direct the playing of (musicians) 3 vt be the path for (electricity, etc.) 4 conduct oneself fml behave ~**ive** adj able to conduct electricity, etc. –**ion** /-ˈdʌkʃən/ n [U] passage of electricity, etc.

con·duct² /ˈkɒndʌkt, -dəkt ‖ ˈkɑːn-/ n [U] 1 fml behaviour 2 management of something

con·duc·tor /kənˈdʌktə ‖ -ər/ n 1 person who conducts musicians 2 person who collects payments on a bus 3 AmE guard on a train 4 substance that conducts electricity, etc.

con·duit /ˈkɒndɪt, ˈkɒndjuːt ‖ ˈkɑːnduːt/ n 1 pipe for water, gas, etc. 2 person carrying information or goods between other people

cone /kəʊn ‖ koʊn/ n 1 hollow or solid object with a round base and pointed top 2 fruit of a PINE or FIR tree

con·fec·tion·e·ry /kənˈfekʃənəri ‖ -neri/ n [U] fml sweets –**ner** n person who makes or sells sweets

con·fed·e·ra·cy /kənˈfedərəsi/ also **confederation** /kənˌfedəˈreɪʃən/ — n union of people, parties, or states

con·fed·e·rate /kənˈfedərət/ n 1 ACCOM-

PLICE 2 member of a confederacy

con·fer /kənˈfɜː ‖ -ˈfɜːr/ v -rr- fml 1 vi talk together 2 vt give (a title, etc.) to

con·fe·rence /ˈkɒnfərəns ‖ ˈkɑːn-/ n meeting for the exchange of ideas

con·fess /kənˈfes/ vi/t admit (one's faults) ~**or** n priest who hears one's confession ~**ion** /-ˈfeʃən/ n [C;U] telling of one's faults

con·fet·ti /kənˈfeti/ n [U] bits of coloured paper thrown at weddings

con·fi·dant /ˈkɒnfɪdænt, ˌkɒnfɪˈdænt ‖ ˈkɑːnfɪdænt/ **confidante** (same pronunciation) fem. — n person to whom one tells secrets

con·fide /kənˈfaɪd/ vt tell (a secret) trustingly

confide in phr vt talk freely to

con·fi·dence /ˈkɒnfɪdəns ‖ ˈkɑːn-/ n 1 [U] faith; trust 2 [U] belief in one's own ability 3 [C] something told secretly 4 **in confidence** secretly –**dent** adj sure

confidence trick /ˈ··· ·/ n trick played in order to cheat a trusting person of money

con·fi·den·tial /ˌkɒnfɪˈdenʃəl◂ ‖ ˌkɑːn-/ adj 1 told in secret 2 trusted with secrets: *confidential secretary* ~**ly** adv

con·fig·u·ra·tion /kənˌfɪgjʊˈreɪʃən/ n shape; arrangement

con·fine /kənˈfaɪn/ vt 1 keep shut in: *confined to bed* 2 keep within the limits ~**ment** n 1 [U] being shut up 2 [C;U] giving birth to a child: *her third confinement* 3 [P] limits

con·firm /kənˈfɜːm ‖ -ˈɜːrm/ vt 1 support; give proof of: *confirm a telephone message in writing* 2 admit (a person) to membership of the Christian Church ~**ed** adj firmly settled; unlikely to change: *confirmed bachelor* ~**ation** /ˌkɒnfəˈmeɪʃən ‖ ˌkɑːnfər-/ n 1 proof 2 religious service in which someone is confirmed

con·fis·cate /ˈkɒnfɪskeɪt ‖ ˈkɑːn-/ vt seize (private property) officially, without payment –**cation** /ˌkɒnfɪˈskeɪʃən ‖ ˌkɑːn-/ n [C;U]

con·flate /kənˈfleɪt/ vi/t combine –**flation** /-ˈfleɪʃən/ n [C;U]

con·flict¹ /ˈkɒnflɪkt ‖ ˈkɑːn-/ n 1 disagreement; argument 2 war

con·flict² /kənˈflɪkt/ vi be in opposition

con·form /kənˈfɔːm ‖ -ˈɔːrm/ vi obey established rules or customs ~**ist** n person who conforms ~**ity** *n* [U]

con·found /kənˈfaund/ *vt* confuse and surprise

con·front /kənˈfrʌnt/ *vt* face; meet: *confront problems* ~**ation** /ˌkɒnfrənˈteɪʃən/ ‖ ˌkɑːn-/ *n* [C;U] angry opposition

con·fuse /kənˈfjuːz/ *vt* **1** cause to be mixed up in the mind: *I'm confused.* **2** be unable to tell the difference between: *to confuse Jack and/with Paul* **3** make less clear: *confusing the issue* –**fusion** /-ˈfjuːʒən/ *n* [U]

con·geal /kənˈdʒiːl/ *vi/t* become solid: *congealed blood*

con·ge·ni·al /kənˈdʒiːniəl/ *adj* pleasant; in agreement with one's tastes ~**ly** *adv*

con·gen·i·tal /kənˈdʒenɪtl/ *adj* (of diseases) existing from one's birth

con·ges·ted /kənˈdʒestɪd/ *adj* too full; blocked –**tion** /-ˈdʒestʃən/ *n* [U]

con·glom·e·rate /kənˈɡlɒmərət ‖ -ˈɡlɑː-/ *n* large business firm producing many kinds of goods –**ration** /kənˌɡlɒməˈreɪʃən ‖-ˌɡlɑː-/ *n*

con·grat·u·late /kənˈɡrætʃʊleɪt/ *vt* express pleasure at (someone's) success or good luck: *I congratulated them on the birth of their daughter.* –**lations** /kənˌɡrætʃʊˈleɪʃənz/ *interj, n* [P] I congratulate you –**latory** /kənˌɡrætʃʊˈleɪtəri ‖ -ˈɡrætʃʊlə-tɔːri/ *adj*

con·gre·gate /ˈkɒŋɡrɪɡeɪt ‖ˈkɑːŋ-/ *vi* gather together –**gation** /ˌkɒŋɡrɪˈɡeɪʃən ‖ ˌkɑːŋ-/ *n* group of people gathered together in church

con·gress /ˈkɒŋɡres ‖ˈkɑːŋɡrɪs/ *n* **1** formal meeting to exchange information **2** (*cap.*) highest lawmaking body of the US, consisting of the Senate and the House of Representatives: *a congressman* –**ional** /kənˈɡreʃənəl/ *adj*

con·i·cal /ˈkɒnɪkəl ‖ˈkɑː-/ *adj* CONE-shaped

co·ni·fer /ˈkəʊnɪfə, ˈkɒ-‖ˈkɑːnɪfər/ *n* tree that bears cones (CONE (2))

con·jec·ture /kənˈdʒektʃə‖-ər/ *vi/t fml* guess ♦ *n* [C;U] –**tural** *adj*

con·ju·gal /ˈkɒndʒʊɡəl ‖ˈkɑːn-/ *adj fml* of marriage

con·ju·gate /ˈkɒndʒʊɡeɪt ‖ˈkɑːn-/ *vt* *gram* give the forms of (a verb) –**gation** /ˌkɒndʒʊˈɡeɪʃən ‖ˌkɑːn-/ *n* class of verbs conjugated in the same way

con·junc·tion /kənˈdʒʌŋkʃən/ *n* **1** *gram* word such as 'but' or 'while' **2** **in conjunction with** in combination with

con·junc·ti·vi·tis /kənˌdʒʌŋktɪˈvaɪtɪs/ *n* painful eye disease

con·jure /ˈkʌndʒə‖ˈkɑːndʒər, ˈkʌn-/ **1** *vi* do clever tricks that seem magical **2** *vt* cause to appear as if by magic: (fig.) *conjure up memories of the past* **3 a name to conjure with** name of a very influential and/or important person or thing –**jurer**, -**juror** *n* person who does conjuring tricks

con·nect /kəˈnekt/ *v* **1** *vt/i* join together: *connect two pipes* **2** *vt* think of as related

con·nec·tion also **connexion** *BrE* /kəˈnekʃən/ *n* **1** [C;U] being connected; relationship **2** [C] plane, train, etc. planned to take passengers arriving by another one **3** [C] person connected to others by family or business **4 in connection with** *fml* with regard to

con·nive /kəˈnaɪv/ *v* **connive at** *phr vt* make no attempt to stop (something wrong) –**nivance** *n* [U]

con·nois·seur /ˌkɒnəˈsɜː ‖ˌkɑːnəˈsɜːr/ *n* person with special knowledge of art, wine, etc.

con·note /kəˈnəʊt ‖-ˈnoʊt/ *vt fml* (of a word) suggest something more than its ordinary meaning –**notation** /ˌkɒnəˈteɪʃən ‖ˌkɑː-/ *n*: *'Skinny' has bad connotations.*

con·quer /ˈkɒŋkə‖ˈkɑːŋkər/ *vt* **1** defeat (enemies): (fig.) *conquer one's fear* **2** take (a place) by force: *a conquered city* ~**or** *n*

con·quest /ˈkɒŋkwest ‖ˈkɑːŋ-/ *n* **1** [U] conquering **2** [C] something conquered, esp. land gained in war

con·science /ˈkɒnʃəns ‖ˈkɑːn-/ *n* **1** [C;U] knowledge of right and wrong: *to have a guilty conscience* **2 on one's conscience** causing one to feel guilty

con·sci·en·tious /ˌkɒnʃiˈenʃəs◂ ˌkɑːn-/ *adj* careful and honest: *conscientious work/workers* ~**ly** *adv* ~**ness** *n* [U]

conscientious ob·jec·tor /ˌ···· ·ˈ··/ *n* person who refuses to serve in the armed forces because of moral or religious beliefs

con·scious /ˈkɒnʃəs ‖ˈkɑːn-/ *adj* **1** awake and able to think **2** knowing; AWARE **3** intentional: *conscious effort* ~**ly** *adv* ~**ness** *n* [S;U]

con·script¹ /kənˈskrɪpt/ *vt* make

someone serve in the armed forces ~ion
/kənˈskrɪpʃən/ n [U] practice of
conscripting people

con·script² /ˈkɒnskrɪpt ‖ ˈkɑːn-/ n
conscripted person

con·se·crate /ˈkɒnsɪ̯kreɪt ‖ ˈkɑːn-/ vt
1 declare as holy: *consecrated wine* 2 set
apart solemnly for a particular purpose:
consecrate one's life to helping the poor
–cration /ˌkɒnsɪ̯ˈkreɪʃən ‖ ˌkɑːn-/ n [U]

con·sec·u·tive /kənˈsekjɪ̯tɪv/ adj
following in unbroken order ~ly adv

con·sen·sus /kənˈsensəs/ n general
agreement

con·sent /kənˈsent/ vi give permission ♦
n [U] permission

con·se·quence /ˈkɒnsəˌkwəns ‖ ˈkɑːnsə̯-
kwens/ n 1 [C] result 2 [U] fml importance:
It's of no consequence to me.

con·se·quent /ˈkɒnsɪ̯kwənt ‖ ˈkɑːn-/
adj following as a result ~ly adv

con·se·quen·tial /ˌkɒnsɪ̯ˈkwenʃəl◂
ˌkɑːn-/ adj fml 1 consequent 2 important

con·ser·va·tion /ˌkɒnsəˈveɪʃən ‖
ˌkɑːnsər-/ n [U] 1 protection of animals,
plants, ancient buildings, etc. 2 careful use
of a limited supply, to prevent waste ~ist n
~ism n [U]

con·ser·va·tive /kənˈsɜːvətɪv ‖ -ɜːr-/
adj 1 not liking change 2 kept rather low: *a
conservative estimate* 3 (cap.) of a British
political party opposed to sudden change ♦
n 1 person who dislikes change 2 (cap.)
member of the Conservative Party ~ly adv
–tism n [U]

Conservative Party /·ˈ··· ˌ··/ n [the]
British political party which tends to be
opposed to sudden change

con·ser·va·to·ry /kənˈsɜːvətəri ‖ -ˈsɜːr-
vətɔːri/ n 1 GREENHOUSE 2 school of music
or acting

con·serve /kənˈsɜːv ‖ -ɜːrv/ vt use
carefully; preserve: *conserve one's energy*

con·sid·er /kənˈsɪdə ‖ -ər/ v 1 vi/t think
about 2 vt take into account; remember: *you
have to consider your wife.* 3 vt believe to be:
consider him suitable ~ed reached after
careful thought ~ing if one takes into
account: *She did well, considering her age.*

con·sid·er·a·ble /kənˈsɪdərəbəl/ adj
fairly large ~bly adv much

con·sid·er·ate /kənˈsɪdərɪ̯t/ adj kind
and thoughtful ~ly adv

con·sid·er·a·tion /kənˌsɪdəˈreɪʃən/ n
1 [U] thoughtful attention 2 [C] fact to be
remembered when deciding something
3 [C] payment; reward 4 **take something
into consideration** remember when
making a judgment

con·sign /kənˈsaɪn/ vt 1 send (goods) for
sale 2 fml give into someone's care ~ment n
1 [C] goods consigned 2 [U] act of
consigning

con·sist /kənˈsɪst/ v

consist in phr vt fml have as a base;
depend on

consist of phr vt be made up of

con·sis·ten·cy /kənˈsɪstənsi/ n 1 [U]
state of always behaving in the same way
2 [C] degree of thickness of a liquid –tent
adj 1 not changing 2 in agreement –tently
adv

con·sole¹ /kənˈsəʊl ‖ -ˈsoʊl/ vt make less
unhappy –solation /ˌkɒnsəˈleɪʃən ‖ ˌkɑːn-/
n [C;U] (person or thing giving) comfort

con·sole² /ˈkɒnsəʊl ‖ ˈkɑːnsoʊl/ n
surface containing the controls for a
machine

con·sol·i·date /kənˈsɒlɪ̯deɪt ‖ -ˈsɑː-/ vi/t
1 (cause to) become stronger 2 combine
into one –dation /kənˌsɒlɪ̯ˈdeɪʃ ən ‖ -ˌsɑː-/ n

con·som·mé /kənˈsɒmeɪ, ˈkɒnsəmeɪ ‖
ˌkɑːnsəˈmeɪ/ n [U] clear soup

con·so·nant¹ /ˈkɒnsənənt ‖ ˈkɑːn-/ n
(letter representing) a speech sound such as
b, m, s, made by stopping the breath

consonant² adj fml in agreement

con·sort¹ /ˈkɒnsɔːt ‖ ˈkɑːnsɔːrt/ n wife
or husband of a ruler

con·sort² /kənˈsɔːt ‖ -ɔːrt/ v consort
with phr vi spend time in company of

con·sor·ti·um /kənˈsɔːtiəm ‖ -ɔːr-/ n
-tiums or -tia /-tiə/ combination of a
number of companies, banks, etc.

con·spic·u·ous /kənˈspɪkjuəs/ adj
easily seen; noticeable ~ly adv

con·spir·a·cy /kənˈspɪrəsi/ n [C;U] (plan
made by) conspiring

con·spir·a·tor /kənˈspɪrətə ‖ -ər/ n
person who conspires

con·spire /kənˈspaɪə ‖ -ˈspaɪr/ vi 1 plan
something bad together secretly 2 (of
events) combine in a bad way

con·sta·ble /ˈkʌnstəbəl ‖ ˈkɑːn-/ n
British policeman or police officer

con·stab·u·la·ry /kənˈstæbjɪ̯ləri ‖ -leri/

n police force of an area

con·stant /'kɒnstənt ‖ 'kɑ:n-/ *adj*
1 happening all the time 2 unchanging: *a
constant speed* 3 continuous 4 loyal ♦
something that never varies ~**ly** *adv*
–**stancy** *n* [U] 1 freedom from change 2 *fml*
loyalty

con·stel·la·tion /ˌkɒnstəˈleɪʃən ‖ ˌkɑ:n-/
n named group of stars

con·ster·na·tion /ˌkɒnstəˈneɪʃən ‖
ˌkɑ:nstər-/ *n* [U] great shock and fear

con·sti·pa·tion /ˌkɒnstɪˈpeɪʃən ‖ ˌkɑ:n-/
n [U] being unable to empty the bowels
properly –**ted** /'kɒnstɪpeɪtɪd ‖ 'kɑ:n-/ *adj*

con·sti·tu·en·cy /kənˈstɪtʃuənsi/ *n*
(voters in) an area that elects a
representative to Parliament

con·sti·tu·ent /kənˈstɪtʃuənt/ *n* 1 voter
2 necessary part: *the constituents of cement*
♦ *adj* helping to make a whole

con·sti·tute /'kɒnstɪtju:t ‖
'kɑ:nstətu:t/ *vt* 1 form when added
together 2 establish

con·sti·tu·tion /ˌkɒnstɪˈtju:ʃən ‖
ˌkɑ:nstəˈtu:-/ *n* 1 laws and principles by
which a country is governed 2 person's
physical condition 3 structure of
something ~**al** *adj* 1 by or of a political
constitution 2 of a person's constitution
~**ally** *adv*

con·strain /kənˈstreɪn/ *vt fml* force
(someone) to do something

con·straint /kənˈstreɪnt/ *n* [C;U]
something that limits freedom: *acted under
constraint*

con·strict /kənˈstrɪkt/ *vt* make narrower
or tighter –**ion** /-ˈstrɪkʃən/ *n* [C;U]

con·struct /kənˈstrʌkt/ *vt* make out of
parts; build

con·struc·tion /kənˈstrʌkʃən/ *n* 1 [U]
building: *the building industry* 2 [C]
something built 3 [C] meaning given to
something: *put the wrong construction on
his behaviour* –**tive** /-tɪv/ *adj* helpful:
constructive suggestions

con·strue /kənˈstru:/ *vt* place a certain
meaning on

con·sul /'kɒnsəl ‖ 'kɑ:n-/ *n* representative
of a government in a foreign city ~**ar**
/-sjələ ‖ -sələr/ *adj* ~**ate** *n* consul's office

con·sult /kənˈsʌlt/ *vt* go to (a person,
book, etc.) for advice ~**ation** /ˌkɒnsəl-
ˈteɪʃən ‖ ˌkɑ:n-/ *n* [C;U]

con·sul·tant /kənˈsʌltənt/ *n* 1 person
who gives professional advice 2 *BrE* high
ranking hospital doctor who gives
specialist advice –**tancy** *n* company that
gives advice or training –**tative** *adj* giving
advice

con·sume /kənˈsju:m ‖ -ˈsu:m/ *vt fml*
1 eat or drink 2 use up; destroy –**suming**
adj main: *a consuming interest in trains*
–**sumer** *n* person who buys goods
–**sumption** /kənˈsʌmpʃən/ *n* [U]

consumer dur·a·ble /·ˌ·· '···/ *n* large
article that is bought only infrequently, e.g.
a car

con·sum·mate¹ /kənˈsʌmət/ *adj* perfect;
complete

con·sum·mate² /'kɒnsəmeɪt ‖ 'kɑ:n-/
vt fml 1 complete (a marriage) by having
sex 2 make perfect –**mation** /ˌkɒnsə-
ˈmeɪʃən ‖ ˌkɑ:n-/ *n* [C;U]

cont *written abbrev. for:* continued

con·tact /'kɒntækt ‖ 'kɑ:n-/ *n* 1 [U]
meeting; relationship: *Have you been in
contact with the disease?* 2 [C] person one
knows who can help one: *some useful
contacts in Spain* 3 [C] electrical part that
touches another to carry electric current ♦
vt reach (someone) by telephone, etc.

contact lens /'·· ·/ *n* plastic LENS (1)
shaped to fit over the eye to improve
eyesight

con·tain /kənˈteɪn/ *vt* 1 have within
itself: *Beer contains alcohol.* 2 keep under
control: *I can't contain myself.*

con·tain·er /kənˈteɪnə ‖ -ər/ *n* 1 box,
bottle, etc. used to contain something
2 large metal box in which goods are packed
to be carried on ships, etc.

con·tam·i·nate /kənˈtæmɪneɪt/ *vt* make
impure or dirty: *contaminated water*
–**nation** /kənˌtæmɪˈneɪʃən/ *n* [U]

con·tem·plate /'kɒntəmpleɪt ‖ 'kɑ:n-/
vt 1 think about; consider as possible 2 look
solemnly at –**plation** /ˌkɒntəmˈpleɪʃən ‖
ˌkɑ:n-/ *n* [U] deep thought –**plative**
/kənˈtemplətɪv, 'kɒntəmpleɪtɪv ‖ kən-,
'kɑ:ntem-/ *adj*

con·tem·po·ra·ry /kənˈtempərəri,
-pəri ‖ -pəreri/ *adj* 1 modern; of the present
2 of the same time ♦ *n* person of the same
age, or living at the same time

con·tempt /kənˈtempt/ *n* [U] complete
lack of respect ~**ible** *adj* deserving

contempt ~**tuous** *adj* showing contempt

contempt of court /·.· '·/ *n* [U] offence of disobeying a judge in court

con·tend /kən'tend/ *v* **1** *vi* compete; struggle **2** *vt fml* claim; declare ~**er** *n* competitor

con·tent[1] /kən'tent/ *adj* satisfied; happy ♦ *vt* make happy ~**ed** *adj* quietly happy ~**edly** *adv* ~**ment** *n* [U] quiet happiness

con·tent[2] /'kɒntent/ *n* **1** [U] subject matter of a book **2** [S] amount contained in something: *a high fat content* ~**contents** *n* [P] what something contains

con·ten·tion /kən'tenʃən/ *n* **1** [C] claim; point of view **2** [U] struggle –**tious** *adj* **1** causing argument **2** quarrelsome

con·test[1] /'kɒntest/ *n* struggle; competition

con·test[2] /kən'test/ *vt fml* **1** compete for **2** argue about the rightness of ~**ant** *n* competitor

con·text /'kɒntekst/ *n* **1** words that surround a word or phrase **2** surrounding conditions

con·ti·nent /'kɒntɪnənt/ *n* **1** [C] large land mass; Europe, Asia, etc. **2** [*the*] (*cap.*) Europe without Britain ~**al** /ˌkɒntɪ'nentl◄/ *adj*

con·tin·gen·cy /kən'tɪndʒənsi/ *n* possible event that might cause problems

con·tin·gent[1] /kən'tɪndʒənt/ *adj* **1** dependent on something uncertain **2** happening by chance

contingent[2] *n* **1** part of a larger force of soldiers, ships, etc. **2** part of a larger gathering of people

con·tin·u·al /kən'tɪnjuəl/ *adj* regular; frequent ~**ly** *adv*

con·tin·ue /kən'tɪnjuː/ *vi/t* **1** go on doing something **2** start again after stopping –**uation** /kənˌtɪnju'eɪʃən/ *n* **1** [U] act of continuing **2** [C] something which continues from something else

con·ti·nu·i·ty /ˌkɒntɪ'njuːɪti/, ˌkɑːn-tʃ'nuː-/ *n* [U] uninterrupted connection

con·tin·u·ous /kən'tɪnjuəs/ *adj* continuing unbroken: *The brain needs a continuous supply of blood.* ~**ly** *adv*

con·tin·u·um /kən'tɪnjuəm/ *n* -**uums** or -**ua** /-juə/ **1** something which is without parts and the same from beginning to end **2** something that changes gradually without sudden breaks

con·tort /kən'tɔːt ‖ -ɔːrt/ *vt* twist out of shape ~**ion** /-'tɔːʃən ‖ -'tɔːr-/ *n* [C;U]

con·tour /'kɒntuə ‖ 'kɑːntur/ *n* **1** shape of the edges of something, such as a coast **2** line on a map showing the edges of areas above a certain height

con·tra·band /'kɒntrəbænd ‖ 'kɑːn-/ *n* [U] goods that it is not legal to bring into a country

con·tra·cep·tion /ˌkɒntrə'sepʃən ‖ ˌkɑːn-/ *n* [U] (methods for) preventing sex from resulting in PREGNANCY –**tive** /-'septɪv/ *n, adj* (drug, etc.) used for contraception

con·tract[1] /'kɒntrækt ‖ 'kɑːn-/ *n* formal agreement to do something ~**ual** /kən'træktʃuəl/ *adj*

contract[2] *v* contract **in/out** *phr vi* promise, esp. officially to or not to take part

con·tract[3] /kən'trækt/ *v* **1** *vi/t* arrange by formal agreement **2** *vt fml* get (a disease) –**ion** /-'trækʃən/ *n* **1** [U] process of getting smaller **2** [C] shortened form of a word **3** [C] strong tightening of a muscle

con·trac·tor /kən'træktə ‖ 'kɑːntræk-tər/ *n* firm that provides supplies and/or workers, esp. for building work

con·tra·dict /ˌkɒntrə'dɪkt ‖ ˌkɑːn-/ *v* **1** *vt/i* say the opposite of; declare to be wrong **2** *vt* (of a statement, fact, etc.) be opposite to (another) –**ory** *adj*: *contra-dictory reports* ~**ion** /-'dɪkʃən/ *n* [C;U]

con·tra·flow /'kɒntrəfləʊ ‖ 'kɑːntrəfloʊ/ *n* [U] arrangement by which traffic in both directions on a road can use only one side

con·tral·to /kən'træltəʊ ‖ -toʊ/ *n* -**tos** female ALTO

con·trap·tion /kən'træpʃən/ *n* strange-looking apparatus

con·tra·ry[1] /'kɒntrəri ‖ 'kɑːntreri/ *n* [S] **1** opposite **2 on the contrary** no, not at all **3 to the contrary** to the opposite effect ♦ *adj* completely different; opposed

con·tra·ry[2] /kən'treəri ‖ -'treri/ *adj* (of a person) unreasonable

con·trast[1] /kən'trɑːst ‖ -'træst/ *v* **1** *vt* compare so that differences are made clear **2** *vi* show a difference: *sharply contrasting attitudes*

con·trast[2] /'kɒntrɑːst ‖ 'kɑːntræst/ *n* [C;U] noticeable difference

con·tra·vene /ˌkɒntrə'viːn ‖ ˌkɑːn-/ *vt fml* break (a law) –**vention** /-'venʃən/ *n*

[C;U]

con·tre·temps /'kɒntrətɒn ‖ 'ka:ntrə-
ta:n/ n -temps /-tɒŋz ‖ -ta:nz/ unlucky and
unexpected event

con·trib·ute /kən'trɪbju:t/ v 1 vt/i join
with others in giving something 2 vi help in
causing: *contribute to good health* 3 vt write
(an article) for a magazine –**utor** n person
who contributes –**utory** adj –**ution**
/ˌkɒntrɪ'bju:ʃən ‖ ˌka:n-/ n [C;U]

con·trite /'kɒntraɪt ‖ 'ka:n-/ adj fml
sorry for having done wrong ~**ly** adv
–**trition** /kən'trɪʃən/ n [U]

con·trive /kən'traɪv/ vt succeed in doing
something: *contrive to escape* –**trivance** n
clever plan or invention –**trived** adj
unnatural and forced

con·trol /kən'trəʊl ‖ -'troʊl/ vt -ll-
1 direct; have power over 2 hold back;
RESTRAIN ♦ n 1 [U] power to control: *lose
control of oneself* 2 [C;U] means of
controlling: *wage control(s)* 3 [C] place
where something is controlled: *controls of a
plane* 4 [C] standard against which the
results of a study are measured 5 **out of
control** in(to) a state of not being
controlled 6 **under control** working
properly ~**ler** n person who directs
something

con·tro·ver·sy /'kɒntrəvɜ:si, kən-
'trɒvəsi ‖ 'ka:ntrəvɜ:rsi/ n [C;U] fierce
argument –**sial** /ˌkɒntrə'vɜ:ʃəl◄ ‖ ˌka:n-
trə'vɜ:rʃəl◄/ adj causing controversy
–**sially** adv

co·nun·drum /kə'nʌndrəm/ n 1 RIDDLE
2 difficult problem

con·ur·ba·tion /ˌkɒnɜː'beɪʃən ‖ ˌka:n-
ɜ:r-/ n number of towns joined into one
large city or network

con·va·lesce /ˌkɒnvə'les ‖ ˌka:n-/ vi
spend time getting well after an illness
–**lescence** n [S;U] time spent getting well
–**lescent** n, adj (person) spending well
getting well

con·vene /kən'vi:n/ v 1 vi meet together
2 vt call (a group) to meet –**vener**, –**venor** n
person who convenes meetings

con·ve·ni·ence /kən'vi:niəns/ n 1 [U]
fitness; suitableness 2 [C] useful tool or
apparatus 3 [C] TOILET 4 [U] personal
comfort –**ent** adj 1 suited to one's needs
2 near –**ently** adv

con·vent /'kɒnvənt ‖ 'ka:nvent/ n place
where NUNS live

con·ven·tion /kən'venʃən/ n 1 [C;U]
accepted social custom 2 [C] meeting of a
group with a shared purpose 3 [C] formal
political agreement ~**al** adj following
accepted customs ~**ally** adv

con·verge /kən'vɜ:dʒ ‖ -ɜ:r-/ vi come
together and meet: *roads converging at the
station* –**vergence** n [U]

con·ver·sant /kən'vɜ:sənt ‖ -ɜ:r-/ adj
fml having knowledge or experience

con·ver·sa·tion /ˌkɒnvə'seɪʃən ‖
ˌka:nvər-/ n [C;U] informal talk ~**al** adj (of
language) used in conversation

con·verse¹ /kən'vɜ:s ‖ -ɜ:rs/ vi fml talk
informally

con·verse² /'kɒnvɜ:s ‖ kən'vɜ:rs/ adj, n
[S] fml opposite: *the converse opinion* ~**ly**
adv

con·ver·sion /kən'vɜ:ʃən ‖ -'vɜ:rʒən/ n
[C;U] act of converting

con·vert¹ /kən'vɜ:t ‖ -ɜ:rt/ vt/i 1 change
into another form: *convert dollars into
pounds* 2 change to a particular religious
belief, etc. ~**er** n apparatus that converts
something, esp. information to be put into a
computer ~**ible** adj (esp. of money) able to
be converted ~**ible** n car with a roof that
can be folded back

con·vert² /'kɒnvɜ:t ‖ 'ka:nvɜ:rt/ n
person who has accepted a particular belief

con·vex /ˌkɒn'veks◄, kən- ‖ ˌka:n-
'veks◄, kən-/ adj curved outwards

con·vey /kən'veɪ/ vt 1 take; carry 2 make
(feelings, etc.) known ~**er**, ~**or** n

con·vey·ance /kən'veɪəns/ n 1 [C] fml
vehicle 2 [U] legal paper giving the right to
property –**ancing** n [U] branch of law
concerned with legal conveyances

conveyer belt, **conveyor belt** /·'·· ·/ n
endless moving belt carrying objects from
one place to another

con·vict¹ /kən'vɪkt/ vt prove (someone)
to be guilty of a crime

con·vict² /'kɒnvɪkt ‖ 'ka:n-/ n convicted
person who is sent to prison

con·vic·tion /kən'vɪkʃən/ n [C;U]
1 being convicted of a crime 2 firm belief

con·vince /kən'vɪns/ vt cause to feel sure
of something –**vincing** adj: *a convincing
argument* –**vincingly** adv

con·viv·i·al /kən'vɪviəl/ adj merry and
friendly ~**ity** /kənˌvɪvi'ælɪti/ n [U]

con·vo·lut·ed /ˈkɒnvəluːtɪd ‖ ˈkɑːn-/ adj fml 1 twisted 2 difficult to understand –lution /ˌkɒnvəˈluːʃən ‖ ˌkɑːn-/ n twist

con·voy /ˈkɒnvɔɪ ‖ ˈkɑːn-/ n 1 group of ships or vehicles travelling together, esp. for safety 2 protecting force of warships, etc. ♦ vt go with and protect

con·vulse /kənˈvʌls/ vt shake violently –vulsive adj –vulsion /-ˈvʌlʃən/ n

coo /kuː/ vi 1 make the soft cry of a DOVE 2 speak lovingly

cook /kʊk/ v 1 vi/t prepare (food) by using heat 2 vi (of food) be cooked 3 vt change (accounts, etc.) dishonestly ♦ n person who cooks food –er n STOVE for cooking on

cook·e·ry /ˈkʊkəri/ n [U] art of cooking

cook·ie /ˈkʊki/ n esp AmE 1 BISCUIT 2 person: a smart/tough cookie.

cool¹ /kuːl/ adj 1 pleasantly cold 2 calm; unexcited: a **cool-headed** decision 3 not very friendly 4 infml used about something one admires: a really cool computer game ♦ n 1 cool temperature: the cool of the evening 2 calmness: lose one's cool ♦ adv play it cool act calmly ~ness n [U] ~ly /ˈkuːl-li/ adv

cool² vi/t make or become cool

cool down/off phr vi become calmer

coop¹ /kuːp/ n cage for small creatures

coop² coop up phr vt shut into a small space

co·op·e·rate /kəʊˈɒpəreɪt ‖ kəʊˈɑːp-/ vi work together for a shared purpose –rative /-rətɪv/ adj helpful -rative n firm, farm, etc. owned by its workers –ration /kəʊˌɒpəˈreɪʃən ‖ kəʊˌɑːp-/ n

co-opt /kəʊ ˈɒpt ‖ kəʊ ˈɑːpt/ vt (of an elected group) choose as a fellow member

co·or·di·nate /kəʊˈɔːdɪneɪt ‖ kəʊˈɔːr-/ vt cause to work together effectively: coordinate our efforts –nation /kəʊˌɔːdɪˈneɪʃən ‖ kəʊˌɔːr-/ n [U] –nator /kəʊˈɔːdɪneɪtə ‖ kəʊˈɔːrdɪneɪtər/ n

co·or·di·nates /kəʊˈɔːdɪnəts ‖ kəʊˈɔːr-/ n [P] 1 garments in matching colours that can be worn together 2 tech numbers or letters on a map that give an exact position

cop¹ /kɒp/ n sl policeman

cop² v/vt -pp- **cop it** sl esp. BrE be in serious trouble

cop out phr vi sl avoid responsibility **cop-out** /ˈ· ·/ n

cope /kəʊp ‖ koʊp/ vi deal with some-

thing successfully

cop·i·er /ˈkɒpiə ‖ ˈkɑːpiər/ n machine for making paper copies (COPY (1))

co·pi·ous /ˈkəʊpiəs ‖ ˈkoʊ-/ adj plentiful ~ly adv

cop·per¹ /ˈkɒpə ‖ ˈkɑːpər/ n 1 [U] a soft reddish-brown metal **b** its colour 2 [C] copper coin

copper² n sl policeman

copse /kɒps ‖ kɑːps/ n small group of trees

cop·u·late /ˈkɒpjʊleɪt ‖ ˈkɑːp-/ vi fml have sex –lation /ˌkɒpjʊˈleɪʃən ‖ ˌkɑːp-/ n [U]

cop·y /ˈkɒpi ‖ ˈkɑːpi/ n 1 thing made to be like another 2 single example of a book, newspaper, etc. 3 **good copy** interesting news —see also HARD COPY, SOFT COPY ♦ v 1 vt make a copy of 2 vt do the same as 3 vi/t cheat in an examination, etc. by copying

cop·y·cat /ˈkɒpikæt ‖ ˈkɑː-/ n derog infml person who copies other people's behaviour, dress, work, etc.

cop·y·right /ˈkɒpiraɪt ‖ ˈkɑː-/ n [C;U] legal right to be the only seller of a book, etc.

cor·al /ˈkɒrəl ‖ ˈkɔː-, ˈkɑː-/ n [U] white, pink, or red substance formed by small sea creatures

cord /kɔːd ‖ kɔːrd/ n [C;U] 1 thick string or thin rope 2 electric wire

cor·di·al¹ /ˈkɔːdiəl ‖ ˈkɔːrdʒəl/ adj warm and friendly ~ly adv

cordial² n [U] nonalcoholic fruit drink

cord·less /ˈkɔːdləs ‖ ˈkɔːrd-/ adj not permanently connected to an electricity supply: a cordless kettle/iron/phone

cor·don /ˈkɔːdn ‖ ˈkɔːrdn/ n ring of police, etc. surrounding an area ♦ v **cordon off** phr vt protect with a cordon

cords /kɔːdz ‖ kɔːrdz/ n [P] infml trousers made from corduroy

cor·du·roy /ˈkɔːdʒərɔɪ, -dʒ ̃ ‖ ˈkɔːrdə-/ n strong cotton cloth with raised lines on it

core /kɔː ‖ kɔːr/ n 1 central part: core of an apple 2 **to the core** thoroughly ♦ vt remove the core of (a fruit)

cork /kɔːk ‖ kɔːrk/ n 1 [U] BARK of a tree (the **cork oak**) 2 [C] piece of this used for closing a bottle ♦ vt close with a cork

cork·screw /ˈkɔːkskruː ‖ ˈkɔːrk-/ n tool used to remove CORKS (2)

corn¹ /kɔːn ‖ kɔːrn/ n [U] 1 BrE (seed of)

various grain plants, esp. wheat 2 *AmE* (seed of) a tall plant with long bunches of yellow seeds

corn[2] *n* painful lump of hard skin on the foot

cor·ne·a /ˈkɔːniə ‖ ˈkɔːr-/ *n* protective covering on the front of the eye

corned beef /ˌ· ˈ·◂/ *n* [U] kind of pressed cooked BEEF in tins

cor·ner /ˈkɔːnə ‖ ˈkɔːrnər/ *n* 1 point where two lines, edges, or roads meet 2 part of the world: *remote corners of England* 3 also **corner kick** (in football) kick taken from the corner of the field 4 **around/round the corner** near 5 **in a tight corner** in a difficult position 6 **turn the corner** become better after a period of difficulties, etc. ♦ *v* 1 *vt* force into a difficult position 2 *vt* gain control of (by buying, building, or production of goods) 3 *vi* (of a vehicle) turn a corner

cor·ner·stone /ˈkɔːnəstəʊn ‖ ˈkɔːrnərstoʊn/ *n* 1 stone set at one bottom corner of a building 2 something of great importance, on which everything else is based

cor·net /ˈkɔːnt ‖ kɔːrˈnet/ *n* 1 musical instrument like a TRUMPET 2 *BrE* CONE-shaped eatable container for ice-cream

corn·flakes /ˈkɔːnfleɪks ‖ ˈkɔːrn-/ *n* [P] bits of crushed CORN[1] (2) to be eaten with milk at breakfast

cor·nice /ˈkɔːnɪs ‖ ˈkɔːr-/ *n* decorative border at the top edge of the front of a building, a column, or the walls of a room

corn·y /ˈkɔːni ‖ ˈkɔːrni/ *adj* (of jokes, stories, etc.) not entertaining because unoriginal, sentimental, or PREDICTABLE

co·rol·la·ry /kəˈrɒləri ‖ ˈkɔːrələri, ˈkɑː-/ *n fml* something that naturally follows from something else

cor·o·nary[1] /ˈkɒrənəri ‖ ˈkɔːrəneri, ˈkɑː-/ *n* stopping of the blood flowing to the heart; kind of HEART ATTACK

coronary[2] *adj tech* relating to the heart: *coronary disease*

cor·o·na·tion /ˌkɒrəˈneɪʃən ‖ ˌkɔː-, ˌkɑː-/ *n* ceremony of crowning a king or queen

cor·o·ner /ˈkɒrənə ‖ ˈkɔːrənər, ˈkɑː-/ *n* official who enquires into the cause of a person's death if it is not clearly known

cor·o·net /ˈkɒrənɪt ‖ ˈkɔːrəˈnet, ˌkɑː-/ *n* small crown worn by nobles, etc.

cor·po·ral /ˈkɔːpərəl ‖ ˈkɔːr-/ *n* person of low rank in an army or air force

corporal pun·ish·ment /ˌ··· ˈ··/ *n* [U] punishment by hitting someone

cor·po·rate /ˈkɔːpərɪt ‖ ˈkɔːr-/ *adj* 1 shared by a whole group: *corporate responsibility* 2 of a CORPORATION (1)

cor·po·ra·tion /ˌkɔːpəˈreɪʃən ‖ ˌkɔːr-/ *n* 1 large business organization 2 town COUNCIL

corps /kɔː ‖ kɔːr/ *n* 1 **a** trained army group **b** branch of the army equal to two DIVISIONS 2 group with the same activity: *the press corps*

corpse /kɔːps ‖ kɔːrps/ *n* dead body

cor·pus·cle /ˈkɔːpəsəl, kɔːrˈpʌ- ‖ ˈkɔːrpə-/ *n* any of the red and white cells in the body

cor·ral /kɒˈrɑːl, kə- ‖ kəˈræl/ *n* enclosed area (esp. in Western America) for cattle and horses ♦ *vt* put in a corral

cor·rect[1] /kəˈrekt/ *adj* 1 without mistakes; true 2 proper: *correct behaviour* ~**ly** *adv* ~**ness** *n* [U]

correct[2] *vt* make right; show the mistakes in ~**ive** *adj*, *n* ~**ion** /kəˈrekʃən/ *n* 1 [U] correcting 2 [C] change that improves something 3 [U] punishment

cor·re·late /ˈkɒrəleɪt ‖ ˈkɔː-, ˈkɑː-/ *vi/t* (show to) have a close connection –**ation** /ˌkɒrəˈleɪʃən ‖ ˌkɔː-, ˌkɑː-/ *n* close connection

cor·re·spond /ˌkɒrəˈspɒnd ‖ ˌkɔːrəˈspɑːnd, ˌkɑː-/ *vi* 1 be equal; match 2 exchange letters ~**ing** *adj* matching; equal

cor·re·spon·dence /ˌkɒrəˈspɒndəns ‖ ˌkɔːrəˈspɑːn-, ˌkɑː-/ *n* [S;U] 1 letter-writing; letters 2 equality between things; likeness –**dent** /n 1 person with whom one exchanges letters 2 someone employed by a newspaper, television, or radio station, etc. to report news from a distant place

cor·ri·dor /ˈkɒrədɔː ‖ ˈkɔːrədɔːr, ˈkɑː-/ *n* passage between rows of rooms

cor·rob·o·rate /kəˈrɒbəreɪt ‖ kəˈrɑː-/ *vt* support (an opinion, etc.) by proof –**ration** /kəˌrɒbəˈreɪʃən ‖ kəˌrɑː-/ *n* [U]

cor·rode /kəˈrəʊd ‖ -ˈroʊd/ *vt/i* destroy slowly, esp. by chemical action

cor·ro·sion /kəˈrəʊʒən ‖ -ˈroʊ-/ *n* [U] 1 corroding 2 RUST, etc. produced by corroding –**sive** /-sɪv/ *adj*

cor·ru·gated /ˈkɒrəgeɪtɪd ‖ ˈkɔː-, ˈkɑː-/

adj having wavelike folds –**gation**
/ˌkɔrəˈɡeiʃən ‖ ˌkɔ:-, ˌka:-/ *n*

cor·rupt /kəˈrʌpt/ *adj* **1** morally bad, esp.
dishonest **2** containing mistakes ♦ *vt/i*
make or become corrupt **~ly** *adv* **~ion**
/-ˈrʌpʃən/ *n* [U]

cor·set /ˈkɔːsət ‖ ˈkɔːr-/ also **corsets** *pl. n*
— tight-fitting undergarment worn esp. by
women

cor·tege /kɔːˈteiʒ ‖ kɔːrˈteʒ/ *n* funeral
procession

cos·met·ic /kɒzˈmetik ‖ kɑːz-/ *n* cream,
powder, etc. for the skin or hair ♦ *adj* **1** of,
related to, or causing increased beauty
2 dealing only with the outside appearance
rather than the central part of something

cos·mic /ˈkɒzmik ‖ ˈkɑːz-/ *adj* of the
whole universe

cos·mo·naut /ˈkɒzmənɔːt ‖ ˈkɑːzmənɔːt/
n a Soviet ASTRONAUT

cos·mo·pol·i·tan /ˌkɒzməˈpɒlɨtən◂ ‖
ˌkɑːzməˈpɑː-/ *adj* **1** consisting of people
from many parts of the world **2** not narrow-
minded ♦ *n* cosmopolitan person

cos·mos /ˈkɒzmɒs ‖ ˈkɑːzməs/ *n* the
whole universe

cos·set /ˈkɒsɨt ‖ ˈkɑː-/ *vt* **-tt-** treat too
kindly

cost¹ /kɒst ‖ kɔːst/ *n* **1** [C] price of
something **2** [U] what is needed to gain
something **3 at all costs** whatever it may
cost **4 to one's cost** from one's own
unpleasant experience **~ly** *adj* expensive
costs [P] cost of taking a matter to a court
of law

cost² *vt* **1** (*past t. and p.* **cost**) have as a
price: *It cost me £5.* | (fig.) *The mistake cost
him his job.* **2** (*past t. and p.* **costed**)
calculate the price to be charged for (a job)

co-star /ˈkou stɑː ‖ ˈkou stɑːr/ *n* famous
actor or actress who appears with another
famous actor or actress in a film, etc. ♦ **co-
star** *vi*

cost-ef·fec·tive /ˈ· ·ˌ··◂/ *adj* bringing the
best possible profits or advantages for the
lowest possible price **~ly** *adv* **~ness** *n* [U]

cos·tume /ˈkɒstjum ‖ ˈkɑːstuːm/ *n* [C;U]
clothes, esp. as worn in plays

costume jew·el·lery /ˈ·· ˌ··/ *n* [U]
precious-looking jewellery made from
cheap materials

co·sy *BrE* ‖ **-zy** *AmE* /ˈkəuzi ‖ ˈkouzi/ *adj*
warm and comfortable **–sily** *adv* **–siness** *n*
[U]

cot /kɒt ‖ kɑːt/ *n* **1** *BrE* bed for a small
child **2** *AmE* light narrow bed which folds
flat

cot death /ˈ· ·/ *n* [C;U] unexplained death
of a healthy baby

cot·tage /ˈkɒtɪdʒ ‖ ˈkɑː-/ *n* small house,
esp. in the country

cottage cheese /ˌ·· ˈ·/ *n* [U] soft lumpy
white cheese

cot·ton¹ /ˈkɒtn ‖ ˈkɑːtn/ *n* [U] **1** soft
white hair of a tropical plant **2** thread or
cloth made from this **3** *AmE* COTTON WOOL

cotton² *v* **cotton on** *phr vi infml*
understand

cotton wool /ˌ·· ˈ·/ *n* [U] *BrE* soft mass of
cotton for cleaning wounds, etc.

couch¹ /kautʃ/ *n* long seat like a bed

couch² *vt fml* express: *His refusal was
couched in unfriendly terms.*

couch potato /ˈ· ·ˌ··/ *n* inactive person,
esp. one who watches a lot of television

cou·chette /kuːˈʃet/ *n* folding bed on a
train

cou·gar /ˈkuːɡə ‖ -ər/ *n* large American
wild cat

cough¹ /kɒf ‖ kɔːf/ *v* **1** *vi* push air out
noisily from the lungs **2** *vt* produce by doing
this: *cough up blood* ♦ *n* **1** [C] act of
coughing **2** [S] illness that makes a person
cough

cough up *phr vt infml* produce (money
or information) unwillingly

could /kəd; *strong* kud/ *v aux* **1** (describes
can in the past): *He could read when he was
four.* **2** (used to describe what someone has
said): *She asked if she could smoke.* **3** (used
to show what is possible): *I think the
accident could have been prevented.* **4** (used
to make a request): *Could you help me?*

could·n't /ˈkudnt/ *v short for:* could not

coun·cil /ˈkaunsəl/ *n* group of people
appointed or elected to manage something
♦ *adj* owned by British local government:
council flats **~lor** *n* member of a council

council tax /ˈ·· ·/ *n* [U] *BrE* tax paid to
local government

coun·sel /ˈkaunsəl/ *n* **counsel 1** [C] *law*
BARRISTER acting for someone **2** [C] *fml*
advice ♦ *v* **-ll-** *BrE* ‖ **-l-** *AmE fml* advise
~lor *BrE* ‖ **¯lor** *AmE* — *n* adviser **~ling**
BrE ‖ **¯ing** *AmE* — *n* [U] giving or
receiving advice, esp. about personal

count¹ /kaʊnt/ v 1 vi/t name (numbers)
in order: count (to) 20 2 vt find the total of
3 vt include: six people, counting me 4 vt
consider to be: count yourself lucky 5 vi
have value: Every moment counts. ♦ n 1 act
of counting; total 2 one of a number of
crimes of which a person is thought to be
guilty: guilty on all counts 3 be out for the
count (in BOXING) be COUNTED out; be
unconscious 4 keep/lose count know/no
longer know the exact number ~able adj
that can be counted: Egg is a countable
noun. ~less adj very many

count down phr vt count backwards to
zero, esp. before sending a spacecraft into
space **countdown** /'kaʊntdaʊn/ n

count in phr vt include

count on/upon phr vt depend on;
expect

count out phr vt 1 put down in turn
while counting 2 not include 3 declare (a
BOXER who fails to get up after 10 seconds) to
be the loser of a fight

count² n European nobleman

coun·te·nance /'kaʊntɪnəns/ n fml
1 [C] face 2 [U] support; approval ♦ vt fml
give approval to

coun·ter¹ /'kaʊntə ‖ -ər/ n 1 table where
people in a shop, etc. are served 2 **over the
counter** (when buying drugs) without a
PRESCRIPTION 3 **under the counter** secretly
and often unlawfully

counter² n 1 object used in some games
instead of money 2 machine that counts

counter³ vt/i meet an attack; oppose:
counter her proposal

counter⁴ adv, adj opposed; opposite: act
counter to all advice

coun·ter·act /ˌkaʊntər'ækt/ vt reduce
the effect of: counteract a poison

coun·ter·at·tack /'kaʊntərəˌtæk/ vi/t,
n (make) an attack to oppose another

coun·ter·bal·ance /'kaʊntəˌbæləns ‖
-tər-/ vt, n (act as) a force that balances
another

coun·ter·feit /'kaʊntəfɪt ‖ -tər-/ n, adj
(thing) made as a copy of something else, to
deceive: counterfeit money ♦ vt make a
counterfeit of

coun·ter·foil /'kaʊntəfɔɪl ‖ -tər-/ n part
of a cheque, etc. kept as a record

coun·ter·part /'kaʊntəpɑːt ‖ -ərpɑːrt/ n
person or thing that matches another, but in
a different system

coun·ter·pro·duc·tive /ˌkaʊntəprə-
'dʌktɪv◄ ‖ -tər-/ adj having an opposite
effect from the one intended

coun·ter·sign /'kaʊntəsaɪn ‖ -ər-/ vt add
another signature to (a paper already
signed)

coun·tess /'kaʊntɪs/ n a woman who
holds the rank of COUNT or EARL for herself
b wife of a COUNT or EARL

coun·try /'kʌntri/ n 1 [C] nation, with its
land and population 2 [S;U] also
countryside /'kʌntrisaɪd/ — land outside
towns 3 **go to the country** esp. BrE (of a
government) call a general election ♦ adj
of, in, or from the country

country and west·ern /ˌ·· · ·'··/ also
country mu·sic /ˌ· '··/ — n [U] popular
music in the style of the southern and
western US

coun·try·man /'kʌntrimən/ -woman
/-ˌwʊmən/ fem. — n -men /-mən/
1 COMPATRIOT 2 person who does not live in
a town

coun·ty /'kaʊnti/ n area divided from
others for purposes of local government

coup /kuː/ n 1 clever effective action
2 also **coup d'état** /ˌkuː deɪˈtɑː ‖ -deˈtɑː/ —
sudden and violent seizure of state power
by a small group

cou·pé /'kuːpeɪ ‖ kuːˈpeɪ/ n closed car
with two doors and a sloping back

cou·ple /'kʌpəl/ n 1 two things of the
same kind 2 two people, esp. a husband and
wife 3 a few ♦ v 1 vt join (two things)
together 2 vi (of animals) MATE –**pling** n
something that joins two things, esp. two
railway carriages

cou·pon /'kuːpɒn ‖ -pɑːn/ n ticket
showing the right of the holder to receive
something

cour·age /'kʌrɪdʒ ‖ 'kɜː-/ n [U] ability to
control fear; bravery –**ageous** /kəˈreɪdʒəs/
adj brave –**ageously** adv

cour·gette /kʊəˈʒet ‖ kʊr-/ n BrE small
green MARROW

cou·ri·er /'kʊriə ‖ -ər/ n 1 person who
looks after travellers on a tour 2 official
messenger

course /kɔːs ‖ kɔːrs/ n 1 path along which
something moves 2 area for races or certain
sports: a golf course 3 plan of action 4 a set

court 100

of lessons, treatments, etc. **b** university studies: *a 4-year course* **5** any of several parts of a meal **6 a matter of course** that which one expects to happen **7 in due course** at the right time **8 in the course of** during **9 of course** certainly **10 run/take its/their course** (of an illness, etc.) continue to its natural end **11 stay the course** continue something through to the end in spite of difficulty ♦ *vi* (of liquid) flow quickly

court¹ /kɔːt ‖ kɔːrt/ *n* **1 a** [C] room (**courtroom**) or building where law cases are judged **b** [U] people gathered together there **2** [C] area for certain ball games such as tennis **3** [C] king or queen with the royal family, officials, etc. **4** [C] **a** short street surrounded by buildings on three sides **b** block of flats **c** also **courtyard** /'kɔːtjɑːd ‖ 'kɔːrtjɑːrd/ — open space surrounded by buildings

court² *vt* **1** try to win the favour of **2** visit and pay attention to (a woman a man hopes to marry) **3** risk foolishly: *to court disaster*

cour·te·ous /'kɜːtiəs ‖ 'kɜːr-/ *adj fml* polite and kind ~**ly** *adv*

cour·te·sy /'kɜːtɪsi ‖ 'kɜːr-/ *n* **1** [C;U] polite behaviour **2 by courtesy of** with the permission of

court·ier /'kɔːtiə ‖ 'kɔːrtɪr/ *n* person in attendance at a royal court

court-mar·tial /ˌ· '··◄ ‖ ˌ· ·/ *n* (trial before) a court for offences against military law ♦ *vt* -ll- *BrE* ‖ -l- *AmE* try (someone) in a court-martial

court·ship /'kɔːt-ʃɪp ‖ 'kɔːrt-/ *n* [U] (period of time) trying to attract someone to oneself, esp. with the aim of marriage

cous·in /'kʌzən/ *n* **1** child of one's uncle or aunt **2** related person or thing —see also FIRST COUSIN, SECOND COUSIN

cove /kəʊv ‖ koʊv/ *n* small BAY¹

cov·e·nant /'kʌvənənt/ *n* **1** formal agreement **2** written promise to pay a fixed regular sum of money to a church, CHARITY (3), etc.

cov·er¹ /'kʌvə ‖ -ər/ **1** *vt* spread something over; hide in this way: *cover the body with a sheet* **2** *vt* lie on the surface of; spread over (something): *furniture covered in dust* | *The town covers five square miles.* **3** *vt* travel (a distance) **4** *vt* include: *a talk covering the whole history of medicine* **5** *vt*

report (an event) for a newspaper **6** *vt* be enough money for **7** *vt* protect from loss; insure **8** *vt* keep a gun aimed at **9** *vi/t* act in place of (someone who is absent)

cover up *phr vt* prevent (something) from being noticed **cover-up** /'·· ·/ *n*

cover up for *phr vt* hide something wrong or shameful in order to save (someone else) from punishment, blame, etc.

cover² *n* **1** [C] anything that protects or hides by covering: *cushion covers* | (fig.) *The business is a cover for illegal activity.* **2** [C] outside of a book or magazine **3** [U] shelter; protection **4** [U] insurance against loss, etc. **5 under plain/separate cover** in a plain/separate envelope ~**ing** *n* something that covers or hides

cov·er·age /'kʌvərɪdʒ/ *n* [U] time and space given to reporting an event

cov·er·alls /'kʌvərɔːlz ‖ -ɒːlz/ *n* [P] *AmE for* OVERALLS

cover charge /'·· ·/ *n* charge made by a restaurant in addition to the cost of the food and drinks or of the service

covering let·ter /ˌ··· '··/ *n* letter or note containing an explanation or additional information, sent with a parcel or another letter

cov·ert /'kʌvət ‖ 'koʊvərt/ *adj* hidden; secret ~**ly** *adv*

cov·et /'kʌvɪt/ *vt* desire (esp. someone else's possessions) eagerly ~**ous** *adj*

cow¹ /kaʊ/ *n* female of cattle and some other large animals

cow² *vt* frighten into obedience

cow·ard /'kaʊəd ‖ -ərd/ *n* person afraid of pain or danger ~**ly** *adj*

cow·ard·ice /'kaʊədɪs ‖ -ər-/ *n* [U] lack of courage

cow·boy /'kaʊbɔɪ/ *n* **1** man who looks after cattle on horseback in N America **2** *BrE sl* someone who is careless and dishonest in business

cow·er /'kaʊə ‖ -ər/ *vi* bend low from fear or shame

cow·pat /'kaʊpæt/ *n* lump of cow DUNG

cox /kɒks ‖ kɑːks/ *n* person who guides and controls a rowing boat, esp. in races ♦ *vi/t* act as cox

coy /kɔɪ/ *adj* pretending not to be self-confident ~**ly** *adv*

co·zy /'kəʊzi ‖ 'koʊzi/ *AmE for* COSY

coy·ote /'kɔɪ-əʊt, kɔɪ'əʊti‖'kaɪ-oʊt, kaɪ'oʊti/ small WOLF

CPU /ˌsiː piː 'juː/ *abbrev. for* CENTRAL PROCESSING UNIT

crab /kræb/ *n* 10-legged shellfish that can be eaten

crab·by /'kræbi/ *adj* bad-tempered

crack¹ /kræk/ *v* **1** *vi/t* break without dividing into pieces: *cracked cups* **2** *vi/t* make a sudden explosive sound: *crack a whip* **3** *vi/t* cause to break open: *crack a safe* **4** *vi* (of a voice) change suddenly in level **5** *vi/t* hit suddenly **6** *vi* lose strength or control: *crack (up) under the strain* **7** make (a joke) **8** discover the secret of (a CODE (1)) **9** (cause to) strike with a sudden blow **10 cracked up to be** believed to be **11 get cracking** be or become busy doing something in a hurried way

    crack down *phr vi* take strong action against something **crackdown** /'krækdaʊn/ *n*

crack² *n* **1** thin line caused by breaking **2** explosive sound: *crack of thunder* **3** sudden sharp blow **4** sudden change in the level of the voice **5** quick joke; clever remark **6 at the crack of dawn** very early in the morning ♦ *adj* very skilful: *crack troops*

crack³ *n* [U] *sl* extremely pure form of COCAINE, taken illegally for pleasure

cracked /krækt/ *adj infml* slightly mad

crack·er /'krækə‖-ər/ *n* **1** unsweetened BISCUIT **2** paper tube that makes a noise when pulled apart

crack·le /'krækəl/ *vi* make small sharp sounds: *The fire crackled.* **crackle** *n* [S;U]

crack·pot /'krækpɒt‖-pɑːt/ *adj* strange; mad ♦ *n* crackpot person

cra·dle /'kreɪdl/ *n* **1** small bed for a baby **2** origin of something: *the cradle of Western civilization* **3** frame to support something ♦ *vt* hold gently

craft¹ /krɑːft‖kræft/ *n* trade needing skill, esp. with one's hands

craft² *n* craft boat, aircraft, or spacecraft

crafts·man /'krɑːftsmən‖'kræ-/ craftswoman /-wʊmən/ *fem.* — *n* **-men** /-mən/ skilled worker **~ship** *n* [U]

craft·y /'krɑːfti‖'kræf-/ *adj* cleverly deceitful **-ily** *adv* **-iness** *n* [U]

crag /kræg/ *n* high steep rock **-gy** *adj* **1** steep and rough **2** (esp. of a man's face) rough in appearance

cram /kræm/ *v* **-mm- 1** *vt* force into a small space; fill too full: *box crammed with letters* **2** *vi* study hard for a short time: *cram for an examination*

cramp /kræmp/ *n* [C;U] sudden painful tightening of a muscle ♦ *vt* **1** cause to have a cramp **2** prevent natural growth or development **3 cramp someone's style** prevent someone from showing their abilities to the full **~ed** *adj* limited in space

cran·ber·ry /'krænbəri‖-beri-/ *n* small red berry: *cranberry sauce*

crane /kreɪn/ *n* **1** machine with a movable arm for lifting heavy objects **2** tall waterbird with long legs ♦ *vi/t* stretch out one's neck to see better

cra·ni·um /'kreɪniəm/ *n* bony part of the head, covering the brain **-al** *adj*

crank /kræŋk/ *n* **1** L-shaped handle for turning **2** person with strange ideas ♦ *vt* **1** move by turning a crank **2** use a CRANK (1) to start a car **~y** *adj* **1** (of people or ideas) peculiar **2** *AmE* bad-tempered

cran·ny /'kræni/ *n* small narrow opening in a wall, etc.

crap /kræp/ *n* [U] *taboo sl* **1** (act of passing) solid waste from the bowel **2** nonsense ♦ **crap** *vi* **-pp-**

crash /kræʃ/ *v* **1** *vi/t* fall or hit violently: *The car crashed into a tree.* **2** *vi* make a sudden loud noise **3** *vi* move violently and noisily: *The elephant crashed through the fence.* **4** *vi/t* (of a computer) (cause to) stop working suddenly **5** *vi* fail suddenly in business ♦ *n* **1** violent vehicle accident: *a car/plane crash* **2** sudden loud noise **3** sudden failure ♦ *adj* intended to get quick results: *a crash diet/course* ♦ *adv* with a crash

crash-land /ˌ· '·/ *vi/t* (cause a plane) to crash in a controlled way **crash landing** *n*

crass /kræs/ *adj fml* showing great stupidity and a complete lack of feeling or respect for others

crate /kreɪt/ *n* large wooden or plastic box for bottles, etc.

cra·ter /'kreɪtə‖-ər/ *n* **1** mouth of a VOLCANO **2** hole made by a bomb, etc. **3** flat-bottomed round hole on the moon's surface

cra·vat /krə'væt/ *n* wide piece of cloth worn like a TIE

crave /kreɪv/ *vi/t* have a very strong

desire for (something) **craving** n

crawl /krɔːl‖ krɔːl/ vi 1 move slowly, esp. with the body close to the ground: *crawling babies*/(fig.) *traffic* 2 be covered by crawling insects, etc. 3 have an unpleasant sensation, as of insects, etc. moving slowly over one's skin: *The idea makes my flesh crawl.* 4 *infml* try to win the favour of someone by being too nice to them ♦ n [S] 1 very slow movement 2 rapid way of swimming ~**er** n 1 something, esp. a vehicle, that goes slowly 2 person who CRAWLS (4)

cray·on /ˈkreɪən, -ɒn‖ -ɑːn, -ən/ n pencil or coloured chalk or wax **crayon** vi/t

craze /kreɪz/ n popular fashion that lasts a short time ♦ vt make excited or mad

cra·zy /ˈkreɪzi/ adj 1 mad; foolish 2 wildly excited –**zily** adv –**ziness** n [U]

creak /kriːk/ vi, n make the sound of a badly oiled door ~**y** adj

cream /kriːm/ n [U] 1 thick liquid that rises to the top of milk 2 soft mixture like this: *face cream* 3 best part: *the cream of the students* ♦ adj yellowish-white ♦ vt 1 make into a soft mixture: *creamed potatoes* 2 take cream from the surface of (milk) ~**y** adj 1 containing cream 2 like cream

cream off phr vt take the best part

crease /kriːs/ n 1 line made by folding 2 line marked on the ground for certain games ♦ vi/t press into CREASES (1)

cre·ate /kriˈeɪt/ vt 1 cause (something new) to exist; make 2 appoint to a rank; *create him a knight* –**ator** n 1 [C] person who creates something 2 [the] (cap.) God –**ation** /-ˈeɪʃən/ n 1 [U] act of creating 2 [C] something created 3 [U] the whole universe

cre·a·tive /kriˈeɪtɪv/ adj able to make new things; inventive ~**ly** adv –**tivity** /ˌkriːeɪˈtɪvəti/ n [U]

crea·ture /ˈkriːtʃə‖ -ər/ n person, animal, or being

creature com·forts /ˌ·· ˈ··/ n [P] things that make life more comfortable: *He missed the creature comforts of home.*

crèche /kreʃ‖ kreʃ, kreɪʃ/ n BrE public NURSERY for babies

cre·dence /ˈkriːdəns/ n fml acceptance as true; belief

cre·den·tials /krɪˈdenʃəlz/ n [P] written proof of a person's ability and trustworthiness

credibility gap /ˌ··ˈ··· ·/ n difference between what someone, esp. a politician, says and what they really mean or do

cred·i·ble /ˈkredəbəl/ adj that can be believed –**bly** adv –**bility** /ˌkredəˈbɪləti/ n [U]

cred·it¹ /ˈkredət/ n 1 [U] system of buying things and paying later: *buy on credit* 2 [U] quality of being likely to repay debts 3 [U] amount of money in someone's bank account 4 [U] belief; trust 5 [C;U] (cause of) public honour: *get credit for an invention* | *He's a credit to his team.* 6 [C] unit of a student's work 7 **to someone's credit a** in someone's favour **b** to/in someone's name ~**able** adj deserving approval ~**ably** adv **credits** n [P] names of actors, etc., which appear at the beginning or end of a film or television show

cred·it² vt 1 believe 2 add to an account

credit card /ˈ·· ·/ n plastic card allowing one to buy goods without paying cash

cred·i·tor /ˈkredətə‖ -ər/ n person to whom money is owed

cred·u·lous /ˈkredjʊləs‖ -dʒə-/ adj too willing to believe –**lity** /krəˈdjuːləti‖ -ˈduː-/ n [U]

creed /kriːd/ n system of (esp. religious) beliefs

creek /kriːk/ n 1 BrE narrow piece of water reaching in from the sea 2 AmE small stream

creep¹ /kriːp/ vi crept /krept/ 1 move slowly and quietly; CRAWL 2 (of a plant) grow along the ground or a surface 3 CRAWL (3) ~**er** n creeping plant ~**y** adj strange and frightening **creeps** n [P] feeling of fear and strangeness

creep² n infml unpleasant SERVILE person

creepy-crawl·y /ˌ·· ˈ··/ n infml esp. BrE creeping insect

cre·mate /krɪˈmeɪt‖ ˈkriːmeɪt/ vt burn (a dead person) –**mation** /krɪˈmeɪʃən/ n [C;U]

crem·a·to·ri·um /ˌkreməˈtɔːriəm‖ ˌkri-/ n place where bodies are cremated

crepe /kreɪp/ n 1 [U] cloth, paper, or rubber with a lined and folded surface 2 [C] very thin PANCAKE

crept /krept/ v past t. and p. of CREEP

cre·scen·do /krəˈʃendəʊ‖ -dou/ n -**dos** gradual increase of force or loudness, esp. in music

cres·cent /ˈkresənt/ n 1 curved shape of

the new moon **2** something shaped like this, e.g. a curved street

cress /kres/ n [U] small green SALAD plant

crest /krest/ n **1** growth of feathers on a bird's head **2** decoration like this on a soldier's HELMET **3** top of a hill, wave, etc. **4** picture used as a personal mark on letters, etc.

crest·fal·len /'krest,fɔːlən ‖ -,fɒː-/ adj disappointed

cret·in /'kretən ‖ 'kriːtn/ n sl very stupid person

cre·vasse /krɪ'væs/ n deep crack in ice

crev·ice /'krevɪs/ n narrow crack in rock, etc.

crew /kruː/ n **1 a** all the people working on a ship or plane **b** all of these except the officers **2** group working together: *a camera crew* ♦ vi act as ship's crew

crib /krɪb/ n **1** AmE for COT **2** book supplying a translation ♦ vt -bb- copy (someone's work) dishonestly

crick /krɪk/ n painful stiffening of the muscles, esp. in the back or neck **crick** vt

crick·et¹ /'krɪkət/ n [U] **1** outdoor ball game played by two teams of 11 players each **2 not cricket** BrE unfair — **er** n cricket player

cricket² n jumping insect that makes a loud noise

cried /kraɪd/ v past t. and p. of CRY

cries /kraɪz/ v pres. t. of CRY ♦ n pl. of CRY

crime /kraɪm/ n **1** [C;U] offence that is punishable by law **2** [S] a shame

crim·i·nal /'krɪmɪnəl/ adj of crime ♦ n person who is guilty of crime — **ly** adv

crim·son /'krɪmzən/ n, adj [U] deep red

cringe /krɪndʒ/ vi **1** bend low from fear; COWER **2** behave without self-respect towards someone

crin·kle /'krɪŋkəl/ n fold made by crushing ♦ vi/t make or get crinkles

crip·ple /'krɪpəl/ n derog person who cannot use the limbs, esp. the legs, properly ♦ vt **1** make into a cripple **2** damage seriously: *crippling debts*

cri·sis /'kraɪsɪs/ n -ses /-siːz/ moment of great danger or difficulty — see also MID-LIFE CRISIS

crisp /krɪsp/ adj **1** hard, dry, and easily broken: *crisp bacon* **2** (of weather) cold and dry **3** (of style, manners, etc.) quick and clear: *crisp reply* ♦ n BrE thin piece of

FRIED potato ♦ vi/t cook until crisp — **ly** adv — **ness** n [U] — **y** adj

criss·cross /'krɪskrɒs ‖ -krɔːs/ vi/t, n (make) a network of crossed lines

cri·te·ri·on /kraɪ'tɪəriən ‖ -'tɪr-/ n -ria /-riə/ standard on which a judgment is based

crit·ic /'krɪtɪk/ n **1** person who gives judgments about art, music, etc. **2** person who expresses disapproval — **al** adj **1** finding fault **2** of a critic's works **3** of or at a CRISIS: *critical decisions* — **ism** /'krɪtɪsɪzəm/ n [C;U] **1** work of a critic **2** disapproval — **ize** also — **ise** BrE — vi/t **1** make judgments **2** find fault

cri·tique /krɪ'tiːk/ n book or article criticizing the work of a writer

croak /krəʊk ‖ krəʊk/ **1** vi/t make the deep low noise a FROG makes **2** vi/t speak with a rough voice as if one has a sore throat **3** vi sl die

cro·chet /'krəʊʃeɪ ‖ krəʊ'ʃeɪ/ vi/t make clothes, etc. from wool, using a special hook ♦ n [U]

crock /krɒk ‖ krɑːk/ n [S] sl something untrue or unbelievable

crock·e·ry /'krɒkəri ‖ 'krɑː-/ n [U] cups, plates, pots, etc.

croc·o·dile /'krɒkədaɪl ‖ 'krɑː-/ n **1** [C] large tropical river REPTILE **2** [U] its skin, used as leather **3** [C] line of people, esp. children, walking in pairs

crocodile tears /'··· ,·/ n [P] insincere sorrow

cro·cus /'krəʊkəs ‖ 'krəʊ-/ n small spring plant with purple, yellow, or white flowers

crois·sant /'krwɑːsɒŋ ‖ krɒː'sɑːnt/ n soft piece of curved bread

cro·ny /'krəʊni ‖ 'krəʊni/ n infml friend or companion

crook /krʊk/ n **1** infml thief **2** bend or curve: *the crook of her arm* ♦ vi/t bend — **ed** /'krʊkɪd/ adj **1** not straight **2** dishonest

croon /kruːn/ vi/t sing gently in a low soft voice

crop¹ /krɒp ‖ krɑːp/ n **1** plant grown by a farmer **2** amount gathered in a season: (fig.) *this year's crop of students*

crop² vt -pp- **1** (of animals) bite off the tops of (grass etc.) **2** cut (hair, etc.) short

  crop up phr vi happen unexpectedly

crop·per /'krɒpə ‖ 'krɑːpər/ n infml

come a **cropper** fall heavily; fail

cro·quet /ˈkrəʊkeɪ, -kɪ ‖ krəʊˈkeɪ/ n [U] garden game in which players knock wooden balls through HOOPs

cross¹ /krɒs ‖ krɔːs/ n 1 the mark X or + 2 a upright post with a bar across it, esp. that on which Christ died b this shape as a sign of the Christian faith 3 sorrow; pain 4 mixture of two things

cross² v 1 vi/t go or put across 2 vt oppose (someone's wishes, etc.) 3 vi (of letters) pass in opposite directions 4 vt mix different breeds of (animals or plants) 5 vt draw two lines across (a cheque) to show that it must be paid into a bank account 6 **cross oneself** make the sign of the cross with the hand 7 **cross one's mind** come into one's thoughts 8 **keep one's fingers crossed** hope that nothing will happen to upset one's plans ~**ing** n 1 journey across the sea 2 place where a road, etc. may be crossed

   cross off/out phr vt draw a line through (writing)

cross³ adj angry ~**ly** adv ~**ness** n [U]

cross·bow /ˈkrɒsbəʊ ‖ ˈkrɔːsbəʊ/ n weapon combining a BOW² (1) and a gun

cross·breed /ˈkrɒsbriːd ‖ ˈkrɔːs-/ n animal or plant of mixed breed –**bred** /-bred/ adj

cross-check /ˌkrɒsˈtʃek ‖ ˌkrɔːs-/ vt test (a calculation, etc.) by using a different method

cross-coun·try /ˌ· ˈ··◂/ adj, adv across the fields or open country

cross-dress·ing /ˈ· ˌ··/ n TRANSVESTISM

cross-ex·am·ine /ˌ· ··ˈ··/ vt question (esp. a witness in court) closely, to test answers given before

cross-eyed /ˈ· ·/ adj with the eyes looking in towards the nose

cross·fire /ˈkrɒsfaɪə ‖ ˈkrɔːsfaɪr/ n [U] gunfire across one's direction of movement

cross-legged /ˌkrɒs ˈlegd◂ ‖ ˌkrɔːs ˈlegɪd◂/ adj having the knees wide apart and ankles crossed

cross-pur·pos·es /ˌ· ˈ····/ n be at cross-purposes misunderstand one another

cross-ref·er·ence /ˌ· ˈ·· ‖ ˈ· ˌ··/ n note directing the reader to another place in the book

cross·roads /ˈkrɒsrəʊdz ‖ ˈkrɔːsrəʊdz/ n -roads 1 place where roads cross 2 point

where a decision must be taken

cross-sec·tion /ˈ· ˌ··/ n 1 (drawing of) a surface made by cutting across 2 typical example of a whole

cross·word /ˈkrɒs·wɜːd ‖ ˈkrɔːs·wɜːrd/ n printed game in which words are fitted into numbered squares

crotch /krɒtʃ ‖ krɑːtʃ/ n place between the tops of a person's legs

crotch·et /ˈkrɒtʃɪt ‖ ˈkrɑː-/ n a musical note

crotch·et·y /ˈkrɒtʃɪti ‖ ˈkrɑː-/ adj infml bad-tempered

crouch /kraʊtʃ/ vi lower the body by bending the knees

crou·pi·er /ˈkruːpɪə ‖ -ər/ n person who collects and pays out money at a CASINO

crow¹ /krəʊ ‖ krəʊ/ n 1 large shiny black bird 2 **as the crow flies** in a straight line

crow² vi 1 make the loud cry of a COCK 2 speak proudly

crow·bar /ˈkrəʊbɑː ‖ ˈkrəʊbɑːr/ n iron bar for raising heavy objects

crowd /kraʊd/ n 1 large number of people together 2 particular social group: *the college crowd* ♦ v 1 vi come together in a crowd 2 vt (esp. of people) fill: *a crowded bus*

crown /kraʊn/ n 1 [C] ring-shaped head decoration, esp. for a king or queen 2 [the+S] royal power 3 [C] top of a head, hat, hill, etc. 4 [C] old British coin ♦ vt 1 place a crown on the head of 2 cover the top of: *mountains crowned with snow* 3 complete worthily 4 **to crown it all** to complete good or bad luck ~**ing** adj above all things

crow's feet /ˈ· ·/ n [P] lines on the skin near the eye; WRINKLES

crow's nest /ˈ· ·/ n small shelter near top of a ship's MAST from which a person can watch for danger, etc.

cru·cial /ˈkruːʃəl/ adj of the greatest importance ~**ly** adv

cru·ci·ble /ˈkruːsɪbəl/ n pot for melting metals in

cru·ci·fix /ˈkruːsɪfɪks/ n cross with a figure of Christ on it

cru·ci·fix·ion /ˌkruːsɪˈfɪkʃən/ n [C;U] death by nailing to a cross

cru·ci·fy /ˈkruːsɪfaɪ/ vt 1 kill by crucifixion 2 be very cruel to, esp. publicly

crude /kruːd/ adj 1 in a natural state;

untreated **2** without sensitive feeling: *crude jokes* **3** badly made ♦ *n* [U] crude oil ~**ly** *adv* **crudity** *n* [C;U]

cru·el /ˈkruːəl/ *adj* **-ll- 1-** liking to cause suffering **2** causing suffering: *cruel disappointment* ~**ly** *adv* ~**ty** *n* [C;U]

cruise /kruːz/ *v* **1** *vi* sail slowly for pleasure **2** *vi* (of a car, etc.) move at a steady speed **3** *vi/t* look (in public places) for a sexual partner, esp. one of the same sex ♦ *n* sea voyage for pleasure **cruiser** *n* **1** fast warship **2** motorboat with a CABIN

cruise mis·sile /ˌ· ˈ··/ *n* GUIDED MISSILE that flies low and can examine the ground

crumb /krʌm/ *n* small piece of dry food, esp. bread: (fig.) *crumbs of information*

crum·ble /ˈkrʌmbəl/ *v* **1** *vi/t* break into small pieces **2** *vi* come to ruin **-bly** *adj* easily crumbled

crum·ple /ˈkrʌmpəl/ *v* **1** *vi/t* crush into irregular folds **2** *vi* lose strength

crunch /krʌntʃ/ *v* **1** *vt* crush (food) noisily with the teeth **2** *vi* make a crushing noise ♦ *n* [S] **1** crunching sound **2** CRISIS: *when it comes to the crunch* ~**y** *adj:* *crunchy carrots*

cru·sade /kruːˈseɪd/ *n* **1** Christian war against the Muslims in the Middle Ages **2** any united struggle: *a crusade for women's rights* ♦ *vi* take part in a crusade **-sader** *n*

crush /krʌʃ/ *v* **1** *vi/t* break or spoil by pressure **2** *vi* press; push: *They crushed through the gates.* **3** *vt* destroy completely: (fig.) *He felt crushed by her cruel remark* ♦ *n* **1** [S] crowd of people pressed together **2** [C] strong, foolish, and short-lived love for someone

crust /krʌst/ *n* [C;U] hard outer surface of something, esp. bread ~**y** *adj* **1** with a hard crust **2** bad-tempered

crus·ta·cean /krʌˈsteɪʃən/ *n* shellfish

crutch /krʌtʃ/ *n* **1** stick to help someone to walk **2** something that gives moral support: *He uses religion as a crutch.* **3** CROTCH

crux /krʌks/ *n* central part of a problem

cry¹ /kraɪ/ *v* **1** *vi* produce tears from the eyes **2** *vi/t* call out loudly: *'Help!' he cried.* **3** *vi* (of a bird or animal) make its natural sound **4 cry one's eyes out** cry very bitterly **5 for crying out loud** *sl* (used to give strength to a demand, etc.): *Oh, for crying out loud, shut that door!*

cry off *phr vi* refuse to fulfil a promise

cry out for *phr vt* need very badly

cry² *n* **1** [C] shout expressing something: *cries of joy* | *a war cry* | *a cry for help* **2** [S] period of crying **3** bird's or animal's natural sound **4 a far cry from** a great deal different from (something)

cry·ba·by /ˈkraɪˌbeɪbi/ *n* [C] person who cries too readily with little cause

crypt /krɪpt/ *n* room under a church

cryp·tic /ˈkrɪptɪk/ *adj* with a hidden meaning

crys·tal /ˈkrɪstl/ *n* **1** [C;U] (piece of) transparent ice-like mineral **2** [U] expensive colourless glass **3** [C] regular shape formed naturally by some substances such as sugar **4** [C] *AmE* transparent cover of a clock or watch face ~**lize** also **-lise** *BrE* — *v* **1** *vi/t* form into crystals **2** *vi/t* make (ideas, etc.) fixed in form **3** *vt* preserve (fruit) with sugar

crystal ball /ˌ·· ˈ·/ *n* ball used by FORTUNE-TELLERS to look into the future: (fig.) *The crystal ball gazers are predicting hard times.*

cub /kʌb/ *n* young lion, bear, etc.

cub·by·hole /ˈkʌbihəʊl ‖ -hoʊl/ *n* small room or cupboard

cube /kjuːb/ *n* **1** solid object with six equal square sides **2** result of multiplying a number by itself twice ♦ *vt* multiply a number by itself twice: *3 cubed is 27.*

cu·bic /ˈkjuːbɪk/ *adj* multiplying length by width and height: *a cubic metre*

cu·bi·cle /ˈkjuːbɪkəl/ *n* small division of a large room

cuck·oo /ˈkʊkuː ‖ ˈkuːkuː, ˈkʊ-/ *n* bird that lays its eggs in other birds' nests and makes a noise like its name

cu·cum·ber /ˈkjuːkʌmbə ‖ -ər/ *n* long green vegetable eaten raw

cud /kʌd/ *n* [U] **1** food swallowed and brought up again by cows, etc. for further eating **2 chew the cud** think deeply before making a decision

cud·dle /ˈkʌdl/ *v* **1** *vt* hold lovingly in one's arms **2** *vi* lie close and comfortably ♦ *n* [S] cuddling; HUG **-dly** *adj* suitable for cuddling

cud·gel /ˈkʌdʒəl/ *n* **1** CLUB (2) **2 take up the cudgels** join in a struggle

cue¹ /kjuː/ *n* **1** signal for the next actor to speak in a play **2** sign of what to do or how to behave

cue² *n* stick for pushing the ball in

BILLIARDS

cuff¹ /kʌf/ *n* 1 end of a SLEEVE 2 **off the cuff** (of an answer, etc.) without preparation

cuff² *vt* hit lightly; SMACK **cuff** *n*

cuff link /'··/ *n* button-like object used for fastening cuffs

cui·sine /kwi'ziːn/ *n* [U] style of cooking

cul-de-sac /'kʌl də ˌsæk, 'kʊl-‖ˌkʌl də 'sæk, ˌkʊl-/ *n* street closed at one end

cul·i·na·ry /'kʌlɪnəri‖'kʌlɪneri, 'kjuːl-/ *adj* of, related to the kitchen or cooking

cull /kʌl/ 1 *vt fml* gather (information, etc.) 2 *vi/t* take from a group and kill (a weak or unproductive animal) ♦ *n* 1 act of CULLing (2) 2 animal killed this way

cul·len·der /'kʌlɪndə‖-ər/ *n* COLANDER

cul·mi·nate /'kʌlmɪneɪt/ *v*

culminate in *phr vt fml* reach the last and highest point: *The battle culminated in victory.* –**nation** /ˌkʌlmɪ'neɪʃən/ *n* [S]

cul·pa·ble /'kʌlpəbəl/ *adj fml* deserving blame –**bly** *adv* –**bility** /ˌkʌlpə'bɪlɪti/ *n* [U]

cul·prit /'kʌlprɪt/ *n* guilty person

cult /kʌlt/ *n* 1 system of worship 2 popular fashion: *cult films*

cul·ti·vate /'kʌltɪveɪt/ *vt* 1 **a** prepare (land) for crops **b** grow (crops) 2 improve or develop by careful attention, study, etc. 3 pay friendly attention to (people) –**vated** *adj* educated and well-mannered –**vation** /ˌkʌltɪ'veɪʃən/ *n* [U]

cul·ture /'kʌltʃə‖-ər/ *n* 1 [C;U] art, thought, and customs of a society: *tribal cultures* 2 [U] high development in art and thought 3 [U] raising animals and growing plants –**tural** *adj*: *cultural activities* –**tured** *adj* 1 cultivated 2 produced by humans: *cultured pearls*

cum·ber·some /'kʌmbəsəm‖-bər-/ *adj* heavy and awkward to carry

cu·mu·la·tive /'kjuːmjʊlətɪv/ *adj* increasing by one addition after another ~**ly** *adv*

cun·ning /'kʌnɪŋ/ *adj* clever in deceiving ♦ *n* [U] quality of being cunning ~**ly** *adv*

cunt /kʌnt/ *n taboo* 1 VAGINA 2 foolish or nasty person

cup /kʌp/ *n* 1 container, usu. with a handle, to drink from 2 cup-shaped thing: *bra cups* 3 gold or silver container given as a prize in competitions 4 *AmE* HOLE (5) in GOLF ♦ *vt* -**pp**- form (one's hands) into a cup shape

cup·board /'kʌbəd‖-ərd/ *n* piece of furniture with doors

cup fi·nal /'·ˌ··/ *n BrE* (esp. in football) last match to decide the winning team in a competition

cu·ra·ble /'kjʊərəbəl‖'kjʊr-/ *adj* that can be cured

cu·rate /'kjʊərɪt‖'kjʊr-/ *n* priest of the lowest rank, who helps another

cu·ra·tor /kjʊ'reɪtə‖-ər/ *n* person in charge of a MUSEUM, etc.

curb /kɜːb‖kɜːrb/ *n* 1 controlling influence; CHECK (2) 2 *AmE for* KERB ♦ *vt* hold back; control

curd /kɜːd‖kɜːrd/ *n* [C;U] thick soft substance that separates from milk when it becomes sour

cur·dle /'kɜːdl‖'kɜːrdl/ *vi/t* (cause to) form into CURDS; (cause to) thicken

cure /kjʊə‖kjʊr/ *vt* 1 **a** bring back to health: (fig.) *a plan to cure unemployment* **b** make (a disease) go away 2 preserve (food, skin, tobacco) by drying, etc. ♦ *n* 1 something that cures a person or disease 2 a return to health after illness

cur·few /'kɜːfjuː‖'kɜːr-/ *n* [C;U] time or signal for people to stay indoors

cu·ri·o /'kjʊəriəʊ‖'kjʊrioʊ/ *n* -os rare or beautiful small object

cu·ri·os·i·ty /ˌkjʊəri'ɒsɪti‖ˌkjʊri'ɑːs-/ *n* 1 [S;U] desire to know 2 [C] interesting rare object

cu·ri·ous /'kjʊəriəs‖'kjʊr-/ *adj* 1 eager to learn 2 peculiar ~**ly** *adv*

curl¹ /kɜːl‖kɜːrl/ *n* 1 hanging twist of hair 2 thing this shape: *curls of smoke* ~**y** *adj* having curls

curl² *vi/t* twist; wind ~**er** *n* object that hair is twisted around to make curls

curl up *phr vi/t* (cause to) lie comfortably with the limbs drawn close to the body: *curl up with a good book*

cur·rant /'kʌrənt‖'kɜːr-/ *n* dried GRAPE

cur·ren·cy /'kʌrənsi‖'kɜːr-/ *n* 1 [C;U] money in use in a country 2 [U] state of being generally believed

cur·rent¹ /'kʌrənt‖'kɜːr-/ *adj* 1 of the present time: *current fashion* 2 commonly accepted 3 (of money) used as currency

current² *n* 1 flow of liquid, gas, or electricity 2 general tendency or course of events

current ac·count /ˈ·· ·ˌ·/ n BrE bank account from which money can be taken out at any time

cur·ric·u·lum /kəˈrɪkjɐ̈ləm/ n -la /-lə/ or -lums course of study in a school, etc.

curriculum vi·tae /kəˌrɪkjɐ̈ləm ˈviːtaɪ/ n cv

cur·ry¹ /ˈkʌri ‖ ˈkɜːri/ n [C;U] hot-tasting Indian dish of meat, vegetables, etc. ♦ vt make into curry

curry² v curry favour try to win approval dishonestly

curse /kɜːs ‖ kɜːrs/ n 1 words calling for evil to come to someone 2 cause of misfortune: Foxes are a curse to farmers. 3 word or words used in swearing ♦ vi/t 1 call down evil upon 2 use violent language (against) 2 **be cursed with** suffer from **cursed** /ˈkɜːsɐ̈d ‖ ˈkɜːr-/ adj hateful; annoying

cur·sor /ˈkɜːsə ‖ ˈkɜːrsər/ n mark which can be moved around a computer SCREEN

cur·so·ry /ˈkɜːsəri ‖ ˈkɜːr-/ adj (of work, reading, etc.) not thorough **-rily** adv

curt /kɜːt ‖ kɜːrt/ adj (of speech) impolitely short **~ly** adv **~ness** n [U]

cur·tail /kɜːˈteɪl ‖ ˈkɜːr-/ vt fml shorten; reduce **~ment** n [C;U]

cur·tain /ˈkɜːtn ‖ ˈkɜːrtn/ n 1 cloth hung over a window, or in front of a theatre stage: (fig.) curtain of smoke 2 [P] sl the end, esp. of a person's life

curt·sy /ˈkɜːtsi ‖ ˈkɜːr-/ vi, n (make) a woman's act of bending the knees and lowering the head to show respect

cur·va·ture /ˈkɜːvətʃə ‖ ˈkɜːrvətʃər/ n [C;U] state of being curved

curve /kɜːv ‖ kɜːrv/ n line that is not straight and has no angles —see also LEARNING CURVE ♦ vi/t: The road curves to the right.

cush·ion /ˈkʊʃən/ n bag filled with something soft, for lying or sitting on: (fig.) a cushion of air ♦ vt 1 lessen the force of 2 protect from hardship

cush·y /ˈkʊʃi/ adj (of a job, style of life, etc.) easy

cus·tard /ˈkʌstəd ‖ -ərd/ n [U] sweet yellow mixture of eggs and milk

cus·to·di·an /kʌˈstəʊdiən ‖ -ˈstoʊ-/ n person in charge of a public building

cus·to·dy /ˈkʌstədi/ n [U] 1 right to look after someone: give him custody of his child

2 being guarded or imprisoned: in police custody

cus·tom /ˈkʌstəm/ n 1 [C;U] established social behaviour 2 [C] something someone does regularly 3 [U] regular support given to a shop by its customers **customs** n [P] 1 taxes on goods entering or leaving a country 2 place where these taxes are collected

cus·tom·a·ry /ˈkʌstəməri ‖ -meri/ adj established by custom; usual

custom-built /ˌ·· ˈ·◂/ adj made especially for someone

cus·tom·er /ˈkʌstəmə ‖ -ər/ n person who buys things from a shop

cus·to·mize also **-ise** BrE /ˈkʌstəmaɪz/ vt change to make suitable for a particular person, job, etc.

cut¹ /kʌt/ v cut, -tt- 1 vt/i something sharp to divide, remove, shorten, make a hole, etc.: cut your fingers/your hair/the corn 2 vi a be able to be cut b (of a knife, etc.) be sharp 3 vt make shorter or smaller: cut a long speech 4 vt make (esp. a public service) less in size, amount, etc.: They're cutting postal deliveries/bus services. 5 vt stay away on purpose: cut a lecture 6 vt put (a film) into final form 7 vt hurt the feelings of (someone): cutting remarks 8 vt (of a line, path, etc.) cross 9 vi stop filming a scene 10 **cut both ways** have both advantages and disadvantages 11 **cut corners** do something quickly and cheaply but not perfectly 12 **cut it fine** leave oneself too little time or money 13 **cut no/not much ice** have no/little influence 14 **cut one's losses** stop doing something before one loses any more money 15 **cut someone dead** refuse to recognize them

cut across phr vt 1 go across instead of round 2 make a different division in: cut across party lines

cut back phr v 1 vt PRUNE (a plant) 2 vi/t reduce **cutback** /ˈkʌtbæk/ n planned reduction

cut down phr vt 1 v bring down by cutting 2 vi/t reduce: cut down (on) smoking 3 knock down or kill (someone) 4 **cut down to size** reduce from too great importance to true or suitable importance

cut in phr vi 1 interrupt 2 drive between moving vehicles

cut off phr vt 1 separate by cutting

2 disconnect (telephone, gas, electricity, etc.) 3 separate from others: *cut off by floods* 4 *lit* kill: *cut off in his prime* 5 DISINHERIT

cut out *phr v* 1 *vt* remove by cutting 2 *vt* make by cutting: *cut out a dress* 3 *vt/i* stop: *cut out smoking | engine keeps cutting out* 4 **not cut out for** not suitable for

cut up *phr vt* 1 cut into little pieces 2 make unhappy

cut² *n* 1 opening made by cutting 2 piece of meat, etc. cut off 3 reduction: *cuts in government spending* 4 way in which clothes, hair, etc. are shaped 5 *infml* someone's share of a profit 6 a act of removing a part, to improve or shorten b part removed 7 **a cut above** better

cut-and-dried /ˌ· · '·◂/ *adj* 1 unlikely to change; fixed

cut and thrust /ˌ· · '·/ *n* [the+S] the strong methods of arguing or behaving typical of a very competitive activity

cute /kjuːt/ *adj* 1 delightfully pretty 2 (too) clever

cu·ti·cle /'kjuːtɪkəl/ *n* skin at the base of one's nails

cut·lass /'kʌtləs/ *n* short sword with a curved blade

cut·ler·y /'kʌtləri/ *n* [U] knives, forks, spoons, etc.

cut·let /'kʌtlɪt/ *n* small piece of meat

cut-price /ˌ· '·◂/ *adj* (of goods) cheap

cut·throat /'kʌtθrəʊt ‖ -θroʊt/ *adj* fierce; unprincipled: *cutthroat competition*

cut·ting /'kʌtɪŋ/ *n* 1 piece cut from a plant to form a new one 2 *BrE* piece cut from a newspaper 3 unroofed passage cut through a hill for a railway, etc.

cut·ting edge /ˌ·· '·/ *n* [S] **at/on the cutting edge** involved in the most important/recent/exciting stage of something **cutting-edge** *adj*: *cutting-edge technology*

CV /ˌsiː 'viː/ *n* short written account of a person's education and past employment

cy·a·nide /'saɪənaɪd/ *n* [U] strong poison

cy·ber·ca·fe /'saɪbəˌkæfeɪ ‖ -bərkæˌfeɪ/ *n* place where one can use computers connected to the INTERNET and buy cups of coffee, etc.

cy·ber·net·ics /ˌsaɪbə'netɪks ‖ -bər-/ *n* [U] science of how information is dealt with by machines, animals, and organizations

cy·ber·space /'saɪbəspeɪs ‖ -bər-/ *n* [U] all the computer connections around the world, considered as a real place where information exists

cy·cle¹ /'saɪkəl/ *n* (time needed for) a set of events in regularly repeated order: *a 50-minute cycle* **cyclical** /'sɪklɪkəl, 'saɪ-/ *adj fml* happening in cycles

cycle² *v, n* bicycle cyclist *n*

cy·clone /'saɪkləʊn ‖ -kloʊn/ *n* very violent wind moving rapidly in a circle

cyl·in·der /'sɪləndə ‖ -ər/ *n* 1 object or container with a circular base and straight sides 2 tube for a PISTON in an engine

cym·bal /'sɪmbəl/ *n* one of a pair of metal plates struck together to make a noise in music

cyn·ic /'sɪnɪk/ *n* person who sees little good in anything and shows it by making unkind remarks ~**al** *adj* ~**ally** /-kli/ *adv* ~**ism** /'sɪnɪsɪzəm/ *n* [U]

cy·press /'saɪprɪs/ *n* EVERGREEN tree with dark green leaves and hard wood

cyst /sɪst/ *n* hollow growth in the body, containing liquid

cyst·i·tis /sɪ'staɪtɪs/ *n* [U] infection of the BLADDER

czar /zɑː ‖ zɑːr/ *n* TSAR

D

D, d /diː/ the 4th letter of the English alphabet

d *written abbrev. for:* 1 died 2 DIAMETER 3 PENNY (2)

DA /ˌdiː 'eɪ/ *n* District Attorney

dab /dæb/ *v* 1 *vt* **-bb-** touch or cover lightly ♦ *n* small quantity of paint, etc.

dab·ble /'dæbəl/ *v* 1 *vi* work at something not professionally: *dabble in politics* 2 *vt* move (one's feet, etc.) playfully about in water

dab hand /ˌ· '·/ *n BrE sl* person who is clever or good at something

dad /dæd/ *n infml* father

dad·dy /'dædi/ n (child's word for) father

daddy-long-legs /ˌ· '·'/ n common long-legged insect

daf·fo·dil /'dæfədɪl/ n bell-shaped yellow spring flower

daft /dɑːft ‖ dæft/ adj BrE silly ~**ly** adv ~**ness** n [U]

dag·ger /'dægə ‖ -ər/ n 1 short knife used as a weapon 2 **look daggers at** look angrily at

dah·li·a /'deɪliə ‖ 'dæliə/ n big brightly coloured garden flower

dai·ly /'deɪli/ adj, adv every day ♦ n 1 newspaper sold every day but Sunday 2 also **daily help** /ˌ· '·/ — infml esp. BrE someone, esp. a woman, who comes to clean a house daily but does not live there

dain·ty /'deɪnti/ adj small, pretty, and delicate –**tily** adv –**tiness** n [U]

dair·y¹ /'deəri ‖ 'deri/ n place where milk, butter, cheese, etc. are produced or sold

dairy² adj relating to (the production of) milk, butter, cheese, etc.

da·is /'deɪɪs, deɪs/ n raised floor at one end of a hall

dai·sy /'deɪzi/ n 1 common small white flower that grows in grass 2 **as fresh as a daisy** not tired

dale /deɪl/ n valley

dam¹ /dæm/ n wall built to keep back water

dam² vt -**mm**- make a dam across **dam up** control (a feeling, esp. of anger) in an unhealthy way

dam·age /'dæmɪdʒ/ n [U] harm; loss: brain damage ♦ vt cause damage to **damages** n [P] money paid for damage done

dame /deɪm/ n 1 AmE sl woman 2 (cap.) British rank of honour for a woman

damn /dæm/ vt 1 (of God) punish 2 declare to be bad 3 ruin: damning evidence 4 **Well, I'll be damned!** infml I'm very surprised ♦ n [S] **not give a damn** not care at all ♦ interj (used in curses): Damn it! **damn** also ~**ed** adj, adv (used for giving force to an expression): run damned (=very) fast | He's a damn fool. **damnedest** /'dæmdɪst/ n **do one's damnedest** do everything possible

damp¹ /dæmp/ adj rather wet ♦ n [U] slight wetness ~**ness** n [U]

damp² also **damp·en** /'dæmpən/ vt 1 wet slightly 2 reduce (eagerness, etc.): damp their spirits

damp down phr vt make (a fire) burn more slowly

damp course /'· ·/ n material built into a wall to stop wetness from coming up

damp·er /'dæmpə ‖ -ər/ n 1 metal plate controlling the flow of air to a fire 2 influence reducing eagerness

damp squib /ˌ· '·/ n something which is intended to be exciting, effective, etc. but which fails and disappoints

dam·son /'dæmzən/ n kind of small PLUM

dance /dɑːns ‖ dæns/ n 1 [C] (music for) a set of movements performed to music 2 [C] party with dances 3 [U] art of dancing —see also SONG AND DANCE ♦ vi/t do a dance **dancer** n

dan·de·li·on /'dændɪlaɪən/ n common bright yellow flower

dan·druff /'dændrəf, -drʌf/ n bits of dead skin in the hair

dan·ger /'deɪndʒə ‖ -ər/ n 1 [U] possibility of harm 2 [C] cause of danger ~**ous** adj not safe ~**ously** adv

dan·gle /'dæŋgəl/ vi/t 1 hang loosely 2 **keep someone dangling** keep someone waiting and not knowing what the result will be

dank /dæŋk/ adj unpleasantly wet and cold

dap·per /'dæpə ‖ -ər/ adj neatly dressed

dap·pled /'dæpəld/ adj having cloudy spots of colour or shadow

dare /deə ‖ der/ v 1 vi be brave enough (to): He didn't dare (to) ask. 2 vt CHALLENGE to do something: I dared her to jump. ♦ n CHALLENGE: She jumped for a dare.

dare·dev·il /'deədevəl ‖ 'der-/ n foolishly adventurous person

daren't /deənt ‖ dernt/ v short for: dare not

dare·say /ˌdeə'seɪ ‖ ˌder-/ v I **daresay** esp. BrE I suppose (that); perhaps

dar·ing /'deərɪŋ ‖ 'der-/ n [U] adventurous bravery ♦ adj brave 2 shocking ~**ly** adv

dark /dɑːk ‖ dɑːrk/ adj 1 without (much) light: dark room 2 tending towards black: dark green 3 secret; hidden: keep it dark 4 evil; sad ♦ n [U] 1 absence of light 2 **after/before dark** after/before night 3 **in the dark** not knowing something ~**en** vi/t make or become darker ~**ly** adv ~**ness** n [U]

Dark Ages /ˈ· ˌ·/ n [the+P] period in Europe between about AD 476 and AD 1000

dark horse /ˌ· ˈ·/ n person who says nothing about his/her experiences, achievements, etc.

dark·room /ˈdɑːkruːm, -rom ‖ ˈdɑːrk-/ n room where photographs are processed

dar·ling /ˈdɑːlɪŋ ‖ ˈdɑːr-/ adj, n dearly loved (person)

darn¹ /dɑːn ‖ dɑːrn/ vt/i mend (holes in cloth) ◆ n darned hole

darn² n, adj, adv, interj DAMN

dart /dɑːt ‖ dɑːrt/ n 1 pointed object to throw, esp. in a game called **darts** 2 quick movement ◆ vi/t move or send suddenly

dash /dæʃ/ v 1 vi run quickly 2 vi/t strike violently: The waves dashed the boat against the rocks. 3 vt destroy (hopes, etc.) ◆ n 1 [C] sudden quick run or short race 2 [C] small amount added: a dash of pepper 3 [C] the mark (-) 4 [U] combination of bravery and style: I admire his dash. ~ing adj having a lot of DASH (4)

dash·board /ˈdæʃbɔːd ‖ -bɔːrd/ n instrument board in a car

da·ta /ˈdeɪtə, ˈdɑːtə/ n [P;U] facts; information, esp. as stored in a computer's **data bank** for **data processing**

da·ta·base /ˈdeɪtəˌbeɪs/ n computer's collection of data

date¹ /deɪt/ n 1 day, month, or year of an event 2 arrangement to meet 3 person of the opposite sex whom one arranges to meet socially 4 **out of date:** a old-fashioned b no longer VALID 5 **to date** up till now 6 **up to date** modern

date² v 1 vt guess the date of 2 vt write the date on 3 vi become old-fashioned 4 vi/t make a social date with **dated** adj old-fashioned

date from also **date back to** phr vt have lasted since

date³ n small tropical fruit with a long stone

daub /dɔːb ‖ dɒːb/ vt cover with something sticky

daugh·ter /ˈdɔːtə ‖ ˈdɒːtər/ n someone's female child

daughter-in-law /ˈ··· ·/ n daughters-in-law son's wife

daunt·ed /ˈdɔːntɪd ‖ ˈdɒːn-/ adj worried; nervous

daunt·ing /ˈdɔːntɪŋ ‖ ˈdɒːn-/ adj worrying; frightening: a daunting prospect

daw·dle /ˈdɔːdl ‖ ˈdɒː-/ vi waste time; be slow

dawn¹ /dɔːn ‖ dɒːn/ n 1 [C;U] first light of morning 2 [S] first appearance: the dawn of civilization

dawn² vi begin to grow light

dawn on phr vt become known to: The truth dawned on me.

day /deɪ/ n 1 [C] period of 24 hours 2 [C;U] time between sunrise and sunset: the **daylight hours** i in the **daytime** 3 [C] hours that one works 4 [C] period; time: the present day 5 [S] period of success 6 **call it a day** finish working for the day 7 **day after day** also **day in, day out** continuously 8 **make someone's day** make someone very happy 9 **one day** at some time 10 **one's days** one's life 11 **the other day** recently 12 **these days** now

day·break /ˈdeɪbreɪk/ n [U] DAWN (1)

day·dream /ˈdeɪdriːm/ vi, n (have) pleasant dreamlike thoughts

day·lights /ˈdeɪlaɪts/ n [P] **beat/knock/scare the (living) daylights out of** hit/frighten (someone) very severely

day re·lease course /ˌ· ·ˈ· ·/ n BrE educational course attended by workers during the usual working day

day re·turn /ˌ· ·ˈ·/ n BrE bus or train ticket that one can use to go and come back on the same day

day-to-day /ˌ· · ˈ·◄/ adj happening each day: our day-to-day routine

daze /deɪz/ vt make unable to think clearly ◆ n dazed condition

daz·zle /ˈdæzəl/ vt 1 make unable to see because of too strong light 2 cause wonder to: dazzled by success

dea·con /ˈdiːkən/ **-ess** /-kənɪs/ fem. — Christian church officer below a priest

dead /ded/ adj 1 no longer alive 2 no longer used or usable: dead languages | The telephone went dead. 3 complete: dead silence 4 without activity: The place seems dead. 5 NUMB: My fingers went dead. 6 (of sound or colour) dull ◆ adv 1 completely: stop dead 2 directly: dead ahead ~en vt cause to lose (strength, feeling, brightness): deaden pain/noise

dead cen·tre /ˌ· ˈ·◄/ n exact centre

dead end /ˌ· ˈ·◄/ n end (of a street) with no way out: (fig.) We've reached a dead end *in our talks.*

dead heat /ˌ· ˈ·/ n race in which the competitors finish together

dead·line /ˈdedlaɪn/ n fixed date for finishing something

dead·lock /ˈdedlɒk ‖ -lɑːk/ n disagreement that cannot be settled

dead·ly /ˈdedli/ adj 1 likely to cause death 2 total: *deadly enemies* 3 *infml* very dull ♦ adv 1 like death: *deadly pale* 2 very: *deadly dull*

dead·pan /ˈdedpæn/ adj, adv with no show of feeling, esp. when telling jokes

dead ring·er /ˌ· ˈ··/ n someone who looks exactly like someone else

dead·weight /ˈdedˌweɪt/ n [S] whole weight of something that does not move

deaf /def/ adj 1 unable to hear 2 **deaf to** unwilling to listen to ~**en** vt (of loud noises) make unable to hear: *The noise was deafening.* (=very loud) ~**ness** n [U]

deal[1] /diːl/ vi/t dealt /delt/ 1 give out (esp. playing cards) as a share 2 strike: *deal someone a blow* ~**er** n 1 person who deals cards 2 trader ~**ing** n [U] methods of business or personal relations ~**ings** n [P] personal or business dealings

deal in phr vt trade in; sell

deal with phr vt 1 trade with 2 take action about 3 be about: *a book dealing with Ireland*

deal[2] n 1 [C] business arrangement 2 [C] one's turn to deal cards 3 **a good/great deal** a fairly/very large amount: *work a good deal faster*

dean /diːn/ n 1 Christian priest in charge of several others 2 important university official

dear /dɪə ‖ dɪr/ adj 1 loved; precious 2 (at the beginning of letters): *Dear Sir* 3 expensive ♦ 1 n loved person 2 a (used when speaking to someone you love): *Yes, dear.* b (used informally as a friendly form of address, esp. by or to a woman): *That's 50 pence, dear.* 3 interj (expressing surprise, sorrow, etc.): *Oh dear!* ~**ly** adv 1 with much feeling 2 at terrible cost

dearth /dɜːθ ‖ dɜːrθ/ n [S] fml lack

death /deθ/ n 1 [C;U] end of life: (fig.) *the death of our hopes* 2 [U] state of being dead 3 cause of death: *Drinking will be the death of him.* 4 **at death's door** in danger of dying; about to die 5 **like death warmed**

up infml very ill or tired 6 **put to death** kill, esp. officially 7 **to death** beyond proper limits: *sick/bored/worried to death* ~**ly** adj, adv like death

death du·ty /ˈ· ˌ··/ n BrE tax paid on property after death

death trap /ˈ· ·/ n very dangerous thing or place

dé·bâ·cle /deɪˈbɑːkəl, dɪ-/ n sudden complete failure

de·bar /dɪˈbɑː ‖ -ˈbɑːr/ v -rr- **debar from** phr vt officially prevent from

de·base /dɪˈbeɪs/ vt make lower in value ~**ment** n [C;U]

de·bate /dɪˈbeɪt/ n [C;U] (process of) DISCUSSION ♦ vi/t 1 hold a debate about 2 think about; wonder **debatable** adj doubtful; questionable

de·bauch /dɪˈbɔːtʃ ‖ dɪˈbɒːtʃ, dɪˈbɑːtʃ/ vt lead away from moral conduct, esp. in relation to sex and alcohol ♦ n ORGY ~**ed** adj ~**ery** n [U]

de·bil·i·tate /dɪˈbɪləteɪt/ vt make weak -**ting** adj -**ty** n [U] fml weakness

deb·it /ˈdebɪt/ n record of money owed ♦ vt charge against an account

deb·o·nair /ˌdebəˈneə◂ ‖ -ˈner◂/ adj cheerful and fashionably dressed

de·brief /ˌdiːˈbriːf/ vt find out information from (someone on one's own side) by thorough questioning after an action

deb·ris /ˈdebriː, ˈdeɪ- ‖ dəˈbriː, deɪ-/ n [U] broken remains; ruins

debt /det/ n [C;U] something owed; state of owing ~**or** n person who owes money

de·bug /ˌdiːˈbʌɡ/ vt search for and remove the BUGS (5) in (a computer PROGRAM)

de·bunk /diːˈbʌŋk/ vt point out the truth about a wrong idea

de·but /ˈdeɪbjuː, ˈdebjuː ‖ deɪˈbjuː, dɪ-/ n first public appearance

dec·ade /ˈdekeɪd, deˈkeɪd/ n period of 10 years

dec·a·dent /ˈdekədənt/ adj falling to a lower level of morals -**dence** n [U]

de·caf·fei·na·ted /diːˈkæfəˌneɪtɪd/ also **de·caf** /ˈdiːkæf/ adj (of coffee, tea, etc.) having had the CAFFEINE removed

de·camp /dɪˈkæmp/ vi go away quickly and esp. secretly

de·cant /dɪˈkænt/ vt pour (liquid) into

another container ~**er** n glass container for liquid, esp. wine

de·cap·i·tate /dɪˈkæpʌteɪt/ vt BEHEAD

de·cath·lon /dɪˈkæθlɒn ‖ -lɑːn, -lən/ n ATHLETIC competition with 10 separate events

de·cay /dɪˈkeɪ/ vi 1 go bad: *decayed teeth* 2 lose health, power, etc. ♦ n [U] process of decaying

de·ceased /dɪˈsiːst/ adj fml dead ♦ n fml the dead person

de·ceit /dɪˈsiːt/ n [U] dishonesty ~**ful** adj dishonest ~**fully** adv

de·ceive /dɪˈsiːv/ vt cause to believe something false **deceiver** n

de·cel·e·rate /ˌdiːˈseləreɪt/ vi/t (cause to) go slower

De·cem·ber /dɪˈsembə ‖ -ər/ n the 12th and last month of the year

de·cent /ˈdiːsənt/ adj 1 socially acceptable; proper 2 good enough: *a decent meal* 3 kind **decency** n [U] being DECENT (1)

de·cen·tral·ize also **-ise** BrE /ˌdiːˈsentrəlaɪz/ vt move (a business, etc.) from a central office or place to several smaller ones

de·cep·tion /dɪˈsepʃən/ n [U] deceiving 2 [C] trick **-tive** /-tɪv/ adj misleading **-tively** adv

dec·i·bel /ˈdesʌbel/ n unit of loudness

de·cide /dɪˈsaɪd/ v 1 vi/t make a choice or judgment: *She decided to go.* 2 vt make (someone) decide 3 vi/t end uncertainty **decided** adj 1 easily seen: *decided improvement* 2 sure of oneself **decidedly** adv certainly

decide on phr vt decide in favour of

de·cid·u·ous /dɪˈsɪdʒuəs/ adj (of trees) losing their leaves in autumn

dec·i·mal /ˈdesʌməl/ adj based on the number 10 ♦ n number such as .5 or .06 ~**ize** also ~**ise** BrE — vi/t change to a decimal system of money, etc.

dec·i·mate /ˈdesʌmeɪt/ vt destroy a large part of

de·ci·pher /dɪˈsaɪfə ‖ -ər/ vt read (something difficult, esp. a CODE)

de·ci·sion /dɪˈsɪʒən/ n 1 [C;U] deciding; choice: *reach a decision* 2 [U] firmness of judgment

de·ci·sive /dɪˈsaɪsɪv/ adj 1 firm in judgment 2 leading to a clear result ~**ly** adv ~**ness** n [U]

deck¹ /dek/ n 1 floor of a ship or bus 2 AmE for PACK of playing cards

deck² vt decorate

deck·chair /ˈdektʃeə ‖ -tʃer/ n folding chair with a cloth seat

de·claim /dɪˈkleɪm/ vt fml say loudly, like an actor

dec·la·ra·tion /ˌdekləˈreɪʃən/ n [C;U] 1 declaring 2 official statement

de·clare /dɪˈkleə ‖ -ˈkler/ vt 1 make known officially: *declare war* 2 state clearly 3 tell CUSTOMS officials about (taxable goods)

de·clas·si·fy /ˌdiːˈklæsʌfaɪ/ vt declare (esp. political and military information) no longer secret

de·cline /dɪˈklaɪn/ v 1 vi become worse or less 2 vt/i refuse (an invitation, etc.) politely ♦ n period of declining (DECLINE (1)): *Interest in the arts is on the decline.*

de·code /ˌdiːˈkəʊd ‖ -ˈkoʊd/ vt read (something written in CODE)

de·col·o·nize also **-ise** BrE /ˌdiːˈkɒlənaɪz ‖ -ˈkɑː-/ vt give political independence to **-nization** /ˌdiːkɒlənaɪˈzeɪʃən ‖ -kɑːlənə-/ n [U]

de·com·pose /ˌdiːkəmˈpəʊz ‖ -ˈpoʊz/ vi go bad; DECAY **-position** /ˌdiːkɒmpəˈzɪʃən ‖ -kɑːm-/ n [U]

de·com·press /ˌdiːkəmˈpres/ vt reduce air pressure on **-ion** /-ˈpreʃən/ n [U]

de·con·tam·i·nate /ˌdiːkənˈtæmʌneɪt/ vt remove dangerous substances from **-nation** /-ˌtæmʌˈneɪʃən/ n [U]

dé·cor /ˈdeɪkɔː ‖ deɪˈkɔːr/ n decoration and furnishings of a place

dec·o·rate /ˈdekəreɪt/ v 1 vt add something beautiful to 2 vi/t paint, put paper, etc. on rooms 3 vt give a mark of honour, such as a MEDAL, etc. to **-rator** n person who paints houses **-rative** /ˈdekərətɪv ‖ ˈdekərə-, ˈdekəreɪ-/ adj beautiful; attractive **-ration** /ˌdekəˈreɪʃən/ n 1 [U] decorating 2 [C] something that decorates 3 [C] mark of honour, MEDAL, etc.

dec·o·rous /ˈdekərəs/ adj (of appearance or behaviour) correct

de·co·rum /dɪˈkɔːrəm/ n [U] fml correct behaviour

de·coy /ˈdiːkɔɪ/ n something used for getting a person or bird into a trap **decoy** /dɪˈkɔɪ/ vt

de·crease¹ /dɪˈkriːs/ vi/t (cause to) become less

de·crease² /'di:kri:s/ n 1 [U] process of decreasing 2 [C] amount by which something decreases

de·cree /dɪ'kri:/ n official command or decision ♦ vt order officially

de·crep·it /dɪ'krepɨt/ adj weak from old age

de·crim·i·nal·ize also **-ise** BrE /di:'krɪmɨnəl-aɪz/ vt make no longer illegal

de·cry /dɪ'kraɪ/ vt fml speak disapprovingly of

ded·i·cate /'dedɨkeɪt/ vt 1 give to a serious purpose: dedicate her life to medical research | a dedicated doctor 2 declare (a book, etc.) to be in honour of someone, by printing their name at the front **-cation** /ˌdedɨ'keɪʃən/ n 1 [C;U] act of dedicating 2 [U] words used in dedicating a book

de·duce /dɪ'dju:s‖dɪ'du:s/ vt reach (a piece of knowledge) by reasoning

de·duct /dɪ'dʌkt/ vt take away (part) from a total **~ible** adj: expenses deductible from tax

de·duc·tion /dɪ'dʌkʃən/ n [C;U] 1 example of deducing; knowledge deduced: a brilliant deduction 2 process of deducting; something deducted: a salary of $10,000 after all deductions

deed /di:d/ n 1 lit something done; action 2 law signed agreement

deed poll /'· ·/ n DEED (2) signed when changing one's name

deem /di:m/ vt fml consider; judge

deep /di:p/ adj 1 going far down from the top, or in from the outside: deep river/wound | ankle-deep in mud 2 (of colour) dark 3 (of sound) low 4 strong; extreme: deep sleep | deep distrust | in deep trouble 5 difficult to understand 6 a wise: a deep thinker b mysterious: a deep secret 7 **go off the deep end** sl lose one's temper 8 **in/into deep water** infml in/into serious trouble 9 **thrown in at the deep end** suddenly and unexpectedly faced with a difficult piece of work ♦ adv far down; far in: ~en vi/t make or become deeper **~ly** adv **~ness** n [U]

deep freeze /ˌ· '·‖'· ·/ vt freeze food quickly in order to preserve it ♦ n FREEZER

deep fry /'· ·/ vt FRY completely under the surface of oil or fat

deep-root·ed /ˌ· '··◂/ also **deep-seated** — adj strongly fixed: deep-rooted habits

deer /dɪə‖dɪr/ n large fast animal of which the males have ANTLERS

de·face /dɪ'feɪs/ vt spoil the surface of **~ment** n [U]

de fac·to /ˌdeɪ 'fæktəʊ‖ˌdɪ 'fæktoʊ, ˌdeɪ-/ adj, adv fml in actual fact, though not by law

de·fame /dɪ'feɪm/ vt fml attack the good REPUTATION of **defamation** /ˌdefə'meɪʃən/ n [U] **defamatory** /dɪ'fæmətəri‖-tɔ:ri/ adj

de·fault /dɪ'fɔ:lt‖-'fɒ:lt/ n [U] failure to fulfil a contract, pay a debt, etc. **default** vi **~er** n

de·feat /dɪ'fi:t/ vt 1 win a victory over 2 cause to fail ♦ n [C;U] (example or act of) defeating **~ism** n [U] practice of thinking or behaving in expectation of defeat **~ist** n

def·e·cate /'defɨkeɪt/ vi fml pass waste matter from the bowels

de·fect¹ /'di:fekt, dɪ'fekt/ n imperfection; fault **~ive** /dɪ'fektɪv/ adj

de·fect² /dɪ'fekt/ vi desert one's political party, country, etc. **~or** n **~ion** /-'fekʃən/ n [C;U]

de·fence also **defense** AmE /dɪ'fens/ n 1 [U] act or process of defending 2 [C] something used in defending 3 [C] law **a** arguments used in defending someone in court **b** lawyers who defend someone **~less** adj unable to defend oneself

de·fend /dɪ'fend/ vt 1 keep safe; protect 2 act as a lawyer for (someone charged with a crime) 3 argue in favour of

de·fen·dant /dɪ'fendənt/ n person against whom a legal charge or claim is brought

de·fen·si·ble /dɪ'fensɨbəl/ adj that can be defended

de·fen·sive /dɪ'fensɪv/ adj 1 used in defence 2 (of someone) who always seems to be expecting attack ♦ n **on the defensive** prepared for attack **~ly** adv **~ness** n [U]

de·fer /dɪ'fɜː‖-'fɜːr/ vt **-rr-** POSTPONE **~ment** n [C;U]

defer to phr vt fml accept the decision of

def·er·ence /'defərəns/ n [U] fml respect for another's wishes

de·fi·ance /dɪ'faɪəns/ n [U] open disobedience **-ant** adj **-antly** adv

de·fi·cien·cy /dɪ'fɪʃənsi/ n [C;U] lack: vitamin deficiency **-cient** adj

def·i·cit /'defɪsɪt/ n amount by which something, esp. money, is too little

de·file /dɪ'faɪl/ vt fml make dirty

de·fine /dɪ'faɪn/ vt 1 give the meaning of; explain exactly 2 set, mark, or show the limits of: a clearly-defined shape

def·i·nite /'defɪnɪt, 'defənɪt/ adj clear; without uncertainty ~ly adv 1 in a clear way 2 certainly

definite ar·ti·cle /'‥ '‥/ n (in English) the word THE

def·i·ni·tion /,defɪ'nɪʃən/ n 1 [C;U] (statement) defining something 2 [U] clearness of shape: The photograph lacks definition.

de·fin·i·tive /dɪ'fɪnɪtɪv/ adj that cannot be questioned; not needing change

de·flate /dɪ'fleɪt, diː-/ v 1 vt let air or gas out of (a tyre, etc.) 2 vi/t reduce the supply of money in a country **deflation** /-'fleɪʃən/ n [U] **deflationary** adj

de·flect /dɪ'flekt/ vi/t turn aside from a straight course: (fig.) to deflect someone from their purpose ~ion /-'flekʃən/ n [C;U]

de·for·est·a·tion /diː,fɒrɪ'steɪʃən ‖ -,fɔː-, -,faː-/ n [U] (process of) cutting down all the trees in an area

de·form /dɪ'fɔːm ‖ -ɔːrm/ vt spoil the shape of ~ity n [C;U] imperfection of the body

de·fraud /dɪ'frɔːd ‖ -'frɔːd/ vt deceive so as to get something: They defrauded him of £50.

de·fray /dɪ'freɪ/ vt fml pay for

de·frost /,diː'frɒst ‖ -'frɔːst/ vt remove ice from; unfreeze

deft /deft/ adj effortlessly skilful ~ly adv

de·funct /dɪ'fʌŋkt/ adj no longer existing or working

de·fuse /,diː'fjuːz/ vt 1 remove the FUSE from (a bomb, etc.) 2 make harmless

de·fy /dɪ'faɪ/ vt 1 refuse to obey 2 CHALLENGE to do something impossible 3 remain unreachable by all efforts at or from: It defies description.

de·gen·e·rate /dɪ'dʒenərɪt/ adj having become worse than before ♦ n degenerate person ♦ vi /-nəreɪt/ become worse –rative /-nərətɪv/ adj –ration /dɪ,dʒenə'reɪʃən/ n [U]

de·grade /dɪ'greɪd/ v 1 vt bring shame to 2 vi/t change to a simpler chemical form **degradation** /,degrə'deɪʃən/ n [C;U]

de·gree /dɪ'griː/ n 1 unit of measurement of angles, or of temperature 2 stage; level: getting better by degrees 3 title given to a university student —see also THIRD DEGREE

de·hy·drate /,diːhaɪ'dreɪt ‖ diː'haɪdreɪt/ vt remove water from

de·i·fy /'diːɪfaɪ, 'deɪ-/ vt make a god of

deign /deɪn/ vt derog CONDESCEND

de·i·ty /'diːɪti, 'deɪ-/ n god or goddess

dé·ja vu /,deɪʒɑː 'vjuː/ n [U] feeling that what is happening now has already happened

de·jec·ted /dɪ'dʒektɪd/ adj low in spirits; sad –tion /-'dʒekʃən/ n [U]

de·lay /dɪ'leɪ/ v 1 vi/t make later 2 vi act slowly ♦ n 1 [U] delaying 2 [C] example or time of being delayed

de·lec·ta·ble /dɪ'lektəbəl/ adj delightful; DELICIOUS

del·e·gate¹ /'delɪgɪt/ n person chosen to act for others

del·e·gate² /'delɪgeɪt/ v 1 vi/t give (power, etc.) to someone else 2 vt appoint (someone) as a delegate –gation /,delɪ'geɪʃən/ n 1 [U] act of delegating 2 [C] group of delegates

de·lete /dɪ'liːt/ vt take out (written words) **deletion** /-'liːʃən/ n [C;U]

de·lib·e·rate¹ /dɪ'lɪbərɪt/ adj 1 done on purpose 2 (of speech, movement, etc.) slow; unhurried ~ly adv

de·lib·e·rate² /dɪ'lɪbəreɪt/ vi/t fml consider carefully –ration /dɪ,lɪbə'reɪʃən/ n fml 1 [C;U] (process of) deliberating 2 [U] being slow and unhurried

del·i·ca·cy /'delɪkəsi/ n 1 [U] being delicate 2 [C] something good to eat

del·i·cate /'delɪkɪt/ adj 1 easily damaged, hurt, or made ill 2 soft and fine: delicate silk 3 needing careful treatment: a delicate situation 4 pleasing but not easy to recognize: a delicate flavour 5 sensitive: delicate instruments ~ly adv

del·i·ca·tes·sen /,delɪkə'tesən/ n shop that sells foreign foods freshly cooked

de·li·cious /dɪ'lɪʃəs/ adj (esp. of taste or smell) delightful ~ly adv

de·light /dɪ'laɪt/ n 1 [U] great pleasure; joy 2 [C] cause of great pleasure ♦ v 1 vt give delight to 2 vi find delight: He delights in scandal. ~ed adj very pleased ~ful adj very pleasing **–fully** adv

de·lin·e·ate /dɪ'lɪnieɪt/ vt fml show by

drawing

de·lin·quent /dɪˈlɪŋkwənt/ n, adj (person) who breaks a law –**quency** n [U]

de·lir·i·ous /dɪˈlɪərɪəs ‖ -ˈlɪr-/ adj excited and dreamy, esp. because of illness ~**ly** adv –**ium** /-rɪəm/ n [U] excited dreamy state

de·liv·er /dɪˈlɪvə ‖ -ər/ vt 1 take (goods, letters, etc.) to people's houses 2 help in the birth of 3 give (a blow, kick, etc.) 4 say (a speech, etc.) 5 fml rescue ~**er** n fml rescuer ~**ance** n [U] fml saving; rescue ~**y** n 1 [C;U] delivering things; things delivered 2 [C] birth of a child 3 [C;U] style of public speaking

del·ta /ˈdeltə/ n land in the shape of a triangle at the mouth of a river

de·lude /dɪˈluːd/ vt mislead; deceive

del·uge /ˈdeljuːdʒ/ n heavy rain; flood **deluge** vt

de·lu·sion /dɪˈluːʒən/ n 1 [U] deluding 2 [C] false belief

deluxe /dəˈlʌks ‖ -ˈlʊks/ adj of very high quality

delve /delv/ vi search deeply

Dem /dem/ abbrev. for: DEMOCRAT

dem·a·gogue /ˈdeməgɒg ‖ -gɑːg/ n leader who gains power by exciting the crowds

de·mand /dɪˈmɑːnd ‖ dɪˈmænd/ n 1 [C] demanding; claim 2 [S;U] desire for things that people can pay for: a great demand for teachers ♦ vt 1 ask for firmly; claim 2 need: problems demanding your attention ~**ing** adj needing a lot of attention or effort

de·mar·ca·tion /ˌdiːmɑːˈkeɪʃən ‖ -ɑːr-/ n [U] limits; separation

de·mean /dɪˈmiːn/ vt fml bring shame to; DEGRADE

de·mea·nour BrE ‖ **-nor** AmE /dɪˈmiːnə ‖ -ər/ n [U] fml behaviour

de·ment·ed /dɪˈmentɪd/ adj mad

de·mer·it /diːˈmerɪt/ n fml fault

de·mil·i·ta·rize also **-ise** BrE /ˌdiːˈmɪlɪtəraɪz/ vt remove armed forces from (an area) –**rization** /ˌdiːmɪlɪtəraɪˈzeɪʃən ‖ -tərə-/ n [U]

de·mise /dɪˈmaɪz/ n [U] law death

de·mist /ˌdiːˈmɪst/ vt remove steam from (car windows) ~**er** n

dem·o /ˈdeməʊ ‖ -moʊ/ n infml demos DEMONSTRATION

de·mo·bi·lize also **-ise** BrE /diːˈməʊbɪlaɪz ‖ -ˈmoʊ-/ vi/t fml send home the

members of (an armed force), usu. at the end of a war

de·moc·ra·cy /dɪˈmɒkrəsi ‖ dɪˈmɑː-/ n 1 [U] government by elected representatives of the people 2 [C] country governed in this way 3 [U] social equality

dem·o·crat /ˈdeməkræt/ n 1 person who believes in democracy 2 (cap.) member of the Democratic Party ~**ic** /ˌdeməˈkrætɪk◂/ adj 1 of or favouring democracy 2 (cap.) of a US political party (the **Democratic Party**) ~**ically** /-kli/ adv

Democrat n member or supporter of the **Democratic Party**, one of the two largest political parties in the US ~**ic** adj

de·mog·ra·phy /dɪˈmɒgrəfi ‖ -ˈmɑː-/ n [U] study of the numbers and movement of human population –**phic** /ˌdeməˈgræfɪk◂, ˌdiː-/ adj

de·mol·ish /dɪˈmɒlɪʃ ‖ dɪˈmɑː-/ vt 1 pull down (buildings, etc.); destroy 2 infml eat up hungrily –**molition** /ˌdeməˈlɪʃən/ n [C;U]

de·mon /ˈdiːmən/ n 1 evil spirit 2 very active skilful person ~**ic** /dɪˈmɒnɪk ‖ dɪˈmɑː-/ adj of, by, or like a demon

de·mon·stra·ble /dɪˈmɒnstrəb əl, ˈdem-ən-‖ dɪˈmɑːn-/ adj fml easily proved –**bly** adv

dem·on·strate /ˈdemənstreɪt/ v 1 vt show clearly 2 vi take part in a public demonstration –**strator** n –**stration** /ˌdemənˈstreɪʃən/ n 1 [C;U] showing something 2 [C;U] also **dem·o** /ˈdeməʊ ‖ -moʊ/ — public show of opinion, by marching, etc.

de·mon·stra·tive /dɪˈmɒnstrətɪv ‖ dɪˈmɑːn-/ adj showing feelings openly

de·mor·al·ize also **-ise** BrE /dɪˈmɒrəlaɪz ‖ dɪˈmɔː-, dɪˈmɑː-/ vt destroy the courage and confidence of –**ization** /dɪˌmɒr-əlaɪˈzeɪʃən ‖ dɪˌmɔːrə-, dɪˌmɑː-/ n [U]

de·mote /dɪˈməʊt ‖ -ˈmoʊt/ vt reduce in rank **demotion** /dɪˈməʊʃən ‖ -ˈmoʊ-/ n [C;U]

de·mure /dɪˈmjʊə ‖ -ˈmjʊr/ adj quiet and MODEST ~**ly** adv

den /den/ n 1 home of a wild animal 2 secret or private place 3 small, quiet room in a house

de·na·tion·al·ize also **-ise** BrE /diːˈnæ-ʃənəlaɪz/ vt remove from state ownership –**ization** /ˌdiːnæʃənəlaɪˈzeɪʃən ‖ -nələ-/ n

[C;U]

de·ni·al /dɪˈnaɪəl/ n 1 [U] denying (DENY) 2 [C] statement that something is false

den·i·grate /ˈdenɪɡreɪt/ vt declare to be worthless

den·im /ˈdenɪm/ n [U] strong cotton cloth used for making JEANS

de·nom·i·na·tion /dɪˌnɒməˈneɪʃən ‖ dɪˌnɑː-/ n 1 religious group 2 unit of value

de·nom·i·na·tor /dɪˈnɒmɪneɪtə ‖ dɪˈnɑːmɪneɪtər/ n —see COMMON DENOMINATOR

de·note /dɪˈnəʊt ‖ -ˈnoʊt/ vt be the name or sign of; mean

de·noue·ment /deɪˈnuːmɒŋ ‖ ˌdeɪnuːˈmɑːŋ/ n end of a story, when everything is explained

de·nounce /dɪˈnaʊns/ vt speak or write publicly against

dense /dens/ adj 1 closely packed 2 hard to see through: dense fog 3 stupid ~ly adv

density n [C;U]

dent /dent/ n 1 small hollow in a surface, made by a blow 2 **make a dent in** make a first step towards success in ♦ vt make a dent

den·tal /ˈdentl/ adj of the teeth

den·tist /ˈdentɪst/ n person trained to treat the teeth ~ry n [U]

den·tures /ˈdentʃəz ‖ -ərz/ n [P] false teeth

de·nude /dɪˈnjuːd ‖ dɪˈnuːd/ vt fml remove the covering from: a hill denuded of trees

de·nun·ci·a·tion /dɪˌnʌnsiˈeɪʃən/ n [C;U] act or example of denouncing (DENOUNCE)

de·ny /dɪˈnaɪ/ vt 1 declare untrue 2 refuse to allow

de·o·do·rant /diːˈəʊdərənt ‖ -ˈoʊ-/ n [C;U] chemical that hides bad smells

de·part /dɪˈpɑːt ‖ -ɑːrt/ vi fml 1 leave; go away 2 **depart this life** lit to die **~ed** adj gone for ever

   depart from phr vt turn or move away from

de·part·ment /dɪˈpɑːtmənt ‖ -ɑːr-/ n 1 division of a government, business, college, etc. 2 infml activity or subject for which a person is responsible ~al /ˌdiːpɑːtˈmentl◂ ‖ -ɑːr-/ adj

department store /·ˈ·· ·/ n large shop divided into departments

de·par·ture /dɪˈpɑːtʃə ‖ -ˈpɑːrtʃər/ n

[C;U] going away: (fig.) a new departure (=change from a usual course of action) in television

de·pend /dɪˈpend/ v 1 [it+vt] vary according to; be decided by: It depends how much you want to spend. 2 **that (all) depends/it all depends** that/it has not yet been decided

   depend on/upon phr vt 1 trust 2 be supported by 3 vary according to

de·pend·a·ble /dɪˈpendəbəl/ adj that can be trusted

de·pen·dant, -dent /dɪˈpendənt/ n person supported by another

de·pen·dence /dɪˈpendəns/ n [U] 1 being dependent: our dependence on oil 2 trust 3 need to have certain drugs regularly

de·pen·dent, -dent /dɪˈpendənt/ adj that depends on

de·pict /dɪˈpɪkt/ vt fml show in a picture, or in words

de·pil·a·to·ry /dɪˈpɪlətəri ‖ -ˈtɔːri/ n, adj (substance) that gets rid of unwanted hair

de·plete /dɪˈpliːt/ vt fml lessen (supplies, etc.) greatly depletion /-ˈpliːʃən/ n [U]

de·plore /dɪˈplɔː ‖ -ˈplɔːr/ vt be very sorry about (and consider wrong) deplorable adj very bad

de·ploy /dɪˈplɔɪ/ vt arrange for effective action ~ment n [U]

de·port /dɪˈpɔːt ‖ -ɔːrt/ vt send (an unwanted foreigner) out of the country ~ation /ˌdiːpɔːˈteɪʃən ‖ -ɔːr-/ n [C;U]

de·port·ment /dɪˈpɔːtmənt ‖ -ɔːr-/ n [U] way a person stands and walks

de·pose /dɪˈpəʊz ‖ -ˈpoʊz/ vt remove (a ruler) from power

de·pos·it¹ /dɪˈpɒzɪt ‖ dɪˈpɑː-/ vt 1 put down 2 (of a river, etc.) leave (soil, etc.) lying 3 put in a bank, etc. to be safe **~or** n person who deposits money

deposit² n 1 [C;U] material deposited by a natural process 2 first part of a payment for something, to show that an agreement will be kept

deposit ac·count /·ˈ·· ·ˌ·/ n BrE bank account which earns interest but from which money cannot be taken out at once

dep·ot /ˈdepəʊ ‖ ˈdiːpoʊ/ n 1 storehouse for goods 2 bus garage 3 AmE railway station

de·praved /dɪˈpreɪvd/ adj wicked

depravity /dɪˈprævəti/ n [C;U]

dep·re·cate /ˈdeprəkeɪt/ vt fml express disapproval of

de·pre·ci·ate /dɪˈpriːʃieɪt/ vi (esp. of money) fall in value –**ation** /dɪˌpriːʃiˈeɪʃən/ n [U]

de·press /dɪˈpres/ vt 1 sadden: *depressing news* 2 make less active 3 fml press down ~**ed** adj 1 sad 2 suffering from low levels of business activity

de·pres·sion /dɪˈpreʃən/ n 1 [C;U] sad feeling 2 [C] period of reduced business activity 3 [C] hollow in a surface 4 [C] area of low air pressure

de·prive /dɪˈpraɪv/ vt prevent from having something: *deprive us of our rights* **deprivation** /ˌdeprɪˈveɪʃən/ n [C;U]

depth /depθ/ n [C;U] 1 (degree of) being deep 2 **in depth** done thoroughly 3 **out of one's depth: a** in water deeper than one's height **b** beyond one's understanding **depths** n [the+P] deepest or most central part of: *the depths of winter/despair*

dep·u·ta·tion /ˌdepjʊˈteɪʃən/ n group sent to act on behalf of others

dep·u·ty /ˈdepjʊti/ n person given power to act for another –**tize** also **-ise** BrE vi act as a deputy

de·rail /ˌdiːˈreɪl, dɪ-/ vt cause (a train) to run off the line –**ment** n [C;U]

de·ranged /dɪˈreɪndʒd/ adj unbalanced in the mind

de·reg·u·late /diːˈregjʊleɪt/ vt remove from control by law –**lation** /ˌdiːregjʊˈleɪʃən/ n [U]

der·e·lict /ˈderəlɪkt/ adj fallen into ruin ♦ n person, esp. an ALCOHOLIC, who has no home and no legal means of support ~**ion** /ˌderəˈlɪkʃən/ n 1 state of being derelict 2 failure to do one's duty

de·ride /dɪˈraɪd/ vt fml laugh unkindly at

de·ri·sion /dɪˈrɪʒən/ n [U] unkind laughter –**sive** /dɪˈraɪsɪv/ adj: *derisive laughter* –**sory** adj deserving derision; ABSURD

de·riv·a·tive /dɪˈrɪvətɪv/ n thing which has been developed from something else ♦ adj derog not original or new

de·rive /dɪˈraɪv/ v 1 vt obtain from somewhere: *derive pleasure from one's work* 2 vi have something as an origin: *words that derive from Latin* **derivation** /ˌderəˈveɪʃən/ n [C;U]

der·ma·ti·tis /ˌdɜːməˈtaɪtəs ‖ ˌdɜːr-/ n [U] skin disease with redness and swelling

de·rog·a·to·ry /dɪˈrɒgətəri ‖ dɪˈrɑːgə-tɔːri/ adj fml (of words) showing disapproval

der·rick /ˈderɪk/ n 1 large CRANE (1) 2 tower over an oil well

de·scend /dɪˈsend/ vi/t 1 go down 2 be **descended from** have as an ANCESTOR ~**ant** n person descended from another

descend on/upon phr vt 1 arrive suddenly 2 attack suddenly

de·scent /dɪˈsent/ n 1 [C;U] going down 2 [C] downward slope 3 [U] family origins: *of German descent*

de·scribe /dɪˈskraɪb/ vt 1 say what something is like 2 fml draw the shape of: *describe a circle*

de·scrip·tion /dɪˈskrɪpʃən/ n 1 [C;U] statement that describes 2 [C] sort: *birds of every description* –**tive** /-tɪv/ adj 1 that describes 2 saying how a language is used

des·e·crate /ˈdesɪkreɪt/ vt spoil (a holy thing or place) –**cration** /ˌdesɪˈkreɪʃən/ n [S;U]

de·seg·re·gate /diːˈsegrɪgeɪt/ vt end racial SEGREGATION in –**gation** /ˌdiːseg-rɪˈgeɪʃən ‖ diːˌseg-/ n [U]

des·ert¹ /ˈdezət ‖ -ərt/ n large area of dry sandy land

de·sert² /dɪˈzɜːt ‖ -ɜːrt/ v 1 vt leave (a place) empty 2 vt leave (people) cruelly 3 vi leave military service without permission ~**er** n person who DESERTS (3) ~**ion** /-ˈzɜːʃən ‖ -ɜːr-/ n [C;U]

de·serts /dɪˈzɜːts ‖ -ɜːrts/ n [P] what someone deserves

de·serve /dɪˈzɜːv ‖ -ɜːrv/ vt be worthy of: *She deserved to win.* **deservedly** /dɪˈzɜːv-ɪdli ‖ -ɜːr-/ adv rightly **deserving** adj

des·ic·cate /ˈdesɪkeɪt/ vi/t fml dry up

de·sign /dɪˈzaɪn/ vt 1 draw a plan for (something to be made) 2 plan (something) for a purpose: *books designed for use in colleges* ♦ n 1 [C] plan drawn for making something 2 [U] art of designing things 3 [C] decorative pattern 4 [C] plan in the mind **designs** n [P] evil plans: *designs on your life*

des·ig·nate /ˈdezɪgneɪt/ vt choose for a particular job or purpose ♦ adj /-nət, -neɪt/ chosen for an office but not yet officially placed in it

de·sign·er¹ /dɪˈzaɪnə ‖ -ər/ n person who makes plans or designs

designer² adj 1 made by a designer: *designer jeans* 2 *humor* or *derog* intended to make the user appear extremely fashionable: *designer stubble/socialism*

de·sir·a·ble /dɪˈzaɪərəbəl ‖ -ˈzaɪr-/ adj worth having; attractive **–bly** adv **–bility** /dɪˌzaɪərəˈbɪləti ‖ -ˌzaɪr-/ n [U]

de·sire /dɪˈzaɪə ‖ -ˈzaɪr/ vt wish for; want very much ♦ n 1 [C;U] strong wish 2 [C;U] strong wish for sexual relations with 3 [C] something desired **desirous** adj feeling or having a desire

de·sist /dɪˈzɪst, dɪˈsɪst/ vi cease doing

desk /desk/ n 1 table at which one writes or works 2 place where a particular type of work is done; the people doing this work: *Contact the information desk.*

desk·top /ˈdesktɒp ‖ -tɑːp/ adj being or using a small computer: *desktop publishing*

des·o·late /ˈdesələt/ adj sad and lonely **–lation** /ˌdesəˈleɪʃən/ n [U]

de·spair /dɪˈspeə ‖ -ˈsper/ vi lose all hope ♦ n loss of hope **~ingly** adv

de·spatch /dɪˈspætʃ/ n, v DISPATCH

des·per·ate /ˈdespərɪt/ adj 1 ready for any wild act because of despair 2 very dangerous and without much hope of success **~ly** adv **–ation** /ˌdespəˈreɪʃən/ n [U]

des·pic·a·ble /dɪˈspɪkəbəl, ˈdespɪ-/ adj deserving to be despised

de·spise /dɪˈspaɪz/ vt regard as worthless

de·spite /dɪˈspaɪt/ prep fml in spite of

de·spon·dent /dɪˈspɒndənt ‖ dɪˈspɑːn-/ adj without hope; discouraged **–dency** n [U]

des·pot /ˈdespɒt, -ət ‖ ˈdespɑt, -ɑːt/ n ruler with total power who governs cruelly **~ic** /dɪˈspɒtɪk, de- ‖ -ˈspɑː-/ adj

des·sert /dɪˈzɜːt ‖ -ɜːrt/ n [C;U] sweet food served at the end of a meal

des·sert·spoon /dɪˈzɜːtspuːn ‖ -ɜːrt-/ n middle-sized spoon

de·sta·bi·lize also **-ise** BrE /diːˈsteɪbəlaɪz/ vt make (a government, etc.) unsteady

des·ti·na·tion /ˌdestəˈneɪʃən/ n place to which someone or something is going

des·tined /ˈdestɪnd/ adj intended, esp. by fate: *He was destined to become famous.*

des·ti·ny /ˈdestɪni/ n [C;U] fate; what must happen

des·ti·tute /ˈdestɪtjuːt ‖ -tuːt/ adj 1 without food, clothes, shelter, etc. 2 fml lacking in: *destitute of feeling* **–tution** /ˌdestɪˈtjuːʃən ‖ -ˈtuː-/ n [U]

de·stroy /dɪˈstrɔɪ/ vt 1 make useless; ruin 2 kill (esp. an animal) **~er** n small fast warship

de·struc·tion /dɪˈstrʌkʃən/ n [U] destroying; ruin **–tive** /-tɪv/ adj 1 causing destruction 2 not helpful: *destructive criticism*

des·ul·to·ry /ˈdesəltəri, ˈdez- ‖ -tɔːri/ adj fml passing from one thing to another without plan or purpose

de·tach /dɪˈtætʃ/ vt separate from something larger **~ed** adj 1 (of a house) not joined to others 2 not influenced by personal feelings **–ment** n 1 [U] being DETACHED (2) 2 [C] group of soldiers, etc.

de·tail /ˈdiːteɪl ‖ dɪˈteɪl/ n 1 small fact about something 2 small working party of soldiers, etc. ♦ vt 1 describe fully: *a detailed account* 2 appoint (soldiers, etc.) for special work

de·tain /dɪˈteɪn/ vt prevent (someone) from leaving

de·tain·ee /ˌdiːteɪˈniː/ n person detained officially in a camp or prison

de·tect /dɪˈtekt/ vt notice; discover **~able** adj **~ive** n person who catches criminals **~or** n instrument for finding something: *a metal detector* **~ion** /-ˈtekʃən/ n [U]

dé·tente /ˈdeɪtɒnt, deɪˈtɒnt ‖ -ɑːnt/ n [C;U] calmer political relations between unfriendly countries

de·ten·tion /dɪˈtenʃən/ n [U] act of preventing a person from leaving

detention cen·tre /·ˈ·· ˌ·ˈ·/ n [C] place where prisoners or REFUGEES are kept until their future is decided

de·ter /dɪˈtɜː ‖ -ˈtɜːr/ vt -rr- discourage from doing something

de·ter·gent /dɪˈtɜːdʒənt ‖ -ɜːr-/ n [C;U] (esp. soapless) product for washing things

de·te·ri·o·rate /dɪˈtɪəriəreɪt ‖ -ˈtɪr-/ vi become worse **–ration** /dɪˌtɪəriəˈreɪʃən ‖ -ˌtɪr/ n [U]

de·ter·mi·na·tion /dɪˌtɜːmɪˈneɪʃən ‖ -ɜːr-/ n [U] 1 strong will to succeed 2 firm intention 3 finding out

de·ter·mine /dɪˈtɜːmɪn ‖ -ɜːr-/ vt 1 form a firm intention 2 limit; fix 3 find out; calculate **–ned** adj full of determination (1)

de·ter·min·er /dɪˈtɜːmɪnə‖ -ˈtɜːrmɪnər/ *n gram* word (such as 'his' in 'his new car') that describes a noun and comes before any adjectives that describe the same noun

de·ter·rent /dɪˈterənt‖ -ˈtɜːr-/ *n, adj* (something) that DETERS

de·test /dɪˈtest/ *vt* hate very much ~**able** *adj*

de·throne /dɪˈθrəʊn‖ -ˈθroʊn/ *vt* remove (a king or queen) from power

det·o·nate /ˈdetəneɪt/ *vi/t* explode –**nator** *n* piece of equipment used for detonating –**nation** /ˌdetəˈneɪʃən/ *n* [C;U]

de·tour /ˈdiːtʊə‖ -tʊr/ *n* way round something

de·tox /ˈdiːtɒks‖ -taːks/ *n* [U] *infml* treatment to stop ADDICTS taking drugs or drinking alcohol: *while she was in detox*

de·tract /dɪˈtrækt/ *v* **detract from** *phr vt* lessen the value of

de·trac·tor /dɪˈtræktə‖ -ər/ *n* person who says bad things about another

det·ri·ment /ˈdetrɪmənt/ *n* [U] *fml* harm; damage ~**al** /ˌdetrɪˈmentl◂/ *adj*

deuce /djuːs‖ duːs/ *n* [U] (in tennis) 40 points to each player

de·val·ue /diːˈvæljuː/ *vi/t* **1** reduce the exchange value of (money) **2** make (a person or action) seem less valuable or important –**uation** /diːˌvæljuːˈeɪʃən/ *n* [C;U]

dev·a·state /ˈdevəsteɪt/ *vt* destroy completely –**stated** *adj* extremely upset –**stating** *adj* **1** destroying completely **2** extremely upsetting –**station** /ˌdevəˈsteɪʃən/ *n* [U]

de·vel·op /dɪˈveləp/ *v* **1** *vi/t* (cause to) grow or become more advanced **2** *vt* (land) for building on **3** *vt* begin to have: *develop measles* **4** *vt* cause (a photograph) to appear on paper ~**er** *n* person who develops land ~**ment** *n* **1** [U] developing **2** [C] new event **3** developed piece of land

de·vel·op·ing coun·try /·,··· ˈ··/ *n* poor country that is trying to improve its industry and living conditions

de·vi·ant /ˈdiːviənt/ *adj* different from an accepted standard –**ance** *n* [U]

de·vi·ate /ˈdiːvieɪt/ *vi* turn away from what is usual –**ation** /ˌdiːviˈeɪʃən/ *n* [C;U] noticeable difference

de·vice /dɪˈvaɪs/ *n* **1** instrument or tool **2** plan; trick **3 leave someone to their**

own **devices** leave (someone) alone. without help

dev·il /ˈdevəl/ *n* **1** evil spirit **2** *sl* person: *You lucky devil!* ~**ish** *adj* evil; like the devil ~**ishly** *adv* very: *devilishly hard work*

devil's ad·vo·cate /ˌ·· ˈ···/ *n* person who opposes an idea or plan to test how good it is

de·vi·ous /ˈdiːviəs/ *adj* not direct; not very honest

de·vise /dɪˈvaɪz/ *vt* plan; invent

de·void /dɪˈvɔɪd/ *adj* devoid of *fml* empty of: *a house devoid of furniture* | *devoid of human feeling*

de·vo·lu·tion /ˌdiːvəˈluːʃən/ *n* [U] giving of power to someone else

de·volve /dɪˈvɒlv‖ dɪˈvɑːlv/ *v* **devolve on/upon** *phr vt* (of power or work) be passed to

de·vote /dɪˈvəʊt‖ -ˈvoʊt/ *vt* give completely to something **devoted** *adj* loyal; loving **devotion** /-ˈvəʊʃən‖ -ˈvoʊ-/ *n* [U] **1** great love **2** devoutness **devotions** *n* [P] prayers

dev·o·tee /ˌdevəˈtiː/ *n* person who admires someone or something

de·vour /dɪˈvaʊə‖ -ˈvaʊr/ *vt* **1** eat up hungrily: (fig.) *I devoured the book.* **2** completely take up the attention of: *devoured by fame*

de·vout /dɪˈvaʊt/ *adj* **1** seriously religious **2** deeply felt: *a devout hope* ~**ly** *adv*

dew /djuː‖ duː/ *n* [U] drops of water that form on cold surfaces in the night ~**y** *adj* wet as if with dew: *a dewy-eyed look*

dex·ter·i·ty /dekˈsterɪti/ *n* [U] quick cleverness, esp. with one's hands –**terous** /ˈdekstərəs/, -**trous** /-trəs/ *adj*

dex·trose /ˈdekstrəʊz, -strəʊs‖ -stroʊz. -stroʊs/ *n* [U] form of sugar found in some fruits

di·a·be·tes /ˌdaɪəˈbiːtiːz, -tɪs/ *n* [U] disease in which there is too much sugar in the blood –**tic** /-ˈbetɪk/ *n, adj* (person) suffering from this

di·a·bol·i·cal /ˌdaɪəˈbɒlɪkəl◂‖ -ˈbɑː-/ *adj* **1** very cruel or bad **2** very unpleasant and annoying: *The train service was diabolical.* ~**ly** /-kli/ *adv*

di·ag·nose /ˈdaɪəgnəʊz‖ -noʊs/ *vt* discover the nature of (a disease)

di·ag·no·sis /ˌdaɪəgˈnəʊsɪs‖ -ˈnoʊ-/ *n*

-ses /-'si:z/ [C;U] (judgment made by) diagnosing **–nostic** /-'nɒstɪk◄/ -'nɑ:-/ adj

di·ag·o·nal /daɪˈægənəl/ adj (of a straight line) joining opposite corners of a square, etc. ~**ly** adv

di·a·gram /ˈdaɪəgræm/ n plan drawn to explain a machine, idea, etc. ~**matic** /ˌdaɪəgrəˈmætɪk◄/ adj

dial /daɪəl/ n 1 marked face of a clock, etc. 2 wheel with holes on a telephone ♦ vi/t -ll- BrE ‖ -l- AmE make a telephone call

di·a·lect /ˈdaɪəlekt/ n [C;U] variety of a language, spoken in one part of a country

di·a·lec·tic /ˌdaɪəˈlektɪk/ n [U] method of arguing according to certain rules

di·a·logue BrE ‖ -log AmE /ˈdaɪəlɒg/ -lɔːg, -lɑːg/ n [C;U] 1 conversation in a book or play 2 exchange of opinion between leaders, etc.

di·am·e·ter /daɪˈæmɪtə ‖ -ər/ n distance across a circle, measured through the centre

di·a·met·ri·cal·ly /ˌdaɪəˈmetrɪkli/ adv completely: diametrically opposed/opposite

di·a·mond /ˈdaɪəmənd/ n 1 [C;U] hard valuable precious stone 2 [C] figure with four equal sides, standing on one of its points 3 [C] red diamond-shaped figure on a playing card —see also ROUGH DIAMOND

di·a·per /ˈdaɪəpə ‖ ˈdaɪpər/ n AmE for NAPPY

di·a·phragm /ˈdaɪəfræm/ n 1 muscle separating the lungs from the stomach 2 rubber object used by a woman as a CONTRACEPTIVE

di·ar·rhoe·a, -rhe·a /ˌdaɪəˈriːə/ n [U] illness in which the bowels are emptied too often

di·a·ry /ˈdaɪəri ‖ ˈdaɪri/ n (book for) a daily record of events in one's life **–rist** n writer of a diary

di·a·tribe /ˈdaɪətraɪb/ n fml violent attack in words

dice /daɪs/ n dice small six-sided block with spots on it, used in games ♦ vt 1 cut (food) into small squares 2 **dice with death** take a great risk ~**y** adj risky and uncertain

di·chot·o·my /daɪˈkɒtəmi ‖ -ˈkɑː-/ n fml division into two opposite parts or groups

dick /dɪk/ n taboo sl PENIS

dick·y /ˈdɪki/ adj infml BrE weak

dic·tate¹ /dɪkˈteɪt ‖ ˈdɪkteɪt/ vi/t 1 say (words) for someone else to write down

2 give (orders)

dic·tate² /ˈdɪkteɪt/ n order (esp. from within ourselves): the dictates of your own conscience

dic·ta·tion /dɪkˈteɪʃən/ n 1 [U] dictating 2 [C] piece of writing dictated

dic·ta·tor /dɪkˈteɪtə ‖ ˈdɪkteɪtər/ n ruler with complete power ~**ship** n [C;U] (country with) government by a dictator ~**ial** /ˌdɪktəˈtɔːriəl◄/ adj

dic·tion /ˈdɪkʃən/ n [U] way in which someone pronounces words

dic·tion·a·ry /ˈdɪkʃənəri ‖ -neri/ n book giving a list of words in A-Z order, with their meanings

dic·tum /ˈdɪktəm/ n -ta /-tə/ or -tums formal statement of opinion

did /dɪd/ v past t. of DO

di·dac·tic /daɪˈdæktɪk, dɪ-/ adj fml intending to teach

did·dle /ˈdɪdl/ vt infml cheat

didn't /ˈdɪdnt/ v short for: did not

die¹ /daɪ/ vi died, pres p. dying /ˈdaɪ-ɪŋ/ 1 stop living; become dead: (fig.) My love will never die. | His secret died with him. 2 **be dying for/to** want very badly 3 **die hard** (of beliefs, customs, etc.) take a long time to disappear

   die away phr vi fade and then cease

   die down phr vi become less: The excitement soon died down.

   die off phr vi die one by one

   die out phr vi become EXTINCT

die² n metal block for shaping coins, etc.

die·hard /ˈdaɪhɑːd ‖ -ɑːrd/ n person who strongly opposes change

die·sel /ˈdiːzəl/ n [U] heavy oil used instead of petrol, esp. in buses and trains

di·et /ˈdaɪət/ n 1 food and drink usually taken 2 limited list of food and drink that someone is allowed for medical reasons 3 **(be/go) on a diet** (be/start) living on a limited list of food usu. in order to lose weight ♦ vi eat according to a DIET (2)

dif·fer /ˈdɪfə ‖ -ər/ vi 1 be different 2 disagree

dif·fe·rence /ˈdɪfərəns/ n 1 [C;U] way or fact of being different 2 [C] slight disagreement 3 **split the difference** agree on an amount halfway between

dif·fe·rent /ˈdɪfərənt/ adj 1 unlike 2 separate: They go to different schools. 3 various: It comes in different colours.

4 unusual **~ly** adv

dif·fe·ren·tial /ˌdɪfəˈrenʃəl◀/ n amount of difference between things: *pay differentials*

dif·fe·ren·ti·ate /ˌdɪfəˈrenʃieɪt/ vi/t see a difference (between)

dif·fi·cult /ˈdɪfɪkəlt/ adj 1 hard to do, understand, etc. 2 (of people) not easily pleased

dif·fi·cul·ty /ˈdɪfɪkəlti/ n 1 [U] being difficult; trouble 2 [C] something difficult; problem

dif·fi·dent /ˈdɪfɪdənt/ adj lacking confidence in oneself **~ly** adv **–dence** n [U]

dif·fuse¹ /dɪˈfjuːz/ vi/t fml spread freely in all directions **–fusion** /-ˈfjuːʒən/ n [U]

dif·fuse² /dɪˈfjuːs/ adj fml 1 DIFFUSED¹ 2 using too many words

dig /dɪg/ vi/t dug /dʌg/, pres p. digging 1 break up and move (earth) 2 make (a hole) in this way: *dig an underground tunnel* 3 sl like or understand 4 **dig somone in the ribs** touch someone with one's elbow, as to share a joke ♦ n 1 quick push 2 place being uncovered by ARCHAEOLOGISTS 3 unpleasant remark **digs** n [P] BrE lodgings

dig at phr vt speak to (someone) in an unpleasant way: *Stop digging at me!*

dig in phr v 1 vi/t dig a protective place for oneself; get firmly settled 2 vi start eating

dig out phr vt get out by digging

dig up phr vt find (something buried) by digging: (fig.) *dig up an old scandal*

di·gest¹ /daɪˈdʒest, dɪ-/ vt 1 change (food) so that the body can use it 2 arrange (facts) in one's mind **~ible** adj **~ive** adj of or helping in digesting food **~ion** /-ˈdʒestʃən/ n ability to digest food

di·gest² /ˈdaɪdʒest/ n short SUMMARY

di·git /ˈdɪdʒɪt/ n 1 any number from 0 to 9 2 fml finger or toe

di·git·al /ˈdɪdʒɪtəl/ adj 1 using a system in which information is shown in the form of changing electrical signals: *a digital recording/digital TV* 2 using numbers: *a digital watch* **~ally** adv **~ize** also **~ise** BrE vt change to a digital (1) system **~ization** /ˌdɪdʒɪtəlaɪˈzeɪʃən ‖ -tələ-/ n [U]

dig·ni·fied /ˈdɪgnɪfaɪd/ adj having dignity

dig·ni·ta·ry /ˈdɪgnɪtəri ‖ -teri/ n fml person of high rank

dig·ni·ty /ˈdɪgnɪti/ n [U] 1 nobleness of character 2 formal grand behaviour 3 **beneath one's dignity** below one's standard of moral or social behaviour

di·gress /daɪˈgres/ vi fml (of a writer or speaker) move away from the subject **~ion** /-ˈgreʃən/ n [C;U]

dike, also **dyke** /daɪk/ n 1 bank to hold back water 2 ditch 3 LESBIAN

di·lap·i·dat·ed /dɪˈlæpɪdeɪtɪd/ adj falling to pieces

di·late /daɪˈleɪt/ vi/t (cause to) become wider by stretching: *eyes dilated with terror* **dilation** /-ˈleɪʃən/ n [U]

di·lem·ma /dɪˈlemə, daɪ-/ n difficult choice between two things

dil·et·tan·te /ˌdɪlɪˈtænti ‖ -ˈtɑːnti/ n, adj (person) who enjoys art or branch of study but does not take it seriously

dil·i·gence /ˈdɪlɪdʒəns/ n [U] steady effort **–gent** adj **–gently** adv

di·lute /daɪˈluːt/ vt make (liquid) weaker and thinner **dilution** /-ˈluːʃən/ n [C;U]

dim /dɪm/ adj **-mm-** 1 (of light) not bright 2 not easy to see 3 sl stupid 4 **take a dim view of** think badly of ♦ vi/t **-mm-** make or become dim **~ly** adv **~ness** n [U]

dime /daɪm/ n coin of US and Canada worth 10 cents

di·men·sion /daɪˈmenʃən, dɪ-/ n 1 measurement of breadth, length, or height 2 particular site or part of a problem, subject, etc. 3 **–dimensional** having (so many) dimensions: *2-dimensional* **dimensions** n [P] size

di·min·ish /dɪˈmɪnɪʃ/ vi/t make or become smaller

dim·i·nu·tion /ˌdɪmɪˈnjuːʃən ‖ -ˈnuː-/ n [C;U] fml diminishing

di·min·u·tive /dɪˈmɪnjʊtɪv/ adj fml very small

dim·ple /ˈdɪmpəl/ n small hollow in the cheek, etc.

dim·wit /ˈdɪmwɪt/ n stupid person **~ted** /ˌdɪmˈwɪtɪd◀/ adj

din¹ /dɪn/ n loud unpleasant noise ♦ v

din² /dɪn/ v **din into** phr vt repeat (something) forcefully over and over again to (someone)

dine /daɪn/ vi fml eat dinner

dine off phr vt eat for dinner

dine out on phr vt gain social success with (news or a story)

di·ner /'daɪnə‖ -ər/ n 1 small informal restaurant 2 customer in a restaurant

din·ghy /'dɪŋgi, 'dɪŋi/ n small open boat

din·gy /'dɪndʒi/ adj dirty and faded

dining car /'·· ·/ n railway carriage where meals are served

dining ta·ble /'·· ,··/ n table for having meals on

din·ner /'dɪnə‖ -ər/ n [C;U] main meal of the day, eaten either at midday or in the evening

dinner jack·et /'·· ,··/ n man's black (or white) coat for formal evening occasions

di·no·saur /'daɪnəsɔː‖ -sɔːr/ n 1 large REPTILE that no longer exists 2 something very large and old-fashioned that no longer works well

dint /dɪnt/ n **by dint of** by means of

di·o·cese /'daɪəsɪs/ n area controlled by a BISHOP –cesan /daɪ'ɒsɪsən‖ -'ɑː-/ adj

dip¹ /dɪp/ v -pp- 1 vt put into a liquid for a moment 2 vi/t drop slightly: dip your headlights

 dip into phr vt 1 read (a book) for a short time 2 use up (money)

dip² n 1 [C] quick bathe 2 [C] downward slope 3 [U] liquid into which food is dipped at parties 4 [C] (liquid for) dipping animals: sheep dip

diph·ther·i·a /dɪf'θɪəriə, dɪp-‖ -'θɪr-/ n [U] serious infectious disease of the throat

diph·thong /'dɪfθɒŋ, 'dɪp-‖ -θɔːŋ/ n compound vowel sound

di·plo·ma /dɪ'pləʊmə‖ -'ploʊ-/ n official paper showing success in studying something

di·plo·ma·cy /dɪ'pləʊməsi‖ -'ploʊ-/ n [U] 1 management of relations between countries 2 skill at dealing with people

dip·lo·mat /'dɪpləmæt/ n person whose profession is DIPLOMACY (1) ~ic /,dɪplə-'mætɪk◄/ adj of or having diplomacy ~ically /-kli/ adv

diplomatic re·la·tions /,···· ·'··/ n [P] connection between two countries that each keep an EMBASSY in the other country

dire /daɪə‖ daɪr/ adj terrible

di·rect¹ /dɪ'rekt, daɪ-/ vt 1 tell (someone) the way to a place 2 control; manage 3 fml command; order 4 aim

direct² adj 1 going straight: direct route 2 with nothing coming between: direct result 3 honest; clearly expressed: direct

answer 4 exact: direct opposite ♦ adv without turning aside ~ly adv 1 in a direct way 2 at once ~ness n [U]

di·rec·tion /dɪ'rekʃən, daɪ-/ n 1 [C] point towards which a person or thing moves or faces 2 [U] control; management **directions** n [P] instructions

di·rec·tive /dɪ'rektɪv, daɪ-/ n official order

direct ob·ject /·,· '··/ n the noun, noun phrase, or PRONOUN that is needed to complete the meaning of a TRANSITIVE verb: In 'I saw Mary', 'Mary' is the direct object.

di·rec·tor /dɪ'rektə, daɪ-‖ -ər/ n 1 senior manager of a firm 2 person who directs a play or film ~ship n company director's position

di·rec·to·ry /daɪ'rektəri, dɪ-/ n book or list of names, facts, etc.: telephone directory

direct speech /·,· '·/ n [U] gram actual words of a speaker

dirge /dɜːdʒ‖ dɜːrdʒ/ n slow sad song

dirt /dɜːt‖ dɜːrt/ n [U] 1 unclean matter; mud, etc. 2 nasty talk 3 **treat someone like dirt** treat someone as worthless ~**y** adj 1 not clean 2 unpleasantly concerned with sex: dirty jokes ~**y** vt make dirty ~**ily** adv

dirt cheap /,· '·◄/ adj extremely cheap

dis·a·bil·i·ty /,dɪsə'bɪlɪti/ n 1 [U] being disabled 2 [C] HANDICAP (1)

dis·a·ble /dɪs'eɪbəl/ vt make unable to use one's body properly –**abled** adj ~**ment** n [C;U]

dis·a·buse /,dɪsə'bjuːz/ vt fml free (someone) from a wrong idea

dis·ad·van·tage /,dɪsəd'vɑːntɪdʒ‖ -'væn-/ n [C;U] unfavourable condition ~**ous** /,dɪsædvən'teɪdʒəs, -væn-/ adj

dis·ad·van·taged /,dɪsəd'vɑːntɪdʒd◄‖ -'væn-/ adj suffering from a disadvantage with regard to one's social position, family background, etc.

dis·af·fect·ed /,dɪsə'fektɪd◄/ adj lacking (esp. political) loyalty –**fection** /-'fekʃən/ n [U]

dis·a·gree /,dɪsə'griː/ vi 1 have different opinions 2 be different ~**able** adj unpleasant ~**ably** adv ~**ment** n [C;U] difference of opinion

 disagree with phr v (of food, etc.) make ill

dis·ap·pear /,dɪsə'pɪə‖ -'pɪr/ vi 1 go out

of sight 2 cease to exist ~ance n [C;U]

dis·ap·point /ˌdɪsəˈpɔɪnt/ vt fail to fulfil hopes ~ed adj sad at not seeing hopes fulfilled ~ing adj ~ingly adv ~ment n 1 [U] being disappointed 2 [C] something disappointing

dis·ap·prove /ˌdɪsəˈpruːv/ vi have an unfavourable opinion –proval n [U]

dis·arm /dɪsˈɑːm‖ -ˈɑːrm/ v 1 vt take away weapons from 2 vi reduce a nation's military strength 3 vt drive away the anger of: a disarming smile ~ingly adv: smile disarmingly

dis·ar·ma·ment /dɪsˈɑːməmənt ‖ -ˈɑːr-/ n [U] act or principle of DISARMING

dis·ar·ray /ˌdɪsəˈreɪ/ n fml disorder

dis·as·so·ci·ate /ˌdɪsəˈsəʊʃieɪt, -sieɪt ‖ -ˈsoʊ-/ vt DISSOCIATE

di·sas·ter /dɪˈzɑːstə‖ dɪˈzæstər/ n [C;U] sudden serious misfortune –trous adj –trously adv

dis·a·vow /ˌdɪsəˈvaʊ/ vt fml refuse to admit (knowledge, etc.)

dis·band /dɪsˈbænd/ vi/t break up (a group)

dis·be·lief /ˌdɪsbɪˈliːf/ n [U] lack of belief

dis·be·lieve /ˌdɪsbɪˈliːv/ vi/t refuse to believe

disc BrE ‖ **disk** AmE /dɪsk/ n 1 anything round and flat, such as a plate or record 2 flat piece of CARTILAGE in one's back: a slipped disc 3 a DISK (2)

dis·card /dɪsˈkɑːd‖ -ɑːrd/ vt get rid of; throw away

di·scern /dɪˈsɜːn‖ -ɜːrn/ vt see or understand esp. with difficulty ~ible adj ~ing adj able to decide and judge; having good taste ~ment n [U]

dis·charge¹ /dɪsˈtʃɑːdʒ‖-ɑːr-/ v 1 vt send (a person) away 2 vt/i let out (gas, liquid, etc.) 3 vt perform (a duty or promise) 4 vt pay (a debt) 5 vt fire (a gun, etc.)

dis·charge² /dɪsˈtʃɑːdʒ, ˈdɪstʃɑːdʒ‖ -ɑːr-/ n 1 [U] discharging 2 [C;U] something discharged

di·sci·ple /dɪˈsaɪpəl/ n follower of a (religious) leader

dis·ci·pli·nar·i·an /ˌdɪsəplɪˈneərɪən‖ -ˈner-/ n person who can make others obey and believes in firm discipline

dis·ci·pli·na·ry /ˈdɪsəplɪnəri, ˌdɪsəˈplɪ-‖ ˈdɪsəpləneri/ adj connected with punishment: take disciplinary action

dis·ci·pline /ˈdɪsəplɪn/ n 1 [U] training to produce obedience and self-control 2 [U] control gained by this training 3 [U] punishment 4 [C] branch of learning ♦ vt 1 train to be obedient 2 punish

disc jock·ey /ˈ· ˌ·/ n broadcaster who introduces records of popular music

dis·claim /dɪsˈkleɪm/ vt say one does not own: disclaim responsibility ~er n written statement which disclaims

dis·close /dɪsˈkləʊz‖ -ˈkloʊz/ vt make (a secret) known

dis·clo·sure /dɪsˈkləʊʒə‖ -ˈkloʊʒər/ n 1 [U] act of disclosing 2 [C] disclosed secret

dis·co /ˈdɪskəʊ‖-koʊ/ n -cos club where people dance to recorded music

dis·col·our BrE ‖ **-or** AmE /dɪsˈkʌlə‖ -ər/ vi/t change colour for the worse –oration /dɪsˌkʌləˈreɪʃən/ n [C;U]

dis·com·fort /dɪsˈkʌmfət ‖ -ərt/ n [C;U] (cause of) being uncomfortable

dis·con·cert /ˌdɪskənˈsɜːt ‖ -ɜːrt/ vt worry; upset ~ed adj ~ingly adv

dis·con·nect /ˌdɪskəˈnekt/ vt undo the connection of ~ed adj (of thoughts and ideas) badly arranged

dis·con·tent /ˌdɪskənˈtent/ n [U] restless unhappiness ~ed adj

dis·con·tin·ue /ˌdɪskənˈtɪnjuː/ vi/t fml stop; end

dis·cord /ˈdɪskɔːd‖ -ɔːrd/ n 1 [U] fml disagreement between people 2 [C;U] lack of musical HARMONY ~ant /dɪsˈkɔːdənt ‖ -ɔːr-/ adj

dis·co·theque /ˈdɪskətek, ˌdɪskəˈtek/ n fml for DISCO

dis·count¹ /ˈdɪskaʊnt/ n reduction in price

dis·count² /dɪsˈkaʊnt ‖ ˈdɪskaʊnt/ vt 1 regard (information) as unimportant or untrue 2 reduce the price of

dis·cour·age /dɪsˈkʌrɪdʒ‖ -ˈkɜːr-/ vt 1 take away hope from 2 persuade not to do something ~ment n [C;U]

dis·course /ˈdɪskɔːs‖ -ɔːrs/ n [C;U] fml serious conversation or speech

dis·cour·te·ous /dɪsˈkɜːtɪəs‖ -ɜːr-/ adj fml not polite ~ly adv

dis·cov·er /dɪsˈkʌvə‖ -ər/ vt find; find out ~er n ~y n 1 [U] discovering 2 [C] something found

dis·cred·it /dɪsˈkredɪt/ vt stop people from believing in ~able adj bringing shame

di·screet /dɪˈskriːt/ adj not saying too much; showing good sense and judgment: a discreet silence ~**ly** adv

di·screp·an·cy /dɪˈskrepənsi/ n difference between amounts, etc.

di·screte /dɪˈskriːt/ adj fml separate; not continuous

di·scre·tion /dɪˈskreʃən/ n [U] **1** being discreet **2** ability to decide what to do: use your own discretion ~**ary** adj

di·scrim·i·nate /dɪˈskrɪmɪneɪt/ v **1** vi/t recognize a difference **2** discriminate against/in favour of treat worse/better than others –**nating** adj (of a person) able to choose the best by seeing small differences –**natory** /-nətəri ‖ -nətɔːri/ adj –**nation** /dɪˌskrɪmɪˈneɪʃən/ n [U] —see also POSITIVE DISCRIMINATION

dis·cus /ˈdɪskəs/ n heavy plate to be thrown as a sport

dis·cuss /dɪˈskʌs/ vt talk about ~**ion** /-ˈskʌʃən/ n [C;U]

dis·dain /dɪsˈdeɪn/ n [U] fml CONTEMPT ♦ vt regard with disdain; be too proud for: She disdained to answer. ~**ful** adj

dis·ease /dɪˈziːz/ n [C;U] illness –**eased** adj: ill

dis·em·bark /ˌdɪsɪmˈbɑːk ‖ -ɑːrk/ vi/t (cause to) leave a ship

dis·em·bod·ied /ˌdɪsɪmˈbɒdid◄ ‖ -ˈbɑː-/ adj existing with no body: a disembodied voice

dis·en·chant·ed /ˌdɪsɪnˈtʃɑːntɪd◄ ‖ -ˈtʃænt-/ adj having lost belief in the value of something –**ment** n [U]

dis·en·fran·chise /ˌdɪsɪnˈfræntʃaɪz/ vt DISFRANCHISE ~**ment** /-tʃɪz- ‖ -tʃaɪz-/ n [U]

dis·en·gage /ˌdɪsɪnˈgeɪdʒ/ vi/t **1** come loose and separate **2** stop fighting

dis·en·tan·gle /ˌdɪsɪnˈtæŋgəl/ vt make free from knots: (fig.) disentangle truth from lies

dis·fig·ure /dɪsˈfɪgə ‖ -ˈfɪgjər/ vt spoil the beauty of ~**ment** n [C;U]

dis·fran·chise /dɪsˈfræntʃaɪz/ vt take away the right to vote from ~**ment** /-tʃɪz- ‖ -tʃaɪz-/ n [U]

dis·gorge /dɪsˈgɔːdʒ ‖ -ɔːr-/ vi/t (cause to) flow out

dis·grace /dɪsˈgreɪs/ n [S;U] (cause of) shame or loss of respect ♦ vt bring disgrace to ~**ful** adj

dis·grun·tled /dɪsˈgrʌntld/ adj annoyed and disappointed

dis·guise /dɪsˈgaɪz/ vt change the appearance of, to hide or deceive ♦ n **1** [C] something worn to disguise someone **2** [U] being disguised

dis·gust /dɪsˈgʌst, dɪz-/ n [U] dislike caused esp. by a bad smell or taste or bad behaviour ♦ vt cause disgust in ~**ing** adj ~**ingly** adv

dish¹ /dɪʃ/ n **1** large plate **2** cooked food of one kind **3** infml, esp. BrE good-looking person

dish² v

dish out phr vt **1** serve out to several people **2** dish it out punish or express disapproval of someone else, esp. thoughtlessly or unjustly

dish up phr vi/t put (a meal) into dishes

dis·heart·en /dɪsˈhɑːtn ‖ -ɑːr-/ vt discourage

di·shev·elled /dɪˈʃevəld/ adj (esp. of someone's hair) untidy

dis·hon·est /dɪsˈɒnɪst ‖ -ˈɑː-/ adj not honest ~**ly** adv ~**y** n [U]

dis·hon·our BrE ‖ -**or** AmE /dɪsˈɒnə ‖ -ˈɑːnər/ n [S;U] fml (person or thing bringing) loss of honour ♦ vt **1** bring dishonour to **2** cause (a cheque) to BOUNCE (3) ~**able** adj

dish·wash·er /ˈdɪʃˌwɒʃə ‖ -ˌwɒʃər, -ˌwɑː-/ n machine that washes dishes

dis·il·lu·sion /ˌdɪsɪˈluːʒən/ vt tell the unpleasant truth to ~**ed** adj –**ment** n [U]

dis·in·cen·tive /ˌdɪsɪnˈsentɪv/ n something that discourages effort

dis·in·clined /ˌdɪsɪnˈklaɪnd/ adj unwilling

dis·in·fect /ˌdɪsɪnˈfekt/ vt make (things and places) free from infection ~**ant** n chemical that disinfects

dis·in·gen·u·ous /ˌdɪsɪnˈdʒenjuəs/ adj not sincere; slightly dishonest

dis·in·her·it /ˌdɪsɪnˈherɪt/ vt take away the right to INHERIT from

dis·in·te·grate /dɪsˈɪntɪgreɪt/ vi/t break up into small pieces –**gration** /dɪsˌɪntɪˈgreɪʃən/ n [U]

dis·in·ter·est·ed /dɪsˈɪntrɪstɪd/ adj not influenced by personal advantage

dis·joint·ed /dɪsˈdʒɔɪntɪd/ adj (of words, ideas, etc.) not well connected ~**ly** adv

disk /dɪsk/ n **1** AmE for DISC **2** also **disc** — flat circular piece of plastic used for storing computer information

disk drive /'· ·/ n piece of electrical equipment used for passing information to and from a DISK (2)

dis·kette /dɪsˈket/ n [U] FLOPPY DISK

dis·like /dɪsˈlaɪk/ vt not like ♦ n [C;U]: have a dislike of cats

dis·lo·cate /ˈdɪsləkeɪt ‖ -loʊ-/ vt 1 put (a bone) out of place 2 put (traffic, plans, etc.) into disorder –**cation** /ˌdɪsləˈkeɪʃən ‖ -loʊ-/ n [C;U]

dis·lodge /dɪsˈlɒdʒ ‖ dɪsˈlɑːdʒ/ vt force out of a position

dis·loy·al /dɪsˈlɔɪəl/ adj not loyal ~**ly** adv ~**ty** n [U]

dis·mal /ˈdɪzməl/ adj sad; hopeless ~**ly** adv

dis·man·tle /dɪsˈmæntl/ vt take to pieces

dis·may /dɪsˈmeɪ/ vt, n [U] (fill with) great fear and hopelessness

dis·mem·ber /dɪsˈmembə ‖ -ər/ vt cut or tear (a body) apart

dis·miss /dɪsˈmɪs/ vt 1 fml remove from a job 2 send away 3 refuse to think seriously about 3 (of a judge) stop (a court case) –**al** n [C;U] ~**ive** adj CONTEMPTUOUS

dis·mount /dɪsˈmaʊnt/ vi get down from (a horse, bicycle, etc.)

dis·o·be·di·ent /ˌdɪsəˈbiːdiənt, ˌdɪsəʊ- ‖ ˌdɪsə-, ˌdɪsoʊ-/ adj refusing to obey ~**ly** adv –**ence** n [U]

dis·o·bey /ˌdɪsəˈbeɪ, ˌdɪsəʊ- ‖ ˌdɪsə-, ˌdɪsoʊ-/ vi/t not obey

dis·or·der /dɪsˈɔːdə ‖ -ˈɔːrdər/ n 1 [U] confusion 2 [C;U] public violence 3 [C;U] illness of the body or mind: She suffered from eating disorders (=ate too little/much because of emotional problems) ♦ vt put into disorder ~**ly** adj

dis·or·gan·ize also -**ise** BrE /dɪsˈɔːɡənaɪz ‖ -ˈɔːr-/ vt throw into confusion

dis·o·ri·en·tate /dɪsˈɔːriənteɪt/ also **dis·o·ri·ent** /-riənt/ — vt cause (someone) to lose sense of time, direction, etc.; confuse

dis·own /dɪsˈəʊn ‖ -ˈoʊn/ vt say that one has no connection with

di·spar·age /dɪˈspærɪdʒ/ vt speak without respect of –**agingly** adv

dis·pa·rate /ˈdɪspərət/ adj fml that cannot be compared; quite different –**rity** /dɪˈspærɪti/ n [C;U] inequality

dis·pas·sion·ate /dɪsˈpæʃənɪt/ adj calm and fair; not taking sides ~**ly** adv

di·spatch, **despatch** /dɪˈspætʃ/ vt 1 send: dispatch invitations 2 finish (work, etc.) quickly ♦ n 1 [C] message sent 2 [U] sending 3 [U] speed and effectiveness

di·spel /dɪˈspel/ vt -ll- drive away; scatter

dis·pen·sa·tion /ˌdɪspenˈseɪʃən, -pen-/ n 1 [C;U] permission to disobey a rule 2 [U] fml dispensing

di·spense /dɪˈspens/ vt 1 give out to people 2 prepare (medicines) –**sary** n place where medicines are dispensed –**ser** machine that dispenses drinks, money, etc.

dispense with phr vt do without

di·sperse /dɪˈspɜːs ‖ -ɜːrs/ vi/t scatter in different directions **dispersal** n [U]

di·spir·it·ed /dɪˈspɪrɪtɪd/ adj lit discouraged –**ting** adj discouraging

dis·place /dɪsˈpleɪs/ vt 1 force out of the proper place 2 take the place of ~**ment** n [U]

di·splay /dɪˈspleɪ/ vt show ♦ n [C;U]: a display of skill

dis·please /dɪsˈpliːz/ vt fml annoy –**pleasure** /-ˈpleʒə ‖ -ər/ n [U] annoyance

dis·pos·a·ble /dɪˈspəʊzəbəl ‖ -ˈspoʊ-/ adj 1 to be used once and then thrown away: disposable plates 2 able to be used: disposable income (=money available to spend)

dis·pos·al /dɪˈspəʊzəl ‖ -ˈspoʊ-/ n [U] 1 removal 2 at one's disposal for one to use

di·spose /dɪˈspəʊz ‖ -ˈspoʊz/ v **dispose of** phr vt get rid of

di·sposed /dɪˈspəʊzd ‖ -ˈspoʊzd/ adj 1 willing: I don't feel disposed to help. 2 having a tendency

dis·po·si·tion /ˌdɪspəˈzɪʃən/ n fml person's natural character

dis·pos·sess /ˌdɪspəˈzes/ vt fml take property away from

dis·pro·por·tion·ate /ˌdɪsprəˈpɔːʃənɪt ‖ -ɔːr-/ adj too much or too little ~**ly** adv

dis·prove /dɪsˈpruːv/ vt prove to be false

di·spute /dɪˈspjuːt/ v 1 vi/t argue (about) 2 vt question the truth of 3 vt struggle over or about (esp. in defence): disputed territory ♦ /dɪˈspjuːt, ˈdɪspjuːt/ n [C;U] argument; quarrel

dis·qual·i·fy /dɪsˈkwɒlɪfaɪ ‖ -ˈkwɑː-/ vt make unfit to do something –**fication** /dɪsˌkwɒlɪfɪˈkeɪʃən ‖ -ˌkwɑː-/ n [C;U]

dis·qui·et /dɪsˈkwaɪət/ *vt fml* make anxious ♦ *n* [U] anxiety

dis·re·gard /ˌdɪsrɪˈɡɑːd ‖ -ˈɑːrd/ *vt* pay no attention to ♦ *n* [U] lack of proper attention

dis·re·pair /ˌdɪsrɪˈpeə ‖ -ˈper/ *n* [U] need for repair

dis·rep·u·ta·ble /dɪsˈrepj̊təbəl/ *adj* having a bad REPUTATION

dis·re·pute /ˌdɪsrɪˈpjuːt/ *n* [U] loss of people's good opinion

dis·re·spect /ˌdɪsrɪˈspekt/ *n* [U] rudeness –**ful** *adj*

dis·rupt /dɪsˈrʌpt/ *vt* throw into disorder ~**ive** *adj*: *disruptive influence* ~**ion** /-ˈrʌpʃən/ *n* [C;U]

dis·sat·is·fy /dɪˈsætɪsfaɪ, dɪsˈsæ-/ *vt* fail to satisfy; displease: *a dissatisfied customer* –**faction** /ˌdɪˌsætɪsˈfækʃən, dɪsˌsæ-/ *n* [U]

dis·sect /dɪˈsekt, daɪ-/ *vt* cut up (a body) so as to study it ~**ion** /-ˈsekʃən/ *n* [C;U]

dis·sem·i·nate /dɪˈsemɪneɪt/ *vt fml* spread (ideas, etc.) widely –**nation** /dɪˌsemɪˈneɪʃən/ *n* [U]

dis·sen·sion /dɪˈsenʃən/ *n* [C;U] disagreement; argument

dis·sent /dɪˈsent/ *vi* disagree with an opinion ♦ *n* [U] refusal to agree ~**er** *n*

dis·ser·ta·tion /ˌdɪsəˈteɪʃən ‖ ˌdɪsər-/ *n* long (written) account of a subject

dis·ser·vice /dɪˈsɜːvɪs, dɪsˈsɜː- ‖ -ˈsɜːr-/ *n* [U] harm or harmful action

dis·si·dent /ˈdɪsɪdənt/ *n, adj* (person) who disagrees: *political dissidents*

dis·sim·i·lar /dɪˈsɪmɪlə, dɪsˈsɪ- ‖ -ər/ *adj* not similar

dis·si·pat·ed /ˈdɪsɪpeɪtɪd/ *adj* wasting one's life in foolish or dangerous pleasure

dis·so·ci·ate /dɪˈsəʊʃieɪt, -sieɪt ‖ -ˈsoʊ-/ also **disassociate** — *n* separate in one's mind –**ation** /dɪˌsəʊʃiˈeɪʃən, -siˈeɪʃən ‖ -ˌsoʊ-/ *n* [U]

dis·so·lute /ˈdɪsəluːt/ *n, adj* (person) who leads a bad or immoral life ~**ly** *adv* ~**ness** *n* [U]

dis·so·lu·tion /ˌdɪsəˈluːʃən/ *n* [U] breaking up of a group

dis·solve /dɪˈzɒlv ‖ dɪˈzɑːlv/ *vi/t* 1 make (a solid) become liquid 2 cause (a group) to break up: *dissolve Parliament* 3 fade out or away gradually: *his strength/the clouds dissolved* 4 lose one's self-control under the influence of strong feeling: *dissolve into tears/laughter*

dis·so·nance /ˈdɪsənəns/ *n* 1 [C;U] combination of musical notes which do not sound pleasant together 2 [S;U] distant place 3 lack of agreement between beliefs and actions –**nant** *adj*

dis·suade /dɪˈsweɪd/ *vt* persuade not to –**suasion** /-ˈsweɪʒən/ *n* [U]

dis·tance /ˈdɪstəns/ *n* 1 [C;U] separation in space between places 2 [S] distant place: *watch from a distance* 3 **go the distance** (in sports) keep playing, etc. till the end of the match 4 **keep one's distance** stay far enough away 5 **keep someone at a distance** treat someone without much friendliness —see also MIDDLE DISTANCE ♦ *vt* separate (esp. oneself) esp. in the mind or feelings

dis·tant /ˈdɪstənt/ *adj* 1 far off 2 not close: *distant relations* 3 unfriendly –**ly** *adv*

dis·taste /dɪsˈteɪst/ *n* [U] dislike ~**ful** *adj* unpleasant

dis·tem·per /dɪˈstempə ‖ -ər/ *n* [U] 1 water-based paint for walls 2 infectious disease of animals

dis·tend /dɪˈstend/ *vi/t fml* swell

dis·til also -**till** *AmE* /dɪˈstɪl/ *vt* -**ll**- 1 make (a liquid) into gas and then make the gas into liquid, as when making alcoholic drinks 2 get or take the most important part(s) of (a book, an idea, etc.) ~**lery** /-ləri/ *n* place where WHISKY, etc. is distilled ~**lation** /ˌdɪstɪˈleɪʃən/ *n* [C;U]

dis·tinct /dɪˈstɪŋkt/ *adj* 1 different; separate 2 clearly noticed ~**ly** *adv*

dis·tinc·tion /dɪˈstɪŋkʃən/ *n* 1 [C;U] difference 2 [S;U] unusual excellence 3 [C] mark of honour –**tive** /-tɪv/ *adj* showing a difference –**tively** *adv*

dis·tin·guish /dɪˈstɪŋɡwɪʃ/ *v* 1 *vi/t* recognize a difference 2 *vi/t* see clearly 3 *vt* make different 4 **distinguish oneself** perform noticeably well ~**able** *adj* ~**ed** *adj* excellent; famous

dis·tort /dɪˈstɔːt ‖ -ɔːrt/ *vt* 1 twist out of the natural shape 2 give a false account of ~**ion** /-ˈstɔːʃən ‖ -ɔːr-/ *n* [C;U]

dis·tract /dɪˈstrækt/ *vt* take (someone's attention) away ~**ed** *adj* anxious and confused ~**ion** /-ˈstrækʃən/ *n* 1 [C] amusement, etc. that distracts 2 [U] anxious confusion

dis·traught /dɪˈstrɔːt ‖ -ˈstrɔːt/ *adj* very anxious and troubled

dis·tress /dɪ'stres/ n [U] **1** great suffering or sorrow **2** serious danger ♦ vt cause suffering to: *distressing news*

dis·trib·ute /dɪ'strɪbjuːt/ vt **1** give out: *distribute prizes* **2** scatter **–utor** n **1** person who distributes goods **2** instrument that distributes electric current in an engine **–ution** /ˌdɪstrɪ'bjuːʃən/ n [C;U]

dis·trict /'dɪstrɪkt/ n area of a country or city

dis·trust /dɪs'trʌst/ vt have no trust in ♦ n [S;U] lack of trust **~fully** adv

dis·turb /dɪ'stɜːb ‖ -ɜːrb/ vt **1** interrupt **2** worry: *disturbing news* **~ance** n [C;U] **1** act of disturbing **2** noisy disorder **~ed** adj having or showing signs of an illness of the mind

dis·use /dɪs'juːs/ n [U] state of no longer being used: *to fall into disuse* **–used** /ˌdɪs'juːzd◂/ adj

ditch /dɪtʃ/ n passage cut for water to flow through ♦ vt sl get rid of

dith·er /'dɪðə ‖ -ər/ vi be unable to decide **dither** n [S]

dit·to /'dɪtəʊ ‖ -toʊ/ n -**tos** the same

dit·ty /'dɪti/ n short simple song

di·van /dɪ'væn ‖ 'daɪvæn/ n bed with no back

dive /daɪv/ vi **dived** or **dove** /dəʊv ‖ doʊv/ AmE, **dived 1** jump head first into water **2** go under water **3** (of a plane or bird) go down steeply and swiftly **4** go down quickly: *dive under the table* **5** enter quickly into some matter or activity ♦ n **1** act of diving **2** not very respectable club, etc. **diver** n person who dives, or works on the sea bottom

di·verge /daɪ'vɜːdʒ, də- ‖ -ɜːr-/ vi separate; get further apart **divergence** n [C;U]

di·verse /daɪ'vɜːs ‖ daɪ'vɜːrs, daɪ-/ adj of different kinds **diversity** /daɪ'vɜːsɪti, də- ‖ -ɜːr-/ n [S;U] variety

di·ver·si·fy /daɪ'vɜːsɪfaɪ ‖ daɪ'vɜːr-, daɪ-/ vi/t make diverse: *diversify our range of products* **–fication** /daɪ,vɜːsɪfə'keɪʃən ‖ daɪ,vɜːr-, daɪ-/ n [U]

di·ver·sion /daɪ'vɜːʃən, də- ‖ -ɜːrʒən/ n **1** [C;U] diverting **2** [C] something that amuses people **~ary** adj intended to DIVERT: *diversionary tactics*

di·vert /daɪ'vɜːt, də- ‖ -ɜːr-/ vt turn to another direction: *divert a river/my attention*

di·vest /daɪ'vest, də-/ vt take away from someone

di·vide /dɪ'vaɪd/ vi/t **1** separate into parts **2** find out how many times one number is contained in another **3** be an important cause of disagreement between ♦ n something that divides

div·i·dend /'dɪvɪdənd, -dend/ n **1** part of profit that is divided among SHAREHOLDERS **2** pay dividends produce an advantage

di·vine¹ /dɪ'vaɪn/ adj **1** of God or a god **2** excellent **divinity** /dɪ'vɪnɪti/ n **1** [U] quality or state of being divine **2** [C] god or goddess **3** [U] THEOLOGY

divine² /dɪ'vaɪn/ vi/t **1** fml find out; guess **2** find (water or minerals) underground using a Y-shaped stick **diviner** n

div·ing board /'···/ n high board off which people DIVE (1) into the water

di·vis·i·ble /dɪ'vɪzəbəl/ adj that can be divided

di·vi·sion /dɪ'vɪʒən/ n **1** [U] separation or sharing **2** [C] one of the parts into which a whole is divided: *the firm's export division* **3** [C] something that separates **4** [U] disagreement **5** [U] process of dividing numbers **~al** adj

di·vi·sive /dɪ'vaɪsɪv/ adj causing disunity

di·vorce /dɪ'vɔːs ‖ -ɔːrs/ n **1** [C;U] legal ending of a marriage **2** [C] separation ♦ v **1** vt/i end a marriage by law **2** vt separate completely **divorcée** /dɪ'vɔːsiː ‖ dɪ,vɔːr-'seɪ, -'siː/ **divorcé** /dɪ'vɔːsiː, -seɪ ‖ -ɔːr-/ masc. — n divorced person

di·vulge /daɪ'vʌldʒ, də-/ vt fml tell (a secret)

DIY /ˌdiː aɪ 'waɪ/ abbrev. for: DO-IT-YOURSELF

diz·zy /'dɪzi/ adj **1** feeling as if things are going round and round **2** causing this feeling: *dizzy heights* **3** silly **–zily** adv **–ziness** n [U]

DJ /ˌdiː 'dʒeɪ◂/ n abbrev. for: **1** DISC JOCKEY **2** DINNER JACKET

DNA /ˌdiː en 'eɪ/ n [U] acid which carries GENETIC information in a cell

do¹ /duː/ v aux **did** /dɪd/, **done** /dʌn/ **1** (used with another verb): *Do you like it?* | *He doesn't know.* | *Do be careful!* **2** (used instead of another verb): *He walks faster than I do.* | *She likes it, and so do I.* | *She sings, doesn't she?*

do² v **1** vt perform (an action); work at or

produce: *do a sum/one's homework/the cooking/business/one's best/one's duty* | *do* (=study) *Science at school* | *do 80 miles an hour* | *It'll do you good.* 2 *vi* a advance: *do well/badly* b behave: *Do as you're told!* 3 *vi/t* be enough or suitable (for): *Will £5 do (you)?* | *That will do!* 4 *vt sl* cheat: *We've been done!* 5 **do well by** treat well 6 **How do you do?** (used when one is introduced to someone) 7 **make do** use (something) even though it may not be perfect or enough 8 **nothing doing** *sl* no 9 **That does it!** (expression showing that enough, or too much has been done) 10 **What do you do (for a living)?** What is your work?

do away with *phr vt* 1 cause to end 2 kill or murder (someone or oneself)

do down *phr vt* 1 cause to feel ashamed or less proud of oneself 2 say bad things about (someone not present)

do for *phr vt* 1 kill or ruin 2 *BrE infml* keep house or do cleaning for (someone) 3 **What will you do for (something)?** What arrangements will you make for (something)?: *What will you do for food?*

do in
phr vt 1 kill someone 2 tire completely

do out of *phr vt* cause to lose, by cheating

do over *phr vt sl* attack and wound

do up *phr vt* 1 fasten or wrap 2 repair; improve

do with *phr vt* 1 need; want 2 cause (oneself) to spend time doing: *I don't know what to do with myself since you've gone.* 3 (in questions with 'what') to do with regard to: *'What have you done with my pen?'* (=where have you put it?) 4 **have/be to do with** be connected with

do without *phr vi/t* succeed without

do³ *n infml* 1 *esp. BrE* a big party 2 **dos and don'ts** rules of behaviour

d.o.b. *abbrev. for:* date of birth

do·cile /'dəʊsaɪl ǁ 'dɑ:səl/ *adj* quiet and easily taught

dock¹ /dɒk ǁ dɑ:k/ *n* 1 place where ships are loaded and unloaded, or repaired: *London's dockland* 2 place in a court of law where prisoner stands ♦ *vi/t* 1 (cause to) sail into, or remain at, a DOCK (1) 2 (cause spacecraft) to join in space ~**er** *n* person who works at a dock, loading and unloading ships

dock² *vt* cut off the end of: (fig.) *dock someone's wages*

dock·yard /'dɒkjɑːd ǁ 'dɑ:kjɑːrd/ *n* SHIPYARD

doc·tor /'dɒktə ǁ 'dɑ:ktər/ *n* 1 person trained in medicine 2 person holding one of the highest university degrees ♦ *vt* 1 change dishonestly: *doctor the accounts* 2 make (an animal) unable to breed

doc·tor·ate /'dɒktərɪt ǁ 'dɑ:k-/ *n* degree of a DOCTOR (2)

doc·tri·naire /ˌdɒktrɪ'neə◄ ǁ ˌdɑ:ktrə'ner◄/ *adj* not questioning a doctrine; not practical: *doctrinaire socialism*

doc·trine /'dɒktrɪn ǁ 'dɑ:k-/ *n* [C;U] belief; set of teachings –**trinal** /dɒk'traɪnəl ǁ 'dɑ:ktrɪnəl/ *adj*

doc·u·ment /'dɒkjʊmənt ǁ 'dɑ:k-/ *n* paper giving information, proof, etc. ♦ /-ment/ *vt* 1 write or record information about 2 prove or support with documents ~**ation** /ˌdɒkjʊmən'teɪʃən, -men- ǁ ˌdɑ:k-/ *n* [U] documents used as proof

doc·u·men·ta·ry /ˌdɒkjʊ'mentəri◄ ǁ ˌdɑ:k-/ *adj* 1 of documents presenting facts through art ♦ *n* film, broadcast, etc. presenting facts

dod·dle /'dɒdl ǁ 'dɑ:dl/ *n infml BrE* something that is very easy to do

dodge /dɒdʒ ǁ dɑ:dʒ/ *v* 1 *vi/t* avoid (something) by suddenly moving aside 2 *vt* avoid dishonestly ♦ *n* clever trick **dodgy** *adj* risky

doe /dəʊ ǁ doʊ/ *n* female of esp. the deer, rat, and rabbit

does /dəz; *strong* dʌz/ *v* 3rd pers. sing. pres. of DO

does·n't /'dʌzənt/ *v short for:* does not

dog /dɒg ǁ dɔ:g/ *n* 1 common four-legged animal, useful to humans 2 male of this and similar animals 3 **a dog's life** a very unhappy life 4 **let sleeping dogs lie** leave something alone —see also TOP DOG ♦ *vt* -gg- follow closely; PURSUE: *dogged by bad luck* **dogs** *n* [P] 1 dog races 2 **go to the dogs** be ruined

dog col·lar /'· ˌ·◄/ *n* 1 neckband for a dog 2 *infml* priest's stiff collar

dog-eared /'· ·◄/ *adj* (of pages) bent down with use

dog·ged /'dɒgɪd ǁ 'dɔ:-/ *adj* refusing to give up; determined ~**ly** *adv*

dog·house /'dɒghaʊs ǁ 'dɔ:g-/ *n* **in the**

doghouse in a state of disfavour or shame

dog·ma /'dɒgmə ‖ 'dɔːgmə, 'dɑːgmə/ n [C;U] (religious) belief to be accepted without reasoning ~**tic** /dɒg'mætɪk ‖ dɔːg-, dɑːg-/ adj trying to force one's beliefs on other people ~**tically** /-kli/ adv

do-good·er /ˌ· '··‖'·, ·ˌ·/ n person who tries to do good things for others

dogs·bod·y /'dɒgz,bɒdi ‖ 'dɔːgz,bɑːdi/ n BrE person in a low position who does the dull work

dog-tired /ˌ· '·◄/ adj very tired

do-it-your·self /ˌ· · ·'·/ n [U] doing repairs, painting the house, etc. oneself, rather than paying workmen

dol·drums /'dɒldrəmz ‖ 'doʊl-, 'dɑːl-, 'dɔːl-/ n [P] **in the doldrums** sad and dull

dole¹ /dəʊl ‖ doʊl/ n **on the dole** receiving money from the government because one is unemployed

dole² v dole out phr vt give in small shares

dole·ful /'dəʊlfəl ‖ 'doʊl-/ adj unhappy ~**ly** adv

doll¹ /dɒl ‖ dɑːl, dɔːl/ n small toy figure of a person

doll² v doll up phr vt dress prettily

dol·lar /'dɒlə ‖ 'dɑːlər/ n 1 unit of money, as used in the US, Canada, and other countries 2 piece of paper, coin, etc. of this value

dol·lop /'dɒləp ‖ 'dɑː-/ n shapeless mass, esp. of food

dol·phin /'dɒlfɪn ‖ 'dɑːl-, 'dɔːl-/ n sea-animal, two to three metres long, which swims in groups

do·main /də'meɪn, dəʊ-‖ də-, doʊ-/ n 1 area of interest or knowledge 2 land controlled by one ruler

dome /dəʊm ‖ doʊm/ n rounded roof domed adj like or covered with a dome

do·mes·tic /də'mestɪk/ adj 1 of the house, home, or family 2 not foreign: domestic policies 3 (of animals) not wild ~**ally** /-kli/ adv ~**ticity** /ˌdəʊme'stɪsti ‖ ˌdoʊ-/ family life

dom·i·cile /'dɒmɪsaɪl ‖ 'dɑː-, 'doʊ-/ n fml place where one lives domicile vt

dom·i·nant /'dɒmɪnənt ‖ 'dɑː-/ adj most noticeable or important; dominating ~**nance** n [U] controlling influence; importance

dom·i·nate /'dɒmɪneɪt ‖ 'dɑː-/ vi/t

1 have power (over); control 2 have the most important place (in) 3 rise or be higher than: The castle dominated the whole town. -**nation** /ˌdɒmɪ'neɪʃən ‖ ˌdɑː-/ n [U]

dom·i·neer /ˌdɒmɪ'nɪə ‖ ˌdɑːmɪ'nɪr/ vi try to control others unpleasantly

do·min·ion /də'mɪnjən/ n 1 [U] lit power to rule 2 [C] land under one government

dom·i·no /'dɒmɪnəʊ ‖ 'dɑːmɪnoʊ/ n -**noes** small flat piece of wood with spots on it, used with others in a game (**dominoes**)

domino ef·fect /'··· ·ˌ·/ n [S] situation in which one event causes similar ones to happen one after another

don /dɒn ‖ dɑːn/ n BrE university teacher

do·nate /dəʊ'neɪt ‖ 'doʊneɪt/ vt give (money, etc.), esp. for a good purpose donation /dəʊ'neɪʃən ‖ doʊ-/ n [C;U]

done /dʌn/ v 1 past p. of DO 2 finished 3 esp. BrE socially acceptable

don·key /'dɒŋki ‖ 'dɑːŋki/ n 1 animal like a small horse, with long ears 2 **donkey's years** a very long time

donkey work /'·· ˌ·/ hard or boring part of a job

do·nor /'dəʊnə ‖ 'doʊnər/ n person who gives or donates: blood donor

don't /dəʊnt ‖ doʊnt/ v short for: do not

do·nut /'dəʊnʌt ‖ 'doʊ-/ n —see DOUGHNUT

doo·dle /'duːdl/ vi/t draw lines, figures, etc. aimlessly while thinking of something else doodle n

doom /duːm/ n 1 unavoidable destruction 2 **doom and gloom** hopelessness ~**ed** DESTINED to something bad

Dooms·day /'duːmzdeɪ/ n [S] end of the world

door /dɔː ‖ dɔːr/ n 1 thing that closes an entrance: bedroom/cupboard/car door 2 DOORWAY 3 (in some fixed phrases) house or building: live next door/two doors away 4 **be on the door** have some duty at the door, such as collecting tickets 5 **by the back door** secretly or by a trick 6 **shut/close the door to/on** make impossible 7 **out of doors** OUTDOORS

door·step /'dɔːstep ‖ 'dɔːr-/ n step in front of a door

door·way /'dɔːweɪ ‖ 'dɔːr-/ n opening for a door

dope /dəʊp ‖ doʊp/ n [U] harmful drug ♦ vt give dope to ~**y** adj 1 sleepy and unable to think clearly, (as if) caused by drugs

2 stupid

dork /dɔːk ‖ dɔːrk/ *n infml derog* strange or stupid person

dor·mant /'dɔːmənt ‖ 'dɔːr-/ *adj* inactive: *dormant volcano*

dor·mi·to·ry /'dɔːmətəri ‖ 'dɔːrmɨtɔːri/ *n* bedroom for several people

dor·mouse /'dɔːmaʊs ‖ 'dɔːr-/ *n* -**mice** /-maɪs/ small mouse

DOS /dɒs ‖ daːs/ *n* [U] *tdmk abbrev. for:* Disk Operating System; SOFTWARE that makes the different parts of a computer system work together

dos·age /'dəʊsɪdʒ ‖ 'doʊ-/ *n fml* amount of a dose

dose /dəʊs ‖ doʊs/ *n* measured amount of medicine to be taken at a time ♦ *vt* give medicine to

doss /dɒs ‖ daːs/ *v* **doss down** *phr vi sl, esp. BrE* sleep, esp. not in a proper bed ~**er** *n* **1** person who sleeps in dosshouses **2** *infml* lazy person

doss·house /'dɒshaʊs ‖ 'daːs-/ *n* -**houses** /-haʊzɨz/ *esp. BrE* very cheap lodging-house

dos·si·er /'dɒsieɪ ‖ 'dɔːsjeɪ, 'daː-/ *n* set of papers containing facts about a person or subject

dot /dɒt ‖ daːt/ *n* **1** small spot **2 on the dot** at the exact moment —see also YEAR DOT ♦ *vt* -**tt- 1** mark with a dot **2** cover with dots **3 dotted about** scattered **4 sign on the dotted line** agree to something quickly and unconditionally ~**ty** *adj* slightly mad

do·tage /'dəʊtɪdʒ ‖ 'doʊ-/ *n* [U] weakness of the mind caused by old age

dote /dəʊt ‖ doʊt/ *v* **dote on** *phr vt* be too fond of **doting** *adj: a doting wife*

dou·ble¹ /'dʌbəl/ *adj* **1** with two parts or uses: *double doors* | *a double meaning* **2** for two people: *a double bed* ♦ *adv, predeterminer* twice: *cloth folded double* | *buy double the amount* **doubly** *adv* twice as: *doubly careful*

double² *n* **1** [C;U] twice the amount: *I'll have a double (vodka) please.* **2** [C] person who looks just like another **3 at the double** quickly **doubles** *n* [P] match between two pairs of players

double³ *v* **1** *vi/t* make or become twice as much **2** *vt* fold in half

double as *phr vt* have as a second use or job

double back *phr vi* return along the same path

double up *phr vi/t* bend (the body) at the waist: *doubled up with pain*

double bass /ˌdʌbəl 'beɪs/ *n* largest stringed musical instrument of the VIOLIN family, with a very deep sound

double-breast·ed /ˌ·· '··◄/ *adj* (of a coat) crossing over in front, with two rows of buttons

double-check /ˌ·· '·/ *vi/t* examine (something) twice for exactness or quality

double chin /ˌ·· '·/ *n* fold of loose skin between the face and neck

double-cross /ˌ·· '·/ *vt* cheat; BETRAY ~**er** *n*

double-deck·er /ˌ·· '··◄/ *n* bus with two levels

double-dutch /ˌ·· '·/ *n* [U] speech or writing that one cannot understand

double-glaz·ing /ˌ·· '·/ *n* [U] two thicknesses of glass in a window –**glaze** *vt*

double-quick /ˌ·· '·◄/ *adj, adv* very quick(ly)

doubt /daʊt/ *vt* **1** feel uncertain about **2** consider unlikely: *I doubt he'll come.* ♦ *n* **1** [C;U] (feeling of) uncertainty **2 in doubt** in a condition of uncertainty **3 no doubt** probably ~**ful** *adj* **1** uncertain **2** not likely ~**less** *adv* without doubt **2** probably

dough /dəʊ ‖ doʊ/ *n* [U] **1** mixture for making bread **2** *sl* money

dough·nut also **donut** /'dəʊnʌt ‖ 'doʊ-/ *n* ring-shaped cake cooked in fat

dour /dʊə ‖ daʊər, dʊr/ *adj* hard and cold in one's nature; unfriendly ~**ly** *adv*

douse /daʊs/ *vt* **1** throw water over **2** put out (a light)

dove¹ /dʌv/ *n* **1** kind of PIGEON **2** person in favour of peace

dove² /dəʊv ‖ doʊv/ *v past t. (esp. AmE)* of DIVE

dove·tail /'dʌvteɪl/ *n* close-fitting joint for two pieces esp. of wood ♦ *v* **1** *vt* join two pieces of wood with a dovetail **2** *vi* fit skilfully or perfectly together

dow·a·ger /'daʊədʒə ‖ -ər/ *n* grand old lady

dow·dy /'daʊdi/ *adj* **1** dully dressed **2** (of clothes) dull

down¹ /daʊn/ *adv* **1** to or at a lower level: *The sun's going down.* | *Please sit down.* **2** to the south: *come down from Scotland* **3** on paper: *write/copy it down* **4** from the past: *jewels handed down in the family* **5** (shows reduction): *Profits are down.* | *Turn the radio down.* **6 Down with...** Let's get rid of... ♦ *prep* **1** to or at a lower level on: *run down the hill* | *swim down the river* **2** along: *They live down the road.* **3** to: *I'm just going down to the shops.* ♦ *adj* **1** at a lower level, esp. lying on the ground: *The telephone wires are down.* | *Prices are down.* **2** directed down: *the down escalator* **3** finished: *8 down and 2 to go* **4** sad **5** not working: *The computer/phone is down.* **6 down on** having a low opinion or dislike for ♦ *vt* **1** knock down; defeat **2** drink quickly ~**er** *n sl* **1** drug that reduces activity **2** experience or state of affairs which is saddening

down² *n* [U] soft feathers or hair ~**y** *adj*

down-and-out /ˌ· · '·◄/ *adj, n* (person who is) suffering from bad fortune, lack of money, etc.

down·cast /'daʊnkɑːst ‖ -kæst/ *adj* **1** downhearted **2** (of eyes) looking down

down·fall /'daʊnfɔːl ‖ -fɒːl/ *n* sudden ruin

down·grade /'daʊngreɪd, ˌdaʊn'greɪd ‖ 'daʊngreɪd/ *vt* reduce to a lower position

down·heart·ed /ˌdaʊn'hɑːtɪd◄ ‖ -ɑːr-/ *adj* low in spirits; sad

down·hill /ˌdaʊn'hɪl◄/ *adj, adv* **1** down a slope **2 go downhill** become worse

Down·ing Street /'daʊnɪŋ striːt/ *n* the government of Great Britain

down·load /'daʊnləʊd ‖ -loʊd/ *vt* move (information) from one part of a computer system to another using a MODEM

down pay·ment /ˌ· '··/ *n* part of the full price paid at the time of buying, with the rest to be paid later

down·play /ˌdaʊn'pleɪ/ *vt* cause (a situation, etc.) to seem less serious than it is

down·pour /'daʊnpɔː ‖ -pɔːr/ *n* heavy fall of rain

down·right /'daʊnraɪt/ *adj* **1** plain; honest **2** (of something bad) complete ♦ *adv*: *downright rude*

downs /daʊnz/ *n* [P] low grassy hills

down·shif·ting /'daʊnˌʃɪftɪŋ/ *n* [U] moving to a job with less money, responsibility, etc. in order to improve the quality of one's life **downshift** *vi*

down·side /'daʊnsaɪd/ *n* [the+S] the negative side of a situation

down·size /'daʊnsaɪz/ *vi/t* reduce the number of people working in (a company) –**ing** *n* [U]

Down's Syndrome /'daʊnz ˌsɪndrəʊm ‖ -droʊm/ also **Down's** /daʊnz/ *n* [U] medical condition that someone is born with, which prevents normal development

down·stairs /ˌdaʊn'steəz◄ ‖ -erz◄/ *adv, adj* on or to a lower floor

down·stream /ˌdaʊn'striːm◄/ *adv, adj* moving with the current of a river

down·time /'daʊntaɪm/ *n* [U] time during which a computer is not operating

down-to-earth /ˌ· · '·◄/ *adj* practical; sensible

down·town /ˌdaʊn'taʊn◄/ *adv, adj* to or in the (business) centre of a town

down·trod·den /'daʊnˌtrɒdn ‖ -ˌtrɑː-/ *adj* treated badly by those in power

down·turn /'daʊntɜːn ‖ -tɜːrn/ *n* [U] start of an unsuccessful period: *a downturn in the economy*

down·ward /'daʊnwəd ‖ -wərd/ *adj* going down –**wards** *adv*

dow·ry /'daʊəri ‖ 'daʊri/ *n* property that a woman's father gives to her husband when she marries

dowse /daʊz/ *vi* search for water or other substances under the ground using special sticks

doze /dəʊz ‖ doʊz/ *vi* sleep lightly **doze** *n* [S] –**zy** *adj* **1** sleepy **2** stupid

doz·en /'dʌzən/ *determiner, n* **dozen** or **dozens 1** twelve **2 talk, speak, etc. nineteen/twenty/forty to the dozen** talk quickly and continuously

Dr *written abbrev. for*: Doctor

drab /dræb/ *adj* dull ~**ness** *n* [U]

draft /drɑːft ‖ dræft/ *n* **1** first rough plan of something **2** written order for money from a bank **3** *AmE for* DRAUGHT **4** *AmE for* CONSCRIPTION ♦ *vt* **1** make a DRAFT (1) of **2** *AmE for* CONSCRIPT¹

drafts·man /'drɑːftsmən ‖ 'dræfts-/ -**woman** /-wʊmən/ *fem. n* — -**men** /-mən/ **1** person who drafts new laws **2** *AmE for* DRAUGHTSMAN

drag /dræg/ *v* -**gg**- **1** *vt* pull (something heavy) along **2** *vi* move too slowly: *The meeting dragged on for hours.* **3** *vt* cause to come or go unwillingly: *They dragged me to a party.* **4** *vi* move along while touching the

dragon

5 *vt* search the bottom of (water) with a net
6 **drag one's feet/heels** act intentionally
in a slow or ineffective way ♦ *n* 1 [C]
someone or something that makes progress
hard 2 [S] *sl* dull event or person 3 [U] *sl* the
clothing of one sex worn by the other 4 [C]
sl act of breathing in cigarette smoke

drag on *phr vi* last an unnecessarily
long time

drag out *phr v* 1 *vi/t* (cause) to last an
unnecessarily long time 2 *vt* force
(something) to be told

drag up *phr vt* raise (a subject)
unnecessarily

drag·on /ˈdrægən/ *n* 1 imaginary fire-
breathing animal 2 fierce old woman

dra·gon·fly /ˈdrægənflaɪ/ *n* large insect
found esp. over water

drain /dreɪn/ *vi/t* 1 (cause to) flow away
2 make or become dry by removing liquid:
drain a field | *wet plates on the* **draining-
board** 3 empty by drinking the contents of
4 make weak and tired ♦ *n* 1 ditch or pipe
to carry water away 2 something that uses
up money, etc. 3 **down the drain** used
wastefully or brought to nothing ~**age** *n* [U]
system for draining

drake /dreɪk/ *n* male duck

dra·ma /ˈdrɑːmə ‖ ˈdrɑːmə, ˈdræmə/ *n*
1 [C] theatrical play 2 [U] plays as a group
3 [C;U] exciting situation ~**tic** /drəˈmætɪk/
adj 1 of the theatre 2 exciting ~**tically**
/-kli/ *adv* ~**tist** /ˈdræmətɪst/ *n* writer of
plays ~**tize** also ~**tise** *BrE vt* 1 turn (a story,
etc.) into a play 2 present (facts) in an
exciting way

drank /dræŋk/ *v past t. of* DRINK

drape /dreɪp/ *vt* 1 hang (cloth) in folds
2 cause to hang or stretch out loosely or
carelessly: *He draped his legs over the arm
of the chair.* ~**ry** /ˈdreɪpəri/ also **drapes**
AmE — *n* [U] cloth, curtains, etc.

dras·tic /ˈdræstɪk/ *adj* sudden and
violent ~**ally** /-kli/ *adv*

draught /drɑːft ‖ dræft/ *n* 1 current of
air 2 amount of liquid swallowed 3 depth of
water a ship needs 4 *BrE* round object used
in playing a board game (**draughts**) ♦ *adj*
1 (of beer, etc.) drawn from a barrel 2 (of
animals) used for pulling loads ~**y** *adj* with
cold DRAUGHTS (1)

draughts·man /ˈdrɑːftsmən ‖ ˈdræfts-/

-**woman** /-wʊmən/ *fem.* — -**men** /-mən/
1 person who draws parts of a new machine
or building 2 person who draws well

draw[1] /drɔː ‖ drɔː/ *v* **drew** /druː/, **drawn**
/drɔːn ‖ drɔːn/ 1 *vi/t* make (pictures) with a
pen or pencil 2 *vt* cause to come, go, or move
by pulling: *get drawn into an argument* |
horse-drawn cart | *She drew me aside.* 3 *vt*
take or pull out: *draw his sword* | *draw £100
from the bank* | *draw blood* (=cause to flow)
4 *vt* attract: *The play drew big crowds.* 5 *vi*
move steadily: *The car drew ahead.* 6 *vt*
make or get by reasoning: *draw a
comparison/lesson/conclusion* 7 *vi* end a
game without either side winning 8 *vi/t*
take (breath) in 9 **draw the curtains/the
blinds** close or open the curtains or blinds
10 **draw the line (at)** refuse to do or accept
drawn *adj* stretched out of shape: *face
drawn with sorrow* **drawing** *n* 1 [U] art of
drawing pictures 2 [C] picture

draw away *phr v* 1 *vi/t* move
(something) away 2 *vi* get further and
further ahead

draw back *phr vi* be unwilling to fulfil
something

draw in *phr vi* 1 (of days) become
shorter 2 arrive

draw into *phr vt* encourage (someone
unwilling) to join in

draw on *phr vt* 1 make use of 2 come
near in time

draw out *phr v* 1 *vi* (of days) become
longer 2 *vt* persuade to talk

draw up *phr v* 1 *vt* DRAFT (a plan, etc.)
2 *vi* (of a vehicle) arrive and stop 3 **draw
oneself up** stand up straight

draw[2] *n* 1 result with neither side
winning 2 LOTTERY 3 person or thing that
attracts the public

draw·back /ˈdrɔːbæk ‖ ˈdrɔː-/ *n* disadvantage

drawer /drɔː ‖ drɔːr/ *n* sliding container
in a piece of furniture

drawing board /ˈ·· ·/ *n* **go back to the
drawing board** start again, because the
first plan, etc. failed

drawing pin /ˈ·· ·/ *n BrE* flat-topped pin,
used for fixing paper to a board

drawl /drɔːl ‖ drɔːl/ *vi/t* speak or say
slowly **drawl** *n*

drawn /drɔːn ‖ drɔːn/ 1 *v past p. of* DRAW
2 *adj* looking tired and ill

dread /dred/ *vt* fear greatly ♦ *n* [S;U] great fear **~ful** *adj* terrible **~fully** *adv*

dread·locks /'dredlɒks ‖ -lɑːks/ *n* [P] hair hanging in long ropelike pieces

dream[1] /driːm/ *n* 1 image experienced during sleep 2 something hopefully desired 3 something very beautiful —see also WET DREAM **~less** *adj* (of sleep) peaceful

dream[2] *vi/t* dreamed *or* dreamt /dremt/ 1 have a dream 2 imagine (something) 3 **not dream of** refuse to consider **~er** *n* 1 person who dreams 2 impractical person **~y** *adj* 1 seeming half asleep 2 peaceful and beautiful

   dream up *phr vt* invent (esp. something silly)

drear·y /'drɪəri ‖ 'drɪri/ *adj* sad and dull **-ily** *adv* **-iness** *n* [U]

dredge /dredʒ/ *vi/t* bring up mud, etc. from the bottom of water

   dredge up *phr vt* 1 bring to the surface of water 2 produce *or* bring up (usu. something unpleasant): *dredge up the past*

dregs /dregz/ *n* [P] 1 bits of matter that sink to the bottom of liquid 2 worthless part: *the dregs of society*

drench /drentʃ/ *vt* make thoroughly wet

dress /dres/ *v* 1 *vi/t* put clothes on 2 *vi* put on formal evening clothes 3 *vt* clean and cover (a wound) 4 *vt* arrange; prepare: *dress a salad/a shop window* 5 **dressed to kill** dressed in one's best clothes ♦ *n* 1 [C] woman's one-piece outer garment 2 [U] clothing —see also EVENING DRESS, MORNING DRESS **~ing** *n* 1 covering for a wound 2 SAUCE, etc. —see also WINDOW DRESSING **~y** showy or too ornamental

   dress up *phr v* 1 *vi/t* put special clothes on 2 *vt* make (something *or* someone) seem different *or* more attractive

dressing gown /'·· ·/ *n* loose coat for wearing indoors

dressing ta·ble /'·· ,··/ *n* table with a mirror, in a bedroom

dress·mak·er /'dres,meɪkə ‖ -ər/ *n* person who makes clothes

drew /druː/ *v past t. of* DRAW

drib·ble /'drɪbəl/ *v* 1 *vi* let SALIVA flow out slowly from the mouth 2 *vi/t* let (liquid) flow slowly 3 *vi/t* move (a ball) by many short kicks *or* strokes **dribble** *n*

dried /draɪd/ *v past t. and p. of* DRY

drift /drɪft/ *n* 1 mass of something blown together: *snowdrifts* 2 aimless movement 3 general meaning: *the drift of his argument* ♦ *vi* 1 be driven by wind *or* water 2 move *or* live aimlessly **~er** person who DRIFTS (2)

drift net /'· ·/ *n* type of very long fishing net

drill[1] /drɪl/ *n* tool for making holes ♦ *vi/t* use a drill (on)

drill[2] *n* [C;U] training by repeating *and* following orders: *army drill* ♦ *vi/t* do *or* give drill

dri·ly /'draɪli/ *adv* in a DRY[1] (4) manner

drink /drɪŋk/ *v* drank /dræŋk/, drunk /drʌŋk/ 1 *vi/t* swallow (liquid) 2 *vi* take in (too much) alcohol ♦ *n* [C;U] 1 liquid to drink 2 alcohol to drink **~able** *adj* **~er** *n* person who drinks too much alcohol

   drink to *phr vt* wish (someone *or* something) good health *or* success

drip /drɪp/ *vi/t* 1 fall *or* let fall in drops 2 overflow with *or* as if with liquid: (fig.) *She was dripping with diamonds.* ♦ *n* 1 (sound of) liquid falling in drops 2 dull person **~ping** *adj* very wet

drip-dry /ˌ· '·◄/ *adj* (of clothes) that will dry smooth if hung while wet

drive[1] /draɪv/ *v* drove /drəʊv ‖ droʊv/, driven /'drɪvən/ 1 *vi/t* guide (a wheeled vehicle) 2 *vt* take (someone) in a vehicle 3 *vt* force (animals, etc.) to go 4 *vt* be the power for 5 *vt* send by hitting 6 *vt* force (someone) into a bad state: *The pain's driving me mad.* 7 *vi* (esp. of rain) move violently 8 **be driving at** mean; HINT **driver** *n* person who drives vehicles *or* animals

drive[2] *n* 1 [C] journey in a vehicle 2 [C] road through a park *or* garden 3 [C] stroke in a ball game 4 [C] CAMPAIGN 5 [U] force of mind: *He lacks drive.* 6 [C] important natural need which must be fulfilled

drive-in /'· ·/ *n, adj* (place) that people can use while remaining in their cars: *a drive-in restaurant/cinema/bank*

driv·el /'drɪvəl/ *n* [U] nonsense

drive-through /'· ·/ *n, adj* (restaurant, bank, etc.) that people can use while remaining in their cars

driz·zle /'drɪzəl/ *n* [U] fine misty rain **drizzle** *vi*

droll /drəʊl ‖ droʊl/ *adj* odd *and* amusing: *a droll person/expression*

drom·e·da·ry /'drɒmədəri ‖ 'drɑːməderi/ n camel with one HUMP (1)

drone /drəʊn ‖ droʊn/ vi make a continuous low dull sound **drone** n [S]

drone on phr vi speak for a long time in an uninteresting manner

drool /druːl/ vi let liquid flow from the mouth: (fig.) *Stop drooling* (=show pleasure in a foolish way) *over that singer*.

droop /druːp/ vi hang downwards **droop** n [S]

drop¹ /drɒp ‖ drɑːp/ n 1 [C] small round mass of liquid 2 [C] small round sweet 3 [S] a distance or fall straight down b fall in quantity: *a drop in sales* 4 **at the drop of a hat** suddenly **drops** n liquid medicine taken drop by drop

drop² v -pp- 1 vi/t fall or let fall 2 vi/t (cause) to become less: *The temperature dropped.* 3 vt let (someone) get out of a vehicle 4 vt stop; give up: *drop a subject* 5 vt say or write informally: *drop a hint/a note* 6 vt leave out (from a team)

drop back/behind phr vi get further away by moving more slowly

drop in/by/round phr vi make an unexpected visit

drop off phr vi 1 get less 2 fall asleep

drop out phr vi stop taking part **dropout** /ˈdrɒpaʊt ‖ ˈdrɑːp-/ n person who leaves a college, etc. without finishing the course

drop·pings /ˈdrɒpɪŋz ‖ ˈdrɑː-/ n [P] waste matter from the bowels of animals or birds

dross /drɒs ‖ drɑːs, drɔːs/ n [U] 1 *infml* (used to say that something is of poor quality) 2 waste or impure matter

drought /draʊt/ n [C;U] long period of dry weather when there is not enough water

drove¹ /drəʊv ‖ droʊv/ v past t. of DRIVE

drove² n group; crowd: *droves of tourists*

drown /draʊn/ v 1 vi/t die or kill by being under water 2 vt cover completely with water 3 vt cover up (a sound) with a louder one 4 **drown one's sorrows** drink alcohol in an attempt to forget one's troubles

drow·sy /ˈdraʊzi/ adj sleepy –**sily** adv –**siness** n [U]

drudge /drʌdʒ/ vi do hard dull work ♦ n person who drudges –**ry** /ˈdrʌdʒəri/ n [U] hard uninteresting work

drug /drʌg/ n 1 medicine 2 substance taken for pleasure: *a drug addict* ♦ vt -**gg**- 1 add harmful drugs to 2 give drugs to

drug·store /ˈdrʌgstɔː ‖ -stɔːr/ n AmE PHARMACY that also sells simple meals

drum¹ /drʌm/ n 1 musical instrument made of a skin stretched over a circular frame 2 container, etc. shaped like this: *oil drum*

drum² vi -**mm**- 1 beat a drum 2 make drumlike noises 3 **drum something into someone** make someone remember something by saying it often ~**mer** n person who plays a drum

drum out phr vt send away formally and disapprovingly

drum up phr vt obtain by continuous effort and noise by advertising

drum·stick /ˈdrʌmˌstɪk/ n 1 cooked leg of a chicken, etc. 2 stick for playing drums

drunk¹ /drʌŋk/ v past p. of DRINK

drunk² adj under the influence of alcohol

drunk³ n also **drunkard** /ˈdrʌŋkəd ‖ -ərd/ — person who is (habitually) drunk

drunk·en /ˈdrʌŋkən/ adj 1 DRUNK² 2 resulting from or connected with too much drinking: *a drunken sleep* ~**ly** adv ~**ness** n [U]

dry¹ /draɪ/ adj 1 not wet: *dry clothes/climate* 2 (of wine) not sweet 3 not allowing the sale of alcohol 4 amusing without appearing to be so; quietly IRONIC: *dry wit* 5 uninteresting ~**ly**, **drily** adv ~**ness** n [U]

dry² v 1 vi/t make or become dry 2 vt preserve (food) by removing liquid ~**er**, **drier** n machine that dries

dry out phr vi/t 1 (cause to) give up dependence on alcohol 2 (cause to) become completely dry

dry up phr vi 1 (of a supply) stop coming 2 sl SHUT UP (1)

dry-clean /ˌ· ˈ·/ vt clean (clothes) with chemicals instead of water ~**er's** n CLEANER'S ~**ing** n [U] 1 action or industry of dry-cleaning clothes 2 clothes that need to be or have just been dry-cleaned

dry dock /ˌ· ˈ·/ n place where a ship is held while water is pumped out

dry rot /ˌ· ˈ·/ n [U] disease that turns wood into powder

du·al /ˈdjuːəl ‖ ˈduːəl/ adj having two parts; double: *a dual carriageway* ~**ity** /djuˈæləti ‖ duː-/ n [U]

dub /dʌb/ vt -**bb**- 1 give (a name) to 2 change the spoken language of (a film)

du·bi·ous /'dju:biəs‖'du:-/ *adj* feeling or causing doubt ~**ly** *adv*

duch·ess /'dʌtʃəs/ *n* **a** wife of a DUKE **b** woman who holds the rank of DUKE in her own right

duch·y /'dʌtʃi/ *n* lands of a DUKE or DUCHESS

duck /dʌk/ *n* **1** [C] common swimming bird **2** [U] its meat **3** [C] *infml, esp. BrE* (used for addressing) a person one likes **4** [C] (in cricket) failure to make any runs at all **5 take to something like a duck to water** learn or get used to something very easily ♦ *v* **1** *vi/t* lower (one's head) quickly **2** *vt* push (someone) under water **3** *vt* try to avoid responsibility —see also LAME DUCK, SITTING DUCK

duck·ling /'dʌklɪŋ/ *n* young duck —see also UGLY DUCKLING

duck·y /'dʌki/ [C] *infml, esp. BrE* (used for addressing) a person one likes

duct /dʌkt/ *n* tube that carries liquids, air, etc.

dud /dʌd/ *n sl* useless person or thing: *a dud cheque*

due /dju:‖du:/ *adj* **1** owed **2** *fml* suitable; proper **3** expected: *The train is due any minute.* **4 due to** because by ♦ *adv* (before **north, south, east, west**) exactly ♦ *n* something that rightfully belongs to one: *give him his due* **dues** *n* [P] official payments

du·el /'dju:əl‖'du:əl/ *n* fight arranged between two people **duel** *vi* **-ll-** *BrE* ‖ **-l-** *AmE*

du·et /dju:'et‖du:'et/ *n* piece of music for two performers

duffel coat /'dʌfəl kəut‖kout/ *n* loose heavy coat, often with a HOOD

dug /dʌg/ *v past t. and p. of* DIG

dug·out /'dʌgaut/ *n* **1** boat made of a hollow log **2** shelter dug in the ground

duke /dju:k‖du:k/ *n* British nobleman of the highest rank ~**dom** *n* rank or lands of a duke

dull /dʌl/ *adj* **1** not bright or shining **2** slow in thinking **3** not sharp: *a dull pain* **4** uninteresting ♦ *vt* make dull ~**ness** *n* [U]

du·ly /'dju:li‖'du:li/ *adv* properly; as expected

dumb /dʌm/ *adj* **1** unable to speak **2** unwilling to speak; silent **3** *sl* stupid ~**ly** *adv* ~**ness** *n* [U]

dumb·found /dʌm'faund/ *vt* make dumb from surprise

dum·my /'dʌmi/ *n* **1** object made to look like a real thing or person **2** *BrE* baby's rubber TEAT for sucking

dump /dʌmp/ *vt* **1** drop carelessly **2** sell (goods) abroad more cheaply than at home ♦ *n* **1** place for dumping waste **2** stored supply **3** *sl* dirty untidy place **4 in the dumps** sad ~**er** *n* large vehicle for carrying earth and stones ~**y** *adj* short and fat

dump·ling /'dʌmplɪŋ/ *n* ball of boiled DOUGH

dune /dju:n‖du:n/ *n* long low sandhill built up by the wind

dung /dʌŋ/ *n* [U] animal MANURE

dun·ga·rees /ˌdʌŋgə'ri:z/ *n* [P] **1** *BrE* trousers with a BIB (2), usu. made of heavy cotton **2** *AmE* JEANS for working in

dun·geon /'dʌndʒən/ *n* underground prison

dunk /dʌŋk/ *vt* dip (esp. food) into liquid while eating

du·o /'dju:əu‖'du:ou/ *n* a pair, esp. of musicians

dupe /dju:p‖du:p/ *vt* trick; deceive ♦ *n fml* person who is duped

du·pli·cate[1] /'dju:plɪkət‖'du:-/ *n, adj* (something that is) exactly like another

du·pli·cate[2] /'dju:plɪkeɪt‖'du:-/ *vt* copy exactly ~**cator** *n* machine that copies ~**cation** /ˌdju:plɪ'keɪʃən‖ˌdu:-/ *n* [U]

du·plic·i·ty /dju:'plɪsɪti‖du:-/ *n* [U] *fml* dishonesty

du·ra·ble /'djuərəbəl‖'dur-/ *adj* long-lasting **durables** *n* [P] goods expected to last for years

du·ra·tion /dju'reɪʃən‖du-/ *n* [U] *fml* **1** time during which something lasts **2 for the duration** as long as something lasts

du·ress /dju'res‖du-/ *n* [U] *fml* threats: *promise under duress*

dur·ing /'djuərɪŋ‖'dur-/ *prep* **1** all through (a length of) time) **2** at some moment in: *He was ill during the night.*

dusk /dʌsk/ *n* [U] time when daylight fades

dusk·y /'dʌski/ *adj* rather dark in colour

dust[1] /dʌst/ *n* [U] powder made of earth or other matter ~**y** *adj* covered with dust

dust[2] *vt* **1** clean the dust from: *dust beds* **2** cover with powder: *dust crops* ~**er** *n* cloth for removing dust

dust off _phr vt_ begin to use or practise again, after a period of not doing so

dust·bin /'dʌstbɪn/ _n BrE_ container for waste materials

dust·cart /'dʌstkɑːt ‖ -kɑːrt/ _n BrE_ vehicle that collects the contents of dustbins

dust·man /'dʌstmən/ _n_ -men /-mən/ _BrE_ person employed to empty dustbins

dust·pan /'dʌstpæn/ _n_ flat container into which house dust is swept

Dutch /dʌtʃ/ _adj_ of the Netherlands (Holland)

du·ty /'djuːti ‖ 'duːti/ _n_ [C;U] 1 something one must do 2 tax: _customs duties_ 3 **heavy duty** (of machines, etc.) able to do hard work 4 **on/off duty** required/not required to work **dutiful** _adj_ showing respect and obedience **dutifully** _adv_

duty-free /ˌ·· '·◂/ _adj, adv_ (of goods) allowed to enter a country without tax

du·vet /'duːveɪ/ _n_ large bag of feathers used as a bed covering

dwarf /dwɔːf ‖ dwɔːrf/ _n_ **dwarfs** or **dwarves** /dwɔːvz ‖ dwɔːrvz/ 1 (in children's stories) small ugly man with magic powers 2 (now considered offensive) person who is much smaller than normal 3 type of small star ♦ _adj_ (of plants) smaller than normal ♦ _vt_ cause to look small

dwell /dwel/ _vi_ **dwelled** or **dwelt** /dwelt/ _lit_ live (in a place) ~**er** _n_ person or animal that lives somewhere: _city-dwellers_ ~**ing** _n fml_ home

dwell on _phr vt_ think or speak a lot about

dwin·dle /'dwɪndl/ _vi_ become gradually fewer or smaller

dye /daɪ/ _n_ [C;U] substance used to colour cloth, etc. ♦ _vi/t_ **dyes, dyed, dyeing** colour with dye

dyed-in-the-wool /ˌ··· '·◂/ _adj_ impossible to change (as to the stated or known quality): _a dyed-in-the-wool Republican_

dy·ing /'daɪ-ɪŋ/ _v present p. of_ DIE

dyke /daɪk/ _n_ 1 _infml derog_ LESBIAN 2 —see DIKE

dy·nam·ic /daɪ'næmɪk/ _adj_ 1 powerful and active 2 of force that causes movement ~**ally** /-kli/ _adv_ **dynamics** _n_ [U] 1 science that deals with matter in movement 2 [P] the way in which people or systems affect one another ~**ism** /'daɪnəmɪzəm/ _n_ [U] being DYNAMIC (1)

dy·na·mite /'daɪnəmaɪt/ _n_ [U] 1 powerful explosive 2 something or someone that will cause great shock, admiration, etc. ♦ _vt_ blow up with dynamite

dy·na·mo /'daɪnəməʊ ‖ -moʊ/ _n_ -**mos** machine that turns movement into electricity

dyn·a·sty /'dɪnəsti ‖ 'daɪ-/ _n_ line of rulers of the same family

dys·en·te·ry /'dɪsəntəri ‖ -teri/ _n_ [U] painful bowel disease

dys·func·tion·al /dɪs'fʌŋkʃənəl/ _adj_ not behaving or existing together normally: _a dysfunctional family_

dys·lex·i·a /dɪs'leksiə/ _n_ [U] inability to read, from difficulty in recognizing letter shapes –**ic** _adj_

E, e /iː/ the 5th letter of the English alphabet

E[1] _written abbrev. for:_ east(ern)

E[2] _n_ [U] Ecstasy; illegal drug giving great energy and happiness

each /iːtʃ/ _determiner, pron_ every one separately: _each child_ | _each of the children_ ♦ _adv_ for or to each: _They cost fifty cents each._

each oth·er /ˌ· '··/ _pron_ with each doing something to the other: _kiss each other_ | _hold each other's hands_

ea·ger /'iːgə ‖ -ər/ _adj_ keen; wanting very much ~**ly** _adv_ ~**ness** _n_ [U]

ea·gle /'iːgəl/ _n_ large meat-eating bird with a hooked beak ~-**eyed** /ˌ·· '·◂/ _adj_ having very good eyesight

ear[1] /ɪə ‖ ɪr/ _n_ 1 [C] either of the two parts of the head with which we hear 2 [S] good recognition of sounds: _an ear for music_ 3 **all ears** listening eagerly 4 **play by ear** play music without written notes 5 **up to one's ears in** deep in; very busy with

ear² n head of a grain-producing plant

ear·ache /ˈɪəreɪk‖ˈɪr-/ n [C;U] pain inside the ear

ear·drum /ˈɪədrʌm‖ˈɪr-/ n tight skin inside the ear which allows one to hear sound

earl /ɜːl‖ɜːrl/ n British nobleman of high rank ~**dom** /ˈɜːldəm‖ˈɜːrl-/ n rank or lands of an earl

ear·ly /ˈɜːli‖ˈɜːrli/ adv, adj **1** sooner than usual or expected: The train arrived early. | an early supper **2** near the beginning: It happened early in the morning/in the early morning. **3** at **the earliest** and not sooner

early bird /ˌ·· ˈ·/ n person who gets up or arrives early

early warn·ing sys·tem /ˌ·· ˈ·· ˌ·/ n RADAR network that gives advance information of enemy air attack

ear·mark /ˈɪəmɑːk‖ˈɪrmɑːrk/ vt set aside (money, etc.) for a particular purpose

earn /ɜːn‖ɜːrn/ v **1** vi/t get (money) by working **2** vt deserve (what one has worked for) ~**er** n ~**ings** n [P] money earned

ear·nest /ˈɜːnɪst‖ˈɜːrl-/ adj determined and serious ♦ n **in earnest: a** in a determined way **b** not joking ~**ly** adv ~**ness** n [U]

ear·plug /ˈɪəplʌg‖ˈɪr-/ n soft thing put into the ear to keep out noise, etc.

ear·ring /ˈɪərɪŋ‖ˈɪr-/ n decoration for the ear

ear·shot /ˈɪəʃɒt‖ˈɪrʃɑːt/ n **within/out of earshot** within/beyond the distance at which a sound can be heard

earth /ɜːθ‖ɜːrθ/ n **1** [S;U] (often cap.) the world we live on: the planet Earth **2** [U] its surface, as opposed to the sky: The rocket fell to earth. **3** [U] soil: a bucket of earth **4** [C] wild animal's hole **5** [C] BrE safety wire carrying electricity to the ground ♦ vt BrE connect (electrical apparatus) to the ground ~**ly** adj **1** of this world, not heaven **2** possible: no earthly reason ~**y** adj like soil **2** concerned with the body, not the mind

earth·en·ware /ˈɜːθənweə, -ðən-‖ˈɜːrθənwer, -ðən-/ n [U] (pots, etc. made of) baked clay

earth·quake /ˈɜːθkweɪk‖ˈɜːrθ-/ n sudden violent shaking of the earth's surface

earth·work /ˈɜːwɜːk‖ˈɜːrwɜːrk/ n large structure of earth used as a protection against enemies

ear·wig /ˈɪəˌwɪg‖ˈɪr-/ n insect with two curved parts on its tail

ease¹ /iːz/ n [U] **1** ability to do something easily **2** state of being comfortable **3** ill at ease uncomfortable

ease² v **1** vi/t make or become less painful or difficult **2** vt make less anxious **3** vt move slowly and carefully into a different position

ease off/up phr vi become less active or severe

ea·sel /ˈiːzəl/ n wooden frame to support a picture or BLACKBOARD

east /iːst/ n [the+S] (often cap.) direction from which the sun rises ♦ adj **1** in the east **2** (of wind) from the east ♦ adv to the east ~**ward** adj, adv

Eas·ter /ˈiːstə‖-ər/ n holy day in memory of Christ's death and RESURRECTION (3)

eas·ter·ly /ˈiːstəli‖-ərli/ adj east

east·ern /ˈiːstən‖-ərn/ adj of the east part of the world or of a country

eas·y /ˈiːzi/ adj **1** not difficult **2** comfortable; without worry ♦ adv go **easy on: a** be less severe with **b** not use too much of ~**ily** adv **1** without difficulty **2** without doubt: easily the best

easy chair /ˌ·· ˈ·/ n an ARMCHAIR

eas·y-go·ing /ˌiːzi'gəʊɪŋ◂‖-ˈgoʊ-/ adj pleasantly calm and unhurried

easy lis·ten·ing /ˌ·· ˈ···/ n [U] (pleasant) music that is not CLASSICAL and not the most modern popular music

eat /iːt/ v ate /et, eɪt‖eɪt/, eaten /ˈiːtn/ **1** vi/t take in (food) through the mouth **2** vt [(away, into)] destroy by chemical action **3** be eaten up with be full of (violent feeling) **4** eat one's words admit that one was wrong **5** eat your heart out infml be very jealous ~**able** adj ~**er** n

eaves /iːvz/ n [P] edges of a roof, beyond the walls

eaves·drop /ˈiːvzdrɒp‖-drɑːp/ vi -**pp**- listen secretly to conversation ~**per** n

ebb /eb/ vi grow less or lower: His courage ebbed away. ♦ n [S] **at a low ebb** in a bad state

ebb tide /ˌ· ˈ·/ n [C;U] outward flow of the sea

eb·o·ny /ˈebəni/ adj, n [U] (of the colour of) hard black wood

e·bul·li·ent /ɪ'bʌliənt, ɪ'bʊ-/ adj fml full of happy excitement –**ence** n [U]

ec·cen·tric /ɪk'sentrɪk/ adj 1 (of people) unusual; peculiar 2 (of circles) not having the same centre ♦ n eccentric person ~**ity** /,eksen'trɪsəti, -sən-/ n [C;U]

ec·cle·si·as·ti·cal /ɪ,kliːzi'æstɪkəl/ adj of the Christian Church

ech·e·lon /'eʃəlɒn‖-lɑːn/ n level within an organization

ech·o /'ekəʊ‖'ekoʊ/ n -**oes** sound sent back from a surface ♦ v 1 vi come back as an echo 2 vt copy or repeat (words, ideas, etc.)

éclair /ɪ'kleə, eɪ-‖ɪ'kler, eɪ-/ n finger-shaped cake with cream inside

e·clec·tic /ɪ'klektɪk/ adj fml using ideas from many different systems ~**ism** /-tɪsɪzəm/ n [U]

e·clipse /ɪ'klɪps/ n disappearance of the sun's light (cut off by the moon) or of the moon's light (cut off by the Earth) ♦ vt 1 cause an eclipse of 2 make (something) less important by comparison

eco-friend·ly /'iːkəʊ ,frendli‖'iːkoʊ-/ adj not harmful to the environment

e·col·o·gy /ɪ'kɒlədʒi‖ɪ'kɑː-/ n [U] the way in which living things are related to each other and to their surroundings –**gist** n –**gical** /,iːkə'lɒdʒɪkəl◄‖-'lɑː-/ adj 1 involving ecology 2 concerned with keeping the environment healthy –**gically** /-kli/ adv

ec·o·nom·ic /,ekə'nɒmɪk◄, ,iː-‖-'nɑː-/ adj 1 connected with trade, industry, and wealth 2 profitable ~**al** adj not wasteful ~**ally** /-kli/ adv

ec·o·nom·ics /,ekə'nɒmɪks, ,iː-‖-'nɑː-/ n [U] study of the way in which wealth is produced and used –**nomist** /ɪ'kɒnəmɪst‖ɪ'kɑː-/ n

e·con·o·mize /ɪ'kɒnəmaɪz‖ɪ'kɑː-/ also -**mise** BrE vi avoid waste

e·con·o·my /ɪ'kɒnəmi‖ɪ'kɑː-/ n 1 [C] economic system of a country 2 [C;U] avoidance of waste —see also BLACK ECONOMY, MIXED ECONOMY ♦ adj cheap: an economy class air ticket

e·co·sys·tem /'iːkəʊ,sɪstəm‖'iːkoʊ-/ n all the living things in an area and the relationship between them

eco-war·ri·or /'iːkəʊ,wɒriə‖'iːkoʊ-,wɔːriər, -,wɑː-/ n person who tries to

prevent damage to the environment by protesting against new roads, etc.

ec·sta·sy /'ekstəsi/ n [C;U] great joy **ecstatic** /ɪk'stætɪk, ek-/ adj **ecstatically** /-kli/ adv

Ecstasy n [U] type of drug; E[2]

e·cu·men·i·cal /,iːkjʊ'menɪkəl◄,ek-/ adj favouring Christian unity

ec·ze·ma /'eksəmə‖'eksəmə, 'egzəmə, ɪg'ziːmə/ n [U] red swollen condition of the skin

ed·dy /'edi/ n circular movement of water, smoke, etc. ♦ vi move in eddies

edge /edʒ/ n 1 cutting part of a knife, etc. 2 narrowest part along the outside of an object: the edge of a coin 3 place where something begins or ends: the water's edge 4 **have the edge on** be better than 5 **on edge** nervous 6 **set someone's teeth on edge** infml give an unpleasant feeling to someone 7 **take the edge off** infml make less severe ♦ v 1 vt put a border on 2 vi/t move gradually, esp. sideways **edging** n [C;U] border **edgy** adj nervous

ed·i·ble /'edəbəl/ adj that can be eaten

e·dict /'iːdɪkt/ n official public command

ed·i·fice /'edəfəs/ n fml large fine building

ed·it /'edət/ vt prepare (a newspaper, film, etc.) for printing or showing –**or** n person who edits

e·di·tion /ɪ'dɪʃən/ n 1 one printing, esp. of a book 2 form in which a book is printed: a paperback edition

ed·i·to·ri·al /,edə'tɔːriəl◄/ adj of an editor ♦ n newspaper article giving the paper's opinion

ed·u·cate /'edjʊkeɪt‖'edʒə-/ vt teach; train

ed·u·ca·tion /,edjʊ'keɪʃən, ,edʒə-/ n [S;U] (knowledge resulting from) teaching or training –**al** adj

eel /iːl/ n long snake-like fish

ee·rie /'ɪəri‖'ɪri/ adj frightening because of being strange: an eerie silence **eerily** adv

ef·face /ɪ'feɪs/ vt fml rub out

ef·fect /ɪ'fekt/ n [C;U] 1 result; what happens because of a cause 2 **in effect: a** in operation **b** in fact 3 **take effect** come into operation —see also SIDE EFFECT ♦ vt fml produce; cause **effects** n [P] 1 sounds, etc. produced in a film or play 2 fml personal belongings

ef·fec·tive /ɪˈfektɪv/ adj 1 producing the desired result: *very effective new laws* 2 fml actual: *the effective strength of our army* ~ly adv -ness n [U]

ef·fem·i·nate /ɪˈfemənət/ adj (of a man) too like a woman -nacy n [U]

ef·fer·vesce /ˌefəˈves/ vi form bubbles of gas -vescence n [U] -vescent adj

ef·fete /ɪˈfiːt/ adj weak; EFFEMINATE

ef·fi·ca·cy /ˈefɪkəsi/ n [U] fml effectiveness

ef·fi·cient /ɪˈfɪʃənt/ adj working well; *an efficient secretary/machine* ~ly adv -ciency n [U]

ef·fi·gy /ˈefɪdʒi/ n fml wooden, stone, etc. likeness of someone

ef·flu·ent /ˈefluənt/ n [C;U] liquid chemical or human waste

ef·fort /ˈefət/ n 1 [U] use of strength 2 [C] attempt: *a good effort* ~less adj successful without effort ~lessly adv

ef·fron·te·ry /ɪˈfrʌntəri/ n [U] rudeness without any feeling of shame

ef·fu·sive /ɪˈfjuːsɪv/ adj showing too much feeling ~ly adv

EFL /ˌiː ef ˈel/ n [U] abbrev. for: English as a foreign language

e.g. /ˌiː ˈdʒiː/ abbrev. for example

e·gal·i·tar·i·an /ɪˌɡælɪˈteəriən/ adj believing in social equality ~ism n [U]

egg¹ /eɡ/ n 1 [C] round object with a shell, containing a baby bird, snake, etc. 2 [C;U] (the contents of) an egg when used as food: *a boiled egg* 3 [C] female cell producing young 4 **have egg on one's face** seem foolish

egg² v **egg on** phr vt encourage someone, esp. to do wrong

egg·cup /ˈeɡ-kʌp/ n container for a boiled egg

egg·plant /ˈeɡplɑːnt/ n large purple vegetable

e·go /ˈiːɡəʊ/ n egos 1 one's opinion of oneself: *an enormous ego* 2 tech one's conscious self —see also ALTER EGO

e·go·cen·tric /ˌiːɡəʊˈsentrɪk/ adj thinking only about oneself; selfish

e·go·is·m /ˈiːɡəʊɪzəm/ n [U] selfishness -ist n

e·go·tis·m /ˈiːɡətɪzəm/ n [U] believing that one is more important than other people -tist n -tistic /ˌiːɡəˈtɪstɪk/,

-e-/, -tistical adj

ego trip /ˈ·· ·/ n act or set of acts done mainly because it makes one feel proud of oneself

ei·der·down /ˈaɪdədaʊn/ n bed covering filled with feathers

eight /eɪt/ determiner, n, pron 8 **eighth** determiner, adv, n, pron 8th

eigh·teen /ˌeɪˈtiːn/ determiner, n, pron 18 ~th determiner, adv, n, pron 18th

eigh·ty /ˈeɪti/ determiner, n, pron 80 -tieth determiner, adv, n, pron 80th

ei·ther¹ /ˈaɪðə/ determiner, pron, conj 1 one or the other: *I haven't seen either John or Sam. | I haven't met either (of them). | He either drives or walks.* 2 each of two: *houses on either side of the road*

either² adv (used with negative expressions) also: *I haven't been to France, or Germany either.*

e·jac·u·late /ɪˈdʒækjʊleɪt/ vi/t 1 throw out (SPERM) suddenly from the body 2 fml cry out suddenly -lation /ɪˌdʒækjʊˈleɪʃən/ n [C;U]

e·ject /ɪˈdʒekt/ vt fml throw out ~ion /ɪˈdʒekʃən/ n [U].

eke /iːk/ v **eke out** phr vt make (supplies) last as long as possible

e·lab·o·rate¹ /ɪˈlæbərət/ adj full of detail ~ly adv

e·lab·o·rate² /ɪˈlæbəreɪt/ vi add more detail -ration /ɪˌlæbəˈreɪʃən/ n [C;U]

e·lapse /ɪˈlæps/ vi fml (of time) pass

e·las·tic /ɪˈlæstɪk/ adj able to spring back into shape after stretching or bending ♦ n elastic material ~ity /ˌiːlæsˈtɪsəti/ n [U]

elastic band /·,·· ˈ·/ n BrE for RUBBER BAND

e·lat·ed /ɪˈleɪtɪd/ adj proud and happy -ion /ɪˈleɪʃən/ n [U]

el·bow /ˈelbəʊ/ n joint where the arm bends ♦ vt push with the elbows

elbow grease /ˈ·· ·/ n [U] hard work with the hands

elbow room /ˈ·· ·/ n [U] space to move freely

el·der /ˈeldə/ adj (of a family member) older: *my elder sister* ♦ n 1 older of two people 2 person in a respected official position ~ly adj rather old

elder states·man /ˌ·· ˈ··/ n old and respected person who is asked for advice because of his or her experience

el·dest /ˈeldɪst/ n, adj (person who is) the oldest of three or more

e·lect /ɪˈlekt/ vt 1 choose by voting 2 fml decide: She elected to go. ♦ adj fml chosen, but not yet at work; president elect ~**or** n person with the right to vote ~**oral** adj ~**orally** adv

e·lec·tion /ɪˈlekʃən/ n [C;U] (occasion of) choosing representatives by voting —see also GENERAL ELECTION

e·lec·tion·eer·ing /ɪˌlekʃəˈnɪərɪŋ ‖ -ˈnɪr-/ n [U] activity of persuading people to vote for a political party

e·lec·to·rate /ɪˈlektərɪt/ n all the electors

e·lec·tric /ɪˈlektrɪk/ adj 1 worked by or producing electricity: an electric razor 2 infml very exciting ~**al** adj concerned with or using electricity: an electrical fault ~**ally** /-kli/ adv

electric chair /ˌ·· ˈ·/ n [the+S] punishment of electrocuting a criminal

el·ec·tri·cian /ɪˌlekˈtrɪʃən/ n person who fits and repairs electrical apparatus

e·lec·tri·ci·ty /ɪˌlekˈtrɪsɪti/ n [U] power supply, carried usu. by wires, for heating, lighting, etc.

e·lec·tri·fy /ɪˈlektrɪfaɪ/ vt 1 use electric power for 2 excite greatly

e·lec·tro·cute /ɪˈlektrəkjuːt/ vt kill by passing electric current through the body ~**cution** /ɪˌlektrəˈkjuːʃən/ n [C;U]

e·lec·trode /ɪˈlektrəʊd ‖ -troʊd/ n point at which current enters or leaves a BATTERY (1)

e·lec·trol·y·sis /ɪˌlekˈtrɒlɪsɪs ‖ -ˈtrɑː-/ n [U] the use of electricity a for separation of a liquid into its chemical parts or b for destruction of hair roots

e·lec·tron /ɪˈlektrɒn ‖ -trɑːn/ n small piece of matter that moves round the NUCLEUS of an atom

el·ec·tron·ic /ɪˌlekˈtrɒnɪk ‖ -ˈtrɑː-/ adj of, using, or produced by equipment that works by means of an electric current passing through CHIPS[1] (4), TRANSISTORS, etc. (for example, televisions, computers, etc.): electronic music/mail ~**ally** /-kli/ adv **electronics** n [U] study or making of such equipment

el·e·gant /ˈeləgənt/ adj graceful; stylish ~**ly** adv –**gance** n [U]

el·e·ment /ˈeləmənt/ n 1 [C] simple substance consisting of only one kind of atom 2 [S] small amount: an element of truth in what you say 3 [C] part of a whole: Honesty is an important element in his character. 4 [C] heating part of a piece of electric apparatus 5 **in/out of one's element** doing/not doing what one is best at **elements** [the+P] 1 (bad) weather 2 first things to study in a subject **elemental** /ˌeləˈmentl◂/ adj of the forces of nature

el·e·men·ta·ry /ˌeləˈmentəri◂/ adj 1 easy: elementary questions 2 concerned with the beginning of something: elementary arithmetic

elementary school /··ˈ·· ˌ·/ n AmE school for the first 6 to 8 years of a child's education

el·e·phant /ˈeləfənt/ n very large animal with TUSKs and a long round nose (TRUNK) —see also WHITE ELEPHANT

el·e·vate /ˈeləveɪt/ vt fml 1 raise 2 improve (the mind)

el·e·va·tion /ˌeləˈveɪʃən/ n 1 [U] fml act of elevating 2 [S] height above sea-level 3 [C] drawing of one side of a building 4 [S] angle made with the horizon, e.g. by a gun

el·e·va·tor /ˈeləveɪtər ‖ -ər/ n 1 AmE for LIFT[2] (2) 2 machine for raising grain, etc.

e·lev·en /ɪˈlevən/ determiner, n, pron 11 ~**th** determiner, adv, n, pron 11th

e·lev·en·ses /ɪˈlevənzɪz/ n BrE infml coffee, tea, or a light meal at about 11 o'clock in the morning

eleventh hour /ɪˌ·· ˈ·/ n [the+S] the very last moment

elf /elf/ n elves /elvz/ small usu. male fairy ~**in** adj

e·li·cit /ɪˈlɪsɪt/ vt fml get (information, etc.) from someone

e·lide /ɪˈlaɪd/ vt leave out (a sound) in pronunciation

el·i·gi·ble /ˈelədʒəbəl/ adj fulfilling the conditions; suitable –**bility** /ˌelədʒəˈbɪlɪti/ n [U]

e·lim·i·nate /ɪˈlɪmɪneɪt/ vt remove; get rid of –**nation** /ɪˌlɪmɪˈneɪʃən/ n [U]

e·lite /eɪˈliːt, ɪ-/ n favoured powerful group in society –**tism** n [U] –**tist** adj

elk /elk/ n very large deer

el·lipse /ɪˈlɪps/ n OVAL shape

el·lip·ti·cal /ɪˈlɪptɪkəl/ adj 1 OVAL 2 (of speech) with hidden meaning

elm /elm/ n large broad-leaved tree

el·o·cu·tion /ˌeləˈkjuːʃən/ n [U] good clear speaking

e·lon·gate /ˈiːlɒŋɡeɪt ‖ ɪˈlɔːŋ-/ vt make longer

e·lope /ɪˈləʊp ‖ ɪˈloʊp-/ vi run away to get married ~ment n [C;U]

el·o·quent /ˈeləkwənt/ adj 1 able to influence people by using language well 2 fml showing something very strongly: an eloquent reminder of the horrors of wars –quence n [U]

else /els/ adv 1 more; as well: What else can I say? 2 apart from (what is mentioned): He's here. Everyone else has gone home. 3 otherwise: You must pay or else go to prison.

else·where /elsˈweə, ˈelsweə ‖ ˈelswer/ adv at, in, from, or to another place

ELT /ˌiː el ˈtiː/ n [U] abbrev. for: English Language Teaching

e·lu·ci·date /ɪˈluːsɪdeɪt/ vt fml explain –dation /ɪˌluːsɪˈdeɪʃən/ n [U]

e·lude /ɪˈluːd/ vt escape from

e·lu·sive /ɪˈluːsɪv/ adj hard to find or remember

elves /elvz/ pl. of ELF

e·ma·ci·a·ted /ɪˈmeɪʃieɪtɪd/ adj extremely thin –ation /ɪˌmeɪsiˈeɪʃən/ n [U]

e-mail also email /ˈiːmeɪl/ n [U] electronic mail; system for sending messages by computer ♦ vt

em·a·nate /ˈeməneɪt/ v emanate from phr vi fml come out (from somewhere) –nation /ˌeməˈneɪʃən/ n [C;U]

e·man·ci·pate /ɪˈmænsɪpeɪt/ vt make (slaves, etc.) free –pation /ɪˌmænsɪˈpeɪʃən/ n [U]

e·mas·cu·late /ɪˈmæskjʊleɪt/ vt 1 weaken 2 CASTRATE –lation /ɪˌmæskjʊˈleɪʃən/ n [U]

em·balm /ɪmˈbɑːm/ vt preserve (a dead body) with chemicals, etc. ~er n

em·bank·ment /ɪmˈbæŋkmənt/ n wall that holds back water or carries a road or railway

em·bar·go /ɪmˈbɑːɡəʊ ‖ -ɑːrɡoʊ/ n -goes official order forbidding trade ♦ vt put an embargo on

em·bark /ɪmˈbɑːk ‖ -ɑːrk/ vi/t go or put onto a ship ~ation /ˌembɑːˈkeɪʃən ‖ -bɑːr-/ n [C;U]

    embark on/upon phr vt start (something new)

em·bar·rass /ɪmˈbærəs/ vt make ashamed or socially uncomfortable: an embarrassing question/silence ~ingly adv ~ment n [C;U]

em·bas·sy /ˈembəsi/ n offices of an AMBASSADOR

em·bat·tled /ɪmˈbætld/ adj surrounded by enemies or difficulties

em·bed /ɪmˈbed/ vt -dd- fix firmly in surrounding material

em·bel·lish /ɪmˈbelɪʃ/ vt 1 decorate 2 add (esp. untrue) details to ~ment n [C;U]

em·ber /ˈembə ‖ -ər/ n [usu. pl.] piece of red-hot coal, etc. in a dying fire

em·bez·zle /ɪmˈbezəl/ vi/t steal (money placed in one's care) ~ment n [U] ~r n

em·bit·ter /ɪmˈbɪtə ‖ -ər/ vt make sad and angry

em·bla·zon /ɪmˈbleɪzən/ vt show (a decoration, etc.) noticeably

em·blem /ˈembləm/ n sign representing something: The emblem of England is a rose.

em·bod·y /ɪmˈbɒdi ‖ ɪmˈbɑːdi/ vt fml give physical expression to –iment n: She's the embodiment of evil.

em·boss /ɪmˈbɒs ‖ ɪmˈbɑːs, -ˈbɔːs/ vt decorate with a raised pattern

em·brace /ɪmˈbreɪs/ v 1 vi/t take (someone) lovingly in one's arms 2 vt fml include 3 vt fml become a believer in: embrace the Muslim faith ♦ n: a warm embrace

em·broi·der /ɪmˈbrɔɪdə ‖ -ər/ vi/t 1 decorate (cloth) with needlework 2 EMBELLISH ~y n [U]

em·broiled /ɪmˈbrɔɪld/ adj mixed up in something troublesome: to get embroiled in an argument

em·bry·o /ˈembriəʊ ‖ -brioʊ/ n -os 1 creature in its first state before birth 2 in embryo still incomplete ~nic /ˌembriˈɒnɪk ‖ -ˈɑːnɪk/ adj

em·bry·ol·o·gy /ˌembriˈɒlədʒi ‖ -ˈɑːl-/ n [U] study of embryos

em·e·rald /ˈemərəld/ n [C;U] (colour of) a bright green precious stone

e·merge /ɪˈmɜːdʒ ‖ -ɜːr-/ vi 1 come out 2 (of facts) become known **emergence** n [U] **emergent** adj beginning to develop: emergent nations

e·mer·gen·cy /ɪˈmɜːdʒənsi ‖ -ɜːr-/ n dangerous happening which must be dealt with at once

em·e·ry /'eməri/ *n* [U] hard powder used for polishing

em·i·grant /'emɪgrənt/ *n* person who emigrates

em·i·grate /'emɪ̱greɪt/ *vi* leave one's own country to live in another ~**gration** /ˌemɪ̱'greɪʃən/ *n* [C;U]

ém·i·gré /'emɪ̱greɪ/ *n fml* a REFUGEE

em·i·nence /'emɪnəns/ *n* [U] great importance

ém·i·nence grise /ˌemɪnəns 'griːz/ *n* someone who secretly has great influence, but does not have an official position of power

em·i·nent /'emɪnənt/ *adj* (of a person) famous and admired ~**ly** *adv fml* extremely

e·mir /e'mɪə‖e'mɪr/ *n* Muslim ruler ~**ate** /'emɪrət/ *n* lands, etc. of an emir

em·is·sa·ry /'emɪsəri‖-seri/ *n fml* person sent with a message or to do special work

e·mis·sion /ɪ'mɪʃən/ *n fml* 1 [U] act of emitting 2 [C] something emitted

e·mit /ɪ'mɪt/ *vt* -tt- *fml* send out: *to emit smoke/a humming sound*

e·mo·tion /ɪ'məʊʃən‖ɪ'moʊ-/ *n* 1 [C] strong feeling, such as love, sorrow, etc. 2 [U] strength of feeling: *a voice shaking with emotion* ~**al** *adj* 1 concerning the emotions 2 having feelings that are (too) strong ~**ally** *adv*

e·mo·tive /ɪ'məʊtɪv‖ɪ'moʊ-/ *adj* causing strong feeling

em·pa·thy /'empəθi/ *n* [S;U] ability to imagine oneself in the position of another person ~**thize**, -**thise** *vi*

em·pe·ror /'empərə‖-ər/ *n* ruler of an empire

em·pha·sis /'emfəsɪ̱s/ *n* -ses /-siːz/ [C;U] special force or attention given to something important

em·pha·size also -**sise** *BrE* /'emfəsaɪz/ *vt* place emphasis on

em·phat·ic /ɪm'fætɪk/ *adj* strongly emphasized ~**ally** /-kli/ *adv*

em·pire /'empaɪə‖-paɪr/ *n* group of countries under one government

em·pir·i·cal /em'pɪrɪ̱kəl/ *adj* based on practical experience rather than ideas: *empirical evidence*

em·ploy /ɪm'plɔɪ/ *vt* 1 give paid work to 2 *fml* use ~**able** *adj* suitable as a worker ~**er**

n person who employs others ~**ment** *n* 1 [U] paid work 2 [C] *fml* useful activity

em·ploy·ee /ɪm'plɔɪ-iː, ˌemplɔɪ'iː/ *n* employed person

em·pow·er /ɪm'paʊə‖-'paʊr/ *vt* give power to

em·press /'emprɪ̱s/ *n* female ruler of an empire, or the wife of an emperor

emp·ty /'empti/ *adj* 1 containing nothing 2 insincere: *empty promises* ♦ *n* [*usu. pl.*] empty container ♦ *vt/i* make or become empty ~**tiness** *n* [U]

empty-hand·ed /ˌ·· '··◀/ *adj* having gained nothing

empty-head·ed /ˌ·· '··◀/ *adj* silly

e·mu /'iːmjuː/ *n* large Australian flightless bird

em·u·late /'emjɪ̱leɪt/ *vt* try to do as well as or better than ~**lation** /ˌemjɪ̱'leɪʃən/ *n* [U]

e·mul·sion /ɪ'mʌlʃən/ *n* [U] creamy liquid mixture, esp. paint

en·a·ble /ɪ'neɪbəl/ *vt* make able: *to enable them to walk again*

en·act /ɪ'nækt/ *vt* make (a law)

e·nam·el /ɪ'næməl/ *n* [U] 1 glassy covering on metal, etc. 2 hard surface of the teeth ♦ *vt* -ll- *BrE*‖ -l- *AmE* cover with enamel

en·am·oured *BrE*‖ —**ored** *AmE* /ɪ'næməd‖-ərd/ *adj* very fond (of an idea, etc.)

en bloc /ɒn 'blɒk‖ɑːn 'blɑːk/ *adv* all together as a single unit

en·camp·ment /ɪn'kæmpmənt/ *n* military camp

en·cap·su·late /ɪn'kæpsjɪ̱leɪt‖-sə-/ *vt* express in a short form

en·case /ɪn'keɪs/ *vt* cover completely

en·chant /ɪn't ʃɑːnt‖ɪn't ʃænt/ *vt* 1 delight 2 use magic on ~**ing** *adj* delightful ~**ingly** *adv* ~**ment** *n* [C;U]

en·cir·cle /ɪn'sɜːkəl‖-ɜːr-/ *vt* surround

en·clave /'enkleɪv, 'en-/ *n* a part of a country surrounded by another **b** area where an ETHNIC or religious group lives, surrounded by an area in which a different group lives

en·close /ɪn'kləʊz‖-'kloʊz/ *vt* 1 surround with a fence, etc. 2 put (something else) into an envelope

en·clo·sure /ɪn'kləʊʒə‖-'kloʊʒər/ *n* 1 enclosed place 2 something put in with a

en·com·pass /ɪn'kʌmpəs/ vt include; be concerned with

en·core /'ɒŋkɔː‖'ɑːŋkɔːr/ interj, n (word calling for) a repeated performance

en·coun·ter /ɪn'kaʊntə‖-ər/ vt fml meet (something dangerous or unexpected) ♦ n sudden (esp. unpleasant) meeting

en·cour·age /ɪn'kʌrɪdʒ‖ɪn'kɜːr-/ vt give approval to; urge: He encouraged her to try. ~ment n [C;U]

en·cour·ag·ing /ɪn'kʌrɪdʒɪŋ‖ɪn'kɜːr-/ adj causing feelings of hope and confidence: encouraging trade figures

en·croach /ɪn'krəʊtʃ‖-'krəʊtʃ/ vi go beyond what is right or usual: encroach on their territory ~ment n [C;U]

en·crust·ed /ɪn'krʌstɪ̇d/ adj thickly covered: encrusted with jewels/mud

en·cum·ber /ɪn'kʌmbə‖-ər/ vt load; BURDEN –brance n

en·cy·clo·pe·di·a, -paedia /ɪn,saɪklə-'piːdiə/ n book of many facts in alphabetical order –dic adj wide and full

end¹ /end/ n 1 point where something stops or finishes: the end of the road/of August 2 little piece remaining: cigarette ends 3 fml aim; purpose 4 **at a loose end** having nothing to do 5 **in the end** at last 6 **make ends meet** get just enough money 7 **no end of** an endless amount of 8 **on end**: a continuously: for hours on end b upright 9 **put an end to** stop —see also SHARP END ~less adj never finishing ~lessly adv

end² /vi t/ finish ~ing n end (of a story, etc.)

end up phr vi finish one's journey

en·dan·ger /ɪn'deɪndʒə‖-ər/ vt cause danger to

en·dear /ɪn'dɪə‖-'dɪr/ vt **endear oneself** to make oneself loved by ~ment n expression of love

en·deav·our BrE ‖ **-or** AmE /ɪn'devə‖-ər/ vi fml try ♦ n [C;U] fml effort

en·dem·ic /en'demɪk, ɪn-/ adj (esp. of something bad) often happening in a place

en·dorse /ɪn'dɔːs‖-'ɔːrs/ vt 1 express approval of (a statement, etc.) 2 write one's name on (a cheque) 3 record a driving offence on (a driver's LICENCE) ~ment n [C;U]

en·dow /ɪn'daʊ/ vt 1 give a continuing income to (a school, etc.) 2 **be endowed**

with fml have (a good quality) from birth ~ment n [C;U]

en·dur·ance /ɪn'djʊərəns‖ɪn'dʊr-/ n [U] power of enduring

en·dure /ɪn'djʊə‖ɪn'dʊr/ v 1 vt suffer (pain, etc.) patiently 2 vi continue to exist

en·e·ma /'enɪmə/ n putting of a liquid, esp. a medicine, into the bowels through the RECTUM

en·e·my /'enəmi/ n 1 person who hates or opposes another person 2 country with which one is at war

en·er·get·ic /,enə'dʒetɪk◄‖-ər-/ adj very active ~ally /-kli/ adv

en·er·gy /'enədʒi‖-ər-/ n [U] 1 ability to be active and work hard 2 power that drives machines, etc.: nuclear energy

en·fant ter·ri·ble /,ɒnfɒn te'riːblə‖,ɑːnfɑːn-/ n shocking but also often interesting and amusing person

en·fold /ɪn'fəʊld‖-'foʊld/ vt take into one's arms

en·force /ɪn'fɔːs‖-ɔːrs/ vt cause (a law etc.) to be obeyed ~able adj ~ment n [U]

en·fran·chise /ɪn'fræntʃaɪz/ vt give the right to vote to ~ment /-tʃɪz-‖-tʃaɪz-/ n [U]

en·gage /ɪn'geɪdʒ/ v fml 1 vt arrange to employ 2 vi/t lock (machine parts) together

engaged adj 1 having agreed to marry 2 busy or in use ~ment n 1 agreement to marry 2 arrangement to meet someone 3 fml battle

engage in phr vt fml make (someone) busy in

en·gag·ing /ɪn'geɪdʒɪŋ/ adj charming ~ly adv

en·gen·der /ɪn'dʒendə‖-ər/ vt fml cause; produce

en·gine /'endʒɪ̇n/ n 1 machine that turns power into movement 2 machine that pulls a train

en·gi·neer /,endʒɪ̇'nɪə‖-'nɪr/ n 1 person who plans machines, roads, bridges, etc. 2 person who controls engines ♦ vt cause by secret planning ~ing n [U] profession of an ENGINEER (1)

en·grave /ɪn'greɪv/ vt cut (words, etc.) on a hard surface **engraver** n **engraving** n 1 [C] picture printed from an engraved piece of metal 2 [U] work of an engraver

en·gross /ɪn'grəʊs‖-'groʊs/ vt completely fill the attention of

en·gulf /ɪn'gʌlf/ vt swallow up: a house

engulfed in flames

en·hance /ɪnˈhɑːns ‖ ɪnˈhæns/ *vt* increase (something good) ~**ment** *n* [C;U]

e·nig·ma /ɪˈnɪgmə/ *n* mystery ~**tic** /ˌenɪgˈmætɪk◂/ *adj* ~**tically** /-kli/ *adv*

en·joy /ɪnˈdʒɔɪ/ *vt* **1** get pleasure from **2** *fml* possess (something good) **3** ~ **oneself** be happy ~**able** *adj* pleasant ~**ably** *adv* ~**ment** *n* [C;U]

en·large /ɪnˈlɑːdʒ ‖ -ɑːr-/ *vt/i* (cause to) become larger ~**ment** *n* [C;U]

enlarge on/upon *phr vt* say more about

en·light·en /ɪnˈlaɪtn/ *vt* make free from false beliefs ~**ment** *n* [U]

en·light·ened /ɪnˈlaɪtənd/ *adj* with a modern attitude; sensible

en·list /ɪnˈlɪst/ *v* **1** *vi/t* (cause to) join the armed forces **2** *vt* obtain (help, etc.) ~**ment** *n* [C;U]

en·liv·en /ɪnˈlaɪvən/ *vt* to make more active or cheerful

en masse /ˌɒn ˈmæs ‖ ˌɑːn-/ *adv* all together

en·mesh /ɪnˈmeʃ/ *vt* catch as if in a net

en·mi·ty /ˈenmɪti/ *n* [C;U] *fml* hatred

e·nor·mi·ty /ɪˈnɔːmɪti ‖ -ɔːr-/ *n* **1** [U] enormous size **2** [C;U] *fml* great wickedness

e·nor·mous /ɪˈnɔːməs ‖ -ɔːr-/ *adj* very large ~**ly** *adv* extremely

e·nough /ɪˈnʌf/ *determiner, pron, adv* **1** as much or as many as is needed: *enough food/chairs* | *not big enough* **2** *fair enough infml* all right **3** *oddly/strangely enough...* and this is strange, but... **4** *sure enough* as expected

en·quire /ɪnˈkwaɪə ‖ -ˈkwaɪr/ *vi/t* INQUIRE **enquiry** *n* [C;U]

en·rage /ɪnˈreɪdʒ/ *vt* make very angry

en·rich /ɪnˈrɪtʃ/ *vt* **1** make rich **2** improve by adding something ~**ment** *n* [U]

en·rol, enroll /ɪnˈrəʊl ‖ -ˈroʊl/ *vi/t* -**ll**- (cause to) join a group officially ~**ment** *n* [C;U]

en route /ˌɒn ˈruːt ‖ ˌɑːn-/ *adv* on the way; travelling

en·sconced /ɪnˈskɒnst ‖ ɪnˈskɑːnst/ *adj* comfortably seated

en·sem·ble /ɒnˈsɒmbəl ‖ ɑːnˈsɑːm-/ *n* **1** small group of musicians **2** *fml* set of things

en·shrine /ɪnˈʃraɪn/ *vt fml* preserve as if holy

en·sign /ˈensaɪn, -sən ‖ ˈensən/ *n* **1** ship's flag **2** US naval officer

en·slave /ɪnˈsleɪv/ *vt* make into a slave ~**ment** *n* [U]

en·sue /ɪnˈsjuː ‖ ɪnˈsuː/ *vi fml* happen afterwards or as a result

en·sure /ɪnˈʃʊə ‖ -ˈʃʊr/ *vt* make (something) certain to happen

en·tail /ɪnˈteɪl/ *vt* make necessary

en·tan·gle /ɪnˈtæŋgəl/ *vt* cause to become twisted with something else ~**ment** *n* [C;U]

en·ter /ˈentə ‖ -ər/ *v* **1** *vi/t* come or go in or into **2** *vt* become a member of **3** *vt* put into a book, list, etc.

enter into *phr vt* take part in

enter on/upon *phr vt fml* begin

en·ter·prise /ˈentəpraɪz ‖ -ər-/ *n* **1** [C] plan that needs courage **2** [U] willingness to take risks **3** [U] way of organizing business: *private enterprise* —see also FREE ENTERPRISE –**prising** *adj* having ENTERPRISE (2)

en·ter·tain /ˌentəˈteɪn ‖ -ər-/ *v* **1** *vi/t* amuse and interest **2** *vi/t* provide food and drink for (guests) **3** *vt fml* be willing to consider (ideas) ~**er** person who amuses people professionally ~**ment** *n* **1** [U] act of entertaining **2** [C] public amusement

en·thral, enthrall /ɪnˈθrɔːl ‖ -ˈθrɒːl/ *vt* -**ll**- hold the complete attention of

en·throne /ɪnˈθrəʊn ‖ -ˈθroʊn/ *vt* put (a ruler) on a THRONE

en·thuse /ɪnˈθjuːz ‖ ɪnˈθuːz/ *vi* speak with enthusiasm

en·thu·si·as·m /ɪnˈθjuːziæzəm ‖ ɪnˈθuː-/ *n* [C;U] great interest and admiration ~**ast** *n* person who is keen on something -**astic** /ɪnˌθjuːziˈæstɪk◂ ‖ ɪnˌθuː-/ *adj* full of enthusiasm -**astically** /-kli/ *adv*

en·tice /ɪnˈtaɪs/ *vt* persuade, esp. to do wrong ~**ment** *n* [C;U] –**cing** *adj* attractive

en·tire /ɪnˈtaɪə ‖ -ˈtaɪr/ *adj* complete ~**ly** *adv* ~**ty** /ɪnˈtaɪərəti ‖ -ˈtaɪr-/ *n* [U]

en·ti·tle /ɪnˈtaɪtl/ *vt* **1** give a right (to) **2** give a title to (a book, etc.) ~**ment** *n* [U]

en·ti·ty /ˈentɪti/ *n* thing with separate existence

en·tou·rage /ˈɒntʊrɑːʒ ‖ ˈɑːn-/ *n* people who surround someone important

en·trails /ˈentreɪlz/ *n* bowels

en·trance¹ /ˈentrəns/ *n* **1** [C] door, etc. by which one enters **2** [C] act of entering **3** [U] right to enter

en·trance² /ɪn'trɑːns ‖ ɪn'træns/ *vt* fill with delight

en·trant /'entrənt/ *n* person who enters a race, profession, etc.

en·treat /ɪn'triːt/ *vt fml* beg; IMPLORE ~**y** *n* [C;U] act of entreating

en·trée /'ɒntreɪ ‖ 'ɑːn-/ *n* **1** freedom to enter **2 a** *esp. BrE* small meat dish eaten before the main dish of a meal **b** *esp. AmE* main dish of a meal

en·trenched /ɪn'trentʃt/ *adj* (of beliefs, etc.) firmly established

en·tre·pre·neur /ˌɒntrəprə'nɜː ‖ ˌɑːntrəprə'nɜːr/ *n* person who starts a firm, etc. and takes business risks –**ial** *adj*

en·trust /ɪn'trʌst/ *vt* give to someone to take care of

en·try /'entri/ *n* **1** [C;U] act of coming or going in **2** [C] something written in a list

en·twine /ɪn'twaɪn/ *vt* twist together or round

E num·ber /'iː nʌmbə ‖ -ər/ *n* number with the letter E in front of it, used to show the chemicals contained in food

e·nu·me·rate /ɪ'njuːməreɪt ‖ ɪ'nuː-/ *vt fml* name one by one –**ration** /ɪˌnjuːmə'reɪʃən ‖ ɪˌnuː-/ *n* [C;U]

e·nun·ci·ate /ɪ'nʌnsieɪt/ *vt/i* pronounce (words) clearly –**ation** /ɪˌnʌnsi'eɪʃən/ *n* [U]

en·vel·op /ɪn'veləp/ *vt* cover completely: *enveloped in flames* –**ment** *n* [U]

en·ve·lope /'envələʊp ‖ -loʊp/ *n* paper container for a letter

en·vi·a·ble /'enviəbəl/ *adj* very desirable –**bly** *adv*

en·vi·ous /'enviəs/ *adj* feeling envy ~**ly** *adv*

en·vi·ron·ment /ɪn'vaɪərənmənt ‖ -'vaɪr-/ *n* conditions in which people, animals, etc. live ~**al** /ɪnˌvaɪərən'mentl◀ ‖ -ˌvaɪr-/ *adj* ~**ally** *adv* ~**alist** *n* person who tries to keep our natural surroundings from being spoilt **environmentally friendly** /·ˌ····· '··/ *adj* ECO-FRIENDLY

en·vis·age /ɪn'vɪzɪdʒ/ also **envision** /ɪn'vɪʒən/ *AmE* — *vt* see in the mind; expect

en·voy /'envɔɪ/ *n* messenger; representative

en·vy /'envi/ *n* [U] **1** bad feeling one has towards someone who has better luck than oneself **2 the envy of (someone)** something which other people want to have or to be ♦ *vt* feel envy towards or because of

en·zyme /'enzaɪm/ *n* substance produced by living cells that causes chemical change

e·on /'iːən/ *n* an AEON

ep·au·let , **-lette** /ˌepə'let/ *n* shoulder decoration on a uniform

e·phem·er·al /ɪ'femərəl/ *adj* lasting only a short time

ep·ic /'epɪk/ *n* **1** long poem, film, etc. about the deeds of gods or great men **2** *derog* event needing a lot of time and energy ♦ *adj* (of stories) full of bravery and excitement

ep·i·cu·re·an /ˌepɪkjʊ'riːən◀/ *n* person who believes pleasure is very important

ep·i·dem·ic /ˌepə'demɪk◀/ *n* many cases of an infectious disease at the same time

ep·i·gram /'epəgræm/ *n* short amusing poem or saying

ep·i·lep·sy /'epəlepsi/ *n* disease of the brain causing sudden unconsciousness -**leptic** /ˌepə'leptɪk◀/ *adj*, *n*

ep·i·logue /'epəlɒg ‖ -lɔːg, -lɑːg/ *n* last part of a play or book

e·pis·co·pal /ɪ'pɪskəpəl/ *adj* of or governed by BISHOPS

ep·i·sode /'epɪsəʊd ‖ -soʊd/ *n* one separate event or period of time

ep·i·taph /'epɪtɑːf ‖ -tæf/ *n* words written above a grave

ep·i·thet /'epɪθet/ *adj* adjective, esp. used of a person

e·pit·o·me /ɪ'pɪtəmi/ *n* something that perfectly shows a particular quality: *My son is the epitome of laziness.* –**mize**, –**mise** *vt* be typical of

e·poch /'iːpɒk ‖ 'epək/ *n* period of historical time, esp. one in which some remarkable event happened ~~**making** *adj* extremely important

eq·ua·ble /'ekwəbəl/ *adj* even and regular: *an equable climate* –**bly** *adv*

e·qual /'iːkwəl/ *adj* **1** the same in size, value, etc. **2 equal to** having enough ability, etc. for ♦ *n* person equal to another ♦ *vt* -**ll-** *BrE* ‖ -**l-** *AmE* be the same as ~**ize**, ~**ise** *vt* make equal ~**ly** *adv*: *equally fit* | *to share the work equally* ~**ity** /ɪ'kwɒlɪti ‖ ɪ'kwɑː-/ *n* [U]: *the equality of women*

eq·ua·nim·i·ty /ˌiːkwə'nɪmɪti, ˌekwə-/ *n* [U] *fml* calmness of mind

e·quate /ɪ'kweɪt/ *vt* consider as equal

e·qua·tion /ɪ'kweɪʒən/ *n* statement that two quantities are equal: $2x + 1 = 7$ *is an* *equation.*

e·qua·tor /ɪ'kweɪtə ‖ -ər/ *n* [*the*+S] imaginary line round the world, halfway between the North and South POLES ~**ial** /ˌekwə'tɔːriəl◂/ *adj*

e·ques·tri·an /ɪ'kwestriən/ *adj* of horse-riding

e·qui·lib·ri·um /ˌiːkwɪ'lɪbriəm/ *n* [U] *fml* BALANCE (1)

eq·ui·nox /'iːkwɪnɒks, 'e-‖-nɑːks/ *n* time of year when day and night are of equal length

e·quip /ɪ'kwɪp/ *vt* -pp- provide with what is necessary ~**ment** *n* [U] things needed for an activity

eq·ui·ta·ble /'ekwɪtəbəl/ *adj* fair and just: -**bly** *adv*

eq·ui·ties /'ekwɪtiz/ *n* [P] *tech* firm's ordinary SHARES, on which no fixed amount of interest is paid

eq·ui·ty /'ekwɪti/ *n* [U] *fml* fairness

e·quiv·a·lent /ɪ'kwɪvələnt/ *n*, *adj* (something) the same in value

e·quiv·o·cal /ɪ'kwɪvəkəl/ *adj* doubtful in meaning; questionable -**cate** *vi fml* speak in an equivocal way on purpose

e·ra /'ɪərə ‖ 'ɪrə/ *n* period of historical time, marked esp. by particular developments

e·rad·i·cate /ɪ'rædɪkeɪt/ *vt* put an end to (something bad) -**cation** /ɪˌrædɪ'keɪʃən/ *n* [U]

e·rase /ɪ'reɪz ‖ ɪ'reɪs/ *vt fml* rub out **eraser** *n* RUBBER[1] (2)

e·rect /ɪ'rekt/ *adj* upright ♦ *vt* **1** put upright: *erect a tent* **2** *fml* build: *erect a monument* ~**ion** /ɪ'rekʃən/ *n* **1** [U] the act of erecting something **2** [C] *fml* a building **3** [C;U] (an example of) the state of the PENIS when upright ~**ly** *adv* ~**ness** *n* [U]

er·go /'ɜːgəʊ ‖ 'ɜːrgoʊ/ *adv* therefore

er·go·nom·ics /ˌɜːgə'nɒmɪks ‖ ˌɜːrgə'nɑː-/ *n* [U] study of how people work best with machines -**ic** *adj* -**ically** /-kli/ *adv*

er·mine /'ɜːmən ‖ 'ɜːr-/ *n* [C;U] (white fur of) the STOAT

e·rode /ɪ'rəʊd ‖ ɪ'roʊd/ *vt* (of acids, water, etc.) wear away; reduce **erosion** /ɪ'rəʊʒən ‖ ɪ'roʊ-/ *n* [U]

e·ro·ge·nous /ɪ'rɒdʒənəs ‖ ɪ'rɑː-/ *adj* sexually sensitive

e·rot·ic /ɪ'rɒtɪk ‖ ɪ'rɑː-/ *adj* of sexual love ~**ism** /-təsɪzəm/ *n* [U]

err /ɜː ‖ ɜːr/ *vi fml* make a mistake

er·rand /'erənd/ *n* short journey to do or esp. buy something

er·rant /'erənt/ *adj fml* wandering away and misbehaving

er·rat·ic /ɪ'rætɪk/ *adj* changeable; not regular ~**ally** /-kli/ *adv*

er·ro·ne·ous /ɪ'rəʊniəs ‖ ɪ'roʊ-/ *adj fml* (of a belief) incorrect ~**ly** *adv*

er·ror /'erə ‖ 'erər/ *n* **1** [C] mistake **2** [U] state of being mistaken

er·satz /'eəzæts ‖ 'erzɑːts/ *adj derog* used instead of something else; artificial

erst·while /'ɜːstwaɪl ‖ 'ɜːr-/ *adj lit* former

er·u·dite /'erʊdaɪt/ *adj fml* full of learning

e·rupt /ɪ'rʌpt/ *vi* (of a VOLCANO) explode suddenly: (fig.) *The crowd erupted.* ~**ion** /ɪ'rʌpʃən/ *n* [C;U]

es·ca·late /'eskəleɪt/ *vi/t* (cause to) grow greater or more serious -**lation** /ˌeskə'leɪʃən/ *n* [U]

es·ca·la·tor /'eskəleɪtə ‖ -ər/ *n* set of moving stairs

es·ca·pade /'eskəpeɪd/ *n* wild dangerous act

es·cape /ɪ'skeɪp/ *v* **1** *vi/t* get out; get free (from) **2** *vt* avoid (something dangerous): *to escape death* **3** *vt* be forgotten by: *His name escapes me.* ♦ *n* [C;U] (act of) getting free

es·cap·is·m /ɪ'skeɪpɪzəm/ *n* [U] activity providing escape from dull reality -**ist** *adj*, *n*

e·scarp·ment /ɪ'skɑːpmənt ‖ -ɑːr-/ *n* long cliff

es·chew /ɪs'tʃuː/ *vt fml* avoid

es·cort[1] /'eskɔːt ‖ -ɔːrt/ *n* **1** person or people who go with another as a protection or honour **2** social companion

es·cort[2] /ɪ'skɔːt ‖ -ɔːrt/ *vt* go with as an escort

Es·ki·mo /'eskɪməʊ ‖ -moʊ/ *n* (*now considered offensive by some people*) INUIT

es·o·ter·ic /ˌesə'terɪk◂, ˌiːsə-/ *adj* having deep and secret meanings understood only by a few people ~**ally** /-kli/ *adv*

es·pe·cial·ly /ɪ'speʃəli/ *adv* **1** to a particularly great degree: *not especially hot* **2** in particular: *I like fruit, especially apples.*

es·pi·o·nage /'espiənɑːʒ/ *n* [U] spying (SPY)

es·pouse /ɪˈspaʊz/ vt fml support (an aim, etc.) **espousal** n [C;U]

es·say /ˈeseɪ/ n short piece of writing on a subject ~**ist** n writer of essays

es·sence /ˈesəns/ n 1 [U] most important quality of something 2 [C;U] liquid, etc. with some particular strong taste or smell: *coffee essence* 3 **of the essence** extremely important

es·sen·tial /ɪˈsenʃəl/ adj 1 necessary 2 FUNDAMENTAL: *the essential difference between us* ♦ n [usu. pl.] something necessary ~**ly** adv basically: *She's essentially kind.*

es·tab·lish /ɪˈstæblɪʃ/ vt 1 begin; CREATE (an organization, set of rules, etc.) 2 settle (esp. oneself) firmly in a particular state or position: *the film which established her reputation as a director* 3 make certain of (a fact, etc.) ~**ment** n 1 [U] act of establishing 2 [C] fml place run as a business 3 [the+S] (cap.) often derog the powerful people who control public life

es·tate /ɪˈsteɪt/ n 1 piece of land in the country, with one owner 2 BrE piece of land built on in a planned way: *a housing estate* 3 law whole of a person's property, esp. as left after death 4 BrE ESTATE CAR —SEE ALSO REAL ESTATE

estate a·gent /·ˈ· ˌ·/ n BrE person who buys and sells houses and land for people

estate car /·ˈ· ·/ n BrE car with a door at the back and folding back seats

es·teem /ɪˈstiːm/ n [U] fml respect: *I hold him in high esteem.* ♦ vt 1 respect greatly 2 fml consider to be **estimable** /ˈestɪməbəl/ adj worthy of respect

es·ti·mate[1] /ˈestɪmeɪt/ vt/i calculate; form an opinion about (cost, etc.) ~**mation** /ˌestɪˈmeɪʃən/ n [U] judgment; opinion

es·ti·mate[2] /ˈestɪmət/ n calculation of cost, number, etc.

es·tranged /ɪˈstreɪndʒd/ adj fml 1 no longer living with one's husband or wife 2 no longer communicating with one's family, etc. because of an argument **estrangement** n [C;U]

es·tu·a·ry /ˈestʃuəri, -tʃəri‖-tʃueri/ n mouth of a river, into which the sea flows

etc. also et cet·e·ra /etˈsetərə/ adv and the rest; and other things

etch /etʃ/ vt/i draw with a needle and acid on metal ~**ing** n [C;U]

e·ter·nal /ɪˈtɜːnl‖-ɜːr-/ adj lasting for ever ~**ly** adv

e·ter·ni·ty /ɪˈtɜːnəti‖-ɜːr-/ n 1 [U] endless time after death 2 [C] an extremely long time

e·ther /ˈiːθə‖-ər/ n [U] 1 liquid that easily changes to a gas 2 upper levels of the air

e·the·re·al /ɪˈθɪəriəl‖-ˈθɪr-/ adj extremely light and delicate

eth·ic /ˈeθɪk/ n system of moral behaviour: *the Christian ethic* ~**al** adj 1 of morals 2 morally good ~**ally** /-kli/ adv **ethics** n 1 [U] science of morals 2 [P] moral rules

eth·nic /ˈeθnɪk/ adj of or related to a racial, national, or tribal group ~**ally** /-kli/ adv

ethnic clean·sing /ˌ·· ˈ··/ n euph killing or removal of people of a particular ethnic group

e·thos /ˈiːθɒs‖-ˈθɑːs/ n [S] characteristic moral beliefs of a person or group

et·i·quette /ˈetɪket‖-kət/ n [U] formal rules of manners

et·y·mol·o·gy /ˌetɪˈmɒlədʒi‖-ˈmɑː-/ n [U] study of the origins of words

EU /ˌiː ˈjuː/ n [the] abbrev. for: European Union; European political and economic organization encouraging trade and friendship between member countries

eu·ca·lyp·tus /ˌjuːkəˈlɪptəs/ n tree whose oil is used as medicine for colds

eu·lo·gy /ˈjuːlədʒi/ n fml speech in praise of someone –**gize** vt praise highly –**gistic** /ˌjuːləˈdʒɪstɪk◂/ adj full of praise

eu·nuch /ˈjuːnək/ n man who has been castrated (CASTRATE)

eu·phe·mis·m /ˈjuːfɪmɪzəm/ n [C;U] (use of) a pleasanter, less direct word for something unpleasant –**mistic** /ˌjuːfɪˈmɪstɪk◂/ adj

eu·pho·ri·a /juːˈfɔːriə‖ juː-/ n [U] state of happiness and cheerful excitement –**ric** /juːˈfɒrɪk‖ -ˈfɔːrɪk, -ˈfɑː-/ adj

eu·ro /ˈjʊərəʊ‖ˈjʊroʊ/ n unit of money used in most EU member countries

Eu·ro·pe·an U·nion /ˌjʊərəpiːən ˈjuːnjən‖ˌjʊr-/ n [the] the EU

eu·tha·na·si·a /ˌjuːθəˈneɪziə‖-ˈneɪʒə/ n [U] painless killing of very ill or very old people

e·vac·u·ate /ɪˈvækjueɪt/ vt take all the people away from (a dangerous place)

–ation /ɪ,vækju'eɪʃən/ n [C;U] **-ee** /-'kjuː'/ n person who has been evacuated

e·vade /ɪ'veɪd/ vt avoid; escape from

e·val·u·ate /ɪ'væljueɪt/ vt calculate the value of –ation /ɪ,vælju'eɪʃən/ n [C;U]

e·van·gel·i·cal /,iːvæn'dʒelɪkəl◄/ n, adj (often cap.) **1** (member) of those Christian churches that believe in studying the Bible rather than in ceremonies **2** (person) showing very great eagerness in spreading certain beliefs

e·van·ge·list /ɪ'vændʒəlٕ\ِst/ n travelling Christian religious teacher –**lism** n [U] ~**ic** /ɪ,vændʒə'lɪstɪk◄/ adj

e·vap·o·rate /ɪ'væpəreɪt/ vi/t change into steam and disappear –**ration** /ɪ,væpə'reɪʃən/ n [U]

e·va·sion /ɪ'veɪʒən/ n [C;U] the act of evading (EVADE): tax evasion –**sive** /-sɪv/ adj

eve /iːv/ n [S] **1** (usu. cap.) day before a (religious) holiday **2** time just before any event: on the eve of the election

even[1] /'iːvən/ adv **1** (shows that something is unexpected and surprising): John's a very good swimmer, but even he doesn't swim in the river. (=so certainly nobody else does) **2** (makes comparisons stronger): It's even colder than yesterday. **3 even if** it does not matter if **4 even now/so/then** in spite of that: I explained, but even then he didn't understand. **5 even though** though

even[2] adj **1** smooth and regular: an even surface/temperature **2** (of things that can be compared) equal: an even chance **3** (of numbers) that can be divided by two ~**ly** adv ~**ness** n [U]

even[3] v **even out** phr vi/t (cause to) become level or equal

even-hand·ed /,· '··◄/ adj giving fair and equal treatment to all sides

eve·ning /'iːvnɪŋ/ n time between afternoon and bedtime

e·vent /ɪ'vent/ n **1** (important) happening **2** one race, etc. in a day's sports **3 at all events** in spite of everything **4 in the event** when it actually happened **5 in the event of...** if (something) happens ~**ful** adj full of important events

e·ven·tu·al /ɪ'ventʃuəl/ adj happening at last ~**ly** adv in the end: They eventually succeeded. ~**ity** /ɪ,ventʃu'ælٕ\ti/ n fml possible event

ev·er /'evə ‖ 'evər/ adv **1** at any time: Does

it ever snow? | Nothing ever annoys him. | colder than ever **2** always: ever since Christmas | the ever-increasing population **3** (gives force to a question): What ever is that? **4 ever so/such** infml very

ev·er·green /'evəgriːn ‖ -ər-/ n, adj (tree) that does not lose its leaves in winter

ev·er·last·ing /,evə'lɑːstɪŋ◄ ‖ ,evər'læ-/ adj lasting for ever

ev·ery /'evri/ determiner **1** each: I enjoy every minute of it. **2** (of things that can be counted) once in each; I go every three days. **3** as much as is possible: I have every reason to trust him. **4 every other** the 1st, 3rd, 5th, etc., or the 2nd, 4th, 6th, etc.: Take the pills every other day **5 every now and then** also **every so often** — sometimes, but not often

ev·ery·bod·y /'evribɒdi ‖ -bɑːdi/ pron everyone

ev·ery·day /'evrideɪ/ adj ordinary; common

ev·ery·one /'evriwʌn/ pron **1** every person: Everyone was pleased. **2** all the people usually here: Where is everyone?

ev·ery·thing /'evriθɪŋ/ pron **1** each thing; They've eaten everything. **2** all that matters: Money isn't everything.

ev·ery·where /'evriweə ‖ -wer/ also ev·ery·place /-pleɪs/ AmE— adv at or to every place

every which way /,·· '· ·/ adv AmE in every direction

e·vict /ɪ'vɪkt/ vt force to leave a house, etc. by law ~**ion** /ɪ'vɪkʃən/ n [C;U]

ev·i·dence /'evٕ\dəns/ n [U] **1** proof **2** answers given in a court of law **3 in evidence** present and easily seen

ev·i·dent /'evٕ\dənt/ adj plain and clear ~**ly** adv

e·vil /'iːvəl/ adj harmful; wicked ♦ n [C;U] fml wickedness or misfortune ~**ly** /'iːvəl-li/ adv

e·voc·a·tive /ɪ'vɒkətɪv ‖ ɪ'vɑː-/ adj bringing memories: an evocative smell

e·voke /ɪ'vəʊk ‖ ɪ'voʊk/ vt fml produce (a memory)

ev·o·lu·tion /,iːvə'luːʃən, ,evə- ‖ ,evə-/ n [U] gradual development, esp. of living things from earlier and simpler forms ~**ary** adj

e·volve /ɪ'vɒlv ‖ ɪ'vɑːlv/ vi/t develop gradually

ewe /juː/ n female sheep

ex /eks/ n *infml* former husband, wife, BOYFRIEND, etc.

ex·a·cer·bate /ɪgˈzæsəbeɪt ‖ -ər-/ *vt fml* make (something bad) worse

ex·act¹ /ɪgˈzækt/ *adj* 1 correctly measured; PRECISE: *the exact time* **~ly** *adv* 1 correctly 2 (as a reply) I agree! 3 **not exactly** not really **~ness** also **~itude** /ɪgˈzæktɪtjuːd ‖ -tuːd/ *n* [U]

exact² *vt fml* demand and obtain by force **~ing** *adj* demanding great effort

ex·ag·ge·rate /ɪgˈzædʒəreɪt/ *vi/t* make (something) seem larger, etc. than it is **-ration** /ɪg,zædʒəˈreɪʃən/ *n* [C;U]

ex·al·ta·tion /,egzɔːlˈteɪʃən, ,eksɔːl- ‖ -oːl-/ *n* great joy because of success

ex·alt·ed /ɪg,zɔːltʃd ‖ -ˈzɔːl-/ *adj* of high rank

ex·am /ɪgˈzæm/ *n* test of knowledge

ex·am·i·na·tion /ɪg,zæmʃˈneɪʃən/ *n* 1 [C] *fml* exam 2 [C;U] act of examining

ex·am·ine /ɪgˈzæmʃn/ *vt* 1 look carefully at 2 ask questions, to find out something or test knowledge **-iner** *n*

ex·am·ple /ɪgˈzɑːmpəl ‖ ɪgˈzæm-/ *n* 1 something that shows a general rule: *a typical example* 2 something to be copied: *Her courage is an example to us all.* 3 **for example** (*abbrev.* **e.g.**) here is one of the things just spoken of 4 **make an example of someone** punish someone to frighten others

ex·as·pe·rate /ɪgˈzɑːspəreɪt ‖ ɪgˈzæ-/ *vt* annoy very much **-ratedly** *adv* **-ratingly** *adv* **-ration** /ɪg,zɑːspəˈreɪʃən ‖ ɪg,zæ-/ *n* [U]

ex·ca·vate /ˈekskəveɪt/ *vt* 1 dig (a hole) 2 uncover by digging **-vator** *n* person or machine that excavates **-vation** /,ekskəˈveɪʃən/ *n* [C;U]

ex·ceed /ɪkˈsiːd/ *vt* 1 be greater than 2 do more than: *to exceed the speed limit* **~ingly** *adv fml* extremely

ex·cel /ɪkˈsel/ *vi* **-ll-** *fml* be extremely good (at something)

Ex·cel·len·cy /ˈeksələnsi/ *n* (title of some people of high rank in the state or church)

ex·cel·lent /ˈeksələnt/ *adj* very good **-lence** *n* [U]

ex·cept /ɪkˈsept/ *prep* not including; but not: *Everyone except John was tired.* ♦ *vt fml* leave out; not include

ex·cep·tion /ɪkˈsepʃən/ *n* 1 [C;U] (a case of) leaving out or being left out: *Everyone, without exception, must attend. | I don't usually see people after 5.00, but I'll make an exception in your case.* 2 **take exception to** be made angry by **~al** *adj* unusual, esp. because very good **~ally** *adv*

ex·cerpt /ˈeksɜːpt ‖ -ɜːr-/ *n* piece taken from a book, etc.

ex·cess /ɪkˈses, ˈekses/ *n, adj* [S;U] (an amount that is) greater than is usual or allowed: *an excess of violence in the film* **~ive** *adj* too much **~ively** *adv* **excesses** *n* [P] extremely bad, cruel, etc. behaviour

ex·change /ɪksˈtʃeɪndʒ/ *vt* give and receive in return: *I exchanged my dollars for pounds.* ♦ *n* 1 [C;U] act of exchanging 2 [U] changing of money: *the rate of exchange* 3 [C] place where **a** telephone wires meet **b** business people meet: *the Stock Exchange* 4 [C] short period of fighting or talking —see also FOREIGN EXCHANGE

ex·cise¹ /ˈeksaɪz/ *n* [U] tax on goods produced inside a country

ex·cise² /ɪkˈsaɪz/ *vt fml* remove by cutting

ex·cite /ɪkˈsaɪt/ *vt* 1 cause to have strong (pleasant) feelings: *an excited little boy* 2 *fml* cause (feelings): *to excite interest* **~ment** *n* [C;U] **excitable** *adj* easily excited **exciting** *adj*: *exciting films*

ex·claim /ɪkˈskleɪm/ *vi/t* speak or say suddenly

ex·cla·ma·tion /,ekskləˈmeɪʃən/ *n* word(s) exclaimed

exclamation mark /·ˈ·· ·/ *BrE ‖* **exclamation point** *AmE* — *n* PUNCTUATION MARK (!) written after an exclamation

ex·clude /ɪkˈskluːd/ *vt* 1 keep out or leave out 2 shut out from the mind: *Don't exclude that possibility.* **excluding** *prep* not including **exclusion** /ɪkˈskluːʒən/ *n* [U]

ex·clu·sive /ɪkˈskluːsɪv/ *adj* 1 keeping out unsuitable people 2 not shared ♦ *n* story appearing in only one newspaper **~ly** *adv* only: *exclusively for women*

ex·com·mu·ni·cate /,ekskəˈmjuːnʃkeɪt/ *vt* exclude from the Christian Church **-cation** /,ekskəmjuːnʃˈkeɪʃən/ *n* [C;U]

ex·cre·ment /ˈekskrʃmənt/ *n* [U] *fml* solid waste from the bowels

ex·crete /ɪkˈskriːt/ *vt* pass out (waste

matter)

ex·cru·ci·at·ing /ɪkˈskruːʃieɪtɪŋ/ adj (of pain) very bad ~**ly** adv

ex·cul·pate /ˈekskʌlpeɪt/ vt fml free from blame

ex·cur·sion /ɪkˈskɜːʃən ‖ ɪkˈskɜːrʒən/ n short journey for pleasure

ex·cuse[1] /ɪkˈskjuːz/ vt 1 forgive: *Please excuse my bad handwriting.* 2 make (bad behaviour) seem less bad 3 free from a duty 4 **Excuse me** (said when starting to speak to a stranger, or when one wants to get past a person, or to APOLOGIZE for something) 5 **excuse oneself** ask permission to be absent **excusable** adj that can be forgiven

ex·cuse[2] /ɪkˈskjuːs/ n reason given when asking to be excused

ex·e·cute /ˈeksɪkjuːt/ vt 1 kill as a legal punishment 2 fml carry out; perform: *execute a plan* –**cution** /ˌeksɪˈkjuːʃən/ n 1 [C;U] legal killing 2 [U] fml carrying out; performance –**cutioner** n official who executes criminals

ex·ec·u·tive /ɪɡˈzekjʊtɪv/ 1 adj concerned with managing, or carrying out decisions 2 suitable for important people; expensive: *executive homes* ♦ n 1 [C] person in an executive position in business 2 [the+S] branch of government that carries out the law

ex·ec·u·tor /ɪɡˈzekjʊtə ‖ -ər/ n person who carries out the orders in a WILL[2] (5)

ex·em·pla·ry /ɪɡˈzempləri/ adj fml suitable to be copied

ex·em·pli·fy /ɪɡˈzemplɪfaɪ/ vt be or give an example of –**fication** /ɪɡˌzemplɪfɪˈkeɪʃən/ n [C;U]

ex·empt /ɪɡˈzempt/ adj freed from a duty, etc. ♦ vt make exempt ~**ion** /ɪɡˈzempʃən/ n [C;U]

ex·er·cise /ˈeksəsaɪz ‖ -ər-/ n 1 [U] use of the powers of the body to improve it: *go swimming for exercise* 2 [C] something done for training; *naval exercises* 3 [S;U] use (of a power or right) ♦ 1 vi/t take or give EXERCISE (1) 2 vt use (a power or right)

ex·ert /ɪɡˈzɜːt ‖ -ɜːrt/ vt 1 use (strength, etc.) 2 **exert oneself** make an effort ~**ion** /ɪɡˈzɜːʃən ‖ -ɜːr-/ n [C;U]

ex gra·tia /ˌeks ˈɡreɪʃə/ adj (of a payment) made as a favour, and not because one has a legal duty to make it

ex·hale /eksˈheɪl/ vi/t breathe out

exhalation /ˌekshəˈleɪʃən/ n [U]

ex·haust /ɪɡˈzɔːst ‖ -ˈzɒːst/ vt 1 tire out 2 use up completely ♦ n pipe by which gases escape from an engine ~**ed** adj very tired ~**ive** adj thorough ~**ively** adv ~**ion** /ɪɡˈzɔːstʃən ‖ -ˈzɒːs-/ n [U]

ex·hib·it /ɪɡˈzɪbɪt/ vt 1 show publicly for sale, etc. 2 fml show that one has (a quality) ♦ n something shown in a MUSEUM, etc. ~**or** n person showing exhibits

ex·hi·bi·tion /ˌeksɪˈbɪʃən/ n 1 public show of objects 2 act of exhibiting ~**ism** n behaviour of someone who wants to be looked at ~**ist** n

ex·hil·a·rate /ɪɡˈzɪləreɪt/ vt make cheerful and excited –**ration** /ɪɡˌzɪləˈreɪʃən/ n [U]

ex·hort /ɪɡˈzɔːt ‖ -ɔːrt/ vt fml urge strongly ~**ation** /ˌeksɔːˈteɪʃən ‖ -ɔːr-/ n [C;U]

ex·hume /ɪɡˈzjuːm, eksˈhjuːm ‖ ɪɡˈzuːm, ɪkˈsjuːm/ vt dig up (a dead body) **exhumation** /ˌeksjʊˈmeɪʃən/ n [U]

ex·i·gen·cy /ˈeksɪdʒənsi, ɪɡˈzɪ-/ n fml urgent need

ex·ile /ˈeksaɪl, ˈeɡzaɪl/ n 1 unwanted absence from one's country 2 [C] someone forced into this ♦ vt send into exile

ex·ist /ɪɡˈzɪst/ vi have life; be real: *The problems she talks about simply don't exist.* ~**ence** n 1 [U] state of being real 2 [S] way of living: *lead a miserable existence* ~**ent** adj existing; present

ex·is·ten·tial /ˌeɡzɪˈstenʃəl/ adj related to existence

ex·it /ˈeɡzɪt, ˈeksɪt/ n 1 way out of a building 2 act of leaving ♦ vi (used as a stage direction) he/she/it goes out

ex·o·dus /ˈeksədəs/ n [S] going away of many people

ex·on·e·rate /ɪɡˈzɒnəreɪt ‖ ɪɡˈzɑː-/ vt fml free (someone) from blame –**ration** /ɪɡˌzɒnəˈreɪʃən ‖ ɪɡˌzɑː-/ n [U]

ex·or·bi·tant /ɪɡˈzɔːbɪtənt ‖ -ɔːr-/ adj (of cost) too much ~**ly** adv

ex·or·cize also –**cise** /ˈeksɔːsaɪz ‖ -ɔːr-/ vt drive out (an evil spirit, etc.) by prayers –**cism** n act or art of exorcizing –**cist** n

ex·ot·ic /ɪɡˈzɒtɪk ‖ ɪɡˈzɑː-/ adj pleasantly strange: *exotic flowers/food* ~**ally** /-kli/ adv

ex·pand /ɪkˈspænd/ vi/t (cause to) grow larger or more detailed

expand on/upon phr vt make more

detailed

ex·panse /ɪkˈspæns/ n wide open space

ex·pan·sion /ɪkˈspænʃən/ n [C;U] act of expanding or expanding of expanding one's land, etc. ~**ist** n, adj

ex·pan·sive /ɪkˈspænsɪv/ adj friendly and willing to talk ~**ly** adv

ex·pat·ri·ate /ek·ˈspætriət, -trieɪt ‖ ek·ˈspeɪ-/ also **ex·pat** /ˌeksˈpæt/ n, adj (person) living abroad

ex·pect /ɪkˈspekt/ vt think or believe that something will happen ~**ing** adj infml PREGNANT ~**ation** /ˌekspekˈteɪʃən/ n 1 [U] state of expecting 2 [C] something expected

ex·pec·tant /ɪkˈspektənt/ adj 1 waiting hopefully 2 PREGNANT ~**ly** adv –**tancy** n [U] hope

ex·pe·di·ent /ɪkˈspiːdiənt/ adj (of an action) useful, esp. for one's own purposes ♦ n useful plan, esp. one thought of in a hurry because of urgent need –**ency** n [U]

ex·pe·dite /ˈekspɪ̈daɪt/ vt fml make (a plan) go faster

ex·pe·di·tion /ˌekspɪ̈ˈdɪʃən/ n (people making) a journey for a purpose: an expedition to the North Pole ~**ary** adj (of an army) sent abroad to fight

ex·pel /ɪkˈspel/ vt -ll- 1 dismiss officially from a school, etc. 2 fml force out from a container

ex·pend /ɪkˈspend/ vt spend; use up ~**able** adj that can be used up without worrying

ex·pen·di·ture /ɪkˈspendɪtʃə ‖ -ər/ n [S;U] fml spending

ex·pense /ɪkˈspens/ n [U] 1 cost 2 **at someone's expense: a** with someone paying **b** (of a joke) against someone **expenses** n [P] money for a purpose: We'll pay his travelling expenses.

ex·pen·sive /ɪkˈspensɪv/ adj costing a lot ~**ly** adv

ex·pe·ri·ence /ɪkˈspɪəriəns ‖ -ˈspɪr-/ n 1 [U] knowledge gained by practice 2 [C] something that happens and has an important effect on someone: a fascinating experience ♦ vt suffer or learn by experience: to experience defeat –**enced** adj having EXPERIENCE (1)

ex·per·i·ment /ɪkˈsperɪ̈mənt/ n [C;U] test carried out to learn something ♦ /-ment/ vi perform experiments –**al** /ɪkˌsperɪ̈ˈmentl◂/ adj used for or based on

experiments ~**ation** /ɪkˌsperɪ̈menˈteɪʃən/ n [U]

ex·pert /ˈekspɜːt ‖ -ɜːrt/ n, adj (person) with special skill or training ~**ly** adv

ex·per·tise /ˌekspɜːˈtiːz ‖ -ɜːr-/ n [U] skill in a particular field

ex·pire /ɪkˈspaɪə ‖ -ˈspaɪr/ vi 1 (of something that lasts for a time) come to an end 2 lit die **expiry** also **expiration** /ˌekspɪ̈ˈreɪʃən/ n [U]

ex·plain /ɪkˈspleɪn/ v 1 vi/t make (a meaning) clear 2 vt be the reason for **explanation** /ˌekspləˈneɪʃən/ n 1 [U] act of explaining 2 [C] something that explains **explanatory** /ɪkˈsplænətəri ‖ -tɔːri/ adj (of a statement) explaining

  explain away phr vt give an excuse for (something) to avoid blame

ex·ple·tive /ɪkˈspliːtɪv ‖ ˈeksplətɪv/ n fml word used for swearing

ex·pli·ca·ble /ek·ˈsplɪkəbəl/ adj fml (of behaviour, etc.) understandable

ex·plic·it /ɪkˈsplɪs̈t/ adj (of a statement, etc.) clearly and fully expressed ~**ly** adv ~**ness** n [U]

ex·plode /ɪkˈspləʊd ‖ -ˈsploʊd/ v 1 vi/t blow up; burst 2 vi show violent feeling

ex·ploit[1] /ɪkˈsplɔɪt/ vt 1 use (people) unfairly for profit 2 use (things) fully for profit ~**er** n ~**ation** /ˌeksplɔɪˈteɪʃən/ n [U] ~**ative** /ɪkˈsplɔɪtətɪv/ adj tending to exploit

ex·ploit[2] /ˈeksplɔɪt/ n brave successful act

ex·plore /ɪkˈsplɔː ‖ -ɔːr/ vt 1 travel through (a place) for discovery 2 examine (a subject) carefully **explorer** n **explor·ation** /ˌeksplɔːˈreɪʃən/ n [C;U] **exploratory** /ɪkˈsplɔrətəri ‖ ɪkˈsplɔːrətɔːri/ adj

ex·plo·sion /ɪkˈspləʊʒən ‖ -ˈsploʊ-/ n 1 (noise of) exploding 2 sudden increase: the population explosion

ex·plo·sive /ɪkˈspləʊsɪv ‖ -ˈsploʊ-/ n, adj (substance) that explodes ~**ly** adv

ex·po·nent /ɪkˈspəʊnənt ‖ -ˈspoʊ-/ n someone who expresses or supports a belief

ex·port[1] /ˈekspɔːt ‖ -ɔːrt/ vi/t send (goods) abroad for sale ~**er** n

ex·port[2] /ˈekspɔːt ‖ -ɔːrt/ n 1 [U] (business of) exporting 2 [C] something exported

ex·pose /ɪkˈspəʊz ‖ -ˈspoʊz/ vt 1 uncover; leave without protection 2 make known (a secret crime, etc.) 3 uncover (photographic film) to the light 4 **expose oneself** show one's sexual parts on purpose, in the hope of shocking people **exposure** /ɪkˈspəʊʒə ‖ -ˈspəʊʒər/ n [C;U]

ex·po·sé /ekˈspəʊzeɪ ‖ ˌekspəˈzeɪ/ n public statement of something shameful

ex·po·si·tion /ˌekspəˈzɪʃən/ n [C;U] fml explaining; explanation

ex·pound /ɪkˈspaʊnd/ vt fml describe (a belief, etc.) in detail

ex·press¹ /ɪkˈspres/ vt 1 make known by words or looks: *She expressed surprise at his decision.* 2 **express oneself** speak or write one's thoughts or feelings

express² adj 1 going quickly 2 clearly stated: *her express wish* ♦ n express train ♦ adv by express post ~**ly** adv 1 clearly 2 on purpose

ex·pres·sion /ɪkˈspreʃən/ n 1 [C;U] act of expressing: *political expression* 2 [C] word or phrase: *an odd expression to use* 3 [C] look on someone's face: *a surprised expression* 4 [U] quality of showing feeling: *singing without much expression* ~**less** adj without EXPRESSION (4)

ex·pres·sive /ɪkˈspresɪv/ adj showing feelings ~**ly** adv

ex·press·way /ɪkˈspreswei/ n AmE very fast road in a city

ex·pro·pri·ate /ɪkˈsprəʊprieɪt ‖ -ˈsprəʊ-/ vt fml take away for public use ~**ation** /ɪkˌsprəʊpriˈeɪʃən ‖ -ˌsprəʊ-/ n [C;U]

ex·pul·sion /ɪkˈspʌlʃən/ n [C;U] act of expelling (EXPEL)

ex·qui·site /ɪkˈskwɪzət, ˈekskwɪ-/ adj beautifully made or done ~**ly** adv

ex·tant /ɪkˈstænt/ adj fml still existing

ex·tend /ɪkˈstend/ v 1 vt make longer or larger: *extend the car park* 2 vt stretch out (part of one's body) to the limit 3 vt offer, give: *extend a welcome* 4 vi [(to)] (of land) reach

ex·ten·sion /ɪkˈstenʃən/ n 1 [U] act of extending 2 [C] part added 3 [C] telephone line inside a set of offices, etc.

ex·ten·sive /ɪkˈstensɪv/ adj large in amount or area ~**ly** adv

ex·tent /ɪkˈstent/ n 1 [U] amount or length: *the extent of the damage* 2 [S] degree: *to a large extent*

ex·ten·u·a·ting /ɪkˈstenjueɪtɪŋ/ adj giving good reasons (for bad behaviour): *extenuating circumstances*

ex·te·ri·or /ɪkˈstɪəriə ‖ -ˈstɪriər/ n outside

of something **exterior** adj

ex·ter·mi·nate /ɪkˈstɜːmɪneɪt ‖ -ɜːr-/ vt kill all of ~**nation** /ɪkˌstɜːmɪˈneɪʃən ‖ -ɜːr-/ n [U]

ex·ter·nal /ɪkˈstɜːnl ‖ -ɜːr-/ adj outside ~**ly** adv

ex·tinct /ɪkˈstɪŋkt/ adj 1 (of a kind of animal) no longer existing 2 (of a VOLCANO) no longer active ~**ion** /ɪkˈstɪŋkʃən/ n [U] state of being or becoming extinct

ex·tin·guish /ɪkˈstɪŋgwɪʃ/ vt fml 1 put out (a fire, etc.) 2 destroy (hope, etc.) ~**er** n apparatus for putting out fires

ex·tol /ɪkˈstəʊl ‖ -ˈstoʊl/ vt -ll- praise highly

ex·tort /ɪkˈstɔːt ‖ -ɔːrt/ vt obtain by force or threats ~**ion** /ɪkˈstɔːʃən ‖ -ɔːr-/ n [C;U] ~**ionist** n

ex·tor·tion·ate /ɪkˈstɔːʃənət ‖ -ɔːr-/ adj EXORBITANT

ex·tra /ˈekstrə/ adj, adv beyond what is usual or necessary: *extra money* | *pay extra* ♦ n 1 extra thing 2 film actor in a crowd scene 3 special EDITION (1) of a newspaper

ex·tract¹ /ɪkˈstrækt/ vt 1 pull out, esp. with difficulty 2 get (a substance) from another substance ~**ion** /ɪkˈstrækʃən/ n 1 [C;U] act or example of extracting 2 [U] family origin: *of Russian extraction*

ex·tract² /ˈekstrækt/ n 1 piece of writing taken from a book, etc. 2 product obtained by extracting: *beef extract*

ex·tra·cur·ric·u·lar /ˌekstrəkəˈrɪkjələ◄ ‖ -lər◄/ adj outside the ordinary course of work in a school or college

ex·tra·dite /ˈekstrədaɪt/ vt send (a foreign criminal) home for trial ~**dition** /ˌekstrəˈdɪʃən/ n [C;U]

ex·tra·mar·i·tal /ˌekstrəˈmærɪtl◄/ adj (of sexual relationships) outside marriage

ex·tra·mu·ral /ˌekstrəˈmjʊərəl◄ ‖ -ˈmjʊr-/ adj connected with but outside an organization

ex·tra·ne·ous /ɪkˈstreɪniəs/ adj not directly connected

extra·or·di·na·ry /ɪkˈstrɔːdənəri ‖ ɪkˈstrɔːrdneri, ˌekstrəˈɔːr-/ adj 1 very strange 2 beyond what is ordinary: *a man of extraordinary ability* ~**narily** adv

ex·trap·o·late /ɪkˈstræpəleɪt/ vi/t guess from facts already known

ex·tra·ter·res·tri·al /ˌekstrətəˈrestriəl◄/ adj (from) outside the Earth

ex·trav·a·gant /ɪkˈstrævəgənt/ adj
1 wasteful of money, etc. 2 (of ideas, behaviour, etc.) beyond what is reasonable –gance n [C;U]

ex·trav·a·gan·za /ɪkˌstrævəˈgænzə/ n very grand and expensive piece of entertainment

ex·treme /ɪkˈstriːm/ adj 1 furthest or greatest possible: extreme cold | the extreme south of the country 2 often derog beyond the usual limits: extreme opinions ♦ n furthest possible degree: He's gone from one extreme to the other. ~ly adv very

ex·trem·is·m /ɪkˈstriːmɪzəm/ n [U] derog holding of (politically) extreme opinions –ist n, adj

ex·trem·i·ty /ɪkˈstreməti/ n [S;U] highest degree extremities n [P] human hands and feet

ex·tri·cate /ˈekstrɪkeɪt/ vt free from something that is hard to escape from

ex·tro·vert, extravert /ˈekstrəvɜːt ‖ -ɜːrt/ n cheerful person who likes to be with others

ex·u·be·rant /ɪgˈzjuːbərənt ‖ ɪgˈzuː-/ adj overflowing with life and excitement ~ly adv –rance n [U]

ex·ude /ɪgˈzjuːd ‖ ɪgˈzuːd/ vi/t (cause to) flow out slowly in all directions

ex·ult /ɪgˈzʌlt/ vi fml show great delight ~ant adj ~antly adv ~ation /ˌegzʌlˈteɪʃən/ n [U]

eye /aɪ/ n 1 either of the two parts of the head with which we see 2 way of seeing: an experienced eye 3 hole in a needle 4 ring into which a hook fits 5 be in the public eye be often seen by the public 6 have an eye for be able to judge 7 in one's mind's eye in one's imagination 8 in the eyes of in the opinion of 9 keep an eye on watch carefully 10 one in the eye for infml a defeat for 11 see eye to eye agree completely 12 up to one's eyes in infml very busy with ♦ vt look at closely

eye·ball /ˈaɪbɔːl ‖ -bɒːl/ n the whole of the EYE (1), including the part inside the head

eye·brow /ˈaɪbraʊ/ n line of hairs above each eye

eye·catch·ing /ˈ· ˌ·/ adj unusual and attractive to look at

eye·lash /ˈaɪlæʃ/ n hair on the edge of the eyelid

eye·lid /ˈaɪlɪd/ n piece of skin that moves to close the eye

eye·o·pen·er /ˈ· ˌ·/ n something surprising that changes one's ideas about something

eye·sha·dow /ˈ· ˌ·/ n [U] coloured substance put on the eyelids

eye·sight /ˈaɪsaɪt/ n [U] power of seeing

eye·sore /ˈaɪsɔː ‖ -sɔːr/ n something ugly to look at

eye·wit·ness /ˈaɪˌwɪtnəs/ n WITNESS (1)

ey·rie, eyry /ˈɪəri, ˈeəri, ˈaɪəri ‖ ˈɪri, ˈeri, ˈaɪri/ n high nest of an EAGLE

F

F, f /ef/ the 6th letter of the English alphabet

F abbrev. for: FAHRENHEIT

fa·ble /ˈfeɪbəl/ n short story that teaches a lesson fabled adj spoken of as true; famous

fab·ric /ˈfæbrɪk/ n [C;U] 1 woven cloth 2 structure of a building, etc.

fab·ri·cate /ˈfæbrɪkeɪt/ vt invent (something false) –cation /ˌfæbrɪˈkeɪʃən/ n [C;U]

fab·u·lous /ˈfæbjələs/ adj 1 existing in fables 2 unbelievable: fabulous wealth 3 excellent ~ly adv very: fabulously rich

fa·cade /fəˈsɑːd, fæ-/ n 1 front of a building 2 false appearance

face¹ /feɪs/ n 1 [C] front part of the head 2 [C] expression on the face 3 [C] front; surface: miners at the coal face 4 [U] position of respect: afraid of losing face 5 face to face in someone's direct presence 6 in the face of in opposition to 7 on the face of it APPARENTLY 8 make/pull a face/faces make an expression with the face 9 to someone's face openly in their presence ~less adj impersonal: faceless bureaucrats

face² v 1 vi/t turn the face towards 2 vt meet and oppose: face danger 3 vt cover the front of: *a building faced with stone*

face up to *phr vt* be brave enough to deal with

face·lift /'feɪslɪft/ *n* medical operation to make the face look younger

face-sav·ing /'· ,·/ *adj* allowing self-respect to be kept

fac·et /'fæsɪt/ *n* 1 one of the flat sides of a cut jewel 2 ASPECT of a subject

fa·ce·tious /fəˈsiːʃəs/ *adj* using silly jokes ~**ly** *adv*

face val·ue /,· '·/ *n* 1 [C;U] value shown on a postage stamp, etc. 2 [U] value of something as it first appears

fa·cial /'feɪʃəl/ *adj* of the face ♦ *n* facial beauty treatment

fa·cile /'fæsaɪl ‖ 'fæsəl/ *adj* (of words) too easy; not deep

fa·cil·i·tate /fəˈsɪlɪteɪt/ *vt fml* make easy **facilitator** *n*

fa·cil·i·ty /fəˈsɪlɪti/ *n* [U] ability to do things easily **-ties** [P] useful things: *shopping/sporting facilities*

fac·ing /'feɪsɪŋ/ *n* [U] 1 outer covering of a wall, etc. 2 material sewn in to stiffen a garment

fac·sim·i·le /fæk'sɪmɪli/ *n* exact copy of a picture, etc.

fact /fækt/ *n* 1 [C] something known to be true 2 [U] truth 3 **in fact** really

fac·tion /'fækʃən/ *n* group within a larger (political) one

fac·tor /'fæktə ‖ -ər/ *n* influence that helps to produce a result

fac·to·ry /'fæktəri/ *n* place where goods are made by machinery

facts of life /,· · '·/ *n* [P] the details of sex and birth

fac·tu·al /'fæktʃuəl/ *adj* based on fact ~**ly** *adv*

fac·ul·ty /'fækəlti/ *n* 1 natural power of the mind or body: *the faculty of hearing* 2 **a** university department **b** teachers in such a department

fad /fæd/ *n* short-lived interest in something

fad·dy /'fædi/ *adj derog* only wanting certain foods

fade /feɪd/ *v* 1 *vi/t* (cause to) lose colour or freshness 2 *vi* disappear gradually

fade in/out *phr vi/t* (in film making and broadcasting) (cause to) appear/disappear slowly

fae·ces also **feces** *AmE* /'fiːsiːz/ *n* [P] solid waste from the bowels

fag /fæg/ *n* BrE 1 [S] *infml* tiring job 2 [C] *sl* cigarette 3 *AmE derog sl* for HOMOSEXUAL

fag·got also **fagot** *AmE* /'fægət/ *n* 1 ball of cut-up meat 2 bunch of sticks for burning 3 *AmE* FAG (3)

Fah·ren·heit /'færənhaɪt/ *n* scale of temperature in which water freezes at 32° and boils at 212°

fail /feɪl/ *v* 1 *vi/t* be unsuccessful or unable 2 *vi* not do what is wanted: *The crops/business failed.* 3 *vt* judge to be unsuccessful in a test 4 *vt* disappoint or leave (someone) at a bad time: *My courage failed me.* 5 *vi* lose strength: *His health is failing.* ♦ *n* **without fail** certainly

fail·ing /'feɪlɪŋ/ *n* fault; weakness ♦ *prep* in the absence of

fail-safe /,· '·◁/ *adj* made so that any failure will stop the machine

fail·ure /'feɪljə ‖ -ər/ *n* 1 [U] lack of success 2 [C] person or thing that fails 3 [C;U] non-performance; inability: *heart failure*

faint /feɪnt/ *adj* 1 likely to lose consciousness 2 lacking strength or courage 3 not clear or bright 4 slight: *faint chance* ♦ *vi* lose consciousness ♦ *n* act of fainting ~**ly** *adv* ~**ness** *n* [U]

faint-heart·ed /,· '·◁/ *adj* cowardly

fair¹ /feə ‖ fer/ *adj* 1 just and honest: *fair play* 2 quite good: *a fair knowledge of French* 3 having a good, clean appearance: *a fair copy of the report* 4 (of skin or hair) not dark 5 (of weather) not stormy ♦ *adv* 1 honestly: *play fair* 2 **fair and square:** a honestly b directly 3 **fair enough** *infml* all right ~**ly** *adv* 1 honestly 2 rather: *fairly warm*

fair² *n* 1 BrE FUNFAIR 2 large show of goods: *book fair*

fair game /,· '·/ *n* [U] person, idea, etc. that can easily be laughed at and CRITICIZEd

fair·ground /'feəgraʊnd ‖ 'fer-/ *n* open space for a FUNFAIR

fair·way /'feəweɪ ‖ 'fer-/ *n* part of a GOLF COURSE along which one hits the ball

fair-weath·er friend /,· ·· '·/ *n* friend who is absent in times of trouble

fai·ry /'feəri ‖ 'feri/ *n* 1 small imaginary person with magical powers 2 *derog* HOMOSEXUAL man

fairy god·moth·er /ˌ· '···/ n person who helps, and esp. saves, someone who is in trouble

fai·ry·land /'feərilænd ‖ 'feri-/ n [S] 1 land where fairies live 2 place of magical beauty

fairy light /'·· ·/ n small coloured light for decorating a Christmas tree

fairy tale /'·· ·/ n 1 story about magic 2 untrue story **fairy-tale** adj magically wonderful

fait ac·com·pli /ˌfeɪt ə'kɒmpli ‖ -ˌækɑːm'pliː/ n faits accomplis /ˌfeɪt ə'kɒmpliːz ‖ -ˌækɑːm'pliːz/ something that has happened and cannot be changed

faith /feɪθ/ n 1 [U] confident trust 2 [C;U] religious belief 3 [U] loyalty to a promise: *keep faith with them* ~**ful** adj 1 loyal 2 true to the facts: *faithful copy* ◆ n [the+P] religious people ~**fully** adv **Yours faithfully** (used for ending letters to strangers) ~**less** adj fml disloyal

faith heal·ing /'· ·/ n [U] method of treating diseases by prayer, etc.

fake /feɪk/ n person or thing that is not what he/she/it looks like or pretends to be ◆ vi/t make or copy (e.g. a work of art) to deceive

fal·con /'fɔːlkən ‖ 'fæl-/ n bird that can be trained to hunt ~**er** n person who trains falcons ~**ry** n [U] hunting with falcons

fall¹ /fɔːl ‖ fɔːls/ vi fell /fel/, fallen /'fɔːlən ‖ 'fɒl-/ 1 come or go down freely: *She fell into the lake.* | *The house fell down.* 2 hang loosely: *Her hair falls over her shoulders.* 3 become lower: *The temperature fell.* 4 (of land) slope down 5 happen: *Christmas falls on a Friday.* 6 become: *fall asleep/in love* 7 be wounded or killed in battle 8 be defeated 9 (of the face) take on a look of sadness, etc. 10 **fall flat** produce no result 11 **fall short** fail to reach a standard

fall about phr vi lose control of oneself (with laughter)

fall back phr vi RETREAT

fall back on phr vt use when there is failure or lack of other means

fall behind phr vi/t not keep level (with)

fall for phr vt 1 be attracted by 2 accept and be cheated by

fall off phr vi become less

fall on phr vt attack eagerly

fall out phr vi quarrel

fall through phr vi (of a plan) fail

fall² n 1 act of falling 2 something that has fallen: *a heavy fall of snow* 3 AmE for AUTUMN **falls** n [P] WATERFALL

fal·la·cy /'fæləsi/ n [C;U] false belief or reasoning –**lacious** /fə'leɪʃəs/ adj fml based on fallacy

fall guy /'· ·/ n infml esp. AmE someone who is punished for another person's crime, mistake, etc.

fal·li·ble /'fæləbəl/ adj able to make mistakes –**bility** /ˌfæləˈbɪləti/ n [U]

falling star /ˌ·· '·/ n SHOOTING STAR

fal·lo·pi·an tube /fəˌləʊpiən 'tjuːb ‖ fəˌloʊpiən tuːb/ n tube through which eggs pass to the WOMB

fall·out /'fɔːlaʊt ‖ 'fɒl-/ n [U] 1 dangerous dust left in the air after a NUCLEAR explosion 2 unpleasant effects of something that happens

fal·low /'fæləʊ ‖ -loʊ/ adj (of land) dug but left unplanted

false /fɔːls ‖ fɔːls/ adj 1 not true or correct 2 disloyal: *false friend* 3 not real: *a false nose* 4 careless; unwise: *One false move and I'll shoot you!* ~**ly** adv ~**ness** n [U] ~**hood** n [C;U] lying; lie

false a·larm /ˌ· ·'·/ n warning of something bad that does not happen

false pre·tenc·es /ˌ· ·'·· ‖ ˌ· '···/ n [P] behaviour intended to deceive

false start /ˌ· '·/ n unsuccessful beginning that means one must start again

fal·set·to /fɔːl'setəʊ ‖ fɔːl'setoʊ/ n [C;U] **-tos** (man with an) unnaturally high voice

fal·si·fy /'fɔːlsəfaɪ ‖ 'fɒl-/ vt make false –**fication** /ˌfɔːlsəfɪ'keɪʃən ‖ ˌfɒl-/ n [C;U]

fal·si·ty /'fɔːlsəti/ n [U] fml falseness

fal·ter /'fɔːltə ‖ 'fɔːltər/ vi 1 move or behave uncertainly 2 speak unsteadily ~**ingly** adv

fame /feɪm/ n [U] condition of being well known **famed** adj famous

fa·mil·i·ar /fə'mɪliə ‖ -ər/ adj 1 often seen; common 2 too friendly 3 **familiar with** knowing thoroughly ~**ly** adv ~**ity** /fəˌmɪliˈærəti/ n [C;U]

fa·mil·i·ar·ize also -ise /fə'mɪliəraɪz/ vt make well informed

fam·i·ly /'fæməli/ n 1 one's parents, children, aunts, etc. 2 one's children

3 people descended from the same ANCESTOR
4 division of living creatures or languages:
the cat family ♦ *adj* suitable for children: *a family film*

family plan·ning /ˌ··· '··/ *n* [U] controlling of the number of children in a family by CONTRACEPTION

family tree /ˌ··· '·/ *n* drawing showing the relationship of family members

fam·ine /'fæmɪn/ *n* [C;U] serious lack of food

fam·ished /'fæmɪʃt/ *adj* very hungry

fa·mous /'feɪməs/ *adj* very well known ~**ly** *adv* very well

fan[1] /fæn/ *n* instrument for making a flow of air ♦ *v* -**nn**- 1 *vt* send cool air onto 2 *vi* spread in a half circle

fan[2] /fæn/ *n* keen supporter: *football fans*

fa·nat·ic /fə'nætɪk/ *n* person who is too keen on something: *religious fanatics* ~**al** *adj* ~**ally** /-kli/ *adv* ~**ism** /-tˌsɪzəm/ *n* [U]

fan belt /'· ·/ *n* belt driving a FAN[1] to cool an engine

fan·ci·ful /'fænsɪfəl/ *adj* showing imagination rather than reason ~**ly** *adv*

fan·cy /'fænsi/ *n* 1 [U] imagination 2 [C] opinion not based on fact 3 **take a fancy to** become fond of ♦ *vt* 1 wish for; like 2 imagine: *Fancy that!* 3 believe: *I fancy he's Dutch.* 4 **fancy oneself** have a very high opinion of oneself ♦ *adj* 1 decorative and unusual 2 higher than the usual or reasonable price

fancy dress /ˌ·· '·/ *n* [U] clothes that make one look like a different person, worn esp. for a party

fan·fare /'fænfeə ‖ -fer/ *n* short loud piece of TRUMPET music to introduce a person or event

fang /fæŋ/ *n* long sharp tooth

fan·light /'fænlaɪt/ *n* small window over a door

fan mail /'· ·/ *n* [U] letters to a famous person from FANS[2]

fan·ny /'fæni/ *n* *sl* 1 *AmE* BOTTOM[1] (2) 2 *BrE taboo* women's outer sex organs

fan·tas·ize also -**ise** *BrE* /'fæntəsaɪz/ *vi/t* have fantasies (about)

fan·tas·tic /fæn'tæstɪk/ *adj* 1 *sl* wonderful 2 (of ideas) not practical 3 wild and strange ~**ally** /-kli/ *adv*

fan·ta·sy /'fæntəsi/ *n* [C;U] (something made by) imagination: *sexual fantasies*

FAQ /fæk/ *n abbrev. for:* frequently asked questions; list of answers to frequent questions

far /fɑː ‖ fɑːr/ *adv, adj* **farther** /'fɑːðə ‖ 'fɑːrðər/ *or* **further** /'fɜːðə ‖ 'fɜːrðər/, **farthest** /'fɑːðɪst ‖ 'fɑːr-/ *or* **furthest** /'fɜːðɪst ‖ 'fɜːr-/ 1 a long way: *too far to walk* | *the far distance* 2 very much: *far better* 3 (of a political position) very much to the LEFT or RIGHT: *the far left* 4 **as/so far as** to the degree that: *So far as I know, he's coming.* 5 **far and away** by a great deal or amount: *She's far and away the best actress.* 6 **far be it from me to** (used esp. to show disagreement or disapproval) I certainly would not want to 7 **far from:** a very much not: *I'm far from pleased.* b instead of: *Far from being angry, he's delighted.* 8 **so far** until now 9 **So far, so good** Things are satisfactory up to this point, at least

far·a·way /'fɑːrəweɪ/ *adj* 1 (of a look in someone's eyes) dreamy

farce /fɑːs ‖ fɑːrs/ *n* 1 light funny play 2 set of silly events **farcical** *adj*

fare /feə ‖ fer/ *n* 1 [C] money charged for a journey 2 [U] *fml* food ♦ *vi* get on; succeed: *fare badly*

Far East /ˌ· '·◂/ *n* [S] countries east of India

fare·well /feə'wel ‖ fer-/ *interj, n fml* goodbye

far·fetched /ˌfɑː'fetʃt◂ ‖ ˌfɑːr-/ *adj* hard to believe

far-flung /ˌ· '·◂/ *adj* spread over a great distance

far-gone /ˌ· '·/ *adj* in an advanced state, esp. of something bad

farm /fɑːm ‖ fɑːrm/ *n* area of land and buildings where crops are grown and animals raised ♦ *vi/t* use (land) as a farm ~**er** *n* person who farms ~**ing** *n* [U]

farm out *phr vt* send (work) for other people to do

farm·house /'fɑːmhaʊs ‖ 'fɑːrm-/ *n* main house on a farm

farm·yard /'fɑːmjɑːd ‖ 'fɑːrmjɑːrd/ *n* yard surrounded by farm buildings

far-off /ˌ· '·◂/ *adj* distant

far-reach·ing /ˌ· '··◂/ *adj* having a wide influence

far·sight·ed /ˌfɑː'saɪtɪd◂ ‖ ˌfɑːr-/ *adj* able to judge future effects

fart /fɑːt ‖ fɑːrt/ *vi taboo* send out air from

the bowels **fart** *n taboo* escape of air from
the bowels

far·ther /ˈfɑːðə‖ˈfɑːrðər/ *adv, adj*
FURTHER

far·thest /ˈfɑːðɪst‖ˈfɑːr-/ *adv, adj*
FURTHEST ◂

fas·ci·nate /ˈfæsɪneɪt/ *vt* attract and
interest strongly –**nating** *adj* –**nation**
/ˌfæsɪˈneɪʃən/ *n* [S;U]

fas·cis·m /ˈfæʃɪzəm/ *n* [U] political
system marked by total state control under
a single leader, and support of one's own
nation and race –**cist** *n, adj*

fash·ion /ˈfæʃən/ *n* 1 [C;U] way of
dressing or behaving that is popular at a
certain time 2 [S] *fml* manner of doing
something: *in an orderly fashion* 3 **after a
fashion** not very well ◆ *vt fml* make; shape
~**able** according to the latest fashion ~**ably**
adv

fast¹ /fɑːst‖fæst/ *adj* 1 quick: *fast cars*
2 firmly fixed: *fast colours* 3 (of a clock)
showing time later than the right time ◆
adv 1 quickly 2 firmly 3 **fast asleep**
sleeping deeply 4 **pull a fast one (on)**
infml deceive (someone) with a trick

fast² *vi* eat no food, esp. for religious
reasons ◆ *n* period of fasting

fas·ten /ˈfɑːsən‖ˈfæ-/ *vi/t* make or
become firmly fixed ~**er** *n* thing that
fastens things together –**ing** *n* something
that holds things shut

fast food /ˌ· ·/ *n* [U] hot food (e.g.
HAMBURGERS) that a restaurant cooks and
serves quickly

fast-for·ward /ˌ· ˈ··/ *vi/t* wind (a VIDEO,
etc.) quickly forward

fas·tid·i·ous /fæˈstɪdiəs/ *adj* difficult to
please; disliking anything dirty or nasty
~**ly** *adv* ~**ness** *n* [U]

fat /fæt/ *n* [U] 1 material under the skins of
animals and human beings which helps
keep them warm 2 this substance used in
cooking ◆ *adj* -tt- 1 having a lot of FAT (1)
on the body 2 thick and well-filled: *fat book*
~**ness** *n* [U]

fa·tal /ˈfeɪtl/ *adj* causing death or ruin ~**ly**
adv

fa·tal·is·m /ˈfeɪtl-ɪzəm/ *n* [U] belief in
FATE (1) –**ist** *n*

fa·tal·i·ty /fəˈtæləti/ *n* 1 [C] violent death
2 [U] being fatal

fate /feɪt/ *n* 1 [U] power beyond human

control that decides events 2 [C] end, esp.
death 3 [S] the future ~**ful** *adj* important
(esp. in a bad way) for the future: *fateful
decision* ~**fully** *adv* **fated** *adj* 1 caused by
fate 2 *infml* very unlucky

fat-free /ˌ· ˈ·◂/ *adj* containing no fat: *a fat-
free diet*

fa·ther /ˈfɑːðə‖-ər/ *n* 1 male parent
2 (*usu. cap.*) priest ◆ *vt* become the father
of ~**hood** *n* [U] ~**less** *adj* ~**ly** *adj* like a good
father **fathers** *n* [P] FOREFATHERS

Father Christ·mas /ˌ·· ˈ··/ *n esp. BrE* for
SANTA CLAUS

father fig·ure /ˈ·· ˌ··/ *n* older man on
whom one depends for advice

father-in-law /ˈ·· · ·/ *n* fathers-in-law
father of one's wife or husband

fath·om /ˈfæðəm/ *n* unit of measurement
(6 feet) for the depth of water ◆ *vt*
understand fully

fa·tigue /fəˈtiːg/ *n* 1 [U] tiredness 2 [U]
weakness in metals caused by repeated
bending 3 [C] (in the army) a job of
cleaning or cooking ◆ *vt fml* make tired

fat·ten /ˈfætn/ *vt* make fatter

fat·ty /ˈfæti/ *adj* containing fat

fat·u·ous /ˈfætʃuəs/ *adj* silly: *fatuous
remarks* ~**ly** *adv*

fau·cet /ˈfɔːsɪt‖ˈfɔː-/ *n AmE* for TAP¹

fault /fɔːlt‖fɒlt/ *n* 1 mistake or
imperfection 2 crack in the Earth's surface
3 **at fault** in the wrong 4 **find fault with**
complain about 5 **one's fault** something
one can be blamed for 6 **to a fault** (of good
qualities) too; too much ◆ *vt* find mistakes
in ~**less** *adj* perfect ~**y** *adj*

fau·na /ˈfɔːnə‖ˈfɒ-/ *n* [U] animals of a
particular area or period

faux pas /ˌfəʊ ˈpɑː‖ˌfəʊ-/ *n* **faux pas**
/ˌfəʊ ˈpɑːz‖ˌfəʊ-/ social mistake

fa·vour *BrE* ‖ **-vor** *AmE* /ˈfeɪvə‖-ər/ *n*
1 [U] approval: *gain widespread favour* 2 [C]
kind act: *do me a favour* 3 **in favour of: a** in
support of **b** (of a cheque) payable to 4 **in
one's favour** to one's advantage ◆ *vt*
1 approve of 2 be unfairly fond of; treat
with favour ~**able** *adj* 1 showing or
winning approval 2 advantageous ~**ably**
adv

fa·vou·rite *BrE* ‖ **-vorite** *AmE* /ˈfeɪvərɪt/
n 1 person or thing loved above all others
2 horse expected to win a race ◆ *adj* most
loved –**ritism** *n* [U] unfairly generous

treatment of one person

fawn[1] /fɔːn‖fɔːn/ n 1 [C] young deer 2 [U] light yellowish-brown colour

fawn[2] v fawn on phr vt try to gain the favour of, by being too attentive

fax /fæks/ n 1 [C] document sent down a telephone line and printed on a machine (**fax** (**machine**)) 2 [U] system of sending faxes: *send it by fax.* ♦ vt

faze /feɪz/ vt shock into silence

FBI /ˌef biː ˈaɪ/ n abbrev. for: Federal Bureau of Investigation; US police department under central control

fear /fɪə‖fɪr/ n 1 [C;U] feeling that danger is near 2 [U] danger 3 **No fear!** Certainly not! ♦ vi/t fml be afraid (of) ~**ful** adj 1 terrible; shocking 2 fml afraid ~**less** adj not afraid ~**lessly** adv ~**some** adj lit frightening

fea·si·ble /ˈfiːzəbəl/ adj able to be done; possible –**bility** /ˌfiːzəˈbɪlɪti/ n [U]

feast /fiːst/ n 1 splendid meal 2 religious FESTIVAL ♦ vi 1 eat and drink very well 2 **feast one's eyes on** look at with delight

feat /fiːt/ n difficult action successfully done

fea·ther /ˈfeðə‖-ər/ n 1 one of a bird's many light skin coverings 2 **a feather in one's cap** honour to be proud of ♦ vt 1 put feathers on or in 2 **feather one's nest** make oneself dishonestly rich while in a trusted position ~**y** adj soft and light

fea·ture /ˈfiːtʃə‖-ər/ n 1 noticeable quality 2 part of the face 3 **a** newspaper article **b** part of a radio or television programme, dealing with a particular subject 4 film being shown at a cinema ♦ v 1 vt include as a performer 2 vi play an important part ~**less** adj uninteresting features n [P] face

Feb·ru·a·ry /ˈfebruəri, ˈfebjuəri‖ ˈfebjueri/ n the second month of the year

fe·ces /ˈfiːsiːz/ n AmE for FAECES

feck·less /ˈfekləs/ adj worthless and irresponsible

fec·und /ˈfekənd, ˈfiːkənd/ adj fml FERTILE

fed /fed/ v past t. and p. of FEED

fed·e·ral /ˈfedərəl/ adj 1 of or being a federation 2 of the central US government as opposed to the States

fed·e·ra·tion /ˌfedəˈreɪʃən/ n 1 [C] united group of states, organizations, etc.

fed up /ˌ· ˈ·/ adj sl tired and discontented

fee /fiː/ n money paid for professional services, to join a club, etc.

fee·ble /ˈfiːbəl/ adj weak **feebly** adv

fee·ble-mind·ed /ˌfiːbəlˈmaɪndɪd◂/ adj with low INTELLIGENCE

feed /fiːd/ v fed /fed/ 1 vt give food to 2 vi (esp. of animals) eat 3 vt supply; provide: *feed information into a computer* ♦ n 1 animal's or baby's meal 2 [U] food for animals 3 [C] pipe, etc. through which a machine is fed

feed·back /ˈfiːdbæk/ n information as to how good a piece of work, etc. is, given to the person who did it

feel[1] /fiːl/ v felt /felt/ 1 vt learn about with the fingers 2 vt experience (the touch of something): *feel the wind* 3 vi search with the fingers: *feel for a pencil* 4 be consciously: *feel hungry/happy* 5 vt suffer because of: *feel the cold* 6 give a sensation: *This sheet feels wet.* 7 vt believe without reasoning: *I feel they won't come.* 8 **feel like** wish for; want

feel for phr vt be sorry for

feel[2] n [S] 1 sensation caused by touching 2 act of feeling 3 **get the feel of** become used to and skilled at

feel·er /ˈfiːlə‖-ər/ n 1 thread-like part of an insect's head, with which it touches things 2 suggestion made to test opinion

feel·ing /ˈfiːlɪŋ/ n 1 [S] consciousness of something felt 2 [S] belief not based on reason 3 [U] power to feel 4 [U] excitement of mind: *cause ill feeling* 5 [U] sympathy **feelings** n [P] EMOTIONS

feet /fiːt/ n pl. of FOOT

feign /feɪn/ vt fml pretend to have or be

feint /feɪnt/ n false attack or blow ♦ vi make a feint

feist·y /ˈfaɪsti/ adj excited and quarrelsome

fe·li·ci·ty /fɪˈlɪsɪti/ n [U] fml happiness

fe·line /ˈfiːlaɪn/ adj of or like a cat

fell[1] /fel/ v past t. of FALL

fell[2] vt cut or knock down: *fell a tree/a man*

fell[3] n high rocky country in the north of England

fel·ler /ˈfelə‖-ər/ n sl fellow; man

fel·low /ˈfeləʊ‖-loʊ/ n 1 man 2 member of a learned society or college 3 companion: *schoolfellows* ♦ adj another of the

same group: *fellow prisoners/students*
~**ship** n 1 [C] group or society 2 [U] companionship 3 [C] position of a college fellow
fellow feel·ing /ˌ·· '·-/ n [S;U] sympathy
for someone like oneself
fel·o·ny /'feləni/ n [C;U] serious crime
(e.g. murder) **felon** n person guilty of
felony
felt[1] /felt/ v past t. and p. of FEEL
felt[2] n [U] thick cloth made of pressed
wool
felt-tip pen /ˌ·· '·/ n pen with felt at the
end instead of a NIB
fe·male /'fiːmeɪl/ adj 1 of the sex that
produces young 2 (of plants) producing
fruits 3 having a hole into which something
fits: *female plug* ♦ n woman or female
animal
fem·i·nine /'femənɪn/ adj 1 having
qualities thought to be typical of women
2 *gram* of the class of words for females
–**ninity** /ˌfemɪ'nɪnəti/ n [U] being FEMININE
(1)
fem·i·nis·m /'femɪnɪzəm/ n [U] principle
that women should have the same rights as
men –**nist** n, adj
fen /fen/ n area of low wet land
fence[1] /fens/ n 1 wall made of wood or
wire 2 someone who buys and sells stolen
goods 3 **sit on the fence** avoid taking sides
in an argument ♦ vt surround or separate
with a fence
fence[2] vi 1 fight with a long thin sword as
a sport 2 avoid giving an honest answer
fencer n
fenc·ing /'fensɪŋ/ n [U] 1 sword-fighting
as a sport 2 material for making fences
fend /fend/ vi
fend for oneself look after oneself
fend off phr vt push away
fend·er /'fendə ‖ -ər/ n 1 low wall round a
fireplace 2 AmE for WING (4)
fer·ment[1] /fə'ment ‖ fər-/ vi/t 1 change
chemically so that sugar becomes alcohol
2 make or become excited ~**ation** /ˌfɜː-
men'teɪʃən ‖ ˌfɜːrmən-/ n
fer·ment[2] /'fɜːment ‖ 'fɜːr-/ n [U]
trouble and excitement
fern /fɜːn ‖ fɜːrn/ n plant with feathery
green leaves
fe·ro·cious /fə'rəʊʃəs ‖ -'roʊ-/ adj fierce;
violent ~**ly** adv
fe·ro·ci·ty /fə'rɒsəti ‖ fə'rɑː-/ n [U]
ferociousness

fer·ret[1] /'ferət/ n small fierce animal that
hunts rats and rabbits
ferret[2] vi infml search, esp. in a drawer,
box, etc.
ferret out phr vt infml succeed in
finding (information)
fer·rous /'ferəs/ adj of or containing iron
fer·ry /'feri/ n boat that carries people and
things across a narrow piece of water ♦ vt
take from one place to another
fer·tile /'fɜːtaɪl ‖ 'fɜːrtl/ adj 1 producing
young, crops, etc. 2 (of a person's mind)
inventive –**tility** /fɜː'tɪləti ‖ fɜːr-/ n [U]
fer·ti·lize also –**ise** /'fɜːtəlaɪz ‖ 'fɜːrtl-aɪz/
vt make fertile –**lizer** plant food –**lization**
/ˌfɜːtəlaɪ'zeɪʃən ‖ ˌfɜːrtələ-/ n [U]
fer·vent /'fɜːvənt ‖ 'fɜːr-/ adj feeling
strongly: *fervent hope/believer* ~**ly** adv
fer·vid /'fɜːvɪd ‖ 'fɜːr-/ adj fml sharing
too strong feeling
fer·vour BrE ‖ **-vor** AmE /'fɜːvə ‖ 'fɜːrvər/
n [U] quality of being fervent: ZEAL
fes·ter /'festə ‖ -ər/ vi (of a wound)
become infected
fes·ti·val /'festəvəl/ n 1 time for public
happiness: *Christmas is a festival of the
Church.* 2 group of musical, etc.
performances held regularly
fes·tive /'festɪv/ adj joyful
fes·tiv·i·ty /fe'stɪvəti/ n [C;U] festive
activity
fes·toon /fe'stuːn/ vt decorate with
chains of flowers, RIBBONS, etc.
fetch /fetʃ/ vt 1 go and get and bring back
2 be sold for: *The house fetched £30,000.*
3 **fetch and carry** do the small duties of a
servant
fetch·ing /'fetʃɪŋ/ adj attractive
fete /feɪt/ n day of public amusement held
esp. to collect money ♦ vt honour publicly
fet·id /'fiːtɪd ‖ 'fetɪd/ adj smelling bad
fet·ish /'fetɪʃ, 'fiː-/ n 1 something
unusual that a person gets sexual pleasure
from 2 something to which one pays too
much attention
fet·ter /'fetə ‖ -ər/ n chain for a prisoner's
foot: (fig.) *the fetters of an unhappy
marriage* ♦ vt tie; prevent from moving
fe·tus /'fiːtəs/ n FOETUS
feud /fjuːd/ n violent continuing quarrel
♦ vi have a feud
feud·al /'fjuːdl/ adj of the system of

fever

practised in Europe from the 9th to the 15th
century ~ism *n* [U]

fe·ver /ˈfiːvə‖-ər/ *n* [S;U] 1 (disease
causing) high body temperature —see also
YELLOW FEVER 2 excited state ~ish *adj* 1 of
or having fever 2 unnaturally fast ~ishly
adv

few /fjuː/ *determiner, pron, n* [P] 1 (with a)
some: *Let's invite a few friends.* 2 (without
a) not many: *She has few friends.*

fi·an·cé, fiancée *fem.* /fiˈɒnseɪ‖
ˌfiːɑːnˈseɪ/ *n* person one is ENGAGED to

fi·as·co /fiˈæskəʊ‖-koʊ/ *n* -cos complete
failure

fib /fɪb/ *vi, n* -bb- (tell) a small lie ~ber *n*

fi·bre *BrE*‖ fiber *AmE* /ˈfaɪbə‖-ər/ *n*
1 [C] thin thread-like plant or animal
growth 2 [U] mass of threads 3 [U] person's
inner character **fibrous** *adj*

fi·bre·glass *BrE*‖ fiberglass *AmE*
/ˈfaɪbəɡlɑːs‖-bərɡlæs/ *n* [U] material of
glass fibres used for making boats, etc.

fibre optics *BrE*‖ fiber optics *AmE*
/ˌfaɪbər ˈɒptɪks/ *n* [U] use of long glass or
plastic threads to carry information in the
form of light, esp. on a telephone line
-**optic** *adj*

fick·le /ˈfɪkəl/ *adj* not loyal; often
changing

fic·tion /ˈfɪkʃən/ *n* 1 [U] stories 2 [S;U]
untrue story -**al** *adj*

fic·ti·tious /fɪkˈtɪʃəs/ *adj* untrue:
invented

fid·dle /ˈfɪdl/ *n* 1 dishonest practice
2 VIOLIN 3 (as) **fit as a fiddle** perfectly
healthy 4 **play second fiddle (to)** play a
less important part (than) ♦ *v* 1 *vi* move
things aimlessly 2 *vi* play the VIOLIN 3 *vt sl*
lie about: *fiddle one's taxes* -**dler** *n*

fid·dling /ˈfɪdlɪŋ/ *adj* small and silly

fid·dly /ˈfɪdli/ *adj* needing delicate use of
the fingers

fi·del·i·ty /fɪˈdelɪti/ *n* [U] 1 faithfulness
2 closeness to an original

fid·get /ˈfɪdʒɪt/ *vi* move one's body around
restlessly ♦ *n* someone who fidgets

field¹ /fiːld/ *n* 1 [C] piece of farming land
2 [C] open area: *a football field* | *an oil
field* | *a battlefield* 3 [C] branch of knowl-
edge 4 [S] place where practical operations
actually happen: *study tribal languages in
the field* 5 [C] area where a force is felt:

gravitational field

field² *v* 1 *vi/t* (in cricket, etc.) catch or stop
(the ball) 2 *vt* produce (a team or army) ~er
n

field day /ˈ· ·/ *n* **have a field day** enjoy
oneself very much

field e·vent /ˈ· ·,·/ *n* competitive sports
event, such as weight-throwing or jumping

field glass·es /ˈ· ,··/ *n* [P] BINOCULARS

field mar·shal /ˈ· ,··/ *n* British army
officer of highest rank

field of vi·sion /ˌ· · ˈ··/ *n* whole space
within seeing distance

field·work /ˈfiːldwɜːk‖-wɜːrk/ *n* [U]
study done in the FIELD¹ (4)

fiend /fiːnd/ *n* 1 evil person 2 *infml*
someone very keen on something ~ish *adj*
~ishly *adv*

fierce /fɪəs‖fɪrs/ *adj* 1 angry, violent, and
cruel 2 severe: *fierce heat/competition* ~ly
adv ~ness *n* [U]

fi·er·y /ˈfaɪəri‖ˈfaɪri/ *adj* 1 like fire
2 violent: *fiery temper*

fi·es·ta /fiˈestə/ *n* religious holiday with
public dancing, etc.

fif·teen /ˌfɪfˈtiːn◂/ *determiner, n, pron* 15
~th *determiner, adv, n, pron* 15th

fifth /fɪfθ, fɪftθ/ *determiner, adv, n, pron*
5th

fifth col·umn /ˌ· ˈ··/ *n* group of people
who secretly help the enemies of their
country in war

fif·ty /ˈfɪfti/ *determiner, n, pron* 50 ~tieth
determiner, adv, n, pron 50th

fifty-fif·ty /ˌ·· ˈ··◂/ *adj, adv* (of shares or
chances) equal(ly)

fig /fɪɡ/ *n* (tree that bears) a soft sweet fruit
with small seeds

fig. *written abbrev. for:* 1 FIGURATIVE
2 FIGURE¹ (5)

fight¹ /faɪt/ *vi/t* fought /fɔːt‖fɔːt/ 1 use
violence (against); struggle 2 argue ~er *n*
1 person who fights professionally: (fig.) *a
tireless fighter against racism* 2 small
military aircraft

fight back 1 recover from a bad or
losing position 2 defend oneself by fighting

fight off *phr vt* keep away with an effort

fight out *phr vt* settle (a quarrel) by
fighting

fight² *n* 1 [C] battle 2 [U] power or wish to
fight 3 [C] boxing (BOX²) match

fighting chance /ˌ·· ˈ·/ *n* small but real

chance if great effort is made

fig leaf /'· ·/ n something that hides something else, esp. dishonestly

fig·ment /'fɪgmənt/ n a figment of one's imagination something not real

fig·u·ra·tive /'fɪgjͧrətɪv, -gə-/ adj (of words, phrases, etc.) used in some way other than the main or usual meaning, to suggest a picture in the mind or make a comparison ~ly adv: She's up to her eyes in paperwork — figuratively speaking, of course!

fig·ure¹ /'fɪgə‖'fɪgjər/ n 1 (shape of) a human body: a good figure 2 person: a leading political figure 3 (sign for) a number 4 price 5 DIAGRAM

figure² v 1 vi take a part 2 vt esp. AmE believe 3 **That figures** infml That seems reasonable

figure on phr vt esp. AmE plan on; include in one's plans

figure out phr vt discover by thinking

fig·ure·head /'fɪgəhed‖'fɪgjər-/ n someone who is the chief in name only

figure of speech /ˌ· · ·/ n figurative expression

fil·a·ment /'fɪləmənt/ n thin thread, esp. in an electric light BULB (2)

filch /fɪltʃ/ vt steal secretly (something of small value)

file¹ /faɪl/ n steel tool for rubbing or cutting hard surfaces ♦ vt rub or cut with a file: file one's nails

file² n 1 arrangement for storing papers 2 store of papers on one subject

file³ vt put in a file

file for phr vt law request officially

file⁴ n line of people one behind the other ♦ vi walk in a file

fi·li·al /'fɪliəl/ adj fml suitable to a son or daughter

fil·i·bus·ter /'fɪlɪbʌstə‖-ər/ vi AmE delay parliamentary action by making long speeches **filibuster** n

fil·i·gree /'fɪlɪɡriː/ n [U] decorative wire work

filing cab·i·net /'·· ,··/ n piece of office furniture for storing papers in

fil·ings /'faɪlɪŋz/ n [P] very small sharp bits that have been rubbed off a metal surface with a FILE¹

fill /fɪl/ v 1 vt/i make or become full 2 vt go or be put into: fill a vacancy 3 fulfil ♦ n full

supply ~**er** n substance added to increase size ~**ing** n 1 material to fill a hole, esp. in a tooth 2 food mixture folded inside pastry, SANDWICHes, etc.

fill in phr vt 1 put in (what is necessary): fill in a form 2 supply the most recent information 3 take someone's place

fill out phr v 1 vi get fatter 2 vt FILL in (1)

fill up phr vi/t make or become full

fil·let /'fɪlɪt‖'fɪlɪt, -leɪ, fɪ'leɪ/ n piece of meat or fish without bones ♦ vt remove bones from

filling sta·tion /'·· ,··/ also **petrol station** BrE‖ **gas station** AmE — n place that sells petrol and oil

fil·ly /'fɪli/ n young female horse

film /fɪlm/ n 1 [C;U] (roll of) thin material used in photography 2 [C] esp. BrE cinema picture 3 [S;U] thin covering: film of oil ♦ vi/t make a FILM (2) (of) ~**y** adj very thin: filmy silk

film star /'· ·/ n famous cinema actor or actress

film·strip /'fɪlm,strɪp/ n [C;U] length of photographic film that shows drawings, etc. separately as still pictures

fil·ter /'fɪltə‖-ər/ n 1 apparatus through which liquids are passed to clean them 2 glass that changes the colour or amount of light ♦ v 1 vi/t go or send through a filter 2 vi move or go slowly: People filtered out of the cinema.

filth /fɪlθ/ n [U] 1 very nasty dirt 2 something rude or unpleasant ~**y** adj

fin /fɪn/ n winglike part of a fish 2 thing shaped like this on a car, etc.

fi·nal /'faɪnl/ adj 1 last 2 (of a decision, etc.) that cannot be changed ♦ also **finals** pl. n 1 last of a set of matches 2 last and most important examinations in a college course ~**ly** adv 1 at last 2 allowing no further change ~**ist** n player in a final match ~**ize**, ~**ise** vt give final form to

fi·na·le /fɪ'nɑːli‖fɪ'næli/ n last division of a piece of music

fi·nance /'faɪnæns, fəˈnæns‖fəˈnæns, 'faɪnæns/ n [U] 1 management of (public) money 2 money, esp. provided by a bank, to help run an organization or buy something ♦ vt provide money for **finances** n [P] money owned or provided **financial** /fəˈnænʃəl, faɪ-/ adj **financially** adv

fi·nan·cier /fɪˈnænsɪə, faɪˈnæn-‖ ˌfɪnən-
ˈsɪr/ n someone who controls large sums of
money

finch /fɪntʃ/ n small songbird

find /faɪnd/ vt **found** /faʊnd/ **1** get
(something lost or not known) by searching
2 learn by chance or effort: find (out) where
he lives **3** obtain by effort: find time to study
4 (of a thing) arrive at: Water finds its own
level. **5** know to exist: Elephants are found
in Africa. **6** law decide to be: find someone
guilty ♦ n something good or valuable that
is found ~**ing** n **1** what is learnt by enquiry
2 law decision made in court **3** something
learnt as the result of an official enquiry

fine¹ /faɪn/ adj **1** good; beautiful **2** very
thin or small: fine thread/dust | (fig.) fine
distinction **3** (of weather) bright; not wet
4 healthy ♦ adv **1** very well **2** very thin
3 cut it fine allow only just enough time
~**ly** adv **1** into small bits **2** delicately: finely
tuned

fine² n money paid as a punishment ♦ vt
take a fine from

fine arts /ˌ· ˈ·/ n [P] painting, music, etc.

fi·ne·ry /ˈfaɪnəri/ n [U] beautiful clothes

fi·nesse /fɪˈnes/ n [U] delicate skill

fin·ger /ˈfɪŋɡə ‖ -ər/ n **1** any of the five
end parts of the hand **2** part of a glove
made to fit one of these parts **3 be/feel all
fingers and thumbs** (be/feel that) one is
unable to control one's hands **4 (have) a
finger in every pie** (have) a part in
everything that is going on **5 keep one's
fingers crossed** hope for the best **6 lay a
finger on** harm **7 not lift a finger** make
no effort to help **8 pull one's finger out** sl
start working hard **9 put one's finger on**
find —see also GREEN FINGERS ♦ vt feel with
one's fingers ~**ing** n [U] use of the fingers
when playing music

fin·ger·nail /ˈfɪŋɡəneɪl ‖ -ər-/ n one of
the hard flat pieces at the ends of the
fingers

fin·ger·print /ˈfɪŋɡəˌprɪnt ‖ -ər-/ n mark
made by a finger pressed onto a surface ♦
vt take (someone's) fingerprints

fin·ger·tip /ˈfɪŋɡəˌtɪp ‖ -ər-/ n **1** end of a
finger **2 have something at one's
fingertips** know it well

fin·i·cky /ˈfɪnɪki/ adj disliking many
things

fin·ish /ˈfɪnɪʃ/ v **1** vi/t come or bring to an

end **2** vt eat or drink the rest of **3** take all
one's powers, hopes of success, etc. ♦ n
1 [C] last part **2** [S;U] appearance or
condition of having been properly polished,
painted, etc.

finish with phr vt have no more use for

fi·nite /ˈfaɪnaɪt/ adj **1** limited **2** gram (of a
verb) changing according to tense and
subject ~**ly** adv

fi·ord /ˈfiːɔːd, fjɔːd ‖ fiːˈɔːrd, fjɔːrd/ n
FJORD

fir /fɜː ‖ fɜːr/ n straight tree with leaves
like needles

fire¹ /faɪə ‖ faɪr/ n **1** [U] condition of
burning: afraid of fire **2** [C] something
burning, on purpose or by accident: light a
fire | forest fires **3** [C] gas or electrical
apparatus for warming a room **4** [U]
destruction by fire **5** [U] shooting from guns
6 catch fire start to burn **7 on fire** burning
8 open/cease fire start/stop shooting **9 set
fire to** cause to burn **10 under fire** being
shot at —see also **hang fire** (HANG¹)

fire² v **1** vi/t shoot off (bullets or arrows)
2 vt dismiss from a job **3** vt excite: fire one's
imagination **4** vt bake (clay things) in a KILN

fire a·larm /ˈ· ·ˌ·/ n signal that warns
people of fire

fire·arm /ˈfaɪərɑːm ‖ ˈfaɪrɑːrm/ n gun

fire·bomb /ˈfaɪəbɒm ‖ ˈfaɪrbɑːm/ n
INCENDIARY bomb

fire·brand /ˈfaɪəbrænd ‖ ˈfaɪr-/ n trouble-
maker; AGITATOR

fire brigade /ˈ· ˌ··/ BrE ‖ **fire department** /ˈ· ˌ··/ AmE — n organization that
FIREFIGHTERS work for

fire drill /ˈ· ·/ n [C;U] practice in leaving a
burning building safely

fire en·gine /ˈ· ˌ··/ n vehicle that carries
FIREFIGHTERS and their equipment

fire es·cape /ˈ· ·ˌ·/ n outside stairs for
leaving a burning building

fire·fight·er /ˈfaɪəˌfaɪtə ‖ ˈfaɪrˌfaɪtər/ n
person whose job is to stop fires

fire·guard /ˈfaɪəɡɑːd ‖ ˈfaɪrɡɑːrd/ n
protective framework round a fireplace

fire·light·er /ˈfaɪəˌlaɪtə ‖ ˈfaɪrˌlaɪtər/ n
small white block of FUEL used for lighting
fires

fire·man /ˈfaɪəmən ‖ ˈfaɪr-/ n **-men** /-mən/
male FIREFIGHTER

fire·place /ˈfaɪəpleɪs ‖ ˈfaɪr-/ n opening
for a fire in a room

fire·pow·er /'faɪə,paʊə ‖ 'faɪr,paʊr/ n [U] ability to deliver gunfire

fire·proof /'faɪəpruːf ‖ 'faɪr-/ adj unable to be damaged by fire **fireproof** vt

fire·side /'faɪəsaɪd ‖ 'faɪr-/ n area around the fireplace

fire sta·tion /'· ,·/ n building for a FIRE BRIGADE

fire·wood /'faɪəwʊd ‖ 'faɪr-/ n [U] wood cut to be used on fires

fire·work /'faɪəwɜːk ‖ 'faɪrwɜːrk/ n container of explosive powder, burnt to make coloured lights **fireworks** n [P] 1 show of FIREWORKS 2 show of anger

firing line /'·· ·/ n in the firing line being attacked or criticized

firing squad /'·· ,·/ n group of soldiers ordered to shoot an offender

firm¹ /fɜːm ‖ fɜːrm/ adj, adv 1 solidly fixed 2 not likely to change 3 determined; RESOLUTE **~ly** adv **~ness** n [U]

firm² n business company

fir·ma·ment /'fɜːməmənt ‖ 'fɜːr-/ n lit the sky

first /fɜːst ‖ fɜːrst/ determiner, adv 1 before the others 2 for the first time: my first visit 3 rather than do something else 4 **first thing** at the earliest time in the morning ♦ n, pron [S] 1 person or thing before others: the first to arrive 2 BrE university examination result of highest quality 3 **at first** at the beginning 4 **the first** the slightest: They haven't the first idea what it means. **~ly** adv before anything else

first aid /,· '·/ n [U] treatment given by an ordinary person to someone hurt in an accident, etc.

first-born /'fɜːstbɔːn ‖ 'fɜːrstbɔːrn/ adj, n **firstborn** eldest (child)

first-class /,· '·◄/ adj of the best quality

first floor /,· '·◄/ n 1 BrE floor above the GROUND FLOOR 2 AmE ground floor

first·hand /,fɜːst'hænd◄ -ɜːr-/ adj, adv (of information) directly from its origin

first la·dy /,· '·/ n [the] (in the US) wife of the President

first name /'·· ·/ n name that stands before one's family name

first-rate /,· '·◄/ adj of the best quality

first re·fus·al /,· ·'··/ n [U] the right to decide whether to buy something before it is offered to other people

first school /'· ·/ n BrE school for children between 5 and 9 years old

firth /fɜːθ ‖ fɜːrθ/ n Scottish river ESTUARY

fis·cal /'fɪskəl/ adj fml of public money, taxes, etc.

fish /fɪʃ/ n fish or fishes 1 [C] cold-blooded creature that lives in water 2 [U] its flesh as food 3 **drink like a fish** drink too much alcohol ♦ v 1 vi try to catch fish 2 vi search indirectly: fish for compliments 3 vt bring out or up: He fished a key from his pocket. **~y** adj 1 like fish 2 seeming false: a fishy story

fish·er·man /'fɪʃəmən ‖ -ʃər-/ n -men /-mən/ man who catches fish, esp. as a job

fish·e·ry /'fɪʃəri/ also -ries pl. part of the sea where fishing is practised

fish·ing /'fɪʃɪŋ/ n [U] sport or job of catching fish

fish·mon·ger /'fɪʃmʌŋgə ‖ -maːŋgər, -mʌŋ-/ n BrE someone who sells fish in a shop

fis·sion /'fɪʃən/ n [U] splitting of a cell or atom

fis·sure /'fɪʃə ‖ -ər/ n deep crack in rock

fist /fɪst/ n hand when closed tightly: holding a **fistful** of coins

fit¹ /fɪt/ v -tt- 1 vi/t be the right size and shape (for): The lid doesn't fit. 2 vt put in place: fit a new lock 3 vt make suitable for ♦ n [S] quality of fitting well 2 way that something fits: a tight fit **~ted** adj fixed in place: fitted carpet **~ter** n 1 person who fits machine parts 2 person who cuts out and fits clothes —see also GAS FITTER

fit in phr v 1 vi match; HARMONIZE 2 vt make room or time for

fit out phr vt supply; FURNISH

fit² adj 1 suitable, right: fit to eat | Do as you think fit. 2 physically healthy 3 ready to: laugh fit to burst **~ness** n [U]

fit³ n 1 short attack of illness, etc.: fit of coughing/of pique 2 sudden loss of consciousness 3 **by fits and starts** not regularly 4 **have a fit** be very angry

fit·ful /'fɪtfəl/ adj restlessly irregular **~ly** adv

fit·ting /'fɪtɪŋ/ adj fml suitable ♦ n 1 something fixed into a building 2 occasion of trying whether clothes fit

five /faɪv/ determiner, n, pron 5 **fiver** n £5 note

fix¹ /fɪks/ vt 1 fasten firmly 2 arrange; decide on: fix a price 3 repair 4 tidy: I must *fix my hair* **5** *esp. AmE* prepare (food or drink) **6** arrange the result of (something) dishonestly ~**ative** *n* chemical for sticking things in position ~**ation** /fɪk'seɪʃən/ *n* OBSESSION

fix on *phr vt* choose

fix up *phr vt* **1** provide **2** repair, change or improve

fix² *n* **1** awkward situation **2** *sl* amount of something, a drug, that one needs: *a caffeine fix*

fix·er /'fɪksə ‖ -ər/ *n* person who is good at arranging that something happens, esp. by using influence or dishonesty

fix·ture /'fɪkstʃə ‖ -ər/ *n* **1** something fixed into a building **2** sports event on an agreed date

fizz /fɪz/ *vi, n* [S] (make) a sound of BUBBLES in a liquid ~**y** *adj*

fiz·zle /'fɪzəl/ *v* **fizzle out** *phr vi* end disappointingly

fjord /fiːɔːd, fjɔːd ‖ fiːˈɔːrd, fjɔːrd/ *n* narrow arm of the sea between steep cliffs, esp. in Norway

flab /flæb/ *n* [U] *infml* soft loose flesh

flab·ber·gast·ed /'flæbəgɑːstɪd ‖ -ərgæs-/ *adj* surprised and shocked

flab·by /'flæbi/ *adj* **1** (of muscles) too soft **2** lacking force or effectiveness –**biness** *n* [U]

flac·cid /'flæsɪd, 'flæksɪd/ *adj* not firm enough

flag¹ /flæg/ *n* piece of cloth used as the sign of a country, etc., or to make signals —see also WHITE FLAG ♦ *vt* -**gg**- put a flag on

flag down *phr vt* signal (a vehicle) to stop

flag² *vi* -**gg**- become weak

flag·on /'flægən/ *n* large container for liquids

flag·pole /'flægpəʊl ‖ -poʊl/ *n* long pole to raise a flag on

fla·grant /'fleɪɡrənt/ *adj* openly bad ~**ly** *adv*

flag·ship /'flæɡ.ʃɪp/ *n* **1** chief naval ship in a group **2** most important of a company's products

flag·staff /'flæɡstɑːf ‖ -stæf/ *n* flagpole

flag·stone /'flæɡstəʊn ‖ -stoʊn/ *n* flat stone for a floor or path

flag-wav·ing /'· ˌ··/ *n* [U] noisy expression of national military feeling

flail /fleɪl/ *vi* wave violently but aimlessly about

flair /fleə ‖ fler/ *n* [S] natural ability to do something

flak /flæk/ *n* **1** gunfire directed at enemy aircraft **2** criticism

flake¹ /fleɪk/ *n* small leaf-like bit: *soap flakes* **flaky** *adj* **1** made up of flakes or tending to flake **2** *AmE infml* ECCENTRIC **flakiness** *n* [U]

flake² *vi* fall off in flakes

flake out *phr vi* fall asleep or faint because of great tiredness

flam·boy·ant /flæm'bɔɪənt/ *adj* **1** brightly coloured **2** (of a person) showy and bold

flame¹ /fleɪm/ *n* [C;U] **1** (tongue of) burning gas **2 in flames** burning —see also OLD FLAME

flame² *vt* send (someone) an unpleasant message in capital letters on the INTERNET

fla·men·co /flə'meŋkəʊ ‖ -koʊ/ *n* [C;U] fast, exciting Spanish dance

fla·min·go /flə'mɪŋɡəʊ ‖ -ɡoʊ/ *n* tall pink tropical water bird

flam·ma·ble /'flæməbəl/ *adj AmE* INFLAMMABLE (1)

flan /flæn/ *n* open pastry case filled with fruit, cheese, etc.

flange /flændʒ/ *n* edge of a wheel, etc. that sticks out

flank /flæŋk/ *n* side of an animal, person, or moving army ♦ *vt* be placed beside

flan·nel /'flænl/ *n* **1** [U] loosely woven woollen cloth **2** [C] FACECLOTH **3** *infml, esp. BrE* meaningless words used to avoid giving a direct answer

flap /flæp/ *n* **1** [C] flat part of anything that covers an opening **2** [S] sound of flapping **3 in a flap** excited and anxious ♦ *vi/t* **1** wave slowly up and down: *flap its wings* **2** get excited and anxious

flap·jack /'flæpdʒæk/ *n* [C;U] type of BISCUIT containing OATS

flare¹ /fleə ‖ fler/ *vi* burn brightly but unsteadily ♦ *n* **1** [S] flaring light **2** [C] bright light used as a signal

flare up *phr vi* become suddenly hotter, more violent, etc. **flare-up** /'· ·/ *n*

flare² *vi/t* widen towards the bottom: *flared skirt* **flare** *n* **flares** *n* [P] flared trousers

flash¹ /flæʃ/ *v* **1** *vi/t* shine for a moment **2** *vi* move very fast **3** *vt* send by radio, etc.:

flash news to London

flash² n 1 sudden bright light: (fig.) *a flash of inspiration* 2 short news report 3 FLASHLIGHT (1) 4 **in a flash** at once ♦ *adj* 1 sudden: *flash flood* 2 modern and expensive-looking ~**y** *adj* unpleasantly big, bright, etc.

flash·back /'flæʃbæk/ n [C;U] scene in a film, etc. that goes back in time

flash·bulb /'flæʃbʌlb/ n bright electric lamp for photography

flash·light /'flæʃlaɪt/ n 1 apparatus for taking photographs in the dark 2 *esp. AmE* for TORCH (1)

flash point /'· ·/ n point or place at which violence may be expected

flask /flɑːsk ‖ flæsk/ n 1 narrow-necked bottle 2 flat bottle for carrying drinks in one's pocket 3 bottle with a VACUUM between its two walls, for keeping liquids hot or cold

flat¹ /flæt/ n 1 low level plain 2 flat part or side (of) 3 (in music) flat note 4 flat piece of stage scenery 5 *BrE* set of rooms on one floor of a building 6 *esp. AmE* a flat tyre

flat² *adj* -tt- 1 smooth and level 2 spread out fully: *lie down flat* 3 not very thick: *flat cakes* 4 (of a tyre) without enough air in it 5 (of a BATTERY) having lost electrical power 6 (of beer, etc.) having lost its gas 7 dull and lifeless 8 (in music) below the right note 9 firm; with no more argument: *a flat refusal* ~**ly** *adv* 1 firmly: *He flatly denied it.* 2 without emotion

flat³ *adv* 1 into a flat or level position 2 below the right note: *sing flat* 3 and no more: *3 minutes flat* 4 **flat out** at full speed

flat feet /ˌ· '·/ n feet that rest too flat on the ground **flat-footed** /ˌ· '··◄/ *adj*

flat rate /ˌ· '·◄/ n one charge including everything

flat·ten /'flætn/ vi/t make or become flat

flat·ter /'flætə ‖ -ər/ vt/i 1 praise too much or insincerely 2 give pleasure to 3 (of a picture) show (a person) as more beautiful ~**er** n ~**y** n [U] flattering remarks

flat·u·lence /'flætjʊləns ‖ -tʃə-/ n [U] *fml* WIND¹ (3)

flaunt /flɔːnt ‖ flɔːnt, flɑːnt/ vt *derog* show for admiration: *flaunt her wealth*

flau·tist /'flɔːtɪst ‖ 'flɔː-/ n *BrE* FLUTE-player

fla·vour *BrE* ‖ **flavor** *AmE* /'fleɪvə ‖ -ər/ n 1 [C;U] taste: *6 popular flavours | not*

much flavour 2 [S] particular characteristic ♦ *vt* give taste to ~**ing** n [C;U] something added to improve the taste ~**less** *adj*

flaw /flɔː ‖ flɔː/ n fault or weakness ~**less** *adj* ~**lessly** *adv* ♦ *vt* make a flaw in

flax /flæks/ n [U] (thread made from the stem of) a plant with blue flowers used for making LINEN

flax·en /'flæksən/ *adj* lit (of hair) pale yellow

flay /fleɪ/ vt 1 remove the skin from 2 attack fiercely in words

flea /fliː/ n wingless jumping insect that feeds on blood

flea mar·ket /'· ˌ··/ n street market where used goods are sold

flea·pit /'fliːˌpɪt/ n *BrE* cheap dirty cinema or theatre

fleck /flek/ n small spot or grain ♦ *vt* mark with flecks

fledg·ling /'fledʒlɪŋ/ n 1 young bird learning to fly 2 inexperienced person

flee /fliː/ vi/t fled /fled/ *fml* hurry away (from); escape

fleece¹ /fliːs/ n 1 [C] sheep's woolly coat 2 [U] artificial soft material used for making clothes 3 [C] also **fleecy** JACKET made of fleece (2) **fleecy** *adj*

fleece² vt *infml* charge too much money

fleet /fliːt/ n 1 number of ships under one command 2 group of buses, etc. under one control

fleet·ing /'fliːtɪŋ/ *adj* not lasting long: *fleeting glimpse*

flesh /fleʃ/ n 1 [U] soft part of a person or animal that covers the bones 2 [U] soft part of a fruit 3 [S] the body as opposed to the soul 4 **flesh and blood a** human beings **b** one's relatives 5 **in the flesh** in real life ~**y** *adj* fat

flew /fluː/ *past t. of* FLY

flex¹ /fleks/ n [C;U] *BrE* electric wire in a protective covering

flex² vt bend or stretch (one's muscles)

flex·i·ble /'fleksəbəl/ *adj* 1 easily bent 2 easily changed: *flexible plans* ~**bility** /ˌfleksəˈbɪləti/ n [U]

flex·i·time /'fleksitaɪm/ n [U] British system by which people can choose their hours of work

flick /flɪk/ n light sudden blow or movement ♦ *vt* touch or strike lightly

flick·er /'flɪkə ‖ -ər/ vi 1 burn unsteadily

2 move backwards and forwards ♦ *n* [S]
1 flickering 2 short-lived feeling: *flicker of interest*

fli·er /'flaɪə‖-ər/ *n* piece of paper advertising something

flies /flaɪz/ *n* [P] covered front opening on trousers

flight[1] /flaɪt/ *n* 1 [C;U] flying: *birds in flight* | (fig.) *His account contained some amazing flights of fancy.* 2 [C] journey by air 3 [C] aircraft making a journey: *Flight Number 347 to Geneva* 4 [C] group of birds or aircraft 5 [C] set of stairs ~**less** *adj* unable to fly

flight[2] *n* [C;U] (an example of) the act of running away; escape

flight at·tend·ant /'· ·,··/ *n* STEWARD (2) on a plane

flight deck /'· ·/ *n* part of a plane where the pilot sits

flight path /'· ·/ *n* course through the air of an aircraft, etc.

flight·y /'flaɪti/ *adj* (of a person) too influenced by sudden desires or ideas

flim·sy /'flɪmzi/ *adj* light and thin; easily destroyed ~**sily** *adv*

flinch /flɪntʃ/ *vi* move back in pain or fear

fling /flɪŋ/ *vt* **flung** /flʌŋ/ throw violently ♦ *n* [S] short time of enjoyment, often with no sense of responsibility

flint /flɪnt/ *n* 1 [C;U] hard stone that makes SPARKS (1) 2 bit of metal in a cigarette lighter that lights the gas or petrol

flip /flɪp/ 1 *vt* send spinning into the air 2 *vi* become mad or very angry ♦ *n* quick light blow

flip chart /'· ·/ *n* large block of paper used to write down information in a meeting, class, etc.

flip·pant /'flɪpənt/ *adj* disrespectful about serious subjects ~**ly** *adv* –**pancy** *n* [U]

flip·per /'flɪpə‖-ər/ *n* 1 flat limb of a SEAL[2], etc. 2 rubber shoe shaped like this, for swimming

flip side /'· ·/ *n* [*the*] other side of a situation, argument, etc.

flirt /flɜːt‖flɜːrt/ *vi* behave as if sexually attracted ♦ *n* person who flirts ~**ation** /flɜː'teɪʃən‖flɜːr-/ *n* [C;U] ~**atious** *adj* liking to flirt

flirt with *phr vt* 1 consider, but not seriously 2 risk, esp. needlessly or lightly

flit /flɪt/ *vi* **-tt-** fly or move quickly and lightly

float /fləʊt‖floʊt/ *v* 1 *vi/t* (cause to) stay on the surface of liquid or be held up in air 2 *vt* establish (a business) by selling SHARES 3 *vi/t* (allow to) vary in exchange value: *float the pound* 4 suggest ♦ *n* 1 light object that floats 2 flat vehicle drawn in a procession 3 money kept for use if an unexpected need arises ~**ing** *adj* not fixed

floating vo·ter /,·· '··/ *n* person who does not always vote for the same political party

flock /flɒk‖flɑːk/ *n* 1 group of sheep, goats, or birds 2 crowd 3 priest's CONGREGATION ♦ *vi* move in large numbers

flog /flɒɡ‖flɑːɡ/ *vt* **-gg-** 1 beat severely 2 *sl* sell 3 **flog a dead horse** waste time with useless efforts 4 **flog to death** *infml* spoil (a story, idea, etc.) by repeating too often

flood /flʌd/ also **floods** *pl.* — *n* 1 water covering a place that is usu. dry 2 large quantity: *floods of tears* ♦ *vi/t* 1 fill or cover with water 2 overflow 3 arrive in large numbers

flood·gate /'flʌdɡeɪt/ *n* 1 gate for controlling water 2 **open the floodgates** suddenly let loose something that was held back

flood·light /'flʌdlaɪt/ *n* powerful light thrown on the outside of buildings, etc. ♦ *vt* **-lit** /-lɪt/ light with floodlights

flood tide /'· ·/ *n* [C;U] flow of the TIDE inwards

floor /flɔː‖flɔːr/ *n* 1 [C] surface one stands on indoors: *dance floor* 2 [C] level of a building —see also FIRST FLOOR, GROUND FLOOR 3 [S] part of a parliament, etc. where members sit and speak 4 **go through the floor** *infml* (of a price) sink to a very low level 5 **take the floor: a** speak in a DEBATE **b** start dancing at a party, etc. ♦ *vt* 1 provide with a floor 2 knock down; defeat 3 confuse ~**ing** *n* material for covering a FLOOR (1)

floor·board /'flɔːbɔːd‖'flɔːrbɔːrd/ *n* board in a wooden floor

floor show /'· ·/ *n* CABARET

flop /flɒp‖flɑːp/ *vi* **-pp-** 1 fall awkwardly 2 fail ♦ *n* 1 [S] awkward fall 2 [C] failure ~**py** *adj* soft and loose: *floppy hat* ~**piness** *n* [U]

flop·house /'flɒphaʊs‖'flɑːp-/ *n* AmE cheap hotel

flop·py disk /ˌ·· '·/ also **floppy** — n plastic circle on which computer information is stored

flo·ra /'flɔːrə/ n [U] plants of a particular area or period

flo·ral /'flɔːrəl/ adj of flowers

flor·id /'flɒrɪd ‖ 'flɔː-, 'flɑː-/ adj 1 over-decorated 2 having a red face

flor·ist /'flɒrɪst ‖ 'flɔː-/ n person who sells flowers

floss /flɒs ‖ flɑːs, flɔːs/ vi/t clean between the teeth using special thin string (**dental floss**)

flo·ta·tion /fləʊ'teɪʃən ‖ floʊ-/ n [C;U] act of FLOATing (2) a business

flo·til·la /flə'tɪlə ‖ floʊ-/ n group of small ships

flot·sam and jet·sam /ˌflɒtsəm ən 'dʒetsəm ‖ ˌflɑːt-/ n 1 [U] collection of broken unwanted things lying about in an untidy way 2 [P] people without homes or work, who move helplessly through life

flounce /flaʊns/ vi move violently to express anger or attract attention

floun·der /'flaʊndə ‖ -ər/ vi 1 make wild movements, esp. in water 2 lose control when speaking, etc.

flour /flaʊə ‖ flaʊr/ n [U] powder of crushed grain, used for making bread, etc.

flour·ish /'flʌrɪʃ ‖ 'flɜːrɪʃ/ v 1 vi grow healthily: (fig.) *Business is flourishing*. 2 vt BRANDISH ♦ n noticeable fancy movement

flout /flaʊt/ vt treat (rules, etc.) without respect

flow /fləʊ ‖ floʊ/ vi (of liquid) move smoothly: (fig.) *traffic flowed past* ♦ n [S;U] steady stream or supply ~**ing** adj curving or hanging gracefully

flow·chart /'fləʊtʃɑːt ‖ 'floʊtʃɑːrt/ n drawing showing how the parts of a process are connected

flow·er /'flaʊə ‖ -ər/ n 1 [C] part of a plant that produces seeds 2 [S] *lit* best part: *the flower of the nation's youth* ~**less** adj ~**y** adj 1 decorated with flowers 2 (of language) FLORID (1) ♦ vi produce flowers

flow·er·bed /'flaʊəbed ‖ -ər-/ n small piece of ground where flowers are grown

flow·er·pot /'flaʊəpɒt ‖ -ərpɑːt/ n pot in which a plant is grown

flown /fləʊn ‖ floʊn/ v past p. of FLY

flu /fluː/ also **influenza** *fml* — n [U] infectious disease like a bad cold but more serious

fluc·tu·ate /'flʌktʃueɪt/ vi *fml* (of levels. etc.) change continually –**ation** /ˌflʌktʃu-'eɪʃən/ n [C;U]

flue /fluː/ n pipe through which smoke or heat passes

flu·ent /'fluːənt/ adj 1 able to speak easily 2 (of speech) coming easily ~**ly** adv –**ency** n [U]

fluff /flʌf/ n [U] 1 soft light pieces from woolly material 2 soft fur or hair on a young animal or bird ♦ vt 1 shake or brush out: *fluff out its feathers* 2 do (something) badly or unsuccessfully ~**y** adv covered with fluff: *fluffy kitten*

flu·id /'fluːɪd/ adj 1 able to flow 2 unsettled: *Our ideas on the subject are still fluid.* ♦ n [C;U] liquid

fluke /fluːk/ n [S] piece of accidental good luck

flum·mox /'flʌməks/ vt confuse completely

flung /flʌŋ/ v past t. and p. of FLING

flunk /flʌŋk/ vt esp. AmE 1 fail (an examination, etc.) 2 mark as unsatisfactory (someone's examination answers)

flunk·ey /'flʌŋki/ n someone who is always with an important person and does/says what he/she wants

flu·o·res·cent /fluə'resənt ‖ flɔːr-, flɔːr-/ adj giving out bright light when certain waves have passed through

flu·o·ride /'fluəraɪd ‖ 'flɔːr-/ n [U] chemical compound said to protect teeth against decay –**ridate** /'fluərɪdeɪt ‖ 'flɔːr-, 'flɔːr-/ vt add fluoride to –**ridation** /ˌfluərɪ'deɪʃən ‖ ˌflɔːr-, ˌflɔːr-/ n [U]

flur·ry /'flʌri ‖ 'flɜːri/ n 1 [C] sudden rush of rain, snow, etc. 2 [S] nervous excitement ♦ vt make nervous

flush /flʌʃ/ n 1 [C] (cleaning with) a rush of water 2 [S] redness of the face 3 [S] feeling of eager excitement ♦ v 1 vt clean with a rush of water 2 vi BLUSH 3 vt make (someone) leave a hiding place ♦ adj 1 level 2 *sl* having plenty of money ~**ed** adj proud and excited

flus·ter /'flʌstə ‖ -ər/ vt make nervous ♦ n [S] nervous state

flute /fluːt/ n WOODWIND musical instrument played by blowing sideways across it

flut·ter /'flʌtə ‖ -ər/ vi/t 1 a move (wings) quickly and lightly **b** fly by doing this

2 move in a quick irregular way: *flags fluttering* ♦ *n* **1** [S;U] fluttering or shaking movement **2** [S] state of excitement

flux /flʌks/ *n* [U] *fml* continual change

fly¹ /flaɪ/ *v* flew /fluː/, flown /fləʊn/ floʊn/ **1** *vi* move through the air as a bird or aircraft does **2** *vt* control (an aircraft) **3** raise (a flag) **4** FLEE **5** *vi* go fast: *Time flies. | I must fly.* (=I have to leave in a hurry) **6 fly in the face of** DEFY **7 fly into a rage/temper** become suddenly angry **8 fly off the handle** *infml* become suddenly and unexpectedly angry **9 let fly** attack

fly² *n* **1** winged insect **2** hook that is made to look like a fly, used in fishing **3 fly in the ointment** *infml* something that spoils the perfection of something **4 like flies** *infml* in very large numbers **5 there are no flies on someone** *BrE infml* someone is not a fool and cannot be tricked

fly³ *n* in FLIES

fly-by-night /ˌ·· ˌ·/ *adj* (of a company) unable to be trusted; not likely to last

fly·er /ˈflaɪə ‖ -ər/ *n* FLIER

flying col·ours /ˌ·· ˈ··/ *n* [P] **with flying colours** very successfully; splendidly

flying sau·cer /ˌ·· ˈ··/ *n* spacecraft believed to come from another world

flying squad /ˈ·· ·/ *n* special police kept ready for quick action

flying start /ˌ·· ˈ·/ *n* very good beginning

flying visit /ˌ·· ˈ··/ *n* very short visit

fly·leaf /ˈflaɪliːf/ *n* -leaves /-liːvz/ empty page at the beginning or end of a book

fly·o·ver /ˈflaɪ-əʊvə ‖ -oʊvər/ *n* BrE place where two roads cross at different levels

fly·past /ˈflaɪpɑːst ‖ -pæst/ *n* BrE ceremonial low flight by aircraft over a public gathering

foal /fəʊl ‖ foʊl/ *n* young horse ♦ *vi* give birth to a foal

foam /fəʊm ‖ foʊm/ *n* [U] **1** mass of BUBBLES **2** *infml* FOAM RUBBER ♦ *vi* produce foam **~y** *adj*

foam rub·ber /ˌ· ˈ··◀/ *n* [U] soft rubber full of BUBBLES

fob /fɒb ‖ fɑːb/ *v* -bb- **fob off** *phr vt* deceive (someone) into accepting (something)

fo·cus /ˈfəʊkəs ‖ ˈfoʊ-/ *n* -cuses *or* -ci /-kaɪ, -saɪ/ **1** [C] point at which beams of light, etc. meet **2** [S] centre of attention **3 in/out of focus** (not) giving a clear

picture because LENS is not correctly placed ♦ *vi/t* -s- *or* -ss- **1** come or bring to a focus **2** direct (attention) **focal** *adj*

fod·der /ˈfɒdə ‖ ˈfɑːdər/ *n* [U] **1** food for farm animals **2** anything that supplies a continuous demand

foe /fəʊ ‖ foʊ/ *n* lit enemy

foe·tus /ˈfiːtəs/ *n* creature before birth, at a later stage than an EMBRYO

fog /fɒɡ ‖ fɑːɡ, fɔːɡ/ *n* [C;U] (period of) thick mist ♦ *vi/t* -gg- (cause to) become covered with fog **~gy** *adj* **1** misty **2** not clear: *I haven't the foggiest idea.*

fog·bound /ˈfɒɡbaʊnd ‖ ˈfɑːɡ-, ˈfɔːɡ-/ *adj* prevented by fog from travelling

fo·gey, fogy /ˈfəʊɡi ‖ ˈfoʊ-/ *n* old fogey person with fixed, old-fashioned ideas

fog·horn /ˈfɒɡhɔːn ‖ ˈfɑːɡhɔːrn, ˈfɔːɡ-/ *n* horn used for warning ships in fog

foi·ble /ˈfɔɪbəl/ *n* foolish little personal habit

foil¹ /fɔɪl/ *vt* prevent (someone) from succeeding in a plan

foil² *n* **1** [U] thin sheet metal **2** [C] person or thing that provides a CONTRAST to another

foil³ *n* thin sword for fencing (FENCE² (1))

foist /fɔɪst/ *vt* force someone to accept: *He tried to foist his company on them.*

fold¹ /fəʊld ‖ foʊld/ *v* **1** *vt* bend back on itself **2** *vi* be able to be folded: *folding table* **3** *vt* cross (one's arms) **4** *vi* (of a business) fail ♦ *n* line made by folding **~er** *n* cardboard holder for papers

fold² *n* enclosure for sheep

fo·li·age /ˈfəʊli-ɪdʒ ‖ ˈfoʊ-/ *n* [U] *fml* leaves

folk /fəʊk ‖ foʊk/ *n* **1** [P] people **2** also **folk music** [U] traditional music ♦ *adj* of traditional music, art, etc. **folks** *n* [P] one's relatives

folk·lore /ˈfəʊklɔː ‖ ˈfoʊklɔːr/ *n* [U] beliefs long preserved among a tribe or nation

folk·sy /ˈfəʊksi ‖ ˈfoʊk-/ *adj* (old-fashioned in a way that seems) typical of areas away from big towns: *his folksy manner*

fol·li·cle /ˈfɒlɪkəl ‖ ˈfɑː-/ *n* small hole from which hair grows

fol·low /ˈfɒləʊ ‖ ˈfɑːloʊ/ *v* **1** *vi/t* come or go after **2** *vt* go along: *follow the river* **3** *vt* attend or listen to carefully **4** *vi/t* understand: *I don't quite follow (you).* **5** *vt* act according to: *follow instructions* **6** *vi* be a necessary result **7 as follows** as now to be told **8 follow suit** do what someone else has done **~er** *n* someone who follows or supports **~ing** *adj* **1** next: *the following day* **2** to be mentioned now **~ing** *n* group of supporters

follow through *phr vt* carry out to the end

follow up *phr vt* take action to continue or add to the effect of something done before **follow-up** /'·· ·/ *n: The paper's doing a follow-up next week.*

fol·ly /'fɒli ‖ 'fɑːli/ *n* [C;U] *fml* foolishness

fo·ment /fəʊ'ment ‖ foʊ-/ *vt fml* help (something bad) to develop

fond /fɒnd ‖ fɑːnd/ *adj* **1** loving **2** foolishly hopeful: *fond belief* **3** having a great liking or love (for) **~ly** *adv* **~ness** *n* [C;U]

fon·dle /'fɒndl ‖ 'fɑːndl/ *vt* touch lovingly

font /fɒnt ‖ fɑːnt/ *n* **1** container for water for BAPTISM **2** printed letters of a particular shape and size

food /fuːd/ *n* [C;U] **1** something, esp. solid, that creatures eat **2 food for thought** something to think about carefully

food chain /'· ·/ *n* [*the*+S] living things considered as a group in which one thing eats another and then is itself eaten by another

food pro·ces·sor /,· '···/ *n* machine that cuts, liquidizes, etc. food very quickly

food·stuff /'fuːdstʌf/ *n* substance used as food

fool /fuːl/ *n* **1** silly person **2 make a fool of oneself** behave in a silly way ♦ *v* **1** *vt* deceive **2** *vi* behave in a silly way **3** *vi* joke **~ish** *adj* silly **~ishly** *adv* **~ishness** *n* [U]

fool·har·dy /'fuːlˌhɑːdi ‖ -ɑːr-/ *adj* taking unwise risks

fool·proof /'fuːlpruːf/ *adj* that cannot fail

foot¹ /fʊt/ *n* **feet** /fiːt/ **1** [C] end part of the leg **2** [S] bottom: *foot of the stairs* **3** [C] (measure of length equal to) 12 inches (INCH) **4 a foot in the door** favourable position from which to advance, gain influence, etc. **5 on foot** walking **6 put one's feet up** rest **7 put one's foot down** speak firmly **8 put one's foot in it** esp. *BrE* ‖ **put one's foot in one's mouth** esp. *AmE*

— *infml* say the wrong thing **9 set foot in/on** enter; visit **~age** *n* [U] length of cinema film **~ing** *n* **1** firm placing of the feet: *lose one's footing* **2** position in relation to others: *on an equal footing*

foot² *vt* **foot the bill** *infml* pay the bill

foot·ball /'fʊtbɔːl ‖ -bɒːl/ *n* **1** [U] *BrE* field game for two teams of 11 players using a round ball that is kicked **2** [C] ball used in this game **3** [U] *AmE* AMERICAN FOOTBALL **~er** *n*

foot·bridge /'fʊtˌbrɪdʒ/ *n* narrow bridge to be used only by people walking

foot·hills /'fʊtˌhɪlz/ *n* [P] low hills near a range of mountains

foot·hold /'fʊthəʊld ‖ -hoʊld/ *n* **1** place where a foot can stand **2** position from which to advance

foot·lights /'fʊtlaɪts/ *n* [P] lights along the front of a stage floor

foot·loose /'fʊtluːs/ *adj* **footloose and fancy free** not married and free to do what one wants

foot·man /'fʊtmən/ *n* **-men** /-mən/ uniformed servant who opens doors, etc.

foot·note /'fʊtnəʊt ‖ -noʊt/ *n* note at the bottom of a page

foot·path /'fʊtpɑːθ ‖ -pæθ/ *n* **-paths** /-pɑːðz ‖ -pæðz/ narrow path for walking on

foot·print /'fʊtˌprɪnt/ *n* mark made by a foot

foot·step /'fʊtstep/ *n* **1** sound of a person's step **2 follow in someone's footsteps** follow an example set by someone else in the past

foot·wear /'fʊtweə ‖ -wer/ *n* [U] shoes, etc.

foot·work /'fʊtwɜːk ‖ -wɜːrk/ *n* [U] use of the feet in sports, etc.

for¹ /fə; *strong* fɔː; ‖ fər; *strong* fɔːr/ *prep* **1** intended to be given to, used by, or used in: *a present for you* ‖ *cake for tea* **2** to help: *lift it for you* ‖ *medicine for a cold* **3** (shows purpose): *What's this knife for?* **4** in support of: *play football for England* **5** towards: *set off for school* **6** so as to get: *wait for the bus* ‖ *no demand for coal* **7** (shows price or amount): *buy it for £1* **8** meaning: *Red is for danger.* **9** (shows distance or time): *stay for a week* **10** because of: *rewarded for his bravery* **11** in regard to: *an ear for music* ‖ *good for his health* **12** considering: *tall for his age* **13** (introducing phrases): *no need*

for

for you to go

for² *conj fml* and the reason is that

for·age /'fɒrɪdʒ ‖ 'fɑː-, 'fɔː-/ *n* [U] food for horses and cattle ♦ *vi* search about

foray /'fɒreɪ ‖ 'fɒː-, 'fɑː-/ *n* sudden rush into enemy country: (fig.) *his unsuccessful foray into politics*

for·bear¹ /fɔː'beə fə- ‖ fɔːr'ber, fər-/ *vi* **-bore** /-'bɔː ‖ -'bɔːr/, **-borne** /-'bɔːn ‖ -'bɔːrn/ *fml* hold oneself back from doing something **~ance** *n* [U] patient forgiveness

for·bear² /'fɔːbeə ‖ 'fɔːrber/ *n* FOREBEAR

for·bid /fə'bɪd ‖ fər-/ *vt* **-bade** /-'beɪd ‖ -'bæd/ *or* **-bad** /-'bæd/, **-bidden** /-'bɪdn/ **1** refuse to allow (a person) **2 God forbid (that)** I very much hope it will not happen (that) **~ding** *adj* looking dangerous

force /fɔːs ‖ fɔːrs/ *n* **1** [U] strength; violence **2** [C;U] influence **3** [C] power that produces change: *the force of gravity* **4** [C] group of soldiers, police, etc. —see also FORCES **5 in force** in large numbers **6 in(to) force** in/into operation **7 join forces (with)** unite (with) for a purpose ♦ *vt* **1** use (physical) force on **2** produce with effort: *forced laughter* **3** hasten the growth of (plants) **4 force someone's hand** make someone act as one wishes or before they are ready **~ful** *adj* (of people, words, etc.) powerful **~fully** *adv* **forcible** *adj* done by physical force **forcibly** *adv*

for·ceps /'fɔːseps, -sɪps ‖ 'fɔːr-/ *n* [P] medical instrument for holding objects

forc·es /'fɔːsɪz ‖ 'fɔːr-/ *n* [(*the*)P] (*often cap.*) the army, navy, and air force of a country

ford /fɔːd ‖ fɔːrd/ *n* place where one can cross a river without a bridge ♦ *vt* cross at a ford

fore /fɔː ‖ fɔːr/ *adj* front ♦ *n* **come to the fore** become well-known; noticeable

fore·arm /'fɔːrɑːm ‖ -ɑːrm/ *n* arm between the hand and elbow

fore·bear /'fɔːbeə ‖ 'fɔːrber/ *n fml* ANCESTOR

fore·bod·ing /fɔː'bəʊdɪŋ ‖ fɔːr'boʊ-/ *n* [C;U] feeling of coming evil

fore·cast¹ /'fɔːkɑːst ‖ 'fɔːrkæst/ *vt* **-cast** *or* **-casted** say in advance (what will happen in future) ♦ *n* statement of future events: *weather forecast*

fore·close /fɔː'kləʊz ‖ fɔːr'kloʊz/ *vi/t* take back property because a MORTGAGE has

not been repaid

fore·court /'fɔːkɔːt ‖ 'fɔːrkɔːrt/ *n* courtyard in front of a building

fore·fa·thers /'fɔː,fɑːðəz ‖ 'fɔːr,fɑːðərz/ *n* [P] ANCESTORS

fore·fin·ger /'fɔː,fɪŋgə ‖ 'fɔːr,fɪŋgər/ *n* finger next to the thumb

fore·front /'fɔːfrʌnt ‖ 'fɔːr-/ *n* [S] leading position

fore·go /fɔː'gəʊ ‖ fɔːr'goʊ/ *vt* FORGO

foregone con·clu·sion /,·· ·'··/ *n* result that is certain from the start

fore·ground /'fɔːgraʊnd ‖ 'fɔːr-/ *n* nearest part of a view

fore·hand /'fɔːhænd ‖ 'fɔːr-/ *n, adj* (tennis stroke) with the inner part of hand and arm turned forward

fore·head /'fɒrɪd, 'fɔːhed ‖ 'fɔːrɪd, 'fɑːrɪd, 'fɔːrhed/ *n* face above the eyes

for·eign /'fɒrɪn ‖ 'fɔː-, 'fɑː-/ *adj* **1** of a country that is not one's own **2** coming or brought in from outside: *a foreign body in her eye* **3** **foreign to** not natural in **~er** *n* foreign person

foreign affairs /,·· ·'·◄/ *n* [P] matters concerning international relations and the interests of one's own country in foreign countries

foreign ex·change /,·· ·'·/ *n* [U] (practice of buying and selling) foreign money

fore·man /'fɔːmən ‖ 'fɔːr-/ **forewoman** /-,wʊmən/ *fem.* — *n* **-men** /-mən/ **1** worker in charge of others **2** leader of a JURY

fore·most /'fɔːməʊst ‖ 'fɔːrmoʊst/ *adj* most important

fo·ren·sic /fə'rensɪk, -zɪk/ *adj* used in the law and the tracking of criminals: *forensic medicine*

fore·run·ner /'fɔː,rʌnə ‖ -ər/ *n* person or thing that prepares the way for another

fore·see /fɔː'siː ‖ fɔːr-/ *vt* **-saw** /-'sɔː ‖ -'sɒː/, **-seen** /-'siːn/ see in advance **~able** *adj* **1** that can be foreseen **2 in the foreseeable future** soon

fore·shad·ow /fɔː'ʃædəʊ ‖ fɔːr'ʃædoʊ/ *vt* be a sign of (what will happen)

fore·shore /'fɔːʃɔː ‖ 'fɔːrʃɔːr/ *n* [S] shore between the sea and ordinary land

fore·sight /'fɔːsaɪt ‖ 'fɔːr-/ *n* [U] ability to imagine the future happening

fore·skin /'fɔː,skɪn ‖ 'fɔːr-/ *n* [C] skin covering the end of a man's PENIS

for·est /'fɒrɪst ‖ 'fɔː-, 'fuː-/ *n* [C;U] area covered with trees **~er** *n* person who works in a forest **~ry** *n* [U] work of planting and caring for trees

fore·stall /fɔːˈstɔːl ‖ fɔːrˈstɔːl/ *vt* prevent (a person or plan) by acting first

fore·taste /'fɔːteɪst ‖ 'fɔːr-/ *n* [S] first experience of something that will come later

fore·tell /fɔːˈtel ‖ fɔːr-/ *vt* **-told** /-ˈtəʊld ‖ -ˈtoʊld/ PROPHESY

fore·thought /'fɔːθɔːt ‖ 'fɔːrθɒt/ *n* [U] wise planning for the future

for·ev·er /fərˈevə ‖ -vər/ *adv* **1** for all future time **2** continually **3 take forever** take an extremely long time

fore·warn /fɔːˈwɔːn ‖ fɔːrˈwɔːrn/ *vt* warn of coming danger

fore·went /fɔːˈwent ‖ fɔːr-/ *past t. of* FOREGO

fore·word /'fɔːwɜːd ‖ 'fɔːrwɜːrd/ *n* short introduction to a book

for·feit /'fɔːfɪt ‖ 'fɔːr-/ *vt* lose as a punishment ♦ *n* something forfeited

for·gave /fəˈgeɪv ‖ fər-/ *v past t. of* FORGIVE

forge[1] /fɔːdʒ ‖ fɔːrdʒ/ *vt* **1** copy in order to deceive: *a forged passport* **2** form (metal) by heating and hammering: (fig.) *forge a new political party*

forge ahead *phr vi* move with a sudden increase of speed and power

forge[2] *n* place where metal is forged **forger** *n* person who forges papers, etc. **~ry** /'fɔːdʒəri ‖ 'fɔːr-/ *n* **1** [U] forging of papers, etc. **2** [C] forged paper, etc.

for·get /fəˈget ‖ fər-/ *vi/t* **-got** /-ˈgɒt ‖ -ˈgɑːt/, **-gotten** /-ˈgɒtn ‖ -ˈgɑːtn/ **1** fail to remember: *Don't forget to lock the door.* **2** stop thinking about: *Let's just forget it.* **~ful** *adj* in the habit of forgetting

for·give /fəˈgɪv ‖ fər-/ *vi/t* **-gave** /-ˈgeɪv/, **-given** /-ˈgɪvn/ stop blaming (someone for something) **-givable** *adj*: *forgivable mistake* **-giving** *adj* willing to forgive **~ness** *n* [U] act of forgiving

for·go, **fore-** /fɔːˈgəʊ ‖ fɔːrˈgoʊ/ *vt* **-went** /-ˈwent/, **-gone** /-ˈgɒn ‖ -ˈgɔːn/ *fml* give up

fork[1] /fɔːk ‖ fɔːrk/ *n* **1** instrument with points, for lifting food to the mouth **2** farm or gardening tool like this **3** place where a road, etc. divides; one of the divisions

fork[2] *v* **1** *vt* lift, etc. with a fork **2** *vi* divide into branches **3** *vi* (of a person) turn (left or right) **~ed** *adj* that divides into two or more points at the end

fork out *phr vi/t* pay (money) unwillingly

fork·lift truck /ˌfɔːklɪft ˈtrʌk ‖ ˌfɔːrk-/ *n* small vehicle with a movable apparatus for lifting goods

for·lorn /fəˈlɔːn ‖ fərˈlɔːrn/ *adj lit* alone and unhappy **~ly** *adv*

form[1] /fɔːm ‖ fɔːrm/ *n* **1** [C;U] shape **2** [C] plan; kind: *forms of government* **3** [U] way in which a work of art is put together **4** [C] official paper with spaces for answering questions **5** [C] class in a British school: *the sixth form* **6** [C] long seat with no back **7** [U] degree of skill, fitness, etc.: *to be on form* **8** [U] correct practice: *a matter of form* **~less** *adj* shapeless

form[2] *v* **1** *vi* begin to exist: *A cloud formed.* **2** *vt* make from parts: *form a government* **3** *vt* make the shape or substance of: *The buildings form a square.*

for·mal /'fɔːməl ‖ 'fɔːr-/ *adj* **1** suitable for official occasions: *formal dress/language* **2** regular in shape: *formal garden* **3** stiff in manner and behaviour **~ly** *adv* **~ize** *vt* make formal **~ity** /fɔːˈmælɪti ‖ fɔːr-/ *n* **1** [U] attention to rules **2** [C] act in accordance with custom: *legal formalities*

for·mat /'fɔːmæt ‖ 'fɔːr-/ *n* size, shape, or arrangement of something ♦ *vt* **-tt-** arrange (a book, computer information, etc.) in a particular format

for·ma·tion /fɔːˈmeɪʃən ‖ fɔːr-/ *n* **1** [U] shaping of something **2** [C;U] arrangement; structure

for·ma·tive /'fɔːmətɪv ‖ 'fɔːr-/ *adj* giving shape: *a child's formative years*

for·mer /'fɔːmə ‖ 'fɔːrmər/ *adj* of an earlier period: *her former husband* ♦ *n* **former** *fml* first of two things mentioned **~ly** *adv* in earlier time

For·mi·ca /fɔːˈmaɪkə ‖ fɔːr-/ *n* [U] *tdmk* hard plastic work surface used in kitchens

for·mi·da·ble /'fɔːmɪdəbəl, fəˈmɪd- ‖ 'fɔːr-/ *adj* **1** large and frightening **2** hard to defeat **-bly** *adv*

for·mu·la /'fɔːmjʊlə ‖ 'fɔːr-/ *n* **-las** *or* **-lae** /-liː/ **1** rule expressed in a short form by letters, numbers, etc.: *chemical formulae* **2** list of substances used in making something: (fig.) *a formula for trouble*

3 combination of suggestions, plans, etc.: *a peace formula*

for·mu·late /'fɔːmjɨleɪt ‖ 'fɔːr-/ *vt* 1 express exactly 2 invent (a plan) –**lation** /ˌfɔːmjɨ'leɪʃən ‖ ˌfɔːr-/ *n* [C;U]

for·ni·cate /'fɔːnɨkeɪt ‖ 'fɔːr-/ *vi esp. law* have sex outside marriage –**cation** /ˌfɔːnɨ'keɪʃən ‖ ˌfɔːr-/ *n* [U]

for·sake /fə'seɪk ‖ fər-/ *vt* **-sook** /-'sʊk/, **-saken** /-'seɪkən/ *lit* DESERT² (2)

fort /fɔːt ‖ fɔːrt/ *n* 1 building for military defence 2 **hold the fort** look after everything while someone is away

for·te /'fɔːteɪ ‖ fɔːrt/ *n* something someone does particularly well

forth /fɔːθ ‖ fɔːrθ/ *adv lit* 1 forward 2 **and (so on and) so forth** etc.

forth·com·ing /ˌfɔːθ'kʌmɪŋ◂ ‖ ˌfɔːrθ-/ *adj* 1 happening soon 2 supplied when needed: *No answer was forthcoming.* 3 ready to be helpful

forth·right /'fɔːθraɪt ‖ 'fɔːrθ-/ *adj* speaking plainly; direct

forth·with /fɔːθ'wɪθ, -'wɪθ ‖ fɔːrθ-/ *adv fml* at once

for·ti·eth /'fɔːtiəθ ‖ 'fɔːr-/ *determiner, n, pron, adj* 40th

for·ti·fy /'fɔːtɨfaɪ ‖ 'fɔːr-/ *vt* 1 strengthen against attack 2 make stronger: *fortified wine* –**fication** /ˌfɔːtɨfɨ'keɪʃən ‖ ˌfɔːr-/ *n* 1 [C] towers, etc. for defence 2 [U] act of fortifying

for·ti·tude /'fɔːtɨtjuːd ‖ 'fɔːrtɨtuːd/ *n* [U] uncomplaining courage

fort·night /'fɔːtnaɪt ‖ 'fɔːrt-/ *n BrE* two weeks ~**ly** *adj, adv* happening once a fortnight

for·tress /'fɔːtrɨs ‖ 'fɔːrt-/ *n* large fort

for·tu·i·tous /fɔː'tjuːɨtəs ‖ fɔːr'tuː-/ *adj fml* accidental

for·tu·nate /'fɔːtʃənət ‖ 'fɔːr-/ *adj* lucky ~**ly** *adv*

for·tune /'fɔːtʃən ‖ 'fɔːr-/ *n* 1 [C;U] good or bad luck 2 [C] that which will happen to a person in the future: *tell someone's fortune* 3 [C] great sum of money: *diamonds worth a fortune* 4 **a small fortune** a lot of money

fortune-tell·er /'·· ˌ·/ *n* person who claims to be able to tell people their future

for·ty /'fɔːti ‖ 'fɔːrti/ *determiner, n, pron* 40

forty winks /ˌ·· '·/ *n* [P] short sleep in the day time

for·um /'fɔːrəm/ *n* place for public argument

for·ward¹ /'fɔːwəd ‖ 'fɔːrwərd/ *adj* 1 towards the front or future 2 advanced in development 3 too bold often in sexual matters ♦ *vt* 1 send (letters, etc.) to a new address 2 *fml* send (goods) ♦ *n* attacking player in football, etc. ~**ness** *n* [U] being FORWARD¹ (2, 3)

forward² *adv* also **forwards** — towards the front or future

for·went /fɔː'went ‖ fɔːr-/ *past t. of* FORGO

fos·sil /'fɒsəl ‖ 'fɑː-/ *n* 1 part or print of an ancient animal or plant, preserved in rock, ice, etc. 2 old person with unchanging ideas ~**ize**, **-ise** *vi/t* 1 change into a fossil 2 (cause to) become very fixed (in ideas, etc.)

fossil fuel /ˌ·· '·/ *n* [C,U] fuel such as coal, formed from decayed plant or animal remains

fos·ter¹ /'fɒstə ‖ 'fɔːstər, 'fɑː-/ *vt* 1 *fml* encourage to develop 2 take (a child) into one's home for a while

foster² *adj* (used to indicate that a child is being fostered): *the foster parents/child*

fought /fɔːt ‖ fɔːt/ *v past t. and p. of* FIGHT

foul¹ /faʊl/ *adj* 1 very unpleasant: *foul smell/language/weather* 2 **fall foul of** get into trouble with ~**ly** *adv*

foul² *n* act that is against the rules

foul³ *vi/t* 1 make dirty 2 be guilty of a FOUL².

foul up *phr vt infml* spoil (an occasion, etc.) **foul-up** /'·‿·/ *n*

foul play /ˌ· '·/ *n* [U] 1 (in sports) unfair play 2 criminal violence, esp. murder

found¹ /faʊnd/ *v past t. and p. of* FIND

found² *vt* 1 establish; build 2 base: *stories founded on fact* ~**er** *n* person who establishes something

foun·da·tion /faʊn'deɪʃən/ *n* 1 [U] founding of an organization 2 [U] BASIS: *rumours without foundation* 3 [C] organization that gives out money

foundations *n* [P] base that supports a building: (fig.) *the foundations of her success*

foundation stone /·'·· ‿·/ *n* first stone of a new building, often laid with public ceremony

found·er /'faʊndə ‖ -ər/ *vi* 1 *lit* (of ship)

sink 2 *fml* (of a plan) fail

foun·dry /'faʊndri/ *n* place where metal is melted and poured into shapes

fount /faʊnt/ *n lit* SOURCE

foun·tain /'faʊntən/ *n* 1 decorative structure from which water springs up 2 flow of liquid

fountain pen /'·· ·/ *n* pen that one fills with ink

four /fɔː‖fɔːr/ *determiner, n, pron* 4

four·teen /ˌfɔː'tiːn◂‖ˌfɔːr-/ *determiner, n, pron* 14 ~**th** *determiner, adv, n, pron* 14th

fourth /fɔːθ‖fɔːrθ/ *determiner, adv, n, pron* 4th

fowl /faʊl/ *n* **fowls** *or* **fowl** 1 farmyard bird, esp. a hen 2 any bird

fox /fɒks‖fɑːks/ *n* doglike wild animal, said to be clever ♦ *vt* confuse; deceive

fox·hole /'fɒks͵həʊl‖'fɑːks͵hoʊl/ *n* hole where soldiers hide from the enemy

fox·hunt·ing /'fɒkshʌntɪŋ‖'fɑːks-/ *n* [U] hunting of foxes by special dogs (**foxhounds**) and people on horses

foy·er /'fɔɪeɪ‖'fɔɪər/ *n* entrance hall of a theatre, etc.

frac·as /'frækɑː‖'freɪkəs/ *n fml* noisy quarrel

frac·tion /'frækʃən/ *n* 1 division of a whole number (e.g. ⅓) 2 small part: *a fraction of the cost* ~**al** *adj* so small as to be unimportant

frac·tious /'frækʃəs/ *adj* restless and complaining

frac·ture /'fræktʃə‖-ər/ *n* [C;U] *fml* breaking of a bone, etc. ♦ *vi/t fml* break

fra·gile /'frædʒaɪl‖-dʒəl/ *adj* 1 easily broken 2 having a small thin body or weak in health ~**gility** /frə'dʒɪlɪti/ *n* [U]

frag·ment¹ /'frægmənt/ *n* piece broken off ~**ary** *adj* incomplete

frag·ment² /fræg'ment‖'frægment/ *vi/t* break into pieces ~**ation** /ˌfrægmən'teɪʃən, -men-/ *n* [U]

fra·grant /'freɪgrənt/ *adj* sweet-smelling ~**ly** *adv* -**grance** *n* [C;U]

frail /freɪl/ *adj* weak, esp. in body ~**ty** *n* 1 [U] quality of being frail 2 [C] fault of character

frame /freɪm/ *n* 1 border into which something fits: *a window frame* 2 structure on which something is built 3 human or animal body 4 single photograph in a cinema film 5 **frame of mind** state of mind at a particular time ♦ *vt* 1 put in a FRAME (1) 2 give shape to; express: *frame a question* 3 *infml* make (a guiltless person) seem guilty of a crime

frame-up /'· ·/ *n infml* carefully prepared plan to FRAME (3) someone

frame·work /'freɪmwɜːk‖-wɜːrk/ *n* supporting structure

fran·chise /'fræntʃaɪz/ *n* 1 [S] the right to vote 2 [C] the right to sell a product

frank¹ /fræŋk/ *adj* open and honest ~**ly** *adv* ~**ness** *n* [U]

frank² *vt* stamp (a letter) by machine

fran·tic /'fræntɪk/ *adj* wildly anxious, afraid, happy, etc. ~**ally** /-kli/ *adv*

fra·ter·nal /frə'tɜːnl‖-ɜːr-/ *adj* BROTHERLY

fra·ter·ni·ty /frə'tɜːnɪti‖-ɜːr-/ *n* 1 [C] people joined by common interests 2 [U] *fml* brotherly feeling

frat·er·nize, **-ise** /'frætənaɪz‖-ər-/ *vi* meet and be friendly -**nization** /ˌfrætənaɪ-'zeɪʃən‖-tərnə-/ *n* [U]

fraud /frɔːd‖frɔːd/ *n* 1 [C;U] criminal deceit to make money 2 [C] person who falsely claims to be something

fraud·u·lent /'frɔːdʒələnt‖'frɔːdʒə-/ *adj* deceitful; got or done by fraud ~**ly** *adv*

fraught /frɔːt‖frɔːt/ *adj* 1 full of: *fraught with danger* 2 *infml* **a** (of a person) worried **b** (of conditions) difficult

fray¹ /freɪ/ *vi/t* develop loose threads by rubbing: *frayed collar* | (fig.) *frayed nerves*

fray² *n* [S] *lit* battle

freak¹ /friːk/ *n* 1 strange unnatural creature or event 2 person who takes a special interest in the stated thing: *a health freak* ♦ *adj* very unusual: *a freak accident* ~**ish** *adj* unreasonable; unusual

freak² *vi/t* also **freak out** *phr vi/t* (cause to) become very angry or frightened

freck·le /'frekəl/ *n* small brown spot on the skin **freckled** *adj*

free /friː/ *adj* 1 able to act as one wants: not in prison or controlled by rules: *free speech* | *You are free to go.* 2 not busy or being used: *Is this seat free?* | *free time* 3 without payment: *free tickets* 4 (of a way or passage) not blocked 5 not tight; loose 6 **free and easy** unworried 7 **free from/of** untroubled by; without: *free from dirt* | *tax free* 8 **free with** ready to give 9 **make free with** use (something) without respect or as if it is one's own ♦ *adv* 1 without payment

2 without control **3** in a loose position ♦ *vt*

freed /fri:d/ set free **~ly** *adv* **1** readily; openly **2** in great amounts

free·bie -bee /'fri:bi/ *n infml* something that is given or received without payment

free·dom /'fri:dəm/ *n* [U] **1** state of being free (1) **2** [*the*+S] certain rights, often given as an honour: *the freedom of the city*

free en·ter·prise /ˌ· '···/ *n* [U] social system in which private trade, business, etc. is carried on without much government control

free-for-all /ˌ· · '·/ *n* quarrel, etc. involving a lot of people

free hand /ˌ· '·/ *n* [S] unlimited freedom of action

free·hand /'fri:hænd/ *adj, adv* drawn without instruments

free·hold /'fri:həʊld ‖ -hoʊld/ *adj, adv, n* [C;U] (with) ownership of land or buildings without conditions

free·lance /'fri:lɑ:ns ‖ -læns/ *adj, adv, n* (done by) a writer, etc. who works for many employers **freelance** *vi* **-lancer** *n*

Free·ma·son /'fri:ˌmeɪsən, ˌfri:'meɪsən/ *n* man belonging to an ancient society whose members help each other

free-range /ˌ· '·◂/ *adj* being (produced by animals) kept under natural conditions

free rein /ˌ· '·/ *n* [U] complete freedom of action

free speech /ˌ· '·/ *n* [U] right to express one's ideas in public

free trade /ˌ· '·◂/ *n* [U] system of allowing foreign goods freely into a country

free verse /ˌ· '·/ *n* [U] poetry that does not follow the usual rules

free·way /'fri:weɪ/ *n AmE for* MOTORWAY

free·wheel /ˌfri:'wi:l/ *vi* travel downhill without using power **~ing** *adj infml* not greatly worrying about rules, responsibilities, etc.

free will /ˌ· '·/ *n* [U] **1** ability to decide freely what to do **2** belief that human effort can influence events, and they are not fixed in advance by God

freeze /fri:z/ *v* **froze** /frəʊz ‖ froʊz/, **frozen** /'frəʊzən ‖ 'froʊ-/ **1** *vi/t* harden into ice **2** *vi* (of weather) be at the temperature at which ice forms **3** *vi/t* stop working properly because of cold **4** *vi* feel very cold **5** *vt* preserve (food) at low temperatures **6** *vi/t* stop moving **7** *vt* fix

(prices, wages, etc.) ♦ *n* [U] **1** period of freezing weather **2** fixing of prices or wages **-zer** *n* machine that freezes food **-zing** *adj* very cold

freeze over *phr vi* turn to ice on the surface

freight /freɪt/ *n* [U] goods carried by ship, plane, etc. **~er** *n* ship or plane that carries goods

French fries /ˌfrentʃ 'fraɪz/ *n* [P] *esp. AmE* CHIPS (3)

French win·dows /ˌ· '··/ *n* [P] glass doors opening onto a garden, etc.

fre·net·ic /frəˈnetɪk/ *adj* overexcited; feverish

fren·zy /'frenzi/ *n* [S;U] violent excitement **-zied** *adj*

fre·quen·cy /'fri:kwənsi/ *n* **1** [U] the happening of something a large number of times **2** [C;U] rate at which something happens or is repeated **3** [C] particular number of radio waves per second

fre·quent¹ /'fri:kwənt/ *adj* happening often **~ly** *adv*

fre·quent² /frɪˈkwent ‖ frɪˈkwent, 'fri:kwənt/ *vt fml* go to (a place) often

fres·co /'freskəʊ ‖ -koʊ/ *n* **-coes** *or* **-cos** picture painted on wet PLASTER¹ (1)

fresh /freʃ/ *adj* **1** recently made, found, etc.; not STALE: *fresh flowers* **2** (of food) not frozen or tinned **3** (of water) not salt **4** new and different: *make a fresh start* **5 a** (of wind) rather strong **b** (of weather) cool and windy **6** not tired ♦ *adv* **1** just; newly **2 fresh out of** *infml, esp. AmE* having just used up one's supplies of **~ly** *adv* **~ness** *n* [U]

fresh·en /'freʃən/ *vi/t* **1** make or become fresh **2** (of wind) become stronger

freshen up *phr vi/t* (cause to) feel less tired, look more attractive, etc.

fresh·er /'freʃə ‖ -ər/ *n BrE* student in the first year at university or college

fresh·man /'freʃmən/ *n* **-men** /-mən/ *AmE* student in the first year at HIGH SCHOOL or college

fresh·wa·ter /ˌfreʃˈwɔ:tə◂ ‖ -ˈwɔːtər◂, -ˈwɑː-/ *adj* of a river or lake, not the sea

fret /fret/ *vi/t* **-tt-** worry about small things **~ful** *adj* anxious and complaining **~fully** *adv*

fri·ar /'fraɪə ‖ -ər/ *n* man belonging to a Christian religious group

fric·tion /'frɪkʃən/ n [U] 1 rubbing of one surface against another 2 disagreement within a group

Fri·day /'fraɪdi/ n the 5th day of the week —see also GOOD FRIDAY

fridge /frɪdʒ/ n cupboard where food is kept cold

fried /fraɪd/ past t. & p. of FRY

friend /frend/ n 1 person whom one likes but who is not related 2 helper; supporter 3 **make friends** form a friendship ~**less** adj without friends ~**ly** adj 1 acting as a friend 2 not causing unpleasant feelings in competitions, etc.: a friendly game ~**liness** n [U] ~**ship** n [C;U] friendly relationship

fries /fraɪz/ n —see FRENCH FRIES

frieze /fri:z/ n decorative border along a wall

frig·ate /'frɪgɪt/ n small fast warship

fright /fraɪt/ n [C;U] feeling of fear

fright·en /'fraɪtn/ vt fill with fear ~**ed** adj ~**ingly** adv

fright·ful /'fraɪtfəl/ adj terrible; very bad ~**ly** adv

fri·gid /'frɪdʒɪd/ adj 1 (of a woman) disliking sex 2 very cold ~**ly** adv –**gidity** /frɪ'dʒɪdɪti/ n [U]

frill /frɪl/ n 1 decorative wavy edge on cloth 2 unnecessary decoration ~**y** adj

fringe /frɪndʒ/ n 1 decorative edge of hanging threads on a curtain, etc. 2 BrE hair hanging over the forehead 3 edge: the fringe(s) of the crowd 4 not official; not CONVENTIONAL: fringe theatre ♦ vt be the border of

fringe ben·e·fit /'· ˌ··/ n something given with a job, besides wages

frisk /frɪsk/ v 1 vi jump about playfully 2 vt search (someone) with the hands, for hidden weapons ~**y** adj joyfully playful

fris·son /'fri:sɒn ‖ fri:'soun/ n feeling of excitement caused by fear

frit·ter[1] /'frɪtə ‖ -ər/ n piece of cooked BATTER[2] with fruit, meat, etc. inside

fritter[2] v fritter away phr vt waste: He fritters away his money.

fri·vol·i·ty /frɪ'vɒlɪti ‖ -'vɑ:-/ n 1 [U] quality of being frivolous 2 [C] frivolous act or remark

friv·o·lous /'frɪvələs/ adj not serious enough; silly ~**ly** adv

frizz·y /'frɪzi/ adj (of hair) very curly, like wool

fro /frəʊ ‖ froʊ/ adv —see TO AND FRO

frock /frɒk/ n woman's dress

frog /frɒg ‖ frɑ:g, frɔ:g/ n 1 small jumping creature that lives on land and in water 2 **a frog in the/one's throat** difficulty in speaking because of roughness in the throat

frog·man /'frɒgmən ‖ 'frɑ:g-, 'frɔ:g-/ n -**men** /-mən/ skilled underwater swimmer who uses breathing apparatus

frog·march /'frɒgmɑ:tʃ ‖ 'frɑ:gmɑ:rtʃ, 'frɔ:g-/ vt force (a person) to move forward with the arms held together firmly from behind

frol·ic /'frɒlɪk ‖ 'frɑ:-/ vi -**ck**- jump about happily **frolic** n

from /frəm; strong frɒm ‖ frəm; strong frʌm, frɑ:m/ prep 1 starting at (a place or time): fly from London to Paris | work from Monday till Friday 2 given or sent by: a letter from John 3 away: subtract 10 from 15 4 using: Bread is made from flour. 5 because of: suffer from heart disease 6 out of: He took a knife from his pocket. 7 in a state of protection or prevention with regard to: She saved the child from drowning. 8 judging by: From what John tells me, they're very rich.

frond /frɒnd ‖ frɑ:nd/ n leaf of a FERN or PALM[1]

front /frʌnt/ n 1 [C] part in the direction that something moves or faces: the front of the aircraft/of the house | his front teeth 2 [C] line where fighting takes place in war 3 [the+S] road beside the sea in a holiday town 4 [C] line dividing cold from warmer air 5 [C] (often false) outward appearance: present a smiling front 6 [C] combined effort or movement against opposing forces: present a united front 7 [C] particular area of activity: They have made little progress on the employment front. 8 [C] infml person, group, or thing used for hiding the real nature of a secret or unlawful activity 9 **in front: a** ahead **b** in the most forward position 10 **in front of: a** ahead of **b** in the presence of 11 **up front** infml as payment in advance ♦ vi/t face (towards): The hotel fronts onto the lake. ~**al** adj at, of, or from the front

front·age /'frʌntɪdʒ/ n front width of a building or piece of land

front·bench /ˌfrʌnt'bentʃ◄/ n either of

the two rows of seats in the British parliament on which the most important politicians of the two major parties sit **frontbencher** n

fron·tier /'frʌntɪə ‖ frʌn'tɪr/ n edge of a country **frontiers** n [P] furthest limit: *the frontiers of knowledge*

front line /,· '·◄/ n [S] 1 military FRONT (2) 2 most advanced position **front-line** adj

front man /'· ·/ n someone who explains the views or future plans of esp. a large company to the public

front-page /'· ·/ adj worthy of being on the front page of a newspaper: *front-page news*

front-run·ner /,· '··/ n person who has the best chance of success in competing for something

frost /frɒst ‖ frɔːst/ n 1 [U] white powder that forms on things below freezing point 2 [C;U] (period of) freezing weather ♦ v 1 vi/t (cause to) become covered with frost 2 vt roughen the surface of (glass) **~y** adj 1 very cold 2 unfriendly: *a frosty greeting*

frost·bite /'frɒstbaɪt ‖ 'frɔːst-/ n [U] harmful swelling etc. of the limbs, caused by cold **–bitten** adj

froth /frɒθ ‖ frɔːθ/ n [U] 1 mass of small BUBBLES on beer, etc. 2 derog light empty show of talk or ideas ♦ vi produce froth **~y** adj covered with froth

frown /fraʊn/ vi draw the EYEBROWS together in anger or effort **frown** n

froze /frəʊz ‖ froʊz/ v past t. of FREEZE

fro·zen /'frəʊzən ‖ 'froʊ-/ v past p. of FREEZE

fru·gal /'fruːgəl/ adj 1 not wasteful 2 small and cheap: *frugal supper*

fruit /fruːt/ n 1 [C;U] seed-containing part of a plant, often eatable 2 [C] also **fruits** pl. result or reward ♦ vi bear fruit **~ful** adj useful; successful **~fully** adv **~less** adj unsuccessful **–lessly** adv **~y** adj 1 like fruit 2 (of a voice) rich and deep

fru·i·tion /fruː'ɪʃən/ n [U] fml fulfilment of plans, etc.

fruit ma·chine /'· ·,·/ n BrE ONE-ARMED BANDIT

frus·trate /frʌ'streɪt ‖ 'frʌstreɪt/ vt 1 disappoint and annoy 2 prevent the fulfilment of (plans) **–tration** /frʌ'streɪ-ʃən/ n [C;U]

fry /fraɪ/ vi/t cook in hot fat or oil **fry** n

—see SMALL FRY

frying pan /'·· ·/ n 1 flat pan for frying 2 **out of the frying pan into the fire** out of a bad position into an even worse one

ft written abbrev. for: FOOT¹ (3)

fuck /fʌk/ vi/t taboo have sex (with) ♦ n taboo sl 1 act of having sex 2 **not give a fuck** not to care at all

fuck off phr vi taboo sl go away

fuck up phr vt taboo sl spoil; ruin ♦ **fuck-up** /'· ·/ n

fudge¹ /fʌdʒ/ n [U] creamy brown sweet made of sugar, milk, butter, etc.

fudge² v 1 vt put together roughly or dishonestly 2 vi/t avoid taking firm action (on)

fuel /fjʊəl ‖ 'fjuːəl/ n [C;U] material (e.g. coal) that produces heat or power ♦ v **-ll-** BrE **-l-** AmE 1 vt provide with fuel 2 vi take in fuel

fugitive /'fjuːdʒətɪv/ n person escaping from something

ful·crum /'fʊlkrəm, 'fʌl-/ n **-crums** or **-cra** /-krə/ point on which a LEVER turns

ful·fil also **-fill** AmE /fʊl'fɪl/ vt **-ll-** 1 perform (a promise, duty, etc.) 2 develop fully the character and abilities of (oneself) **~ment** n [U]

full /fʊl/ adj 1 holding as much or as many as possible: *full bottle/train* 2 well fed 3 complete: *your full name* 4 highest possible: *full speed* 5 (of a garment) loose: *full skirt* 6 rounded; PLUMP 7 **full of** thinking only of ♦ n 1 **in full** completely 2 **to the full** thoroughly ♦ adv 1 straight; directly: *The sun shone full on her face.* 2 very: *They knew full well he wouldn't keep his promise.* **-ly** adv 1 at least: *It's fully an hour since he left.* 2 completely **~ness, fulness** n [U]

full-blown /,· '·◄/ adj 1 (of a flower) completely open 2 fully developed: *a full-blown war*

full-grown /,· '·◄/ adj completely developed

full-length /,· '·◄/ adj 1 (of a painting, etc.) showing someone from head to foot 2 not shorter than usual

full moon /,· '·/ n the moon when seen as a full round shape

full-scale /,· '·◄/ adj 1 (of a model, etc.) as big as the object represented 2 (of an activity) not lessened: *full-scale war*

full stop /ˌ· '·/ n 1 a mark (.) showing esp. the end of a sentence 2 **come to a full stop** stop completely

full-time /ˌ· '·◄/ adj working or studying all the usual hours

fully-fledged /ˌ·· '·◄/ adj 1 (of a bird) having grown all its feathers 2 completely trained

ful·some /'fulsəm/ adj praising too much

fum·ble /'fʌmbəl/ vi use the hands awkwardly

fume /fjuːm/ vi show great anger

fumes /fjuːmz/ n [P] strong-smelling gas or smoke

fu·mi·gate /'fjuːmɪɡeɪt/ vt disinfect by means of smoke or gas

fun /fʌn/ n [U] 1 playfulness 2 (cause of) amusement; enjoyment 3 **for fun** also **for the fun of it** — for pleasure 4 **in fun** not seriously 5 **make fun of** laugh unkindly at

func·tion /'fʌŋkʃən/ n 1 natural purpose of something or someone 2 important social gathering ♦ vi be in action; work ~**al** adj 1 made for use, not decoration 2 functioning

fund /fʌnd/ n supply of money for a purpose ♦ vt provide money for

fun·da·men·tal /ˌfʌndə'mentl◄/ adj central; very important: *fundamental difference* ♦ n basic rule ~**ly** adv ~**ism** n [U] belief in the exact truth of the Bible ~**ist** n, adj

fu·ne·ral /'fjuːnərəl/ n ceremony of burying or burning a dead person

fun·fair /'fʌnfeə‖-fer/ n esp. BrE travelling show, with amusements and machines to ride on

fun·gi·cide /'fʌndʒɪsaɪd/ n [C;U] chemical for destroying fungus

fun·gus /'fʌŋɡəs/ n -**gi** /-dʒaɪ, -ɡaɪ/ or -**guses** [C;U] leafless plant that grows on wood, etc.

fu·nic·u·lar /fjʊ'nɪkjʊlə‖-ər/ n mountain railway worked by a rope

funk·y /'fʌŋki/ adj infml 1 (of music) having a strong beat 2 AmE attractive and fashionable

fun·nel /'fʌnl/ n 1 wide-mouthed tube for pouring liquids through 2 chimney on a steam engine or steamship ♦ vi/t -**ll**- BrE ‖-**l**- AmE pass (as if) through a FUNNEL (1)

fun·ny /'fʌni/ adj 1 amusing 2 strange -**nily** adv

funny bone /'·· ·/ n tender part of the elbow

fur /fɜː‖fɜːr/ n 1 [U] soft thick hair of a cat, rabbit, etc. 2 [C] (garment made of) the fur-covered skin of an animal 3 [U] hard covering on the inside of pots, hot-water pipes, etc. ~**ry** adj

fu·ri·ous /'fjʊəriəs‖'fjʊr-/ adj 1 very angry 2 wild; uncontrolled ~**ly** adv

fur·long /'fɜːlɒŋ‖'fɜːrlɔːŋ/ n a measure of length equal to 220 yards (201 metres)

fur·nace /'fɜːnɪs‖'fɜːr-/ n 1 enclosed space where metals, etc. are heated 2 enclosed fire to make hot water

fur·nish /'fɜːnɪʃ‖'fɜːr-/ vt 1 put furniture in 2 fml supply ~**ings** n [P] furniture, etc. for a room

fur·ni·ture /'fɜːnɪtʃə‖'fɜːrnɪtʃər/ n [U] beds, chairs, etc.

fu·ro·re /fjʊ'rɔːri, 'fjʊərɔː‖'fjʊrɔːr/ n [S] sudden burst of public interest

fur·row /'fʌrəʊ‖'fɜːroʊ/ n 1 track cut by a PLOUGH 2 WRINKLE ♦ vt make furrows in

fur·ther /'fɜːðə‖'fɜːrðər/ adv, adj 1 (comparative of FAR) at or to a greater distance or more distant point: *too tired to walk any further* 2 more: *any further questions* 3 **further to** continuing the subject of 4 **go further** give, do, or say more ♦ vt help to advance ~**ance** n [U] fml advancement ~**most** adj farthest

further ed·u·ca·tion /ˌ·· ··''/ n [U] BrE education for people who have left school but are not at university

fur·ther·more /ˌfɜːðə'mɔː‖ 'fɜːrðərmɔːr/ adv fml also

fur·thest /'fɜːðɪst‖'fɜːr-/ adv, adj (superlative of FAR) at or to the greatest distance or degree

fur·tive /'fɜːtɪv‖'fɜːr-/ adj trying to escape notice ~**ly** adv ~**ness** n [U]

fu·ry /'fjʊəri‖'fjʊri/ n 1 [S;U] great anger 2 [U] wild force

fuse¹ /fjuːz/ n wire that melts to break an electric connection ♦ vi/t 1 stop working because a fuse has melted 2 join by melting

fuse² n part of a bomb, etc. that makes it explode

fu·se·lage /'fjuːzəlɑːʒ‖-sə-/ n body of an aircraft

fu·sil·lade /ˌfjuːzɪ'leɪd‖-sə-/ n rapid continuous firing of shots

fu·sion /'fjuːʒən/ n [C;U] join together by

melting: (fig.) *a fusion of different styles of music*

fuss /fʌs/ *n* [S;U] **1** unnecessary show of excitement or annoyance **2 make a fuss of** pay loving attention to ♦ *vi* show unnecessary anxiety **~y** *adj* **1** too concerned about details **2** (of dress, etc.) overdecorated

fus·ty /ˈfʌsti/ *adj* **1** old and smelling bad **2** old-fashioned

fu·tile /ˈfjuːtaɪl‖-tl/ *adj* unsuccessful; useless: *futile attempts* **futility** /fjuːˈtɪlɪti/ *n* [U]

fu·ton /ˈfuːtɒn‖-tɑːn/ *n* soft MATTRESS used as a bed or folded into a seat

fu·ture /ˈfjuːtʃə‖-ər/ *n* **1** [S] time after the present: *in the future* **2** [C] that which will happen to someone or something: *an uncertain future* **3** [U] likelihood of success **4 in future** from now on **future** *adj*: *his future wife* | *the future tense*

fu·tur·is·tic /ˌfjuːtʃəˈrɪstɪk◄/ *adj* of strange modern design

fuzz /fʌz/ *n* [U] FLUFF **~y** *adj* **1** (of hair) standing up in a light short mass **2** (of cloth, etc.) having a raised soft hairy surface **–ily** *adv* **-iness** *n* [U] **3** not clear in shape

FYI *AmE abbrev. for:* For Your Information

G

G, g /dʒiː/ the 7th letter of the English alphabet

g *written abbrev. for:* GRAM(s)

gab /gæb/ *n* —see **the gift of the gab** (GIFT)

gab·ar·dine, **-erdine** /ˈgæbədiːn, ˌgæbəˈgæbərdiːn/ *n* **1** [U] strong cloth **2** [C] raincoat made from this

gab·ble /ˈgæbəl/ *vi/t* speak or say too quickly to be heard **gabble** *n* [S]

ga·ble /ˈgeɪbəl/ *n* three-cornered top of a wall between sloping roofs

gad /gæd/ *v* **gad about** *phr vi* travel for enjoyment

gad·get /ˈgædʒɪt/ *n* small useful machine or tool **~ry** *n* [U] gadgets

Gae·lic /ˈgeɪlɪk, ˈgælɪk/ *adj, n* [U] (of or being) any of the CELTIC languages, esp. those of Scotland, Ireland, or the Isle of Man

gaffe /gæf/ *n* social mistake

gaf·fer /ˈgæfə‖-ər/ *n* man in charge, esp. of lighting for a film

gag /gæg/ *n* **1** something put over someone's mouth to stop them from talking **2** joke ♦ *vt* **-gg-** put a GAG (1) on

ga·ga /ˈgɑːgɑː/ *adj* SENILE

gage /geɪdʒ/ *n, v AmE for* GAUGE

gag·gle /ˈgægəl/ *n* [S] **1** group of GEESE **2** group of noisy people

gai·e·ty /ˈgeɪɪti/ *n* [U] cheerfulness

gai·ly /ˈgeɪli/ *adv* cheerfully

gain¹ /geɪn/ *v* **1** *vi/t* obtain (something useful) **2** *vi* (of a clock) go too fast **3** *vt fml* reach (a place) with effort

   gain on/upon *phr vt* get close to (someone ahead in a race)

gain² *n* [C;U] increase in wealth or amount **~ful** *adj* paid for: *gainful employment* **~fully** *adv*

gain·say /ˌgeɪnˈseɪ/ *vt* **-said** /-ˈsed/ *fml* DENY

gait /geɪt/ *n* way of walking

gal /gæl/ *n* girl

ga·la /ˈgɑːlə‖ˈgeɪlə, ˈgælə/ *n* special public entertainment

gal·ax·y /ˈgæləksi/ *n* large group of stars **–actic** /gəˈlæktɪk/ *adj*

gale /geɪl/ *n* **1** strong wind **2** noisy burst of laughter, etc.

gall¹ /gɔːl‖gɒːl/ *n* [U] daring rudeness

gall² *vt* cause to feel annoyed disappointment or anger

gal·lant /ˈgælənt/ *adj* **1** brave **2** /gəˈlænt, ˈgælənt‖gəˈlænt, gəˈlɑːnt/ (of a man) polite to women **~ly** *adv* **~ry** /ˈgæləntri/ *n* [U]

gall blad·der /ˈ ˌ-/ *n* baglike organ in which BILE is stored

gal·le·on /ˈgæliən/ *n* (esp. Spanish) sailing ship of the 15th to 18th centuries

gal·le·ry /ˈgæləri/ *n* **1** place where works of art are shown **2** upper floor of a hall or church **3** passage in a mine **4** top floor in a theatre

gal·ley /ˈgæli/ *n* **1** ancient ship rowed by slaves **2** ship's kitchen

Gal·lic /'gælɪk/ *adj* typical of France

gal·li·vant /'gælɪvænt/ *vi* GAD about

gal·lon /'gælən/ *n* a (measure for liquids equal to) **a** (in Britain) 4 QUARTS **b** (in America) 231 CUBIC inches

gal·lop /'gæləp/ *n* [S] movement of a horse at its fastest speed **gallop** *vi/t*

gal·lows /'gæləʊz ‖ -loʊz/ *n* **gallows** wooden frame on which criminals were once killed by hanging

gallows hu·mour /'·· ,·'·/ *n* [U] *lit* jokes about the unpleasant side of life

gall·stone /'gɔːlstəʊn ‖ 'gɔːlstoʊn/ *n* hard stone or grain that forms in the GALL BLADDER

ga·lore /gə'lɔː ‖ -'lɔːr/ *adj* in plenty: *bargains galore*

gal·va·nize, **-nise** /'gælvənaɪz/ *vt* 1 cover (another metal) with ZINC **2** shock into action

gam·bit /'gæmbɪt/ *n* action done to produce a future advantage, esp. an opening move in a game, conversation, etc.

gam·ble /'gæmbəl/ *v* 1 *vi/t* BET (1) **2** *vi* take a risk ♦ *n* [S] risky matter **–bler** *n*

gam·bol /'gæmbəl/ *vi* **-ll-** *BrE* ‖ **-l-** *AmE* jump about in play

game /geɪm/ *n* 1 [C] form of play or sport **2** [C] single part of a match in tennis, etc. **3** [U] wild animals and birds hunted for food and sport **4** [C] *infml* secret trick: *give the game away* (=let a secret plan be known) **5** [C] *infml* profession or activity: *the advertising game* —see also FAIR GAME ♦ *adj* brave and willing **~ly** *adv* **games** *n* [P] sports competitions

game·keep·er /'geɪm,kiːpə ‖ -ər/ *n* man who looks after GAME (3), esp. birds

games·man·ship /'geɪmzmənʃɪp/ *n* [U] art of winning by using rules to one's own advantage but without cheating

gam·mon /'gæmən/ *n* [U] smoked or salted HAM (1)

gam·ut /'gæmət/ *n* [S] whole range of a subject

gan·der /'gændə ‖ -ər/ *n* male GOOSE

gang¹ /gæŋ/ *n* 1 group of people working together, esp. criminals **2** group of friends

gang² *v* **gang up** *phr vi* work together (against someone); CONSPIRE

gang·land /'gæŋlænd/ *adj* connected with organized groups of criminals: *gangland killings*

gang·ling /'gæŋglɪŋ/ *adj* tall, thin, and awkward

gang·plank /'gæŋplæŋk/ *n* movable bridge for getting into or out of a ship

gan·grene /'gæŋgriːn/ *n* [U] decay of a body part because blood has stopped flowing there **–grenous** /-grɪnəs/ *adj*

gang·ster /'gæŋstə ‖ -ər/ *n* member of a criminal GANG (1)

gang·way /'gæŋweɪ/ *n* 1 large gangplank **2** *BrE* passage between rows of seats

gan·try /'gæntri/ *n* frame supporting movable heavy machinery

gaol /dʒeɪl/ *n, v BrE for* JAIL **~er** *n*

gaol·bird /'dʒeɪlbɜːd ‖ -bɜːrd/ *n BrE for* JAILBIRD

gap /gæp/ *n* empty space between two things: (fig.) *gaps in my knowledge*

gape /geɪp/ *vi* 1 look hard in surprise **2** come apart: *gaping hole*

gar·age /'gærɑːʒ, -ɪdʒ ‖ gə'rɑːʒ/ *n* 1 building in which motor vehicles are kept **2** place that repairs them, and sells petrol and oil ♦ *vt* put in a garage

garb /gɑːb ‖ gɑːrb/ *n* [U] *fml* clothes

gar·bage /'gɑːbɪdʒ ‖ 'gɑːr-/ *n* [U] *esp. AmE for* RUBBISH

garbage can /'·· ·/ *n AmE for* DUSTBIN

gar·ble /'gɑːbəl ‖ 'gɑːr-/ *vt* give a confused description of

gar·den /'gɑːdn ‖ 'gɑːr-/ *n* 1 piece of land for growing flowers and vegetables **2** also **gardens** *pl.* — public park **3** lead someone up the garden path trick someone into believing what is not true and acting on it ♦ *vi* work in a garden **~er** *n*

garden par·ty /'·· ,·/ *n* formal party held in a garden

gar·gan·tu·an /gɑː'gæntʃuən ‖ gɑːr-/ *adj* extremely large

gar·gle /'gɑːgəl ‖ 'gɑːr-/ *vi* wash the throat by blowing through liquid ♦ *n* 1 [S] act of gargling **2** [C;U] liquid for gargling

gar·goyle /'gɑːgɔɪl ‖ 'gɑːr-/ *n* hollow figure of an ugly creature on a church roof, through which rain water runs away

gar·ish /'geərɪʃ ‖ 'ger-/ *adj* unpleasantly bright **~ly** *adv*

gar·land /'gɑːlənd ‖ 'gɑːr-/ *n* circle of flowers for decoration ♦ *vt* put garlands on

gar·lic /'gɑːlɪk ‖ 'gɑːr-/ *n* [U] plant like an onion, used in cooking

gar·ment /'gɑːmənt ‖ 'gɑːr-/ *n fml* article

of clothing

gar·ner /'gɑːnə ‖ 'gɑːrnər/ vt lit collect

gar·net /'gɑːnɪt ‖ 'gɑːr-/ n red jewel

gar·nish /'gɑːnɪʃ ‖ 'gɑːr-/ vt decorate (food) ♦ n something used to garnish

gar·ret /'gærɪt/ n lit small usu. unpleasant room at the top of a house

gar·ri·son /'gærɪsən/ n 1 soldiers living in a town or fort 2 fort or camp where such soldiers live ♦ vt (send a group of soldiers to) guard (a place)

gar·rotte /gə'rɒt ‖ gə'rɑːt/ vt STRANGLE, esp. with a metal collar or wire

gar·ru·lous /'gærələs/ adj fml talking too much ~ly adv

gar·ter /'gɑːtə ‖ 'gɑːrtər/ n elastic band to keep a STOCKING up

gas /gæs/ n -ss- or -s- 1 [C;U] substance like air 2 [U] gas used for heating, cooking, poisoning, etc. 3 [U] AmE petrol ♦ v 1 vt kill with gas 2 vi infml talk a long time ~eous /'gæsɪəs/ adj of or like gas

gas·bag /'gæsbæg/ n infml person who talks too much

gas fit·ter /'· ͵·· / n workman who puts in gas pipes, repairs cookers, etc.

gash /gæʃ/ vt, n (wound with) a long deep cut

gas·ket /'gæskɪt/ n flat piece of material placed between surfaces to prevent oil, etc. from escaping

gas·man /'gæsmæn/ n -men /-men/ official who visits houses to see how much gas has been used

gas mask /'·· / n breathing apparatus that protects the wearer against poisonous gas

gas·o·line, -lene /'gæsəliːn/ n [U] AmE for PETROL

gasp /gɑːsp ‖ gæsp/ v 1 vi breathe quickly and with effort 2 vt say while gasping **gasp** n

gas sta·tion /'· ͵·· / n AmE for FILLING STATION

gas·sy /'gæsi/ adj full of gas –**siness** n [U]

gas·tric /'gæstrɪk/ adj of the stomach: gastric juices

gas·tri·tis /gæ'straɪtɪs/ n [U] painful swelling of the lining of the stomach

gas·tro·en·te·ri·tis /͵gæstrəʊ-entə'-raɪtɪs ‖ -trou-/ n [U] swelling of the stomach lining and bowels

gas·tro·nom·ic /͵gæstrə'nɒmɪk◂/ adj connected with cooking and eating good food **gastronomy** n [U]

gas·works /'gæswɜːks ‖ -wɜːrks/ n gasworks place where gas is made from coal

gate /geɪt/ n 1 frame closing an opening in a wall, fence, etc. 2 way in or out at an airport 3 (money paid by) the number of people attending a match, etc.

gâ·teau /'gætəʊ ‖ gɑː'toʊ/ n -teaux /-təʊz ‖ -'toʊz/ [C;U] large rich cake

gate·crash /'geɪtkræʃ/ vi/t go to (a party) uninvited ~**er** n

gate·post /'geɪtpəʊst ‖ -poʊst/ n post from which a gate is hung

gate·way /'geɪt-weɪ/ n 1 [C] opening for a gate 2 [S] way of finding: the gateway to success

gath·er /'gæðə ‖ -ər/ v 1 vi/t come or bring together 2 vt obtain gradually: gather facts/speed 3 vt collect (flowers, crops, etc.) 4 vt understand: I gather she's ill. 5 vt draw (cloth) into small folds: gathered skirt ~**ing** n meeting

gauche /gəʊʃ ‖ goʊʃ/ adj socially awkward

gau·dy /'gɔːdi ‖ 'gɔːdi/ adj too bright; overdecorated –**dily** adv

gauge also **gage** AmE /geɪdʒ/ n 1 instrument for measuring 2 thickness or width of e.g. a gun barrel 3 distance between the RAILS of a railway ♦ vt 1 measure 2 make a judgment about

gaunt /gɔːnt ‖ gɔːnt/ adj 1 thin, as if ill or hungry 2 (of a place) bare and unattractive ~**ness** n [U]

gaunt·let /'gɔːntlɪt ‖ 'gɔːnt-/ n long GLOVE protecting the wrist

gauze /gɔːz ‖ gɔːz/ n [U] thin net-like cloth

gave /geɪv/ v past t. of GIVE

gav·el /'gævəl/ n small hammer used by a chairman, etc. to get attention

gawk /gɔːk ‖ gɔːk/ vi infml GAWP

gaw·ky /'gɔːki ‖ 'gɔːki/ adj awkward in movement –**kiness** n [U]

gawp /gɔːp ‖ gɔːp/ vi look at something in a foolish way

gay /geɪ/ adj 1 HOMOSEXUAL 2 bright: gay colours 3 cheerful ♦ n GAY (1) person

gaze /geɪz/ vi look steadily ♦ n [S] steady fixed look

ga·zette /gə'zet/ n official government newspaper giving important notices, etc.

ga·zump /gə'zʌmp/ vt BrE cheat

(someone who has agreed to buy a house) by selling it to someone else who offers more money

GB /ˌdʒiː ˈbiː/ *abbrev. for:* GREAT BRITAIN

GCSE /ˌdʒiː siː es ˈiː/ *n abbrev. for:* General Certificate of Secondary Education; examination taken by students aged 15 or 16 in Britain

GDP /ˌdʒiː diː ˈpiː/ *n [the+S] abbrev. for:* Gross Domestic Product; the total value of everything produced in a country, usu. in a single year, except for income received from abroad

gear[1] /ɡɪə‖ɡɪr/ *n* 1 [C;U] set of toothed wheels in a machine 2 [U] equipment: *football gear* 3 [U] apparatus of wheels, etc.: *the landing gear of an aircraft*

gear[2] *v*

gear to *phr vt* allow (an activity or action) to be influenced by (a particular fact): *education geared to the needs of industry*

gear up *phr vt infml* put (esp. oneself) into a state of excited or anxious expectation

gear·box /ˈɡɪəbɒks‖ˈɡɪrbɑːks/ *n* case containing the gears of a vehicle

gear le·ver /ˈ· ˌ··/ *n* rod that controls the gears of a vehicle

geese /ɡiːs/ *n pl. of* GOOSE

Gei·ger count·er /ˈɡaɪɡə ˌkaʊntə‖ -ɡər ˌkaʊntər/ *n* instrument that measures RADIOACTIVITY

gei·sha /ˈɡeɪʃə/ *n* Japanese woman whose job is to entertain men

gel[1] /dʒel/ *n* [C; U] thick wet JELLYlike substance, esp. one used to fix a hairstyle

gel[2] *vi* -ll- 1 (of liquid) become thicker 2 (of ideas) become more definite 3 (of people) begin to work together

gel·a·tine /ˈdʒelətiːn‖ -tn/ also **-tin** /-tn‖ -tn/ *AmE* — *n* [U] gluey material used in making jelly

geld /ɡeld/ *vt* remove the sexual organs of (certain male animals) ~**ing** *n* gelded animal, esp. a horse

gel·ig·nite /ˈdʒelɪɡnaɪt/ *n* [U] powerful explosive

gem /dʒem/ *n* 1 jewel 2 very valuable thing or person

gen /dʒen/ *n* [U] *BrE infml* information

gen·der /ˈdʒendə‖ -ər/ *n* [C;U] 1 (in grammar) (division into) MASCULINE, FEMININE, or NEUTER 2 division into male and female; sex

gene /dʒiːn/ *n* material in a cell controlling HEREDITY

ge·ne·al·o·gy /ˌdʒiːniˈælədʒi/ *n* [C;U] (study of) the history of a family, often shown in a drawing like a tree –**gical** /ˌdʒiːniəˈlɒdʒɪkəl◂‖ -ˈlɑː-/ *adj*

gen·e·ra /ˈdʒenərə/ *n pl. of* GENUS

gen·e·ral /ˈdʒenərəl/ *adj* 1 concerning all: *the general feeling* 2 not detailed: *a general idea* 3 (in titles) chief: *Postmaster-General ♦ n* 1 army or airforce officer of very high rank 2 **in general** usually ~**ly** *adv* 1 usually 2 by most people 3 without considering details –**rality** /ˌdʒenəˈræləti/ *n* 1 [C] general statement 2 [U] being general

general e·lec·tion /ˌ··· ˈ··/ *n* election in which the whole country takes part

gen·e·ral·ize -**ise** /ˈdʒenərəlaɪz/ *vi* make a general statement –**ization** /ˌdʒenərəlaɪˈzeɪʃən‖ -lə-/ *n* [C;U] (statement formed by) generalizing

gen·e·rate /ˈdʒenəreɪt/ *vt* produce: *generate heat* –**rator** *n* machine that generates esp. electricity –**rative** /ˈdʒenərətɪv/ *adj* able to produce

gen·e·ra·tion /ˌdʒenəˈreɪʃən/ *n* 1 [C] length of time in which a child grows up and has children 2 [C] people of about the same age 3 [U] act of generating

ge·ner·ic /dʒɪˈnerɪk/ *adj* shared by a whole class –**ally** /-kli/ *adv*

gen·e·ros·i·ty /ˌdʒenəˈrɒsəti‖ -ˈrɑː-/ *n* 1 [U] quality of being generous 2 [C] generous act

gen·e·rous /ˈdʒenərəs/ *adj* 1 giving freely 2 more than enough ~**ly** *adv*

gen·e·sis /ˈdʒenəsəs/ *n* [S] origin

genetic /dʒɪˈnetɪk/ *adj* relating to GENES or GENETICS –**ically** *adv*

genetic en·gin·eer·ing /·ˌ··· ··ˈ··/ *n* [U] science of changing plant or animal GENES

ge·net·ics /dʒɪˈnetɪks/ *n* [U] study of how the development of living things is affected by their GENES **geneticist** *n*

ge·ni·al /ˈdʒiːniəl/ *adj* cheerful and kind ~**ly** *adv*

ge·nie /ˈdʒiːni/ *n* (in stories) magic character who makes wishes come true

gen·i·tals /ˈdʒenətlz/ *n* [P] outer sex organs **genital** *adj*

ge·ni·us /ˈdʒiːniəs/ n 1 [U] great and rare powers of thought, skill, or imagination 2 [C] person with this ability 3 [S] special ability or skill: *She has a genius for saying the wrong thing.*

gen·o·cide /ˈdʒenəsaɪd/ n [U] killing of a whole race of people

gen·re /ˈʒɒnrə ‖ ˈʒɑːnrə/ n fml class; kind

gent /dʒent/ n sl gentleman **gents** n BrE men's public TOILET

gen·teel /dʒenˈtiːl/ adj extremely polite

gen·tile /ˈdʒentaɪl/ n, adj (sometimes cap.) (person who is) not Jewish

gen·til·i·ty /dʒenˈtɪləti/ n [U] being genteel

gen·tle /ˈdʒentl/ adj not rough or violent ~ness n [U] -tly adv

gen·tle·man /ˈdʒentlmən/ n -men /-mən/ 1 man who behaves well and can be trusted 2 any man 3 lit man of good but not noble family ~ly adj like a GENTLEMAN (1)

gentleman's a·gree·ment /ˌ··· ·ˈ·/ n unwritten agreement made between people who trust each other

gen·tle·wo·man /ˈdʒentlˌwʊmən/ n -women /-ˌwɪmɪn/ lady

gen·try /ˈdʒentri/ n [P] people of high social class

gen·u·flect /ˈdʒenjɵflekt/ vi fml bend one's knee in worship ~ion /ˌdʒenjɵˈflekʃən/ n [C;U]

gen·u·ine /ˈdʒenjuɵn/ adj real; true ~ly adv ~ness n [U]

ge·nus /ˈdʒiːnəs/ n genera /ˈdʒenərə/ division of plants or animals

ge·og·ra·phy /dʒiˈɒgrəfi, ˈdʒɒgrəfi ‖ dʒiˈɑːg-/ n [U] study of the countries of the world and of seas, towns, etc. -pher n -phical /ˌdʒiːəˈgræfɪkəl◄/ adj -phically /-kli/ adv

ge·ol·o·gy /dʒiˈɒlɒdʒi ‖ -ˈɑːli-/ n [U] study of the Earth's history as recorded in rocks -gist n -gical /ˌdʒiːəˈlɒdʒɪkəl◄ ‖ -ˈlɑː-/ adj -gically /-kli/ adv

ge·om·e·try /dʒiˈɒmɪtri ‖ -ˈɑːm-/ n [U] study of lines, angles, and surfaces and their relationships **geometric** /ˌdʒiːəˈmetrɪk◄/ adj **geometrical** /-kli/ adv

Geord·ie /ˈdʒɔːdi ‖ ˈdʒɔːr-/ n person from northeast England

ge·ri·at·rics /ˌdʒeriˈætrɪks/ n [U] medical care of old people **geriatric** adj

germ /dʒɜːm ‖ dʒɜːrm/ n 1 bacterium

carrying disease 2 beginning of an idea, etc.

ger·mane /dʒɜːˈmeɪn ‖ dʒɜːr-/ adj fml RELEVANT

german mea·sles /ˌdʒɜːmən ˈmiːzəlz ‖ ˌdʒɜːr-/ n [U] infectious disease causing red spots

ger·mi·cide /ˈdʒɜːmɪsaɪd ‖ ˈdʒɜːr-/ n [C;U] chemical for killing germs

ger·mi·nate /ˈdʒɜːmɪneɪt ‖ ˈdʒɜːr-/ vi/t cause (a seed) to start growing **-nation** /ˌdʒɜːmɪˈneɪʃən ‖ ˌdʒɜːr-/ n [U]

ger·und /ˈdʒerənd/ n VERBAL NOUN

ges·ta·tion /dʒeˈsteɪʃən/ n [S;U] carrying of a young creature inside the mother's body

ges·tic·u·late /dʒeˈstɪkjɵleɪt/ vi wave the hands and arms about to express something **-lation** /dʒeˌstɪkjɵˈleɪʃən/ n [C;U]

ges·ture /ˈdʒestʃə ‖ -ər/ n 1 [C;U] movement of the body to express something 2 [C] action done to show one's feelings ♦ vi make a GESTURE (1)

get /get/ v got /gɒt ‖ gɑːt/, got esp. BrE ‖ gotten /ˈgɒtn ‖ ˈgɑːtn/ AmE; pres. p. getting 1 vt receive; obtain: get permission 2 vt collect; bring 3 vt catch (an illness) 4 vi/t (cause to) go or arrive: get home ‖ get my boots off 5 [+adj] become: get wed/married 6 vi come or bring to the stated degree of success: Now we're getting somewhere. 7 vt succeed in or be allowed: He's nice when you get to know him. ‖ I never get to drive the car. 8 vt prepare (a meal) 9 vt hear or understand: I don't get you. 10 vt confuse; PUZZLE: That's got you! 11 vt annoy: It's his attitude that gets me. 12 vt infml a punish or harm (someone) in return for harm they have done you: I'll get you for this! b catch or attack: The crocodiles will get them. 13 get (something) done: a cause something to be done: I must get these shoes mended. b experience something that happens to one: I got my hand caught in the door. 14 have got have: He's got red hair. 15 you get infml there is/are

get about/around phr vi 1 be able to move again after an illness 2 travel 3 also **get round** BrE — (of news, etc.) spread

get across/over phr vi/t (cause to) be understood

get along phr vi 1 make progress;

manage 2 GET on (2)

get around/round to *phr vt* find time for; do at last

get at *phr vt* 1 reach 2 mean; IMPLY 3 say unkind things

get away *phr vi* escape

get away with *phr vt* escape punishment for

get back *phr vi* 1 return 2 return to power after having lost it 3 speak or write to a person at a later time: *I can't tell you now, but I'll get back to you tomorrow.* 4 **get back at someone** also **get one's own back on someone** — punish someone in return for a wrong done to oneself

get by *phr vi* 1 continue to live; SURVIVE 2 be acceptable; be good enough but not very good

get down *phr vt* 1 swallow: *get the medicine down* 2 write down 3 DEPRESS: *This weather gets me down.*

get down to *phr vt* begin to work at

get in *phr v* 1 vi arrive: *The plane got in late.* 2 vt call (someone) to help 3 vt collect a supply of 4 vt enter (a vehicle) 5 vt say (something), esp. by interrupting a conversation

get into *phr vt* 1 develop (a bad condition): *get into trouble* 2 become accustomed to

get off *phr v* 1 vi leave; start 2 vi/t (cause to) escape punishment 3 vt leave a (public vehicle) 4 vt DISMOUNT

get off with *phr vt sl* start a (sexual) relationship with

get on *phr v* 1 vi progress 2 vi be friendly: *They don't get on together.*

get onto *phr vt* 1 CONTACT 2 begin to talk about something: *How did we get onto that subject?*

get out *phr v* 1 vi/t (cause to) escape 2 vi become known 3 gain from

get over *phr vt* 1 get better from (illness, etc.) 2 manage to deal with 3 reach the end of (usu. something unpleasant) 4 make clear; cause to be understood 5 I can't/couldn't get over I am/was very much surprised at

get round *phr vt* 1 avoid; CIRCUMVENT 2 persuade to do something

get through *phr v* 1 vi/t pass (an examination, etc.) 2 vi reach someone by telephone 3 vi finish 4 vi/t (cause to) be understood by someone

get together *phr vi* have a meeting or party

get up *phr v* 1 vi rise from bed 2 vt ORGANIZE 3 vt decorate or change the appearance of in the stated way

get up to *phr vt* 1 do (something bad) 2 reach

get·a·way /ˈɡetəweɪ/ *n* [S] escape

get-to·geth·er /ˈ··ˌ··/ *n* friendly informal meeting for enjoyment

get·up /ˈɡetʌp/ *n* set of clothes

get-up-and-go /ˌ···ˈ·/ *n* [U] *infml* forceful active quality of mind

gey·ser /ˈɡiːzə/ ‖ ˈɡaɪzər/ *n* 1 natural spring of hot water 2 *BrE* bathroom apparatus for heating water by gas

ghast·ly /ˈɡɑːstli ‖ ˈɡæstli/ *adj* 1 very bad; terrible 2 pale and ill-looking

gher·kin /ˈɡɜːkɪn ‖ ˈɡɜːr-/ *n* small green CUCUMBER

ghet·to /ˈɡetəʊ ‖ -toʊ/ *n* -tos *or* -toes part of a city where poor people or foreigners live

ghetto-blast·er /ˈ·· ˌ··/ *n* large TAPE RECORDER that can be carried around

ghost /ɡəʊst ‖ ɡoʊst/ *n* 1 (spirit of) a dead person who appears again 2 also **ghost writer** /ˈ· ˌ··/ — person who writes material which another person gives out as his own 3 **give up the ghost** die 4 **the ghost of a** the slightest ~**ly** *adj* like a ghost ♦ *vt* write (something) as a GHOST (2)

ghost town /ˈ· ·/ *n* empty town that was once busy

ghoul /ɡuːl/ *n* person who likes thinking about dead bodies and nasty things ~**ish** *adj*

GI /ˌdʒiː ˈaɪ/ *n* US soldier

gi·ant /ˈdʒaɪənt/ *n* big strong person or creature ♦ *adj* very large

gib·ber /ˈdʒɪbə ‖ -ər/ *vi* talk very fast and meaninglessly

gib·ber·ish /ˈdʒɪbərɪʃ/ *n* [U] meaningless talk

gib·bet /ˈdʒɪbɪt/ *n* GALLOWS

gib·bon /ˈɡɪbən/ *n* animal like a monkey with no tail and long arms

gibe, jibe /dʒaɪb/ *n* remark that makes someone look foolish ♦ *v* **gibe at** *phr vt*

gib·lets /ˈdʒɪblɪts/ *n* [P] bird's heart, etc. taken out before cooking

gid·dy /ˈɡɪdi/ *adj* 1 having a feeling of unsteady movement 2 (of a person) not serious **–diness** n [U]

gift /gɪft/ n **1** something given freely **2** TALENT: *a gift for music* **3 the gift of the gab** *infml* the ability to speak well continuously, and esp. to persuade people **~ed** *adj* TALENTED

gift horse /ˈ· ·/ n look a gift horse in the mouth complain about a gift

gig /gɪg/ n musician's performance

gi·gan·tic /dʒaɪˈgæntɪk/ adj very large

gig·gle /ˈgɪgəl/ vi laugh in a silly way **giggle** n **1** [C] act of giggling **2** [S] *infml, esp. BrE* something that amuses: *We only did it for a giggle.*

gig·o·lo /ˈʒɪgələu, ˈdʒɪ- ‖ -lou/ n woman's paid lover and companion

gild /gɪld/ vt **1** cover with gold or gold paint **2 gild the lily** to try to improve something that is already good enough, so spoiling the effect

gill¹ /gɪl/ n organ through which a fish breathes

gill² /dʒɪl/ n measure of liquid

gilt /gɪlt/ n [U] material with which things are gilded

gilt-edged /ˌ· ˈ·◂/ adj (of government SHARES (2)) having a fixed interest rate and therefore safe

gim·let /ˈgɪmlɪt/ n tool for making holes for screws

gim·mick /ˈgɪmɪk/ n trick, phrase, etc. used to draw attention **–y** adv

gin /dʒɪn/ n [U] colourless alcoholic drink

gin·ger /ˈdʒɪndʒə ‖ -ər/ n [U] **1** plant whose hot-tasting root is used in cooking **2** orange-brown colour: *ginger hair*

ginger ale /ˌ· ·ˈ· ‖ ˈ·· ·/ n [C;U] gassy alcoholic drink

ginger beer /ˌ· ·ˈ· ‖ ˈ·· ·/ n [C;U] gassy non-alcoholic drink

gin·ger·bread /ˈdʒɪndʒəbred ‖ -dʒər-/ n [U] cake with ginger in it

gin·ger·ly /ˈdʒɪndʒəli ‖ -ər-/ adv carefully

ging·ham /ˈgɪŋəm/ n [U] cotton cloth with a pattern of squares

gip·sy, gypsy /ˈdʒɪpsi/ n member of a dark-haired people who often travel about in CARAVANS (1, 2)

gi·raffe /dʒɪˈrɑːf ‖ -ˈræf/ n long-necked African animal

gir·der /ˈgɜːdə ‖ ˈgɜːrdər/ n metal beam supporting a roof, bridge, etc.

gir·dle /ˈgɜːdl ‖ ˈgɜːr-/ n **1** woman's light

CORSET **2** *lit* something that surrounds something: *a girdle of islands* ♦ vt lit go all round

girl /gɜːl ‖ gɜːrl/ n young female person **~hood** n time of being a girl **~ish** adj like a girl

girl·friend /ˈgɜːlfrend ‖ ˈgɜːrl-/ n **1** man's female companion **2** woman's female friend

gi·ro /ˈdʒaɪərəu ‖ ˈdʒaɪrou/ n **1** [U] banking system handled by one central computer **2** [C] *BrE* SOCIAL SECURITY payment (by cheque)

girth /gɜːθ ‖ gɜːrθ/ n **1** [C] band round a horse's middle to hold the SADDLE firm **2** [U] *fml* thickness measured round something: *the girth of a tree*

gist /dʒɪst/ n [S] main points of something

give¹ /gɪv/ v gave /geɪv/, given /ˈgɪvən/ **1** vt cause or allow someone to have: *give him a present/a job* | *Give me time.* **2** pay in exchange: *I'll give £3000 for the car.* **3** vi supply money: *give generously to charity* **4** vt provide: *Cows give milk.* **5** vt perform (an action): *give an order/a sign* **6** vt offer (an amusement, etc.): *give a party* **7** vi bend or stretch under pressure **8** vt *fml* cause to believe, esp. wrongly: *I was given to understand that he was ill.* **9** vt call on (people present) to drink a TOAST (2) to: *I give you the President!* **10 give or take (a certain amount)** more or less (a certain amount) **11 give way (to): a** admit defeat in an argument or fight **b** break **c** become less useful or important than **d** allow oneself to show (esp. a feeling) **e** allow other traffic to go first **giver** n

give away *phr vt* **1** give freely **2** show the truth about

give back *phr vt* return (something) to the owner

give in *phr v* **1** *vi* SURRENDER **2** *vt* deliver

give off *phr vt* send out (a smell, etc.)

give out *phr v* **1** *vt* DISTRIBUTE **2** *vi* come to an end: *The petrol/My strength gave out.*

give up *phr v* **1** *vi/t* stop: *give up smoking* **2** *vi* stop trying to guess, etc. **3** *vt* regard as lost or hopeless **4** *vt* offer as a prisoner **5** *vt* deliver to someone: *give up one's seat in the train*

give² n [U] quality of bending or stretching under pressure

give-and-take /ˌ· · ˈ·/ n [U] willingness to COMPROMISE (=give way to another's wishes)

give·a·way /'gɪvəweɪ/ n [S] something unintentional that makes a secret known ♦ adj (of a price) very low

giv·en /'gɪvən/ adj 1 fixed and stated: a given time 2 **be given to** have a tendency to ♦ prep if one takes into account: Given her inexperience, she's done a good job.

given name /'·· ·/ n AmE for FIRST NAME

gla·cial /'gleɪʃəl/ adj of ice or an ICE AGE

gla·ci·er /'glæsɪə ‖ 'gleɪʃər/ n mass of ice that flows slowly down a valley

glad /glæd/ adj -dd- 1 pleased 2 lit causing happiness ~ly adv willingly ~ness n [U]

glad·den /'glædn/ vt make glad

glade /gleɪd/ n lit open space in a forest

glad·i·a·tor /'glædieɪtə ‖ -ər/ n (in ancient Rome) man who fought in public as an entertainment

glam·o·rize also **-rise** BrE /'glæməraɪz/ vt make (something) appear more attractive than it really is

glam·our BrE ‖ **-or** AmE /'glæmə ‖ -ər/ n 1 the charm of something unusual 2 sexual attraction ~ous adj

glance /glɑːns ‖ glæns/ vi give a rapid look ♦ n 1 rapid look 2 **at a glance** at once

  glance off phr vi/t (of a blow, etc.) hit and move off at an angle

gland /glænd/ n body organ that treats materials from the bloodstream to produce various liquid substances

glan·du·lar /'glændjələ ‖ -dʒələr/ adj of the glands

glare /gleə ‖ gler/ vi 1 look fiercely 2 shine too strongly **glare** n [S] **glaring** adj 1 too bright 2 noticeably bad: glaring injustice

glass /glɑːs ‖ glæs/ n 1 [U] hard transparent material used in windows, etc. 2 [C] something made of this, esp. a container for drinking from 3 [C] amount held by such a container —see also GLASSES ~y adj like glass: a glassy stare

glass·es /'glɑːsɪz ‖ 'glæ-/ n [P] two pieces of specially-cut glass in a frame, worn in front of the eyes for improving a person's ability to see

glass fi·bre /,· '··◂/ n [U] FIBREGLASS

glass·house /'glɑːshaʊs ‖ 'glæs-/ n BrE GREENHOUSE

glass·ware /'glɑːsweə ‖ 'glæswer/ n [U] glass objects generally

glass·works /'glɑːswɜːks ‖ 'glæswɜːrks/ n glassworks factory where glass is made

glau·co·ma /glɔːˈkəʊmə ‖ glɔːˈkoʊ-/ n [U] eye disease marked by increased pressure within the eyeball

glaze /gleɪz/ v 1 vt put a shiny surface on (pots, etc.) 2 vt fit (a window, etc.) with glass 3 vi (of the eyes) become dull ♦ n [U] shiny surface

gla·zi·er /'gleɪzɪə ‖ -ʒər/ n workman who fits glass into windows

gleam /gliːm/ n 1 a gentle light 2 sudden sign of something: a gleam of interest ♦ vi send out a gleam

glean /gliːn/ vt gather (facts, etc.) in small amounts

glee /gliː/ n [U] joyful satisfaction ~ful adj ~fully adv

glen /glen/ n narrow valley, esp. in Scotland

glib /glɪb/ adj -bb- speaking or spoken too easily: glib excuses ~ly adv ~ness n [U]

glide /glaɪd/ vi 1 move smoothly and noiselessly 2 fly in a glider ♦ n gliding movement **glider** n plane with no engine

glim·mer /'glɪmə ‖ -ər/ vi shine faintly ♦ n 1 faint light 2 small uncertain sign: a glimmer of hope

glimpse /glɪmps/ n quick incomplete view of something ♦ vt see for a moment

glint /glɪnt/ vi, n (give out) a small flash of light

glis·ten /'glɪsən/ vi shine as if wet

glitch /glɪtʃ/ n small fault in the operation of something

glit·ter /'glɪtə ‖ -ər/ vi flash brightly: glittering diamonds ♦ n [S;U] brightness

glit·te·ra·ti /,glɪtəˈrɑːti/ n [(the) P] fashionable people whose social activities are widely reported

gloat /gləʊt ‖ gloʊt/ vi look at something with unpleasant satisfaction ~ingly adv

glo·bal /'gləʊbəl ‖ 'gloʊ-/ adj 1 of the whole world 2 taking account of all considerations ~ly adv

global war·ming /,·· '··/ n [U] increase in world temperatures, because gases caused by POLLUTION trap the sun's heat

globe /gləʊb ‖ gloʊb/ n 1 [C] object in the shape of a ball; esp. one with a map of the Earth painted on it 2 [the+S] the Earth

globe·trot·ter /'gləʊbtrɒtə ‖ 'gloʊb-trɑːtər/ n person who travels widely –ting adj, n

glob·u·lar /'glɒbjʊ̈lə‖'glɑːbjʊ̈lər/ *adj* shaped like a ball

glob·ule /'glɒbjuːl‖'glɑː-/ *n* drop of liquid

gloom /gluːm/ *n* 1 [U] darkness 2 [S;U] sadness; hopelessness ~y *adj* ~ily *adv*

glo·ri·fy /'glɔːrɪfaɪ/ *vt* 1 praise; worship 2 cause to seem more important: *Her cottage is just a glorified hut.* –**fication** /ˌglɔːrɪfɪ'keɪʃən/ *n* [U]

glo·ri·ous /'glɔːrɪəs/ *adj* 1 having great honour: *glorious victory* 2 splendid ~ly *adv*

glo·ry¹ /'glɔːri/ *n* [U] 1 great honour 2 splendid beauty

glory² *v* **glory in** *phr vt* enjoy, often selfishly

gloss /glɒs‖glɔːs, glɑːs/ *n* [S;U] 1 shiny brightness 2 pleasant but deceiving outer appearance 3 explanation of a piece of writing ♦ *vt* write an explanation of ~y *adj* shiny

gloss over *phr vt* hide (faults)

glos·sa·ry /'glɒsəri‖'glɔː-, 'glɑː-/ *n* list of explanations of words

glossy mag·a·zine /ˌ·· ··'·‖ˌ·· '··/ *n* magazine printed on shiny paper with lots of pictures, esp. of clothes

glove /glʌv/ *n* 1 covering for the hand 2 **fit like a glove** fit perfectly —see also KID GLOVES

glow /gləʊ‖gloʊ/ *vi* 1 give out heat or light without flames 2 be warm and red in the face ♦ *n* [S] glowing light —**ing** *adj* strongly approving: *a glowing account*

glow·er /'glaʊə‖-ər/ *vi* look with an angry expression —**ingly** *adv*

glow-worm /'·· ·/ *n* insect that gives out a greenish light

glu·cose /'gluːkəʊs‖-koʊs/ *n* [U] sugar found in fruit

glue /gluː/ *n* [U] sticky substance for joining things ♦ *vt pres. p.* **gluing** or **glueing** 1 join with glue 2 **glued to** close to: *children glued to the television* ~y *adj*

glue-snif·fing /'· ·/ *n* [U] harmful breathing in of FUMES of glue to produce a state of excitement

glum /glʌm/ *adj* -mm- sad; GLOOMY ~ly *adv*

glut /glʌt/ *vt* -tt- supply with too much: *shops glutted with fruit* ♦ *n* [S] too large a supply

glu·ti·nous /'gluːt̬ɪ̈nəs/ *adj fml* sticky

glut·ton /'glʌtn/ *n* 1 person who eats too much 2 person who is always ready to do more of something hard or unpleasant: *a glutton for punishment* ~**ous** *adj* GREEDY ~y *n* [U] *fml* habit of eating too much

gly·ce·rine /'glɪsəriːn‖-rə̈n/ also **glycerin** /-rə̈n/ — *n* [U] colourless liquid used in making soap, medicines, and explosives

GM /ˌdʒiː 'em◂/ *adj* (of food) genetically modified; containing GENES that have been deliberately changed

gm *written abbrev. for:* GRAM

GMT /ˌdʒiː em 'tiː/ *n* [U] Greenwich Mean Time; the time in Greenwich in London, used as an international standard

gnarled /nɑːld‖nɑːrld/ *adj* rough and twisted: *gnarled tree trunks*

gnash /næʃ/ *n* strike (one's teeth) together

gnat /næt/ *n* small flying insect that stings

gnaw /nɔː‖nɔː/ *vi/t* bite steadily (at): (fig.) *gnawing anxiety*

gnome /nəʊm‖noʊm/ *n* 1 (in stories) little (old) man who lives under the ground 2 (stone or plastic) figure representing this 3 **the gnomes of Zurich** certain powerful bankers, esp. Swiss ones

GNP /ˌdʒiː en 'piː/ *n* [the+S] *abbrev. for:* Gross National Product; total value of everything produced in a country, usu. in a single year

go¹ /gəʊ‖goʊ/ *v* went /went/, gone /gɒn ‖gɔːn/ 1 *vi* leave a place: *I must go now.* 2 *vi* move; travel: *go by bus* | *go shopping* 3 *vi* lead; reach: *This road goes to London.* 4 *vi* start an action: *Ready, steady, go!* 5 **a** become: *go mad* **b** be or remain: *Her protests went unnoticed.* 6 *vi* match; fit: *Blue and green don't go (together).* | *4 into 3 won't go.* | *Your dress goes with your eyes.* 7 *vi* belong: *The knives go in this drawer.* 8 *vi* (of machines) work: *This clock doesn't go.* 9 *vi* be sold: *The house is going cheap.* 10 *vt* have (certain words or sounds): *Ducks go 'quack'.* 11 *vi* become weak or worn out: *My voice is going.* 12 *vi* lose one's usual powers of control: *let oneself go* | *He's pretty far gone.* 13 *vi* state or do up to or beyond a limit: *go too far* 14 *vi* be accepted or acceptable: *What she says goes.* 15 *vi* happen or develop in the stated way: *The party went well.* 16 **as someone/something goes** compared with the average person or thing of that type:

He's not a bad cook, as cooks go, but he's no expert. **17 be going** be present for use: *Is there any good going?* **18 be going to** (shows the future): *Is it going to rain?* **19 go a long way** also **go far: a** (of money) buy a lot **b** (of a person) succeed **20 go and: a** go in order to: *go and fetch it* **b** (shows surprise): *She went and bought it!* **21 go for it** *infml* make every effort to succeed at something **22 go it alone** act independently **23 to go** left; remaining: *only 3 more days to go* **24 -goer** person who goes somewhere regularly: *churchgoers*

go about *phr v* **1** *vt* perform; work at: *go about one's business* **2** *vi* GO AROUND (1, 3)

go after *phr vt* try to get; chase

go against *phr vt* **1** oppose **2** be unfavourable to: *The case may go against you.*

go ahead *phr vi* **1** begin **2** continue

go along *phr vi* continue

go along with *phr vt* agree with

go around/round *phr vi* **1** (of an illness) spread **2** be enough for everyone: *not enough chairs to go round* **3** be often out in public (with someone)

go at *phr vt* attack; TACKLE

go back *phr vi* **1** return **2** stretch back in time

go back on *phr vt* break (a promise, etc.)

go by *phr v* **1** *vi* pass (in place or time): *A year went by.* **2** *vt* act according to **3** *vt* judge by **4 go by the name of** be called

go down *phr vi* **1** become lower **2** sink: *The sun/The ship went down.* **3** become less swollen **4** (of food) be swallowed **5** be accepted: *His speech went down well with the crowd.* **6** be recorded: *This day will go down in history.* **7** (of computers) stop working

go down with *phr vt* catch (an illness)

go for *phr vt* **1** attack **2** GO AFTER **3** like or be attracted to **4 go for nothing** be wasted

go in *phr vi* **1** (of the sun, etc.) become covered by clouds **2** join

go in for *phr vt* **1** enter (a competition) **2** have a habit of: *go in for football*

go into *phr vt* **1** enter (a profession) **2** explain or examine thoroughly

go off *phr v* **1** *vi* **a** explode **b** ring or sound loudly **2** *vi* succeed or fail: *The conference went off well.* **3** *vi* go bad **4** *vt* lose interest in **5** *vi* stop operating

go off with *phr vt* take away without permission

go on *phr v* **1** *vi* happen: *What's going on?* **2** *vi* (of time) pass **3** *vi* **a** continue: *go on with your work* **b** talk, complain, or behave in a certain way continually **4** *vi* be put into operation **5** *vt* use as proof, etc.: *I'm going on what you told me.* **6 go on (with you)!** *BrE infml* I don't believe you! **7 to be going/go on with** *infml, esp. BrE* for the moment

go out *phr vi* **1** leave the house **2** spend time with someone **3** stop burning **4** become unfashionable **5** (of the sea) go back to its low level **6** (of feelings) be in sympathy (with)

go over *phr vt* **1** examine **2** repeat

go round *phr vi* GO AROUND

go through *phr v* **1** *vi* be approved officially **2** *vt* suffer or experience **3** *vt* finish; spend **4** *vt* search

go through with *phr vt* complete

go to *phr vt* **1** take oneself have: *go to a lot of trouble* **2** start experiencing or causing (a state or action)

go under *phr vi* **1** (of a ship) sink **2** fail

go up *phr vi* **1** rise **2** be built **3** be destroyed in fire, etc.

go with *phr vt* **1** match **2** be often found with

go without *phr vi/t* **1** DO without **2 it goes without saying** it is clear without needing to be stated

go² *n* **1** [U] quality of being very active **2** [C] attempt **3** [C] turn, esp. in a game **4 from the word go** from the beginning **5 have a go** *infml, esp. BrE* **a** to complain **b** attempt to catch or stop a wrongdoer by force **6 it's all go** it's very busy **7 make a go of** *infml* make a success of **8 on the go** very busy

goad /gəʊd ‖ goʊd/ *vt* urge by continuous annoyance ♦ *n* stick for driving cattle

go·a·head¹ /ˈ·ˌ·,·ˈ/ *n* [(*the*)S] permission to take action

go-ahead² *adj* active in using new methods

goal /gəʊl ‖ goʊl/ *n* **1** one's aim or purpose **2 a** place where the ball must go to gain a point in football, etc. **b** point gained by sending the ball there —see also OWN GOAL

goal·keep·er /ˈgəʊlˌkiːpə ‖ ˈgoʊlˌkiːpər/

n player responsible for keeping the ball out of a team's goal

goal·post /'gəulpəust ‖ 'goulpoust/ *n* one of the two posts between which the ball must go to gain a goal

goat /gəut ‖ gout/ *n* **1** horned animal like a sheep **2 get one's goat** annoy me

goa·tee /gəu'ti: ‖ gou-/ *n* small pointed beard

gob /gɒb ‖ gɑ:b/ *n BrE sl* mouth

gob·ble /'gɒbəl ‖ 'gɑ:-/ *vi/t* eat quickly and often noisily

gob·ble·dy·gook /'gɒbəldigu:k ‖ 'gɑ:bəldiguk, -gu:k/ *n* [U] meaningless official language

go-be·tween /'· ·ˌ·/ *n* person who takes messages, etc. from one person or side to another

gob·let /'gɒblɪt ‖ 'gɑ:b-/ *n* glass or metal drinking cup with a stem and no handle

gob·lin /'gɒblɪn ‖ 'gɑ:b-/ *n* unkind fairy that plays tricks on people

god /gɒd ‖ gɑ:d/ **goddess** /'gɒdɪs ‖ 'gɑ:-/ *fem. — n* being who is worshipped — see also GODS ~**less** *adj fml* wicked; not showing respect for or belief in God ~**like** *adj* like a god: *godlike beauty* ~**ly** *adj fml* religious; leading a good life

God *n* (in the Christian, Jewish, and Muslim religions) the maker and ruler of the world

god·child /'gɒdtʃaɪld ‖ 'gɑ:d-/ *n* boy (**godson**) or girl (**goddaughter**) for whom someone makes promises at BAPTISM

god·fa·ther /'gɒdˌfɑːðə ‖ 'gɑ:dˌfɑːðər/ *n* male godparent

god-fear·ing /'· ˌ·ⁿ/ *adj fml* good and well-behaved

god·for·sak·en /'gɒdfəseɪkən ‖ 'gɑ:d-fər-/ *adj* (of places) sad and empty

god·moth·er /'gɒdˌmʌðə ‖ 'gɑ:dˌmʌðər/ *n* female godparent

god·pa·rent /'gɒdˌpeərənt ‖ 'gɑ:dˌper-/ *n* person who takes responsibility for a new Christian at BAPTISM

gods /gɒdz ‖ gɑ:dz/ *n [the*+S] seats high up at the back of a theatre

god·send /'gɒdsend ‖ 'gɑ:d-/ *n* unexpected lucky chance or thing

go·fer /'gəufə ‖ 'goufər/ *n* person whose job is to fetch or take things for other people

go-get·ter /ˌ· '··, '· ˌ··‖ ·ˌ·/ *n* someone who is forceful and determined, and likely to succeed

gog·gle /'gɒgəl ‖ 'gɑ:-/ *vi* STARE with the eyes wide open **goggles** *n* [P] glasses to protect the eyes

go·ing /'gəuɪŋ ‖ 'gou-/ *n* [U] speed or condition of travel: *fast/rough going* ♦ *adj* operating at present: *the going rate | a going concern*

goings-on /ˌ·· '·/ *n* [P] undesirable activities

goi·tre *BrE* ‖ **-ter** *AmE* /'gɔɪtə ‖ -ər/ *n* swelling in the neck caused by lack of certain chemicals

go-kart /'gəu kɑ:t ‖ 'gou kɑ:rt/ *n* small low racing car

gold /gəuld ‖ gould/ *n* **1** [U] valuable yellow metal **2** [U] gold coins **3** [U] the colour of gold: *gold paint* **4** [C] GOLD MEDAL **5 as good as gold** very well behaved

gold·en /'gəuldən ‖ 'goul-/ *adj* **1** of or like gold **2** very favourable: *a golden opportunity*

golden hand·shake /ˌ·· '··/ *n* large amount of money given to someone leaving a firm

golden rule /ˌ·· '·/ *n* [S] very important rule of behaviour

gold·fish /'gəuld,fɪʃ ‖ 'gould-/ *n* goldfish small orange fish kept as a pet

gold leaf /ˌ· '·/ *n* [U] thin sheets of gold

gold·mine /'gəuldmaɪn ‖ 'gould-/ *n* **1** mine where gold is found **2** profitable business

gold rush /'· ·/ *n* rush to newly discovered goldmines

gold·smith /'gəuld,smɪθ ‖ 'gould-/ *n* person who makes things out of gold

golf /gɒlf ‖ gɑ:lf, gɔ:lf/ *n* game in which people hit a ball into holes with GOLF CLUBS ~**er** *n*

golf club /'· ·/ *n* **1** long-handled stick for hitting the ball in golf **2** club for golfers with buildings and land they can use

gone /gɒn ‖ gɔ:n/ *v past p. of* GO: *George has gone to Paris.* (=he is there now)

gong /gɒŋ ‖ gɑ:ŋ, gɔ:ŋ/ *n* **1** round piece of metal that makes a ringing sound when struck **2** *BrE sl* MEDAL

gon·or·rhe·a, **-rhoea** /ˌgɒnə'ri:ə ‖ ˌgɑ:-/ *n* [U] disease passed on during sexual activity

goo /gu:/ *n* [U] **1** sticky material **2** SENTIMENTALISM

gossip

good[1] /gʊd/ *adj* **better** /ˈbetə ‖ -ər/, **best** /best/ **1** satisfactory: *good food/brakes* **2** pleasant: *good news* | *have a good time* **3** useful; suitable: *Milk is good for you.* **4** clever: *good at maths* **5** well-behaved **6** morally right: *good deeds* **7** *fml* kind: *Be good enough to hold this.* **8** thorough: *have a good cry* **9 a good: a** at least: *a good 3 hours* **b** large in size, amount: *a good distance* **10 a good deal** quite a lot **11 all in good time** (it will happen) at a suitable later time; be patient **12 as good as** almost the same as **13 Good!** I agree, I'm glad, etc. **14 good and ... infml** completely: *I'll do it when I'm good and ready.* **15 good for a** effective in use: *The ticket is good for a month.* **b** likely to produce: *She's always good for a few pounds/a laugh.* **16 in good time** early **17 make good** be successful

good[2] *n* [U] **1** something that is good **2** something that causes gain or improvement: *It'll do you good.* | *It's no good.* (=it's useless) | *What's the good of/What good is it having a car if you don't drive?* **3 for good** forever **4 good for you** (used to express approval and pleasure at someone's success, etc.) **5 up to no good** doing or intending doing something bad —see also GOODS

good af·ter·noon /·ˌ·ˈ·/ *interj* (used when meeting someone in the afternoon)

good·bye /ɡʊdˈbaɪ/ *interj* (used when leaving someone)

good eve·ning /·ˈ··/ *interj* (used when meeting someone in the evening)

good-for-noth·ing /ˈ·· ·ˌ·/ *adj, n* useless (person)

Good Fri·day /ˌ· ˈ··/ *n* the Friday before EASTER

good-hu·moured /ˌ· ˈ···◂/ *adj* cheerful and friendly

good-look·ing /ˌ· ˈ··◂/ *adj* attractive; beautiful

good·ly /ˈɡʊdli/ *adj* **1** large **2** satisfying

good morn·ing /·ˈ··/ *interj* (used when meeting someone in the morning)

good-na·tured /ˌ· ˈ··◂/ *adj* kind

good·ness /ˈɡʊdnɪs/ *n* [U] **1** quality of being good **2** the best part of food, etc. **3** (used in expressions of surprise and annoyance): *Goodness me!* | *for goodness' sake*

good·night /ɡʊdˈnaɪt/ *interj* (used when leaving someone at night, or going to sleep)

goods /ɡʊdz/ *n* [P] **1** things for sale **2** things carried by train, etc. **3** possessions **4 come up with/deliver the goods** produce in full what is expected

good Sam·ar·i·tan /ˌ· ·ˈ···/ *n* person who kindly helps people in trouble

good·will /ˌɡʊdˈwɪl/ *n* [U] **1** kind feelings **2** popularity of a business, as part of its value

good·y /ˈɡʊdi/ *n* something very pleasant, esp. to eat

goo·ey /ˈɡuːi/ *adj* **1** sticky and sweet **2** SENTIMENTAL

goof /ɡuːf/ *n infml* **1** foolish person **2** silly mistake ♦ *vi infml, esp. AmE* make a silly mistake

goof off *phr vi AmE infml* waste time or avoid work

goose /ɡuːs/ *n* **geese** /ɡiːs/ **1** bird like a large duck **2** silly person

goose·ber·ry /ˈɡʊzbəri, ˈɡuːz-, ˈɡuːs- ‖ ˈɡuːsberi/ *n* **1** garden bush with hairy green berries **2** (of a third person) present with a man and woman who would rather be alone

goose·flesh /ˈɡuːsfleʃ/ *n* [U] condition in which the skin rises up in small points

goose-step /ˈɡuːs-step/ *n* [S] way of marching with stiff straight legs

gore[1] /ɡɔː ‖ ɡɔːr/ *vt* wound with horns or TUSKS

gore[2] *n* [U] *lit* (esp. thick) blood **gory** *adj*

gorge[1] /ɡɔːdʒ ‖ ɡɔːrdʒ/ *n* **1** steep narrow valley **2 make someone's gorge rise** make someone feel sickened

gorge[2] *vi/t* eat or feed eagerly

gor·geous /ˈɡɔːdʒəs ‖ ˈɡɔːr-/ *adj* wonderful; beautiful ~**ly** *adv*

go·ril·la /ɡəˈrɪlə/ *n* the largest of the APES

gorse /ɡɔːs ‖ ɡɔːrs/ *n* [U] prickly wild bush with yellow flowers

gosh /ɡɒʃ ‖ ɡɑːʃ/ *interj* (expressing surprise)

gos·ling /ˈɡɒzlɪŋ ‖ ˈɡɑː-/ *n* young GOOSE

go-slow /ˌ· ˈ·◂/ *n BrE* decision to work slowly, as a kind of STRIKE[2] (1)

gos·pel /ˈɡɒspəl ‖ ˈɡɑː-/ *n* **1** [U] something completely true **2** [C] (*cap.*) any of four accounts of Christ's life in the Bible

gos·sa·mer /ˈɡɒsəmə ‖ ˈɡɑːsəmər/ *n* [U] thin silky thread

gos·sip /ˈɡɒsɪp ‖ ˈɡɑː-/ *n* **1** [S;U] talk

about other people's private lives **2** [C] person who likes this kind of talk ♦ *vi* spend time in gossip

got /gɒt ‖ gɑːt/ *v past t. and p. of* GET

Goth·ic /'gɒθɪk ‖ 'gɑː-/ *adj* **1** of a style of building common from the 12th to the 16th centuries, with pointed arches and tall pillars **2** of a style of writing in the 18th century which produced NOVELs set in lonely fearful places

got·ten /'gɒtn ‖ 'gɑːtn/ *v AmE past p. of* GET

gou·ache /ɡʊ'ɑːʃ, ɡwɑːʃ/ *n* [C;U] (picture painted by) a method using colours mixed with water and a sort of glue

gouge /ɡaʊdʒ/ *v* **gouge out** *phr vt* push or dig out violently

gourd /ɡʊəd ‖ ɡɔːrd, ɡʊrd/ *n* hard outer shell of a fruit

gour·met /'ɡʊəmeɪ ‖ ɡʊr-, ɡʊr'meɪ/ *n* person who knows a lot about food and drink ♦ *relating to* good food and drink

gout /ɡaʊt/ *n* [U] disease that makes the toes and fingers swell painfully

gov·ern /'ɡʌvən ‖ -ərn/ *v* **1** *v/t* rule (a country, etc.) **2** *vt* control: *The price is governed by the quantity produced.* ~**ance** *n* [U] *fml* governing

gov·ern·ess /'ɡʌvənɪs ‖ -ər-/ *n* woman who teaches children in their home

gov·ern·ment /'ɡʌvənmənt, 'ɡʌvəmənt ‖ 'ɡʌvərn-/ *n* **1** [C] group of people who govern: *the Swiss government* **2** [U] act or process of governing: *the art of government* **3** [U] form or method of governing: *a return to democratic government* ~**al** /ˌɡʌvən-'mentl◄ ‖ ˌɡʌvərn-/ *adj*

gov·er·nor /'ɡʌvənə ‖ -ər/ *n* person who controls various sorts of place or organization: *the governor of the prison/of California* ~**ship** *n* [U]

gown /ɡaʊn/ *n* **1** woman's dress **2** outer garment worn by judges, members of universities, etc. **3** loose garment worn for some special purpose: *a nightgown/dressing gown*

GP /ˌdʒiː 'piː/ *n abbrev. for:* general practitioner; local doctor who is trained in general medicine

grab /ɡræb/ *vt/i* -**bb**- seize suddenly and roughly ♦ *n* **1** sudden attempt to seize something **2 up for grabs** ready for anyone to take or win

grace /ɡreɪs/ *n* [U] **1** beauty of movement

or shape **2** delay allowed as a favour: *give them a week's grace* **3** prayer of thanks before or after meals **4** God's favour towards people **5 a saving grace** pleasing quality for which the person's faults are forgiven him **6 with (a) good/bad grace** willingly/unwillingly ♦ *vt fml* give honour or beauty to ~**ful** *adj* **1** having GRACE (1) **2** suitably expressed ~**fully** *adv* ~**less** *adj* awkward

gra·cious /'ɡreɪʃəs/ *adj* **1** polite and pleasant **2** having those qualities made possible by wealth: *gracious living* ~**ly** *adv* ~**ness** *n* [U]

gra·da·tion /ɡrə'deɪʃən/ *n fml* stage; degree: *gradations of colour*

grade /ɡreɪd/ *n* **1** level of quality **2** *AmE* a FORM[1] (5) **b** mark given for schoolwork **c** gradient **3 make the grade** succeed; reach the necessary standard ♦ *vt* separate into levels of quality

grade school /'·ˌ·/ *n AmE* ELEMENTARY SCHOOL

gra·di·ent /'ɡreɪdiənt/ *n* degree of slope, as on a road

grad·u·al /'ɡrædʒuəl/ *adj* happening slowly; not sudden ~**ly** *adv* ~**ness** *n* [U]

grad·u·ate[1] /'ɡrædʒuɪt/ *n* **1** person with a university degree **2** *AmE* person who has completed any school or college course

grad·u·ate[2] /'ɡrædʒueɪt/ *v* **1** *vi* become a graduate **2** *vt* GRADE **3** *vt* mark with degrees for measurement -**ation** /ˌɡrædʒu'eɪʃən/ *n* **1** [U] (ceremony of) becoming a graduate **2** [C] mark of measurement

graf·fi·ti /ɡræ'fiːti, ɡrə-/ *n* [P;U] drawings or writings on a wall

graft /ɡrɑːft ‖ ɡræft/ *n* **1** [C] piece from one plant fixed inside another to grow there **2** [C] piece of skin or bone similarly fixed into the body **3** [U] *esp. AmE* practice of obtaining money or advantage by the dishonest use of esp. political influence **4** [U] *BrE infml* work ♦ *vt* put onto as a graft

grain /ɡreɪn/ *n* **1** [C] single seed of rice, wheat, etc. **2** [U] crops from food plants like these **3** [C] small hard piece: *grains of sand* | (fig.) *a grain of truth* **4** [U] natural arrangement of threads or FIBREs in wood, cloth, etc. **5 be/go against the grain** it is not what one wishes (to do, know, etc.)

gram, gramme /ɡræm/ *n* (measure of

weight equal to) 1/1000 of a kilogram

gram·mar /'græmə‖-ər/ n [U] (book that teaches) rules for the use of words

gram·mar·i·an /grə'meəriən‖-'mer-/ n person who studies and knows about grammar

grammar school /'·· ·/ n British school, esp. formerly, for children over 11 who study for higher examinations

gram·mat·i·cal /grə'mætıkəl/ adj 1 concerning grammar 2 correct according to the rules of grammar

gran /græn/ n BrE infml grandmother

gra·na·ry /'grænəri‖'greı-, 'græ-/ n storehouse for grain ♦ tdmk adj (of bread) containing whole grains

grand /grænd/ adj 1 splendid; IMPRESSIVE 2 (of people) important 3 pleasant; delightful ♦ n 1 GRAND PIANO 2 (pl. grand) sl 1,000 pounds or dollars

gran·dad /'grændæd/ n infml grandfather

grand·child /'græntʃaıld/ n grandchildren /-,tʃıldrən/ boy (grandson) or girl (granddaughter) who is the child of the stated person's son or daughter

gran·dee /græn'di:/ n Spanish or Portuguese nobleman

gran·deur /'grændʒə‖-ər/ n [U] quality of being grand; MAGNIFICENCE

grand·fa·ther /'grænd,fɑ:ðə‖-ər/ n male grandparent

grandfather clock /'··· ·, ,··· '·/ n tall clock that stands on the floor

gran·di·ose /'grændiəus‖-ous/ adj intended to seem splendid and important

grand·ma /'grænmɑ:/ n infml grandmother

grand·moth·er /'græn,mʌðə‖-ər/ n female grandparent

grand·par·ent /'græn,peərənt‖-,per-/ n parent of someone's father or mother

grand pi·a·no /, ·'··/ n large piano with strings set parallel to the ground

grand slam /, '·/ n the winning of all of a set of important sports competitions

grand·stand /'grændstænd/ n seats arranged in rising rows, for people watching races, etc.

grand to·tal /, '··/ n complete amount

gran·ite /'grænát/ n [U] hard usu. grey rock

gran·ny, -nie /'græni/ n infml grandmother

♦ adj for old people: a granny flat

grant /grɑ:nt‖grænt/ vt 1 fml give: grant permission 2 admit the truth of 3 take something for granted accept it without question ♦ n money granted esp. officially

gran·u·lar /'grænjələ‖-ər/ adj made of grains

gran·u·lat·ed /'grænjəleıtád/ adj (of sugar) in the form of not very fine powder

gran·ule /'grænju:l/ n small grain

grape /greıp/ n green or purple fruit from which wine is made —see also SOUR GRAPES

grape·fruit /'greıpfru:t/ n large yellow fruit like a sour orange

grape·vine /'greıpvaın/ n [S] unofficial way of spreading news: hear about it through the office grapevine

graph /grɑ:f, græf‖græf/ n drawing showing the relationship between two changing values

graph·ic /'græfık/ adj 1 clear and detailed: a graphic description 2 of drawing, printing, etc. ~ally /-kli/ adv 1 clearly 2 using graphs **graphics** n [P] drawings, etc.

graphic de·sign /, ·· ·'·/ n [U] art of combining pictures and words in the production of books, magazines, etc. **graphic designer** n

graph·ite /'græfaıt/ n [U] black substance used in pencils, etc.

grap·ple /'græpəl/ v **grapple with** phr vt seize and struggle with: (fig.) grapple with a problem

grasp /grɑ:sp‖græsp/ vt 1 take firm hold of 2 succeed in understanding ♦ n [S] 1 firm hold 2 understanding **~ing** adj too eager for money

grass /grɑ:s‖græs/ n 1 [U] common wild green plants that cows, etc. eat 2 [C] one of these plants: tall grasses 3 sl someone who GRASSES 4 out to grass: a feeding on this plant b no longer working **~y** adj ♦ vi BrE sl (esp. of a criminal) inform the police about the action of (other) criminals

grass·hop·per /'grɑ:s,hopə‖'græs-,hɑ:pər/ n insect which can jump high and makes a sharp noise by rubbing parts of its body together

grass roots /, '·/ n [P] ordinary people, not those with political power

grass wid·ow /, '··/ n woman whose husband is away for a period of time

grate¹ /greɪt/ n metal frame in a fireplace

grate² v 1 vt rub into pieces on a rough surface: grated cheese 2 vi make a sharp unpleasant sound 3 vi annoy **grater** n tool for grating food, etc.

grate·ful /ˈgreɪtfəl/ adj feeling or showing thanks ~**ly** adv ~**ness** n [U]

grat·i·fy /ˈgrætɪfaɪ/ vt please; satisfy ~**ing** adj pleasing **–fication** /ˌgrætɪfɪˈkeɪʃən/ n [C;U]

grat·ing /ˈgreɪtɪŋ/ n network of bars to protect an opening

gra·tis /ˈgrætɪs, ˈgreɪtɪs/ adv, adj fml without payment; free

grat·i·tude /ˈgrætɪtjuːd ‖ -tuːd/ n [U] gratefulness

gra·tu·i·tous /grəˈtjuːɪtəs ‖ -ˈtuː-/ adj fml not deserved or necessary: gratuitous insults ~**ly** adv

gra·tu·i·ty /grəˈtjuːɪti ‖ -ˈtuː-/ n 1 fml TIP³ for a service done 2 money given to someone leaving a job

grave¹ /greɪv/ n hole where a dead person is buried

grave² adj serious; solemn ~**ly** adv

grav·el /ˈgrævəl/ n [U] small stones used for making paths, etc. 1 covered with gravel 2 having a low hard sound ~**ly** adj

grave·stone /ˈgreɪvstəʊn ‖ -stoʊn/ n stone over a grave

grave·yard /ˈgreɪvjɑːd ‖ -ɑːrd/ n CEMETERY

grav·i·tate /ˈgrævɪteɪt/ vi be attracted (as if) by gravity **–tation** /ˌgrævɪˈteɪʃən/ n [U]

grav·i·ty /ˈgrævɪti/ n [U] 1 force by which objects are drawn towards each other 2 seriousness: the gravity of his illness

gra·vy /ˈgreɪvi/ n [U] juice that comes out of meat in cooking

gravy train /ˈ·· ·/ n [the+S] something from which many people can make money or profit without much effort

gray /greɪ/ adj, n, v AmE for GREY

graze¹ /greɪz/ vi (of animals) eat growing grass

graze² vt 1 rub the skin from 2 rub lightly while passing ♦ n surface wound

grease /griːs/ n [U] soft fat or oil ♦ vt 1 put grease on 2 **grease someone's palm** BRIBE someone 3 **like greased lightning** infml extremely fast **greasy** adj

grease·proof pa·per /ˌgriːs-pruːf

ˈpeɪpə ‖ -ər/ n BrE paper used in cooking, etc. that does not let grease pass through it

great /greɪt/ adj 1 excellent and important: great writers 2 large: great pleasure | a great many people 3 keen; active: a great filmgoer 4 sl splendid: a great idea 5 **great-:** a parent of someone's GRANDPARENT: his great-grandfather b child of someone's GRANDCHILD: his great-granddaughter ~**ly** adv very much ~**ness** n [U]

Great Brit·ain /ˌgreɪt ˈbrɪtn/ n England, Scotland, and Wales (but not any part of Ireland)

greed /griːd/ n [U] desire for too much food, money, etc. ~**y** adj ~**ily** adv

green /griːn/ adj 1 of a colour between yellow and blue; the colour of leaves and grass 2 unhealthily pale in the face 3 (of fruit, plants, etc.) young or unripe 4 inexperienced and easily deceived 5 very jealous: green with envy ♦ n 1 [U] green colour 2 [C] smooth piece of grass: village green | bowling green ~**ness** n [U] **greens** n [P] green vegetables

green belt /ˈ· ·/ n [C;U] stretch of land round a town where building is not allowed, so that fields, etc. remain

green card /ˈ· ·/ n document allowing a foreigner to live and work in the US

green·e·ry /ˈgriːnəri/ n [U] green leaves and plants

green-eyed mon·ster /ˌ· ˈ· ·/ n [the+S] jealousy

green fin·gers /ˌ· ˈ··/ n [P] esp. BrE natural skill in making plants grow

green·gage /ˈgriːngeɪdʒ/ n kind of green PLUM

green·gro·cer /ˈgriːnˌgrəʊsə ‖ -ˌgroʊsər/ n esp. BrE person who sells fruit and vegetables

green·house /ˈgriːnhaʊs/ n glass building for growing plants in

greenhouse ef·fect /ˈ·· ·ˌ·/ n [the+S] warming of the air around the Earth because gases caused by POLLUTION (**greenhouse gases**) trap the sun's heat

green light /ˌ· ˈ·/ n [the+S] permission: They've just got the green light to start testing.

greet /griːt/ vt 1 welcome 2 be suddenly seen or heard ~**ing** n 1 words used on meeting or writing to someone 2 a good wish: *Christmas greetings*

gre·gar·i·ous /grɪ'geərɪəs ‖ -'ger-/ *adj* fond of companionship

gre·nade /grɔ'neɪd/ *n* small bomb to be thrown by hand

grew /gru:/ *v past t. of* GROW

grey /greɪ/ *adj* 1 of the colour of black mixed with white 2 having grey hair ♦ *n* [U] grey colour ♦ *vi* become grey

grey·hound /'greɪhaʊnd/ *n* thin dog with long legs, which can run swiftly

grey mat·ter /'· ,··/ *n* [U] 1 the brain 2 *infml* power of thought

grid /grɪd/ *n* 1 GRATING 2 *BrE* network of electricity supply wires 3 system of numbered squares on a map

grid·i·ron /'grɪdaɪən ‖ -ərn/ *n* 1 frame for cooking meat over a fire 2 field marked for AMERICAN FOOTBALL

grid·lock /'grɪdlɒk ‖ -lɑːk/ *n* [U] 1 situation in which cars, etc. cannot move because there are so many on the street 2 DEADLOCK ~ed *adj*

grief /gri:f/ *n* [U] 1 (cause of) great sorrow 2 come to grief suffer harm; fail 3 Good grief! (expression of surprise and some dislike)

griev·ance /'gri:vəns/ *n* cause for complaint

grieve /gri:v/ *v* 1 *vi* suffer grief 2 *vt* make unhappy

griev·ous /'gri:vəs/ *adj fml* very harmful; severe ~ly *adv*

grill /grɪl/ *v* 1 *vi/t* cook under or over direct heat 2 *vt* question severely ♦ *n BrE* 1 shelf under direct heat, for grilling food 2 meat cooked this way: *a mixed grill*

grille /grɪl/ *n* bars filling a space, esp. in a bank or post office

grim /grɪm/ *adj* -mm- 1 serious; terrible: *grim news* 2 showing determination: *grim smile* ~ly *adv* ~ness *n* [U]

gri·mace /grɪ'meɪs, 'grɪməs ‖ 'grɪməs, grɪ'meɪs/ *vi* twist the face to express pain, etc. grimace *n*

grime /graɪm/ *n* [U] black dirt on a surface grimy *adj*

grim reap·er /,· '··/ *n [the]* (a name for death, considered as a person)

grin /grɪn/ *vi* -nn- 1 smile widely 2 grin and bear it suffer without complaint grin *n*

grind /graɪnd/ *vt* **ground** /graʊnd/

1 crush into powder: *grind coffee beans* 2 rub (the teeth) together 3 make smooth or sharp by rubbing: *grind knives* 4 press upon with a strong twisting movement 5 **grind to a halt** stop noisily ♦ *n infml* 1 [S] hard dull work 2 [C] *AmE for* SWOT ~**er** *n* person or machine that grinds

grind down *phr vt* keep in a state of suffering and hopelessness

grind out *phr vt derog* produce (esp. writing or music) continually, but like a machine

grind·stone /'graɪndstəʊn ‖ -stoʊn/ *n* 1 round stone that is turned to sharpen tools 2 one's nose to the grindstone in a state of continuous hard work

grip /grɪp/ *vi/t* -pp- 1 seize tightly 2 hold someone's attention: *a gripping story* ♦ *n* 1 tight hold 2 thing that grips: *hairgrip* 3 *AmE* traveller's small bag 4 come/get to grips with deal seriously with

gripe /graɪp/ *vi sl* complain continuously ♦ gripe *n*

gris·ly /'grɪzli/ *adj* shocking and sickening

gris·tle /'grɪsəl/ *n* [U] CARTILAGE in cooked meat

grit /grɪt/ *n* [U] 1 small stones and sand 2 lasting courage: determination ♦ *vt* -tt- 1 put grit on (esp. a road) 2 grit one's teeth show determination ~ty *adj*

griz·zled /'grɪzəld/ *adj* grey-haired

groan /grəʊn ‖ groʊn/ *vi, n* (make) a loud deep sound of suffering

gro·cer /'grəʊsə ‖ 'groʊsər/ *n* shopkeeper who sells dry foods and other things for the home

gro·cer·ies /'grəʊsəriz ‖ 'groʊ-/ *n* [P] goods sold by a grocer

grog·gy /'grɒgi ‖ 'grɑːgi/ *adj* weak and unsteady from illness, etc. –giness *n* [U]

groin /grɔɪn/ *n* place where the legs meet the front of the body

groom /gru:m, grʊm/ *n* 1 person who looks after horses 2 BRIDEGROOM ♦ *vt* 1 brush and clean (horses) 2 make (oneself) neat and tidy 3 prepare (someone) for special work

groove /gru:v/ *n* long hollow in a surface

grope /grəʊp ‖ groʊp/ 1 *vi* search about with the hands as in the dark 2 *vt sl* (try to) feel the body of (a person) to get sexual pleasure grope *n*

gross¹ /grəʊs‖groʊs/ *adj* **1** *infml* very unpleasant **2** unpleasantly fat **3** clearly wrong: *gross negligence* **4** total: *gross income* ◆ *vt* gain as total profit ~**ly** *adv* ~**ness** *n* [U]

gross² *determiner, n* **gross** *or* **grosses** 144

gro·tesque /grəʊˈtesk‖groʊ-/ *adj* strange and ugly ~**ly** *adv*

grot·to /ˈgrɒtəʊ‖ˈgrɑːtoʊ/ *n* -**toes** *or* -**tos** cave

grot·ty /ˈgrɒti‖ˈgrɑː-/ *adj infml BrE* unattractive

grouch /graʊtʃ/ *n* **1** person who often complains **2** thing complained about ◆ *vi:* *Stop grouching.* ~**y** *adj*

ground¹ /graʊnd/ *v past t. and p. of* GRIND

ground² *n* **1** [S;U] surface of the earth **2** [U] soil **3** [C] piece of land used for a particular purpose: *a playground* **4** [U] **a** base for argument: *You're on safe ground as long as you avoid the subject of politics.* **b** area of knowledge or experience: *It was absurd to try to cover so much ground in such a short course.* **5** [U] position of advantage to be won or defended: *The army has lost ground.* | *The idea is gaining ground.* (=becoming more popular) **6** [C] *AmE for* EARTH (5) **7 get off the ground** make a successful start **8 to ground** into hiding to escape —see also GROUNDS ~**less** *adj* without reason: *groundless fears* ~**lessly** *adv*

ground³ *v* **1** *vi* (of a boat) strike against the bottom of the sea, a river, etc. **2** *vt* cause (a plane or pilot) to stay on the ground **3** *vt* base: *arguments grounded on experience* ~**ing** *n* [S] first necessary training in something

ground floor /ˌ· ·◄/ *n* **1** *BrE* part of a building at ground level **2 get/be in on the ground floor** be part of an activity, business operation, etc. from the time it starts

ground·nut /ˈgraʊndnʌt/ *n* PEANUT

ground rule /ˈ· ·/ *n* basic rule

grounds /graʊndz/ *n* [P] **1** solid bits at the bottom of a liquid **2** gardens, etc. round a building **3** reason: *grounds for divorce*

ground·sheet /ˈgraʊndʃiːt/ *n* WATER-PROOF sheet to spread on the ground

ground·work /ˈgraʊndwɜːk‖-wɜːrk/ *n* [U] work on which further study, etc. is based

group /gruːp/ *n* connected set of people or things ◆ *vi/t* form into groups

grouse¹ /graʊs/ *vi, n* GRUMBLE

grouse² *n* **grouse** smallish fat bird which is shot for food and sport

grove /grəʊv‖groʊv/ *n lit* small group of trees

grov·el /ˈgrɒvəl‖ˈgrɑː-, ˈgrʌ-/ *vi* -**ll-** *BrE*‖ -**l-** *AmE* **1** lie flat in fear or obedience **2** be shamefully humble and eager to please ~**ler** *n*

grow /grəʊ‖groʊ/ *v* **grew** /gruː/, **grown** /grəʊn‖groʊn/ **1** *vi* get bigger **2** *vi* (of plants) live and develop **3** *vt* cause (plants, etc.) to grow **4** *fml* become: *grow old* **grown** *adj* ADULT: *grown men*

grow on *phr vt* become more pleasing to: *This music will grow on you.*

grow out of *phr vt* get too big or old for

grow up *phr vi* **1** develop from child to man or woman **2** start to exist: *customs that have grown up*

growl /graʊl/ *vi, n* (make) the threatening noise of an angry dog

grown-up /ˌ· ·◄/ *adj, n* ADULT

growth /grəʊθ‖groʊθ/ *n* **1** [S;U] process of growing; increase **2** [C] something that has grown, esp. an unnatural lump in the body

grub¹ /grʌb/ *n* **1** [C] insect in the wormlike stage **2** [U] *sl* food

grub² *vi/t* -**bb-** dig with the hands or PAWS

grub·by /ˈgrʌbi/ *adj* rather dirty ~**biness** *n* [U]

grub·stake /ˈgrʌbˌsteɪk/ *n* money provided to develop a new business

grudge /grʌdʒ/ *vt* be unwilling to give: *He grudged paying so much.* ◆ *n* continuing feeling of anger against someone **grudgingly** *adv*

gru·el·ling *BrE*‖ **grueling** *AmE* /ˈgruːəlɪŋ/ *adj* very tiring

grue·some /ˈgruːsəm/ *adj* very shocking and sickening ~**ly** *adv*

gruff /grʌf/ *adj* (of the voice) deep and rough ~**ly** *adv* ~**ness** *n* [U]

grum·ble /ˈgrʌmbəl/ *vi* complain ◆ *n* complaint

grump·y /ˈgrʌmpi/ *adj* bad-tempered ~**ily** *adv* ~**iness** *n* [U]

grunge /grʌndʒ/ *n* [U] *infml* dirt ~**gy** *adj*

grunt /grʌnt/ *vi, n* (make) the short rough sound that pigs make

guar·an·tee /ˌgærən'tiː/ *n* **1** written promise to replace an article if it is found to be imperfect **2** agreement to be responsible for a debt ♦ *vt* **1** give a guarantee about **2** promise: *I guarantee you'll enjoy it.*

guar·an·tor /ˌgærən'tɔː‖ -'tɔːr/ *n law* person who agrees to be responsible for a debt

guard /gɑːd‖ gɑːrd/ *n* **1** [U] state of watching against attack: *soldiers on guard* **2 a** [C] person keeping guard **b** [S] group of these people **3** [C] protective apparatus: *a fireguard* **4** [C] *BrE* railway official on a train —see also OLD GUARD ♦ *vt* **1** defend **2** watch (prisoners) to prevent escape **~ed** *adj* not saying too much

guard against *phr vt* prevent by care: *guard against infection*

guard·i·an /'gɑːdiən‖ 'gɑːr-/ *n* person responsible for a child **~ship** *n* [U]

guer·ril·la /gə'rɪlə/ *n* member of an unofficial army which attacks in small groups

guess /ges/ **1** *vi/t* form an opinion (on) without knowing all the facts **2** *vt infml, esp. AmE* suppose; consider likely ♦ *n* **1** opinion formed by guessing **2** attempt to guess

guess·work /'geswɜːk‖ -wɜːrk/ *n* [U] guessing

guest¹ /gest/ *n* **1** person invited to someone's home, or staying in a hotel **2** person, esp. an entertainer, invited to take part in a show, etc. **3 be my guest!** please feel free to do so ♦ *vi esp. AmE* take part as a guest performer

guest·house /'gesthaʊs/ *n* small private hotel

guf·faw /gə'fɔː‖ -'fɔː/ *vi* laugh loudly and esp. rudely **guffaw** *n*

guid·ance /'gaɪdəns/ *n* [U] help; advice

guide /gaɪd/ *n* **1** person who shows the way **2** something that influences behaviour **3** also **guide book** — book describing a place **4** instruction book **5** member of an association (the **Guides**) for training girls in character and self-help ♦ *vt* act as a guide to

guided mis·sile /ˌ·· '··/ *n* MISSILE whose flight is controlled by electrical means

guide dog /'· ·/ *n BrE* dog trained to help a blind person

guide·lines /'gaɪdlaɪnz/ *n* [P] main points on how to deal with something

guild /gɪld/ *n* association of people with the same interests

guile /gaɪl/ *n* [U] deceit **~ful** *adj* **~less** *adj*

guil·lo·tine /'gɪlətiːn/ *n* **1** machine for cutting off the heads of criminals **2** machine for cutting paper **3** time limit fixed for argument in Parliament ♦ *vt* use a GUILLOTINE on

guilt /gɪlt/ *n* [U] **1** fact of having done wrong; blame **2** shame **~y** *adj* having done wrong

guin·ea /'gɪni/ *n* £1.05 in British money

guinea pig /'·· ·/ *n* **1** small tailless furry animal kept as a pet **2** person on whom something is tested

guise /gaɪz/ *n fml* outer appearance

gui·tar /gɪ'tɑː‖ -'tɑːr/ *n* stringed musical instrument played with the fingers

gulf /gʌlf/ *n* **1** piece of sea partly surrounded by land **2** division, esp. between opinions

gull /gʌl/ *n* any of several kinds of large seabirds

gul·let /'gʌlɪt/ *n* foodpipe in the throat

gul·li·ble /'gʌlɪbəl/ *adj* easily tricked **~bility** /ˌgʌlɪ'bɪlɪti/ *n* [U]

gulp /gʌlp/ *vi/t* swallow hastily **gulp** *n*

gum¹ /gʌm/ *n* flesh in which the teeth are fixed

gum² *n* **1** [U] sticky plant substance **2** [C] hard jelly-like sweet **3** [U] CHEWING GUM ♦ *vt* **-mm-** stick with gum (1) **~my** *adj* sticky

gum·boot /'gʌmbuːt/ *n* WELLINGTON

gump·tion /'gʌmpʃən/ *n* [U] practical good sense

gun¹ /gʌn/ *n* weapon that fires bullets or SHELLS through a tube —see also **stick to one's guns** (STICK²)

gun² *v*

gun down *phr vt* shoot, causing to fall to the ground dead or wounded

gun for *phr vt* search for in order to attack

gun·boat /'gʌnbəʊt‖ -boʊt/ *n* small heavily armed warship

gun·fire /'gʌnfaɪə‖ -faɪr/ *n* [U] (sound of) shooting

gung-ho /ˌgʌŋ 'həʊ‖ -'hoʊ/ *adj* showing extreme, often foolish, eagerness, esp. to attack an enemy

gun·man /'gʌnmən/ *n* **-men** /-mən/ armed criminal

gun·ner /'gʌnə‖-ər/ n soldier who uses heavy guns

gun·point /'gʌnpɔɪnt/ n **at gunpoint** under a threat of death by shooting

gun·pow·der /'gʌn,paʊdə‖-ər/ n [U] explosive powder

gun·run·ner /'gʌn,rʌnə‖-ər/ n person who unlawfully and secretly brings guns into a country **-ning** n [U]

gun·shot /'gʌnʃɒt‖-ʃɑːt/ n **1** [C] sound made by a gun **2** [U] bullets fired from a gun

gur·gle /'gɜːgəl‖'gɜːr-/ vi, n (make) the sound of water flowing unevenly

gu·ru /'ɡʊruː/ n **-rus 1** Indian religious teacher **2** greatly respected person whose ideas are followed

gush /gʌʃ/ v **1** vi flow out: *oil gushing from a pipe* **2** vt send out (liquid) in large quantities **3** vi express admiration foolishly ♦ n [S] sudden flow

gust /gʌst/ n sudden rush of wind ♦ vi **~y** adj

gus·to /'gʌstəʊ‖-toʊ/ n [U] eager enjoyment

gut /gʌt/ n [U] thread made from animal bowels ♦ vt **1** take out the inner organs of: *gut a fish* **2** destroy the inside of (a building) ♦ adj coming from feelings rather than thought: *gut reactions* **guts** n [P] **1** bowels **2** bravery and determination **gutsy** adj brave

gut·ter /'gʌtə‖-ər/ n **1** [C] ditch or pipe that carries away rainwater **2** [the+S] the poorest level of society

gutter press /'·· ,·/ n derog newspapers which tend to be full of shocking stories

gut·tur·al /'gʌtərəl/ adj (of speech) coming from deep in the throat

guy /ɡaɪ/ n **1** sl **a** man **b** esp. AmE person, male or female: *Come on, you guys!* **2** figure of a man burnt in Britain on November 5th

guz·zle /'ɡʌzəl/ vi/t eat or drink eagerly

gym /dʒɪm/ n **1** [C] gymnasium **2** [U] gymnastics

gym·kha·na /dʒɪm'kɑːnə/ n esp. BrE local sports meeting, esp. for horse riding by children

gym·na·si·um /dʒɪm'neɪziəm/ n hall with apparatus for indoor exercise

gym·nas·tics /dʒɪm'næstɪks/ n [U] training of the body by physical exercises **-tic** adj **gym·nast** n /'dʒɪmnæst, -nəst/ n person trained in this

gy·nae·col·o·gy usu. gynecology AmE /,gaɪn⅛'kɒlədʒi‖-'kɑː-/ n [U] medical study and treatment of the female sex organs **-gist** n **-gical** /,gaɪn⅛kə'lɒdʒɪkəl◄‖-'lɑː-/ adj **-gically** /-kli/ adv

gyp·sy /'dʒɪpsi/ n GIPSY

gy·rate /dʒaɪ'reɪt‖'dʒaɪreɪt/ vi fml swing round and round **gyration** /dʒaɪ'reɪʃən/ n [C;U]

gy·ro·scope /'dʒaɪrəskəʊp‖-skoʊp/ n wheel that spins inside a frame, used for keeping ships, etc. steady

H

H, h /eɪtʃ/ the 8th letter of the English alphabet

ha·be·as cor·pus /,heɪbiəs 'kɔːpəs‖-'kɔːr-/ n [U] written order that a person must be brought before a court

hab·er·dash·er /'hæbədæʃə‖-bərdæʃər/ n **1** BrE shopkeeper who sells thread, etc. used in sewing **2** AmE shopkeeper who sells men's hats, GLOVES, etc. **~y** n [U] haberdasher's goods

hab·it /'hæb⅛t/ n **1** [C;U] person's usual behaviour **2** [C] clothes worn by a MONK or NUN

hab·i·ta·ble /'hæb⅛təbəl/ adj fit to be lived in

hab·i·tat /'hæb⅛tæt/ n natural home of an animal or plant

hab·i·ta·tion /,hæb⅛'teɪʃən/ n fml [U] living in: *houses fit for habitation*

ha·bit·u·al /hə'bɪtʃuəl/ adj **1** usual **2** (done) by habit **~ly** adv

hack¹ /hæk/ vi/t cut roughly

hack² n writer who does a lot of poor quality work

   hack into phr vt use, change, etc. (a computer system) without permission

hack·er /'hækə‖-ər/ n **1** someone who HACKS INTO a computer **2** someone who uses computers a lot

hacking cough /ˌ·· ˈ·/ *n* cough with a rough, unpleasant sound
hack·les /ˈhækəlz/ *n* **make someone's hackles rise** make someone very angry
hack·neyed /ˈhæknid/ *adj* (of a saying) meaningless because used too often
hack·saw /ˈhæksɔː ‖ -sɒː/ *n* tool with a fine-toothed blade used esp. for cutting metal
had /d, əd, həd; *strong* hæd/ *v past t. and p. of* HAVE
had·dock /ˈhædək/ *n* **haddock** common fish, used as food
had·n't /ˈhædnt/ *v short for:* had not
hag /hæg/ *n derog* ugly old woman
hag·gard /ˈhægəd ‖ -ərd/ *adj* (of the face) lined and hollow from tiredness
hag·gis /ˈhægɨs/ *n* Scottish food made of parts of a sheep
hag·gle /ˈhægəl/ *vi* argue over a price
hail¹ /heɪl/ *n* [U] frozen rain drops: (fig.) *a hail of bullets* ♦ *vi* (of hail) fall
hail² *vi* 1 call out to: *hail a taxi* 2 recognize (someone) as important: *They hailed him king.*
hail as *phr vt* recognize as (something good)
hail from come from: *She hails from Liverpool.*
hail·stone /ˈheɪlstəʊn ‖ -stoʊn/ *n* single piece of HAIL
hair /heə ‖ her/ *n* 1 [C] threadlike growth from the skin 2 [U] mass of these growths 3 **let one's hair down** behave as one likes after being formal 4 **make someone's hair curl** *infml* shock someone 5 **make one's hair stand on end** frighten one badly 6 **not turn a hair** show no fear or worry (when in difficulty) ~**y** *adj* 1 covered with hair 2 *infml* exciting in a way that causes fear; dangerous ~**iness** *n* [U]
hair·cut /ˈheəkʌt ‖ ˈher-/ *n* 1 hairdo 2 cutting of someone's hair
hair·do /ˈheədu: ‖ ˈher-/ *n* **-dos** style a person's hair is shaped into
hair·dress·er /ˈheəˌdresə ‖ ˈherˌdresər/ *n* person who cuts and shapes hair
hair·grip /ˈheəgrɪp ‖ ˈher-/ *n BrE* flat hairpin with the ends pressed together
hair·line /ˈheəlaɪn ‖ ˈher-/ *n* 1 edge of the area of one's head covered in hair 2 **hairline crack/fracture** very thin crack
hair·piece /ˈheəpiːs ‖ ˈher-/ *n* piece of false hair used to make one's own hair seem thicker or longer
hair·pin bend /ˌheəpɪn ˈbend ‖ ˌher-/ *n* U-shaped curve on a road
hair-rais·ing /ˈ· ˌ··/ *adj* very frightening
hair's breadth /ˈ· ·/ *n* very short distance
hair-split·ting /ˈ· ˌ··/ *n* [U] *derog* act or habit of paying too much attention to unimportant differences and details
hair·style /ˈheəstaɪl ‖ ˈher-/ *n* HAIRDO
hal·cy·on /ˈhælsiən/ *adj lit* peaceful and happy: *halcyon days*
hale /heɪl/ *adj* **hale and hearty** very healthy
half¹ /hɑːf ‖ hæf/ *n* **halves** /hɑːvz ‖ hævz/ 1 either of two equal parts: ½ *Half of 50 is 25.* 2 either of two parts into which something is divided: *He's in the bottom half of the class.* 3 coin, ticket, drink, etc. of ½ the value or amount: *A pint of beer and two halves please.* 4 **by halves** incompletely 5 **go halves** share something equally 6 **my/your/his/her better half** one's husband or wife
half² *predeterminer, adj* ½ in amount: *She bought half a kilo of rice.*
half³ *adv* 1 partly: *half cooked* | *half French* 2 **half and half** ½ one and ½ the other 3 **not half** *BrE infml* **a** very: *It isn't half windy today.* **b** not at all: *This food's not half bad.* **c** very much: *'Did you like the show?' 'Not half.'* 4 **not half as** not nearly as
half-baked /ˌ· ˈ·◂/ *adj* (esp. of ideas) not sensible
half board /ˌ· ˈ·/ *n* [U] *esp. BrE* (price of) a hotel room with an evening meal and breakfast
half-broth·er /ˈ· ˌ··/ *n* brother related through only one parent
half-caste /ˈ· ·/ *n, adj derog* (person) with parents of different races
half-heart·ed /ˌ· ˈ··◂ ‖ ˈ· ˌ··/ *adj* showing not much interest
half-life /ˈ· ·/ *n* time it takes for half the atoms in a RADIOACTIVE substance to decay
half-mast /ˌ· ˈ·/ *n* 1 point near the middle of a flag-pole where the flag flies as a sign of sorrow 2 **(at) half-mast** too short: *His trousers are always at half-mast.*
half·penny /ˈheɪpni/ *n* 1 (in Great Britain before 1985) small BRONZE coin, two of which made a penny 2 **not have two**

halfpennies to rub together be very poor

half-sis·ter /'· ·/ n sister related through only one parent

half term /ˌ· '·◂/ n [C;U] BrE short holiday in the middle of the school TERM

half time /ˌ· '·◂/ n [U] rest between the two parts of a game, eg. football

half·way /ˌhɑːf'weɪ◂ ‖ ˌhæf-/ adj, adv 1 at the midpoint between two things 2 **meet someone halfway** make an agreement with someone which partly satisfies the demands of both sides

half-wit /'· ·/ n weak-minded, stupid person ~**ted** /ˌ· '·◂/ adj

hall /hɔːl ‖ hɒːl/ n 1 passage inside the entrance of a house 2 large room for meetings, etc. 3 place where university students live or eat together

hal·le·lu·ja /ˌhælɪ'luːjə/ interj (expression of praise to God)

hall·mark /'hɔːlmɑːk ‖ 'hɒːlmɑːrk/ n mark proving that something is really silver or gold: (fig.) Clear expression is the hallmark of a good writer.

hal·lo /hə'ləʊ, he-, hæ-‖-'loʊ/ interj, n -los BrE for HELLO

hal·lowed /'hæləʊd ‖-loʊd/ adj fml holy

Hal·low·e·en /ˌhæləʊ'iːn ‖-loʊ-/ n October 31, when children play tricks and dress in strange clothes

hal·lu·ci·nate /hə'luːsɪneɪt/ vi see things that are not there –**natory** /-nətəri ‖ -nətɔːri/ adj –**nation** /hə,luːsɪ'neɪʃən/ n [C;U] (experience of seeing) something which is not really there, because of illness or drugs

ha·lo /'heɪləʊ ‖-loʊ/ n -loes or -los 1 circle representing light round the heads of holy people in pictures 2 circle of light round the sun or moon

halt /hɔːlt ‖ hɒːlt/ vi/t fml stop **halt** n [S]

hal·ter /'hɔːltə ‖ 'hɒːltər/ n rope for leading a horse

halt·ing /'hɔːltɪŋ ‖ 'hɒːl-/ adj stopping and starting unconfidently

halve /hɑːv ‖ hæv/ vt 1 reduce by half: halve the time 2 divide into halves

halves /hɑːvz ‖ hævz/ n pl. of HALF

ham /hæm/ n 1 [C;U] (preserved meat from) the upper part of a pig's leg 2 [C] actor whose performance is unnatural 3 [C] non-professional radio operator ♦ vi/t perform like a HAM (2)

ham·burg·er /'hæmbɜːgə ‖ -bɜːrgər/ n flat round cake of small bits of meat, eaten in a bread ROLL² (3)

ham-fisted /ˌ· '·◂/ adj awkward in using the hands

ham·let /'hæmlɪt/ n small village

ham·mer /'hæmə ‖ -ər/ n 1 tool with a metal head for driving nails into wood 2 part of a piano, etc. that hits another part 3 **be/go at it hammer and tongs** fight or argue violently 4 **come under the hammer** be offered for sale at an AUCTION 5 **throwing the hammer** sport in which a heavy metal ball on a chain is thrown

hammer² v 1 vi/t hit with a hammer 2 vt defeat thoroughly 3 vi work continuously: hammer away at the problem 4 vt force: hammer the facts into their heads

hammer out phr vt talk about in detail and come to a decision about

ham·mock /'hæmək/ n cloth or net hung up to sleep in

ham·per¹ /'hæmpə ‖-ər/ vt cause difficulty in movement

hamper² n large basket with a lid

ham·ster /'hæmstə ‖ -ər/ n small mouselike animal often kept as a pet

ham·string /'hæm,strɪŋ/ n cordlike TENDON at the back of the leg ♦ vt –**strung** /-,strʌŋ/ make powerless

hand¹ /hænd/ n 1 [C] movable part at the end of the arm 2 [C] pointer on a clock, etc. 3 [C] set of playing cards held by one player 4 [S] handwriting 5 [C] worker; someone with a skill: factory hands —see also OLD HAND 6 [S] help: give/lend a hand 7 [C;U] control: get out of hand ǀ have the matter in hand ǀ in the hands of the police 8 [S] APPLAUSE: Give the singer a big hand. 9 **at first hand** by direct experience 10 **at hand** near in time or place 11 **at second/third/fourth hand** as information passed on through 1, 2, or 3 people 12 **by hand** a not typed or printed b delivered directly, not by post 13 **change hands** go from the possession of one person to that of another 14 **get/keep one's hand in** get/stay used to an activity 15 **get the upper hand (of)** get control or power (over something/somebody difficult) 16 **give someone a free hand** let them do things in their own way 17 **hand in glove (with)** closely connected (with someone), esp. in something bad **18 hand in hand: a** holding each other's hands **b** in close connection **19 hand over fist** very quickly and successfully **20 have a hand in** be partly responsible for **21 have one's hands full** be very busy **22 in hand** ready for use **23 live from hand to mouth** have just enough money, food, etc. to live **24 on hand** ready for use or to take part **25 on the one/other hand** (used for comparing two things) **26 (out of/off) one's hands** (no longer) one's responsibility **27 play into someone's hands** do something which gives (one's opponent) an advantage **28 raise one's hand to/against** (make a movement) to hit **29 show one's hand** make one's power or intentions clear, esp. after keeping them secret **30 throw in one's hand** accept defeat **31 to hand** within reach **32 try one's hand (at)** attempt (an activity) **33 turn one's hand to** begin to practise (a skill) **34 wait on (someone) hand and foot** do every little thing for (someone)

hand² vt **1** give with one's hand(s) **2 (have to) hand it to someone** (have to) admit the high quality or success of someone

   hand down phr vt give to those who come later

   hand in phr vt deliver

   hand on phr vt give to someone else

   hand out phr vt **1** give out to several people **2** give freely: *He's always ready to hand out advice.*

   hand over phr vt give control of: *We handed him over to the police.*

hand·bag /'hændbæg/ n woman's small bag for money and personal things

hand·book /'hændbʊk/ n book of instructions

hand·brake /'hændbreɪk/ n BRAKE worked by the driver's hand, not by the foot

hand·cuffs /'hændkʌfs/ n [P] pair of metal rings for fastening a criminal's wrists **handcuff** vt put handcuffs on

hand·ful /'hændfʊl/ n **1** as much as can be held in one hand **2** small number (of people) **3** *infml* person or animal that is hard to control

hand·gun /'hændgʌn/ n small gun held in one hand to shoot

hand·i·cap /'hændɪkæp/ n **1** disability of the body or mind **2** disadvantage given to

the stronger competitors in a sport ♦ vt **-pp- 1** give a disadvantage to **2** (of a disability of body or mind) prevent (someone) from acting or living as most people do

hand·i·craft /'hændɪkrɑːft‖-kræft/ n skill such as weaving, which uses the hands

hand·i·work /'hændɪwɜːk‖-wɜːrk/ n [U] **1** work demanding the skilful use of the hands **2** result of someone's action

hand·ker·chief /'hæŋkətʃɪf‖-kər-/ n cloth or paper for drying the nose, etc.

han·dle¹ /'hændl/ n part of a door, cup, etc. that one holds

handle² vt **1** touch or move with the hands **2** control; deal with: *handle the accounts* **3** (of a car, boat, etc.) obey controlling movements in the stated way **–dler** n person who controls an animal

han·dle·bars /'hændlbɑːz‖-bɑːrz/ n [P] curved bar above the front wheel of a bicycle, etc., which controls the direction it goes in

hand·out /'hændaʊt/ n **1** something given free **2** printed sheet of information given out

hand·picked /ˌhænd'pɪkt◁/ adj carefully chosen

hand·shake /'hændʃeɪk/ n act of taking each other's hand as a greeting

hand·some /'hænsəm/ adj **1** of good appearance: *a handsome boy* **2** plentiful; *a handsome reward* **–ly** adv

hands-on /ˌ· '·◁/ adj (of training, etc.) gained by doing something rather than studying it

hand·stand /'hændstænd/ n position in which the body is supported upside down on the hands

hand-to-mouth /ˌ· · '·◁/ adj (of a way of life) with just enough food, money, etc. to live

hand·writ·ing /'hænd,raɪtɪŋ/ n [U] (style of) writing done by hand **–written** /ˌhænd'rɪtn◁/ adj written by hand

hand·y /'hændi/ adj **1** useful **2** clever with one's hands **3** easily reached **4 come in handy** be useful **–ily** adv

hand·y·man /'hændimæn/ n **-men** /-men/ person who does small repairs

hang¹ /hæŋ/ v hung /hʌŋ/ **1** vi/t fix or be fixed from above so that the lower part is free **2** vi/t (of certain kinds of meat) be kept in this position until ready to eat **3** *vt* stick (wallpaper) on a wall **4** *vt* (*past t. and p.* **hanged**) kill by dropping with a rope round the neck **5 hang fire** be delayed **6 hang one's head** appear ashamed

hang about/around *phr vi* **1** wait without purpose **2** delay

hang back *phr vi* be unwilling to move

hang on *phr vi* **1** keep hold of something **2** wait **3** pay close attention to **4** depend on

hang onto *phr vt* try to keep

hang out *phr vi infml* **1** live or spend a lot of time **2 let it all hang out** *sl* behave exactly as you want to

hang up *phr vi* **1** finish a telephone conversation **2** put something on a hook **3 be hung up on/about** *sl* be anxious or have a fixed idea about

hang² *n* **get/have the hang of something** understand how a machine, etc. works

hang·ar /'hæŋə∥-ər/ *n* building where aircraft are kept

hang·er /'hæŋə∥-ər/ *n* hook and crosspiece to hang a garment from

hanger-on /ˌ·· '·/ *n* **hangers-on** person who tries to be friendly in the hope of advantage

hang glid·ing /'· ˌ··/ *n* [U] the sport of gliding (GLIDE (2)) using a large KITE (1) instead of a plane

hang·ings /'hæŋɪŋz/ *n* [P] curtains, etc. that hang

hang·man /'hæŋmən/ *n* **-men** /-mən/ man whose work was hanging criminals

hang·o·ver /'hæŋəʊvə∥-oʊvər/ *n* **1** feeling of sickness, etc. the day after drinking too much alcohol **2** condition or effect resulting from an earlier event or state

hang-up /'hæŋʌp/ *n sl* something about which a person gets unusually worried

han·ker /'hæŋkə∥-ər/ *v* **hanker after/for** *phr vt* desire stongly **hankering** *n* [S]

han·kie, **-ky** /'hæŋki/ *n* handkerchief

hank·y-pank·y /ˌhæŋki 'pæŋki/ *n* [U] improper behaviour, esp. deceit of a not very serious kind

hap·haz·ard /ˌhæp'hæzəd◀∥-ərd◀/ *adj* unplanned; disorderly

hap·less /'hæpləs/ *adj lit* unlucky

hap·pen /'hæpən/ *vi* **1** (of an event) take place: *When did the accident happen?* **2** be or do by chance: *We happened to meet.* **3** be true by or as if by chance: *As it happens, we do know each other.* **~ing** *n* event

happen on *phr vt* find by chance

hap·py /'hæpi/ *adj* **1** pleased; contented **2** causing pleasure: *a happy occasion* **3** (of thoughts, etc.) suitable: *a happy remark* **4** (used in good wishes): *Happy Birthday!* **–pily** *adv* **–piness** *n* [U]

happy-go-luck·y /ˌ··· ˌ·◀/ *adj* unworried; CAREFREE

happy hour /'·· ·/ *n* limited period in the day when alcoholic drinks are sold at lower than usual prices in a bar, etc.

ha·rangue /həˈræŋ/ *vt* attack or try to persuade with a long angry speech **harangue** *n*

har·ass /'hærəs, həˈræs∥həˈræs, 'hærəs/ *vt* worry repeatedly **~ment** *n* [U]

har·bour *BrE*∥ **-bor** *AmE* /'hɑːbə∥ 'hɑːrbər/ *n* sheltered area where ships are safe ♦ *vt* **1** give protection to **2** keep (thoughts or feelings) in the mind

hard¹ /hɑːd∥hɑːrd/ *adj* **1** firm and stiff: *hard skin* **2** difficult: *hard question* **3** needing or using effort: *hard work/ worker* **4** unpleasant; severe: *hard winter* | *Don't be too hard on him.* **5** containing minerals that stop soap from forming LATHER easily **6** (of drugs) dangerous and ADDICTIVE **~ness** *n* [U]

hard² *adv* **1** with great effort: *push hard* **2** heavily: *raining hard* **3 hard at it** working hard **4 hard by** *fml* near **5 hard done by** unfairly treated **6 hard hit** suffering loss **7 hard put (to it)** having great difficulty **8 hard up** *infml* not having enough (esp. money) **9 take (it) hard** suffer deeply

hard-and-fast /ˌ·· '·◀/ *adj* (of rules) fixed

hard·back /'hɑːdbæk∥'hɑːrd-/ *n* book with a stiff cover

hard·ball /'hɑːdbɔːl∥'hɑːrdbɔːl/ *n* [U] *AmE* BASEBALL **2 play hardball** use methods that are not gentle, and may be unfair

hard-bit·ten /ˌ· '··◀/ *adj* (of a person) made firm in argument and decision by hard experience

hard·board /'hɑːdbɔːd∥'hɑːrdbɔːrd/ *n* [U] stiff cardboard, used like wood

hard-boiled /ˌ· ˈ·◂/ *adj* **1** (of eggs) boiled till the yellow part is hard **2** (of people) not showing feeling

hard cop·y /ˈ· ˌ·/ *n* [U] printed information from a computer

hard·core /ˌhɑːˈdkɔː‖ˌhɑːrdkɔːr/ *n* [U] small unchanging group within an organization **hard-core** *adj* **1** very strongly following a particular belief or activity **2** showing or describing sexual activity in a very detailed way: *hard-core pornography*

hard cur·ren·cy /ˌ· ˈ···/ *n* [C;U] money that can be freely exchanged

hard disk also **hard drive** /ˈ· ·/ *n* part of a computer used for permanently keeping information

hard·en /ˈhɑːdn‖ˈhɑːrdn/ *vi/t* make or become hard or firm

  harden to *phr vt* make (someone) less sensitive to (something)

hard-head·ed /ˌhɑːˈdhedᶻd◂‖ˌhɑːrd-/ *adj* tough and practical

hard-heart·ed /ˌ· ˈ··◂/ *adj* not kind or gentle

hard-hit·ting /ˌ· ˈ··◂/ *adj* criticizing in a strong, effective way

hard la·bour /ˌ· ˈ··/ *n* [U] (punishment which consists of) hard bodily work such as digging, etc.

hard-line /ˌ· ˈ·◂/ *adj* unwilling to change one's extreme opinions **hard-liner** *n*

hard-luck /ˌ· ˈ·◂/ *n* [U] bad luck

hard·ly /ˈhɑːdli‖ˈhɑːrdli/ *adv* **1** almost not: *I can hardly wait.* **2** not at all: *You can hardly blame me.*

hard-nosed /ˌ· ˈ·◂/ *adj* determined; not affected by emotion

hard of hear·ing /ˌ· · ˈ··/ *adj* rather DEAF

hard-pressed /ˌ· ˈ·◂/ *adj* experiencing severe or continual difficulties

hard sell /ˌ· ˈ·◂/ *n* [U] method of selling by putting pressure on buyers

hard·ship /ˈhɑːdʃɪp‖ˈhɑːrd-/ *n* [C;U] difficult conditions of life, such as lack of money, food, etc.

hard shoul·der /ˌ· ˈ··/ *n esp. BrE* hard surface beside a MOTORWAY where cars may stop if in difficulty

hard up /ˌ· ˈ·/ *adj infml* not having enough (money)

hard·ware /ˈhɑːdweə‖ˈhɑːrdwer/ *n* [U] **1** pans, tools, etc. for the home **2** machinery which makes up a COMPUTER **3** machinery used in war

hard·wear·ing /ˌhɑːdˈweərɪŋ◂‖ˌhɑːrd-ˈwer-/ *adj* (of clothes, etc.) that last a long time

hard·wood /ˈhɑːdwʊd‖ˈhɑːrd-/ *n* [U] strong wood from trees such as the OAK

har·dy /ˈhɑːdi‖ˈhɑːrdi/ *adj* able to bear cold, hard work, etc. **–diness** *n* [U]

hare /heə/ *n* fast-running animal like a large rabbit ♦ *vi* run fast

hare·brained /ˈheəbreɪnd‖ˈher-/ *adj* impractical; foolish

hare·lip /ˌheəˈlɪp‖ˌher-/ *n* top lip divided into two parts

har·em /ˈheərəm, hɑːˈriːm‖ˈhɑːrəm/ *n* (women living in) the women's part of a Muslim house

hark /hɑːk‖hɑːrk/ *vi lit* listen

  hark at *phr vi infml esp. BrE* listen to (something or something that is disapproved of)

  hark back *phr vi* talk about the past

harm /hɑːm‖hɑːrm/ *n* [U] **1** damage; INJURY **2 out of harm's way** safe ♦ *vt* cause harm to **~ful** *adj* **~less** *adj* not dangerous

har·mon·i·ca /hɑːˈmɒnɪkə‖hɑːrˈmɑː-/ *n* MOUTHORGAN

har·mo·nize, ise /ˈhɑːmənaɪz‖ˈhɑːr-/ *vi/t* **1** (cause to) be in agreement, esp. in style, colour, etc. **2** sing or play in musical HARMONY

har·mo·ny /ˈhɑːməni‖ˈhɑːr-/ *n* **1** [C;U] musical notes pleasantly combined **2** [U] peaceful agreement **3** [C;U] pleasant combination of colours, etc.

har·ness /ˈhɑːnɨs‖ˈhɑːr-/ *n* [C;U] **1** leather bands, etc. that fasten a horse to a cart **2** similar arrangement for tying someone to something: *safety harness* ♦ *vt* **1** fasten with a harness **2** use (wind, water, etc.) to produce esp. electrical power

harp¹ /hɑːp‖hɑːrp/ *n* large stringed musical instrument played with the fingers **~ist** *n*

harp² *v* **harp on** *phr vt* talk a lot about (one's misfortunes)

har·poon /hɑːˈpuːn‖hɑːr-/ *vt, n* (strike with) a spear on a rope, for hunting WHALES, etc.

harp·si·chord /ˈhɑːpsɪkɔːd‖ˈhɑːrpsɪkɔːrd/ *n* kind of early piano

har·row·ing /ˈhærəʊɪŋ‖-roʊ-/ *adj* causing painful feelings

har·ry /'hæri/ *vt fml* trouble continually

harsh /hɑːʃ ‖ hɑːrʃ/ *adj* **1** painful to the senses: *harsh light* **2** cruel ~**ly** *adv* ~**ness** *n* [U]

har·vest /'hɑːvɪst ‖ 'hɑːr-/ *n* **1** (time of) gathering the crops **2** amount of crops gathered ♦ *vt* gather (crops)

has /s, z, əz, həz; *strong* hæz/ *v 3rd pers. sing. pres. t. of* HAVE

has-been /'· ·/ *n* formerly well-known or successful person

hash /hæʃ/ *n* [U] **1** meal of (re-cooked) cut up meat **2** **make a hash of something** do something badly

hash·ish /'hæʃiːʃ, -ɪʃ/ *n* [U] strongest form of the drug CANNABIS

has·n't /'hæzənt/ *v short for:* has not

has·sle /'hæsəl/ *n infml* a lot of trouble ♦ *vi/t* cause trouble or difficulties to

haste /heɪst/ *n* [U] quick movement, or action

has·ten /'heɪsən/ *vi/t* **1** *fml* hurry **2** be quick (to say): *I hasten to add that no one was hurt.*

hast·y /'heɪsti/ *adj* **1** done (too) quickly **2** (of people) too quick in acting or deciding —**ily** *adv*

hat /hæt/ *n* **1** covering for the head **2** **keep (something) under one's hat** keep (something) secret **3** **take one's hat off to** show admiration for **4** **talking through one's hat** saying something stupid —see also OLD HAT —**ter** *n* maker of hats

hatch¹ /hætʃ/ *v* **1** *vi/t* (cause to) be born from an egg **2** *vt* form (a plan)

hatch² *n* (cover over) a hole in a wall or floor

hatch·back /'hætʃbæk/ *n* car with a door at the back that opens upwards

hatch·et /'hætʃət/ *n* **1** small AXE **2** **bury the hatchet** become friends again after a bad quarrel

hatchet job /'·· ,·/ *n* cruel attack in speech or writing

hate /heɪt/ *vt* **1** dislike very much **2** be sorry: *I hate to tell you.* ♦ *n* [C;U] strong dislike ~**ful** *adj* very unpleasant ~**fully** *adv*

ha·tred /'heɪtrəd/ *n* [S;U] hate

hat trick /'· ·/ *n* (in sport) three successes of the same kind one after the other

haugh·ty /'hɔːti ‖ 'hɔː-/ *adj* too proud; ARROGANT —**tily** *adv* —**tiness** *n* [U]

haul /hɔːl ‖ hɔːl/ *vi/t* pull with effort ♦ *n*

1 a amount of fish caught **b** amount of something gained, esp. stolen goods **2** distance that something travels or is carried: *the long haul home*

haul·age /'hɔːlɪdʒ ‖ hɔː-/ *n* [U] **1** carrying of goods by road **2** charge for this

haunch /hɔːntʃ ‖ hɔːntʃ/ *n* fleshy part of the body between the waist and knee

haunt /hɔːnt ‖ hɔːnt/ *vt* **1** (of a spirit) appear in **2** visit regularly **3** remain in the thoughts of: *haunted by the memory* | *haunting tune* ♦ *n* place often visited

have¹ /v, əv, həv; *strong* hæv/ *v aux, pres. t. I/you/we/they* have, *he/she/it* has /z, əz, həz; *strong* hæz/; *past t.* had /d, əd, həd; *strong* hæd/ **1 a** (forms perfect tenses): *I've/I have finished* **b** Had (I, he, etc.) if (I, he, etc.) had: *Had I known, I would have stayed.* **2** had better (do/not do) ought (not) to: *You'd better tell him about it.* **3** have (got) to be forced to; must: *I'll have to wash it.* **4** have had it *infml* have experienced, worked, etc. all one can: *I've had it! Let's go home.*

have² *vt* **1** also **have got** — possess: *She has/has got blue eyes.* **2** experience or enjoy: *to have a party/a holiday* **3** receive: *I had some good news today.* **4** eat, drink, or smoke: *I had a cigarette.* **5** ask (someone) to one's home: *We're having some people round/over for drinks.* **6** allow: *I won't have all this noise.* **7** cause to be done: *You should have your hair cut.* **8** give birth to: *to have twins* **9** have done with finish **10** have it in for be as unkind as possible to **11** have it off/away with *BrE infml* have sex with **12** have to do with have a connection with

have on *phr vt* **1** be wearing **2** have arranged to do **3** play a trick on: *She's just having you on.* **4** have (unfavourable information) recorded against (someone) **5** have nothing on be not nearly as good as

have out *phr vt* **1** get (a tooth or organ) removed **2** settle by argument: *have the whole thing out with Bill*

have up *phr vt BrE* take to court: *had up for dangerous driving*

ha·ven /'heɪvən/ *n* calm safe place

have·n't /'hævənt/ *v short for:* have not

hav·er·sack /'hævəsæk ‖ -ər-/ *n* RUCKSACK

hav·oc /'hævək/ *n* [U] widespread damage

hawk¹ /hɔːk ‖ hɔːk/ *n* **1** bird that catches

creatures for food **2** person who believes in use of force, esp. military

hawk² *vt* sell (goods) on the street or at doors of houses

haw·thorn /'hɔːθɔːn ‖ 'hɔːθɔːrn/ *n* [C;U] small prickly tree with small white flowers and red berries

hay /heɪ/ *n* [U] dried grass for animal food

hay fe·ver /'· ˌ··/ *n* [U] illness like a bad cold, caused by breathing in POLLEN from the air

hay·stack /'heɪstæk/ *n* large pile of stored hay

hay·wire /'heɪwaɪə ‖ -waɪr/ *adj* go haywire (of plans, etc.) become badly disordered

haz·ard /'hæzəd ‖ -ərd/ *n* danger; risk ♦ *vt* **1** offer (a guess or suggestion) **2** put in danger ~**ous** *adj* dangerous

haze /heɪz/ *n* [S;U] light mist **hazy** *adj* **1** misty **2** uncertain: *I'm hazy about the details.*

ha·zel /'heɪzəl/ **1** *n, adj* light greenish brown: *hazel eyes* **2** *n* [C;U] small nut tree

H-bomb /'eɪtʃ bɒm ‖ -bɑːm/ *n* HYDROGEN BOMB

he /i, hi; *strong* hiː/ *pron* (used for the male subject of a sentence)

head¹ /hed/ *n* **1** [C] part of the body containing the eyes, mouth, and brain **2** [*the*+S] end where this rests: *the head of the bed* **3** [C] mind: *Don't put ideas into his head.* **4** [S] **a** ability: *no head for figures* **b** the power to be in control of oneself: *to keep/lose one's head in a crisis* **5** ruler; chief: *heads of state* [(*the*)S] **a** top: *head of a hammer/a page/the stairs* **b** front: *head of a procession* **7** [S] pressure of steam or water **8** **a/per head** for each person: *cost £5 a head* **9** **above/over one's head** too hard to understand **10** **bring/come to a head** reach a point where something must be done **11** **eat/shout, etc. one's head off** *infml* eat/shout, etc. too much, loudly, etc. **12** **go to one's head: a** make one drunk **b** over-excite someone **c** make someone too proud **13** **head and shoulders above** very much better than **14** **head over heels: a** turning over headfirst **b** completely: *head over heels in love* **15** **make head or tail of** manage to understand **16** **off one's head** *infml* mad **17** **put our/your/their heads together** think out a plan with other people

18 **turn someone's head: a** make someone too proud **b** make someone fall in love

heads *n* [U] front of a coin

head² *v* **1** *vt* be at the top or front of: *head a procession* **2** *vt* strike (a ball) with the head **3** *vi* go somewhere: *head north/towards Rome/for the bar*

 head off *phr vt* **1** cause to change direction **2** prevent

head·ache /'hedeɪk/ *n* **1** pain in the head **2** problem

head·dress /'hed-dres/ *n* decorative head covering

head·first /ˌhed'fɜːst◂ ‖ -'fɜːrst◂/ *adj, adv* with the rest of the body following the head

head·gear /'hedgɪə ‖ -gɪr/ *n* [U] covering for the head

head·hunt·er /'hedˌhʌntə ‖ -ər/ *n* person who tries to find suitable people for important jobs

head·ing /'hedɪŋ/ *n* words written as a title at the top of a page

head·land /'hedlənd/ *n* piece of land sticking out into the sea

head·light /'hedlaɪt/ also **head·lamp** /-læmp/ *n* strong light on the front of a vehicle

head·line /'hedlaɪn/ *n* **1** heading above a newspaper story **2** main point of the news on radio

head·long /'hedlɒŋ ‖ -lɔːŋ/ *adj, adv* **1** HEADFIRST **2** in foolish haste

head·mas·ter /ˌhed'mɑːstə ‖ 'hedˌmæstər/ **-mistress** /ˌhed'mɪstrɪs ‖ 'hedˌmɪstrɪs/ *fem.* — *n* head teacher in a school

head-on /ˌ· '·◂/ *adv, adj* with the front parts meeting, usu. violently: *a head-on collision*

head·phones /'hedfəʊnz ‖ -foʊnz/ *n* [P] listening apparatus that fits over the ears

head·quar·ters /'hedˌkwɔːtəz, ˌhed'kwɔːtəz ‖ -ɔːrtərz/ *n* **-ters** central office of an organization

head·rest /'hed-rest/ *n* support for the head

head·room /'hed-rʊm, -ruːm/ *n* [U] space to stand or move under something

head start /ˌ· '·/ *n* [S] advantage in a race or competition

head·stone /'hedstəʊn ‖ -stoʊn/ *n* stone marking the top end of a grave

head·strong /'hedstrɒŋ ‖ -strɔːŋ/ *adj*

uncontrollable; impatient

head·way /'hedweɪ/ n **make headway** advance; make PROGRESS

head·wind /'hed,wɪnd, ,hed'wɪnd/ n wind blowing directly against one

head·y /'hedi/ adj 1 making one drunk 2 exciting

heal /hiːl/ vi/t make or become healthy again ~er n

health /helθ/ n [U] 1 state of being well, without disease 2 condition of body or mind: in poor health 3 TOAST (2): to drink someone's health ~y adj 1 physically strong 2 producing good health 3 showing good health: (fig.) healthy profits

health centre /'· ,··/ n BrE place where doctors and nurses give advice and treatment

health club /'· ·/ n club where one can use exercise equipment, swim, etc.

health farm /'· ·/ n hotel for people who want to get fit

health food /'· ·/ n [C;U] food containing only natural substances: a health food shop

heap /hiːp/ n untidy pile ♦ vt pile up: heap food on the plate **heaps** n [P] infml lots: heaps of time

hear /hɪə ‖ hɪr/ v **heard** /hɜːd ‖ hɜːrd/ 1 vi/t receive (sounds) with the ears 2 vt be told or informed: I hear they're married. 3 vt listen to with attention: A priest heard my confession. 4 Hear! Hear! (shout of agreement) 5 won't/wouldn't hear of refuse(s) to allow

hear from phr vt receive news from, esp. by letter

hear of phr vt know about: I've never heard of him.

hear out phr vt listen to, till the end

hear·ing /'hɪərɪŋ ‖ 'hɪr-/ n 1 [U] ability to hear sound 2 [U] distance at which one can hear 3 [C;U] act or experience of hearing 4 [C] chance to explain 5 [C] law trial of a case

hearing aid /'·· ·/ n small electric machine to improve hearing

hearing im·paired /'·· ·,·/ adj unable to hear well or at all

hear·say /'hɪəseɪ ‖ 'hɪr-/ n [U] things heard but unproved

hearse /hɜːs ‖ hɜːrs/ n car for carrying a body to a funeral

heart /hɑːt ‖ hɑːrt/ n 1 [C] organ that pumps blood round the body 2 [C] centre of a person's feelings: a kind heart | My heart bled (=I was very sorry) for him. 3 [C] something shaped like a heart 4 [C] centre: heart of a lettuce/of the city/of the matter 5 [C] red heart-shaped figure on a playing card 6 [U] courage: take/lose heart 7 after one's own heart of the kind that one likes 8 break someone's/one's heart make/become very unhappy 9 by heart from memory 10 eat one's heart out be very troubled 11 from the (bottom of one's) heart with real feeling 12 have one's heart in the right place be a kind person 13 lose one's heart to fall in love with 14 set one's heart on want very much 15 take something to heart feel it deeply

heart·ache /'hɑːteɪk ‖ 'hɑːrt-/ n [U] deep sorrow

heart at·tack /'·· ,·/ n dangerous condition in which the heart beats irregularly and painfully

heart·beat /'hɑːtbiːt ‖ 'hɑːrt-/ n [C;U] pumping movement of the heart

heart·break /'hɑːtbreɪk ‖ 'hɑːrt-/ n terrible sorrow ~ing adj causing heartbreak

heart·brok·en /'hɑːt,brəʊkən ‖ 'hɑːrt-,broʊ-/ adj BROKEN-HEARTED

heart·burn /'hɑːtbɜːn ‖ 'hɑːrtbɜːrn/ n [U] unpleasant feeling of burning in the chest, caused by INDIGESTION

heart·en /'hɑːtn ‖ 'hɑːr-/ vt encourage

heart·felt /'hɑːtfelt ‖ 'hɑːrt-/ adj sincere

hearth /hɑːθ ‖ hɑːrθ/ n area round the fire in a home

heart·land /'hɑːtlənd ‖ 'hɑːrt-/ n central and most important area

heart·less /'hɑːtləs ‖ 'hɑːrt-/ adj cruel ~ly adv ~ness n [U]

heart·rend·ing /'hɑːt,rendɪŋ ‖ 'hɑːrt-/ adj causing great pity ~ly adv

heart·strings /'hɑːt,strɪŋz ‖ 'hɑːrt-/ n [P] deepest feelings of love and pity

heart·throb /'hɑːtθrɒb ‖ 'hɑːrtθrɑːb/ n infml man who is very attractive and with whom girls fall in love

heart-to-heart /,· · '·◁/ n open talk about personal details **heart-to-heart** adj

heart·warm·ing /'hɑːt,wɔːmɪŋ ‖ 'hɑːrt,wɔːr-/ adj causing pleasant feelings: heartwarming response

heart·y /'hɑːti ‖ 'hɑːrti/ adj 1 friendly

and cheerful **2** healthy **3** (of meals) large **4** *BrE* (too) cheerful in a loud way **–ily** *adv* **1** in a hearty way **2** very: *I'm heartily sick of your questions.*

heat¹ /hiːt/ n **1** [U] (degree of) hotness **2** [U] hot weather: *I don't like the heat much.* **3** [U] great excitement **4** [C] part of a race, whose winners will then race against others **5 on heat** (of female dogs, etc.) in a state of sexual excitement —see also WHITE HEAT

heat² *vi/t* make or become hot **–ed** *adj* excited and angry **–er** *n* machine for heating air or water **~ing** *n* [U] system for keeping rooms warm

heath /hiːθ/ n piece of open wild land

hea·then /ˈhiːðən/ n, adj (person) not belonging to one of the large established religions

heath·er /ˈheðə‖ -ər/ n [U] plant which grows on MOORS and has small pink or purple flowers

heat wave /ˈ· ·/ n period of unusually hot weather

heave¹ /hiːv/ v **1** *vi/t* pull or lift with effort **2** *vt* throw (something heavy) **3** *vi* rise and fall regularly **4** *vi infml* VOMIT **5 heave a sigh** SIGH

heave² *vi* hove /həʊv‖ hoʊv/ **1** (esp. of a ship) move; come **2 heave into sight/view** come into one's view

  heave to *phr vi* hove (of a ship) stop moving

heav·en /ˈhevən/ n **1** [U] home of God or the gods **2** (*usu. cap.*) God: *Heaven help you!* | *Good heavens!* **3** [C *usu. pl.*] the sky **4** [U] wonderful place or state **5 move heaven and earth** do everything possible (to cause or prevent something) —see also SEVENTH HEAVEN

heav·en·ly /ˈhevənli/ adj **1** of heaven: *The moon is a* **heavenly** *body.* **2** wonderful

heav·y¹ /ˈhevi/ adj **1** of great weight **2** of unusual amount: *heavy rain/traffic* | *a heavy smoker* (=someone who smokes a lot) **3** needing effort: *heavy work* **4** serious and dull: *heavy reading* **5** (of food) too solid **6** (of the sea) with big waves **7 find it heavy going** find it very difficult **8 make heavy weather of something** make a job or problem seem more difficult than it really is ♦ *adv* in a troublesome, dull way **–ily** *adv* **–iness** *n* [U]

heavy² n serious usu. male part in a play, etc., esp. a bad character

heavy-du·ty /ˌ·· ˈ··◄/ adj (of clothes, machines, etc.) strong enough for rough treatment

heavy-hand·ed /ˌ·· ˈ··◄/ adj awkward; not careful

heav·y-heart·ed /ˌhevi·hɑːtˈɪd◄‖ -ˈhɑːr-/ adj sad

heavy in·dus·try /ˌ·· ˈ···/ n [U] industry that produces large goods, or materials such as coal, steel, etc. that are used in the production of other goods

heavy met·al /ˌ·· ˈ··/ n [C] type of loud ROCK¹ (6) music

heav·y·weight /ˈheviweɪt/ n, adj **1** (a FIGHTER) of the heaviest class in boxing (BOX²) **2** (a person or thing) **a** of more than average weight **b** having great importance or influence

He·brew /ˈhiːbruː/ n [U] language of the ancient Jews and of modern Israel

heck·le /ˈhekəl/ vi/t interrupt (a speaker) disapprovingly at a meeting **–ler** n

hec·tare /ˈhektɑː, -teə‖ -ter/ n (a measure of area of land equal to) 10,000 square metres

hec·tic /ˈhektɪk/ adj full of hurry and excitement

hec·tor /ˈhektə‖ -ər/ vt BULLY

he'd /id, hiːd; *strong* hiːd/ *short for:* **1** he would **2** he had

hedge /hedʒ/ n **1** row of bushes dividing gardens or fields **2** protection: *a hedge against inflation* ♦ v **1** *vt* make a hedge round **2** *vi* refuse to answer directly **3 hedge one's bets** protect oneself against loss by favouring or supporting more than one side in a competition, etc.

hedge·hog /ˈhedʒhɒg‖ -hɔːg/ n small prickly animal

hedge·row /ˈhedʒrəʊ‖ -roʊ/ n row of bushes, esp. along roads, separating fields

he·don·is·m /ˈhiːdənɪzəm/ n [U] idea that pleasure is the only important thing in life **–ist** n **–istic** /ˌhiːdəˈnɪstɪk◄/ adj

heed /hiːd/ vt fml give attention to ♦ n [U] fml attention **~less** adj

heel /hiːl/ n **1** back of the foot **2** part of a shoe, sock, etc. which covers this, esp. the raised part of shoe under the foot **3** esp. AmE unpleasant person, who treats others badly **4 at/on one's heels** close behind one

5 bring to heel bring under control **6 come to heel: a** (of a dog) follow close to its owner **b** (of a person) obey without question **7 down at heel** (of people) untidy and poor-looking **8 kick one's heels** not have anything particular to do ◆ *vt* put a heel on (a shoe)

hef·ty /'hefti/ *adj* big and powerful

he·gem·o·ny /hɪ'gemənɪ, 'hedʒəmənɪ ‖ hɪ'dʒemənɪ, 'hedʒəmoʊnɪ/ *n* [U] *fml* power of one state over others

heif·er /'hefə ‖ -ər/ *n* young cow

height /haɪt/ *n* 1 [C;U] (degree of) being high 2 [C] measurement from top to bottom 3 [C] also **heights** *pl.* — high place 4 [S] a highest degree: *the height of fashion* b the main or most active point: *the height of the storm.*

height·en /'haɪtn/ *vi/t* make or become greater in degree

hei·nous /'heɪnəs/ *adj fml* (of wickedness) extreme

heir /eə ‖ er/ **heiress** /'eərɪs, 'eəres ‖ 'er-/ *fem.* — *n* person with the legal right to receive property, etc. when the owner dies

heir·loom /'eəluːm ‖ 'er-/ *n* valuable object given by older members of a family to younger ones over many years

held /held/ *v past t. and p. of* HOLD

hel·i·cop·ter /'helɪkɒptə ‖ -kɑːptər/ *n* aircraft that flies by means of fast-turning blades on top

he·li·um /'hiːlɪəm/ *n* [U] very light gas used in AIRSHIPS, etc.

hell /hel/ *n* 1 [U] place where the wicked are said to be punished after death 2 [C] terrible place 3 [U] *sl* (used in anger or to give force): *What the hell's that?* | *That's a hell of a good car.* 4 **for the hell of it** for fun 5 **give someone hell** treat them roughly 6 **hell to pay** *sl* serious trouble or punishment 7 **like hell: a** very much!: *I worked like hell all week.* b not at all: *'He paid, didn't he?' 'Like hell he did.'* 8 **play hell with** cause damage to ◆ *interj* (an expression of) anger or disappointment ~**ish** *adj* terrible

he'll /iːl, hiːl; *strong* hiːl/ *short for:* he will

hel·lo /hə'ləʊ, he- ‖ -loʊ/ *interj, n* **-los** 1 (used in greeting) 2 *esp. BrE* (an expression of surprise): *Hello! She's left something behind.*

helm /helm/ *n* 1 wheel or TILLER that

guides a ship 2 **at the helm** in control

hel·met /'helmɪt/ *n* protective head covering

help¹ /help/ *v* 1 *vi/t* make it possible for (someone) to do something; be useful (to) 2 *vt* avoid; prevent: *I can't help laughing.* | *It can't be helped.* (=these things happen) 3 *vt* give food, etc. to: *Help yourself to sugar.* | *He just helped himself to the money.* (=took) ~**er** *n* person who helps ~**ing** *n* serving of food

help out *phr vi/t* give help (to someone) at a time of need

help² *n* 1 [U] act of helping; AID 2 [C] someone or something that helps 3 [C] person employed to do housework 4 **there's no help for it** there's no way of avoiding it 5 **Help!** Please bring help. ~**ful** *adj* useful ~**fully** *adv* ~**less** *adj* unable to look after oneself ~**lessly** *adv*

help·line /'helplaɪn/ *n* telephone service giving information or advice

hem¹ /hem/ *n* edge of a skirt, etc. turned under and sewn

hem² *vt* **-mm-** put a hem on

hem in *phr vt* surround closely

hem·i·sphere /'hemɪsfɪə ‖ -sfɪr/ *n* 1 half a SPHERE 2 half of the Earth: *the southern hemisphere*

hem·line /'hemlaɪn/ *n* length of a skirt or dress

he·mo·phil·i·a /ˌhiːmə'fɪlɪə/ *n* [U] disease that makes the sufferer bleed badly after only a small cut

hem·or·rhage /'hemərɪdʒ/ *n* [C;U] flow of blood, esp. long and unexpected

hem·or·rhoid /'hemərɔɪd/ *n* swollen blood vessel at the lower end of the bowel

hemp /hemp/ *n* [U] plant used for making rope, rough cloth, and the drug CANNABIS

hen /hen/ *n* female bird, esp. the kind kept for its eggs on farms

hence /hens/ *adv fml* 1 for this reason 2 from here or now

hence·forth /ˌhens'fɔːθ, 'hensfɔːθ ‖ -ɔːrθ/, **-forward** /-'fɔːwəd ‖ -'fɔːrwərd/ *adv fml* from now on

hench·man /'hentʃmən/ *n* **-men** /-mən/ faithful supporter

hen·na /'henə/ *n* [U] reddish-brown DYE

hen·pecked /'henpekt/ *adj* (of a man) too obedient to his wife

hep·a·ti·tis /ˌhepə'taɪtɪs/ *n* [U] serious

disease of the LIVER

her /ə, hə; *strong* hɜː‖ ər, hər; *strong* hɜːr/ *pron* (used for the female object of a sentence) ♦ *determiner* of her: *her car* **hers** *pron* of her; her one(s): *It's hers.*

her·ald /'herəld/ *n* (in former times) person who brought important news ♦ *vt fml* be a sign of (something coming)

her·ald·ry /'herəldri/ *n* [U] study of COATS OF ARMS

herb /hɜːb ‖ ɜːrb, hɜːrb/ *n* any plant used in medicine or to improve the taste of food ~**al** *adj* of herbs ~**alist** *n* person who uses herbs, esp. to treat disease

her·ba·ceous /hɜːˈbeɪʃəs ‖ ɜːr-, hɜːr-/ *adj* (of a plant) soft-stemmed: *a herbaceous border* (=border of such plants)

her·bi·vore /'hɜːbɪvɔː ‖ 'hɜːrbɪvɔːr, 'ɜːr-/ *n* plant-eating animal ~**vorous** ‖ *adj*

Her·cu·le·an /,hɜːkjʊˈliːən, hɜːˈ-kjuːliən ‖ -ɜːr-/ *adj* needing great strength or determination

herd /hɜːd ‖ hɜːrd/ *n* **1** group of animals together **2** people generally, thought of as acting all alike ♦ *vt* drive in a herd: (fig.) *to herd tourists into a bus*

here /hɪə ‖ hɪr/ *adv* **1** at, in, or to this place: *'It's Professor Worth here.'* (=speaking on the telephone) **2** at this point: *Here we agree.* **3** **here and there** scattered about **4** **Here goes!** Now I'm going to have a try. **5** **Here's to** (said when drinking a TOAST (2)) **6** **neither here nor there** not connected with the matter being talked about

here·a·bouts /,hɪərəˈbauts, 'hɪərəbauts ‖ ,hɪr-/ *adv* somewhere near here

here·af·ter /,hɪərˈɑːftə ‖ hɪrˈæftər/ *adv fml* in the future ♦ *n* [S] life after death

here·by /,hɪəˈbaɪ, 'hɪəbaɪ ‖ ,hɪr-/ *adv fml* by this means

he·red·i·ta·ry /həˈredɪtəri ‖ -teri/ *adj* passed down from parent to child

he·red·i·ty /həˈredɪti/ *n* [U] fact that qualities are passed on from parent to child

here·in /,hɪərˈɪn ‖ ,hɪr-/ *adv fml* in this

her·e·sy /'herəsi/ *n* [C;U] belief that goes against what is officially accepted

her·e·tic /'herətɪk/ *n* person guilty of heresy ~**al** /həˈretɪkəl/ *adj*

here·with /,hɪəˈwɪð ‖ ,hɪr-/ *adv fml* with this

her·i·tage /'herɪtɪdʒ/ *n* something passed down within a family or nation

her·mit /'hɜːmɪt ‖ 'hɜːr-/ *n* person who lives alone away from other people, esp. for religious reasons

her·mit·age /'hɜːmɪtɪdʒ ‖ 'hɜːr-/ *n* hermit's home

her·ni·a /'hɜːniə ‖ 'hɜːr-/ *n* [C;U] conditions in which an organ, esp. the bowel, pushes through its covering wall

he·ro /'hɪərəʊ ‖ 'hɪroʊ/ **heroine** /'herəʊɪn ‖ -roʊ-/ *fem.* — *n* —**roes 1** someone admired for bravery etc. **2** most important character in a story ~**ic** /hɪˈrəʊɪk ‖ -'roʊ-/ *adj* very brave ~**ically** /-kli/ *adv* ~**ics** *n* [P] grand speech or actions that mean nothing ~**ism** /'herəʊɪzəm ‖ -roʊ-/ *n* [U] courage

her·o·in /'herəʊɪn ‖ -roʊ-/ *n* [U] drug made from MORPHINE

her·pes /'hɜːpiːz ‖ 'hɜːr-/ *n* [U] very infectious skin disease

her·ring /'herɪŋ/ *n* sea fish used for food —see also RED HERRING

her·ring·bone /'herɪŋbəʊn ‖ -boʊn/ *n* [U] V-shaped pattern

her·self /əˈself, hə-; *strong* hɜː- ‖ ər-, hər-; *strong* hɜːr-/ *pron* **1** (*reflexive form of* she): *She hurt herself.* **2** (*strong form of* she): *She ate it herself.* **3** (all) **by herself**: **a** alone **b** without help **4** **to herself** not shared

he's /ɪz, hɪz; *strong* hiːz/ *short for:* **1** he is **2** he has

hes·i·tant /'hezɪtənt/ *adj* tending to hesitate ~**tancy** *n* [U]

hes·i·tate /'hezɪteɪt/ *vi* **1** pause because one is uncertain **2** be unwilling ~**tation** /,hezɪˈteɪʃən/ *n* [C;U]

hes·si·an /'hesiən ‖ 'heʃən/ *n* [U] thick cloth used for SACKS (SACK(1))

het·e·ro·dox /'hetərədɒks ‖ -dɑːks/ *adj* (of beliefs, etc.) against accepted opinion

het·e·ro·ge·ne·ous /,hetərəʊˈdʒiːniəs ‖ -roʊ-/ *adj fml* of many different kinds

het·e·ro·sex·u·al /,hetərəˈsekʃuəl ◂/ *adj* attracted to people of the other sex ~**ity** /,hetərəsekʃuˈælɪti/ *n* [U]

het up /,het ˈʌp/ *adj BrE* anxious

hew /hjuː/ *vi/t* **hewed**, **hewed** *or* **hewn** /hjuːn/ *fml* cut with a heavy tool

hex·a·gon /'heksəgən ‖ -gɑːn/ *n* figure with six sides ~**al** /hekˈsægənəl/ *adj*

hey·day /'heɪdeɪ/ *n* [S] time of greatest success

hi·a·tus /haɪˈeɪtəs/ *n fml* space where

something is missing

hi·ber·nate /'haibəneit ‖ -ər-/ vi (of some animals) sleep during the winter –**nation** /ˌhaibə'neiʃən ‖ -ər-/ n [U]

hic·cup, **hiccough** /'hikʌp, -kəp/ n 1 sudden stopping of the breath with a sharp sound 2 small problem ♦ vi have HICCUPS (1)

hide¹ /haid/ v hid /hid/, hidden /'hidn/ 1 vt put out of sight 2 vi keep oneself from being seen

hide² n 1 animal's skin 2 **hide or/nor hair of** infml any sign of

hide³ n place where one may watch animals, birds, etc. without being seen by them

hid·e·ous /'hidiəs/ adj very ugly; horrible ~**ly** adv

hide·out /'haidaut/ also **hide·a·way** /'haidəwei/ — n place where one can go to avoid people

hid·ing¹ /'haidiŋ/ n beating

hiding² n [U] state of being hidden: go into hiding

hi·er·ar·chy /'haiərɑːki ‖ 'hairɑːr-/ n [C;U] organization with higher and lower ranks

hi·e·ro·glyph·ics /ˌhaiərə'glifiks ‖ ˌhair-/ n [P] writing that uses pictures, as in ancient Egypt

hi-fi /'hai fai, ˌhai 'fai/ n **hi-fis** high-quality equipment for reproducing recorded sound

high¹ /hai/ adj 1 far above the ground: a high mountain | 4 metres high 2 great: high cost 3 good: high standards 4 (of a musical note) not deep 5 (of time) as the mid-point: high summer | It's high time we were going. (=we should go at once) 6 (of food) not fresh 7 infml drunk or drugged ♦ n 1 high point or level: Sales are at an all-time high. 2 state of great excitement: on a high ~**ly** adv 1 very: highly amused 2 very well: highly paid

high² adv 1 to or at a high level: aim high 2 **feelings ran high** people got excited and angry 3 **high and dry** deserted 4 **high and low** everywhere

high-and-mighty /ˌ··'··◀/ adj infml too proud and certain of one's own importance

high·brow /'haibrau/ n, adj (person) knowing a lot about art, books, etc.

high-class /ˌ· '·◀/ adj 1 of good quality

2 of high social position

high com·mis·sion·er /ˌ· ·'···/ n person representing one COMMONWEALTH country in another

high court /ˌ· '·◀/ n most important court of justice

higher ed·u·ca·tion /ˌ·· ··'··/ n [U] education at a university or college

high-fli·er, -flyer /ˌ· '··/ n clever person who has high aims

high-hand·ed /ˌ· '··◀/ adj using power too forcefully

high jump /'· ·/ n [S] 1 sport of jumping over a bar 2 **be for the high jump** BrE be about to get a bad punishment or scolding

High·lands /'hailəndz/ n [the+P] mountainous area

high·light /'hailait/ n 1 most important detail 2 lightest area on a picture, or in the hair ♦ vt throw attention onto ~**er** n bright pen used for highlighting words on a page

highly-strung /ˌ·· '·◀/ adj nervous; excitable

high-mind·ed /ˌ· '··◀/ adj having high principles

High·ness /'hainis/ n (title of some royal persons)

high-pitched /ˌ· '·◀/ adj (of a voice, etc.) high and sharp

high-pow·ered /ˌ· '··◀/ adj having great force or ability

high-pro·file /ˌ· '··◀/ adj attracting a lot of attention

high-rise /'· ·/ adj (of buildings) with many floors

high school /'· ·/ n esp. AmE school for children over 14

high-spir·it·ed /ˌ· '···◀/ adj active and adventurous

high spot /'· ·/ n most enjoyable part of an activity

high street /'· ·/ n BrE main street of a town

high tea /ˌ· '·/ n [U] BrE early-evening meal

high-tech /ˌhai 'tek/ adj using the most modern equipment, methods, etc.: a new high-tech camera

high tide /ˌ· '·/ n [C;U] time when the sea reaches its highest level at the coast

high·way /'haiwei/ n broad main road

high·way·man /'haiweimən/ n -**men** /-mən/ (in former times) man who used to stop people on the roads and rob them

hi·jack /'haɪdʒæk/ vt 1 take control of (esp. an aircraft) by force 2 stop and rob (a train, etc.) **~er** n

hike /haɪk/ vi, n (go for) a long country walk **hiker** n

hi·lar·i·ous /hɪ'leərɪəs ‖ -'ler-/ adj full of or causing laughter **~ly** adv

hi·lar·i·ty /hɪ'lærəti/ n [U] cheerful laughter

hill /hɪl/ n 1 raised piece of land, not as high as a mountain 2 slope on a road, etc. **~y** adj

hilt /hɪlt/ n 1 handle of a sword 2 **(up) to the hilt** completely

him /ɪm; strong hɪm/ pron (used for the male object of a sentence)

him·self /ɪm'self; strong hɪm-/ pron 1 (reflexive form of he): He shot himself. 2 (strong form of he): He made it himself. 3 **(all) by himself: a** alone **b** without help 4 **to himself** not shared

hind¹ /haɪnd/ adj (of animals' legs) back

hind² n hinds or hind female deer

hin·der /'hɪndə ‖ -ər/ vt delay the progress of **–drance** n [C;U]

hind·most /'haɪndməʊst ‖ -moʊst/ adj furthest behind

hind·quar·ters /'haɪnd,kwɔːtəz ‖ -,kwɔːr-tərz/ n [P] animal's back legs

hind·sight /'haɪndsaɪt/ n [U] ability to understand the past, and esp. what went wrong

Hin·du /'hɪnduː, hɪn'duː/ n **-dus** person whose religion is Hinduism **Hindu** adj

Hin·du·is·m /'hɪnduː-ɪzəm/ n [U] chief religion of India, notable for its CASTE system and belief in REINCARNATION

hinge¹ /hɪndʒ/ n metal joint on which a door, etc. swings

hinge² vt fix on hinges

hinge on/upon phr vt depend on

hint /hɪnt/ n 1 small or indirect suggestion: (fig.) There's a hint of summer in the air. 2 useful advice ♦ vi/t suggest indirectly

hin·ter·land /'hɪntəlænd ‖ -ər-/ n [S] inner part of a country

hip¹ /hɪp/ n fleshy part where the legs join the body

hip² adj infml modern; fashionable

hip·pie, -py /'hɪpi/ n (young) person who is against the standards of ordinary society

hip·po·pot·a·mus /,hɪpə'pɒtəməs ‖ -'pɑː-/ -muses or -mi /-maɪ/ also **hip·po** /'hɪpəʊ ‖ -poʊ/ — n large African river animal

hire /haɪə ‖ haɪr/ vt get the use or services of someone or someone for a limited time, for payment: hire a car ♦ n [U] (money for) being hired

hire pur·chase /,· '··/ n [U] BrE system of paying small sums regularly for goods already received

his /ɪz; strong hɪz/ determiner of him: his shoes ♦ pron of him; his one(s): It's his.

hiss /hɪs/ vi, t make a sound like 's', esp. to show disapproval **hiss** n

his·to·ri·an /hɪ'stɔːrɪən/ n person who studies history

his·tor·ic /hɪ'stɒrɪk ‖ -'stɔː-, -'stɑː-/ adj important in history: an historic event

his·tor·i·cal /hɪ'stɒrɪkəl ‖ -'stɔː-, -'stɑː-/ adj about history: historical research/novels **~ly** /-kli/ adv

his·to·ry /'hɪstəri/ n 1 [U] study of past events 2 [C] account of past events 3 [C] record of someone's past: her medical history 4 **make history** do something important which will be remembered —see also NATURAL HISTORY

his·tri·on·ics /,hɪstri'ɒnɪks, ‖ -'ɑːn-/ n [P] insincere behaviour, like a theatrical performance **histrionic** adj

hit¹ /hɪt/ vt hit, pres. p. hitting 1 come, or bring something, hard against: He hit the ball with the bat. | The car hit the wall. 2 reach: hit the main road 3 have a bad effect on 4 **hit it off** have a good relationship 5 **hit the bottle** infml drink too much alcohol 6 **hit the nail on the head** say or do the right thing 7 **hit the road** infml start on a journey 8 **hit the roof** show or express great anger

hit back phr vi reply forcefully to an attack on oneself

hit on/upon phr vt find by chance

hit out at/against phr vt attack in words

hit² n 1 blow 2 successful song, film, play, etc.

hit-and-miss /,· · '·/ adj depending on chance

hit-and-run /,· · '◂/ n, adj (accident) in which the driver does not stop after hitting someone/something

hitch /hɪtʃ/ v 1 vt fasten by hooking a rope or metal part on something 2 vi hitchhike 3 **get hitched** get married ♦ n 1 difficulty or delay 2 kind of knot

hitch up phr vt pull up into place

hitch·hike /'hɪtʃhaɪk/ vi travel by getting rides in other people's cars **hitchhiker** n

hi-tech /ˌhaɪ 'tek◂/ adj HIGH-TECH

hith·er·to /ˌhɪðə'tuː◂ ‖ -ər-/ adv fml until now

hit list /'· ·/ n infml list of people or organizations against whom some (bad) action is planned

hit man /'· ·/ n infml, esp. AmE criminal who is employed to kill someone

hit-or-miss /ˌ·· '·/ adj HIT-AND-MISS

HIV /ˌeɪtʃ aɪ 'viː◂/ n [(the)S] VIRUS carried in the blood that often develops into the disease AIDS: *He's HIV positive.* (=he has the HIV virus)

hive¹ /haɪv/ n 1 box, etc. where bees are kept 2 crowded busy place

hive² v **hive off** phr vt make separate from a larger organization

HMS /ˌeɪtʃ em es/ abbrev. for: His/Her Majesty's Ship; title for a ship in the British Navy

hoard /hɔːd ‖ hɔːrd/ n (secret) store of something valuable ♦ vt save; store, esp. secretly

hoard·ing /'hɔːdɪŋ ‖ 'hɔːr-/ n BrE high fence, esp. for sticking advertisements on

hoarse /hɔːs ‖ hɔːrs/ adj (of a voice) sounding rough ~**ly** adv ~**ness** n [U]

hoar·y /'hɔːri/ adj (of hair) white with age: (fig.) *hoary old jokes*

hoax /həʊks ‖ hoʊks/ n trick to deceive someone **hoax** vt

hob /hɒb ‖ hɑːb/ n flat COOKER top

hob·ble /'hɒbəl ‖ 'hɑː-/ n 1 vi walk with difficulty 2 vt tie two legs of (a horse)

hob·by /'hɒbi ‖ 'hɑː-/ n pleasant activity for one's free time

hob·by·horse /'hɒbihɔːs ‖ 'hɑːbihɔːrs/ n 1 children's toy like a horse's head on a stick 2 fixed idea to which a person keeps returning

hob·nail /'hɒbneɪl ‖ 'hɑːb-/ n heavy nail in the SOLE of a boot or shoe

hob·nob /'hɒbnɒb ‖ 'hɑːbnɑːb/ vi -bb- have a social relationship with (with)

hock vt sl for PAWN²

hock·ey /'hɒki ‖ 'hɑːki/ n [U] 1 BrE field team game played with sticks and a ball 2 esp. AmE for ICE HOCKEY

hod /hɒd ‖ hɑːd/ n box on a stick, for carrying bricks

hoe /həʊ ‖ hoʊ/ n garden tool for breaking up the soil **hoe** vi/t

hog /hɒg ‖ hɑːg, hɔːg/ n 1 pig 2 person who eats too much 3 **go the whole hog** infml do something thoroughly —see also ROAD HOG ♦ vt take and keep (all of something) for oneself

Hog·ma·nay /'hɒgmáneɪ ‖ ˌhɑːgmə'neɪ/ n NEW YEAR'S EVE in Scotland

hoist /hɔɪst/ vt pull up on a rope ♦ n 1 upward push 2 apparatus for lifting heavy goods

hold¹ /həʊld ‖ hoʊld/ v **held** /held/ 1 vt keep in the hands, etc. 2 vt keep in a particular position: *hold one's head up* | *Hold it!* (=don't move) 3 vt support: *The branch won't hold me.* 4 vt not allow to leave: *The police held two men.* 5 vt not use: *hold one's breath* 6 vt defend against attack 7 vi remain unchanged: *What I said still holds.* 8 vt have room for: *The cinema holds 500.* 9 vt possess: *hold the office of chairman* 10 vt believe 11 vt cause to happen: *hold an election* 12 vt keep (the interest or attention) of (someone) 13 **hold court** receive admirers in a group 14 **hold good** be true 15 **Hold it!** infml Don't move. 16 **hold one's own** keep one's (strong) position 17 **hold one's tongue** not talk 18 **hold the line** keep a telephone connection 19 **hold water** seem to be true

hold against phr vt allow (something bad) to influence one's feelings about (someone)

hold back phr v 1 vt control 2 vt keep secret 3 vi be unwilling to act

hold down phr vt 1 keep in a low position 2 keep (a job)

hold forth phr vi talk at length

hold off phr v 1 vt keep at a distance 2 vi/t delay

hold on phr vi 1 wait (esp. on the telephone) 2 continue in spite of difficulties

hold onto phr vt keep possession of

hold out phr vi 1 continue to exist; last 2 offer

hold out for phr vt demand firmly and wait in order to get

hold over phr vt POSTPONE

hold to phr vt keep to: I'll hold you to your promise.

hold up phr vt 1 delay 2 rob by force

hold with phr vt approve of

hold[2] n 1 [U] holding 2 [C] something to hold, esp. in climbing 3 [C] influence

hold[3] n bottom of a ship, where goods are stored

hold·all /'həʊld-ɔːl ‖ 'hoʊld-ɒːl/ n bag for travelling

hold·er /'həʊldə ‖ 'hoʊldər/ n 1 person who possesses something 2 container

hold·ing /'həʊldɪŋ ‖ 'hoʊl-/ n land, etc. that one possesses

hold·up /'həʊld-ʌp ‖ 'hoʊld-/ n 1 delay, as in traffic 2 attempt at armed robbery

hole[1] /həʊl ‖ hoʊl/ n 1 empty space in something solid 2 a home of a small animal b small unpleasant living-space 3 infml difficult position 4 (in GOLF) hollow place in the ground into which the ball must be hit: an 18-hole golf course 5 make a hole in infml use up a large part of 6 pick holes in find faults in —see also BLACK HOLE

hole[2] vt 1 make a hole in 2 vi/t hit (the ball) into a hole in GOLF

hole up phr vi sl hide as a means of escape

hol·i·day /'hɒlɪdi ‖ 'haːlɪdeɪ/ n 1 time of rest from work 2 on holiday having a holiday ♦ vi have a period of holiday ~maker n person on holiday

hol·i·er-than-thou /ˌ··· · '·/ adj derog thinking oneself to be morally better than other people

hol·i·ness /'həʊlinɪs ‖ 'hoʊ-/ n [U] 1 being holy 2 (cap.) (title of the Pope)

ho·lis·tic /həʊ'lɪstɪk ‖ hoʊ-/ adj concerning the whole of something or someone, not just certain parts: holistic medicine

hol·low /'hɒləʊ ‖ 'haːloʊ/ adj 1 having an empty space inside 2 lacking flesh: hollow cheeks 3 (of sounds) as if made by striking an empty container 4 insincere ♦ n wide hole ♦ vt make hollow

hol·ly /'hɒli ‖ 'haːli/ n [C;U] tree whose leaves and red berries are used for Christmas decoration

hol·o·caust /'hɒləkɔːst ‖ 'haːləkɒːst/ n great destruction and the loss of many lives, esp. by burning

hol·o·gram /'hɒləgræm ‖ 'hoʊ-, 'haː-/ n

picture made with laser light so that it appears to be solid rather than flat

hol·o·graph·y /hɒ'lɒgrəfi ‖ hoʊ'lɑː-/ n [U] science of producing holograms

hol·ster /'həʊlstə ‖ 'hoʊlstər/ n leather holder for a PISTOL

ho·ly /'həʊli ‖ 'hoʊli/ adj 1 connected with, or serving, religion 2 leading a pure and blameless life

hom·age /'hɒmɪdʒ ‖ 'haː-/ n [U] fml signs of great respect

home[1] /həʊm ‖ hoʊm/ n 1 [C] place where one lives 2 [C;U] one's house and family: She came from a poor home. 3 [S] a place where a plant or animal is found b place where something was originally discovered, made or developed 4 [C] place for the care of people or animals: an old people's home 5 [U] (in sports) place which a player must try to reach 6 be/feel at home feel comfortable 7 make oneself at home behave freely 8 nothing to write home about nothing special ~less adj

home[2] adv 1 to or at one's home: go home 2 to the right place: strike a nail home 3 bring/come home to one make/become clearly understood 4 home and dry infml, esp. BrE having safely or successfully completed something

home[3] adj 1 of or related to one's home or origin 2 not foreign 3 prepared or made in the home: home grown 4 (of a sports match) played at the place, sports field, etc. of one's home area

home[4] v home in on phr vt aim exactly towards —see also HOMING

home·com·ing /'həʊmˌkʌmɪŋ ‖ 'hoʊm-/ n arrival home, esp. after a long absence

home help /ˌ· '·/ n someone sent in by the British Social Services to clean, etc.

home·land /'həʊmlænd, -lənd ‖ 'hoʊm-/ n 1 country where one was born 2 area formerly set aside for the South African black population

home·ly /'həʊmli ‖ 'hoʊm-/ adj 1 simple and plain 2 AmE not good-looking

home·mak·er /'həʊmˌmeɪkə ‖ 'hoʊm-ˌmeɪkər/ n person, esp. a woman, who cooks, cleans, etc. at home and has no other job

ho·me·op·athy homoeo- /ˌhəʊmi-'ɒpəθi ‖ ˌhoʊmi'ɑːp-/ n [U] system of treating disease with small amounts of substances that in larger amounts would produce a similar illness –**opath** /'həʊmiəpæθ ‖ 'hoʊ-/ n person who treats diseases in this way –**opathic** /,həʊmi-ə'pæθɪk◂ ‖ ,hoʊ-/ adj

home-page /'··/ n place on the INTERNET with information about a person, company, etc. and part of a WEBSITE

home-sick /'həʊm,sɪk ‖ 'hoʊm-/ adj unhappy because away from home ~**ness** n [U]

home truth /,· '·/ n unpleasant fact about someone

home-ward /'həʊmwəd ‖ 'hoʊmwərd/ adj going towards home **homewards** also **homeward** AmE —adv

home-work /'həʊmwɜːk ‖ 'hoʊmwɜːrk/ n [C] **1** schoolwork done outside the classroom **2** preparations done before taking part in an important activity

hom-ey /'həʊmi ‖ 'hoʊmi/ adj AmE infml pleasant, like home

hom-i-cide /'hɒmɪsaɪd ‖ 'hɑː-/ n [C;U] fml murder –**cidal** /,hɒmɪ'saɪdl◂ ‖ ,hɑː-/ adj

hom-i-ly /'hɒmɪli ‖ 'hɑː-/ n long speech on moral behaviour

hom-ing /'həʊmɪŋ ‖ 'hoʊ-/ adj of or having the ability to a guide oneself home b (of machines) guide themselves towards the place they are aimed at

ho-mo-ge-ne-ous /,həʊmə'dʒiːniəs ‖ ,hoʊ-/ adj formed of parts of the same kind

ho-mo-ge-nize, -**nise** /hə'mɒdʒənaɪz ‖ -'mɑː-/ vt make (the parts of a whole, esp. a mixture) become evenly spread

ho-mo-pho-bi-a /,həʊmə'fəʊbiə ,hɒ-‖ ,hoʊmə'foʊ- / n [U] hatred and fear of HOMOSEXUALs –**phobic** adj

ho-mo-sex-u-al /,həʊmə'sekʃuəl, ,hɒ-‖ ,hoʊ-/ n, adj (person) sexually attracted to people of the same sex –**ity** /,həʊmə‖ ,sekʃu'æləti, ,hɒ-‖ ,hoʊ-/ n [U]

hone /həʊn ‖ hoʊn/ vt **1** improve (a skill) **2** sharpen (a knife)

hon-est /'ɒnɪst ‖ 'ɑːn-/ adj **1** not likely to lie or cheat **2** (of actions, etc.) showing these qualities ~**ly** adv **1** in an honest way **2** really

hon-es-ty /'ɒnɪsti ‖ 'ɑːn-/ n [U] quality of being honest

hon-ey /'hʌni/ n **1** [U] sweet substance that bees make **2** [C] esp. AmE for DARLING

hon-ey-comb /'hʌnikəʊm ‖ -koʊm/ n wax structure that bees make to store honey

hon-ey-moon /'hʌnimuːn/ n **1** holiday taken by two people who have just got married **2** short period of good relations, etc. at the beginning of a period in office, etc. ♦ vi spend one's honeymoon **honeymooner** n

honk /hɒŋk ‖ hɑːŋk, hɔːŋk/ vi, n (make) the sound of a car horn

hon-or-ar-y /'ɒnərəri ‖ 'ɑːnəreri/ adj **1** (of a rank, etc.) given as an honour **2** unpaid: honorary chairman

hon-our BrE ‖ **honor** AmE /'ɒnə ‖ 'ɑːnər/ n **1** [U] great public respect **2** [U] high standards of behaviour: men of honour **3** [S] person or thing that brings pride: He's an honour to his parents. **4** [C] (cap.) (used as a title for a judge) ♦ vt **1** bring honour to **2** keep (an agreement)

honours n [P] **1** marks of respect: full military honours **2** specialized university degree or a level gained in it

hon-our-a-ble BrE ‖ **honorable** AmE /'ɒnərəbəl ‖ 'ɑːn-/ adj **1** bringing or showing honour **2** (cap.) (title for certain high officials, children of noblemen, etc.) –**bly** adv

hood /hʊd/ n **1** covering for the head and neck a except the face, so that it can be pushed back b including the face, to avoid recognition **2** folding cover over a car, etc. **3** AmE for BONNET (2)

hood-wink /'hʊdwɪŋk/ vt deceive

hoof /huːf ‖ hʊf/ n **hoofs** or **hooves** /huːvz ‖ hʊfs/ horny foot of a horse, etc.

hook /hʊk/ n **1** curved piece of metal or plastic for catching, hanging, or fastening things **2** (in boxing (BOX²)) blow given with the elbow bent **3** by **hook or by crook** by any means possible **4** off the **hook** no longer in a difficult situation ♦ vt catch, hang, or fasten with a hook ~**ed** adj **1** hook-shaped **2** dependent on drugs, etc.)

hoo-li-gan /'huːlɪɡən/ n noisy violent person who breaks things, etc. ~**ism** n [U]

hoop /huːp ‖ hʊp, huːp/ n circular band of wood or metal

hoo-ray /hʊ'reɪ/ interj, n HURRAY

hoot /huːt/ n **1** sound made by an OWL or a car's horn **2** shout of dislike **3** not **care/ give a hoot/two hoots** not care at all ♦

vi/t (cause to) make a hoot ~**er** *n* horn, whistle, etc.

hoo·ver /'huːvə ‖ -ər/ *n tdmk BrE* (type of) VACUUM CLEANER ♦ *vi/t* clean with any VACUUM CLEANER

hooves /huːvz ‖ hʊfs/ *pl. of* HOOF

hop[1] /hɒp ‖ haːp/ *vi* -**pp**- 1 (of people) jump on one leg 2 (of small creatures) jump 3 get into or onto a vehicle 4 **Hop it!** Go away! ♦ *n* 1 jump 2 distance flown by a plane without landing 3 **catch someone on the hop** meet someone when they are unprepared

hop[2] *n* climbing plant used for giving taste to beer

hope /həʊp ‖ hoʊp/ *n* 1 [C;U] expectation that something good will happen 2 [C] person or thing that may bring success 3 **beyond/past hope** with no chance of success 4 **hold out hope** give encouragement —see also WHITE HOPE ♦ *vi/t* wish and expect ~**ful** *adj* feeling or giving hope ~**fully** *adv* 1 in a hopeful way 2 if our hopes succeed ~**less** *adj* 1 feeling or giving no hope 2 not skilled: *hopeless at maths* ~**lessly** *adv*

hop·per /'hɒpə ‖ 'haːpər/ *n* large FUNNEL for grain or coal

hop·scotch /'hɒpskɒtʃ ‖ 'haːpskaːtʃ/ *n* [U] children's game of jumping along squares marked on the ground to pick up stones

horde /hɔːd ‖ hɔːrd/ *n* large moving crowd

ho·ri·zon /həˈraɪzən/ *n* 1 line where the sky seems to meet the earth or sea 2 **broaden one's horizons** increase the range of one's experience

hor·i·zon·tal /ˌhɒrɪˈzɒntl◀ ‖ ˌhɔːrəˈzaːntl◀/ *adj* flat; level ♦ *n* [C;U] a horizontal line, surface or position ~**ly** *adv*

hor·mone /'hɔːməʊn ‖ 'hɔːrmoʊn/ *n* substance produced in the body that influences growth, etc.

horn /hɔːn ‖ hɔːrn/ *n* 1 [C] pointed growth on an animal's head 2 [U] material that this is made of: *horn-rimmed glasses* 3 [C] apparatus, e.g. in a car, that makes a warning sound 4 [C] musical instrument played by blowing ~**y** *adj* 1 hard and rough 2 *taboo sl* sexually excited

hor·net /'hɔːnɪt ‖ 'hɔːr-/ *n* large stinging insect

hor·o·scope /'hɒrəskəʊp ‖ 'haːrəskoʊp, 'hɔː-/ *n* set of ideas about someone's character, life, and future gained by knowing the position of the stars or PLANETS at time of birth

hor·ren·dous /hɒˈrendəs ‖ haː-, hɔː-/ *adj* really terrible ~**ly** *adv*

hor·ri·ble /'hɒrəbəl ‖ 'hɔː-, 'haː-/ *adj* 1 causing horror 2 very unpleasant –**bly** *adv*

hor·rid /'hɒrɪd ‖ 'hɔː-, 'haː-/ *adj* nasty

hor·rif·ic /hɒˈrɪfɪk ‖ hɔː-, haː-/ *adj* horrifying ~**ally** /-kli/ *adv*

hor·ri·fy /'hɒrɪfaɪ ‖ 'hɔː-, 'haː-/ *vt* fill with horror: *horrifying news*

hor·ror /'hɒrər ‖ 'hɔːrər, 'haː-/ *n* 1 [C;U] (something causing) great shock and fear 2 [C] unpleasant person, usu. a child 3 **have a horror of** hate ♦ *adj* frightening: *horror films* –**s** *n infml* [*the*+P] state of great fear, worry, or sadness

horror-strick·en /'·· ˌ·/ *also* **horror-struck** /'·· ·/ — *adj* deeply shocked

hors d'oeu·vre /ˌɔː ˈdɜːv ‖ ˌɔːr ˈdɜːrv/ *n* -**d'oeuvres** /-ˈdɜːvz ‖ -ˈdɜːrvz/ small things served at the beginning of a meal

horse[1] /hɔːs ‖ hɔːrs/ *n* 1 large four-legged animal that people ride on, etc. 2 apparatus for jumping over 3 **eat like a horse** eat a lot 4 **(straight) from the horse's mouth** (of information) directly from the person concerned —see also DARK HORSE, HIGH HORSE, TROJAN HORSE

horse[2] *v* **horse around/about** *phr vi infml* play roughly or waste time in rough play

horse·back /'hɔːsbæk ‖ 'hɔːrs-/ *n* **on horseback** riding a horse ♦ *adj, adv esp. AmE* on the back of a horse: *horseback riding*

horse·box /'hɔːsbɒks ‖ 'hɔːrsbaːks/ *n* vehicle in which a horse can travel

horse·play /'hɔːspleɪ ‖ 'hɔːrs-/ *n* [U] rough noisy behaviour

horse·pow·er /'hɔːsˌpaʊə ‖ 'hɔːrsˌpaʊr/ *n* horsepower unit measuring the power of an engine

horse·rad·ish /'hɔːsˌrædɪʃ ‖ 'hɔːrs-/ *n* [U] (root used in) a strong-tasting sauce

horse·shoe /'hɔːʃ·ʃuː, 'hɔːs- ‖ 'hɔːr-/ *n* U-shaped shoe for a horse, believed to bring good luck

hors·y /'hɔːsi ‖ 'hɔːrsi/ *adj* 1 interested in horses 2 looking like a horse

hor·ti·cul·ture /ˈhɔːtɪˌkʌltʃə‖ˈhɔːrtɪˌkʌltʃər/ — n [U] science of growing fruit, flowers, and vegetables –**tural** /ˌhɔːtɪˈkʌltʃərəl◁‖ˌhɔːr-/ adj

hose /həʊz‖həʊz/ also **hose·pipe** /ˈhəʊzpaɪp‖ˈhəʊz-/ — n tube used for watering gardens, etc. ♦ vt use a hose on

ho·sier·y /ˈhəʊzjəri‖ˈhəʊʒəri/ n [U] socks, stockings, etc.

hos·pice /ˈhɒspɪs‖ˈhɑː-/ n hospital for people with incurable illnesses

hos·pi·ta·ble /ˈhɒspɪtəbəl, hɒˈspɪ-‖hɑːˈspɪ-, ˈhɑːspɪ-/ adj offering a friendly welcome to guests –**bly** adv

hos·pi·tal /ˈhɒspɪtl‖ˈhɑː-/ n place where people who are ill or injured are treated ~**ize**, ~**ise** vt put into hospital

hos·pi·tal·i·ty /ˌhɒspɪˈtæləti‖ˌhɑː-/ n [U] being hospitable

host¹ /həʊst‖həʊst/ n 1 man who receives guests 2 person who introduces performers, e.g. on a TV show ♦ vt act as a host

host² n large number: a host of difficulties

hos·tage /ˈhɒstɪdʒ‖ˈhɑː-/ n prisoner kept by an enemy so that the other side will obey demands, etc.

hos·tel /ˈhɒstl‖ˈhɑː-/ n building where students, etc. can live and eat

host·ess /ˈhəʊstəs‖ˈhəʊ-/ n 1 female host 2 AIRHOSTESS 3 young woman who acts as companion, dancing partner, etc. in a social club

hos·tile /ˈhɒstaɪl‖ˈhɑːstl, ˈhɑːstaɪl/ adj 1 unfriendly 2 belonging to an enemy

hos·til·i·ty /hɒˈstɪləti‖hɑː-/ n unfriendliness –**ties** n [P] war

hot¹ /hɒt‖hɑːt/ adj -**tt**- 1 having a high temperature 2 having a burning taste: hot pepper 3 fierce; excitable: hot temper 4 (of news) very recent 5 well-informed on and interested in: She's very hot on jazz. 6 hot **and bothered** worried by a feeling that things are going wrong 7 **hot on someone's trail** following someone closely 8 **not so hot** infml not very good ~**ly** adv 1 angrily 2 eagerly: hotly pursued

hot² v -**tt**- **hot up** phr vi become more exciting or dangerous

hot air /ˌ· ˈ·/ n [U] meaningless talk

hot·bed /ˈhɒtbed‖ˈhɑːt-/ n place where something bad can develop: a hotbed of crime

hot-blood·ed /ˌ· ˈ·◁/ adj PASSIONATE

hotch·potch /ˈhɒtʃpɒtʃ‖ˈhɑːtʃpɑːtʃ/ n confused mixture

hot dog /ˌ· ˈ·‖ˈ· ·/ n SAUSAGE in a long bread ROLL² (3)

ho·tel /həʊˈtel‖həʊ-/ n building where people can stay in return for payment

ho·tel·i·er /həʊˈtelieɪ, -liə‖ˌhəʊtəlˈjeɪ/ n hotel manager

hot·head /ˈhɒthed‖ˈhɑːt-/ n person who acts in haste, without thinking ~**ed** /ˌhɒtˈhedʌd◁‖ˌhɑːt-/ adj

hot·house /ˈhɒthaʊs‖ˈhɑːt-/ n heated GREENHOUSE

hot·line /ˈhɒtlaɪn‖ˈhɑːt/ n 1 telephone number that one calls to give or receive information on a particular subject 2 telephone line between heads of government

hot·plate /ˈhɒtpleɪt‖ˈhɑːt-/ n metal surface on which food is cooked

hot seat /ˈ· ·/ n infml position of difficulty from which one must make important decisions

hot·shot /ˈhɒtʃɒt‖ˈhɑːt-/ adj, n infml very successful and confident (person): hotshot lawyers

hotspot /ˈhɒtspɒt‖ˈhɑːtspɑːt/ n 1 place where there is likely to be unrest and perhaps war 2 area on a computer screen where one CLICKs (4) to see pictures or information

hot-tem·pered /ˌ· ˈ··◁/ adj easily made angry

hot wa·ter /ˌ· ˈ··/ n [U] trouble: get into hot water

hot-water bot·tle /ˌ· ˈ·· ˌ·/ n rubber container for hot water, to warm a bed

hound /haʊnd/ n hunting dog ♦ vt chase and worry

hour /aʊə‖aʊr/ n 1 period of 60 minutes 2 time when a new hour starts: arrive on the hour 3 distance one can travel in this period of time: It's only an hour away. 4 period of time: my lunch hour 5 **after hours** later than the usual times of work or business 6 **at all hours** (at any time) during the whole day and night —see also ELEVENTH HOUR, HAPPY HOUR, SMALL HOURS ~**ly** adj, adv once every hour

house¹ /haʊs/ n houses /ˈhaʊzɪz/ 1 a building for people to live in, esp. on more than one level **b** people in such a building:

You'll wake the whole house. **2** building for a stated purpose: *a hen house* | *the Houses of Parliament* | *the House of Lords* **3** *(often cap.)* noble or royal family **4 a** a division of a school **b** business firm: *the house magazine* **5** people voting after a DEBATE **6** theatre, or the people in it **7 bring the house down** cause loud admiration **8 get on like a house on fire** be very friendly **9 on the house** (of drinks) paid for by the people in charge **10 (as) safe as houses** *BrE* very safe

house² /haʊz/ *vt* provide a home, or space, for

house ar·rest /ˈ· ·,·/ *n* **under house arrest** officially ordered not to leave one's house

house·bound /ˈhaʊsbaʊnd/ *adj* unable to leave one's home

house·break·er /ˈhaʊs,breɪkə ‖ -ər/ *n* thief who enters a house by force

house·bro·ken /ˈhaʊs,brəʊkən ‖ -,broʊ-/ *adj AmE for* HOUSE-TRAINED

house·hold /ˈhaʊshəʊld ‖ -hoʊld/ *n* all the people living in a house ♦ *adj* concerned with the management of a house: *household expenses* ~**er** *n* person who owns or is in charge of a house

household name /,·· ˈ·/ *also* **household word** — *n* person or thing that is very well known or talked about by almost everyone

house hus·band /ˈ· ,·/ *n* man who works at home for his family, cleaning, cooking, etc.

house·keep·er /ˈhaʊs,kiːpə ‖ -ər/ *n* person paid to run a house

house·keep·ing /ˈhaʊs,kiːpɪŋ/ *n* **1** work of running a house **2** money set aside for food, etc.

house·man /ˈhaʊsmən/ *n* -men /-mən/ *BrE* low-ranking doctor completing hospital training

House of Com·mons /,· · ˈ··/ *n* [*the*] the lower but more powerful of the two parts of the British or Canadian parliament

House of Lords /,·· · ˈ·/ *n* [*the*] the upper but less powerful of the two parts of the British parliament, the members of which are not elected

House of Rep·re·sen·ta·tives /,·· ··ˈ···/ *n* [*the*] the larger and lower of the two parts of the central law-making body in such countries as New Zealand, Australia,

and the US

house-proud /ˈ· ·/ *adj* keeping one's home very clean and tidy

house-trained /ˈ· ·/ *adj BrE* (of pets) trained to empty the bowels and BLADDER outside the house

house·warm·ing /ˈhaʊs,wɔːmɪŋ ‖ -,wɔːr-/ *n* party given for friends when one has moved into a new house

house·wife /ˈhaʊs-waɪf/ *n* -wives /-waɪvz/ woman who works at home for her family, cleaning, cooking, etc.

house·work /ˈhaʊswɜːk ‖ -wɜːrk/ *n* [U] cleaning, etc. in a house

hous·ing /ˈhaʊzɪŋ/ *n* **1** [U] places to live **2** [C] protective cover for a machine

hove /həʊv ‖ hoʊv/ *v past t. and p. of* HEAVE² (2)

hov·el /ˈhɒvəl ‖ ˈhʌ-, ˈhɑː-/ *n* dirty little house or hut

hov·er /ˈhɒvə ‖ ˈhʌvər, ˈhɑː-/ *vi* **1** (of birds, etc.) stay in the air in one place **2** (of people) wait around

hov·er·craft /ˈhɒvəkrɑːft ‖ ˈhʌvərkræft, ˈhɑː-/ *n* -craft *or* -crafts boat that moves over land or water supported by a strong force of air

how /haʊ/ *adv* **1** (used in questions) **a** in what way: *How do you spell it?* **b** in what state of health: *How are you?* **c** (in questions about number, size, etc.): *How big is it?* **2** (showing surprise): *How kind of you!* **3 How come...?** *infml* Why is it that...? **4 How do you do?** (used when formally introduced to someone; this person replies with the same phrase) ♦ *conj* the way in which; the fact that: *I remember how they laughed.*

how·ev·er /haʊˈevə ‖ -ər/ *adv* **1** in whatever degree or way: *We'll go, however cold it is.* **2** in spite of this **3** in what way (showing surprise): *However did you get here?*

howl /haʊl/ *vi/t, n* (make) a long loud cry ~**er** *n* silly laughable mistake

HP /,eɪtʃ ˈpiː/ *abbrev. for:* **1** HORSEPOWER **2** HIRE PURCHASE

HQ /,eɪtʃ ˈkjuː/ *n* [C;U] *abbrev. for:* HEADQUARTERS

hr, hrs *written abbrev. for:* hour

HRH *abbrev. for:* His/Her Royal Highness; title for certain members of the British royal family

hub /hʌb/ n 1 centre of a wheel 2 centre of activity

hub·bub /'hʌbʌb/ n [S] mixture of loud noises

hub·cap /'hʌbkæp/ n metal covering for the centre of a wheel on a car

hud·dle /'hʌdl/ vi/t crowd together ♦ n crowded group

hue /hju:/ n fml colour

hue and cry /ˌ··'·/ n expression of worry, anger, etc. by noisy behaviour

huff /hʌf/ n [S] bad temper ~y adj

hug /hʌg/ vt -gg- 1 hold tightly in one's arms 2 travel along beside: The boat hugged the coast. hug n

huge /hju:dʒ/ adj very big ~ly adv very much

huh /hʌh/ interj (used for asking a question or for expressing surprise or disapproval)

hulk /hʌlk/ n 1 old broken ship 2 heavy, awkward person or creature

hulk·ing /'hʌlkɪŋ/ adj big and awkward

hull /hʌl/ n body of a ship or aircraft

hul·lo /hʌ'ləʊ ‖ -'loʊ/ interj, n -los BrE for HELLO

hum /hʌm/ v -mm- 1 vi BUZZ (1) 2 vi/t sing with closed lips 3 vi be full of activity hum n [U]

hu·man /'hju:mən/ adj 1 of people 2 kind, etc., as people should be: He's really very human. ♦ n also human being noun ~ism n [U] system of belief based on people's needs, and not on religion, ~ize, ~ise vt make human or humane ~ly adv according to human powers: not humanly possible

hu·mane /hju:'meɪn/ adj 1 showing human kindness and the qualities of a civilized person 2 trying not to cause pain: a humane method of killing animals ~ly adv

hu·man·i·tar·i·an /hju:ˌmænɪ'teəriən ‖ -'ter-/ n, adj (person) trying to improve life for human beings by improving their living conditions, etc. ~ism n [U]

hu·man·i·ty /hju:'mænɪti/ n [U] 1 being human or humane 2 people in general

human race /ˌ·· '·/ n [the+S] all people

human rights /ˌ·· '·/ n [P] basic rights of all people

hum·ble /'hʌmbəl/ adj 1 low in rank; unimportant 2 having a low opinion of

oneself and a high opinion of others; not proud ♦ vt make humble –bly adv

hum·bug /'hʌmbʌg/ n 1 [U] insincere nonsense 2 [C] BrE hard boiled sweet

hum·drum /'hʌmdrʌm/ adj dull and ordinary

hu·mid /'hju:mɪd/ adj (of air) DAMP ~ify /hju:'mɪdɪfaɪ/ vt make humid ~ity n [U]

hu·mil·i·ate /hju:'mɪlieɪt/ vt cause to feel ashamed –ation /hju:ˌmɪli'eɪʃən/ n [C;U]

hu·mil·i·ty /hju:'mɪlɪti/ n [U] quality of being HUMBLE (2)

hu·mor·ist /'hju:mərɪst ‖ 'hju:-, 'ju:-/ n person who makes jokes in speech or writing

hu·mor·ous /'hju:mərəs ‖ 'hju:-, 'ju:-/ adj funny ~ly adv

hu·mour BrE ‖ humor AmE /'hju:mə ‖ 'hju:mər, 'ju:-/ n [U] ability to be amused or cause amusement ♦ vt keep (someone) happy by acceptance of their foolish wishes, behaviour, etc.

hump /hʌmp/ n 1 [C] round lump, esp. on a camel's back 2 [the+S] BrE infml feeling of bad temper: She took the hump (=got angry). ♦ v 1 vt infml carry (something heavy), esp. with difficulty 2 vi/t taboo sl have sex with

hunch[1] /hʌntʃ/ n idea based on feeling rather than reason

hunch[2] vt pull (part of the body) into a rounded shape: hunched shoulders

hunch·back /'hʌntʃbæk/ n (person with) a back mis-shaped by a round lump ~ed adj

hun·dred /'hʌndrɪd/ determiner, n, pron -dred or -dreds 100 ~th determiner, adv, n, pron 100th

hun·dred·weight /'hʌndrɪdweɪt/ n -weight (a measure of weight equal to) a 45.36 kilograms or b 50.8 kilograms

hung /hʌŋ/ v past t. and p. of HANG —see also be hung up (HANG up)

hun·ger /'hʌŋgə ‖ -ər/ n 1 [U] need for food 2 [S] strong wish ♦ vi feel hunger –gry adj feeling hunger

hunger strike /'·· ·/ n refusal to eat as a sign of strong dissatisfaction

hung·o·ver /hʌŋ'əʊvə ‖ -'oʊvər/ adj feeling ill after drinking too much alcohol the day before

hunk /hʌŋk/ n 1 thick piece of food, etc. 2 infml good-looking man

hunt /hʌnt/ vi/t 1 chase (animals) for food

or sport **2** search (for) ♦ *n* **1** chasing or searching **2** people hunting foxes ~**er** *n*

hunt down/out/up *phr vt* find by searching

hur·dle /'hɜːdl ‖ 'hɜːr-/ *n* **1** frame to jump over in a race **2** difficulty to be dealt with

hurl /hɜːl ‖ hɜːrl/ *vt* throw violently: (fig.) *He hurled abuse at the other driver.*

hur·ly-bur·ly /ˈhɜːli ˌbɜːli ‖ ˌhɜːrli ˈbɜːrli/ *n* [S;U] noisy activity

hur·ray, **hooray** /hʊˈreɪ/ *interj*, *n* (shout of joy or approval)

hur·ri·cane /'hʌrɪkən ‖ 'hɜːrɪˌkeɪn/ *n* violent storm with a strong fast circular wind

hur·ry /'hʌri ‖ 'hɜːri/ *vi/t* (cause to) go or do something (too) quickly: *Hurry up!* (=Be quick!) ♦ *n* [S;U] **1** quick activity **2** need to hurry **–ried** *adj* done (too) quickly **–riedly** *adv*

hurt /hɜːt ‖ hɜːrt/ *v* **hurt 1** *vt* cause pain or damage to **2** *vt* cause pain (to the feelings of (a person)) **3** *vi* feel pain **3** *vi/t* matter (to): *It won't hurt (you) to wait.* ♦ *n* [C;U] harm; damage ~**ful** *adj* **–fully** *adv*

hur·tle /'hɜːtl ‖ 'hɜːrt-/ *vi* move or rush with great force

hus·band /'hʌzbənd/ *n* man to whom a woman is married

hush /hʌʃ/ *vi/t* (cause to) be silent ♦ *n* [S;U] silence

  hush up *phr vt* keep secret

husk /hʌsk/ *n* dry outer covering of some fruits and seeds

hus·ky /'hʌski/ *adj* **1** (of a voice) HOARSE **2** (of a person) big and strong **–kily** *adv*

hus·tings /'hʌstɪŋz/ *n* [P] speeches, etc. before an election

hus·tle /'hʌsəl/ *vt* **1** push or drive hurriedly **2** persuade someone forcefully, esp. to buy something ♦ *n* [U] hurried activity **hustler** *n infml* busy, active person, esp. one who tries to persuade people to buy things, etc.

hut /hʌt/ *n* small simple building

hutch /hʌtʃ/ *n* cage for rabbits, etc.

hy·brid /'haɪbrɪd/ *n* animal or plant of mixed breed

hy·drant /'haɪdrənt/ *n* water pipe in the street

hy·draul·ic /haɪˈdrɒlɪk, -'drɔː- ‖ -'drɔː-/ *adj* using water pressure

hy·dro·e·lec·tric /ˌhaɪdrəʊ-ɪ'lektrɪk ‖ -droʊ-/ *adj* producing electricity by water power

hy·dro·foil /'haɪdrəfɔɪl/ *n* large motor boat which raises itself out of the water as it moves

hy·dro·gen /'haɪdrədʒən/ *n* [U] light gas that burns easily

hydrogen bomb /'··· ·/ *n* bomb made using hydrogen which explodes when the central parts of the atoms join together

hy·e·na /haɪˈiːnə/ *n* doglike wild animal that makes a sound like laughter

hy·giene /'haɪdʒiːn/ *n* [U] cleanness, to prevent the spreading of disease **hygienic** /haɪˈdʒiːnɪk ‖ -'dʒe-, -'dʒiː-/ *adj*

hymn /hɪm/ *n* song of praise to God

hype /haɪp/ *vt infml* try to get a lot of public attention for, esp. more than is deserved **hype** *n* [U] attempts to do this

hyped up /ˌ·ˈ·/ *adj infml* very excited and anxious

hy·per /'haɪpə ‖ -ər/ *adj infml* very excited or with a lot of energy

hy·per·ac·tive /ˌhaɪpərˈæktɪv◂/ *adj* unable to rest or be quiet

hy·per·bo·le /haɪˈpɜːbəli ‖ -ɜːr-/ *n* EXAGGERATION

hy·per·mar·ket /'haɪpəˌmɑːkət ‖ -pər-ˌmɑːr-/ *n BrE* very large SUPERMARKET

hy·phen /'haɪfən/ *n* (in joining words or word parts ~**ate** *vt* join with a hyphen

hyp·no·sis /hɪpˈnəʊsɪs ‖ -'noʊ-/ *n* [U] sleep-like state in which a person can be influenced by the person who produced the state **–notic** /-'nɒtɪk ‖ -'nɑː-/ *adj* **–tism** /'hɪpnətɪzəm/ *n* [U] production of hypnosis **–tist** *n* **–tize**, **–ise** *vt* produce hypnosis in

hy·po·chon·dri·ac /ˌhaɪpəˈkɒndriæk ‖ -'kɑːn-/ *n* someone who worries unnecessarily about their health

hy·poc·ri·sy /hɪ'pɒkrɪsi ‖ -'pɑː-/ *n* [U] pretending to be different from and usu. better than one is

hyp·o·crite /'hɪpəkrɪt/ *n* person who practises hypocrisy **–critical** /ˌhɪpəˈkrɪtɪkəl◂/ *adj*

hy·po·der·mic /ˌhaɪpəˈdɜːmɪk◂ ‖ -ɜːr-/ *adj*, *n* (of a needle for putting drugs into the body

hy·pot·e·nuse /haɪˈpɒtənjuːz ‖ -'pɑːtə-njuːs, -nuːz/ *n* longest side of a right-angled TRIANGLE which is opposite the right angle

TRIANGLE which is opposite the right angle

hy·poth·e·sis /haɪˈpɒθəsəs ‖ -ˈpɑː-/ n idea that may explain facts **–etical** /ˌhaɪpəˈθetɪkəl◁/ adj not yet proved

hys·te·ri·a /hɪˈstɪəriə ‖ -ˈsteriə/ n [U] uncontrolled nervous excitement **–rical** /hɪˈsterɪkəl/ adj 1 in a state of hysteria 2 extremely amusing **–rics** n [P] 1 attack(s) of hysteria 2 uncontrollable laughter

I¹, **i** /aɪ/ the 9th letter of the English alphabet

I² pron (used for the person speaking, as the subject of a sentence)

ice¹ /aɪs/ n 1 [U] frozen water 2 [C] frozen sweet food 3 **skating on thin ice** taking risks 4 **keep something on ice** take no immediate action about something —see also BLACK ICE

ice² vt 1 make cold with ice 2 cover with ICING

ice over/up phr vi become covered with ice

ice age /ˈ· ·/ n period when ice covered many northern countries

ice·berg /ˈaɪsbɜːɡ ‖ -bɜːrɡ/ n 1 mass of floating ice in the sea 2 **the tip of the iceberg** a small sign of a much larger situation, problem, etc.

ice·box /ˈaɪsbɒks ‖ -bɑːks/ n 1 box where food is kept cool with ice 2 AmE old-fash for FRIDGE

ice·break·er /ˈaɪsˌbreɪkə ‖ -ər/ n 1 ship that cuts through floating ice 2 action which makes people who have just met more relaxed

ice cap /ˈ· ·/ n lasting covering of ice, e.g. at the POLES² (1)

ice cream /ˌ· ˈ·◁ ‖ ˈ· ·/ n [C;U] frozen creamy food mixture

ice floe /ˈaɪs fləʊ ‖ -floʊ/ n large area of floating ice

ice hock·ey /ˈ· ˌ··/ n [U] game like HOCKEY¹ played on ice

ice lol·ly /ˌ· ˈ··/ n BrE piece of ICE¹ (2) on a stick

ice pack /ˈ· ·/ n bag of ice to put on the body

ice pick /ˈ· ·/ n tool for breaking ice

ice-skate /ˈ· ·/ n SKATE (1) ♦ vi

i·ci·cle /ˈaɪsɪkəl/ n pointed stick of ice, formed when water freezes as it runs down

ic·ing /ˈaɪsɪŋ/ n [U] mixture of powdery sugar with liquid, used to decorate cakes

i·con /ˈaɪkɒn ‖ -kɑːn/ n 1 much admired person or thing connected with an important idea: a feminist icon 2 small picture on a computer screen that one CLICKS (4) on to carry out a command 3 also **ikon** picture of a holy person

i·con·o·clast /aɪˈkɒnəklæst ‖ -ˈkɑː-/ n person who attacks established beliefs **~ic** /aɪˌkɒnəˈklæstɪk◁ ‖ -ˌkɑː-/ adj

ic·y /ˈaɪsi/ adj 1 very cold 2 covered with ice **icily** adv

ID /ˌaɪ ˈdiː/ n [U] IDENTIFICATION (2)

I'd /aɪd/ short for: 1 I would 2 I had

i·dea /aɪˈdɪə/ n 1 [C] plan, thought, or suggestion for a possible course of action 2 [C;U] picture in the mind; CONCEPTION 3 [C] opinion or belief: strange ideas 4 understanding: They've got no idea how to run a house. 5 [C] guess; feeling of probability: I've an idea she doesn't like him.

i·deal /aɪˈdɪəl/ adj 1 perfect 2 too good to exist ♦ n 1 [often pl.] (belief in) high principles or perfect standards 2 perfect example **~ize**, **~ise** vt imagine as perfect **~ly** adv 1 in an ideal way: ideally suited 2 if things were perfect

i·deal·ism /aɪˈdɪəlɪzəm/ n [U] quality or habit of living according to one's ideals, or the belief that such a way of life is possible **–ist** n **–istic** adj /ˌaɪdɪəˈlɪstɪk◁/ **–istically** /-kli/

i·den·ti·cal /aɪˈdentɪkəl/ adj 1 exactly alike 2 the same **~ly** /-kli/ adv

i·den·ti·fy /aɪˈdentɪfaɪ/ vt show the identity of **–fication** /aɪˌdentɪ̥fɪˈkeɪʃən/ n [U] 1 identifying 2 paper, etc. that proves who one is

identify with phr vt 1 consider (someone) to be connected with 2 feel sympathy for

i·den·ti·ty /aɪˈdentɪ̥ti/ n 1 [C;U] who or

what a person or thing is **2** [U] sameness

i·de·ol·o·gy /ˌaɪdiˈɒlədʒi ‖ -ˈɑːlə-/ n [C;U] set of (political or social) ideas **–ogical** /ˌaɪdiəˈlɒdʒɪkəl◄ ‖ -ˈlɑː-/ adj

id·i·o·cy /ˈɪdiəsi/ n **1** [U] stupidity **2** [C] stupid act

id·i·om /ˈɪdiəm/ n phrase that means something different from the meanings of its separate words: *'Kick the bucket' is an idiom meaning 'die'.*

id·i·o·mat·ic /ˌɪdiəˈmætɪk◄/ adj typical of natural speech **–ally** /-kli/ adv

id·i·o·syn·cra·sy /ˌɪdiəˈsɪŋkrəsi/ n personal peculiarity **–tic** /ˌɪdiəsɪnˈkrætɪk◄/ adj **–tically** /-kli/ adv

id·i·ot /ˈɪdiət/ n **1** fool **2** weak-minded person **~ic** /ˌɪdiˈɒtɪk◄ ‖ -ˈɑːt-/ adj

i·dle¹ /ˈaɪdl/ adj **1** not working **2** lazy **3** useless: *idle threats* **~ness** n [U] **idly** adv

idle² vi **1** waste time **2** (of an engine) run slowly because it is disconnected **idler** n

idle away phr vt waste (time)

i·dol /ˈaɪdl/ n **1** image worshipped as a god **2** someone greatly admired **~ize**, **~ise** vt worship as an idol

i·dol·a·try /aɪˈdɒlətri ‖ -ˈdɑː-/ n [U] worshipping of idols **–trous** adj idolater n

id·yl·lic /ɪˈdɪlɪk ‖ aɪ-/ adj very pleasant and peaceful **idyll** /ˈɪdəl, ˈɪdɪl ‖ ˈaɪdl/ n idyllic place

i.e. /ˌaɪ ˈiː/ that is; by which is meant: *open to adults, i.e. people over 18*

if /ɪf/ conj **1** on condition that: *I'll come if I can.* **2** even though: *It was nice, if expensive.* **3** whether: *I don't know if he'll come.* **4** (after words expressing feeling): *I'm sorry if she's annoyed.* **5** **if I were you** (used when giving advice): *If I were you, I'd burn it.* **6** **it isn't/it's not as if** it's not true that ♦ n **ifs and buts** reasons given for delay

ig·loo /ˈɪɡluː/ n house made of snow

ig·nite /ɪɡˈnaɪt/ vi/t fml start to burn

ig·ni·tion /ɪɡˈnɪʃən/ n **1** [C] electrical apparatus that starts an engine **2** [U] fml action of igniting

ig·no·ble /ɪɡˈnəʊbəl ‖ -ˈnoʊ-/ adj fml not honourable **–bly** adv

ig·no·mi·ny /ˈɪɡnəmɪni/ n [C;U] (act of) shame **–nious** /ˌɪɡnəˈmɪniəs◄/ adj

ig·no·ra·mus /ˌɪɡnəˈreɪməs/ n ignorant person

ig·no·rant /ˈɪɡnərənt/ adj **1** without knowledge **2** rude, esp. because of lack of

social training **–rance** n [U]

ig·nore /ɪɡˈnɔː ‖ -ˈnɔːr/ vt refuse to notice

ill /ɪl/ adj **worse** /wɜːs ‖ wɜːrs/, **worst** /wɜːst ‖ wɜːrst/ **1** sick **2** bad: *ill luck* ♦ adv **1** badly: *The child was ill-treated.* **2** not enough: *ill fed* ♦ n bad thing: *the social ills of poverty and unemployment*

I'll /aɪl/ short for: I will or I shall

ill-ad·vised /ˌ· ·'·◄/ adj unwise

il·le·gal /ɪˈliːɡəl/ adj against the law **~ly** adv **~ity** /ˌɪlɪˈɡælɪti/ n [C;U]

il·le·gi·ble /ɪˈledʒəbəl/ adj impossible to read

il·le·git·i·mate /ˌɪlɪˈdʒɪtɪmɪt◄/ adj **1** born to unmarried parents **2** against the rules **–ly** adv

ill-got·ten /ˌ· '··◄/ adj dishonestly obtained

il·li·cit /ɪˈlɪsɪt/ adj against the law or the rules **~ly** adv

il·lit·e·rate /ɪˈlɪtərɪt/ adj unable to read or write **–racy** n [U]

ill-na·tured /ˌ· '··◄/ adj bad-tempered

ill·ness /ˈɪlnəs/ n [C;U] disease

il·lo·gi·cal /ɪˈlɒdʒɪkəl ‖ -ˈlɑː-/ adj against LOGIC; not sensible **~ly** /-kli/ adv

il·lu·mi·nate /ɪˈluːmɪneɪt, ɪˈljuː- ‖ ɪˈluː-/ vt **1** give light to **2** decorate with lights **3** (esp. in former times) decorate with gold and bright colours **–nating** adj helping to explain: *illuminating remark* **–nation** /ɪˌluːmɪˈneɪʃən, ɪˌljuː- ‖ ɪˌluː-/ n [U] act of illuminating or state of being illuminated **–nations** n [P] coloured lights to decorate a town

il·lu·sion /ɪˈluːʒən/ n something seen wrongly; false idea **–sory** /ɪˈluːsəri/ adj fml unreal

il·lus·trate /ˈɪləstreɪt/ vt **1** add pictures to **2** explain by giving examples **–trator** n person who draws pictures for a book, etc. **–tration** /ˌɪləˈstreɪʃən/ n **1** [C] picture **2** [C] example **3** [U] act of illustrating **–trative** /ˈɪləstreɪtɪv, -strət- ‖ ɪˈlʌstrətɪv/ adj used as an example

il·lus·tri·ous /ɪˈlʌstriəs/ adj famous

ill will /ˌ· '·/ n [U] unfriendly feeling

I'm /aɪm/ short for: I am

im·age /ˈɪmɪdʒ/ n **1** picture in the mind, or seen in a mirror **2** general opinion about a person, etc. that has been formed or intentionally created in people's minds **3** copy; likeness: *He's the image of his father.* **4** IDOL (1) **~ry** n [U] METAPHORS, etc. in literature

i·ma·gi·na·ry /ɪˈmædʒɪ̈nəri ‖ -dʒɪ̈neri/ *adj* unreal

i·ma·gine /ɪˈmædʒɪ̈n/ *vt* 1 form (an idea) in the mind: *imagine a world without cars* 2 believe; suppose: *I imagine they've forgotten.* **-ginable** *adj* that can be imagined **-ginative** *adj* good at imagining **-gination** /ɪ̈ˌmædʒɪ̈ˈneɪʃən/ *n* 1 [C;U] ability to imagine 2 [U] something only imagined

im·bal·ance /ɪmˈbæləns/ *n* lack of balance or equality

im·be·cile /ˈɪmbɪ̈siːl ‖ -səl/ *n* IDIOT **-cility** /ˌɪmbɪ̈ˈsɪlɪ̈ti/ *n* 1 [U] being an imbecile 2 [C] foolish act

im·bibe /ɪmˈbaɪb/ *vi/t fml* drink or take in

im·bue /ɪmˈbjuː/ *v* imbue with *phr vt* fill with (a feeling, etc.)

im·i·tate /ˈɪmɪ̈teɪt/ *vt* 1 copy 2 take as an example **-tator** *n* **-tative** /-tətɪv ‖ -teɪtɪv/ *adj* following an example; not inventive **-tation** /ˌɪmɪ̈ˈteɪʃən/ *n* 1 [C;U] act or act of imitating 2 [C] copy of the real thing

im·mac·u·late /ɪˈmækjɪ̈lɪ̈t/ *adj* clean; pure **~ly** *adv*

im·ma·te·ri·al /ˌɪmɪ̈ˈtɪəriəl◂ ‖ -ˈtɪr-/ *adj* 1 unimportant 2 without physical substance

im·ma·ture /ˌɪmɪ̈ˈtʃʊə◂ ‖ -ˈtjʊr-/ *adj* not fully formed or developed **-turity** *n* [U]

im·mea·sur·a·ble /ɪˈmeʒərəbəl/ *adj* too big to be measured **-bly** *adv*

im·me·di·ate /ɪˈmiːdiət/ *adj* 1 done or needed at once: *an immediate reply* 2 nearest: *the immediate future* **-ly** *adv* 1 at once 2 with nothing between: *immediately in front* **-ly** *conj* as soon as: *Immediately your application is accepted, you will be informed* **-acy** *n* [U] nearness or urgent presence of something

im·me·mo·ri·al /ˌɪmɪ̈ˈmɔːriəl◂/ *adj* —see TIME IMMEMORIAL

im·mense /ɪˈmens/ *adj* very large **~ly** *adv* very much **immensity** *n* [U]

im·merse /ɪˈmɜːs ‖ -ɜːrs/ *vt* put deep into liquid: (fig.) *immersed in my work* **immersion** /ɪˈmɜːʃən, -ʒən ‖ -ɜːr-/ *n* [U] **immersion heat·er** /·ˈ·· ˌ··/ *n* electric water heater in a TANK

im·mi·grate /ˈɪmɪ̈greɪt/ *vi* come to live in a country **-grant** *n* person who does this **-gration** /ˌɪmɪ̈ˈgreɪʃən/ *n* [U]

im·mi·nent /ˈɪmɪ̈nənt/ *adj* going to happen soon **~ly** *adv*

im·mo·bile /ɪˈməʊbaɪl ‖ ɪˈmoʊbəl/ *adj* unmoving; unable to move **-bility** /ˌɪməʊˈbɪlɪ̈ti ‖ ˌɪmoʊ-/ *n* [U] **-bilize, -bilise** /ɪˈməʊbɪ̈laɪz ‖ ɪˈmoʊ-/ *vt* make immobile **-bilizer** *n*

im·mor·al /ɪˈmɒrəl ‖ ɪˈmɔː-/ *adj* 1 not good or right 2 sexually improper **~ity** /ˌɪməˈrælɪ̈ti/ *n* [C;U]

im·mor·tal /ɪˈmɔːtl ‖ -ɔːr-/ *adj* living or remembered for ever ♦ *n* immortal being **~ize, ~ise** *vt* give endless life or fame to **~ity** /ˌɪmɔːˈtælɪ̈ti ‖ -ɔːr-/ *n* endless life

im·mune /ɪˈmjuːn/ *adj* unable to be harmed; protected **immunity** *n* [U] **immunize, -ise** /ˈɪmjɪ̈naɪz/ *vt* protect from disease

immune sys·tem /·ˈ· ˌ··/ *n* bodily system that fights substances that cause disease

imp /ɪmp/ *n* 1 little devil 2 troublesome child **~ish** *adj*

im·pact /ˈɪmpækt/ *n* 1 force of one object hitting another 2 influence; effect 3 on impact at the moment of hitting ♦ /ɪmˈpækt/ *vi/t* 1 hit with force 2 also impact on *phr vt* influence

im·pair /ɪmˈpeə ‖ -ˈper/ *vt* spoil; weaken

im·pale /ɪmˈpeɪl/ *vt* run something sharp through: *impaled on the spikes*

im·part /ɪmˈpɑːt ‖ -ɑːrt/ *vt fml* give (knowledge, etc.)

im·par·tial /ɪmˈpɑːʃəl ‖ -ɑːr-/ *adj* fair; just **~ly** *adv* **~ity** /ɪmˌpɑːʃiˈælɪ̈ti ‖ -ɑːr-/ *n* [U]

im·pass·a·ble /ɪmˈpɑːsəbəl ‖ ɪmˈpæ-/ *adj* (of roads, etc.) impossible to travel over

im·passe /æmˈpæs ‖ ˈɪmpæs/ *n* point where further movement is blocked

im·pas·sioned /ɪmˈpæʃənd/ *adj* full of deep feelings: *impassioned speech*

im·pas·sive /ɪmˈpæsɪv/ *adj* showing no feelings; calm **~ly** *adv*

im·pa·tient /ɪmˈpeɪʃənt/ *adj* 1 not patient 2 eager: *impatient to go* **~ly** *adv* **-tience** *n* [U]

im·peach /ɪmˈpiːtʃ/ *vt* charge (a politician, official, etc.) with a crime committed whilst in office **~ment** *n* [C;U]

im·pec·ca·ble /ɪmˈpekəbəl/ *adj* faultless **-bly** *adv*

im·pe·cu·ni·ous /ˌɪmpɪ̈ˈkjuːniəs◂/ *adj fml* without money: poor

im·pede /ɪmˈpiːd/ *vt* get in the way of

im·ped·i·ment /ɪmˈpedɪmənt/ *n* something that makes action difficult or impossible: *a speech impediment*

im·pel /ɪmˈpel/ *vt* -ll- (of an idea, etc.) cause (someone) to act

im·pend·ing /ɪmˈpendɪŋ/ *adj* (esp. of something bad) about to happen

im·pen·e·tra·ble /ɪmˈpenɪtrəbəl/ *adj* 1 that cannot be gone through 2 impossible to understand

im·per·a·tive /ɪmˈperətɪv/ *adj* urgent; that must be done ♦ *n gram* verb form expressing a command (e.g. 'Come!') ~**ly** *adv*

im·per·fect /ɪmˈpɜːfɪkt ‖ -ˈɜːr-/ *adj* not perfect ♦ *n gram* verb form showing incomplete action in the past (e.g. *was walking*) ~**ly** *adv* ~**ion** /ˌɪmpəˈfekʃən ‖ -pər-/ *n* [C;U] 1 [U] imperfect state 2 [C] fault

im·pe·ri·al /ɪmˈpɪəriəl ‖ -ˈpɪr-/ *adj* of an EMPIRE or its ruler ~**ly** *adv* ~**ism** *n* [U] (belief in) the making of an EMPIRE ~**ist** *n, adj*

im·per·il /ɪmˈperɪl/ *vt* -ll- *BrE* ‖ -l- *AmE* put in danger

im·pe·ri·ous /ɪmˈpɪəriəs ‖ -ˈpɪr-/ *adj fml* (too) commanding; expecting obedience from others

im·per·son·al /ɪmˈpɜːsənəl ‖ -ɜːr-/ *adj* without personal feelings: *large impersonal organizations* ~**ly** *adv*

im·per·so·nate /ɪmˈpɜːsəneɪt ‖ -ɜːr-/ *vt* pretend to be (another person) –**nation** /ɪmˌpɜːsəˈneɪʃən ‖ -ˌpɜːr-/ *n* [C;U]

im·per·ti·nent /ɪmˈpɜːtɪnənt ‖ -ɜːr-/ *adj* not properly respectful ~**ly** *adv* –**nence** *n* [U]

im·per·tur·ba·ble /ˌɪmpəˈtɜːbəbəl ‖ -pərˈtɜːr-/ *adj* unworried; calm –**bly** *adv*

im·per·vi·ous /ɪmˈpɜːviəs ‖ -ɜːr-/ *adj* 1 not letting water, etc. through 2 not easily influenced: *impervious to criticism*

im·pet·u·ous /ɪmˈpetʃuəs/ *adj* acting quickly but without thought ~**ly** *adv* –**osity** /ɪmˌpetʃuˈɒsɪti ‖ -ˈɑːs-/ *n* [U]

im·pe·tus /ˈɪmpɪtəs/ *n* 1 [U] force of something moving 2 [S;U] STIMULUS: *a fresh impetus to industry*

im·pinge /ɪmˈpɪndʒ/ *v* impinge on/upon *phr vt* have an effect on

im·plac·a·ble /ɪmˈplækəbəl/ *adj* impossible to satisfy or PLACATE

im·plant[1] /ɪmˈplɑːnt ‖ ɪmˈplænt/ *vt* fix deeply into

im·plant[2] /ˈɪmplɑːnt ‖ ˈɪmplænt/ *n* thing put into a person's body in a medical operation

im·plau·si·ble /ɪmˈplɔːzəbəl ‖ -ˈplɔː-/ *adj* seeming to be untrue or unlikely

im·ple·ment[1] /ˈɪmplɪmənt/ *n* tool or instrument

im·ple·ment[2] /ˈɪmplɪment/ *vt* carry out (plans, etc.)

im·pli·cate /ˈɪmplɪkeɪt/ *vt fml* show (someone) to be concerned: *a letter implicating him in the crime*

im·pli·ca·tion /ˌɪmplɪˈkeɪʃən/ *n* 1 [C;U] (example of) the act of implying 2 [C] possible later effect of something 3 [U] act of implicating

im·pli·cit /ɪmˈplɪsɪt/ *adj* 1 meant though not expressed 2 unquestioning: *implicit trust* ~**ly** *adv*

im·plode /ɪmˈpləʊd ‖ -ˈploʊd/ *vi fml* explode inwards because of outside pressure: (fig.) *fears that the organization would implode*

im·plore /ɪmˈplɔː ‖ -ˈplɔːr/ *vt* beg; request strongly: *implore them to go*

im·ply /ɪmˈplaɪ/ *vt* 1 express indirectly: *He implied that he had not yet made a decision* 2 make necessary

im·po·lite /ˌɪmpəˈlaɪt◂/ *adj* rude

im·pon·de·ra·ble /ɪmˈpɒndərəbəl ‖ -ˈpɑːn-/ *n, adj* (thing) whose effects cannot be measured exactly

im·port[1] /ɪmˈpɔːt ‖ -ɔːrt/ *vt* bring in (goods) from abroad ~**er** *n* ~**ation** /ˌɪmpɔːˈteɪʃən ‖ -pɔːr-/ *n* [C;U]

im·port[2] /ˈɪmpɔːt ‖ -ɔːrt/ *n* 1 [C] something imported 2 [U] *fml* importance

im·por·tant /ɪmˈpɔːtənt ‖ -ɔːr-/ *adj* mattering very much ~**ly** *adv* –**tance** *n* [U]

im·pose /ɪmˈpəʊz ‖ -ˈpoʊz/ *v* 1 *vt* establish (a tax, etc.) 2 *vt* force the acceptance of 3 *vi* take unfair advantage **imposing** *adj* large and IMPRESSIVE **imposition** /ˌɪmpəˈzɪʃən/ *n* [C;U] act of imposing

im·pos·si·ble /ɪmˈpɒsəbəl ‖ ɪmˈpɑː-/ *adj* 1 not possible 2 hard to bear: *make life impossible* –**bly** *adv* –**bility** /ɪmˌpɒsəˈbɪlɪti ‖ ɪmˌpɑː-/ *n* [U]

im·pos·tor /ɪmˈpɒstə ‖ ɪmˈpɑːstər/ *n*

someone who deceives by pretending to be someone else

im·po·tent /'ɪmpətənt/ adj 1 powerless 2 (of a man) unable to perform the sex act -ly adv -tence n [U]

im·pound /ɪm'paʊnd/ vt take away officially

im·pov·er·ish /ɪm'pɒvərɪʃ ‖ ɪm'pɑː-/ vt make poor

im·prac·ti·ca·ble /ɪm'præktɪkəbəl/ adj that cannot be used in practice

im·prac·ti·cal /ɪm'præktɪkəl/ adj not practical; not sensible or reasonable

im·preg·na·ble /ɪm'pregnəbəl/ adj impossible to enter by attack

im·preg·nate /'ɪmpregneɪt ‖ ɪm'preg-/ vt 1 make wet; SATURATE: cloth impregnated with polish 2 fml make PREGNANT

im·pre·sa·ri·o /ˌɪmprɪ'sɑːriəʊ ‖ -riəʊ/ n -os person who arranges theatre or concert performances

im·press /ɪm'pres/ vt 1 fill with admiration 2 tell (someone) that something matters: impress on them that they must work ~ive adj causing admiration ~ively adv ~ion /-'preʃən/ n 1 effect produced on the mind 2 mark left by pressing 3 attempt to copy a person's appearance or behaviour, esp. in theatre, etc. ~ionable adj easily influenced ~ionistic /ɪm,preʃə'nɪstɪk/ adj based on an IMPRESSION (1)

im·print¹ /ɪm'prɪnt/ vt press (a mark) on

im·print² /'ɪmprɪnt/ n mark left on or in something

im·pris·on /ɪm'prɪzən/ vt put in prison ~ment n [U]

im·prob·a·ble /ɪm'prɒbəbəl ‖ -'prɑː-/ adj unlikely -bly adv -bility /ɪm,prɒbə'bɪləti ‖ -,prɑː-/ n [C;U]

im·promp·tu /ɪm'prɒmptjuː ‖ 'prɑːmptuː/ adj, adv without preparation

im·prop·er /ɪm'prɒpə ‖ -'prɑːpər/ adj 1 not suitable or correct 2 socially unacceptable ~ly adv **impropriety** /ˌɪmprə'praɪəti/ n [U]

im·prove /ɪm'pruːv/ vi/t make or become better ~ment n [C;U] (sign of) improving

im·pro·vise /'ɪmprəvaɪz/ vi/t 1 do (something one has not prepared for) 2 invent (music) while one plays -visation /ˌɪmprəvaɪ'zeɪʃən ‖ ɪm,prʌvə-/ n [C;U]

im·pu·dent /'ɪmpjʃdənt/ adj shamelessly disrespectful ~ly adv -dence n [U]

im·pulse /'ɪmpʌls/ n 1 [C;U] sudden urge 2 sudden force: nerve impulse **impulsive** /ɪm'pʌlsɪv/ adj acting on IMPULSE (1)

im·pu·ni·ty /ɪm'pjuːnɪti/ n [U] **with impunity** without being punished

im·pure /ɪm'pjʊə ‖ -'pjʊr/ adj 1 mixed with something else 2 morally bad **impurity** n [C;U]

in¹ /ɪn/ prep 1 contained or surrounded by: in a box | in a field | in France 2 (of time) a during: in the summer b at the end of: finish in 5 minutes 3 included as part of: people in a story 4 wearing: the girl in red 5 using: write in pencil | pay in dollars 6 (shows an area of employment): a job in insurance 7 (shows direction): the sun in my eyes 8 (shows the way something is done or happens): in public | in a hurry | in danger 9 divided or arranged: in rows 10 for each: a slope of 1 in 3 11 with regard to: weak in judgment 12 as a/an: What did you give him in return? 13 **in all** as the total

in² adv 1 (in order to be) contained or surrounded; away from the outside: Open the bag and put the money in. 2 towards or at home or the usual place: Let's stay in tonight. 3 into a surface: knock a nail in 4 from lots of people or places: Letters came pouring in. 5 so as to be added: Fill in your name. 6 (in sport) a having a turn to BAT b (of a ball) inside the line 7 fashionable: Long hair is in again. 8 so as to have a position of power: The Nationalist Party are sure to get in. 9 **be in for** be about to have (esp. something bad) 10 **be in on** take part in 11 **be in with** infml be friendly with

in³ adj 1 directed inwards: a letter in my in tray 2 infml fashionable: the in place to go 3 shared by only a few favoured people: an in joke

in⁴ n **the ins and outs (of something)** infml the details (of a difficult situation, etc.)

in·a·bil·i·ty /ˌɪnə'bɪləti/ n [S;U] lack of power or skill

in·ac·ces·si·ble /ˌɪnək'sesəbəl/ adj impossible to reach

in·ac·cu·rate /ɪn'ækjərɪt/ adj not correct ~ly adv -racy n [C;U]

in·ad·e·quate /ɪn'ædɪkwət/ adj not good enough ~ly adv

in·ad·ver·tent /ˌɪnəd'vɜːtənt ‖ -ɜːr-/ adj done by accident ~ly adv

in·a·li·en·a·ble /ɪn'eɪlɪənəbəl/ *adj fml* (of rights, etc.) that cannot be taken away

i·nane /ɪ'neɪn/ *adj* stupid **~ly** *adv* **inanity** /ɪ'nænɪti/ *n* [C;U]

in·an·i·mate /ɪn'ænɪmɪt/ *adj* not living: *Stones are inanimate.*

in·ap·pro·pri·ate /ˌɪnə'prəʊpri-ɪt‖ -'proʊ-/ *adj* not suitable **~ly** *adv* **~ness** *n* [U]

in·ar·tic·u·late /ˌɪnɑː'tɪkjəlɪt‖ -ɑːr-/ *adj* **1** (of speech) not clear **2** (of people) not speaking clearly **~ly** *adv*

in·as·much as /ˌɪnəz'mʌtʃ əz/ *conj fml* to the degree that; because

in·au·gu·rate /ɪ'nɔːɡjʊreɪt‖-'nɒː-/ *vt* **1** start or introduce with a special ceremony **2** be the beginning of (a period of time) **–ral** *adj*: *his inaugural speech* **–ration** /ɪˌnɔːɡjə'reɪʃən‖ɪˌnɒː-/ *n* [C;U]

in·born /ˌɪn'bɔːn‖ -ɔːrn/ *adj* present from one's birth

in·bred /ˌɪn'bred/ *adj* **1** inborn **2** produced by inbreeding

in·breed·ing /'ɪnbriːdɪŋ/ *n* [U] breeding between closely related family members

in·built /ˌɪn'bɪlt/ *adj* INHERENT

Inc /ɪŋk/ *adj* incorporated; (of a US firm) formed into a legal CORPORATION

in·cal·cu·la·ble /ɪn'kælkjələbəl/ *adj* too great to be counted **–bly** *adv*

in·can·des·cent /ˌɪnkæn'desənt‖ -kən-/ *adj* shining brightly when heated **–cence** *n* [U]

in·can·ta·tion /ˌɪnkæn'teɪʃən/ *n* [C;U] words used in magic

in·ca·pa·ble /ɪn'keɪpəbəl/ *adj* not able: *He's incapable of doing the simplest thing.*

in·ca·pa·ci·tate /ˌɪnkə'pæsɪteɪt/ *vt* make unable (to do something) **–ty** *n* [S;U] lack of ability

in·car·ce·rate /ɪn'kɑːsəreɪt‖ -ɑːr-/ *vt fml* imprison **–ration** /ɪnˌkɑːsə'reɪʃən‖ -ɑːr-/ *n* [U]

in·car·nate /ɪn'kɑːnɪt‖ -ɑːr-/ *adj* in human form: *the devil incarnate* **–nation** /ˌɪnkɑː'neɪʃən‖-ɑːr-/ *n* **1** [U] state of being incarnate **2** [C] any of a person's many lives **3** [*the*] (*cap.*) the coming of God to Earth in the body of Jesus Christ

in·cen·di·a·ry /ɪn'sendɪəri‖ -dieri/ *adj* **1** causing fires: *incendiary bomb* **2** causing violence: *incendiary speech*

in·cense /'ɪnsens/ *n* [U] substance burnt to make a sweet smell

in·censed /ɪn'senst/ *adj fml* extremely angry

in·cen·tive /ɪn'sentɪv/ *n* [C;U] encouragement to get things done

in·ces·sant /ɪn'sesənt/ *adj* (of something bad) never stopping **~ly** *adv*

in·cest /'ɪnsest/ *n* [U] sexual relationship between close relatives **~uous** /ɪn'sestʃʊəs/ *adj*

inch /ɪntʃ/ *n* **1** a measure of length equal to 2.54 centimetres **2** small amount **3** **every inch** completely **4** **within an inch of** very near ♦ *vi/t* move slowly

in·ci·dence /'ɪnsɪdəns/ *n* [S] rate of happening: *a high incidence of disease*

in·ci·dent /'ɪnsɪdənt/ *n* **1** event, esp. one that is unusual **2** event that includes or leads to violence, danger, or serious disagreement: *The spy scandal caused a diplomatic incident.*

in·ci·dent·al /ˌɪnsɪ'dentl/ *adj* **1** happening in connection with something else: *incidental expenses* **2** something (esp. a fact or detail) that is unimportant **~ally** *adv* (used to introduce a new subject in talking)

in·cin·e·rate /ɪn'sɪnəreɪt/ *vt fml* burn (unwanted things) **–rator** *n* machine for burning things

in·cip·i·ent /ɪn'sɪpiənt/ *adj fml* at an early stage

in·cise /ɪn'saɪz/ *vt* cut into **incisor** *n* front cutting tooth **incisive** *adj* going directly to the point: *incisive comments* **incision** /ɪn'sɪʒən/ *n* [C;U] (act of making) a cut, done with a special tool

in·cite /ɪn'saɪt/ *vt* encourage (violence, or people to be violent) **~ment** *n* [U]

in·cline¹ /ɪn'klaɪn/ *v* **1** *vt* encourage to feel or think **2** *vi* tend: *I incline to take the opposite view.* **3** *vi/t* slope **4** *vt* (cause to) move downward: *He inclined his head (in greeting).* **inclined** *adj* tending: *The handle is inclined to stick.* **inclination** /ˌɪnklɪ-'neɪʃən/ *n* **1** [C;U] liking **2** [C] tendency **3** [C] act of inclining

in·cline² /'ɪnklaɪn/ *n* slope

in·clude /ɪn'kluːd/ *vt* **1** have as a part **2** put in with something else **–ding** *prep* having as a part **inclusion** /ɪn'kluːʒən/ *n* [U] **inclusive** /-'kluːsɪv/ *adj* including everything

in·cog·ni·to /ˌɪnkɒɡ'niːtəʊ‖ ˌɪnkɑːɡ'niːtoʊ/ *adj, adv* taking another name

in·co·her·ent /ˌɪnkəʊˈhɪərənt ‖-kəʊˈhɪr-/ *adj* not clearly expressed **~ly** *adv* **~ence** *n* [U]

in·come /ˈɪŋkʌm, ˈɪn-/ *n* money received regularly

income tax /ˈ·· ·/ *n* tax on one's income

in·com·ing /ˈɪnkʌmɪŋ/ *adj* coming in, starting a period in office

in·com·mu·ni·ca·do /ˌɪnkəmjuːnɪˈkɑːdəʊ ‖-dəʊ/ *adv* (of people) prevented from giving or receiving messages

in·com·pa·ra·ble /ɪnˈkɒmpərəbəl ‖-ˈkɑːm-/ *adj* unequalled; very great **-bly** *adv*

in·com·pat·i·ble /ˌɪnkəmˈpætəbəl◄/ *adj* not suitable to be together **-bility** /ˌɪnkəmpætəˈbɪləti/ *n* [U]

in·com·pe·tent /ɪnˈkɒmpətənt ‖-ˈkɑːm-/ *adj* not skilful **-tence** *n* [U]

in·com·pre·hen·si·ble /ɪnˌkɒmprɪˈhensəbəl ‖-ˌkɑːm-/ *adj* impossible to understand **-sion** /-ˈhenʃən/ *n* [U] failure to understand **-bility** /ɪnˌkɒmprɪhensəˈbɪləti ‖-ˌkɑːm-/ *n* [U]

in·con·ceiv·a·ble /ˌɪnkənˈsiːvəbəl◄/ *adj* impossible to imagine

in·con·gru·ous /ɪnˈkɒŋgruəs ‖-ˈkɑːŋ-/ *adj* out of place **-ity** /ˌɪnkɒnˈgruːəti/ *n* [C;U]

in·con·se·quen·tial /ɪnˌkɒnsɪˈkwenʃəl◄‖-ˌkɑːn-/ *adj* 1 unimportant 2 not RELEVANT **~ly** *adv*

in·con·sid·er·a·ble /ˌɪnkənˈsɪdərəbəl◄/ *adj* not inconsiderable large

in·con·sid·er·ate /ˌɪnkənˈsɪdərət◄/ *adj* not thinking of other people **~ly** *adv*

in·con·so·la·ble /ˌɪnkənˈsəʊləbəl◄‖-ˈsəʊ-/ *adj* too sad to be comforted **-bly** *adv*

in·con·ti·nent /ɪnˈkɒntɪnənt ‖-ˈkɑːn-/ *adj* unable to control one's bowels and BLADDER **-nence** *n* [U]

in·con·tro·vert·i·ble /ɪnˌkɒntrəˈvɜːtəbəl ‖ ɪnˌkɑːntrəˈvɜːr-/ *adj fml* which cannot be disproved **-bly** *adv*

in·con·ve·ni·ence /ˌɪnkənˈviːniəns/ *n* (cause of) state of difficulty when things do not suit one ♦ *vt* cause inconvenience to **-ent** *adj* causing inconvenience **-ently** *adv*

in·cor·po·rate /ɪnˈkɔːpəreɪt ‖-ɔːr-/ *vt* include in something larger **-ration** /ɪnˌkɔːpəˈreɪʃən ‖-ɔːr-/ *n* [U]

in·cor·ri·gi·ble /ɪnˈkɒrɪdʒəbəl ‖-ˈkɔː-/ *adj* bad, and impossible to improve **-bly** *adv*

in·crease /ɪnˈkriːs/ *vi/t* (cause to) become larger **increasingly** *adv* more and more

increase /ˈɪŋkriːs/ *n* rise in amount, numbers, or degree

in·cred·i·ble /ɪnˈkredəbəl/ *adj* 1 unbelievable 2 *infml* wonderful **-bly** *adv*

in·cred·u·lous /ɪnˈkredjələs ‖-dʒə-/ *adj* not believing **~ly** *adv* **-lity** /ˌɪnkrɪˈdjuːləti ‖-ˈduː-/ *n* [U] disbelief

in·cre·ment /ˈɪŋkrəmənt/ *n* increase in money or value

in·crim·i·nate /ɪnˈkrɪməneɪt/ *vt* cause (someone) to seem guilty of a crime or fault

in·cu·bate /ˈɪŋkjʊbeɪt/ *vt* keep (eggs) warm until they HATCH **-bator** *n* apparatus for keeping eggs warm, or for keeping PREMATURE babies alive **-bation** /ˌɪŋkjʊˈbeɪʃən/ *n* [U] 1 act of incubating 2 period between infection and the appearance of a disease

in·cul·cate /ˈɪŋkʌlkeɪt ‖ɪnˈkʌl-/ *vt* fix (ideas) in someone's mind

in·cum·bent /ɪnˈkʌmbənt/ *adj* **be incumbent on** *fml* be the moral duty of ♦ *n* person holding a (political) office

in·cur /ɪnˈkɜː/ *vt* **-rr-** bring (esp. something bad) on oneself: *incur expenses*

in·cur·a·ble /ɪnˈkjʊərəbəl ‖-ˈkjʊr-/ *adj* that cannot be cured **-bly** *adv*

in·debt·ed /ɪnˈdetəd/ *adj* grateful **~ness** *n* [U]

in·de·cent /ɪnˈdiːsənt/ *adj* 1 sexually offensive 2 unsuitable **~ly** *adv* **-cency** *n* [U]

in·de·ci·sion /ˌɪndɪˈsɪʒən/ *n* [U] inability to decide **-sive** /-ˈsaɪsɪv◄/ *adj*

in·deed /ɪnˈdiːd/ *adv* 1 certainly; really: *'Did you see him?' 'Indeed I did.'* 2 (used with **very** to make the meaning stronger): *It's very cold indeed.* 3 (showing surprise): *Did he, indeed?*

in·de·fat·i·ga·ble /ˌɪndɪˈfætɪgəbəl◄/ *adj* tireless **-bly** *adv*

in·de·fen·si·ble /ˌɪndɪˈfensəbəl◄/ *adj* that cannot be defended: *indefensible behaviour*

in·de·fin·a·ble /ˌɪndɪˈfaɪnəbəl◄/ *adj* impossible to describe **-bly** *adv*

in·def·i·nite /ɪnˈdefənət/ *adj* not clear or fixed **~ly** *adv* for an unlimited period

indefinite ar·ti·cle /·,·· ˈ··/ (in English) A or AN

in·del·i·ble /ɪnˈdeləbəl/ *adj* that cannot be rubbed out **-bly** *adv*

in·del·i·cate /ɪnˈdeləkət/ *adj* not polite or modest **~ly** *adv* **-cacy** *n* [U]

in·dem·ni·fy /ɪn'demnᵻfaɪ/ vt pay (someone) in case of loss –**nity** n [C;U] protection against loss; payment for loss

in·dent /ɪn'dent/ vi/t start (a line of writing) further into the page than the others –**ation** /ˌɪnden'teɪʃən/ n 1 [C;U] (act of making) a space at the beginning of a line of writing 2 space pointing inwards: *the indentations of a coastline*

in·de·pen·dent /ˌɪndᵻ'pendənt◂/ adj 1 self-governing 2 not depending on advice, money, etc. from others ♦ n (often cap.) person who does not always favour the same political party ~**ly** adv –**dence** n [U]

in·depth /' ⋅ '/ adj very thorough

in·de·scrib·a·ble /ˌɪndɪs'kraɪbəbəl◂/ adj that cannot be described –**bly** adv

in·de·struc·ti·ble /ˌɪndɪ'strʌktᵻbəl◂/ adj too strong to be destroyed

in·de·ter·mi·nate /ˌɪndɪ'tɜːmᵻnᵻt◂ ‖ -ɜːr-/ adj not fixed as one thing or another

in·dex /'ɪndeks/ n -**dexes** or -**dices** /-dᵻsiːz/ **1 a** alphabetical list of subjects mentioned in a book **b** also **card index** – similar alphabetical list, e.g. of books and writers that can be found in a library, written on separate cards **2 a** sign by which something can be measured **b** system of comparing prices with their former level: *the cost of living index* ♦ vt make, include in, or provide with an INDEX (1)

index fin·ger /' ⋅ ⋅ / n FOREFINGER

In·di·an /'ɪndiən/ n, adj 1 (person) from India 2 NATIVE AMERICAN

in·di·cate /'ɪndᵻkeɪt/ **1** vt point at; show **2** vi/t show (the direction in which one is turning in a vehicle) by hand signals, lights, etc. –**cator** n 1 flashing light on a car that shows which way it will turn 2 event, fact, etc. showing the existence or development of something: *economic indicators* –**cation** /ˌɪndᵻ'keɪʃən/ n [C;U] sign or suggestion indicating something –**cative** /ɪn'dɪkətɪv/ adj showing

in·di·ces /'ɪndᵻsiːz/ n pl. of INDEX

in·dict /ɪn'daɪt/ vt charge officially with a crime ~**able** adj for which one can be indicted: *indictable offence* ~**ment** n [U]

in·dig·e·nous /ɪn'dɪdʒənəs/ adj NATIVE to a place: *indigenous flowers*

in·di·ges·tion /ˌɪndɪ'dʒestʃən/ n [U]

illness from not being able to DIGEST food

in·dig·nant /ɪn'dɪgnənt/ adj angry, esp. at something unjust ~**ly** adv –**nation** /ˌɪndɪg'neɪʃən/ n [U] indignant feeling

in·dig·ni·ty /ɪn'dɪgnᵻti/ n [C;U] treatment that makes one feel ashamed

in·di·rect /ˌɪndᵻ'rekt◂/ adj 1 not straight; not directly connected to: *indirect route* ‖ *indirect result* 2 (of taxes) paid by increasing the cost of goods or services 3 meaning something which is not directly mentioned: *an indirect answer* ~**ly** adv

indirect ob·ject /ˌ⋅⋅ '⋅⋅/ n person or thing that the DIRECT OBJECT is given to, made for, done to, etc.: *In 'I asked him a question', 'him' is the indirect object.*

indirect speech /ˌ⋅⋅ '⋅/ n [U] gram speech reported without repeating the actual words (e.g. *She said, 'I'm coming.'* becomes *She said she was coming.*)

in·dis·creet /ˌɪndɪ'skriːt◂/ adj not acting carefully or politely ~**ly** adv –**cretion** /-'kreʃən/ n 1 [U] state or quality of being indiscreet 2 [C] indiscreet act: *youthful indiscretions*

in·dis·crim·i·nate /ˌɪndɪ'skrɪmᵻnᵻt◂/ adj not choosing or chosen carefully ~**ly** adv

in·dis·pen·sa·ble /ˌɪndɪ'spensəbəl◂/ adj necessary

in·dis·posed /ˌɪndɪ'spəʊzd ‖ -'spoʊzd/ adj fml 1 not very well 2 unwilling

in·dis·pu·ta·ble /ˌɪndɪ'spjuːtəbəl◂/ adj beyond doubt: *indisputable proof* –**bly** adv

in·dis·tin·guish·a·ble /ˌɪndɪ'stɪŋgwɪʃəbəl/ adj impossible to tell apart: *indistinguishable from silk*

in·di·vid·u·al /ˌɪndᵻ'vɪdʒuəl◂/ adj 1 single; separate 2 (of a manner, style, or way of doing things) particular to a person, thing, etc. ♦ n single person (in a group) ~**ly** adv separately –**ism** n [U] belief in the rights of each person in society –**ist** n, adj (person) independent and unlike other people –**istic** /ˌɪndᵻ'vɪdʒuə'lɪstɪk/ adj –**ity** /ˌɪndᵻˌvɪdʒu'ælᵻti/ n [U] qualities that make a person unusual

in·doc·tri·nate /ɪn'dɒktrᵻneɪt ‖ ɪn'dɑːk-/ vt train to accept ideas without question –**nation** /ɪnˌdɒktrᵻ'neɪʃən ‖ -ˌdɑːk-/ n [U]

in·do·lent /'ɪndələnt/ adj fml lazy –**lence** n [U]

in·dom·i·ta·ble /ɪn'dɒmᵻtəbəl ‖ ɪn'dɑː-/

adj too strong to be discouraged

in·door /'ındɔ:‖-dɔ:r/ *adj* inside a building **indoors** /ın'dɔ:z‖-'dɔ:rz/ *adv*

in·du·bi·ta·ble /ın'dju:bₐtəbəl‖ ın'du:-/ *adj fml* unquestionable **–bly** *adv*

in·duce /ın'dju:s‖-ın't/ *vt* **1** persuade **2** cause; produce **~ment** *n* [C;U] (something, esp. money, which provides) encouragement to do something

in·duc·tion /ın'dʌkʃən/ *n* **1** [U] act or ceremony of introducing a person to a new job, organization, etc. **2** [C;U] (action of causing) birth of a child which has been hastened by the use of drugs **3** [U] way of reasoning using known facts to produce general laws

in·dulge /ın'dʌldʒ/ *v* **1** *vt* allow to do or have something nice **2** *vi* allow oneself pleasure: *indulge in a cigar* **indulgence** *n* [U] indulging **2** [C] something in which one indulges **indulgent** *adj* (too) kind

in·dus·tri·al /ın'dʌstriəl/ *adj* of or having INDUSTRY (1) **~ly** *adv* **~ism** *n* [U] system in which industries are important **~ist** *n* owner or manager of an industry **~ize**, **~ise** *vi/t* (cause to) become industrially developed

industrial action /·,··· '··/ *n* [U] *esp. BrE* action by workers to try to make their employers agree to their demands

industrial park /·'·· ·/ *also* **industrial es·tate** /·,··· ·'·/ *n BrE* area where factories are built

in·dus·tri·ous /ın'dʌstriəs/ *adj* hardworking **~ly** *adv*

in·dus·try /'ındəstri/ *n* **1** [C;U] (branch of) the production of goods for sale: *the clothing industry* **2** [U] continual hard work

i·ne·bri·at·ed /ı'ni:brieıtₐd/ *adj fml* drunk

in·ed·i·ble /ın'edₐbəl/ *adj* unsuitable for eating

in·ef·fec·tive /,ınₐ'fektıv◄/ *adj* unable to produce the right results **~ly** *adv* **~ness** *n* [U]

in·ef·fec·tu·al /,ınₐ'fektʃuəl◄/ *adj* which does not give a good enough effect, or who is not able to get things done **~ly** *adv*

in·ef·fi·cient /,ınₐ'fıʃənt◄/ *adj* not working well **~ly** *adv* **–ciency** *n* [U]

in·el·i·gi·ble /ın'elₐdʒₐbəl/ *adj* not fulfilling the conditions **–bility** /ın,elₐdʒₐ'bılₐti/ *n* [U]

in·ept /ı'nept/ *adj* **1** foolishly unsuitable **2** totally unable to do things **~ly** *adv* **~itude** *n* [C;U]

in·e·qual·i·ty /,ını'kwɒlₐti‖-'kwɑ:-/ *n* [C;U] lack of fairness or equality

in·ert /ı'nɜ:t‖-ɜ:rt/ *adj* **1** unable to move **2** not acting chemically: *inert gases*

in·er·tia /ı'nɜ:ʃə‖-ɜ:r-/ *n* [U] **1** force that keeps a thing in the same state until pushed **2** laziness

in·es·ca·pa·ble /,ını'skeıpəbəl◄/ *adj* unavoidable

in·es·ti·ma·ble /ın'estₐməbəl/ *adj fml* too good to be measured **–bly** *adv*

in·ev·i·ta·ble /ın'nevₐtəbəl/ *adj* **1** unavoidable **2** *infml* expected and familiar: *The head teacher made her inevitable joke about school food.* **–bly** *adv* **–bility** /ı,nevₐtə'bılₐti/ *n* [U]

in·ex·cu·sa·ble /,ınık'skju:zəbəl◄/ *adj* unforgivable **–bly** *adv*

in·ex·pli·ca·ble /,ınık'splıkəbəl◄/ *adj* too strange to be explained **–bly** *adv*

in·ex·tri·ca·ble /ın'ekstrıkəbəl, ,ınık-'strı-/ *adj fml* impossible to escape from, or to untie **–bly** *adv*

in·fal·li·ble /ın'fælₐbəl/ *adj* **1** never making mistakes **2** always effective: *infallible cure* **–bility** /ın,fælₐ'bılₐti/ *n* [U]

in·fa·mous /'ınfəməs/ *adj* wicked **–my** *n* [C;U] wickedness

in·fan·cy /'ınfənsi/ *n* [S;U] early childhood

in·fant /'ınfənt/ *n* very young child

in·fan·tile /'ınfəntaıl/ *adj* childish

in·fan·try /'ınfəntri/ *n* [U] foot soldiers

in·fat·u·at·ed /ın'fætʃueıtₐd/ *adj* foolishly loving **–ation** /ın,fætʃu'eıʃən/ *n* [C;U]

in·fect /ın'fekt/ *vt* give disease to: (fig.) *She infected the whole class with her laughter.* (=everyone laughed) **~ion** /-'fekʃən/ *n* [C;U] (disease spread by) infecting **~ious** *adj* able to infect: (fig.) *infectious laughter*

in·fer /ın'fɜ:‖-ɜ:r/ *vt* **-rr-** draw (meaning) from facts: *I inferred from his letter that he had not made a decision* **~ence** /'ınfərəns/ *n* [C;U]

in·fe·ri·or /ın'fıəriə‖-'fıriər/ *adj* less good; low(er) in rank ♦ *n* inferior person **~ity** /ın,fıəri'ɒrₐti‖-,fıri'ɔ:rₐ-/ *n* [U]

in·fer·nal /ın'fɜ:nl‖-ɜ:r-/ *adj* terrible:

like HELL

in·fer·no /ɪnˈfɜːnəʊ ‖ -ɜːrnoʊ/ n -nos place of very great heat and large uncontrollable flames

in·fer·tile /ɪnˈfɜːtaɪl ‖ -ɜːrtəl/ adj not FERTILE: infertile eggs

in·fest /ɪnˈfest/ vt (of something bad) be present in large numbers

in·fi·del·i·ty /ˌɪnfɪˈdeləti/ n [C;U] 1 (act of) disloyalty 2 (act of) sex with someone other than one's marriage partner

in·fight·ing /ˈɪnfaɪtɪŋ/ n [U] disagreement between members of a group

in·fil·trate /ˈɪnfɪltreɪt ‖ ɪnˈfɪltreɪt, ˈɪnfɪl-/ vt enter secretly, with an unfriendly purpose -tration /ˌɪnfɪlˈtreɪʃən/ n [U]

in·fi·nite /ˈɪnfənət/ adj without limits; endless ~ly adv

in·fin·i·tes·i·mal /ˌɪnfɪnəˈtesəməl◂/ adj extremely small

in·fin·i·tive /ɪnˈfɪnətɪv/ n gram verb form that can follow other verbs and be used with to (e.g. 'go' in I can go and I want to go)

in·fin·i·ty /ɪnˈfɪnəti/ n [U] endless space or quantity

in·firm /ɪnˈfɜːm ‖ -ɜːrm/ adj fml weak in body or mind ~ity n [C;U]

in·fir·ma·ry /ɪnˈfɜːməri ‖ -ɜːr-/ n 1 hospital 2 room where sick people are given treatment

in·flame /ɪnˈfleɪm/ vt make violent inflamed red and swollen: inflamed eyes

in·flam·ma·ble /ɪnˈflæməbəl/ adj 1 which can easily be set on fire and which burns quickly 2 easily excited or made angry

in·flam·ma·tion /ˌɪnfləˈmeɪʃən/ n [C;U] inflamed condition

in·flam·ma·to·ry /ɪnˈflæmətəri ‖ -tɔːri/ adj likely to inflame: inflammatory speeches

in·flate /ɪnˈfleɪt/ v 1 vt fill (a tyre, etc.) with air 2 vi/t increase the supply of money in a country inflated adj too big: inflated prices | an inflated opinion of oneself -table n, adj (thing) that has to be filled with air to be used

in·fla·tion /ɪnˈfleɪʃən/ n [U] 1 act of inflating or state of being inflated 2 rise in prices caused by increased production costs or an increase in money supply ~ary adj likely to cause INFLATION (2)

in·flec·tion /ɪnˈflekʃən/ n [C;U] a gram change in the form of a word to show

difference in its use b movement up or down of the voice **inflect** /ɪnˈflekt/ vi/t

in·flex·i·ble /ɪnˈfleksəbəl/ adj impossible to bend or change –bly adv –bility /ɪnˌfleksəˈbɪləti/ n [U]

in·flict /ɪnˈflɪkt/ vt force (punishment, etc.) on ~ion /-ˈflɪkʃən/ n [C;U]

in·flu·ence /ˈɪnfluəns/ n [C;U] 1 (power to have) an effect 2 someone with this power: She's a bad influence on you. 3 under the influence drunk ♦ vt have an influence on

in·flu·en·tial /ˌɪnfluˈenʃəl◂/ adj having great influence

in·flu·en·za /ˌɪnfluˈenzə/ n [U] fml FLU

in·flux /ˈɪnflʌks/ n [C;U] arrival in large numbers or quantities

in·fo /ˈɪnfəʊ ‖ -foʊ/ n [U] infml information

in·form /ɪnˈfɔːm ‖ -ɔːrm/ vt fml give information to ~ant n person who gives information ~ed adj 1 knowing things: well-informed 2 having and using suitable knowledge: an informed guess ~er n person who tells the police about someone

    inform against/on phr vt tell the police that (someone) is guilty

in·for·mal /ɪnˈfɔːməl ‖ -ɔːr-/ adj not formal; without ceremony: an informal meeting | informal clothes ~ly adv ~ity /ˌɪnfɔːˈmæləti ‖ -ɔːr-/ n [U]

in·for·ma·tion /ˌɪnfəˈmeɪʃən ‖ -fər-/ n [U] knowledge given; facts

information su·per·high·way /ˌɪnfə-meɪʃən suːpəˈhaɪweɪ ‖ -fər-, -pər-/ n [the+S] the INTERNET

information tech·nol·o·gy /ˌ···· ·ˈ···/ n [U] science of collecting and using information by means of computer systems

in·for·ma·tive /ɪnˈfɔːmətɪv ‖ -ɔːr-/ adj telling one useful things

in·fra·red /ˌɪnfrəˈred◂/ adj of the heat-giving light RAYS of longer wavelength than those we can see

in·fra·struc·ture /ˈɪnfrəˌstrʌktʃə ‖ -ər/ n underlying systems (e.g. of power, roads, laws, banks) needed to keep a country going

in·fringe /ɪnˈfrɪndʒ/ vt/i fml go against (a law, or someone's rights) ~ment n [C;U]

in·fu·ri·ate /ɪnˈfjʊərieɪt ‖ -ˈfjʊr-/ vt make very angry

in·fuse /ɪnˈfjuːz/ vt 1 fill (someone) with a quality 2 put (tea, etc.) into hot water to make a drink **infusion** /-'fju:ʒən/ *n* [C;U] (liquid made by) infusing

in·ge·ni·ous /ɪn'dʒi:niəs/ *adj* clever at making or inventing: *ingenious person/ excuse* ~**ly** *adv* –**nuity** /ˌɪndʒɪ'nju:ɪti ‖ -'nu:-/ *n* [U]

in·gen·u·ous /ɪn'dʒenjuəs/ *adj* simple and inexperienced ~**ly** *adv*

in·got /'ɪŋgət/ *n* (brick-shaped) lump of metal

in·grained /ɪn'greɪnd/ *adj* deeply fixed: *ingrained dirt/habits*

in·gra·ti·ate /ɪn'greɪʃieɪt/ *vt* make (oneself) pleasant, so as to gain favour –**ating** *adj* –**atingly** *adv*

in·grat·i·tude /ɪn'grætɪtju:d ‖ -tu:d/ *n* [U] ungratefulness

in·gre·di·ent /ɪn'gri:diənt/ *n* one of a mixture of things, esp. in baking

in·hab·it /ɪn'hæbɪt/ *vt fml* live in (a place) ~**ant** *n* person living in a place

in·hale /ɪn'heɪl/ *vi/t* breathe in **inhaler** *n* apparatus for inhaling medicine to make breathing easier **inhalant** *n* medicine inhaled **inhalation** /ˌɪnhə'leɪʃən/ *n* [C;U]

in·her·ent /ɪn'hɪərənt ‖ -'hɪr-/ *adj* necessarily present; *problems inherent in the system* ~**ly** *adv*

in·her·it /ɪn'herɪt/ *vi/t* receive (property, etc.) from someone who has died: (fig.) *He's inherited his father's meanness* ~**ance** *n* 1 [C] something inherited 2 [U] inheriting ~**or** *n* person who inherits

in·hib·it /ɪn'hɪbɪt/ *vt* prevent; HINDER ~**ed** *adj* too nervous, worried, etc. to do what one wants ~**ion** /ˌɪnhɪ'bɪʃən/ *n* feeling of worry, etc that prevents one from doing what one wants

in-house /ˌ· '·◀/ *adj, adv* within a company rather than outside it: *an in-house training department*

in·hu·man /ɪn'hju:mən/ *adj* cruel ~**ity** /ˌɪnhju:'mænɪti/ *n* [C;U]

in·hu·mane /ˌɪnhju:'meɪn/ *adj* unkind; not HUMANE *n* [C;U] ~**ly** *adv*

in·im·i·ta·ble /ɪ'nɪmɪtəbəl/ *adj* too good to be copied –**bly** *adv*

in·iq·ui·tous /ɪ'nɪkwɪtəs/ *adj fml* very unjust or wicked ~**ly** *adv* –**ty** *n* [C;U]

i·ni·tial /ɪ'nɪʃəl/ *adj* at the beginning ♦ *n* first letter of someone's name ♦ *vt* **-ll-** *BrE* ‖ **-l-** *AmE* write one's initials on ~**ly** *adv* at first

i·ni·ti·ate[1] /ɪ'nɪʃieɪt/ *vt* 1 start (something) working 2 introduce (someone) into a group, etc. –**ation** /ˌɪˌnɪʃi'eɪʃən/ *n* [C;U]

i·ni·ti·ate[2] /ɪ'nɪʃiɪt/ *n* person instructed or skilled in some special field

i·ni·tia·tive /ɪ'nɪʃətɪv/ *n* 1 [U] ability to act without help or advice 2 [C] first step: *take the initiative*

in·ject /ɪn'dʒekt/ *vt* put (a drug, etc.) into someone with a needle: (fig.) *inject new life, interest, etc. into something* ~**ion** /-'dʒekʃən/ *n* 1 (an act of) injecting a drug 2 [C] act of putting money into an organization, plan, etc. [C;U]

in·junc·tion /ɪn'dʒʌŋkʃən/ *n fml* official order

in·jure /'ɪndʒə ‖ -ər/ *vt* hurt; damage **injured** *adj*, *n* hurt (people) **injury** *n* 1 [U] harm; damage 2 [C] wound, etc.

in·jus·tice /ɪn'dʒʌstɪs/ *n* [C;U] (act of) unfairness

ink /ɪŋk/ *n* [C;U] coloured liquid for writing, printing, etc. ~**y** *adj* black

ink·ling /'ɪŋklɪŋ/ *n* [S;U] slight idea

in·laid /ˌɪn'leɪd◀/ *adj* set ornamentally into another substance: *inlaid gold*

in·land /'ɪnlənd/ *adj, adv* inside a country: *inland trade*

Inland Rev·e·nue /ˌ·· '···/ *n* [the] (in Britain) office that collects taxes

in-laws /'· ·/ *n* [P] relatives by marriage

in·let /'ɪnlet, 'ɪnlɪt/ *n* narrow piece of water reaching into the land

in·mate /'ɪnmeɪt/ *n* person living in a prison, hospital, etc.

in·most /'ɪnməʊst ‖ -məʊst/ also **in·ner·most** /'ɪnəməʊst ‖ -nər -məʊst/ *adj* furthest inside; most well-hidden

inn /ɪn/ *n* small pub or hotel, esp. one built many centuries ago

in·nards /'ɪnədz ‖ -ər-/ *n* [P] inside parts, esp. of the stomach

in·nate /ˌɪ'neɪt◀/ *adj* (of a quality) present from birth ~**ly** *adv*

in·ner /'ɪnə ‖ -ər/ *adj* 1 on the inside; close to the middle 2 secret, esp. if of the spirit: *inner meaning/life*

inner cir·cle /ˌ·· '··/ *n* [S] the few people in an organization who control it or share power with its leader

inner ci·ty /ˌ·· '··◀/ *adj, n* (found in) the part of a city near the middle, usu. with poor living conditions

in·ning /'ɪnɪŋ/ n period of play in BASEBALL **innings** n 1 period when a cricket team or player BATS 2 BrE infml time when one is active

in·no·cent /'ɪnəsənt/ adj 1 not guilty 2 harmless 3 unable to recognize evil; simple ~ly adv **-cence** n [U]

in·noc·u·ous /ɪ'nɒkjuəs ‖ ɪ'nɑːk-/ adj harmless

in·no·va·tion /ˌɪnə'veɪʃən/ n 1 [C] new idea 2 [U] introducing new things **-vate** /'ɪnəveɪt/ vi make changes **-tor** n **-tive** /'ɪnəˌveɪtɪv/ also **-tory** /-təri/ adj

in·nu·en·do /ˌɪnjuˈendəʊ ‖ -doʊ/ n **-does** or **-dos** [C;U] unpleasant indirect remark(s)

in·nu·me·ra·ble /ɪ'njuːmərəbəl ‖ ɪ'nuː-, ɪ'njuː-/ adj too many to count

in·nu·mer·ate /ɪ'njuːmərət ‖ ɪ'njuː-, ɪ'nuː-/ adj BrE unable to calculate with numbers -acy n [U]

i·noc·u·late /ɪ'nɒkjʊleɪt ‖ ɪ'nɑː-/ vt introduce a weak form of a disease into (someone) as a protection **-lation** /ɪˌnɒkjʊ'leɪʃən ‖ ɪˌnɑː-/ n [C;U]

in·of·fen·sive /ˌɪnə'fensɪv◂/ adj not causing dislike; not rude ~ly adv

in·op·por·tune /ɪn'ɒpətjuːn ‖ ˌɪnɑːpər-'tuːn/ adj fml at the wrong time ~ly adv

in·or·di·nate /ɪ'nɔːdɪnət ‖ -ɔːr-/ adj fml beyond reasonable limits ~ly adv

in·put /'ɪnpʊt/ n [S;U] something put in for use, esp. information into a computer ♦ vt **-tt-**; past t. & p. **inputted** or **input** put (information) into a computer

in·quest /'ɪŋkwest/ n official inquiry, esp. when someone dies unexpectedly

in·quire /ɪn'kwaɪə ‖ -'kwaɪr/ vi/t ask for information (about) **inquiring** adj that shows an interest in knowing **inquiry** n 1 [C;U] (act of) inquiring 2 [C] set of meetings, etc. to find out why something happened

   inquire after phr vt ask about the health of

   inquire into phr vt look for information about

in·qui·si·tion /ˌɪŋkwʌ'zɪʃən/ n thorough and esp. cruel inquiry

in·quis·i·tive /ɪn'kwɪzÌtɪv/ adj asking too many questions ~ly adv

in·roads /'ɪnrəʊdz ‖ -roʊdz/ n 1 attack upon or advance into a new area 2 effort or activity that lessens the quantity or difficulty of what remains afterwards

ins and outs /ˌ· · '·/ n [the+P] details (of a situation, problem, etc.)

in·sane /ɪn'seɪn/ adj mad ~ly adv **insanity** /ɪn'sænÌti/ n [U]

in·san·i·ta·ry /ɪn'sænÌtəri ‖ -teri/ adj dirty enough to cause disease

in·sa·ti·a·ble /ɪn'seɪʃəbəl/ adj impossible to satisfy **-bly** adv

in·scribe /ɪn'skraɪb/ vt fml write (words) on **inscription** /ɪn'skrɪpʃən/ n piece of writing inscribed, esp. on stone

in·scru·ta·ble /ɪn'skruːtəbəl/ adj mysterious: inscrutable smile **-bly** adv

in·sect /'ɪnsekt/ n small creature with six legs

in·sec·ti·cide /ɪn'sektÌsaɪd/ n [C;U] chemical used to kill insects

in·se·cure /ˌɪnsɪ'kjʊə◂ ‖ -'kjʊr◂/ adj 1 not safe 2 not sure of oneself ~ly adv **-curity** n [U]

in·sem·i·na·tion /ɪnˌsemɪ'neɪʃən/ n [U] putting of male seed into a female

in·sen·si·ble /ɪn'sensÌbəl/ adj 1 unconscious 2 lacking knowledge of **-bility** /ɪnˌsensÌ'bɪlÌti/ n [U]

in·sen·si·tive /ɪn'sensÌtɪv/ adj not SENSITIVE ~ly adv **-tivity** /ɪnˌsensÌ'tɪvÌti/ n [S;U]

in·sep·a·ra·ble /ɪn'sepərəbəl/ adj impossible to separate

in·sert[1] /ɪn'sɜːt ‖ -'sɜːrt/ vt put into something: insert a key in a lock ♦ /'ɪnsɜːt ‖ -'sɜːrt/ n written or printed material put in between pages of a book ~**ion** /-'sɜːʃən ‖ -'sɜːr-/ n [C;U]

in·ser·vice /ˌ· '··◂/ adj (taking place) during one's work: in-service training

in·side /ɪn'saɪd, 'ɪnsaɪd/ n 1 [the+S] a part nearest to the middle, or that faces away from the open air b infml position in which one is able to know special or secret information 2 [C] also **insides** pl. — infml one's stomach 3 **inside out**: a with the inside parts on the outside b thoroughly: know it inside out ♦ adj 1 facing or at the inside: the inside pages of a newspaper 2 from someone closely concerned: inside information ♦ adv to or in the inside, esp. indoors: The children are playing inside. ♦ prep to or on the inside of: inside the car 2 in less time than: inside an hour **insider** /ɪn'saɪdə ‖ -ər/ n person accepted in a social group, esp. someone with special information or influence

in·sid·er dealing /-‚· ‘-·/, also **insider trad·ing** n [U] illegal practice of buying and selling business shares by people who use their knowledge of the business affairs of the companies they work for

in·sid·i·ous /ɪnˈsɪdiəs/ adj secretly harmful ~**ly** adv

in·sight /ˈɪnsaɪt/ n [C;U] understanding: *insight into their lives*

in·sig·ni·a /ɪnˈsɪgniə/ n [P] objects worn as signs of rank

in·sig·nif·i·cant /‚ɪnsɪgˈnɪfɪkənt◄/ adj not important ~**ly** adv –**cance** n [U]

in·sin·u·ate /ɪnˈsɪnjueɪt/ vt 1 suggest (something unpleasant) indirectly 2 gain acceptance for (esp. oneself) by secret means –**ation** /ɪnˌsɪnjuˈeɪʃən/ n [C;U]

in·sip·id /ɪnˈsɪpɪd/ adj derog lacking a strong character, taste, or effect

in·sist /ɪnˈsɪst/ vt/i 1 order: *insist that he should go* 2 declare firmly: *He insists he wasn't there.* ~**ent** adj repeatedly insisting ~**ence** n [U]

in si·tu /‚ɪn ˈsɪtjuː ‖ ‚ɪn ˈsaɪtuː/ adv in its original place

in so far as /‚·· ‘· ·/ conj to the degree that

in·sole /ˈɪnsəʊl ‖ -səʊl/ n removable shoe lining

in·so·lent /ˈɪnsələnt/ adj disrespectful; rude –**lence** n [U]

in·sol·u·ble /ɪnˈsɒljᵿbəl ‖ ɪnˈsɑː-/ adj 1 impossible to answer 2 impossible to DISSOLVE

in·sol·vent /ɪnˈsɒlv ənt ‖ ɪnˈsɑːl-, ɪnˈsɒːl-/ n, adj (someone) unable to pay their debts –**vency** n [U]

in·som·ni·a /ɪnˈsɒmniə ‖ -ˈsɑːm-/ n [U] inability to sleep **insomniac** /-niæk/ n, adj (someone) who habitually cannot sleep

in·spect /ɪnˈspekt/ vt examine closely ~**or** n 1 official who inspects something 2 police officer of middle rank ~**ion** /-ˈspekʃən/ n [C;U]

in·spire /ɪnˈspaɪə ‖ -ˈspaɪr/ vt 1 encourage to act 2 fill with a feeling: *inspire them with confidence* **inspiration** /ˌɪnspᵿˈreɪʃən/ n 1 [U] act of inspiring or state of being inspired 2 [C] something that inspires 3 [C] sudden good idea **inspired** /ɪnˈspaɪəd ‖ -ˈspaɪrd/ adj very clever

in·sta·bil·i·ty /ˌɪnstəˈbɪlᵻti/ n [U]

1 unsteadiness 2 (of people) tendency to act in changeable ways

in·stall /ɪnˈstɔːl ‖ -ˈstɔːl/ vt 1 put (a machine, etc.) somewhere 2 settle (someone) in a position ~**ation** /ˌɪnstəˈleɪʃən/ n 1 [U] installing 2 [C] apparatus, etc. installed

in·stal·ment /ɪnˈstɔːlmənt ‖ -/ n 1 single part of a story, etc. that appears in regular parts 2 single regular payment

in·stance /ˈɪnstəns/ n 1 EXAMPLE (1) 2 **for instance** for example ♦ vt give as an example

in·stant /ˈɪnstənt/ n moment of time ♦ adj happening or produced at once ~**ly** adv at once

in·stan·ta·ne·ous /ˌɪnstənˈteɪniəs◄/ adj happening at once ~**ly** adv

in·stead /ɪnˈsted/ adv 1 in place of that 2 **instead of** in place of: *You go instead of me.*

in·step /ˈɪnstep/ n upper surface of the foot

in·sti·gate /ˈɪnstᵻgeɪt/ vt fml cause to do or happen –**gator** n –**gation** /ˌɪnstᵻˈgeɪʃən/ n [U]

in·stil /ɪnˈstɪl/ vt -**ll**- put (ideas) into someone's mind

in·stinct /ˈɪnstɪŋkt/ n [C;U] natural tendency to act in a certain way ~**ive** adj: *instinctive fear of snakes* ~**ively** adv

in·sti·tute /ˈɪnstᵻtjuːt ‖ -tuːt/ n society formed for a special purpose ♦ vt fml start; establish

in·sti·tu·tion /ˌɪnstᵻˈtjuːʃən ‖ -ˈtuː-/ n 1 [C] (building for) a hospital, school, etc. where people are looked after 2 [C] established custom 3 [U] act of instituting ~**al** adj ~**alize**, **-alise** 1 make into an INSTITUTION (2) 2 (of people) to become unable to live or work anywhere except in an INSTITUTION (1)

in·struct /ɪnˈstrʌkt/ vt 1 give orders to 2 teach 3 *law* inform officially ~**ive** adj teaching something useful ~**or** n teacher

in·struc·tion /ɪnˈstrʌkʃən/ n 1 [C] order 2 [U] act of instructing; teaching **instructions** n [P] advice on how to do something: *Follow the instructions on the packet.*

in·stru·ment /ˈɪnstrᵿmənt/ n 1 thing that helps in work 2 apparatus for playing music ~**al** /ˌɪnstrᵿˈment◄/ adj 1 for musical instruments 2 helpful; causing: *His* *information was instrumental in catching the thief.* **~alist** *n* player of a musical instrument

in·sub·or·di·nate /ˌɪnsəˈbɔːdənɪt◂ -ɔːr-/ *adj* disobedient **–nation** /ˌɪnsəbɔːdʒˈneɪʃən‖ -ɔːr-/ *n* [C;U]

in·sub·stan·tial /ˌɪnsəbˈstænʃəl◂/ *adj* not firm or solid

in·suf·fer·a·ble /ɪnˈsʌfərəbəl/ *adj* unbearable

in·suf·fi·cient /ˌɪnsəˈfɪʃənt◂/ *adj* not enough **~ly** *adv* **–ciency** *n* [S;U]

in·su·lar /ˈɪnsjʊlə‖ ˈɪnsələr/ *adj* 1 narrow-minded 2 of an island **~ity** /ˌɪnsjʊˈlærɪti‖ -sə-/ *n* [U]

in·su·late /ˈɪnsjʊleɪt‖ ˈɪnsə-, ˈɪnʃə-/ *vt* 1 cover, to prevent the escape of heat, electricity, etc. 2 protect from experiences **–lator** *n* thing that insulates **–lation** /ˌɪnsjʊˈleɪʃən‖ ˌɪnsə-/ *n* [U] (material for) insulating

in·su·lin /ˈɪnsjʊlɪn‖ ˈɪnsə-/ *n* [U] substance which controls the level of sugar in the blood

in·sult¹ /ɪnˈsʌlt/ *vt* be rude to

in·sult² /ˈɪnsʌlt/ *n* 1 rude remark or action 2 **add insult to injury** do or say something more against someone when one has already harmed them enough

in·su·pe·ra·ble /ɪnˈsjuːp ərəb əl‖ ɪnˈsuː-/ *adj* impossible to deal with

in·sur·ance /ɪnˈʃʊərəns‖ -ˈʃɔr-/ *n* 1 [U] agreement to pay money in case of misfortune 2 [U] money paid by or to an insurance company for this 3 [S;U] protection against anything

in·sure /ɪnˈʃʊə‖ -ˈʃɔr/ *vt* protect by insurance: *insured against fire*

in·sur·gent /ɪnˈsɜːdʒənt‖ -ɜːr-/ *n, adj* REBEL **–gency** *n* [C;U]

in·sur·mount·a·ble /ˌɪnsəˈmaʊntəb əl‖ -sɔr-/ *adj* too large, difficult, etc. to be dealt with

in·sur·rec·tion /ˌɪnsəˈrekʃən/ *n* [C;U] REBELLION

in·tact /ɪnˈtækt/ *adj* undamaged

in·take /ˈɪnteɪk/ *n* 1 [S] amount or number taken in 2 [C] pipe to let in gas, water, etc.

in·tan·gi·ble /ɪnˈtændʒɪbəl/ *adj* 1 which cannot be known by the senses or described: *an intangible quality* 2 which is hidden or not material, but known to be

real: *intangible assets of the business, such as the loyalty of its customers* **–bly** *adv* **–bility** /ɪnˌtændʒɪˈbɪlɪti/ *n* [U]

in·te·gral /ˈɪntɪgrəl/ *adj* necessary to complete something: *an integral part of the argument*

in·te·grate /ˈɪntɪgreɪt/ *vi/t* (cause to) mix with other races or people **–gration** /ˌɪntɪˈgreɪʃən/ *n* [U] **–grationist** *n* believer in integration

integrated circuit /ˌ···· ˈ··/ *n* set of electrical connections printed esp. on a CHIP¹ (4)

in·teg·ri·ty /ɪnˈtegrɪti/ *n* [U] 1 honesty; trustworthiness 2 wholeness

in·tel·lect /ˈɪntɪlekt/ *n* [C;U] ability to think **~ual** /ˌɪntɪˈlektʃuəl◂/ *adj* 1 of the intellect 2 clever and well-educated **~ual** *n* intellectual person **~ually** *adv*

in·tel·li·gence /ɪnˈtelɪdʒəns/ *n* [U] 1 ability to learn and understand 2 (people who gather) information about enemies **–gent** *adj* clever **–gently** *adv*

in·tel·li·gent·si·a /ɪnˌtelɪˈdʒentsiə/ *n* [P] intellectuals as a social group

in·tel·li·gi·ble /ɪnˈtelɪdʒəbəl/ *adj* understandable **–bly** *adv* **–bility** /ɪnˌtelɪdʒɪˈbɪlɪti/ *n* [U]

in·tend /ɪnˈtend/ *vt* have as one's purpose; mean

in·tense /ɪnˈtens/ *adj* strong (in quality or feeling) **~ly** *adv* **intensity** *n* [U] quality or appearance of being intense

in·ten·si·fy /ɪnˈtensɪfaɪ/ *vi/t* make or become more intense **–fication** /ɪnˌtensɪfɪˈkeɪʃən/ *n* [U]

in·ten·sive /ɪnˈtensɪv/ *adj* giving a lot of attention **~ly** *adv*

in·tent¹ /ɪnˈtent/ *n* [U] 1 purpose: *enter with intent to steal* 2 **to all intents and purposes** in almost every way

intent² *adj* 1 with fixed attention 2 determined

in·ten·tion /ɪnˈtenʃən/ *n* 1 [C;U] plan; purpose 2 **good intentions** wish to bring about a good result **~al** *adj* done on purpose **~ally** *adv*

in·ter /ɪnˈtɜː‖ -ɜːr/ *vt* **-rr-** *fml* bury

in·ter·act /ˌɪntərˈækt/ *vi* have an effect on each other **~ion** /-ˈækʃən/ *n* [C;U]

in·ter·act·ive /ˌɪntərˈæktɪv◂/ *adj* 1 that interacts 2 allowing the exchange of information between a computer and a user while a PROGRAM is in operation

in·ter·cede /ˌɪntəˈsiːd ‖ -ər-/ vi speak in favour of someone

in·ter·cept /ˌɪntəˈsept ‖ -ər-/ vt stop (someone or something moving between two places) ~**ion** /-ˈsepʃən/ n [C;U]

in·ter·ces·sion /ˌɪntəˈseʃən ‖ -tər-/ n 1 [U] act of interceding 2 [C;U] prayer which asks for other people to be helped

in·ter·change /ˌɪntəˈtʃeɪndʒ ‖ -ər-/ vi/t exchange ~**able** adj ♦ n /ˈɪntətʃeɪndʒ ‖ -tər-/ 1 [C;U] (act of) interchanging 2 [C] system of smaller roads connecting main roads

in·ter·com /ˈɪntəkɒm ‖ ˈɪntərkɑːm/ n system for talking through a machine to people fairly near

in·ter·course /ˈɪntəkɔːs ‖ ˈɪntərkɔːrs/ n [U] 1 SEXUAL INTERCOURSE 2 fml conversation, etc. between people

in·ter·de·pen·dent /ˌɪntədɪˈpendənt ‖ -tər-/ adj depending on each other

in·ter·est /ˈɪntrəst/ n 1 [S;U] willingness to give attention: take an interest 2 [U] quality that makes people give attention: That's of no interest to her. 3 [C] activity or subject that one likes to give time to 4 [C] also **interests** pl. — advantage: It's in your interest to go. 5 [U] money paid for the use of money: 10% interest 6 [C] share in a business ♦ vt cause to feel INTEREST (1) ~**ed** adj 1 feeling INTEREST (1) 2 personally concerned ~**ing** adj having INTEREST (2)

in·ter·face /ˈɪntəfeɪs ‖ -ər-/ n point where two systems meet and act on each other ♦ vi/t connect or be connected by means of an interface

in·ter·fere /ˌɪntəˈfɪə ‖ -tərˈfɪr/ vi 1 enter into a matter that does not concern one and in which one is not wanted 2 prevent something from working properly –**ference** n [U] 1 act of interfering 2 noises, etc. that stop radio or television from working properly

interfere with phr vt 1 get in the way of 2 touch or move (something) in a way that is not allowed 3 annoy or touch sexually

in·ter·ga·lac·tic /ˌɪntəgəˈlæktɪk◄ ‖ -tər-/ adj between the galaxies (GALAXY)

in·ter·im /ˈɪntərɪm/ adj done as part of something to follow later: interim report

in·te·ri·or /ɪnˈtɪərɪə ‖ -ˈtɪriər/ n inside of

something **interior** adj

interior de·sign /·,·· ·ʹ·/ n [U] (job of) choosing colours, materials, furniture, etc. for the inside of people's houses ~**er** n

in·ter·ject /ˌɪntəˈdʒekt ‖ -ər-/ vi/t fml make (a sudden remark) between others ~**ion** /-ˈdʒekʃən/ n 1 [C] word or phrase, such as 'Good heavens!' interjected 2 [U] act of interjecting

in·ter·lock /ˌɪntəˈlɒk ‖ ˌɪntərˈlɑːk/ vi/t fasten or be fastened together

in·ter·lop·er /ˈɪntələʊpə ‖ -tərloupər/ n person found in a place, esp. among others, with no right to be there

in·ter·lude /ˈɪntəluːd ‖ -ər-/ n period of time between two parts or activities

in·ter·mar·ry /ˌɪntəˈmæri ‖ -ər-/ vi (of groups of people) become connected by marriage –**marriage** n [U]

in·ter·me·di·a·ry /ˌɪntəˈmiːdiəri ‖ ˌɪntərˈmiːdieri/ n person who persuaded opposing sides to agree

in·ter·me·di·ate /ˌɪntəˈmiːdiət◄ ‖ -tər-/ adj between two others; halfway

in·ter·ment /ɪnˈtɜːmənt ‖ -ɜːr-/ n [C;U] fml burial

in·ter·mi·na·ble /ɪnˈtɜːmɪnəbəl ‖ -ɜːr-/ adj long and dull; (seeming) endless –**bly** adv

in·ter·mis·sion /ˌɪntəˈmɪʃən ‖ -tər-/ n esp. AmE for INTERVAL (2)

in·ter·mit·tent /ˌɪntəˈmɪtənt◄ ‖ -tər-/ adj not continuous ~**ly** adv

in·tern¹ /ɪnˈtɜːn ‖ -ɜːrn/ vt put in prison, esp. in wartime ~**ment** n [U]

in·tern² /ˈɪntɜːn ‖ -ɜːrn/ n esp. AmE person who has recently completed professional training, esp. in medicine, and is gaining practical experience, esp. in a hospital

in·ter·nal /ɪnˈtɜːnl ‖ -ɜːr-/ adj 1 inside 2 not foreign: internal trade ~**ly** adv

Internal Rev·e·nue Service /·,·· ·ʹ·· ,·ʹ/ n [the] (in the US) office that collects taxes

in·ter·na·tion·al /ˌɪntəˈnæʃənəl◄ ‖ -tər-/ adj between nations ♦ n 1 international sports match 2 person who plays for his or her country's team in such a match ~**ly** adv ~**ism** n [U] principle that nations should work together

In·ter·net /ˈɪntənet ‖ ˈɪntər-/ n [the+S] system that allows people using computers around the world to exchange information

in·ter·per·son·al /ˌɪntəˈpɜːsənəl◄ ‖ -tərˈpɜːr-/ adj involving relationships between people

in·ter·play /ˈɪntəpleɪ ‖ -ər-/ n [U] INTERACTION

in·ter·po·late /ɪnˈtɜːpəleɪt ‖ -ɜːr-/ vt fml put in (words); interrupt –lation /ɪn,tɜːpəˈleɪʃən ‖ -ɜːr-/ n [C;U]

in·ter·pose /ˌɪntəˈpəʊz ‖ -tərˈpoʊz/ vt fml put or say between things

in·ter·pret /ɪnˈtɜːprət ‖ -ɜːr-/ v 1 vt understand or explain the meaning of 2 vi/t turn (spoken words) into another language ~er n person who INTERPRETS (2) ~ation /ɪn,tɜːprəˈteɪʃən ‖ -ɜːr-/ n [C;U] 1 explanation 2 (example of) performance of music, theatre, etc. by someone giving their own idea of the COMPOSER's, writer's, etc. intentions

in·ter·ro·gate /ɪnˈterəɡeɪt/ vt 1 question formally esp. for a long time and often with the use of threats or violence 2 (try to) get direct information from: to interrogate a computer –gation /ɪn,terəˈɡeɪʃən/ n [C;U] –gative /ˌɪntəˈrɒɡətɪv◄ ‖ -ˈrɑː-/ adj asking a question

in·ter·rupt /ˌɪntəˈrʌpt/ vi/t break the flow of (speech, etc.) –ion /-ˈrʌpʃən/ n [C;U]

in·ter·sect /ˌɪntəˈsekt ‖ -ər-/ vi/t cut across: intersecting paths –ion /-ˈsekʃən/ n 1 [U] act of intersecting 2 [C] CROSSROADS

in·ter·sperse /ˌɪntəˈspɜːs ‖ -ntərˈspɜːrs/ vt put here and there among other things

in·ter·twine /ˌɪntəˈtwaɪn ‖ -ər-/ vi/t twist together

in·ter·val /ˈɪntəvəl ‖ -tər-/ n 1 time between events 2 BrE time between the parts of a play, etc. 3 distance between things

in·ter·vene /ˌɪntəˈviːn ‖ -ər-/ vi 1 interrupt so as to stop something 2 (of time) happen between events –vention /-ˈvenʃən/ n [C;U]

in·ter·view /ˈɪntəvjuː ‖ -ər-/ n meeting where a person is asked questions ♦ vt ask (someone) questions in an interview ~ee n person who is being or is to be interviewed, esp. for a job ~er n person who interviews

in·tes·tate /ɪnˈtesteɪt, -stət/ adj law not having made a WILL2 (5)

in·tes·tine /ɪnˈtestɪn/ also -tines pl n

bowels –tinal adj

in·ti·ma·cy /ˈɪntəməsi/ n 1 [U] state of being intimate 2 [C] remark or action of a kind that happens only between people who know each other very well 3 [U] the act of sex

in·ti·mate¹ /ˈɪntəmət/ adj 1 having a close relationship: intimate friends 2 private: her intimate thoughts 3 resulting from close study: intimate knowledge ~ly adv

in·ti·mate² /ˈɪntəmeɪt/ vt fml make known; suggest –mation /ˌɪntəˈmeɪʃən/ n [C;U]

in·tim·i·date /ɪnˈtɪmədeɪt/ vt frighten by threats –dation /ɪn,tɪməˈdeɪʃən/ n [U]

in·to /ˈɪntə; before vowels ˈɪntʊ; strong ˈɪntuː/ prep 1 so as to be in: jump into the water | get into trouble 2 so as to be: translate it into French 3 against; bump into a tree 4 (used when dividing): 7 into 11 won't go.

in·tol·e·ra·ble /ɪnˈtɒlərəbəl ‖ -ˈtɑː-/ adj unbearable –bly adv

in·tol·e·rant /ɪnˈtɒlərənt ‖ -ˈtɑː-/ adj not TOLERANT –rance n [U]

in·to·na·tion /ˌɪntəˈneɪʃən/ n [C;U] rise and fall of the voice in speech

in·tone /ɪnˈtəʊn ‖ -ˈtoʊn/ vi/t say (a prayer, etc.) in a level voice

in·tox·i·cate /ɪnˈtɒksɪkeɪt ‖ ɪnˈtɑːk-/ vt make drunk; (fig.) intoxicated by success –cation /ɪn,tɒksɪˈkeɪʃən ‖ -,tɑːk-/ n [U]

in·trac·ta·ble /ɪnˈtræktəbəl/ adj difficult to control or deal with

in·tran·si·gent /ɪnˈtrænsɪdʒənt/ adj fml refusing to change; STUBBORN –gence n [U]

in·tran·si·tive /ɪnˈtrænsətɪv/ adj (of a verb) having a subject but no object: 'Break' is intransitive in the sentence 'My cup fell and broke' but transitive in 'I broke my cup'.

in·tra·ve·nous /ˌɪntrəˈviːnəs◄/ adj into a VEIN: intravenous injection

in·trep·id /ɪnˈtrepɪd/ adj fml fearless ~ly adv

in·tri·ca·cy /ˈɪntrɪkəsi/ n 1 [U] being intricate 2 [C] something intricate

in·tri·cate /ˈɪntrɪkət/ adj having many details; COMPLICATED ~ly adv

in·trigue /ɪnˈtriːɡ/ v 1 vt interest greatly 2 vi make PLOTS ♦ n /ˈɪntriːɡ, ɪnˈtriːɡ/ 1 [U] act or practice of secret planning 2 [C] PLOTS intriguing adj very interesting, esp. because of some strange quality

in·trin·sic /ɪn'trɪnsɪk, -zɪk/ adj belonging naturally; INHERENT ~ally /-klɪ/ adv

in·tro·duce /ˌɪntrə'djuːs ‖ -'duːs/ vt 1 make (people) known to each other 2 bring or put in –duction /-'dʌkʃən/ n 1 [U] act of introducing 2 [C] occasion of telling people each other's names 3 [C] explanation at the beginning of a book, etc. 4 [C] simple book about a subject –ductory /-'dʌktəri◁/ adj happening or said at the beginning

in·tro·spec·tion /ˌɪntrə'spekʃən/ n [U] thinking about one's own thoughts and feelings –tive adj

in·tro·vert /'ɪntrəvɜːt ‖ -ɜːrt/ n quiet introspective person ~ed adj

in·trude /ɪn'truːd/ vi come in when not wanted **intruder** n person who intrudes, esp. intending to steal **intrusive** /-'truːsɪv/ adj intruding **intrusion** /-'truːʒən/ n [C;U]

in·tu·i·tion /ˌɪntjuː'ɪʃən ‖ -tu-, -tju-/ n 1 [U] power of knowing something without reasoning or learned skill 2 [C] something known in this way –tive /ɪn'tjuːətɪv ‖ -'tuː-, -'tjuː-/ adj –tively adv

In·u·it /'ɪnjuɪt/ n member of a race of people living in the icy far north of N America

in·un·date /'ɪnəndeɪt/ vt flood: (fig.) *inundated with letters* –**dation** /ˌɪnən-'deɪʃən/ n [U]

in·ured /ɪ'njʊəd ‖ ɪ'njʊrd/ adj accustomed (by long experience): *inured to the smell*

in·vade /ɪn'veɪd/ vt 1 attack and take control of (a country) 2 crowd into **invader** n **invasion** /-'veɪʒən/ n [C;U]

in·val·id¹ /ɪn'vælɪd/ adj not VALID: *invalid argument/ticket* ~**ate** vt make invalid ~**ation** /ɪnˌvælɪ'deɪʃən/ n [U]

in·va·lid² /'ɪnvəlɪd, -lɪd ‖ -lɪd/ n person weakened by illness

invalid³ v **invalid out** phr vt allow to leave the armed forces because of ill-health

in·val·ua·ble /ɪn'væljʊəbəl/ adj too valuable for the worth to be measured

in·var·i·a·ble /ɪn'veəriəbəl ‖ -'ver-/ adj unchanging –**bly** adv always

in·veigh /ɪn'veɪ/ v **inveigh against** phr vt fml attack in words

in·vei·gle /ɪn'veɪgəl, -'viː- ‖ -'veɪ-/ v **inveigle into** phr vt trick (someone) into (doing something)

in·vent /ɪn'vent/ vt 1 produce for the first time 2 think of (something untrue) ~**ive** adj able to invent ~**or** n –**ion** /-'venʃən/ n 1 [U] act of inventing 2 [C] something invented

in·ven·to·ry /'ɪnventri ‖ -tɔːri/ n list, esp. one of all the goods in a place

in·verse /ˌɪn'vɜːs◁ ‖ -ɜːrs◁/ n, adj opposite

in·vert /ɪn'vɜːt ‖ -ɜːrt/ vt fml turn upside down **inversion** /-'vɜːʃən ‖ -'vɜːrʒən/ n [C;U]

in·ver·te·brate /ɪn'vɜːtɪbrət, -breɪt ‖ -ɜːr-/ n animal without a BACKBONE

inverted com·ma /·,·· '··/ n BrE for QUOTATION MARK

in·vest /ɪn'vest/ vt use (money) to make more money ~**ment** n 1 [U] act of investing 2 [C] (something bought with) money invested ~**or** n

invest in phr vt buy

invest with phr vt fml give officially to: *power invested in him* ‖ (fig.) *Don't invest his words with too much meaning!* (=take them too seriously)

in·ves·ti·gate /ɪn'vestɪgeɪt/ vi/t inquire carefully (about): *investigate a crime* –**gator** n –**gative** /-gətɪv ‖ -geɪtɪv/ adj –**gation** /ɪnˌvestɪ'geɪʃən/ n [C;U]

in·ves·ti·ture /ɪn'vestɪtʃə ‖ -tʃʊr/ n ceremony of investing someone with rank

in·vet·e·rate /ɪn'vetərət/ adj fixed in a bad habit: *inveterate liar*

in·vid·i·ous /ɪn'vɪdiəs/ adj tending to cause ill-will or make people unnecessarily offended or jealous

in·vi·gi·late /ɪn'vɪdʒɪleɪt/ vi/t BrE watch over (students in an examination) –**lator** n

in·vig·o·rate /ɪn'vɪgəreɪt/ vt give health and strength: *an invigorating swim*

in·vin·ci·ble /ɪn'vɪnsɪbəl/ adj too strong to be defeated –**bly** adv

in·vi·o·la·ble /ɪn'vaɪələbəl/ adj fml impossible to VIOLATE: *inviolable rights*

in·vis·i·ble /ɪn'vɪzəbəl/ adj that cannot be seen –**bly** adv –**bility** /ɪnˌvɪzə'bɪləti/ n [U]

in·vite /ɪn'vaɪt/ vt 1 ask to come 2 ask politely for: *invite questions* **inviting** adj attractive **invitingly** adv **invitation** /ˌɪnvɪ'teɪʃən/ n 1 [C] request to come: *invitations to a wedding* 2 [U] act of inviting: *entrance by invitation only* 3 [C] encouragement to an action

in vi·tro /ɪn 'viːtrəʊ ‖ -troʊ/ adj (done)

outside a living body, in a piece of scientific equipment

in·vo·ca·tion /ˌɪnvəˈkeɪʃən/ n fml 1 [U] act of invoking 2 [C] prayer for help

in·voice /ˈɪnvɔɪs/ vt, n (send) a bill for goods received

in·voke /ɪnˈvəʊk ‖ -ˈvoʊk/ vt fml 1 call to (God, the law) for help 2 beg for 3 cause to appear by magic

in·vol·un·ta·ry /ɪnˈvɒləntəri ‖ ɪnˈvɑː-lənteri/ adj done without intention: an involuntary smile –**rily** adv

in·volve /ɪnˈvɒlv ‖ ɪnˈvɑːlv/ vt 1 have as a necessary result 2 cause to become concerned **involved** adj 1 COMPLICATED 2 (of a person) closely concerned in relationships and activities with others, esp. in a personal or sexual way ~**ment** n [U]

in·vul·ne·ra·ble /ɪnˈvʌlnərəbəl/ adj that cannot be harmed

in·ward /ˈɪnwəd ‖ -ərd/ adj, adv 1 on or towards the inside 2 of the mind or spirit: inward peace ~**ly** adv **inwards** adv

i·o·dine /ˈaɪədiːn ‖ -daɪn/ n [U] chemical used to prevent infection in wounds

i·on /ˈaɪən ‖ ˈaɪən, ˈaɪɑːn/ n atom with an electrical CHARGE ~**izer** /ˈaɪənaɪzə ‖ -ər/ n machine that produces negative ions, believed to make the air more healthy

i·on·o·sphere /aɪˈɒnəsfɪə ‖ aɪˈɑːnəsfɪr/ n [the+S] part of the atmosphere which is used in helping to send radio waves around the Earth

i·o·ta /aɪˈəʊtə ‖ -ˈoʊ-/ n [S] very small amount

IOU /ˌaɪ əʊ ˈjuː ‖ -oʊ-/ n 'I owe you'; signed piece of paper saying one owes money

ip·so fac·to /ˌɪpsəʊ ˈfæktəʊ ‖ -soʊ ˈfæktoʊ/ adv fml (proved) by the fact itself

IQ /ˌaɪ ˈkjuː/ n intelligence quotient; measure of INTELLIGENCE

IRA /ˌaɪ ɑːr ˈeɪ/ n Irish Republican Army; illegal Irish military organization

i·ras·ci·ble /ɪˈræsəbəl/ adj fml easily made angry

i·rate /aɪˈreɪt◂/ adj fml angry –**ly** adv

ir·i·des·cent /ˌɪrɪˈdesənt◂/ adj changing colour as light falls on it –**cence** n [U]

i·ris /ˈaɪərɪs ‖ ˈaɪrɪs/ n 1 tall yellow or purple flower 2 coloured part of the eye

irk /ɜːk ‖ ɜːrk/ vt annoy ~**some** adj annoying

i·ron¹ /ˈaɪən ‖ ˈaɪərn/ n 1 [U] common hard

metal used in making steel, etc. 2 [C] heavy object for making cloth smooth 3 **have several irons in the fire** have various different interests, activities, or plans at the same time ♦ adj very firm: iron will **irons** n [P] chains for a prisoner

iron² vt make smooth with an iron

iron out phr vt remove (difficulties, etc.)

Iron Age /ˈ·· ·/ n [the+R] time in the history of mankind when iron was used for tools, etc.

Iron Cur·tain /ˌ·· ˈ··/ n border between western Europe and the former COMMUNIST countries of eastern Europe

i·ron·ic /aɪˈrɒnɪk ‖ aɪˈrɑː-/ also ~**al** /-kəl/ — adj expressing IRONY ~**ally** /-kli/ adv

ironing board /ˈ··· ·/ n narrow table for ironing clothes on

iron lung /ˌ·· ˈ·/ n machine fitted over the body which helps one breathe in and out

i·ron·mon·ger /ˈaɪənˌmʌŋgə ‖ ˈaɪərn-ˌmʌŋgər, -ˌmɑːŋ-/ n BrE person who sells HARDWARE (1)

i·ron·y /ˈaɪərəni ‖ ˈaɪr-/ n 1 [U] intentional use of words which are opposite to one's real meaning, in order to be amusing or to show annoyance 2 [C;U] event or situation which is the opposite of what one expected

ir·ra·di·ate /ɪˈreɪdieɪt/ vt 1 fml throw bright light on 2 treat with X-RAYS or similar beams of force 3 treat (food) with X-RAYS to kill bacteria and make last longer

ir·ra·tion·al /ɪˈræʃənəl/ adj not reasonable ~**ly** adv

ir·rec·on·ci·la·ble /ɪˌrekənˈsaɪləbəl/ adj impossible to bring into agreement –**bly** adv

ir·re·fu·ta·ble /ˌɪrɪˈfjuːtəbəl/ adj fml too strong to be disproved

ir·reg·u·lar /ɪˈregjələ ‖ -ər/ adj 1 uneven 2 fml against the usual rules 3 gram not following the usual pattern ~**ly** adv ~**ity** /ɪˌregjəˈlærəti/ n [C;U]

ir·rel·e·vant /ɪˈreləvənt/ adj not RELEVANT –**vance** n [C;U]

ir·rep·a·ra·ble /ɪˈrepərəbəl/ adj too bad to be put right –**bly** adv

ir·re·place·a·ble /ˌɪrɪˈpleɪsəbəl◂/ adj too special for anything else to REPLACE it

ir·re·proach·a·ble /ˌɪrɪˈprəʊtʃəbəl ‖ -ˈproʊ-/ adj fml faultless –**bly** adv

ir·re·sis·ti·ble /ˌɪrɪˈzɪstəbəl◂/ adj so nice,

powerful, etc., that one cannot RESIST it **–bly** *adv*

ir·res·o·lute /ɪˈrezəluːt/ *adj fml* unable to make decisions **~ly** *adv*

ir·re·spec·tive /ˌɪrɪˈspektɪv/ *adv* irrespective of without regard to

ir·re·spon·si·ble /ˌɪrɪˈspɒnsəbəl◂‖ -ˈspɑːn-/ *adj* not trustworthy; careless **–bly** *adv* **–bility** /ˌɪrɪspɒnsəˈbɪləti‖ -spɑːn-/ *n* [U]

ir·re·triev·a·ble /ˌɪrɪˈtriːvəbəl◂/ *adj* impossible to get back or put right **–bly** *adv*

ir·rev·e·rent /ɪˈrevərənt/ *adj* not respectful, esp. of holy things **~ly** *adv* **–rence** *n* [U]

ir·rev·o·ca·ble /ɪˈrevəkəbəl/ *adj* unchangeable once made or started: *irrevocable decision* **–bly** *adv*

ir·ri·gate /ˈɪrɪgeɪt/ *vt* supply water to (land) **–gation** /ˌɪrɪˈgeɪʃən/ *n* [U]

ir·ri·ta·ble /ˈɪrɪtəbəl/ *adj* easily annoyed **–bly** *adv* **–bility** /ˌɪrɪtəˈbɪləti/ *n* [U]

ir·ri·tate /ˈɪrɪteɪt/ *vt* 1 annoy 2 make sore **–tant** *n* **–tation** /ˌɪrɪˈteɪʃən/ *n* [C;U]

is /s, z, əz; *strong* ɪz/ *v* 3rd person sing. present tense of BE

Is·lam /ˈɪslɑːm, ˈɪz-, ɪsˈlɑːm/ *n* (people and countries that practise) the Muslim religion **~ic** /ɪzˈlæmɪk, ɪs-/ *adj*

is·land /ˈaɪlənd/ *n* 1 piece of land surrounded by water 2 raised place where people can wait in the middle of a road for traffic to pass **~er** *n* person living on an island

isle /aɪl/ *n lit* island

is·n't /ˈɪzənt/ *v short for:* is not

i·so·late /ˈaɪsəleɪt/ *vt* keep separate from others **–lated** *adj* alone; only: *an isolated case* **–lation** /ˌaɪsəˈleɪʃən/ *n* [U]

is·sue /ˈɪʃuː, ˈɪsjuː‖ ˈɪʃuː/ *n* 1 [C] subject to be talked about or argued about —see also SIDE ISSUE 2 [C] printing at one time of a magazine, etc. 3 [U] *law* children ♦ *vt* produce or provide officially: *issue a statement/new uniforms*

ISA /ˈaɪsə/ *n* Individual Savings Account; type of tax-free ACCOUNT (3)

isth·mus /ˈɪsməs/ *n* narrow piece of land joining two larger pieces

it /ɪt/ *pron* 1 that thing already mentioned: *'Where's my dinner?' 'The cat ate it.'* 2 that person: *'Who's that?' 'It's me.'* 3 (used in statements about weather, time, or

distance): *It's raining.* | *It's Thursday.* | *It's not far to Paris.* 4 (used when the real subject comes later): *It's a pity you forgot.* 5 (making part of a sentence more important): *It was Jane who told me.* ♦ *n* 1 *infml* a very important person: *He thinks he's it.* b the important point: *This is it, I have to decide.* 2 **That's it: a** That's complete; there's nothing more to come **b** That's right

IT /ˌaɪ ˈtiː/ *n abbrev. for:* INFORMATION TECHNOLOGY

i·tal·ics /ɪˈtælɪks/ *n* [P] sloping printed letters **–icize** /-ləsaɪz/ *vt* print in italics

itch /ɪtʃ/ *vi* 1 have the feeling of wanting to SCRATCH the skin 2 **be itching to/for** want very much ♦ *n* 1 itching feeling 2 strong desire —see also SEVEN-YEAR ITCH **~y** *adj*

itchy feet /ˌ· ˈ·/ *n* [P] *infml* desire to travel

it'd /ˈɪtəd/ *short for:* 1 it would 2 it had

i·tem /ˈaɪtəm/ *n* 1 single thing on a list, etc. 2 piece of news **~ize**, **–ise** *vt* make a detailed list of

i·tin·e·rant /aɪˈtɪnərənt/ *adj* travelling from place to place

i·tin·e·ra·ry /aɪˈtɪnərəri‖ -nəreri/ *n* plan for a journey

it'll /ˈɪtl/ *short for:* it will

its /ɪts/ *determiner* of it: *its ears*

it's /ɪts/ *short for:* 1 it is 2 it has

it·self /ɪtˈself/ *pron* 1 (*reflexive form* of it): *The cat washed itself.* 2 (*strong form* of it): *I had the copy, but the letter itself was missing.* 3 (all) by itself: a alone b without help 4 in itself without considering the rest 5 to itself not shared

IUD /ˌaɪ juː ˈdiː/ *n* plastic or metal object fitted inside a woman's WOMB as a form of CONTRACEPTION

I've /aɪv/ *short for:* I have

i·vo·ry /ˈaɪvəri/ *n* [U] 1 hard white substance of which elephants' TUSKS are made 2 creamy white colour of this

ivory tow·er /ˌ·· ˈ··/ *n* place where people avoid the difficult realities of ordinary life

i·vy /ˈaɪvi/ *n* [U] climbing plant with shiny leaves **ivied** *adj* covered with ivy

Ivy League /ˌ·· ˈ·/ *adj AmE* belonging to or typical of a group of old and respected universities of the eastern US

J

J, j /dʒeɪ/ the 10th letter of the English alphabet

jab /dʒæb/ *vi/t* **-bb-** push with force (something pointed) ♦ *n* **1** sharp forceful push **2** *infml, esp. BrE* INJECTION

jab·ber /'dʒæbə‖-ər/ *vi/t* talk or say quickly **jabber** *n* [S;U]

jack¹ /dʒæk/ *n* **1** apparatus for lifting a car, etc. **2** playing card between the 10 and the queen

jack² *v*

jack in *phr vt BrE sl* stop; be unwilling to continue

jack up *phr vt* lift with a jack

jack·al /'dʒækɔ:l, -kəl‖-kəl/ *n* kind of wild dog

jack·boot /'dʒækbu:t/ *n* **1** [C] high military boot **2** [S] cruel military rule

jack·et /'dʒækɪ̵t/ *n* **1** short coat with SLEEVES **2** potato skin **3** cover for a machine, pipe, etc. **4** loose paper book cover

jack knife /'· ·/ *n* large pocket knife, the blade of which folds into the handle

jack-knife /'· ·/ *vi* (of a vehicle) bend suddenly in the middle

jack·pot /'dʒækpɒt‖-pɑ:t/ *n* biggest money prize to be won in a game

ja·cuz·zi /dʒə'ku:zi/ *n tdmk* bath fitted with a system of hot water currents

jade /dʒeɪd/ *n* [U] (colour of) a green precious stone

ja·ded /'dʒeɪdɪ̵d/ *adj* tired because of having had too much of something, esp. experience

jag·ged /'dʒægɪ̵d/ *adj* with a rough uneven edge

jag·u·ar /'dʒægjuə‖'dʒægwɑ:r/ *n* large spotted wild cat of S America

jail /dʒeɪl/ *n* [C;U] prison ♦ *vt* put in jail ~**er** *n* person in charge of prisoners

jam¹ /dʒæm/ *n* [U] fruit boiled in sugar, for spreading on bread

jam² *v* **-mm-** **1** *vt* crush or press tightly: *jam clothes into a bag | jam the brakes on* **2** *vi* get stuck: *The door jammed.* **3** *vt* block (radio messages) ♦ *n* **1** closely jammed mass: *traffic jam* **2** **in a jam** in a difficult situation

jam·bo·ree /ˌdʒæmbə'ri:/ *n* large party or gathering

jam-packed /ˌ· '·◂/ *adj* with many people or things very close together

jan·gle /'dʒæŋgəl/ *vi/t* (cause to) make the noise of metal striking metal

jan·i·tor /'dʒænɪ̵tə‖-ər/ *n* CARETAKER

Jan·u·a·ry /'dʒænjuəri, -njʊri‖-jueri/ *n* the 1st month of the year

jar¹ /dʒɑ:‖dʒɑ:r/ *n* short wide pot or bottle

jar² *vi/t* **-rr-** **1** *vi* make a nasty sound **2** *vt* give a nasty shock to **3** *vi* go badly together: *jarring colours*

jar·gon /'dʒɑ:gən‖'dʒɑ:rgən, -gɑ:n/ *n* [U] language used by a particular group: *computer jargon*

jaun·dice /'dʒɔ:ndɪ̵s‖'dʒɒn-, 'dʒɑ:n-/ *n* [U] disease that makes the skin yellow **jaundiced** *adj* mistrustful and CYNICAL: *jaundiced opinions*

jaunt /dʒɔ:nt‖dʒɒnt, dʒɑ:nt/ *n* short pleasure trip ~**y** *adj* cheerful and confident

jav·e·lin /'dʒævəlɪ̵n/ *n* light spear for throwing

jaw /dʒɔ:‖dʒɒ:/ *n* one of the two bony structures where the teeth are fixed ♦ *vi/t infml* talk (to) for a long time **jaws** *n* [P] **1** animal's mouth **2** two parts of a tool, etc. that hold things tightly: (fig.) *the jaws of death*

jay·walk /'dʒeɪwɔ:k‖-wɒ:k/ *vi* cross streets carelessly

jazz¹ /dʒæz/ *n* [U] music with a strong beat, originated by black Americans ~**y** *adj* brightly coloured

jazz² *v* **jazz up** *phr vt* make brighter or more interesting

jeal·ous /'dʒeləs/ *adj* **1** unhappy at not being liked as much as someone else: *jealous husband* **2** very ENVIOUS **3** wanting to keep what one has ~**ly** *adv*

jeal·ous·y /'dʒeləsi/ *n* [C;U] jealous feeling

jeans /dʒi:nz/ *n* [P] strong cotton trousers

jeep /dʒi:p/ *n tdmk* (military) car for travelling on rough ground

jeer /dʒɪə‖dʒɪr/ *vi/t* laugh rudely (at) **jeer** *n* ~**ingly** *adv*

jel·ly /'dʒeli/ *n* **1** [C;U] soft gluey food made with GELATINE, or from fruit juice boiled with sugar **2** [S;U] any material beteen a liquid and a solid state

jel·ly·fish /'dʒeli,fɪʃ/ n transparent sea animal with long hanging parts: *She got stung by a jellyfish.*

jeop·ar·dize, -dise /'dʒepədaɪz ‖ -ər-/ vt *fml* put in danger

jeop·ar·dy /'dʒepədi ‖ -ər-/ n [U] *fml* danger: *put one's future in jeopardy*

jerk[1] /dʒɜːk ‖ dʒɜːrk/ n sudden quick pull or movement ♦ vi/t pull or move with a jerk ~y adj not smooth in movement

jerk[2] n *sl* foolish and ungraceful person

jerry-built /'dʒeri bɪlt/ adj built cheaply and badly

jerry-can /'dʒeri kæn/ n flat-sided container, e.g. for petrol

jer·sey /'dʒɜːzi ‖ -ɜːr-/ n SWEATER

jest /dʒest/ vi *fml* joke **jest** n [C;U] **~er** n man kept formerly to amuse a ruler

jet[1] /dʒet/ n 1 narrow stream of gas or liquid forced out of a hole 2 hole from which this comes 3 aircraft whose engine (**jet engine**) works on this principle ♦ vi 1 come in a JET (1) 2 travel by JET (3)

jet[2] n [U] hard shiny black mineral: (fig.) *jet-black hair*

jet·foil /'dʒetfɔɪl/ n HYDROFOIL

jet lag /'· ·/ n [U] tiredness after flying to a place where the time is different

jet·sam /'dʒetsəm/ n [U] —see FLOTSAM AND JETSAM

jet set /'· ·/ n [S] international social group of rich fashionable people

jet·ti·son /'dʒetɪsən, -zən/ vt throw away

jet·ty /'dʒeti/ n small PIER

Jew /dʒuː/ n person descended from the people of ancient Israel whose history is told in the Bible **~ish** adj

jew·el /'dʒuːəl/ n 1 (real or artificial) precious stone 2 very valuable person or thing **~ler** BrE ‖ **ˉer** AmE person who sells jewels **~lery** BrE ‖ **ˉry** AmE [U] jewels worn as decoration

jibe /dʒaɪb/ n, v GIBE

jif·fy /'dʒɪfi/ n [S] moment: *I'll come in a jiffy.*

jig /dʒɪg/ n (music for) a quick merry dance ♦ vi jump up and down

jig·gle /'dʒɪgəl/ vi/t shake from side to side

jig·saw /'dʒɪgsɔː ‖ -sɒː/ also **jigsaw puz·zle** /'·· ,··/ n picture cut into pieces to be fitted together for fun

jilt /dʒɪlt/ vt unexpectedly refuse (an accepted lover)

jin·gle /'dʒɪŋgəl/ n 1 sound as of small bells ringing 2 simple poem used esp. for advertisement ♦ vi/t (cause to) sound with a jingle

jin·go·is·m /'dʒɪŋgəʊɪzəm ‖ -goʊ-/ n [U] *derog* extreme warlike NATIONALISM

jinx /dʒɪŋks/ n something that brings bad luck

jit·ters /'dʒɪtəz ‖ -ərz/ n [P] anxiety before an event **–tery** adj

jive /dʒaɪv/ n [U] (dance performed to) a kind of popular music with a strong beat ♦ vi dance to jive music

Jnr *written abbrev. for:* JUNIOR

job /dʒɒb ‖ dʒɑːb/ n 1 [C] regular paid employment: *out of a job* (=unemployed) 2 [C] piece of work 3 [C] *sl* crime, esp. a robbery —see also INSIDE JOB 4 [S] something hard to do: *You'll have a job to open it.* 5 [S] one's affair; duty: *It's not my job to interfere.* 6 [C] *infml* example of a certain type: *That new Rolls of yours is a beautiful job.* 7 [C] *infml* a PLASTIC SURGERY operation: *a nose job* 8 **a good/bad job** *infml* a good/bad thing 9 **just the job** exactly the thing wanted or needed 10 **make the best of a bad job** do as much or as well as possible in unfavourable conditions 11 **on the job** while working; at work **~ber** n member of the STOCK EXCHANGE who does not deal directly with the public **~bing** adj paid by the JOB (2) **~less** adj unemployed

job cen·tre /'· ,··/ n BrE government office where one can find out about available jobs

job lot /'· ·, ,· '·/ n group of things of different kinds bought or sold together

job·share /'dʒɒbʃeə ‖ 'dʒɑːbʃer/ n arrangement in which a full-time job is shared between two part-time workers ♦ v **–ring** n [U]

jock·ey /'dʒɒki ‖ 'dʒɑːki/ n professional rider in horse races ♦ vi/t try by all possible means to get into a good position: *jockey for position*

joc·u·lar /'dʒɒkjʊlə ‖ 'dʒɑːkjʊlər/ adj *fml* joking; not serious **~ly** adv

joc·und /'dʒɒkənd ‖ 'dʒɑː-/ adj *lit* merry

jodh·purs /'dʒɒdpəz ‖ 'dʒɑːdpərz/ n [P] trousers for horse riding

jog /dʒɒg ‖ dʒɑːg/ v -gg- **1** vt knock slightly **2** vi run slowly for exercise **3 jog someone's memory** make someone remember ♦ n ~ger n someone who JOGS (2)
    jog along
    phr vi move slowly and uneventfully

join /dʒɔɪn/ v **1** vt fasten; connect: *join two ropes* **2** vi/t come together (with); meet: *Join me for a drink.* | *The stream joins the river.* **3** vt become a member of: *join the army* ♦ n place where two things are joined
    join in phr vi/t take part (in an activity)
    join up phr vi offer oneself for military service

join·er /ˈdʒɔɪnə ‖ -ər/ n woodworker who makes doors, etc. inside buildings ~y n [U] trade of a joiner

joint[1] /dʒɔɪnt/ n **1** place where things join (esp. bones) join **2** BrE large piece of meat **3** sl public place for drinking, etc. **4** sl cigarette containing CANNABIS

joint[2] adj shared: *joint bank account* ~ly adv

joist /dʒɔɪst/ n beam supporting a floor

joke /dʒəʊk ‖ dʒoʊk/ n **1** something said or done to amuse people **2 play a joke on someone** do something to make other people laugh at someone ♦ vi tell jokes
    joker n **1** person who makes jokes **2** additional playing card with no fixed value

jol·ly[1] /ˈdʒɒli ‖ ˈdʒɑːli/ adj happy; pleasant

jolly[2] infml persuade; urge gently
    jolly along phr vt encourage in a joking or friendly way
    jolly up phr vt make (esp. a place) bright and cheerful

jolly[3] adv infml very: *jolly difficult*

jolt /dʒəʊlt ‖ dʒoʊlt/ vi/t shake or shock **jolt** n

joss stick /ˈdʒɒs ˌstɪk ‖ ˈdʒɑːs-/ n stick of INCENSE

jos·tle /ˈdʒɒsəl ‖ ˈdʒɑː-/ vi/t knock or push (against)

jot /dʒɒt ‖ dʒɑːt/ n [S] very small bit: *not a jot of truth* ♦ vt -tt- write quickly ~ter n notebook ~ting n rough note

jour·nal /ˈdʒɜːnl ‖ -ɜːr-/ n **1** magazine **2** DIARY ~ism n profession of writing for newspapers ~ist n person whose profession is journalism

jour·nal·ese /ˌdʒɜːnəlˈiːz ‖ -ɜːr-/ n [U]

derog language of newspapers

jour·ney /ˈdʒɜːni ‖ -ɜːr-/ n long trip, esp. by land ♦ vi lit travel

jo·vi·al /ˈdʒəʊviəl ‖ ˈdʒoʊ-/ adj friendly and cheerful ~ly adv

jowl /dʒaʊl/ n lower part of the face

joy /dʒɔɪ/ n **1** [U] great happiness **2** [C] something that causes joy **3** [U] BrE infml success: *I tried phoning her but didn't have any joy.* (=I wasn't able to) ~ful adj fml full of or causing joy ~fully adv ~ous adj lit joyful

joy·ride /ˈdʒɔɪraɪd/ n ride for pleasure in a stolen car -der n -ding n [U]

joy·stick /ˈdʒɔɪˌstɪk/ n handle used to control an aircraft or computer game

JP /ˌdʒeɪ ˈpiː/ n abbrev. for: Justice of the Peace; MAGISTRATE

Jr written abbrev. for: JUNIOR

jub·i·lant /ˈdʒuːbɪlənt/ adj joyful; delighted -lation /ˌdʒuːbɪˈleɪʃən/ n [U] rejoicing

ju·bi·lee /ˈdʒuːbɪliː, ˌdʒuːbɪˈliː/ n **1** time of rejoicing at an ANNIVERSARY **2 diamond/golden/silver jubilee** 60th/ 50th/25th return of an important date

Ju·da·is·m /ˈdʒuːdeɪ-ɪzəm, ˈdʒuːdə- ‖ ˈdʒuːdə-, ˈdʒuːdi-/ n [U] religion and civilization of the Jews

jud·der /ˈdʒʌdə ‖ -ər/ vi BrE (of a vehicle) shake violently

judge /dʒʌdʒ/ n **1** public official who decides legal cases **2** person who decides in a competition, etc. **3** person who can give a valuable opinion: *I'm no judge of music.* ♦ vi/t act as a judge (in); form an opinion (about)

judg·ment, judgement /ˈdʒʌdʒmənt/ n **1** [U] ability to decide correctly: *a man of sound judgment* **2** [C] opinion **3** [C;U] decision of a judge or court of law: *She passed (=gave) judgment on the accused man.*

ju·di·cial /dʒuːˈdɪʃəl/ adj of law courts and judges ~ly adv

ju·di·cia·ry /dʒuːˈdɪʃəri ‖ -ʃieri, -ʃəri/ n all the judges, as a group

ju·di·cious /dʒuːˈdɪʃəs/ adj fml sensible ~ly adv

ju·do /ˈdʒuːdəʊ ‖ -doʊ/ n [U] kind of WRESTLING, from Asia

jug /dʒʌg/ n esp. BrE pot for liquids, with a handle and a lip for pouring

jug·ger·naut /'dʒʌgənɔːt ‖ -ərnɔːt/ *n BrE* very large LORRY

jug·gle /'dʒʌgəl/ *vi/t* 1 keep (objects) in the air by throwing and catching them 2 try to fit in two or more jobs, activities, etc. **juggler** *n* entertainer who juggles (1)

jug·u·lar /'dʒʌgjʊlə ‖ -ər/ *also* **jugular vein** /ˌ··· '·/ *n* main VEIN in the neck

juice /dʒuːs/ *n* [C;U] liquid from fruit, vegetables, or meat **juicy** *adj* 1 having a lot of juice 2 *infml* interesting esp. because providing details about improper behaviour

juke·box /'dʒuːkbɒks ‖ -bɑːks/ *n* coin-operated music machine

Ju·ly /dʒʊ'laɪ/ *n* the 7th month of the year

jum·ble /'dʒʌmbəl/ *vi/t* mix in disorder ♦ *n* 1 [S] disorderly mixture 2 [U] *BrE* things for a JUMBLE SALE

jumble sale /'·· ·/ *n BrE* sale of used articles to get money for CHARITY, etc.

jum·bo /'dʒʌmbəʊ ‖ -boʊ/ *adj* very large *a* jumbo jet (=very large passenger aircraft)

jump¹ /dʒʌmp/ *v* 1 *vi* push oneself off the ground with one's leg muscles 2 *vt* cross in this way: *jump a stream* 3 *vi* move suddenly: *The noise made me jump.* 4 *vi* rise sharply: *Oil prices have jumped.* 5 *vt* attack suddenly 6 *vt* leave, pass or escape from (something) illegally 7 **jump down someone's throat** *infml* attack someone in words, strongly and unexpectedly 8 **jump the gun** start something too soon 9 **jump the queue** get something before those who have waited longer 10 **jump to it!** hurry

jump at *phr vt* accept eagerly

jump on *phr vt infml* speak to sharply

jump² *n* 1 act of jumping 2 thing to jump over 3 **be/stay one jump ahead** do the right thing because one knows or guesses what one's competitors are going to do **~y** *adj* nervously excited

jumped-up /ˌ· '·◂/ *adj* having too great an idea of one's own importance

jump·er /'dʒʌmpə ‖ -ər/ *n* 1 *BrE* for SWEATER 2 horse or person that jumps

junc·tion /'dʒʌŋkʃən/ *n* place of joining: *railway junction*

junc·ture /'dʒʌŋktʃə ‖ -ər/ *n fml* point in time

June /dʒuːn/ *n* the 6th month of the year

jun·gle /'dʒʌŋgəl/ *n* [C;U] thick tropical forest

ju·ni·or /'dʒuːniə ‖ -ər/ *n, adj* 1 (someone) younger 2 (someone) of low or lower rank

Junior *adj esp. AmE* the younger (of two men in the same family with the same name)

junior school /'··· ˌ·/ *n BrE* school for children between 7 and 11 years old

junk /dʒʌŋk/ *n* [U] 1 old useless things 2 *sl* dangerous drug, esp. HEROIN ♦ *vt infml* get rid of as worthless

jun·ket /'dʒʌŋkɪt/ *n* [C] *infml, often derog* trip, esp. one made by a government official and paid for with government money

junk food /'· ·/ *n* [U] *infml* unhealthy food

junk·ie, -y /'dʒʌŋki/ *n sl* drug ADDICT: (fig.) *I'm a real sugar junkie.*

junk mail /'· ·/ *n* [U] mail, usu. for advertising, sent to people although they have not asked for it

jun·ta /'dʒʌntə, 'hʊntə/ *n* (military) government that has seized power by armed force

Ju·pi·ter /'dʒuːpɪtə ‖ -ər/ *n* the largest PLANET, 5th in order from the sun

jur·is·dic·tion /ˌdʒʊərɪs'dɪkʃən ‖ ˌdʒʊr-/ *n* [U] legal power

ju·ror /'dʒʊərə ‖ 'dʒʊrər/ *n* member of a jury

ju·ry /'dʒʊəri ‖ 'dʒʊri/ *n* 1 group of people chosen to decide questions of fact in a court of law 2 group of people chosen to judge a competition of any kind

just¹ /dʒəst; *strong* dʒʌst/ *adv* 1 exactly: *sitting just here* 2 completely: *It's just perfect!* 3 at this moment: *I'm just coming.* 4 only a short time (ago): *just after breakfast* | *They've only just left.* 5 almost not: *She arrived just in time.* 6 only: *no dinner, just coffee* 7 **just about** very nearly 8 **just as well:** a lucky or suitable: *It's just as well I brought my coat — it's freezing!* b with good reason, considering the situation: *Since there's no more work to do, we might just as well go home.* 9 **just now:** a at this moment: *We're having dinner just now — come back later.* b a moment ago: *Paul telephoned just now to say he'll be late.* 10 **just yet** quite yet

just² /dʒʌst/ *adj* fair; according to what is deserved **~ly** *adv*

jus·tice /'dʒʌstɪs/ *n* 1 [U] quality of being just; fairness 2 [U] the law: *court of justice* 3 [C] JUDGE (1) 4 **do justice to someone** also **do someone justice** — treat someone

in a fair way
Justice of the Peace /ˌ·· · ·'·/ n
MAGISTRATE
jus·ti·fy /'dʒʌstɪfaɪ/ vt give or be a good
reason for –**fiable** adj –**fiably** adv –**fication**
/ˌdʒʌstɪfɪ'keɪʃən/ n [U] good reason
jut /dʒʌt/ vi -tt- stick out or up further
than the things around it
ju·ve·nile /'dʒuːvənaɪl ‖ -nəl, -naɪl/ n
1 young person 2 actor or actress who plays
such a person ♦ adj 1 of or for juveniles
2 childish or foolish
juvenile de·lin·quen·cy /ˌ··· ·'···/ n [U]
crimes by JUVENILES (1) –**quent** n
jux·ta·pose /ˌdʒʌkstə'pəʊz ‖ 'dʒʌkst-
əpoʊz/ vt fml put side by side –**position**
/ˌdʒʌkstəpə'zɪʃən/ n [U]

K

K, **k** /keɪ/ the 11th letter of the English
alphabet
K written abbrev. for: 1 1024 BYTES of
computer DATA 2 infml one thousand: a £20K
salary
ka·lei·do·scope /kə'laɪdəskəʊp ‖ -skoʊp/
n tube containing mirrors, and often bits of
coloured glass, turned to produce changing
patterns –**scopic** /kə,laɪdə'skɒpɪk ‖
-'skɑː-/ adj changing quickly and often
kan·ga·roo /ˌkæŋɡə'ruː/ n Australian
animal that jumps along on its large back
legs, and carries its baby in a pocket
ka·o·lin /'keɪəlɪn/ n [U] fine white clay
used in medicine, etc.
kar·at /'kærət/ n CARAT
ka·ra·te /kə'rɑːti/ n [U] Asian style of
fighting using the hands and feet
kar·ma /'kɑːmə ‖ -ɑːr-/ n [U] (according to
some religions) the force produced by one's
actions, which influences the future
kay·ak /'kaɪæk/ n light covered CANOE
K.C. /ˌkeɪ 'siː/ n (title, while a king is
ruling, for) a British lawyer of high rank

ke·bab /kə'bæb ‖ kə'bɑːb/ n small pieces
of meat cooked on a stick
keel[1] /kiːl/ n 1 bar along the bottom of a
boat 2 **on an even keel** steady
keel[2] v **keel over** phr vi fall over sideways
keen /kiːn/ adj 1 having a strong interest:
keen students | keen on football 2 (of the five
senses) good, strong, quick, etc.: keen
eyesight 3 (of edges) sharp; cutting: (fig.)
keen wind ~ly adv ~ness n [U]
keep[1] /kiːp/ v kept /kept/ 1 vt continue to
have; not lose or give back 2 vi/t (cause) to
continue being: keep them warm | Keep off
the grass! 3 vi continually do something: He
keeps complaining. 4 vt fulfil (a promise)
5 vt prevent: keep them from knowing 6 vt
not tell (a secret) 7 vt make records of or in:
keep accounts/a diary 8 vt support with
money, etc. 9 vt own or manage: keep
chickens/a shop 10 vi remain fresh: This
fish won't keep. 11 vt take suitable notice of
(a holiday, etc): keep Christmas 12 **keep
(oneself) to oneself** not mix with or talk to
other people very much 13 **keep one's
head** remain calm 14 **keep one's shirt on**
also **keep one's hair on** BrE — infml to
remain calm; not to become upset or angry
15 **keep someone company** remain with
someone
  keep at phr vt continue working at
  (something)
  keep back phr vt not tell or give;
  WITHHOLD
  keep down phr vt 1 prevent from
  increasing 2 OPPRESS
  keep from phr vt 1 not to tell
  (someone) about something 2 prevent
  oneself from (doing something)
  keep in with phr vt remain friendly
  with
  keep on phr vi 1 continue talking
  2 continue to employ (someone) 3 continue
  to have (something)
  keep on at phr vt ask repeatedly
  keep out phr vi/t (cause to) stay away
  or not enter
  keep to phr vt 1 stay in: keep to the left
  2 limit oneself to: keep to the point 3 keep
  (something) private to (oneself)
  keep up phr v 1 vi stay level 2 vt
  continue doing 3 vt prevent from going to
  bed 4 vt prevent from falling or dropping: a
  belt to keep my trousers up | (fig.) keep your

spirits up! (=remain cheerful)

keep² n 1 [U] (cost of) necessary food, etc: *earn one's keep* 2 [C] central tower of a castle 3 **for keeps** *infml* for ever

keep·er /'kiːpə‖-ər/ n person who guards or looks after: *shopkeeper*

keep·ing /'kiːpɪŋ/ n [U] 1 care; charge: *leave her jewels in my keeping* 2 **in/out of keeping with** suitable/not suitable for

keep·sake /'kiːpseɪk/ n thing kept to remind one of the giver

keg /keg/ n small barrel

ken /ken/ n **beyond one's ken** outside one's knowledge

ken·nel /'kenl/ n house for a dog **kennels** n place where dogs are bred (BREED (2)) or looked after

kept /kept/ v past t. and p. of KEEP¹

kerb /kɜːb‖kɜːrb/ n BrE stone edge of a PAVEMENT

ker·nel /'kɜːnl‖'kɜːr-/ n 1 centre of a nut, seed, etc. 2 important part of a subject

ker·o·sene /'kerəsiːn/ n [U] PARAFFIN

kes·trel /'kestrəl/ n red-brown European bird which eats mice, birds, and insects

ketch·up /'ketʃəp/ n [U] thick liquid made from TOMATO juice

ket·tle /'ketl/ n pot with a SPOUT, for boiling water

ket·tle·drum /'ketldrʌm/ n large metal drum

key¹ /kiː/ n 1 shaped piece of metal for locking a door, etc.: *car keys* 2 something that explains or helps one to understand 3 any of the parts of a piano, etc. to be pressed to produce the desired sound or effect: *typewriter keys* 4 musical notes starting at a particular base note: *the key of C* ♦ adj very important; necessary: *key industries* | *a key position in the firm*

key² vt 1 make suitable: *factories keyed to military needs* 2 keyboard (information) 3 keyed up excited and nervous

key·board /'kiːbɔːd‖-bɔːrd/ n row of KEYS (3) ♦ vt put (information) into a machine by working a keyboard ~**er** n someone who puts information into a machine using a keyboard ~**ist** keyboard player in a band

key·hole /'kiːhəʊl‖-hoʊl/ n hole for a KEY (1)

keyhole sur·ger·y /ˌ· '··/ n [U] medical operation in which instruments are put into someone's body through a very small hole

key·note /'kiːnəʊt‖-noʊt/ n central idea (of a speech, etc.)

kg written abbrev. for: KILOGRAM(s)

kha·ki /'kɑːki‖'kæki, 'kɑːki/ n 1 [U] yellowish-brown colour 2 cloth of this colour, esp. as worn by soldiers

kib·butz /kɪ'bʊts/ n -**zim** /-sɪm/ or -**zes** farm or settlement in Israel where many families live and work together

kick¹ /kɪk/ v 1 vt hit with the foot 2 vi move the feet as if to kick 3 vi (of a gun) move violently when fired 4 vt sl stop or give up (a harmful activity) 5 **kick someone in the teeth** infml discourage or disappoint someone very much 6 **kick the bucket** sl die

kick about/around phr v 1 vi/t lie unnoticed in (a place) 2 vt beat roughly

kick against phr vt oppose or dislike

kick off phr vi begin

kick out phr vt remove or dismiss (someone), esp. violently

kick up phr vt make (trouble): *kick up a fuss*

kick² n 1 [C] act of kicking 2 [C] sl excitement: *drive fast for kicks* 3 [S;U] infml strength 4 [C] extremely strong new interest: *She's on a health food kick.*

kick·back /'kɪkbæk/ n money paid for dishonestly helping someone

kick·off /'kɪk-ɒf‖-ɔːf/ n first kick in football

kid¹ /kɪd/ n 1 [C] child or young person 2 [C;U] (leather from) a young goat

kid² vi/t -**dd**- sl pretend; deceive

kid gloves /ˌ· '·/ n [P] gentle methods of dealing with people

kid·nap /'kɪdnæp/ vt -**pp**- take (someone) away by force, so as to demand money, etc. ~**per** n

kid·ney /'kɪdni/ n organ that separates waste liquid from the blood

kidney ma·chine /'·· ·ˌ·/ n hospital machine that can do the work of human kidneys

kill /kɪl/ vt 1 cause to die: *My feet are killing me.* (=hurting very much) | (fig.) *The boss will kill me* (=be very angry) *when she finds out.* 2 destroy; spoil 3 **kill time** make time pass quickly 4 **kill two birds with one stone** get two good results from one action ♦ *n* [S] **1** bird or animal killed **2** act or moment of killing ~**er** *n* ~**ing** *n* **1** murder **2 make a killing** make a lot of money suddenly

kill·joy /'kɪldʒɔɪ/ *n* person who spoils other people's pleasure

kiln /kɪln/ *n* apparatus for baking pots, bricks, etc.

ki·lo /'kiːləʊ ‖ -loʊ/ *n* **kilos** kilogram

kil·o·byte /'kɪləbaɪt/ *n* 1000 or 1024 BYTES of computer information

kil·o·gram , **-gramme** /'kɪləgræm/ *n* (a measure of weight equal to) 2.2 pounds

kil·o·me·tre *BrE* ‖ **-ter** *AmE* /'kɪlə-,miːtə, kɪ'lɒmɪtə ‖ kɪ'lɑːmətər/ *n* (a measure of length equal to) 0.62 of a mile

kil·o·watt /'kɪləwɒt ‖ -wɑːt/ *n* 1000 WATTS

kilt /kɪlt/ *n* short skirt worn esp. by Scotsmen

ki·mo·no /kɪ'məʊnəʊ ‖ -'moʊnoʊ/ *n* **-nos** **1** long loose Japanese garment **2** loose DRESSING GOWN

kin /kɪn/ *n* [P] **next of kin** one's closest relative(s)—see also KITH AND KIN

kind¹ /kaɪnd/ *n* **1** type; sort: *all kinds of people* **2 a kind of** unclear or unusual sort of: *I had a kind of feeling she'd phone.* **3 in kind** (of payment) in goods, not money **4 kind of** *infml* in a certain way; rather **5 of a kind: a** of the same kind: *They're two of a kind.* **b** of a not very good kind: *It was coffee of a kind, but we couldn't drink it.*

kind² *adj* helpful and friendly ~**ness** *n* **1** [U] quality of being kind **2** [C] kind act

kin·der·gar·ten /'kɪndəgɑːtn ‖ -dərgɑːr tn/ *n* school for young children, usu. between the ages of 4 and 6

kind-heart·ed /,· '··◄‖·,··/ *adj* having a kind nature ~**ly** *adv* ~**ness** *n* [U]

kin·dle /'kɪndl/ *vt/i* (cause to) start burning **-dling** *n* [U] materials for starting a fire

kind·ly /'kaɪndli/ *adv* **1** in a kind way **2** (showing annoyance) please **3 take kindly to** accept willingly ♦ *adj fml* kind

kin·dred /'kɪndrɪd/ *adj* **1** related **2 kindred spirit** person with almost the same habits, interests, etc.

ki·net·ic /kɪ'netɪk, kaɪ-/ *adj fml* of or about movement

king /kɪŋ/ *n* **1** (title of) the male ruler of a country **2** most important man or animal **3** playing card with a picture of a king

king·dom /'kɪŋdəm/ *n* **1** country governed by a king or queen **2** any of the three divisions of natural objects: *the animal/plant/mineral kingdom*

king·fish·er /'kɪŋ,fɪʃə ‖ -ər/ *n* brightly coloured bird that lives near rivers

king-size /'· ·/ *adj* above the standard size

kink /kɪŋk/ *n* **1** twist in hair, a pipe, etc. **2** strangeness of character ~**y** *adj* sexually unnatural

kins·man /'kɪnzmən/ **kins·wom·an** /-,wʊmən/ *fem.* — *n* **-men** /-mən/ *fml* relative

ki·osk /'kiːɒsk ‖ -ɑːsk/ *n* **1** small open hut for selling newspapers, etc. **2** *BrE fml* public telephone box

kip /kɪp/ *vi* **-pp-** *BrE sl* sleep **kip** *n* [S;U]

kip·per /'kɪpə ‖ -ər/ *n* salted HERRING treated with smoke

kiss /kɪs/ *vi/t* touch with the lips as a sign of love or a greeting **kiss** *n* act of kissing

kiss of death /,· · '·/ *n* [*the*+S] *infml* something that makes failure certain

kiss of life /,· · '·/ *n* [*the*+S] *esp. BrE* method of preventing death of a person by breathing into his/her mouth

kit¹ /kɪt/ *n* **1** necessary clothes, tools, etc.: *a sailor's/carpenter's kit* **2** set of pieces to be put together: *model aircraft kit*

kit² *v* **-tt- kit out/up** *phr vt* supply with necessary clothes, etc.

kit bag /'· ·/ *n* bag for carrying a soldier's or sailor's kit

kitch·en /'kɪtʃən/ *n* room for cooking in

kitch·en·ette /,kɪtʃɪ'net/ *n* very small kitchen

kite /kaɪt/ *n* **1** frame covered with paper or cloth, for flying in the air **2** kind of HAWK¹ (1)

kith and kin /,kɪθ ən 'kɪn/ *n* one's friends and relatives

kitsch /kɪtʃ/ *n* objects, works of literature which pretend to be art but are considered silly, funny, or worthless

kit·ten /'kɪtn/ *n* **1** young cat **2 have kittens** *BrE infml* be in a very nervous anxious condition

kit·ty /'kɪti/ *n* money collected by several people for an agreed purpose

ki·wi /'kiːwiː/ *n* **1** flightless New Zealand bird **2** *infml* New Zealander **3** also **kiwi fruit** *n* [C;U] small green fruit with rough brown skin

Kleen·ex /'kli:neks/ n [C;U] tdmk paper handkerchief

klep·to·ma·ni·a /ˌkleptə'meiniə/ n [U] disease of the mind that makes one steal **-ac** /-niæk/ n person with kleptomania

klutz /klʌts/ n esp. AmE infml CLUMSY (1) person **~y** adj

km written abbrev. for: kilometre(s)

knack /næk/ n infml special skill

knack·ered /'nækəd‖-ərd/ adj BrE sl very tired

knead /ni:d/ vt mix (flour and water, etc.) by pressing with the hands **2** press and rub (muscles) to cure pain, stiffness, etc.

knee /ni:/ n **1** middle joint of the leg **2** part of a pair of trousers, etc. that covers the knee **3 bring someone to his knees** defeat someone completely ♦ vt hit with the knee

knee·cap¹ /'ni:kæp/ n bone at the front of the knee

kneecap² vt **-pp-** shoot the kneecaps of (someone), usu. as an unofficial punishment

knee-deep /ˌ· '·◂/ adj deep enough to reach the knees: (fig.) knee-deep in debt (=in trouble over debt)

knee-jerk /'· ·/ adj derog (of opinion) held without thought

kneel /ni:l/ vi knelt /nelt/ or (esp. AmE) kneeled go down on one's knees

knell /nel/ n sound of a bell rung slowly for a death

knew /nju:‖nu:/ v past t. of KNOW¹

knick·ers /'nɪkəz‖-ərz/ n [P] BrE women's UNDERPANTS

knick-knack /'nɪk næk/ n small decorative object

knife /naif/ n knives /naivz/ **1** blade with a handle, for cutting **2 have/get one's knife into someone** treat someone as an enemy and try to harm them ♦ vt wound with a knife

knife-edge /'· ·/ n **1** something sharp and narrow **2 on a knife-edge** in an extremely uncertain position

knight /nait/ n **1** (in former times) noble soldier **2** man who has been given the British title SIR **3** piece in chess **~hood** n [C;U] rank of a knight ♦ vt make (someone) a KNIGHT (2)

knit /nit/ vi/t knitted or knit **1** make (clothes, etc.) by forming a network of threads with long needles **(knitting needles) 2** join closely; grow together **~ting** n something being knitted

knit·wear /'nit-weə‖-wer/ n [U] knitted clothing

knives /naivz/ n pl. of KNIFE

knob /nɒb‖na:b/ n **1** round handle or control button **2** round lump: knob of butter

knob·bly /'nɒbli‖'na:-/ BrE ‖ **knob·by** /'nɒbi‖'na:-/ AmE — adj having KNOBS (2): knobbly knees

knock¹ /nɒk‖na:k/ v **1** vi/t hit: knock on the door **2** vt sl say bad things about **3** (of a car engine) make a noise like hitting **4 knock spots off** BrE infml defeat easily

knock about/around /ˌ· '·/ **1** vi/t be present or active (in) **2** vt treat roughly **3** infml travel continuously **4** infml be seen in public (with someone); have a relationship (with someone)

knock back phr vt **1** drink quickly **2** shock

knock down phr vt **1** destroy (a building) with blows **2** strike to the ground: knocked down by a bus **3** reduce (a price)

knock off phr v **1** vi/t stop (work) **2** vt take from a total payment: knock £2 off the price **3** vt sl steal **4** vt finish quickly **5** vt sl murder

knock out phr vt **1** make unconscious by hitting **2** (of a drug) make (someone) go to sleep **3** cause someone to be dismissed from a competition **4** sl fill with great admiration

knock up phr v **1** vt BrE make quickly **2** vt BrE awaken by knocking **3** vt AmE sl make PREGNANT **4** vi BrE practice before beginning a real game

knock² n **1** sound of knocking **2** infml piece of bad luck

knock·down /'nɒkdaun‖'na:k-/ adj (of a price) the lowest possible

knock·er /'nɒkə‖'na:kər/ n instrument fixed to a door, for knocking

knock-kneed /ˌ· '·◂‖·ˈ·/ adj with knees that touch when walking

knock-on /'· ·/ adj marked by a set of events, actions, etc. each of which is caused by the one before: price rises which will have a knock-on effect throughout the economy

knock·out /'nɒk-aut‖'na:k-/ n **1** also KO — act of knocking a BOXER unconscious **2** competition from which losers are dismissed **3** person or thing causing admiration ♦ *adj infml* causing great admiration

knoll /nəʊl ‖ noʊl/ *n* small round hill

knot /nɒt ‖ nɑːt/ *n* 1 fastening made by tying rope, etc. 2 hard lump in wood, etc. 3 small group of people 4 a measure of the speed of a ship, about 1853 metres per hour 4 **get tied (up) into knots (over)** become confused (about) ♦ *vt* **-tt-** make a knot in; join with a knot ~**ty** *adj* 1 (of wood) with KNOTS (2) 2 difficult: *knotty problem*

know[1] /nəʊ ‖ noʊ/ *v* **knew** /njuː ‖ nuː/, **known** /nəʊn ‖ noʊn/ 1 *vi/t* have (information) in the mind 2 *vt* have learnt 3 *vt* be familiar with: *Do you know Paris well?* 4 *vt* be able to recognize: *You'll know him by his red hair.* 5 [*only in past and perfect tenses*] see, hear, etc.: *I've known him to run 10 miles before breakfast.* —see also **let someone know** (LET)

know apart *phr vt* be able to tell the difference between

know backwards *phr vt* know or understand perfectly

know of *phr vt* have heard of or about: *I know of him, but I've never met him.*

know[2] *n* **in the know** well-informed

know-all /ˈ· ·/ *n* person who behaves as if he/she knew everything

know-how /ˈ· ·/ *n* [U] practical ability

know·ing /ˈnəʊɪŋ ‖ ˈnoʊ-/ *adj* having secret understanding ~**ly** *adv* 1 in a knowing way 2 intentionally

knowl·edge /ˈnɒlɪdʒ ‖ ˈnɑː-/ *n* [S;U] 1 understanding 2 learning 3 information about something 4 **to the best of one's knowledge** so far as one knows —see also WORKING KNOWLEDGE

knowl·edge·a·ble /ˈnɒlɪdʒəbəl ‖ ˈnɑː-/ *adj* well-informed

known[1] /nəʊn ‖ noʊn/ *past p. of* KNOW[1]

known[2] *adj* 1 publicly recognized: *known criminals* 2 **known as:** a generally recognized as b also publicly called

knuck·le[1] /ˈnʌkəl/ *n* 1 finger joint 2 **near the knuckle** *infml* almost improper

knuckle[2] *v*

knuckle down *phr vi* start working hard

knuckle under *phr vi* be forced to accept the orders of someone more powerful

ko·a·la /kəʊˈɑːlə ‖ koʊ-/ *n* type of small Australian animal like a bear

kook·y /ˈkuːki/ *adj AmE infml* behaving in a silly unusual manner

Ko·ran /kɔːˈrɑːn, kə- ‖ kəˈræn, -ˈrɑːn/ *n* [*the*] the holy book of the Muslims

ko·sher /ˈkəʊʃə ‖ ˈkoʊʃər/ *adj* 1 (of food) prepared according to Jewish law 2 *infml* honest and trustworthy

kow·tow /ˌkaʊˈtaʊ/ *vi* obey without question

kph *written abbrev. for:* kilometres per hour

Krem·lin /ˈkremlɪn/ *n* (buildings containing) the government of Russia or of the former Soviet Union

ku·dos /ˈkjuːdɒs ‖ ˈkuːdɑːs/ *n* [U] public admiration and glory (for something done)

kung fu /ˌkʌŋ ˈfuː/ *n* [U] Chinese style of fighting, like KARATE

kw *written abbrev. for:* KILOWATT(s)

L

L, l /el/ the 12th letter of the English alphabet

l *written abbrev. for:* 1 litre(s) 2 line 3 (*often cap.*) lake

lab /læb/ *n* laboratory

Lab *written abbrev. for:* LABOUR PARTY

la·bel /ˈleɪbəl/ *n* piece of paper, etc. fixed to something to say what it is, who owns it, etc. ♦ *vt* **-ll-** *BrE* ‖ **-l-** *AmE* 1 fix a label on 2 describe as: *They labelled him a thief.*

la·bor·a·tory /ləˈbɒrətri ‖ ˈlæbrətɔːri/ *n* building or room where a scientist works

la·bo·ri·ous /ləˈbɔːriəs/ *adj* needing great effort ~**ly** *adv*

la·bour[1] *BrE* ‖ **labor** *AmE* /ˈleɪbə ‖ -ər/ *n* 1 [U] hard work 2 [U] workers as a group 3 [S;U] act of giving birth ♦ *adj* (*cap.*) of the LABOUR Party ~**er** *n* man who does heavy unskilled work

labour under *phr vt* suffer from: *labour under a delusion*

labour² _BrE_ ‖ **labor** _AmE_ v **1** _vi_ work hard **2** _vt_ work something out in too great detail: _labour the point_

labour camp _BrE_ ‖ **labor camp** _AmE_ /'·· ·/ _n_ prison where prisoners do hard physical work

Labour Par·ty /'·· ,·/ _n_ [_the_] political party in favour of social improvement for esp. workers and less wealthy people

la·bra·dor /'læbrədɔː ‖ -ɔːr/ _n_ large black or golden dog

lab·y·rinth /'læbərɪnθ/ _n_ MAZE

lace /leɪs/ _n_ **1** [U] netlike decorative cloth **2** [C] cord for fastening shoes, etc. ♦ _vt_ **1** fasten with a lace **2** make (a drink) stronger by adding alcohol **lacy** _adj_ like LACE (1)

la·ce·rate /'læsəreɪt/ _vt fml_ cut; wound –ration /,læsə'reɪʃən/ _n_ [C;U]

lack /læk/ _vt_ be without (enough of) ♦ _n_ [S;U] absence; need ~**ing** _adj_ **1** missing **2 be lacking in** without the usual or needed amount of

lack·a·dai·si·cal /,lækə'deɪzɪkəl/ _adj_ without enough effort; careless

lack·ey /'læki/ _n derog_ person who obeys without question

lack·lus·tre _BrE_ ‖ **-ter** _AmE_ /'læk,lʌstə ‖ -ər/ _adj_ lifeless; dull

la·con·ic /lə'kɒnɪk ‖ -'kɑː-/ _adj fml_ using few words ~**ally** /-kli/ _adv_

lac·quer /'lækə ‖ -ər/ _n_ [U] transparent substance that makes a hard shiny surface, or keeps hair in place ♦ _vt_ cover with lacquer

lad /læd/ _n_ **1** boy; youth **2** _infml_ playfully rude man: _a bit of a lad_ **lads** _n_ [_the_+P] _BrE infml_ group of men one knows and likes

lad·der /'lædə ‖ -ər/ _n_ **1** frame with steps for climbing: (fig.) _the promotion ladder_ **2** _BrE_ ladder-shaped fault in a STOCKING, etc. ♦ _vi/t_ develop a LADDER (2) (in)

la·den /'leɪdn/ _adj_ heavily loaded: (fig.) _laden with sorrow_

la·dle /'leɪdl/ _n_ large spoon for serving liquids ♦ _vt_ serve with a ladle
    ladle out _phr vt_ give out freely

la·dy /'leɪdi/ _n_ **1** woman **2** woman of good manners or high social rank **3** (_cap._) (title for) a woman of noble rank ~**like** _adj_ (of a woman) behaving like a LADY (1) ~**ship** _n_ (title for) a woman called LADY (3): _your ladyship_

la·dy·bird /'leɪdɪbɜːd ‖ -bɜːrd/ _BrE_ ‖ –**bug** /-bʌɡ/ _AmE_ – _n_ small red insect with black spots

lag¹ /læɡ/ _vi_ -**gg**- move too slowly: _lag behind the others_

lag² _vt_ -**gg**- cover (water pipes, etc.) to prevent heat loss ~**ging** _n_ [U] material for this

la·ger /'lɑːɡə ‖ -ər/ _n_ [U] light kind of beer

la·goon /lə'ɡuːn/ _n_ lake of sea water, (partly) separated from the sea

laid /leɪd/ _v_ past t. and p. of LAY²

laid-back /,· '·◄/ _adj infml_ cheerfully informal and unworried

lain /leɪn/ _v_ past p. of LIE²

lair /leə ‖ ler/ _n_ home of a wild animal

la·i·ty /'leɪɪti/ _n_ [P] LAY³ people

lake /leɪk/ _n_ large mass of water surrounded by land

lamb /læm/ _n_ **1** [C] young sheep **2** [U] its meat **3** [C] harmless gentle person ♦ _vi_ give birth to lambs

lam·baste /'læmbeɪst/ also **lam·bast** /-bæst/ _vt infml_ beat or attack fiercely

lame /leɪm/ _adj_ **1** unable to walk properly **2** (of excuses, etc.) weak ♦ _vt_ make lame ~**ly** _adv_ ~**ness** _n_ [U]

lame duck /,· '·◄/ _n_ **1** helpless person or business **2** _esp. AmE_ political official whose period in office will soon end

la·ment /lə'ment/ _vi/t_ **1** express grief or sorrow (for) **2 the late lamented** the recently dead (person) ♦ _n_ song, etc. expressing sorrow ~**able** /'læməntəbəl, lə'mentəbəl/ _adj fml_ **1** unsatisfactory **2** worthy of blame ~**ation** /,læmən'teɪʃən/ _n_ [C;U] _fml_

lam·i·nated /'læmɪneɪtɪd/ _adj_ made by joining thin sheets of a material

lamp /læmp/ _n_ **1** apparatus for giving light **2** apparatus for producing health-giving sorts of heat: _an INFRARED lamp_

lam·poon /læm'puːn/ _n_ written attack that makes someone look foolish ♦ _vt_

lamp·post /'læmp-pəʊst ‖ -poʊst/ _n_ post supporting a street lamp

lamp·shade /'læmpʃeɪd/ _n_ cover for a lamp

lance /lɑːns ‖ læns/ _n_ long spearlike weapon ♦ _vt_ cut open with a lancet

lan·cet /'lɑːnsɪt ‖ 'læn-/ _n_ doctor's knife for cutting flesh

land¹ /lænd/ _n_ **1** [U] solid dry part of the

Earth's surface **2** [C] country; nation **3** [U] earth for farming **4** [U] also **lands** *pl.* — ground owned as property **5 see how the land lies** try to discover the present state of affairs before taking action ~**ed** *adj* owning a lot of land

land² *v* **1** *vi/t* come or bring to land **2** *vi* succeed in getting: *land the top job*

land in *phr vt* bring (someone) into (an undesirable state or position): *Her resignation landed us in a real mess.*

land up *phr vt* reach the stated (often undesirable) state or position: *He landed up in prison.*

land with *phr vt* give (someone) (something unwanted): *I got landed with organizing the Christmas party.*

land·ing /ˈlændɪŋ/ *n* **1** level space at the top of a set of stairs **2** arrival on land: *crash landing* **3** place where people and goods are loaded, esp. from a ship

landing craft /ˈ·· ·/ *n* flat boat for landing soldiers and their vehicles on shore

landing gear /ˈ·· ·/ *n* [U] wheels and UNDERCARRIAGE of an aircraft

land·la·dy /ˈlænd,leɪdi/ *n* **1** woman **a** who runs a small hotel **b** from whom one rents a room **2** a female LANDLORD

land·locked /ˈlændlɒkt ‖ -lɑːkt/ *adj* surrounded by dry land

land·lord /ˈlændlɔːd ‖ -lɔːrd/ *n* **1** person from whom one rents land or buildings **2** man who owns or runs a pub, etc.

land·mark /ˈlændmɑːk ‖ -mɑːrk/ *n* **1** recognizable object from which one can tell one's position **2** important event, discovery, etc.

land·mine /ˈlændmaɪn/ *n* bomb placed under the ground

land·scape /ˈlændskeɪp/ *n* (picture of) country scenery ♦ *vt* make (land) into a garden

land·slide /ˈlændslaɪd/ *n* **1** sudden fall of earth and rocks **2** great success in an election

lane /leɪn/ *n* **1** narrow road **2** division of a wide road, to keep fast and slow vehicles apart **3** path used regularly by ships or aircraft **4** path marked for each competitor in a race

lan·guage /ˈlæŋgwɪdʒ/ *n* [C;U] **1** system of human expression by means of words: *the origins of language* **2** particular system

as used by a people or nation: *the English language* **3** system of signs: *computer languages* **4** particular style or manner of expression: *poetic language* **5** words and phrases considered shocking: *bad language*

language la·bor·a·tory /ˈ·· ·,···‖ ˈ·· ,··/ *n* room where foreign languages are taught using TAPE RECORDERs, etc.

lan·guid /ˈlæŋgwɪd/ *adj* lacking strength, will ~**ly** *adv*

lan·guish /ˈlæŋgwɪʃ/ *vi fml* **1** experience long suffering **2** become weak

lan·guor /ˈlæŋgə ‖ -ər/ *n* **1** tiredness of mind or body **2** pleasant or heavy stillness

lank /læŋk/ *adj* (of hair) straight and lifeless

lank·y /ˈlæŋki/ *adj* ungracefully tall and thin

la·no·lin /ˈlænəl-ɪn/ *n* [U] oily substance in wool, used in some COSMETICS

lan·tern /ˈlæntən ‖ -ərn/ *n* container round the flame of a light

lap¹ /læp/ *n* front of a seated person between the waist and the knees

lap² *v* -**pp**- **1** *vt* drink as a cat does **2** *vi* (of water) move with soft sounds ♦ *n* act or sound of lapping

lap³ *n* single journey round a racing track ♦ *vt* -**pp**- **1** pass (another racer) so as to be one lap ahead **2** race completely round the track

la·pel /ləˈpel/ *n* part of the front of a coat that is joined to the collar and folded back

lapse /læps/ *n* **1** small fault or mistake **2** failure in correct behaviour, belief, etc. **3** passing away of time ♦ *vi* **1** sink gradually: *lapse into silence* **2** (of time) pass **3** (of business agreements, etc.) come to an end **lapsed** *adj* **1** no longer practising, esp. one's religion **2** *law* no longer in use

lap·top /ˈlæptɒp ‖ -tɑːp/ *n* small computer that can be carried around

lard /lɑːd ‖ lɑːrd/ *n* [U] pig's fat used in cooking ♦ *vt* **1** put lard on **2** use lots of noticeable phrases in one's speech or writing

lar·der /ˈlɑːdə ‖ ˈlɑːrdər/ *n* storeroom or cupboard for food

large /lɑːdʒ ‖ lɑːrdʒ/ *adj* **1** big **2 at large**: **a** free **b** as a whole: *the country at large* ~**ly** *adv* mostly

lar·gesse /lɑːˈʒes ‖ lɑːrˈdʒes/ *n* [U] money given generously

lark[1] /lɑːk ‖ lɑːrk/ *n* bit of fun; joke

lark[2] *v* **lark about/around** *phr vi* play rather wildly

lar·va /'lɑːvə ‖ 'lɑːrvə/ *n* **-vae** /-viː/ wormlike young of an insect

lar·yn·gi·tis /ˌlærən'dʒaɪtɪs/ *n* [U] painful swelling of the larynx

lar·ynx /'lærɪŋks/ *n* hollow boxlike part in the throat, where voice is produced by the VOCAL CORDS

la·sa·gne *BrE* lasagna /lə'sænjə, -'zæn- ‖ -'zɑːn-/ *AmE* — *n* [C;U] flat pieces of PASTA baked with sauce

las·civ·i·ous /lə'sɪviəs/ *adj* causing, showing, or feeling uncontrolled sexual desire ~**ly** *adv*

la·ser /'leɪzə ‖ -ər/ *n* (apparatus producing) a strong narrow beam of light: *laser surgery*

lash[1] /læʃ/ *v* **1** *vi/t* whip **2** *vi/t* move about violently **3** *vt* tie firmly

lash out *phr vi* **1** attack violently **2** give out (esp. money) in large quantities: *We lashed out on a new car.*

lash[2] *n* **1** (a hit with) the thin striking part of a whip: (fig.) *the lash of the waves* **2** EYELASH

lass /læs/ *n* girl

las·si·tude /'læsɪtjuːd ‖ -tjuːd, -tuːd/ *n* [U] *fml* tiredness

las·so /lə'suː, 'læsəʊ ‖ -soʊ/ *n* **-s** rope for catching horses and cattle ♦ *vt* catch with a lasso

last[1] /lɑːst ‖ læst/ *determiner, adv* **1** after the others / only remaining: *my last £5* **3** most recent(ly): *When did we last meet?* **4** least suitable or likely: *He's the last person I'd have expected to see here.* **5** every last every, not leaving out any ♦ *n, pron* [(*the*) S] **1** person or thing after all others: *the last to leave* **2** the only remaining: *the last of the wine* **3** the one or ones before the present one: *the week before last* (=two weeks ago) **4** at (long) last in the end ~**ly** *adv* in the end

last[2] *v* **1** *vi* continue **2** *vi/t* be enough (for): *The food will last (us) a week.* ~**ing** *adj* continuing for a long time

last-ditch /ˌ· '·◁/ *adj* done as one last effort before accepting defeat

last straw /ˌ· '·/ *n* [*the*+S] the difficulty, etc. that makes the total unbearable when it is added to one's present difficulties

last word /ˌ· '·/ *n* [*the*+S] **1** remark that ends an argument **2** most modern example of something

latch[1] /lætʃ/ *n* **1** small bar for fastening a door, gate, window, etc. **2** spring lock for a house door which can be opened from outside with a key

latch[2] *vt*

latch on *phr vi* understand

latch onto *phr vt* **1** LATCH on **2** refuse to leave (someone)

late /leɪt/ *adj, adv* **1** after the usual time: *The train was late.* **2** near the end: *in late September* **3** recently dead: *his late wife* **4** recent: *the latest fashions* | *Have you heard the latest?* (=most recent news) **5** at the latest and not later **6** of late lately ~**ly** *adv* not long ago

la·tent /'leɪtənt/ *adj* existing but not yet noticeable or developed: *latent talent* **latency** *n* [U]

lat·e·ral /'lætərəl/ *adj* of, from, or to the side ~**ly** *adv*

lateral thinking /ˌ··· '··/ *n* [U] making of unusual connections in the mind to find a new and clever answer to a problem

la·tex /'leɪteks/ *n* [U] liquid from which natural rubber is made

lathe /leɪð/ *n* machine that turns a piece of wood or metal to be shaped

la·ther /'lɑːðə ‖ 'læðər/ *n* [S;U] **1** FROTH made with soap and water **2** in a lather *infml* worried ♦ *v* **1** *vi* make a lather **2** *vt* cover with lather

Lat·in /'lætɪn ‖ lætn/ *n, adj* (of) the language of the ancient Romans

Latin A·mer·i·can /ˌ··· ·'···◁/ *adj* of the Spanish- or Portuguese-speaking countries of Central and S America

lat·i·tude /'lætɪtjuːd ‖ -tuːd/ *n* [S;U] **1** distance north or south of the EQUATOR, measured in degrees **2** freedom of choice **latitudes** *n* [P] area at a particular latitude

la·trine /lə'triːn/ *n* outdoor TOILET in a camp, etc.

lat·ter /'lætə ‖ -ər/ *adj* of a later period: *his latter years* ♦ *n fml* second of two things mentioned ~**ly** *adv* recently

latter-day /'··· ·/ *adj* modern

lat·tice /'lætɪs/ *n* wooden or metal frame used as a fence, etc.

laud /lɔːd ‖ lɔːd/ *vt lit* praise ~**able** *adj* deserving praise

laugh /lɑːf ‖ læf/ vi 1 express amusement, happiness, etc. by breathing out forcefully so that one makes sounds with the voice, usu. while smiling 2 **no laughing matter** serious ♦ n 1 act or sound of laughing 2 something done for a joke 3 **have the last laugh** win after earlier defeats 4 **laugh up one's sleeve** infml laugh secretly and often unkindly –**able** adj foolish

laugh·ing-stock /'·· ·/ n someone or something regarded as foolish

laugh·ter /'lɑːftə ‖ 'læftər/ n [U] laughing

launch /lɔːntʃ ‖ lɔːntʃ/ vt 1 send (a newly built boat) into the water 2 send (a ROCKET, etc.) into the sky 3 begin (an activity): launch an attack/a company ♦ n 1 act of launching 2 large motorboat ~**er** n

launch into phr vt begin with eagerness, force, etc.

launch out phr vi begin something new

launch·ing pad /'·· ·/ n base from which spacecraft, etc. are launched

laun·der /'lɔːndə ‖ 'lɔːndər/ 1 vt wash and iron (clothes) 2 make (money) seem to come from a legal origin

laun·derette /lɔːn'dret ‖ lɔːn-/ n place where the public pay to wash their clothes in machines

laun·dry /'lɔːndri ‖ 'lɔːn-/ n 1 [C] place where clothes are laundered 2 [U] clothes (needing to be) laundered

laur·e·ate /'lɔːriɪt/ adj —see POET LAUREATE

laur·el /'lɒrəl ‖ 'lɔː-, 'lɑː-/ n EVERGREEN bush with shiny leaves **laurels** n [P] 1 honour gained for something done 2 **rest on one's laurels** be satisfied with what one has done already, and not do any more 3 **look to one's laurels** guard against competition

la·va /'lɑːvə/ n [U] melted rock that flows from a VOLCANO

lav·a·to·ry /'lævətəri ‖ -tɔːri/ n TOILET

lav·en·der /'lævəndə ‖ -ər/ n [U] (pale purple colour of) a plant with strong-smelling flowers

lav·ish /'lævɪʃ/ adj 1 generous 2 given or produced in (too) great quantity: lavish praise ♦ vt give freely: She lavishes money on them. ~**ly** adv

law /lɔː ‖ lɒː/ n 1 [C] rule made by a government 2 [U] all these rules: Stealing is

against the law. 3 [C] statement of what always happens in certain conditions: the laws of physics 4 [the+S] infml police or a policeman 5 **be a law unto oneself** do exactly what one wishes 6 **law and order** respect for the law 7 **lay down the law** give an opinion in an unpleasant commanding manner ~**ful** adj allowed or recognized by law ~**fully** adv ~**less** adj not governed by laws ~**lessness** n [U]

law·a·bid·ing /'··,·/ adj obeying the law

lawn /lɔːn ‖ lɒːn/ n area of closely cut grass

law·suit /'lɔːsuːt, -sjuːt ‖ 'lɒːsuːt/ n non-criminal case in a law court

law·yer /'lɔːjə ‖ 'lɒːjər/ n person whose profession is the LAW (2)

lax /læks/ adj careless and uncontrolled ~**ity** n [C;U]

lax·a·tive /'læksətɪv/ n, adj (medicine) helping the bowels to empty

lay¹ /leɪ/ v past t. of LIE²

lay² v laid /leɪd/ 1 vt **a** put, esp. carefully, in a flat position: She laid his coat on the bed. **b** set in proper order or position: to lay bricks 2 vt arrange for use: lay the table for dinner 3 vt cause to settle or disappear: lay his fears to rest 4 vi/t of a bird, insect, etc.) produce (eggs) 5 vt make (a statement, claim, etc.) in a serious or official way: lay charges against someone 6 vt sl have sex with: He only goes to parties to **get laid**. 7 **lay hold of** catch and hold firmly 8 **lay waste** destroy completely

lay down phr vt 1 state firmly: lay down the law 2 give up (one's life) 3 store (esp. wine) for the future

lay in phr vt get and store a supply of

lay into phr vt attack with words or blows

lay low phr vt 1 knock down 2 make ill

lay off phr vt 1 stop employing 2 give up

lay on phr vt 1 provide: lay on lunch 2 **lay it on** tell something in a way that goes beyond the truth

lay out phr vt 1 arrange or plan: lay out a garden 2 knock (someone) down 3 spend (money)

lay up phr vt 1 keep in bed with an illness: laid up with flu 2 collect and store for future use

lay³ adj 1 of or by people who are not priests 2 not professional

lay·a·bout /ˈleɪəbaʊt/ n lazy person

lay-by /ˈ··/ n -bys BrE space next to a road where vehicles may park

lay·er /ˈleɪə‖-ər/ n 1 thickness of some substance laid over a surface: layers of rock 2 bird that lays eggs

lay·man /ˈleɪmən/ n -men /-mən/ LAY³ person

lay-off /ˈ· ·/ n stopping of a worker's employment

lay·out /ˈleɪaʊt/ n (planned) arrangement: the layout of the room

laze /leɪz/ vi rest lazily

la·zy /ˈleɪzi/ adj 1 avoiding work 2 spent in inactivity **lazily** adv **laziness** n [U]

la·zy·bones /ˈleɪzibəʊnz‖-boʊnz/ n lazy person

lb written abbrev. for: POUND¹ (1)

LCD /ˌel siː ˈdiː/ n abbrev. for: Liquid Crystal Display; part of an apparatus on which numbers, etc. are shown by passing an electric current through a special liquid

L-driver /ˈel ˌdraɪvə‖-ər/ n BrE person learning to drive

lead¹ /liːd/ v led /led/ 1 vi/t guide, esp. by going first 2 vi (of a road, etc.) go somewhere: (fig.) The plan led to trouble. 3 vt influence: What led you to do it? 4 vt control or govern: lead an army 5 vi/t be ahead (of) in sports 6 vt experience (a kind of life) 7 vi (of a newspaper) have as a main story **~ing** adj most important; chief

lead on phr vt influence (someone) to do something wrong or believe something untrue

lead up to phr vt be a preparation for

lead² /liːd/ n 1 [C] guiding suggestion 2 [S] a chief or front position b distance by which one competitor is ahead 3 [C] (person playing) the chief acting part in a play or film 4 [C] main or most important article in a newspaper 5 [C] chain, etc. for leading a dog 6 [C] wire carrying electrical power

lead³ /led/ n 1 [U] heavy greyish metal used for water pipes, etc. 2 [C;U] (stick of) GRAPHITE used in pencils

lead·en /ˈledn/ adj 1 dull grey 2 heavy and sad

lead·er /ˈliːdə‖-ər/ n 1 person who leads 2 BrE for EDITORIAL **~ship** n [U] position or qualities of a leader

leading ar·ti·cle /ˌliːdɪŋ ˈɑːtɪk əl‖-ˈɑːr-/ n BrE for EDITORIAL

leading light /ˌliːdɪŋ ˈlaɪt/ n person of importance

leading ques·tion /ˌliːdɪŋ ˈkwestʃən/ n question formed so as to suggest the answer

leaf¹ /liːf/ n leaves /liːvz/ 1 flat green part of a plant, joined to its stem 2 sheet of paper or metal 3 part of a tabletop that can be slid or folded out 4 **take a leaf out of someone's book** follow someone's example 5 **turn over a new leaf** begin a new course of improved behaviour, habits, etc. **~y** adj

leaf² v leaf through phr vt turn the pages (of a book, etc.) quickly without reading much

leaf·let /ˈliːflət/ n small sheet of printed matter ♦ v give out (political) leaflets

league /liːg/ n 1 group of people, countries, etc. joined together for a shared aim 2 group of sports clubs that play against each other 3 level of quality: They're not in the same league. 4 **in league (with)** working together secretly

leak /liːk/ n 1 accidental hole through which something flows 2 spreading of secret news: security leak ♦ v 1 vi/t (allow to) pass through a leak 2 vt make (secrets) publicly known **~y** adj

leak·age /ˈliːkɪdʒ/ n [C;U] process or amount of leaking

lean¹ /liːn/ v leant /lent/ or leaned 1 vi bend from an upright position 2 vi/t support or rest in a sloping position: lean a ladder against a tree 3 **lean over backwards** make every possible effort (to) **~ing** n tendency: have artistic leanings

lean on/upon phr vt 1 depend on 2 infml influence (someone) by threats

lean towards phr vt favour (a plan or opinion)

lean² adj 1 not fat 2 producing little profit: a lean year for business

leap /liːp/ v leapt /lept/ or leaped /lept‖ liːpt/ 1 jump 2 sudden increase in number, quantity, etc. 3 **by leaps and bounds** very quickly 4 **a leap in the dark** action or risk taken without knowing what will happen ♦ n sudden jump

leap·frog /ˈliːpfrɒg‖-frɔːg, -frɑːg/ n [U] game in which players jump over each other ♦ vi/t -gg- go ahead of (each other) in turn

leap year /ˈ· ·/ n a year, every fourth year, in which February has 29 days

learn /lɜːn ‖ lɜːrn/ *vi/t* **learned** *or* **learnt** /lɜːnt ‖ lɜːrnt/ **1** gain (knowledge or skill): *learn French* | *learn to swim* **2** fix in the memory: *learn a poem* **3** become informed (of): *learn of his success* ~**er** *n* ~**ing** *n* [U] knowledge gained by study ~**ed** /'lɜːnɪd ‖ 'lɜːr-/ *adj* having great knowledge

learning curve /'·· ‚·/ *n* [usu. S] **steep learning curve** period of learning a lot very quickly

lease /liːs/ *n* **1** contract for the use of a place in return for rent **2 a new lease of life** (*BrE*)/**on life** (*AmE*) new strength or desire to be happy, etc. ♦ *vt* give or take (a place) on a lease

lease·hold /'liːshəʊld ‖ -hoʊld/ *adj, adv* (of a place) held on a lease ~**er** *n* person who has a place on a lease

leash /liːʃ/ *n* LEAD³ (5)

least¹ /liːst/ *determiner, pron* **1** smallest number, amount, etc.: *Buy the one that costs (the) least.* **2 at least: a** not less than: *at least £100* **b** if nothing else: *At least it's legal.* **3 in the least** at all

least² *adv* (*superlative of* LITTLE) **1** less than anything else or than any others **2 not least** partly, and quite importantly

leath·er /'leðə ‖ -ər/ *n* preserved animal skin used for making shoes, etc. ~**y** *adj* stiff like leather

leave¹ /liːv/ *v* **left** /left/ **1** *vi/t* go away (from) **2** *vt* allow to remain: *leave the door open* | *Is there any coffee left?* **3** *vt* fail to take or bring: *I've left my coat behind.* **4** *vt* give by a WILL² (5) **5** *vt* allow something to be the responsibility of (someone) *I'll leave you to buy the tickets.* **6** *vt* have remaining in a sum: *2 from 8 leaves 6.* **7 leave go/hold of** stop holding **8 leave it at that** do or say no more **9 leave someone/something alone** stop behaving annoyingly in someone's presence or touching something **10 leave someone/something standing** *infml* be much better than someone or something **leaver** *n: school leavers*

    leave off *phr vi/t* stop (doing something)

    leave out *phr vt* not include

leave² *n* **1** [C;U] time spent away from work **2** [U] *fml* permission **3 take leave of** say goodbye to: *She must have taken leave of her senses.* (=gone mad)

leaves /liːvz/ *n pl. of* LEAF¹

lech·er·ous /'letʃərəs/ *adj derog* wanting continual sexual pleasure ~**ly** *adv*

lech·er·y /'letʃəri/ *n* [U] *derog* being lecherous

lec·tern /'lektən ‖ -ərn/ *n* sloping table to hold a book

lec·ture /'lektʃə ‖ -ər/ *n* **1** speech given as a method of teaching **2** long solemn scolding or warning ♦ *vi/t* give a lecture (to) ~**turer** *n* person who gives (university) lectures

led /led/ *v. past t. and p. of* LEAD¹

ledge /ledʒ/ *n* shelf sticking out from a wall, rock, etc.

ledg·er /'ledʒə ‖ -ər/ *n* account book of a business

lee /liː/ *n fml* shelter from the wind ♦ *adj* on the side away from the wind

leech /liːtʃ/ *n* **1** wormlike creature that sucks blood **2** person who makes profit from others

leek /liːk/ *n* vegetable with long fleshy stem and broad leaves that tastes slightly of onions

leer /lɪə ‖ lɪr/ *vi, n* (look with) an unpleasant smile

lee·ward /'liːwəd, *tech* 'luːəd ‖ -ərd/ *adj* **1** with or in the direction of the wind: *a leeward engine* **2** away from the wind: *the leeward side of the ship*

lee·way /'liːweɪ/ *n* additional time, money, etc., allowing the chance of success

left¹ /left/ *past t. and p. of* LEAVE¹

left² *adj* **1** on the side of the body that contains the heart **2** in the direction of one's left side **3** belonging to or favouring the LEFT³ (2) in politics

left³ *n* [U] **1** left side or direction **2** political parties that favour more change and more state control ♦ *adv* towards the left ~**ist** *n, adj* (a supporter) of the political left

left-hand /‚· '·◄/ *adj* on the left side ~**ed** *adj* using the left hand for most actions ~**er** *n* left-handed person

left·o·vers /'left‚əʊvəz ‖ -‚oʊvərz/ *n* [P] food remaining uneaten after a meal

left wing /‚· '·◄/ *n* [U] LEFT³ (2)

leg /leg/ *n* **1** limb that includes the foot, used for walking **2** part of a garment that covers this **3** support of a table, etc. **4** single stage of a journey **5 give someone a leg up** *BrE* help someone to climb onto something by supporting the lower part of their leg **6 not have a leg to stand on** have no good reason or excuse **7 on one's/its last legs: a** very tired **b** nearly worn out **c** nearly dead **8 pull someone's leg** make fun of a person in a playful way

leg·a·cy /'legəsi/ n **1** money, etc. left in someone's WILL **2** something left behind: *Disease is often a legacy of war.*

le·gal /'liːgəl/ adj of, allowed, or demanded by the law ~**ly** adv ~**ize**, ~**ise** vt make legal ~**ity** /liˈgælɪti/ n [U]

le·gal·ist·ic /ˌliːgəˈlɪstɪk◄/ adj derog placing too great an importance on keeping exactly to what the law says

legal ten·der /ˌ•• ˈ••/ n fml money that must by law be accepted in payment

le·gend /'ledʒənd/ n **1** [C] old story which may not be true **2** [U] such stories collectively **3** [C] famous person or act **4** [C] words that explain a picture, etc. in a book ~**ary** adj famous

leg·gings /'legɪŋz/ n [P] women's clothing that fits tightly around the legs

le·gi·ble /'ledʒəbəl/ adj that can be read easily –**bly** adv –**bility** /ˌledʒəˈbɪləti/ n [U]

le·gion /'liːdʒən/ n **1** division of an army, esp. in ancient Rome **2** large group of people ♦ adj fml very many ~**ary** n member of a legion (1)

le·gion·naire's dis·ease /ˌliːdʒəˈneəz dɪˌziːz‖-ˈnerz-/ n [U] serious infectious disease of the lungs

le·gis·late /'ledʒəsleɪt/ vi make laws –**lator** n –**lation** /ˌledʒəsˈleɪʃən/ n [U] **1** law or set of laws **2** act of making laws

le·gis·la·tive /'ledʒəslətɪv‖-leɪtɪv/ adj having the power and duty to make laws: *a legislative assembly*

le·gis·la·ture /'ledʒəsleɪtʃə, -lətʃ‖-ər/ n body of people who make the laws

le·git·i·mate /lɪˈdʒɪtəmət/ adj **1** legally correct **2** born of parents married to each other **3** reasonable: *legitimate conclusion* ~**ly** adv –**macy** n [U]

le·git·i·mize also –**mise** BrE /lɪˈdʒɪtəmaɪz/ also **le·git·i·ma·tize, -tise** BrE /lɪˈdʒɪtəmətaɪz/ vt **1** make legal; make acceptable **2** make (a child) legitimate

leg·less /'legləs/ adj infml, esp. BrE very drunk

lei·sure /'leʒə‖'liːʒər/ n [U] **1** free time **2 at one's leisure** at a convenient time

leisured adj **1** having leisure **2** leisurely

leisure cen·tre /'•• ˌ••/ n BrE place where one can swim, do exercise classes, etc.

lei·sure·ly /'leʒəli‖'liːʒərli/ adj unhurried

lem·on /'lemən/ n **1** [C] sour fruit with a hard yellow skin **2** [U] light bright yellow **3** [C] BrE sl foolish person **4** [C] sl something unsatisfactory or worthless

lem·on·ade /ˌleməˈneɪd◄/ n [U] **1** drink made of lemons, sugar, and water **2** BrE FIZZY drink tasting of lemons

lend /lend/ v lent /lent/ **1** vt/i give something for a limited time: *lend him £10 till tomorrow* **2** vt give; add: *The flags lent colour to the streets.* **3 lend a hand** give help **4 lend itself to** be suitable for ~**er** n

length /leŋθ/ n **1** [C;U] measurement of something from one end to the other, or of its longest side **2** [U] quality or condition of being long: *the length of the exam paper* **3** [C] distance from front to back of a horse or boat in a race: *win by 3 lengths* **4** [C] amount of time from beginning to end **5** [C] piece of something: *a length of string* **6 at length: a** in many words **b** fml finally **7 go to any/great lengths** be prepared to do anything ~**y** adj (too) long

length·en /'leŋθən/ vi/t make or become longer

length·ways /'leŋθweɪz/ also **length·wise** /-waɪz/ — adv in the direction of the longest side

le·ni·ent /'liːniənt/ adj not severe in judgment ~**ly** adv –**ence**, –**ency** n [U]

lens /lenz/ n **1** curved piece of glass in a camera, microscope, etc. **2** part of the eye that can FOCUS light **3** CONTACT LENS

lent /lent/ v past t. and p. of LEND

Lent n the 40 days before EASTER

len·til /'lentl/ n small beanlike seed used for food

leop·ard /'lepəd‖-ərd/ **leopardess** /'lepədes‖-pər-/ fem. — n large spotted catlike animal

le·o·tard /'liːətɑːd‖-ɑːrd/ n close fitting one-piece garment worn by dancers, etc.

lep·er /'lepə‖-ər/ n **1** person with leprosy **2** person avoided by other people for social or moral reasons

lep·ro·sy /'leprəsi/ n [U] disease in which the skin becomes rough, flesh and nerves are destroyed, and fingers, toes, etc. drop off

-rous *adj*

les·bi·an /'lezbɪən/ *adj, n* (of or being) a woman HOMOSEXUAL ~**ism** *n* [U]

le·sion /'liːʒən/ *n fml* wound

less[1] /les/ *determiner, pron,* (*comparative of* LITTLE) **1** smaller amount: *less noise* | *less than a mile* **2 less and less** (an amount) that continues to become smaller **3 less than no time** a very short time **4 none the less** but in spite of everything **5 think (the) less of** have a lower opinion of

less[2] *adv* **1** not so; to a smaller degree (than): *less cold* **2** not so much: *to work less* **3 less and less** increasingly rarely **4** much/still less and certainly not

less[3] *prep* but we subtract; MINUS: *I earned $100, less tax.*

less·en /'lesən/ *vi/t* make or become less

less·er /'lesə‖-ər/ *adj, adv* smaller: *the lesser of two evils*

les·son /'lesən/ *n* **1** (period of) teaching something in school, etc. **2** experience from which to learn: *The accident taught him a lesson.* **3** short piece read from the Bible

lest /lest/ *conj fml* for fear that

let /let/ *vt* let; *pres. p.* **letting 1** allow (to do or happen): *He let his beard grow.* **2** (the named person) must, should, or can: *Let each man decide for himself.* | (when suggesting a plan) *'Let's have a party!'* **3** give the use of (a place) for rent **4 let alone** and certainly not: *He can't walk, let alone run.* **5 let/leave go** stop holding **6 let oneself go: a** behave freely **b** stop taking care of one's appearance **7 let someone go:** a set someone free **b** dismiss someone from a job **8 let someone know** tell someone, esp. at a later date **9 let someone/ something alone** stop behaving annoyingly in someone's presence or touching something **10 let well (enough) alone** allow existing conditions to remain as they are, for fear of making things worse

let down *phr vt* **1** make (clothes) longer **2** disappoint

let in for *phr vt* cause (esp. oneself) to have (something unwanted)

let into/in on *phr vt* allow to share (a secret)

let off *phr vt* **1** excuse from punishment **2** explode; fire off *fireworks*

let on *phr vi* tell a secret

let out *phr vt* **1** give (a shout, etc.)

2 make (clothes) wider

let up *phr vi* lessen or stop

let·down /'letdaʊn/ *n* disappointment

le·thal /'liːθəl/ *adj* causing death

leth·ar·gy /'leθədʒi ‖-ər-/ *n* [U] tiredness and laziness **–gic** /lɪ'θɑːdʒɪk ‖-ɑːr-/ *adj*

let·ter /'letə ‖-ər/ *n* **1** [C] written message sent to someone **2** [C] sign representing a sound **3** [(the)S] actual words of something: *the letter of the law* ~**ing** *n* [U] style and size of written letters **letters** *n* [U] *fml* literature

let·ter·box /'letəbɒks ‖ 'letərbɑːks/ *n esp. BrE* **1** hole in a door for letters **2** box in a post office or street, in which letters may be posted

let·ter·head /'letəhed ‖-ər-/ *n* name and address printed at the top of the owner's writing paper

let·ting /'letɪŋ/ *n esp. BrE* house or flat to be rented

let·tuce /'letɪs/ *n* [C;U] green leafy vegetable, eaten raw

let·up /'letʌp/ *n* [C;U] lessening of activity

leu·ke·mia also **-kae-** *BrE* /luː'kiːmɪə/ *n* [U] serious disease in which the blood has too many white cells

lev·el[1] /'levəl/ *adj* **1** flat; HORIZONTAL **2** equal: *The teams finished level.* **3 (at) level pegging** *infml* having the same score **4 one's level best** all that one can do

level[2] *n* [C;U] **1** line or surface parallel with the ground; position of height in relation to a flat surface: *The garden is on two levels.* | (fig.) *The decision was taken at ministerial level.* **2** standard of quality or quantity: *increase production levels* **3 on the level** honest(ly)

level[3] *vt/i* **-ll-** *BrE* ‖ **-l-** *AmE* make or become level

level at/against *phr vt* **1** aim (a weapon) at **2** bring (a charge) against (someone)

level off/out *phr vi* stop rising or falling

level with *phr vt infml* speak truthfully to

level[4] *adv* so as to be level: *a missile flying level with the ground*

level cross·ing /ˌ·· '··/ *n BrE* place where a road and a railway cross, usu. protected by gates

level-head·ed /ˌ·· '··◂/ *adj* calm and sensible

le·ver /'liːvə ‖ 'levər, 'liː-/ *n* **1** bar that turns on its middle point, to lift things **2** rod that works a machine **3** something which may be used for influencing ♦ *vt* move with a lever: *Lever it into position.*

le·ver·age /'liːvərɪdʒ ‖ 'le-, 'liː-/ *n* [U] power of a lever: (fig.) *use political leverage*

lev·i·tate /'levɪteɪt/ *vi* rise into the air as if by magic –**tation** /ˌlevɪ'teɪʃən/ *n* [U]

lev·i·ty /'levɪti/ *n* [U] *fml* lack of proper seriousness

lev·y /'levi/ *vt* demand and collect (esp. taxes) officially

lewd /luːd/ *adj* sexually dirty: *lewd songs* ~**ly** *adv* ~**ness** *n* [U]

lex·i·cal /'leksɪkəl/ *adj* of words ~**ly** /-kli/ *adv*

lex·i·con /'leksɪkən ‖ -kɑːn, -kən/ *n* dictionary or wordlist

li·a·bil·i·ty /ˌlaɪə'bɪlɪti/ *n* **1** [U] condition of being liable **2** [C] debt that must be paid **3** [C] someone or something that limits one's activities or freedom

li·a·ble /'laɪəbəl/ *adj* **1** responsible in law **2** liable to have a tendency to

li·aise /li'eɪz/ *vi* form a LIAISON (1)

li·ai·son /li'eɪzən ‖ 'liːəzɑːn, li'eɪ-/ *n* **1** [S;U] working association between groups **2** [C] sexual relationship between an unmarried couple

li·ar /'laɪə ‖ -ər/ *n* person who tells lies

Lib *written abbrev. for:* LIBERAL PARTY

li·bel /'laɪbəl/ *n* [C;U] damaging written statement about someone ♦ *vt* **-ll-** *BrE* ‖ **-l-** *AmE* make a libel against ~**lous** *BrE* ‖ ~**ous** *AmE adj: a libellous remark*

lib·e·ral /'lɪbərəl/ *adj* **1** willing to respect the opinions of others **2** (of education) leading to wide general knowledge **3** given freely: *liberal supplies* **4** (*cap.*) of the LIBERAL PARTY ♦ *n* (*cap.*) member of the LIBERAL PARTY ~**ism** *n* [U] LIBERAL (1) opinions ~**ize**, ~**ise** *vt* remove limits on freedom: *liberalize the divorce laws* ~**ization**, ~**isation** /ˌlɪbərəlaɪ'zeɪʃən ‖ -rələ-/ *n*

Liberal Dem·o·crats /ˌ··· '···/ *n* [*the*] political party that favours liberal opinions, esp. a British party that has a position between the CONSERVATIVE PARTY and the LABOUR PARTY

lib·e·rate /'lɪbəreɪt/ *vt fml* set free –**rated** *adj* socially and sexually free –**rator** *n* –**ration** /ˌlɪbə'reɪʃən/ *n* [U]

lib·er·tar·i·an /ˌlɪbə'teəriən ‖ -bər'ter-/ *n* believer in freedom of thought ~**ism** *n* [U]

lib·er·ty /'lɪbəti ‖ -ər-/ *n* [U] **1** personal or political freedom **2** chance or permission to do or use something **3** **at liberty** free **4** **take liberties** behave too freely

li·bid·i·nous /lɪ'bɪdɪnəs/ *adj fml* LASCIVIOUS ~**ly** *adv*

li·bi·do /lɪ'biːdəʊ ‖-doʊ/ *n* **-dos** *tech* the sexual urge

li·brar·i·an /laɪ'breəriən ‖ -'brer-/ *n* person in charge of a library ~**ship** *n* [U]

li·bra·ry /'laɪbrəri, -bri ‖ -breri/ *n* (room or building with) a collection of books, records, etc.

lice /laɪs/ *n pl. of* LOUSE

li·cence usu. **license** *AmE* /'laɪsəns/ *n* **1** [C;U] (paper showing) official permission to do something **2** [U] *fml* uncontrolled freedom

li·cense also **licence** *AmE* /'laɪsəns/ *vt* give a LICENCE (1) to **licensee** /ˌlaɪsən'siː/ *n* person with a licence, esp. to sell alcohol

lick /lɪk/ *vt* **1** move the tongue across **2** (of flames or waves) pass lightly over **3** *infml* defeat ♦ *n* **1** [C] act of licking **2** [C] small amount (of paint, etc.) **3** [S] *BrE infml* speed

lic·o·rice /'lɪkərɪs, -rɪʃ/ *n* [U] LIQUORICE

lid /lɪd/ *n* **1** movable cover of a container **2** EYELID

li·do /'liːdəʊ, 'laɪ- ‖ 'liːdoʊ/ *n* **-dos** place for swimming and lying in the sun

lie¹ /laɪ/ *vi*, *n* **lied**, *pres. p.* **lying** (make) a false statement —see also WHITE LIE

lie² *vi* **lay** /leɪ/, **lain** /leɪn/, *pres. p.* **lying** /'laɪ-ɪŋ/ **1** be or remain in a flat position on a surface **2** be or remain in a particular position or state: *The town lies two miles to the east.* ‖ *The machinery was lying idle.* **3** be the responsibility of: *The decision lies with you.* **4** **lie low** be in hiding or avoid being noticed ♦ *n* [S] **1** way something lies **2** **the lie of the land** *BrE* **a** appearance, slope, etc. of a piece of land **b** the state of affairs at a particular time

  lie about *phr vi* be lazy; do nothing

  lie behind *phr vt* be the reason for

  lie down *phr vi* **1 lie down on the job** do work that is not good enough in quantity or quality **2 take something lying down**

suffer something bad without complaining or trying to stop it

lie in *phr vi* stay in bed late

lie de·tec·tor /'· ·,··/ *n* instrument that is said to show when someone is telling LIES¹

lie-down /'· ·/ *n BrE infml* a short rest

lie-in /'· ·/ *n infml, esp. BrE* a stay in bed later than usual in the morning

lieu /lju:, lu:‖lu:/ *n* **in lieu (of)** instead (of)

lieu·ten·ant /lef'tenənt‖lu:'ten-/ *n* officer of low rank in the armed forces

life /laɪf/ *n* **lives** /laɪvz/ **1** [U] active force that makes animals and plants different from stones or machines **2** [U] living things: *There is no life on the moon.* **3** [U] human existence: *Life is full of surprises.* **4** [C] period or way of being alive: *their busy lives* | (fig.) *during the life of this government* | (fig.) *The machine has a life of 10 years.* **5** [C] person: *No lives were lost.* **6** [U] activity; movement; strength: *full of life* **7** [U] existence as a collection of widely different experiences: *You see life in the navy.* **8** [U] also **life imprisonment** — punishment of being put in prison for a long time **9** [C] BIOGRAPHY **10** [*the*+S] person or thing that is the cause of enjoyment in a group: *the life and soul of the party* **11** [U] using a living person as the subject of a painting, etc.: *painted from life* **12 as large as life** unexpectedly but unmistakably the real person **13 come to life: a** regain one's senses after fainting **b** show or develop interest, excitement, etc. **14 for dear life** with the greatest effort **15 Not on your life!** Certainly not! **16 take one's life** kill oneself **17 take one's life in one's (own) hands** be in continual danger **18 take someone's life** kill them ~**less** *adj* **1** dead **2** not active; dull ~**lessly** *adv* ~**like** *adj* like a real person

life belt /'· ·/ *n* belt worn to keep a person from sinking in water

life·blood /'laɪfblʌd/ *n* [U] something that gives continuing strength

life·boat /'laɪfbəʊt‖-boʊt/ *n* boat for saving people in danger at sea

life buoy /'· ·/ *n* floating ring to hold onto in the water

life cy·cle /'· ,··/ *n* all the stages of development through which a creature passes during its life

life ex·pec·tan·cy /'· ·,···/ *n* [C;U] length of time someone is likely to live for

life·guard /'laɪfgɑːd‖-gɑːrd/ *n* swimmer employed to help other swimmers in danger

life jack·et /'· ,··/ *n* garment worn to support a person in water

life·line /'laɪflaɪn/ *n* **1** rope for saving life **2** something on which one's life depends

life·long /'laɪflɒŋ‖-lɔːŋ/ *adj* lasting all one's life

life of Ri·ley /,laɪf əv 'raɪli/ *n* [*the*+S] *infml* a very easy untroubled life

life-size, life-sized /'· ·/ *adj* (of a work of art) as big as what it represents

life·span /'laɪfspæn/ *n* length of a creature's life

life·style /'laɪfstaɪl/ *n* way of living

life·time /'laɪftaɪm/ *n* time during which someone is alive

lift¹ /lɪft/ *v* **1** *vt* raise to a higher level **2** *vt* improve: *lift my spirits* **3** *vi* (of clouds, etc.) disappear **4** *vt* bring to an end: *lift a ban* **5** *vt* steal

lift off *phr vi* (of an aircraft or spacecraft) leave the ground **lift-off** /'· ·/ *n*

lift² *n* **1** act of lifting **2** *BrE* apparatus in a building for taking people and goods from one floor to another **3** free ride in a vehicle **4** feeling of increased strength, higher spirits, etc.

lig·a·ment /'lɪgəmənt/ *n* band that joins bones together

lig·a·ture /'lɪgətʃə‖-ər/ *n* thread used for tying, esp. in medicine

light¹ /laɪt/ *n* **1** [U] force by which we see things: *sunlight* **2** [C] lamp, etc. that gives light **3** [C] (something that will make) a flame **4** [C] bright part of a painting, etc. **5** [S;U] brightness in the eyes **6** [C] way in which something is regarded: *see it in a different light* **7 bring/come to light** make or become known **8 in a good/bad light** in a favourable/unfavourable way **9 in the light of** taking into account **10 see the light: a** be born **b** be made public **c** understand or accept an idea or truth **11 throw/shed light on** explain

light² *v* **lit** /lɪt/ *or* **lighted 1** *vi/t* (cause to) start burning **2** *vt* give light to: *lighted streets* ~**ing** *n* system or quality of lights in a place

light up *phr v* **1** *vi/t* make or become bright **2** *vi* start smoking

light³ adj 1 not dark: a light room 2 pale: light green

light⁴ adj 1 not heavy 2 small in amount: light meals/traffic 3 easy to bear or do: light duties 4 gentle: light touch 5 quick and graceful 6 (of wine, etc.) not very strong 7 not serious: light reading 8 (of sleep) not deep 9 **make light of** treat as of little importance ♦ adv with few travelling cases or possessions: to travel light ~**ly** adv 1 gently 2 slightly 3 not seriously ~**ness** n [U]

light⁵ vt lit or lighted come down from flight and settle: (fig.) I finally lit on the idea of going to Paris.

light bulb /'· ·/ n BULB (2)

light·en /'laɪtn/ vi/t make or become a brighter b less heavy, or c more cheerful

light·er /'laɪtə/ -ər/ n instrument for lighting cigarettes, etc.

light-fin·gered /ˌ· '··◂/ adj infml having the habit of stealing small things

light-head·ed /ˌ· '··◂/ adj 1 unable to think clearly 2 not sensible

light-heart·ed /ˌ· '··◂/ adj cheerful

light·house /'laɪthaʊs/ n tower with a powerful light to guide ships

light·ning /'laɪtnɪŋ/ n [U] 1 electric flash of light in the sky 2 very quick, short, or sudden: a lightning visit

lightning con·duc·tor /'·· ·ˌ··/ n BrE wire leading from the top of a building to the ground, as a protection against lightning

light·weight /'laɪt-weɪt/ n 1 person or thing of less than average weight 2 someone who does not think deeply or seriously ♦ adj

light year /'· ·/ n 1 distance that light travels in a year 2 infml a very long time

li·ka·ble, **likeable** /'laɪkəbəl/ adj (esp. of people) pleasant

like¹ /laɪk/ vt 1 regard with pleasure or fondness 2 be willing (to): I don't like to ask. 3 (with **should** or **would**) wish or choose (to have): I'd like a boiled egg. | Would you like to read it? 4 **How do you like...?** (used when asking for an opinion) 5 **I'd like to...** I would be surprised/interested to 6 **I like that!** That's very annoying! 7 **if you like** if that is what you want **liking** n [S] 1 fondness 2 **to one's liking** which suits one's ideas or expectations **likes** n [P]

things that one likes

like² prep 1 in the same way as; similar to: Do it like this. 2 typical of: It's not like her to be late. 3 such as: Houses like that are expensive. 4 **something like** about ♦ n 1 something of the same kind: running, swimming, and the like 2 **the likes of** people or things of the stated type ♦ adj fml similar ♦ conj infml as: Make it like you make tea.

like·li·hood /'laɪklihʊd/ n [U] probability

like·ly /'laɪkli/ adj 1 probable 2 **(That's a) likely story!** infml (said to show that one disbelieves what someone has said) ♦ adv 1 **most/very likely** probably 2 **Not likely!** infml Certainly not!

like-mind·ed /ˌ· '··◂/ adj having the same ideas, interests, etc.

lik·en /'laɪkən/ v **liken to** phr vt to compare to

like·ness /'laɪknəs/ n [C;U] sameness in appearance: a family likeness

like·wise /'laɪk-waɪz/ adv similarly; also

li·lac /'laɪlək/ n 1 [C] bush with pinkish-purple or white flowers 2 [U] pinkish-purple

lilt /lɪlt/ n [S] pleasant pattern of rising and falling sound ~**ing** adj

lil·y /'lɪli/ n plant with large esp. white flowers: her lily-white skin

limb /lɪm/ n 1 leg, arm, or wing 2 branch of a tree 3 **out on a limb** alone without support 4 **tear limb from limb** tear (a person) apart

lim·bo /'lɪmbəʊ‖ -boʊ/ n [U] state of uncertainty

lime¹ /laɪm/ n [U] white substance used in making cement

lime² n tree with sweet-smelling yellow flowers

lime³ n sour fruit like a LEMON

lime·light /'laɪmlaɪt/ n [the+S] the centre of public attention

lim·e·rick /'lɪmərɪk/ n funny poem with five lines

lime·stone /'laɪmstəʊn‖ -stoʊn/ n [U] type of rock containing CALCIUM

lim·it /'lɪmɪt/ n 1 farthest point or edge 2 infml someone or something too bad to bear 3 **off limits** where one is not allowed to go 4 **within limits** up to a reasonable point —see also TIME LIMIT ♦ vt keep below a limit ~**ed** adj 1 small; having limits

2 (*abbrev.* **Ltd**) (of a British firm) having a reduced duty to pay back debts: *a limited company* ~**less** *adj* endless

lim·i·ta·tion /ˌlɪmɪˈteɪʃən/ *n* **1** [U] limiting **2** [C] condition that limits

lim·ou·sine /ˈlɪməziːn, ˌlɪməˈziːn/ *n* expensive car with the driver's seat separated from the back

limp¹ /lɪmp/ *vi, n* [S] (walk with) an uneven step

limp² *adj* lacking firmness; not stiff ~**ly** *adv*

lim·pet /ˈlɪmpɪt/ *n* kind of SHELLFISH that holds tightly to the rock: (fig.) *cling to him like a limpet*

lim·pid /ˈlɪmpɪd/ *adj lit* clear and transparent

linch·pin /ˈlɪntʃˌpɪn/ *n* person or thing that keeps something together

linc·tus /ˈlɪŋktəs/ *n* [U] *BrE* liquid cough medicine

line¹ /laɪn/ *n* **1** long narrow mark on a surface: *a line drawing* (=done with pen or pencil) **2** limit; border: *the finishing line in a race* —see also BOTTOM LINE **3** a row: *boys standing in (a) line* **b** row of words on a printed page: *The actor forgot his lines.* **4** row of military defences **5** a direction followed: *the line of fire* **6** piece of string, wire, etc.: *fishing line* **7** telephone connection: *Hold the line, please.* **8** railway **9** system of travel: *airline* **10** method of action: *new line of approach* | *You're on the right lines.* (=following the right method) **11** an official POLICY (1): *the party line* **12** trade or profession **13** family following one another: *line of kings* **14** a short letter **15** area of interest **16** type of goods: *a new line in hats* **17** in line for being considered for **18** in line with in accordance with **19** (step) out of line (act) differently from others or from what is expected **20** (reach) the end of the line (reach) the last stages, esp. a point of failure **21** read between the lines find hidden meanings

line² *vt* **1** mark with lines or WRINKLES: *lined paper* | *His face is very lined.* **2** form rows along: *crowds lining the streets*

line up *phr v* **1** *vi/t* form into a row **2** *vt* arrange (an event)

line³ *vt* **1** cover the inside of (something) with material: *fur-lined boots* **2** line one's pocket(s)/purse make money for oneself

lining *n* [C;U]: *brake linings*

lin·e·age /ˈlɪni-ɪdʒ/ *n* [C;U] *fml* line of descent from one person to another in a family

lin·e·ar /ˈlɪniə‖-ər/ *adj* **1** in lines **2** of length: *linear measurements*

lin·en /ˈlɪnɪn/ *n* [U] **1** cloth made from FLAX **2** sheets, tablecloths, etc.

lin·er /ˈlaɪnə‖-ər/ *n* **1** large passenger ship **2** something used to LINE³ something

lines·man /ˈlaɪnzmən/ *n* -men /-mən/ (in sport) official who says whether a ball has gone outside the limits

line-up /ˈlaɪn-ʌp/ *n* **1** collection of people, esp. side by side in a line **2** competitors in a race or game **3** set of events

lin·ger /ˈlɪŋgə‖-ər/ *vi* be slow to disappear; delay going: *lingering illness*

lin·ge·rie /ˈlænʒəri‖ˌlɑːnʒəˈreɪ, ˈlænʒəriː/ *n* [U] *fml* women's underclothes

lin·go /ˈlɪŋgəʊ‖-goʊ/ *n* -goes *sl* language

lin·guist /ˈlɪŋgwɪst/ *n* **1** person who studies and is good at foreign languages **2** person who studies language in general ~**ic** /lɪŋˈgwɪstɪk/ *adj* of language ~**ics** *n* [U] study of language

lin·i·ment /ˈlɪnɪmənt/ *n* [U] liquid for rubbing on stiff muscles

link /lɪŋk/ *n* **1** connection **2** one ring of a chain —see also LINKS ♦ *vt/i* join; connect

link·age /ˈlɪŋkɪdʒ/ *n* [C;U] system or way of connection

links /lɪŋks/ *n* links GOLF COURSE

li·no·le·um /lɪˈnəʊliəm‖-ˈnoʊ-/ also **li·no** /ˈlaɪnəʊ‖-noʊ/ *BrE* — *n* [U] smooth hard floor-covering

lint /lɪnt/ *n* [U] soft material for protecting wounds

li·on /ˈlaɪən/, **lioness** /ˈlaɪənes, -nɪs/ *fem.* — *n* **1** large yellow catlike animal **2** famous and important person: *a literary lion* **3** the lion's share the biggest part ~**ize**, ~**ise** *vt* treat (someone) as important

lip /lɪp/ *n* **1** edge of the mouth **2** edge of a cup, etc. —see also STIFF UPPER LIP

lip-read /ˈlɪp riːd/ *vi/t* understand speech by watching lip movements

lip ser·vice /ˈ· ˌ·/ *n* [U] pay lip service to support in words, but not in fact

lip·stick /ˈlɪpˌstɪk/ *n* [C;U] (stick of) coloured substance put on the lips

liq·ue·fy /ˈlɪkwɪfaɪ/ *vi/t fml* make or

become liquid –**faction** /ˌlɪkwəˈfækʃən/ n [U]

li·queur /lɪˈkjʊə‖lɪˈkɜːr/ n [C;U] strong sweet alcoholic drink

liq·uid /ˈlɪkwəd/ n [C;U] a substance which is not a solid or a gas, which flows freely and is wet ♦ adj 1 in the form of a liquid 2 clear and wet-looking 3 (of sounds) pure and flowing 4 easily exchanged for money: *liquid assets* ~**ize,** ~**ise** vt crush into juice ~**izer,** ~**iser** n BrE for BLENDER

liq·ui·date /ˈlɪkwədeɪt/ v 1 vt kill 2 vi/t arrange the end of (an unsuccessful company) –**dation** /ˌlɪkwəˈdeɪʃən/ n [U]

liq·uid·i·ty /lɪˈkwɪdəti/ n [U] 1 state of being liquid 2 state of having LIQUID (4) money

liq·uor /ˈlɪkə‖-ər/ n [U] alcoholic drink

liq·uo·rice /ˈlɪkərɪs, -rɪʃ/ n [U] black substance used in medicine and sweets

lisp /lɪsp/ vi pronounce /s/ to sound like /θ/ ♦ n [S]

list¹ /lɪst/ n set of things written in order: *shopping list* —see also HIT LIST ♦ vt put into a list –**ing** n (name on) a printed list

list² vi (of a ship) lean or slope to one side ♦ n

lis·ten /ˈlɪsən/ vi 1 give attention in hearing 2 **Don't listen to someone** Don't believe or do what someone says ~**er** n

listen in phr vt 1 listen to (a broadcast on) the radio 2 listen to other people's conversation when one should not

list·less /ˈlɪstləs/ adj tired and not interested ~**ly** adv ~**ness** n [U]

lit /lɪt/ v past t. and p. of LIGHT² or LIGHT⁵

lit·a·ny /ˈlɪtəni/ n form of long Christian prayer: (fig.) *a long litany of complaints*

li·ter /ˈliːtə‖-ər/ n AmE for LITRE

lit·e·ra·cy /ˈlɪtərəsi/ n [U] state or condition of being literate

lit·e·ral /ˈlɪtərəl/ adj 1 giving one word for each word: *a literal translation* 2 following the usual meaning of words ~**ly** adv 1 really 2 word by word

lit·e·ra·ry /ˈlɪtərəri‖ˈlɪtəreri/ adj of literature or writers

lit·e·rate /ˈlɪtərət/ adj 1 able to read and write 2 well-educated

lit·e·ra·ture /ˈlɪtərətʃə‖-tʃʊr/ n [U] 1 written works of artistic value 2 printed material giving information: *sales literature*

lithe /laɪð/ adj (of people or animals) able to bend easily

lith·o·graph /ˈlɪθəgrɑːf‖-græf/ n picture printed from stone or metal

lit·i·ga·tion /ˌlɪtɪˈɡeɪʃən/ n [U] fml process of taking action in law, in non-criminal matters

li·ti·gious /lɪˈtɪdʒəs/ adj often derog fond of litigation

lit·mus /ˈlɪtməs/ n [U] substance that turns red in acid and blue in ALKALI

li·tre BrE ‖ **-ter** AmE /ˈliːtə‖-ər/ n (a measure of liquid equal to) 1.76 PINTS

lit·ter /ˈlɪtə‖-ər/ n 1 [U] paper, etc. scattered untidily: *a litter bin* 2 [C] family of young animals ♦ vt scatter litter on

lit·tle¹ /ˈlɪtl/ adj 1 small: *little birds* 2 short: *a little while* 3 young 4 unimportant ♦ adv 1 not much: *little-known facts* 2 fml not at all: *They little thought that I was watching.*

little² determiner, pron, n less, least 1 [U] (without **a** or **only**) not much: *I have very little (money) left.* 2 [S] (with **a** or **the**) a small amount, but at least some: *a little milk* | *stay a little longer* 3 **little by little** gradually

lit·ur·gy /ˈlɪtədʒi‖-ər-/ n form of Christian worship –**gical** /lɪˈtɜːdʒɪkəl‖ -ɜːr-/ adj

live¹ /lɪv/ v 1 vi be alive 2 vi remain alive: *The doctor says he'll live.* 3 vi have one's home: *live in Paris* 4 vt lead (a kind of life) 5 **live and let live** be TOLERANT 6 **live it up** infml have a lot of fun

live down phr vt cause (a bad action) to be forgotten, by later good behaviour

live off phr vt 1 produce one's food or income from 2 get money for one's needs from

live on phr v 1 vt have as one's food or income 2 vi continue in life or use

live out phr v 1 vt live till the end of 2 vt experience in reality: *live out one's fantasies* 3 vi (esp. of a servant) live in a place away from one's place of work

live through phr vt remain alive during: *live through two world wars*

live together phr vi live as if married

live up to phr vt keep to the high standards of

live with phr vt 1 live as if married with 2 accept (an unpleasant thing)

live² /laɪv/ adj 1 alive 2 able to explode or shock: *live bomb/wire* 3 (of broadcasting) seen or heard as it happens

live·li·hood /'laɪvlihʊd/ n way one earns one's money

live·ly /'laɪvli/ adj 1 full of quick movement and thought 2 bright: *lively colours* –liness n [U]

liv·en /'laɪvən/ v liven up phr vi/t make or become lively

liv·er /'lɪvə ‖ -ər/ n 1 [C] organ in the body that cleans the blood 2 [U] animal's liver as food

liv·e·ry /'lɪvəri/ n uniform worn by servants, etc.

lives /laɪvz/ n pl. of LIFE

live·stock /'laɪvstɒk ‖ -stɑːk/ n [P] farm animals

live wire /ˌlaɪv 'waɪə ‖ -'waɪr/ n very active person

liv·id /'lɪvɪd/ adj 1 bluish-grey 2 very angry

liv·ing¹ /'lɪvɪŋ/ adj 1 alive still in use: *living language*

living² n 1 [S] LIVELIHOOD 2 [U] manner of life

living room /'···/ n main room for general use in a house

liz·ard /'lɪzəd ‖ -ərd/ n four-legged REPTILE with a long tail

ll written abbrev. for: lines

lla·ma /'lɑːmə/ n South American animal with thick woolly hair

load /ləʊd ‖ loʊd/ n 1 something being carried 2 a amount the stated vehicle can carry b weight borne by the frame of a building 3 amount of work to be done 4 a load off someone's mind the removing of a great worry 5 loads of infml a lot of ♦ v 1 vt/i put a load on or in 2 vt put a bullet, etc. into (a gun) or film into (a camera) –ed adj 1 containing a hidden trap: *a loaded question* 2 sl very rich 3 sl drunk

loaf¹ /ləʊf ‖ loʊf/ n loaves /ləʊvz ‖ loʊvz/ 1 [C] single mass of baked bread 2 [C;U] food prepared in a solid piece: *meat loaf* 3 [C] sl head: *Use your loaf!* (=think!)

loaf² vi waste time ~er n

loan /ləʊn ‖ loʊn/ n 1 something lent 2 amount of money lent 3 on loan being borrowed ♦ vt lend

loan shark /'· ·/ n money lender who charges very high INTEREST (5)

loath, loth /ləʊθ ‖ loʊθ/ adj unwilling

loathe /ləʊð ‖ loʊð/ vt hate very much

loathing n [S;U]

loath·some /'ləʊðsəm ‖ 'loʊð-/ adj DISGUSTING

loaves /ləʊvz ‖ loʊvz/ n pl. of LOAF

lob /lɒb ‖ lɑːb/ vt -bb- send (a ball) in a high curve ♦ n lobbed ball

lob·by /'lɒbi ‖ 'lɑːbi/ n 1 hall or passage in a public building 2 group of people who try to influence those in power: *the clean-air lobby* ♦ vi/t 1 meet (a Member of Parliament) in order to persuade him/her to support one's actions, etc. 2 be publicly active in trying to bring about change ~ist n

lobe /ləʊb ‖ loʊb/ n 1 lower fleshy part of the ear 2 division of the brain or lungs

lob·ster /'lɒbstə ‖ 'lɑːbstər/ n 1 [C] eight-legged sea animal with CLAWS 2 [U] its meat as food

lo·cal /'ləʊkəl ‖ 'loʊ-/ adj 1 of a certain place: *our local doctor* 2 limited to one part: *local anaesthetic* ♦ n 1 person living in a place 2 BrE local pub ~ly adv

local au·thor·i·ty /ˌ··'···/ n BrE group of people elected or paid to the government of a particular area

lo·cal·i·ty /ləʊ'kælɪti ‖ loʊ-/ n fml place; area

lo·cal·ize also –ise /'ləʊkəlaɪz ‖ 'loʊ-/ vt keep inside a small area

lo·cate /ləʊ'keɪt ‖ 'loʊkeɪt/ vt fml 1 learn the position of 2 fix in a particular place: *offices located in the town centre* **location** /ləʊ'keɪʃən ‖ loʊ-/ n [C] position 2 [U] act of locating 3 on location in a town, country, etc. to make a film

loch /lɒx, lɒk ‖ lɑːk, lɑːx/ n ScotE lake

lock¹ /lɒk ‖ lɑːk/ n 1 apparatus for fastening a door, etc. 2 piece of water closed off by gates, so that the level can be raised or lowered 3 BrE amount that a STEERING WHEEL can be turned 4 lock, stock, and barrel completely

lock² v 1 vi/t fasten with a lock 2 vi become fixed or blocked

lock away phr vt keep safe or secret, as by putting in a locked place

lock in/out phr vt keep (a person or criminal) inside/outside a place by locking the door

lock onto phr vt (esp. of a MISSILE) find and follow (the object to be attacked) closely

lock up phr v 1 vi/t make (a building)

safe by locking the doors **2** *vt* put in a safe place and lock the door: *He should be locked up!* (=in prison)

lock³ *n* small piece of hair: *his curly locks*

lock·er /'lɒkə ‖ 'lɑːkər/ *n* small cupboard for clothes, etc., esp. at school, in a sports building, etc.

lock·et /'lɒkɪt ‖ 'lɑː-/ *n* case for a small picture, etc. worn on a chain round the neck

lo·co·mo·tion /ˌləʊkə'məʊʃən ‖ ˌloʊkə-'moʊ-/ *n* [U] movement from place to place

lo·co·mo·tive /ˌləʊkə'məʊtɪv ‖ ˌloʊkə-'moʊ-/ *adj* of movement ♦ *n fml* railway engine

lo·cum /'ləʊkəm ‖ 'loʊ-/ *n esp. BrE* doctor or priest doing the work of another who is away

lo·cust /'ləʊkəst ‖ 'loʊ-/ *n* large flying insect that destroys crops

lodge¹ /lɒdʒ ‖ lɑːdʒ/ *v* **1** *vi* stay somewhere and pay rent **2** *vi/t* (cause to) become fixed: *The chicken bone lodged in his throat.* **3** *vt* make (a report, etc.) officially: *lodge a complaint* **4** *vt* put in a safe place: *papers lodged with the bank* **lodger** *n* person who pays to live in someone's house

lodge² *n* **1** small house on the land of a larger one **2** house in wild country for hunters, etc.: *skiing lodge*

lodg·ing /'lɒdʒɪŋ ‖ 'lɑː-/ *n* [S;U] place to stay **lodgings** *n* [P] rented furnished rooms

loft /lɒft ‖ lɔːft/ *n* ATTIC

loft·y /'lɒfti ‖ 'lɔːfti/ *adj* **1** (of ideas, etc.) noble **2** proud **3** *lit* high **–ily** *adv*

log¹ /lɒg ‖ lɔːg, lɑːg/ *n* **1** thick piece of wood from a tree **2** official record of a journey **3 sleep like a log** sleep deeply without moving

log² *vt* **-gg-** record in a LOG¹ (2)

log in/on *phr vi* begin a period of using a computer system by performing a fixed set of operations

log off/out *phr vi* finish a period of using a computer system by performing a fixed set of operations

log·book /'lɒgbʊk ‖ 'lɔːg-, 'lɑːg-/ *n* **1** LOG¹ (2) **2** *BrE for* REGISTRATION DOCUMENT

log·ger·heads /'lɒgəhedz ‖ 'lɔːg-, 'lɑː-/ *n* **at loggerheads** always disagreeing

lo·gic /'lɒdʒɪk ‖ 'lɑː-/ *n* [U] **1** science of formal reasoning **2** good sense **–al** *adj* **~ally** /-kli/ *adv*

lo·gis·tics /lə'dʒɪstɪks ‖ loʊ-/ *n* [P]

detailed planning of an operation

log·o /'ləʊgəʊ ‖ 'loʊgoʊ/ *n* **-os** sign, pattern, etc. representing a business firm

loin /lɔɪn/ *n* [C;U] (piece of) meat from the lower part of an animal **loins** *n* [P] human body between the waist and legs

loin·cloth /'lɔɪnklɒθ ‖ -klɔːθ/ *n* cloth worn round the loins

loi·ter /'lɔɪtə ‖ -ər/ *vi* stand somewhere for no clear reason **~er** *n*

loll /lɒl ‖ lɑːl/ *vi* **1** lie lazily **2** (allow to) hang down loosely

lol·li·pop /'lɒlipɒp ‖ 'lɑːlipɑːp/ *n* hard sweet made of boiled sugar or frozen fruit juice on a stick

lol·ly /'lɒli ‖ 'lɑːli/ *n BrE* **1** [C] ICE LOLLY **2** [U] *sl* money

lone /ləʊn ‖ loʊn/ *adj fml* alone; single

lone·ly /'ləʊnli ‖ 'loʊn-/ *adj* **1** alone and unhappy **2** (of places) without people **–liness** *n* [U]

lon·er /'ləʊnə ‖ 'loʊnər/ *n* person who likes to be alone

lone·some /'ləʊnsəm ‖ 'loʊn-/ *adj* LONELY (1)

long¹ /lɒŋ ‖ lɔːŋ/ *adj* **1** large when measured from beginning to end: *long hair | a long time | 2 metres long* **2** (of a drink) cool, containing little or no alcohol, and served in a long glass **3 long on** with a lot of

long² *adv* **1** (for) a long time: *long ago | Will you be long?* **2 as/so long as** on condition that **3 no longer/(not) any longer** (not) any more **4 so long** goodbye for now ♦ *n* **1** a long time: *It won't take long.* **2 before long** soon **3 the long and (the) short of it** *infml* the general result, expressed in a few words

long³ *vi* wish very much: *longing to go* **~ing** *adj, n* [C;U] (showing) a strong wish **~ingly** *adv*

long for *phr vt* want very much

long-dis·tance /ˌ· '·◄/ *adj* covering a long distance ♦ *adv* to or from a distant point

lon·gev·i·ty /lɒn'dʒevɪti ‖ lɑːn-, lɔːn-/ *n* [U] *fml* long life

long·hand /'lɒŋhænd ‖ 'lɔːŋ-/ *n* [U] ordinary writing by hand

lon·gi·tude /'lɒndʒɪtjuːd ‖ 'lɑːndʒɪtuːd/ *n* [C;U] distance east or west of Greenwich, measured in degrees **–tudinal** /ˌlɒndʒɪ-**

'tʃuːdənəl◀‖ˌlɑːndʒəˈtuː-/ *adj* going along, not across

long jump /'· ·/ *n* [S] sport of jumping as far as possible along the ground

long-range /ˌ· '·◀/ *adj* covering a long distance or time

long shot /'· ·/ *n* something one tries although it is unlikely to succeed

long·sight·ed /ˌlɒŋˈsaɪtəd◀‖ˌlɔːŋ-/ *adj* able to see things only when they are far away

long-stand·ing /ˌ· '··◀/ *adj* having existed for a long time: *long-standing rivalry*

long-suf·fer·ing /ˌlɒŋˈsʌfərɪŋ◀‖ˌlɔːŋ-/ *adj* patient under continued difficulties

long-term /ˌ· '·◀/ *adj* for or in the distant future

long wave /ˌ· '·◀/ *n* [U] radio broadcasting on waves of more than 1000 metres

long-wind·ed /ˌlɒŋˈwɪndəd◀‖ˌlɔːŋ-/ *adj* saying too much; dull

loo /luː/ *n* **loos** *BrE infml for* TOILET

look¹ /lʊk/ *v* **1** *vi* use the eyes to see something **2** seem; appear: *You look tired.* **3** *vi* face: *The window looks east.* **4 look as if/like** seem probably: *It looks as if he's gone.* **5 (not) look oneself** (not) appear healthy **6 look well** *fml* be attractive

   look after *phr vt* take care of

   look ahead *phr vi* plan for the future

   look around/round *phr vi* search

   look at *phr vt* **1** watch **2** consider; examine **3 not much to look at** not attractive in appearance

   look back *phr vi* **1** remember **2 never look back** continue to succeed

   look down on *phr vt* DESPISE

   look for *phr vt* try to find

   look forward to *phr vt* expect to enjoy

   look in *phr vi infml* make a short visit

   look into *phr vt* examine; INVESTIGATE

   look on *phr v* **1** *vi* watch **2** *vt* regard as

   look out *phr vi* take care; keep watching

   look over *phr vt* examine quickly

   look round *phr vi/t* examine (a place)

   look through *phr vt* examine for points to be noted

   look to *phr vt* **1** depend on: *I look to you for support.* **2** pay attention to

   look up *phr v* **1** *vi* improve **2** *vt* find (information) in a book **3** *vt* find and visit

   look up to *phr vt* respect

look² *n* **1** act of looking **2** appearance **3 I don't like the look of it/the looks of this.** This (state of affairs, etc.) suggests something bad to me **looks** *n* [P] person's (attractive) appearance

look·a·like /'lʊkəlaɪk/ *n* (used to say that someone looks very similar to a famous person): *a Prince Charles lookalike*

look-in /'· ·/ *n* [S] chance to take part or succeed

look·out /'lʊk-aʊt/ *n* [S] **1** state of watching **2** person who keeps watch **3** one's personal problem: *It's your own lookout if you're caught.*

loom¹ /luːm/ *n* machine for weaving cloth

loom² *vi* appear in a threatening way: *Fear of failure loomed large in his life.*

loon·y /'luːni/ *n, adj sl* LUNATIC

loop /luːp/ *n* (shape of) a piece of string, etc. curved back on itself ♦ *vi/t* make (into) a loop

loop·hole /'luːphəʊl‖-hoʊl/ *n* way of escape: *loopholes in the tax laws*

loose /luːs/ *adj* **1** not firmly fixed: *a loose tooth* **2** free from control: *loose cattle* **3** not packed together: *loose biscuits* **4** (of clothes) too wide **5** not exact: *a loose translation* **6** without sexual morals: *loose living* **7 at a loose end** having nothing to do **8 cut loose** break away from a group or situation ~**ly** *adv*

loose end /ˌ· '·/ *n* [*usu. pl.*] **1** part not properly completed **2 at a loose end** *BrE ‖* **at loose ends** *AmE* having nothing to do

loos·en /'luːsən/ *vi/t* make or become looser

loot /luːt/ *n* [U] goods taken illegally by soldiers, etc. ♦ *vi/t* take loot (from) ~**er** *n*

lop /lɒp‖lɑːp/ *vt* **-pp-** cut (branches) from a tree

lop-sid·ed /ˌ· '··◀/ *adj* with one side lower than the other

loq·ua·cious /ləʊˈkweɪʃəs‖loʊ-/ *adj fml* talking a great deal ~**ly** *adv* ~**city** /-ˈkwæsəti/ *n* [U]

lord /lɔːd‖lɔːrd/ *n* **1** ruler; master **2** nobleman: *the Lords* (=members of the HOUSE OF LORDS) **3** (*cap.*) God **4** (*cap.*) (title for certain official people): *Lord Mayor* ~**ship** *n* (title for) a Lord: *your lordship*

lord·ly /'lɔːdli‖-ɔːr-/ *adj* proud; grand

lor·ry /'lɒri‖'lɔːri, 'lɑːri/ *n BrE* heavy

motor vehicle; TRUCK[1]

lose /luːz/ v lost /lɒst ‖ lɔːst/ 1 vt be unable to find: lose a book/one's way 2 vt have taken away: lose one's job 3 vi/t fail to win: lose a battle 4 vt have less of: lose weight/money 5 vi (of a clock) go too slowly 6 vt (cause to) fail to hear, see, or understand: You've lost me; could you explain that again? 7 lose oneself in something give all one's attention to something so as not to notice anything else 8 lose sight of forget loser n 1 person who loses 2 infml unsuccessful person

 lose out phr vi 1 make a loss 2 be defeated

loss /lɒs ‖ lɔːs/ n 1 [U] act of losing; failure to keep 2 [C] person, thing, or amount lost: The army suffered heavy losses. 3 [C] failure to make a profit 4 at a loss uncertain what to do or say 5 be a dead loss infml have no worth or value

lost /lɒst ‖ lɔːst/ v past t. and p. of LOSE

lost cause /ˌ· ˈ·/ n something which has no chance of success

lot[1] /lɒt ‖ lɑːt/ n 1 a great number or amount: a lot of people | lots (and lots) of money 2 group or amount: a new lot of students 3 a lot much: a lot better 4 a fat lot infml none at all 5 the lot the whole; all

lot[2] n 1 [C] article sold at an AUCTION 2 [C] esp. AmE piece of land 3 [C;U] (use of) different objects to make a decision by chance: choose the winner by lot 4 [S] fml one's fate 5 a bad lot a bad person

loth /ləʊθ ‖ loʊθ/ adj LOATH

lo·tion /ˈləʊʃən ‖ ˈloʊ-/ n [C;U] liquid mixture for the skin or hair to make it clean and healthy

lot·te·ry /ˈlɒtəri ‖ ˈlɑː-/ n system of giving prizes to people who bought numbered tickets, chosen by chance: (fig.) It's a lottery. (=a matter of chance)

loud /laʊd/ adj 1 producing a lot of sound 2 unpleasantly colourful ♦ adv in a loud way ~ly adv ~ness n [U]

loud·speak·er /ˌlaʊdˈspiːkə, ˈlaʊd-
ˌspiːkə ‖ -ər/ n piece of equipment that makes sound louder

lounge /laʊndʒ/ vi stand or sit lazily ♦ n comfortable room to sit in

lounge bar /ˈ· ·/ n BrE comfortably furnished room in a **pub**, with more expensive drinks than in the PUBLIC BAR

louse /laʊs/ n lice /laɪs/ 1 insect that lives on people's and animals' bodies 2 worthless person

lou·sy /ˈlaʊzi/ adj very bad: lousy weather

lout /laʊt/ n rough awkward man or boy ~ish adj

lov·a·ble /ˈlʌvəbəl/ adj deserving, causing, or worthy of love

love /lʌv/ n 1 [U] great fondness for someone 2 [S;U] warm interest: a love of music 3 [C] loved person or thing 4 [U] (in tennis) NIL 5 give/send someone one's love send friendly greetings 6 make love (to) have sex (with) 7 not for love or/nor money infml not by any means ♦ v 1 vi/t feel love (for) 2 vt like very much: I'd love a drink. loving adj fond

love af·fair /ˈ· ·ˌ·/ n sexual relationship: (fig.) a love affair with Russian literature (=a great interest and liking)

love·ly /ˈlʌvli/ adj 1 beautiful: lovely girl/view 2 very pleasant: lovely dinner

lov·er /ˈlʌvə ‖ -ər/ n 1 person who has a sexual relationship with another person 2 person who is fond of the stated thing: art lovers

love·sick /ˈlʌvˌsɪk/ adj sad because of unreturned love

low /ləʊ ‖ loʊ/ adj 1 not high: low wall/cost/standards 2 (of a supply) nearly finished 3 (of sounds) a deep b not loud 4 unhappy 5 not fair or honest: a low trick 6 for a slow speed: a low gear ♦ adv to or at a low level: bend low ♦ n low point or level

low·down /ˈləʊdaʊn ‖ ˈloʊ-/ n [S] sl the plain facts

low-down /ˈ··/ adj worthless; dishonourable

low·er[1] /ˈləʊə ‖ ˈloʊər/ adj at or nearer the bottom: the lower leg

lower[2] vt 1 make less high 2 lower oneself bring oneself down in people's opinion

low·er[3] /ˈlaʊə ‖ -ər/ vi 1 be dark and threatening 2 FROWN severely

lower class /ˌ·· ˈ·/ n social class of lowest rank **lower-class** adj

low-fat /ˌ· ˈ·/ adj (of foods) containing little fat

low-key /ˌ· ˈ·/ adj quiet and controlled

low-life /ˈləʊlaɪf ‖ ˈloʊ-/ n infml unpleasant person, esp. a criminal

low·lands /ˈləʊləndz ‖ ˈloʊ-/ n [P] land

low·ly /'ləʊli ‖ 'loʊ-/ adj low in rank;
HUMBLE **–liness** n [U]

loy·al /'lɔɪəl/ adj faithful to one's friends,
country, etc. **~ist** n person who remains
loyal to a ruler **~ly** adv

loy·al·ty /'lɔɪəlti/ n 1 [U] being loyal 2 [C
usu P] loyal feeling: *political loyalties*

loyalty card /'··· ·/ n card shown by a
regular customer in a store in order to
receive advantages

loz·enge /'lɒzɪndʒ ‖ 'lɑː-/ n medical
sweet: *cough lozenge*

LP /ˌel 'piː/ n record that plays for about 25
minutes each side

L-plate /'el pleɪt/ n letter L, fixed to a
British vehicle to show that the driver is a
learner

LSD /ˌel es 'diː/ n [U] illegal drug that
causes HALLUCINATIONS

Ltd written abbrev. for: LIMITED (2)

lu·bri·cant /'luːbrɪkənt/ n [C;U]
substance that lubricates; oil, etc.

lu·bri·cate /'luːbrɪkeɪt/ vt make
(machine parts) work without rubbing

lu·cid /'luːsɪd/ adj 1 easy to understand
2 able to think clearly **~ly** adv **~ity**
/luːˈsɪdɪti/ n [U]

luck /lʌk/ n [U] 1 what happens to
someone by chance 2 success: *wish them
luck* 3 **be down on one's luck** have bad
luck, esp. be without money 4 **be in/out of
luck** have/not have good fortune **~y** adj
having or bringing good fortune **~ily** adv

lu·cra·tive /'luːkrətɪv/ adj profitable

lud·dite /'lʌdaɪt/ n (often cap.) derog
someone who is opposed to change, esp. the
introduction of new work methods and
machinery

lu·di·crous /'luːdɪkrəs/ adj causing
laughter; foolish **~ly** adv

lug /lʌg/ vt **-gg-** pull or carry with
difficulty

lug·gage /'lʌgɪdʒ/ n [U] bags, etc. of a
traveller

lu·gu·bri·ous /luːˈguːbriəs/ adj fml
sorrowful **~ly** adv

luke·warm /ˌluːkˈwɔːm◂ ‖ -ˌɔːrm◂/ adj
1 (of liquid) neither warm nor cold 2 not
eager

lull /lʌl/ vt cause to rest ♦ n [S] calm period

lul·la·by /'lʌləbaɪ/ n song to make a child
go to sleep

lum·ba·go /lʌmˈbeɪgəʊ ‖ -goʊ/ n [U] pain
in the lower back

lum·ber[1] /'lʌmbə ‖ -ər/ v 1 vi move
heavily and awkwardly 2 vt give (someone)
an unwanted object or job

lumber[2] n 1 useless articles stored away
2 AmE for TIMBER

lu·mi·na·ry /'luːmɪnəri ‖ -neri/ n fml
famous respected person

lu·mi·nous /'luːmɪnəs/ adj shining in the
dark **–nosity** /ˌluːmɪˈnɒsɪti ‖ -'nɑː-/ n [U]

lump /lʌmp/ n 1 solid mass: *lump of
coal/sugar* 2 hard swelling 3 **lump in the
throat** tight sensation in the throat caused
by unexpressed pity, sorrow, etc. ♦ v **lump
it** accept bad conditions without complaint
~y adj: *lumpy sauce*

lump together phr vt consider (two or
more things) as a single unit

lump sum /ˌ· '·/ n money given as a single
payment rather than in parts

lu·na·cy /'luːnəsi/ n madness

lu·nar /'luːnə ‖ -ər/ adj of the moon

lu·na·tic /'luːnətɪk/ adj, n mad or foolish
(person)

lunch /lʌntʃ/ also **lunch·eon** fml
/'lʌntʃən/ n [C;U] meal eaten at about
midday ♦ vi

lung /lʌŋ/ n either of the two breathing
organs in the chest

lunge /lʌndʒ/ vi, n (make) a sudden
forward movement

lurch[1] /lɜːtʃ ‖ lɜːrtʃ/ vi move irregularly
lurch n

lurch[2] n 1 lurching movement 2 **leave
someone in the lurch** leave them when
they are in difficulty

lure /lʊə, ljʊə ‖ lʊr/ n something that
attracts: *the lure of wealth* ♦ vt attract into
trouble

lu·rid /'lʊərɪd, 'ljʊərɪd ‖ 'lʊrɪd/ adj
1 unnaturally bright: *lurid colours* 2 shocking; unpleasant

lurk /lɜːk ‖ lɜːrk/ vi wait in hiding, esp. for
a bad purpose

lus·cious /'lʌʃəs/ adj 1 having a ripe
sweet taste 2 sexually attractive

lush /lʌʃ/ adj (of plants) growing thickly

lust /lʌst/ n [C;U] strong (sexual) desire:
lust for power ♦ vi **~ful** adj

lus·tre BrE ‖ **-ter** AmE /'lʌstə ‖ -ər/ n
[S;U] 1 brightness of a polished surface
2 glory

lust·y /'lʌsti/ *adj* strong and healthy

lute /luːt/ *n* old stringed musical instrument

lux·u·ri·ant /lʌg'zjuəriənt, ləg'ʒuəri-ənt ‖ ləg'ʒur-/ *adj* growing well and thickly ~**ly** *adv* –**ance** *n* [U]

lux·u·ri·ate /lʌg'zjuərieit, ləg'ʒuəri-ləg'ʒur-/ *v* **luxuriate in** *phr vt* enjoy oneself lazily in

lux·u·ri·ous /lʌg'zjuəriəs, ləg'ʒuəriəs ‖ ləg'ʒur-/ *adj* comfortable and esp. expensive

lux·u·ry /'lʌkʃəri/ *n* **1** [U] great comfort, as provided by wealth **2** [C] something pleasant, but not necessary and not often had or done

ly·cra /'laikrə/ *n* [U] *tdmk* (cloth made from) stretchy FIBRE (2), used for (sports) clothes

ly·ing /'lai-iŋ/ *v pres. p. of* LIE¹ and LIE²

lynch /lintʃ/ *vt* (esp. of a crowd) kill without a legal trial

lynch·pin /'lintʃpin/ *n* LINCHPIN

lyr·ic /'lirik/ *n, adj* (short poem) expressing strong feelings in songlike form ~**al** *adj* full of joyful feeling **lyrics** *n* [P] words of a popular song

M

M, m /em/ the 13th letter of the English alphabet

m *written abbrev. for:* **1** metre(s) **2** mile(s) **3** million **4** married **5** male

ma /mɑː/ *n sl* mother

ma'am /mæm, mɑːm, məm ‖ mæm/ *n AmE* (polite way of addressing a woman)

mac /mæk/ *n BrE* coat that keeps out the rain

ma·ca·bre /mə'kɑːbrə, -bə ‖ -brə, -bər/ *adj* causing fear, esp. because connected with death

ma·caw /mə'kɔː ‖ -'kɔː/ *n* large S American PARROT

ma·ca·ro·ni /ˌmækə'rəuni◀ ‖ -'rou-/ *n* [U] small tubes of PASTA

mace /meis/ *n* ceremonial rod carried by an official

ma·chet·e /mə'ʃeti, mə'tʃeti/ *n* large heavy knife

Mach·i·a·vel·li·an /ˌmækiə'veliən/ *adj* skilful in using indirect means to get what one wants; CUNNING

mach·i·na·tions /ˌmækɨ'neiʃənz, ˌmæʃɨ-/ *n* [P] secret efforts or plans to do harm

ma·chine /mə'ʃiːn/ *n* **1** instrument or apparatus that uses power to work **2** group that controls and plans activities of a political party ♦ *vt* make or produce by machine

ma·chine·gun /mə'ʃiːngʌn/ *n* gun that fires continuously

ma·chin·e·ry /mə'ʃiːnəri/ *n* [U] **1** machines: *farm machinery* **2** working parts of a machine or engine **3** operation of a system or organization

ma·chis·mo /mə'tʃizməu, -'kiz- ‖ mɑː'tʃiz-mou, mə-/ *n* [U] *usu. derog* quality of being macho

ma·cho /'mætʃəu ‖ 'mɑːtʃou/ *adj* (trying to seem) strong and brave

mack·e·rel /'mækərəl/ *n* mackerel *or* mackerels sea fish, often eaten

mack·in·tosh /'mækɨntɒʃ ‖ -tɑːʃ/ *n esp. BrE* MAC

mad /mæd/ *adj* -**dd**- **1** ill in the mind **2** very foolish **3** angry **4** filled with strong interest: *She's mad about politics.* **5** like mad very hard, fast, loud, etc. **6** mad keen *BrE infml* extremely keen ~**ly** *adv*: *madly* (=very much) *in love* ~**ness** *n* [U] ~**den** *vt* annoy extremely

mad·am /'mædəm/ *n* (*often cap.*) (polite way of addressing a woman)

mad cow disease /ˌ· '· ·ˌ·/ *n* [U] BSE

made /meid/ *v past t. and p. of* MAKE

ma·don·na /mə'dɒnə ‖ -'dɑː-/ *n* (in the Christian religion) (picture or figure of) Mary, the mother of Christ

mad·ri·gal /'mædrigəl/ *n* song for several singers without instruments

mael·strom /'meilstrəm/ *n lit* **1** violent WHIRLPOOL **2** destructive force of events

maes·tro /'maistrəu ‖ -trou/ *n* -**tros** great or famous musician

maf·i·a /'mɑːfiə ‖ 'mɑː-, 'mæː-/ *n* **1** (*usu.*

cap.) organization of criminals, esp. in the US **2** influential group who support each other without any concern for people outside the group: *the medical mafia*

mag·a·zine /ˌmægəˈziːn ‖ ˈmægəziːn/ *n* **1** sort of book with a paper cover, which contains writing, photographs, and advertisements, that is printed every week or month and is of interest to a particular group of people **2** part of a gun in which bullets are stored

ma·gen·ta /məˈdʒentə/ *adj* dark purplish red

mag·got /ˈmægət/ *n* wormlike young of flies and other insects

ma·gic /ˈmædʒɪk/ *n* **1** use of strange unseen forces, or of tricks, to produce effects **2** special wonderful quality: *the magic of the theatre* —see also BLACK MAGIC ♦ *adj* caused by or used in magic: *a magic trick/ring* **-al** *adj* strange and wonderful ~**ly** /-kli/ *adv*

ma·gi·cian /məˈdʒɪʃən/ *n* person who practises magic

ma·gis·te·ri·al /ˌmædʒɪˈstɪəriəl ‖ -ˈstɪr-/ *adj fml* showing complete and undoubted control

ma·gis·trate /ˈmædʒɪˌstreɪt, -strɪt/ *n* official who judges cases in the lowest law courts

mag·nan·i·mous /mægˈnænɪməs/ *adj fml* very generous ~**ly** *adv* **-mity** /ˌmæg-nəˈnɪmɪti/ *n* [U]

mag·nate /ˈmægneɪt, -nɪt/ *n* wealthy and powerful person

mag·ne·si·um /mægˈniːziəm/ *n* silver-white metal

mag·net /ˈmægnɪt/ *n* **1** piece of iron or steel that draws other metal objects towards it **2** person or thing that attracts or interests people greatly ~**ism** *n* [U] magnetic force ~**ize**, ~**ise** *vt* ~**ic** /mægˈnetɪk/ *adj*: *a magnetic personality* ~**ically** /-kli/ *adv*

magnetic tape /ˌ·ˈ· ‖ ·ˈ· ·/ *n* [C;U] TAPE on which sound or other information can be recorded

mag·nif·i·cent /mægˈnɪfɪsənt/ *adj* extremely fine or good **-cence** *n* [U] ~**ly** *adv*

mag·ni·fy /ˈmægnɪfaɪ/ *vt* cause to look or seem larger **-fication** /ˌmægnɪfɪˈkeɪʃən/ *n* [U]

magnifying glass /ˈ···· ˌ·/ *n* curved LENS

(1) for magnifying things

mag·ni·tude /ˈmægnɪtjuːd ‖ -tuːd/ *n* [U] *fml* degree of size or importance

mag·pie /ˈmægpaɪ/ *n* noisy black and white bird which likes to steal bright objects

ma·hog·a·ny /məˈhɒgəni ‖ məˈhɑː-/ *n* [U] dark reddish wood used for furniture

maid /meɪd/ *n* female servant

maid·en /ˈmeɪdn/ *n lit* young unmarried woman ♦ *adj* **1** first: *the ship's maiden voyage* **2** unmarried: *my maiden aunts*

maiden name /ˈ·· ·/ *n* family name a woman has or had before marriage

mail¹ /meɪl/ *n* [U] **1** the postal system: *It came by airmail.* **2** letters, etc. that one posts or receives **3** E-MAIL ♦ *vt* **1** *esp. AmE* for POST² (1, 2) **2** E-MAIL

mail² *n* [U] soldiers' protective clothing in former times, made of small metal rings

mail or·der /ˌ· ˈ··/ *n* [U] buying things by MAIL¹ (1)

mail·shot /ˈmeɪlʃɒt ‖ -ʃɑːt/ *n* sending of advertisements, etc. to large numbers of people by post

maim /meɪm/ *vt* wound very seriously and usu. lastingly

main¹ /meɪn/ *adj* chief; most important: *its main function* ~**ly** *adv*: *His money comes mainly from investments.*

main² *n* **1** large pipe or wire supplying water, gas, or electricity **2 in the main** mainly; mostly

main chance /ˌ· ˈ·/ *n* [*the*+S] possibility of making money or other personal gain

main·frame /ˈmeɪnfreɪm/ *n* the largest and most powerful kind of computer

main·land /ˈmeɪnlənd, -lænd/ *n* a land mass, considered without its islands **mainland** *adj*

main line /ˌ· ˈ·/ *n* important railway between cities

main·spring /ˈmeɪnˌsprɪŋ/ *n* **1** chief spring in a watch **2** chief force or reason that makes something happen

main·stay /ˈmeɪnsteɪ/ *n* someone or something which provides the chief means of support

main·stream /ˈmeɪnstriːm/ *n* main or usual way of thinking or acting in relation to a subject

main·tain /meɪnˈteɪn, mən-/ *vt* **1** keep in good condition **2** support with money

3 continue to have or do 4 continue to say, believe, or argue

main·te·nance /'meɪntənəns/ n [U] 1 keeping in good condition 2 money given to wives and/or children by a husband/father who does not live with them

mai·son·ette /ˌmeɪzə'net/ n flat that is part of a larger house

maize /meɪz/ n [U] esp. BrE for CORN (2)

ma·jes·ty /'mædʒəsti/ n 1 (cap.) (used as a title for kings and queens) 2 [U] fml grandness –**tic** /mə'dʒestɪk/ adj: majestic scenery –**tically** /-kli/ adv

ma·jor¹ /'meɪdʒə‖ -ər/ adj of great importance or seriousness: a major problem | major surgery

major² n army officer, above CAPTAIN —see also SERGEANT MAJOR

major³ v major in phr vt esp. AmE study as the chief subject(s) for a university degree

ma·jor·i·ty /mə'dʒɒrəti‖ mə'dʒɔː-, mə'dʒɑː-/ n 1 [(the)S] most 2 [C] difference in number between a large and small group: win by a majority of 300 votes

make¹ /meɪk/ vt made /meɪd/ 1 produce: make a cake/a noise/a decision | a bag made of leather | wine made from local grapes 2 cause to be: It made me happy. 3 force; cause: I can't make him understand. 4 earn (money) 5 calculate or be counted as: What time do you make it? | That makes the fourth glass you've had! 6 add up to: 2 and 2 make 4 7 tidy (a bed that has been slept in) 8 have the qualities of: That story makes good reading. 9 reach: We made harbour by night fall. 10 complete: That picture really makes the room. 11 make believe pretend 12 make do use something for lack of any better: We had to make do with water. 13 make it: a arrive in time b succeed 14 make one's way go: I made my way home. 15 make or break which will cause success or complete failure **maker** n 1 person who or company that makes something: the three big US car makers 2 (usu. cap.) God –**making** 1 be the making of cause to improve greatly 2 have the makings of have the possibility of developing into

make for phr vt 1 move in the direction of: I made for the exit. 2 result in: Large print makes for easy reading.

make into phr vt use in making: He made the bottle into an interesting ornament.

make of phr vt 1 understand by: I don't know what to make of the situation. 2 give (the usu. stated importance) to: She makes too much of her problems.

make off phr vi leave in a hurry

make off with phr vt steal

make out phr v 1 vt write in complete form 2 vt see, hear, or understand properly 3 vt claim; pretend 4 vi succeed 5 vt argue as proof: make out a case (=give good reasons)

make over phr vt 1 pass over to someone else, esp. legally 2 esp. AmE remake

make up phr v 1 vt invent (a story, etc.), esp. to deceive 2 vi/t use special paint and powder on the face to look beautiful or change the appearance 3 vt prepare for use: A pharmacist made up the doctor's prescriptions. 4 vt form as a whole: Oil makes up half of our exports. 5 vi become friends again after a quarrel

make up for phr vt give something good to take away disappointment: I bought him a present to make up for my bad behaviour.

make² n 1 type of product 2 on the make searching for personal gain

make-be·lieve /'·· ·,·/ n [U] pretending

make·o·ver /'meɪkəʊvə‖ -oʊvər/ n complete change of appearance for a person, building, etc.

make·shift /'meɪkˌʃɪft/ adj used because there is nothing better

make-up /'·· ·/ n [C;U] 1 paint, powder, etc. worn on the face 2 combination of members or qualities

mal·ad·just·ed /ˌmæləˈdʒʌstɪd◄/ adj not fitting in well with other people or with life generally

ma·laise /məˈleɪz/ n [C;U] 1 failure to be active and successful 2 feeling of not being well

mal·a·prop·is·m /'mæləprɒpɪzəm‖ -prɑː-/ n often amusing misuse of a word

ma·lar·i·a /məˈleəriə‖ -ˈler-/ n [U] tropical disease passed on by MOSQUITOes

mal·con·tent /'mælkəntent, ˌmælkənˈtent/ n fml dissatisfied person who is likely to make trouble

male /meɪl/ *n, adj* (person or animal) of the sex that does not give birth

male chau·vin·ist /ˌ· ·—◄/ *n derog* man who behaves unreasonably towards women because he thinks they are less able, strong, etc. than men

ma·lev·o·lent /məˈlevələnt/ *adj lit* wishing to do evil to others ~**ly** *adv* –**lence** *n* [U]

mal·formed /ˌmælˈfɔːmd◄ ‖ -ɔːr-/ *adj* made or shaped badly: *a malformed limb* –**formation** /ˌmælfɔːˈmeɪʃən ‖ -ɔːr-/ *n* [C;U]

mal·func·tion /mælˈfʌŋkʃən/ *n* fault in operation ♦ **malfunction** *vi*

mal·ice /ˈmælɪs/ *n* [U] desire to hurt or harm –**icious** /məˈlɪʃəs/ *adj*: *a malicious attack* –**iciously** *adv*

ma·lign /məˈlaɪn/ *adj fml* bad; causing harm ♦ *vt* say bad things about

ma·lig·nant /məˈlɪgnənt/ *adj* **1** (of disease) likely to kill **2** *fml* malign ~**ly** *adv*

ma·lin·ger /məˈlɪŋgə ‖ -ər/ *vi* avoid work by pretending to be ill ~**er** *n*

mall /mɔːl, mæl ‖ mɔːl/ *n AmE* area of streets with no cars, where one can shop

mal·le·a·ble /ˈmæliəbəl/ *adj* (of metal) easy to shape; soft: (fig.) *a malleable personality*

mal·let /ˈmælɪt/ *n* wooden hammer

mal·nour·ished /ˌmælˈnʌrɪʃt ‖ -ˈnɜːr-, -ˈnʌr-/ *adj* ill or weak because of MALNUTRITION

mal·nu·tri·tion /ˌmælnjuːˈtrɪʃən ‖ -nuː-/ *n* [U] lack of (proper) food

mal·prac·tice /ˌmælˈpræktɪs/ *n* [C;U] failure to do one's professional duty properly or honestly

malt /mɔːlt ‖ mɒːlt/ *n* [U] partly grown grain used esp. for making beer and WHISKY

mal·treat /mælˈtriːt/ *vt fml* treat roughly and/or cruelly ~**ment** *n* [U]

ma·ma¹ /ˈmɑːmə/ *n AmE infml* mother

ma·ma² /məˈmɑː/ *n BrE lit* mother

mam·mal /ˈmæməl/ *n* animal of the sort fed on the mother's milk when young

mam·moth /ˈmæməθ/ *adj* extremely large

man /mæn/ *n* **men** /men/ **1** [C] adult male person **2** [U] the human race: *Man must change in a changing world.* **3** [C] person: *All men must die.* **4** [C] male of low rank: *officers and men* **5** [C] male member of a team **6** [C] object used in board games: *chess*

men 7 a man of the world man with a lot of experience **8 man and wife** *fml* married **9 one's own man** independent in action **10 the man in the street** the average person **11 to a man** every person: *They agreed, to a man.* —see also BEST MAN, FRONT MAN ♦ *vt* -**nn**- provide with people for operation ~**hood** *n* [U] quality or time of being a (brave) man

man·a·cle /ˈmænəkəl/ *n* metal ring for fastening a prisoner's hands or feet

man·age /ˈmænɪdʒ/ *v* **1** *vt* be in charge of; run **2** *vi/t* succeed in doing: *I only just managed to get out of the way.* **3** *vi* succeed in living, esp. on a small amount of money: *We don't earn much, but we manage.* ~**able** *adj* easy or possible to deal with ~**ment** *n* [U] **1** managing **2** people in charge **manager, manageress** /ˌmænɪdʒəˈres ‖ ˈmænɪdʒɔːrəs-/ *fem.* — *n* person who runs a business, hotel, sports team, etc. –**agerial** /ˌmænəˈdʒɪəriəl◄ ‖ -ˈdʒɪr-/ *adj*: *managerial responsibilities*

man·da·rin /ˈmændərɪn/ *n* **1** high-ranking official in the former Chinese empire **2** *derog* high-ranking official **3** type of small orange

man·date /ˈmændeɪt/ *n* government's right or duty to act according to the wishes of the electors

man·da·to·ry /ˈmændətəri ‖ -tɔːri/ *adj fml* which must be done

man·do·lin /ˌmændəˈlɪn/ *n* eight-stringed musical instrument

mane /meɪn/ *n* long hair on a horse's or lion's neck

ma·neu·ver /məˈnuːvə ‖ -ər/ *n, v AmE for* MANOEUVRE

man·ful·ly /ˈmænfəli/ *adv* bravely and determinedly

man·ger /ˈmeɪndʒə ‖ -ər/ *n* long open container for animals' food

man·gle /ˈmæŋgəl/ *vt* crush and tear so as to ruin

man·go /ˈmæŋgəʊ ‖ -goʊ/ *n* -**goes** *or* -**gos** tropical fruit with sweet yellow flesh

mang·y /ˈmeɪndʒi/ *adj* of bad appearance, esp. because of loss of hair or fur

man·han·dle /ˈmænˌhændl/ *vt* hold or move forcefully or roughly

man·hole /ˈmænhəʊl ‖ -hoʊl/ *n* opening in the road leading to underground pipes, wires, etc.

ma·ni·a /'meɪniə/ n [C;U] **1** madness
2 extreme interest or desire: *a mania for
collecting matchboxes* | *soccer mania*
maniac /-niæk/ n ~**cal** /mə'naɪəkəl/ adj:
maniacal laughter

man·i·cure /'mænɨkjʊə‖-kjʊr/ vt, n
(give) treatment for the hands, esp. the
fingernails, including cleaning, cutting, etc.
–curist n

man·i·fest¹ /'mænɨfest/ adj fml plain to
see or understand ~**ly** adv

manifest² vt show plainly ~**ation**
/ˌmænɨfe'steɪʃən‖-fə-/ n [C;U]

man·i·fes·to /ˌmænɨ'festəʊ‖-toʊ/ n -
tos or -toes statement of intentions or
opinions, esp. as made by a political party
before an election

man·i·fold¹ /'mænɨfəʊld‖-foʊld/ adj
many in number or kind

manifold² n tech pipe with holes

ma·nip·u·late /mə'nɪpjɨleɪt/ vt **1** fml
handle skilfully **2** control and influence for
one's own purposes **–lative** /-lətɪv/ adj
–lation /mə,nɪpjɨ'leɪʃən/ n [U]

man·kind /ˌmæn'kaɪnd/ n [U] human
beings

man·ly /'mænli/ adj having qualities
(believed to be) suitable to a man **–liness** n
[U]

man-made /ˌ· '·◂/ adj **1** produced by
people **2** (of materials) not made from
natural substances

man·ner /'mænə‖-ər/ n **1** fml way: *a
meal prepared in the Japanese manner*
2 way of behaving towards people: *a rude
manner* **3** all manner of fml every sort of
4 –mannered having the stated way of
behaving: *bad-mannered* **5** (as) to the
manner born as if one is used to
(something, esp. social position) from birth
manners n [U] (polite) social practices: *It's
bad manners to make a noise while you eat.*

man·ner·is·m /'mænərɪzəm/ n (bad or
strange) way of behaving that has become a
habit

ma·noeu·vre BrE ‖ **maneuver** AmE
/mə'nuːvə‖-ər/ n **1** skilful movement
2 secret trick to gain a purpose **3** on
manoeuvres doing battle training ♦ vt
move or turn, esp. skilfully or deceivingly:
The car manoeuvres well in wet weather.
–vrable BrE ‖ **verable** AmE adj

man·or /'mænə‖-ər/ n area of land

owned by the local lord in former times

man·pow·er /'mæn,paʊə‖-,paʊr/ n [U]
number of workers needed

man·qué /'mɒŋkeɪ‖mɑːŋ'keɪ/ adj fml
that failed to become the stated thing

man·sion /'mænʃən/ n large grand house

man-sized /'· ·/ adj large

man·slaugh·ter /'mæn,slɔːtə‖-slɔːtər/
n [U] crime of killing someone unintentionally

man·tel·piece /'mæntlpiːs/ n shelf
above a fireplace

man·tle /'mæntl/ n **1** covering: *a mantle
of snow* **2** (sign of) general or official
recognition: *He took over the mantle of
world heavyweight champion.*

man-to-man /ˌ· · '·◂/ adj, adv open(ly)
and honest(ly)

man·tra /'mæntrə/ n word or phrase that
is often repeated, esp. when praying in
some religions

man·u·al¹ /'mænjuəl/ adj of or using the
hands ~**ly** adv

manual² n book giving information or
instructions

man·u·fac·ture /ˌmænjɨ'fæktʃə‖-ər/ vt
make in large quantities using machinery
♦ n [U] manufacturing: *goods of foreign
manufacture* ~**turer** n

ma·nure /mə'njʊə‖mə'nʊr/ n [U] animal
waste matter put on land to make crops
grow ♦ vt put manure on

man·u·script /'mænjɨskrɪpt/ n **1** first
copy of a book, etc., handwritten or typed
2 old book written by hand

man·y /'meni/ determiner, pron **1** a large
number (of): *I haven't got as many as you.* |
many people **2** a good/great many many
3 one too many infml too much (alcohol) to
drink

map¹ /mæp/ n **1** representation of (part
of) the Earth's surface as if seen from
above: *a map of France* **2** (put something)
on the map (cause something to be)
considered important

map² vt -pp- make a map of
map out phr vt plan details of

mar /mɑː/ vt fml spoil

mar·a·thon /'mærəθən‖-θɑːn/ n
1 running race of about 26 miles (42
kilometres) **2** (hard) activity that lasts a
long time: *a marathon speech of 6 hours*

ma·raud·ing /mə'rɔːdɪŋ‖-'rɔː-/ adj

moving around looking for things or people to attack **-er** n

mar·ble /'maːbəl ‖ 'maːr-/ n [U] 1 hard smooth usu. white stone used for STATUES or buildings 2 small glass ball rolled against others in a game (**marbles**)

march /maːtʃ ‖ maːrtʃ/ v 1 vi walk with regular forceful steps like a soldier 2 vt force to go: *They marched him off to prison.*
♦ n act of marching: (fig.) *the march* (=steady advance) *of history*

March n the third month of the year

marching or·ders /'·· ‚·/ n [P] BrE being told that one must leave

mare /meə ‖ mer/ n female horse

mar·ga·rine /‚maːdʒə'riːn, ‚maːgə- ‖ 'maːrdʒərən/ n butter-like food substance

mar·gin /'maːdʒɪn ‖ 'maːr-/ n 1 space down the edge of a page, with no writing or printing in it 2 amount by which one thing is greater than another: *We won by a decisive margin.* 3 area on the outside edge of a larger area: *the margin of the stream*

mar·gin·al /'maːdʒɪnəl ‖ 'maːr-/ adj 1 small in importance or amount: *a marginal difference* 2 (of a SEAT (3) in parliament) in danger of being lost to another party in an election **~ly** adv **~ize** vt push out to the edge of (a group)

mar·i·jua·na /‚mærɪ'waːnə, -'hwaːnə/ n [U] form of the drug CANNABIS

ma·ri·na /mə'riːnə/ n small harbour for pleasure boats

mar·i·nade /‚mærɪ'neɪd/ n [C;U] mixture of oil, wine, etc. into which food is put for a time before being cooked **–nate** /'mærɪneɪt/ vt keep in a marinade

ma·rine /mə'riːn/ adj 1 of the sea 2 of ships and sailing ♦ n soldier who serves on a naval ship

mar·i·ner /'mærɪnə ‖ -ər/ n sailor

mar·i·o·nette /‚mæriə'net/ n PUPPET with strings

mar·i·tal /'mærɪtl/ adj of marriage

mar·i·time /'mærɪtaɪm/ adj 1 MARINE 2 near the sea

mark¹ /maːk ‖ maːrk/ n 1 something on or put onto a surface: *dirty marks on the wall* | *tyre marks in the snow* 2 a number that represents a judgment of quality: *The top mark in the test was 8 out of 10.* 3 something that shows a quality: *They all stood as a mark of respect.* 4 printed or

written sign: *punctuation mark* 5 particular type of machine: *the new Mark 4 gun* 6 **make one's mark (on)** gain success, fame, etc. (in) 7 **quick/slow off the mark** infml quick/slow in understanding or acting 8 **up to the mark**: a of an acceptable standard b in good health 9 **wide of the mark** not correct or close to the subject

mark² 1 vi/t spoil with marks: *Hot cups have marked the table.* | *The table marks easily.* 2 vt give MARKS¹ (2) to 3 vt stay close to (an opposing player) to spoil their play 4 vt be a sign of: *A cross marks his grave.* | *The election marks a turning point in our affairs.* 5 **mark time** spend time on work, etc. without making any advance 6 **(You) mark my words!** You will see later that I am right. **~ed** adj noticeable **~edly** /'maːkɪdli ‖ 'maːr-/ adv

mark down/up phr vt lower/raise the price of

mark out phr vt 1 also **mark off** — draw lines round (an area) 2 [(for)] show or choose as likely to become (successful) or gain (success)

mark³ n German unit of money

mark·er /'maːkə ‖ 'maːrkər/ n 1 tool for making marks 2 object for marking a place

mar·ket¹ /'maːkɪt ‖ 'maːr-/ n 1 (place for) a gathering of people to buy and sell goods 2 desire to buy; demand: *There's no market for coats at this time of year.* 3 area where goods are sold: *the foreign/domestic market* 4 trade: *the tea market* 5 **in the market** wishing to buy 6 **on the market** (of goods) for sale 7 **play the market** buy and sell business shares to try to make a profit —see also BLACK MARKET, COMMON MARKET

market² vt present and offer for sale **~ing** n [U] 1 skills of advertising, supplying, and selling goods 2 AmE shopping **~able** adj: (fig.) *marketable skills* **~ability** /‚maːkɪt-ə'bɪlɪti ‖ ‚maːr-/ n [U]

market gar·den /‚·· '··/ n BrE area for growing vegetables and fruit for sale

mar·ket·place /'maːkɪtpleɪs ‖ 'maːr-/ n 1 place where a market is held 2 activities of buying and selling

market re·search /‚·· ·'·, ‚·· '··/ n [U] study of what people buy and why

mark·ing /'maːkɪŋ ‖ 'maːr-/ n [C;U] (any

of a set of) coloured marks on an animal's fur or feathers

marks·man /'mɑːksmən‖'mɑːrks-/ **marks·woman** /-,wʊmən/ *fem.* *n* **-men** /-mən/ person who can shoot well ~**ship** *n* [U]

mark·up /'mɑːk-ʌp‖'mɑːrk-/ *n* price increase by a seller

mar·ma·lade /'mɑːməleɪd‖'mɑːr-/ *n* [U] JAM made from oranges

ma·roon¹ /mə'ruːn/ *vt* put or leave in a lonely or dangerous place, without help

maroon² *adj* dark red

mar·quee /mɑː'kiː‖mɑːr-/ *n* very large tent

mar·riage /'mærɪdʒ/ *n* [C;U] **1** ceremony to marry people **2** state of being husband and wife ~**able** *adj* suitable for marriage

mar·row /'mærəʊ‖-roʊ/ *n* **1** [C] very large long round dark green vegetable **2** [U] soft fatty substance inside bones

mar·ry /'mæri/ *v* **1** *vi/t* take (as) a husband or wife: *He never married.* | *She married a soldier.* **2** *vt* join in marriage: *The priest married them.* **3** *vt* [(off)] cause to get married: *They married their daughter (off) to a young diplomat.* **married** *adj* **1** having a husband or wife: *a married man* **2** of MARRIAGE (2): *married life* **3** **married to** having as a husband or wife: *She's married to a doctor.*

Mars /mɑːz‖mɑːrz/ *n* the PLANET fourth in order from the sun

marsh /mɑːʃ‖mɑːrʃ/ *n* [C;U] (area of) soft wet land ~**y** *adj*

mar·shal¹ /'mɑːʃəl‖'mɑːr-/ *n* **1** US law official, like a SHERIFF (1) **2** military officer of very high rank **3** organizer of an event, such as a ceremony or race

marshal² *vt* **-ll-** *BrE*‖ **-l-** *AmE* **1** arrange (esp. facts) in good order **2** lead (people) carefully

marsh·mal·low /,mɑːʃ'mæləʊ‖'mɑːrʃ-,melоʊ/ *n* type of soft round sweet

mar·su·pi·al /mɑː'sjuːpiəl‖mɑːr'suː-/ *n* animal, esp. Australian, that carries its young in a pocket of skin

mar·tial /'mɑːʃəl‖'mɑːr-/ *adj fml* of war, soldiers, etc.

martial art /,·· '·/ *n* Eastern fighting sport: *Judo is a martial art.*

martial law /,·· '·/ *n* [U] government by the army under special laws

Mar·tian /'mɑːʃən‖'mɑːr-/ *n, adj*

(creature) from MARS

mar·ti·net /,mɑːtɪ'net‖,mɑːr-/ *n* very STRICT person

mar·tyr /'mɑːtə‖'mɑːrtər/ *n* **1** someone who dies or suffers for their (religious) beliefs **2** **make a martyr of oneself** give up one's own wishes to help others, or in the hope of being praised ♦ *vt* kill as a martyr

mar·vel /'mɑːvəl‖'mɑːr-/ *n* wonderful thing or example: *the marvels of modern science* ♦ *vi* **-ll-** *BrE*‖ **-l-** *AmE fml* be filled with surprise and admiration ~**lous** *BrE*‖ ~**ous** *AmE adj* very pleasing or good ~**lously** *adv*

Marx·is·m /'mɑːksɪzəm‖'mɑːr-/ *n* [U] teaching of Karl Marx on which COMMUNISM is based ~**ist** *n, adj*

mar·zi·pan /'mɑːzɪpæn‖'mɑːrtsɪ-, 'mɑːrzə-/ *n* [U] sweet paste made from ALMONDS

mas·ca·ra /mæ'skɑːrə‖mæ'skærə/ *n* [U] dark substance for colouring the EYELASHes

mas·cot /'mæskət‖-ɑːt/ *n* object, animal, or person thought to bring good luck

mas·cu·line /'mæskjʊlɪn/ *adj* **1** (in grammar) referring to males **2** of or like a man ~**linity** /,mæskjʊ'lɪnɪti/ *n* [U]

mash /mæʃ/ *vt* [(UP)] crush into a soft substance ♦ *n* [U] mashed potatoes

mask /mɑːsk‖mæsk/ *n* covering for the face, to hide or protect it ♦ *vt* hide ~**ed** *adj* wearing a mask

mas·o·chis·m /'mæsəkɪzəm/ *n* [U] **1** gaining pleasure from being hurt **2** wish to be hurt so as to gain sexual pleasure ~**chist** *n* ~**chistic** /,mæsə'kɪstɪk◄/ *adj*

ma·son /'meɪsən/ *n* **1** STONEMASON **2** (*usu. cap.*) FREEMASON ~**ic** /mə'sɒnɪk‖-'sɑː-/ *adj*

ma·son·ry /'meɪsənri/ *n* [U] stone building blocks

mas·que·rade /,mæskə'reɪd/ *vi* pretend: *thieves masquerading as bank employees* ♦ *n* **1** hiding of the truth **2** dance where people wear MASKs

mass /mæs/ *n* **1** [C] large lump, heap, or quantity: *a mass of clouds* **2** [C] also **masses** *pl.* — *infml* lots: *masses of work to do* **3** [U] (in science) amount of matter in a body ♦ *vi/t* gather in large numbers or quantity ~**masses** *n* [*the+*P] ordinary people in society

Mass n (in the Catholic and Orthodox churches) important religious ceremony

mas·sa·cre /ˈmæsəkə ‖ -ər/ n killing of large numbers of people ♦ **massacre** vt

mas·sage /ˈmæsɑːʒ ‖ məˈsɑːʒ/ n [C;U] (act of) pressing and rubbing someone's body, esp. to cure pain or stiffness ♦ vt 1 give a massage to 2 change (facts, figures, etc.) usu. in a dishonest way

mas·seur /mæˈsɜː, mə- ‖ -ˈsɜːr/ **masseuse** /mæˈsɜːz, mə-/ fem. — n person who gives massages

mas·sive /ˈmæsɪv/ adj extremely big ~**ly** adv ~**ness** n [U]

mass-pro·duce /ˌ··ˈ·/ vt produce (goods) in large numbers to the same pattern **mass production** n [U]

mast /mɑːst ‖ mæst/ n 1 long upright pole for carrying sails 2 tall framework for AERIALS

mas·tec·to·my /mæˈstektəmi/ n operation for the removal of a breast

mas·ter¹ /ˈmɑːstə ‖ ˈmæstər/ n 1 **mistress** fem. — person in control of people, animals, or things **mistress** fem. — teacher 3 great artist, writer, etc. —see also OLD MASTER 4 captain of a ship 5 something from which copies are made: a master tape ~**ful** adj able or eager to control others ~**fully** adv ~**ly** adj showing great skill.

master² vt 1 learn or gain as a skill: master the art of public speaking 2 control and defeat: He mastered his fear of heights.

master key /ˈ·· ˌ·/ n key that opens all the doors in a building

mas·ter·mind /ˈmɑːstəmaɪnd ‖ ˈmæstər-/ vt plan cleverly: mastermind a crime ♦ n very clever person

master of ce·re·mo·nies /ˌ·· · ˈ····/ n person who introduces speakers or performers at a public event

mas·ter·piece /ˈmɑːstəpiːs ‖ ˈmæstər-/ n piece of work, esp. of art, done with extreme skill

mas·ter·y /ˈmɑːstəri ‖ ˈmæ-/ n [U] 1 power to control 2 great skill or knowledge

mas·tur·bate /ˈmæstəbeɪt ‖ -ər-/ vi/t excite the sex organs (of) by handling, rubbing, etc. –**bation** /ˌmæstəˈbeɪʃən ‖ -tər-/ n [U]

mat /mæt/ n 1 piece of strong material for covering part of a floor 2 small piece of material for putting under objects on a table

mat·a·dor /ˈmætədɔː ‖ -dɔːr/ n person who kills the BULL in a BULLFIGHT

match¹ /mætʃ/ n 1 sports or other competition between two people or sides; game: a football match 2 one who is equal to or better than another: I'm no match for her at maths. 3 good combination: The hat and shoes are a perfect match. 4 marriage: Both her daughters made good matches. ♦ v 1 vi/t be similar (to) or combine well (with): The curtains and carpets don't match. 2 vt be equal to or find an equal for: a restaurant that can't be matched for service

match² n short thin stick that burns when its end is rubbed against a rough surface ~**box** n box for holding matches

match·mak·er /ˈmætʃˌmeɪkə ‖ -ər/ n person who tries to arrange other's love affairs

mate¹ /meɪt/ n 1 friend, or person one works or lives with: We're mates/schoolmates/flatmates. 2 either of a male-female pair 3 officer on a non-navy ship 4 BrE sl (used for addressing a man)

mate² vi (esp. of animals) join sexually to produce young

mate³ n, v CHECKMATE

ma·te·ri·al /məˈtɪəriəl ‖ -ˈtɪr-/ n 1 [C;U] substance of which things are or can be made 2 [U] cloth 3 [U] knowledge of facts from which a (written) work may be produced: She's collecting material for a book. ♦ adj 1 of matter or substance, not spirit 2 fml important or necessary ~**ly** adv

ma·te·ri·al·is·m /məˈtɪəriəlɪzəm ‖ -ˈtɪr-/ n [U] (too) great interest in the pleasures of the world, money, etc. ~**ist** n ~**istic** /məˌtɪəriəˈlɪstɪk◀ ‖ tɪr-/ adj

ma·te·ri·al·ize, **-ise** /məˈtɪəriəlaɪz ‖ -ˈtɪr-/ vi 1 become able to be seen 2 become real or actual: Her hopes never materialized. 3 come; arrive –**ization** /məˌtɪəriəˈlaɪzeɪʃən ‖ -uriələ-/ n [U]

ma·ter·nal /məˈtɜːnl ‖ -ɜːr-/ adj 1 of or like a mother 2 related through the mother's part of the family: my maternal grandmother

ma·ter·ni·ty /məˈtɜːnɨti ‖ -ɜːr-/ n [U] motherhood ♦ adj for women who are going to give birth: a maternity hospital/dress

math·e·mat·ics /ˌmæθəˈmætɪks/ also **maths** /mæθs/ *BrE* ‖ **math** /mæθ/ *AmE* — *n* [U] science of numbers –**ical** *adj* –**ically** /-kli/ *adv* –**ician** /ˌmæθəməˈtɪʃən/ *n*

mat·i·née /ˈmætɪneɪ ‖ ˌmætɪˈneɪ/ *n* afternoon performance of a play, film, etc.

ma·tri·arch /ˈmeɪtriɑːk ‖ -ɑːrk/ *n* woman who controls a (family) group ~**al** /ˌmeɪtriˈɑːkəl ‖ -ˈɑːrk-/ *adj*

ma·tric·u·late /məˈtrɪkjəleɪt/ *vi* become a member of a university –**ation** /məˌtrɪkjəˈleɪʃən/ *n* [U]

mat·ri·mo·ny /ˈmætrɪməni ‖ -mouni-/ *n* [U] being married –**nial** /ˌmætrɪˈməuniəl ◂ ‖ -ˈmou-/ *adj*

ma·tron /ˈmeɪtrən/ *n* **1** chief nurse **2** woman in charge of living arrangements in a school **3** *lit* older married woman, esp. of quiet behaviour ~**ly** *adj* **1** (of a woman) rather fat **2** with the DIGNITY of a MATRON (3)

matt /mæt/ *adj* not shiny

mat·ted /ˈmætəd/ *adj* twisted in a thick mass

mat·ter¹ /ˈmætə ‖ -ər/ *n* **1** [C] subject; affair: *several important matters to discuss* **2** [*the*+S] trouble; cause of pain, illness, etc.: *Is anything the matter?* **3** [U] substance of which things are made: *all the matter in the universe* —see also GREY MATTER **4** [U] things of a particular kind or for a particular purpose: *reading matter* (=magazines, books, etc.) **5 a matter of: a** a little more or less than: *It's only a matter of hours before the doctor arrives.* **b** needing as a part: *Learning is a matter of concentration.* **6 a matter of course** a usual event **7 as a matter of fact** in fact; really **8 for that matter** (used when mentioning another possibility) **9 no matter ...** it makes no difference: *No matter how hard I tried, I couldn't move it.* **10 That's a matter of opinion.** My opinion is different from yours.

matter² *vi* be important

matter-of-fact /ˌ· · · ·◂/ *adj* without feelings or imagination

mat·ting /ˈmætɪŋ/ *n* [U] rough woven material, esp. for the floor

mat·tress /ˈmætrəs/ *n* large filled cloth case for sleeping on

ma·ture /məˈtʃuə ‖ -tʃur/ *adj* **1** fully developed **2** sensible, like a mature person **3** *fml* carefully thought about ♦ *vi/t*

become or make mature –**turity** *n* [U]

maud·lin /ˈmɔːdlɪn ‖ ˈmɔː-/ *adj* stupidly sad, esp. when drunk

maul /mɔːl ‖ mɔːl/ *vt* hurt by handling roughly: *mauled by a lion*

mau·so·le·um /ˌmɔːsəˈliːəm ‖ ˌmɔː-/ *n* grand building containing a grave

mauve /məuv ‖ mouv/ *adj* pale purple

mav·e·rick /ˈmævərɪk/ *n* person who acts differently from the rest of a group

mawk·ish /ˈmɔːkɪʃ ‖ ˈmɔː-/ *adj* expressing love and admiration in a silly way

max /mæks/ *abbrev. for:* MAXIMUM

max·im /ˈmæksəm/ *n* rule for sensible behaviour

max·i·mize, **-ise** /ˈmæksəmaɪz/ *vt* make as big as possible

max·i·mum /ˈmæksəməm/ *n, adj* -**ma** /-mə/ *or* -**mums** largest (amount, number, etc.): *our maximum offer | He smokes a maximum of 10 cigarettes a day.* –**mal** *adj*

may /meɪ/ *v aux* **1** (shows a possibility): *He may come and he may not. | She may have missed the train.* (=perhaps she has missed it) **2** have permission to; be allowed to: *You may come in now. | May we go home, please?* **3** (used when expressing a wish): *May you live happily ever after!* **4 may as well** have no strong reason not to: *It's late, so I may as well go to bed.*

May *n* the fifth month of the year

may·be /ˈmeɪbi/ *adv* perhaps

may·hem /ˈmeɪhem/ *n* [U] violent disorder and confusion

may·on·naise /ˌmeɪəˈneɪz ‖ ˈmeɪəneɪz/ *n* [U] thick liquid made from eggs and oil, poured on food

mayor /meə ‖ ˈmeɪər/ *n* person elected each year by a town council to be head of that city or town

mayor·ess /ˈmeərəs ‖ ˈmeɪərəs/ *n* **1** woman who is a MAYOR **2** wife of a MAYOR

maze /meɪz/ *n* arrangement of twisting paths in which one becomes lost

MC /ˌem ˈsiː/ *n abbrev. for:* **1** MASTER OF CEREMONIES **2** Member of Congress

MD /ˌem ˈdiː/ *n abbrev. for:* **1** Doctor of Medicine **2** Managing Director

me /mi; *strong* miː/ *pron* (object form of I)

ME /ˌem ˈiː/ *n* [U] myalgic encephalomyelitis; medical condition causing painful muscles and weakness over a long period

mead·ow /'medəʊ ‖ -doʊ/ n field of grass
mea·gre BrE ‖ -ger AmE /'miːgə ‖ -ər/ adj not big enough ~ly adv ~ness n [U]
meal¹ /miːl/ n (food eaten at) an occasion for eating
meal² n [U] crushed grain
mealy-mouthed /,·· ·-◂/ adj expressing (unpleasant) things too indirectly
mean¹ /miːn/ vt meant /ment/ 1 (of words, signs, etc.) represent an idea: 'Melancholy' means 'sad'. | The red light means 'stop'. 2 intend: He said Tuesday, but meant Thursday. | I said I'd help and I meant it. (=I am determined to do so) 3 be a sign of: This could mean war. 4 be of importance to the stated degree: Her work means a lot/everything to her. 5 be meant to esp. BrE ought to; be supposed to 6 mean business act with serious intentions 7 mean well act with good intentions ~ing n [C;U] 1 idea intended to be understood, esp. from words: 'Measure' has several meanings. 2 importance or value: His life lost its meaning when his wife died. ~ing adj suggesting a hidden thought: a meaning look ~ingful adj: a meaningful look ~ingless adj
mean² adj 1 ungenerous 2 unkind; nasty 3 esp. AmE bad-tempered 4 no mean very good: He's no mean cook.
mean³ n, adj average
me·an·der /mi'ændə ‖ -ər/ vi 1 wander 2 (of a stream) flow slowly and twistingly
means /miːnz/ n means 1 [C] method; way 2 [P] money, esp. enough to live on 3 by all means (a polite way of giving permission) 4 by means of using; with 5 by no means fml not at all 6 live beyond/within one's means spend more than/not more than one can afford
means test /'· ·/ n inquiry into the amount of money someone has to find out if they need money from the state
meant /ment/ v past t. and p. of MEAN¹
mean·time /'miːntaɪm/ n in the meantime MEANWHILE (1)
mean·while /'miːnwaɪl/ adv 1 in the time between two events 2 during the same period of time
mea·sles /'miːzəlz/ n [U] infectious disease in which the sufferer has small red spots on the skin
meas·ly /'miːzli/ adj sl too small

mea·sure¹ /'meʒə ‖ -ər/ vt 1 find or show the size, amount, degree, etc. of: Measure the (height of the) cupboard first. | A clock measures time. 2 be of the stated size: The river measured 200 metres from side to side. –surable adj –surably adv

  measure off/out phr vt take from a longer length or larger quantity

  measure up phr vi show good enough qualities (for)
measure² n 1 [U] measuring system 2 [C] unit in such a system 3 [S;U] fml amount: She's had a certain measure of success. 4 [C] act to bring about an effect: The government was forced to take strong measures. 5 for good measure in addition 6 take someone's measure/get the measure of someone judge what someone is like –sured adj careful and steady ~ment n 1 [U] act of measuring 2 [C] length, height, etc. measured
meat /miːt/ n [U] 1 flesh of animals (not fish) for eating 2 valuable matter, ideas, etc.: It was a clever speech, but there was no real meat in it. ~y adj
mec·ca /'mekə/ n place that many people wish to reach
me·chan·ic /mɪ'kænɪk/ n person skilled in using or repairing machines
me·chan·i·cal /mɪ'kænɪkəl/ adj 1 of or worked or produced by machinery 2 without new thought or strong feeling ~ly /-kli/ adv
me·chan·ics /mɪ'kænɪks/ n 1 [U] science of the action of forces on objects 2 [U] science of machinery 3 [P] way in which something works
mech·a·nis·m /'mekənɪzəm/ n machine or the way it works: (fig.) the mechanism of the brain
mech·a·nize, -ise /'mekənaɪz/ vt (start to) use machines for or in –ization /,mekənaɪ'zeɪʃən ‖ -nə-/ n [U]
med·al /'medl/ n usu. coinlike object given as a mark of honour, esp. for bravery ~list BrE ‖ ~ist AmE — n person who has won a medal, esp. in sport
me·dal·li·on /mɪ'dæliən/ n large medal, or piece of jewellery like a medal
med·dle /'medl/ vi take action in a matter which does not concern one ~dler n
me·di·a /'miːdɪə/ n [U;P] television, radio, newspapers, etc. —see also MEDIUM²

me·di·ate /ˈmiːdieit/ *vi* act so as to bring agreement after a quarrel **–ator** *n* **–ation** /ˌmiːdiˈeɪʃən/ *n* [U]

med·ic /ˈmedɪk/ *n infml* doctor or medical student

med·ic·aid /ˈmedɪkeɪd/ *n* [U] (*often cap.*) (in the US) system by which the government helps to pay the medical costs of people on low incomes

med·i·cal /ˈmedɪkəl/ *adj* of or for the treatment of illness, esp. with medicine rather than operations ♦ *n* medical examination of the body **–ly** /-kli/ *adv*

med·i·care /ˈmedɪkeə‖ -ker/ *n* [U] (*often cap.*) (in the US) system of medical care provided by the government, esp. for old people

med·i·ca·tion /ˌmedɪˈkeɪʃən/ *n* [C;U] medicine, esp. a drug

me·di·ci·nal /məˈdɪsənəl/ *adj* as medicine; curing **–ly** *adv*

medi·cine /ˈmedsən‖ˈmedsən/ *n* 1 [C;U] substance for treating illness 2 [U] science of treating illness 3 **a taste/dose of one's own medicine** deserved punishment

med·i·e·val /ˌmedɪˈiːvəl‖ˌmiː-/ *adj* of the MIDDLE AGES

me·di·o·cre /ˌmiːdiˈoʊkə◂‖-ˈoʊkər◂/ *adj* rather bad **–crity** /ˌmiːdiˈɒkrʃti‖-ˈɑːk-/ *n* [U]

med·i·tate /ˈmedɪteɪt/ *v* 1 *vi* think deeply, esp. to gain calmness or before making a decision 2 *vt* plan or consider carefully **–tation** /ˌmedʃˈteɪʃən/ *n* [C;U]

me·di·um¹ /ˈmiːdiəm/ *adj* of middle size, amount, quality, etc.

medium² *n* **-dia** /-diə/ *or* **-diums** 1 method of artistic expression or of giving information 2 condition or surroundings in which things exist 3 middle position: *a happy medium between eating all the time and not eating at all*

medium³ *n* **-diums** person who claims to receive messages from the spirits of the dead

med·ley /ˈmedli/ *n* mass of different types mixed together

meek /miːk/ *adj* gentle and uncomplaining **–ly** *adv* **–ness** *n* [U]

meet¹ /miːt/ *v* met /met/ 1 *vi/t* come together (with): *I met an old friend in the street.* | *Our lips met (in a kiss).* 2 *vi/t* be

introduced (to) 3 *vt* find or experience: *She met her death in a plane crash.* 4 *vt* follow (as if) in answer: *His speech was met with boos.* 5 *vt* satisfy: *Their offer meets all our needs.* 6 *vt* pay: *Have you enough money to meet your debts?* 7 **meet someone halfway** make an agreement which partly satisfies both sides 8 **more (in/to something) than meets the eye** hidden facts or reasons (in or for something) **~ing** *n* occasion of coming together, esp. to talk

meet up *phr vi infml* meet, esp. by informal arrangements

meet with *phr vt* 1 experience: *I met with an accident.* 2 *esp. AmE* have a meeting with

meet² *n* gathering of people for (*BrE*) FOXHUNTING or (*AmE*) sports events

meg·a·byte /ˈmegəbaɪt/ *n* unit of computer information equal to a million BYTES

meg·a·lo·ma·ni·a /ˌmegələʊˈmeɪniə‖-loʊ-/ *n* [U] belief that one is more important, powerful, etc. than one really is **-niac** /-niæk/ *n*

meg·a·phone /ˈmegəfəʊn‖-foʊn/ *n* horn-shaped instrument to make the voice louder

mel·an·chol·y /ˈmelənkəli‖-kɑːli/ *adj, n* [U] sad(ness) **-ic** /ˌmelənˈkɒlɪk◂‖-ˈkɑː-/ *adj*

mel·ee /ˈmeleɪ‖ˈmeɪleɪ, meɪˈleɪ/ *n* struggling or disorderly crowd

mel·low /ˈmeloʊ‖-loʊ/ *adj* 1 suggesting gentle ripeness 2 (of colour) soft and warm ♦ *vi/t* become or make mellow **~ness** *n* [U]

mel·o·dra·mat·ic /ˌmelədrəˈmætɪk◂/ *adj* too full of excited feeling **~ally** /-kli/ *adv*

mel·o·dy /ˈmelədi/ *n* 1 tune 2 song **–dic** /məˈlɒdɪk‖-ˈlɑː-/ *adj* of or having melody **–dious** /məˈləʊdiəs‖-ˈloʊ-/ *adj* tuneful

mel·on /ˈmelən/ *n* large round juicy fruit

melt /melt/ *v* 1 *vi/t* become or make liquid: *The sun melted the ice.* 2 *vi* go away: disappear 3 *vi* become more sympathetic

melt down *phr vt* make (a metal object) liquid by heating

melt·down /ˈmeltdaʊn/ *n* 1 dangerous situation in which material burns through the bottom of an atomic REACTOR 2 sudden complete failure

melting pot /ˈ··· ·/ *n* 1 place where many

different things are mixed together **2 in the melting pot** not fixed or decided

mem·ber /'membə ‖ -ər/ n **1** someone who belongs to a club, group, etc. **2** part of the body, such as an organ or limb ~**ship** n **1** [U] state of being a MEMBER (1) **2** [C] all the members of a club, society, etc.

Member of Par·lia·ment /, · · '··/ n BrE person elected to serve in parliament

mem·brane /'membreɪn/ n [C;U] soft thin skin

me·men·to /mɪ'mentəʊ ‖ -too/ n -tos object that brings back pleasant memories

mem·o /'meməʊ ‖ -mou/ n -os also **memorandum** – note from one person or office to another within an organization

mem·oirs /'memwɑːz ‖ -ɑːrz/ n [P] AUTO-BIOGRAPHY

mem·o·ra·bil·i·a /,memərə'bɪliə/ n [P] interesting things connected with a famous person or event

mem·o·ra·ble /'memərəbəl/ adj worth remembering, esp. because good –**bly** adv

mem·o·ran·dum /,memə'rændəm/ n -da /-də-/ fml MEMO

me·mo·ri·al /mɪ'mɔːriəl/ n something, esp. a stone MONUMENT, in memory of a person, event, etc.

mem·o·rize also -**rise** BrE /'meməraɪz/ vt learn and remember, on purpose

mem·o·ry /'meməri/ n **1** [C;U] ability to remember: *She's got a good memory.* **2** [C] example of remembering: *one of my earliest memories* **3** [U] time during which things happened which can be remembered: *within living memory* **4** [U] opinion held of someone after their death: *to praise his memory* **5** [C] part of a computer in which information is stored **6 in memory of** as a way of remembering or being reminded of

men /men/ n pl. of MAN

men·ace /'menɪs/ n **1** [C;U] threat; danger **2** [C] troublesome person or thing ♦ vt threaten

me·na·ge·rie /mɪ'nædʒəri/ n collection of wild animals kept privately or for the public to see

mend /mend/ v **1** vt repair **2** vi regain one's health **3 mend one's ways** improve one's behaviour ♦ n **1** repaired place **2 on the mend** regaining one's health ~**er** n

me·ni·al /'miːniəl/ adj (of a job) humble and not interesting or important ♦ n

someone who does menial work

men·in·gi·tis /,menɪn'dʒaɪtɪs/ n [U] serious brain illness

men·o·pause /'menəpɔːz ‖ -pɔːz/ n [the+S] time of life when a woman's PERIOD(S)[1] (3) stop

men·stru·al /'menstruəl/ adj of a woman's PERIOD(s)

men·stru·ate /'menstrueɪt/ vi have a PERIOD –**ation** /,menstru'eɪʃən/ n [U]

men·tal /'mentl/ adj **1** of or in the mind: *mental illness* | *a mental picture* **2** of or for illness of the mind: *a mental hospital* **3** infml mad ~**ly** adv

men·tal·i·ty /men'tælɪti/ n **1** [U] abilities and powers of the mind **2** [C] person's character and way of thought

men·thol /'menθɒl ‖ -θɒːl, -θɑːl/ n [U] substance which smells and tastes of MINT[1] ~**ated** /-θəleɪtɪd/ adj

men·tion /'menʃən/ vt **1** tell of or about, esp. in a few words **2 Don't mention it** (polite reply to thanks) **3 not to mention** and in addition there's ... ♦ n **1** short remark about **2** naming of someone, esp. to honour them

men·tor /'mentɔː ‖ -tɔːr/ n person who habitually advises another

men·u /'menjuː/ n list of food one can order in a restaurant

MEP /,em iː 'piː/ abbrev. for: Member of the European Parliament

mer·ce·na·ry /'mɜːsənəri ‖ 'mɜːrsəneri/ adj influenced by the wish for money ♦ n soldier who fights for whoever will pay him

mer·chan·dise /'mɜːtʃəndaɪz, -daɪs ‖ 'mɜːr-/ n [U] things for sale

mer·chant /'mɜːtʃənt ‖ 'mɜːr-/ n person who buys and sells goods in large amounts ♦ adj used in trade, not war: *the merchant navy*

merchant bank /,·· '·/ n bank that provides banking services for businesses rather than for ordinary people

mer·cu·ry /'mɜːkjʊri ‖ 'mɜːr-/ n [U] **1** silvery liquid metal **2** (cap.) the PLANET nearest the sun –**rial** /mɜː'kjʊəriəl ‖ mɜːr'kjʊr-/ adj quick, active, and often changing

mer·cy /'mɜːsi ‖ 'mɜːrsi/ n [U] **1** willingness to forgive, not to punish; kindness and pity **2** fortunate event **3 at the mercy of** defenceless against **merciful** adj

merciless *adj*

mere /mɪə ‖ mɪr/ *adj* only; nothing more than: *a mere child* **~ly** *adv* only

merge /mɜːdʒ ‖ mɜːrdʒ/ *v* **1** *vi* combine, esp. gradually, so as to become a single thing **2** *vi/t* join together: *The two companies merged.* **merger** *n* joining together of two or more companies

me·rid·i·an /məˈrɪdiən ‖ -ɪən/ *n* **1** imaginary line over the Earth's surface from the top to the bottom, used on maps **2** highest point, esp. of a star

me·ringue /məˈræŋ/ *n* [C;U] (light cake made from) a mixture of sugar and the white part of eggs

mer·it /ˈmerɪt/ *n* [C;U] good quality ♦ *vt fml* deserve

mer·i·toc·ra·cy /ˌmerɪˈtɒkrəsi ‖ -ˈtɑː-/ *n* social system which gives the highest positions to those with the most ability

mer·maid /ˈmɜːmeɪd ‖ ˈmɜːr-/ *n* (in stories) woman with a fish's tail

mer·ry /ˈmeri/ *adj* **1** full of or causing laughter and fun **2** *BrE infml* rather drunk **~rily** *adv* **~riment** *n* [U]

merry-go-round /ˈ··· ·ˌ·/ *n* machine with large model animals on which children ride round and round

mesh[1] /meʃ/ *n* [C;U] **1** net, esp. with small holes **2** threads in such a net

mesh[2] *vi* (of the teeth of GEARS) connect: (fig.) *Their characters just don't mesh.* (=fit together suitably)

mes·mer·ize, -ise /ˈmezməraɪz/ *vt* hold the complete attention of, as if by a strong force

mess[1] /mes/ *n* **1** [S;U] (state of) untidiness or dirt **2** [S] bad situation; trouble **3** [C] room where soldiers, etc. eat **4 make a mess of** ruin; spoil **~y** *adj*

mess[2] *v*

mess about/around *phr v* **1** *vi* act or speak stupidly **2** *vi* spend time with no particular plan or purpose **3** *vt* treat badly

mess up *phr vt* ruin; spoil

mes·sage /ˈmesɪdʒ/ *n* **1** piece of information passed from one person to another **2** main moral idea of a story, picture, etc. **3 get the message** understand what is meant

mes·sen·ger /ˈmesəndʒə ‖ -ər/ *n* person who brings a message

mes·si·ah /məˈsaɪə/ *n* **1** new leader in a religion **2** (*cap.*) Jesus Christ

met /met/ *v past t. and p. of* MEET[1]

me·tab·o·lis·m /məˈtæbəlɪzəm/ *n* process by which a body lives, esp. by changing food into ENERGY **-lic** /ˌmetəˈbɒlɪk◄ ‖ -ˈbɑː-/ *adj*

met·al /ˈmetl/ *n* [C;U] usu. solid shiny material, such as iron, copper, or silver **~lic** /məˈtælɪk/ *adj*

met·al·lur·gy /məˈtælədʒi ‖ ˈmetələːrdʒi/ *n* [U] scientific study of metals **-gist** *n* **-gical** /ˌmetəˈlɜːdʒɪkəl◄ ‖ -ˈlɜːr-/ *adj*

met·al·work /ˈmetlwɜːk ‖ -wɜːrk/ *n* [U] making of metal objects

met·a·mor·pho·sis /ˌmetəˈmɔːfəsɪs ‖ -ɔːr-/ *n* **-ses** /-siːz/ complete change from one form to another

met·a·phor /ˈmetəfə, -fɔː ‖ -fɔːr/ *n* [C;U] (use of) a phrase which describes one thing by stating another thing with which it can be compared (as in *the roses in her cheeks*) — see also MIXED METAPHOR **~ical** /ˌmetəˈfɒrɪkəl◄ ‖ -ˈfɔː-, -ˈfɑː-/ *adj* **~ically** /kli/ *adv*

met·a·phys·i·cal /ˌmetəˈfɪzɪkəl◄/ *adj* **1** concerned with the science of being and knowing **2** (of ideas) at a high level and difficult to understand

mete /miːt/ *v*

mete out *phr vt fml* or *lit* give (esp. punishment)

me·te·or /ˈmiːtɪə ‖ -ər/ *n* small piece of matter that flies through space and can be seen burning if it comes near the Earth **~ic** /ˌmiːtiˈɒrɪk◄ ‖ -ˈɔːrɪk◄, -ˈɑːrɪk◄/ *adj* very fast: *a meteoric rise to fame* **~ically** /-kli/ *adv*

me·te·o·rite /ˈmiːtɪəraɪt/ *n* meteor that lands on the Earth

me·te·o·rol·o·gy /ˌmiːtɪəˈrɒlədʒi ‖ -ˈrɑː-/ *n* [U] scientific study of weather **-gist** *n* **-gical** /ˌmiːtɪərəˈlɒdʒɪkəl◄ ‖ -ˈlɑː-/ *adj*

me·ter[1] /ˈmiːtə ‖ -ər/ *n* machine that measures something: *a gas meter*

meter[2] *n AmE for* METRE

meth·a·done /ˈmeθədəʊn ‖ -doʊn/ *n* [U] drug given to people who want to stop using HEROIN

me·thane /ˈmiːθeɪn ‖ ˈme-/ *n* [U] gas that burns easily

meth·od /ˈmeθəd/ *n* **1** [C] way of doing something **2** [U] proper planning and arrangement **~ical** /məˈθɒdɪkəl ‖ məˈθɑː-/

adj careful; using an ordered system
~**ically** /-kli/ *adv*

meth·o·dol·o·gy /ˌmeθəˈdɒlədʒi ǁ -ˈdɑː-/ *n* set of methods

meth·yl·at·ed spir·its /ˌmeθɪˈleɪtɪd ˈspɪrɪts/ also **meths** /meθs/ *BrE infml* — *n* alcohol for burning in lamps, heaters, etc.

me·tic·u·lous /mɪˈtɪkjɪˌləs/ *adj* very careful, with great attention to detail ~**ly** *adv*

me·tre¹ *BrE* ǁ **meter** *AmE* /ˈmiːtə ǁ -ər/ *n* a measure of length equal to 39.37 inches

metre² *BrE* ǁ **meter** *AmE* — *n* [C;U] arrangement of beats in poetry

met·ric /ˈmetrɪk/ *adj* using a measured system (**metric system**) based on the metre and kilogram ~**ation** /ˌmetrɪˈkeɪʃən/ *n* [U] changing to a metric system

met·ro /ˈmetrəʊ -troʊ/ *n* -**ros** underground railway system: *the Paris metro*

me·trop·o·lis /mɪˈtrɒpəlɪs ǁ mɪˈtrɑː-/ *n* main or capital city —**litan** /ˌmetrəˈpɒlɪtən◂ -ˈpɑː-/ *adj*

met·tle /ˈmetl/ *n* **1** *fml* will to continue bravely in spite of difficulties **2 be on one's mettle/put someone on their mettle** have to make/force someone to make the best possible effort

mew /mjuː/ *vi, n* (make) the crying sound a cat makes

mews /mjuːz/ *n* **mews** small city street with houses and flats, at the back of larger houses

mez·za·nine /ˈmezəniːn, ˈmetsə- ˈmezə-/ *n* floor that comes between two other floors of a building

mg *written abbrev. for* MILLIGRAM(s)

mi·aow /miˈaʊ/ *vi, n* (make) the crying sound a cat makes

mice /maɪs/ *pl. of* MOUSE (1)

mick·ey /ˈmɪki/ *n* **take the mickey (out of)** *sl for* TEASE

mi·crobe /ˈmaɪkrəʊb ǁ -kroʊb/ *n* very small living creature that can only be seen with a MICROSCOPE

mi·cro·bi·ol·o·gy /ˌmaɪkrəʊbaɪˈɒlədʒi ǁ -kroʊbaɪˈɑː-/ *n* [U] scientific study of very small living creatures —**gist** *n*

mi·cro·chip /ˈmaɪkrəʊˌtʃɪp ǁ -kroʊ-/ *n* CHIP¹ (4)

mi·cro·com·put·er /ˈmaɪkrəʊkəmˌpjuːtə ǁ -kroʊkəmˈpjuːtər/ also **micro** /ˈmaɪkrəʊ ǁ -kroʊ-/ *infml* — *n* the smallest

type of computer, used esp. in the home, in schools, or by small businesses

mi·cro·cosm /ˈmaɪkrəʊˌkɒzəm ǁ -kroʊˌkɑː-/ *n* something small that represents all the qualities, activities, etc. of something larger

mi·cro·film /ˈmaɪkrəʊˌfɪlm ǁ -kroʊ-/ *n* [C;U] film for photographing something in a very small size ♦ *vt*

mi·cro·or·gan·is·m /ˌmaɪkrəʊˈɔːgənɪzəm ǁ -kroʊˈɔːr-/ *n* bacterium

mi·cro·phone /ˈmaɪkrəfəʊn ǁ -foʊn/ *n* electrical instrument for collecting sound, so as to make it louder or broadcast it

mi·cro·pro·ces·sor /ˌmaɪkrəʊˈprəʊsesə ǁ -kroʊˈprɑːsər/ *n* central controlling CHIP¹ (4) in a small computer

mi·cro·scope /ˈmaɪkrəskəʊp ǁ -skoʊp/ *n* scientific instrument that makes things look larger, used for studying extremely small things —**scopic** /ˌmaɪkrəˈskɒpɪk◂ -ˈskɑː-/ *adj* **1** very small **2** using a microscope —**scopically** /-kli/ *adv*

mi·cro·wave /ˈmaɪkrəweɪv/ also **micro·wave ov·en** /ˌ··· ˈ··/ — *n* box that cooks food using very short electric waves *vt* cook in a microwave

mid-air /ˌmɪdˈeə◂ -ˈer◂/ *n* [U] point up in the sky

mid·day /ˌmɪdˈdeɪ◂ ˈmɪd-deɪ/ *n* [U] 12 o'clock NOON

mid·dle /ˈmɪdl/ *adj, n* [S;U] (in or at) the centre or a point halfway between two ends

middle age /ˌ·· ˈ·◂/ *n* [U] period between youth and old age **middle-aged** *adj*

Middle Ag·es /ˌ·· ˈ·◂/ *n* [the+P] period between about AD 1100 and 1500 in Europe

middle class /ˌ·· ˈ·◂/ *n* social class of business and professional people, office workers, etc. **middle-class** *adj*

middle dis·tance /ˌ·· ˈ·◂/ *n* [U] part of a view between what is close and what is far away

Middle East /ˌ·· ˈ·◂/ *n* [the+S] countries in Asia west of India ~**ern** *adj*

mid·dle·man /ˈmɪdlmæn/ *n* -**men** /-men/ someone who buys from a producer and sells to a customer

middle name /ˌ·· ˈ·/ *n* **1** name coming between the FIRST NAME and the SURNAME **2** *infml* something for which a person is well known: *'Generosity's my middle name.'*

middle-of-the-road /ˌ·· · · ˈ·◂/ *adj*

favouring a course of action that most people would agree with

middle school /ˈ·· ·/ n school for children **a** BrE between 8 and 12 years old **b** AmE between 11 and 14 years old

mid·dling /ˈmɪdəlɪŋ/ adj average

midge /mɪdʒ/ n small winged insect that bites

midg·et /ˈmɪdʒɪt/ adj, n very small (person)

Mid·lands /ˈmɪdləndz/ n [the+P] central parts of England, between the North and the South

mid-life cri·sis /ˌ· · ˈ··/ n feeling of unhappiness, etc. suffered by a MIDDLE-AGED person

mid·night /ˈmɪdnaɪt/ n [U] 12 o'clock at night

mid·riff /ˈmɪdrɪf/ n front of the body below the chest

midst /mɪdst/ n **in the midst of** in the middle of; among

mid·sum·mer /ˌmɪdˈsʌmə◄ ‖ -ər◄/ n [U] middle of the summer

mid·way /ˌmɪdˈweɪ◄ ‖ ˈmɪdweɪ/ adj, adv halfway

mid·wife /ˈmɪdwaɪf/ n -wives /-waɪvz/ nurse who helps women giving birth –wifery /ˈmɪdˌwɪfəri ‖ -ˌwaɪfəri/ n [U]

miffed /mɪft/ adj infml slightly angry

might¹ /maɪt/ v aux **1** (used for expressing slight possibility): He might come, but it's unlikely. **2** past t. of MAY: I thought it might rain. **3** ought; should: You might have offered to help! **4 might well** be likely to **5 might as well** have no strong reason not to

might² n [U] power; strength ~y adj very great: a mighty blow

mi·graine /ˈmiːgreɪn, ˈmaɪ- ‖ ˈmaɪ-/ n [C;U] very severe headache

mi·grant /ˈmaɪgrənt/ n migrating person or bird: migrant workers

mi·grate /maɪˈgreɪt ‖ ˈmaɪgreɪt/ vi **1** (of birds or fish) travel regularly from one part of the world to another, according to the season **2** move from one place to another, esp. for a limited period –gration /maɪˈgreɪʃən/ n [C;U] –gratory /maɪˈgreɪtəri ‖ ˈmaɪgrəˌtɔːri/ adj

mike /maɪk/ n sl for MICROPHONE

mild /maɪld/ adj not strong, forceful, or severe; gentle ~ly adv ~ness n [U]

mil·dew /ˈmɪldjuː ‖ -duː/ n [U] whitish growth on plants and on things kept a long time in slightly wet conditions ~ed adj

mile /maɪl/ n **1** a measure of length equal to 1.609 kilometres **2** also **miles** pl. — infml a lot: I feel miles better now.

mile·age /ˈmaɪlɪdʒ/ n [C;U] **1** distance travelled, measured in miles **2** fixed amount of money paid for each mile travelled **3** amount of use: The press were getting a lot of mileage out of the affair.

mile·om·e·ter /maɪˈlɒmɪtə ‖ -ˈlɑːmətər/ n BrE instrument that tells how far a car, etc. has travelled

mile·stone /ˈmaɪlstəʊn ‖ -stoʊn/ n **1** stone beside the road, saying how far to the next town **2** important event

mi·lieu /ˈmiːljɜː ‖ miːˈljɜː, -ˈljuː/ n -s or -x /-ljɜːz, -ljɜː ‖ -ˈljɜːz, -ˈljuːz, -ˈljɜː, -ˈljuː/ person's social surroundings

mil·i·tant /ˈmɪlɪtənt/ n, adj (person) taking a strong active part in a struggle ~ly adv –tancy n [U]

mil·i·ta·rism /ˈmɪlɪtərɪzəm/ n [U] derog belief in the use of armed force –rist n –ristic /ˌmɪlɪtəˈrɪstɪk◄/ adj

mil·i·ta·ry /ˈmɪlɪtəri ‖ -teri/ adj of, for, or by soldiers, armies, or war ♦ n [the+P] the army

mil·i·tate /ˈmɪlɪteɪt/ n, adj **militate against** phr vt act, serve, or have importance as a reason against

mi·li·tia /məˈlɪʃə/ n force trained to be soldiers in time of special need

milk /mɪlk/ n [U] **1** white liquid produced by human or animal females to feed their young **2** white liquid produced by certain plants: coconut milk ♦ v **1** vt take milk from (a cow, etc.) **2** vi (of a cow, etc.) give milk **3** vt get money or advantages from (someone or something) ~y adj

milk·man /ˈmɪlkmən/ n -men /-mən/ person who delivers milk to houses

milk shake /ˌ· ˈ· ‖ ˈ· ·/ n drink of milk with an added taste of fruit, chocolate, etc.

milk tooth /ˈ· ·/ n one of a child's early teeth that fall out when the permanent teeth appear

mill¹ /mɪl/ n **1** (building containing) a machine for crushing grain to flour **2** factory: a cotton mill **3** small machine for crushing: a coffee mill **4 put someone through/go through the mill** (cause someone to) pass through (a time of) hard training, hard experience, etc. ♦ *vt* crush or produce in a mill

mill² *v* **mill about/around** *phr vi* move purposelessly in large numbers

mil·len·ni·um /mɪˈleniəm/ *n* **-nia** /-niə/ **1** [C] 1000 years **2** [*the*+S] time when a new 1000-year period begins

mil·let /ˈmɪlɪt/ *n* [U] small seeds of a grasslike plant, used as food

mil·li·gram, **-gramme** /ˈmɪlɪɡræm/ *n* measure of weight equal to 0.001 GRAMS

mil·li·li·tre *BrE* ‖ **-ter** *AmE n* /ˈmɪlɪˌliːtə ‖ -ər/ measure of liquid equal to 0.001 LITRES

mil·li·me·tre *BrE* ‖ **-ter** *AmE* /ˈmɪlɪˌ-miːtə ‖ -ər/ *n* measure of length equal to 0.001 METRES

mil·li·ner /ˈmɪlɪnə ‖ -ər/ *n* maker of women's hats ~**y** *n* [U] (making of) women's hats

mil·lion /ˈmɪljən/ *determiner, n, pron* **million** *or* **millions 1** 1,000,000 **2** also **millions of** — very large number ~**th** *determiner, n, pron, adv*

mil·lion·aire /ˌmɪljəˈneə◂ ‖ -ˈner◂/ **mil·lionairess** /-rɪs/ *fem.* — *n* person who has a million or more pounds or dollars; very wealthy person

mil·li·pede /ˈmɪlɪpiːd/ *n* small wormlike creature with many legs

mill·stone /ˈmɪlstəʊn ‖ -stoʊn/ *n* **1** circular crushing stone in a flourmill **2** cause of great trouble and anxiety

mime /maɪm/ *n* [C;U] use of actions without language to show meaning, esp. as a performance ♦ *n* actor who does this ♦ *vi/t* act in mime

mim·ic /ˈmɪmɪk/ *vt* **-ck- 1** copy (someone or something) amusingly **2** appear very like (something else) ♦ *n* person who mimics others ♦ *adj* not real

min·a·ret /ˌmɪnəˈret, ˈmɪnəret/ *n* tall thin tower in a MOSQUE

mince /mɪns/ *v* **1** *vt* cut (esp. meat) into very small pieces **2** *vi* walk in a silly unnatural way **3** **not mince one's words** speak of something sad or unpleasant using plain direct language ♦ *n* [U] **1** *BrE* meat that has been cut into very small pieces **2** *AmE* MINCEMEAT

mince·meat /ˈmɪns-miːt/ *n* [U] **1** mixture of dried fruit used as a filling for pastry **2** **make mincemeat of** defeat or

destroy (a person, belief, etc.) completely

mince pie /ˌ· ˈ·/ *n* small pastry case filled with mincemeat

mind¹ /maɪnd/ *n* **1** [C;U] person's (way of) thinking or feeling; thoughts: *She has a very quick mind.* **2** [U] memory: *I'll* **bear/keep** *it* **in mind**. (=not forget it) | *I can't* **call** *it* **to mind**. (=remember it) | *You* **put** *me* **in mind of** (=remind me of) *my brother.* **3** [C] attention: **Keep your mind on** *your work.* | *You need something to* **take your mind off** *the problem.* **4** [C;U] intention: *Nothing was further from my mind. I've* **got a good mind to** (=I think I may) *report you.* **5** [C;U] opinion: *We are of one/ of the same mind on this matter.* | **To my mind** (=in my opinion) *you're quite wrong.* **6** [C] person considered for his/her ability to think well: *She's one of the finest minds in the country.* **7** **be in two minds (about something)** be unable to reach a decision **8** **change one's mind** change one's intentions or opinions **9** **have half a mind** have a desire or intention that is not firmly formed **10** **in one's right mind** not mad **11** **know one's own mind** know what one wants **12** **make up one's mind** reach a decision **13** **mind over matter** control over events or material objects by the power of the mind **14** **on one's mind** causing anxiety **15** **out of one's mind** mad **16** **speak one's mind** express plainly one's thoughts and opinions ~**ful** *adj* giving attention ~**less** *adj* not needing or using thought; stupid ~**lessly** *adv* ~**lessness** *n* [U]

mind² *v* **1** *vi/t* be opposed to (a particular thing): *'Coffee or tea?' 'I don't mind.'* (=I'd like either) | *Would you mind opening* (=please open) *the window?* **2** *vi/t* be careful (of): *Mind the step!* **3** *vt* take care of; look after **4** **Do you mind!** I am offended and annoyed **5** **mind one's own business** not INTERFERE **6** **mind you** also **mind** — take this into account also **7** **never mind: a** don't worry **b** it doesn't matter **8** **never you mind** it is not your business ~**er** *n* person who looks after someone or something: *a childminder*

mind-bog·gling /ˈ· ˌ··/ *adj sl* very surprising

mind-set /ˈmaɪndset/ *n* way a person thinks, esp. if unlikely to change

mind's eye /ˌ· ˈ·/ *n* [U] imagination;

memory

mine[1] /main/ *pron* of me; my one(s): *This pen's mine, not yours.*

mine[2] *n* 1 place where coal or metal is dug from the ground: *a goldmine* | (fig.) *He's a mine of information.* (=can tell you a lot) 2 bomb placed under the ground or in the sea ♦ *v* 1 *vi/t* dig or get from a MINE[2] (1) 2 *vt* put MINES[2] (2) in or under 3 *vt* destroy by MINES[2] (2) **miner** *n* worker in a MINE[2] (1)

mine·field /'mainfi:ld/ *n* 1 place where MINES[2] (2) have been put 2 something full of hidden dangers

min·e·ral /'minərəl/ *n* substance formed naturally in the earth, such as stone, metal, coal, salt, or oil

mineral wa·ter /'··· ,··/ *n* [U] water from under the ground, containing minerals

mine·sweep·er /'main,swi:pə ‖ -ər/ *n* ship for finding and destroying MINES[2] (2)

min·gle /'miŋgəl/ 1 *vi/t* mix so as to form an undivided whole 2 *vi infml* talk to different people at a party

min·i·a·ture /'miniətʃə, 'minitʃə ‖ 'miniətʃur/ *adj, n* very small (thing, esp. a copy of a bigger one) **–turize, –ise** *vt*

min·i·bus /'minibʌs/ *n* small bus for between 6 and 12 people

min·i·mal /'miniməl/ *adj* as little as possible **~ly** *adv*

min·i·mize, –ise /'minimaiz/ *vt* 1 reduce as much as possible 2 treat as if not serious

min·i·mum /'miniməm/ *n, adj* **-ma** /-mə/ *or* **-mums** smallest (amount, number, etc.)

min·ing /'mainiŋ/ *n* [U] digging minerals out of the earth

min·ion /'minjən/ *n* slavelike helper

miniscule /'miniskju:l/ *adj* MINUSCULE

min·i·skirt /'mini,skɜ:t ‖ -,skɜ:rt/ *n* very short skirt

min·is·ter[1] /'ministə ‖ -ər/ *n* 1 politician in charge of a government department: *the Minister of Defence* 2 Christian priest **~ial** /,mini'stiəriəl◄ ‖ -'stir-/ *adj*

minister[2] *v* **minister to** *phr vt fml* help: *ministering to the sick*

min·is·tra·tion /,mini'streiʃən/ *n* [C;U] giving of help and service

min·is·try /'ministri/ *n* 1 [C] government department 2 [*the*+S] job of being a priest: *to enter the ministry* (=become a priest)

mink /miŋk/ *n* mink [C;U] (valuable brown fur of) a small fierce animal

mi·nor[1] /'mainə ‖ -ər/ *adj* of small importance or seriousness: *a minor problem* | *minor surgery*

minor[2] *n law* person too young to be held responsible

mi·nor·i·ty /mai'nɒrəti ‖ mə'nɔ:-, -nɒ:-, mə'nɑ:-/ *n* 1 [C] less than half: *A minority of people favour it.* 2 [C] small part of a population different from the rest: *minority rights* | *minority interest* (=supported by a small number of people) 3 [U] *law* state or time of being a minor

min·ster /'minstə ‖ -ər/ *n* great or important church: *Westminster*

min·strel /'minstrəl/ *n* travelling singer in former times

mint[1] /mint/ *n* 1 [C] PEPPERMINT 2 [U] plant with fresh-smelling leaves used in food **~y** *adj*

mint[2] *n* 1 place where coins are made 2 **make a mint** earn a lot of money ♦ *vt* make (a coin) ♦ *adj* (of a stamp, coin, etc.) unused and in perfect condition

min·u·et /,minju'et/ *n* (music for) a slow graceful dance

mi·nus /'mainəs/ *prep* 1 made less by: *10 minus 4 is 6.* 2 below freezing point: *It was minus 10 today.* (=−10°) 3 *infml* without ♦ *n* also **minus sign** — sign (−) showing a number less than zero, or that one number is to be taken away from another ♦ *adj* less than zero

min·us·cule, miniscule /'miniskju:l/ *adj* extremely small

min·ute[1] /'minit/ *n* 1 60th part of an hour 2 short time: *Wait a minute!* 3 60th part of a degree of angle 4 a short note of an official nature, such as on a report **b minutes** *pl.* written record of a meeting 5 **the minute (that)** as soon as ♦ *vt* record in the MINUTES[1] (4b)

mi·nute[2] /mai'nju:t ‖ -'nu:t/ *adj* very small **~ness** [U]

mi·nu·ti·ae /mai'nju:ʃiai, mə- ‖ mə'nu:-/ *n* [P] small exact details

mir·a·cle /'mirəkəl/ *n* 1 unexplainable but wonderful act or event, esp. as done by a holy person: (fig.) *It's a miracle the explosion didn't kill her.* 2 wonderful example (of a quality, ability, etc.): *a miracle of modern science* **–culous** /mi'rækjələs/ *adj*

mi·rage /'mirɑ:ʒ ‖ mə'rɑ:ʒ/ *n* something

seen that is not really there, esp. as caused by the hot desert air

mire /maɪə‖maɪr/ n [U] esp. lit deep mud

mir·ror /'mɪrə‖-ər/ n piece of glass in which one can see oneself ♦ vt show truly (as if) in a mirror

mirth /mɜːθ‖mɜːrθ/ n [U] laughter

mis·ad·ven·ture /,mɪsəd'ventʃə‖-ər/ n [C;U] esp. lit accident or piece of bad luck

mis·an·throp·ic /,mɪsən'θrɒpɪk◂ -'θrɑː-/ adj disliking everyone ~ally /-kli/ adv –ist n /'mɪsænθrəpəst/ n

mis·ap·pre·hen·sion /,mɪsæprɪ'henʃən/ n fml mistaken belief; misunderstanding

mis·ap·pro·pri·ate /,mɪsə'prəuprieɪt‖-'prou-/ vt take dishonestly (and use)

mis·be·have /,mɪsbɪ'heɪv/ vi/t behave (oneself) badly

misc. written abrev. for: MISCELLANEOUS

mis·cal·cu·late /,mɪs'kælkjǝleɪt/ vi/t calculate wrongly; form a wrong judgment of something –lation /,mɪs,kælkjǝ'leɪʃən/ n

mis·car·riage /'mɪs'kærɪdʒ, 'mɪskærɪdʒ/ n giving birth to a child too early for it to live

miscarriage of justice /·,··'··/ n unjust legal decision

mis·car·ry /mɪs'kæri/ vi 1 have a miscarriage 2 fml (of a plan) go wrong

mis·cel·la·ne·ous /,mɪsə'leɪniəs◂/ adj of many different kinds

mis·chief /'mɪstʃɪf/ n 1 slightly bad behaviour, esp. by children 2 damage; harm

mis·chie·vous /'mɪstʃǝvəs/ adj 1 playfully troublesome 2 causing harm, esp. intentionally ~ly adv

mis·con·ceive /,mɪskən'siːv/ vt make (a plan) badly

mis·con·cep·tion /,mɪskən'sepʃən/ n case of wrong understanding

mis·con·duct /,mɪs'kɒndʌkt‖-'kɑːn-/ n [U] fml bad behaviour, esp. sexual

mis·con·strue /,mɪskən'struː/ vt wrongly understand

mis·deed /,mɪs'diːd/ n fml wrong act

mis·de·mea·nour BrE ‖ -nor AmE /,mɪsdɪ'miːnə‖-ər/ n crime or wrong act which is not very serious

mi·ser /'maɪzə‖-ər/ n person who hates spending money ~liness n [U] ~ly adj

mis·e·ra·ble /'mɪzərəbəl/ adj 1 very unhappy 2 causing lack of cheerfulness:

miserable weather 3 very low in quality or very small in amount: a few miserable pounds –bly adv

mis·e·ry /'mɪzəri/ n 1 [C;U] great unhappiness or suffering 2 [C] esp. BrE complaining person

mis·fire /,mɪs'faɪə‖-'faɪr/ vi 1 (of a gun) not fire properly 2 (of a plan or joke) not have the intended effect

mis·fit /'mɪs,fɪt/ n someone who cannot live or work happily in their surroundings

mis·for·tune /mɪs'fɔːtʃən‖-ɔːr-/ n [C;U] 1 bad luck, esp. of a serious nature 2 very unfortunate event, condition, etc.

mis·giv·ing /mɪs'gɪvɪŋ/ n [C;U] feeling that it might be better not to do a thing

mis·guid·ed /,mɪs'gaɪdǝd/ adj showing bad judgment; foolish ~ly adv

mis·hap /'mɪshæp/ n slight unfortunate happening

mis·in·form /,mɪsɪn'fɔːm‖-ɔːrm/ vt give wrong information to

mis·in·ter·pret /,mɪsɪn'tɜːprǝt‖-ɜːr-/ vt wrongly understand

mis·judge /,mɪs'dʒʌdʒ/ vt judge wrongly, esp. form a wrong or unfairly bad opinion –judgment n [C;U]

mis·lay /mɪs'leɪ/ vt -laid /-'leɪd/ lose for a short time

mis·lead /mɪs'liːd/ vt -led /-'led/ cause to think or act mistakenly

mis·man·age /,mɪs'mænɪdʒ/ vt control or deal with (private, public, or business affairs) badly ~ment n [U]

mis·no·mer /mɪs'nəumə‖-'noumər/ n unsuitable name

mi·so·gy·nist /mǝ'sɒdʒǝnǝst‖mǝ'sɑː-/ n woman-hater

mis·place /,mɪs'pleɪs/ vt 1 put in the wrong place: (fig.) misplaced trust 2 mislay

mis·print /'mɪs,prɪnt/ n mistake in printing

mis·quote /,mɪs'kwəut‖-'kwout/ vt wrongly report what someone has said/written

mis·rep·re·sent /,mɪsreprɪ'zent/ vt give an intentionally untrue account or explanation of ~ation /,mɪsreprɪzen'teɪʃən/ n [C;U]

miss¹ /mɪs/ v 1 vi/t fail to hit, catch, meet, see, hear, etc.: He shot at me, but missed. | I missed the train. | She narrowly missed being killed. 2 vt feel unhappy at the absence or loss of ♦ *n* **1** failure to hit, etc. **2** **give something a miss** *esp. BrE* not do, take, etc. something —see also NEAR MISS **~ing** *adj* not in the proper place; lost

miss out *phr v* **1** *vt* fail to include **2** *vi* lose a chance to gain advantage or enjoyment

miss² *n* (*usu. cap.*) (title of a girl or unmarried woman): *Miss Browne*

mis·shap·en /ˌmɪsˈʃeɪpən, mɪˈʃeɪ-/ *adj* not having a normal shape

mis·sile /ˈmɪsaɪl ‖ ˈmɪsəl/ *n* **1** explosive flying weapon **2** object or weapon thrown: *They threw bottles and other missiles at the police.*

mis·sion /ˈmɪʃən/ *n* **1** special job, duty, or purpose: *He felt his mission in life was to help others.* | *They were sent on a secret mission.* **2** group of people sent abroad: *a trade mission* **3** place where missionaries work

mis·sion·a·ry /ˈmɪʃənəri ‖ -neri/ *n* person sent abroad to spread religion

mis·spent /ˌmɪsˈspent◄/ *adj* wasted

mist /mɪst/ *n* [C;U] thin FOG: (fig.) *lost in the mists of time* ♦ *vi/t* cover with mist: *The windscreen had misted up.* **~y**: (fig.) *misty memories*

mis·take /mɪˈsteɪk/ *vt* **-took** /mɪˈstʊk/, **-taken** /mɪˈsteɪkən/ **1** have a wrong idea about: *He mistook my meaning.* **2** fail to recognize ♦ *n* [C;U] something done through carelessness, lack of knowledge or skill, etc.: *I made a terrible mistake.* | *I did it by mistake.*

mistake for *phr vt* think wrongly that (a person or thing) is (someone or something else): *I mistook him for his brother.*

mis·tak·en /mɪˈsteɪkən/ *adj* wrong; incorrect **~ly** *adv*

mis·tle·toe /ˈmɪsəltəʊ ‖ -toʊ/ *n* [U] plant with white berries, used for Christmas decorations

mis·took /mɪˈstʊk/ *past t. of* MISTAKE

mis·tress /ˈmɪstrɪs/ *n* **1** woman in control **2** married man's sexual partner who is not his wife

mis·trust /ˌmɪsˈtrʌst/ *vt* not trust ♦ *n* [U] lack of trust **~ful** *adj*

mis·un·der·stand /ˌmɪsʌndəˈstænd ‖ -ər-/ *vi/t* **-stood** /stʊd/ understand wrongly **~ing** *n* [C;U] failure of correct understanding,

esp. with slight disagreement

mis·use /mɪsˈjuːs/ *n* [C;U] wrong use: *the misuse of power* ♦ *vt* /ˌmɪsˈjuːz/

mite /maɪt/ *n* **1** very small insect: *dust mites* **2** (used to show sympathy for) a small child

mit·i·gate /ˈmɪtɪɡeɪt/ *vt fml* lessen the severity of: *mitigating circumstances* (=which help to explain why something bad was done) **-gation** /ˌmɪtɪˈɡeɪʃən/ *n* [U]

mi·tre *BrE* ‖ **miter** *AmE* /ˈmaɪtə ‖ -ər/ *n* BISHOP's tall pointed hat

mitt /mɪt/ *n* type of protective mitten

mit·ten /ˈmɪtn/ *n* GLOVE without separate finger parts

mix /mɪks/ *v* **1** *vi/t* combine so that the parts no longer have a separate shape, appearance, etc.: *Oil and water don't mix.* | *Mix blue and yellow to make green.* | *She mixed herself a cocktail.* **2** *vi* be or enjoy being in the company of others **~ed** *adj* **1** of different kinds **2** for both sexes **3** **mixed up in** connected with (something bad) **~er** *n* ♦ *n* [C;U] MIXTURE (1): *cake mix*

mixed bag /ˌ· ˈ·/ *n* [S] collection of things of many different kinds (and qualities)

mixed bles·sing /ˌ· ˈ·/ *n* [S] something that is bad as well as good

mixed e·con·o·my /ˌ· ·ˈ···/ *n* operation of a country's money supply, industry, and trade by a mixture of CAPITALIST and SOCIALIST principles

mixed met·a·phor /ˌ· ˈ···/ *n* use of two METAPHORs together with a foolish or funny effect

mix·ture /ˈmɪkstʃə ‖ -ər/ *n* **1** [C;U] set of substances (to be) mixed together **2** [S] combination: *a mixture of amusement and disbelief* **3** [U] act of mixing

mix-up /ˈ· ·/ *n* state of disorder and confusion

ml *written abbrev. for* MILLILITRE(s)

mm *written abbrev. for* MILLIMETRE(s)

mne·mon·ic /nɪˈmɒnɪk ‖ nɪˈmɑː-/ *adj, n* (something) used for helping one to remember

MO /ˌem ˈəʊ ‖ -ˈoʊ/ *n abbrev. for:* **1** medical officer **2** MODUS OPERANDI

moan /məʊn ‖ moʊn/ *vi, n* (make a) **a** low sound of pain **b** discontented complaint

moat /məʊt ‖ moʊt/ *n* long deep usu. water-filled hole round esp. a castle

mob /mɒb ‖ mɑːb/ *n* **1** noisy (violent)

crowd 2 group of criminals ♦ vt -bb- gather round a to attack b because of interest or admiration

mo·bile¹ /'məubail ‖ 'moubəl, -biːl/ adj (easily) movable; not fixed –**bility** /məu'biləti ‖ mou-/ n [U]

mo·bile² /'məubail ‖ 'moubiːl/ n 1 decoration made of small hanging objects 2 BrE also **mobile phone** BrE CELLULAR PHONE

mo·bil·ize, -ise /'məubəlaiz ‖ 'maː-/ vt bring into action, esp. ready for war –**ization, -isation** /,məubəlai'zeiʃən ,moubələ-/ n [U]

moc·ca·sin /'mɒkəsin ‖ 'maː-/ n simple soft leather shoe

mock¹ /mɒk ‖ maːk/ vt laugh at unkindly or unfairly

mock² adj not real; pretended: a mock battle

mock·er·y /'mɒkəri ‖ 'maː-/ n 1 [U] mocking 2 [S] something unworthy of respect 3 **make a mockery of** show to be foolish or untrue

mock-up /'·· ·/ n full-size model of something to be built

modal aux·il·i·a·ry /,·· ·'····/ n verb that goes in front of another, such as can, may, or would

mod con /,mɒd 'kɒn ‖ ,maːd 'kaːn/ n all mod cons with all modern conveniences (such as hot water, central heating, etc.)

mode /məud ‖ moud/ n way of doing something

mod·el /'mɒdl ‖ 'maːdl/ n 1 small copy: a model aeroplane 2 person who models clothes 3 person to be painted or photographed 4 person or thing of the highest quality: a model student 5 type of vehicle, machine, weapon, etc.: His car is the latest model. ♦ v -ll- BrE ‖ -l- AmE 1 vt make a small copy 2 vi/t wear (clothes) to show them to possible buyers

model on phr vt form as a copy of: She modelled herself on her mother.

mo·dem /'məudəm ‖ 'mou,dem/ n equipment for sending information from one computer to another down a telephone line

mod·e·rate¹ /'mɒdərət ‖ 'maː-/ adj 1 neither too much nor too little; middle 2 not politically extreme ~**ly** adv not very –**ration** /,mɒdə'reiʃən ‖ ,maː-/ n [U] 1 self-control 2 reduction in force or degree 3 **in**

moderation within sensible limits

mod·e·rate² /'mɒdəreit ‖ 'maː-/ vi/t lessen in force, degree, etc.

mod·e·rate³ /'mɒdərət ‖ 'maː-/ n person whose opinions are MODERATE¹ (2)

mod·ern /'mɒdn ‖ 'maːdərn/ adj 1 of the present time 2 new and different from the past ~**ize, -ise** v 1 vt make suitable for modern use 2 vi start using more modern methods ~**ization, ~isation** /,mɒdənai-'zeiʃən ‖ ,maːdərnə-/ n [C;U]

mod·est /'mɒdɪst ‖ 'maː-/ adj 1 not too proud 2 not large 3 not sexually improper ~**ly** adv ~**y** n [U]

mod·i·cum /'mɒdɪkəm ‖ 'maː-/ n small amount

mod·i·fy /'mɒdɪfai ‖ 'maː-/ vt 1 change, esp. slightly 2 make (a claim, condition, etc.) less hard to accept or bear 3 (esp. of an adjective or adverb) go with and describe (another word) –**fication** /,mɒdɪfə'keiʃən ‖ ,maː-/ n [C;U]

mod·u·late /'mɒdjʊleit ‖ 'maːdʒə-/ vt vary the strength, nature, etc. of (a sound) –**lation** /,mɒdjʊ'leiʃən ‖ ,maːdʒə-/ n [C;U]

mod·ule /'mɒdjuːl ‖ 'maːdʒuːl/ n 1 standard part used in building, making furniture, etc. 2 part of a spacecraft for independent use 3 BrE one of the parts that a course of study is divided into –**ular** /'mɒdjʊlə ‖ 'maːdʒələr/ adj

mo·dus **op·e·ran·di** /,məudəs ,ɒpə'rændi ‖ ,moudəs ,aːpə-/ n [S] method of doing something

modus vi·ven·di /,məudəs vɪ'vendi ‖ ,mou-/ n [S] way of living (together)

mo·gul /'məugəl ‖ 'mou-/ n person of very great power and wealth

mo·hair /'məuheə ‖ 'mouher/ n [U] (cloth from) the long silky hair of a sort of goat

Mo·ham·me·dan /məu'hæmɪdən, mə- ‖ mou-, mə-/ n, adj Muslim

moist /mɔist/ adj slightly wet ~**en** /'mɔisən/ vi/t make or become moist ~**ure** /'mɔistʃə ‖ -ər/ n [U] liquid in or on something ~**urize, ~urise** /'mɔistʃəraiz/ vt ~**urizer, ~uriser** n liquid, cream, etc. used to soften the skin

mo·lar /'məulə ‖ 'moulər/ n large back tooth

mold /məuld ‖ mould/ n, v AmE for MOULD

mol·der /'məuldə ‖ 'mouldər/ v AmE for MOULDER

mole[1] /məʊl‖moʊl/ *n* **1** small furry animal that lives underground **2** *BrE* SPY who works inside an organization

mole[2] *n* small, dark brown mark on the skin

mol·e·cule /'mɒlɪkjuːl‖'maː-/ *n* very small piece of matter, made of two or more atoms –**cular** /məˈlekjʃlə‖-ər/ *adj*

mole·hill /'məʊl‚hɪl‖'moʊl-/ *n* small pile of earth thrown up by a mole –see also **make a mountain out of a molehill** (MOUNTAIN)

mo·lest /məˈlest/ *vt* **1** attack; harm **2** attack (esp. a woman or child) sexually

mol·li·fy /'mɒlɪfaɪ‖'maː-/ *vt* make less angry

mol·lusc also **mollusk** *AmE* /'mɒləsk‖'maː-/ *n* sort of soft-bodied limbless animal, usu. with a shell

mol·ly·cod·dle /'mɒli‚kɒdl‖'maːliˌkɑːdl/ *vt* take too much care of (a person or animal)

molt /məʊlt‖moʊlt/ *v AmE for* MOULT

mol·ten /'məʊltən‖'moʊl-/ *adj* (of metal or rock) melted

mo·ment /'məʊmənt‖'moʊ-/ *n* **1** very short period of time **2** particular point in time **3** importance: *a matter of great moment* **4** **the moment (that)** as soon as ~**ary** *adj* lasting a moment –**arily** /'məʊməntərʃli‖‚mooʊmənˈterʃli/ *adv* **1** for just a very short time **2** *esp. AmE* very soon; in a moment

mo·men·tous /məʊˈmentəs, mə-‖ moʊ-, mə-/ *adj* extremely important ~**ness** *n* [U]

mo·men·tum /məʊˈmentəm, mə-‖ moʊ-, mə-/ *n* [U] measurable quantity of movement in a body: (fig.) *The campaign had lost its momentum.*

mon·arch /'mɒnək‖'maːnərk, -aːrk/ *n* non-elected ruler; king, queen, etc. ~**y** *n* **1** [U] rule by a monarch **2** [C] country ruled by a monarch ~**ist** *n* person who supports monarchy (1)

mon·as·tery /'mɒnəstri‖'maːnəsteri/ *n* building in which MONKs live

mo·nas·tic /məˈnæstɪk/ *adj* of MONKs or monasteries

Mon·day /'mʌndi/ *n* the first day of the week, between Sunday and Tuesday

mon·e·ta·ris·m /'mʌnɪtərɪzəm‖'maː-/ *n* [U] (in ECONOMICS) belief that the best way

of controlling the ECONOMY of a country is to control its money supply –**rist** *n, adj*

mon·e·ta·ry /'mʌnɪtəri‖'maːnəteri/ *adj* of or about money

mon·ey /'mʌni/ *n* [U] **1** something used for paying, esp. coins or paper money **2** wealth: *We're in the money.* (=rich) **3** **for my money** in my opinion **4** **one's money's worth** full value for the money one has spent

money mar·ket /'·· ‚··/ *n* financial organizations that buy and sell BONDS (2), CURRENCY (1), etc.

money-spin·ner /'·· ‚·'/ *n* something that brings in a lot of money

money sup·ply /'·· ·‚/ *n* [*the*+S] all the money that exists and is being paid and spent in a country in the form of coins, notes, and CREDIT

mon·grel /'mʌŋgrəl‖'maːŋ-, 'mʌŋ-/ *n* dog of mixed breed

mon·i·tor /'mɒnɪtə‖'maːnɪtər/ *vt* watch or listen to carefully for a special purpose ♦ *n* **1** television used to show the view seen by a television camera **2** instrument for monitoring a bodily condition: *a heart monitor* **3** **a** screen for use with a computer **b** parts of a computer operation that make sure that the computer system is working properly **4** person who listens to foreign radio news, etc. and reports on its content **5** pupil chosen to help the teacher: *dinner money monitor*

monk /mʌŋk/ *n* member of an all-male religious group that lives together

mon·key[1] /'mʌŋki/ *n* **1** small tree-climbing long-tailed animal **2** *infml* child full of playful tricks **3** **make a monkey (out) of someone** *infml* make someone appear foolish

monkey[2] *v* **monkey about/around** *phr vi* play foolishly

monkey busi·ness /'·· ‚··/ *n* [U] *infml* secret behaviour which causes trouble

mon·o·chrome /'mɒnəkrəʊm‖'maːnə-kroʊm/ *adj* **1** in only one colour **2** in black and white only

mon·o·cle /'mɒnəkəl‖'maː-/ *n* LENS for one eye only, to help the sight

mo·nog·a·my /məˈnɒgəmi‖məˈnaː-/ *n* [U] having only one husband or wife at a time –**mous** *adj*

mon·o·gram /'mɒnəgræm‖'maː-/ *n*

combined letters, esp. someone's INITIALs ~**med** adj

mon·o·lith·ic /ˌmɒnəˈlɪθɪk◁ ‖ ˌmɑː-/ adj 1 like a large stone pillar 2 often derog forming a large unchangeable whole

mon·o·logue /ˈmɒnəlɒg ‖ ˈmɑːnəlɔːg, -lɑːg/ n long speech by one person

mo·nop·o·ly /məˈnɒpəli ‖ məˈnɑː-/ n unshared control or right to do or produce something: (fig.) He thinks he's got a monopoly on brains. (=that he alone is clever) –**lize**, –**lise** vt keep unshared control of

mon·o·rail /ˈmɒnəʊreɪl, -nə- ‖ ˈmɑːnoʊ-/ n railway with one rail

mon·o·sod·i·um glu·tam·ate /ˌmɒnəʊˌsəʊdiəm ˈgluːtəmeɪt ‖ ˌmɑːnə,soʊ-/ n [U] chemical compound added to certain foods, to make their taste stronger

mon·o·syl·la·ble /ˈmɒnəˌsɪləbəl ‖ ˈmɑː-/ n word of one SYLLABLE –**bic** /ˌmɒnəsɪˈlæb-ɪk◁ ‖ ˌmɑː-/ adj

mon·o·tone /ˈmɒnətəʊn ‖ ˈmɑːnətoʊn/ n [S] way of speaking or singing in which the voice continues on the same note

mo·not·o·ny /məˈnɒtəni ‖ məˈnɑː-/ n [U] dull sameness –**onous** adj dull; boring (BORE²) –**onously** adv

mon·soon /mɒnˈsuːn ‖ mɑːn-/ n (time of) very heavy rains in and near India

mon·ster /ˈmɒnstə ‖ ˈmɑːnstər/ n 1 strange usu. large and frightening creature 2 very evil person ♦ adj unusually large: a monster potato —see also GREEN-EYED MONSTER

mon·stros·i·ty /mɒnˈstrɒsəti ‖ mɑːnˈstrɑː-/ n something very ugly and usu. large

mon·strous /ˈmɒnstrəs ‖ ˈmɑːn-/ adj 1 extremely bad; shocking 2 unnaturally large, strange, etc. ~**ly** adv

mon·tage /ˈmɒntɑːʒ ‖ mɑːnˈtɑːʒ/ n [C;U] picture made from separate parts combined

month /mʌnθ/ n 12th part of a year; four weeks ~**ly** adj

mon·u·ment /ˈmɒnjəmənt ‖ ˈmɑː-/ n 1 something built in honour of a person or event 2 historical old building or place 3 work, esp. a book, worthy of lasting fame ~**al** /ˌmɒnjʉˈmentl◁ ‖ ˌmɑː-/ adj 1 intended as a monument 2 very large 3 (esp. of something bad) very great in degree ~**ally** adv extremely

moo /muː/ vi,n (make) the sound that a cow makes

mooch /muːtʃ/ vt AmE sl get by asking for it

mooch about/around phr vi wander about rather unhappily with no purpose

mood¹ /muːd/ n 1 state of feeling: in a cheerful mood 2 state of feeling in which one is bad-tempered or angry ~**y** adj often having bad moods ~**ily** adv

mood² n any of the three sets of verb forms that express **a** a fact or action (INDICATIVE), **b** a command (IMPERATIVE), or **c** a doubt, wish, etc. (SUBJUNCTIVE)

moon¹ /muːn/ n 1 large body that moves round the Earth and shines at night 2 body that moves round a PLANET other than the Earth 3 infml over the moon very happy —see also BLUE MOON

moon² v moon about/around phr vi wander about in an aimless unhappy way

moon·beam /ˈmuːnbiːm/ n beam of light from the moon

moon·light¹ /ˈmuːnlaɪt/ [U] light of the moon

moonlight² vi -ed have a second job in addition to a regular one, esp. without the knowledge of a government department

moor¹ /mʊə ‖ mʊr/ also **moors** pl., **moorland** /ˈmʊələnd ‖ ˈmʊr-/ esp. BrE (area of) high hilly usu. treeless land

moor² vi/t fasten (a boat) to land, etc. by means of ropes, etc. ~**ings** n [P] 1 ropes, ANCHORS, etc. for mooring 2 also **mooring** — place where a boat is moored

moose /muːs/ n moose large North American deer

moot /muːt/ vt state (a question, matter, etc.) for consideration

moot point /ˌ· ˈ·/ n undecided matter, on which people have different opinions

mop¹ /mɒp ‖ mɑːp/ n 1 long stick with thick string or a SPONGE at one end, for washing floors 2 thick untidy mass of hair

mop² vt -pp- wash or dry (as if) with a mop: She mopped her brow.

mop up phr vt 1 remove liquid, dirt, etc. with a mop 2 finish dealing with: mop up small enemy groups

mope /məʊp ‖ moʊp/ vi be continuously sad

mo·ped /ˈməʊped ‖ ˈmoʊ-/ n small motorcycle

mor·al /'mɒrəl ‖ 'mɔːr-/ *adj* **1** of or based on the difference between good and evil or right and wrong: *She has high moral principles.* **2** pure and honest in character and behaviour ♦ *n* lesson that can be learnt from a story or event ~**ize** /-ize/ *vi* give one's opinions on right and wrong, esp. when unwelcome **morals** *n* [P] standards of (sexual) behaviour ~**ity** /məˈrælɪti/ *n* [U] rightness or pureness of behaviour or of an action

mo·rale /məˈrɑːl ‖ məˈræl/ *n* [U] pride and confidence, esp. in relation to a job to be done

moral sup·port /,·· ·'·/ *n* [U] encouragement

mo·rass /məˈræs/ [C] *esp. lit* MARSH: (fig.) bogged down in a morass of detail

mor·a·to·ri·um /,mɒrəˈtɔːriəm ‖ ,mɔː-/ *n* -**ria** /-riə/ official period during which a particular thing is not done

mor·bid /'mɔːbɪd ‖ 'mɔːr-/ *adj* unhealthily interested in death ~**ly** *adv* ~**ity** /mɔːˈbɪdɪti ‖ mɔːr-/ *n* [U]

mor·dant /'mɔːdənt ‖ 'mɔːr-/ *adj fml* cruel and cutting in speech

more¹ /mɔː ‖ mɔːr/ *adv* **1** (forms COMPARATIVES): *more difficult* **2** to a greater degree: *He likes this one more than that one.* **3** again: *Do it just once more.*

more² *determiner, pron* (*comparative of* **many, much**) **1** a greater or additional number or quantity (of): *He wants more food.* | *I can't eat any more.* **2** **more and more** increasingly **3** **more or less**: a nearly **b** about

more·o·ver /mɔːrˈəʊvə ‖ -ˈoʊvər/ *adv fml* in addition; besides

mo·res /'mɔːreɪz/ *n* [P] *fml* fixed moral customs in a social group

morgue /mɔːg ‖ mɔːrg/ *n* MORTUARY

mor·i·bund /'mɒrɪbʌnd ‖ 'mɔːr-, 'mɑːr-/ *adj* completely inactive and near to the end of existence

morn·ing /'mɔːnɪŋ ‖ 'mɔːr-/ *n* **1** time between sunrise and midday **2** **in the morning** tomorrow morning

morning-af·ter pill /,·· '·· ,·/ *n* drug taken by mouth by a woman within 72 hours of having sex, to prevent her from having a baby

morning dress /'·· ·/ *n* [U] formal dress worn by men, e.g. at weddings

mo·ron /'mɔːrɒn ‖ 'mɔːrɑːn/ *n* very stupid person ~**ic** /məˈrɒnɪk ‖ məˈrɑː-/ *adj*

mo·rose /məˈrəʊs ‖ -ˈroʊs/ *adj* angry and silent ~**ly** *adv*

mor·phine /'mɔːfiːn ‖ 'mɔːr-/ *n* [U] powerful drug for stopping pain

Morse code /,mɔːs ˈkəʊd ‖ ,mɔːrs ˈkoʊd/ *n* [U] system of sending messages with letters represented by combinations of long and short signals

mor·sel /'mɔːsəl ‖ 'mɔːr-/ *n* small piece, esp. of food

mor·tal /'mɔːtl ‖ 'mɔːrtl/ *adj* **1** that will die **2** of human beings **3** causing death: *a mortal wound* ♦ *n* human being ~**ly** *adv* **1** so as to cause death **2** very much: *mortally offended* ~**ity** /mɔːˈtælɪti ‖ mɔːr-/ *n* [U] **1** rate or number of deaths **2** state of being mortal

mor·tar¹ /'mɔːtə ‖ 'mɔːrtər/ *n* [U] mixture of lime, sand, and water, used in building

mortar² *n* **1** apparatus for firing small bombs **2** thick bowl in which things are crushed

mort·gage /'mɔːgɪdʒ ‖ 'mɔːr-/ *n* **1** agreement to borrow money to buy esp. a house, which belongs to the lender until the money is repaid **2** the amount borrowed ♦ *vt* give up the ownership of (a house, etc.) for a time in return for money lent

mor·ti·cian /mɔːˈtɪʃən ‖ mɔːr-/ *AmE for* UNDERTAKER

mor·ti·fy /'mɔːtɪfaɪ ‖ 'mɔːr-/ *vt* make ashamed -**fication** /,mɔːtɪfɪˈkeɪʃən ‖ ,mɔːr-/ *n* [U]

mor·tu·a·ry /'mɔːtʃuəri ‖ 'mɔːrtʃueri/ *n* place where dead bodies are kept until a funeral

mo·sa·ic /məʊˈzeɪ·ɪk ‖ moʊ-/ *n* pattern or picture formed by small pieces of coloured stone or glass

Mos·lem /'mɒzləm ‖ 'mɑːz-/ *n, adj* Muslim

mosque /mɒsk ‖ mɑːsk/ *n* building in which Muslims worship

mos·qui·to /məˈskiːtəʊ ‖ -toʊ/ *n* -**tos** *or* -**toes** small blood-sucking flying insect

moss /mɒs ‖ mɔːs/ *n* [U] (thick flat mass of) a small usu. green plant of wet places

most¹ /məʊst ‖ moʊst/ *adv* **1** (forms SUPERLATIVES): *the most difficult question* **2** more than anything else: *He likes bananas most of all.* **3** *fml* very: *I was most* *upset.*

most² *determiner, pron (superlative of* many, much) **1** nearly all: *Most people dislike him.* **2 at (the) most** not more than **3 for the most part** mainly **4 make the most of** get the best advantage from ~**ly** *adv* mainly

MOT /,em əʊ 'tiː ‖ -oʊ-/ *n* (in Britain) regular official examination of cars to make sure they are in good enough condition to be driven

mo·tel /məʊ'tel ‖ moʊ-/ *n* hotel specially built for MOTORISTS

moth /mɒθ ‖ mɔːθ/ *n* large-winged insect that flies mainly at night

moth·ball /'mɒθbɔːl ‖ 'mɔːθbɒːl/ *n* **1** ball of strong-smelling chemical for keeping moths away from clothes **2 in mothballs** stored and not used

moth-eat·en /'· ·ˌ·◂/ *adj* **1** (of clothes) eaten by the young of moths **2** very worn out

moth·er /'mʌðə ‖ -ər/ *n* **1** female parent **2** (*usu. cap.*) female head of a CONVENT: *mother superior* **the mother of all** *infml* very bad or extreme example of: *the mother of all headaches* ♦ *vt* care for or protect (too) lovingly ~**hood** *n* [U] ~**ly** *adj* like a good mother

mother coun·try /'·· ·ˌ·/ *n* country one was born in or came from originally

mother-in-law /'·· · ·/ *n* mothers-in-law *or* mother-in-laws wife's or husband's mother

mother-of-pearl /,·· · '·◂/ *n* [U] shiny substance from inside certain shells, used decoratively

mother tongue /,·· '·/ *n* first language one spoke

mo·tif /məʊ'tiːf ‖ moʊ-/ *n* (repeated) artistic or musical pattern

mo·tion /'məʊʃən ‖ moʊ-/ *n* **1** [U] act, way, or process of moving: *the ship's rolling motion* **2** [C] single movement **3** [C] suggestion formally made at a meeting **4 go through the motions** do something without care or interest **5 put/set in motion** start (a machine or process) ♦ *vi/t* signal or direct by a movement of esp. the hand ~**less** *adj* unmoving

mo·ti·vate /'məʊtɪveɪt ‖ 'moʊ-/ *vt* **1** give (someone) a (strong) reason for doing something; encourage **2** be the reason why

(something) was done –**vation** /,məʊtɪ- 'veɪʃən ‖ ,moʊ-/ *n* [U]

mo·tive /'məʊtɪv ‖ moʊ-/ *n* reason for action

mot·ley /'mɒtli ‖ 'mɑːtli/ *adj usu. derog.* of many different kinds and qualities

mo·to·cross /'məʊtəʊkrɒs ‖ 'moʊtoʊ- krɒːs/ *n* [U] motorcycle racing across rough country

mo·tor /'məʊtə ‖ 'moʊtər/ *n* **1** machine that changes power into movement: *an electric motor* **2** *BrE infml* a car ♦ *adj* **1** driven by an engine: *a motor mower* **2** of cars, etc.: *the motor trade* ♦ *vi* go by car –**ist** *n* car driver

mo·tor·cade /'moʊtəkeɪd ‖ 'moʊtər-/ *n* group of cars surrounding an important person's car

mo·tor·car /'məʊtəkɑː ‖ 'moʊtərkɑːr/ *n* *BrE fml* car

mo·tor·cycle /'məʊtəˌsaɪkəl ‖ 'moʊtər-/ *n* also **mo·tor·bike** /-ˌbaɪk/ *BrE infml* — large heavy bicycle driven by an engine

mo·tor·way /'məʊtəweɪ ‖ 'moʊtər-/ *n* *BrE* wide road for fast long-distance travel

mot·tled /'mɒtld ‖ 'mɑː-/ *adj* irregularly marked with colours and/or shapes

mot·to /'mɒtəʊ ‖ 'mɑːtoʊ/ *n* -toes *or* -tos phrase or short sentence used as a guiding principle

mould¹ *BrE* ‖ **mold** *AmE* /məʊld ‖ moʊld/ *n* container into which a soft substance is poured, to take on the shape of the container when it sets ♦ *vt* shape or form (something solid): (fig.) *influences that moulded her character* ~**ing** *n* [C;U] decorative stone, plastic, or wood band(s)

mould² *BrE* ‖ **mold** *AmE* — *n* [U] soft often greenish growth on old food, etc. ~**y** *adj: mouldy cheese*

moul·der *BrE* ‖ **molder** *AmE* /'məʊldə ‖ 'moʊldər/ *vi* decay gradually

moult *BrE* ‖ **molt** *AmE* /məʊlt ‖ moʊlt/ *vi* (of a bird or animal) lose most of its feathers, fur, etc.

mound /maʊnd/ *n* **1** pile **2** small hill

mount¹ /maʊnt/ *v* **1** *vi* rise: *Costs mounted.* **2** *vt* get on (a horse, bicycle, etc.) **3** *vt* provide with a horse, etc.: *the mounted police* **4** *vt* prepare and produce: *mount an exhibition/an attack* **5** *vt* fix on a support or in a frame **6** *vt* go up; climb ♦ *n* animal for riding

mount² n (usu. cap.) (used before names of mountains): *Mount Everest*

moun·tain /'maʊntɪn/ n 1 very high rocky hill 2 very large amount 3 **make a mountain out of a molehill** make a problem seem more difficult than it is ~**ous** adj 1 full of mountains 2 extremely large

moun·tain·eer /ˌmaʊntɪˈnɪə ‖ -tnˈɪr/ n mountain climber ~**ing** n [U]

mourn /mɔːn ‖ mɔːrn/ vi/t feel or express grief (for), esp. when someone dies ~**er** n ~**ful** adj (too) sad ~**ing** n [U] 1 grief 2 funeral clothes, usu. black

mouse /maʊs/ n 1 mice /maɪs/ long-tailed furry animal, like a rat but smaller 2 **mouses** small object connected to a computer, which is moved around and pressed to give commands **mousy** adj 1 (of hair) dull pale brown 2 (of a person) unattractively plain and quiet

mouse mat BrE ‖ **mouse pad** AmE /'· ·/ n flat piece of plastic, rubber, etc. on which a computer MOUSE (2) is moved around

mousse /muːs/ n [C;U] 1 dish made from flavoured cream and eggs 2 substance used to keep hair in place

mous·tache /məˈstɑːʃ ‖ ˈmʌstæʃ/ n hair on the upper lip

mouth¹ /maʊθ/ n mouths /maʊðz/ 1 opening in the face for eating and speaking 2 opening; entrance: *the mouth of the cave* 3 **down in the mouth** not cheerful 4 **keep one's mouth shut** keep silent

mouth² /maʊð/ vt 1 say by moving the lips soundlessly 2 repeat without understanding or sincerity

mouth·ful /'maʊθfʊl/ n 1 amount put into the mouth 2 long word or phrase, difficult to say

mouth·or·gan /'maʊθˌɔːɡən ‖ -ˌɔːr-/ n musical instrument played by moving the mouth up and down it and blowing

mouth·piece /'maʊθpiːs/ n 1 part of a musical instrument, telephone, etc. held in or near the mouth 2 person, newspaper, etc. that only expresses the opinions of others

mouth·wash /'maʊθwɒʃ ‖ -wɒʃ, -wɑːʃ/ n [C;U] liquid used to freshen or clean inside the mouth

mouth-wa·ter·ing /'· ˌ·· / adj (of food) very attractive

mov·a·ble /'muːvəbəl/ adj able to be moved

move¹ /muːv/ v 1 vi/t (cause to) change place or position: *Sit still and don't move!* 2 vi act: *I had to move fast to clinch the deal.* 3 vi also **move house** — change one's home 4 vt cause to have strong feelings, esp. of pity: *a very moving story* 5 vi/t make (a formal suggestion) at a meeting ~**ment** n 1 [C;U] (act of) moving: *Police are watching his movements.* (=activities) 2 [C] group of people in a united effort: *the trade-union movement* —see also WOMEN'S MOVEMENT 3 [C] separate part of a large piece of music

move in phr vi 1 take possession of a new home 2 (prepare to) take control, attack, etc.

move off phr vi leave

move on phr v 1 vi change (to something new) 2 vi/t go away to another place or position

move out phr vi leave one's former home

move over phr vi change position in order to make room for someone or something else

move² n 1 change of position or place, esp. in games like CHESS 2 set of actions to bring about a result: *new moves to settle the dispute* 3 **get a move on** infml hurry up 4 **make a move: a** (start to) leave **b** begin to take action 5 **on the move: a** travelling about **b** having started to move or happen

mov·ie /'muːvi/ n esp. AmE for FILM (2) **movies** n [the+P] esp. AmE for CINEMA

mow /məʊ/ mowed, mowed or **mown** /məʊn ‖ moʊn/ cut (grass, corn, etc.) ~**er** n

mow down phr vt knock down or kill, esp. in large numbers

MP /ˌem ˈpiː/ n abbrev. for: Member of Parliament

mpg written abbrev. for: miles per GALLON

mph written abbrev. for: miles per hour

Mr /'mɪstə ‖ -ər/ n (ordinary man's title): *Mr Smith*

Mrs /'mɪsɪz/ n (married woman's title)

Ms /mɪz, məz/ n (unmarried or married woman's title)

MS /ˌem ˈes/ n [U] abbrev. for: MULTIPLE SCLEROSIS

Mt written abbrev. for: MOUNT²

much¹ /mʌtʃ/ adv 1 a lot: *much better* | *much too small* 2 to the stated degree: *I liked it very much.* | *She would so much like to go.*

3 in most ways: *much the same as usual*
4 **much as** although

much² *determiner, pron* **more, most**
1 large amount or part (of): *He gave me too much cake.* | *How much is it?* (=what does it cost?) | *I didn't get much.* | (fig.) *I don't think much of that.* (=I have a low opinion of it) 2 **I thought as much** I had expected that the stated usu. bad thing would happen 3 **make much of**: a treat as important b understand 4 **much as** although 5 **not much of a** not a very good 6 **not up to much** not very good 7 **so much for** that is the end of 8 **too much for** too difficult for

muck¹ /mʌk/ *n* [U] 1 dirt 2 worthless or improper material 3 MANURE ~y *adj*

muck² *v*
  muck about/around *phr vi esp. BrE*
1 behave in a silly way 2 treat without consideration
  muck in *phr vi* join in work or activity (with others)
  muck up *phr vt* 1 spoil or do wrong 2 make dirty

muck·rak·ing /ˈmʌk-reɪkɪŋ/ *n* [U] *derog* finding and telling unpleasant stories about well-known people –**ing** *adj* –**er** *n*

mu·cus /ˈmjuːkəs/ *n* [U] slippery body liquid, as produced in the nose

mud /mʌd/ *n* [U] 1 very wet earth 2 **one's name is mud** one is spoken badly of after causing trouble –**dy** *adj*

mud·dle¹ /ˈmʌdl/ *n* state of confusion and disorder

muddle² *vt* 1 put into disorder 2 confuse the mind of
  muddle along *phr vi* continue confusedly, with no plan
  muddle through *phr vi* succeed in spite of having no plan or good method

mud·guard /ˈmʌdɡɑːd ‖ -ɡɑːrd/ *n* protective cover over a cycle wheel

mues·li /ˈmjuːzli/ *n* [U] breakfast dish of grain, nuts, fruit, etc., with milk

muff¹ /mʌf/ *n* fur or cloth cover to keep the hands or ears warm

muff² *vt* spoil a chance to do (something) well

muf·fle /ˈmʌfəl/ *vt* make (sound) less easily heard

muf·fler /ˈmʌflə ‖ -ər/ *n* 1 scarf worn to keep one's neck warm 2 *AmE for* SILENCER

mug¹ /mʌɡ/ *n* 1 **a** large straight-sided drinking cup with a handle **b** the contents of this: *a mug of tea* 2 *BrE sl* foolish person 3 *sl* face

mug² *vt* -gg- rob violently ~**ger** *n*

mug·gy /ˈmʌɡi/ *adj* (of weather) unpleasantly warm with heavy wet air

mulch /mʌltʃ/ *n* [U] decaying plant material put around plants to feed and protect them ♦ *v*

mule /mjuːl/ *n* animal that is the young of a donkey and a horse **mulish** *adj* unwilling to change or agree; STUBBORN

mull /mʌl/ *vt* heat (wine) with sugar, SPICES, etc.
  mull over *phr vt* consider carefully

mul·ti·cul·tur·al /ˌmʌltɪˈkʌltʃərəl◂/ *adj* of many different religions, races, etc.: *a multicultural society* ~**ism** *n* [U]

mul·ti·lat·e·ral /ˌmʌltɪˈlætərəl◂/ *adj* including more than two groups, countries, etc. ~**ly** *adv*

mul·ti·me·di·a /ˌmʌltɪˈmiːdiə◂/ *adj, n* [U] (using) a mixture of sounds, pictures, etc. to give information, esp. on a computer

mul·ti·na·tion·al /ˌmʌltɪˈnæʃənəl◂/ *adj* having factories, offices, etc. in many different countries **multinational** *n*

mul·ti·ple /ˈmʌltɪpəl/ *adj* of many different types or parts ♦ *n* number which contains a smaller number an exact number of times

multiple scle·ro·sis /ˌ··· ·ˈ··◂/ *n* [U] serious nerve disease in which one can no longer control one's bodily movements

mul·ti·plex /ˈmʌltɪpleks/ *n* cinema showing several different films at the same time

mul·ti·pli·ci·ty /ˌmʌltɪˈplɪsɪti/ *n* [S;U] large number or great variety

mul·ti·ply /ˈmʌltɪplaɪ/ *v* 1 *vt* add (a number) to itself the stated number of times: *2 multiplied by 3 is 6.* 2 *vi/t* increase in number or amount 3 *vi* breed –**plication** /ˌmʌltɪpləˈkeɪʃən/ *n* [C;U]

mul·ti·ra·cial /ˌmʌltɪˈreɪʃəl◂/ *adj* involving many different races of people

mul·ti·tude /ˈmʌltɪtjuːd ‖ -tuːd/ *n* 1 large number 2 large crowd

mum¹ /mʌm/ *n* mother

mum² *adj infml* not saying or telling anything: *Mum's the word.* (=silence must/will be kept about this)

mum·ble /'mʌmbəl/ *vi/t* speak or say unclearly

mum·bo jum·bo /ˌmʌmbəʊ 'dʒʌmbəʊ ‖ -boʊ 'dʒʌmboʊ/ *n* [U] *derog* meaningless talk or actions, esp. in religion

mum·mi·fy /'mʌmɪfaɪ/ *vt* preserve as a MUMMY²

mum·my¹ /'mʌmi/ *n BrE* (child's word for) mother

mummy² *n* dead body preserved from decay, esp. in ancient Egypt

mumps /mʌmps/ *n* [U] infectious illness with swelling in the throat

munch /mʌntʃ/ *vi/t* eat (something hard) with a strong jaw movement

mun·dane /mʌn'deɪn/ *adj* ordinary; with nothing exciting or interesting in it

mu·ni·ci·pal /mjuː'nɪsɪpəl ‖ mjʊ-/ *adj* of a town or its local government

mu·ni·ci·pal·i·ty /mjuːˌnɪsɪ'pælɪti ‖ mjʊ-/ *n* town, city, etc. with its own local government

mu·ni·tions /mjuː'nɪʃənz ‖ mjʊ-/ *n* [P] bombs, guns, etc.; war supplies

mu·ral /'mjʊərəl ‖ 'mjʊr-/ *n* painting done directly on a wall

mur·der /'mɜːdə ‖ 'mɜːrdər/ *n* [C;U] 1 crime of killing someone intentionally 2 very difficult or tiring experience —see also BLUE MURDER ♦ *vt* kill illegally and intentionally ~**er** *n* ~**ous** *adj* 1 intending or likely to cause murder 2 violent (in appearance)

murk·y /'mɜːki ‖ 'mɜːr-/ *adj* unpleasantly dark

mur·mur /'mɜːmə ‖ 'mɜːrmər/ *n* 1 [C] soft low continuous sound 2 [S] complaint ♦ *vi/t* make or express in a murmur: *She murmured her approval.*

mus·cle¹ /'mʌsəl/ *n* 1 [C;U] (one of) the pieces of elastic material in the body which can tighten to produce movement 2 [U] strength 3 **not move a muscle** stay quite still

muscle² *v* **muscle in** *phr vi* force one's way into (esp.) a group activity, so as to gain a share in what is produced

muscle-bound /'·· ·/ *adj* having large stiff muscles

mus·cu·lar /'mʌskjʊlə ‖ -ər/ *adj* 1 of muscles 2 with large muscles; strong

muse¹ /mjuːz/ *vi* think deeply

muse² *n* (*often cap.*) any of nine ancient Greek goddesses representing an art or science 2 force or person that seems to help someone write, paint, etc.

mu·se·um /mjuː'ziːəm ‖ mjʊ-/ *n* building where objects of historic, scientific, or artistic interest are kept and shown

mush /mʌʃ/ *n* [U] soft mass of half-liquid, half-solid material ~**y** *adj*

mush·room /'mʌʃruːm, -rʊm/ *n* type of FUNGUS that is often eaten ♦ *vi* grow and develop fast

mu·sic /'mjuːzɪk/ *n* [U] 1 sounds arranged in patterns, usu. with tunes 2 art of making music 3 printed representation of music 4 **face the music** admit to blame, responsibility, etc. and accept the results, esp. punishment or difficulty ~**ian** /mjuː'zɪʃən ‖ mjʊ-/ *n*

mu·sic·al /'mjuːzɪkəl/ *adj* 1 of music 2 skilled at music ♦ *n* play or film with songs and usu. dances ~**ly** /-kli/ *adv*

music hall /'·· ·/ *n* [C;U] (in Britain in former times) (theatre for) performances of songs, jokes, acts of skill, etc.

musk /mʌsk/ *n* [U] strong-smelling substance used in PERFUMES ~**y** *adj*

mus·ket /'mʌskɪt/ *n* early type of long-barrelled gun

Mus·lim /'mʌzləm, 'mʊz-, 'mʊs-/ *n, adj* (follower) of the religion started by Mohammed

mus·lin /'mʌzlən/ *n* [U] very fine thin cotton

mus·sel /'mʌsəl/ *n* sea animal with a black shell, often eaten

must /məst; *strong* mʌst/ *vi 3rd person sing.* **must** 1 (shows what is necessary): *It's an order; you must obey.* 2 (shows what is likely): *You must be cold.* ♦ *n* something that should be done, seen, etc.

mus·tache /mə'stɑːʃ ‖ 'mʌstæʃ/ *n AmE for* MOUSTACHE

mus·tard /'mʌstəd ‖ -ərd/ *n* [U] hot-tasting yellow substance made from a plant and usu. eaten with meat

mus·ter /'mʌstə ‖ -ər/ *vt* gather; collect

must·n't /'mʌsənt/ *short for:* must not

must·y /'mʌsti/ *adj* with an unpleasant smell as if old –**iness** *n* [U]

mu·tant /'mjuːtənt/ *n, adj* (animal or plant that is) unusual because of GENETIC changes

mu·tate /mjuːˈteɪt/ *vi/t* (cause) to become different from others of the same kind because of GENETIC changes ~**tion** /-ˈteɪʃən/ *n* [C;U]

mute /mjuːt/ *adj* not speaking or spoken; silent ♦ *n* **1** person who cannot speak **2** object put on or in a musical instrument to make it sound softer ~**ly** *adv* **muted** *adj* (of sound or colour) softer than usual

mu·ti·late /ˈmjuːtəleɪt/ *vt* wound and make ugly or useless –**lation** /ˌmjuːtə-ˈleɪʃən/ *n* [C;U]

mu·ti·neer /ˌmjuːtəˈnɪə∥ -tnˈɪr/ *n* person who mutinies

mu·ti·ny /ˈmjuːtəni∥ -tn-/ *n* [C;U] (an example of) the act of taking power from the person in charge, esp. on a ship –**nous** *adj* **1** taking part in a mutiny **2** angrily disobedient –**nously** *adv* ♦ *vi* take part in a mutiny

mutt /mʌt/ *n* dog of no particular breed

mut·ter /ˈmʌtə∥ -ər/ *vi/t* speak or say quietly and unclearly

mut·ton /ˈmʌtn/ *n* [U] meat from a sheep

mu·tu·al /ˈmjuːtʃuəl/ *adj* **1** equal for both sides: *their mutual dislike* (=they dislike each other) **2** shared by both: *mutual interests/friends* ~**ly** *adv*

mu·zak /ˈmjuːzæk/ *n* [U] *tdmk* (dull) recorded music played in restaurants, shops, etc.

muz·zle /ˈmʌzəl/ *n* **1** animal's nose and mouth **2** covering for an animal's muzzle, to stop it biting **3** front end of a gun barrel ♦ *vt* **1** put a muzzle on (an animal) **2** force to keep silent

my /maɪ/ *determiner* of me: *my parents* ♦ *interj* (expresses surprise)

my·o·pi·a /maɪˈəʊpiə∥ -ˈoʊ-/ *n* [U] inability to see distant objects clearly –**pic** /maɪˈɒpɪk∥ -ˈɑːpɪk/ *adj*

myr·i·ad /ˈmɪriəd/ *n, adj* large and varied number (of)

my·self /maɪˈself/ *pron* **1** (*reflexive form of* I): *I hurt myself.* **2** (*strong form of* I): *I'll do it myself.* **3** (in) my usual state of mind or body: *I'm not myself today.* (=I feel ill) **4** (all) by myself: a alone b without help **5** to myself not shared

mys·te·ry /ˈmɪstəri/ *n* **1** [C] something which cannot be explained or understood **2** [U] strange secret quality –**rious** /mɪˈstɪəriəs∥ -ˈstɪr-/ *adj* **1** unexplainable:

his mysterious disappearance **2** hiding one's intentions –**riously** *adv* –**riousness** *n* [U]

mys·tic /ˈmɪstɪk/ *n* person who practises mysticism

mys·ti·cis·m /ˈmɪstɪsɪzəm/ *n* gaining of secret religious knowledge **mystical**, **mystic** *adj* **mystically** /-kli/ *adv*

mys·ti·fy /ˈmɪstɪfaɪ/ *vt* cause (someone) to wonder or be unsure: *her mystifying disappearance*

mys·tique /mɪˈstiːk/ *n* special quality that makes a person or thing seem mysterious and different, esp. causing admiration

myth /mɪθ/ **1** story from ancient times **2** widely believed false story or idea ~**ical** *adj* **1** of myths **2** not real

my·thol·o·gy /mɪˈθɒlədʒi∥ -ˈθɑː-/ *n* [U] myths: *heroes of Greek mythology* –**gical** /ˌmɪθəˈlɒdʒɪkəl∥ -ˈlɑː-/ *adj*

myx·o·ma·to·sis /ˌmɪksəməˈtəʊsɪs∥ -ˈtoʊ-/ *n* [U] disease in rabbits

N

N, n /en/ the 14th letter of the English alphabet

N *written abbrev. for:* north(ern)

nab /næb/ *vt* -**bb**- *sl* **1** ARREST **2** get; take

na·dir /ˈneɪdɪə∥ -dər/ *n* lowest point of misfortune, failure, etc.

naff /næf/ *adj BrE sl* (of things, ideas, behaviour, etc.) foolish or worthless, esp. in a way that shows a lack of good TASTE (3)

nag[1] /næg/ *vi/t* -**gg**- continuously complain (at) ~**ging** *adj* continuously hurting or worrying: *a nagging headache*

nag[2] *n* old horse

nail[1] /neɪl/ *n* **1** thin pointed piece of metal for hammering into a piece of wood **2** hard flat piece at the end of each finger and toe **3** hard as nails without any tender feelings **4** hit the nail on the head do or say exactly the right thing

nail² *vt* 1 fasten with a nail 2 *sl* catch; trap

nail down *phr vt* force to tell plans or wishes clearly

nail-bit·ing /ˈ·ˌ··/ *adj* causing excitement and anxiety

nail pol·ish also **nail var·nish** *BrE* /ˈ· ˌ··/ *n* [U] liquid painted onto finger and toenails

na·ive, **naïve** /naɪˈiːv‖ naːˈiːv/ *adj* 1 without experience of life 2 too willing to believe without proof **–ly** *adv* **–ty** /naɪˈiːv-ti‖ naːˌiːvəˈteɪ/ *n* [U] quality of being naive

na·ked /ˈneɪkɪd/ *adj* 1 with no clothes on 2 uncovered: *a naked light* | (fig.) *the naked truth* 3 **with the naked eye** without a microscope, TELESCOPE, etc. **–ness** *n* [U]

nam·by-pam·by /ˌnæmbi ˈpæmbi◄/ *adj* too weak, childish, or easily frightened

name /neɪm/ *n* 1 [C] what someone (or something) is called: *Her name is Mary.* 2 [C] usu. offensive title for someone: *to call someone names* 3 [S;C] opinion others have of one; REPUTATION: *The restaurant has a good name.* | *He made a name for himself* (=became famous) *in show business.* 4 [C] *sl* well-known person: *There were several big names* (=famous people) *at the party.* 5 **in name only** in appearance or by title but not in fact 6 **in the name of** by the right or power of: *Open up, in the name of the law!* 7 **the name of the game** quality or object which is most necessary or important 8 **to one's name** (esp. of money) as one's property: *He hasn't a penny to his name.* ♦ *vt* 1 give a name to: *They named their daughter Mary.* 2 say what the name of (someone or something) is: *Can you name this plant?* 3 appoint; choose **~less** *adj* 1 whose name is not known or told 2 too terrible to mention **~ly** *adv* and that is/they are: *There are two factors, namely cost and availability.*

name·drop /ˈneɪmdrɒp‖ -drɑːp/ *vi* -**pp**- mention famous people as if one knew them well **~per** *n* **~ping** *n* [U]

name·sake /ˈneɪmseɪk/ *n* person with the same name

nan·ny /ˈnæni/ *n* woman employed to take care of children

nanny goat /ˈ·· ·/ *n* female goat

nap¹ /næp/ *n* short sleep ♦ *vi* 1 have a nap 2 **catch someone napping** find or take advantage of someone unprepared

nap² *n* soft furry surface of cloth

na·palm /ˈneɪpɑːm‖ -pɑːm, -pɑːlm/ *n* [U] fiercely burning petrol jelly, used in bombs

nape /neɪp/ *n* back (of the neck)

nap·kin /ˈnæpkɪn/ *n* piece of cloth or paper used at meals for protecting clothes and cleaning the lips and fingers

nap·py /ˈnæpi/ *n BrE* cloth worn by a baby to take up waste matter from its body

nar·cis·sis·m /ˈnɑːsɪsɪzəm‖ ˈnɑːr-/ *n* [U] too great love for one's own appearance or abilities **–sist** *n* **–sistic** /ˌnɑːsɪˈsɪstɪk◄‖ ˌnɑːr-/ *adj*

nar·cot·ic /nɑːˈkɒtɪk‖ nɑːrˈkɑː-/ *n* sleep-producing drug, harmful in large amounts

nar·rate /nəˈreɪt‖ ˈnæreɪt, næˈreɪt, nə-/ *vt* tell (a story) or describe (events) **–rator** *n* **–ration** /nəˈreɪʃən‖ næ-, nə-/ *n* [C;U]

nar·ra·tive /ˈnærətɪv/ *n* 1 [C;U] *fml* story 2 [U] art of narrating

nar·row¹ /ˈnærəʊ‖ -roʊ/ *adj* 1 small from one side to the other 2 limited 3 only just successful: *a narrow escape* 4 not open to new ideas: *a narrow mind* —see also STRAIGHT AND NARROW **~ly** *adv* only just **~ness** *n* [U]

nar·row² *vi/t* become or make narrower

narrow down *phr vt* reduce, limit

narrow-mind·ed /ˌ·· ˈ··◄‖ ˈ·· ˌ··◄/ *adj* unwilling to respect the opinions of others when different from one's own **~ness** *n* [U]

na·sal /ˈneɪzəl/ *adj* of the nose

nas·ty /ˈnɑːsti‖ ˈnæsti/ *adj* 1 not nice; unpleasant 2 dangerous or painful: *a nasty cut* —see also VIDEO NASTY **–tily** *adv* **–tiness** *n* [U]

na·tion /ˈneɪʃən/ *n* (all the people belonging to) a country

na·tion·al /ˈnæʃənəl/ *adj* 1 of or being a nation, esp. as opposed to **a** any of its parts: *a national newspaper* (=one read everywhere in the country) **b** another nation or other nations: *The national news comes after the international news.* 2 owned or controlled by the central government of a country: *a national bank* | *the National Health Service* ♦ *n* person from a usu. stated country **~ly** *adv* **~ism** *n* [U] love of and pride in one's country 2 desire to become a separate independent country **~ist** *adj*, *n* **~istic** /ˌnæʃənəˈlɪstɪk◄/ *adj* showing too great nationalism **~ity** /ˌnæʃəˈnælɪti/ *n* [U] being from a particular country: *a man of Italian nationality*

national in·sur·ance /ˌ··· ·'··/ *n* [U] government system of collecting money from workers and employers so that it can pay old, ill, and unemployed people

na·tion·al·ize also **-ise** *BrE* /'næʃənəlaɪz/ *vt* take (a business or industry) into government control **-ization, -isation** /ˌnæʃənəlaɪ'zeɪʃən ‖ -nələ-/ *n* [U]

national park /ˌ··· ·'·/ *n* large area of beautiful land, protected by the government for people to visit

national ser·vice /ˌ··· '··/ *n* [U] (period of) forced service in the army, etc.

na·tion·wide /ˌneɪʃən'waɪd◄/ *adj, adv* happening over the whole country

na·tive /'neɪtɪv/ *adj* **1** of or being one's place of birth **2** found naturally in a place: *native species* **3** not learned: *native ability* ♦ *n* **1** person born in a place **2** *now often considered offensive* local person, esp. non-European **3** native animal or plant

Native A·mer·i·can /ˌ·· ·'···/ *n, adj* (person) belonging to one of the groups of people living in North, Central, or South America before Europeans arrived

Na·tiv·i·ty /nə'tɪvɪti/ *n* the birth of Christ

NATO /'neɪtəʊ ‖ -toʊ/ *n abbrev. for:* the North Atlantic Treaty Organisation; a group of countries which give military help to each other

nat·ter /'nætə ‖ -ər/ *vi, n* [S] *BrE* (have) a long unimportant talk

nat·u·ral /'nætʃərəl/ *adj* **1** existing or happening ordinarily in the world, esp. not made by people: *death from natural causes* **2** usual; to be expected: *It's natural to feel nervous.* **3** existing from birth; not learned: *a natural talent* **4** having natural skill: *a natural musician* **5** ordinary; not AFFECTED ♦ *n* person with natural skill **~ly** *adv* **1** as a natural skill: *Swimming comes naturally to her.* **2** in an ordinary way **3** of course **~ist** *n* person who studies animals and plants **~istic** /ˌnætʃərə'lɪstɪk◄/ *adj* showing things exactly as they are: *a naturalistic painting* **-istically** /-kli/ *adv*

nat·u·ral·ize also **-ise** *BrE* /'nætʃərəlaɪz/ *vt* make (someone born elsewhere) a citizen of a country **-ization, -isation** /ˌnætʃərəl-aɪ'zeɪʃən ‖ -rələ-/ *n* [U]

natural his·to·ry /ˌ··· '··/ *n* [U] study of

animals and plants

natural se·lec·tion /ˌ··· ·'··/ *n* [U] process by which creatures well suited to their conditions live and those less well suited die

na·ture /'neɪtʃə ‖ -ər/ *n* **1** [U] everything that exists in the world independently of people, such as animals and plants, the land, and the weather **2** [C;U] character: *She has a very kind nature.* —see also SECOND NATURE **3** [S] *fml* kind; sort

naugh·ty /'nɔːti ‖ 'nɒːti, 'nɑːti/ *adj* **1** (esp. of a child) behaving badly **2** sexually improper **-tily** *adv* **-tiness** *n* [U]

nau·se·a /'nɔːziə, -sɪə ‖ 'nɒːziə, -ʃə/ *n* [U] feeling of sickness and desire to VOMIT **-ous** *adj* **-ate** /'nɔːzieɪt, -sɪ- ‖ 'nɒːzi-, -ʒi-/ *vt* cause to feel nausea: (fig.) *nauseating hypocrisy*

nau·ti·cal /'nɔːtɪkəl ‖ 'nɒː-/ *adj* of ships or sailing

na·val /'neɪvəl/ *adj* of a navy or warships

nave /neɪv/ *n* long central part of a church

na·vel /'neɪvəl/ *n* small sunken place in the middle of the stomach

nav·i·ga·ble /'nævɪɡəbəl/ *adj* (of a river, etc.) deep and wide enough to let ships pass

nav·i·gate /'nævɪɡeɪt/ *vi/t* direct the course of (a ship, aircraft, etc. or a car) **-gator** *n* **-gation** /ˌnævɪ'ɡeɪʃən/ *n* [U]

na·vy /'neɪvi/ *n* ships and sailors for fighting

navy blue /ˌ·· '·◄/ *n* [U] dark blue

NB (used in writing) take notice (of this)

near /nɪə ‖ nɪr/ *adj* **1** at a short distance; close: *Christmas/My office is near.* **2** nearest and dearest one's family ♦ *adv, prep* not far (from): *Don't go near the edge.* ♦ *vi/t* come closer (to) **~ly** *adv* **1** almost **2 not nearly** not at all **~ness** *n* [U]

near·by /ˌnɪə'baɪ◄, ˌnɪr-/ *adj, adv* near

near miss /ˌ· '·/ *n* something that almost succeeds, happens, etc.

near·side /'nɪəsaɪd ‖ 'nɪr-/ *adj, n* (on) the left-hand side, esp. of a vehicle

near·sight·ed /ˌnɪə'saɪtɪd◄ ‖ 'nɪrsaɪtɪd/ *adj esp. AmE for* SHORTSIGHTED

neat /niːt/ *adj* **1** tidy **2** simple and effective: *a neat trick* **3** (of an alcoholic drink) with no water, etc. added **~ly** *adv* **~ness** *n* [U]

neb·u·lous /'nebjʊləs/ *adj* not clear, esp. in meaning or expression **~ly** *adv*

ne·ces·sa·ry /'nesɨsəri ‖ -seri/ *adj* that is needed or must be done –**rily** *adv* in a way that must be so: *Food that looks good doesn't necessarily taste good.*

ne·ces·si·tate /nɨ'sesɨteɪt/ *vt fml* make necessary

ne·ces·si·ty /nɨ'sesɨti/ *n* **1** [S;U] condition of being necessary; need: *There's no necessity to stay.* **2** [C] something necessary, esp. for life

neck /nek/ *n* **1** part of the body joining the head to the shoulders **2** part of a garment that goes round this **3** narrow part sticking out from a broader part: *the neck of a bottle* **4** **get it in the neck** *infml* be severely scolded and punished **5** **neck and neck** doing equally well in a competition **6** **neck of the woods** *infml* area or part of the country **7** **up to one's neck (in)** deeply concerned (with or by): *He's up to his neck in debt.* (=he owes a lot of money)

neck·lace /'nek-lɨs/ *n* decorative chain or string of jewels, worn round the neck

neck·tie /'nektaɪ/ *n esp. AmE* TIE¹ (1)

nec·tar /'nektə ‖ -ər/ *n* [U] **1** sweet liquid collected by bees from flowers **2** sweet and good-tasting drink

nec·tar·ine /'nektəriːn/ *n* PEACHlike fruit with smooth skin

née /neɪ/ *adj* (used to show a woman's name before she married): *Sheila Smith, née Brown*

need¹ /niːd/ *n* **1** [S;U] condition in which something necessary or desirable is missing: *a need for better medical services* **2** [S;U] necessary duty: *There's no need for you to come.* **3** [C] something one must have **4** [U] state of lacking food, money, etc.: *children in need* **5** **if need be** if necessary ~**less** *adj* **1** unnecessary **2** **needless to say** of course ~**lessly** *adv* ~**y** *adj* poor

need² *vt* have a need for; want: *To survive, plants need water.*

need³ *v,* negative short form **needn't** have to; must: *'Was he late?' 'Need you ask!'* (=of course he was) | *Do you think I need go to the meeting?*

nee·dle /'niːdl/ *n* **1** thin pointed pin or rod used in sewing or knitting (KNIT) **2** something long, thin, and sharp, such as the part of a HYPODERMIC which is pushed into someone's skin ♦ *vt* annoy

nee·dle·work /'niːdlwɜːk ‖ -wɜːrk/ *n* [U] sewing

ne·gate /nɪ'geɪt/ *vt* cause to have no effect

ne·ga·tion /nɪ'geɪʃən/ *n* [U]

neg·a·tive /'negətɪv/ *adj* **1** saying or meaning 'no': *a negative reply* **2** not useful or encouraging: *negative advice* **3** less than zero **4** (of electricity) of the type carried by ELECTRONS ♦ *n* **1** word, expression, or statement saying or meaning 'no': *The answer was in the negative.* **2** film showing dark areas as light and light as dark

ne·glect /nɪ'glekt/ *vt* **1** give too little attention or care to **2** fail (to do something) esp. because of carelessness ♦ *n* [U] neglecting or being neglected ~**ful** *adj* tending to neglect things ~**fully** *adv* ~**fulness** *n* [U]

neg·li·gee /'neglɨʒeɪ ‖ ,neglɨ'ʒeɪ/ *n* light thin NIGHTDRESS

neg·li·gent /'neglɨdʒənt/ *adj* not taking enough care ~**ly** *adv* –**gence** *n* [U]

neg·li·gi·ble /'neglɨdʒɨbəl/ *adj* too slight or unimportant to worry about

ne·go·ti·a·ble /nɪ'gəʊʃiəbəl, -ʃə- ‖ -'goʊ-/ *adj* **1** that can be settled or changed by being negotiated: **2** *infml* that can be travelled through, along, etc.

ne·go·ti·ate /nɪ'gəʊʃieɪt ‖ -'goʊ-/ *v* **1** *vi/t* talk to someone in order to try to get (an agreement) **2** *vt* travel safely along or through –**ator** *n* –**ation** /nɪ,gəʊʃi'eɪʃən ‖ -,goʊ-/ *n* [C;U]

Ne·gro /'niːgrəʊ ‖ -groʊ/ *n.* -**es** *tech; now often considered offensive* black person

neigh /neɪ/ *vi, n* (make) the sound of a horse

neigh·bour *BrE* ‖ -**bor** *AmE* /'neɪbə ‖ -ər/ *n* someone who lives next door, or near ~**hood** *n* **1** area in a town **2** the area around a point or place: (fig.) *a price in the neighbourhood of* (=about) *£500* ~**ing** *adj* (of a place) near ~**ly** *adj* friendly

nei·ther /'naɪðə ‖ 'niːðər/ *determiner, pron, conj* not one and not the other: *Neither book/Neither of the books is very good.* ♦ *adv* also not: *I can't swim and neither can my brother.*

nem·e·sis /'nemɨsɨs/ *n* [U] *lit* (force bringing) just and unavoidable punishment

ne·o·clas·sic·al /,niːəʊ'klæsɪkəl◄ ‖ ,niːoʊ-/ *adj* done recently, but in the style of ancient Greece and Rome

ne·o·co·lo·ni·al·is·m /,niːəʊkə-

'ləʊniəlızəm‖ˌniːoʊkəˈlou-/ n [U] *derog*
indirect control of smaller countries by
more powerful ones

ne·o·lith·ic /ˌniːəˈlɪθɪk◂/ *adj* of a period
about 10,000 years ago

ne·ol·o·gis·m /niːˈɒlədʒɪzəm‖-ˈɑːl-/ *n*
new word or expression

ne·on /ˈniːɒn‖-ɑːn/ *n* [U] gas used in
making bright electric lights

neph·ew /ˈnefjuː, ˈnev-‖ˈnef-/ *n* son of
one's brother or sister

nep·o·tis·m /ˈnepətɪzəm/ *n* [U] giving
unfair favour and advantages to one's
relatives

Nep·tune /ˈneptjuːn‖-tuːn/ *n* the PLANET
eighth in order from the sun

nerd /nɜːd‖ˈnɜːrd/ *n infml* 1 stupid person
2 computer nerd person who spends too
much time using or talking about
computers

nerve /nɜːv‖nɜːrv/ *n* 1 [C] threadlike
part in the body that carries feelings and
messages to and from the brain 2 [U]
courage: *I meant to do it, but I lost my
nerve.* 3 [S;U] disrespectful rudeness: *He
had the nerve to say I was a fool!* ♦ *vt* give
courage to (someone, esp. oneself) **nerves** *n*
[P] 1 great nervousness 2 **get on
someone's nerves** make someone annoyed
or bad-tempered **nervous** *adj* 1 a rather
frightened b easily excited and worried 2 of
the nerves: *The brain is at the centre of the
nervous system.* **nervously** *adv*
nervousness *n* [U]

nerve cen·tre /ˈ· ˌ·/ *n* place from which
a system, organization, etc. is controlled

nerve-rack·ing /ˈ· ˌ·/ *adj* that causes
great worry or fear

nervous break·down /ˌ·· ˈ·/ *n* serious
medical condition of deep worrying,
anxiety, and tiredness which stops one
working

nest /nest/ *n* 1 hollow place built or used
by a bird as a home and a place to keep its
eggs 2 group of similar objects which fit
closely into or inside one another: *a nest of
tables* ♦ *vi* build or use a nest

nest egg /ˈ· ·/ *n* amount of money saved
for special future use

nes·tle /ˈnesəl/ *vi/t* settle, lie, or put in a
close comfortable position: *She nestled
down (into the big chair) and began to read.*

nest·ling /ˈnestlɪŋ, ˈneslɪŋ/ *n* very young

bird

net¹ /net/ *n* 1 [C;U] (piece of) material
made of strings, wires, etc. tied together
with regular spaces between them: *the
fisherman's nets* 2 also **Net** [the+S] the
INTERNET —see also SAFETY NET ♦ *vt* -tt-
catch in a net ~**ting** *n* string, wire, etc.
made into a net

net² also **nett** *adj* left after nothing further
is to be taken away: *a net profit* ♦ *vt* -tt- gain
as a profit

net·ball /ˈnetbɔːl‖-bɒːl/ *n* [U] women's
team game in which points are gained by
throwing a ball into a net

neth·er /ˈneðə‖-ər/ *adj lit* lower; under

net·tle /ˈnetl/ *n* wild plant with stinging
leaves

net·work¹ /ˈnetwɜːk‖-wɜːrk/ *n* 1 large
system of lines, wires, etc. that cross or
meet each other 2 group of radio or
television stations —see also OLD-BOY
NETWORK

network² *v* 1 *vi* meet people in similar
work to share information, help each other,
etc. 2 *vt vi/t* connect (computers) into a
NETWORK¹ (1) to share information ~**ing** *n*
[U]

neu·rol·o·gy /njʊˈrɒlədʒi‖nʊˈrɑː-/ *n* [U]
scientific study of nerves and their diseases
-**gist** *n*

neu·ro·sis /njʊˈrəʊsɪs‖nʊˈrou-/ *n* -**ses**
/-siːz/ a disorder of the mind in which one
suffers from strong unreasonable fears and
has troubled relations with other people
-**rotic** /njʊˈrɒtɪk‖nʊˈrɑː-/ *adj* of or
suffering from a neurosis

neu·ter /ˈnjuːtə‖ˈnuːtər/ *adj* (in
grammar) belonging to the class of words
that mainly includes things rather than
males or females ♦ *vt* remove part of the
sex organs of (an animal)

neu·tral¹ /ˈnjuːtrəl‖ˈnuː-/ *adj* 1 not
supporting either side in a war, argument,
etc. 2 having no strong or noticeable
qualities: *a neutral colour* ~**ize**, ~**ise** *vt*
cause to have no effect ~**ity** /njuːˈtrælɪti‖
nuː-/ *n* [U]

neutral² *n* [U] the position of a car's
GEARS in which the engine is not connected
to the wheels

neu·tron /ˈnjuːtrɒn‖ˈnuːtrɑːn/ *n* a very
small piece of matter that is part of an
atom and carries no electricity

nev·er /'nevə ‖ -ər/ *adv* not ever: *It never snows in the desert.*

nev·er·the·less /ˌnevəðə'les ‖ -vər-/ *adv* in spite of that; yet: *It was a cold day but nevertheless very pleasant.*

new /nju: ‖ nu:/ *adj* **1** only recently made or begun: *a new film* **2** different from the one before: *She's looking for a new job.* **3** having only recently arrived or started: *I'm new here.* **4** new newly; recently: *a new-laid egg* **5** new to just beginning to know about or do; unfamiliar with ~**ly** *adv* that has just happened or been done; recently: *a newly-built house* ~**ness** *n* [U]

New Age /ˌ· '·/ *adj* relating to (beliefs about) ALTERNATIVE (2) religions, medicine, and ways of life

new·born /'nju:bɔ:n ‖ 'nu:bɔ:rn/ *adj* born recently

new broom /ˌ· '·/ *n esp. BrE* newly appointed person who is eager to make changes

new·com·er /'nju:kʌmə ‖ 'nu:kʌmər/ *n* someone who has just arrived

new·fan·gled /ˌnju:'fæŋgəld◄ ‖ ˌnu:-/ *adj* new but neither necessary nor better

new·ly·wed /'nju:liwed ‖ 'nu:-/ *n* recently married person

news /nju:z ‖ nu:z/ *n* **1** [U] facts that are reported about a recent event: *a piece of news* **2** [*the*+S] regular report of recent events on radio or television

news·a·gent /'nju:z,eɪdʒənt ‖ 'nu:z-/ *BrE* ‖ **news deal·er** /'·ˌ·/ *AmE* — *n* someone who sells newspapers in a shop

news·cast·er /'nju:z,kɑ:stə ‖ 'nu:z-,kæstər/ also **newsreader** /-ˌri:də ‖ -ər/ *BrE* — *n* person who reads the news on television

news·hound /'nju:zhaʊnd ‖ 'nu:z-/ *n* very eager newspaper reporter

news·let·ter /'nju:z,letə ‖ 'nu:z,letər/ *n* sheet of printed news about an organization

news·pa·per /'nju:s,peɪpə ‖ 'nu:z,peɪpər/ *n* paper printed with news, notices, advertisements, etc., that comes out every day or every week

news·print /'nju:z,prɪnt ‖ 'nu:z-/ *n* [U] paper on which newspapers are printed

news·wor·thy /'nju:z,wɜ:ði ‖ 'nu:z-,wɜːrði/ *adj* important or interesting enough to be reported as news

newt /nju:t ‖ nu:t/ *n* four-legged animal living both on land and in water

new wave /ˌ· '·/ *n, adj* (people) trying to introduce new ideas in art, films, politics, etc.

new year /ˌ· '·/ *n* (*often caps.*) a year which has just begun or will soon begin

next /nekst/ *adj* **1** with nothing before or between; nearest: *the house next to mine* **2** the one following or after: *I'm coming next week.* ♦ *adv* **1** just afterwards: *First, heat the oil; next, add the onions.* **2** the next time: *when next we meet* **3** next to almost: *next to impossible*

next door /ˌ· '·/ *adv* in the next room or building: *She lives next door.*

NHS /ˌen eɪtʃ 'es/ *n* [*the*+S] *abbrev. for:* National Health Service; the British system of medical treatment for everyone, paid for by taxes

nib /nɪb/ *n* pointed piece on the end of a pen, out of which ink flows

nib·ble /'nɪbəl/ *vi/t* eat with small bites ♦ *n* small bite

nice /naɪs/ *adj* **1** good; pleasant: *a nice holiday* **2** showing or needing careful understanding; SUBTLE: *a nice distinction* **3** *infml* bad: *He got us into a nice mess.* **4** nice and pleasantly; as was wanted: *The soup was nice and hot.* ~**ly** *adv* ~**ness** *n* [U]

ni·ce·ty /'naɪsəti/ *n* fine or delicate point; detail

niche /nɪtʃ, ni:ʃ ‖ nɪtʃ/ *n* **1** hollow place in a wall, where something is put **2** suitable place, job, etc.

nick[1] /nɪk/ *n* **1** small cut **2** *BrE infml* prison **3** in the nick of time only just in time; almost too late ♦ *vt* **1** make a small cut in **2** *BrE sl* ARREST **3** *BrE infml* steal

nick[2] *n* [U] *BrE sl* a stated condition: *The car's in good nick.*

nick·el /'nɪkəl/ *n* **1** [U] hard silver-white metal **2** [C] US five-cent coin

nick·name /'nɪkneɪm/ *n* informal name used instead of someone's real name ♦ *vt:* *They nicknamed him 'Baldy'.*

nic·o·tine /'nɪkəti:n/ *n* [U] poisonous chemical found in tobacco

niece /ni:s/ *n* daughter of one's brother or sister

nif·ty /'nɪfti/ *adj infml* very good, attractive, or effective

nig·gard·ly /'nɪgədli ‖ -ər-/ *adj* very

ungenerous

nig·gle /'nɪgəl/ vi be continually annoying or troubling

night /naɪt/ n 1 [C;U] dark part of the day, between sunrise and sunset: *Did you have a good night?* (=sleep well) **2 at night: a** during the night **b** at the end of the day **3 by night** during the night **4 make a night of it** spend all or most of the night in enjoyment **5 night after night** every night **6 night and day** also **day and night** — all the time

night·cap /'naɪtkæp/ n drink before going to bed

night·club /'naɪtklʌb/ n place where people can drink and dance, open late at night

night·dress /'naɪtdres/ also **night·ie** /'naɪti/ n woman's garment worn in bed

night·fall /'naɪtfɔːl‖-fɔːl/ n [U] beginning of night

nigh·tin·gale /'naɪtɪŋgeɪl/ n bird with a beautiful song

night·life /'naɪtlaɪf/ n [U] evening entertainment or social activity

night·ly /'naɪtli/ adj, adv (happening, done, etc.) every night

night·mare /'naɪtmeə‖-mer/ n 1 frightening dream **2** terrible experience or event

night·shirt /'naɪt-ʃɜːt‖-ʃɜːrt/ n long loose shirt worn in bed

night watch·man /ˌ· '·-/ n man who guards a building at night

ni·hil·is·m /'naɪɪlɪzəm/ n [U] belief that nothing has meaning or value —**ist** n

nil /nɪl/ n nothing; zero

nim·ble /'nɪmbəl/ adj 1 quick, light, and neat in movement **2** quick in thought or understanding —**bly** adv ~**ness** n [U]

nine /naɪn/ determiner, n, pron 9 **ninth** determiner, adv, n, pron 9th

nine·pins /'naɪn,pɪnz/ n like ninepins (falling or being destroyed) quickly and in large numbers

nine·teen /ˌnaɪn'tiːn◂/ determiner, n, pron 19 —**th** determiner, adv, n, pron 19th

nine·ty /'naɪnti/ determiner, n, pron 90–**tieth** determiner, adv, n, pron 90th

nip /nɪp/ v -**pp**- 1 vt catch in a sharp tight usu. painful hold **2** vi BrE go quickly; hurry **3 nip something in the bud** stop something before it has properly started ♦ n [S] **1** sharp tight hold or bite **2** coldness: *a*

nip in the air

nip·per /'nɪpə‖-ər/ n infml child

nip·ple /'nɪpəl/ n round pointed dark-skinned area on a breast

nip·py /'nɪpi/ adj 1 cold **2** quick in movement

nir·va·na /nɪə'vɑːnə, nɜː-‖nɪr-, nɜːr-/ n [U] (usu. cap.) (in Buddhism and Hinduism) calm state of union with the spirit of the universe

nit /nɪt/ n BrE silly person

nit·pick·ing /'nɪt,pɪkɪŋ/ n [U] habit of paying too much attention to small unimportant details **nitpicking** adj

ni·trate /'naɪtreɪt, -trɪt/ n chemical used esp. to improve the soil for growing crops

ni·tric ac·id /ˌ· '·-/ n [U] powerful acid which destroys other materials

ni·tro·gen /'naɪtrədʒən/ n [U] gas that forms most of the Earth's air

ni·tro·gly·ce·rine /ˌnaɪtrəʊ'glɪsərɪn, -trə-, -riːn‖-trəʊ'glɪsərɪn/ n [U] powerful liquid explosive

nit·ty-grit·ty /ˌnɪti 'grɪti/ n **get down to the nitty-gritty** sl deal with the difficult, practical, and important part of a matter

nit·wit /'nɪt,wɪt/ n silly person

no /nəʊ/ adv **1** (used for refusing or disagreeing): *'Do you like it?' 'No!'* **2** not any: *He felt no better.* ♦ determiner **1** not a; not any: *She felt no fear.* **I** *I'm no fool!* **2** (shows what is not allowed): *No smoking* (on a sign) ♦ n answer or decision of no: *a clear no*

no. written abbrev. for: number

No. 10 NUMBER TEN

nob·ble /'nɒbəl/ vt BrE sl **1** prevent (a racehorse) from winning by using drugs **2** get or persuade dishonestly

no·bil·i·ty /nəʊ'bɪlɪti, nə-‖nɒu-/ n [U] **1** people of high social rank with titles **2** state of being noble

no·ble /'nəʊbəl‖'nɒu-/ adj **1** of high moral quality; fine and unselfish **2** grand **3** of high social rank ♦ n lord in former times –**bly** adv

no·ble·man /'nəʊbəlmən‖'nɒu-/, -**woman** /-,wʊmən/ fem. — n -**men** /-mən/ member of the nobility

no·bod·y /'nəʊbədi‖'nɒu,bɑːdi, -bədi/ pron no one ♦ n unimportant person

no-claims bo·nus /ˌ· '·-/ n reduction in the payments made to an insurance company when someone has not made any claims within a particular period

noc·tur·nal /nɒk'tɜ:nl ‖ nɑ:k'tɜ:rn-/ adj happening or active at night

nod /nɒd ‖ nɑ:d/ vi/t -dd- bend (one's head) forward and down, esp. to show agreement or give a sign ♦ n act of nodding

    nod off phr vi fall asleep unintentionally

nod·ding ac·quaint·ance /ˌ·· ·'··/ n [S] slight familiarity

nod·ule /'nɒdju:l ‖ 'nɑ:dʒu:l/ n small round lump or swelling

no-frills /ˌ· '·◄/ adj without unnecessary features; basic: a no-frills airline

noise /nɔɪz/ n [C;U] sound, esp. loud and unpleasant **noisy** adj making a lot of noise **noisily** adv **noisiness** n [U]

no·mad /'nəʊmæd ‖ 'nəʊ-/ n member of a tribe that does not settle long in one place **~ic** /nəʊ'mædɪk/ adj

no-man's-land /'·· ·,·/ n [S;U] land no one owns or controls, esp. between two armies or borders

no·men·cla·ture /nəʊ'meŋklətʃə ‖ 'nəʊmənkleɪ-/ n [C;U] system of naming things

nom·i·nal /'nɒmɪnəl ‖ 'nɑ:-/ adj **1** not really what the name suggests: He's only the nominal head of the business; his son really runs it. **2** (of an amount of money) very small **3** of or being a noun **~ly** adv

nom·i·nate /'nɒmɪneɪt ‖ 'nɑ:-/ vt to suggest officially that (someone) should be chosen or elected **–nation** /ˌnɒmɪ'neɪʃən ‖ ˌnɑ:-/ n [C;U]

nom·i·nee /ˌnɒmɪ'ni: ‖ ˌnɑ:-/ n person who has been nominated

non-a·ligned /ˌnɒn-ə'laɪnd◄ ‖ ˌnɑ:n-/ adj (of a country) not supporting any particular powerful nation

non·cha·lant /'nɒnʃələnt ‖ ˌnɑ:nʃə'lɑ:nt/ adj calm and usu. uninterested **~ly** adv **–lance** n [U]

non-com·mis·sion·ed of·fi·cer /ˌnɒnkəmɪʃənd 'ɒfɪsə ‖ ˌnɑ:n-, -'fɪsər-, -'ɑ:f-/ n person in the army, navy, etc. below the rank of officer but with some power to command others

non-com·mit·tal /ˌnɒnkə'mɪtl◄ ‖ ˌnɑ:n-/ adj not showing what you really think or intend **~ly** adv

non-con·form·ist /ˌnɒnkən'fɔ:mɪst◄ ‖ ˌnɑ:nkən'fɔ:r-/ n, adj **1** (person) not

following customary ways of living, thinking, etc. **2** (cap.) (member) of a Christian group separated from the Church of England

non·de·script /'nɒndɪˌskrɪpt ‖ ˌnɑ:ndɪ'skrɪpt/ adj very ordinary-looking and dull

none /nʌn/ pron not any: She has several, but I have none. | None of the wine was drinkable. ♦ adv **1 none the not at all:** My car is none the worse for (=not damaged by) its accident. **2 none too** not very

non·en·ti·ty /nɒ'nentɪti ‖ nɑ:-/ n person without much ability, character, or importance

none·the·less /ˌnʌnðə'les◄/ adv in spite of that; NEVERTHELESS

non-e·vent /ˌ· ·'·/ n something much less important, interesting, etc. than expected

non-ex·ist·ent /ˌnɒnɪg'zɪstənt◄ ‖ ˌnɑ:n-/ adj not existing at all

non-fic·tion /ˌnɒn'fɪkʃən ‖ ˌnɑ:n-/ n [U] writing about facts, not stories

no-non·sense /ˌ· '··/ adj practical and direct

non·plussed /ˌnɒn 'plʌst ‖ ˌnɑ:n-/ adj so surprised that one does not know what to say or do

non-pro·lif·er·a·tion /ˌnɒnprəˌlɪfə'reɪʃən ‖ ˌnɑ:n-/ n [U] limiting the number of NUCLEAR or chemical weapons being produced

non·sense /'nɒnsəns ‖ 'nɑ:nsens/ n [U] **1** meaningless words **2** foolish words, ideas, or actions **–sensical** /nɒn'sensɪkəl ‖ nɑ:n-/ adj foolish

non seq·ui·tur /ˌnɒn 'sekwɪtə ‖ ˌnɑ:n-'sekwɪtər/ n statement that does not follow by correct reasoning from what has been said before

non-start·er /ˌnɒn'stɑ:tə ‖ ˌnɑ:n'stɑ:rtər/ n BrE person or idea with no chance of success

non-stick /ˌnɒn'stɪk◄ ‖ ˌnɑ:n-/ adj with a special surface that food will not stick to when cooked

non-stop /ˌnɒn'stɒp◄ ‖ ˌnɑ:n'stɑ:p◄/ adj, adv without a pause or interruption

noo·dle /'nu:dl/ n long thin piece of paste made from flour, cooked in soup or boiling water

nook /nʊk/ n **1** sheltered private place **2 nooks and crannies** hidden or little-known places

noon /nuːn/ n [U] 12 o'clock in the daytime

no one /'· ·/ pron not anyone; no person

noose /nuːs/ n ring formed by the end of a rope, which closes tighter as it is pulled

nor /nɔː‖ nɔːr/ conj 1 (used after **neither** or **not**) also not; or: neither hot nor cold — just warm 2 and also not: 'I don't like it.' 'Nor do I.'

norm /nɔːm‖ nɔːrm/ n usual or average way of happening or behaving

nor·mal /'nɔːməl‖ 'nɔːr-/ adj according to what is usual, expected, or average ~**ly** adv: Normally I go to bed at 11 o'clock. ~**ity** also ~**cy** AmE —n [U]

nor·mal·ize also **-ise** BrE /'nɔːməlaɪz‖ 'nɔːr-/ vi/t (cause to) become normal, esp. to bring or come back to a good or normal state **-ization**, **-isation** /ˌnɔːməlaɪˈzeɪʃən‖ ˌnɔːrmələ-/ n [U]

north /nɔːθ‖ nɔːrθ/ n (often cap.) direction which is on the left of a person facing the rising sun ♦ adj 1 in the north 2 (of wind) from the north ♦ adv 1 towards the north 2 **up north** to or in the north ~**ward** adj, adv

north·east /ˌnɔːθˈiːst◄‖ ˌnɔːrθ-/ n, adj, adv (direction) halfway between north and east ~**ern** adj

nor·ther·ly /'nɔːðəli‖ 'nɔːrðərli/ adj towards or in the north

nor·thern /'nɔːðən‖ 'nɔːrðərn/ adj of the north part of the world or of a country ~**er** n person who lives in or comes from the northern part of a country

north·west /ˌnɔːθˈwest◄‖ ˌnɔːrθ-/ n, adj, adv (direction) halfway between north and west ~**ern** adj

nos. written abbrev. for: numbers

nose /nəʊz‖ noʊz/ n 1 [C] the part of the face above the mouth that is used for breathing and smelling 2 [C] (pointed) front end: the nose of the rocket 3 [S] ability to find out: I have a nose for trouble. | Just follow your nose. (=use this ability) 4 [C] too great an interest in things which do not concern one: Stop **poking your nose** into my affairs! 5 **get up someone's nose** BrE infml annoy someone very much 6 **keep one's nose clean** keep out of trouble 7 **pay through the nose (for)** pay a great deal too much money (for) 8 **put someone's nose out of joint** make someone jealous by

taking their place as the centre of attention 9 **turn one's nose up at** consider (something) not good enough to enjoy 10 **under someone's (very) nose** quite openly in front of someone ♦ vi 1 move ahead slowly and carefully 2 try to find out about things that do not concern you

nose·bleed /'nəʊzbliːd‖ 'noʊz-/ n case of bleeding from the nose

nose·cone /'nəʊzkəʊn‖ 'noʊzkoʊn/ n pointed front part of a spacecraft or MISSILE

nose·dive /'nəʊzdaɪv‖ 'noʊz-/ vi 1 (of a plane) drop suddenly, front end first 2 fall suddenly and greatly: Prices nosedived. nosedive n

nosh /nɒʃ‖ nɑːʃ/ n [S;U] BrE sl meal, food

nos·tal·gia /nɒˈstældʒə‖ nɑː-/ n [U] fondness for past things **-gic** adj

nos·tril /'nɒstrɪl‖ 'nɑː-/ n either of the two openings in the nose

nos·y , **nosey** /'nəʊzi‖ 'noʊ-/ adj interested in things that do not concern one

nosy park·er /ˌ·· '··/ n BrE infml nosy person

not /nɒt‖ nɑːt/ adv 1 (used for showing the opposite meaning): He's happy, but I'm not. | It's a cat, not a dog! | Will he come, or not? | Not one (=none) remained. 2 **not at all** (a polite answer to thanks) 3 **not that** I don't mean that: Not that it matters, but where were you last night?

no·ta·ble /'nəʊtəbəl‖ 'noʊ-/ adj unusual or good enough to be especially noticed **-bly** adv particularly

no·ta·ry /'nəʊtəri‖ 'noʊ-/ n public official who watches the signing of written statements and makes them official

no·ta·tion /nəʊˈteɪʃən‖ noʊ-/ n [C;U] system of signs for writing something down: musical notation

notch /nɒtʃ‖ nɑːtʃ/ n V-shaped cut ♦ vt 1 make a notch in 2 win: We notched up our third victory.

note /nəʊt‖ noʊt/ n 1 [C] short written record to remind one of something 2 [C] short piece of additional information in a book 3 [C] short informal letter 4 [C] piece of paper money 5 [C] (sign representing) a musical sound 6 [S] stated quality or feeling: a note of anger in his voice 7 [U] fml fame; importance: a composer of some note 8 **compare notes** tell one's experiences and opinions of something to 9 **take note of**

pay attention to ♦ vt 1 record in writing: *The policeman noted down his address.* 2 notice and remember **noted** *adj* famous

note·book /'nəʊtbʊk || 'nout-/ *n* book of plain paper in which one writes NOTES¹ (1)

note·pa·per /'nəʊt,peɪpə || 'nout,peɪpər/ *n* [U] paper for writing letters on

note·wor·thy /'nəʊt,wɜːði || 'nout,wɜːr-/ *adj* NOTABLE

noth·ing /'nʌθɪŋ/ *pron* 1 not any thing: *There's nothing in this box — it's empty.* 2 something of no importance: *My shoes are nothing to* (=much less than) *his.* 3 for **nothing: a** free **b** with no good result 4 **nothing but** nothing other than: *He's nothing but a criminal.* 5 **nothing doing: a** I won't! **b** no result, interest, etc. 6 **nothing for it** no other way 7 **nothing like** not nearly: *It's nothing like as cold as yesterday.* 8 **think nothing of** treat as easy or unimportant

no·tice /'nəʊtɪs || 'nou-/ *n* 1 [C] written or printed sign giving information 2 [U] information that something is going to happen; warning: *The rules may be changed without notice.* 3 [U] attention: *Don't* **take any notice of** (=pay no attention to) *him.* ♦ *vi/t* see, hear, etc. so as to be conscious and remember: *She was wearing a new dress, but he didn't even notice (it).* **~able** *adj* big enough to be noticed **~ably** *adv*

no·ti·fy /'nəʊtɪfaɪ || 'nou-/ *vt* tell (someone), esp. formally **–fication** /,nəʊtɪfɪ'keɪʃən || ,nou-/ *n* [U]

notice board /'·· ·/ *n* BrE board for information

no·tion /'nəʊʃən || 'nou-/ *n* idea; opinion

no·to·ri·ous /nəʊ'tɔːrɪəs, nə- || nou-, nə-/ *adj* famous for something bad: *a notorious liar* **~ly** *adv* **notoriety** /,nəʊtə'raɪɪti || ,nou-/ *n* [U]

not·with·stand·ing /,nɒtwɪθ'stændɪŋ, -wɪð- || ,nɑːt-/ *adv fml* in spite of that

nou·gat /'nuːgɑː || -gət/ *n* [U] sweet made of sugar, nuts, fruit, etc.

nought /nɔːt || nɒːt/ *n* BrE zero

noun /naʊn/ *n* word that is the name of a thing, quality, action, etc. and can be used as the subject or object of a verb

nour·ish /'nʌrɪʃ || 'nɜːrɪʃ, 'nʌ-/ *vt* 1 keep alive and healthy by giving food **b** keep (a feeling, plan, etc.) alive **~ment** *n* [U] food

nous /naʊs || nuːs/ *n* [U] BrE good practical judgment

nou·velle cuis·ine /,nuːvel kwɪ'ziːn/ *n* [U] style of cooking in which (small amounts of) unusual combinations of food are attractively arranged

nov·el¹ /'nɒvəl || 'nɑː-/ *n* long written story **~ist** *n* novel writer

novel² *adj* new and rather clever

nov·el·ty /'nɒvəlti || 'nɑː-/ *n* 1 [U] interesting newness 2 [C] something new and unusual 3 [C] small cheap object, usu. not very useful

No·vem·ber /nəʊ'vembə, nə- || nou'vem-bər, nə-/ *n* the 11th month of the year

nov·ice /'nɒvɪs || 'nɑː-/ *n* person who has just begun and has no experience

now /naʊ/ *adv* 1 at this present time: *He used to be fat, but now he's slim.* 2 next; at once: *Now for* (=now we will have) *the next question.* 3 (used for attracting attention or giving a warning): *Now then, what's all this?* 4 **(every) now and again/then** at times; sometimes ♦ *conj* because: *Now (that) you've arrived, we can begin.*

now·a·days /'naʊədeɪz/ *adv* in these modern times

no way /,· '·/ *adv, interj sl* no; certainly not

no·where /'nəʊweə || 'nouwer/ *adv* 1 not anywhere 2 **nowhere near** not at all near or nearly

nox·ious /'nɒkʃəs || 'nɑːk-/ *adj* harmful; poisonous

noz·zle /'nɒzəl || 'nɑː-/ *n* short tube at the end of a pipe for controlling the flow of a liquid

nth /enθ/ *adj* **to the nth degree** to the highest, greatest, furthest, etc. degree

nu·ance /'njuːɑːns || 'nuː-/ *n* slight delicate difference in meaning, colour, etc.

nub /nʌb/ *n* most important point

nu·bile /'njuːbaɪl || 'nuːbəl/ *adj* (of a young woman) sexually attractive

nu·cle·ar /'njuːklɪə || 'nuːklɪər/ *adj* being, using, or producing the great power you get by breaking up atoms: *nuclear energy | nuclear warfare* (=with nuclear bombs)

nuclear fam·i·ly /,·· '···/ *n* family unit that consists only of husband, wife, and children, without grandmothers, uncles, etc.

nu·cle·us /'njuːklɪəs || 'nuː-/ *n* **-clei** /-klɪaɪ/ 1 central part of **a** an atom **b** a CELL

(2) **2** original part round which the rest is built

nude /njuːd ‖ nuːd/ *adj* with no clothes on ♦ *n* **1** (piece of art showing a) nude person **2 in the nude** with no clothes on

nudge /nʌdʒ/ *vt* push gently, esp. with the elbow **nudge** *n*

nud·is·m /'njuːdɪzəm ‖ 'nuː-/ *n* [U] practice of going around with no clothes on, usu. in a special place (**nudist camp**) **nudist** *n*

nu·di·ty /'njuːdɪti ‖ 'nuː-/ *n* [U] state of being nude

nug·get /'nʌɡɪt/ *n* small rough lump: *gold nuggets* | (fig.) *a nugget of information*

nui·sance /'njuːsəns ‖ 'nuː-/ *n* annoying person, animal, thing, or situation

nuke /njuːk/ *vt infml* attack with NUCLEAR weapons

null and void /ˌnʌl ənd 'vɔɪd/ *adj* having no legal effect

nul·li·fy /'nʌlɪfaɪ/ *vt* cause to have no effect

numb /nʌm/ *adj* unable to feel: *fingers numb with cold* **numb** *vt* **~ness** *n* [U]

num·ber /'nʌmbə ‖ -ər/ *n* **1** [C] (written sign for) a member of the system used in counting and measuring: *1, 2, and 3 are numbers.* **2** [C;U] quantity; amount: *A large number of people came.* **3** [C] (copy of) a magazine printed at a particular time —see also BACK NUMBER **4** [C] piece of music **5 have someone's number** have knowledge useful in annoying or defeating someone —see also E NUMBER, OPPOSITE NUMBER ♦ *vt* **1** give a number to: *numbered pages* **2** reach as a total: *The audience numbered over 5000.* **3** *fml* include: *I number him among my friends.* **4 someone's days are numbered** someone cannot continue or live much longer **~less** *adj* too many to count

number one /ˌ·· '·/ *n* **1** chief person or thing **2** oneself and no one else: *Look after number one.*

Number Ten /ˌ·· '·/ *n* home of the British PRIME MINISTER, in London

nu·me·ral /'njuːmərəl ‖ 'nuː-/ *n* sign that represents a number —see also ROMAN NUMERAL

nu·me·rate /'njuːmərət ‖ 'nuː-/ *adj* able to calculate with numbers

nu·mer·i·cal /njuː'merɪkəl ‖ nuː-/ *adj* of

or using numbers **~ly** /-kli/ *adv*

nu·me·rous /'njuːmərəs ‖ 'nuː-/ *adj* many

nun /nʌn/ *n* member of an all-female religious group that lives together **~nery** building where they live

nurse /nɜːs ‖ nɜːrs/ *n* person who takes care of sick, hurt, or old people, esp. in hospital ♦ *vt* **1** take care of as or like a nurse **2** hold in the mind: *nurse a grudge* **3** handle carefully or lovingly: *He nursed the battered plane home.* **4** feed (a baby) with breast milk **nursing** *n* [U] job of being a nurse

nur·se·ry /'nɜːsəri ‖ 'nɜːr-/ *n* **1** place where young children are taken care of **2** area where garden plants are grown to be sold

nursery rhyme /'··· ·/ *n* song or poem for young children

nursery school /'··· ·/ *n* school for young children of 2 to 5 years of age

nursing home /'·· ·/ *n* place where old or sick people can live and be looked after

nur·ture /'nɜːtʃə ‖ 'nɜːrtʃər/ *vt lit* give care and food to, so as to help development

nut /nʌt/ *n* **1** fruit with a hard shell and a softer dry seed inside which is eaten **2** small piece of metal with a hole through it for screwing onto a BOLT (2) **3** *sl* mad person **4 a hard/tough nut to crack** a difficult question, person, etc. to deal with **5 do one's nut** *infml* be very worried and/or angry **6 off one's nut** *sl* mad **nuts** *adj sl* mad **~ty** *adj* **1** like or full of nuts **2** *sl* mad

nut·crack·er /'nʌt,krækə ‖ -ər/ *n* tool for cracking the shell of a nut

nu·tri·ent /'njuːtriənt ‖ 'nuː-/ *n, adj* (a chemical or food) providing for life or growth

nu·tri·tion /njuː'trɪʃən ‖ nuː-/ *n* [U] process of giving or getting food **–tious** *adj* valuable to the body as food

nuts and bolts /ˌ· · '·/ *n* [(*the*)P] the simple facts or skills of a subject or job

nut·shell /'nʌt-ʃel/ *n* **in a nutshell** described in as few words as possible

nuz·zle /'nʌzəl/ *vi/t* press closely, esp. with the nose

ny·lon /'naɪlɒn ‖ -lɑːn/ *n* [U] strong man-made material made into cloth, plastic, etc.

nymph /nɪmf/ *n* (in Greek and Roman

literature) goddess of nature living in trees, streams, mountains, etc.

nym·pho·ma·ni·a /ˌnɪmfəˈmeɪnɪə/ *n* [U] strong sexual desire in a woman to a degree considered as unhealthy or socially unacceptable –**niac** /-nɪæk/ *n* woman with nymphomania

O

O, o /əʊ‖oʊ/ **1** the 15th letter of the English alphabet **2** (in speech) zero

oaf /əʊf‖oʊf/ *n* rough stupid awkward person

oak /əʊk‖oʊk/ *n* large broad tree with hard wood and curly leaves

OAP /ˌəʊ eɪ ˈpiː‖ˌoʊ-/ *n BrE abbrev. for:* old age pensioner; person old enough to receive an OLD AGE PENSION

oar /ɔː‖ɔːr/ *n* **1** long pole with a flat blade, used for rowing a boat **2 put/shove/stick one's oar in** *sl for* INTERFERE

o·a·sis /əʊˈeɪsɪs‖oʊ-/ *n* **-ses** /-siːz/ place with water and trees in a desert

oath /əʊθ‖oʊθ/ *n* **oaths** /əʊðz‖oʊðz/ **1** solemn promise **2 be on/under oath** have promised to tell the truth, in a court of law

oat·meal /ˈəʊtmiːl‖ˈoʊt-/ *n* [U] crushed oats

oats /əʊts‖oʊts/ *n* [P] sort of grain used as food —see also WILD OATS

ob·du·rate /ˈɒbdʒʊrət‖ˈɑːbdə-/ *adj fml* unwilling to think or act differently ~**ly** *adv* –**racy** *n* [U]

o·be·di·ent /əˈbiːdɪənt/ *adj* doing what one is told to do ~**ly** *adv* –**ence** *n* [U]

ob·e·lisk /ˈɒbəlɪsk‖ˈɑː-, ˈoʊ-/ *n* tall pointed stone pillar

o·bese /əʊˈbiːs‖oʊ-/ *adj fml* unhealthily fat **obesity** *n* [U]

o·bey /əʊˈbeɪ, ə-‖oʊ-, ə-/ *vi/t* do what one is told to do (by someone in a position of power)

o·bit·u·a·ry /əˈbɪtʃʊəri‖-tʃʊeri/ *n* report in a newspaper, etc. of someone's death

ob·ject¹ /ˈɒbdʒɪkt‖ˈɑːb-/ *n* **1** thing that can be seen or felt **2** purpose **3** *gram* word or words that represent **a** the person or thing (the **direct object**) that something is done to (such as *door* in *She closed the door.*) or **b** the person (the **indirect object**) who is concerned in the result of an action (such as *her* in *I gave her the book.*) **4** person or thing that produces the stated feeling: *She has become an object of pity.* **5 be no object** not be a difficulty

ob·ject² /əbˈdʒekt/ *vi* be against something or someone: *I object to paying so much.*

ob·jec·tion /əbˈdʒekʃən/ *n* **1** statement or feeling of dislike or opposition **2** reason or argument against

ob·jec·tion·a·ble /əbˈdʒekʃənəbəl/ *adj* unpleasant –**bly** *adv*

ob·jec·tive¹ /əbˈdʒektɪv/ *adj* **1** not influenced by personal feelings; fair **2** existing outside the mind; real –**tivity** /ˌɒbdʒekˈtɪvəti‖ˌɑːb-/ *n* [U]

objective² *n* purpose of a plan

ob·jet d'art /ˌɒbʒeɪ ˈdɑː‖ˌɑːbʒeɪ ˈdɑːr/ *n* **objets d'art** small object of some value as art

ob·li·ga·tion /ˌɒblɪˈɡeɪʃən‖ˌɑːb-/ *n* [C;U] duty: *You're under* **no obligation** *to buy.* (=you don't have to) –**tory** /əˈblɪɡətəri‖-tɔːri/ *adj*

o·blige /əˈblaɪdʒ/ *vt fml* **1** make it necessary for (someone) to do something: *We were obliged to* (=had to) *leave.* **2** do a favour for **3 (I'm) much obliged (to you)** (used for thanking someone politely)

o·blig·ing /əˈblaɪdʒɪŋ/ *adj* kind and eager to help ~**ly** *adv*

o·blique /əˈbliːk/ *adj* **1** indirect: *an oblique hint* **2** sloping

o·blit·er·ate /əˈblɪtəreɪt/ *vt* remove all signs of; destroy –**ation** /əˌblɪtəˈreɪʃən/ *n* [U]

o·bliv·i·on /əˈblɪvɪən/ *n* [U] **1** state of being completely forgotten **2** state of being unconscious or not noticing one's surroundings

o·bliv·i·ous /əˈblɪvɪəs/ *adj* not noticing: *He was oblivious of/to the danger.*

ob·long /ˈɒblɒŋ‖ˈɑːblɔːŋ/ *n* right-angled figure with four sides, two long and two shorter ones **oblong** *adj*

ob·nox·ious /əbˈnɒkʃəs ‖ -ˈnɑːk-/ *adj* extremely unpleasant ~**ly** *adv*

o·boe /ˈəʊbəʊ ‖ ˈoʊboʊ/ *n* musical instrument made of a black wooden tube, played by blowing **oboist** *n* player of an oboe

ob·scene /əbˈsiːn/ *adj* very offensive or shocking, esp. sexually **obscenity** /əbˈsenʒti/ *n* [C;U] obscene word or behaviour

ob·scure /əbˈskjʊə ‖ -ˈskjʊr/ *adj* 1 hard to understand; not clear 2 not well known ♦ *vt* hide **obscurity** *n* [U] state of being obscure

ob·se·qui·ous /əbˈsiːkwiəs/ *adj fml* too eager to obey or serve ~**ly** *adv* ~**ness** *n* [U]

ob·ser·vance /əbˈzɜːvəns ‖ -ɜːr-/ *n fml* 1 [U] doing something in accordance with a law, custom, etc. 2 [C] part of a religious ceremony

ob·ser·vant /əbˈzɜːvənt ‖ -ɜːr-/ *adj* quick at noticing things

ob·ser·va·tion /ˌɒbzəˈveɪʃən ‖ ˌɑːbzər-/ *n* 1 [C;U] action of noticing 2 [U] ability to notice things 3 [C] remark, esp. about something noticed 4 **under observation** being carefully watched during a period of time

ob·ser·va·to·ry /əbˈzɜːvətəri ‖ əbˈzɜːrvətɔːri/ *n* place where scientists look at and study the stars, moon, etc.

ob·serve /əbˈzɜːv ‖ -ɜːrv/ *vt* 1 watch carefully 2 *fml* act in accordance with (a law, custom, etc.) 3 *fml* say **observer** *n* 1 someone who observes 2 someone who attends meetings, etc. only to listen, not take part

ob·sess /əbˈses/ *vt* completely fill (someone's) mind, so they cannot think about anything else: *She was obsessed by the fear of failure.* ~**ive** *adj* that is an obsession ~**ion** /-ˈseʃən/ *n* fixed and often unreasonable idea or pattern of behaviour

ob·so·lete /ˈɒbsəliːt ‖ ˌɑːbsəˈliːt◄/ *adj* no longer used; out of date

ob·sta·cle /ˈɒbstəkəl ‖ ˈɑːb-/ *n* something that prevents action, movement, or success

ob·ste·tri·cian /ˌɒbstɨˈtrɪʃən ‖ ˌɑːb-/ *n* doctor concerned with obstetrics

ob·stet·rics /əbˈstetrɪks/ *n* [U] branch of medicine concerned with the birth of children

ob·sti·nate /ˈɒbstɨnɨt ‖ ˈɑːb-/ *adj* 1 not willing to obey or change one's opinion

2 difficult to control or defeat: *obstinate resistance* ~**ly** *adv* ~**nacy** *n* [U]

ob·struct /əbˈstrʌkt/ *vt* 1 block 2 put difficulties in the way of ~**ive** *adj* intentionally obstructing ~**ion** /əbˈstrʌkʃən/ *n* 1 [C] act of obstructing 2 [U] something that obstructs

ob·tain /əbˈteɪn/ *vt fml* get: *How did you obtain this information?* ~**able** *adj*

ob·tru·sive /əbˈtruːsɪv/ *adj fml* unpleasantly noticeable ~**ly** *adv*

ob·tuse /əbˈtjuːs ‖ -ˈtuːs/ *adj* 1 *fml* annoyingly slow to understand 2 (of an angle) more than 90° ~**ly** *adv* ~**ness** *n* [U]

ob·verse /ˈɒbvɜːs ‖ ˈɑːbvɜːrs/ *n* 1 front side of a coin, etc. 2 opposite

ob·vi·ous /ˈɒbviəs ‖ ˈɑːb-/ *adj* easy to see and understand; clear: *an obvious lie* ~**ly** *adv*

oc·ca·sion /əˈkeɪʒən/ *n* 1 [C] time when something happens: *May I take this occasion* (=this chance) *to thank you for your help.* 2 [U] *fml* reason: *He had no occasion to be so rude.* 3 [C] special event or ceremony 4 **on occasion** *fml* occasionally —see also SENSE OF OCCASION ♦ *vt fml* cause

oc·ca·sion·al /əˈkeɪʒənəl/ *adj* happening sometimes; not regular ~**ly** *adv*

oc·ci·den·tal /ˌɒksɨˈdentəl◄ ‖ ˌɑːk-/ (person) of the western part of the world

oc·cult /ˈɒkʌlt, əˈkʌlt ‖ əˈkʌlt, ˈɑː-/ *adj* magical and mysterious ♦ *n* [the+S]

oc·cu·pant /ˈɒkjʊ̆pənt ‖ ˈɑːk-/ *n* person who is living in a house, room, etc. ~**pancy** *n* [U] (period of) being an occupant

oc·cu·pa·tion /ˌɒkjʊ̆ˈpeɪʃən ‖ ˌɑːk-/ *n* 1 [C] job 2 [C] something done to pass time 3 [U] taking possession of ~**al** *adj* of one's job

oc·cu·py /ˈɒkjʊ̆paɪ ‖ ˈɑːk-/ *vt* 1 be in: *The seat was occupied.* (=someone was sitting in it) 2 fill (space or time): *Writing occupies most of my spare time.* 3 take possession of: *an occupied country* 4 keep busy —**pier** *n*

oc·cur /əˈkɜː ‖ əˈkɜːr/ *vi* -**rr**- 1 happen 2 be found; exist: *a disease that occurs in children* ~**rence** /əˈkʌrəns ‖ əˈkɜː-/ *n* 1 [C] event 2 [U] process of occurring

occur to *phr vt* (of an idea) come to (someone's) mind

o·cean /ˈəʊʃən ‖ ˈoʊ-/ *n* 1 [U] great mass of salt water that covers most of the Earth 2 [C] any of the great seas into which this is divided: *the Atlantic Ocean ~ic* /ˌəʊʃiˈænɪk/ *adj*

o·clock /əˈklɒk ‖ əˈklɑːk/ *adv* (used in telling the time when it is exactly a numbered hour): *at 5 o'clock*

oc·ta·gon /ˈɒktəgən ‖ ˈɑːktəgɑːn/ *n* flat figure with eight sides and eight angles

oc·tane /ˈɒkteɪn ‖ ˈɑːk-/ *n* number showing the power and quality of petrol: *high-octane fuel*

oc·tave /ˈɒktɪv, -teɪv ‖ ˈɑːk-/ *n* space of eight degrees between musical notes

Oc·to·ber /ɒkˈtəʊbə ‖ ɑːkˈtoʊbər/ *n* the 10th month of the year

oc·to·ge·nar·ian /ˌɒktəʊdʒəˈneəriən, -tə- ‖ ˌɑːktoʊdʒəˈner-/ *n* a person who is between 80 and 90 years old

oc·to·pus /ˈɒktəpəs ‖ ˈɑːk-/ *n* deep-sea creature with eight limbs

odd /ɒd ‖ ɑːd/ *adj* 1 strange; unusual 2 (of a number) that cannot be exactly divided by two 3 separated from its pair or set: *an odd shoe* 4 not regular: *doing odd jobs* 5 rather more than the stated number: *20-odd years ago* **~ly** *adv* strangely **~ity** *n* 1 [C] strange thing, person, etc. 2 [U] strangeness

odd·ment /ˈɒdmənt ‖ ˈɑːd-/ *n* something left over: *a few oddments of cloth*

odds /ɒdz ‖ ɑːdz/ *n* [P] 1 probability of something happening: *The odds are* (=it is likely) *that she will fail.* 2 **at odds** in disagreement 3 **it/that makes no odds** *BrE* it/that makes no difference; has no importance

odds and ends /ˌ· · ˈ·/ *n* [P] small articles of various kinds

ode /əʊd ‖ oʊd/ *n* long poem

o·di·ous /ˈəʊdiəs ‖ ˈoʊ-/ *adj fml* very unpleasant

o·dour *BrE* ‖ **-dor** *AmE* /ˈəʊdə ‖ ˈoʊdər/ *n fml* smell

oe·soph·a·gus /ɪˈsɒfəgəs ‖ ɪˈsɑː-/ *n* med food tube from the mouth to the stomach

oes·tro·gen /ˈiːstrədʒən ‖ ˈes-/ *n* [U] substance in females that changes the body ready for the production of young

of /əv, ə; *strong* ɒv ‖ əv, ə; *strong* ɑːv/ *prep* 1 belonging to: *the wheels of the car* 2 made from: *a crown of gold* 3 containing: *a bag of potatoes* 4 (shows a part or amount): *2 pounds of sugar* 5 a that is/are: *a friend of mine* | *some fool of a boy* (=some foolish boy) b happening in or on: *the Battle of Waterloo* 6 in relation to; in connection with: *a teacher of English* | *fond of swimming* 7 a done by: *the plays of Shakespeare* b done about: *a picture of Shakespeare* 8 with; having: *a matter of no importance* 9 (shows what someone or something is or does): *the laughter of the children* | *How kind of you!* 10 (used in dates): *the 27th of February* 11 during: *We often go there of an evening.*

off¹ /ɒf ‖ ɒːf/ *adv, adj* 1 disconnected; removed: *The handle fell off.* 2 (esp. of electrical apparatus) not lit or working: *The TV is off.* 3 away: *She drove off.* | *2 miles off* 4 away or free from work: *She's taken this week off.* 5 so as to be finished or destroyed: *They were all killed off.* 6 not going to happen after all: *The party's off!* 7 no longer good to eat or drink 8 provided with what you need: *They're not well off.* (=have not got much money) | *You'd be better off with a bike than that old car!* 9 a *infml* not quite right; not as good as usual: *It was a bit off, not answering my letter.* | *having an off day* b quiet and dull: *the off season* 10 **off and on** sometimes 11 **on the off chance** just in case 12 **right/straight off** at once

off² *prep* 1 away from: *I jumped off the bus.* | *I cut a piece off the loaf.* | *The ship was blown off course.* 2 (of a road) turning away from (a larger one) 3 in the sea near: *an island off the coast* 4 not wanting: *She's off her food.*

of·fal /ˈɒfəl ‖ ˈɒː-, ˈɑː-/ *n* [U] the inside organs of an animal used as food

off·beat /ˌɒfˈbiːt◄ ‖ ˌɒːf-/ *adj* not CONVENTIONAL

off col·our /ˌ· ˈ·◄/ *adj* 1 slightly ill 2 sexually improper

of·fence *BrE* ‖ **offense** *AmE* /əˈfens/ *n* 1 [C] wrong act, esp. a crime 2 [U] cause for hurt feelings: *Don't take offence.* (=feel offended)

of·fend /əˈfend/ *v* 1 *vt* hurt the feelings of; upset 2 *vt* displease greatly 3 *vi* do wrong: *to offend against good manners* **~er** *n* person who offends, esp. a criminal: *a first offender* (=someone found guilty of a crime for the first time) **~ing** *adj* causing displeasure, discomfort, or inconvenience

of·fen·sive /əˈfensɪv/ *adj* 1 extremely unpleasant 2 for attacking ♦ *n* 1 continued military attack 2 **on the offensive**

attacking ~**ly** *adv* ~**ness** *n* [U]

of·fer /'ɒfə‖'ɔːfər, 'ɑː-/ *v* *vt/i* say one will give or do: *The police are offering a big reward.* | *She offered to drive me there.* **2** *vt* provide; give: *The situation doesn't offer much hope.* | *He offered no resistance.* **3** give (to God): *She offered (up) a prayer.* ♦ *n* **1** statement offering something **2** what is offered ~**ing** *n* something offered

off·hand /ˌɒf'hænd◀‖ˌɒːf-/ *adv, adj* **1** careless; disrespectful **2** without time to think or prepare

of·fice /'ɒfɪs‖'ɒː-, 'ɑː-/ *n* **1** [C] room or building where written work is done **2** [C] place where a particular service is provided: *a ticket office* **3** [C] government department: *the Foreign Office* **4** [C;U] important job or position of power: *the office of president*

of·fi·cer /'ɒfɪsə‖'ɒːfɪsər, 'ɑː-/ *n* **1** person in command in the army, navy, etc. **2** person in a government job: *a local government officer* **3** policeman

of·fi·cial /ə'fɪʃəl/ *adj* of, from, or decided by someone in a position of power and responsibility: *official permission* ♦ *n* person who holds an OFFICE (4) ~**ly** *adv* **1** formally as stated by an official **2** as stated publicly (but perhaps not really) ~**dom** *n* [U] officials as a group ~**ese** /əˌfɪʃəˈliːz/ *n* [U] *infml* language of government officials, considered unnecessarily hard to understand

of·fi·ci·ate /ə'fɪʃieɪt/ *vi* perform official duties

of·fi·cious /ə'fɪʃəs/ *adj* too eager to give orders ~**ly** *adv* ~**ness** *n* [U]

off·ing /'ɒfɪŋ‖'ɒː-, 'ɑː-/ *n* **in the offing** coming soon

off·li·cence /'· ··/ *n* *BrE* shop where alcoholic drink is sold to be taken away

off·load /ˌ·'·/ *vt* *BrE* get rid of (something unwanted)

off·peak /ˌ·'·◀/ *adj* **1** less busy **2** existing during less busy periods

off·put·ting /'· ˌ··/ *adj* *esp. BrE* unpleasant and making one not want to continue

off·set /'ɒfset, ˌɒf'set‖'ɒːfset, ˌɒːf'set/ *vt* **-set**; *present p.* **-setting** make up for; balance: *They offset the cost by charging higher prices.*

off·shoot /'ɒfʃuːt‖'ɒːf-/ *n* new stem or branch: (fig.) *an offshoot of a large company*

off·shore /ˌɒf'ʃɔː◀‖ˌɒːf'ʃɔːr◀/ *adj* **1** in the sea near the coast: *offshore islands* **2** away from the coast: *offshore winds* **3** (of banks, companies, etc.) in another country, where less tax has to be paid ♦ *adv*

off·side /ˌɒf'saɪd◀‖ˌɒːf-/ *adj, adv* **1** (in certain sports) ahead of the ball, which is against the rules **2** (on) the right-hand side, esp. of a vehicle

off·spring /'ɒf,sprɪŋ‖'ɒː-/ *n* **offspring** *fml* someone's child or children

off·the·rec·ord /ˌ· ·'··◀/ *adj, adv* unofficial and not to be formally recorded

off·the·wall /ˌ· ·'·◀/ *adj* *esp. AmE* amusingly foolish

off·white /ˌ· '·◀/ *adj* greyish or yellowish white

of·ten /'ɒfən, 'ɒftən‖'ɒː-/ *adv* **1** many times: *He was often ill.* **2** in many cases: *Very fat people are often unhealthy.* **3 as often as not** at least 50% of the time **4 every so often** sometimes **5 more often than not** more than 50% of the time

o·gle /'əʊɡəl‖'oʊ-/ *vi/t* look (at) with great sexual interest

o·gre /'əʊɡə‖'oʊɡrəs‖'oʊ-/ *fem.* — *n* **1** fierce creature in fairy stories, like a very large person **2** frightening person

oh /əʊ‖oʊ/ *interj* (expresses surprise, fear, etc.)

oil /ɔɪl/ *n* [U] thick fatty liquid that burns easily, esp. PETROLEUM ♦ *vt* put oil on or into ~**y** *adj* **1** like or covered with oil **2** too polite **oils** *n* [P] paints containing oil

oil·field /'ɔɪlfiːld/ *n* area with oil underneath it

oil·rig /'ɔɪl,rɪɡ/ *n* large apparatus for getting oil up from under the sea

oil·skin /'ɔɪl,skɪn/ *n* [C;U] (garment made of) cloth treated with oil so as not to let water through

oil well /'· ·/ *n* hole made in the ground to get oil

oint·ment /'ɔɪntmənt/ *n* **1** [C;U] oily usu. medicinal substance rubbed on the skin **2 a/the fly in the ointment** one small unwanted thing that spoils the happiness of an occasion

o·kay /'əʊ'keɪ‖oʊ-/ *adj, adv* **1** all right; satisfactory **2** (expresses agreement or permission) ♦ *n* approval; permission ♦ *vt* give permission for

old /əʊld ‖ oʊld/ adj 1 having lived or existed a long time 2 of a particular age: *The baby is 2 years old.* 3 having been so a long time: *an old friend* 4 former: *He got his old job back.* | *an old boy/girl* (=former pupil of a school) 5 of **old**: a in the past **b** for a long time ♦ *n* [the+S] old people

old age /ˌ· '·◂/ *n* [U] part of one's life when one is old

old age pen·sion /ˌ· · '··/ *n* money paid regularly by the state to old people ~**er** *n*

old-boy net·work /ˌ· · ˌ··/ *n BrE* tendency of former pupils of the same school (esp. PUBLIC SCHOOLs) to favour each other, esp. in gaining positions of importance

olde worl·de /ˌəʊldi 'wɜːldi ‖ ˌoʊldi 'wɜːr-/ *adj BrE* of a perhaps too consciously old-fashioned style

old-fash·ioned /ˌ· '·◂/ *adj* once usual or fashionable but now less common

old flame /ˌ· '·/ *n* someone with whom one used to be in love

old guard /ˌ· '·/ *n* [the+S] group of people with old-fashioned ideas who are against change

old hand /ˌ· '·/ *n* very experienced person

old mas·ter /ˌ· '··/ *n* (picture by) an important painter of esp. the 15th to 18th centuries

old tim·er /ˌ· '··/ *n* 1 person who has been somewhere or done something for a long time 2 *AmE* old man

old wives' tale /ˌ· '· ·/ *n* ancient and not necessarily true belief

ol·i·gar·chy /'ɒlɪgɑːki ‖ 'ɑːlɪgɑːrki, 'oʊ-/ *n* 1 [U] government by a small usu. unrepresentative group 2 [C] state governed in this way

ol·ive /'ɒlɪv ‖ 'ɑː-/ *n* 1 [C] small fruit of the **olive tree**, grown in Mediterranean countries and eaten raw or made into **olive oil** for cooking 2 [U] dull pale green

olive branch /'·· ·/ *n* sign of a wish for peace

om·buds·man /'ɒmbʊdzmən ‖ 'ɑːm-/ *n* -men /-mən/ person who deals with complaints about an organization

ome·lette /'ɒmlət ‖ 'ɑːm-/ *n* flat round mass of eggs beaten together and cooked

o·men /'əʊmən ‖ 'oʊ-/ *n* sign of something that will happen

om·i·nous /'ɒmɪnəs ‖ 'ɑː-/ *adj* seeming to show that something bad will happen ~**ly** *adv*

o·mis·sion /əʊ'mɪʃən, ə- ‖ oʊ-, ə-/ *n* 1 [U] act of omitting 2 [C] something left out

o·mit /əʊ'mɪt, ə- ‖ oʊ, ə-/ *vt* 1 not include: *An important detail was omitted.* 2 *fml* not do; fail: *They omitted to tell me.*

om·ni·bus /'ɒmnɪbəs, -,bʌs ‖ 'ɑːm-/ *n* **a** book containing several works **b** television programme including two or more programmes

om·nip·o·tent /ɒm'nɪpətənt ‖ ɑːm-/ *adj fml* having unlimited power -**tence** *n* [U]

om·nis·ci·ent /ɒm'nɪʃənt, -'nɪsiənt ‖ ɑːm'nɪʃənt/ *adj* knowing everything -**ence** *n* [U]

om·niv·o·rous /ɒm'nɪvərəs ‖ ɑːm-/ *adj* (esp. of an animal) eating anything

on¹ /ɒn ‖ ɒːn, ɑːn/ *prep* 1 touching, supported by, hanging from, or connected with: *a lamp on the table* 2 towards; in the direction of 3 directed towards: *a tax on beer* 4 in (a large vehicle): *on a train* 5 (shows when something happens): *She's coming on Tuesday.* 6 about: *a book on golf* 7 by means of: *A car runs on petrol.* 8 in a state of: *on fire* | *on holiday* 9 working for; belonging to: *She's on the committee.* 10 directly after and because of: *I acted on your advice.* 11 paid for by: *The drinks are on me!*

on² *adv, adj* 1 continuously, instead of stopping: *He kept on talking.* 2 further; forward: *We walked on to the next one.* 3 (so as to be) wearing: *He put his coat on.* | *He had nothing on.* 4 with the stated part in front: *They crashed head on.* 5 in(to) a vehicle: *The bus stopped and we got on.* 6 (esp. of electrical apparatus) lit or working: *The TV was on.* 7 (of something arranged) happening or going to happen: *What's on at the cinema?* | *I've got nothing on on Tuesday.* (=I'm not doing anything) 8 with the stated part forward: *Look at it sideways on.* 9 **and so on** etc. 10 **be on about/at** keep talking (about something/to someone) in a dull, complaining way: *What's he on about now?* | *She's always on at me to* (=trying to persuade me to) *have my hair cut.* 11 **not on** impossible; not acceptable 12 **on and off** from time to time

13 on and on without stopping

once /wʌns/ *adv* **1** one time: *We've only met once.* **2** formerly: *He was once a famous singer.* **3 all at once** suddenly **4 at once: a** now; without delay: *Come at once!* **b** together: *Don't all speak at once!* **5 for once** for this one time only: *Just for once he was telling the truth.* **6 once and for all** now, so as to be settled, with no further change **7 once in a while** sometimes, but not often **8 once more** again ♦ *conj* from the moment that: *Once he's arrived, we can start.*

once·o·ver /'wʌns,əʊvə‖-,oʊvər/ *n infml* a quick look or examination

on·com·ing /'ɒn,kʌmɪŋ‖'ɔːn-, 'ɑːn-/ *adj* coming towards you: *oncoming traffic*

one¹ /wʌn/ *determiner, n* **1** (the number) 1 **2** a certain: *They'll come back one day.* | *The victim was one Roy Malkin.* **3** the same: *They all ran in one direction.* **4** particular type or example (of): *He can't tell one tree from another.* **5 at one** *fml* in agreement **6 be one up (on)** have the advantage (over) **7 for one** as one (person, thing, reason, etc.) out of several **8 in one** combined: *It's a table and desk all in one.* **9 one and all** every one **10 one and the same** exactly the same **11 one of** a member of: *Our dog's like one of the family.* **12 one or two** a few

one² *pron* **1** single thing or person of the sort mentioned: *Have you any books on gardening? I'd like to borrow one.* **2** *fml* any person; you: *One should do one's duty.*

one an·oth·er /ˌ··'··/ *pron* EACH OTHER

one-armed ban·dit /ˌ· · '··/ *n* machine with a long handle, into which people put money to try to win more money

one-night stand /ˌ· · '·/ *n* sexual relationship which lasts only one night

one-off /ˌ· '·◂/ *adj esp. BrE* **1** happening or done only once **2** made as a single example **one-off** *n*

o·ner·ous /'ɒnərəs, 'əʊ-‖'ɑː-, 'oʊ-/ *adj fml* difficult; hard to bear: *an onerous duty*

one·self /wʌn'self/ *pron* **1** (*reflexive form of* ONE² (2)): *to wash oneself* **2** (*strong form of* ONE² (2)): *One shouldn't try and do everything oneself.* **3 (all) by oneself: a** alone **b** without help **4 to oneself** not shared

one-sid·ed /ˌ· '··◂/ *adj* with one side stronger or more favoured than the other: *a*

one-sided football match

one-time /'wʌntaɪm/ *adj* former

one-to-one /ˌ· · '·◂/ *adj, adv* between only two people

one-up·man·ship /wʌn'ʌpmənʃɪp/ *n* [U] art of getting an advantage without actually cheating

one-way /ˌ· '·◂/ *adj* moving or allowing movement in one direction only: *a one-way street*

on·go·ing /'ɒn,gəʊɪŋ‖'ɑːn,goʊ-/ *adj* continuing: *an ongoing problem*

on·ion /'ʌnjən/ *n* strong-smelling round white vegetable

on·line /'ɒnlaɪn‖'ɔːn-, 'ɑːn-/ *adj* connected to other computers, esp. ones on the INTERNET ♦ *adv*

on·look·er /'ɒn,lʊkə‖'ɔːn,lʊkər, 'ɑːn-/ *n* person watching something happen

on·ly¹ /'əʊnli‖'oʊn-/ *adj* **1** with no others in the same group: *my only friend* **2** best: *She's the only person for this job.*

only² *adv* **1** and no one or nothing else: *There were only five left.* **2 if only** (expresses a strong wish): *If only she were here!* **3 only just: a** a moment before **b** almost not **4 only too** very; completely: *I'm afraid it's only too true.*

only³ *conj* except that; but: *She wants to go, only she hasn't got enough money.*

on·set /'ɒnset‖'ɔːn-, 'ɑːn-/ *n* start, esp. of something bad

on·shore /ˌɒn'ʃɔː◂‖ˌɔːn'ʃɔːr◂, ˌɑːn-/ *adv, adj* towards the coast: *onshore winds*

on·slaught /'ɒnslɔːt‖'ɔːnslɔːt, 'ɑːn-/ *n* fierce attack

on·to /'ɒntʊ, -tə‖'ɔːn-, 'ɑːn-/ *prep* **1** to a position or point on: *He jumped onto the train.* **2 be onto someone** have found out that someone is doing something bad

o·nus /'əʊnəs‖'oʊ-/ *n* [S] duty; responsibility: *The onus is on you to do it.*

on·ward /'ɒnwəd‖'ɔːnwərd, 'ɑːn-/ *adj, adv* forward in space or time

oo·dles /'uːdlz/ *n* [P] *infml* lots

ooze /uːz/ *v* **1** *vi* (of thick liquid) pass or flow slowly **2** *vt* have (liquid) oozing out: (fig.) *He oozes charm.* ♦ *n* [U] mud or thick liquid

o·pal /'əʊpəl‖'oʊ-/ *n* white precious stone with colours in it

o·paque /əʊ'peɪk‖oʊ-/ *adj* which you cannot see through ~ness *n* [U]

OPEC /ˈəʊpek ‖ ˈoʊ-/ n abbrev. for: Organization of Petroleum Exporting Countries

o·pen¹ /ˈəʊpən ‖ ˈoʊ-/ adj **1** not shut: an open window/book | (fig.) an open mind (=not closed to new ideas) **2** not surrounded by anything: open country **3** without a roof: an open boat **4** not fastened or folded: with his shirt open **5** not completely decided or answered: an open question **6** that one can go into as a visitor or customer: Is the bank open yet? **7** (of a job) not filled **8** not hiding or hidden; honest **9** that anyone can enter: an open competition **10** spread out: The flowers are open. **11** (of a cheque) payable in actual money to the person whose name is written on it **12** **keep open house** encourage visitors to come at any time **13** **open to**: **a** not safe from: open to criticism **b** willing to receive: open to suggestions **14** **with open arms** in a very friendly way ~**ly** adv not secretly ~**ness** n [U]

open² vi/t **1** make or become open: Open your mouth! **2** spread; unfold: open a map **3** (cause to) start: The story opens in a country village. **4** (cause to) begin business: The shops open at 9 o'clock. **5** **open fire** start shooting **6** **open someone's eyes (to something)** make someone know or understand something ~**er** n

   open into/onto phr vt provide a means of entering or reaching

   open out phr vi speak more freely

   open up phr v **1** vt make possible the development of **2** vi open the door **3** vi speak more freely

open³ n [the+S] **1** the outdoors **2** **in(to) the open** (of opinions, secrets, etc.) in(to) the consciousness of the people around one

open-air /ˌ·· ˈ·◂/ adj of or in the outdoors: an open-air theatre

open-and-shut /ˌ·· ·ˈ·◂/ adj easy to prove

open-cast /ˈ·· ·/ adj where coal is dug from an open hole in the ground

open-end·ed /ˌ·· ˈ··◂/ adj with no limit set in advance

open-hand·ed /ˌ·· ˈ··◂/ adj generous

o·pen·ing /ˈəʊpənɪŋ ‖ ˈoʊ-/ n **1** hole or clear space **2** favourable set of conditions **3** unfilled job ♦ adj first; beginning

open-plan /ˌ·· ˈ·◂/ adj (of a large room) not divided into a lot of little rooms

op·e·ra /ˈɒpərə ‖ ˈɑː-/ n musical play in which (most of) the words are sung ~**tic** /ˌɒpəˈrætɪk◂ ‖ ˌɑː-/ adj

op·e·ra·ble /ˈɒpərəbəl ‖ ˈɑː-/ adj (of a disease, etc.) that can be cured by an operation

op·e·rate /ˈɒpəreɪt ‖ ˈɑː-/ v **1** vi/t (cause to) work: learning to operate the controls **2** vi carry on trade or business: We operate throughout Europe. **3** vi cut the body to cure or remove diseased parts, usu. in a special room (**operating theatre**) **4** vi produce effects: The new law operates in our favour.

op·e·ra·tion /ˌɒpəˈreɪʃən ‖ ˌɑː-/ n **1** [U] condition or process of working **2** [C] thing (to be) done; activity **3** [C] cutting of the body to cure or remove a diseased part **4** [C] planned military movement ~**al** adj **1** of operations: operational costs **2** ready for use

op·e·ra·tive /ˈɒpərətɪv ‖ ˈɑːpərə-, ˈɑːpəreɪ-/ adj **1** (of a plan, law, etc.) working; producing effects **2** most important: 'Fast' is the operative word. ♦ n worker

op·e·ra·tor /ˈɒpəreɪtə ‖ ˈɑːpəreɪtər/ n person who works a machine, apparatus, or esp. telephone SWITCHBOARD

o·pin·ion /əˈpɪnjən/ n **1** [C] what someone thinks about something, based on personal judgment rather than facts: In my opinion, it's crazy. **2** [U] what people in general think about something **3** [C] professional judgment or advice ~**ated** adj too sure that what one thinks is right

o·pi·um /ˈəʊpiəm ‖ ˈoʊ-/ n [U] sleep-producing drug

op·po·nent /əˈpəʊnənt ‖ əˈpoʊ-/ n **1** person who takes the opposite side in a competition or fight **2** person who opposes someone or something

op·por·tune /ˈɒpətjuːn ‖ ˌɑːpərˈtuːn◂/ adj fml **1** (of time) right for a purpose **2** coming at the right time ~**ly** adv

op·por·tun·is·m /ˈɒpətjuːnɪzəm ‖ ˌɑːpərˈtuː-/ n [U] taking advantage of every chance for success, sometimes to other people's disadvantage –**ist** n

op·por·tu·ni·ty /ˌɒpəˈtjuːnɪti ‖ ˌɑːpərˈtuː-/ n [C;U] favourable moment; chance

op·pose /əˈpəʊz ‖ əˈpoʊz/ vt be or act against

op·posed /əˈpəʊzd ‖ əˈpoʊzd/ adj **1** against: I'm opposed to abortion. **2** **as opposed to** and not

op·po·site /'ɒpəzɪt ‖ 'ɑː-/ *adj* **1** as different as possible from: *at opposite ends of the room* **2** facing: *the houses opposite* ♦ *n* opposite thing or person: *Black and white are opposites.* ♦ *prep* facing: *She sat opposite me.*

opposite num·ber /ˌ··· '··/ *n* person with the same job, rank, etc. but working in a different group or organization

op·po·si·tion /ˌɒpə'zɪʃən ‖ ˌɑː-/ *n* **1** [U] act or state of opposing **2** [U] people who are against one **3** [C] (*often cap.*) political parties opposed to the government

op·press /ə'pres/ *vt* **1** rule in a hard cruel way **2** cause to feel ill or sad ~**ive** *adj* **1** cruel; unjust **2** causing feelings of illness and unhappiness: *oppressive heat* ~**or** *n* ~**ion** /ə'preʃən/ *n* [U]

opt /ɒpt ‖ ɑːpt/ *vi* make a choice: *I opted for the smaller one.*

   opt out *phr vi* decide not to take part

op·tic /'ɒptɪk ‖ 'ɑː-/ *adj* of the eyes: *the optic nerve*

op·ti·cal /'ɒptɪkəl ‖ 'ɑːp-/ *adj* **1** of or about the sense of sight: *She thought she saw it, but it was an optical illusion.* (=something that deceives the sense of sight) **2** of or using light: *optical character recognition*

op·ti·cian /ɒp'tɪʃən ‖ ɑːp-/ *n* person who makes and sells glasses, etc. for people's eyes

op·ti·mist /'ɒptəmɪst ‖ 'ɑːp-/ *n* person who expects good things to happen –**mism** *n* [U] ~**ic** /ˌɒptə'mɪstɪk◀‖ ˌɑːp-/ *adj*

op·ti·mize also -**mise** *BrE* /'ɒptəmaɪz ‖ 'ɑːp-/ *vt* make as perfect or effective as possible

op·ti·mum /'ɒptəməm ‖ 'ɑːp-/ also **op·ti·mal** /'ɒptəməl ‖ 'ɑːp-/ *adj* most favourable: *optimum conditions for growing rice*

op·tion /'ɒpʃən ‖ 'ɑːp-/ *n* **1** [U] freedom to choose: *I had to do it; I had no option.* **2** [C] possible course of action that can be chosen **3** [C] right to buy or sell something at a stated time in the future —*see also* SOFT OPTION ~**al** *adj* which you can choose to have or not to have

op·u·lent /'ɒpjʊlənt ‖ 'ɑːp-/ *adj* **1** showing great wealth **2** in good supply –**lence** *n* [U]

o·pus /'əʊpəs ‖ 'oʊ-/ *n* piece of work done, esp. a piece of music written

or /ə; *strong* ɔː ‖ ər; *strong* ɔːr/ *conj* **1** (shows different possibilities): *Will you have tea or coffee?* **2** if not: *Wear your coat or you'll be cold.* **3** (describes the same thing in a different way): *a kilometre, or one thousand metres* **4 or else** *infml* (used as a threat) or something bad will happen **5 or so** about: *We waited for 5 minutes or so.*

or·a·cle /'ɒrəkəl ‖ 'ɔːr-, 'ɑː-/ *n* **1** (in ancient Greece) person through whom a god answered human questions **2** person thought to be, or who believes himself to be, wise and able to give good advice

o·ral /'ɔːrəl/ *adj* **1** spoken, not written: *an oral exam* **2** *med* of the mouth ~**ly** *adv*

or·ange /'ɒrɪndʒ ‖ 'ɔːr-, 'ɑː-/ *n* common round reddish-yellow fruit ♦ *adj* of the colour of an orange

o·rang·u·tan /ɔː,ræŋuː'tæŋ ‖ ə'ræŋətæŋ/ *n* large monkey with reddish hair and no tail

o·ra·tion /ə'reɪʃən, ɔː-/ *n* solemn formal public speech

or·a·tor /'ɒrətə ‖ 'ɔːrətər, 'ɑː-/ *n* public speaker

or·a·to·ry /'ɒrətri ‖ 'ɔːrətɔːri, 'ɑː-/ *n* [U] language highly decorated with long or formal words

or·bit /'ɔːbɪt ‖ 'ɔːr-/ *n* **1** path of something going round something else, esp. in space **2** area of power or influence ♦ *vi/t* go round in an orbit: *The satellite orbits the Earth.* ~**al** *adj*

or·chard /'ɔːtʃəd ‖ 'ɔːrtʃərd/ *n* place where fruit trees are grown

or·ches·tra /'ɔːkɪstrə ‖ 'ɔːr-/ *n* large group of musicians playing different instruments **orchestral** /ɔː'kestrəl ‖ ɔːr-/ *adj*

or·ches·trate /'ɔːkəstreɪt ‖ 'ɔːr-/ *vt* **1** arrange (music) to be played by an orchestra **2** plan (something with many parts) for best effect –**tration** /ˌɔːkə'streɪʃən ‖ ˌɔːr-/ *n* [C;U]

or·chid /'ɔːkɪd ‖ 'ɔːr-/ *n* plant with bright strange-shaped flowers

or·dain /ɔː'deɪn ‖ ɔːr-/ *vt* **1** make (someone) a priest **2** *fml* (of God, the law, etc.) order

or·deal /ɔː'diːl, 'ɔːdiːl ‖ ɔːr'diːl, 'ɔːrdiːl/ *n* difficult or painful experience

or·der¹ /'ɔːdə ‖ 'ɔːrdər/ *n* **1** [U] way in which things are arranged: *in alphabetical* *order* | *in order of importance* | *Leave everything in good order.* (=tidily) **2** [U] fitness for use: *The phone's out of order.* (=doesn't work) **3** [U] condition in which laws and rules are obeyed: *That new teacher can't keep order in his class.* | *Your papers are in order.* (=acceptable according to the rules) **4** [C] command: *An officer gives orders.* **5** [C] request to supply goods: *The waiter took our order.* **6** [C] (MEDAL, etc. given to someone in) a group of specially honoured people: *the Order of Merit* **7** [C] *fml* kind; sort: *courage of the highest order* **8** [P] state of being a priest, etc.: *to take (holy) orders* **9 in order that** *fml* so that **10 in order to** with the purpose of **11 in the order of** about **12 on order** asked for but not yet supplied —see also TALL ORDER

order² *v* **1** *vt* command: *He ordered them to attack.* **2** *vt/i* ask for (something) to be supplied: *I ordered chicken soup.* **3** *vt* arrange

order about *phr vt* give many commands to, unpleasantly

or·der·ly /ˈɔːdəli ‖ ˈɔːrdərli/ *adj* **1** well-arranged **2** liking tidy arrangement **3** peaceful and well-behaved: *an orderly crowd* ♦ *n* helper in a hospital –**liness** *n* [U]

or·di·nal num·ber /ˌɔːdɪnəl ˈnʌmbə ‖ ˌɔːrdənəl ˈnʌmbər/ *n* one of the numbers (1st, 2nd, 3rd, etc.) that show order rather than quantity

or·di·nary /ˈɔːdənri ‖ ˈɔːrdəneri/ *adj* **1** not unusual; common **2 out of the ordinary** unusual –**narily** /ˈɔːdənərəli ‖ ˌɔːrdənˈerəli/ *adv* usually

or·di·na·tion /ˌɔːdɪˈneɪʃən ‖ ˌɔːrdn-/ *n* [U;C] act of ORDAINing a priest

ore /ɔː ‖ ɔːr/ *n* [U] rock from which metal is obtained

or·gan /ˈɔːgən ‖ ˈɔːr-/ *n* **1** part of an animal or plant that has a special purpose, such as the heart **2** organization with a special purpose within a larger one: *Parliament is an organ of government.* **3** large musical instrument played by blowing air through pipes –**ist** *n* ORGAN (2) player

or·gan·ic /ɔːˈgænɪk ‖ ɔːr-/ *adj* **1** grown without chemicals ~**ally** /-kli/ *adv* **2** of living things or bodily organs **3** made of parts with related purposes

or·gan·is·m /ˈɔːgənɪzəm ‖ ˈɔːr-/ *n*

1 living creature **2** whole made of related parts

or·gan·i·za·tion, **-sation** /ˌɔːgənaɪ ˈzeɪ ʃən ‖ ˌɔːrgənə-/ *n* **1** [C] group of people with a special purpose, such as a business or club **2** [U] organizing; arrangement

or·gan·ize, **-ise** /ˈɔːgənaɪz ‖ ˈɔːr-/ *vt* **1** arrange into a good system: *a well-organized office* **2** make necessary arrangements for: *to organize a party* –**izer**, **-iser** *n*

or·gas·m /ˈɔːgæzəm ‖ ˈɔːr-/ *n* [C;U] highest point of sexual pleasure

or·gy /ˈɔːdʒi ‖ ˈɔːr-/ *n* **1** wild party where people get drunk and have sex **2** *infml* a set (of usu. pleasant activities) close together in time

O·ri·ent /ˈɔːriənt, ˈɒri-‖ ˈɔːr-/ *n* [*the*] the eastern part of the world; Asia

o·ri·en·tal /ˌɔːriˈentl◀, ˌɒ-‖ˌɔːri-/ *n, adj* (person) of or from the Orient

o·ri·en·ta·tion /ˌɔːriənˈteɪʃən, ˌɒ-‖ˌɔːri-/ *n* **1** [C;U] beliefs, ideas, etc. that a person or group has: *right-wing political orientation* **sexual orientation** whether a person is HETEROSEXUAL or HOMOSEXUAL **2** [2] direction in which something faces; position

o·ri·en·ted /ˈɔːrientɪd, ˈɒ-‖ ˈɔːr-/ also **o·ri·en·tat·ed** /ˈɔːrienteɪtɪd, ˈɒ-‖ ˈɔːr-/ *BrE* – *adj* chiefly concerned with or aimed at: *The magazine had become too politically oriented.*

or·i·fice /ˈɒrɪfɪs ‖ ˈɔː-, ˈɑː-/ *n fml* opening, esp. in the body

or·i·gin /ˈɒrɪdʒɪn ‖ ˈɔː-, ˈɑː-/ *n* **1** [C;U] starting point **2** [U] also **origins** *pl.* — parents and conditions of early life: *a woman of humble origin*

o·rig·i·nal /əˈrɪdʒɪnəl, -dʒənəl/ *adj* **1** first; earliest **2** new and different **3** not copied ♦ *n* the one from which copies have been made ~**ly** *adv* **1** in the beginning, before changing **2** in a new and different way –**ity** /əˌrɪdʒɪˈnælɪti/ *n* [U] quality of being ORIGINAL (2)

o·rig·i·nate /əˈrɪdʒɪneɪt/ *vi/t* (cause to) begin –**nator** *n*

or·na·ment /ˈɔːnəmənt ‖ ˈɔːr-/ *n* [C;U] decorative object(s) ♦ *vt* /-ment/ decorate ~**al** /ˌɔːnəˈmentl◀ ‖ ˌɔːr-/ *adj* ~**ation** /ˌɔːnəmenˈteɪʃən ‖ ˌɔːr-/ *n* [U]

or·nate /ɔːˈneɪt ‖ ɔːr-/ *adj* having (too) much ornament

or·ni·thol·o·gy /ˌɔːnɪˈθɒlədʒi ‖ ˌɔːrnɪˈθɑː-/

n [U] scientific study of birds –**gist** *n*

or·phan /'ɔːfən ‖ 'ɔːrf-/ *n* child with no parents ♦ *vt* cause to be an orphan ~**age** *n* place where orphans live

or·tho·dox /'ɔːθədɒks ‖ 'ɔːrθədɑːks/ *adj* 1 generally or officially accepted or used: *orthodox methods* 2 holding orthodox opinions ~**y** *n* [U]

or·tho·pae·dic , -**pedic** /ˌɔːθə'piːdɪk◂ ‖ ˌɔːr-/ *adj* of the branch of medicine (**orthopaedics**) that puts bones straight

os·cil·late /'ɒsɪleɪt ‖ 'ɑː-/ *vi* 1 move regularly from side to side 2 vary between opposing choices –**lation** /ˌɒsɪ'leɪʃən ‖ ˌɑː-/ *n* [C;U]

os·mo·sis /ɒz'məʊsɪs ‖ ɑːz'moʊ-/ *n* [U] gradual passing of liquid through a skinlike wall –**tic** /ɒz'mɒtɪk ‖ ɑːz'mɑː-/ *adj*

os·ten·si·ble /ɒ'stensɪbəl ‖ ɑː-/ *adj* (of a reason) seeming or pretended, but perhaps not really true –**bly** *adv*

os·ten·ta·tion /ˌɒsten'teɪʃən, -ten- ‖ ˌɑː-/ *n* [U] unnecessary show of wealth, knowledge, etc. –**tious** *adj*

os·te·o·path /'ɒstiəpæθ ‖ 'ɑː-/ *n* person who treats diseases by moving and pressing bones and muscles

os·tra·cize , -**cise** /'ɒstrəsaɪz ‖ 'ɑː-/ *vt* stop accepting (someone) into one's group –**cism** *n* [U]

os·trich /'ɒstrɪtʃ ‖ 'ɒ-, 'ɑː-/ *n* extremely large long-legged African bird that cannot fly

oth·er /'ʌðə ‖ -ər/ *determiner, pron* 1 the remaining one of a set; what is left as well as that mentioned: *She held on with one hand and waved with the other.* 2 additional: *Have you any other questions?* 3 not this, not oneself, not one's own, etc.: *He likes spending other people's money.* 4 **one after the other** first one, then the next, etc. 5 **other than** a except: *no one other than me* b anything but: *I can't be other than grateful.* 6 **the other day/night/afternoon/ evening** on a recent day/night/afternoon/evening

oth·er·wise /'ʌðəwaɪz ‖ 'ʌðər-/ *adv* 1 differently 2 apart from that: *The soup was cold, but otherwise that was excellent.* 3 if not: *Go faster, otherwise we'll be late.*

ot·ter /'ɒtə ‖ -ər/ *n* small animal with brown fur that swims and eats fish

ouch /aʊtʃ/ *interj* (expresses sudden pain)

ought /ɔːt ‖ ɒːt/ *v aux* 1 have a (moral)

duty: *You ought to look after them better.* 2 (shows what is right or sensible): *You ought to see a doctor.* 3 will probably: *Prices ought to come down soon.*

ounce /aʊns/ *n* 1 [C] a measure of weight equal to 28.35 grams 2 [S] a small amount

our /aʊə ‖ aʊr/ *determiner* of us: *our house*

ours /aʊəz ‖ aʊrz/ *pron* of us; our one(s)

our·selves /aʊə'selvz ‖ aʊr-/ *pron* 1 (*reflexive form of* **we**): *We saw ourselves on TV.* 2 (*strong form of* **we**): *We built the house ourselves.* 3 (**all**) **by ourselves:** a alone b without help 4 **to ourselves** not shared

oust /aʊst/ *vt* force (someone) out

out[1] /aʊt/ *adv* 1 away from the inside: *Open the bag and take the money out.* 2 away from home or the usual place: *Let's go out tonight.* 3 away from a surface: *The nail stuck out.* 4 to lots of people or places: *Hand out the drinks.* 5 (of a fire or light) no longer burning 6 completely: *I'm tired out.* 7 aloud: *Call the names out.* 8 so as to be clearly seen, understood, etc.: *Their secret is out.* | *Are the daffodils out* (=flowering) *yet?* 9 wrong in guessing, etc.: *I was two years out in my estimation.* 10 (of the ball in a game, e.g. tennis) outside the line 11 no longer fashionable 12 (of the TIDE) away from the coast 13 **out of:** a from inside; away from: *I jumped out of bed.* | (fig.) *We're out of danger* (=safe) *now.* | (fig.) *It's out of sight.* (=can't be seen) b from among: *four out of five people preferred it.* c not having; without: *We're out of petrol.* d because of: *I came out of interest.* e (shows what something is made from): *made out of wood* 14 **out of it (all):** a lonely and unhappy because one is not included in something b *infml* not thinking clearly 15 **out to** trying to

out[2] *adj* 1 directed outward 2 **out-and-out** complete; total

out[3] *vt* say publicly that a person is HOMOSEXUAL, against his/her wishes ~**ing** *n* [C;U]

out[4] *n infml* excuse not to do something

out·board mo·tor /ˌaʊtbɔːd 'məʊtə ‖ -bɔːrd'moʊtər/ *n* motor fixed to the back end of a small boat

out·break /'aʊtbreɪk/ *n* sudden appearance or start of something bad

out·burst /'aʊtbɜːst ‖ -bɜːrst/ *n* sudden powerful expression of feeling

out·cast /'aʊtkɑːst‖-kæst/ *n* someone forced from their home or friendless

out·class /aʊt'klɑːs‖-'klæs/ *vt* be very much better than

out·come /'aʊtkʌm/ *n* effect; result

out·crop /'aʊtkrɒp‖-krɑːp/ *n* rock or rocks on the surface of the ground

out·cry /'aʊtkraɪ/ *n* public show of anger

out·dat·ed /ˌaʊt'deɪtᵻd◂/ *adj* no longer in general use

out·do /aʊt'duː/ *vt* -**did** /-'dɪd/, -**done** /-'dʌn/, 3rd person sing. pres. t. -**does** /-'dʌz/ do or be better than

out·door /ˌaʊt'dɔː‖-'dɔːr/ *adj* existing, happening, or used outside **outdoors** *adv*

out·er /'aʊtə‖-ər/ *adj* on the outside; furthest from the middle

outer space /ˌ··'·/ *n* [U] area where the stars and other heavenly bodies are

out·fit /'aʊtˌfɪt/ *n* 1 set of things esp. clothes for a particular purpose 2 group of people working together ♦ *vt* -**tt**- provide with a set of esp. clothes ~**ter** *n*

out·flank /aʊt'flæŋk/ *vt* go round the side of (an enemy) to attack

out·go·ing /ˌaʊt'ɡəʊɪŋ◂‖-'ɡoʊ-/ *adj* 1 finishing a period in office 2 friendly **outgoings** *n* [P] money spent

out·grow /aʊt'ɡrəʊ‖-'ɡroʊ/ *vt* -**grew** /-'ɡruː/, -**grown** /-'ɡrəʊn‖-'ɡroʊn/ grow too big, too old, or too fast for

out·house /'aʊthaʊs/ *n* small building near a larger main building

out·ing /'aʊtɪŋ/ *n* 1 [C] short journey for pleasure, esp. by a group 2 see OUT³

out·land·ish /aʊt'lændɪʃ/ *adj* strange and unpleasing ~**ly** *adv* ~**ness** *n* [U]

out·last /aʊt'lɑːst‖-'læst/ *vt* last longer than

out·law /'aʊtlɔː‖-lɒː/ *n* (in former times) criminal being hunted ♦ *vt* declare (something) illegal

out·lay /'aʊtleɪ/ *n* money spent on something

out·let /'aʊtlet, -lᵻt/ *n* way out for liquid or gas: (fig.) *an outlet for his energy*

out·line /'aʊtlaɪn/ *n* 1 line showing the shape of something 2 main ideas or facts, without details ♦ *vt: She outlined her plans.*

out·live /aʊt'lɪv/ *vt* live longer than

out·look /'aʊtlʊk/ *n* 1 view from a place 2 future probabilities 3 one's general point of view

out·ly·ing /'aʊtˌlaɪ-ɪŋ/ *adj* distant; far from a city, etc.

out·mod·ed /aʊt'məʊdᵻd‖-'moʊ-/ *adj* no longer in fashion or use

out·num·ber /aʊt'nʌmbə‖-ər/ *vt* be more in numbers than: *outnumbered by the enemy*

out-of-date /ˌ·· '·◂/ *adj* no longer in use or in fashion

out-of-the-way /ˌ·· '·◂/ *adj* distant

out·pa·tient /'aʊtˌpeɪʃənt/ *n* person treated at a hospital but not staying there

out·post /'aʊtpəʊst‖-poʊst/ *n* group of people or settlement far from the main group or settlement

out·pour·ing /'aʊtˌpɔːrɪŋ/ *n* sudden expression of strong feelings

out·put /'aʊtpʊt/ *n* [C;U] production: *The factory's output is 200 cars a day.*

out·rage /'aʊtreɪdʒ/ *n* 1 [C] very wrong or cruel act 2 [U] anger caused by such an act ♦ *vt* offend greatly ~**ous** /aʊt'reɪdʒəs/ *adj* 1 very offensive 2 wildly unexpected and unusual

out·right /ˌaʊt'raɪt◂/ *adv* 1 completely: *She won outright.* 2 without delay: *He was killed outright.* 3 openly: *Tell him outright what you think.* ♦ *adj* complete and clear: *an outright lie*

out·set /'aʊtset/ *n* beginning: *There was trouble from/at the outset.*

out·shine /aʊt'ʃaɪn/ *vt* -**shone** /-'ʃɒn‖-'ʃoʊn/ 1 shine more brightly than 2 be much better than

out·side /aʊt'saɪd, 'aʊtsaɪd/ *n* 1 [(the)S] the part furthest from the middle, or that faces away from one or towards the open air: *to paint the outside of a house* 2 **at the outside** at the most ♦ *adj* 1 facing or at the outside: *the outside wall* 2 from elsewhere: *an outside broadcast* 3 (of a chance or possibility) slight ♦ *adv* to or on the outside, esp. in the open air: *go outside* ♦ *prep* 1 to or on the outside of: *Wait just outside the door.* 2 beyond the limits of: *outside my experience*

out·sid·er /aʊt'saɪdə‖-ər/ *n* 1 person not accepted in a social group 2 person or animal not expected to win

out·size /'aʊtsaɪz/ *adj* larger than the standard sizes

out·skirts /'aʊtskɜːts‖-ɜːr-/ n [P] outer areas or limits of a town

out·smart /aʊt'smɑːt‖-ɑːr-/ vt defeat by being cleverer

out·spo·ken /aʊt'spəʊkən‖-'spoʊ-/ adj expressing thoughts or feelings openly ~ly adv ~ness n [U]

out·stand·ing /aʊt'stændɪŋ/ adj 1 much better than others 2 not yet done or paid ~ly adv

out·stay /aʊt'steɪ/ vt stay longer than: to outstay one's welcome (=stay too long as a guest so as to be no longer welcome)

out·stretched /ˌaʊt'stretʃt◂/ adj (of arms, hands, etc.) stretched out as far as possible

out·strip /aʊt'strɪp/ vt -pp- do better than: to outstrip one's competitors

out·ward /'aʊtwəd‖-ərd/ adj, adv 1 away: the outward journey 2 on the outside but perhaps not really: outward cheerfulness ~ly adv outwards adv

out·weigh /aʊt'weɪ/ vt be more important than

out·wit /aʊt'wɪt/ vt -tt- defeat by being cleverer

o·val /'əʊvəl‖'oʊ-/ n, adj (something) egg-shaped

o·va·ry /'əʊvəri‖'oʊ-/ n part of a female that produces eggs

o·va·tion /əʊ'veɪʃən‖oʊ-/ n joyful expression of public approval

ov·en /'ʌvən/ n closed box for cooking, baking clay, etc.: (fig.) It's like an oven in here. (=uncomfortably hot)

over¹ /'əʊvə‖'oʊvər/ prep 1 higher than but not touching: the clock over the fireplace 2 so as to cover: Put a cloth over the jug. 3 from side to side of, esp. by going up and down: to climb over a wall │ a bridge over the river 4 down across the edge of: It fell over the cliff. 5 in; through: There's snow over most of Europe. 6 in control of: I don't want anyone over me, telling me what to do. 7 more than: over 10 years ago 8 while doing, eating, etc.: We held a meeting over lunch. 9 by means of: I heard it over the radio. 10 about: an argument over money 11 over and above as well as

over² adv 1 downwards from an upright position: I fell over. 2 across an edge or distance: The milk boiled over. │ We flew over to America. 3 so that another side is seen:

Turn the page over. 4 beyond: children of seven and over (=older) 5 so as to be covered: The windows are boarded over. 6 remaining: Was there any money over? 7 (shows something is repeated): I had to do it (all) over again. 8 in all details: Think it over carefully. ◆ adj ended: The party's over.

o·ver·all¹ /ˌəʊvər'ɔːl◂‖ˌoʊvər'ɔːl◂/ adj, adv including everything: overall costs

o·ver·all² /'əʊvərɔːl‖'oʊvərɔːl/ n 1 BrE loose coat worn to protect clothes 2 AmE for OVERALLS (1)

o·ver·alls /'əʊvərɔːlz‖'oʊvərɔːlz/ n [P] 1 BrE garment for the whole body, to protect one's clothes 2 AmE for DUNGAREES

o·ver·arm /'əʊvərɑːm‖'oʊvərɑːrm/ adj, adv (in sport) with the hand above the shoulder

o·ver·awe /ˌəʊvər'ɔː‖ˌoʊvər'ɔː/ vt make quiet because of respect and fear

o·ver·bal·ance /ˌəʊvə'bæləns‖ˌoʊvər-/ vi become unbalanced and fall over

o·ver·bear·ing /ˌəʊvə'beərɪŋ‖ˌoʊvər-'ber-/ adj forcefully trying to tell others what to do

o·ver·board /'əʊvəbɔːd‖'oʊvərbɔːrd/ adv 1 over the side of a boat into the water 2 go overboard become very or too keen

o·ver·cast /ˌəʊvə'kɑːst◂‖ˌoʊvər'kæst◂/ adj dark with clouds

o·ver·coat /'əʊvəkəʊt‖'oʊvərkoʊt/ n long warm coat

o·ver·come /ˌəʊvə'kʌm‖ˌoʊvər-/ vt -came /-'keɪm/, -come 1 defeat 2 make helpless: overcome with grief

o·ver·crowd /ˌəʊvə'kraʊd‖ˌoʊvər-/ vt put or allow too many people or things in (one place)

o·ver·do /ˌəʊvə'duː‖ˌoʊvər-/ vt -did /-'dɪd/, -done /-'dʌn/, 3rd person sing. pres. t. -does /-'dʌz/ do, decorate, perform, etc. too much: I've been overdoing it (=working too hard) lately.

o·ver·dose /'əʊvədəʊs‖'oʊvərdoʊs/ n too much of a drug

o·ver·draft /'əʊvədrɑːft‖'oʊvərdræft/ n money lent by a bank to an overdrawn person

o·ver·drawn /ˌəʊvə'drɔːn◂‖ˌoʊvər-'drɔːn◂/ adj having taken more money from your bank account than it contains

o·ver·drive /'əʊvədraɪv‖'oʊvər-/ n [U] GEAR that allows a car to go fast on less than full power

o·ver·due /ˌəuvə'djuː◂‖ˌouvər'duː◂/ *adj* late

o·ver·flow /ˌəuvə'fləu‖ˌouvər'flou/ *vi/t* 1 flow over the edge (of): *The water's/The bath's overflowing.* 2 go beyond the limits (of): *The crowd overflowed into the street.* ♦ /'əuvəfləu‖'ouvərflou/ *n* (pipe for carrying away) something that overflows

o·ver·grown /ˌəuvə'grəun◂‖ˌouvər-groun◂/ *adj* 1 covered with plants growing uncontrolled 2 grown too large

o·ver·hang /ˌəuvə'hæŋ‖ˌouvər-/ *vi/t* -hung /-'hʌŋ/ hang or stick out over (something) ♦ /'əuvəhæŋ‖'ouvər-/ *n* overhanging rock, roof, etc.

o·ver·haul /ˌəuvə'hɔːl‖ˌouvər'hɔːl/ *vt* 1 examine thoroughly (and repair) 2 OVERTAKE ♦ /'əuvəhɔːl‖'ouvərhɔːl/ *n* thorough examination: *The car needs an overhaul.*

o·ver·head /ˌəuvə'hed◂‖ˌouvər-/ *adj*, *adv* above one's head: *overhead cables*

o·ver·heads /'əuvəhedz‖'ouvər-/ *n* [P] money spent regularly to keep a business running

o·ver·hear /ˌəuvə'hɪə‖ˌouvər'hɪr/ *vi/t* -heard /-'hɜːd‖-'hɜːrd/ hear (what others are saying) without them knowing

o·ver·joyed /ˌəuvə'dʒɔɪd‖ˌouvər-/ *adj* extremely pleased

o·ver·kill /'əuvəkɪl‖'ouvər-/ *n* [U] something that goes beyond the desirable or safe limits

o·ver·la·den /ˌəuvə'leɪdn‖ˌouvər-/ *past p. of* OVERLOAD

o·ver·land /ˌəuvə'lænd◂‖ˌouvər-/ *adj*, *adv* across land and not by sea or air

o·ver·lap /ˌəuvə'læp‖ˌouvər-/ *vi/t* -pp- cover (something) partly and go beyond it: (fig.) *Our interests overlap.* (=are partly the same) ♦ /'əuvəlæp‖'ouvər-/ *n* part that overlaps

o·ver·leaf /ˌəuvə'liːf‖'ouvərliːf/ *adv* on the other side of the page

o·ver·load /ˌəuvə'ləud‖ˌouvər'loud/ *vt* -loaded *or* -laden /-'leɪdn/ 1 load too heavily 2 put too much electricity through **overload** /'əuvələud‖'ouvərloud/ *n*

o·ver·look /ˌəuvə'luk‖ˌouvər-/ *vt* 1 give a view of from above 2 not notice; miss 3 forgive

o·ver·ly /'əuvəli‖'ouvər-/ *adv* more than normal or necessary; especially

o·ver·much /ˌəuvə'mʌtʃ‖ˌouvər-/ *adv*, *determiner*, *pron* 1 *fml* too much 2 very much: *I don't like him overmuch.*

o·ver·night /ˌəuvə'naɪt◂‖ˌouvər-/ *adj*, *adv* 1 for or during the night 2 sudden(ly): *an overnight success*

o·ver·play /ˌəuvə'pleɪ‖ˌouvər-/ *vt* make (something) appear more important than it really is

o·ver·pow·er /ˌəuvə'pauə‖ˌouvər'paur/ *vt* defeat by using greater power ~ing *adj* very strong: *an overpowering desire*

o·ver·ran /ˌəuvə'ræn‖ˌou-/ *past tense of* OVERRUN

o·ver·rate /ˌəuvə'reɪt‖ˌou-/ *vt* give too high an opinion of

o·ver·re·act /ˌəuvəri'ækt‖ˌou-/ *vi* act too strongly as a result of (something)

o·ver·ride /ˌəuvə'raɪd‖ˌou-/ *vt* -rode /-'rəud‖-'roud/, -ridden /-'rɪdn/ forbid obedience to or acceptance of (and take the place of): *My orders were overridden.* -riding *adj* greater than anything else: *of overriding importance*

o·ver·rule /ˌəuvə'ruːl‖ˌou-/ *vt* decide against (something already decided) by official power

o·ver·run /ˌəuvə'rʌn‖ˌou-/ *v* -ran /-'ræn/, -run 1 *vt* spread over and cause harm 2 *vi/t* continue beyond (a time limit)

o·ver·seas /ˌəuvə'siːz◂‖ˌouvər-/ *adv*, *adj* in, to, or from a foreign country across the sea

o·ver·see /ˌəuvə'siː‖ˌouvər-/ *vt* -saw /-'sɔː‖-'sɒː/, -seen /-'siːn/ watch to see that work is properly done -seer /'əuvəsɪə‖'ouvərsiːər/ *n*

o·ver·shad·ow /ˌəuvə'ʃædəu‖ˌouvər-'ʃædou/ *vt* 1 make worried and sadder 2 make appear less important

o·ver·shoot /ˌəuvə'ʃuːt‖ˌouvər-/ *vi/t* -shot /-'ʃɒt‖-'ʃɑːt/ go too far or beyond, and miss

o·ver·sight /'əuvəsaɪt‖'ouvər-/ *n* unintended failure to notice or do something

o·ver·sleep /ˌəuvə'sliːp‖ˌouvər-/ *vi* -slept /-'slept/ wake up too late

o·ver·spill /'əuvəspɪl‖'ouvər-/ *n esp. BrE* people who leave a crowded city and settle elsewhere

o·ver·state /ˌəuvə'steɪt‖ˌouvər-/ *vt* EXAGGERATE

o·ver·step /ˌəuvə'step‖ˌouvər-/ *vt* -pp-go beyond (the limits of what is proper or allowed)

o·vert /'əʊvɜːt, əʊ'vɜːt‖'oʊvɜːrt, oʊ-'vɜːrt/ adj not hidden; open: overt resistance ~ly adv

o·ver·take /ˌəʊvə'teɪk‖ˌoʊvər-/ v -took /-'tʊk/, -taken /-'teɪkən/ **1** vi/t pass (a vehicle in front) **2** vt (of something unpleasant) reach suddenly and unexpectedly

o·ver·throw /ˌəʊvə'θrəʊ‖ˌoʊvər'θroʊ/ vt -threw /-'θruː/, -thrown /-'θrəʊn‖ -'θroʊn/ remove from power ♦ /'əʊvəθrəʊ ‖'oʊvərθroʊ/ n: the violent overthrow of the government

o·ver·time /'əʊvətaɪm‖'oʊvər-/ n, adv [U] (money paid for or time spent working) beyond the usual working time: to work overtime to do something (=use much effort)

o·ver·tones /'əʊvətəʊnz‖'oʊvərtoʊnz/ n [P] things suggested but not stated clearly

o·ver·took /ˌəʊvə'tʊk‖ˌoʊvər-/ past tense of OVERTAKE

o·ver·ture /'əʊvətjʊə, -tʃʊə, -tʃə‖ 'oʊvərtjʊr, -tʃʊr, -tʃər/ n musical introduction, esp. to an OPERA **overtures** n [P] offer to begin talks

o·ver·turn /ˌəʊvə'tɜːn‖ˌoʊvər'tɜːrn/ v **1** vi/t turn over **2** vt bring (esp. a government) to an end suddenly

o·ver·view /'əʊvəvjuː‖'oʊvər-/ n usu. short account (of something) which gives a general picture but no details

o·ver·weight /ˌəʊvə'weɪt◄‖ˌoʊvər-/ adj weighing too much

o·ver·whelm /ˌəʊvə'welm‖ˌoʊvər-/ vt **1** defeat or make powerless by much greater numbers **2** (of feelings) make completely helpless

o·ver·worked /ˌəʊvə'wɜːkt◄‖ˌoʊvər-'wɜːrkt◄/ adj working too hard **overwork** vi

o·ver·wrought /ˌəʊvə'rɔːt◄‖ˌoʊvər-'rɔːt◄/ adj too nervous and excited

ov·u·late /'ɒvjʊleɪt‖'ɑːv-/ vi produce eggs from the OVARY **–lation** /ˌɒvjʊ'leɪʃən‖ ˌɑːv-/ n [U]

ow /aʊ/ interj (expresses sudden slight pain)

owe /əʊ‖oʊ/ vt **1** have to pay: I owed her £5. **2** feel grateful for: We owe a lot to our parents.

ow·ing /'əʊɪŋ‖'oʊ-/ adj **1** still to be paid **2** owing to /'·· ·/ because of

owl /aʊl/ n night bird with large eyes

own¹ /əʊn‖oʊn/ determiner, pron **1** belonging to the stated person and no one else: At last I had my own room/a room of my own. **2 come into one's own** begin to be properly respected for one's qualities **3 have/get one's own back (on someone)** succeed in doing harm (to someone) in return for harm done to oneself **4 hold one's own (against)** avoid defeat (by) **5 on one's own: a** alone **b** without help

own² vt possess, esp. by legal right **~er** n **~ership** n [U]

own to phr vt admit

own up phr vi admit a fault or crime

own goal /ˌ· '·/ n esp. BrE **1** (in football) a GOAL SCORED by mistake against one's own team **2** infml mistake that makes one look foolish

ox /ɒks‖ɑːks/ n **oxen** /'ɒksən‖'ɑːk-/ large animal of the cattle type, esp. male

ox·y·gen /'ɒksɪdʒən‖'ɑːk-/ n [U] gas present in the air, necessary for life

oy·ster /'ɔɪstə‖-ər/ n **1** flat shellfish, often eaten **2 the world is one's/someone's oyster** there are no limits on where one/someone can go, etc.

oz written abbrev. for: OUNCE(s)

o·zone lay·er /'əʊzəʊn ˌleɪə‖'oʊzoʊn ˌleɪər/ n [the+S] layer of gases that stops the sun's heat from damaging the Earth

P

P, p /piː/ **1** the 16th letter of the English alphabet **2 mind one's p's and q's** be careful in what one says so as to avoid displeasing others

p abbrev. for: **1** page **2** BrE penny/pence

P.A. /ˌpiː'eɪ/ n **1** abbrev. for: personal assistant; secretary working for one person only **2** public address system; equipment that makes it possible to hear someone talking to a crowd of people

pace /peɪs/ n 1 speed, esp. of walking or running: *She works so fast I can't keep pace with* (=go as fast as) *her.* 2 (distance moved in) a single step 3 **put someone through his/her paces** make someone do something in order to show his/her abilities, qualities, etc. 4 **set the pace** fix the speed for others to copy 5 **show one's paces** show one's abilities/qualities ♦ v 1 vi/t walk (across) with slow regular steps 2 vt set the speed of movement for

pace out/off phr vt measure by taking steps

pace·mak·er /'peɪsˌmeɪkə‖-ər/ n 1 person who sets a speed or pace for others to follow 2 machine used to make weak or irregular heartbeats regular

pac·i·fist /'pæsɪfɪst/ n person who believes war is wrong and refuses to fight –**fism** n [U]

pac·i·fy /'pæsɪfaɪ/ vt make calm and quiet, esp. less angry –**fication** /ˌpæsɪfɪ-'keɪʃən/ n [U]

pack¹ /pæk/ n 1 number of things wrapped or tied together or put in a case 2 esp. AmE packet 3 group of hunting animals 4 collection, group: *a pack of lies/thieves* 5 complete set of playing cards

pack² v 1 vi/t put (things) into cases, boxes, etc. for taking somewhere or storing 2 vi/t fit or push into a space: *Crowds of people packed into the hall.* 3 vt cover, fill, or surround closely with protective material 4 **send someone packing** infml cause someone undesirable to leave quickly ~**ed** adj full of people

pack in phr vt infml 1 stop doing 2 attract in large numbers: *That film is really packing them in.*

pack off phr vt infml BUNDLE off

pack up phr v infml 1 vi finish work 2 vi esp. BrE (of a machine) stop working 3 vt stop

pack·age /'pækɪdʒ/ n 1 number of things packed together; parcel 2 set of related things offered as a unit ♦ vt 1 make into a package 2 put in a box, bag, etc. for selling –**ging** n [U] box, bag, etc. in which something is sold

package tour /'·· ·/ also **package hol·i·day** /'·· ,···/ BrE — n holiday where travel, hotels, food, etc. are paid for together

pack·et /'pækɪt/ n 1 small container or parcel: *a packet of cigarettes* 2 sl large amount of money

pack·ing /'pækɪŋ/ n [U] 1 putting things in cases or boxes 2 protective material for packing things

pact /pækt/ n solemn agreement

pad¹ /pæd/ n 1 something made or filled with soft material, for protection or to give shape 2 many sheets of paper fastened together: *a writing pad* 3 LAUNCHING PAD 4 sl one's house or home 5 usu. thick-skinned underpart of foot of some four-footed animals ♦ vt -dd- 1 protect, shape, or make more comfortable with a pad or pads 2 make longer by adding unnecessary words ~**ding** /'pædɪŋ/ n [U] 1 material used to pad something 2 unnecessary words or sentences

pad² vi -dd- walk steadily and usu. softly

pad·dle¹ /'pædl/ n short pole with a wide blade at one end or both ends, for rowing a small boat ♦ vi/t 1 row with a paddle 2 **paddle one's own canoe** infml depend on oneself and no one else

paddle² vi walk about in water a few inches deep ♦ n [S] act of paddling

pad·dock /'pædək/ n small field where horses are kept

pad·dy /'pædi/ n field where rice is grown in water

pad·lock /'pædlɒk‖-lɑːk/ n removable lock fastened with a U-shaped bar, for locking gates, bicycles, etc. ♦ vi/t fasten or lock with a padlock

pae·di·at·rics /ˌpiːdi'ætrɪks/ n [U] PEDIATRICS

pa·gan /'peɪgən/ n person who does not believe in one's religion, or in any of the main religions ♦ adj: *pagan tribes* ~**ism** n [U]

page¹ /peɪdʒ/ n one or both sides of a sheet of paper in a book, newspaper, etc.

page² vt get the attention of, using a LOUDSPEAKER or a **pager** (small machine that receives messages)

pag·eant /'pædʒənt/ n splendid public show or ceremony ~**ry** n [U] splendid show of ceremonial grandness

pa·go·da /pə'gəʊdə‖-'goʊ-/ n temple (esp. Buddhist or Hindu) built on several floors

paid /peɪd/ past t. and p. of PAY —see also **put paid to** (PUT (6))

paid-up /ˌ· '·◂/ *adj* having paid in full (esp. so as to continue being a member)

pail /peɪl/ *n* bucket

pain /peɪn/ *n* 1 [U] suffering in body or mind; hurting: *Are you in pain?* 2 [C] case of such suffering in a particular part: *a pain in my stomach* 3 [S] also **pain in the neck** /ˌ· ·'·◂/ — *sl* person, thing, or happening that makes one angry or tired 4 **on/under pain of** *fml* at the risk of suffering (a punishment) if something is not done ♦ *vt fml* cause pain to ~**ed** *adj* displeased or hurt in one's feelings ~**ful** *adj*: *a painful cut* ~**less** *adj* **pains** *n* [P] effort; trouble: *I went to great pains to get the one you wanted.* **painstaking** *adj* very careful and thorough

paint /peɪnt/ *n* [U] liquid colouring matter for decorating surfaces or making pictures ♦ *vi/t* 1 put paint on (a surface) 2 make a picture (of) with paint 3 describe in clear, well-chosen words 4 **paint the town red** go out and have a good time ~**ing** *n* 1 [U] act or art of painting 2 [C] painted picture —see also OIL PAINTING **paints** *n* [P] set of small containers of different-coloured paint, for painting pictures

paint·er¹ /'peɪntə‖-ər/ *n* person who paints pictures, or houses, rooms, etc.

painter² *n* rope for tying up a small boat

paint·work /'peɪntwɜːk‖-wɜːrk/ *n* [U] painted surface

pair /peə‖per/ *n* 1 two of the same kind: *a pair of gloves* 2 something made of two similar parts: *a pair of scissors* 3 two people closely connected ♦ *vi/t* form into one or more pairs: *Jane and David paired off at the party.*

 pair up *phr vi/t* (cause to) join in pairs, esp. for work or sport

pa·ja·mas /pəˈdʒɑːməz‖-ˈdʒɑː-, -ˈdʒæ/ *n* [P] *esp. AmE* PYJAMAS

pal /pæl/ *n infml* friend

pal·ace /'pælɪs/ *n* large grand house, esp. where a king or president lives

pal·a·ta·ble /'pælətəbəl/ *adj fml* 1 good to taste 2 acceptable; pleasant: *not a palatable suggestion*

pal·ate /'pælɪt/ *n* 1 the top inside part of the mouth 2 ability to judge good food or wine

pa·la·tial /pəˈleɪʃəl/ *adj* (of a building) large and splendid

pa·la·ver /pəˈlɑːvə‖-ˈlævər/ *n* [U] trouble over unimportant matters; FUSS

pale¹ /peɪl/ *adj* 1 not bright or dark: *pale blue* 2 (of a face) rather white ♦ *vi* 1 become pale 2 seem less important, clever, etc. when compared with

pale² *n* limit of proper behaviour: *beyond the pale*

pal·e·on·tol·o·gy /ˌpælɪɒnˈtɒlədʒi‖ ˌpeɪliːɑːnˈtɑː-/ *n* [U] study of FOSSILS **-gist** *n*

pal·ette /'pælɪt/ *n* board on which a painter mixes colours

pall¹ /pɔːl‖pɒːl/ *vi* become uninteresting or dull

pall² *n* 1 [S] heavy or dark covering: *a pall of smoke* 2 [C] cloth spread over a COFFIN

pall·bear·er /'pɔːlˌbeərə‖'pɒːlˌberər/ *n* person who walks beside or helps carry a COFFIN

pallet /'pælɪt/ *n* large flat frame used with a FORKLIFT for lifting heavy goods

pal·ette /'pælɪt/ *n* board on which a painter mixes colours

pal·li·ate /'pælieɪt/ *vt fml* cause to be or seem less unpleasant or wrong **-ative** /'pæliətɪv/ *n, adj*: *only a palliative, not a cure*

pal·lid /'pælɪd/ *adj* (of skin) unhealthily pale ~**ness** *n* [U]

pal·lor /'pælə‖-ər/ *n* [S] pallidness

palm¹ /pɑːm‖pɑːm/ *n* tall tropical tree with no branches and a mass of large leaves at the top

palm² *n* lower surface of the hand

palm³ *v* **palm off** *phr vt* 1 get rid of by deception 2 deceive into accepting

palm·ist /'pɑːmɪst‖'pɑːm-, 'pɑːlm-/ *n* person who tells someone's future by looking at their PALM² **-ry** *n* [U] palmist's art

palm·y /'pɑːmi‖'pɑːmi, 'pɑːlmi/ *adj* (of past periods) most pleasant and successful

pal·pa·ble /'pælpəbəl/ *adj fml* easily and clearly known: *a palpable lie* **-bly** *adv*

pal·pi·tate /'pælpɪteɪt/ *vi* (of the heart) beat fast and irregularly **-tations** /ˌpælpɪˈteɪʃənz/ *n* [P]

pal·try /'pɔːltri‖'pɒːl-/ *adj* worthlessly small or unimportant

pam·pas /'pæmpəz, -pəs/ *n* [U] wide treeless plains in South America

pam·per /'pæmpə‖-ər/ *vt* treat too kindly

pam·phlet /'pæmflɪt/ *n* small book with

paper covers

pan¹ /pæn/ n 1 round metal container for cooking, usu. with a long handle 2 esp. BrE bowl of a LAVATORY 3 container with holes in the bottom used for separating precious metals from other material

pan² v -nn- 1 vt infml CRITICIZE very severely 2 vi/t move (a camera) to follow the action being recorded on film or television

pan out phr vi happen in a particular way

pan·a·ce·a /ˌpænəˈsiːə/ n something that will put right all troubles

pa·nache /pəˈnæʃ, pæ-/ n [U] showy splendid way of doing things

pan·cake /ˈpænkeɪk/ n thin flat cake cooked in a pan

pan·cre·as /ˈpænkriəs/ n bodily organ that helps in changing food chemically for use by the body

pan·da /ˈpændə/ n black-and-white bearlike animal from China

Panda car /ˈ··ˌ·/ n BrE police car

pan·de·mo·ni·um /ˌpændɪˈməʊniəm ‖ -ˈmoʊ-/ n [U] wild and noisy disorder

pan·der /ˈpændə ‖ -ər/ v **pander to** phr vt satisfy unworthily: The newspapers pander to people's interest in sex scandals.

Pan·do·ra's box /pænˌdɔːrəz ˈbɒks ‖ -ˈbɑːks/ n open Pandora's box unintentionally cause or discover a large number of problems

p & p /ˌpiː ənd ˈpiː/ abbrev. for: postage and packing; cost of this, added to the cost of goods bought through the post

pane /peɪn/ n sheet of glass in a window

pan·e·gyr·ic /ˌpænɪˈdʒɪrɪk/ n fml speech or writing full of great praise

pan·el /ˈpænl/ n 1 flat piece of wood in a door or on a wall 2 board with instruments fixed in it: an aircraft's control panel 3 small group of people who answer questions on esp. a radio or television show 4 piece of cloth of a different colour or material, set in a dress —see also SOLAR PANEL ♦ vt -ll- BrE ‖ -l- AmE decorate with PANELS (1): oak-panelled walls ~ling BrE ‖ ~ing AmE — n [U] PANELS (1)

pang /pæŋ/ n sudden sharp feeling of pain

pan·ic /ˈpænɪk/ n [C;U] sudden uncontrollable quickly spreading fear or terror ♦ vi/t -ck- (cause to) feel panic ~ky

adj suddenly afraid

panic sta·tions /ˈ·· ˌ··/ n [U] state of confused anxiety because something needs to be done in a hurry

panic-strick·en /ˈ·· ˌ·/ adj filled with panic

pan·ni·er /ˈpæniə ‖ -ər/ n basket, esp. either of a pair on a bicycle

pan·o·ply /ˈpænəpli/ n [U] splendid ceremonial show or dress

pan·o·ra·ma /ˌpænəˈrɑːmə ‖ -ˈræmə/ n 1 complete view of a wide stretch of land 2 general representation in words or pictures –ramic /-ˈræmɪk/ adj

pan-pipes /ˈpæn paɪps/ n [P] musical instrument made of wooden pipes of different lengths tied together

pan·sy /ˈpænzi/ 1 small flowering garden plant 2 infml derog a EFFEMINATE young man b male HOMOSEXUAL

pant /pænt/ vi breathe quickly, with short breaths ♦ n quick short breath

pan·the·is·m /ˈpænθiˌɪzəm/ n [U] religious idea that God and the universe are the same thing –ist n

pan·ther /ˈpænθə ‖ -ər/ n LEOPARD, esp. a black one

pan·ties /ˈpæntiz/ n [P] women's or children's short undergarment worn below the waist

pan·to·mime /ˈpæntəmaɪm/ also **pan·to** /ˈpæntəʊ ‖ -toʊ/ infml — n [C;U] play for children based on a fairy story, produced at Christmas

pan·try /ˈpæntri/ n small room with shelves where food is kept

pants /pænts/ n [P] 1 BrE for panties or UNDERPANTS 2 esp. AmE trousers 3 **with one's pants down** sl awkwardly unprepared 4 **by the seat of one's pants** infml guided by one's experience rather than by a formal plan

pap /pæp/ n [U] 1 soft liquid food for babies or sick people 2 reading matter or entertainment intended only for amusement, which does not instruct or contain ideas of any value

pap·a¹ /ˈpɑːpə/ n AmE father

pa·pa² /pəˈpɑː/ n BrE lit father

pa·pa·cy /ˈpeɪpəsi/ n power and office of the POPE

pa·pal /ˈpeɪpl/ adj of the POPE

pap·a·raz·zi /ˌpæpəˈrætsi/ newspaper

writers or photographers who follow famous people about hoping to find out interesting or shocking stories about them

pa·per /'peɪpə‖-ər/ n 1 [U] material in thin sheets for writing or printing on, wrapping things in, etc. 2 [C] newspaper 3 [C] set of questions to be answered in an examination 4 [C] piece of writing for specialists, often read aloud **5 on paper** as written down, but not yet tried out in reality —see also WHITE PAPER ♦ vt cover with WALLPAPER **papers** n [P] pieces of paper written or printed, esp. used for official purposes

pa·per·back /'peɪpəbæk‖-ər-/ n book with a thin cardboard cover

pa·per·boy /'peɪpəbɔɪ‖-ər-/ n boy who delivers newspapers

paper clip /'···/ n piece of curved wire for holding papers together

pa·per·weight /'peɪpəweɪt‖-ər-/ n heavy object put on papers to stop them being scattered

pa·per·work /'peɪpəwɜːk‖-pərwɜːrk/ n [U] writing reports and letters, keeping records, etc.

pa·pier-mâ·ché /ˌpæpieɪ 'mæʃeɪ, ˌpeɪpə-‖ˌpeɪpər məˈʃeɪ/ n [U] mixture of wet paper and glue, used to make various objects and left to harden

pap·ri·ka /'pæprɪkə‖pəˈpriːkə/ n [U] hot-tasting red powder from a plant, used in cooking

par /pɑː‖pɑːr/ n 1 [S] (nearly) equal level: *Her skill is on a par with mine.* 2 [U] average number of hits in GOLF 3 **under par** infml not in the usual or average condition of health

par·a·ble /'pærəbəl/ n short simple story which teaches a moral lesson

pa·rab·o·la /pəˈræbələ/ n curved line, like a thrown ball rising and falling –**bolic** /ˌpærəˈbɒlɪk◀‖-ˈbɑː-/ adj

par·a·chute /'pærəʃuːt/ n piece of cloth on long ropes, fastened to someone to allow them to fall slowly and safely from an aircraft ♦ vi/t drop by means of a parachute

pa·rade /pəˈreɪd/ n 1 informal procession 2 ceremonial gathering of soldiers to be officially looked at —see also HIT PARADE ♦ v 1 vi walk or gather in a parade 2 vi walk showily 3 vt show in order to be admired: *parading her knowledge*

par·a·dise /'pærədaɪs/ n 1 [U] (usu. cap.) Heaven 2 [S;U] place or state of perfect happiness —see also FOOL'S PARADISE

par·a·dox /'pærədɒks‖-dɑːks/ n 1 statement that says two opposite things but has some truth in it 2 strange combination of opposing qualities, ideas, etc. ~**ical** /ˌpærəˈdɒksɪkəl◀‖-ˈdɑːk-/ adj ~**ically** /-kli/ adv 1 in a paradoxical way 2 it is a paradox that

par·af·fin /'pærəfɪn/ n [U] BrE sort of oil burned for heating and lighting

par·a·gon /'pærəgən‖-gɑːn/ n person who is or seems to be a perfect model to copy

par·a·graph /'pærəgrɑːf‖-græf/ n division of a piece of writing that begins a new line

par·a·keet /'pærəkiːt/ n small PARROT

par·al·lel /'pærəlel/ adj 1 (of lines) always the same distance apart 2 comparable ♦ n 1 [C;U] comparable person or thing 2 [C] similarity (point of) 3 [C] line of LATITUDE ♦ vt -ll- BrE ‖ -l- AmE be similar to

par·al·lel·o·gram /ˌpærəˈleləgræm/ n four-sided figure with opposite sides equal and parallel

par·a·lyse BrE ‖ -**lyze** AmE /'pærəlaɪz/ vt 1 cause paralysis in 2 cause to stop working: *The strike paralysed the industry.*

pa·ral·y·sis /pəˈræləsɪs/ n [U] loss of movement in (some of) the body muscles

paralytic /ˌpærəˈlɪtɪk◀/ adj 1 suffering from paralysis 2 esp. BrE infml very drunk

par·a·med·ic /ˌpærəˈmedɪk/ n person who is trained to help injured or sick people, but is not a doctor or nurse

pa·ram·e·ter /pəˈræmətə‖-ər/ n (usu. pl.) any of the established limits within which something must operate

par·a·mil·i·tary /ˌpærəˈmɪlɪtri◀-teri◀/ adj acting like an army, esp. illegally

par·a·mount /'pærəmaʊnt/ adj fml greater than all others in importance

par·a·noi·a /ˌpærəˈnɔɪə/ n [U] disease of the mind in which you think esp. that other people are trying to harm you –**noid** /'pærənɔɪd/ adj (as if) suffering from paranoia

par·a·nor·mal /ˌpærəˈnɔːməl◀‖-ˈnɔːr-/ adj having no sensible explanation;

involving unknown forces ♦ *n* [*the*+S]
par·a·pet /'pærəpɪt, -pet/ *n* low
protective wall at the edge of a roof, bridge,
etc.

par·a·pher·na·li·a /ˌpærəfəˈneɪliə
-fər-/ *n* [U] small articles of various kinds

par·a·phrase /'pærəfreɪz/ *vt, n* (make) a
re-expression of (something written or
said) in different words

par·a·ple·gic /ˌpærəˈpliːdʒɪk◂/ *n, adj*
(person) unable to move their lower body

par·a·site /'pærəsaɪt/ *n* 1 animal or plant
that lives and feeds on another 2 useless
person supported by others' efforts –**sitic**
/ˌpærəˈsɪtɪk◂/ *adj*

par·a·sol /'pærəsɒl ‖ -sɔːl, -sɑːl/ *n*
SUNSHADE

par·a·troops /'pærətruːps/ , –**troopers**
/-truːpəz ‖ -ərz/ *n* [P] soldiers who drop
from aircraft using PARACHUTES

par·cel[1] /'pɑːsəl ‖ 'pɑːr-/ *n* 1 something
wrapped up in paper and fastened 2 **part
and parcel of** a most important part that
cannot be separated from the whole of

parcel[2] *v* -ll- *BrE* ‖ -l- *AmE* **parcel out** *phr
vt* divide into parts or shares **parcel up** *phr
vt* wrap and tie

parch /pɑːtʃ ‖ pɑːrtʃ/ *vt* make hot and dry

parch·ment /'pɑːtʃmənt ‖ 'pɑːr-/ *n* [C;U]
treated animal skin, used formerly for
writing on

par·don /'pɑːdn ‖ 'pɑːrdn/ *n* 1 [C;U] (act
of) forgiving, esp. of a guilty person, so they
will no longer be punished 2 **I beg your
pardon**, also **pardon me** — **a** 'Please
excuse me for having accidentally
touched/pushed you.' **b** 'Please repeat what
you said.' ♦ *vt* give pardon to ♦ *interj* (ask
for something not fully heard to be
repeated) ~**able** *adj* that can be forgiven

pare /peə ‖ per/ *vt* cut off the edge or thin
covering of: (fig.) *We must pare down*
(=reduce) *costs.*

par·ent /'peərənt ‖ 'per-/ *n* father or
mother ~**tal** /pəˈrentl/ *adj*

pa·ren·the·sis /pəˈrenθəsɪs/ *n* -**ses**
/-siːz/ *fml* 1 (*usu. pl.*) *BrE fml* or *AmE* for
BRACKET (2c) 2 words introduced as an
added explanation or thought

pa·ri·ah /pəˈraɪə, ˈpæriə ‖ pəˈraɪə/ *n fml*
person not accepted by society

par·ish /'pærɪʃ/ *n* area for which a priest
has responsibility: *the parish church*

pa·rish·io·ner /pəˈrɪʃənə ‖ -ər/ *n* person
who lives in a parish

par·i·ty /'pærɪti/ *n* [U] *fml* being equal

park[1] /pɑːk ‖ pɑːrk/ *n* large usu. grassy
enclosed piece of land in a town, used by
the public for pleasure and rest —see also
SCIENCE PARK

park[2] *vi/t* put (a vehicle) for a time: (fig.)
*He just came in and parked himself on the
sofa.*

parking me·ter /'·· ˌ·/ *n* apparatus into
which you put money, allowing you to park
near it for a time

Par·kin·son's di·sease /'pɑːkɪnsənz
dɪˌziːz ‖ 'pɑːr-/ *n* [U] disease causing
uncontrollable shaking

park·land /'pɑːk-lænd ‖ 'pɑːrk-/ *n* [U]
large grassy area surrounding a large
country house

par·lance /'pɑːləns ‖ 'pɑːr-/ *n* [U] *fml*
particular way of speaking or use of words

par·lia·ment /'pɑːləmənt ‖ 'pɑːr-/ *n*
body of people elected or appointed to make
laws –**ary** /ˌpɑːləˈmentəri◂ ‖ ˌpɑːr-/ *adj*

par·lour *BrE* ‖ -**lor** *AmE* /'pɑːlə ‖
'pɑːrlər/ *n esp. AmE* shop: *an ice-cream
parlour*

pa·ro·chi·al /pəˈrəʊkiəl ‖ -'roʊ-/ *adj*
1 only interested in one's own affairs 2 of a
PARISH

par·o·dy /'pærədi/ *n* [C;U] copy of a
writer's or musician's style, made to amuse
♦ *vt* make a parody of

pa·role /pəˈrəʊl ‖ -'roʊl/ *n* [U] letting
someone out of prison before their official
period of imprisonment has ended ♦ *vt* let
out of prison on parole

par·quet /'pɑːkeɪ, 'pɑːki ‖ pɑːrˈkeɪ/ *n* [U]
small wooden blocks making a floor

par·rot /'pærət/ *n* tropical bird with a
curved beak and usu. brightly coloured
feathers ♦ *vt* repeat (someone else's words
or actions) without thought or understanding

par·ry /'pæri/ *vt* turn aside (a blow or
weapon): (fig.) *parrying awkward questions*

pars·ley /'pɑːsli ‖ 'pɑːr-/ *n* [U] small plant
used in cooking

pars·nip /'pɑːsnɪp ‖ 'pɑːr-/ *n* plant with a
long white root used as a vegetable

part[1] /pɑːt ‖ pɑːrt/ *n* 1 [C] any of the
pieces into which something is divided: *an
engine with 100 moving parts* ‖ *The travel is*

the best part of my job **2** [S;U] share in an activity: *Did you take part in the fighting?* **3** [U] side; position: *He took my part* (=supported me) *in the quarrel.* **4** [C] (words of) a character acted in a play or film **5 for my part** as far as I am concerned **6 for the most part: a** mostly **b** in most cases **7 in part** partly **8 on the part of** of or by (someone) **9 play a part in** have an influence on **10 in good part** without being offended ♦ *adv* partly: *The exams are part written, part practical* **~ly** *adv* **1** not completely **2** in some degree **parts** *n* [P] **1** area of a country: *We don't have much rain in these parts.* **2** *fml* **a man/woman of parts** with many different abilities

part² *v* **1** *vi/t* separate: *They parted as friends.* | *She parted the curtains.* **2** *vt* separate (hair on the head) along a line **3 part company (with): a** end a relationship (with) **b** no longer be together (with) **c** disagree (with) **~ing** *n* **1** [U] leaving **2** [C] line on the head where the hair is parted

  part with *phr vt* give away; stop having
par·take /pɑːˈteɪk ‖ pɑːr-/ *vi* **-took** /-ˈtʊk/, **-taken** /-ˈteɪkən/ *fml* eat or drink something offered
par·tial /ˈpɑːʃəl ‖ ˈpɑːr-/ *adj* **1** not complete **2** (unfairly) favouring one more than another **3 partial to** very fond of **~ly** *adv* **~ity** /ˌpɑːʃiˈælɪti ‖ ˌpɑːr-/ *n* **1** [U] being PARTIAL (2) **2** [S] fondness: *a partiality for cream cakes*
par·tic·i·pant /pɑːˈtɪsɪpənt ‖ pɑːr-/ *n* person who participates
par·tic·i·pate /pɑːˈtɪsɪpeɪt ‖ pɑːr-/ *vi* take part or have a share in an activity **-pation** /pɑːˌtɪsɪˈpeɪʃən ‖ pɑːr-/ *n* [U]
par·ti·ci·ple /ˈpɑːtɪsɪpəl ‖ ˈpɑːr-/ *n* PAST PARTICIPLE or PRESENT PARTICIPLE
par·ti·cle /ˈpɑːtɪkəl ‖ ˈpɑːr-/ *n* very small piece
par·tic·u·lar /pəˈtɪkjʊlə ‖ pərˈtɪkjʊlər/ *adj* **1** special; unusual: *of no particular importance* **2** single and different from others: *this particular case* **3** showing (too) much care over small matters **4 in particular** especially ♦ *n* small single part of a whole; detail **~ly** *adv* especially
parting shot /ˌ·· ˈ·/ *n* remark or action made when leaving
par·ti·san /ˌpɑːtɪˈzæn ‖ ˈpɑːrtɪzən, -sən/

n, adj **1** (person) giving strong unreasoning support to one side **2** member of an armed group that fights in secret against an enemy that has conquered its country
par·ti·tion /pɑːˈtɪʃən ‖ pər-, pɑːr-/ *n* **1** [C] thin wall indoors **2** [U] division, esp. of a country ♦ *vt* divide up

  partition off *phr vt* separate with a partition
part·ner /ˈpɑːtnə ‖ ˈpɑːrtnər/ *n* **1** person or organization one is doing something with: *a dancing/business partner* **2** person one is married to or having a relationship with **~ship** *n* **1** [U] being a partner **2** [C] business owned by two or more partners
part of speech /ˌ· · ˈ·/ *n* class of word, such as 'noun' or 'verb'
par·took /pɑːˈtʊk ‖ pɑːr-/ *v* past t. of PARTAKE
part-time /ˌ· ˈ·◂/ *adj, adv* (working) during only part of the regular working time
par·ty /ˈpɑːti ‖ ˈpɑːrti/ *n* **1** gathering of people for food and amusement: *a birthday party* **2** association of people with the same political aims: *the Democratic party* **3** group of people doing something together: *a search party* —see also WORKING PARTY **4** *esp. law* person or group concerned in a matter **5 be (a) party to** take part in or know about (some action or activity) **6 (follow) the party line** act according to the official opinion of a political party —see also THIRD PARTY ♦ *vi infml, esp. AmE* enjoy oneself, esp. at a party or parties
party piece /ˈ·· ˌ·/ *n* song, poem, etc. that is someone's usual choice when asked to give a performance, e.g. at a party
pass¹ /pɑːs ‖ pæs/ *v* **1** *vi/t* reach and move beyond: *Several cars passed (us).* **2** *vi/t* go through or across: *A cloud passed across the sun.* **3** *vi/t* (cause to) go: *I passed a rope around the tree.* **4** *vi* come to an end: *Summer is passing.* **5** *vt* give: *Please pass me the salt.* **6** *vt* (in sport) kick, throw, etc. (esp. a ball) to a member of one's own side **7 a** *vi* (of time) go by **b** *vt* spend (time) **8** *vt* accept officially: *Parliament passed a new law.* **9** *vi/t* succeed in (an examination) **10** *vt* give (a judgment, opinion, etc.): *The judge passed a heavy sentence on him.* **11 let something pass** leave (a wrong statement, mistake, etc.) without putting it right

12 pass the time of day (with) give a greeting (to), and/or have a short conversation (with)

pass away *phr vi* die

pass by *phr vt* disregard

pass for *phr vt* be (mistakenly) accepted or considered as

pass off *phr v* **1** *vt* present falsely: *passing herself off as a doctor* **2** *vi* take place and be completed

pass on *phr vi* **1** PASS AWAY **2** move on

pass out *phr vi* faint

pass over *phr vt* fail to choose

pass up *phr vt* fail to take advantage of; miss

pass² *n* **1** successful result in an examination **2** official paper showing that one is allowed to do something: *a travel pass* **3** act of giving the ball to someone else in sport **4** way by which one can travel through or over a place, esp. a range of mountains **5** act of trying to interest someone sexually: *He made a pass at me.*

pass·a·ble /ˈpɑːsəbəl ‖ ˈpæ-/ *adj* **1** (just) good enough **2 a** (of a road) fit to be used **b** (of a river) fit to be crossed **—bly** *adv*

pas·sage /ˈpæsɪdʒ/ *n* **1** [C] long narrow connecting way, esp. a CORRIDOR **2** [C] way through: *We forced a passage through the crowd.* **3** [U] *fml* going across, through, etc.: *the bill's passage through Parliament* **4** [U] onward flow (of time) **5** [S] (cost of) a journey by sea or air **6** [C] short part of a speech, piece of music, etc.

pas·sé /ˈpɑːseɪ, ˈpæseɪ ‖ pæˈseɪ/ *adj* old-fashioned

pas·sen·ger /ˈpæsɪndʒə, -sən- ‖ -ər/ *n* person being taken in a vehicle

pass·er·by /ˌpɑːsəˈbaɪ ‖ ˌpæsər-/ *n* passersby person who is going past a place

pass·ing /ˈpɑːsɪŋ ‖ ˈpæ-/ *n* [U] **1** going by **2** ending; disappearance **3** death **4 in passing** while talking about something else ♦ *adj* **1** moving or going by: *passing traffic* **2** not lasting long: *I didn't give it a passing thought.*

pas·sion /ˈpæʃən/ *n* **1** [C;U] strong deep feeling, esp. of love or anger **2** [S] a strong liking: *a passion for tennis* **3 the Passion** the suffering and death of Christ

pas·sion·ate /ˈpæʃənət/ *adj* filled with passion **—ly** *adv*

pas·sive¹ /ˈpæsɪv/ *adj* **1** suffering something bad without (enough) opposition **2** (of verbs or sentences) expressing an action which is done to the subject of a sentence **—ly** *adv* **~ness**, also *n* [U] **—sivity** /pæˈsɪvəti/

passive² *n* [*the*+S] passive form of a verb

passive smo·king /ˌ·· ˈ··/ *n* [U] breathing in other people's cigarette smoke

pass·key /ˈpɑːskiː ‖ ˈpæs-/ *n* **1** key given to only a few people **2** key that will open many different locks

pass·port /ˈpɑːspɔːt ‖ ˈpæspɔːrt/ *n* **1** small official book allowing you to enter foreign countries **2** something that lets you get something else easily: *Is money a passport to happiness?*

pass·word /ˈpɑːswɜːd ‖ ˈpæswɜːrd/ *n* secret word which you have to know to be allowed into a building, etc.

past¹ /pɑːst ‖ pæst/ *adj* **1** (of time) earlier than the present: *the past few days* **2** ended: *Winter is past.* **3** *gram* expressing past time: *the past tense* **4** former: *a past president of our club* ♦ *n* [S] **1** (what happened in) the time before the present: *It happened in the past.* | *our country's glorious past* **2** *derog* secret former life containing wrong-doing of some kind: *a woman with a past*

past² *prep* **1** up to and beyond: *They rushed past us.* **2** beyond in time or age: *It's 10 minutes past four.* **3** beyond the possiblity of: *I'm past caring.* (=no longer care) **4 past it** *infml* no longer able to do the things one could formerly do ♦ *adv* by: *The children ran past.*

pas·ta /ˈpæstə ‖ ˈpɑː-/ *n* [U] food made in different shapes from flour paste

paste /peɪst/ *n* [U] **1** soft mixture of powder and liquid **2** liquid mixture, usu. with flour, for sticking paper together ♦ *vt* fasten with paste

pas·tel /ˈpæstl ‖ pæˈstel/ *adj* soft and light in colour

pas·teur·ize, **-ise** /ˈpæstʃəraɪz, -stə-/ *vt* heat (a liquid) to destroy bacteria **—ization**, **-isation** /ˌpæstʃəraɪˈzeɪʃən, -stə- ‖ -rə-/ *n* [U]

pas·tiche /pæˈstiːʃ/ *n* work of art made of, or in the style of, other works of art

pas·tille /ˈpæstiːl/ *n* small hard sweet, esp. containing throat medicine

pas·time /ˈpɑːstaɪm ‖ ˈpæs-/ *n* something done to pass one's time pleasantly

past mas·ter /ˌ ˈ ··/ n very skilled person

pas·tor /ˈpɑːstə ‖ ˈpæstər/ n Christian priest in charge of a church

pas·tor·al /ˈpɑːstərəl ‖ ˈpæ-/ adj 1 of a priest's duties amongst his religious group 2 of simple country life

past par·ti·ci·ple /ˌ ˈ····/ n form of a verb used in compounds to show the passive or the PERFECT[1] (5) tenses (such as broken in The cup was broken.)

pas·try /ˈpeɪstri/ n 1 [U] a mixture of flour, fat, and liquid, eaten when baked 2 [C] article of food made from this

pas·ture /ˈpɑːstʃə ‖ ˈpæstʃər/ n [C;U] grassy land where farm animals feed

pas·ty[1] /ˈpæsti/ n small pastry case filled usu. with meat

past·y[2] /ˈpeɪsti/ adj (of the face) unhealthily white

pat[1] /pæt/ vt -tt- strike gently and repeatedly with a flat hand ♦ n 1 light friendly stroke with the hand 2 small shaped mass of butter 3 **a pat on the back** expression of praise or satisfaction for something done

pat[2] adj, adv (too) easily or quickly answered or known

patch /pætʃ/ n 1 irregularly shaped part of a surface different from the rest: damp patches on the wall 2 small piece of material to cover a hole 3 small piece of ground: a cabbage patch 4 piece of material worn to protect a damaged eye 5 period: He's going through **a bad patch**. (=a time of trouble or misfortune) 6 **not a patch on** BrE infml not nearly as good as ♦ vt put a PATCH (2) on phr vt 1 repair 2 become friends again after (a quarrel)

patch·work /ˈpætʃwɜːk ‖ -wɜːrk/ n [C;U] (piece of) sewn work made by joining small bits of different materials: (fig.) the patchwork of fields seen from an aircraft

patch·y /ˈpætʃi/ adj 1 in or having patches (PATCH (1)): patchy fog 2 incomplete or only good in parts **–ily** adv **–iness** n [U]

pât·é /ˈpæteɪ ‖ pɑːˈteɪ, pæ-/ n [U] food made by crushing meat, esp. LIVER, into a soft mass

pa·tent /ˈpeɪtnt, ˈpæ-‖ ˈpæ-/ n (official paper giving someone) the unshared right to make or sell a new invention ♦ adj 1 protected by a patent 2 fml clear to see: his patent annoyance ♦ vt obtain a patent for

~ly adv fml clearly

patent leath·er /ˌpeɪtnt ˈleθə◂ ‖ˌpætnt ˈleðər/ n [U] very shiny leather, usu. black

pa·ter·nal /pəˈtɜːnl ‖ -ɜːr-/ adj 1 of or like a father 2 protecting people like a father but allowing them no freedom 3 related to a person through the father's side of the family **~ly** adv

pa·ter·nal·ism /pəˈtɜːnəl-ɪzəm ‖ -ɜːr-/ n [U] a PATERNAL (2) way of controlling people **–istic** /pəˌtɜːnəlˈɪstɪk◂ ‖ -ɜːr-/ adj **–istically** /-kli/ adv

pa·ter·ni·ty /pəˈtɜːnəti ‖ -ɜːr-/ n [U] esp. law origin from the male parent

path /pɑːθ ‖ pæθ/ n paths /pɑːðz ‖ pæðz/ 1 track or way where you can walk 2 line along which something moves: the path of an arrow

pa·thet·ic /pəˈθetɪk/ adj 1 causing pity or sorrow 2 derog hopelessly unsuccessful **~ally** /-kli/ adv

pa·thol·o·gy /pəˈθɒlədʒi ‖ -ˈθɑː-/ n [U] study of disease **–gist** n specialist in pathology, esp. one who examines a dead body to find out how the person died **-gical** /ˌpæθəˈlɒdʒɪkəl◂ ‖ -ˈlɑː-/ adj 1 of pathology 2 caused by disease, esp. of the mind 3 great and unreasonable: pathological jealousy **-gically** /-kli/ adv

pa·thos /ˈpeɪθɒs ‖ -θɑːs/ n [U] quality that causes pity and sorrow

path·way /ˈpɑːθweɪ ‖ ˈpæθ-/ n PATH (1)

pa·tience /ˈpeɪʃəns/ n [U] 1 ability to wait calmly, to control oneself when angered, or to accept unpleasant things without complaining 2 card game for one player

pa·tient[1] /ˈpeɪʃənt/ adj showing patience **~ly** adv

patient[2] n person being treated medically

pat·i·na /ˈpætɪnə/ n pleasingly smooth shiny surface

pat·i·o /ˈpætɪəʊ ‖ -tiʊʊ/ n **-os** stone-floored space next to a house, for sitting out on in fine weather

pa·tois /ˈpætwɑː/ n **-tois** /-twɑːz/ [C;U] local form of speech

pa·tri·arch /ˈpeɪtriɑːk ‖ -ɑːrk/ n 1 old and much-respected man 2 chief BISHOP of the Eastern Churches **~al** /ˌpeɪtriˈɑːkəl◂ ‖ -ˈɑːr-/ adj 1 ruled only by men 2 of a patriarch

pat·ri·ot /ˈpætriət, -triɒt, ˈpeɪ-‖

'peɪtrɪət, -trɪɑːt/ *n* someone who loves their country ~**ism** *n* [U] ~**ic** /ˌpætriˈɒtɪk◄, ˌpeɪ-‖ˌpeɪtriˈɑːtɪk◄/ *adj* ~**ically** /-kli/ *adv*

pa·trol /pəˈtrəʊl‖-troʊl/ *n* 1 [U] (period of) patrolling: *warships on patrol in the Channel* 2 [C] small group on patrol ♦ *vi/t* go round (an area, building, etc.) repeatedly to see there is no trouble

pa·tron /ˈpeɪtrən/ *n* 1 person who gives money for support: *a patron of the arts* 2 *fml* customer in a shop, pub, etc., esp. regularly ~**age** /ˈpætrənɪdʒ/ *n* [U] 1 support given by a PATRON (1) 2 right to appoint people to important positions

pat·ron·ize , **-ise** /ˈpætrənaɪz‖ˈpeɪ-, ˈpæ-/ *vt* 1 act towards (someone) as if you were better or more important than them 2 *fml* be a PATRON of (2)

patron saint /ˌ·· ˈ·/ *n* SAINT giving special protection to a particular place, activity, etc.

pat·ter¹ /ˈpætə‖-ər/ *vi*, *n* (run with or make) the sound of something striking lightly, quickly, and repeatedly

patter² *n* [U] fast continuous amusing talk

pat·tern /ˈpætn‖ˈpætərn/ *n* 1 regularly repeated arrangement, esp. with a decorative effect: *cloth with a pattern of red and white squares* 2 way in which something develops: *the usual pattern of the illness* 3 shape used as a guide for making something: *a dress pattern* ♦ *vt* 1 make a decorative pattern on 2 make according to a PATTERN (3)

paunch /pɔːntʃ‖pɔːntʃ/ *n* fat stomach ~**y** *adj*

pau·per /ˈpɔːpə‖ˈpɔːpər/ *n* very poor person

pause /pɔːz‖pɔːz/ *n* short but noticeable break in activity, speech, etc. ♦ *vi* make a pause

pave /peɪv/ *vt* 1 cover with a hard level surface, esp. of PAVING STONES 2 **pave the way (for/to)** prepare for or make possible

pave·ment /ˈpeɪvmənt/ *n* BrE paved path at the side of a road

pa·vil·ion /pəˈvɪljən/ *n* 1 esp. BrE building beside a sports field, for the players and watchers 2 large public building usu. put up for only a short time, used for EXHIBITIONS, etc.

pav·ing /ˈpeɪvɪŋ/ *n* 1 [U] (material for making) a paved surface 2 [C] paving stone

paving stone /ˈ·· ·/ *n* flat stone for making pavements, etc.

paw /pɔː‖pɔː/ *n* 1 animal's foot with CLAWS 2 *infml* human hand: *Keep your paws off me!* ♦ *vi/t* 1 (of an animal) touch or strike with the foot 2 handle rudely or roughly

pawn¹ /pɔːn‖pɔːn/ *n* 1 least valuable piece in CHESS 2 unimportant person used for someone else's advantage

pawn² *vt* leave with a pawnbroker in return for money lent ♦ *n* [U]: *My watch is in pawn.*

pawn·bro·ker /ˈpɔːnˌbrəʊkə‖ˈpɔːn-ˌbroʊkər/ *n* person who lends money in return for things one brings, which he keeps if one does not repay the money

pay /peɪ/ *v* **paid** /peɪd/ 1 *vi/t* give (money) to (someone) in return for goods bought, work done, etc. 2 *vt* settle (a bill, debt, etc.) 3 *vi/t* be profitable (to); be worth the trouble (to): *It doesn't pay (you) to argue with him.* 4 *vt* give, offer, or make: *Pay attention to what I say.* | *We paid them a visit.* 5 **pay one's way** pay money for things as one buys them so as not to get into debt 6 **pay through the nose (for)** *infml* pay far too much (for) ♦ *n* [U] 1 money received for work 2 **in the pay of** employed by ~**er** *n*

pay back *phr vt* 1 return (what is owing) to (someone) 2 return bad treatment, rudeness, etc. to

pay for *phr vt* receive suffering or punishment for

pay off *phr v* 1 *vt* pay all of (a debt) 2 *vt* pay and dismiss 3 *vt* pay (someone) to keep silent about a wrong act 4 *vi* be successful

pay out *phr v* 1 *vi/t* make (a large payment) 2 *vt* allow (a rope) to be pulled out gradually

pay up *phr vi* pay a debt in full, esp. unwillingly or late

pay·a·ble /ˈpeɪəbəl/ *adj* that must or can be paid

pay dirt /ˈ· ·/ *n* [U] AmE valuable discovery

pay·ee /peɪˈiː/ *n tech* person to whom money is or should be paid

pay·load /ˈpeɪləʊd‖-loʊd/ *n* amount carried in a vehicle, esp. a spacecraft

pay·mas·ter /ˈpeɪˌmɑːstə‖-ˌmæstər/ *n* person who pays someone, and can therefore control their actions

pay·ment /'peɪmənt/ n 1 [U] act of paying 2 [C] amount of money (to be) paid —see also BALANCE OF PAYMENTS, DOWN PAYMENT

pay·off /'peɪɒf ‖ -ɔːf/ n 1 payment made to settle matters 2 ending to something, when everything is explained

pay pack·et /'· ‚·/ n (envelope containing) wages

pay·roll /'peɪrəʊl ‖ -roʊl/ n 1 list of workers employed 2 wages paid in a particular company

PC[1] /ˌpiː 'siː/ n abbrev. for: 1 personal computer; small computer used by one person at a time 2 BrE police constable; policeman of the lowest rank

PC[2] adj abbrev. for: POLITICALLY CORRECT

PE /ˌpiː 'iː/ n [U] abbrev. for: physical education; development of the body by games, exercises, etc.

pea /piː/ n large round green seed used as food

peace /piːs/ n [U] 1 period free of war 2 calmness; quietness 3 good order in a country: The job of the police is to keep the peace. 4 lack of anxiety: peace of mind 5 hold one's peace remain silent 6 make one's peace with settle a quarrel with ~ful adj 1 quiet; untroubled 2 without war ~fully adv ~fulness n [U]

peace·keep·ing /'piːsˌkiːpɪŋ/ adj (of military forces/activities) intended to stop the fighting in an area where there is war

peace·time /'piːstaɪm/ n [S] time when a nation is not at war

peach /piːtʃ/ n round soft juicy yellowish-red fruit

pea·cock /'piːkɒk ‖ -kɑːk/ n large bird with long beautifully coloured tail feathers

peak /piːk/ n 1 highest point, level, etc. 2 sharply pointed mountain top 3 part of a cap which sticks out in front ♦ adj highest; greatest: at peak fitness ♦ vi reach a PEAK (1)

peal /piːl/ n 1 loud long sound: peals of laughter 2 sound of bells ringing ♦ vi (of a bell) ring loudly

pea·nut /'piːnʌt/ n nut that grows in a shell underground **peanuts** n [P] sl very little money

pear /peə ‖ per/ n sweet, juicy fruit, narrow at the stem end and wide at the other

pearl /pɜːl ‖ pɜːrl/ n round silvery-white jewel formed in the shell of OYSTERS

peas·ant /'pezənt/ n 1 person who works on the land in a poor country or in former times 2 infml derog uneducated or bad-mannered person

peas·ant·ry /'pezəntri/ n all the PEASANTS (1) in a place

peat /piːt/ n [U] partly decayed plant material in the earth, used for growing things or burning ~y adj

peb·ble /'pebəl/ n small stone —**bly** adj

pe·can /pɪ'kæn, 'piːkən ‖ pɪ'kɑːn, -'kæn/ n type of nut that can be eaten

pec·ca·dil·lo /ˌpekə'dɪləʊ ‖ -loʊ/ n -loes or -los unimportant wrongdoing

peck /pek/ v 1 (of a bird) strike with the beak 2 vt kiss hurriedly ♦ n 1 stroke or mark made by pecking 2 hurried kiss

pecking or·der /'·· ‚·/ n social order, showing who is more and less important

peck·ish /'pekɪʃ/ adj slightly hungry

pe·cu·li·ar /pɪ'kjuːlɪə ‖ -ər/ adj 1 strange, esp. in a displeasing way 2 belonging only to a particular place, time, etc.: a plant peculiar to these islands 3 rather mad 4 rather ill ~**ly** adv 1 especially 2 strangely ~**ity** /pɪˌkjuːli'ærʌti/ n 1 [U] being peculiar 2 [C] something PECULIAR (2) 3 [C] strange or unusual habit, etc.

ped·a·gog·i·cal /ˌpedə'gɒdʒɪkəl ‖ -'gɑː-, -'goʊ-/ adj of teaching or the study of teaching methods ~**ly** /-kli/ adv

ped·a·gogue /'pedəgɒg ‖ -gɑːg/ n teacher who is too much concerned with rules

ped·al /'pedl/ n part pushed with the foot to drive or control a machine: a bicycle pedal ♦ v -ll- BrE ‖ -l- AmE 1 vi work pedals 2 vi/t ride (a bicycle)

ped·ant /'pednt/ n person who overvalues small details and formal rules ~**ic** /pɪ'dæntɪk/ adj ~**ically** /-kli/ adv

ped·dle /'pedl/ vt try to sell by going from place to place

ped·dler /'pedlə ‖ -ər/ n person who peddles illegal drugs

ped·es·tal /'pedʌstl/ n 1 base on which a pillar or STATUE stands 2 put someone on a pedestal treat someone as better or nobler than anyone else

pe·des·tri·an[1] /pʌ'destriən/ n walker

pedestrian[2] 1 dull and ordinary 2 for pedestrians: a pedestrian crossing

pe·di·at·rics, paediatrics /ˌpiːdiˈætrɪks/ *n* [U] branch of medicine concerned with children –**rician** /ˌpiːdiəˈtrɪʃən/ *n* children's doctor

ped·i·gree /ˈpedɪɡriː/ *n* [C;U] (an official description of) the set of people or animals from whom a person or animal is descended ♦ *adj* (of an animal) specially bred from a high-quality family of animals

pee /piː/ *vi infml for* URINATE ♦ *n infml* 1 [S] act of peeing 2 [U] URINE

peek /piːk/ *vi, n* (take) a quick look

peel /piːl/ *v* 1 *vt* remove (the outer covering) from (esp. a fruit or vegetable): (fig.) *They peeled off their clothes and jumped in the water.* 2 *vi* come off in small pieces: *My skin is peeling.* 3 **keep one's eyes peeled** keep careful watch ♦ *n* [U] outer covering of fruits and vegetables

peep[1] /piːp/ *vi, n* (take) a quick often secret look

peep[2] *n* 1 [C] short weak high sound 2 [S] sound, esp. something spoken

peer[1] /pɪə ‖ pɪr/ *n* 1 lord or lady 2 *fml* one's equal in rank, quality, etc.

peer[2] *vi* look very carefully or hard: *peering through the mist*

peer·age /ˈpɪərɪdʒ ‖ ˈpɪr-/ *n* 1 rank of a PEER[1] (1) 2 all the PEERS[1] (1)

peeve /piːv/ *vt* annoy

peev·ish /ˈpiːvɪʃ/ *adj* bad-tempered ~**ly** *adv* ~**ness** *n* [U]

peg[1] /peɡ/ *n* short piece of wood, metal, etc. for fastening things, hanging things on, etc.

peg[2] *vt* -gg- fasten with a peg: (fig.) *Prices have been pegged at this year's levels.* —see also **at level pegging** (LEVEL[1])

peg out *phr vi infml, esp. BrE* die

pe·jo·ra·tive /pɪˈdʒɒrətɪv ‖ -ˈdʒɔː-, -ˈdʒɑː-/ *adj* (of a word or expression) saying that something is bad or worthless

pe·kin·ese /ˌpiːkɪˈniːz◀/ *n* small dog with long silky hair

pel·i·can /ˈpelɪkən/ *n* **pelicans** *or* **pelican** large water bird with a large beak in which it stores fish to eat

pelican cross·ing /ˈˌˌ ˈˌ◀/ *n* (in Britain) place where PEDESTRIANS[2] wishing to cross the road can stop the traffic by working special TRAFFIC LIGHTS

pel·let /ˈpelɪt/ *n* 1 small ball of soft material 2 small metal ball fired from a gun

pel·met /ˈpelmɪt/ *n esp. BrE* strip above a window to hide curtain tops

pelt[1] /pelt/ *v* 1 *vt* attack by throwing things 2 *vi* (of rain) fall very heavily 3 *vi* run very fast ♦ *n* (**at**) **full pelt** very fast

pelt[2] *n* animal's skin with its fur

pel·vis /ˈpelvɪs/ *n* bowl-shaped frame of bones at the base of the SPINE –**vic** *adj*

pen[1] /pen/ *n* instrument for writing with ink

pen[2] *n* enclosed piece of land for keeping animals in ♦ *vt* -**nn**- shut in a pen or small space

pe·nal /ˈpiːnl/ *adj* of or being legal punishment, esp. in prison

pe·nal·ize , -**ise** /ˈpiːnəl-aɪz ‖ ˈpiː-, ˈpe-/ *vt* put in an unfavourable or unfair situation

pen·al·ty /ˈpenlti/ *n* 1 punishment or disadvantage suffered, esp. for doing wrong 2 (in sports) disadvantage suffered by a player or team for breaking a rule

pen·ance /ˈpenəns/ *n* [U] willing self-punishment, to show one is sorry for doing wrong

pence /pens/ *n pl. of* PENNY

pen·chant /ˈpɒnʃɒn, ˈpentʃənt ‖ ˈpentʃɑːnt/ *n* liking for something

pen·cil[1] /ˈpensəl/ *n* narrow pointed writing instrument containing a thin stick of black material

pencil *v* -**ll**- *BrE* ‖ -**l**- *AmE* **pencil in** *phr vi* include for now, with the possibility of being changed later

pen·dant /ˈpendənt/ *n* hanging piece of jewellery, esp. round the neck

pend·ing /ˈpendɪŋ/ *adj* waiting to be decided ♦ *prep* until

pen·du·lous /ˈpendjʊləs ‖ -dʒə-/ *adj fml* hanging down loosely

pen·du·lum /ˈpendjʊləm ‖ -dʒə-/ *n* weight hanging so as to swing freely, esp. as used to control a clock

pen·e·trate /ˈpenɪtreɪt/ *v* 1 *vi/t* go (into or through): *The knife didn't penetrate his skin.* 2 *vt* see into or through –**trating** *adj* 1 (of sight, a question, etc.) sharp and searching 2 able to understand clearly and deeply –**tration** /ˌpenɪˈtreɪʃən/ *n* [U] 1 act of penetrating 2 ability to understand clearly and deeply

pen friend /ˈˌ ˈ/ *n usu.* foreign friend that you write to but have usu. never met

pen·guin /'peŋgwɨn/ n black-and-white seabird of the ANTARCTIC that cannot fly

pen·i·cil·lin /ˌpenɨ'sɪlɨn/ n [U] medicine that kills bacteria

pe·nin·su·la /pɨ'nɪnsjɨlɨ ‖ -sələ/ n piece of land almost surrounded by water

pe·nis /'piːnɨs/ n male sex organ

pen·i·tent /'penɨtɨnt/ adj feeling sorry and intending not to do wrong again –**tence** n [U]

pen·i·ten·tia·ry /ˌpenɨ'tenʃəri/ n prison, esp. in the US

pen·knife /'pen-naɪf/ n -**knives** /-naɪvz/ small knife with a folding blade

pen name /'· ·/ n false name used by a writer instead of his/her real name

pen·nant /'penənt/ n long narrow pointed flag

pen·ni·less /'penɪlɨs/ adj having no money

pen·ny /'peni/ n pennies or pence /pens/ 1 British coin worth 1/100th of a pound 2 **a pretty penny** a rather large amount of money 3 **in for a penny, in for a pound** if something has been begun it should be finished whatever the cost may be 4 **spend a penny** infml URINATE 5 **the penny (has) dropped** BrE infml the meaning (of something said) has at last been understood

penny-far·thing /ˌpeni 'faːðɪŋ ‖ -'faːr-/ n bicycle with a very large front wheel and very small back wheel

pen·sion¹ /'penʃən/ n money paid regularly to someone who can no longer earn (enough) money by working esp. because of old age or illness ~**er** n person receiving a pension

pension² v **pension off** phr vt dismiss from work and pay a pension to

pen·si·on³ /'pɒnsɪɒn ‖ ˌpaːnsi'oʊn/ n house in a non-English speaking country where one can get a room and meals

pen·sive /'pensɪv/ adj deeply or sadly thoughtful ~**ly** adv ~**ness** n [U]

pen·ta·gon /'pentəgən ‖ -gaːn/ n 1 [C] five-sided shape 2 [the+S] (cap.) building from which the US army, navy, etc. are controlled

pen·tath·lon /pen'tæθlən/ n sports event in which the competitors take part in five different sports

pent·house /'penthaʊs/ n set of rooms built on top of a tall building

pent up /ˌ· '·◄/ adj not allowed to be free or freely expressed: pent-up emotions

pe·nul·ti·mate /pɪ'nʌltɨmɨt/ adj next to the last

pen·u·ry /'penjʊri/ n fml being very poor –**rious** /pɨ'njʊəriəs ‖ -'nʊr-/ adj

peo·ple /'piːpəl/ n 1 [P] persons other than oneself; persons in general: How many people were at the meeting? | That sort of thing annoys people. 2 [(the)P] all the ordinary members of a nation 3 [C] race; nation: the peoples of Africa 4 [P] persons from whom one is descended ♦ vt 1 live in (a place) 2 fill with PEOPLE (1)

pep¹ /pep/ n [U] infml keen activity and forcefulness

pep² v -**pp- pep up** sl make more active or interesting

pep·per¹ /'pepə ‖ -ər/ n 1 [U] hot-tasting powder made from the fruit (**peppercorns**) of a tropical plant 2 [C] hollow slightly hot-tasting vegetable: green peppers

pepper² vt hit repeatedly with shots

pep·per·mint /'pepə-mɪnt ‖ -ər-/ n 1 MINT¹ (2) plant with a special strong taste 2 [C] sweet with this taste

pep talk /'· ·/ n talk intended to make people work harder, more quickly, etc.

per /pə; strong pɜː ‖ pər; strong pɜːr/ prep 1 for each: apples at 90 pence per kilo 2 infml according to: as per your instructions

per an·num /pər 'ænəm/ adv each year

per·ceive /pə'siːv ‖ pər-/ vt fml (come to) have knowledge of, esp. by seeing or understanding

per cap·i·ta /pə 'kæpɨtə ‖ pər-/ adj, adv fml for each person in the population

per cent /pə'sent ‖ pər-/ n, adv, adj (one part) in or for each 100: a 10 per cent pay increase

per·cen·tage /pə'sentɨdʒ ‖ pər-/ n 1 [C] number stated as if it is part of a whole which is 100: a high percentage of babies 2 [U] infml advantage; profit

per·cep·ti·ble /pə'septɨbəl ‖ pər-/ adj fml noticeable –**bly** adv

per·cep·tion /pə'sepʃən ‖ pər-/ n [U] fml 1 action of perceiving 2 keen natural understanding

per·cep·tive /pə'septɪv ‖ pər-/ adj having or showing PERCEPTION (2) –**ly** adv

perch /pɜːtʃ ‖ pɜːrtʃ/ n 1 branch, rod, etc. where a bird sits 2 high position or place ♦

v **1** *vi* (of a bird) sit **2** *vi/t* put or be in a high or unsafe place: *a house perched on top of the cliff*

per·cip·i·ent /pəˈsɪpiənt ‖ pər-/ *adj fml* perceptive **-ence** *n* [U]

per·co·late /ˈpɜːkəleɪt ‖ ˈpɜːr-/ *vi* pass slowly through a material with small holes: (fig.) *The news gradually percolated through to us.* **-lator** *n* pot in which coffee is made by hot water percolating through the crushed beans

per·cus·sion /pəˈkʌʃən ‖ pər-/ *n* [U] musical instruments played by being struck: *The drum is a percussion instrument.*

per·di·tion /pəˈdɪʃən ‖ pər-/ *n* [U] *fml* everlasting punishment after death

pe·remp·to·ry /pəˈremptəri/ *adj fml* **1** impolitely quick and unfriendly **2** (of a command) that must be obeyed **-rily** *adv*

pe·ren·ni·al /pəˈreniəl/ *adj* **1** lasting forever or for a long time **2** (of a plant) living for more than two years ♦ *n* perennial plant **-ly** *adv*

per·fect¹ /ˈpɜːfɪkt ‖ ˈpɜːr-/ *adj* **1** of the very best possible kind, standard, etc. **2** as good or suitable as possible: *Your English is almost perfect.* **3** with nothing missing; full: *a perfect set of teeth* **4** complete: *a perfect fool* **5** *gram* expressing an action that has happened and finished: *The perfect tense is formed with 'have' in English.* **~ly** *adv*

per·fect² /pəˈfekt ‖ pər-/ *vt* make perfect **~ible** *adj*

per·fec·tion /pəˈfekʃən ‖ pər-/ *n* [U] **1** being perfect **2** making perfect **3** perfect example: *His performance was sheer perfection.*

per·fec·tion·ist /pəˈfekʃənɪst ‖ pər-/ *n* someone not satisfied with anything not perfect

per·fid·i·ous /pəˈfɪdiəs ‖ pər-/ *adj fml* disloyal **-ly** *adv* **~ness** *n* [U]

per·fo·rate /ˈpɜːfəreɪt ‖ ˈpɜːr-/ *vt* **1** make a hole through **2** make a line of holes in (paper) to make it easier to tear **-ration** /ˌpɜːfəˈreɪʃən ‖ ˌpɜːr-/ *n* [C;U]

per·form /pəˈfɔːm ‖ pərˈfɔːrm/ *v* **1** *vt* do (a piece of work, ceremony, etc.): *to perform an operation* **2** *vi/t* act or show (a play, piece of music, etc.), esp. in public **3** *vi* work or carry out an activity (in the stated way): *a car that performs well on hills* **~ance** *n* **1** [U]

action or manner of performing **2** [C] (public) show of music, a play, etc. **~er** *n* actor, musician, etc.

per·fume /ˈpɜːfjuːm ‖ ˈpɜːr-/ *n* [C;U] (liquid having) a sweet smell ♦ /ˈpɜːfjuːm ‖ pərˈfjuːm/ *vt* cause to smell sweet

per·func·to·ry /pəˈfʌŋktəri ‖ pər-/ *adj fml* done hastily and without interest or care

per·haps /pəˈhæps, præps ‖ pər-, præps/ *adv* it may be; possibly

per·il /ˈperəl/ *n* [C;U] (something that causes) great danger **~ous** *adj*

pe·rim·e·ter /pəˈrɪmɪtə ‖ -ər/ *n* (length of) the border round an enclosed area, esp. a camp or airfield

pe·ri·od¹ /ˈpɪəriəd ‖ ˈpɪr-/ *n* **1** stretch of time **2** division of a school day **3** monthly flow of blood from a woman's body **~ic** /ˌpɪəriˈɒdɪk◀ ‖ ˌpɪriˈɑː-/ *adj* repeated and regular **~ical** *n* magazine that comes out regularly **~ically** /-kli/ *adv*

period² *adv infml* (used at end of a sentence) and that is all I'm going to say on the matter: *I'm not going, period.*

pe·ri·o·di·cal /ˌpɪəriˈɒdɪkəl ‖ ˌpɪriˈɑː-/ *n* magazine (on a technical subject)

per·i·pa·tet·ic /ˌperɪpəˈtetɪk◀/ *adj fml* travelling about, esp. to work

pe·riph·e·ry /pəˈrɪfəri/ *n* outside edge **-ral** *adj* **1** on the periphery **2** slight: *of peripheral interest*

per·i·scope /ˈperɪskəʊp ‖ -skoʊp/ *n* long tube with mirrors so that people lower down can see what is above them, esp. in SUBMARINES

per·ish /ˈperɪʃ/ *vi fml* **1** die **2** (cause to) decay or lose natural qualities **~able** *adj* (of food) that will decay quickly **~ing, ~ed** *adj* very cold

per·jure /ˈpɜːdʒə ‖ ˈpɜːrdʒər/ *vt* **perjure oneself** tell lies in a court of law **-jury** *n* [U] lying in court

perk¹ /pɜːk ‖ pɜːrk/ *n* money, goods, etc. that one gets from an employer in addition to one's pay: *Having Tuesdays free is one of the perks of the job.*

perk² *v* **perk up** *phr vi/t* make or become more cheerful

perk·y /ˈpɜːki ‖ ˈpɜːrki/ *adj* confidently cheerful **-iness** *n* [U]

perm /pɜːm ‖ pɜːrm/ *n BrE* act of putting artificial curls into hair using chemicals

♦ *vt*

per·ma·nent /'pɜːmənənt ‖ 'pɜːr-/ *adj* lasting a long time or for ever **~ly** *adv* **~ence** *n* [U]

per·me·a·ble /'pɜːmiəbəl ‖ 'pɜːr-/ *adj* that can be permeated

per·me·ate /'pɜːmieɪt ‖ 'pɜːr-/ *vt* spread or pass through or into every part of

per·mis·si·ble /pə'mɪsɪbəl ‖ pər-/ *adj fml* allowed **–bly** *adv*

per·mis·sion /pə'mɪʃən ‖ pər-/ *n* [U] act of allowing

per·mis·sive /pə'mɪsɪv ‖ pər-/ *adj* allowing (too) much freedom, esp. in sexual matters **~ly** *adv* **~ness** *n* [U]

per·mit¹ /pə'mɪt ‖ pər-/ *vi/t* **-tt-** allow

per·mit² /'pɜːmɪt ‖ 'pɜːr-/ *n* offical paper allowing something

per·mu·ta·tion /ˌpɜːmjʊ'teɪʃən ‖ ˌpɜːr-/ *n* one of the possible ways of arranging things

per·ni·cious /pə'nɪʃəs ‖ pər-/ *adj fml* very harmful **~ly** *adv* **~ness** *n* [U]

per·nick·e·ty /pə'nɪkɪti ‖ pər-/ *adj* worrying too much about small things

per·pen·dic·u·lar /ˌpɜːpən'dɪkjəl◄ ‖ ˌpɜːrpən'dɪkjələr◄/ *adj* 1 exactly upright 2 at an angle of 90° to another line or surface ♦ *n* [C;U] perpendicular line or position

per·pe·trate /'pɜːpɪtreɪt ‖ 'pɜːr-/ *vt fml* be guilty of **–trator** *n*

per·pet·u·al /pə'petʃuəl ‖ pər-/ *adj* lasting (as if) for ever **~ly** *adv*

per·pet·u·ate /pə'petʃueɪt ‖ pər-/ *vt fml* make (something) continue to exist for a long time **–ation** /pəˌpetʃu'eɪʃən ‖ pər-/ *n* [U]

per·pe·tu·i·ty /ˌpɜːpɪ'tjuːɪti ‖ ˌpɜːrpɪ'tuː-/ *n* in perpetuity *fml* for ever

per·plex /pə'pleks ‖ pər-/ *vt* make (someone) feel confused by being difficult to understand: *a perplexing problem* **~ity** *n* [U]

per se /ˌpɜː 'seɪ ‖ ˌpɜːr 'siː, ˌpɜːr 'seɪ, ˌper 'seɪ/ *adv* considered alone and not in connection with other things

per·se·cute /'pɜːsɪkjuːt ‖ 'pɜːr-/ *vt* 1 cause to suffer, esp. for religious beliefs 2 trouble or harm continually **–cutor** *n* **–cution** /ˌpɜːsɪ'kjuːʃən ‖ ˌpɜːr-/ *n* [C;U]

per·se·vere /ˌpɜːsɪ'vɪə ‖ ˌpɜːrsɪ'vɪr/ *vi* continue firmly in spite of difficulties **–verance** *n* [U]

per·sist /pə'sɪst ‖ pər-/ *vi* 1 continue firmly in spite of opposition or warning: *Do not persist in this unwise action.* 2 continue to exist **~ent** *adj* persisting: *persistent rudeness/coughing* **~ently** *adv* **~ence** *n* [U]

per·son /'pɜːsən ‖ 'pɜːr-/ *n* 1 single human being 2 *gram* form of verb or PRONOUN, showing the speaker (**first person**), the one spoken to (**second person**), or the one spoken about (**third person**) 3 in person personally; oneself 4 on/about one's person carried around with one

per·so·na /pə'səʊnə ‖ pər'soʊ-/ *n* outward character a person takes on

per·son·a·ble /'pɜːsənəbəl ‖ 'pɜːr-/ *adj fml* attractive

per·son·age /'pɜːsənɪdʒ ‖ 'pɜːr-/ *n* character in a play or book, or in history

per·son·al /'pɜːsənəl ‖ 'pɜːr-/ *adj* 1 of, for, or by a particular person: *It's a personal* (=private) *matter.* 2 rude 3 *fml* of the body: *personal cleanliness* **~ly** *adv* 1 directly and not through a representative 2 giving one's own opinion 3 privately

personal col·umn /'··· ˌ··/ *n* part of a newspaper that gives or asks for messages, news, etc. about particular people

personal com·pu·ter /ˌ··· ·'··/ *n* PC¹ (1)

per·son·al·i·ty /ˌpɜːsə'nælɪti ‖ ˌpɜːr-/ *n* 1 [C;U] whole nature or character of a person 2 [U] unusual, strong, exciting character: *She's got lots of personality.* 3 [C] well-known person

personality cult /-'··· ˌ·/ *n* practice of giving too great admiration to a particular person, esp. a political leader

per·son·a·lize also **-ise** *BrE* /'pɜːsənəlaɪz ‖ 'pɜːr-/ *vt* 1 make suitable for a particular person 2 mark with the owner's name 3 consider in a personal, not general, way

personal or·gan·i·zer , **-iser** /ˌ··· '····/ *n* small computer or book with loose pages, for recording addresses, times of meetings, etc.

personal pro·noun /ˌ··· '·/ *n* PRONOUN showing the PERSON (2), such as *I* or *you*

personal ster·e·o /ˌ··· '···/ *n* small machine for playing CASSETTES, which has EARPHONES and is carried around with the user

per·son·i·fy /pə'sɒnɪfaɪ ‖ pər'sɑː-/ *vt* 1 be a good example of (a quality)

2 represent as being human –**fication** /pə₁sɒnɪfɪ'keɪʃən ‖ pər₁sɑː-/ n [C;U]

per·son·nel /₁pɜːsə'nel ‖ ₁pɜːr-/ n 1 [P] all employed people in a company, army, etc. 2 [U] department that deals with these people and their problems

per·spec·tive /pə'spektɪv ‖ pər-/ n 1 [U] effect of depth, distance, and solidity in drawing and painting 2 [C;U] proper relationship of each part of a matter: *We must get the problem in perspective; it's not really that serious.*

per·spex /'pɜːspeks ‖ 'pɜːr-/ n [U] strong glasslike plastic

per·spire /pə'spaɪə ‖ pər'spaɪr/ vi fml for SWEAT –**spiration** /₁pɜːspə'reɪʃən ‖ ₁pɜːr-/ n [U] fml 1 SWEAT 2 act of sweating

per·suade /pə'sweɪd ‖ pər-/ vt make (someone) do something by reasoning, arguing, begging, etc.

per·sua·sion /pə'sweɪʒən ‖ pər-/ n 1 [U] (skill in) persuading 2 [C] particular belief: *her political persuasions*

per·sua·sive /pə'sweɪsɪv ‖ pər-/ adj able to persuade others ~**ly** adv ~**ness** n [U]

pert /pɜːt ‖ pɜːrt/ adj amusingly disrespectful ~**ly** adv ~**ness** n [U]

per·tain /pə'teɪn ‖ pər-/ v **pertain to** phr vt fml be about or connected with

per·ti·na·cious /₁pɜːtɪ'neɪʃəs◄ ‖ ₁pɜːr-/ adj fml holding firmly to an opinion or action

per·ti·nent /'pɜːtɪnənt ‖ 'pɜːr-/ adj fml directly connected; RELEVANT ~**ly** adv –**nence** n [U]

per·turb /pə'tɜːb ‖ pər'tɜːrb/ vt fml worry –**ation** /₁pɜːtə'beɪʃən ‖ ₁pɜːrtər-/ n [U]

pe·ruse /pə'ruːz/ vt fml read carefully **perusal** n [C;U]

per·vade /pə'veɪd ‖ pər-/ vt fml spread all through

per·va·sive /pə'veɪsɪv ‖ pər-/ adj pervading; widespread ~**ly** adv ~**ness** n [U]

per·verse /pə'vɜːs ‖ pər'vɜːrs/ adj 1 purposely doing wrong or unreasonable things 2 awkward and annoying ~**ly** adv

per·ver·sion /pə'vɜːʃən, -ʒən ‖ pər-'vɜːrʒən/ n 1 [C] perverted form of what is true, reasonable, etc. 2 [C] unnatural sexual act 3 [U] act of perverting

per·ver·si·ty /pə'vɜːsɪti ‖ pər'vɜːr-/ n 1 [U] being perverse 2 [C] perverse act

per·vert¹ /pə'vɜːt ‖ pər'vɜːrt/ vt 1 lead into wrong or unnatural (sexual) behaviour 2 use for a bad purpose

per·vert² /'pɜːvɜːt ‖ 'pɜːrvɜːrt/ n person who does unnatural sexual acts

pes·si·mist /'pesɪmɪst/ n person who expects bad things to happen –**mism** n [U] –**mistic** /₁pesɪ'mɪstɪk◄/ adj

pest /pest/ n 1 animal or insect that harms food products 2 annoying person

pes·ter /'pestə ‖ -ər/ vt annoy continually, esp. with demands

pes·ti·cide /'pestɪsaɪd/ n [C;U] chemical to kill PESTS (1)

pes·tle /'pesəl, 'pestl/ n instrument for crushing things in a thick bowl

pet /pet/ n 1 animal kept as a companion: *my pet cat* 2 person specially favoured ♦ v -tt- 1 vi kiss and touch sexually 2 vt touch lovingly

pet·al /'petl/ n coloured leaflike part of a flower

pet·er /'piːtə ‖ -ər/ v **peter out** phr vi gradually end

pe·tite /pə'tiːt/ adj (esp. of a woman) having a small and neat figure

pe·ti·tion /pə'tɪʃən/ n request or demand to a government, etc., signed by many people ♦ vi/t make or send a petition ~**er** n

pet name /'· ·/ n name for someone you like, instead of their real name

pet·ri·fy /'petrɪfaɪ/ vt 1 frighten extremely 2 turn into stone

pet·ro·dol·lar /'petrəʊ₁dɒlə ‖ 'petroʊ-₁dɑːlər/ n US dollar earned by the sale of oil, esp. by oil-producing countries in the Middle East

pet·rol /'petrəl/ n [U] BrE liquid obtained from petroleum and used for producing power in engines

pe·tro·le·um /pə'trəʊliəm ‖ -'troʊ-/ n [U] mineral oil obtained from below the ground

petrol sta·tion /'·· ₁··/ n BrE FILLING STATION

pet·ti·coat /'petikəʊt ‖ -koʊt/ n skirtlike undergarment

pet·ty /'peti/ adj 1 unimportant (by comparison) 2 showing a narrow and ungenerous mind –**tiness** n [U]

petty cash /₁·· '·/ n [U] money kept for small payments

petty of·fi·cer /₁·· '···◄/ n person of middle rank in the navy

pet·u·lant /'petʃ‿lənt/ adj showing childish bad temper ~ly adv —lance n [U]

pew /pjuː/ n seat in a church: (fig.) Take a pew. (=sit down)

pew·ter /'pjuːtə‖-ər/ n [U] greyish metal made from lead and tin

PG /ˌpiː 'dʒiː/ abbrev. for: parental guidance; (of a film) which may in parts be unsuitable for children

pha·lanx /'fælæŋks‖'feɪ-/ n group packed closely together, esp. for attack or defence

phal·lus /'fæləs/ n image of the male sex organ —lic adj

phan·tom /'fæntəm/ n 1 GHOST 2 something that is not really there

pha·raoh /'feərəʊ‖'ferou/ n ruler of ancient Egypt

phar·ma·ceu·ti·cal /ˌfaːməˈsjuːtɪkəl‖ˌfaːrməˈsuː-/ adj of (the making of) medicine

phar·ma·cist /'faːməsɨst‖'faːr-/ n 1 person who makes medicines 2 BrE for CHEMIST (2)

phar·ma·col·o·gy /ˌfaːməˈkɒlədʒi‖ˌfaːrməˈkaː-/ n [U] study of medicine and drugs —gist n

phar·ma·cy /'faːməsi‖'faːr-/ n 1 [C] shop where medicines are sold 2 [U] making or giving out of medicines

phase /feɪz/ n 1 stage of development 2 way the moon looks at a particular time ♦ vt arrange in separate phases

  phase in/out phr vt introduce/remove gradually

pheas·ant /'fezənt/ n large bird often shot for food

phe·nom·e·nal /fɨˈnɒmɨnəl‖-ˈnaː-/ adj very unusual ~ly adv: phenomenally strong

phe·nom·e·non /fɨˈnɒmɨnən‖fɨˈnaːmɨnaːn, -nən/ n —na /-nə/ 1 fact or event in the world as it appears or is experienced by the senses, esp. an unusual one 2 very unusual person, thing, etc.

phi·al /'faɪəl/ n small glass tube containing medicine

phi·lan·der·er /fɨˈlændərə‖-ər/ n old-fash man who has too many love affairs

phi·lan·thro·pist /fɨˈlænθrəpɨst/ n kind person who gives money to those who are poor or in trouble —py n [U] —pic /ˌfɨlən-ˈθrɒpɪk◀‖-ˈθra-/ adj

phi·lat·e·ly /fɨˈlætəli/ n [U] stamp collecting —list n

phil·is·tine /'fɨlɨstaɪn‖-stiːn/ n person who does not understand and actively dislikes art, music, beautiful things, etc.

phi·los·o·pher /fɨˈlɒsəfə‖-ˈlaːsəfər/ n 1 person who studies philosophy 2 PHILOSOPHICAL (2) person

phi·los·o·phize also **-phise** BrE /fɨˈlɒsəfaɪz‖-ˈlaː-/ vi talk or write like a philosopher

phi·los·o·phy /fɨˈlɒsəfi‖-ˈlaː-/ n 1 [U] study of the nature and meaning of existence, reality, morals, etc. 2 [C] system of thought —ophical /ˌfɨləˈsɒfɪkəl◀‖-ˈsaː-/ adj 1 of philosophy 2 accepting things with calm courage —ophically /-kli/ adv

phlegm /flem/ n [U] 1 thick liquid produced in the nose and throat 2 fml calmness

phleg·mat·ic /flegˈmætɪk/ adj calm and unexcitable ~ally /-kli/ adv

pho·bi·a /'fəʊbiə‖'fou-/ n strong (unreasonable) fear and dislike

phoe·nix /'fiːnɨks/ n imaginary bird that burnt itself up and was born again from its ashes

phone /fəʊn‖foun/ n, vi/t telephone

phone book /'·‿·/ n book with a list of all telephone numbers in an area

phone box /'·‿·/ n hut containing a public telephone

phone-in /'·‿·/ n show in which telephoned questions, etc. from the public are broadcast

pho·net·ic /fəˈnetɪk/ adj 1 of the sounds of human speech 2 (of a language) with all the sounds spelled very much as they sound ~ally /-kli/ adv

pho·net·ics /fəˈnetɪks/ n [U] study and science of speech sounds —ician /ˌfəʊnɨˈtɪʃən‖ˌfou-/ n

pho·ney /'fəʊni‖'fou-/ n, adj sl (someone or something) pretended or false

pho·nol·o·gy /fəˈnɒlədʒi‖-ˈnaː-/ n [U] study of the system of speech sounds in a language —ogical /ˌfəʊnəˈlɒdʒɪkəl◀‖ˌfəʊnəˈlaː-/ adj

phos·phate /'fɒsfeɪt‖'faːs-/ n [C;U] chemical made from phosphoric acid, esp. as used for making plants grow better

phos·pho·res·cent /ˌfɒsfəˈresənt‖ˌfaːs-/ adj shining faintly in the dark by a natural process —cence n [U]

phos·pho·rus /'fɒsfərəs ‖ 'fɑːs-/ n [U] yellowish waxlike chemical that burns when brought into the air –**phoric** /fɒs'fɒrɪk ‖ fɑːs'fɔːr-, fɑːs'fɑː-, 'fɑːsfərɪk/ adj

pho·to /'fəʊtəʊ ‖ 'foʊtoʊ/ n -tos photograph

pho·to·cop·y /'fəʊtəʊˌkɒpɪ ‖ 'foʊtəˌkɑːpi/ vi/t, n (make) a photographic copy –**pier** n

photo fin·ish /ˌ·· '··/ n very close finish to a race, etc. where a photograph is needed to show the winner

pho·to·gen·ic /ˌfəʊtəʊ'dʒenɪk◄, ˌfəʊtə'- ‖ ˌfoʊtoʊ-, -tə-/ adj that looks good when photographed

pho·to·graph /'fəʊtəɡrɑːf ‖ 'foʊtəɡræf/ n picture taken with a camera and film ♦ vt take a photograph of –**er** /fə'tɒɡrəfə ‖ -'tɑːɡrəfər/ n ~**y** n [U] art or business of producing photographs or films ~**ic** /ˌfəʊtə'ɡræfɪk◄, ˌfoʊ-/ adj

pho·to·sen·si·tive /ˌfəʊtəʊ'sensɪtɪv ‖ ˌfoʊtə'sen-/ adj changing under the action of light

pho·to·syn·the·sis /ˌfəʊtəʊ'sɪnθəsɪs ‖ ˌfoʊtə'sɪn-/ n [U] process by which plants make food using sunlight

phras·al /'freɪzəl/ adj of or being a phrase: 'Blow up' is a phrasal verb.

phrasal verb /ˌ·· '·/ n group of words that acts like a verb and consists usu. of a verb with an adverb and/or a PREPOSITION: 'Set off' and 'put up with' are phrasal verbs.

phrase /freɪz/ n 1 group of words without a FINITE verb 2 short (suitable) expression ♦ vt express in the stated way

phrase·book /'freɪzbʊk/ n book explaining foreign phrases, for use abroad

phra·se·ol·o·gy /ˌfreɪzi'ɒlədʒi ‖ -'ɑː-/ n [U] choice and use of words

phys·i·cal /'fɪzɪkəl/ adj 1 of or being matter or material things (not the mind, etc.) 2 of the body: physical strength –**ly** /-kli/ adv 1 with regard to the body 2 according to the laws of nature: physically impossible

phy·si·cian /fɪ'zɪʃən/ n fml doctor

phys·i·cist /'fɪzɪsɪst/ n person who studies or works in physics

phys·ics /'fɪzɪks/ n [U] science dealing with matter and natural forces

phys·i·ol·o·gy /ˌfɪzi'ɒlədʒi ‖ -'ɑː-/ n [U] science of how living bodies work –**gist** n

-**gical** /ˌfɪziə'lɒdʒɪkəl◄ ‖ -'ɑː-/ adj

phys·i·o·ther·a·py /ˌfɪziəʊ'θerəpi ‖ -zioʊ-/ n [U] exercises, rubbing, etc. to treat sick people –**pist** n

phy·sique /fɪ'ziːk/ n shape and quality of a person's body

pi·an·o /pi'ænəʊ ‖ -noʊ/ n -os large musical instrument with wire strings, played by pressing black and white bars

pi·az·za /pi'ætsə/ n public square, esp. in Italy

pic·co·lo /'pɪkələʊ ‖ -loʊ/ n -los small FLUTE

pick¹ /pɪk/ vt 1 choose 2 pull off from a plant: picking fruit 3 take up with the fingers, a beak, or a pointed instrument 4 remove unwanted pieces from: picking her teeth 5 steal from: I had my pocket picked. 6 open (a lock) without a key 7 cause (a fight, etc.) intentionally 8 **pick and choose** choose very carefully 9 **pick holes in** find the weak points in 10 **pick one's way** walk carefully 11 **pick someone's brains** make use of someone's knowledge ~**er** n ~**ings** n [P] additional money or profits

pick at phr vt eat (a meal) with little interest

pick off phr vt shoot one by one

pick on phr vt choose unfairly for punishment or blame

pick out phr vt 1 choose specially 2 see among others, esp. with difficulty

pick up phr v 1 vt take hold of and lift up 2 vt gather together: Pick up your toys. 3 vi/t (cause to) start again 4 vt get: I picked up a cold last week. 5 vt go and meet or collect: I'll pick you up at the station. 6 vi improve, esp. in health 7 vt become friendly with for sexual purposes 8 vt catch: The police picked up the criminals at the airport. 9 vt be able to hear or receive (on a radio)

pick² n [U] 1 choice: Take your pick! 2 best: It's the pick of the new films.

pick³ n 1 PICKAXE 2 sharp, pointed, usu. small instrument

pick·axe also -**ax** AmE /'pɪk-æks/ n large tool with two sharp points, for digging up roads, etc.

pick·et /'pɪkɪt/ n 1 person or group outside a place of work trying to persuade others not to work there during a quarrel with employers 2 soldier guarding a camp

3 strong pointed stick fixed in the ground —see also FLYING PICKET ♦ *vt* surround with or as PICKETS (1)

pick·le /'pɪkəl/ *n* **1** [U] VINEGAR or salt water for preserving foods **2** [C;U] vegetable preserved in this **3** [S] dirty, difficult, or confused condition: *in a pickle* ♦ *vt* preserve in pickle –led *adj infml* drunk

pick-me-up /'· ·ˌ·/ *n infml* something, esp. a drink or medicine, that makes one feel stronger, happier, etc.

pick·pock·et /'pɪk,pɒkɪt ‖ -ˌpɑːk-/ *n* person who steals from people's pockets

pick-up /'· ·/ *n* **1** needle and arm of a record player **2** light VAN having an open body with low sides

pic·nic /'pɪknɪk/ *n* informal outdoor meal ♦ *vi* -ck- have a picnic

pic·to·ri·al /pɪk'tɔːriəl/ *adj* having or expressed in pictures ~ly *adv*

pic·ture /'pɪktʃə‖ -ər/ *n* **1** [C] representation made by painting, drawing, or photography **2** [C] what is seen on the television screen: *We don't get a very good picture.* **3** [C] cinema film **4** [C] image in the mind **5** [S] person or thing that is beautiful **6** [S] perfect example: *He's the picture of health.* (=very healthy) **7 in the picture: a** knowing all the facts **b** receiving much attention ♦ *vt* **1** imagine: *Just picture the frightful scene.* **2** paint or draw pictures *n* [P] **1** the cinema **2** the film industry

pic·tur·esque /ˌpɪktʃə'resk◂/ *adj* **1** charming to look at **2** (of language) unusually forceful and descriptive

pid·dling /'pɪdlɪŋ/ *adj infml* small and unimportant

pid·gin /'pɪdʒɪn/ *n* language which is a mixture of other languages

pie /paɪ/ *n* baked dish of pastry filled with meat or fruit

pie·bald /'paɪbɔːld ‖ -bɒːld/ *n, adj* (horse) coloured black and white

piece[1] /piːs/ *n* **1** separate part or bit: *pieces of broken glass* **2** single object that is an example of its kind or class: *a piece of paper/music/*(fig.) *advice* **3** small object used in board games: *a chess piece* **4** BrE coin: *a 50p piece* **5 give someone a piece of one's mind** *infml* tell someone angrily what you think of them **6 go to pieces** *infml* lose the ability to think or act clearly **7 in one piece** unharmed **8 of a piece**

similar; in agreement **9 say one's piece** say what one wants to or has planned to, esp. in a way that is annoying or unwelcome to others —see also PARTY PIECE

piece[2] *v* **piece together** *phr vt* complete by finding all the bits and putting them together

pi·èce de ré·sis·tance /piːˌes də rezi:'stɑ:ns/ *n* **pièces de résistance** *(same pronunciation)* the best or most important thing or event

piece·meal /'piːsmiːl/ *adj, adv* (done) only one part at a time

piece of cake /ˌ· · '·/ *n* [S] *infml* something very easy to do

piece·work /'piːswɜːk ‖ -wɜːrk/ *n* [U] work paid for by the amount done rather than by the hours worked

pie chart /'· ˌ·/ *n* circle divided into several showing the way in which something, e.g. money or population, is divided up

pied /paɪd/ *adj* marked with different colours

pi·ed-à-terre /ˌpjeɪd æ 'teə ‖ pɪˌed ə 'ter/ *n* **pieds-à-terre** *(same pronunciation)* small additional home

pier /pɪə ‖ pɪr/ *n* **1** long structure built out into the sea, esp. with entertainments on it **2** supporting pillar

pierce /pɪəs ‖ pɪrs/ *vt* make a hole in or through with a point: (fig.) *A cry of fear pierced the silence.* **piercing** *adj* **1** (of wind) very strong and cold **2** (of sound) unpleasantly sharp and clear **3** searching: *a piercing look*

pi·e·ty /'paɪəti/ *n* [U] *fml* deep respect for God and religion

pif·fling /'pɪflɪŋ/ *adj infml* useless; worthless

pig /pɪg/ *n* **1** fat short-legged animal with no fur, kept on farms for food **2** *infml* person who is dirty or rude or eats too much **3 make a pig of oneself** *infml* eat (or drink) too much

pi·geon /'pɪdʒɪn/ *n* **1** quite large light-grey bird **2** responsibility: *It's not my pigeon.*

pi·geon·hole /'pɪdʒɪnhəʊl ‖ -hoʊl/ *n* **1** boxlike division for putting papers in **2** neat division which separates things too simply ♦ *vt* **1** put aside and do nothing about **2** put in a PIGEONHOLE (2)

pigeon-toed /ˈ·· ·/ adj having feet that point inwards

pig·gy·back /ˈpɪgibæk/ n, adv (act of) carrying someone on one's back

pig·gy·bank /ˈpɪgibæŋk/ n small usu. pig-shaped container used by children for saving coins

pig·head·ed /ˌpɪgˈhedɪd◄/ adj very unwilling to agree or obey

pig·let /ˈpɪglɪt/ n young pig

pig·ment /ˈpɪgmənt/ n 1 [C;U] dry coloured powder for making paint 2 [U] natural colouring matter in plants and animals ~**ation** /ˌpɪgmənˈteɪʃən/ n [U]

pig·my /ˈpɪgmi/ n PYGMY

pig·sty /ˈpɪgstaɪ/ n 1 small building for pigs 2 very dirty room or house

pig·swill /ˈpɪgˌswɪl/ n [U] waste food given to pigs

pig·tail /ˈpɪgteɪl/ n length of twisted hair hanging down the back

pike[1] /paɪk/ n **pikes** or **pike** large fish-eating river fish

pike[2] n long-handled spear

pil·chard /ˈpɪltʃəd ‖ -ərd/ n small sea fish, often eaten

pile[1] /paɪl/ n 1 tidy heap: a pile of books 2 also **piles** pl. — infml lots: I've got piles of work to do. 3 infml very large amount of money 4 large tall building —see also PILES ♦ v 1 vt make a pile of 2 vi come or go in a (disorderly) crowd: The children piled into the car.

pile up phr vi form into a mass or large quantity

pile[2] n [C;U] soft surface of short threads on CARPETS or cloth

pile[3] n heavy supporting post hammered into the ground

piles /paɪlz/ n [P] HEMORRHOIDS

pile-up /ˈpaɪlʌp/ n traffic accident with many vehicles

pil·fer /ˈpɪlfə ‖ -ər/ vi/t steal (small things)

pil·grim /ˈpɪlgrɪm/ n person on a journey to a holy place ~**age** n [C;U] pilgrim's journey

pill /pɪl/ n 1 [C] small ball of medicine 2 [the+S] (often cap.) pill taken as birth control

pil·lage /ˈpɪlɪdʒ/ vi/t fml steal things violently from (a place taken in war)

pil·lar /ˈpɪlə ‖ -ər/ n 1 tall upright round post, usu. of stone, used esp. as a support

for a roof 2 important member and active supporter: a pillar of the church

pillar-box /ˈ·· ·/ n BrE large round box in the street for posting letters

pill·box /ˈpɪlbɒks ‖ -bɑːks/ n 1 small round box for PILLS (1) 2 CONCRETE shelter with a gun inside it

pil·lion /ˈpɪljən/ n passenger seat on a motorcycle

pil·lo·ry /ˈpɪləri/ vt attack with words, esp. in public

pil·low /ˈpɪləʊ ‖ -loʊ/ n filled cloth bag for supporting the head in bed ♦ vt rest (esp. one's head) on something

pil·low·case /ˈpɪləʊkeɪs ‖ -loʊ-/ n cloth cover for a pillow

pi·lot /ˈpaɪlət/ n 1 person who flies a plane 2 person who guides ships into a harbour, etc. ♦ adj intended to try something out: a pilot survey ♦ vt act as the pilot of

pilot light /ˈ·· ·/ n small gas flame to light a main flame

pimp /pɪmp/ n man who controls and gets money from PROSTITUTES

pim·ple /ˈpɪmpəl/ n small raised diseased spot on the skin

pin /pɪn/ n 1 short thin pointed piece of metal for fastening things 2 AmE BROOCH 3 infml leg ♦ vt **-nn-** 1 fasten with a pin 2 keep in one position, esp. by weight from above 3 **pin one's hopes on someone** depend on someone for help, etc.

pin down phr vt 1 force to give clear details, make a firm decision, etc. 2 prevent from moving

PIN /pɪn/ n also **PIN num·ber** /ˈ· ˌ··/ abbrev. for: Personal Identification Number; secret number used when taking money from a CASHPOINT

pin·a·fore /ˈpɪnəfɔː ‖ -fɔːr/ n loose garment worn over (the front of) a dress to keep it clean

pin·cer /ˈpɪnsə ‖ -ər/ n footlike part of a CRAB, LOBSTER, etc. for seizing things

pincers n [P] tool for holding things tightly

pinch /pɪntʃ/ v 1 vt press tightly between two surfaces or between finger and thumb 2 vi hurt by being too tight 3 vt infml steal 4 vt infml for ARREST ♦ n 1 [C] act of pinching 2 [C] amount picked up with finger and thumb: a pinch of salt 3 [the+S] suffering through not having enough, esp. of money: We're beginning to feel the pinch.

4 at a pinch if necessary

pin·cush·ion /ˈpɪnˌkʊʃən/ n small filled bag for sticking pins into until needed

pine¹ /paɪn/ n tall tree with thin sharp leaves that do not drop off in winter

pine² vi **1** lose strength and health through grief **2** have a strong desire, esp. that is impossible to fulfil

pine·ap·ple /ˈpaɪnæpəl/ n [C;U] large tropical fruit with sweet juicy yellow flesh

ping /pɪŋ/ vi, n (make) a short sharp ringing sound

ping-pong /ˈ· ·/ n [U] TABLE TENNIS

pin·ion¹ /ˈpɪnjən/ vt prevent from moving by tying or holding the limbs

pinion² n small wheel fitting against a larger one for turning

pink /pɪŋk/ adj pale red ♦ n **in the pink** in perfect health

pin mon·ey /ˈ· ˌ·/ n [U] money earned by doing small jobs

pin·na·cle /ˈpɪnəkəl/ n highest point or degree: *the pinnacle of success*

pin·point /ˈpɪnpɔɪnt/ vt find or describe exactly

pins and nee·dles /ˌ· ˈ ·/ n [P] slight pricking pains in a limb

pin·stripe /ˈpɪnstraɪp/ n **1** [C] any of a pattern of parallel pale lines on dark cloth **2** [P] also **pinstripe suit** — suit made of cloth with a pattern of pinstripes

pint /paɪnt/ n **1** a measure of liquids equal to 20 fluid ounces **2** pint of beer

pin-up /ˈpɪnʌp/ n picture of an attractive or admired person such as a popular singer, esp. as stuck up on a wall

pi·o·neer /ˌpaɪəˈnɪə ‖ -ˈnɪr/ n person who does something first, preparing the way for others ♦ vt act as a pioneer in

pi·ous /ˈpaɪəs/ adj **1** having deep respect for God and religion **2** unlikely to be fulfilled: *a pious hope* ~**ly** adv

pip¹ /pɪp/ n small seed of an apple, orange, etc.

pip² n short high-sounding note, esp. as given on the radio to show the exact time

pip³ vt BrE **pipped at the post** just beaten at the end of some struggle

pipe¹ /paɪp/ n **1** tube carrying liquid or gas **2** small tube with a bowl-like container, for smoking tobacco **3** simple tubelike musical instrument **pipes** n [P] BAGPIPES

pipe² vt **1** carry in pipes **2** play music on a

PIPE (3) or PIPES **piper** n player of BAGPIPES

pipe down phr vi infml stop talking or being noisy

pipe up phr vi suddenly start to speak

piped mu·sic /ˌ· ˈ·/ n [U] quiet recorded music played continuously in public places

pipe dream /ˈ· ·/ n impossible hope, plan, or idea

pipe·line /ˈpaɪp-laɪn/ n **1** line of joined pipes, esp. for carrying oil or gas **2 in the pipeline** about to arrive or appear; being prepared

pi·pette /pɪˈpet ‖ paɪ-/ n small glass tube for sucking up and measuring liquids

pip·ing¹ /ˈpaɪpɪŋ/ n [U] PIPES¹ (1)

piping² adv **piping hot** very hot

pi·quant /ˈpiːkənt/ adj **1** having a pleasant sharp taste **2** interesting and exciting to the mind –**quancy** n [U]

pique /piːk/ n [U] annoyance and displeasure because of hurt pride ♦ vt offend

pi·ra·nha /pəˈrɑːnjə, -nə/ n fierce S. American flesh-eating river fish

pi·rate /ˈpaɪərət ‖ ˈpaɪrət/ n **1** person who sails around robbing ships **2** person who pirates things ♦ vt make and sell (a VIDEO, CD, etc.) by someone else) without permission or payment ♦ adj: *pirate videos* –**cy** n [U]

pir·ou·ette /ˌpɪruˈet/ n very fast turn on one foot by a dancer **pirouette** vi

piss¹ /pɪs/ vi taboo sl URINATE ~**ed** adj taboo sl **1** drunk **2** AmE annoyed

piss about/around phr vi taboo sl waste time; act in a foolish way

piss off phr v taboo sl **1** vi go away **2** vt annoy

piss² n [U] taboo sl **1** URINE **2 take the piss out of** make fun of

pis·ta·chi·o /pɪstəˈʃiəʊ ‖ -ˈstɑːʃiəʊ/ n small green nut that can be eaten

pis·tol /ˈpɪstl/ n small gun held in one hand

pis·ton /ˈpɪstən/ n short pipe-shaped part of an engine that goes up and down inside a tube and sends power to the engine

pit¹ /pɪt/ n **1** hole in the ground **2** coal mine **3** small hollow mark on a surface **4** space in front of a stage where musicians sit **5** esp. AmE hard central part of certain fruit **6 pit of the stomach** place where fear is thought to be felt **pits** n [P] **1** place beside the track where cars are repaired during a race **2** *infml* the worst possible example of something

pit² *vt* **-tt-** mark with PITS¹ (3)

pit against *phr vt* set against in competition or fight

pitch¹ /pɪtʃ/ *v* **1** *vt* set up (a camp or tent) **2** *vi* (of a ship or aircraft) move along with the front and back going up and down **3** *vt* set the PITCH² (2) of (a sound, music, etc.) **4** *vt* throw **5** *vi/t* (cause to) fall suddenly forwards

pitch in *phr vi* **1** start eagerly **2** add one's help or support

pitch² *n* **1** *BrE* marked-out area for playing sport **2** degree of highness and lowness of a (musical) sound **3** level; degree: *a high pitch of excitement* **4** place in a market, etc. where somebody regularly performs, sells, etc. **5** *infml* salesman's special way of talking about goods he/she is trying to sell: *a good sales pitch*

pitch³ *n* [U] black substance used for keeping out water: (fig.) a **pitch-black** (=very dark) *night*

pitched bat·tle /ˌ· ˈ··/ *n* *infml* fierce and long quarrel or argument

pitch·er¹ /ˈpɪtʃə‖-ər/ *n* **1** *BrE* large old-fashioned container for holding and pouring liquids **2** *AmE* JUG

pitch·er² *n* (in BASEBALL) player who throws the ball towards the BATTER³

pitch·fork /ˈpɪtʃfɔːk‖-fɔːrk/ *n* long-handled fork for lifting dried grass on a farm ♦ *vt* put without warning or against someone's will

pit·e·ous /ˈpɪtiəs/ *adj fml* causing pity **~ly** *adv*

pit·fall /ˈpɪtfɔːl‖-fɔːl/ *n* unexpected difficulty or danger

pith /pɪθ/ *n* [U] soft white substance in the stems of some plants and under the skin of oranges, etc. **~y** *adj* **1** full of pith **2** strongly and cleverly stated in few words

pit·i·a·ble /ˈpɪtiəbəl/ *adj* **1** deserving pity **2** PITIFUL **-bly** *adv*

pit·i·ful /ˈpɪtɪfəl/ *adj* **1** causing or deserving pity **2** worthless; weak **~ly** *adv*

pit·i·less /ˈpɪtɪləs/ *adj* merciless; cruel **~ly** *adv*

pit·tance /ˈpɪtəns/ *n* very small amount of pay or money

pi·tu·i·ta·ry /pəˈtjuːɪtəri‖pəˈtuːɪteri/ *n* small organ near the brain which helps to control growth

pit·y /ˈpɪti/ *n* **1** [U] sympathy and sorrow for others' suffering or unhappiness: *We took pity on* (=felt pity for and helped) *the homeless family.* **2** [S] unfortunate state of affairs: *It's a pity you have to go now.* **3 for pity's sake** (used to add force to a request) please **4 more's the pity** unfortunately ♦ *vt* feel pity for

piv·ot /ˈpɪvət/ *n* **1** central point on which something turns **2** most important thing in a situation ♦ *vi/t* **~al** *adj*: *Education is pivotal to success.*

pix·el /ˈpɪksəl/ *n tech* smallest unit in a computer image

pix·ie , **pixy** /ˈpɪksi/ *n* small fairy that plays tricks

piz·za /ˈpiːtsə/ *n* [C;U] flat round pastry baked with cheese, TOMATOES, etc. on top

pizz·azz /pəˈzæz/ *n* [U] *sl* exciting, forceful quality

plac·ard /ˈplækɑːd‖-ərd/ *n* board put up or carried around publicly, with information on it

pla·cate /pləˈkeɪt‖ˈpleɪkeɪt/ *vt* cause to stop feeling angry

place¹ /pleɪs/ *n* **1** [C] particular position in space: *the place where the accident happened* | (fig.) *Sport never had a place in his life.* **2** [C] particular town, building, etc.: *Is London a nice place to live in?* **3** [C] usual or proper position: *Put it back in its place.* **4** position in the result of a competition, race, etc.: *I took first place in the exam.* **5** [C] position of employment, etc.: *She got a place at university.* **6** [S] numbered point in an argument, etc.: *In the first place, I can't afford it.* **7** [S] duty: *It's not my place to tell them what to do.* **8** [S] *infml* home: *Come back to my place.* **9 go places** *infml* be increasingly successful **10 in/out of place: a** in/not in the usual or proper position **b** suitable/unsuitable **11 in place of** instead of **12 know one's place** consider oneself of low rank and behave respectfully **13 lay/set a place** put knives, forks, spoons, etc. in position on the main table (for one person) **14 put someone in his/her place** show someone that he/she is not as important as he/she would like to be **15 take place** happen **16 take the place of** act or be used instead of; REPLACE

place² vt **1** put in the stated place **2** make (an order for goods one wants to buy) **3** remember fully who (someone) is ~**ment** n [U] act or example of placing someone or something in position

pla·ce·bo /plə'si:bəʊ‖-boʊ/ n -**bos** or -**boes** substance given instead of real medicine, without the person who takes it knowing that it is not real

pla·cen·ta /plə'sentə/ n -**tas** or -**tae** /-ti:/ thick mass inside the WOMB joining the unborn child to its mother

plac·id /'plæsɪd/ adj not easily angered or excited ~**ly** adv

pla·gia·rize , -**rise** /'pleɪdʒəraɪz/ vt take (words, ideas, etc.) from (someone else's work) and use them in one's own writings without admitting that one has done so –**rism** n [C;U]

plague /pleɪg/ n **1** [C;U] quickly spreading disease that kills many people **2** [C] widespread uncontrollable mass or number: *a plague of locusts* ♦ vt trouble or annoy continually

plaice /pleɪs/ n **plaice** flat fish, often eaten

plaid /plæd/ n (piece of) thick cloth with a pattern of coloured squares

plain¹ /pleɪn/ adj **1** without decoration or pattern; simple **2** easy to see, hear, or understand **3** expressing thoughts clearly, honestly, and exactly **4** rather ugly ♦ adv completely: *plain daft* ~**ly** adv ~**ness** n [U]

plain² n large stretch of flat land

plain sail·ing /, · ' ··/ n [U] something easy to do

plain·spo·ken /,pleɪn'spəʊkən◄‖ -'spoʊ-/ adj (too) direct and honest in speech

plain·tiff /'pleɪntɪf/ n person who brings a legal charge or claim

plain·tive /'pleɪntɪv/ adj sad-sounding ~**ly** adv

plait /plæt‖ pleɪt/ vt esp. BrE twist together into a ropelike length ♦ n esp. BrE plaited length of esp. hair

plan /plæn/ n **1** arrangement for carrying out a (future) activity **2** (maplike drawing showing) an arrangement of parts in a system ♦ vi/t -**nn-** make a plan (for) ~**ner** n

plane¹ /pleɪn/ n **1** aircraft **2** level; standard: *Let's keep the conversation on a friendly plane.* **3** maths flat surface ♦ adj maths completely flat

plane² n tool with a sharp blade for making wood smooth ♦ vt use a plane on

plane³ n broad-leaved tree common in towns

plan·et /'plænɪt/ n large body in space that moves round a star, esp. the sun ~**ary** adj

plank /plæŋk/ n **1** long narrow wooden board **2** main principle of a political party's stated aims ~**ing** n [U] (floor) planks

plank·ton /'plæŋktən/ n [U] extremely small sea animals and plants

plant¹ /plɑːnt‖ plænt/ n **1** [C] living thing with leaves and roots **2** [C] factory or other industrial building **3** [U] industrial machinery **4** [C] infml **a** person placed secretly in a group in order to discover facts about them **b** thing hidden on a person to make him seem guilty

plant² vt **1** put (plants or seeds) in the ground **2** infml hide (illegal goods) on someone to make them seem guilty **3** infml put (a person) secretly in a group **4** place firmly or forcefully ~**er** n

plan·ta·tion /plæn'teɪʃən, plɑːn-‖ plæn-/ n area where large plants are grown as a business: *a rubber plantation*

plaque /plæk/ n flat metal or stone plate with writing on it, usu. fixed to a wall

plas·ma /'plæzmə/ n [U] liquid part of blood, containing the cells

plas·ter¹ /'plɑːstə‖ 'plæstər/ n **1** [U] mixture of lime, water, sand, etc. which hardens when dry **2** [C;U] (a thin band of) material that can be stuck to the skin to protect small wounds **3 in plaster** in a PLASTER CAST (2)

plaster² vt **1** put plaster on (a wall, etc.) **2** cover too thickly ~**ed** adj infml drunk ~**er** n

plaster cast /,·· '·, '·· ·/ n **1** copy of a STATUE in plaster of paris **2** case of plaster of Paris supporting a broken bone

plaster of Par·is /,plɑːstər əv 'pærɪs‖ ,plæs-/ n [U] white powder which is mixed with water to form a hard substance, used esp. for making STATUES

plas·tic /'plæstɪk/ n [C;U] light artificial material used for making various things ♦ adj fml **1** easily formed into various shapes **2** connected with the art of shaping forms in clay, wood, etc. ~**ity** /plæ'stɪsɪti/ n [U]

plas·ti·cine /'plæstɪsiːn/ n [U] tdmk

coloured claylike substance played with by children

plastic sur·ge·ry /ˌ·· ˈ···/ *n* [U] medical treatment to improve the way someone's face or body looks

plate /pleɪt/ *n* 1 [C] **a** flat dish from which food is eaten or served **b** also **plate·ful** /-fʊl/ — amount of food this will hold 2 [C] flat, thin, usu. large piece of something hard 3 [U] metal covered with gold or silver 4 [C] picture in a book, usu. coloured 5 **on a plate** with too little effort 6 **on one's plate** to deal with ♦ *vt* cover (a metal article) thinly with gold, silver, or tin

plat·eau /ˈplætəʊ ‖ plæˈtoʊ/ *n* -eaus *or* -eaux /-təʊ ‖ -toʊ/ 1 large area of level high land 2 steady unchanging level, period, or condition

plate glass /ˌ· ˈ·◄/ *n* [U] clear glass in large thick sheets

plat·form /ˈplætfɔːm ‖ -fɔːrm/ *n* 1 raised area beside the track at a railway station 2 raised floor for speakers or performers 3 main ideas and aims of a political party, esp. as stated before an election

plat·i·num /ˈplætʌnəm/ *n* [U] very valuable greyish-white metal

plat·i·tude /ˈplætʌtjuːd ‖ -tuːd/ *n* statement that is true but not new or interesting

pla·ton·ic /pləˈtɒnɪk ‖ -ˈtɑː-/ *adj* (of friendship, esp. between a man and woman) not sexual

pla·toon /pləˈtuːn/ *n* small group of soldiers

plat·ter /ˈplætə ‖ -ər/ *n* 1 *AmE for* DISH¹ (1) 2 large flat esp. wooden dish

plat·y·pus /ˈplætɪpəs/ *n* small Australian animal that has a beak and lays eggs

plau·dits /ˈplɔːdɪts ‖ ˈplɔː-/ *n* [P] show of pleased approval

plau·si·ble /ˈplɔːzʌbəl ‖ ˈplɔː-/ *adj* seeming true; believable —**bly** *adv*

play¹ /pleɪ/ *n* 1 [U] activity for fun, esp. by children 2 [C] story written to be acted 3 [U] action in a sport: *Rain stopped play.* 4 [U] action; effect: *He had to* **bring** *all his experience* **into play**. (=use it)

play² *v* 1 *vi* amuse oneself with a game, toys, etc. 2 *vi/t* produce sounds or music (from) 3 *vi/t* take part in (a sport or game) 4 *vi/t* perform (in): *Who played the part of Hamlet?* 5 *vt* plan and carry out: *They*

played a trick on me. 6 pretend to be: *Stop playing the fool!* (=being foolish) 7 *vt* strike and send (a ball) 8 *vt* place (a playing card) face upwards on the table 9 *vt* aim; direct: *The firemen played their hoses on the blaze.* 10 *vi* move lightly and quickly: *A smile played across her lips.* 11 **play ball** *infml* COOPERATE 12 **play for time** delay in order to gain time 13 **play into someone's hands** behave in a way that gives someone an advantage over one 14 **play it by ear** act according to changing conditions, rather than making fixed plans in advance 15 **play (it) safe** act so as to avoid trouble ~**er** *n* person playing a sport or a musical instrument

play along *phr vi* pretend to agree, esp. to avoid trouble

play at *phr vt* 1 PLAY² (6) 2 do in a way that is not serious

play back *phr vt* listen to or look at (something just recorded) **playback** /ˈpleɪbæk/ *n* playing of something just recorded, esp. on television

play down *phr vt* cause to seem less important

play off *phr v* 1 *vt* set (people or things) in opposition, esp. for one's own advantage 2 *vi* play another match in order to decide who wins **play-off** /ˈ· ·/ *n* second match played to decide who wins

play on *phr vt* try to use or encourage (others' feelings) for one's own advantage

play up *phr v* 1 *vi/t* cause trouble or suffering (to) 2 *vt* give special importance to

play up to *phr vt* act so as to win the favour of

play with *phr vt* 1 consider (an idea) not very seriously 2 **play with oneself** MASTURBATE 3 **to play with** that one can use; AVAILABLE

play·act /ˈ· ·/ *vi* behave with an unreal show of feeling

play·boy /ˈpleɪbɔɪ/ *n* wealthy (young) man who lives for pleasure

play·ful /ˈpleɪfəl/ *adj* 1 full of fun 2 not intended seriously ~**ly** *adv* ~**ness** *n* [U]

play·ground /ˈpleɪgraʊnd/ *n* piece of ground for children to play on

play·group /ˈpleɪgruːp/ *n* organized group where young children learn through play

playing card /ˈ·· ·/ n fml for CARD (1a)

playing field /ˈ·· ·/ n level playing field fair situation in which neither side has special advantages

play·mate /ˈpleɪmeɪt/ n child's friend who shares in games

play·pen /ˈpleɪpen/ n enclosed frame for a baby to play in

play·thing /ˈpleɪˌθɪŋ/ n 1 toy 2 person treated without consideration

play·wright /ˈpleɪraɪt/ n writer of plays

pla·za /ˈplɑːzə‖ˈplæzə/ n public square or marketplace

plc /ˌpiː el ˈsiː/ abbrev. for public LIMITED company

plea /pliː/ n 1 fml urgent or serious request 2 law statement by someone in a court saying whether they are guilty or not

plea bar·gain·ing /ˈ· ˌ··/ n [U] practice of agreeing to say in a court of law that one is guilty of a small crime in exchange for not being charged with a greater one

plead /pliːd/ v 1 vi make continual and deeply felt requests 2 vt law say officially in court that one is (guilty or not guilty) 3 vt offer as an excuse: He pleaded ignorance

pleas·ant /ˈplezənt/ adj pleasing; nice ~**ly** adv

pleas·ant·ry /ˈplezəntri/ n fml politely amusing remark

please /pliːz/ v 1 vi/t make (someone) happy or satisfied 2 vi want; like: They can appoint whoever they please. ♦ interj (used when asking politely for something) **pleased** adj happy; satisfied: Are you pleased with your new car?

plea·sur·a·ble /ˈpleʒərəbəl/ adj fml enjoyable ~**bly** adv

plea·sure /ˈpleʒə‖-ər/ n 1 [U] happy feeling; enjoyment 2 [C] something that gives one pleasure 3 [S] something that is not inconvenient and that one is pleased to do: 'Thank you for helping me.' 'My pleasure.'

pleat /pliːt/ n flattened narrow fold in cloth ♦ vt make pleats in

ple·be·ian /plɪˈbiːən/ n, adj (member) of the lower social classes

pleb·is·cite /ˈplebɪsɪt‖-saɪt/ n vote by the people of a country to decide a matter

plec·trum /ˈplektrəm/ n small piece of plastic, metal, etc. for picking the strings of a GUITAR

pledge /pledʒ/ n 1 solemn promise 2 something valuable left with someone as a sign that one will fulfil an agreement 3 something given as a sign of love ♦ vt make a solemn promise of

ple·na·ry /ˈpliːnəri/ adj fml (of powers or rights) full; limitless

plen·i·po·ten·tia·ry /ˌplenɪpəˈtenʃəri‖-ˈʃeri/ n fml official or representative with full powers

plen·ti·ful /ˈplentɪfəl/ adj in large enough quantities: plentiful supplies ~**ly** adv

plen·ty /ˈplenti/ pron as much as or more than is needed: There's plenty (of food) for everyone.

pleth·o·ra /ˈpleθərə/ n [S] fml too much

pli·a·ble /ˈplaɪəbəl/ adj 1 easily bent 2 able and willing to change; ADAPTABLE 3 PLIANT (1) ~**bility** /ˌplaɪəˈbɪlɪti/ n [U]

pli·ant /ˈplaɪənt/ adj 1 (too) easily influenced 2 PLIABLE (1) ~**ancy** n [U]

pli·ers /ˈplaɪəz‖-ərz/ n [P] small tool for holding small things or cutting wire

plight /plaɪt/ n bad or serious condition or situation

plim·soll /ˈplɪmsəl, -səʊl‖-səl, -soʊl/ n BrE light shoe with a cloth top

Plimsoll line /ˈ·· ·/ n line on a ship showing the depth to which it can go down in the water when loaded

plinth /plɪnθ/ n square block which a STATUE stands on

plod /plɒd‖plɑːd/ vi -dd- 1 walk slowly and with effort 2 work steadily, esp. at something dull ~**der** n slow, steady, not very clever worker

plonk¹ /plɒŋk‖plɑːŋk, plɔːŋk/ vt infml put, esp. heavily or with force

plonk² n [U] infml BrE cheap wine

plop /plɒp‖plɑːp/ vi, n -pp- [S] (make or fall with) a sound like something falling smoothly into liquid

plot¹ /plɒt‖plɑːt/ n 1 set of connected events on which a story is based 2 secret plan to do something bad 3 small piece of ground for building or growing things

plot² v -tt- 1 vi/t plan together secretly (something bad) 2 vt mark (the course of a ship or aircraft) on a map 3 vt mark (a line showing facts) on special paper with squares ~**ter** n

plough also **plow** AmE /plaʊ/ n farming

tool for breaking up earth and turning it over ♦ v 1 vi/t break up and turn over (earth) with a plough 2 vi go forcefully or roughly

plough back phr vt put (money earned) back into a business

ploy /plɔɪ/ n something done to gain an advantage, sometimes deceivingly

pluck[1] /plʌk/ vt 1 pull the feathers off (a bird to be cooked) 2 pull out or pick up sharply 3 play an instrument by pulling (its strings) 4 esp. lit. pick (a flower)

pluck up phr vt show (courage) in spite of fear

pluck[2] n [U] courage ~y adj brave

plug /plʌg/ n 1 small usu. round thing for blocking a hole, esp. in a bath, etc. 2 small object for connecting an apparatus with a supply of electricity 3 publicly stated favourable opinion about a product on radio, television, etc. intended to make people want to buy it ♦ vt -gg- 1 block or fill with a PLUG (1) 2 give a PLUG (3) to

plug in phr vt connect to a supply of electricity

plug·hole /'plʌghəʊl ‖ -hoʊl/ n BrE hole in a bath, etc. where a PLUG (1) fits

plum /plʌm/ n roundish usu. dark red fruit with a hard seed in the middle ♦ adj very desirable: a plum job

plum·age /'pluːmɪdʒ/ n [U] feathers on a bird

plumb[1] /plʌm/ vt 1 (try to) find the meaning of 2 **plumb the depths** reach the lowest point

plumb[2] adv exactly: plumb in the centre

plumb·er /'plʌmə ‖ -ər/ n person who fits and repairs water pipes

plumb·ing /'plʌmɪŋ/ n [U] 1 all the water pipes and containers in a building 2 work of a plumber

plumb line /'· ·/ n string with a weight on it, for finding the depth of water or whether something is upright

plume /pluːm/ n 1 (large or showy) feather 2 rising feathery shape: a plume of smoke **plumed** adj

plum·met /'plʌmɪt/ vi fall steeply or suddenly

plump[1] /plʌmp/ adj pleasantly fat ~**ness** n [U]

plump[2] v **plump for** phr vt BrE infml choose

plump up phr vt make rounded and soft by shaking

plun·der /'plʌndə ‖ -ər/ vi/t steal or rob in time of war ♦ n [U] (goods seized by) plundering ~**er** n

plunge /plʌndʒ/ vi/t 1 move suddenly forwards and/or downwards 2 (of the neck of a woman's garment) have a low front or v-neck showing quite a large area of chest: a plunging neckline ♦ n 1 act of plunging 2 **take the plunge** at last do something one had delayed doing **plunger** n part of a machine that moves up and down

plu·per·fect /pluː'pɜːfɪkt ‖ -ɜːr-/ n verb tense that expresses action completed before a particular time, formed in English with had

plu·ral /'plʊərəl ‖ 'plʊr-/ n, adj (word or form) that expresses more than one

plus /plʌs/ prep with the addition of: 3 plus 2 is 5. ♦ adj 1 greater than zero 2 additional and desirable ♦ n 1 sign (+) for adding 2 infml welcome or favourable addition

plush /plʌʃ/ adj looking very splendid and expensive

Plu·to /'pluːtəʊ ‖ -toʊ/ n the PLANET ninth in order from the sun

plu·to·ni·um /pluː'təʊniəm ‖ -'toʊ-/ n [U] substance used in producing atomic power

ply[1] /plaɪ/ n [U] measure of the number of threads in wool, rope, etc. or the number of sheets in plywood

ply[2] v 1 vi travel regularly for hire or other business 2 vt work at (a trade)

ply with phr vt keep giving (esp. food) to

ply·wood /'plaɪwʊd/ n [U] material made of thin sheets of wood stuck together

pm , **PM** /ˌpiː 'em/ abbrev. for: post meridiem (= (Latin) after midday) (used after numbers expressing time)

PM /ˌpiː 'em◂/ n infml esp. BrE abbrev. for: PRIME MINISTER

PMT /ˌpiː em 'tiː/ also **PMS** /ˌpiː em 'es/ n [U] abbrev. for: premenstrual tension/-syndrome; pain, anger, and sadness felt by some women before their PERIOD

pneu·mat·ic /njuː'mætɪk ‖ nʊ-/ adj 1 worked by air pressure 2 filled with air: a pneumatic tyre

pneu·mo·ni·a /njuː'məʊniə ‖ nʊ'moʊ-/ n [U] serious lung disease

P.O. Box /ˌpiː 'əʊ bɒks ‖ -'oʊ bɒks/ n

Post Office Box; a box with a number, to which mail is sent

poach¹ /pəʊtʃ‖pəʊtʃ/ *vi/t* catch or kill (animals) illegally on someone else's land: (fig.) *poaching* (=stealing) *my ideas* ~**er** *n*

poach² *vt* cook in gently boiling water

pock·et /'pɒkɪt‖'pɑːkɪt/ *n* **1** small baglike part in or on a garment **2** container for thin things in a case, inside a car door, etc. **3** small separate area or group: *pockets of mist* **4** (supply of) money: *beyond my pocket* (=too expensive) **5 be/live in each other's pockets** *infml* (of two people) to be always together **6 out of pocket** *BrE* having spent money without any good result ♦ *adj* small enough to put into one's pocket: *a pocket camera* ♦ *vt* **1** put into one's pocket **2** take (money) dishonestly

pocket mon·ey /'·· ,··/ *n* [U] money given regularly to a child by its parents

pock·mark /'pɒkmɑːk‖'pɑːkmɑːrk/ *n* hollow mark on the skin where a diseased spot has been ~**ed** *adj*

pod /pɒd‖pɑːd/ *n* long narrow seed container of PEAs and beans

podg·y /'pɒdʒi‖'pɑː-/ *adj* short and fat

po·di·um /'pəʊdiəm‖'poʊ-/ *n* -**ums** *or* -**dia** /-diə/ raised part for a speaker or performer to stand on

po·em /'pəʊɪm‖'poʊ-/ *n* piece of writing in patterns of lines and sounds

po·et /'pəʊɪt‖'poʊ-/ *n* writer of poetry ~**ic** /pəʊ'etɪk‖poʊ-/ *adj* **1** of poetry **2** graceful ~**ical** *adj* **1** written as poetry **2** poetic ~**ically** /-kli/ *adv*

poetic jus·tice /ˌ·· '··/ *n* [U] something suitably bad happening to a wrong-doer

poetic li·cence /ˌ·· '··/ *n* [U] poet's freedom to change facts, not to obey the usual rules of grammar, etc.

poet laur·e·ate /ˌ· '··/ *n* (often caps.) poet appointed to the British royal court, who writes poems on important occasions

po·et·ry /'pəʊɪtri‖'poʊ-/ *n* [U] **1** art of a poet **2** poems **3** graceful quality

po-faced /ˌpəʊ 'feɪst◀‖ˌpoʊ-/ *adj BrE infml* looking solemn

pog·rom /'pɒgrəm‖pə'grɑːm/ *n* planned killing of large numbers of people

poig·nant /'pɔɪnjənt/ *adj* sharply sad ~**ly** *adv* **poignancy** *n* [U]

point¹ /pɔɪnt/ *n* **1** [C] sharp end: *the point of a needle* **2** [C] particular place or

moment: *a weak point in the plan* | *At that point I left*. **3** [C] unit for recording the SCORE in a game **4** [C] single particular idea or part of an argument or statement: *You've made* (=expressed) *an important point*. **5** [C] main idea, which gives meaning to the whole: *That's beside the point*. (=is unimportant) **6** [U] purpose; advantage: *There's no point in waiting any longer.* **7** [C] place on a measuring system: *the boiling point of water* | *the 32 points of the compass* **8** [C] particular quality or ability: *Spelling isn't her strong point.* **9** [C] sign (.) to the left of decimals: *4.2 is read as '4 point 2'.* **10** [C] SOCKET: *a power point* **11 case in point** something that proves or is an example of the subject under consideration **12 in point of fact** actually **13 make a point of** take particular care to **14 on the point of** just about to **15 to the point of** so as to be almost **16 when it comes/came to the point** when the moment for action or decision comes/came **points** *n* [P] *BrE* short rails for moving a train from one track to another

point² *v* **1** *vi* show or draw attention to something by holding out a finger, stick, etc. in its direction **2** *vi/t* aim or be aimed: *The gun was pointed/pointing at his head.* **3** *vt* fill in and make smooth the spaces between bricks (of a wall, etc.) with CEMENT ~**ed** *adj* **1** having a sharp end **2** directed against a particular person: *a pointed remark* ~**edly** *adv*

point out *phr vt* draw attention to

point-blank /ˌ· '·◀/ *adj, adv* **1** fired from a very close position **2** forceful and direct: *a point-blank refusal*

point·er /'pɔɪntə‖-ər/ *n* **1** stick for pointing at things **2** thin piece that points to numbers on a measuring apparatus **3** piece of helpful advice **4** type of hunting dog

point·less /'pɔɪntləs/ *adj* meaningless; useless ~**ly** *adv* ~**ness** *n* [U]

point of view /ˌ· · '·/ *n* particular way of considering something

poise /pɔɪz/ *n* [U] **1** quiet confidence and self-control **2** well-balanced way of moving ♦ *vt* put lightly in a place where it is hard to be steady **poised** *adj* **1** ready: *poised to attack* **2** showing poise

poi·son /'pɔɪzən/ *n* [C;U] substance that can kill or cause illness ♦ *vt* **1** give poison to or put poison in **2** have a damaging or evil effect on ~**ous** *adj*

poke /pəʊk ‖ poʊk/ *vi/t* **1** push out sharply: *She poked her head round the corner.* **2** push a pointed thing (into) **3** **poke fun at** cause (unkind) laughter at **4** **poke one's nose into something** enquire into something which does not concern one ♦ *n* act of poking

pok·er¹ /'pəʊkə ‖ 'poʊkər/ *n* thin metal rod for poking a fire to make it burn better

po·ker² *n* [U] card game

poker face /'·· ·/ *n* face that hides someone's thoughts or feelings

pok·y /'pəʊki ‖ 'poʊ-/ *adj* uncomfortably small and unattractive

po·lar /'pəʊlə ‖ 'poʊlər/ *adj* of or near the North or South Poles

polar bear /,·· '· ‖ '·· ·/ *n* large white bear that lives near the North Pole

po·lar·i·ty /pəˈlærəti/ *n* [C;U] *fml* having or developing two opposite qualities

po·lar·ize , **-ise** /'pəʊləraɪz ‖ 'poʊ-/ *vi/t* form into groups based on two directly opposite principles –**ization**, –**isation** /ˌpəʊləraɪˈzeɪʃən ‖ ˌpoʊlərə-/ *n* [U]

Po·lar·oid /'pəʊlərɔɪd ‖ 'poʊ-/ *n tdmk* **1** [U] substance that makes sunshine less bright, used in SUNGLASSES **2** [C] camera that produces finished photographs in seconds

pole¹ /pəʊl ‖ poʊl/ *n* long straight thin stick or post

pole² *n* **1** (*often cap.*) point furthest north or south on the Earth **2** either end of a MAGNET **3** either of the points on a BATTERY where wires are fixed **4** either of two positions that are as far apart as they can be **5** **poles apart** widely separated in opinion, etc.

pole·axe /'pəʊlæks ‖ 'poʊl-/ *vt* cause to fall (as if) by a heavy blow

pole·cat /'pəʊlkæt ‖ 'poʊl-/ *n* small fierce animal with an unpleasant smell

po·lem·ic /pəˈlemɪk/ *n* [C;U] *fml* fierce argument defending or attacking ideas or opinions ~**al** *adj*

pole vault /'· ·/ *n* jump over a high bar using a long pole

po·lice /pəˈliːs/ *n* [P] official body for making people obey the law, catching criminals, etc. ♦ *vt* control or keep a watch on with policemen: (fig.) *a new committee to police the nuclear industry*

police of·fi·cer /·'· ,··/ **po·lice·man** *masc* /pəˈliːsmən/ **po·lice·wom·an** *fem* /pəˈliːsˌwʊmən/ *n* member of the police

police state /·'· ·/ *n* country where people are controlled by (secret) political police

pol·i·cy /'pɒlɪsi ‖ 'pɑː-/ *n* **1** what a government, company, political party, etc. intends to do about a particular matter **2** insurance contract

po·li·o /'pəʊliəʊ ‖ 'poʊlioʊ/ *n* [U] serious infectious nerve disease, esp. of the SPINE, which often prevents movement

pol·ish¹ /'pɒlɪʃ ‖ 'pɑː-/ *vt* **1** make smooth and shiny by rubbing **2** make as perfect as possible: *a polished performance* ♦ *n* **1** [U] liquid, paste, etc. for polishing **2** [S] act of polishing **3** [U] fine quality ~**ed** *adj* **1** (of a piece of artistic work, a performance, etc.) done with great skill and control **2** polite and graceful ~**er** *n*

polish off *phr vt* finish (food, work, etc.) quickly or easily

polish up *phr vt* improve by practising

po·lit·bu·ro /pəˈlɪtbjʊərəʊ, 'pɒlɪt- ‖ 'pɑːlɪtbjʊroʊ, pəˈlɪt-/ *n* -**ros** chief Communist decision-making committee, esp, in the former Soviet Union

po·lite /pəˈlaɪt/ *adj* having good manners ~**ly** *adv* ~**ness** *n* [U]

pol·i·tic /'pɒlɪtɪk ‖ 'pɑː-/ *adj fml* sensible; advantageous

po·lit·i·cal /pəˈlɪtɪkəl/ *adj* **1** of or concerning government and public affairs **2** of (party) politics **3** very interested in or active in politics ~**ly** /-kli/ *adv* ~**ize** *vt*

political a·sy·lum /·,··· ·'·/ *n* [U] official protection given to someone who has left their country because they oppose his government

politically cor·rect /·,··· ·'·/ *adj* not likely to offend e.g. women, other races, or DISABLED people

pol·i·ti·cian /ˌpɒlɪˈtɪʃən ‖ ˌpɑː-/ *n* person whose business is politics

pol·i·tics /'pɒlɪtɪks ‖ 'pɑː-/ *n* **1** [U] the activity of winning and using government power, in competition with other parties: *active in local politics* **2** [U] art and science of government: *studying politics at university* **3** [P] political opinions **4** [U] activity within a group by which some members try to gain an advantage: *office* *politics*

pol·ka /'pɒlkə, 'pəʊlkə ‖ 'poʊlkə/ n quick simple dance for people dancing in pairs

poll /pəʊl ‖ poʊl/ n 1 [C] also **opinion poll** — attempt to find out the general opinion about something by questioning a number of people chosen by chance 2 [C;U] election 3 [S] number of votes given ♦ vt 1 receive (a stated number of votes) 2 question in a POLL (1)

pol·len /'pɒlən ‖ 'pɑː-/ n [U] yellow dust that makes plants produce seeds

pollen count /'·· ·/ n amount of POLLEN in the air

pol·li·nate /'pɒləneɪt ‖ 'pɑː-/ vt bring pollen to (a flower) –**nation** /ˌpɒlə'neɪʃən ‖ ˌpɑː-/ n [U]

poll·ing sta·tion /'·· ˌ··/ also **poll·ing place** /'·· ·/ AmE — n place where people vote in an election

poll·ster /'pəʊlstə ‖ 'poʊlstər/ n person who carries out POLLs (1)

pol·lut·ant /pə'luːtənt/ n substance that pollutes

pol·lute /pə'luːt/ vt make dangerously impure or unfit for use: *polluted rivers* –**lution** /pə'luːʃən/ n [U] 1 act of polluting 2 polluting substances

po·lo /'pəʊləʊ ‖ 'poʊloʊ/ n [U] game played on horses by hitting a ball with a long-handled hammer —see also WATER POLO

polo neck /'·· ·/ n round rolled collar

pol·ter·geist /'pɒltəgaɪst ‖ 'poʊltər-/ n spirit that makes noises and throws things around

pol·y·es·ter /'pɒliestə, ˌpɒli'estə ‖ 'pɑːliestər/ n [U] artificial material used for cloth

po·lyg·a·my /pə'lɪɡəmi/ n [U] having two or more wives at one time –**mist** n –**mous** adj

pol·y·glot /'pɒlɪɡlɒt ‖ 'pɑːlɪɡlɑːt/ adj fml speaking or including many languages

pol·y·gon /'pɒlɪɡən ‖ 'pɑːlɪɡɑːn/ n figure with five or more straight sides

pol·y·graph /'pɒlɪɡrɑːf ‖ 'pɑːlɪɡræf/ n LIE DETECTOR

pol·y·math /'pɒlɪmæθ ‖ 'pɑː-/ n fml person who knows a lot about many subjects

pol·y·mer /'pɒlɪmə ‖ 'pɑːlɪmər/ n simple chemical compound with large MOLECULEs

pol·yp /'pɒlɪp ‖ 'pɑː-/ n 1 very simple small water animal 2 small diseased bodily growth

pol·y·sty·rene /ˌpɒlɪ'staɪəriːn◂ ‖ ˌpɑː-stair-/ n [U] light plastic that keeps heat in

pol·y·tech·nic /ˌpɒlɪ'teknɪk◂ ‖ ˌpɑː-/ n place of higher education giving training in science, industry, etc.

pol·y·the·is·m /'pɒlɪθiːɪzəm ‖ 'pɑː-/ n [U] belief in many gods

pol·y·thene /'pɒləθiːn ‖ 'pɑː-/ n [U] strong plastic used for making many common articles

pol·y·un·sat·u·ra·ted /ˌpɒliʌn-'sætʃəreɪtɪd ‖ ˌpɑː-/ adj (of fat or oil) having chemicals combined in a way that is thought to be good for the health when eaten

pom·e·gran·ate /'pɒmɪˌɡrænət ‖ 'pʌm-ˌɡrænɪt, 'pɑːm-/ n fruit with small red seeds inside

pom·my /'pɒmi ‖ 'pɑː-/ n AustrE sl English person

pomp /pɒmp ‖ pɑːmp/ n [U] grand solemn ceremonial show

pom·pom /'pɒmpɒm ‖ 'pɑːmpɑːm/ n small decorative woollen ball

pom·pous /'pɒmpəs ‖ 'pɑːm-/ adj foolishly solemn and thinking oneself important ~**ly** adv ~**ness**, **-posity** /pɒm'pɒsəti ‖ pɑːm'pɑː-/ n [U]

ponce /pɒns ‖ pɑːns/ n sl man who behaves foolishly, showily, or womanishly ♦ v **ponce about/around** phr vi BrE sl behave like a PONCE

pon·cho /'pɒntʃəʊ ‖ 'pɑːntʃoʊ/ n -chos cloth worn over the shoulders, with a hole for the head

pond /pɒnd ‖ pɑːnd/ n small area of still water

pon·der /'pɒndə ‖ 'pɑːndər/ vi/t spend time considering

pon·der·ous /'pɒndərəs ‖ 'pɑːn-/ adj 1 heavy, slow, and awkward 2 dull and solemn

pong /pɒŋ ‖ pɑːŋ/ vi, n BrE sl (make) a bad smell ~**y** adj

pon·tiff /'pɒntəf ‖ 'pɑːn-/ n POPE

pon·tif·i·cate /pɒn'tɪfəkeɪt ‖ pɑːn-/ vi give one's opinion as if it were the only right one

pon·toon[1] /pɒn'tuːn ‖ pɑːn-/ n floating hollow container connected with others to support a floating bridge

pontoon[2] *n* [U] *BrE* card game

po·ny /'pəʊni ‖ 'poʊni/ *n* small horse

po·ny·tail /'pəʊniteɪl ‖ 'poʊ-/ *n* hair tied in a bunch at the back of the head

pooch /puːtʃ/ *n infml* dog

poo·dle /'puːdl/ *n* dog with curling hair, often cut in shapes

poof /puːf, pʊf/ *n BrE derog sl* male HOMOSEXUAL

pooh /puː/ *interj* (used when something smells bad)

pooh-pooh /ˌ· '·/ *vt* treat as not worth considering

pool[1] /puːl/ *n* **1** small area of water in a hollow place **2** small amount of liquid on a surface **3** SWIMMING POOL

pool[2] *n* **1** [C] shared supply of money, goods, workers, etc. —see also CAR POOL **2** [U] game like SNOOKER ♦ *vt* combine; share **pools** *n* [*the*+P] arrangement (esp. in Britain) for risking money on the results of football matches

poor /pʊə ‖ pʊr/ *adj* **1** having very little money **2** less or worse than usual or than expected: *a poor harvest/essay* | *poor weather/health* **3** unlucky; deserving pity: *Poor David has failed his exams.* **~ness** *n* [U] low quality

poor·ly /'pʊəli ‖ 'pʊrli/ *adv* not well; badly: *poorly paid* ♦ *adj infml* ill

poor re·la·tion /ˌ· ·'··/ *n* one regarded as the least important among a group of similar ones

pop[1] /pɒp ‖ pɑːp/ *vi/t* **-pp-** **1** (cause to) make a small explosive sound **2** come, go, or put quickly: *A button popped off his shirt.* **3** pop the question *infml* make an offer of marriage

pop up *phr vi* happen or appear suddenly

pop[2] *n* **1** [C] small explosive sound **2** [U] sweet FIZZY drink

pop[3] *n* [U] modern popular music with a strong beat: *a pop group/concert*

pop[4] *n esp. AmE* **1** father **2** (used as a form of address to an old man)

pop[5] *abbrev. for:* population

pop·a·dum /'pɒpədəm ‖ 'pɑː-/ *n* thin Indian bread

pop art /ˌ· '·◂/ *n* [U] modern art showing objects from everyday life

pop·corn /'pɒpkɔːn ‖ 'pɑːpkɔːrn/ *n* [U] MAIZE seeds heated so that they swell

pope /pəʊp ‖ poʊp/ *n* (*often cap.*) the head of the Roman Catholic Church

pop·lar /'pɒplə ‖ 'pɑːplər/ *n* tall straight thin tree

pop·lin /'pɒplɪn ‖ 'pɑːp-/ *n* [U] strong cotton cloth

pop·py /'pɒpi ‖ 'pɑːpi/ *n* plant with bright flowers, usu. red

pop·py·cock /'pɒpikɒk ‖ 'pɑːpikɑːk/ *n* [U] nonsense

pop·si·cle /'pɒpsɪkəl ‖ 'pɑː-/ *n AmE tdmk for* ICE LOLLY

pop·u·lace /'pɒpjələs ‖ 'pɑː-/ *n* [U] all the (ordinary) people of a country

pop·u·lar /'pɒpjələ ‖ 'pɑːpjələr/ *adj* **1** liked by many people: *a popular restaurant* **2** common; widespread: *a popular name* **3** of the general public: *popular opinion* **~ly** *adv* by most people **~ize, -ise** *vt* **~ity** /ˌpɒpjʊ'lærɪti ‖ ˌpɑː-/ *n* [U]

pop·u·late /'pɒpjəleɪt ‖ 'pɑː-/ *vt* live in as a population

pop·u·la·tion /ˌpɒpjʊ'leɪʃən ‖ ˌpɑː-/ *n* (number of) people (or animals) living in a particular area or country

pop·u·list /'pɒpjələst ‖ 'pɑː-/ *n* person who claims to support the aims of ordinary people in politics

pop·u·lous /'pɒpjələs ‖ 'pɑː-/ *adj fml* having a large population

porce·lain /'pɔːsləŋ ‖ 'pɔːrsəlŋn/ *n* [U] (cups, plates, etc. made from) fine hard thin claylike substance

porch /pɔːtʃ ‖ pɔːrtʃ/ *n* roofed entrance built out from a house or church

por·cu·pine /'pɔːkjʊpaɪn ‖ 'pɔːr-/ *n* animal with long needle-like hairs on its back

pore[1] /pɔː ‖ pɔːr/ *n* small hole in the skin, through which SWEAT passes

pore[2] *v* pore over *phr vt* read with close attention

pork /pɔːk ‖ pɔːrk/ *n* [U] meat from pigs

porn /pɔːn ‖ pɔːrn/ *n* [U] *infml, esp. BrE* pornography

por·nog·ra·phy /pɔː'nɒgrəfi ‖ pɔːr'nɑːg-/ *n* [U] *derog* (books, films, etc.) showing or describing sexually exciting scenes **~graphic** /ˌpɔːnə'græfɪk◂ ‖ ˌpɔːr-/ *adj*

po·rous /'pɔːrəs/ *adj* allowing liquid to pass through

por·poise /'pɔːpəs ‖ 'pɔːr-/ *n* large

fishlike sea animal

por·ridge /'pɒrɪdʒ ‖ 'pɑ:-, 'pɔ:-/ *n* [U] soft breakfast food of OATMEAL

port¹ /pɔ:t ‖ pɔ:rt/ *n* harbour

port² *n* [U] left side of a ship or aircraft

port³ *n* [U] strong sweet red wine from Portugal

por·ta·ble /'pɔ:təbəl ‖ 'pɔ:rt-/ *adj* that can be carried

por·tals /'pɔ:tlz ‖ 'pɔ:rtlz/ *n* [P] grand entrance to a building

port·cul·lis /pɔ:t'kʌlɪs ‖ pɔ:rt-/ *n* castle gate that can be raised and lowered

por·tent /'pɔ:tent ‖ 'pɔ:r-/ *n fml* sign of a future strange or undesirable event

por·ten·tous /pɔ:'tentəs ‖ pɔ:r-/ *adj fml* 1 threatening 2 solemnly self-important

por·ter /'pɔ:tə ‖ 'pɔ:rtər/ *n esp. BrE* 1 person who carries loads, esp. travellers' bags, or goods in a market 2 person in charge of the entrance to a hotel, hospital, etc.

port·fo·li·o /pɔ:t'fəʊliəʊ ‖ pɔ:rt'fəʊliəʊ/ *n* 1 **a** flat case for carrying drawings, etc. **b** drawings, etc. carried in this 2 collection of business shares owned 3 office and duties of a government minister

port·hole /'pɔ:thəʊl ‖ 'pɔ:rthoʊl/ *n* window in a ship or aircraft

por·tion¹ /'pɔ:ʃən ‖ 'pɔ:r-/ *n* 1 part: *the front portion of the train* 2 share 3 quantity of food for one person

portion² *v* portion out *phr vt* share

port·ly /'pɔ:tli ‖ 'pɔ:r-/ *adj* (of a person) fat

port of call /,· · '·/ *n* 1 port where a ship stops 2 place one visits

por·trait /'pɔ:trɪt ‖ 'pɔ:r-/ *n* 1 picture of a person 2 lifelike description in words

por·tray /pɔ:'treɪ ‖ pɔ:r-/ *vt* 1 represent, describe 2 act the part of ~**al** *n* [C;U]

pose /pəʊz ‖ poʊz/ *v* 1 *vi* stand or sit in a particular position to be drawn, photographed, etc. 2 *vt* cause (a problem) 3 *vt* ask (a question) ♦ *n* 1 position when posing (POSE (1)) 2 pretended way of behaving

   pose as *phr vt* pretend to be

pos·er /'pəʊzə ‖ 'poʊzər/ *n* 1 hard question 2 poseur

po·seur /pəʊ'zɜ: ‖ poʊ'zɜ:r/ *n* person who behaves unnaturally to produce an effect

posh /pɒʃ ‖ pɑ:ʃ/ *adj* 1 fashionable and splendid 2 of the upper social classes

po·si·tion /pə'zɪʃən/ *n* 1 [C;U] place where something is 2 [U] proper place: *Is everyone in position?* 3 [C] way in which something is placed or stands, sits, etc. 4 [C] situation; state: *the company's current financial position* 5 [C] place in a rank or group: *He finished in second position.* 6 [C] *fml* job 7 [C] *fml* opinion ♦ *vt* place

pos·i·tive /'pɒzətɪv ‖ 'pɑ:-/ *adj* 1 leaving no possibility of doubt: *positive proof* 2 having no doubt; sure 3 effective; actually helpful 4 more than zero 5 (of electricity) of the type carried by PROTONS 6 complete; real: *a positive delight* ~**ly** *adv* 1 in a POSITIVE (1, 2) way 2 really; indeed

positive di·scrim·i·na·tion /,··· ···'··/ *n* [U] practice or principle of favouring people who are often treated unfairly, esp. because of their sex or race

pos·se /'pɒsi ‖ 'pɑ:si/ *n* group of people gathered together to help find a criminal

pos·sess /pə'zes/ *vt* 1 *fml* have; own 2 (of a feeling or idea) seem to control all (someone's) actions ~**ed** *adj* wildly mad ~**or** *n*

pos·ses·sion /pə'zeʃən/ *n* 1 [U] state of possessing; ownership 2 [C] something one owns 3 [U] control by an evil spirit

pos·ses·sive /pə'zesɪv/ *adj* 1 unwilling to share one's own things 2 wanting all of someone's love and attention for oneself 3 *gram* showing ownership: *'My' is a possessive adjective.* ~**ly** *adv* ~**ness** *n* [U]

pos·si·bil·i·ty /,pɒsə'bɪləti ‖ ,pɑ:-/ *n* 1 [S;U] (degree of) likelihood 2 [U] fact of being possible 3 [C] something possible: *The house is in bad condition but it has possibilities.* (=can be improved)

pos·si·ble /'pɒsəbəl ‖ 'pɑ:-/ *adj* 1 that can exist, happen, or be done 2 acceptable; suitable ♦ *n* 1 [the+S] that which can exist, happen, or be done 2 [C] person or thing that might be suitable ~**bly** *adv* 1 in accordance with what is possible: *I'll do all I possibly can.* 2 perhaps

pos·sum /'pɒsəm ‖ 'pɑ:-/ *n* small tree-climbing animal from America and Australia

post¹ /pəʊst ‖ poʊst/ *n* 1 strong thick upright pole fixed in position 2 finishing place in a race ♦ *vt* 1 put up a notice about

2 report as being: *The ship was posted missing.*

post² *n* [U] *esp. BrE* 1 official system for carrying letters, parcels, etc. 2 (a single official collection or delivery of) letters, parcels, etc. sent by this means ♦ *vt* 1 send by post 2 **keep someone posted** continue to give someone all the latest news about something

post³ *n* 1 job 2 special place of duty, esp. of a soldier 3 military base ♦ *vt* 1 place (soldiers, policemen, etc.) on duty 2 send to a job, esp. abroad

post·age /'pəustidʒ ‖ 'pou-/ *n* [U] charge for carrying a letter, parcel, etc. by post

postage stamp /'·· ·/ *n fml for* STAMP

post·al /'pəustl ‖ 'pou-/ *adj* 1 of the POST² (1, 2) 2 sent by post

postal or·der /'·· ,··/ *n* official paper sent by post, to be exchanged for money by the receiver

post·bag /'pəustbæg ‖ 'poust-/ *n* 1 postman's bag 2 number of letters received

post·box /'pəustbɒks ‖ 'poustba:ks/ *n* box into which people put letters for posting

post·card /'pəustka:d ‖ 'poustka:rd/ *n* card for sending messages by post without an envelope

post·code /'pəustkəud ‖ 'poustkoud/ *n* BrE letters and numbers added to an address to make it more exact for delivering letters

post·date /,pəust'deit ‖ ,poust-/ *vt* write a date later than the actual date of writing (esp. on a cheque)

post·er /'pəustə ‖ 'poustər/ *n* large printed notice or picture

pos·te·ri·or /pɒ'stiəriə ‖ pɑ:'stririər/ *adj fml* nearer the back ♦ *n* BOTTOM¹ (2)

pos·te·ri·ty /pɒ'sterəti ‖ pɑ:-/ *n* [U] people or times after one's death

poster paint /'·· ·/ *n* [C;U] bright-coloured artist's paints

post·grad·u·ate /,pəust'grædjuət ‖ ,poust'grædʒuət/ *n, adj* (person doing university studies) after getting a first degree

post·haste /,pəust'heist ‖ ,poust-/ *adv fml* very quickly

post·hu·mous /'pɒstjʊməs ‖ 'pɑ:stʃə-/ *adj* after death ~ly *adv*

post·man /'pəustmən ‖ 'poust-/ *n* -men /-mən/ person who delivers letters, etc.

post·mark /'pəustmɑ:k ‖ 'poustmɑ:rk/ *n* official mark on a letter, etc. showing where and when it was posted **postmark** *vt*

post·mor·tem /,pəust'mɔ:təm ‖ ,poust-'mɔ:r-/ *n* 1 tests to find out why someone died 2 finding out why something failed

post of·fice /'· ,··/ *n* place where stamps are sold, letters can be posted, and various sorts of government business are done

post·pone /pəus'pəun ‖ pous'poun/ *vt* move to a later time ~**ment** *n* [C;U]

post·script /'pəust,skript ‖ 'poust-/ *n* additional information at the end of a piece of writing, esp. a letter

pos·ture /'pɒstʃə ‖ 'pɑ:stʃər/ *n* 1 bodily position 2 manner of behaving or thinking on some occasion *vi* 1 place oneself in fixed bodily positions, esp. in order to make other people admire one 2 pretend to be something one is not

po·sy /'pəuzi ‖ 'pou-/ *n* small bunch of flowers

pot¹ /pɒt ‖ pɑ:t/ *n* [C] round container: *a paint pot | a cooking pot* 2 [U] *sl for* MARIJUANA 3 **go to pot** *infml* become ruined or worthless **pots** *n* [P] *infml* (of money) large amount

pot² *v* -tt- 1 *vi/t* shoot, esp. for food or sport 2 *vt* plant in a pot ~**ted** *adj* 1 (of meat, fish, etc.) made into a paste 2 (of a book) in a short simple form

pot·ash /'pɒtæʃ ‖ 'pɑ:-/ *n* [U] sort of potassium used in farming and industry

po·tas·si·um /pə'tæsiəm/ *n* [U] soft silver-white metal common in nature and necessary for life

po·ta·to /pə'teitəu ‖ -tou/ *n* -toes common roundish brown or yellowish vegetable that grows underground

pot·bel·ly /'pɒt,beli ‖ 'pɑ:t-/ *n infml* fat stomach

pot·boil·er /'pɒt,bɔilə ‖ 'pɑ:t,bɔilər/ *n* book, etc. produced quickly just to earn money

po·tent /'pəutənt ‖ 'pou-/ *adj* powerful: *a potent drug* ~**ly** *adv* **potency** *n* [U]

po·ten·tial /pə'tenʃəl/ *adj* that may become so; not (yet) actual: *potential danger* ♦ *n* [U] possibility for developing ~**ly** *adv* ~**ity** /pə,tenʃi'æləti/ *n* [C;U]

pot·hole /'pɒthəul ‖ 'pɑ:thoul/ *n* 1 deep hole going far underground 2 unwanted hole in the road ~**holing** *n* [U] sport of climbing down POTHOLES (1)

po·tion /'pəʊʃən‖'poʊ-/ n liquid mixture intended as a medicine, poison, or magic charm

pot·luck /ˌpɒt'lʌk‖ˌpɑːt-/ n take potluck choose without enough information; take a chance

pot plant /'··/ n plant grown (indoors) in a pot

pot·shot /'pɒt-ʃɒt‖'pɑːt-ʃɑːt/ n carelessly aimed shot

pot·ter¹ /'pɒtə‖'pɑːtər/ n person who makes pottery

potter² vi move or act slowly or purposelessly

potter about/around phr vi spend time in activities that demand little effort

pot·ter·y /'pɒtəri‖'pɑː-/ n [U] (pots, dishes, etc. made of) baked clay

pot·ty¹ /'pɒti‖'pɑːti/ adj BrE infml 1 slightly mad 2 having a strong uncontrolled interest in or admiration for: He's potty about her.

potty² n pot for children to URINATE into

pouch /paʊtʃ/ n 1 small leather bag 2 baglike part of an animal

poul·tice /'pəʊltɪs‖'poʊl-/ n soft wet heated mass placed on the skin to lessen pain

poul·try /'pəʊltri‖'poʊl-/ n [U] (meat from) farmyard birds such as hens, ducks, etc.

pounce /paʊns/ vi fly down or jump suddenly to seize

pounce on phr vt seize or accept eagerly

pound¹ /paʊnd/ n 1 a standard unit of money, in Britain containing 100 pence 2 a measure of weight equal to 0.4536 kilograms

pound² v 1 vt crush 2 vi/t strike repeatedly and heavily 3 vi move with quick heavy steps

pound³ n place where lost animals and cats are kept until their owners take them back

pour /pɔː‖pɔːr/ v 1 vi/t (cause to) flow fast and steadily 2 vi rush together in large numbers 3 vi (of rain) fall hard

pour out phr vt tell freely and with feeling

pout /paʊt/ vi push the lips forwards, esp. to show displeasure **pout** n

pov·er·ty /'pɒvəti‖'pɑːvərti/ n [U] 1 being poor 2 fml lack

poverty-strick·en /'·· ˌ·/ adj extremely poor

poverty trap /'··· ˌ·/ n earning too much to be able to receive government payments but not enough to live comfortably on

pow·der /'paʊdə‖-ər/ n 1 [C;U] very fine dry grains 2 [U] pleasant-smelling substance like this, used on the skin 3 [U] gunpowder ♦ vt put POWDER (2) on –**ed** adj produced in the form of powder ~**y** adj

pow·er /'paʊə‖paʊr/ n 1 [U] strength 2 [U] force used for driving machines, producing electricity, etc.: nuclear power 3 [S;U] control over others; influence 4 [U] what one can do; (natural) ability: the power of speech 5 [C;U] right to act: The police now have the power to search people in the street. 6 [C] person, nation, etc. that has influence or control 7 [S+of] a large amount: A holiday will do you a power of good. 8 **the powers that be** infml the unknown people in important positions who make decisions that have an effect on one's life —see also BLACK POWER ♦ vt supply power to (a machine)

pow·er·ful /'paʊəfəl‖'paʊr-/ adj 1 full of force: a powerful engine 2 great in degree: a powerful smell 3 having much control or influence 4 having a strong effect: powerful drugs ~**ly** adv

pow·er·less /'paʊələs‖'paʊr-/ adj lacking strength or ability: powerless to help

power of at·tor·ney /ˌ··· ·'··/ n [U] right to act for someone else in business or law

power plant /'·· ·/ n engine supplying power to a factory, aircraft, etc.

power sta·tion /'·· ˌ·/ n building where electricity is made

pox /pɒks‖pɑːks/ n [U] infml for SYPHILIS

pp abbrev. for: pages

PR /ˌpiː 'ɑː‖-'ɑːr/ n [U] abbrev. for: 1 PUBLIC RELATIONS 2 infml for PROPORTIONAL REPRESENTATION

prac·ti·ca·ble /'præktɪkəbəl/ adj that can be done –**bility** /ˌpræktɪkə'bɪləti/ n [U]

prac·ti·cal /'præktɪkəl/ adj 1 concerned with action or actual conditions, rather than ideas 2 effective or convenient in actual use: a practical uniform 3 clever at doing things and dealing with difficulties; sensible ~**ly** /-kli/ adv 1 usefully; suitably

2 almost ~**ity** /ˌpræktɪˈkælɪti/ n [C;U]
practical joke /ˌ··· ˈ·/ n trick played on someone to amuse others
prac·tice also -**tise** AmE /ˈpræktɪs/ n 1 [C;U] regular or repeated doing of something, to gain skill 2 [U] experience gained by this 3 [U] actual doing of something: to put a plan into practice 4 [C] business of a doctor or lawyer 5 [C;U] something regularly done 6 **in/out of practice** having/not having practised enough —see also SHARP PRACTICE
prac·tise also -**tice** AmE /ˈpræktɪs/ v 1 vi/t do (an action) or perform on (esp. a musical instrument) repeatedly to gain skill 2 vi/t do (the work of a doctor, lawyer, etc.) 3 vt act in accordance with (a religion): a practising Jew 4 vt fml do (habitually) 5 **practise what one preaches** do what you advise others to do –**tised** adj skilled through practice
prac·ti·tion·er /prækˈtɪʃənə ‖ -ər/ n person who works in a profession, esp. a doctor —see also GENERAL PRACTITIONER
prag·mat·ic /prægˈmætɪk/ adj concerned with actual effects rather than general principles ~**ally** /-kli/ adv
prai·rie /ˈpreəri ‖ ˈpreri/ n wide grassy plain, esp. in North America
praise /preɪz/ vt 1 speak of with admiration 2 worship ♦ n [U] expression of admiration
praise·wor·thy /ˈpreɪzwɜːði ‖ -ɜːr-/ adj deserving praise
pram /præm/ n small four-wheeled hand-pushed carriage for a baby
prance /prɑːns ‖ præns/ vi 1 (of an animal) jump on the back legs 2 move happily or showily
prank /præŋk/ n playful but foolish trick
prat·tle /ˈprætl/ vi talk continually about unimportant things ♦ n [U] foolish or unimportant talk
prawn /prɔːn ‖ prɒːn/ n small ten-legged sea creature, often eaten
pray /preɪ/ vi 1 speak to God or a god, often silently, often asking for something 2 wish or hope strongly: We're praying for fine weather.
prayer /preə ‖ prer/ n 1 [C] (form of words used in) a solemn request to God or a god 2 [U] praying
preach /priːtʃ/ v 1 vi/t make (a religious

speech) in public 2 vt urge others to accept: preaching revolution 3 vi offer unwanted advice on matters of right and wrong ~**er** n
pre·am·ble /priːˈæmbəl ‖ ˈpriːæmbəl/ n something said or written before getting to the main part
pre·car·i·ous /prɪˈkeəriəs ‖ -ker-/ adj not firm or steady; full of danger ~**ly** adv
pre·cau·tion /prɪˈkɔːʃən ‖ -kɒː-/ n action done to avoid possible trouble ~**ary** adj
pre·cede /prɪˈsiːd/ vt come (just) before –**ceding** adj: the preceding day
pre·ce·dence /ˈpresɪdəns/ n [U] (right to) a particular place before others, esp. because of importance
pre·ce·dent /ˈpresɪdənt/ n 1 [U] what has usu. been done before 2 [C] earlier act which shows what may be done now
pre·cept /ˈpriːsept/ n fml guiding rule of behaviour
pre·cinct /ˈpriːsɪŋkt/ n 1 part of a town limited to the stated use: a shopping precinct 2 AmE division of a town for election or police purposes **precincts** n [P] space around a large (old) building, usu. inside walls
pre·cious /ˈpreʃəs/ adj 1 of great value 2 fml (of words, manners, etc.) unnaturally fine or perfect ♦ adv very: precious few ~**ness** n [U]
pre·ci·pice /ˈpresɪpɪs/ n very steep side of a mountain or cliff
pre·cip·i·tate[1] /prɪˈsɪpɪteɪt/ vt 1 fml make (an unwanted event) happen sooner 2 fml throw down suddenly 3 separate (solid matter) from liquid chemically ♦ n [C;U] precipitated matter –**tation** /prɪˌsɪpɪˈteɪʃən/ n [U] fml 1 precipitating 2 rain, snow, etc. 3 unwise speed
pre·cip·i·tate[2] /prɪˈsɪpɪtət/ adj fml too hasty ~**ly** adv
pre·cip·i·tous /prɪˈsɪpɪtəs/ adj fml 1 dangerously steep 2 precipitate ~**ly** adv ~**ness** n [U]
pré·cis /ˈpreɪsiː ‖ preɪˈsiː/ n précis-/ˈpreɪsiːz ‖ preɪˈsiːz/ shortened form of something written or said
pre·cise /prɪˈsaɪs/ adj 1 exact 2 (too) careful and correct about small details ~**ly** adv 1 exactly 2 yes, that is correct
pre·ci·sion /prɪˈsɪʒən/ n [U] exactness ♦ adj 1 done with exactness: precision

bombing **2** giving exact results: *precision instruments*

pre·clude /prɪˈkluːd/ *vt fml* prevent

pre·co·cious /prɪˈkəʊʃəs‖-ˈkoʊ-/ *adj* developing unusually early **~ly** *adv* **~ness** *n* [U]

pre·con·cep·tion /ˌpriːkənˈsepʃən/ *n* opinion formed in advance without (enough) knowledge **–ceived** /-kənˈsiːvd◂/ *adj: preconceived notions*

pre·con·di·tion /ˌpriːkənˈdɪʃən/ *n* thing that must be agreed to if something is to be done

pre·cur·sor /prɪˈkɜːsə‖-ˈkɜːrsər/ *n* one that came before and led to a later thing

pred·a·to·ry /ˈpredətəri‖-tɔːri/ *adj* **1** killing and eating other animals **2** living by attacking and robbing **predator** *n* predatory animal

pre·de·ces·sor /ˈpriːdɪˌsesə‖ˈpredɪˌsesər/ *n* one that came before: *my predecessor as headmaster*

pre·des·ti·na·tion /prɪˌdestɪˈneɪʃən, ˌpriːdes-/ *n* [U] belief that everything in the world has been decided by God, and that no human effort can change it

pre·des·tine /prɪˈdestɪn/ *vt* settle in advance, esp. as if by fate or the will of God

pre·de·ter·mine /ˌpriːdɪˈtɜːmɪn‖-ɜːr-/ *vt* **1** fix unchangeably from the beginning **2** arrange in advance

pre·de·ter·min·er /ˌpriːdɪˈtɜːmɪnə‖-ˈtɜːrmɪnər/ *n* word that can be used before a DETERMINER (=word such as **the**, **that**, **his**, etc.): *In the phrase 'all the boys', 'all' is a predeterminer.*

pre·dic·a·ment /prɪˈdɪkəmənt/ *n* difficult situation

pred·i·cate /ˈpredɪkət/ *n* part of a sentence which makes a statement about the subject

pre·dic·a·tive /prɪˈdɪkətɪv‖ˈpredɪkeɪt-/ *adj* coming after a verb

pre·dict /prɪˈdɪkt/ *vt* say in advance (what will happen) **~able** *adj* **1** that can be predicted **2** not doing anything unexpected **~ably** *adv* **~ion** /prɪˈdɪkʃən/ *n* [C;U] predicting or something predicted

pre·dis·pose /ˌpriːdɪˈspəʊz‖-ˈspoʊz/ *vt fml* make (someone) likely to do or have **–position** /ˌpriːdɪspəˈzɪʃən/ *n*

pre·dom·i·nant /prɪˈdɒmɪnənt‖-ˈdɑː-/ *adj* most powerful, noticeable, important,

etc. **~ly** *adv* **–nance** *n* [U]

pre·dom·i·nate /prɪˈdɒmɪneɪt‖-ˈdɑː-/ *vi* **1** have the main power or influence **2** be greatest in numbers

pre·em·i·nent /priːˈemɪnənt/ *adj* better than any others **~ly** *adv* **–nence** *n* [U]

pre·empt /priːˈempt/ *vt* prevent by taking action in advance **~ive** *adj*

preen /priːn/ *vi/t* (of a bird) clean (itself or its feathers) with its beak

pre·fab·ri·cate /priːˈfæbrɪkeɪt/ *vt* make (the parts of a building, ship, etc.) in advance in a factory and put them together later

pref·ace /ˈprefɪs/ *n* introduction to a book ♦ *vt* introduce (speech or writing) in the stated way

pre·fect /ˈpriːfekt/ *n* **1** older pupil who keeps order among younger ones **2** (esp. in France) public official with government or police duties

pre·fer /prɪˈfɜː‖-ˈfɜːr/ *vt* **-rr-** **1** like better; choose rather: *I prefer wine to beer.* **2** *law* make (a charge) officially **~erable** /ˈprefərəbəl/ *adj* better, esp. because more suitable **~ably** *adv*

pref·er·ence /ˈprefərəns/ *n* [C;U] **1** liking for one thing rather than another **2** special favour shown to one person, group, etc.

pref·e·ren·tial /ˌprefəˈrenʃəl◂/ *adj* giving or showing PREFERENCE (2) **~ly** *adv*

pre·fix /ˈpriːfɪks/ *n* wordlike part added at the beginning of a word to change its meaning (as in *untie*) ♦ *vt* **1** add a prefix to **2** add (something) to the beginning (of)

preg·nant /ˈpregnənt/ *adj* **1** having an unborn child or young in the body **2** full of hidden meaning **–nancy** *n* [C;U]

pre·hen·sile /prɪˈhensaɪl‖-səl/ *adj* able to hold things: *a monkey's prehensile tail*

pre·his·tor·ic /ˌpriːhɪˈstɒrɪk◂‖-ˈstɔː-, -ˈstɑː-/ *adj* of times before recorded history **~ally** /-kli/ *adv*

pre·judge /ˌpriːˈdʒʌdʒ/ *vt* form an opinion about before knowing all the facts

prej·u·dice /ˈpredʒʊdɪs/ *n* **1** [C;U] unfair feeling against something **2** [U] *fml* damage; harm ♦ *vt* **1** cause to have a prejudice (1) **2** weaken; harm: *It may prejudice your chances of success.* **–diced** *adj* having a prejudice (1) **–dicial** /ˌpredʒʊˈdɪʃəl◂/ *adj fml* harmful: *Refusing* *to speak could be prejudicial to your case.*

prel·ate /'prelɪt/ *n* priest of high rank

pre·lim·i·na·ry /prɪ'lɪmɪnəri ‖ -neri/ *adj* coming before (and preparing for) esp. the main one ♦ *n* preliminary act or arrangement

prel·ude /'prelju:d/ *n* 1 something that is followed by something larger or more important 2 short piece of music introducing a large musical work

pre·mar·i·tal /pri:'mærɪtəl/ *adj* happening before marriage

pre·ma·ture /'premətʃə, -tʃʊə, ˌpremə'tʃʊə ‖ ˌpri:mə'tʊr/ *adj* happening before the proper time ~**ly** *adv*

pre·med·i·tat·ed /pri:'medɪteɪtɪd ‖ prɪ-/ *adj* planned in advance –**tation** /pri:ˌme-dɪ'teɪʃən ‖ prɪ-/ *n* [U]

prem·i·er /'premiə ‖ prɪ'mɪr/ *n* PRIME MINISTER ♦ *adj fml* first in importance

prem·i·ere , **-ère** /'premiea ‖ prɪ'mɪr/ *n* first public performance of a film or play ♦ *vt* give a premiere of (a play or film)

prem·ise /'premɪs/ *n fml* statement or idea on which reasoning is based

prem·is·es /'premɪsɪz/ *n* [P] building and its land, considered as a piece of property

pre·mi·um /'pri:miəm/ *n* 1 money paid for insurance 2 additional charge 3 **at a premium** rare or difficult to obtain 4 **put a premium on** cause to be an advantage

pre·mo·ni·tion /ˌpremə'nɪʃən, ˌpri:-/ *n* feeling that something is going to happen

pre·oc·cu·pa·tion /pri:ˌɒkjʊ'peɪʃən ‖ -ˌɑ:k-/ *n* 1 [U] being preoccupied 2 [C] something that takes up all one's attention

pre·oc·cu·py /pri:'ɒkjʊpaɪ ‖ -'ɑ:k-/ *vt* fill (someone's) thoughts, taking attention away from other things

prep·a·ra·tion /ˌprepə'reɪʃən/ *n* 1 [U] act or process of preparing 2 [C] arrangement for a future event 3 [C] *fml* (chemical) mixture for a certain purpose

pre·par·a·to·ry /prɪ'pærətəri ‖ -tɔ:ri/ *adj* done to get ready

pre·pare /prɪ'peə ‖ -'per/ *vi/t* 1 get or make ready 2 put (oneself) into a suitable state of mind –**pared** *adj* willing: *not prepared to help*

pre·pon·de·rance /prɪ'pɒndərəns ‖ -'pɑ:n-/ *n* [S] *fml* larger number; state of being more

prep·o·si·tion /ˌprepə'zɪʃən/ *n* word (such as *in* or *by*) used with a noun or PRONOUN to show its connection with another word ~**al** *adj*

pre·pos·ter·ous /prɪ'pɒstərəs ‖ -'pɑ:s-/ *adj* foolishly unreasonable or improbable ~**ly** *adv*

prep·py /'prepi/ *adj AmE infml* typical of (former) students of expensive private schools in the US, esp. in being neat and well-dressed

prep school /'prep sku:l/ also **preparatory school** /·'····, ·/ *n* 1 (in Britain) private school for pupils up to the age of 13 2 (in the US) private school that makes pupils ready for college

pre·req·ui·site /pri:'rekwɪzɪt/ *n fml* something needed before something else can happen

pre·rog·a·tive /prɪ'rɒgətɪv ‖ -'rɑ:-/ *n* special right belonging to someone

Pres·by·te·ri·an /ˌprezbɪ'tɪəriən ‖ -'tɪr-/ *n, adj* (member) of a Protestant church governed by a body of equal-ranking officials

pre·school /'pri:sku:l/ *n AmE* school for children of 2 to 5 years of age

pre·school /ˌpri:'sku:l/ *adj* of or for children who are not old enough for school

pre·scribe /prɪ'skraɪb/ *vt* 1 order as a medicine or treatment 2 *fml* state (what must be done)

pre·scrip·tion /prɪ'skrɪpʃən/ *n* 1 [C] (doctor's written order for) a particular medicine or treatment 2 [U] act of prescribing

pres·ence /'prezəns/ *n* [U] 1 fact of being present 2 *fml* personal appearance and manner, as having a strong effect on others

presence of mind /ˌ·· '·/ *n* [U] ability to act quickly, calmly, and wisely when necessary

pres·ent¹ /'prezənt/ *n* gift

pre·sent² /prɪ'zent/ *vt* 1 give, esp. ceremonially 2 be the cause of: *That presents no difficulties.* 3 offer for consideration: *to present a report* 4 provide for the public to see in a theatre, cinema etc. 5 introduce and take part in (a radio or television show) 6 introduce (someone) esp. to someone of higher rank 7 **present itself** (of something possible) happen ~**er** *n*

pres·ent³ /ˈprezənt/ adj 1 here/there: *I was not present at the meeting.* 2 existing or being considered now: *my present address* 3 gram expressing an existing state or action: *the present tense*

present⁴ n 1 [the+S] the PRESENT³ (2) time 2 **at present** at this time 3 **for the present** now, but not necessarily in the future

pre·sent·a·ble /prɪˈzentəbəl/ adj fit to be seen publicly –bly adv

pre·sen·ta·tion /ˌprezənˈteɪʃən ‖ ˌpriːzen-, -zən-/ n 1 [C;U] act of presenting 2 [U] way something is shown, explained, etc. to others

pres·ent-day /ˌ·· '·◂/ adj existing now; modern

pre·sen·ti·ment /prɪˈzentəmənt/ n strange feeling that something (bad) is going to happen

pres·ent·ly /ˈprezntli/ adv 1 soon 2 esp. AmE now

present par·ti·ci·ple /ˌ·· '···/ n (in grammar) a participle that is formed in English by adding -ing to the verb and can be used in compound forms of the verb to show PROGRESSIVE tenses, or sometimes as an adjective

pres·er·va·tion /ˌprezəˈveɪʃən ‖ -zər-/ n [U] 1 act of preserving 2 condition after a long time

pre·ser·va·tive /prɪˈzɜːvətɪv ‖ -ɜːr-/ n, adj [C;U] (substance) used to PRESERVE (2) food

pre·serve /prɪˈzɜːv ‖ -ɜːrv/ vt 1 keep from decaying or being destroyed or lost: *preserving old customs/one's health* 2 treat (food) so it can be kept a long time ♦ n 1 [C;U] JAM (1) 2 [C] something limited to one person or group

pre·side /prɪˈzaɪd/ vi be in charge, esp. at a meeting

pres·i·den·cy /ˈprezədənsi/ n office of president

pres·i·dent /ˈprezədənt/ n 1 head of state (and government) in countries that do not have a king or queen 2 head of a business firm, government department, club, etc. ~**ial** /ˌprezəˈdenʃəl◂/ adj

press¹ /pres/ v 1 vt push firmly and steadily 2 vt hold firmly as a sign of friendship, etc.: *He pressed my hand warmly.* 3 vt direct weight onto to flatten, shape, get liquid out, etc. 4 vi move strongly,

esp. in a mass 5 vt give (clothes) a smooth surface and a sharp fold by using a hot iron 6 vt urge strongly: *She pressed her guests to say a little longer.* 7 vi make quick action necessary ~**ed** adj not having enough: *pressed for time* ~**ing** adj urgent

press for phr vt demand urgently

press on phr vi continue with determination

press² n 1 [U] (writers for) the newspapers 2 [S] treatment given in the newspapers: *The play got a good press.* 3 [S] act of pushing steadily 4 [C] printing machine 5 [C] business for printing (and sometimes also selling) books, etc. 6 [C] apparatus for pressing something: *trouser press* 7 [C] act of smoothing a garment with a hot iron 8 **go to press** (of a newspaper, etc.) start being printed

press box /ˈ· ·/ n place where newspaper reporters sit at sports events

press con·fer·ence /ˈ· ˌ···/ n meeting where someone answers reporters' questions

press·gang /ˈpresgæn/ vt force to do something unwillingly

press re·lease /ˈ· ·ˌ·/ n official statement to newspapers, radio, television, etc.

press-up /ˈ· ·/ n form of exercise where one lies face down and pushes with one's arms

pres·sure /ˈpreʃə ‖ -ər/ n 1 [C;U] (force produced by) pressing: *Water pressure burst the dam.* 2 [C;U] (force of) the weight of the air 3 [U] forcible influence; strong persuasion 4 [C;U] conditions of anxiety in life or work ♦ vt PRESSURIZE (1)

pressure cook·er /ˈ·· ˌ··/ n closed metal pot in which food is cooked quickly in steam

pressure group /ˈ·· ·/ n group of people trying to influence public and political opinion

pres·sur·ize , -ise /ˈpreʃəraɪz/ vt 1 (try to) make (someone) do something by forceful demands 2 control the air pressure inside

pres·tige /preˈstiːʒ/ n [U] quality of being widely admired, esp. because of being the best or connected with high rank –**tigious** /preˈstɪdʒəs ‖ -ˈstiː-, ˈstɪ-/ adj having or bringing prestige

pre·su·ma·bly /prɪˈzjuːməbli ‖ -ˈzuː-/

adv it may reasonably be supposed that

pre·sume /prɪˈzjuːm ‖ -ˈzuːm/ *v* 1 *vt* take as true without proof 2 *vi fml* be disrespectful enough; dare: *I wouldn't presume to argue.*

pre·sump·tion /prɪˈzʌmpʃən/ *n* [U] 1 act of supposing 2 *fml* disrespectful behaviour

pre·sump·tu·ous /prɪˈzʌmptʃuəs/ *adj* disrespectful and with too high an opinion of oneself **~ly** *adv*

pre·sup·pose /ˌpriːsəˈpəʊz ‖ -ˈpoʊz/ *vt* 1 accept as true in advance without proof 2 need according to reason: *A child presupposes a mother.* **–position** /ˌpriːsʌpəˈzɪʃən/ *n* [C;U]

pre·tence also **-tense** *AmE* /prɪˈtens ‖ ˈpriːtens/ *n* 1 [S;U] false appearance or reason 2 [U] claim to possess: *little pretence to fairness*

pre·tend /prɪˈtend/ *v* 1 *vi/t* give an appearance of (something untrue), to deceive or as a game 2 *vi* attempt; dare

pre·tend·er /prɪˈtendə ‖ -ər/ *n* person who makes a (doubtful or unproved) claim to some high position

pre·ten·sion /prɪˈtenʃən/ *n fml* claim to possess a skill, quality, etc.

pre·ten·tious /prɪˈtenʃəs/ *adj* claiming importance, rank, or artistic value one does not have **~ly** *adv* **–ness** *n* [U]

pre·text /ˈpriːtekst/ *n* false reason

pret·ty /ˈprɪti/ *adj* pleasing to look at ♦ *adv* 1 rather; quite 2 **pretty well** almost **–tily** *adv* —see also **a pretty penny** (PENNY)

pre·vail /prɪˈveɪl/ *vi fml* 1 win 2 exist; be widespread **–ing** *adj* 1 (of wind) that usu. blows 2 common or general (in some place or time)

   prevail upon *phr vt fml* persuade

prev·a·lent /ˈprevələnt/ *adj fml* common in a place or at a time **~ly** *adv* **–lence** *n* [U]

pre·var·i·cate /prɪˈværɪkeɪt/ *vi fml* try to hide the truth **–cation** /prɪˌværɪˈkeɪʃən/ *n* [C;U]

pre·vent /prɪˈvent/ *vt* stop (something) happening or (someone) doing something **~ion** /prɪˈvenʃən/ *n* [U]

pre·ven·tive /prɪˈventɪv/ also **pre·ven·ta·tive** /prɪˈventətɪv/ *adj* that prevents esp. illness

pre·view /ˈpriːvjuː/ *n* private showing or short description of film, show, etc. before

it is publicly seen ♦ *vt* give a preview of

pre·vi·ous /ˈpriːvɪəs/ *adj* before this one: *my previous employer* **~ly** *adv*

prey¹ /preɪ/ *n* [U] 1 animal hunted and eaten by another 2 such hunting and eating: *The eagle is a bird of prey.*

prey² *v* **prey on** *phr vt* 1 hunt and eat as prey 2 trouble greatly

price /praɪs/ *n* 1 money (to be) paid for something: (fig.) *the price of freedom* 2 **at a price** at a high price 3 **not at any price** not at all ♦ *vt* fix the price of

price·less /ˈpraɪsləs/ *adj* 1 extremely valuable 2 *infml* very funny

price tag /ˈ· ·/ *n* 1 small ticket showing the price of an article 2 a (fixed or stated) price: *The government has not yet put a price tag on the plan.*

pric·ey /ˈpraɪsi/ *adj infml, esp. BrE* expensive

prick¹ /prɪk/ *v* 1 *vt* make a small hole in with something sharp-pointed 2 *vi/t* (cause to) feel a light sharp pain on the skin 3 **prick up one's ears** start to listen carefully

prick² *n* 1 small sharp pain 2 mark made by pricking 3 *taboo* PENIS 4 *taboo sl* foolish worthless man

prick·le /ˈprɪkəl/ *n* 1 [C] small sharp point on an animal or plant 2 [S] pricking sensation on the skin ♦ *vi/t* PRICK¹ (2) **–ly** *adj* 1 covered with prickles 2 that gives you a prickling sensation 3 difficult to deal with

pride¹ /praɪd/ *n* 1 [S;U] pleasure in what you (or someone connected with you) can do or have done well 2 [U] reasonable self-respect 3 [U] too high an opinion of yourself 4 [S] most valuable one: *the pride of my collection* 5 **pride of place** *esp. BrE* highest or best position

pride² *v* **pride oneself on** *phr vt* be proud of (oneself) because of

priest /priːst/ *n* 1 (in the Christian Church, esp. in the ROMAN Catholic Church) specially trained person who performs religious ceremonies and other religious duties 2 **priestess** /ˈpriːstes/ *fem.* — specially trained person in certain non-Christian religions **–hood** *n* [U] 1 position of being a priest 2 all the priests

prig /prɪg/ *n* unpleasantly moral person **~gish** *adj*

prim /prɪm/ *adj* **-mm-** easily shocked by

rude things ~**ly** *adv*
pri·ma·cy /ˈpraɪməsi/ *n* [U] *fml* being first in importance, rank, etc.
prima don·na /ˌpriːmə ˈdɒnə ‖ -ˈdɑːnə/ *n* **1** main female OPERA singer **2** someone who thinks they are very important and often gets excited and angry
pri·ma fa·cie /ˌpraɪmə ˈfeɪʃi ‖ -ʃə/ *adj, adv law* based on what seems true
pri·mal /ˈpraɪməl/ *adj* belonging to the earliest times
pri·ma·ri·ly /ˈpraɪmərəli ‖ praɪˈmerəli/ *adv* mainly
pri·ma·ry¹ /ˈpraɪməri ‖ -meri/ *adj* **1** chief; main: *the primary purpose of his visit* **2** earliest in time or order of development: *primary education*
primary² *n* (esp. in the US) election in which the members of a political party in a particular area vote for the person they would like to see as their party's CANDIDATE for a political office
primary col·our *BrE* ‖ **color** *AmE* /ˌ··· ˈ··/ *n* **1** (in art) red, yellow, or blue **2** (in PHYSICS) red, green, or blue
primary school /ˈ··· ˌ·/ *n* **1** *BrE* school for children between 5 and 11 years old **2** *AmE* ELEMENTARY SCHOOL
pri·mate¹ /ˈpraɪmeɪt/ *n* member of the most highly developed group of MAMMALS which includes human beings, monkeys, and related animals
pri·mate² /ˈpraɪmɪ̈t/ *n* priest of the highest rank in the Church of England
prime¹ /praɪm/ *n* [S] time when someone is at their best
prime² *adj* **1** main **2** best
prime³ *vt* **1** put PRIMER¹ (1) on **2** instruct in advance **3** put explosive powder into (a gun)
prime min·is·ter /ˌ· ˈ···/ *n* chief minister and government leader
prime num·ber /ˌ· ˈ··/ *n* number that can only be divided by itself and the number one
prim·er /ˈpraɪmə ‖ -ər/ *n* **1** [U] paint put on before the main painting **2** [C] tube containing explosive, esp. to set off a bomb
prime time /ˈ· ˌ·/ *n* [U] time when most people are thought to watch television
pri·me·val /praɪˈmiːvəl/ *adj* very ancient
prim·i·tive /ˈprɪmɪ̈tɪv/ *adj* **1** of the earliest stage of development **2** roughly made or done **3** old-fashioned and inconvenient *n* member of a PRIMITIVE (1) race or tribe ~**ly** *adv*
pri·mor·di·al /praɪˈmɔːdiəl ‖ -ˈmɔːr-/ *adj* existing from or at the beginning of time
prim·rose /ˈprɪmrəʊz ‖ -roʊz/ *n* pale yellow spring flower
prince /prɪns/ *n* **1** king's son **2** royal ruler of a small country ~**ly** *adj* **1** of a prince **2** splendid; generous
prin·cess /ˌprɪnˈses◂ ‖ ˈprɪnsəs/ *n* **1** king's daughter **2** prince's wife
prin·ci·pal /ˈprɪnsɪ̈pəl/ *adj* main ♦ *n* **1** [C] head of a college, school, etc. **2** [S] money lent, on which interest is paid ~**ly** *adv*
principal boy /ˌ··· ˈ·/ *n* chief male character in a PANTOMIME, played by a woman
prin·ci·pal·i·ty /ˌprɪnsɪ̈ˈpælɪ̈ti/ *n* country ruled by a prince
prin·ci·ple /ˈprɪnsɪ̈pəl/ *n* **1** [C] general truth or belief: *the principle of free speech* **2** [C;U] moral rule which guides behaviour: *She resigned on a matter of principle.* **3** [U] high personal standard of right and wrong: a man of principle **4** [P] general rules on which a skill, etc. is based: *Archimedes' principle* **5 in principle** as an idea, if not in fact **6 on principle** because it would be morally wrong
print¹ /prɪnt/ *n* **1** [U] printed letters, words, etc. **2** [C] mark made on a surface: *a thumbprint* **3** [C] photograph printed on paper **4** [C] picture printed from a metal sheet or copied from a painting by photography **5 in/out of print** (of a book) that can still/no longer be obtained —see also SMALL PRINT
print² *v* **1** *vi/t* produce words or pictures on paper or material, using a machine **2** *vt* produce copies of a book, newspaper, etc. **3** *vt* print (a letter, speech, etc.) in a newspaper, etc. **4** *vi/t* write without joining the letters ~**able** *adj* suitable for reading by anyone ~**er** *n* **1** machine that prints documents from a computer **2** person or company that prints books, etc.
print·out /ˈprɪntˌaʊt/ *n* [C;U] printed information from a computer
pri·or¹ /ˈpraɪə ‖ -ər/ *adj* **1** earlier **2** more important **3 prior to** before
prior² *n* head of a priory
pri·o·ri·tize, -ise /praɪˈɒrɪ̈taɪz ‖ -ˈɔːr-/ *vt*

give (something) priority

pri·or·i·ty /praɪˈɒrəti ‖ -ˈɔːr-/ n 1 [U] (right of) being first in position or earlier in time 2 [C] something that needs attention before others

pri·o·ry /ˈpraɪəri/ n (building for) a religious group

prise /praɪz/ vt esp. BrE for PRIZE[2]

pris·m /ˈprɪzəm/ n transparent three-sided block that breaks up light into different colours

pris·on /ˈprɪzən/ n [C;U] large building where criminals are kept for punishment

prison camp /ˈ·· ·/ n guarded camp for prisoners of war

pris·on·er /ˈprɪzənə ‖ -ər/ n person kept in prison

prisoner of war /ˌ··· ·ˈ·/ n soldier, etc. caught by the enemy in war

pris·sy /ˈprɪsi/ adj infml annoyingly exact or proper

pris·tine /ˈprɪstiːn/ adj fml fresh and clean

priv·a·cy /ˈprɪvəsi, ˈpraɪ- ‖ ˈpraɪ-/ n [U] 1 (the desirable) state of being away from other people 2 secrecy

pri·vate /ˈpraɪvət/ adj 1 not (to be) shared with others; secret 2 just for one person or a small group, not everyone 3 not connected with or paid for by government 4 not connected with one's work or rank; unofficial 5 quiet; without lots of people ♦ n soldier of the lowest rank -ly adv

private de·tec·tive /ˌ·· ·ˈ··/ n person, not a policeman, hired to follow people, report on their actions, etc.

private en·ter·prise /ˌ·· ˈ···/ n [U] CAPITALISM

private eye /ˌ·· ·ˈ/ n infml private detective

private parts /ˌ·· ·ˈ/ n [P] outer sexual organs

private sec·tor /ˌ·· ˈ··◂/ n [the+S] those industries and services that are owned and run by private companies, not by the state

pri·vat·ize also -ise BrE /ˈpraɪvətaɪz/ vt sell (a government-owned industry or organization) into private ownership -ization, -isation /ˌpraɪvətaɪˈzeɪʃən ‖ -tə-/ n [U]: the privatization of the hospital service

priv·et /ˈprɪvət/ n [U] bush often used for HEDGES

priv·i·lege /ˈprɪvəlɪdʒ/ n 1 [C] special advantage limited to a particular person or group 2 [U] unfair possession of such advantages because of wealth, social rank, etc. ~leged adj having (a) privilege

priv·y[1] /ˈprɪvi/ adj fml sharing secret knowledge (of)

privy[2] n old use for TOILET

Privy Coun·cil /ˌ·· ˈ··/ n body of important people who advise the British king or queen

prize[1] /praɪz/ n something you get given for winning, doing well, etc. ♦ vt value highly adj 1 that has gained or is worthy of a prize: a prize hen 2 given as a prize: prize money

prize[2] vt lift or force with a tool or metal bar

prize·fight /ˈpraɪzfaɪt/ n public BOXING match in former times ~er n

pro[1] /prəʊ ‖ proʊ/ n pros infml for PROFESSIONAL

pro[2] n argument or reason in favour (of something)

pro·ac·tive /ˌprəʊˈæktɪv ‖ proʊ-/ adj making things happen instead of just reacting to events

pro-am /ˌprəʊ ˈæm ‖ ˌproʊ-/ n, adj (competition) including both PROFESSIONALS and AMATEURS

prob·a·bil·i·ty /ˌprɒbəˈbɪləti ‖ ˌprɑː-/ n 1 [S;U] likelihood 2 [C] probable event or result

prob·a·ble /ˈprɒbəbəl ‖ ˈprɑː-/ adj that has a good chance of happening or being true; likely -bly adv

pro·bate /ˈprəʊbeɪt, -bət ‖ ˈproʊbeɪt/ n [U] legal process of declaring someone's WILL (5) properly made

pro·ba·tion /prəˈbeɪʃən ‖ proʊ-/ n [U] 1 (period of) testing someone's suitability 2 system of not sending law-breakers to prison if they behave well for a time

probation of·fi·cer /·ˈ·· ˌ··/ n person who watches and advises law-breakers on probation (2)

probe /prəʊb ‖ proʊb/ vi/t search or examine carefully (as if) with a long thin instrument ♦ n 1 metal tool for probing 2 spacecraft for searching through space 3 thorough inquiry

prob·lem /ˈprɒbləm ‖ ˈprɑː-/ n difficulty that needs attention and thought

prob·lem·at·ic /ˌprɒbləˈmætɪk◂/ ˌprɑː-/ adj full of problems or causing problems

pro·ce·dure /prəˈsiːdʒə ‖ -ər/ n 1 [C] set of actions for doing something 2 [U] way a meeting, trial, etc. is (is to be) run –**dural** adj

pro·ceed /prəˈsiːd/ vi fml 1 begin or continue in a course of action 2 walk or travel in a particular direction

pro·ceed·ings /prəˈsiːdɪŋz/ n [P] legal action taken against someone

pro·ceeds /ˈprəʊsiːdz ‖ ˈprou-/ n [P] money gained from the sale of something

pro·cess¹ /ˈprəʊses ‖ ˈprɑː-/ n 1 set of actions that produce continuation, change, or something new 2 method, esp. for producing goods 3 **in the process of** actually doing (the stated thing) at the time ♦ vt 1 treat and preserve (food): processed cheese 2 print a photograph from (film) 3 deal with; examine

pro·cess² /prəˈses/ vi walk in a procession

pro·ces·sion /prəˈseʃən/ n [C;U] line of people or vehicles moving along, esp. ceremonially

pro·ces·sor /ˈprəʊsesə ‖ ˈprɑːsesər/ n MICROPROCESSOR —see also WORD PROCESSOR, FOOD PROCESSOR

pro·claim /prəˈkleɪm ‖ prou-/ vt declare publicly and officially

proc·la·ma·tion /ˌprɒkləˈmeɪʃən ‖ ˌprɑː-/ n 1 [C] official public statement 2 [U] act of proclaiming

pro·cras·ti·nate /prəˈkræstəneɪt/ vi fml delay (annoyingly) –**nation** /prəˌkræst ɪˈneɪʃən/ n [U]

pro·cre·ate /ˈprəʊkrieɪt ‖ ˈprou-/ vi fml produce young –**ation** /ˌprəʊkriˈeɪʃən ‖ ˌprou-/ n [U]

pro·cure /prəˈkjʊə ‖ prouˈkjʊr/ v 1 vt fml obtain 2 vi/t provide (a woman) for sexual pleasure –**curer** n [U]

prod /prɒd ‖ prɑːd/ v -**dd**- 1 vi/t push with a pointed object 2 vt urge sharply **prod** n

prod·i·gal /ˈprɒdɪgəl ‖ ˈprɑː-/ adj fml 1 carelessly wasteful, esp. of money 2 giving or producing (something) freely and in large amounts ~**ity** /ˌprɒdɪˈgælɪti ‖ ˌprɑː-/ n [U]

pro·di·gious /prəˈdɪdʒəs/ adj wonderfully large, powerful, etc. ~**ly** adv

prod·i·gy /ˈprɒdɪdʒi ‖ ˈprɑː-/ n 1 person with unusual abilities: child prodigy 2 a

wonder in nature

pro·duce¹ /prəˈdjuːs ‖ -ˈduːs/ vt 1 bring into existence; give: These trees produce rubber. | Poverty produces ill-health. 2 make (goods for sale) 3 give birth to 4 bring out and show 5 prepare and bring before the public

prod·uce² /ˈprɒdjuːs ‖ ˈprɑːduːs/ n [U] something produced, esp. on a farm

pro·duc·er /prəˈdjuːsə ‖ -ˈduːsər/ n 1 person, company, etc. that produces goods 2 person in charge of the business of putting on a play, film, etc.

prod·uct /ˈprɒdʌkt ‖ ˈprɑː-/ n 1 something made or produced 2 result

pro·duc·tion /prəˈdʌkʃən/ n 1 [U] act of producing 2 [U] process of making products 3 [U] amount produced: a cut in production 4 [C] play, film, or broadcast that is produced

production line /·ˈ·· ·/ n arrangement of factory workers and machines for producing goods

pro·duc·tive /prəˈdʌktɪv/ adj 1 that produces a lot 2 causing or producing (a result) ~**ly** adv

pro·duc·tiv·i·ty /ˌprɒdʌkˈtɪvɪti, -dək- ‖ ˌprɑː-/ n [U] rate of producing goods, crops, etc.

prof /prɒf ‖ prɑːf/ n infml for PROFESSOR

pro·fane /prəˈfeɪn/ adj 1 showing disrespect, esp. for holy things 2 (esp. of language) socially shocking 3 fml concerned with human life in this world; SECULAR: profane art ♦ vt treat disrespectfully ~**ly** adv

pro·fan·i·ty /prəˈfænɪti/ n [C;U] profane behaviour or speech

pro·fess /prəˈfes/ vt fml 1 declare openly 2 claim, usu. falsely 3 have as one's religion ~**ed** adj 1 self-declared 2 pretended

pro·fes·sion /prəˈfeʃən/ n 1 form of employment, esp. a socially respected one like law or medicine 2 people in a particular profession 3 fml open declaration

pro·fes·sion·al /prəˈfeʃənəl/ adj 1 working in a profession 2 doing for payment what others do for fun 3 showing high standards of work ♦ n professional person ~**ism** n [U] skill or quality of professionals

pro·fes·sor /prəˈfesə ‖ -ər/ n university

teacher of highest rank ~**ial** /ˌprəfə'sɔ:-riəl || ˌprɑː-/ *adj*

pro·fi·cient /prə'fɪʃənt/ *adj* very good at doing something ~**ly** *adv* –**ciency** *n* [U]

pro·file /'prəʊfaɪl || 'prəʊ-/ *n* 1 side view, esp. of someone's head 2 state of being noticed by other people around me: *The management is trying to keep a* **low profile** *on this issue.* | *a* **high** *political* **profile** 3 short description ♦ *vt* draw or write a profile of

prof·it¹ /'prɒfɪt || 'prɑː-/ *n* 1 [C;U] money gained 2 [U] advantage gained from some action

profit² *v* profit **by/from** *phr vt* gain advantage or learn from

prof·it·a·bil·i·ty /ˌprɒfɪtə'bɪlɪti || ˌprɑː-/ *n* [U] state of being profitable or the degree to which a business is profitable

prof·it·a·ble /'prɒfɪtəbəl || 'prɑː-/ *adj* producing profit –**bly** *adv*

prof·it·eer /ˌprɒfɪ'tɪə || ˌprɑːfɪ'tɪr/ *n* person who makes unfairly large profits profiteer *vi*

profit mar·gin /'·· ˌ·/ *n* difference between production cost and selling price

profit shar·ing /'·· ˌ·/ *n* [U] workers sharing the profits of a business

pro·found /prə'faʊnd/ *adj* 1 very strongly felt; deep 2 having thorough knowledge and understanding ~**ly** *adv* –**fundity** /prə'fʌndɪti/ *n* [C;U]

pro·fuse /prə'fjuːs/ *adj* produced in great quantity ~**ly** *adv* –**fusion** /prə'fjuːʒən/ *n* [S;U] (too) great amount

pro·ges·ter·one /prəʊ'dʒestərəʊn || prəʊ'dʒestərəʊn/ *n* [U] bodily substance that prepares the UTERUS for its work

prog·no·sis /prɒg'nəʊsɪs || prɑːg'nəʊ-/ *n* -**ses** /-siːz/ 1 doctor's opinion of how an illness will develop 2 description of the future

pro·gram¹ /'prəʊɡræm || 'prəʊ-/ *n* 1 set of instructions for making a computer do something 2 *AmE* a programme

program² *vt* -**mm-** *or* -**m-** 1 supply (a computer) with a PROGRAM¹ 2 *AmE* to programme ~**mable** *adj* controllable by means of a PROGRAM¹ (1) ~**mer** *n*

pro·gramme *BrE* ‖ -**gram** *AmE* /'prəʊɡræm || 'prəʊ-/ *n* 1 list of performers or things to be performed 2 television or radio show 3 plan for future action ♦ *vt* plan or arrange

pro·gress¹ /'prəʊɡres || 'prɑː-/ *n* [U] 1 continual improvement or development 2 forward movement in space 3 **in progress** happening or being done

pro·gress² /prə'ɡres/ *vi* make progress

pro·gres·sion /prə'ɡreʃən/ *n* 1 [S;U] progressing 2 [C] set of numbers that vary in a particular way

pro·gres·sive /prə'ɡresɪv/ *adj* 1 developing continuously or by stages 2 favouring change or new ideas 3 (of a verb form) showing action that is continuing ♦ *n* person with progressive ideas, esp. about social change ~**ly** *adv*

pro·hib·it /prə'hɪbɪt || prəʊ-/ *vt fml* 1 forbid by law or rule 2 prevent

pro·hi·bi·tion /ˌprəʊhɪ'bɪʃən || ˌprəʊ-/ *n* 1 [U] act of prohibiting something, esp. the sale of alcohol 2 [C] *fml* order forbidding something

pro·hib·i·tive /prə'hɪbɪtɪv || prəʊ-/ *adj* preventing or tending to discourage: *prohibitive prices* (=too high) ~**ly** *adv*

proj·ect¹ /'prɒdʒekt || 'prɑː-/ *n* long piece of planned work

pro·ject² /prə'dʒekt/ *v* 1 *vi/t* stick out beyond a surface 2 *vt fml* aim and throw through the air 3 *vt* direct (sound or light) into space or onto a surface 4 *vt* make plans for: *our projected visit to France* 5 *vt* judge or calculate using the information one has: *projected sales figures* 6 *vi/t* express (oneself or one's beliefs, etc.) outwardly, esp. to have a favourable effect on others

pro·jec·tile /prə'dʒektaɪl || -tl/ *n* object or weapon thrown or fired

pro·jec·tion /prə'dʒekʃən/ *n* 1 [U] act of projecting 2 [C] something that sticks out 3 [C] guess of future possibilities based on known facts

pro·jec·tion·ist /prə'dʒekʃənɪst/ *n* person who works a PROJECTOR, esp. in a cinema

pro·jec·tor /prə'dʒektə || -ər/ *n* apparatus for projecting films, etc.

pro·lapse /'prəʊlæps || prəʊ-/ *vi fml* (of an inner body organ) slip out of its right place

pro·le·tar·i·at /ˌprəʊlɪ'teəriət || ˌprəʊlɪ'ter-/ *n* class of unskilled wage-earning workers

pro·lif·e·rate /prə'lɪfəreɪt/ *vi* increase

rapidly in numbers –**ration** /prə,lɪfə-'reɪʃən/ n [S;U]

pro·lif·ic /prə'lɪfɪk/ adj producing a lot –**ally** /-kli/ adv

pro·logue BrE ‖ **-log** AmE /'prəʊlɒg ‖ 'prəʊlɔ:g, -lɑ:g/ n 1 introduction to a play, long poem, etc. 2 event that leads up to another, bigger one

pro·long /prə'lɒŋ ‖ -'lɔ:ŋ/ vt lengthen ~**ed** adv long

prom /prɒm ‖ prɑ:m/ n BrE 1 PROMENADE (1) 2 PROMENADE CONCERT

prom·e·nade /,prɒmə'nɑ:d◄, 'prɒmə-nɑ:d ‖ ,prɑ:mə'neɪd/ n wide path along the coast in a holiday town

promenade con·cert /·'· ,··, '··· ,·/ n (esp. in Britain) concert where some listeners stand

prom·i·nent /'prɒmɪnənt ‖ 'prɑ:-/ adj 1 sticking out 2 noticeable 3 famous ~**ly** adv –**nence** n 1 [U] fact or quality of being prominent 2 [C] fml part that sticks out

pro·mis·cu·ous /prə'mɪskjuəs/ adj not limited to one sexual partner –**cuity** /,prɒmɪ'skju:ɪti ‖ ,prɑ:-/ n [U]

prom·ise /'prɒmɪs ‖ 'prɑ:-/ n 1 [C] statement, which one wishes to be believed, of what one will do 2 [U] signs of future success, good results, etc. ♦ v 1 vi/t make a promise: I promise I won't tell them. 2 vt cause one to expect or hope for –**ising** adj showing PROMISE (2)

Promised Land /,·· '·/ n [(the)S] hoped-for condition which will bring happiness

prom·on·to·ry /'prɒməntəri ‖ 'prɑ:mən-tɔ:ri/ n point of land stretching out into the sea

pro·mote /prə'məʊt ‖ -'moʊt/ vt 1 raise to a higher position or rank 2 help to arrange (a business, concert, etc.) 3 advertise 4 fml help to bring about –**moter** n person whose job is to promote events, activities, etc.

pro·mo·tion /prə'məʊʃən ‖ -'moʊ-/ n [C;U] 1 raising of rank or position 2 advertising activity

prompt¹ /prɒmpt ‖ prɑ:mpt/ vt 1 cause; urge 2 remind (an actor) of forgotten words prompt, ~**er** n person who prompts actors

prompt² adj acting or done quickly or at the right time ~**ly** adv ~**ness** n [U]

prone /prəʊn ‖ proʊn/ adj 1 likely to suffer: prone to colds | accident-prone

2 lying face downwards

prong /prɒŋ ‖ prɔ:ŋ/ n pointed part of a fork: (fig.) a three-pronged attack (=from three directions)

pro·nom·i·nal /prəʊ'nɒmɪnəl ‖ proʊ-'nɑ:-/ adj of a pronoun

pro·noun /'prəʊnaʊn ‖ 'proʊ-/ n word used instead of a noun, such as he or it

pro·nounce /prə'naʊns/ vt 1 make the sound of (a letter, word, etc.) 2 fml declare officially ~**ment** n solemn declaration –**nounced** adj very strong or noticeable

pro·nun·ci·a·tion /prə,nʌnsi'eɪʃən/ n [C;U] way in which a language or word is pronounced

proof¹ /pru:f/ n 1 [C;U] way of showing that something is true 2 [C] a test or trial 3 [C] test copy of something to be printed 4 [U] standard of strength for certain alcoholic drinks

proof² adj having or giving protection: proof against temptation | waterproof

proof·read /'pru:f,ri:d/ vi/t read and put right mistakes in proofs (PROOF¹ (3)) ~**er** n

prop¹ /prɒp/ n support for something heavy ♦ vt -**pp**- support or keep in a leaning position

prop² n small article used on stage

prop·a·gan·da /,prɒpə'gændə ‖ ,prɑ:-/ n [U] information spread to influence public opinion

prop·a·gate /'prɒpəgeɪt ‖ 'prɑ:-/ v 1 vi/t (cause to) increase in number by producing young 2 vt fml spread (ideas, etc.) –**gation** /,prɒpə'geɪʃən ‖ ,prɑ:-/ n [U]

pro·pel /prə'pel/ vt -**ll**- move or push forward

pro·pel·lant /prə'pelənt/ n [C;U] explosive for firing a bullet or ROCKET

pro·pel·ler /prə'pelə/ -ər/ n two or more blades on a central bar that turns to drive an aircraft or ship

pro·pen·si·ty /prə'pensɪti/ n fml natural tendency

prop·er /'prɒpə ‖ 'prɑ:pər/ adj 1 right; suitable; correct 2 socially acceptable 3 complete: a proper fool ~**ly** adv

proper noun /,·· '·/ n name of a particular thing or person, spelt with a CAPITAL letter

prop·er·ty /'prɒpəti ‖ 'prɑ:pərti/ n 1 [U] something owned; possession(s) 2 [C;U] (area of) land and/or building(s) 3 [C] natural quality or power

proph·e·cy /'prɒfɨsi || 'prɑː-/ n [C;U] (statement) telling what will happen in the future

proph·e·sy /'prɒfɨsaɪ || 'prɑː-/ vi/t say what will happen in the future

proph·et /'prɒfɨt || 'prɑː-/ n 1 person who makes known and explains God's will 2 person who tells about the future ~ic /prə'fetɪk/ adj

pro·phy·lac·tic /ˌprɒfɨˈlæktɪk◄||ˌprɑː-/ adj fml for preventing disease ♦ n something prophylactic, esp. a CONDOM

pro·por·tion /prə'pɔːʃən || -'pɔːr-/ n 1 [C;U] relationship between one thing or part and another in size, importance, etc. 2 [C] part of a whole 3 **in/out of proportion** according/not according to real importance ♦ vt fml make in or put into suitable proportion ~al, ~ate adj in correct proportion **proportions** n [P] size and shape

proportional rep·re·sen·ta·tion /ˌ···ˈ····ˌ····/ n [U] system of voting in elections by which parties are represented in parliament according to the proportion of votes they receive, rather than having to get a majority of the votes in each voting area

pro·pos·al /prə'pəʊzəl || -'pou-/ n 1 plan; suggestion 2 offer of marriage

pro·pose /prə'pəʊz || -'pouz/ v 1 vt suggest 2 vt intend 3 vi/t make an offer of (marriage)

prop·o·si·tion /ˌprɒpə'zɪʃən || ˌprɑː-/ n 1 statement giving an unproved judgment 2 suggested offer or arrangement 3 person or situation to be dealt with 4 suggested offer to have sex with someone vt infml make a PROPOSITION (esp. 4) to (someone)

pro·pound /prə'paʊnd/ vt fml put forward (an idea)

pro·pri·e·ta·ry /prə'praɪətəri || -teri/ adj 1 privately owned: a proprietary brand name 2 of or like an owner

pro·pri·e·tor /prə'praɪətə || -ər/ n owner of a business

pro·pri·e·ty /prə'praɪəti/ n [U] fml 1 social or moral correctness 2 rightness or reasonableness

pro·pul·sion /prə'pʌlʃən/ n [U] force that PROPELS ~sive /-sɪv/ adj

pro ra·ta /ˌprəʊ 'rɑːtə || ˌprou 'reɪtə/ adv, adj according to a fair share for each

pro·sa·ic /prəʊˈzeɪ-ɪk, prə- || prou-, prə/ adj dull ~ally /-kli/ adv

pros and cons /ˌprəʊz ən 'kɒnz || ˌprouz ən 'kɑːnz/ n [P] reasons for and against

pro·scribe /prəʊ'skraɪb || prou-/ vt fml forbid, esp. by law

prose /prəʊz || prouz/ n [U] ordinary written language (not poetry)

pros·e·cute /'prɒsɨkjuːt || 'prɑː-/ vi/t bring a criminal charge (against) in court -cutor n -cution /ˌprɒsɨ'kjuːʃən || ˌprɑː-/ n 1 [C;U] prosecuting 2 [the+S] group of people prosecuting someone in court 3 [U] fml the carrying out of something that needs to be done

pros·e·lyt·ize, -ise /'prɒsələtaɪz || 'prɑː-/ vi fml try to persuade people to become proselytes

pros·pect¹ /'prɒspekt || 'prɑː-/ n 1 [C;U] reasonable hope of something happening 2 [S;U] something which is likely soon 3 [C] wide or distant view

pros·pect² /prə'spekt || 'prɑːspekt/ vi try to find gold, oil, etc. ~or n

pro·spec·tive /prə'spektɪv/ adj likely to become

pro·spec·tus /prə'spektəs/ n small book advertising a product, college, new business, etc.

pros·per /'prɒspə || 'prɑːspər/ vi 1 become successful and esp. rich 2 grow well ~ous adj successful and rich ~ity /prɒ'sperɨti || prɑː-/ n [U] success and wealth

pros·tate /'prɒsteɪt || 'prɑː-/ n male bodily organ producing a seed-carrying liquid

pros·the·sis /prɒs'θiːsɨs || prɑːs-/ n artificial body part

pros·ti·tute /'prɒstɨtjuːt || 'prɑːstɨtuːt/ n someone who has sex with people for money ♦ vt fml use dishonourably for money -tution /ˌprɒstɨ'tjuːʃən || ˌprɑːs-tɨ'tuː-/ n [U]

pros·trate /'prɒstreɪt || 'prɑː-/ adj 1 lying face downwards, esp. in worship 2 without any strength or courage ♦ /prɒs'treɪt || 'prɑːstreɪt/ vt make prostrate

pro·tag·o·nist /prəʊ'tægənɨst || prou-/ n 1 main supporter of a new idea 2 someone taking part

pro·tect /prə'tekt/ vt keep safe ~or n

~ion /prə'tekʃən/ n 1 [U] act of protecting or state of being protected 2 [C] something that protects

pro·tec·tion·is·m /prə'tekʃənɪzəm/ n [U] helping one's own country's trade by taxing foreign goods

protection rack·et /·'·· ,··/ n getting money from shop owners, etc. by threatening to damage their property

pro·tec·tive /prə'tektɪv/ adj 1 that protects 2 wishing to protect ~ly adv

pro·tec·tor·ate /prə'tektərət/ n country controlled and protected by another country

prot·é·gé /'prɒtɪʒeɪ ‖ 'prou-/ n person guided and helped by another

pro·tein /'prəutiːn ‖ 'prou-/ n [C;U] food substance that builds up the body and keeps it healthy

pro tem /,prəu 'tem ‖ ,prou-/ adv for the present time only

pro·test¹ /'prəutest ‖ 'prou-/ n [C;U] 1 strong expression of disapproval, opposition, etc. 2 **under protest** unwillingly

pro·test² /prə'test/ v 1 vi make a protest 2 vt declare strongly against opposition ~er n

Prot·es·tant /'prɒtɪstənt ‖ 'prɑː-/ n, adj (member) of a branch of the Christian church that separated from the Roman Catholic Church in the 16th century

prot·es·ta·tion /,prɒtɪ'steɪʃən ,prəu- ‖ ,prɑː-, ,prou-/ n fml 1 [C] solemn declaration 2 [U] protesting

pro·to·col /'prəutəkɒl ‖ 'proutəkɔːl/ n [U] fixed rules of behaviour

pro·ton /'prəutɒn ‖ 'proutɑːn/ n very small piece of matter that is part of an atom and carries POSITIVE (5) electricity

pro·to·type /'prəutətaɪp ‖ 'prou-/ n first form of a machine, afterwards developed

pro·tract /prə'trækt ‖ prou-/ vt cause to last an (unnecessarily) long time ~ion /prə'trækʃən/ n [U]

pro·trac·tor /prə'træktə ‖ prou-'træktər/ n instrument for measuring and drawing angles

pro·trude /prə'truːd ‖ prou-/ vi fml stick out ~trusion /prə'truːʒən/ n [C;U]

pro·tu·ber·ance /prə'tjuːbərəns ‖ prou'tuː-/ n fml swelling; BULGE

proud /praud/ adj 1 showing proper and reasonable self-respect 2 having too high an opinion of oneself 3 having or expressing personal pleasure in something connected with oneself: proud of her new car 4 splendid; glorious ♦ adv: do someone proud treat someone, esp. a guest, splendidly ~ly adv

prove /pruːv/ v 1 vt show to be true 2 be (later) found to be: These revelations could prove highly embarrassing.

prov·en /'pruːvən, 'prəuvən ‖ 'prou-, 'pruː-/ adj tested and shown to be true

prov·e·nance /'prɒvənəns ‖ 'prɑː-/ n fml (place of) origin

prov·erb /'prɒvɜːb ‖ 'prɑːvɜːrb/ n short well-known wise saying ~ial /prə'vɜːbiəl ‖ -'vɜːr-/ adj 1 (used when mentioning part of a well-known saying): Sweep it under the proverbial carpet. 2 widely known and spoken of

pro·vide /prə'vaɪd/ vt arrange for someone to get; supply ~vided conj on condition that ~viding conj provided

provide for phr vt 1 supply with necessary things 2 (of the law) make possible

prov·i·dence /'prɒvɪdəns ‖ 'prɑː-/ n [U] the kindness of fate

prov·i·dent /'prɒvɪdənt ‖ 'prɑː-/ adj fml careful to save for future needs

prov·i·den·tial /,prɒvɪ'denʃəl◄ ‖ ,prɑː-/ adj fml lucky

prov·ince /'prɒvɪns ‖ 'prɑː-/ n 1 main division of a country 2 area of knowledge, activity, etc. ~incial /prə'vɪnʃəl/ adj 1 of a province 2 narrow or old-fashioned in interest, customs, etc. **provinces** n [the+P] parts of a country far from the main city

pro·vi·sion /prə'vɪʒən/ n 1 [U] act of providing 2 [U] preparation against future risks or for future needs 3 [C] condition in an agreement or law **provisions** n [P] food supplies

pro·vi·sion·al /prə'vɪʒənəl/ adj for use now, but likely to be changed ~ly adv

pro·vi·so /prə'vaɪzəu ‖ -zou/ n -sos condition made in advance

prov·o·ca·tion /,prɒvə'keɪʃən ‖ ,prɑː-/ n 1 [U] act of provoking 2 [C] something annoying

pro·voc·a·tive /prə'vɒkətɪv ‖ -'vɑː-/ adj likely to cause a anger b sexual interest ~ly adv

pro·voke /prə'vəʊk ‖ -'voʊk/ vt 1 make angry 2 cause (a feeling or action)

prow /praʊ/ n front part of a ship

prow·ess /'praʊɪs/ n [U] fml great ability or courage

prowl /praʊl/ vi/t move about quietly and threateningly n [S] ♦ ~er n

prox·im·i·ty /prɒk'sɪmɪti ‖ prɑːk-/ n [U] fml nearness

prox·y /'prɒksi ‖ 'prɑːksi/ n 1 [U] right to act for another person, esp. as a voter 2 [C] person given this right

prude /pruːd/ n person easily offended by rude things, esp. connected with sex **prudish** adj

pru·dent /'pruːdənt/ adj sensible and careful **-ly** adv **-dence** n [U]

prune[1] /pruːn/ n dried PLUM

prune[2] vt 1 cut off parts of (a tree or bush) to improve shape and growth 2 remove unwanted parts of

pry[1] /praɪ/ vi try to find out about someone's private affairs

pry[2] vt esp. AmE for PRIZE[2]

P.S. /ˌpiː 'es/ n note added at the end of a letter

psalm /sɑːm ‖ sɑːm, sɑːlm/ n religious song or poem, esp. as in the Bible

pseu·do·nym /'sjuːdənɪm ‖ 'suːdənɪm/ n invented name, esp. of a writer

psst /ps/ interj (used for quietly gaining someone's attention)

psych /saɪk/ v sl, esp. AmE

  psych out phr vt 1 understand by INTUITION 2 frighten

  psych up phr vt make (esp. oneself) keen and ready

psy·che /'saɪki/ n fml human mind or spirit

psy·che·del·ic /ˌsaɪkɪ'delɪk◂/ adj 1 (of a drug) causing strange and powerful feelings 2 having strong patterns of colour, lines, moving lights, noise, etc.

psy·chi·a·try /saɪ'kaɪətri ‖ sə-/ n [U] study and treatment of diseases of the mind **-trist** n **-tric** /ˌsaɪki'ætrɪk◂/ adj

psy·chic /'saɪkɪk/ adj 1 having strange powers, such as the ability to see into the future 2 of the mind 3 connected with the spirits of the dead **~ally** /-kli/ adv

psy·cho·a·nal·y·sis /ˌsaɪkəʊ·ə'nælɪsɪs ‖ ˌsaɪkoʊ-/ n [U] way of treating disorders of the mind by finding their causes in the

patient's past life **–analyse** also **–analyze** AmE /ˌsaɪkəʊ'ænəlaɪz ‖ ˌsaɪkoʊ-/ vt **–analyst** /-'ænəl-ɪst/ n

psy·cho·log·i·cal /ˌsaɪkə'lɒdʒɪkəl◂ ‖ -'lɑː-/ adj 1 of or connected with the way the mind works 2 infml not real **-ly** adv

psy·cho·log·i·cal war·fare /ˌ····· '··/ n [U] spreading fear, different political beliefs, etc. among the enemy

psy·chol·o·gy /saɪ'kɒlədʒi ‖ -'kɑː-/ n [U] study of how the mind works **-gist** n

psy·cho·path /'saɪkəʊpæθ/ n mad person who may be violent **~ic** /ˌsaɪkə'pæθɪk◂/ adj

psy·cho·sis /saɪ'kəʊsɪs ‖ -'koʊ-/ n **-ses** /-siːz/ serious disorder of the mind **–chotic** /saɪ'kɒtɪk ‖ -'kɑː-/ n, adj

psy·cho·so·mat·ic /ˌsaɪkəʊsə'mætɪk ‖ -kəsə-/ adj (of an illness) caused by anxiety, not a real disorder of the body

psy·cho·ther·a·py /ˌsaɪkəʊ'θerəpi ‖ -koʊ-/ n [U] treatment of mind disorders by psychological methods (not drugs, etc.) **–pist** n

pt written abbrev. for: 1 part 2 PINT(s) 3 point 4 port

PTO /ˌpiː tiː 'əʊ ‖ -'oʊ/ abbrev. for: please turn over; look at the next page

pub /pʌb/ n building where alcohol may be bought and drunk

pub-crawl /'·· ˌ·/ n sl, esp. BrE visit to several pubs

pu·ber·ty /'pjuːbəti ‖ -ər-/ n period of change from childhood to the adult state in which one can produce children

pu·bic /'pjuːbɪk/ adj of or near the sexual organs

pub·lic /'pʌblɪk/ adj 1 of or for people in general or everyone; not private: public opinion 2 of the government: public money 3 not secret 4 go public (of a company) become a PUBLIC COMPANY 5 **in the public eye** often seen in public or on television, or mentioned in newspapers ♦ n [S] 1 people in general 2 people interested in the stated thing 3 **in public** openly **~ly** adv

pub·li·can /'pʌblɪkən/ n person who runs a PUB

pub·li·ca·tion /ˌpʌblɪ'keɪʃən/ n 1 [U] act of publishing (PUBLISH) 2 [C] book, magazine, etc.

public bar /ˌ·· '·/ n BrE plainly furnished room in a PUB, where drinks are cheaper than in the LOUNGE BAR

public com·pa·ny /ˌ·· '···/ n business company that offers shares in itself for sale on the STOCK EXCHANGE

public con·ve·nience /ˌ·· ·'··/ n BrE public TOILET

public house /ˌ·· '·/ n fml for PUB

pub·li·cist /'pʌblɪ̇sɪ̇st/ n person who publicizes something or someone

pub·lic·i·ty /pʌ'blɪsɪ̇ti/ n [U] 1 public notice or attention: unwelcome publicity 2 business of publicizing things; advertising

pub·li·cize also **-cise** BrE /'pʌblɪ̇saɪz/ vt bring to public notice

public re·la·tions /ˌ·· ·'··/ n 1 [U] forming of a favourable public opinion of an organization 2 [P] good relations between an organization and the public

public school /ˌ·· '·/ n British school for older children, not run by the state

public sec·tor /ˌ·· '··/ n [the+S] those industries and services that are owned and run by the state

public spir·it /ˌ·· '··/ n [U] willingness to do what is helpful for everyone **public-spirited** adj

pub·lish /'pʌblɪʃ/ vt 1 bring out (a book, newspaper, etc.) 2 make known generally: publishing the exam results ~er n

puce /pjuːs/ adj dark brownish purple

puck /pʌk/ n hard flat piece of rubber used in ICE HOCKEY

puck·er /'pʌkə‖-ər/ vi/t tighten into folds

pud·ding /'pʊdɪŋ/ n [C;U] 1 BrE sweet dish served at the end of a meal 2 British dish with a covering made from flour, fat, etc.: steak and kidney pudding

pud·dle /'pʌdl/ n small amount of water, esp. rain, lying in a hollow place in the ground

pu·er·ile /'pjʊəraɪl‖'pjʊərəl/ adj fml childish; silly

puff¹ /pʌf/ v 1 vi breathe rapidly and with effort 2 vi/t send out or come out as little clouds of smoke or steam: puffing at a cigarette ~ed adj infml out of breath

puff out/up phr vi/t swell

puff² n 1 sudden light rush of air, smoke, etc. 2 piece of light pastry filled with a soft, sweet mixture 3 infml piece of writing praising a person or entertainment ~y adj rather swollen

puf·fin /'pʌfɪ̇n/ n seabird with a large brightly coloured beak

puff pas·try /ˌ· '··/ n [U] light air-filled pastry

pug·na·cious /pʌg'neɪʃəs/ adj fml fond of quarrelling and fighting

puke /pjuːk/ vi infml for VOMIT

puk·ka /'pʌkə/ adj real; GENUINE

pull¹ /pʊl/ v 1 vi/t bring (something) along behind one: The horses pulled the plough. 2 vi/t move (someone or something) towards oneself: She pulled the door open. 3 vt take with force: He had a tooth pulled (out). 4 vt stretch and damage: pull a muscle 5 vi move in or as a vehicle: The train pulled out. (=left) 6 vt attract 7 pull a face make an expression with the face to show rude amusement, disagreement, etc. 8 pull a fast one (on) get the advantage (over) by a trick 9 pull a gun take out a gun and aim it (at someone)

pull away phr vi (esp. of a road vehicle) start to move off

pull down phr vt destroy (a building, etc.)

pull in phr vi 1 (of a train) arrive at a station 2 (of a vehicle) move to one side (and stop)

pull off phr vt succeed in doing (something difficult)

pull out phr vi/t 1 (cause to) stop taking part 2 (of a train) leave a station

pull over phr vi/t PULL in (2)

pull through phr vi/t 1 (cause to) live in spite of illness or wounds 2 (help to) succeed in spite of difficulties

pull together phr v 1 vi work together to help a shared effort 2 vt control the feelings of (oneself)

pull up phr vi (of a vehicle) stop

pull² n 1 [C;U] (act of) pulling 2 [C] rope, handle, etc. for pulling something: a bellpull 3 [S] difficult steep climb 4 [U] special (unfair) influence

pul·let /'pʊlɪ̇t/ n young hen

pul·ley /'pʊli/ n apparatus for lifting things with a rope

pull·o·ver /'pʊl,əʊvə‖-,oʊvər/ n SWEATER pulled on over the head

pul·mo·na·ry /'pʌlmənəri, 'pʊl-‖'pʊlmənəri, 'pʌl-/ adj of the lungs

pulp /pʌlp/ n 1 [S;U] soft almost liquid mass, esp. of plant material 2 [U] book, magazine, etc. cheaply produced and containing matter of bad quality ♦ *vt* make into pulp

pul·pit /'pʊlpɪt/ *n* raised enclosure from which a priest speaks in church

pul·sar /'pʌlsɑːǁ-ɑːr/ *n* starlike object that sends out regular radio signals

pul·sate /pʌl'seɪt‖'pʌlseɪt/ *vi* 1 shake very rapidly and regularly 2 pulse –sation /,pʌl'seɪʃən/ *n* [C;U]

pulse¹ /pʌls/ *n* 1 regular beating of blood in the body's blood tubes 2 strong regular beat 3 short sound or electrical charge ♦ *vi* move or flow with a strong beat

pulse² *n* [C;U] (seeds of) beans, PEAs, etc. used as food

pul·ver·ize , -ise /'pʌlvəraɪz/ *vt* 1 crush to a powder 2 defeat thoroughly

pu·ma /'pjuːmə/ *n* -mas *or* -ma large fierce American wild cat

pu·mice /'pʌmɪs/ *n* [C;U] very light rock from a VOLCANO, rubbed against the skin to soften it

pum·mel /'pʌməl/ *vt* -ll- *BrE* ‖ -l- *AmE* — hit repeatedly

pump¹ /pʌmp/ *n* machine for forcing liquid or gas into or out of something ♦ 1 *vt* empty or fill with a pump 2 *vt* put in or remove with a pump 3 *vi* a work a pump b work like a pump: *My heart was pumping fast.* 4 *vt* try to get information from with questions

pump² *n* light shoe

pump·kin /'pʌmpkɪn/ *n* [C;U] extremely large round dark yellow vegetable

pun /pʌn/ *n* amusing use of a word or phrase with two meanings

punch¹ /pʌntʃ/ *vt* 1 hit hard with the closed hand 2 cut a hole in with a special tool: *The inspector punched my ticket.* ♦ 1 [C] hard blow with the closed hand 2 [U] forcefulness 3 **not pull one's punches** strongly express an unfavourable opinion

punch² *n* [U] mixed sweet fruit drink usu. made with alcohol

punch³ *n* [C] steel tool for cutting holes

punch-drunk /'· ·/ *adj* suffering brain damage from blows in boxing (BOX²)

punch line /'· ·/ *n* funny part at the end of a joke

punch-up /'· ·/ *n BrE infml* fight

punc·tu·al /'pʌŋktʃʊəl/ *adj* coming, happening, etc. at exactly the right time ~ly

adv -ality /,pʌŋktʃu'æləti/ *n* [U]

punc·tu·ate /'pʌŋktʃueɪt/ *vt* 1 divide into sentences, phrases, etc. with punctuation marks 2 repeatedly break the flow of -ation /,pʌŋktʃu'eɪʃən/ *n* [U] 1 act or system of punctuating 2 punctuation marks

punctuation mark /,··'·· ·/ *n* sign used in punctuating, e.g. a FULL STOP or a COMMA

punc·ture /'pʌŋktʃəǁ-ər/ *n* small hole, esp. in a tyre ♦ *vi/t* (cause to) get a puncture

pun·dit /'pʌndɪt/ *n* EXPERT who is often asked to give an opinion

pun·gent /'pʌndʒənt/ *adj* (of a taste or smell) strong and sharp

pun·ish /'pʌnɪʃ/ *vt* 1 cause (someone) to suffer for (a crime or fault) 2 deal roughly with ~**able** *adj* causing the punishment mentioned: *a crime punishable by death* ~**ment** *n* 1 [U] act of punishing 2 [C] way in which someone is punished

pun·ish·ing /'pʌnɪʃɪŋ/ *adj* that makes one thoroughly tired and weak

pu·ni·tive /'pjuːnɪtɪv/ *adj* 1 intended as punishment 2 very severe

punk /pʌŋk/ 1 [U] also **punk rock** /,· '·/ loud violent music popular in the 1970s and 1980s 2 [C] person who liked this music and wore chains and SAFETY PINS 3 *AmE infml* boy or young man who causes trouble, does not respect others, etc.

pun·net /'pʌnɪt/ *n esp. BrE* small square basket in which fruit is sold

punt /pʌnt/ *n* long narrow flat-bottomed river boat moved along with a pole

punt·er /'pʌntəǁ-ər/ *n esp. BrE* 1 person who BETs on horse races 2 customer

pu·ny /'pjuːni/ *adj* small and weak

pup /pʌp/ *n* PUPPY

pu·pa /'pjuːpə/ *n* -pas *or* -pae /-piː/ form of an insect in a covering preparing to become an adult **pupal** *adj*

pu·pil¹ /'pjuːpəl/ *n* person being taught

pupil² *n* small round black opening in the middle of the eye

pup·pet /'pʌpɪt/ *n* 1 toylike figure of a person or animal that is made to move as if it were alive 2 person or group that is controlled by someone else: *a puppet government*

pup·py /'pʌpi/ *n* young dog

puppy love /'·· ·/ *n* [U] young boy's or

girl's love for an older person

pur·chase /'pɜːtʃəs ‖ 'pɜːr-/ vt fml buy ♦ n fml 1 [U] act of buying 2 [C] something bought 3 [U] firm hold on a surface

pur·dah /'pɜːdə, -dɑː ‖ 'pɜːr-/ n [U] system of keeping women out of public view, esp. among Muslims

pure /pjʊə ‖ pjʊr/ adj 1 not mixed with anything else 2 clean 3 free from evil 4 complete; thorough: by pure chance ~ly adv wholly; only

pu·ree /'pjʊəreɪ ‖ pjʊ'reɪ/ n [C;U] soft half-liquid mass of food ♦ vt make (fruit or vegetable) into a puree

pur·ga·tive /'pɜːgətɪv ‖ 'pɜːr-/ n medicine that empties the bowels

pur·ga·to·ry /'pɜːgətəri ‖ 'pɜːrgətɔːri/ n [U] 1 (in the Roman Catholic Church) place where the soul of a dead person is made pure and fit to enter heaven 2 situation of great suffering

purge /pɜːdʒ ‖ pɜːrdʒ/ vt 1 get rid of (an unwanted person) from (a state, group, etc.) by driving out, killing, etc. 2 make clean and free from (something evil) 3 empty the bowels with medicine ♦ n act of purging (PURGE (1))

pu·ri·fy /'pjʊərɪfaɪ ‖ 'pjʊr-/ vt make pure –fication /ˌpjʊərɪfɪ'keɪʃən ‖ ˌpjʊr-/ n [U]

pur·ist /'pjʊərɪst ‖ 'pjʊr-/ n someone who tries to make sure things are always done correctly and not changed, esp. in matters of grammar

pu·ri·tan /'pjʊərɪtən ‖ 'pjʊr-/ n 1 person with hard fixed standards of behaviour who thinks pleasure is wrong 2 (cap.) member of a former Christian group which wanted to make religion simpler and less ceremonial ~ical /ˌpjʊərɪ'tænɪkəl ‖ ˌpjʊr-/ adj

pu·ri·ty /'pjʊərɪti ‖ 'pjʊr-/ n [U] being pure

purl /pɜːl ‖ pɜːrl/ n [U] knitting (KNIT) stitch done backwards ♦ vi/t

pur·loin /pɜː'lɔɪn, 'pɜːlɔɪn ‖ -ɜːr-/ vt fml steal

pur·ple /'pɜːpəl ‖ 'pɜːr-/ adj of a colour that is a mixture of red and blue

pur·port /pɜː'pɔːt, -pət ‖ 'pɜːrpɔːrt/ n [U] fml meaning ♦ /pɜː'pɔːt ‖ pɜːr'pɔːrt/ vt have an intended appearance of being

pur·pose /'pɜːpəs ‖ 'pɜːr-/ n 1 [C] reason for doing something 2 [C] use; effect; result:

It has served its purpose. (=done what is needed) 3 [U] determined quality; willpower 4 **on purpose** intentionally ~**ful** adj determined ~**ly** adv intentionally

purpose-built /ˌ·· '·◀/ adj esp. BrE originally made to be the stated thing

purr /pɜː ‖ pɜːr/ vi make the low continuous sound of a pleased cat

purse[1] /pɜːs ‖ pɜːrs/ n 1 small flat bag for carrying coins 2 amount of money offered, esp. as a prize 3 AmE for HANDBAG

purse[2] vt draw (esp. the lips) together in little folds

purs·er /'pɜːsə ‖ 'pɜːrsər/ n ship's officer responsible for money and traveller's arrangements

purse strings /'· ·/ n hold the purse strings control the spending of money

pur·su·ance /pə'sjuːəns ‖ pər'suː-/ n in the pursuance of fml doing

pur·su·ant /pə'sjuːənt ‖ pər'suː-/ adj pursuant to fml in accordance with

pur·sue /pə'sjuː ‖ pər'suː/ vt 1 follow in order to catch 2 fml continue steadily with: pursuing a policy of neutrality –**suer** n

pur·suit /pə'sjuːt ‖ pər'suːt/ n 1 [U] act of pursuing 2 [C] fml activity, esp. for pleasure

pur·vey·or /pə'veɪə ‖ pər'veɪər/ n fml shop, etc. that sells something: purveyors of fine cheeses

pus /pʌs/ n [U] thick yellowish liquid produced in an infected part of the body

push[1] /pʊʃ/ v 1 vi/t use sudden or steady pressure to move (someone or something) forward, away from oneself, or to a different position: He pushed the drawer shut. 2 vt try to force (someone) by continual urging 3 vt sell (illegal drugs) 4 **be pushing** infml be nearly (a stated age) 5 **push one's luck** take a risk ~**ed** adj not having enough: pushed for time ~**er** n seller of illegal drugs

push around phr vt treat roughly and unfairly

push for phr vt demand urgently and forcefully

push off phr vi infml go away

push[2] n 1 act of pushing 2 large planned attack and advance 3 **at a push** if necessary 4 **if/when it comes to the push** if/when there's a time of special need 5 **give/get the push** infml dismiss/be dismissed from a job

push-but·ton /'· ˌ··/ n small button

pressed to operate something

push·chair /ˈpʊʃ-tʃeə‖-tʃer/ n BrE small chair on wheels for a child

push·o·ver /ˈpʊʃˌəʊvə‖-ˌoʊvər/ n [S] infml 1 something very easy to do or win 2 someone easily influenced or deceived

push·y /ˈpʊʃi/ adj too forceful in getting things done, esp. for one's own advantage

pus·sy[1] /ˈpʊsi/ also **puss** /pʊs/, **pus·sy·cat** /ˈpʊsiˌkæt/ n (child's name for) a cat

pussy[2] n taboo sl the female sex organ

pus·sy·foot /ˈpʊsifʊt/ vi act too carefully

put /pʊt/ vt put, pres. p. -tt- 1 move, place, or fix to, on, or in the stated place 2 cause to be: She put her books in order. | Put your mistakes right at once. 3 express in words 4 express officially for judgment: I'll put your suggestions to the committee. 5 write down 6 **put paid to** BrE RUIN

put about phr vt spread (bad or false news)

put across phr vt cause to be understood

put aside phr vt save (money)

put away phr vt 1 remove to its usual storing place 2 infml eat (usu. large quantities of food) 3 place (someone) in prison or a hospital for mad people

put back phr vt delay

put by phr vt PUT aside

put down phr vt 1 control; defeat: put down a rebellion 2 record in writing 3 allow to leave a vehicle 4 kill (an old or sick animal) 5 cause to feel unimportant 6 pay (an amount) as part of the cost of something with a promise to pay the rest over a period of time n

put down to phr vt state that (something) is caused by

put forward phr vt suggest

put in phr vt 1 do (work) or spend (time) on work 2 interrupt by saying 3 (of a ship) enter a port

put in for phr vt make a formal request for

put into phr vt add (something) to (something): Put more effort into your work!

put off phr vt 1 delay 2 discourage 3 cause to dislike

put on phr vt 1 cover (part of) the body with (esp. clothing) 2 operate (a radio, light, etc.) by pressing or turning a button

3 increase: She's put on weight. 4 provide: They're putting on another train. 5 perform (a play, show, etc.) on stage 6 pretend to have (a feeling, quality, etc.) 7 deceive playfully

put onto phr vt give information about

put out phr vt 1 cause to stop burning 2 trouble or annoy 3 broadcast or print 4 **put oneself out** take trouble

put over phr vt PUT across

put over on phr vt **put one over on** deceive

put through phr vt 1 connect (a telephone caller) 2 cause to suffer or experience

put to phr vt 1 ask (a question) of or make (an offer) to 2 suggest to (someone) that 3 **be hard put to it to** find it difficult to

put up phr vt 1 raise 2 put in a public place: put up a notice 3 provide food and lodging for 4 make; offer: He didn't put up much of a fight. 5 offer for sale 6 supply (money needed)

put up to phr vt give the idea of doing (esp. something bad)

put up with phr vt suffer without complaining

pu·ta·tive /ˈpjuːtətɪv/ adj fml generally supposed to be or to become

put-down /ˈ· ·/ n infml words intended to make someone feel stupid

pu·tre·fy /ˈpjuːtrɪfaɪ/ vi fml decay -faction /ˌpjuːtrɪˈfækʃən/ n [U]

pu·tres·cent /pjuːˈtresənt/ adj fml decaying

pu·trid /ˈpjuːtrɪd/ adj 1 very decayed and bad-smelling 2 worthless; greatly disliked

putsch /pʊtʃ/ n sudden attempt to remove a government by force

putt /pʌt/ vi/t (in GOLF) hit (the ball) along the ground towards or into the hole ~**er** n 1 CLUB[1] (3) for putting 2 person who putts

put·ty /ˈpʌti/ n [U] soft oily paste, esp. for fixing glass to window frames

put-up job /ˈ· · ˌ·/ n infml something dishonestly arranged in advance

put-up·on /ˈ· ·ˌ·/ adj (of a person) used for someone else's advantage

puz·zle /ˈpʌzəl/ v 1 vt cause (someone) difficulty in the effort to understand 2 vi try hard to find the answer ♦ n 1 game or toy to exercise the mind 2 something that puzzles one

puzzle out *phr vt* find the answer to by thinking hard

PVC /ˌpiː viː 'siː/ *n* [U] polyvinyl chloride; type of plastic

pyg·my /'pɪgmi/ *n* 1 (*usu. cap.*) member of a racial group of very small people 2 small SPECIES of animal

py·ja·mas *BrE* ‖ **pajamas** *esp. AmE* /pə'dʒɑːməz ‖ -'dʒæ-, -'dʒɑː-/ *n* [P] soft loose-fitting trousers and short coat worn in bed

py·lon /'paɪlən ‖ -lɑːn, -lən/ *n* tall structure supporting electricity-carrying wires

pyr·a·mid /'pɪrəmɪd/ *n* 1 solid figure with three-angled sides that slope up to meet at a point 2 large stone building in this shape, used as the burial place of kings, etc. in ancient Egypt

pyramid sell·ing /'··· ˌ·/ *n* [U] (practice of) selling goods to DISTRIBUTORS (1) who then sell at a higher price to other distributors who then sell to other distributors, etc.

pyre /paɪə ‖ paɪr/ *n* high mass of wood for burning a dead body

Py·rex /'paɪreks/ *n* [U] *tdmk* strong glass used in making cooking containers

py·ro·ma·ni·ac /ˌpaɪrəʊ'meɪniæk ‖ -rə-/ *n* person who has uncontrollable urges to start fires –**mania** /-'meɪniə/ *n* [U]

py·ro·tech·nics /ˌpaɪrəʊ'tekniks ‖ -rə-/ *n fml* 1 [U] making or displaying FIREWORKS 2 [P] show of great skill

py·thon /'paɪθən ‖ -θɑːn, -θən/ *n* large tropical snake that crushes the animals it eats

Q

Q, q /kjuː/ the 17th letter of the English alphabet

Q.C. /ˌkjuː 'siː/ *n* (title, while a queen is ruling, for) a British lawyer of high rank

QED /ˌkjuː iː 'diː/ there is the proof of my argument

quack¹ /kwæk/ *vi, n* (make) the sound ducks make

quack² *n* 1 person dishonestly claiming to be a doctor 2 *derog BrE* a doctor

quad¹ /kwɒd ‖ kwɑːd/ *n BrE* square open space with buildings round it

quad² *n* QUADRUPLET

quad·ran·gle /'kwɒdræŋgəl ‖ 'kwɑː-/ *n* 1 QUADRILATERAL 2 *fml for* QUAD¹ –**rangular** /kwɒ'dræŋgjᵊlə ‖ kwɑː'dræŋgjᵊlər/ *adj*

quad·rant /'kwɒdrənt ‖ 'kwɑː-/ *n* 1 quarter of a circle 2 instrument for measuring angles

quad·ra·phon·ic /ˌkwɒdrə'fɒnɪk◄ ‖ ˌkwɑːdrə'fɑː-/ *adj* giving sound from four different places

quad·ri·lat·er·al /ˌkwɒdrᵊ'lætərəl◄ ‖ ˌkwɑː-/ *n, adj* (flat figure) with four straight sides

quad·ru·ped /'kwɒdrʊped ‖ 'kwɑːdrə-/ *n* four-legged creature

quad·ru·ple /'kwɒdrʊpəl, kwɒ'druː- ‖ kwɑː'druː-/ *vi/t* multiply by four ♦ *adj, adv* four times as big

quad·ru·plet /'kwɒdrʊplᵊt ‖ kwɑː'druːp-/ *n* any of four children born at the same time

quaff /kwɒf, kwɑːf ‖ kwɑːf, kwæf/ *vt fml* drink deeply

quag·mire /'kwægmaɪə, 'kwɒg- ‖ 'kwægmaɪr/ *n* soft wet ground: (fig.) *a legal quagmire*

quail¹ /kweɪl/ *n* quail *or* quails (meat of) a type of small bird

quail² *vi fml* be afraid; tremble

quaint /kweɪnt/ *adj* charmingly old-fashioned ~**ly** *adv*

quake /kweɪk/ *vi* shake; tremble

Quak·er /'kweɪkə ‖ -ər/ *n* member of a Christian religious group that opposes violence

qual·i·fi·ca·tion /ˌkwɒlᵊfᵊ'keɪʃən ‖ ˌkwɑː-/ *n* 1 [C] something that limits the force of a statement 2 [U] act of qualifying 3 [C *often pl.*] proof that one has passed an examination **qualifications** *n* [P] (proof of having) the necessary ability, experience, or knowledge

qual·i·fy /'kwɒlᵊfaɪ ‖ 'kwɑː-/ *v* 1 *vi/t* (cause to) reach a necessary standard 2 *vt* limit the force or meaning of (a statement)

-fied *adj* 1 having suitable qualifications 2 limited: *qualified approval*

qual·i·ta·tive /'kwɒlɪtətɪv ‖ 'kwɑːlɪteɪ-/ *adj* of or about quality

qual·i·ty /'kwɒlɪti ‖ 'kwɑː-/ *n* 1 [C;U] (high) degree of goodness 2 [C] something typical of a person or thing

qualm /kwɑːm ‖ kwɑːm, kwɑːlm/ *n* uncomfortable feeling of uncertainty

quan·da·ry /'kwɒndəri ‖ 'kwɑːn-/ *n* feeling of not knowing what to do

quan·go /'kwæŋɡəʊ ‖ -ɡoʊ/ *n* -gos (in Britain) independent body with legal powers, set up by the government

quan·ti·fi·er /'kwɒntɪfaɪə ‖ 'kwɑːntɪfaɪr/ *n* (in grammar) a word or phrase that is used with a noun to show quantity, such as *much*, *few*, and *a lot of*

quan·ti·fy /'kwɒntɪfaɪ ‖ 'kwɑːn-/ *vt fml* measure **-fiable** *adj*

quan·ti·ta·tive /'kwɒntɪtətɪv ‖ 'kwɑːntɪteɪ-/ *adj* of or about quantity

quan·ti·ty /'kwɒntɪti ‖ 'kwɑːn-/ *n* 1 [U] the fact of being measurable, amount 2 [C] amount; number —see also UNKNOWN QUANTITY

quan·tum /'kwɒntəm ‖ 'kwɑːn-/ *n* -ta /-tə/ (in PHYSICS) fixed amount

quantum leap /ˌ·· '·/ *n* very large and important advance or improvement

quantum the·o·ry /'·· ˌ··/ *n* [U] idea that ENERGY travels in quanta

quar·an·tine /'kwɒrəntiːn ‖ 'kwɑː-/ *n* [U] period when a sick person or animal is kept away from others so the disease cannot spread ♦ *vt* put in quarantine

quark /kwɑːk, kwɔːk ‖ kwɑːrk, kwɔːrk/ *n* smallest possible piece of material forming the substances of which atoms are made

quar·rel¹ /'kwɒrəl ‖ 'kwɔː-, 'kwɑː-/ *n* 1 angry argument 2 cause for point of disagreement

quarrel² *vi* **-ll-** *BrE* ‖ **-l-** *AmE* have an ARGUMENT (1) ~**some** *adj* likely to argue

quarrel with *phr vt* disagree with

quar·ry¹ /'kwɒri ‖ 'kwɔː-, 'kwɑː-/ *n* place where stone, sand, etc. are dug out ♦ *vt* dig from a quarry

quarry² *n* person or animal being hunted

quart /kwɔːt ‖ kwɔːrt/ *n* a measure of amount equal to two pints

quar·ter /'kwɔːtə ‖ 'kwɔːrtər/ *n* 1 [C] a fourth part of a whole: *a quarter of a mile* 2 [C] 15 minutes: *a quarter to 10* 3 [C] three months of the year 4 [C] part of a town: *the student quarter* 5 [C] person or place from which something comes: *no help from that quarter* 6 [U] *fml* giving of life to a defeated enemy ♦ *vt* 1 divide into four parts 2 provide lodgings for **quarters** *n* [P] 1 lodgings 2 **at close quarters** near together

quar·ter·deck /'kwɔːtədek ‖ 'kwɔːrtər-/ *n* top part of a ship, used only by officers

quar·ter·fi·nal /ˌkwɔːtə'faɪnl ‖ ˌkwɔːrtər-/ *n* any of four matches whose winners play in SEMIFINALS

quar·ter·ly /'kwɔːtəli ‖ 'kwɔːrtər-/ *adj*, *adv* (happening) four times a year ♦ *n* quarterly magazine

quar·ter·mas·ter /'kwɔːtəˌmɑːstə ‖ 'kwɔːrtərˌmæstər/ *n* military officer in charge of supplies

quar·tet /kwɔː'tet ‖ kwɔːr-/ *n* (music for) four musicians

quartz /kwɔːts ‖ kwɔːrts/ *n* [U] hard mineral used in making very exact clocks

qua·sar /'kweɪzɑː ‖ -zɑːr/ *n* very bright very distant starlike object

quash /kwɒʃ ‖ kwɑːʃ, kwɔːʃ/ *vt* 1 officially refuse to accept 2 put an end to: *quash a rebellion*

qua·ver /'kweɪvə ‖ -ər/ *vi* (of a voice or music) shake ♦ *n* a shaking in the voice ~**y** *adj*

quay /kiː/ *n* place in a harbour by which ships stop and unload

quea·sy /'kwiːzi/ *adj* 1 feeling one is going to be sick 2 uncertain about the rightness of doing something

queen /kwiːn/ *n* 1 a female ruler b king's wife 2 leading female: *a beauty queen* 3 leading female insect in a group: *a queen bee* 4 *sl* male homosexual ~**ly** *adj* like, or suitable for, a queen

queen moth·er /ˌ· '··/ *n* mother of a ruler

queer /kwɪə ‖ kwɪr/ *adj* 1 strange 2 *infml derog* HOMOSEXUAL ♦ *n infml derog* male HOMOSEXUAL

quell /kwel/ *vt* defeat; crush

quench /kwentʃ/ *vt* 1 satisfy (thirst) by drinking 2 put out (flames)

quer·u·lous /'kwerʊləs/ *adj* complaining

que·ry /'kwɪəri ‖ 'kwɪri/ *n* question or

doubt ♦ *vt* express doubt or uncertainty about

quest /kwest/ *n fml* long search

ques·tion[1] /'kwestʃən/ *n* 1 [C] sentence or phrase asking for information 2 [C] matter to be settled; problem 3 [C;U] doubt: *His honesty is beyond question.* 4 **in question** being talked about 5 **out of the question** impossible 6 **there's no question of** there's no possibility of

question[2] *vt* 1 ask (someone) questions 2 have doubts about ~**able** *adj* 1 uncertain 2 perhaps not true or honest ~**er** *n*

question mark /'·· ·/ *n* mark (?) written at the end of a question: (fig.) *a question mark over our future*

ques·tion·naire /ˌkwestʃə'neə, ˌkes‖-'ner/ *n* set of questions asked to obtain information

queue /kjuː/ *n BrE* line of people, vehicles, etc. waiting to do something in turn ♦ *vi* wait in a queue

queue-jump /'· ·/ *vi* join a queue in front of others who were there before you

quib·ble /'kwɪbəl/ *vi* argue about small unimportant points **quibble** *n*

quiche /kiːʃ/ *n* flat pastry case filled with eggs, cheese, vegetables, etc.

quick[1] /kwɪk/ *adj* 1 fast 2 easily showing anger: *a quick temper* ♦ *adv* fast ~**ly** *adv* ~**en** *vi/t* make or become quicker ~**ness** *n* [U]

quick[2] *n* 1 [U] flesh to which fingernails and toenails are joined 2 **cut (a person) to the quick** hurt a person's feelings deeply

quick·ie /'kwɪki/ *n* something made or done in a hurry

quick·sand /'kwɪksænd/ *n* [U] wet sand which sucks things away

quick·step /'kwɪkstep/ *n* dance with fast steps

quick-wit·ted /ˌ· '··◄/ *adj* swift to understand and act

quid /kwɪd/ *n* quid *BrE infml* pound in money

quid pro quo /ˌkwɪd prəʊ 'kwəʊ‖-proʊ 'kwoʊ/ *n* something given in fair exchange

qui·es·cent /kwi'esənt, kwaɪ-/ *adj fml* inactive (for the present)

qui·et /'kwaɪət/ *adj* 1 with little noise 2 calm; untroubled: *a quiet life* ♦ *n* [U] 1 quietness 2 **keep something quiet** keep something a secret 3 **on the quiet** secretly

~**en** *vi/t* make or become quiet ~**ly** *adv* ~**ness** *n* [U]

quiff /kwɪf/ *n* hair standing up over the forehead

quill /kwɪl/ *n* 1 long feather 2 pen made from this 3 sharp prickle on some animals, esp. the PORCUPINE

quilt /kwɪlt/ *n* cloth covering for a bed, filled with feathers, etc. ~**ed** made with cloth containing soft material with stitching across it

quin /kwɪn/ *n* QUINTUPLET

quince /kwɪns/ *n* hard apple-like fruit

quin·ine /'kwɪniːn‖ 'kwaɪnaɪn/ *n* [U] drug used for treating MALARIA

quin·tes·sence /kwɪn'tesəns/ *n fml* perfect type or example –**tessential** /ˌkwɪntɪ'senʃəl/ *adj*

quin·tet /kwɪn'tet/ *n* (music for) five musicians

quin·tu·plet /'kwɪntjʊplɪt, kwɪn'tjuː-p‖kwɪn'tʌp-/ *n* any of five children born at the same time

quip[1] /kwɪp/ *n* clever amusing remark ♦ *vi* -**pp**- make a quip

quirk /kwɜːk‖kwɜːrk/ *n* 1 strange happening or accident 2 strange habit or way of behaving ~**y** *adj*

quit /kwɪt/ *vi/t* quitted or quit, pres. p. -**tt**- stop (doing something) and leave ~**ter** *n* person who lacks the courage to finish things when he/she meets difficulties

quite /kwaɪt/ *predeterminer, adv* 1 completely; perfectly: *not quite right* 2 to some degree; rather: *quite cold* 3 esp. *BrE* (used for showing agreement): *Quite (so).* 4 **quite a/an** an unusual: *quite a party* | *It's quite something to be a government minister at 30.*

quits /kwɪts/ *adj* back on an equal level with someone after an argument, repaying money, etc.

quiv·er[1] /'kwɪvə‖-ər/ *vi/t* (cause to) tremble a little **quiver** *n*

quiver[2] *n* container for ARROWS

qui vive /ˌkiː 'viːv/ *n* **on the qui vive** careful to notice; watchful

quix·ot·ic /kwɪk'sɒtɪk‖-'saː-/ *adj* doing foolishly brave things in order to be helpful

quiz /kwɪz/ *n* -**zz**- game where questions are put ♦ *vt* -**zz**- ask questions of (someone). repeatedly

quiz·zi·cal /'kwɪzɪkəl/ *adj* (of a smile or

look) suggesting a question or secret
knowledge ~**ly** /-kli/ *adv*

quoit /kwɔɪt, kɔɪt/ *n* ring to be thrown
over a small post in a game

quo·rate /ˈkwɔːrɪt/ *adj* (of a meeting)
having a quorum present

quo·rum /ˈkwɔːrəm/ *n* number of people
who must be present for a meeting to be
held

quo·ta /ˈkwəʊtə ‖ ˈkwoʊ-/ *n* amount
officially to be produced, received, etc. as
one's share

quo·ta·tion /kwəʊˈteɪʃən ‖ kwoʊ-/ *n*
1 [C] words QUOTEd (1) 2 [U] act of quoting
3 [C] amount QUOTEd (2)

quotation mark /·ˈ·· ·/ *n* mark (' or ', " or
") showing the start or end of a QUOTATION
(1)

quote /kwəʊt ‖ kwoʊt/ *v* 1 *vi/t* repeat the
words of (a person, book, etc.) in speech or
writing 2 *vt* offer as a price for work to be
done ♦ *n* 1 *infml* QUOTATION (1, 3) 2 in
quotes in QUOTATION MARKs

quo·tient /ˈkwəʊʃənt ‖ ˈkwoʊ-/ *n*
number got by dividing

q.v. (used for telling readers to look in
another place in the same book to find
something out)

qwert·y /ˈkwɜːtiː ‖ ˈkwɜːrtiː/ *adj* (of a
KEYBOARD with letters) having the standard
arrangement of letters

R

R, r /ɑː ‖ ɑːr/ the 18th letter of the English
alphabet—see also THREE R's

rab·bi /ˈræbaɪ/ *n* Jewish priest

rab·bit¹ /ˈræbɪt/ *n* common small long-
eared animal, often kept as a pet

rabbit² *vi BrE infml* talk continuously
and annoyingly

rab·ble /ˈræbəl/ *n* disordered noisy crowd

rabble-rous·ing /ˈ·· ,··/ *adj* causing
hatred and violence among a crowd of

listeners

rab·id /ˈræbɪd/ *adj* 1 suffering from rabies
2 (of feelings or opinions) unreasonably
violent

ra·bies /ˈreɪbiːz/ *n* [U] disease passed on
by the bite of an infected animal and
causing madness and death

rac·coon /rəˈkuːn, ræ- ‖ ræ-/ *n* small
North American animal with a black-
ringed tail

race¹ /reɪs/ *n* competition in speed: *a
horse race* ‖ (fig.) *a race against time* ♦ *vi/t*
1 compete in a race (against) 2 (cause to) go
very fast

race² *n* 1 [C;U] (any of) the main divisions
of human beings, each of a different
physical type 2 [C] group of people with the
same history, language, etc.: *the German
race* 3 [C] breed or type of animal or plant

race·course /ˈreɪs-kɔːs ‖ -kɔːrs/ *n* track
round which horses race

race re·la·tions /ˈ· ·ˌ··/ *n* [P]
relationships between people of different
races living in a place

race·track /ˈreɪs-træk/ *n* track round
which horses, runners, cars, etc. race

ra·cial /ˈreɪʃəl/ *adj* 1 of a race 2 between
RACEs²: *racial tension* ~**ly** *adv*

ra·cis·m /ˈreɪsɪzəm/ *n* [U] 1 belief that
one's own RACE² is best 2 dislike or unfair
treatment of other races **racist** *adj, n*

rack¹ /ræk/ *n* 1 frame or shelf with bars,
hooks, etc. for holding things 2 instrument
for hurting people by stretching their
bodies 3 bar with teeth, moved along by a
wheel with similar teeth

rack² *vt* 1 cause great pain or anxiety to
2 rack one's brains think very hard

rack³ *n* rack and ruin ruined condition,
esp. of a building

rack·et¹, racquet /ˈrækɪt/ *n* instrument
with a netlike part for hitting the ball in
games like tennis

racket² *n* 1 [S] loud noise 2 [C] dishonest
business

rack·e·teer /ˌrækəˈtɪə ‖ -ˈtɪr/ *n* someone
who works a RACKET² (2)

rac·on·teur /ˌrækɒnˈtɜː ‖ ˌrækɑːnˈtɜːr/
n someone good at telling stories

rac·y /ˈreɪsiː/ *adj* (of a story, etc.) amusing,
full of life, and perhaps dealing with sex

ra·dar /ˈreɪdɑː ‖ -dɑːr/ *n* [U] apparatus or
method of finding solid objects by receiving

and measuring the speed of radio waves seen as a SCREEN

ra·di·al¹ /'reɪdɪəl/ adj like a wheel

radial² also **radial tyre** /ˌ··· '·/ — n car tyre with cords inside the rubber that go across the edge of the wheel, so as to give better control

ra·di·ant /'reɪdɪənt/ adj 1 sending out light or heat in all directions 2 (of a person) showing love and happiness ~ly adv –ance n [U]

ra·di·ate /'reɪdɪeɪt/ vi/t send out light, heat, etc.: (fig.) She radiates happiness.

ra·di·a·tion /ˌreɪdɪ'eɪʃən/ n [U] 1 (act of) radiating 2 RADIOACTIVITY

ra·di·a·tor /'reɪdɪeɪtə‖-ər/ n 1 apparatus, esp. of hot-water pipes, for heating a building 2 apparatus that keeps a car's engine cool

rad·i·cal /'rædɪkəl/ adj 1 (of a change) thorough and complete 2 in favour of complete political change ♦ n RADICAL (2) person ~ly /-kli/ adv

rad·i·i /'reɪdɪaɪ/ pl. of RADIUS

ra·di·o /'reɪdɪəʊ ‖-dɪoʊ/ n 1 [U] sending or receiving sounds through the air by electrical waves 2 [C] apparatus to receive such sounds 3 [U] radio broadcasting industry 4 **on the radio: a** (of a sound) broadcast **b** (of a person) broadcasting

ra·di·o·ac·tiv·i·ty /ˌreɪdɪəʊæk'tɪvɪti ‖ -dɪoʊ-/ n [U] 1 quality, harmful in large amounts to living things, that some ELEMENTS have of giving out ENERGY by the breaking up of atoms 2 the energy given out in this way: exposed to radioactivity –tive /ˌreɪdɪəʊ'æktɪv◄‖-dɪoʊ-/ adj

ra·di·og·ra·phy /ˌreɪdɪ'ɒɡrəfi ‖ -'a:ɡ-/ n [U] taking of photographs made with X-RAYS, usu. for medical reasons –pher n [C] person who practises radiography

ra·di·ol·o·gy /ˌreɪdɪ'ɒlədʒi ‖ -'a:-/ n [U] study and medical use of radioactivity –gist n [C]

radio tel·e·scope /ˌ··· '···/ n radio receiver for following the movements of stars and other objects in space

ra·di·o·ther·a·py /ˌreɪdɪəʊ'θerəpi ‖ -dɪoʊ-/ n [U] medical treatment using RADIATION (1)

rad·ish /'rædɪʃ/ n small plant with a round red root, eaten raw

ra·di·um /'reɪdɪəm/ n [U] RADIOACTIVE

metal used in the treatment of certain diseases

ra·di·us /'reɪdɪəs/ n -dii /-dɪaɪ/ 1 (length of) a straight line from the centre of a circle to its side 2 stated circular area measured from its centre point: houses within a ten-mile radius of the town

RAF /ˌɑːr eɪ 'ef/ n [the+S] abbrev. for: Royal Air Force; British AIRFORCE

raf·fia /'ræfɪə/ n [U] soft string-like substance from leaves of a PALM tree, used to make baskets, etc.

raf·fish /'ræfɪʃ/ adj (of a person) happy, wild, and not very respectable

raf·fle /'ræfəl/ n way of getting money by selling chances to win prizes ♦ vt offer as a raffle prize

raft /rɑːft ‖ ræft/ n flat, usu. wooden, floating structure, used esp. as a boat

raf·ter /'rɑːftə ‖ 'ræftər/ n large sloping beam that holds up a roof

rag /ræɡ/ n 1 small piece of old cloth 2 old worn-out garment 3 infml derog newspaper

rag·bag /'ræɡbæɡ/ n confused mixture

rage /reɪdʒ/ n [C;U] 1 (sudden feeling of) extreme anger 2 **all the rage** very fashionable ♦ vi 1 be in a rage 2 (of bad weather, pain, etc.) be very violent

rag·ged /'ræɡɪd/ adj 1 old and torn 2 dressed in old torn clothes 3 rough; uneven: a ragged beard | (fig.) a ragged performance ~ly adv

rag·lan /'ræɡlən/ adj (of an arm of a garment) joined at the neck rather than at the shoulder

rag·time /'ræɡtaɪm/ n [U] popular music of the 1920s, in which the strong notes of the tune come just before the main beats

rag trade /'· ·/ n [the+S] infml garment industry

raid /reɪd/ n 1 quick attack on an enemy position 2 unexpected visit by the police in search of crime ♦ vi/t make a raid (on): (fig.) The children raided the kitchen for food. ~er n

rail¹ /reɪl/ n 1 [C] fixed bar, esp. to hang things on or for protection 2 [C] line of metal bars which a train runs on 3 [U] railway ♦ vt enclose or separate with rails ~ing n rail in a fence

rail² /reɪl/ vi fml curse or complain angrily

rail·road /'reɪlrəʊd ‖-roʊd/ vt 1 hurry (someone) unfairly 2 pass (a law) or carry out (a plan) quickly in spite of opposition ♦ *n AmE for* RAILWAY

rail·way /'reɪlweɪ/ *n BrE* 1 track for trains 2 system of such tracks

rain /reɪn/ *n* 1 [U] water falling from the clouds 2 [S] thick fall of anything: *a rain of questions* 3 **as right as rain** in perfect health 4 **(come) rain or shine** whatever happens ♦ *v* 1 *vi* (of rain) fall 2 *vi/t* (cause to) fall thickly, like rain 3 **rain cats and dogs** rain very heavily ~y *adj* 1 with lots of rain 2 **for a rainy day** for a time when money may be needed

rain·bow /'reɪnbəʊ‖-boʊ/ *n* arch of different colours that appears in the sky after rain

rain check /'· ·/ *n* request to claim later something offered now

rain·fall /'reɪnfɔːl‖-fɔːl/ *n* [C;U] amount of rain that falls in a certain time

rain for·est /'· ˌ··/ *n* wet tropical forest

raise /reɪz/ *vt* 1 lift 2 make higher in amount, size, etc. 3 collect together: *raise an army* 4 produce and look after (children, animals, or crops) 5 mention or introduce (a subject) for consideration 6 a make (a noise) b cause people to make (a noise) or have feelings: *raise a laugh/raise doubts* 7 bring to an end (something that controls or forbids): *raise a siege* 8 **raise Cain/hell/the roof** *infml* become very angry ♦ *n AmE for* RISE² (3)

rai·sin /'reɪzən/ *n* dried GRAPE

rai·son d'êt·re /ˌreɪzɒn 'detrə‖-zoʊn-/ *n* reason for existing

raj /rɑːdʒ/ *n the+S* British rule in India

ra·jah /'rɑːdʒə/ *n* (title of) Indian ruler

rake¹ /reɪk/ *n* gardening tool with a row of points at the end of a long handle

rake² *vt* 1 gather, loosen, or level with a rake 2 examine or shoot in a continuous sweeping movement

  rake in *phr vt infml* earn or gain a lot of (money)

  rake out *infml* find by searching

  rake up *phr vt* 1 produce with difficulty by searching 2 remember and talk about (something that should be forgotten)

rake³ /·/ *n* man who has led a wild life with regard to drink and women

rake-off /'· ·/ *n infml* usu. dishonest share of profits

rak·ish /'reɪkɪʃ/ *adj* wild and informal ~**ly** *adv*

ral·ly¹ /'ræli/ *n* 1 large esp. political public meeting 2 motor race over public roads 3 long exchange of hits in tennis

rally² *v* 1 *vi/t* come or bring together (again) for a shared purpose 2 *vi* recover

  rally round *phr vi* help in time of trouble

ram /ræm/ *n* 1 adult male sheep that can be the father of young 2 any machine that repeatedly drops or pushes a weight onto or into something ♦ *vt* **-mm-** 1 run into (something) very hard 2 force into place with heavy pressure: (fig.) *My father keeps ramming his ideas down my throat.*

RAM /ræm/ *n* [U] *abbrev. for:* Random-Access Memory; part of a computer that keeps information temporarily, for immediate use

ram·ble¹ /'ræmbəl/ *n* (long) country walk for pleasure

ramble² *vi* 1 go on a ramble 2 talk or write in a disordered wandering way –**bler** *n* –**bling** *adj* 1 (of speech or writing) disordered and wandering 2 (of a street, house, etc.) of irregular shape; winding 3 (of a plant) growing loosely in all directions

ram·i·fi·ca·tion /ˌræmɪfɪˈkeɪʃən/ *n* 1 branch of a system with many parts 2 any of the results that may follow from an action or decision

ramp /ræmp/ *n* artificial slope connecting two levels

ram·page /ræm'peɪdʒ, 'ræmpeɪdʒ/ *vi* rush about wildly or angrily ♦ *n* **on the rampage** rampaging

ram·pant /'ræmpənt/ *adj* (of crime, disease, etc.) widespread and uncontrollable

ram·part /'ræmpɑːt‖-ɑːrt/ *n* wide bank or wall protecting a fort or city

ram-raid /'ræmreɪd/ *n* robbery in which a stolen car is driven through a shop window and filled with stolen goods ♦ *vi/t* **~er** *n* **~ing** *n* [U]

ram·rod /'ræmrɒd‖-rɑːd/ *n* stick for pushing explosive powder into or cleaning a gun

ram·shack·le /'ræmˌʃækəl/ *adj* (of a building or vehicle) falling to pieces

ran /ræn/ *past t. of* RUN

ranch /rɑːntʃ‖ræntʃ/ *n* large American farm where animals are raised ~**er** *n*

ran·cid /'rænsɪd/ *adj* (of butter, cream, etc.) unpleasant because not fresh

ran·cour *BrE* ‖ **-cor** *AmE* /'ræŋkə ‖ -ər/ *n* [U] *fml* bitter unforgiving hatred **–corous** *adj*

R and D /ˌɑːr ən 'diː/ *n* [U] *abbrev. for:* research and development; part of a business concerned with studying new ideas, planning new products, etc.

ran·dom /'rændəm/ *adj* without any fixed plan ♦ *n* **at random** in a random way **~ly** *adv* **~ness** *n* [U]

rand·y /'rændi/ *adj infml, esp. BrE* full of sexual desire **–iness** *n* [U]

rang /ræŋ/ *past t. of* RING

range¹ /reɪndʒ/ *n* 1 [S;U] distance over which something has an effect or limits between which it varies: *He shot her at close range.* | *a wide range of temperature* 2 [C] area where shooting is practised or MISSILES are tested 3 [C] connected line of mountains or hills 4 [*the*+S] (in N America) stretch of grassy land where cattle feed 5 [C] set of different objects of the same kind, esp. for sale 6 (formerly) iron fireplace and stove set into a chimney in a kitchen

range² *v* 1 *vi* vary between limits 2 *vi* wander freely: *The conversation ranged over many topics.* 3 *vt* put in position

rang·er /'reɪndʒə ‖ -ər/ *n* forest or park guard

rank¹ /ræŋk/ *n* 1 [C;U] position in the army, navy, etc.: *the rank of colonel* 2 [C;U] (high) social position 3 [C] line of people or things 4 **keep/break rank(s)** (of soldiers) stay in line/fail to stay in line 5 **of the first rank** among the best 6 **pull rank (on someone)** use unfairly the advantage of one's higher position —see also TAXI RANK ♦ *v* 1 *vi/t* be or put in a certain class 2 *vt* arrange in regular order **ranks** *n* [P] ordinary soldiers below the rank of SERGEANT

rank² *adj* 1 (of a plant) too thick and widespread 2 (of smell or taste) very strong and unpleasant 3 (of something bad) complete: *a rank beginner at the job*

rank and file /ˌ· · '·/ *n* [S] ordinary people in an organization, not the leaders

ran·kle /'ræŋkəl/ *vi* continue to be remembered with bitterness and anger

ran·sack /'rænsæk/ *vt* 1 search thoroughly and roughly 2 search and rob

ran·som /'rænsəm/ *n* money paid to free a prisoner ♦ *vt* free by paying a ransom

rant /rænt/ *vi* talk wildly and loudly

rap¹ /ræp/ *n* 1 quick light blow 2 **take the rap (for)** *infml* receive the punishment (for someone else's crime) 3 [U] type of popular music in which the words are spoken, not sung ♦ *v* **-pp-** 1 *vi/t* strike quickly and lightly 2 *vt* say sharply and suddenly

rap² *v* **-pp-** 1 *vt* criticize or blame 2 *vi* perform RAP music **–pper** *n* RAP performer also **oilseed rape**

ra·pa·cious /rə'peɪʃəs/ *adj fml* taking all one can, esp. by force **~ness**, **–pacity** /rə'pæsɪti/ *n* [U]

rape¹ /reɪp/ *vt* have sex with (someone) against their will ♦ *n* [C;U] 1 act of raping 2 spoiling **rapist** *n*

rape² *n* [U] plant grown for the oil produced from its seeds

rap·id /'ræpɪd/ *adj* fast **~ly** *adv* **~ity** /rə'pɪdɪti/ *n* [U]

rap·ids /'ræpɪdz/ *n* [P] fast-flowing rocky part of a river

ra·pi·er /'reɪpɪə ‖ -ər/ *n* long thin sharp sword

rap·port /ræ'pɔː ‖ -ər/ *n* [U] close agreement and understanding

rapt /ræpt/ *adj* giving one's whole mind: *rapt attention*

rap·ture /'ræptʃə ‖ -ər/ *n* [U] *fml* great joy and delight **–turous** *adj*

rare¹ /reə ‖ rer/ *adj* uncommon **~ly** *adv* not often **~ness** *n* [U]

rare² *adj* (of meat) lightly cooked

rar·ing /'reərɪŋ ‖ 'rer-/ *adj* very eager: *We're raring to go.*

rar·i·ty /'reərɪti ‖ 'rer-/ *n* 1 [U] being uncommon 2 [C] something uncommon

ras·cal /'rɑːskəl ‖ 'ræs-/ *n* 1 misbehaving child 2 dishonest person

rash¹ /ræʃ/ *adj* without thinking enough of the (possibly bad) results **~ly** *adv* **~ness** *n* [U]

rash² *n* red spots on the skin, caused by illness: *He came out in* (=became covered in) *a rash.* | (fig.) *a rash* (=sudden large number) *of complaints*

rash·er /'ræʃə ‖ -ər/ *n* thin piece of BACON

rasp /rɑːsp ‖ ræsp/ *v* 1 *vt* rub with something rough 2 say in a rough voice ♦ 1 [C] tool for smoothing metal, wood, etc.

2 [S] rasping sound ~ing *adj* (of a sound) unpleasantly rough

rasp·ber·ry /'raːzbəri ‖ 'ræzberi/ *n* 1 red berry, often eaten 2 rude sound made by putting one's tongue out and blowing

ras·ta·fa·ri·an /ˌræstə'feəriən ‖ -'fer-/ also **ras·ta** /'ræstə/ — *n (often cap.)* follower of a religion from Jamaica ~**ism** *n* [U]

rat /ræt/ *n* 1 animal like a large mouse 2 worthless disloyal person ♦ *vi* -tt- act disloyally

ratch·et /'rætʃɪt/ *n* toothed wheel or bar that allows a part of a machine to move past it in one direction only

rate¹ /reɪt/ *n* 1 amount measured in relation to another: *a death rate of 500 a year* 2 payment fixed according to a standard scale 3 of the (numbered) quality: *a first-rate performer* 4 **at any rate** in any case 5 **at this/that rate** if events continue in the same way —see also FLAT RATE

rate² *vt* 1 have the stated opinion about 2 deserve 3 *infml* have a good opinion of: *I really rate her as a singer.*

ra·ther /'rɑːðə ‖ 'ræðər/ *predeterminer, adv* 1 to some degree: *a rather cold day* 2 more willingly: *I'd rather have tea than coffee.* 3 more exactly: *He's done it, or rather he says he has.*

rat·i·fy /'rætɪfaɪ/ *vt* approve (a formal agreement) and make it official –**fication** /ˌrætɪfɪ'keɪʃən/ *n* [U]

rat·ing /'reɪtɪŋ/ *n* British sailor who is not an officer **ratings** *n* [P] list of the positions of popularity given to television shows

ra·tio /'reɪʃiəʊ ‖ 'reɪʃoʊ/ *n* -os way one amount relates to another: *The ratio of adults to children was 4 to 1.*

ra·tion /'ræʃən ‖ 'ræ-, 'reɪ-/ *n* amount of something allowed to one person for a period ♦ *vt* 1 limit (someone) to a fixed ration 2 limit and control (supplies) **rations** *n* [P] supplies of food

ra·tion·al /'ræʃənəl/ *adj* 1 (of ideas and behaviour) sensible 2 (of a person) able to reason ~**ly** *adv* ~**ity** /ˌræʃə'nælɪti/ *n* [U]

ra·tion·ale /ˌræʃə'nɑːl ‖ -'næl/ *n* [C;U] reasons and principles on which a practice is based

ra·tion·al·ize also **-ise** *BrE* /'ræʃənəlaɪz/ *vi/t* 1 give or claim a rational explanation for (esp. strange behaviour) 2 *esp. BrE* make (a system) more modern and sensible

–**ization** /ˌræʃənəlaɪ'zeɪʃən ‖ -lə-/ *n* [C;U]

rat race /'· ·/ *n* endless competition for success in business

rat·tle /'rætl/ *v* 1 *vi/t* (cause to) make continuous quick hard noises 2 *vi* move quickly while making these noises 3 *vt* make anxious or afraid ♦ *n* 1 [C] toy or other instrument that rattles 2 [S] rattling noise

rattle off *phr vt* repeat quickly and easily from memory

rattle on/away *phr vi* talk quickly and continuously

rattle through *phr vt* perform quickly

rattle·snake /'rætlˌsneɪk/ *n* poisonous American snake that rattles its tail

rat trap /'· ·/ *n AmE* dirty old building that is in very bad condition

rau·cous /'rɔːkəs ‖ 'rɒ:-/ *adj* unpleasantly loud and rough ~**ly** *adv* ~**ness** *n* [U]

raunch·y /'rɔːntʃi ‖ 'rɒ:-/ *adj infml* sexy –**ily** *adv* –**iness** *n* [U]

rav·age /'rævɪdʒ/ *vt* 1 ruin and destroy 2 rob (an area) violently **ravages** *n* [P] destroying effects

rave¹ /reɪv/ *vi* 1 talk wildly as if mad 2 talk with extreme admiration ♦ *adj* full of very eager praise: *rave reviews in the papers* **raving** *adj, adv* wildly (mad)

rave² *n* large party where young people dance to electronic music

ra·ven /'reɪvən/ *n* large black bird of the CROW family

rav·e·nous /'rævənəs/ *adj* very hungry ~**ly** *adv*

ra·vine /rə'viːn/ *n* deep narrow steep-sided valley

ra·vi·o·li /ˌrævi'əʊli ‖ -'oʊ-/ *n* [U] small squares of PASTA, filled with meat, etc.

rav·ish /'rævɪʃ/ *vt fml* 1 *lit* RAPE[1]: (fig.) *a country ravished by war* **ravishing** *adj lit* very beautiful

raw /rɔː ‖ rɒː/ *adj* 1 not cooked 2 not treated for use: *raw materials* 3 not yet trained or experienced 4 (of skin) painful; sore 5 (of weather) cold and wet ~**ness** *n* [U]

raw deal /ˌ· '·/ *n* unfair treatment

ray /reɪ/ *n* narrow beam of light or other force: (fig.) *a ray* (=small bit) *of hope*

ray·on /'reɪɒn ‖ -ɑːn/ *n* [U] silklike material made from plant substances

raze /reɪz/ *vt fml* flatten (buildings, cities, etc.)

ra·zor /'reɪzə ‖ -ər/ n sharp instrument for removing hair, esp. from a man's face

razz·ma·tazz /ˌræzmə'tæz/ n [U] infml noisy showy activity

Rd written abbrev. for: Road

re /riː/ prep fml on the subject of; with regard to

-'re /ə ‖ -ər/ short for: are: We're ready.

reach /riːtʃ/ v 1 vi arrive at 2 vi stretch out an arm or hand for some purpose 3 vi/t touch by doing this: It's too high; I can't reach it. 4 vt get by doing this: Reach me my hat. 5 vi/t stretch (as far as): The garden reaches down to the lake. 6 vt get a message to ♦ n 1 [S;U] distance one can reach 2 [C] part of a river

re·act /ri'ækt/ vi 1 act or behave as a result 2 change when mixed with another substance

re·ac·tion /ri'ækʃən/ n 1 [C;U] (way of) reacting 2 [S;U] change back to a former condition 3 [U] quality of being reactionary

re·ac·tion·a·ry /ri'ækʃənəri ‖ -ʃəneri/ n, adj (person) strongly opposed to change

re·ac·tor /ri'æktə ‖ -ər/ n large machine that produces ENERGY from atoms

read /riːd/ v read /red/ 1 vi/t look at and understand (something printed or written): read a newspaper 2 vi/t say (written words) to others: Read me a story. 3 vi (of something written) have (the stated form or meaning) or give (the stated idea): The letter reads as follows… | Her letters always read well. 4 vt (of a measuring instrument) show 5 vt study at university 6 **read between the lines** find hidden meanings 7 **take something as read** accept something as true without any need to consider it further ~**able** adj interesting or easy to read

read·er /'riːdə ‖ -ər/ n 1 someone who reads 2 British university teacher of high rank 3 schoolbook for beginners ~**ship** n [S] number or type of READERS (1)

read·ing /'riːdɪŋ/ n 1 [U] act or practice of reading 2 [C] opinion about the meaning of something 3 [C] figure shown by a measuring instrument 4 [U] something to be read: It makes (=is) interesting reading. 5 [U] knowledge gained through books 6 (in Parliament) one of the three official occasions on which a suggested new law is read and considered

read·out /'riːd-aʊt/ n [U] information produced from a computer in readable form

read·y /'redi/ adj 1 prepared and fit for use 2 willing 3 (of thoughts or their expressions) quick: a ready wit ♦ adv in advance: ready-cut bread ♦ n **at the ready** READY -**ily** adv 1 willingly 2 easily -**iness** n [U]

ready mon·ey /ˌ·· '··/ n [U] coins and notes that can be paid at once

re·a·gent /ri'eɪdʒənt/ n chemical that shows the presence of a particular substance

real /rɪəl/ adj 1 actually existing 2 complete: a real idiot 3 **for real** esp. AmE serious(ly) ♦ adv AmE very ~**ly** adv 1 in fact; truly 2 very 3 (shows interest, doubt, or displeasure)

real es·tate /'· ·ˌ·/ n [U] esp. AmE houses to be bought

re·al·is·m /'rɪəlɪzəm/ n [U] 1 accepting the way things really are in life 2 (in art and literature) showing things as they really are -**list** n -**listic** /rɪə'lɪstɪk/ adj

re·al·i·ty /ri'ælɪti/ n 1 [U] real existence 2 [C;U] something or everything real 3 **in reality** in actual fact

re·a·lize also **-ise** BrE /'rɪəlaɪz/ v 1 vi/t (come to) have full knowledge and understanding (of) 2 vt make (a purpose, fear, etc.) real 3 vt be sold for -**lization** /ˌrɪəlaɪ'zeɪʃən ‖ -lə-/ n [U]

realm /relm/ n 1 fml kingdom 2 area of activity; world

real-time /'· ·/ adj tech (of a computer system) dealing with information as fast as it is received

real·tor /'rɪəltə, -tɔː ‖ -tər, -tɔːr/ n AmE for ESTATE AGENT

ream /riːm/ n 480 pieces of paper **reams** n [P] a lot of writing

reap /riːp/ vi/t cut and gather (a crop of grain): (fig.) He reaped (=gained) the benefit of all his hard work. ~**er** n —see also GRIM REAPER

rear[1] /rɪə ‖ rɪr/ n, adj [only before n] 1 back (part) 2 **bring up the rear** be last

rear[2] v 1 vt care for until fully grown 2 vi rise upright on the back legs 3 vt raise (the head)

rear·guard /'rɪəgɑːd ‖ 'rɪrgɑːrd/ n soldiers protecting the rear of an army

rearguard ac·tion /ˌ·· '··/ n 1 fight by the rearguard of an army being driven back by a victorious enemy **2** attempt (to do or stop something) which is unlikely to succeed

re·ar·ma·ment /riːˈɑːməmənt ‖ -ˈɑːr-/ n [U] providing a nation with weapons again, or with new weapons

rea·son¹ /ˈriːzən/ n **1** [C;U] why something is or was done; cause **2** [U] power to think, understand and form opinions **3** [U] healthy mind that is not mad: *to lose one's reason* (=go mad) **4** [U] good sense **5 stand to reason** be clear to all sensible people **6 within reason** not beyond sensible limits

reason² v **1** vi use one's REASON¹ (2) **2** vt give as an opinion based on REASON¹ (2) ~**ing** n [U] steps in thinking about or understanding something

    reason with phr vt try to persuade by fair argument

rea·son·a·ble /ˈriːzənəbəl/ adj **1** showing fairness or good sense **2** quite cheap –**bly** adv **1** sensibly **2** quite: *in reasonably good health*

re·as·sure /ˌriːəˈʃʊə ‖ -ˈʃʊr/ vt comfort and make free from worry –**surance** n [C;U]

re·bate /ˈriːbeɪt/ n official return of part of a payment

reb·el¹ /ˈrebəl/ n person who rebels

re·bel² /rɪˈbel/ vi -ll- oppose or fight against someone in control

re·bel·lion /rɪˈbeljən/ n [C;U] (act of) rebelling –**lious** adj

re·birth /ˌriːˈbɜːθ ‖ -ˈɜːrθ/ n [S] fml renewal of life; change of spirit

re·born /ˌriːˈbɔːn ‖ -ˈɔːrn/ adj fml as if born again

re·bound /rɪˈbaʊnd/ vi fly back after hitting something ♦ /ˈriːbaʊnd/ n **on the rebound: a** while rebounding **b** while in an unsettled state of mind as a result of failure in a relationship

    rebound on phr vt (of a bad action) harm (the doer)

re·buff /rɪˈbʌf/ n rough or cruel answer or refusal **rebuff** vt

re·buke /rɪˈbjuːk/ vt fml speak to angrily and blamingly **rebuke** n

re·but /rɪˈbʌt/ vt fml prove the falseness of -**tal** n [C;U]

re·cal·ci·trant /rɪˈkælsɪtrənt/ adj fml refusing to obey –**trance** n [U]

re·call /rɪˈkɔːl ‖ -ˈkɔːl/ vt **1** remember **2** send for or take back ♦ /rɪˈkɔːl ‖ rɪˈkɔːl,

ˈriːkɔːl/ n **1** [U] ability to remember **2** [S;U] call to return

re·cant /rɪˈkænt/ vi/t fml say publicly that one no longer holds (a religious or political opinion) ~**ation** /ˌriːkænˈteɪʃən/ n [C;U]

re·cap /ˈriːkæp ‖ riːˈkæp/ vi/t -pp- repeat (the chief points of something said) **recap** /ˈriːkæp/ n

re·ca·pit·u·late /ˌriːkəˈpɪtʃʊleɪt/ vi/t fml recap –**lation** /ˌriːkəpɪtʃʊˈleɪʃən/ n [C;U]

re·cede /rɪˈsiːd/ vi move back or away

re·ceipt /rɪˈsiːt/ n **1** [C] written statement that one has received money **2** [U] fml receiving **receipts** n [P] money received from a business

re·ceive /rɪˈsiːv/ vt **1** get; be given: *receive a letter/a nasty shock* **2** accept as a visitor or member **3** turn (radio waves) into sound or pictures –**ceived** adj generally accepted –**ceiver** n **1** part of a telephone that is held to the ear **2** radio or television set **3** official who looks after the affairs of a BANKRUPT **4** person who buys and sells stolen property

re·cent /ˈriːsənt/ adj that happened or started only a short time ago ~**ly** adv not long ago

re·cep·ta·cle /rɪˈseptəkəl/ n fml container

re·cep·tion /rɪˈsepʃən/ n **1** [C] welcome: *a friendly reception* **2** [C] large formal party **3** [U] place where visitors to a hotel or other large building are welcomed **4** [U] quality of radio or television signals ~**ist** n person who welcomes and deals with visitors to a hotel, shop, etc.

re·cep·tive /rɪˈseptɪv/ adj willing to consider new ideas ~**ness**, –**tivity** /ˌriːsepˈtɪvəti/ n [U]

re·cess /rɪˈses ‖ ˈriːses/ n **1** pause for rest during a working period **2** space in an inside wall for shelves, cupboards, etc. **3** secret inner place ♦ /rɪˈses/ vt make or put into a RECESS (2)

re·ces·sion /rɪˈseʃən/ n **1** period of reduced business activity **2** act of receding

re·cher·ché /rəˈʃeəʃeɪ ‖ rəˈʃer-, rəˌʃerˈʃeɪ/ adj rare and strange

re·ci·pe /ˈresɪpi/ n set of cooking instructions

re·cip·i·ent /rɪˈsɪpiənt/ n fml person who receives something

re·cip·ro·cal /rɪˈsɪprəkəl/ adj fml given and received in return; MUTUAL ~**ly** /-kli/

adv

re·cip·ro·cate /rɪˈsɪprəkeɪt/ *vi/t fml* give or do (something) in return **-cation** /rɪˌsɪprəˈkeɪʃən/ *n* [U]

re·cit·al /rɪˈsaɪtl/ *n* performance of music or poetry by one person or a small group

re·cite /rɪˈsaɪt/ *v* 1 *vi/t* say (something learned) aloud in public 2 *vt fml* give a detailed account or list of **recitation** /ˌresəˈteɪʃən/ *n* [C;U]

reck·less /ˈrekləs/ *adj* not caring about danger **~ly** *adv* **~ness** *n* [U]

reck·on /ˈrekən/ *vt* 1 consider; regard 2 guess; suppose 3 calculate; add up **~ing** *n* [U] 1 calculation 2 punishment: *a day of reckoning*

reckon on *phr vt* make plans in expectation of

reckon with *phr vt* 1 have to deal with 2 take account of in one's plans 3 **to be reckoned with** to be taken seriously as a possible opponent, competitor, etc.

re·claim /rɪˈkleɪm/ *vt* 1 ask for the return of 2 make (land) fit for use **reclamation** /ˌrekləˈmeɪʃən/ *n* [U]

re·cline /rɪˈklaɪn/ *vi fml* lie back or down; rest

re·cluse /rɪˈkluːs ‖ ˈrekluːs/ *n* someone who lives alone on purpose

rec·og·nize, -ise /ˈrekəgnaɪz, ˈrekən-/ *vt* 1 know again (as someone or something one has met before) 2 accept as being legal or real 3 be prepared to admit 4 show official gratefulness for **-nizable** *adj* **-nition** /ˌrekəgˈnɪʃən/ *n* [U]

re·coil /rɪˈkɔɪl/ *vi* 1 move back suddenly in fear or dislike 2 (of a gun) spring back when fired **recoil** /ˈriːkɔɪl, rɪˈkɔɪl/ *n* [S;U]

rec·ol·lect /ˌrekəˈlekt/ *vi/t* remember **~ion** /-ˈlekʃən/ *n* [C;U] memory

rec·om·mend /ˌrekəˈmend/ *vt* 1 praise as being good for a purpose 2 advise: *I'd recommend caution.* 3 (of a quality) to make (someone or something) attractive: *A hotel with little to recommend it.* **~ation** /ˌrekəmenˈdeɪʃən/ *n* [C;U]

rec·om·pense /ˈrekəmpens/ *n* [S;U] *fml* reward or payment for trouble or suffering ♦ *vt fml* give recompense to

rec·on·cile /ˈrekənsaɪl/ *vt* 1 make friendly again 2 find agreement between (two opposing things) **-ciliation** /ˌrekənsɪliˈeɪʃən/ *n* [U]

reconcile to *phr vt* cause (someone) to accept (something unpleasant)

re·con·di·tion /ˌriːkənˈdɪʃən/ *vt* repair and bring back into working order: *a reconditioned engine*

re·con·nais·sance /rɪˈkɒnɪsəns ‖ rɪˈkɑː-/ *n* [C;U] (act of) reconnoitring

re·con·noi·tre *BrE* ‖ **-ter** *AmE* /ˌrekəˈnɔɪtə ‖ ˌriːkəˈnɔɪtər/ *vi/t* go near (the place where an enemy is) to find out information

re·con·sid·er /ˌriːkənˈsɪdə ‖ -ər/ *vi/t* think again and change one's mind (about)

re·cord¹ /rɪˈkɔːd ‖ -ɔːrd/ *v* 1 *vt* write down so that it will be known 2 *vi/t* preserve (sound or a television show) so that it can be heard or seen again 3 *vt* (of an instrument) show by measuring

rec·ord² /ˈrekɔːd ‖ -ərd/ *n* 1 written statement of facts, events, etc. 2 known facts about past behaviour: *his criminal record* 3 best yet done: *the world record for the long jump* 4 circular piece of plastic on which sound is stored for playing back 5 **for the record** to be reported as official 6 **off the record** unofficial(ly) 7 **on the record: a** (of facts or events) (ever) recorded: *the coldest winter on record* **b** (of a person) having publicly said, as if for written records ♦ *adj* better, faster, etc. than ever before: *finished in record time*

re·cord·er /rɪˈkɔːdə ‖ -ˈkɔːrdər/ *n* simple musical instrument played by blowing

re·cord·ing /rɪˈkɔːdɪŋ ‖ -ɔːr-/ *n* recorded performance, speech, or piece of music

record play·er /ˈ‧‧ ˌ‧‧/ *n* machine for producing sounds from RECORDS² (4)

re·count¹ /ˌriːˈkaʊnt/ *vt* count (esp. votes) again **recount** /ˈriːkaʊnt/ *n*

re·count² /rɪˈkaʊnt/ *vt fml* tell

re·coup /rɪˈkuːp/ *vt* get back (something lost, esp. money)

re·course /rɪˈkɔːs ‖ ˈriːkɔːrs/ *n* **have recourse to** *fml* make use of

re·cov·er /rɪˈkʌvə ‖ -ər/ *v* 1 *vt* get back (something lost or taken away) 2 *vi* return to the proper state of health, strength, ability, etc. **~able** *adj* **~y** *n* [U]

rec·re·a·tion /ˌrekriˈeɪʃən/ *n* [C;U] (form of) amusement; way of spending free time **~al** *adj*

re·crim·i·na·tion /rɪˌkrɪməˈneɪʃən/ *n* [C;U] (act of) quarrelling and blaming one another

re·cruit /rɪˈkruːt/ n new member of an organization, esp. the army, navy, etc. ♦ vi/t get recruits or as a recruit ~**ment** n [U]

rec·tan·gle /ˈrektæŋgəl/ n flat shape with four straight sides forming four 90° angles /rek'tæŋgʊlə‖ -ər/ adj

rec·ti·fy /ˈrektɪfaɪ/ vt fml put right

rec·ti·tude /ˈrektɪtjuːd‖ -tuːd/ n [U] fml moral pureness

rec·tor /ˈrektə‖ -ər/ n priest in charge of a PARISH ~**y** n rector's home

rec·tum /ˈrektəm/ n med lowest end of the bowel, where food waste passes out

re·cum·bent /rɪˈkʌmbənt/ adj fml lying down on the back or side

re·cu·pe·rate /rɪˈkjuːpəreɪt, -ˈkuː-/ vi get well again after illness [U] –**rative** /-pərətɪv/ adj helping one to recuperate –**ration** /rɪˌkjuːpəˈreɪʃən, -ˌkuː-/ n

re·cur /rɪˈkɜː‖ -ˈkɜːr/ vi -rr- happen again: a recurring problem –**currence** /rɪˈkʌrəns‖ -ˈkɜːr-/ n [C;U]: frequent recurrence of the fever –**current** adj

re·cy·cle /ˌriːˈsaɪkəl/ vt treat a (used substance) so that it is fit to use again

red /red/ adj -dd- 1 of the colour of blood 2 (of hair) brownish orange 3 (of skin) pink 4 **see red** become angry suddenly and lose control of oneself ♦ n 1 [C;U] red colour 2 [U] red clothes 3 **in the red** in debt –**den** vi/t make or become red

red car·pet /ˌ· ˈ··/ n [S] special ceremonial welcome to a guest

Red Cres·cent /ˌ· ˈ··/ n [the+S] organization like the Red Cross, working in Muslim countries

Red Cross /ˌ· ˈ·/ n [the+S] international organization that looks after the sick and wounded

re·deem /rɪˈdiːm/ vt 1 buy back (something given for money lent) 2 fml make (something bad) slightly less bad 3 fml fulfil (a promise, etc.) **Redeemer** n [the, our+S] Christ

re·demp·tion /rɪˈdempʃən/ n [U] redeeming

re·de·ploy /ˌriːdɪˈplɔɪ/ vt rearrange (soldiers, workers in industry, etc.) in a more effective way ~**ment** n

re·de·vel·op /ˌriːdɪˈveləp/ vt improve (an area) by building, bringing in business, etc. ~**ment** n [C;U]

red-hand·ed /ˌ· ˈ··◀/ adj in the act of doing wrong

red·head /ˈredhed/ n person with RED (2) hair

red her·ring /ˌ· ˈ··/ n something introduced to draw people's attention away from the main point

red-hot /ˌ· ˈ·◀/ adj so hot that it shines red: (fig.) red-hot enthusiasm

red-let·ter day /ˌ· ˈ·· ·/ n specially good day

red-light dis·trict /ˌ· ˈ· ·ˌ·/ n area where PROSTITUTES work

red meat /ˌ· ˈ·/ n [U] meat such as BEEF which is a dark colour after cooking

red·neck /ˈrednek/ n infml, esp. AmE person who lives in the country, esp. one who is uneducated or poor and has strong unreasonable opinions

re·doub·le /riːˈdʌbəl/ vi/t increase greatly

re·doub·ta·ble /rɪˈdaʊtəbəl/ adj greatly respected and feared

re·dress /rɪˈdres/ vt fml 1 put right (a wrong, injustice, etc.) 2 **redress the balance** make things equal again ♦ n [U] something, such as money, that puts right a wrong

red tape /ˌ· ˈ·/ n [U] silly detailed unnecessary rules

re·duce /rɪˈdjuːs‖ rɪˈduːs/ vt 1 make less 2 (of a person) lose weight on purpose –**duction** /rɪˈdʌkʃən/ n [C;U]: price reductions

reduce to phr vt 1 bring to (a less favourable state): The child was reduced to tears. (=made to cry) 2 bring (something) to (a smaller number or amount)

re·dun·dant /rɪˈdʌndənt/ adj esp. BrE no longer employed because there is not enough work 2 fml not needed –**dancy** n [C;U]

red·wood /ˈredwʊd/ n extremely tall American CONIFEROUS tree

reed /riːd/ n 1 grasslike plant growing in wet places 2 thin piece of wood or metal in certain musical instruments, blown across to produce sound ~**y** adj 1 full of reeds 2 (of a sound) thin and high

reef /riːf/ n line of sharp rocks at or near the surface of the sea

reef·er /ˈriːfə/ n infml cigarette containing the drug MARIJUANA

reef knot /ˈ· ·/ n double knot that will not

undo easily

reek /riːk/ *vi, n* (have) a strong unpleasant smell

reel¹ /riːl/ *n* **1** round object on which cotton, cinema film, etc. can be wound **2** length of time it takes to show this amount of film ♦ *vt* bring, take, etc. by winding

   reel off *phr vt* say quickly and easily from memory

reel² *vi* **1** walk unsteadily as if drunk **2** be shocked or confused **3** seem to go round and round

re·en·try /riːˈentri/ *n* [C;U] entering again, esp. into the Earth's ATMOSPHERE

ref /ref/ *n infml for* REFEREE (1)

re·fec·to·ry /rɪˈfektəri/ *n* eating room in a school, college, etc.

refer /rɪˈfɜː ‖ -ˈfɜːr/ *v* **-rr-**

   refer to *phr vt* **1** mention; speak about **2** be about or directed towards **3** look at for information **4** send to (a person or place) for information, a decision, etc.

ref·er·ee /ˌrefəˈriː/ *n* **1** person in charge of a game **2** person who gives a REFERENCE (3)

ref·er·ence /ˈrefərəns/ *n* **1** [C;U] (act of) mentioning **2** [C;U] (act of) looking at something for information **3** [C] **a** information about someone's character and ability, esp. when they are looking for a job **b** person who gives such information **4** in/with reference to *fml* about

reference book /ˈ··· ·/ *n* book for finding information

ref·er·en·dum /ˌrefəˈrendəm/ *n* **-da** /-də/ *or* **-dums** direct vote by all the people to decide something

re·fine /rɪˈfaɪn/ *vt* make pure **–refined** *adj* **1** made pure **2** showing education, delicacy of feeling, and good manners **~ment** *n* **1** [C] clever addition or improvement **2** [U] act of refining **3** [U] quality of being refined

re·fin·e·ry /rɪˈfaɪnəri/ *n* place where oil, sugar, etc. is refined

re·fit /ˌriːˈfɪt/ *vt* **-tt-** repair and put new machinery into (a ship) **refit** /ˈriːfɪt/ *n*

re·flect /rɪˈflekt/ *v* **1** vt throw back (heat, sound, or an image) **2** vt give an idea of; express **3** vi think carefully **~ive** *adj* thoughtful **~or** *n* piece of plastic that reflects light

   reflect on *phr vt* **1** consider carefully **2** cause to be considered in a particular way

re·flec·tion /rɪˈflekʃən/ *n* **1** [C] reflected image **2** [U] reflecting of heat, sound, etc. **3** [C;U] deep and careful thought

re·flex /ˈriːfleks/ *n* unintentional movement made in reply to an outside influence: *quick/slow reflexes*

re·flex·ive /rɪˈfleksɪv/ *n, adj* (word) showing effect on oneself: *In 'I enjoyed myself', 'enjoy' is a reflexive verb.*

re·form /rɪˈfɔːm ‖ -ɔːrm/ *vi/t* make or become (morally) right; improve ♦ *n* [C;U] action to improve conditions, remove unfairness, etc. **~er** *n*

re·form /ˌriːˈfɔːm ‖ -ɔːrm/ *vi/t* (cause to) form again, esp. into ranks

ref·or·ma·tion /ˌrefəˈmeɪʃən ‖ -fər-/ *n* [U] **1** (moral) improvement **2** (*cap.*) 16th-century religious movement leading to the establishment of Protestant churches

re·fract /rɪˈfrækt/ *vt* bend (light passing through) **~ion** /ˈfrækʃən/ *n* [U]

re·frac·to·ry /rɪˈfræktəri/ *adj fml* disobedient and troublesome

re·frain¹ /rɪˈfreɪn/ *vi fml* not do something

refrain² *n* part of a song that is repeated

re·fresh /rɪˈfreʃ/ *vt* **1** cause to feel fresh or active again **2 refresh one's memory** help oneself to remember again **~ing** *adj* **1** producing comfort and new strength **2** pleasingly new and interesting **~ment** *n* [U] **~ments** *n* [P] food and drink

re·frig·e·rate /rɪˈfrɪdʒəreɪt/ *vt* make (food, drink, etc.) cold to preserve it **–ration** /rɪˌfrɪdʒəˈreɪʃən/ *n* [U]

re·frig·e·ra·tor /rɪˈfrɪdʒəreɪtə ‖ -ər/ *n* *fml for* FRIDGE

re·fu·el /ˌriːˈfjuːəl/ *vi/t* fill (a vehicle) with FUEL again before continuing a journey

ref·uge /ˈrefjuːdʒ/ *n* [C;U] (place providing) protection or shelter

ref·u·gee /ˌrefjʊˈdʒiː/ *n* person forced to leave their country because of (political) danger

re·fund /ˈriːfʌnd/ *n* repayment ♦ /rɪˈfʌnd/ *vt* pay (money) back

re·fur·bish /ˌriːˈfɜːbɪʃ ‖ -ɜːr-/ *vt* make fit for use again

re·fus·al /rɪˈfjuːzəl/ *n* [C;U] (a case of) refusing —see also FIRST REFUSAL

re·fuse¹ /rɪˈfjuːz/ *vi/t* not accept, do, or give: *She refused my offer.*

ref·use² /'refjuːs/ n [U] waste material; RUBBISH

re·fute /rɪ'fjuːt/ vt fml prove that (someone or something) is mistaken **refutation** /,refjʊ'teɪʃən/ n [C;U]

re·gain /rɪ'geɪn/ vt get or win back

re·gal /'riːgəl/ adj like a king or queen; very splendid ~**ly** adv

re·gale /rɪ'geɪl/ v regale with phr vt entertain with

re·ga·li·a /rɪ'geɪliə/ n [U] ceremonial clothes and decorations

re·gard¹ /rɪ'gɑːd‖-ɑːrd/ vt 1 look at or consider in the stated way: *I regard him as the finest lawyer in the country.* 2 fml pay respectful attention to ~**ing** prep fml in connection with

regard² n [U] 1 respect 2 respectful attention; concern 3 **in/with regard to** in connection with ~**less** adv 1 whatever may happen 2 **regardless of** without worrying about **regards** n [P] good wishes

re·gat·ta /rɪ'gætə/ n meeting for boat races

re·gen·cy /'riːdʒənsi/ n [C;U] rule by a regent, esp. (cap.) from 1811 to 1820 in Britain

re·gen·e·rate /rɪ'dʒenəreɪt/ vi/t (cause to) grow or develop again –**ration** /rɪ,dʒenə'reɪʃən/ n [U]: *economic regeneration*

re·gent /'riːdʒənt/ n person who governs in place of a king or queen who is ill, still a child, etc.

reg·gae /'regeɪ/ n [U] West Indian popular dance and music

re·gime /reɪ'ʒiːm/ n 1 (system of) government 2 regimen

re·gi·men /'redʒɪmɪn/ n fml fixed plan of food, exercise, etc. to improve health

re·gi·ment /'redʒɪmənt/ n large military group ♦ /'redʒɪment/ vt control too firmly ~**al** /,redʒɪ'mentl◁/ adj

re·gion /'riːdʒən/ n 1 quite large area or part 2 **in the region of** about ~**al** adj **regions** [(the)P] parts of the country away from the capital

re·gis·ter¹ /'redʒɪstə‖-ər/ n 1 (book containing) a record or list 2 range of the voice or a musical instrument 3 words, style, etc. used by speakers and writers in particular conditions

register² v 1 vt put into a REGISTER¹ (1) 2 vi put one's name on a list, esp. of those who will take part 3 vt (of a measuring instrument) show 4 vt (of a person or face) express 5 vt have an effect (on a person)

re·gis·trar /,redʒɪ'strɑː‖'redʒɪstrɑːr/ n keeper of official records

re·gis·tra·tion /,redʒɪ'streɪʃən/ n [U] registering (REGISTER² (2))

registration num·ber /·'·· ,·/ n BrE official number shown on a vehicle

registry of·fice /'redʒɪstri ,ɒfɪs‖ -,ɔːfɪs, -,ɑː-/ also **register office** /'··· ,·/ — n (esp. in Britain) office where marriages can legally take place and where births, marriages, and deaths are officially recorded

re·gress /rɪ'gres/ vi fml go back to a former and usu. worse condition, way of behaving, etc. ~**ion** /-'greʃən/ n [U]

re·gret¹ /rɪ'gret/ vt -tt- be sorry that: *I've never regretted my decision to leave.* ~**table** adj that one should regret ~**tably** adv

regret² n [C;U] unhappiness at the loss of something, because of something one has done or not done, etc. ~**ful** adj

re·group /,riː'gruːp/ vi/t form into new groups

reg·u·lar /'regjʊlə‖-ər/ adj 1 not varying: *a regular pulse | a regular customer* 2 happening (almost) every time: *regular church attendance* 3 correct or usual 4 evenly shaped 5 employed continuously: *a regular soldier* 6 gram following the standard pattern: *regular verbs* 7 infml complete; thorough 8 esp. AmE pleasant and honest: *a regular guy* ♦ n regular visitor, customer, etc. ~**ly** adv at regular times ~**ize**, **-ise** vt make lawful **-lar·ity** /,regjʊ'lærɪti/ n [U]

reg·u·late /'regjʊleɪt/ vt 1 control, esp. by rules 2 make (a machine) work in a certain way **–latory** /-lətəri‖-tɔːri/ adj fml having the purpose of regulating

reg·u·la·tion /,regjʊ'leɪʃən/ n 1 [C] (official) rule 2 [U] control

re·gur·gi·tate /rɪ'gɜːdʒɪteɪt‖-ɜːr-/ vt fml 1 bring back (swallowed food) through the mouth 2 repeat (something heard or read) in one's own work, without thought or change

re·ha·bil·i·tate /,riːhə'bɪlɪteɪt/ vt 1 make able to live an ordinary life again

2 put back into good condition 3 put back to a former high rank, position, etc.

re·hab·il·i·ta·tion /ˌriːhəbɪləˈteɪʃən/ also **re·hab** /ˈriːhæb/ n [U] 1 (process of) treating someone with a drug or alcohol problem 2 —see REHABILITATE

re·hash /riːˈhæʃ/ vt use (old ideas) again **rehash** /ˈriːhæʃ/ n

re·hearse /rɪˈhɜːs/ vi/t practise for later performance **rehearsal** n [C;U]

re·house /ˌriːˈhaʊz/ vt officially provide a new or better home for

reign /reɪn/ n period of reigning ♦ vi 1 be the king or queen 2 exist (noticeably): Silence reigned.

reign of ter·ror /ˌ· · ˈ··/ n period of widespread official killing

re·im·burse /ˌriːɪmˈbɜːs ‖ -ˈɜːrs/ vt pay (money) back to **-ment** n [C;U]

rein /reɪn/ n 1 also **reins** pl. — long narrow (leather) band for controlling a horse 2 **give (free) rein to** give freedom to (feelings or desires) 3 **keep a tight rein on** control firmly —see also FREE REIN **reins** n [P] means of control: take the reins (=become the leader)

re·in·car·nate /ˌriːɪnˈkɑːneɪt ‖ -ɑːr-/ vt cause to return to life in a new form after death **-nation** /ˌriːɪnkɑːˈneɪʃən ‖ -kɑːr-/ n [C;U]

rein·deer /ˈreɪndɪə ‖ -dɪr/ n **reindeer** large deer from northern parts of the world

re·in·force /ˌriːɪnˈfɔːs ‖ -ˈfɔːrs/ vt strengthen with additions **-ment** n [U] **~ments** n [P] more soldiers sent to reinforce an army

reinforced con·crete /ˌ··· ˈ··/ n [U] CONCRETE strengthened by metal bars

re·in·state /ˌriːɪnˈsteɪt/ vt put back into a position formerly held **~ment** n [C;U]

re·it·e·rate /riːˈɪtəreɪt/ vt fml repeat several times **-ration** /riːˌɪtəˈreɪʃən/ n [C;U]

re·ject /rɪˈdʒekt/ vt refuse to accept ♦ /ˈriːdʒekt/ n something thrown away as useless or imperfect **~ion** /rɪˈdʒekʃən/ n [C;U]

re·jig /riːˈdʒɪg/ vt -gg- (rearrange, esp. so as to perform different work or to work more effectively

re·joice /rɪˈdʒɔɪs/ vi 1 feel or show great joy 2 **rejoice in the name of** be called (used when the name sounds foolish)

rejoicing n [C;U] (public) show of joy

re·join[1] /ˌriːˈdʒɔɪn/ vi/t join again

re·join[2] /rɪˈdʒɔɪn/ vt answer, esp. angrily

re·join·der /rɪˈdʒɔɪndə ‖ -ər/ n (rude) answer

re·ju·ve·nate /rɪˈdʒuːvəneɪt/ vt make young again **-nation** /rɪˌdʒuːvəˈneɪʃən/ n [U]

re·lapse /rɪˈlæps/ vi return to a bad state of health or way of life **relapse** n

re·late /rɪˈleɪt/ vt 1 see or show a connection between 2 fml tell (a story) **-related** adj of the same family or kind; connected

   relate to phr vt 1 connect (one thing) with (another) 2 infml understand and accept

re·la·tion /rɪˈleɪʃən/ n 1 [C] member of one's family 2 [C;U] connection 3 **in/with relation to** fml with regard to **~ship** n 1 [C] friendship or connection between people 2 [C;U] connection **relations** n [P] dealings between (and feelings towards) each other

rel·a·tive /ˈrelətɪv/ n RELATION (1) ♦ adj compared to each other or something else: now living in relative comfort **-ly** adv quite

relative clause /ˌ··· ˈ·/ n CLAUSE joined on by a RELATIVE PRONOUN

relative pro·noun /ˌ··· ˈ··/ n PRONOUN which joins a CLAUSE to the rest of a sentence, such as who, which, or that

rel·a·tiv·i·ty /ˌreləˈtɪvəti/ n [U] relationship between time, size, and mass, said to change with increased speed

re·lax /rɪˈlæks/ vi/t make or become a less active and worried b less stiff, tight, or severe **-ation** /ˌriːlækˈseɪʃən/ n 1 [C;U] (something done for) rest and amusement 2 [U] act of making or becoming less severe

re·lay /ˈriːleɪ/ n [C;U] 1 group that takes the place of another to keep work going continuously: In a **relay (race)**, each member of each team runs part of the distance. 2 (broadcast sent out by) an electrical connection for receiving and passing on signals

re·lease /rɪˈliːs/ vt 1 set free 2 allow to be seen or read publicly 3 press (a handle) so as to let something go ♦ n 1 [S;U] setting free 2 [C] new film, record, or piece of information that has been released 3 **on general release** (of a film) able to be seen at all the cinemas in an area

rel·e·gate /'relɪgeɪt/ vt put into a lower or worse place –**gation** /ˌrelɪ'geɪʃən/ n [U]

re·lent /rɪ'lent/ vi become less cruel or severe ~**less** adj continuously cruel or severe

rel·e·vant /'relɪvənt/ adj directly connected with the subject ~**ly** adv –**vance** n [U]

re·li·a·ble /rɪ'laɪəbəl/ adj that may be trusted –**ably** adv –**ability** /rɪˌlaɪə'bɪlɪti/ n [U]

re·li·ant /rɪ'laɪənt/ adj dependent (on) –**ance** n [U] 1 dependence 2 trust

rel·ic /'relɪk/ n 1 something old that reminds us of the past 2 part of or something that belonged to a dead holy person

re·lief /rɪ'li:f/ n 1 [S;U] comfort at the ending of anxiety, pain, or dullness 2 [U] help for people in trouble 3 [C] person who takes over another's duty 4 [C;U] decoration that stands out above the rest of the surface it is on 5 [U] BrE part of one's income on which one does not have to pay tax 6 **light relief** pleasant and amusing change

relief map /·ˈ· ·/ n map showing the height of land

re·lieve /rɪ'li:v/ vt 1 lessen (pain or trouble) 2 take over duties from 3 give variety or interest to 4 **relieve oneself** URINATE or empty the bowels **relieved** adj no longer worried

relieve of phr vt free from

re·li·gion /rɪ'lɪdʒən/ n [C;U] (system of) belief in and worship of one or more gods

re·li·gious /rɪ'lɪdʒəs/ adj 1 of religion 2 obeying the rules of a religion 3 performing the stated duties very carefully ~**ly** adv

re·lin·quish /rɪ'lɪŋkwɪʃ/ vt fml for GIVE up (5)

rel·ish /'relɪʃ/ n [U] 1 great enjoyment 2 substance eaten with a meal, to add taste and interest ♦ vt enjoy

re·live /ˌri:'lɪv/ vt experience again in the imagination

re·lo·cate /ˌri:ləʊ'keɪt ‖ ri:'ləʊkeɪt/ vi/t move to a new place ~**tion** /ˌri:ləʊ'keɪʃən ‖ -'loʊ-/ n

re·luc·tant /rɪ'lʌktənt/ adj unwilling ~**ly** adv –**tance** n [U]

re·ly /rɪ'laɪ/ v **rely on** phr vt 1 trust 2 depend on

re·main /rɪ'meɪn/ v 1 vi stay or be left behind after others have gone 2 continue to be: *remain calm/a prisoner* **remains** n [P] 1 parts which are left 2 fml dead body

re·main·der /rɪ'meɪndə ‖ -ər/ n what is left over ♦ vt sell (esp. books) cheap so as to get rid of them quickly

re·mand /rɪ'mɑ:nd ‖ rɪ'mænd/ vt send back to prison from a court of law, to be tried later ♦ n [C;U]: *He's on remand.* (=in prison waiting for a trial)

re·mark /rɪ'mɑ:k ‖ -ɑ:rk/ n spoken or written opinion ♦ vt say

remark on phr vt fml mention

re·mark·a·ble /rɪ'mɑ:kəbəl ‖ -ɑ:r-/ adj unusual or noticeable –**bly** adv

re·me·di·al /rɪ'mi:diəl/ adj providing a remedy

rem·e·dy /'remɪdi/ n [C;U] way of curing or dealing with something ♦ vt put (something bad) right

re·mem·ber /rɪ'membə ‖ -ər/ v 1 vt call back into the mind 2 vi/t take care not to forget 3 vt give money or a present to

remember to phr vt send greetings from (someone) to

re·mem·brance /rɪ'membrəns/ n [U] 1 act of remembering 2 something given or kept to remind one

re·mind /rɪ'maɪnd/ vt cause to remember ~**er** n something to make one remember

remind of phr vt cause to remember by seeming the same

rem·i·nisce /ˌremɪ'nɪs/ vi talk pleasantly about the past –**niscence** n [U] –**niscences** n [P] written or spoken account of one's past life –**niscent** adj that reminds one (of); like

re·miss /rɪ'mɪs/ adj fml careless about a duty

re·mis·sion /rɪ'mɪʃən/ n [C;U] 1 lessening of the time someone has to stay in prison 2 fml period when an illness is less severe

re·mit /rɪ'mɪt/ vt **-tt-** fml 1 send (money) by post 2 free someone from (a debt or punishment) ~**tance** n [C] money remitted 2 fml act of remitting money

rem·nant /'remnənt/ n part that remains

rem·on·strate /'remənstreɪt ‖ rɪ'mɑ:n-/ vi fml express disapproval

re·morse /rɪ'mɔ:s ‖ -ɔ:rs/ n [U] sorrow

for having done wrong ~**ful** adj ~**less** adj 1 showing no remorse 2 threateningly unstoppable

re·mote /rɪˈməʊt ‖ -ˈməʊt/ adj 1 far distant in space or time 2 quiet and lonely: *a remote village* 3 widely separated; not close: *a remote connection* 4 slight: *a remote chance of success* 5 not showing interest in others ~**ly** adv at all: *not remotely interested* ~**ness** n [U]

remote con·trol /·ˌ· ·ˈ·/ n 1 [U] controlling machinery by radio signals 2 [C] also **remote** piece of equipment used to control a television, VIDEO machine, etc. from a distance

re·move /rɪˈmuːv/ vt 1 take away; get rid of 2 fml dismiss 3 **removed from** distant or different from ♦ n stage; degree: *Their action was only (at) one remove from* (=was nearly) *revolution.* **removal** n [C;U] ~**mover** n [C;U]

re·mu·ne·rate /rɪˈmjuːnəreɪt/ vt fml pay ~**rative** /-rətɪv/ adj well-paid ~**ration** /rɪˌmjuːnəˈreɪʃən/ n [S;U]

re·nais·sance /rɪˈneɪsəns ‖ ˌrenəˈsɑːns/ n renewal of interest in art, literature, etc., esp. (cap.) in Europe between the 15th and 17th centuries

re·nal /ˈriːnl/ adj med of the KIDNEYS

ren·der /ˈrendə ‖ -ər/ vt fml 1 cause to be 2 give 3 perform ~**ing**, also **rendition** /renˈdɪʃən/ n performance

ren·dez·vous /ˈrɒndɪvuː, -deɪ- ‖ ˈrɑːn-/ n -**vous** /-vuːz/ 1 (arrangement for) a meeting 2 meeting place ♦ vi meet by arrangement

ren·e·gade /ˈrenɪɡeɪd/ n person who disloyally leaves one country or belief to join another

re·nege, **renegue** /rɪˈniːɡ, rɪˈneɪɡ ‖ rɪˈnɪɡ, rɪˈniːɡ/ vi fml break a promise

re·new /rɪˈnjuː ‖ rɪˈnuː/ vt 1 repeat: *They renewed their attack.* 2 give new life and freshness to 3 get something new of the same kind to take the place of ~**al** n [C;U]

ren·ew·a·ble /rɪˈnjuːəbəl ‖ rɪˈnuː-/ adj 1 able to be replaced as quickly as it is used: *renewable energy sources* 2 able to be continued after a time limit: *a renewable contract*

ren·net /ˈrenɪt/ n [U] substance for thickening milk to make cheese

re·nounce /rɪˈnaʊns/ vt say formally that

one does not own or has no more connection with

ren·o·vate /ˈrenəveɪt/ vt put back into good condition ~**vation** /ˌrenəˈveɪʃən/ n [C;U]

re·nown /rɪˈnaʊn/ n [U] fame ~**ed** adj famous

rent /rent/ n [C;U] money paid regularly for the use of a house, television set, etc. ♦ vt 1 pay rent for the use of 2 allow to be used in return for rent ~**al** sum of money fixed to be paid as rent

rent boy /ˈ· ·/ n BrE infml young male PROSTITUTE

re·nun·ci·a·tion /rɪˌnʌnsɪˈeɪʃən/ n [C;U] (act of) renouncing (RENOUNCE)

re·or·gan·ize, -ise /riːˈɔːɡənaɪz ‖ -ˈɔːr-/ vi/t ORGANIZE in a new and better way -**ization**, -**isation** n /riːˌɔːɡənaɪˈzeɪʃən ‖ riːˌɔːrɡənə-/ [C;U]

rep¹ /rep/ n infml for SALES REPRESENTATIVE

rep² n [C;U] REPERTORY (company)

Rep written abbrev. for: REPUBLICAN

re·pair /rɪˈpeə ‖ -ˈper/ vt mend ♦ n 1 [C;U] (act or result of) mending 2 [U] condition: *in good repair*

rep·a·ra·tion /ˌrepəˈreɪʃən/ n [C;U] fml repayment for loss or damage

rep·ar·tee /ˌrepɑːˈtiː ‖ ˌrepərˈtiː/ n [U] quick amusing talk

re·past /rɪˈpɑːst ‖ rɪˈpæst/ n fml meal

re·pat·ri·ate /riːˈpætrieɪt ‖ riːˈpeɪ-/ vt send (someone) back to their own country -**ation** /ˌriːpætriˈeɪʃən ‖ ˌriːpeɪ-/ n [U]

re·pay /rɪˈpeɪ/ vt repaid /-ˈpeɪd/ 1 pay (money) back to (someone) 2 reward ~**ment** n [C;U]

re·peal /rɪˈpiːl/ vt end (a law) repeal n [U]

re·peat /rɪˈpiːt/ vt 1 say or do again 2 **repeat oneself** keep saying the same thing ♦ n performance broadcast a second time ~**ed** adj done again and again ~**edly** adv

re·pel /rɪˈpel/ vt -**ll**- 1 drive away (as if) by force 2 cause feelings of extreme dislike in ~**lent** adj extremely nasty ~**lent** n [C;U] substance that repels esp. insects

re·pent /rɪˈpent/ vi/t fml be sorry for (wrongdoing) ~**ant** adj ~**ance** n [U]

re·per·cus·sion /ˌriːpəˈkʌʃən ‖ ˌriːpər-/ n far-reaching effect

rep·er·toire /ˈrepətwɑː ‖ -pərtwɑːr/ n set of things one can perform

rep·er·to·ry /ˈrepətəri ‖ ˈrepərtoːri/ n [U] performing several plays one after the other on different days with the same actors

rep·e·ti·tion /ˌrepɪˈtɪʃən/ n [C;U] repeating **–tious, -tive** /rɪˈpetɪtɪv/ adj containing parts that are repeated too much

re·phrase /riːˈfreɪz/ vt put into different (clearer) words

re·place /rɪˈpleɪs/ vt 1 put back in the right place 2 take the place of 3 get another (better) one instead of **~ment** n 1 [U] act of replacing 2 [C] that replaces someone or something

re·plen·ish /rɪˈplenɪʃ/ vt fill up again

re·plete /rɪˈpliːt/ adj fml very full, esp. of food **–pletion** /-ˈpliːʃən/ n [U]

rep·li·ca /ˈreplɪkə/ n close copy

rep·li·cate /ˈreplɪkeɪt/ vt fml copy exactly

re·ply /rɪˈplaɪ/ vi, n answer

re·port¹ /rɪˈpɔːt ‖ -ɔːrt/ n 1 [C] account of events, business affairs, etc. 2 [C;U] what is said generally but unofficially 3 [C] noise of an explosion

report² v 1 vi/t provide information (about); give an account of, esp. for a newspaper or radio or television 2 vi go somewhere and say that one is there (and ready for work) 3 vt make a complaint about **~er** n person who reports news

re·port·age /rɪˈpɔːtɪdʒ, ˌrepɔːˈtɑːʒ ‖ -ˈpɔːr-, ˌrepərˈtɑːʒ/ n [U] (writing, film, etc. in) the style of reporters

re·port·ed·ly /rɪˈpɔːtɪdli ‖ -ˈpɔːr-/ adv according to what is said

reported speech /·,·· ·/ n [U] INDIRECT SPEECH

re·pose /rɪˈpəʊz ‖ -ˈpoʊz/ n [U] fml rest ♦ vt fml rest; lie

repose in phr vt fml place (trust, hope, etc.) in

re·pos·i·to·ry /rɪˈpɒzɪtəri ‖ rɪˈpɑːzətɔːri/ n place where things are stored

re·pos·sess /ˌriːpəˈzes/ vt take back (something partly paid for), because payments have not been made

rep·re·hen·si·ble /ˌreprɪˈhensɪbəl/ adj fml deserving blame; bad **–bly** adv

rep·re·sent /ˌreprɪˈzent/ v 1 vt act or speak officially for (someone else) 2 vt be a picture or STATUE of; show 3 vt be a sign of; stand for 4 be: *This represents a considerable improvement.* **~ation** /ˌreprɪzen-** 'teɪʃən/ n 1 [U] act of representing or state of being represented 2 [C] something that REPRESENTS (2, 3) something else

rep·re·sen·ta·tive /ˌreprɪˈzentətɪv/ adj 1 typical of 2 (of government) in which the people and their opinions are represented ♦ n person who REPRESENTS (1) others —see also HOUSE OF REPRESENTATIVES

re·press /rɪˈpres/ vt control; hold back **~ive** adj hard and cruel **~ion** /-ˈpreʃən/ n [U] pushing unwelcome feelings into one's unconscious mind, with odd effects on behaviour

re·prieve /rɪˈpriːv/ vt give a reprieve to ♦ n official order not to carry out the punishment of death (yet)

rep·ri·mand /ˈreprɪmɑːnd ‖ -mænd/ vt express severe official disapproval of reprimand n

re·pri·sal /rɪˈpraɪzəl/ n [C;U] (act of) punishing others for harm done to oneself

re·proach /rɪˈprəʊtʃ ‖ -ˈproʊtʃ/ n [C;U] 1 (word of) blame 2 **above/beyond** reproach perfect ♦ vt blame, not angrily but sadly **~ful** adj

rep·ro·bate /ˈreprəbeɪt/ n fml person of bad character

re·pro·duce /ˌriːprəˈdjuːs ‖ -ˈduːs/ vi/t 1 produce the young of (oneself or one's kind) 2 produce a copy (of) **–duction** /-ˈdʌkʃən/ n [C;U] **–ductive** /-ˈdʌktɪv/ adj concerned with producing young

re·proof /rɪˈpruːf/ n [C;U] fml (expression of) blame or disapproval

re·prove /rɪˈpruːv/ vt fml speak blamingly or disapprovingly to

rep·tile /ˈreptaɪl ‖ ˈreptl/ n animal, such as a snake, with blood that changes temperature **–tilian** /repˈtɪliən/ adj

re·pub·lic /rɪˈpʌblɪk/ n state ruled by a president and usu. an elected parliament, not by a king

re·pub·li·can¹ /rɪˈpʌblɪkən/ adj 1 belonging to or supporting a republic

republican² n person who favours republics **~ism** n [U] beliefs or practices of republicans

Republican n member or supporter of the Republican Party, one of the two largest political parties of the US

re·pu·di·ate /rɪˈpjuːdieɪt/ vt fml 1 state that (something) is untrue 2 refuse to accept **–ation** /rɪˌpjuːdiˈeɪʃən/ n [U]

re·pug·nant /rɪˈpʌgnənt/ adj fml causing extreme dislike; nasty **–nance** n [U]

re·pulse /rɪˈpʌls/ vt 1 refuse coldly 2 drive back (an attack) **–pulsive** adj extremely unpleasant **–pulsion** /-ˈpʌlʃən/ n [U] 1 extreme dislike 2 natural force by which one body drives another away from it

rep·u·ta·ble /ˈrepjɐtəbəl/ adj having a good reputation **–bly** adv

rep·u·ta·tion /ˌrepjɐˈteɪʃən/ n [C;U] opinion which people in general have about someone or something

re·pute /rɪˈpjuːt/ n [U] fml 1 reputation 2 good reputation **reputed** adj generally supposed, but with some doubt **reputedly** adv

re·quest /rɪˈkwest/ n 1 [C;U] polite demand 2 [C] something asked for ♦ vt demand politely

req·ui·em /ˈrekwiəm, ˈrekwiem/ n (music for) a Christian ceremony for a dead person

re·quire /rɪˈkwaɪə ‖ -ˈkwaɪr/ vt 1 need 2 fml order, expecting obedience: *You are required to* (=must) *do it.* **~ment** n something needed or demanded

req·ui·site /ˈrekwɪzɪt/ adj needed for a purpose

req·ui·si·tion /ˌrekwɪˈzɪʃən/ n [C;U] formal demand, esp. by the army ♦ vt demand or take officially, esp. for the army

re·route /riːˈruːt ‖ -ˈraʊt, -ˈruːt/ vt cause (vehicles, etc.) to go a different way

re·scind /rɪˈsɪnd/ vt end (a law) or take back (a decision, order, etc.)

res·cue /ˈreskjuː/ vt save or set free from harm or danger **rescue** n **–cuer** n

re·search /rɪˈsɜːtʃ, ˈriːsɜːtʃ ‖ -ɜːr-/ n [C;U] advanced and detailed study, to find out (new) facts ♦ /rɪˈsɜːtʃ ‖ -ɜːr-/ vi/t do research (on or for) **~er** n

re·sem·ble /rɪˈzembəl/ vt look or be like **–blance** n [C;U] likeness

re·sent /rɪˈzent/ vt feel hurt and angry because of **~ful** adj **–ment** n

res·er·va·tion /ˌrezəˈveɪʃən ‖ -zər-/ n 1 [C;U] limiting condition(s): *I accepted every point, without reservation.* 2 [C] private doubt in one's mind 3 [C] arrangement to have or use something: *a hotel reservation* 4 [C] area set apart for particular people to live in

re·serve /rɪˈzɜːv ‖ -ɜːrv/ vt 1 keep apart for a special purpose 2 arrange to have or use: *reserve hotel rooms* ♦ n 1 [C] quantity kept for future use 2 [C] piece of land kept for the stated purpose 3 [C] player who will play if another cannot 4 [U] being reserved 5 [the+S] also **reserves** pl. — military forces kept for use if needed 6 **in reserve** for future use 7 **without reserve** fml completely **reserved** adj not liking to show one's feelings or talk about oneself

res·er·voir /ˈrezəvwɑː ‖ -ərvwɑːr, -vɔːr-/ n 1 artificial lake for storing water 2 large supply (still unused)

re·shuf·fle /riːˈʃʌfəl/ vt change around the positions of people working in **reshuffle** n

re·side /rɪˈzaɪd/ vi fml have one's home

res·i·dence /ˈrezɪdəns/ n fml 1 [C] (large grand) house 2 [U] state of residing 3 **in residence** actually living in a place

res·i·dent /ˈrezɪdənt/ n, adj (person) who lives in a place **~ial** /ˌrezɪˈdenʃəl◄/ adj 1 consisting of private houses 2 for which one must live in a place: *a residential course*

re·sid·u·al /rɪˈzɪdʒuəl/ adj left over; remaining

res·i·due /ˈrezɪdjuː ‖ -duː/ n what is left over

re·sign /rɪˈzaɪn/ vi/t leave (one's job or position) **~ed** adj calmly suffering without complaint **~edly** /rɪˈzaɪnɪdli/ adv

resign to phr vt cause (oneself) to accept calmly (something which cannot be avoided)

res·ig·na·tion /ˌrezɪgˈneɪʃən/ n 1 [C;U] (act or written statement of) resigning 2 [U] state of being resigned

re·sil·i·ent /rɪˈzɪliənt/ adj 1 able to spring back to its former shape 2 able to recover quickly from misfortune **–ence** n [U]

res·in /ˈrezɪn/ n 1 [U] thick sticky liquid from trees 2 [C] man-made plastic substance

re·sist /rɪˈzɪst/ vt 1 oppose; fight against 2 remain unharmed by 3 force oneself not to accept

re·sist·ance /rɪˈzɪstəns/ n [S;U] 1 act of resisting or ability to resist 2 [U] force opposed to movement: *wind resistance* 3 [(the)U] secret army fighting against an enemy in control of its country 4 **the line of least resistance** the easiest way **–ant** adj showing resistance

re·sis·tor /rɪˈzɪstə ‖ -ər/ n piece of wire.

etc. for reducing the power of an electrical current

res·o·lute /'rezəluːt/ adj firm; determined in purpose **~ly** adv

res·o·lu·tion /ˌrezə'luːʃən/ n 1 [C] formal decision at a meeting: a United Nations resolution 2 [C] firm decision: a New Year resolution to eat less 3 [U] quality of being resolute 4 [U] action of resolving (RESOLVE (1))

re·solve /rɪ'zɒlv ‖ rɪ'zɑːlv, rɪ'zɔːlv/ vt 1 find a way of dealing with (a problem); settle 2 decide firmly 3 make a RESOLUTION (1, 2) ♦ n [C;U] fml for RESOLUTION (2, 3)

res·o·nant /'rezənənt/ adj 1 (of a sound) full, clear, and continuing 2 producing RESONANCE (2) **–nance** n [U] 1 quality of being RESONANT (1) 2 sound produced in a body by sound waves from another

res·o·nate /'rezəneɪt/ vi 1 produce RESONANCE (2) 2 be RESONANT (1)

re·sort[1] /rɪ'zɔːt ‖ -ɔːrt/ n 1 holiday place 2 as a/in the last resort if everything else fails

resort[2] v resort to phr vt make use of, esp. when there is nothing else

re·sound /rɪ'zaʊnd/ vi 1 be loud and clearly heard 2 be filled (with sound) **~ing** adj very great: a resounding victory

re·source /rɪ'zɔːs, -'sɔːs ‖ -ɔːrs/ n 1 [C] something useful that one possesses 2 [U] resourcefulness 3 leave someone to his own resources leave someone alone to pass the time as he wishes **~ful** adj able to find a way round difficulties **~fully** adv

re·spect /rɪ'spekt/ n 1 [U] great admiration and honour 2 [U] attention; care 3 [C] detail; point: In some respects (=ways) it is worse. 4 with respect to with regard to; about ♦ vt feel or show respect for **~ing** prep in connection with **respects** n [P] polite formal greetings

re·spec·ta·ble /rɪ'spektəbəl/ adj 1 socially acceptable 2 quite good; a respectable income **–bly** adv **–bility** /rɪˌspektə'bɪləti/ n [U]

re·spect·ful /rɪ'spektfəl/ adj feeling or showing RESPECT (1) **~ly** adv

re·spec·tive /rɪ'spektɪv/ adj particular and separate **~ly** adv each separately in the order mentioned

res·pi·ra·tion /ˌrespə'reɪʃən/ n [U] fml breathing **–piratory** /rɪ'spɪrətəri,

'respəreɪtəri, rɪ'spaɪərə- ‖ 'resprətɔːri, rɪ'spaɪrə-/ adj: the respiratory system (=lungs, etc.)

res·pi·ra·tor /'respəreɪtə ‖ -ər/ n apparatus to help people breathe

res·pite /'respɪt, -paɪt ‖ -pɪt/ n [C;U] 1 short rest from effort, pain, etc. 2 delay before something unwelcome happens

re·splen·dent /rɪ'splendənt/ adj gloriously bright and shining **~ly** adv

re·spond /rɪ'spɒnd ‖ rɪ'spɑːnd/ vi 1 answer 2 act in answer

respond to phr vt (esp. of a disease) get better as a result of

re·sponse /rɪ'spɒns ‖ rɪ'spɑːns/ n 1 [C] answer 2 [C;U] action done in answer

re·spon·si·bil·i·ty /rɪˌspɒnsə'bɪləti ‖ rɪˌspɑːn-/ n 1 [U] condition or quality of being responsible: I take full responsibility for losing it. 2 [C] something for which one is RESPONSIBLE (2) 3 [U] trustworthiness

re·spon·si·ble /rɪ'spɒnsəbəl ‖ rɪ'spɑːn-/ adj 1 having done or caused something (bad); guilty 2 having a duty to do or look after something 3 trustworthy 4 (of a job) needing a trustworthy person to do it 5 be responsible for be the cause of **–bly** adv

re·spon·sive /rɪ'spɒnsɪv ‖ rɪ'spɑːn-/ adj answer readily with words or feelings: (fig.) a disease responsive to treatment

rest[1] /rest/ n 1 [C;U] (period of) freedom from action or something tiring 2 [U] not moving: It came to rest (=stopped) just here. 3 [C] support, esp. for the stated thing: a headrest 4 set someone's mind/fears at rest free someone from anxiety **~ful** adj peaceful; quiet

rest[2] v 1 vi/t (allow to) take a rest 2 vt lean; support 3 vi lie buried: Let him rest in peace. 4 rest assured be certain

rest on phr vt 1 (of a proof, argument, etc.) depend on 2 lean on 3 (of eyes) be directed towards

rest with phr vt be the responsibility of

rest[3] n 1 the rest ones that still remain; what is left 2 for the rest apart from what has already been mentioned

res·tau·rant /'restərɒnt ‖ -rant, -rɑːnt/ n place where meals are sold and eaten

res·tau·ra·teur /ˌrestərə'tɜː ‖ -'tɜːr/ n restaurant owner

res·ti·tu·tion /ˌrestɪ'tjuːʃən ‖ -'tuː-/ n [U] fml giving something back to its owner.

or paying for damage

res·tive /'restɪv/ adj unwilling to keep still or be controlled ~ly adv

rest·less /'restləs/ adj 1 giving no rest or sleep 2 unable to stay still, esp. from anxiety or lack of interest ~ly adv

res·to·ra·tion /ˌrestəˈreɪʃən/ n [C;U] 1 restoring 2 (cap.) period after 1660 in Britain

re·sto·ra·tive /rɪˈstɔːrətɪv/ n, adj (food, medicine, etc.) that brings back health and strength

re·store /rɪˈstɔː‖-ˈstɔːr/ vt 1 give back 2 bring back into existence 3 bring back to a proper state, esp. of health 4 put back into a former position 5 repair (an old painting, building, etc.) **restorer** n

re·strain /rɪˈstreɪn/ vt prevent from doing something; control ~ed adj calm and controlled **restraint** n 1 [U] quality of being restrained or act of restraining oneself 2 [C] something that restrains: *the restraints of life in a small town*

re·strict /rɪˈstrɪkt/ vt keep within a certain limit ~ive adj that restricts type ~ion /-ˈstrɪkʃən/ n [C;U]

re·struc·ture /ˌriːˈstrʌktʃə‖-ər/ vt arrange (a system or organization) in a new way, esp. by getting rid of workers

re·sult /rɪˈzʌlt/ n 1 [C;U] what happens because of an action or event 2 [C;U] (a) noticeable good effect 3 [C] situation of defeat or victory at the end of a game 4 [C] answer to a sum ♦ vi happen as an effect or RESULT (1) ~ant adj resulting

result in phr vt cause

re·sume /rɪˈzjuːm‖-ˈzuːm/ v 1 vi/t begin again after a pause 2 vt fml return to

ré·su·mé /ˈrezjʊmeɪ, ˈreɪ-‖ˌrezʊˈmeɪ/ n 1 shortened form of a speech, book, etc. 2 esp. AmE CURRICULUM VITAE

re·sump·tion /rɪˈzʌmpʃən/ n [U] act of resuming

re·sur·gence /rɪˈsɜːdʒəns‖-ɜːr-/ n [U] becoming active again

res·ur·rect /ˌrezəˈrekt/ vt bring back into use or fashion ~ion /-ˈrekʃən/ n 1 [U] renewal 2 [the+S] return of dead people to life at the end of the world 3 [the] (cap.) return of Christ to life after his death

re·sus·ci·tate /rɪˈsʌsɪteɪt/ vt bring a person back to life ~tation /-rɪˌsʌsɪˈteɪʃən/ n [U]

re·tail¹ /ˈriːteɪl/ n [U] sale of goods in shops to customers, not for reselling to anyone else ♦ adv ~er n ♦ /rɪˈteɪl/ vi/t sell by retail

retail park /'·· ·/ n [U] group of large stores built together, usu. outside a town

re·tain /rɪˈteɪn/ vt 1 keep; avoid losing 2 hold in place 3 employ (esp. a lawyer)

re·tain·er /rɪˈteɪnə‖-ər/ n 1 servant 2 money paid for advice and help

re·tal·i·ate /rɪˈtælieɪt/ vi pay back evil with evil ~atory /-liətəri‖-tɔːri/ adj ~ation /rɪˌtæliˈeɪʃən/ n [U]

re·tard /rɪˈtɑːd‖-ɑːrd/ vt make slow or late ~ed adj often considered offensive slow in development of the mind

retch /retʃ/ vi try unsuccessfully to be sick

re·ten·tion /rɪˈtenʃən/ n [U] state or action of retaining (RETAIN)

re·ten·tive /rɪˈtentɪv/ adj able to remember things well

re·think /ˌriːˈθɪŋk/ vt rethought /ˌriːˈθɔːt ‖-ˈθɒːt/ think again and perhaps change one's mind about rethink /ˈriːθɪŋk/ n [S]

ret·i·cent /ˈretɪsənt/ adj unwilling to say much -cence n [U]

ret·i·na /ˈretɪnə/ n area at the back of the eye which receives light

ret·i·nue /ˈretɪnjuː‖-nuː/ n group travelling with and helping an important person

re·tire /rɪˈtaɪə‖-ˈtaɪr/ vi 1 leave one's job, usu. because of age 2 leave a place of action 3 fml go away, esp. to a quiet place 4 fml go to bed ~ment n [U] retired adj having stopped working retiring adj liking to avoid company

re·tort¹ /rɪˈtɔːt‖-ɔːrt/ n quick or angry reply ♦ vt make a retort

re·tort² n long-necked bottle for heating chemicals

re·touch /ˌriːˈtʌtʃ/ vt improve (a picture) with small additions

re·trace /rɪˈtreɪs, riː-/ vt go back over: *She retraced her steps.* (=went back the way she had come)

re·tract /rɪˈtrækt/ vi/t 1 draw back or in: *The cat retracted its claws.* 2 take back (a statement or offer one has made) ~able adj ~ion /-ˈtrækʃən/ n [U]

re·tread /ˈriːtred/ n tyre with a new covering of rubber

re·treat /rɪˈtriːt/ *vi* **1** move backwards, esp. when forced **2** escape (from something unpleasant) ♦ *n* **1** [C;U] (act of) retreating **2** [*the*+S] military signal for this **3** [C] place one goes to for peace and safety

re·trench /rɪˈtrentʃ/ *vi fml* arrange to lessen (one's spending) ~**ment** *n*[C;U]

re·tri·al /ˈriːtraɪəl/ *n* new trial of a law case

ret·ri·bu·tion /ˌretrɪˈbjuːʃən/ *n fml* deserved punishment

re·trieve /rɪˈtriːv/ *vt* **1** find and bring back **2** *fml* put right **retrieval** *n* [U] retrieving **retriever** *n* dog that retrieves shot birds

ret·ro·grade /ˈretrəɡreɪd/ *adj* moving back to an earlier and worse state

ret·ro·gres·sion /ˌretrəˈɡreʃən/ *n* [U] *fml* going back to an earlier and worse state ~**sive** /-ˈɡresɪv/ *adj*

ret·ro·spect /ˈretrəspekt/ *n* **in retrospect** looking back to the past ~**ive** /ˌretrəˈspektɪv◂/ *adj* **1** thinking about the past **2** (of a law) having an effect on the past **3** also **retrospective exhibition** /ˌ···◂ ···/ — *n* a show of the work of a painter, SCULPTOR, etc. from his or her earliest years up to the present time

re·turn¹ /rɪˈtɜːn ‖ -ˈɜːrn/ *v* **1** *vi* come or go back **2** *vt* give or send back **3** *vt* elect to parliament **4** *vt* give (a VERDICT) **5 return a favour** do a kind action in return for another

return² *n* **1** [C;U] (act of) coming or giving back **2** [C] profit **3** [C] official statement or set of figures: *a tax return* **4 by return of post** by the next post **5 in return for** in exchange (for) **6 Many happy returns (of the day)!** (used as a birthday greeting) ♦ *adj BrE* (of a ticket) for a journey to a place and back again

returning of·fi·cer /·ˈ··· ˌ···/ *n* official who arranges an area's parliamentary election and gives out the result

return match /·ˌ· '·/ *n* second game between the same sides

re·u·ni·fi·ca·tion /ˌriːˌjuːnɪfɪˈkeɪʃən/ *n* [U] act or process of joining together the different parts of a country that has been divided up: *German reunification* **reunify** /riːˈjuːnɪfaɪ/ *vt*

re·u·nion /riːˈjuːnjən/ *n* **1** [C] meeting of former fellow-workers or friends after a

separation **2** [U] state of being brought together again

rev /rev/ *vt* -**vv**- increase the speed of (an engine) ♦ *sl for* REVOLUTION (3)

re·vamp /ˌriːˈvæmp/ *vt* give a new and improved form to

re·veal /rɪˈviːl/ *vt* allow to be seen or known

rev·el /ˈrevəl/ *v* -**ll**- *BrE* ‖ -**l**- *AmE lit* pass the time in dancing, etc. ~**ler** *BrE* ‖ -**er** *AmE* — *n* person taking part in revelry ~**ry** *n* [U] wild noisy dancing and feasting

revel in *phr vt* enjoy greatly

rev·e·la·tion /ˌrevəˈleɪʃən/ *n* **1** [U] making known of something secret: *forced to resign by the revelation of his unpleasant activities* **2** [C] (surprising) fact made known

re·venge /rɪˈvendʒ/ *n* [U] punishment given in return for harm done to oneself ♦ *vt* do something in revenge

rev·e·nue /ˈrevənjuː ‖ -nuː/ *n* [U] income, esp. received by the government

re·ver·be·rate /rɪˈvɜːbəreɪt ‖ -ɜːr-/ *vi* (of sound) be continuously repeated in waves ~**ration** /rɪˌvɜːbəˈreɪʃən ‖ -ɜːr-/ *n* [C;U]

re·vere /rɪˈvɪə ‖ -ˈvɪr/ *vt fml* respect and admire greatly

rev·e·rence /ˈrevərəns/ *n* [U] *fml* great respect and admiration

Rev·e·rend /ˈrevərənd/ *n* (title of respect for) a Christian priest

rev·e·rent /ˈrevərənt/ *adj* showing (religious) reverence ~**ly** *adv*

rev·e·ren·tial /ˌrevəˈrenʃəl◂/ *adj* showing reverence ~**ly** *adv*

rev·e·rie /ˈrevəri/ *n* [C;U] pleasant dreamlike state while awake

re·ver·sal /rɪˈvɜːsəl ‖ -ɜːr-/ *n* **1** [C;U] (case of) being reversed **2** [C] defeat or piece of bad luck

re·verse /rɪˈvɜːs ‖ -ɜːrs/ *adj* opposite in position: *the reverse side* ‖ *in reverse order* ♦ *n* **1** [U] opposite **2** [U] position of a vehicle's controls that causes backward movement **3** [C] REVERSAL (2) **4** [C] back side of a coin, etc. ♦ **1** *vi/t* go or cause (a vehicle) to go backwards **2** *vt* change round or over to the opposite: *reverse the order* ‖ *reverse a decision* **3 reverse the charges** make a telephone call to be paid for by the receiver

re·vers·i·ble /rɪˈvɜːsəbəl ‖ -ɜːr-/ *adj* **1** able to be changed back to how it was

2 able to be worn with either side on the outside

re·ver·sion /rɪˈvɜːʃən ‖ rɪˈvɜːrʒən/ n [U] return to a former condition or habit

re·vert /rɪˈvɜːt ‖ -ɜːrt/ v **revert to** phr vt go back to (a former condition, habit, or owner)

re·view /rɪˈvjuː/ vt 1 consider and judge (an event or situation) 2 hold a REVIEW (2) 3 give a REVIEW (3a) of ♦ n 1 [C;U] (act of) REVIEWing (1) 2 grand show of armed forces, in the presence of a king, queen, general, etc. 3 a [C] (written) expression of judgment on a new book, play, etc. b magazine containing such judgments –**er** n

re·vile /rɪˈvaɪl/ vt fml say bad things about

re·vise /rɪˈvaɪz/ v 1 vt improve and make corrections to (written material) 2 vt change (an opinion, intention, etc.) 3 vi/t esp. BrE restudy (something already learned), esp. before an examination

re·vi·sion /rɪˈvɪʒən/ n 1 [C;U] (act of) revising 2 [C] revised piece of writing

re·vi·sion·is·m /rɪˈvɪʒənɪzəm/ n [U] questioning of the main beliefs of a (Marxist) political system –**ist** n

re·vi·tal·ize, -**ise** /riːˈvaɪtəl-aɪz/ vt put new strength or power into

re·vive /rɪˈvaɪv/ v 1 vi/t become or make conscious or healthy again: (fig.) The photo revived (=brought to mind) old memories. 2 vi/t come or bring back into use or existence 3 perform (an old play) again after many years **revival** n 1 [C;U] renewal 2 [C] new performance of an old play

rev·o·ca·tion /ˌrevəˈkeɪʃən/ n [U] revoking

re·voke /rɪˈvəʊk ‖ -ˈvouk/ vt put an end to (a law, decision, permission, etc.)

re·volt /rɪˈvəʊlt ‖ -ˈvoult/ v 1 vi (try to) take power violently from those in power 2 vt (cause) to feel sick and shocked ♦ n [C;U] (example of) the act of REVOLTing (1) ~**ing** adj extremely nasty ~**ingly** adv: revoltingly dirty

rev·o·lu·tion /ˌrevəˈluːʃən/ n 1 [C;U] (time of) great social change esp. of a political system by force 2 [C] complete change in ways of thinking or acting 3 [C] one complete circular movement ~**ary** adj 1 of a REVOLUTION (1) 2 completely new and different ♦ n person who favours or joins in a REVOLUTION (1) ~**ize**, -**ise** vt cause a

REVOLUTION (2) in

re·volve /rɪˈvɒlv ‖ rɪˈvɑːlv/ vi/t spin round on a central point

   revolve around phr vt have as a centre or main subject

re·volv·er /rɪˈvɒlvə ‖ rɪˈvɑːlvər/ n small gun with a revolving bullet-container

re·vue /rɪˈvjuː/ n theatrical show with short acts, songs, jokes, etc.

re·vul·sion /rɪˈvʌlʃən/ n [U] feeling of being REVOLTed (2)

re·ward /rɪˈwɔːd ‖ -ɔːrd/ n 1 [C;U] (something gained in) return for work or service 2 [C] money given for helping the police ♦ vt give a reward to or for ~**ing** adj giving personal satisfaction

re·work /ˌriːˈwɜːk ‖ -ˈwɜːrk/ vt put (music, writing, etc.) into a new or different form (in order to use again)

rhap·so·dy /ˈræpsədi/ n 1 expression of too great praise and excitement 2 piece of music of irregular form –**dic** /ræpˈsɒdɪk ‖ -ˈsɑː-/ adj

rhet·o·ric /ˈretərɪk/ n [U] 1 art of speaking persuadingly 2 fine-sounding but insincere or meaningless words ~**al** /rɪˈtɒrɪkəl ‖ -ˈtɔː-, -ˈtɑː-/ adj 1 asked or asking only for effect, and not expecting an answer: a rhetorical question 2 of or showing rhetoric ~**ally** /-kli/ adv

rheu·ma·tis·m /ˈruːmətɪzəm/ n [U] disease causing joint or muscle pain -**matic** /ruːˈmætɪk/ adj of, suffering from, or being rheumatism

rheu·ma·toid ar·thri·tis /ˌruːmətɔɪd ɑːˈθraɪtɪs ‖ -ɑːr-/ n [U] long-lasting disease causing pain and stiffness in the joints

rhine·stone /ˈraɪnstəʊn ‖ -stoun/ n diamond-like jewel made from glass or a transparent rock

rhi·no /ˈraɪnəʊ ‖ -nou/ n -**nos** rhinoceros

rhi·no·ce·ros /raɪˈnɒsərəs ‖ -ˈnɑː-/ n large thick-skinned African or Asian animal with either one or two horns on its nose

rho·do·den·dron /ˌrəʊdəˈdendrən ‖ ˌrou-/ n large bush with large bright flowers

rhom·bus /ˈrɒmbəs ‖ ˈrɑːm-/ n figure with four equal straight sides

rhu·barb /ˈruːbɑːb ‖ -ɑːrb/ n [U] large-leaved plant whose thick red stems are eaten

rhyme /raɪm/ v 1 vi (of words or lines in poetry) end with the same sound: *'Cat' rhymes with 'mat'.* 2 vt put together (words) ending with the same sound ♦ n 1 [U] (use of) rhyming words at line-ends in poetry 2 [C] word that rhymes with another 3 [C] short simple rhyming poem 4 **rhyme or reason** (any) sense or meaning

rhyth·m /'rɪðəm/ n [C;U] regular repeated pattern of sounds or movements: (fig.) *the rhythm of the seasons* –**mic** /'rɪðmɪk/, **-mical** adj **-mically** /-kli/ adv

rhythm meth·od /'·· ,··/ n [the+S] method of CONTRACEPTION in which a woman only has sex when she is not likely to CONCEIVE

rib /rɪb/ n 1 any of the curved bones enclosing the chest 2 curved rod for strengthening a frame 3 thin raised line in a pattern ♦ vt **-bb-** laugh at (someone) ~**bed** adj having a pattern of RIBS (3)

rib·ald /'rɪbəld/ adj fml (of jokes or laughter) rude and disrespectful

rib·bon /'rɪbən/ n long narrow band of cloth

rib cage /'· ·/ n all one's RIBS (1)

rice /raɪs/ n [U] (plant with) a seed that is widely eaten

rice pa·per /'· ,··/ n [U] sort of eatable paper

rich /rɪtʃ/ adj 1 having a lot of money or property 2 having a lot: *a city rich in ancient buildings* 3 expensive, valuable, and beautiful 4 (of food) containing a lot of cream, eggs, sugar, etc. 5 (of a sound or colour) deep, strong, and beautiful 6 infml amusing but often rather annoying ♦ n [(the) P] rich people ~**ly** adv 1 splendidly 2 fully: *richly deserved* ~**ness** n [U]

rich·es /'rɪtʃɪz/ n [pl.] esp. lit wealth

rick¹ /rɪk/ vt twist (part of the body) slightly

rick² n large pile of dried grass

rick·ets /'rɪkɪts/ n [U] children's disease in which bones become soft and bent

rick·et·y /'rɪkɪti/ adj weak and likely to break

rick·shaw /'rɪkʃɔː ‖ -ʃɔː/ n small East Asian carriage pulled by a man

ric·o·chet /'rɪkəʃeɪ/ n sudden change of direction by a bullet, stone, etc. when it hits a hard surface ♦ vi **-t-** or **-tt-** change direction in a ricochet

rid /rɪd/ v (**rid** or **ridded**, pres. p. **-dd-**) **rid of** phr vt 1 make free of 2 **get rid of:** a free oneself from b drive or throw away or destroy

rid·dance /'rɪdəns/ n **good riddance** (said when one is glad that someone or something has gone)

rid·dle¹ /'rɪdl/ n 1 difficult and amusing question 2 mystery

riddle² v **riddle with** phr vt make full of holes

ride¹ /raɪd/ v rode /rəʊd ‖ rəʊd/, **ridden** /'rɪdn/ 1 vi/t travel along on (a horse, etc., a bicycle, or a motorcycle) 2 vi travel on a bus 3 vt remain safe and (floating) through: *a ship riding a storm* 4 **let something ride** let something continue, taking no action 5 **ride high** have great success 6 **ride roughshod over** act in a hurtful way towards **rider** n 1 person riding esp. a horse 2 statement added to esp. an official declaration or judgment

ride out phr vt come safely through (bad weather, trouble)

ride up phr vi (of clothing) move upwards or out of place

ride² n 1 journey on an animal, in a vehicle, etc. 2 **take someone for a ride** deceive someone

ridge /rɪdʒ/ n long narrow raised part, where two slopes meet

rid·i·cule /'rɪdɪkjuːl/ n [U] unkind laughter ♦ vt laugh unkindly at

ri·dic·u·lous /rɪ'dɪkjʊləs/ adj silly ~**ly** adv

rife /raɪf/ adj (of a bad thing) widespread; common

rif·fle /'rɪfəl/ v **riffle through** phr vt turn over (papers, etc.) quickly, searching

riff·raff /'rɪfræf/ n [U] derog worthless badly behaved people

ri·fle¹ /'raɪfəl/ n gun with a long barrel, fired from the shoulder

rifle² vt search through and steal from

rift /rɪft/ n crack: (fig.) *a rift in their friendship*

rig¹ /rɪg/ vt **-gg-** fit (a ship) with sails, ropes, etc.

rig out phr vt dress in special or funny clothes

rig up phr vt make quickly and roughly

rig² n 1 way a ship's sails and MASTS are arranged 2 apparatus: *a drilling rig* –**ging**

n [U] all the ropes, etc. holding up a ship's sails

rig³ /rɪg/ *vt* **-gg-** arrange dishonestly for one's own advantage

right¹ /raɪt/ *adj* **1 a** on the side of the body away from the heart **b** in the direction of one's right side: *the right bank of the river* **2** just; proper; morally good **3** correct **4** in a proper or healthy state; *to put the trouble right* | *Are you all right?* **5 right enough** as was expected

right² *n* **1** [U] RIGHT¹ (1) side or direction **2** [U] what is RIGHT¹ (2) **3** [C;U] morally just or legal claim: *You've no right to* (=should not) *say that.* **4** [U] political parties that favour less change and less state control **5 in one's own right** because of a personal claim that does not depend on anyone else **6 in the right** not wrong or deserving blame **~ness** *n* [U]: *the rightness of their claim* —see also RIGHTS

right³ *adv* **1** towards the RIGHT² (1, 2) **2** correctly **3** exactly: *right in the middle* **4** completely: *Go right back to the beginning!* **5** yes; I will: *'See you tomorrow.' 'Right!'* —see also ALL RIGHT **6** *BrE sl or old use* very **7 right away** at once

right⁴ *vt* put back to a correct position or condition

right an·gle /'· ˌ·/ *n* angle of 90 degrees

right·eous /'raɪtʃəs/ *adj* **1** morally good **2** having just cause: *righteous indignation* **~ly** *adv* **~ness** *n* [U]

right·ful /'raɪtfəl/ *adj* according to a just or legal claim **~ly** *adv*

right-hand /ˌ· '·◄/ *adj* on the right side **~ed** *adj* using the right hand for most actions **~er** *n* right-handed person

right-hand man /ˌ· '·/ *n* most useful and valuable helper

right·ly /'raɪtli/ *adv* **1** correctly **2** justly

right-mind·ed /ˌ· '··◄/ *adj* having the right opinions, principles, etc.

right of way /ˌ· ·'·/ *n* **rights of way 1** [U] right of a vehicle to go first **2** [C] (right to follow) a path across private land

rights /raɪts/ *n* [P] **1** political, social, etc. advantages to which someone has a just claim, morally or in law **2 by rights** in justice; if things were done properly **3 set/put someone/something to rights** make someone/something just, healthy, etc. **4 the rights and wrongs of** the true facts

of **5 within one's rights** not going beyond one's just claims

right wing /ˌ· '·◄/ *n* [U] of a political party of the RIGHT (4)

ri·gid /'rɪdʒɪd/ *adj* **1** stiff **2** not easy to change **~ly** *adv* **~ity** /rɪ'dʒɪdʃti/ *n* [U]

rig·ma·role /'rɪgmərəʊl‖-roʊl/ *n* [S;U] long confused story or set of actions

rig·or mor·tis /ˌrɪgə 'mɔːtɪs, ˌraɪgɔː-‖ ˌrɪgər 'mɔːr-/ *n* [U] stiffening of the muscles after death

rig·or·ous /'rɪgərəs/ *adj* **1** careful and exact **2** severe **~ly** *adv*

rig·our *BrE‖* **-or** *AmE* /'rɪgə‖-ər/ *n* [U] **1** severity **2** *fml* exactness and clear thinking

rile /raɪl/ *vt infml* annoy

Ri·ley /'raɪli/ *n* —see LIFE OF RILEY

rim /rɪm/ *n* edge, esp. of a round object ♦ *vt* **-mm-** be round the edge of

rind /raɪnd/ *n* [C;U] thick outer covering of certain fruits, or of cheese or BACON

ring¹ /rɪŋ/ *n* **1** (metal) circle worn on the finger **2** circular band: *smoke rings* **3** circular mark or arrangement: *a ring of troops round the building* **4** enclosed space where things are shown, performances take place, or esp. people BOX or WRESTLE **5** group of people who work together, esp. dishonestly: *a drug ring* **6 make/run rings round** do things much better and faster than ♦ *vt* form or put a ring round

ring² *v* **rang** /ræŋ/, **rung** /rʌŋ/ **1** *vi/t* cause (a bell) to sound **2** *vi* (of a bell, telephone, etc.) sound **3** *vi/t esp. BrE* telephone **4** *vi* be filled with sound **5 ring a bell** remind one of something **6 ring the changes** introduce variety in **7 ring true/false** sound true/untrue ♦ *n* **1** [C] (making) a bell-like sound **2** [S] certain quality: *It had a ring of truth.* (=sounded true) **3** [S] *esp. BrE* telephone call

  ring off *phr vi BrE* end a telephone conversation

  ring out *phr vi* (of a voice, bell, etc.) sound loudly and clearly

  ring up *phr vt* **1** record (money paid) on a CASH REGISTER **2** RING² (3)

ring·er /'rɪŋə‖-ər/ *n* —see DEAD RINGER

ring·lead·er /'rɪŋˌliːdə‖-ər/ *n* person who leads others to do wrong

ring·let /'rɪŋlɪt/ *n* long hanging curl of hair

ring·mas·ter /ˈrɪŋˌmɑːstə‖-ˌmæstər/ n person who directs CIRCUS performances

ring road /ˈ··‖ n BrE road that goes round a town

ring·side /ˈrɪŋsaɪd/ adj, adv, n (at) the edge of a RING¹ (4)

ring·worm /ˈrɪŋwɜːm‖-wɜːrm/ n [U] disease causing red rings on the skin

rink /rɪŋk/ n specially prepared surface for skating (SKATE)

rinse /rɪns/ vt wash in clean water, so as to get rid of soap, dirt, etc. ♦ n 1 [C] act of rinsing 2 [C;U] liquid hair colouring

ri·ot /ˈraɪət/ n 1 [C] noisy violent crowd behaviour 2 [S] plentiful show: *The garden is a riot of colour.* 3 [S] infml very funny and successful occasion or person 4 **run riot: a** become violent and uncontrollable **b** (of a plant) grow too thick and tall ♦ vi take part in a riot ~**er** n ~**ous** adj wild and disorderly

riot act /ˈ··‖·/ n **read the riot act** warn (esp. a child) to behave well

rip¹ /rɪp/ vi/t **-pp-** 1 tear quickly and violently 2 **let something rip** infml remove control and let things develop in their own way ♦ n long tear

rip off phr vt infml 1 charge too much 2 esp. AmE steal **rip-off** /ˈ··/ n

RIP /ˌɑːr aɪ ˈpiː/ abbrev. for: rest in peace (=words written on a gravestone)

rip·cord /ˈrɪpkɔːd‖-kɔːrd/ n cord pulled to open a PARACHUTE

ripe /raɪp/ adj 1 (fully grown and) ready to be eaten: *a ripe apple* 2 ready; suitable: *land ripe for industrial development* 3 grown-up and experienced: (humor.) *He's reached the ripe old age of 20.* ~**ness** n [U]

rip·en /ˈraɪpən/ vi/t make or become ripe

rip·off /ˈrɪpɒf‖-ɔːf/ n infml thing that is unreasonably expensive

ri·poste /rɪˈpɒst, rɪˈpəʊst‖rɪˈpoʊst/ vi, n (make) a quick clever (unfriendly) reply

rip·ple /ˈrɪpəl/ vi/t 1 move in small waves 2 make a sound like gently running water ♦ n [C] 1 very small wave or gentle waving movement 2 sound of or like gently running water

rise¹ /raɪz/ vi rose /rəʊz/rouz/, risen /ˈrɪzən/ 1 go up; get higher: (fig.) *My spirits rose.* (=I became happier) 2 (of the sun, etc.) come above the horizon 3 (of land) slope upward 4 stand up 5 fml get out of bed 6 (of wind) get stronger 7 REBEL¹: *They rose up*

against their leaders. 8 come back to life after being dead 9 (esp. of a river) begin 10 move up in rank 11 **rise to the occasion** show that one can deal with a difficult matter **rising** n UPRISING **rising** prep nearly (the stated age)

rise² n 1 [C] increase 2 [U] act of growing greater or more powerful 3 [C] BrE wage increase 4 [C] upward slope 5 **give rise to** cause

rising damp /ˌ·· ˈ·/ n [U] water that comes up into the walls of a building

risk /rɪsk/ n [C;U] 1 chance that something bad may happen 2 (in insurance) (a person or thing that is) a danger 3 **at risk** in danger 4 **at one's own risk** agreeing to bear any loss or danger 5 **run/take a risk** do dangerous things ♦ vt 1 place in danger 2 take the chance of: *Are you willing to risk failure?* ~**y** adj dangerous

ri·sot·to /rɪˈzɒtəʊ‖-ˈsɔːtoʊ/ n [C;U] rice dish with chicken, vegetables, etc.

ris·qué /ˈriːskeɪ‖riˈskeɪ/ adj (of a joke, etc.) slightly rude

rite /raɪt/ n ceremonial (religious) act with a fixed pattern

rit·u·al /ˈrɪtʃuəl/ n [C;U] (ceremonial) act or acts always repeated in the same form ♦ adj done as a rite: *ritual murder*

ri·val /ˈraɪvəl/ n person with whom one competes ♦ adj competing ♦ vt **-ll-** BrE ‖ **-l-** AmE be as good as ~**ry** n [C;U] competition

riv·er /ˈrɪvə‖-ər/ n wide natural stream of water

riv·et /ˈrɪvət/ n metal pin used for fastening heavy metal plates together ♦ vt 1 fasten with rivets 2 attract and hold (someone's attention) strongly ~**ing** adj very interesting

ri·vi·e·ra /ˌrɪviˈeərə‖-ˈerə/ n stretch of coast where people take holidays

road /rəʊd‖roʊd/ n 1 smooth prepared track for wheeled vehicles: (fig.) *We're on the road to* (=on the way to) *success.* 2 **on the road** travelling

road·block /ˈrəʊdblɒk‖ˈroʊdblɑːk/ n something placed across a road to stop traffic

road hog /ˈ··/ n fast selfish careless driver

road rage /ˈ··/ n [U] extreme anger in a driver, usu. because of heavy traffic, often resulting in violent behaviour

road tax /'· ·/ n [C;U] tax vehicle owners must pay

road works /'rəʊdwɜːks ‖ 'roʊdwɜːrks/ n [P] road repairing

road·wor·thy /'rəʊd,wɜːθi ‖ 'roʊd,wɜːr-/ adj (of a vehicle) in safe condition to drive –**thiness** n [U]

roam /rəʊm ‖ roʊm/ vi/t wander around with no clear purpose

roan /rəʊn ‖ roʊn/ n, adj (horse) of mixed colour

roar /rɔː ‖ rɔːr/ n deep loud continuing sound: *roars of laughter* ♦ v 1 vi give a roar 2 vt say forcefully 3 vi laugh loudly ~**ing** adj, adv 1 very great: *We're doing a roaring trade.* (=doing very good business) 2 very: *roaring drunk*

roast /rəʊst ‖ roʊst/ vt cook (esp. meat) in an OVEN or over a fire ♦ adj roasted ♦ n large piece of roasted meat

roast·ing /'rəʊstɪŋ ‖ 'roʊ-/ adj/ very hot n angry words spoken to someone who has done something wrong

rob /rɒb ‖ rɑːb/ vt -**bb**- steal something from ~**ber** n -**bery** n [C;U] (example of) the crime of robbing

robe /rəʊb ‖ roʊb/ n long flowing garment

rob·in /'rɒbɪn ‖ 'rɑː-/ n small brown bird with a red front —see also ROUND ROBIN

ro·bot /'rəʊbɒt ‖ 'roʊbɑːt, -bət/ n machine that can do some of the work of a human being ~**ics** /rəʊ'bɒtɪks ‖ roʊ'bɑː-/ n [U] study of the making and use of robots

ro·bust /rə'bʌst, 'rəʊbʌst ‖ rə'bʌst, 'roʊ-/ adj strong (and healthy) ~**ly** adv ~**ness** n[U]

rock[1] /rɒk ‖ rɑːk/ n 1 [C;U] stone forming part of the Earth's surface 2 [C] large piece of stone 3 [C] AmE a stone 4 [U] (in Britain) hard sticky kind of sweet made in long round bars 5 [C] sl, esp. AmE a diamond 6 [U] popular music with a strong loud beat 7 **on the rocks**: **a** (of a marriage) likely to fail soon **b** (of a drink) with ice but no water

rock[2] /rɒk ‖ rɑːk/ v 1 vi/t move regularly backwards and forwards or from side to side 2 vt shock greatly 3 **rock the boat** spoil the existing good situation

rock and roll /,· · '·/ n [U] ROCK 'N' ROLL

rock bot·tom /,· '·◂/ n [U] the lowest point

rock·er /'rɒkə ‖ 'rɑːkər/ n 1 curved piece of wood on which something rocks 2 esp.

AmE ROCKING CHAIR 3 **off one's rocker** infml mad

rock·e·ry /'rɒkəri ‖ 'rɑː-/ n (part of) a garden laid out with rocks and small plants

rock·et /'rɒkɪt ‖ 'rɑː-/ n 1 tube-shaped object driven through the air by burning gases, used for travelling into space, or as a MISSILE or FIREWORK 2 **give someone/get a rocket** BrE infml scold someone/be scolded severely ♦ vi rise quickly and suddenly

rock·ing chair /'·· ·/ n chair with rockers

rocking horse /'·· ·/ n wooden horse with rockers, for a child to ride on

rock 'n' roll /,rɒk ən 'rəʊl ‖,rɑːk ən 'roʊl/ n [U] music with a strong loud beat that was popular in the 1950s

rock·y /'rɒki ‖ 'rɑːki/ adj 1 full of rocks 2 infml unsteady; not firm

ro·co·co /rə'kəʊkəʊ ‖ -'koʊkoʊ/ adj with much curling decoration

rod /rɒd ‖ rɑːd/ n long thin stiff pole or bar

rode /rəʊd ‖ roʊd/ past t. of RIDE

ro·dent /'rəʊdənt ‖ 'roʊ-/ n small plant-eating animal with long front teeth, such as a mouse, rat, or rabbit

ro·de·o /ˌrəʊ'deɪ-əʊ,   'rəʊdi-əʊ ‖ roʊ'deɪoʊ, 'roʊdioʊ/ n -**os** (in America) public entertainment with horse riding, cattle catching, etc.

roe /rəʊ ‖ roʊ/ n [C;U] mass of fish eggs, often eaten

roe deer /'· ·/ n small European and Asian deer

ro·ger /'rɒdʒə ‖ 'rɑːdʒər/ interj (used in radio and signalling to say one has understood)

rogue /rəʊg ‖ roʊg/ n dishonest person ♦ adj 1 (of a wild animal) bad-tempered and dangerous 2 not following the usual or accepted standards **roguish** adj playful and fond of playing tricks

rogues' gal·le·ry /,· '···/ n collection of (pictures of) criminal or unpleasant people

role /rəʊl ‖ roʊl/ n 1 character played by an actor 2 part someone takes in an activity

role mo·del /'· ,·/ n person that one admires and tries to copy

roll[1] /rəʊl ‖ roʊl/ v 1 vi/t turn over and over or from side to side: *The ball rolled into the hole.* 2 vt form into esp. a tube by curling round and round 3 vi move steadily and smoothly (as if) on wheels 4 vi swing from side to side on the sea 5 vt flatten with a

ROLLER (1) or ROLLING PIN **6** *vi* make a long deep sound **7** *vt* cause (esp. film cameras) to begin working **8** *vt* cause (the eyes) to move round and round **9 roll in the aisles** (esp. of people at the theatre) laugh uncontrollably **10 roll one's r's** pronounce the sound /r/ with the tongue beating rapidly against the roof of the mouth **11 roll one's own** *BrE infml* make one's own cigarettes instead of buying them ~**ing** *adj* **1** (of land) with long gentle slopes **2 rolling in it** *infml* extremely rich

roll in *phr vi* arrive in large quantities

roll on *phr vi* come soon; hurry up: *Roll on, summer!*

roll out *phr vt* UNROLL

roll up *phr vi* **1** arrive **2** (used esp. asking people to see a show at a CIRCUS, etc.) come in

roll² *n* **1** act of rolling **2** rolled tube **3** small loaf for one person: *a cheese roll* (=one cut and filled with cheese) **4** long deep sound (as if) of a lot of quick strokes: *a roll of drums* **5** official list of names —see also TOILET ROLL

roll call /ˈ· ·/ *n* calling a list of names to see who is there

roll·er /ˈrəʊlə ‖ ˈrəʊlər/ *n* **1** tube-shaped part for pressing, smoothing, shaping, etc. **2** long heavy wave on the coast

Rol·ler·blade /ˈrəʊləbleɪd ‖ ˈrəʊlər-/ *n tdmk* boot with a single row of wheels fixed under it ♦ *vi* ~**ding** *n* [U]

roller coast·er /ˈ·· ˌ·/ *n* small railway with sharp slopes and curves, found in amusement parks

roller skate /ˈ·· ·/ *n* boot with two wheels fixed under it at the front and two at the back ♦ *vi* ~**ing** *n* [U]

rol·lick·ing /ˈrɒlɪkɪŋ ‖ ˈrɑː-/ *adj* noisy and merry ♦ *n BrE infml* act of expresing angry disapproval of someone

rolling pin /ˈ·· ·/ *n* tube-shaped piece of wood, etc. for flattening pastry

rolling stock /ˈ·· ·/ *n* [U] carriages, engines, etc. of a railway

rolling stone /ˌ·· ˈ·/ *n* person with no fixed home or responsibilities

ro·ly-po·ly /ˌrəʊli ˈpəʊli◂ ‖ ˌrəʊli ˈpoʊ-/ *adj infml* (of a person) fat and round

ROM /rɒm ‖ rɑːm/ *n abbrev. for:* Read-Only Memory; part of a computer where permanently needed information is stored

Ro·man /ˈrəʊmən, ‖ ˈroʊ-/ *n, adj* (citizen) of Rome, esp. ancient Rome

Roman Cath·o·lic /ˌ·· ˈ···/ *n, adj* (member) of the branch of the Christian religion led by the POPE ~**ism** /ˌ·· ·ˈ····/ *n* [U]

ro·mance /rəʊˈmæns, rə- ‖ roʊ-, rə-/ *n* **1** [C] love affair **2** [U] ROMANTIC (2) quality **3** [C] story of love, adventure, etc.

Roman nu·me·ral /ˌ·· ˈ···/ *n* any of the signs (such as I, II, V, X, L) used for numbers in ancient Rome and sometimes now

ro·man·tic /rəʊˈmæntɪk, rə- ‖ roʊ-, rə-/ *adj* **1** showing warm feelings of love **2** of or suggesting love, adventure, strange happenings, etc. **3** highly imaginative; not practical: *romantic notions* **4** showing romanticism ♦ *n* romantic person ~**ally** /-kli/ *adv* ~**ism** /-tʃsɪzəm/ *n* [U] admiration of feeling rather than thought in art and literature ~**ize**, ~**ise** *vt* make (something) seem more interesting or ROMANTIC (2) than it really is

Ro·ma·ny /ˈrəʊməni ‖ ˈrɑː-/ *n* **1** [C] GIPSY **2** [U] gipsies' language

Ro·me·o /ˈrəʊmiəʊ ‖ ˈroʊmioʊ/ *n* -**os** romantic male lover

romp /rɒmp ‖ rɑːmp/ *vi* play noisily and roughly ♦ *n* **1** occasion of romping **2** *infml* piece of amusing entertainment with plenty of action

romp through *phr vt* succeed in, quickly and easily

roof /ruːf/ *n* **1** top covering of a building, vehicle, etc. **2** upper part of the inside (of the mouth) ♦ *vt* put or be a roof on ~**ing** *n* [U] roof material

roof rack /ˈ·· ·/ *n* metal frame on top of a car, for carrying things

roof·top /ˈruːftɒp ‖ -tɑːp/ *vt* **1** roof **2 from the rooftops** loudly, so that everyone can hear

rook¹ /rʊk/ *n* large black bird, like a CROW

rook² *vt sl* cheat

rook·e·ry /ˈrʊkəri/ *n* group of rooks' nests

rook·ie /ˈrʊki/ *n esp. AmE* new soldier or policeman

room /ruːm, rʊm/ *n* [C] division of a building, with its own floor, walls, and CEILING **2** [U] (enough) space **3** [U] need or possibility for something to happen: *room for improvement* ♦ *vi AmE* have lodgings; have a room or rooms ~**y** *adj* with plenty of space inside

room ser·vice /'· ,·/ n [U] hotel service providing food, etc. in people's rooms

roost /ruːst/ n 1 place where a bird sleeps 2 **rule the roost** be the leader ♦ vi 1 (of a bird) sit and sleep 2 **come home to roost** (of a bad action) have a bad effect on the doer, esp. after a period of time

roost·er /'ruːstə ‖ -ər/ n esp. AmE for COCK (1)

root[1] /ruːt/ n 1 part of a plant that goes down into the soil for food 2 part of a tooth, hair, etc. that holds it to the body 3 cause; beginning; origin 4 (in grammar) base part of a word to which other parts can be added 5 a number that when multiplied by itself a stated number of times gives another stated number 6 **root and branch** (of something bad) be got rid of thoroughly 7 **take root** (of plants or ideas) become established and begin to grow —**less** adj without a home

roots n [P] 1 (one's connection with) one's place of origin 2 **pull up one's roots** move to a new place from one's settled home 3 **put down (new) roots** establish a (new) place, by making friends, etc. —see also GRASS ROOTS

root[2] v 1 vi/t (cause to) form roots: (fig.) *rooted to the spot* (=unable to move) | *deeply rooted* (=firmly fixed) 2 vi search by turning things over

root for phr vt support strongly

root out phr vt get rid of completely

rope[1] /rəup ‖ roup/ n 1 [C;U] (piece of) strong thick cord 2 [C] fat twisted string (of the stated jewels) 3 [*the*+S] hanging as a punishment 4 **give someone (plenty of) rope** allow someone (plenty of) freedom to act

rope[2] vt tie with a rope **ropes** n [P] rules, customs, and ways of operating

rope in phr vt infml persuade or force to join an activity

rope off phr vt separate or enclose with ropes

rop·y, ropey /'rəupi ‖ 'rou-/ adj BrE infml of bad quality or condition

ro·sa·ry /'rəuzəri ‖ 'rou-/ n string of BEADS used by Roman Catholics for counting prayers

rose[1] /rəuz ‖ rouz/ past t. of RISE

rose[2] n 1 (brightly coloured sweet-smelling flower of) a prickly stemmed bush

2 pale to dark pink colour 3 **be not all roses** infml (of a job, situation, etc.) include some unpleasant things —see also BED OF ROSES

ro·sé /'rəuzeɪ ‖ rou'zeɪ/ n [U] light pink wine

ro·se·ate /'rəuziət ‖ 'rou-/ adj lit pink

rose-col·oured /'· ,·/ also **rose-tinted** — adj **look at/see/view the world through rose-coloured spectacles/ glasses** see the world, life, etc. as better and more pleasant than they really are

ro·sette /rəu'zet ‖ rou-/ n flat flower-like arrangement of cloth, worn as a sign of something

rose win·dow /'· ,·/ n circular decorative church window

ros·ter /'rɒstə ‖ 'raːstər/ n list of people's names and duties

ros·trum /'rɒstrəm ‖ 'raː-/ n **-trums** or **-tra** /-trə/ raised place for a public performer

ros·y /'rəuzi ‖ 'rou-/ adj 1 (esp. of skin) pink 2 (esp. of future) giving hope

rot /rɒt ‖ raːt/ vi/t -tt- decay ♦ n [U] 1 decay 2 process of getting worse or going wrong 3 infml foolish nonsense

ro·ta /'rəutə ‖ 'rou-/ n list of things to be done by different people taking turns

ro·ta·ry /'rəutəri ‖ 'rou-/ adj rotating (ROTATE (1))

ro·tate /rəu'teɪt ‖ 'routeɪt/ vi/t 1 turn round a fixed point 2 (cause to) take turns or come round regularly **rotation** /rəu'teɪʃən ‖ 'rout-/ n 1 [U] action of rotating 2 [C] one complete turn 3 **in rotation** taking regular turns

rote /rəut ‖ rout/ n [U] fml repeated study using memory rather than understanding

ro·tor /'rəutə ‖ 'routər/ n 1 rotating part of a machine 2 set of HELICOPTER blades

rot·ten /'rɒtn ‖ 'raːtn/ adj 1 decayed; gone bad 2 infml nasty or unpleasant 3 **feel rotten** feel ill, tired, or unhappy

rott·weil·er /'rɒtvaɪlə, -waɪ- ‖ 'raːt-waɪlər/ n type of strong dangerous dog

ro·tund /rou'tʌnd/ adj fml (of a person) fat and round

rou·ble /'ruːbəl/ n unit of money in Russia and some other countries of the former USSR

rouge /ruːʒ/ n [U] red substance for colouring the cheeks

rough¹ /rʌf/ *adj* 1 having an uneven surface 2 stormy and violent: *rough weather* 3 lacking gentleness, good manners, or consideration: *rough handling at the airport* 4 (of food and living conditions) not delicate; simple 5 not detailed or exact 6 unfortunate and/or unfair 7 *infml* unwell 8 **rough and ready** simple and without comfort ♦ *adv* 1 in uncomfortable conditions: *sleeping rough* 2 **cut up rough** *infml* become angry ~ly *adv* 1 in a rough manner 2 about; not exactly ~**en** *vi/t* make or become rough ~**ness** *n* [U]

rough² *n* [U] 1 areas of long grass on a GOLF course 2 **in rough** in an incomplete or undetailed form 3 **take the rough with the smooth** accept bad things as well as good things uncomplainingly

rough³ *v* **rough it** *infml* live simply and rather uncomfortably

rough up *phr vt infml* attack roughly, usu. as a threat

rough·age /'rʌfɪdʒ/ *n* [U] coarse matter in food, which helps the bowels to work

rough·cast /'rʌfkɑːst ‖ -kæst/ *n* [U] surface of little stones on the outside of a building

rough dia·mond /ˌ· '··/ *n* very kind person with rough manners

rough-hewn /ˌ· '·◄/ *adj* (of wood or stone) roughly cut

rough pa·per /ˌ· '··/ *n* [U] paper for making informal notes or drawings

rough·shod /'rʌfʃɒd ‖ -ʃɑːd/ *adv* —see ride roughshod over (RIDE¹)

rough stuff /'· ·/ *n* [U] *BrE* violent behaviour

rou·lette /ruːˈlet/ *n* [U] game of chance played with a small ball and a spinning wheel —see also RUSSIAN ROULETTE

round¹ /raʊnd/ *adj* 1 circular 2 ball-shaped 3 (of parts of the body) fat and curved 4 (of a number) expressed to the nearest 10, 100, 1000, etc. ~**ness** *n* [U]

round² *adv* 1 with a circular movement: *The wheels went round.* 2 surrounding a central point: *Gather round.* 3 to various places: *travelling round* 4 so as to face the other way: *Turn it round.* 5 everywhere or to everyone: *Pass the drinks round.* 6 to a particular place: *We invited some friends round* (=to our house) *for drinks.* 7 **all the**

year round during the whole year 8 **round about** a little bit more or less than 9 **the other/opposite way round** in the opposite order

round³ *prep.* 1 with a circular movement about: *The Earth goes round the Sun.* 2 surrounding: *Sit round the table.* 3 into all parts of: *Look round the shop.* 4 not going straight but changing direction: *He went round the corner.* 5 near (a place or amount): *Do you live round here?*

round⁴ *n* 1 number or set (of events): *a continual round of parties* 2 regular delivery journey: *do one's rounds* (=make one's usual visits) 3 number of esp. alcoholic drinks bought for everyone present: *It's my round.* (=I'm paying) 4 a (in GOLF) complete game b (in boxing BOX²) period of fighting in a match c (in tennis, football, etc.) stage in a competition d one single shot from a gun 5 long burst: *a round of applause* 6 type of song for three or four voices, in which each sings the same tune, one starting a line after another has just finished it 7 *esp. BrE* SANDWICH made with two whole pieces of bread

round⁵ *vt* 1 go round: *rounding the corner* 2 make round: *rounding his lips* ~**ed** *adj*

round down *phr vt* reduce to a whole number

round off *phr vt* end suitably and satisfactorily

round on *phr vt* turn and attack

round up *phr vt* 1 gather together (scattered things) 2 increase (an exact figure) to the next highest whole number

round·a·bout /'raʊndəbaʊt/ *n BrE* 1 area of circular traffic flow where several roads meet 2 MERRY-GO-ROUND ♦ *adj* indirect

roun·ders /'raʊndəz ‖ -ərz/ *n* [U] children's game where a player hits the ball and then runs round a square area

round·ly /'raʊndli/ *adv fml* 1 completely 2 forcefully

round rob·in /ˌ· '··/ *n* sports event in which everyone plays against everyone else

round-ta·ble /ˌ· '·◄/ *adj* at which everyone can meet and talk equally

round-the-clock /ˌ· · '·◄/ *adj* happening both day and night

round trip /ˌ· '·◄/ *n* journey to a place and back again

round·up /'raʊndʌp/ *n* gathering

together of scattered things, animals, or people

rouse /raʊz/ vt 1 fml waken 2 make more active, interested, or excited **rousing** adj that makes people excited

rout /raʊt/ n complete defeat ♦ vt

route /ruːt ‖ ruːt, raʊt/ n way from one place to another —see also EN ROUTE ♦ vt send by a particular route

route march /'· ·/ n soldiers' long training march

rou·tine /ˌruːˈtiːn◄/ n 1 [C;U] regular fixed way of doing things 2 [C] set of dance steps, songs, etc. ♦ adj 1 regular; not special 2 dull ~ly adv

rove /raʊv/ vi esp. lit wander

roving eye /ˌ·· '·/ n [S] sexual interest that passes quickly from one person to another

row¹ /raʊ ‖ roʊ/ n 1 neat line of people or things 2 **in a row** one after the other without a break

row² /raʊ ‖ roʊ/ vi/t move (a boat) through the water with OARS

row³ /raʊ/ n 1 [C] noisy quarrel 2 [S] noise ♦ vi quarrel (noisily)

row·dy /'raʊdi/ adj noisy and rough **–dily** adv **–diness** n [U] ~**ism** n [U] rowdy behaviour

row house /'raʊ haʊs ‖ 'roʊ-/ n AmE for TERRACED HOUSE

row·lock /'rɒlɒk ‖ 'rɑː-; not tech 'rəʊlɒk ‖ 'roʊlɑːk/ n fastener for an OAR on the side of a boat

roy·al /'rɔɪəl/ adj of a king or queen ♦ n member of the royal family ~ly adv splendidly

royal blue /ˌ·· '·◄/ adj strong bright blue

roy·al·ist /'rɔɪəlɪst/ n supporter of rule by kings and queens

roy·al·ty /'rɔɪəlti/ n 1 [U] people of the royal family 2 [C] payment made to the writer of a book, piece of music, etc. out of the money from its sales

rpm /ˌɑː piː 'em ‖ ˌɑːr-/ abbrev. for: revolutions per minute

RSVP /ˌɑːr es viː 'piː/ please reply (written on invitations)

rub /rʌb/ vi/t -bb- 1 press against (something or each other) with a repeated up-and-down or round-and-round movement 2 **rub it in** infml keep talking about something that another person wants to forget 3 **rub salt in the wound** make

someone's suffering even worse 4 **rub shoulders with** infml meet socially and treat as equals 5 **rub someone up the wrong way** infml annoy ♦ n 1 [C] act of rubbing 2 [the+S] cause of difficulty: There's the rub. ~**bing** n copy made by rubbing paper laid over the top

rub down phr vt 1 dry by rubbing 2 make smooth by rubbing

rub in phr vt make (liquid) go into a surface by rubbing

rub off phr vi come off a surface (onto another) by rubbing: (fig.) I hope some of her good qualities rub off on you.

rub out phr vt BrE remove with a RUBBER¹ (2)

rub·ber¹ /'rʌbə ‖ -ər/ n 1 [U] elastic substance used for keeping out water, making tyres, etc. 2 [C] BrE piece of this for removing pencil marks ~**y** adj

rubber² n competition, esp. in cards, which usu. consists of an odd number of games

rubber band /ˌ·· '·/ n thin circle of rubber for fastening things together

rubber plant /'·· ·/ n decorative large-leaved house plant

rubber-stamp /ˌ·· '·/ n piece of rubber with raised letters or figures, for printing ♦ vt approve or support (a decision) officially, without really thinking about it

rub·bish /'rʌbɪʃ/ n [U] BrE 1 waste material to be thrown away 2 nonsense

rub·ble /'rʌbəl/ n [U] broken stone and bricks, esp. from a destroyed building

ru·bel·la /ruːˈbelə/ n [U] GERMAN MEASLES

ru·bric /'ruːbrɪk/ n fml set of printed instructions

ru·by /'ruːbi/ n deep red precious stone

ruck·sack /'rʌksæk/ n large bag carried on the back, esp. by walkers, etc.

ruck·us /'rʌkəs/ n AmE for RUMPUS

ruc·tions /'rʌkʃənz/ n [P] infml noisy complaints and anger

rud·der /'rʌdə ‖ -ər/ n blade at the back of a boat or aircraft to control its direction

rud·dy /'rʌdi/ adj (of the face) pink and healthy-looking

rude /ruːd/ adj 1 not polite; bad-mannered 2 concerned with sex: a rude joke 3 sudden and violent: a rude shock 4 old use roughly made ~**ly** adv ~**ness** n [U]

ru·di·men·ta·ry /ˌruːdɪˈmentəri◄/ adj

1 (of facts, knowledge, etc.) at the simplest level 2 small and not fully usable: *rudimentary wings*

ru·di·ments /'ru:dǝmǝnts/ *n* [the+P] simplest parts of a subject, learnt first

rue /ru:/ *vt* be very sorry about ~**ful** *adj* feeling or showing that one is sorry about something

ruff /rʌf/ *n* stiff wheel-shaped white collar

ruf·fi·an /'rʌfiǝn/ *n* unpleasant violent man

ruf·fle /'rʌfǝl/ *vt* 1 make uneven 2 trouble; upset

rug /rʌg/ *n* 1 thick floor mat 2 warm woollen covering to wrap round oneself

rug·by /'rʌgbi/ *n* [U] type of football played with an egg-shaped ball which can be handled

rug·ged /'rʌgǝd/ *adj* large, rough, and strong-looking ~**ly** *adv* ~**ness** *n* [U]

rug·ger /'rʌgǝ ‖ -ǝr/ *n* [U] *infml* rugby

ru·in /'ru:ǝn/ *n* 1 [U] destruction 2 [C] also **ruins** *pl.* remains of a building that has fallen down or been (partly) destroyed ♦ *vt* 1 spoil 2 cause total loss of money to ~**ed** *adj* (of a building) partly or wholly destroyed ~**ous** *adj* causing destruction or total loss of money

ru·in·a·tion /,ru:ǝneiʃǝn/ *n* [U] (cause of) being ruined

rule¹ /ru:l/ *n* 1 [C] something that tells you what you must do: *the rules of the game* 2 [U] period or way of ruling: *under foreign rule* 3 [C] RULER (2) 4 **as a rule** usually

ruling *n* official decision

rule² *v* 1 *vi/t* be in charge of (a country, people, etc.) 2 *vi* give an official decision 3 *vt* draw (a line) with a ruler

rule out *phr vt* 1 remove from consideration 2 make impossible

rule of thumb /, · · '·/ *n* [C;U] quick inexact way of calculating or judging

rul·er /'ru:lǝ ‖ -ǝr/ *n* 1 person who rules 2 narrow flat rod for measuring or drawing straight lines

rum¹ /rʌm/ *n* [U] strong alcoholic drink made from sugar

rum² *adj* -mm- *old-fash infml* strange

rum·ba /'rʌmbǝ/ *n* lively Latin American dance

rum·ble¹ /'rʌmbǝl/ *vi, n* [S] (make) a deep continuous rolling sound

rumble² *vt BrE infml* not be deceived by

rum·bus·tious /rʌm'bʌstʃǝs/ *adj* noisy, cheerful, and full of life

ru·mi·nant /'ru:mǝnǝnt/ *n, adj* (animal) that RUMINATES (2)

ru·mi·nate /'ru:mǝneit/ *vi* 1 think deeply 2 (of an animal) bring food back from the stomach and CHEW it again ~**native** /-nǝtiv ‖ -nei-/ *adj* seeming thoughtful

rum·mage /'rʌmidʒ/ *vi* turn things over untidily in searching

rum·my /'rʌmi/ *n* [U] card game

ru·mour *BrE* ‖ **-mor** *AmE* /'ru:mǝ ‖ -ǝr/ *n* [C;U] (piece of) information, perhaps untrue, spread from person to person ~**ed** *adj* reported unofficially

rump /rʌmp/ *n* part of an animal above the back legs: *rump steak*

rum·ple /'rʌmpǝl/ *vt* make untidy; disarrange

rum·pus /'rʌmpǝs/ *n* [S] noisy angry argument or disagreement

run¹ /rʌn/ *v* ran /ræn/, run, *pres. p.* -nn-
1 *vi* (of people and animals) move faster than a walk 2 *vt* take part in (a race) by running 3 *vi/t* (cause to) move quickly: *The car ran into a tree.* 4 *vi/t* (cause to) work: *This machine runs on/by electricity.* 5 *vi* (of a public vehicle) travel as arranged 6 *vt* control (an organization or system) 7 *vi* go; pass: *The road runs south.* 8 *vi* continue in operation, performance, etc.: *The play ran for two years in London.* 9 *vi* (cause liquid) to flow: *run a bath ǀ running water* 10 *vi* pour out liquid: *The baby's nose is running.* 11 *vi* (melt and) spread by the action of heat or water 12 become 13 *vi esp. AmE* try to get elected 14 *vt* print in a newspaper 15 *vt* bring into a country illegally and secretly 16 *vi esp. AmE for* LADDER 17 *vt* take (someone or something) to somewhere in a vehicle: *I'll run you home.* 18 **run for it** escape by running 19 **run short: a** use almost all one has and not have enough left **b** become less than enough

run across *phr vt* meet or find by chance

run after *phr vt* 1 chase 2 try to gain the attention and company of

run along *phr vi* go away

run away *phr vi* go away (as if) to escape

run away/off with *phr vt* 1 gain control of: *Don't let your temper run away* *with you.* 2 go away with (a lover) 3 steal

run down *phr v* 1 *vt* knock down and hurt with a vehicle 2 *vt* chase and catch 3 *vi* (esp. of a clock or BATTERY) lose power and stop working: (fig.) *The coal industry is being run down.* 4 *vt* say unfair things about

run into *phr vt* 1 meet by chance 2 cause (a vehicle) to meet (something) with force

run off *phr vt* print (copies)

run out *phr vi* 1 come to an end, so there is none left 2 have none left: *We've run out of petrol.*

run over *phr v* 1 *vt* knock down and drive over 2 *vi* overflow

run through *phr vt* 1 repeat for practice 2 read or examine quickly 3 push one's sword right through

run to *phr vt* be or have enough to pay for

run up *phr vt* 1 raise (a flag) 2 make quickly, esp. by sewing 3 cause oneself to have (bills or debts)

run up against *phr vt* be faced with (a difficulty)

run² *n* 1 [C] act of running 2 [C] ship or train journey 3 [S] continuous set of similar events, performances, etc.: *a run of bad luck | The play had a run of three months.* 4 [S] **a** eager demand to buy: *a big run on ice cream* **b** general desire to sell money or take one's money out: *a run on the pound* 5 [S] freedom to use: *He gave me the run of his library.* 6 [C] animal enclosure: *a chicken run* 7 [C] point won in cricket 8 [C] sloping course: *a ski run* 9 [C] *AmE for* LADDER (2) 10 **a (good) run for one's money: a** plenty of opposition in a competition **b** good results for money spent or effort made 11 **in the long run** after a long period; in the end 12 **on the run** trying to escape 13 **the common/ordinary run (of)** the usual sort (of)

run·a·bout /'··,··/ *n* small light car

run·a·round /'·· ··,·/ *n* [the+S] *sl* delaying or deceiving treatment

run·a·way /'rʌnəweɪ/ *adj* 1 out of control: *runaway prices* 2 having escaped by running: *a runaway child*

run·down /'rʌndaʊn/ *n* detailed report

run-down /,· '·◄/ *adj* 1 tired, weak, and ill 2 in bad condition

rune /ruːn/ *n* letter in an alphabet

formerly used in Northern Europe **runic** *adj*

rung¹ /rʌŋ/ *past p. of* RING²

rung² *n* cross-bar in a ladder or on a chair

run-in /'· ·/ *n infml* quarrel or disagreement, esp. with the police

run·ner /'rʌnə-ər/ *n* 1 person or animal that runs 2 SMUGGLER: *a gunrunner* 3 thin blade on which something slides on ice or snow 4 stem with which a plant spreads itself along the ground

runner bean /,·· '·/ *n* bean with long eatable seed container

runner-up /,·· '·/ *n* runners-up one that comes second in a race, etc.

run·ning¹ /'rʌnɪŋ/ *n* 1 act or sport of running 2 **in/out of the running** with some/no hope of winning 3 **make the running** set the speed at which something develops

running² *adj* 1 (of water) flowing 2 continuous: *a running battle | a running commentary* 3 (of money) spent or needed to keep something working: *running costs* 4 **in running order** (of a machine) working properly 5 **take a running jump: a** run to a point where one starts a jump **b** *infml* Go away and don't annoy me! ♦ *adv* in a row: *I won three times running.*

running-mate /'·· ·/ *n* (in US politics) person with whom one is trying to get elected for a pair of political positions of greater and lesser importance

run·ny /'rʌni/ *adj* 1 in a more liquid form than usual 2 (of the nose or eyes) producing liquid

run-of-the-mill /,·· ··· '·◄/ *adj* ordinary; dull

runt /rʌnt/ *n* 1 small badly developed animal 2 *derog* small unpleasant person

run-through /'· ·/ *n* act of repeating (something) for practice

run-up /'· ·/ *n* [S] period leading up to an event

run·way /'rʌnweɪ/ *n* surface on which aircraft land and take off

ru·pee /ruː'piː/ *n* unit of money in India, Pakistan, etc.

rup·ture /'rʌptʃə‖-ər/ *n* 1 [C;U] *fml* sudden breaking 2 [C] HERNIA ♦ *v* 1 *vi/t fml* break suddenly 2 *vt* give (oneself) a HERNIA

ru·ral /'rʊərəl‖'rʊr-/ *adj* of the country (not the town)

ruse /ruːz ‖ ruːs, ruːz/ n deceiving trick

rush[1] /rʌʃ/ v 1 vi/t go or take suddenly and very quickly 2 vi hurry 3 vt deal with (too) hastily 4 vt force (someone) to eat hastily 5 vt attack suddenly and all together 6 **rush someone off his/her feet** make someone hurry too much or work too hard ♦ n 1 [C] sudden rapid movement 2 [U] (need for) (too much) hurrying 3 [S] sudden demand 4 [U] period of great and hurried activity: *the Christmas rush*

rush[2] n grasslike water plant

rush·es /ˈrʌʃɪz/ n [P] (in film making) the first print of a film

rush hour /ˈ··/ n busy period when most people are travelling to or from work

rusk /rʌsk/ n hard BISCUIT for babies

rus·set /ˈrʌsɪt/ adj esp. lit brownish red

Rus·sian rou·lette /ˌrʌʃən ruːˈlet/ n [U] dangerous game in which one fires a gun at one's head without knowing whether it is loaded

rust /rʌst/ n [U] 1 reddish brown surface formed on iron, steel, etc. that has been wet 2 the colour of this ♦ vi/t (cause to) become covered with rust ~**y** adj 1 covered with rust 2 lacking recent practice

rus·tic /ˈrʌstɪk/ adj typical of the country, esp. in being simple ♦ n usu. derog person from the country

rus·tle /ˈrʌsəl/ v 1 vi/t (cause to) make slight sounds like dry leaves moving 2 vt esp. AmE steal (cattle or horses) -**tler** n

rustle up phr vt provide quickly

rut[1] /rʌt/ n 1 [C] deep narrow track left by a wheel 2 [S] dull fixed way of life ~**ted** adj having ruts

rut[2] n (season of) sexual excitement in deer ♦ vi -**tt**- (of an animal) be in a rut

ru·ta·ba·ga /ˌruːtəˈbeɪgə/ n AmE for SWEDE

ruth·less /ˈruːθləs/ adj doing cruel things without pity ~**ly** adv ~**ness** n [U]

rye /raɪ/ n [U] grass plant with grain used esp. for flour

S

S, s /es/ the 19th letter of the English alphabet

S written abbrev. for: south(ern)

Sab·bath /ˈsæbəθ/ n [S] religious day of rest, esp. Saturday (for Jews) or (for Christians) Sunday

sab·bat·i·cal /səˈbætɪkəl/ n, adj period with pay when one is free to leave one's ordinary job to travel and study

sa·ble /ˈseɪbəl/ n [C;U] (dark fur from) a small animal

sab·o·tage /ˈsæbətɑːʒ/ n [U] intentional damage carried out secretly ♦ vt perform sabotage against

sab·o·teur /ˌsæbəˈtɜː ‖ -ˈtɜːr/ n person who practises sabotage

sa·bre BrE ‖ **saber** AmE /ˈseɪbə ‖ -ər/ n heavy military sword, usu. curved

sabre-rat·tling /ˈ·· ˌ·/ n [U] talking about (military) power in a threatening way

sac /sæk/ n tech small bag containing air or liquid inside a plant or animal

sac·cha·rin /ˈsækərɪn/ n [U] very sweet-tasting chemical used instead of sugar ♦ adj too SENTIMENTAL

sach·et /ˈsæʃeɪ ‖ sæˈʃeɪ/ n small plastic bag holding an amount of liquid, etc.

sack[1] /sæk/ n 1 [C] large simple bag of strong material 2 [the+S] BrE dismissal from a job 3 [the+S] infml esp. AmE bed 4 **hit the sack** infml go to bed ♦ vt BrE dismiss from a job ~**ing** n [U] sackcloth (1)

sack[2] vt destroy and rob (a defeated city) sack n [U]: *the sack of ancient Rome*

sack·cloth /ˈsæk-klɒθ ‖ -klɔːθ/ n [U] 1 also **sacking** /ˈsækɪŋ/ — rough cloth for making sacks 2 **sackcloth and ashes** lit sign of sorrow for what one has done

sac·ra·ment /ˈsækrəmənt/ n important Christian ceremony, such as BAPTISM or marriage ~**al** /ˌsækrəˈmentl◁/ adj

sa·cred /ˈseɪkrɪd/ adj 1 connected with religion 2 holy because connected with God or gods 3 that is solemn and must be respected ~**ness** n [U]

sacred cow /ˌ·· ˈ·/ n derog thing so much accepted that not even honest doubts about it are allowed

sac·ri·fice /'sækrɪfaɪs/ n 1 (an offering) to gods, esp. of an animal killed ceremonially 2 loss or giving up of something of value ♦ v 1 vi/t offer (something or someone) as a SACRIFICE (1) 2 vt give up or lose, esp. for some good purpose –**ficial** /ˌsækrɪ'fɪʃəl◄/ adj

sac·ri·lege /'sækrɪlɪdʒ/ n [C;U] treating a holy place or thing without respect –**legious** /ˌsækrɪ'lɪdʒəs◄/ adj

sac·ro·sanct /'sækrəʊsæŋkt ‖ -krəʊ-/ adj often derog or humor too holy or important to be treated disrespectfully or harmed

sad /sæd/ adj -**dd**- 1 unhappy 2 unsatisfactory ~**ly** adv ~**den** vt make or become SAD (1) ~**ness** n [U]

sad·dle¹ /'sædl/ n 1 rider's seat on a horse, bicycle, etc. 2 piece of meat from the back of a sheep or deer 3 **in the saddle:** a sitting on a SADDLE (1) b in control (of a job)

saddle² vt put a saddle on (a horse)

  saddle with phr vt give (someone) (an unpleasant or difficult duty, responsibility, etc.)

sa·dis·m /'seɪdɪzəm/ n [U] unnatural fondness for cruelty to others, (sometimes to gain sexual pleasure) –**dist** n –**distic** /sə'dɪstɪk/ adj

sa·do·mas·o·chis·m /ˌseɪdəʊ'mæsə-kɪzəm ‖ -dəʊ-/ n [U] the gaining of (sexual) pleasure from hurting oneself (or other people)

s.a.e. /ˌes eɪ 'iː/ abbrev. for: stamped addressed envelope

sa·fa·ri /sə'fɑːri/ n [C;U] journey to hunt or photograph animals, esp. in Africa

safari park /·'·· ·/ n park where wild animals are kept and can be looked at

safe¹ /seɪf/ adj 1 out of danger 2 not likely to cause danger or harm 3 (of a seat in Parliament) certain to be won in an election by a particular party 4 **as safe as houses** very free from risk 5 **safe and sound** unharmed 6 **on the safe side** being more careful than may be necessary 7 **play it safe** take no risks ~**ly** adv ~**ness** n [U]

safe² n thick metal box with a lock, for keeping valuable things in

safe-con·duct /ˌ· '··/ n [C;U] official protection given to someone passing through an area

safe-de·pos·it box /· ··ˌ· ˌ/ n small box for storing valuable objects, esp. in a bank

safe·guard /'seɪfgɑːd ‖ -gɑːrd/ n means of protection against something unwanted ♦ vt protect

safe·keep·ing /ˌseɪf'kiːpɪŋ/ n [U] protection from harm or loss

safe·ty /'seɪfti/ n [U] condition of being safe

safety net /'·· ·/ n 1 system or arrangement to help people who have serious problems: the safety net of insurance 2 large net to catch someone performing high above the ground

safety pin /'·· ·/ n bent pin with a cover at one end, used for fastening things

safety valve /'·· ·/ n 1 means of getting rid of possibly dangerous forces (in a machine) 2 something that allows strong feelings to be expressed in a non-violent way

saf·fron /'sæfrən/ n [U] 1 deep orange substance got from a flower, used for giving colour and taste to food 2 orange-yellow colour

sag /sæg/ vi -**gg**- 1 sink or bend downwards out of the usual position 2 become less active, happy, etc.: My spirits sagged when I saw all the work I had to do. sag n [S;U]

sa·ga /'sɑːgə/ n 1 old story, esp. about the Vikings 2 long story

sage /seɪdʒ/ adj lit wise, esp. from long experience ♦ n wise person, esp. an old man

sa·go /'seɪgəʊ ‖ -goʊ/ n [U] white plant substance used for making sweet dishes

sahib /sɑːb ‖ 'sɑː-ɪb/ n (used formerly in India as a title of respect for a European man)

said /sed/ past t. and p. of SAY ♦ adj law just mentioned

sail /seɪl/ n 1 piece of strong cloth that allows the wind to move a ship through the water 2 trip in a boat 3 wind-catching blade of a WINDMILL 4 **set sail** begin a trip at sea 5 **under sail** driven by sails and wind ♦ v 1 vi/t travel (across) by boat 2 vt direct or command (a boat) on water 3 vi be able to control a sailing boat: Can you sail? 4 vi begin a voyage 5 vi move smoothly or easily —see also **sail close to the wind** (CLOSE²) ~**ing** n [U] sport of riding in or directing a small boat with sails

sail·or /'seɪlə ‖ -ər/ n person who works on a ship

saint /seɪnt/ n 1 person officially recognised after death as especially holy by the Christian church 2 *infml* a very good and completely unselfish person ~**ly** *adj* very holy

sake /seɪk/ n 1 **for the sake of: a** in order to help, improve, or bring advantage to **b** for the purpose of 2 **for Christ's/God's/goodness/pity('s) sake** *infml* (used to give force to urgent request or sometimes an expression of annoyance): *For goodness sake, stop arguing!* | *For God's sake, what do you want from me!*

sal·ad /'sæləd/ n [C;U] a mixture of usu. raw vegetables served cold, sometimes with other (stated) food added: *a cheese/chicken salad*

sal·a·man·der /'sæləmændə ‖ -ər/ n small animal like a LIZARD

sa·la·mi /sə'lɑːmi/ n [U] large salty SAUSAGE with a strong taste of garlic

sal·a·ry /'sæləri/ n [C;U] fixed regular pay each month for a job, esp. for workers of higher rank –**ried** *adj* receiving a salary

sale /seɪl/ n 1 [C;U] (act of) selling 2 [C] special offering of goods at low prices 3 **for sale** offered to be sold, esp. privately 4 **on sale: a** offered to be sold, esp. in a shop **b** *AmE* at or in a SALE (2) 5 **(on) sale or return** obtained from seller so that what is used can be paid for and the rest sent back without payment **salable, saleable** *adj* that can be sold

sales /seɪlz/ *adj* of or for selling: *a sales forecast*

sales·clerk /'seɪlzklɑːk ‖ -klɜːrk/ n *AmE* for SHOP ASSISTANT

sales·man /'seɪlzmən/ n -men /-mən/ a male salesperson

sales·man·ship /'seɪlzmənʃɪp/ n [U] skill in selling

sales·per·son /'seɪlzpɜːsən ‖ -pɜːr-/ n –people 1 a sales representative 2 SHOP ASSISTANT, esp. a skilled one

sales rep·re·sen·ta·tive /'· ··,···/ also **sales rep** /'· ·/ n person who goes from place to place, selling and taking orders for their firm's goods

sales talk /'· ·/ n [U] talking intended to persuade people to buy

sales·wo·man /'seɪlz,wʊmən/ n -women /-,wɪmɪn/ a female salesperson

sa·li·ent /'seɪliənt/ *adj fml* most noticeable or important

sa·line /'seɪlaɪn/ *adj* containing salt

sa·li·va /sə'laɪvə/ n [U] natural liquid produced in the mouth ~**ry** *adj*

sal·low /'sæləʊ ‖ -loʊ/ *adj* (of the skin) yellow and unhealthy-looking ~**ness** n [U]

salm·on /'sæmən/ n salmon *or* salmons [C;U] large pink-fleshed fish highly valued as food

sal·mo·nel·la /ˌsælmə'nelə◂/ n [U] bacteria that causes food poisoning

sal·on /'sælɒn ‖ sə'lɑːn/ n stylish or fashionable small shop: *a hairdressing salon*

sa·loon /sə'luːn/ n 1 large grandly furnished room for use of ship's passengers 2 *BrE* large car with a fixed roof 3 *AmE* public drinking place

saloon bar /·'· ·/ n *BrE* LOUNGE BAR

sal·sa /'sælsə ‖ 'sɑː-/ n [U] 1 hot-tasting SAUCE 2 type of South American dance music

salt¹ /sɔːlt ‖ sɒːlt/ n 1 [U] common white substance used for preserving food and improving its taste: *salt water* 2 [C] chemical compound of an acid and a metal 3 [C] *infml* an old, experienced sailor: *an old salt* 4 **the salt of the earth** person or people regarded as admirable and dependable 5 **take something with a pinch/grain of salt** not necessarily believe all of something —see also **worth one's salt** (WORTH)

salt² *vt* put salt on

salt away *phr vt* save money (esp. for the future)

salt·cel·lar /'sɔːlt,selə ‖ 'sɒːlt,selər/ n small pot with a hole for shaking salt onto food

salt·pe·tre *BrE* ‖ -ter *AmE* /ˌsɔːlt'piːtə ‖ ˌsɒːlt'piːtər/ n [U] chemical used in making GUNPOWDER and matches

salt·y /'sɔːlti ‖ 'sɒːl-/ *adj* containing or tasting of salt

sa·lu·bri·ous /sə'luːbriəs/ *adj* 1 socially desirable or RESPECTABLE 2 *fml* health-giving

sal·u·ta·ry /'sæljʊtəri ‖ -teri/ *adj* causing an improvement in character, future behaviour, health, etc.

sal·u·ta·tion /ˌsæljʊ̆ˈteɪʃən/ n 1 [C;U] fml expression of greeting by words or actions 2 [C] word or phrase such as 'Ladies and Gentlemen', 'Dear Sir', 'Dear Miss Jones', at the beginning of a speech or letter

sa·lute /səˈluːt/ n 1 military sign of recognition, esp. raising the hand to the forehead 2 ceremonial firing of guns to honour someone 3 **take the salute** (of a person of high rank) to stand while being SALUTEd by soldiers marching past ♦ v 1 vi/t make a SALUTE (1) (to) 2 vt fml honour and praise 3 vt fml greet

sal·vage /ˈsælvɪdʒ/ vt save (goods or property) from wreck or destruction ♦ n [U] act or process of salvaging

sal·va·tion /sælˈveɪʃən/ n [U] 1 (esp. in the Christian religion) the saving or state of being saved from SIN 2 something or someone that saves one from loss or failure

Salvation Ar·my /ˌ··· ˈ··/ n Christian organization with military uniforms and ranks, that helps poor people

salve /sɑːv ‖ sæv/ n [C;U] medicinal paste for putting on a wound, sore place, etc. ♦ vt fml make (esp. feelings) less painful

sal·ver /ˈsælvə ‖ -ər/ n fine metal plate for serving food, drink, etc. formally

sal·vo /ˈsælvəʊ ‖ -voʊ/ n -vos or -voes firing of several guns together

Sa·mar·i·tan /səˈmærɪtən/ n a member of the **Samaritans**, an organization that people who are sad, lonely, etc. can telephone in order to talk to someone —see also GOOD SAMARITAN

sam·ba /ˈsæmbə/ n quick dance of Brazilian origin

same[1] /seɪm/ adj 1 not changed or different; not another or other 2 alike in (almost) every way 3 **one and the same** exactly the same 4 **same here** infml me too 5 **by the same token** in the same way 6 **in the same boat** in the same unpleasant situation 7 **just/all the same** in spite of this

same[2] pron 1 the same thing, person, condition, etc. 2 **the same again, please** (an order for another drink of the same kind) 3 **same to you** I wish you the same (a greeting or sometimes an angry wish) ~**ness** n [U] 1 very close likeness 2 lack of variety

same[3] adv the same (as) in the same way

(as)

sa·mo·sa /sæˈməʊsə ‖ -ˈmoʊ-/ n small pastry case containing hot-tasting vegetables or meat

sam·o·var /ˈsæməvɑː ‖ -vɑːr/ n Russian water boiler for making tea

sam·ple /ˈsɑːmpəl ‖ ˈsæm-/ n small part representing the whole ♦ vt take and examine a sample of

sam·pler /ˈsɑːmplə ‖ ˈsæmplər/ n piece of cloth with pictures, etc. stitched on it with thread, done to show one's skill at sewing

san·a·to·ri·um /ˌsænəˈtɔːriəm/ n -ums or -a /-riə/ sort of hospital for sick people who are getting better but still need treatment, rest, etc.

sanc·ti·fy /ˈsæŋktɪfaɪ/ vt make holy

sanc·ti·mo·ni·ous /ˌsæŋktɪˈməʊniəs◄ ‖ -ˈmoʊ-/ adj fml disapproving of others because one thinks one is good, right, etc. and they are not ~**ly** adv ~**ness** n [U]

sanc·tion /ˈsæŋkʃən/ n 1 [U] fml formal or official permission, approval, or acceptance 2 [C] action taken against a person or country that has broken a law or rule 3 [C] something that forces people to keep a rule: a moral sanction ♦ vt fml 1 accept, approve, or permit, esp. officially 2 make acceptable: a custom sanctioned by long usage

sanc·ti·ty /ˈsæŋktɪti/ n [U] holiness

sanc·tu·a·ry /ˈsæŋktʃuəri, -tʃəri ‖ -tʃueri/ n 1 [C] part of a (Christian) church considered most holy 2 [C;U] (place of) protection for someone being hunted by officers of the law 3 [C] area where animals are protected

sanc·tum /ˈsæŋktəm/ n 1 holy place inside a temple 2 infml private place or room where one can be quiet and alone

sand /sænd/ n [U] 1 loose material of very small grains, found on seacoasts and in deserts 2 **build on sand** plan or do something with no good reason to believe in its success ♦ vt 1 make smooth by rubbing with esp. SANDPAPER 2 put sand on, esp. to stop slipping **sands** n [P] 1 area of sand 2 moments in time (as if measured by sand in an HOURGLASS): The sands of time are running out. ~**y** adj 1 consisting of sand or having sand on the surface 2 (of hair) yellowish brown

san·dal /'sændl/ n light shoe with a flat bottom and bands to hold it to the foot

sand·bag /'sændbæg/ n sand-filled bag, esp. for forming a protective wall

sand·blast /'sændblɑːst ‖ -blæst/ vt clean or cut with a high-speed stream of sand

sand·cas·tle /'sænd,kɑːsəl ‖ -,kæ-/ n small model, esp. of a castle, built of sand

sand·pa·per /'sænd,peɪpə ‖ -ər/ n [U] paper covered with fine grainy material, for rubbing surfaces to make them smoother ♦ vt rub with sandpaper

sand·stone /'sændstəʊn ‖ -stoʊn/ n [U] soft rock formed from sand

sand·storm /'sændstɔːm ‖ -ɔːrm/ n desert windstorm in which sand is blown about

sand·wich /'sænwɪdʒ ‖ 'sændwɪtʃ, 'sæn-wɪtʃ/ n two pieces of bread with other food between them ♦ vt fit (with difficulty) between two other things

sandwich board /'·· ·/ n advertising signs hung at the front and back of someone who walks about in public

sandwich course /'·· ·/ n BrE course of study including a period of work in business or industry

sane /seɪn/ adj 1 healthy in mind; not mad 2 sensible ♦ **-ly** adv **~ness** n [U]

sang /sæŋ/ past t. of SING

san·guine /'sæŋgwɪn/ adj fml quietly hopeful

san·i·ta·ry /'sænɪtəri ‖ -teri/ adj 1 concerned with preserving health, esp. by removing dirt 2 not dangerous to health; clean

sanitary tow·el /'···· ,··/ n small mass of soft paper worn to take up MENSTRUAL blood

san·i·ta·tion /,sænɪ'teɪʃən/ n [U] methods of protecting public health, esp. by removing and treating waste

san·i·tize also **-tise** BrE /'sænɪtaɪz/ vt derog make less unpleasant, dangerous, strongly expressed, etc. in order not to offend people

san·i·ty /'sænɪti/ n [U] quality of being SANE

sank /sæŋk/ v past t. of SINK[1]

San·ta Claus /'sæntə klɔːz ‖ 'sænti klɔːz, 'sæntə-/ n imaginary old man believed by children to bring presents at Christmas

sap[1] /sæp/ n [U] watery food-carrying liquid in plants

sap[2] vt -pp- weaken or destroy, esp. over a long time

sap·ling /'sæplɪŋ/ n young tree

sap·phire /'sæfaɪə ‖ -faɪr/ n [C;U] bright blue precious stone

sar·cas·m /'sɑːkæzəm ‖ 'sɑːr-/ n [U] saying the clear opposite of what is meant, in order to be (amusingly) offensive **–castic** /sɑːˈkæstɪk ‖ sɑːr-/ adj **-tically** /-kli/ adv

sar·dine /sɑːˈdiːn ‖ sɑːr-/ n 1 small young fish often preserved in oil for eating 2 **like sardines** packed very tightly together

sar·don·ic /sɑːˈdɒnɪk ‖ sɑːrˈdɑː-/ adj seeming to regard oneself as too important to consider a matter, person, etc. seriously **~ally** /-kli/ adv

sarge /sɑːdʒ ‖ sɑːrdʒ/ n infml for SERGEANT

sa·ri /'sɑːri/ n dress consisting of a length of cloth, worn by Hindu women

sa·rong /sə'rɒŋ ‖ sə'rɔːŋ, sə'rɑːŋ/ n Malayan skirt consisting of a length of cloth

sar·to·ri·al /sɑːˈtɔːriəl ‖ sɑːr-/ adj fml of (the making of) men's clothes

sash[1] /sæʃ/ n length of cloth worn round the waist or over one shoulder

sash[2] n window frame, esp. in a sort of window with two frames that slide up and down

sat /sæt/ past t. and p. of SIT

Sa·tan /'seɪtn/ n the Devil

sa·tan·ic /sə'tænɪk/ adj 1 very evil or cruel 2 of satanism **~ally** /-kli/ adv

sat·an·is·m /'seɪtənɪzəm/ n [U] worship of the devil **-ist** n

satch·el /'sætʃəl/ n small bag carried over the shoulders

sat·el·lite /'sætɪlaɪt/ n 1 [C] man-made object moving round the Earth, moon, etc., used esp. for radio/television communication 2 [U] system of broadcasting television signals using a SATELLITE (1): **satellite television/a satellite dish** (=round object that receives SIGNALS) 3 heavenly body that moves round a larger one 4 country, town, or organization controlled by or depending on another

sat·in /'sætɪn/ n [U] smooth shiny cloth made mainly from silk

sat·ire /'sætaɪə -taɪr/ n [C;U] (piece of writing, etc.) showing the foolishness or

evil of something in an amusing way
–**irical** /sə'tɪrɪkəl/ adj –**irize** /'sætɪraɪz/ vt
–**irist** n

sat·is·fac·tion /ˌsætɪs'fækʃən/ n 1 [C;U]
(something that gives) a feeling of pleasure
2 [U] fml fulfilment of a need, desire, etc.
3 [U] fml certainty: It has been proved to my
satisfaction. 4 [U] fml chance to defend
one's honour

sat·is·fac·to·ry /ˌsætɪs'fæktəri◀/ adj
1 pleasing 2 good enough –**rily** adv

sat·is·fy /'sætɪsfaɪ/ vt 1 please 2 fulfil (a
need, desire, etc.) 3 fml fit (a condition, rule,
standard, etc.) 4 persuade fully ~**ing** adj
pleasing

sat·su·ma /sæt'su:mə/ n type of small
orange

sat·u·rate /'sætʃəreɪt/ vt 1 make
completely wet 2 fill completely: The house
market is saturated. –**rated** adj (of fat or oil)
having chemicals unhealthily combined
–**ration** /ˌsætʃə'reɪʃən/ n [U]

Sat·ur·day /'sætədi‖-ər-/ n the sixth day
of the week, between Friday and Sunday

Sat·urn /'sætən‖-ərn/ n the PLANET sixth
in order from the sun, with large rings
round it

sauce /sɔ:s‖sɒ:s/ n 1 [C;U] quite thick
liquid put on food 2 [S;U] rude disrespectful
talk **saucy** adj 1 amusingly disrespectful or
rude 2 producing sexual interest in an
amusing way

sauce·pan /'sɔ:spæn, -pən‖'sɒ:s-/ n
metal cooking pot with a handle

sau·cer /'sɔ:sə‖'sɒ:sər/ n small plate for
putting a cup on —see also FLYING SAUCER

sau·na /'sɔ:nə, 'sɒ:nə‖'saʊnə/ n (a
room or building for) a Finnish type of bath
in steam

saun·ter /'sɔ:ntə‖'sɒ:ntər/ vi walk
unhurriedly

saus·age /'sɒsɪdʒ‖'sɒ:-/ n [C;U] cut-up
meat in a tube of thin skin

sausage roll /ˌ··'·/ n small piece of
sausage in a pastry covering

sav·age /'sævɪdʒ/ adj 1 forcefully cruel
or violent 2 uncivilized ♦ n member of an
uncivilized tribe ♦ vt attack and bite
fiercely ~**ly** adv

sav·ag·e·ry /'sævɪdʒəri/ n [C;U] (act of)
savage behaviour

sa·van·na /sə'vænə/ n [U] flat grassy
land in a warm part of the world

save¹ /seɪv/ v 1 vt make safe from danger
or destruction 2 vi/t keep and add to an
amount of (money) for later use 3 vt avoid
the waste of (money, time, etc.) 4 vt keep for
future use or enjoyment later 5 vt make
unnecessary 6 vt (of a GOALKEEPER) stop
one's opponents from getting the ball in the
net 7 **save one's skin/neck/bacon** infml
escape from a serious danger 8 **to save
one's life** infml even with the greatest
effort: I can't play the piano to save my life.
♦ n act of saving (SAVE (6)) **saver** n **savings**
n [P] money saved, esp. in a bank

save² prep fml except

saving grace /ˌ·· '·/ n the one good thing
that makes something acceptable

savings and loan as·so·ci·a·tion /ˌ··
·'···, ··ˌ···/ n AmE for BUILDING SOCIETY

sa·viour BrE ‖ –**vior** AmE /'seɪvjə‖-ər/
n 1 one who saves from danger or loss
2 (usu. cap.) Jesus Christ

sav·oir-faire /ˌsævwɑː 'feə‖-wɑːr 'fer/
n [U] ability to do or say the proper thing on
every social occasion

sa·vour BrE ‖ –**vor** AmE /'seɪvə‖-ər/ n
[S;U] 1 taste or smell 2 (power to excite)
interest ♦ vt enjoy slowly and purposefully

sa·vour·y BrE ‖ –**vory** AmE /'seɪvəri/ adj
1 not sweet; tasting of meat, cheese, etc.
2 fml morally good ♦ n a small salty dish

saw¹ /sɔ:‖sɒ:/ past t. of SEE

saw² n thin-bladed tool with teeth for
cutting hard materials ♦ vi/t **sawed** or
sawn /sɔ:n‖sɒ:n/ cut (as if) with a saw

saw³ n short well-known saying

saw·dust /'sɔ:dʌst‖'sɒ:-/ n [U] wood
dust made by a saw in cutting

saw·mill /'sɔ:mɪl‖'sɒ:-/factory where
trees are cut into boards

sax·o·phone /'sæksəfəun‖-foun/ also
sax /sæks/ infml – n metal musical
instrument of the WOODWIND family, used
esp. in JAZZ

say¹ /seɪ/ **said** /sed/ 1 vt pronounce (a
sound, word, etc.) 2 vi/t express (a thought,
opinion, etc.) in words 3 vt give as a general
opinion; claim 4 vt suppose; suggest: Let's
say they accept your idea – what then? |
Would you accept, say, (=for example) £500?
5 **go without saying** be clear; not need
stating 6 **hard to say** be difficult to judge 7 **I
say** BrE infml a weak expression of
surprise, concern, etc. b (used for calling

someone's attention): *I say, I've just had a wonderful idea!* **8 I wouldn't say no** *BrE infml* yes, please **9 say for oneself/ something** offer as an excuse or defence: *You're late again. What have you got to say for yourself?* | *The idea has little to be said for it.* **10 say no more!** *infml* your/the meaning is clear **11 say to oneself** think **12 that is to say** expressed another (more exact) way **13 they say** it is usually thought **14 to say nothing of** including **15 when all is said and done** it must be remembered that **16 you don't say!** (an expression of slight surprise)

say² *n* [S;U] **1** power or right of (sharing in) acting or deciding **2 have one's say** (have the chance to) express one's opinion

say·ing /'sei-iŋ/ *n* well-known wise statement

say-so /'· ·/ *n* **1** personal statement without proof **2** permission

scab /skæb/ *n* **1** hard mass of dried blood formed over a wound **2** *derog* one who works while others are on STRIKE

scab·bard /'skæbəd ‖ -ərd/ *n* tube for holding a sword, knife, etc.

sca·bies /'skeibiz/ *n* [U] skin disease

scaf·fold /'skæfəld, -fould ‖ -fəld, -fould/ *n* raised stage for the official killing of criminals ~**ing** /-fəl-/ *n* [U] structure of poles and boards round a building for workmen to stand on

scald /skɔːld ‖ skɔːld/ *vt* burn with hot liquid **scald** *n*

scale¹ /skeil/ *n* **1** [C] set of marks on an instrument, used for measuring **2** [C] set of figures for measuring or comparing: *a temperature scale* **3** [C;U] relationship between a map or model and the thing it represents: *a scale of one inch to the mile* **4** [C;U] size or level in relation to other or usual things: *a large-scale business operation* **5** [C] set of musical notes at fixed separations **6 to scale** according to a fixed rule for reducing the size of something in a drawing, etc.

scale² also **scales** *pl.* — *n* weighing apparatus

scale³ *n* **1** any of the small flat stiff pieces covering fish, snakes, etc. **2** greyish material formed inside hot water pipes, pots in which water is boiled, etc. ♦ *vt* remove the scales from **scaly** *adj*

scale⁴ *vt* **1** climb up **2** increase/reduce, esp. by a fixed rate

scal·lop /'skɒləp ‖ 'skɑː-/ *n* small sea animal (MOLLUSC) with a shell, used for food

scal·ly·wag /'skæliwæg/ *n* trouble-making child

scalp /skælp/ *n* skin on top of the head: (fig.) *He wants the Minister's scalp.* (=wants him to admit defeat and leave his job) ♦ *vt* cut off the scalp of

scal·pel /'skælpəl/ *n* small sharp knife used by SURGEONS in operations

scam /skæm/ *n sl* clever and dishonest plan or course of action

scamp /skæmp/ *n* playfully trouble-making child

scam·per /'skæmpə ‖ -ər/ *vi* run quickly and usu. playfully

scam·pi /'skæmpi/ *n* [U] *BrE* (dish of) large PRAWNS

scan /skæn/ *v* **-nn- 1** *vt* examine closely, esp. using a machine **2** *vt* look at quickly without careful reading **3** *vt* copy from paper onto a computer, using a machine **4** *vi* (of poetry) have a regular pattern of repeated beats ♦ *n* act of scanning ~**ner** *n* machine for SCANNING (1, 3)

scan·dal /'skændl/ *n* **1** [C] (something causing) a public shock **2** [U] talk which brings harm or disrespect to someone ~**ize**, -**ise** *vt* offend (someone's) feelings of what is right or proper ~**ous** *adj* morally shocking

Scan·di·na·vi·an /ˌskændɪˈneɪviən◄/ *adj* of Denmark, Norway, Sweden, Finland, and/or Iceland

scan·sion /'skænʃən/ *n* [U] way a line of a poem SCANS (3)

scant /skænt/ *adj* hardly enough

scant·y /'skænti/ *adj* hardly (big) enough -**ily** *adv*

scape·goat /'skeipgəut ‖ -gout/ *n* one who takes the blame for others' faults

scar /skɑː ‖ skɑːr/ *n* mark left when a wound heals ♦ *vt* -**rr**- mark with a scar

scarce /skeəs ‖ skers/ *adj* **1** less than wanted; hard to find **2 make oneself scarce** *infml* go away or keep away, esp. in order to avoid trouble ~**ly** *adv* **1** hardly; almost not **2** (almost) certainly not **scarcity** *n* [C;U] being scarce; lack

scare /skeə ‖ sker/ *vt* frighten ♦ *n* **1** [S] sudden fear **2** [C] (mistaken or unreasonable) public fear: *scare stories about war in the newspapers* **scary** *adj* frightening

scare·crow /'skeəkrəʊ ‖ 'skerkroʊ/ *n* figure dressed in old clothes set up in a field to scare birds away from crops

scare·mon·ger /'skeə‚mʌŋgə ‖ 'sker-‚mɑːŋgər, -,mʌn-/ *n* person who spreads reports causing public alarm

scarf /skɑːf ‖ skɑːrf/ *n* **scarves** /skɑːvz ‖ skɑːrvz/ *or* **scarfs** piece of cloth worn round the neck or head

scar·let /'skɑːlət ‖ -ɑːr-/ *adj* bright red

scarlet fe·ver /,·· '··/ *n* [U] serious disease marked by a painful throat and red spots on the skin

scar·per /'skɑːpə ‖ 'skɑːrpər/ *vi BrE sl* run away

scath·ing /'skeɪðɪŋ/ *adj* bitterly cruel in judgment **~ly** *adv*

scat·ter /'skætə ‖ -ər/ *v* 1 *vi/t* separate widely 2 *vt* spread widely (as if) by throwing **~ed** *adj* far apart; irregularly separated **~ing** *n*

scat·ter·brain /'skætəbreɪn ‖ -ər-/ *n* careless or forgetful person **~ed** *adj*

scat·ty /'skæti/ *adj BrE* slightly mad or scatterbrained

scav·enge /'skævɪndʒ/ *vi/t* 1 (of an animal) feed on (waste or decaying flesh) 2 search for or find (usable objects) among unwanted things **~enger** *n*

sce·na·ri·o /sɪ'nɑːriəʊ ‖ -'nærioʊ, -'ner-/ *n* **-os** 1 written description of the action in a film or play 2 description of a possible course of events

scene /siːn/ *n* 1 (in a play) division (within an act) 2 single piece of action in one place in a play or film 3 background for action of a play: *There are few scene changes.* 4 place where something happens: *the scene of the crime* 5 event regarded as like something in a play or film: *scenes of merrymaking* 6 show of angry feelings esp. between two people in front of others 7 an area of activity: *He's new to the film/political scene.* 8 **behind the scenes** secretly 9 **on the scene** present: *a report from our man on the scene in Africa* 10 **set the scene** prepare 11 **steal the scene** get all the attention and praise expected by someone else at a show, party, etc.

sce·ne·ry /'siːnəri/ *n* [U] 1 natural surroundings, esp. in the country 2 painted background and other articles used on stage

sce·nic /'siːnɪk/ *adj* showing attractive natural scenery

scent /sent/ *n* 1 [C] pleasant smell 2 [C] smell followed by hunting animals 3 [U] *esp. BrE for* PERFUME ♦ *vt* 1 tell the presence of by smelling 2 get a feeling of the presence of 3 fill with pleasant smells

scep·tic *BrE* ‖ **skep-** *AmE* /'skeptɪk/ *n* sceptical person **~al** *adj* unwilling to believe **~ally** -kli/ *adv* **-ticism** /-tɪsɪzəm/ *n* [U] doubt

scep·tre *BrE* ‖ **-ter** *AmE* /'septə ‖ -ər/ *n* ceremonial rod carried by a ruler

sched·ule /'ʃedjuːl ‖ 'skedʒʊl, -dʒəl/ *n* 1 planned list or order of things to be done 2 **a** list of prices **b** *esp. AmE* timetable of trains, buses, etc. 3 **ahead of/on/behind schedule** before/at/after the planned or expected time ♦ *vt* plan for a certain future time **-uled** *adj* being a regular service

sche·mat·ic /skiː'mætɪk, skɪ-/ *adj* showing the main parts but leaving out details **~ally** -kli/ *adv*

scheme /skiːm/ *n* 1 plan in simple form; system 2 *BrE* official or business plan 3 clever dishonest plan ♦ *vi* make SCHEMES (3)

schis·m /'sɪzəm, 'skɪzəm/ *n* [C;U] separation between parts originally together, esp. in the church **~atic** /sɪz'mætɪk, skɪz-/ *adj*

schiz·oid /'skɪtsɔɪd/ *adj* of schizophrenia

schiz·o·phre·ni·a /,skɪtsəʊ'friːniə, -sə- ‖ -soʊ-, -sə-/ *n* [U] disorder in which the mind becomes separated from the feelings **-phrenic** /-'frenɪk/ *adj, n* (of) someone with schizophrenia

schlep /ʃlep/ *v* **-pp-** *AmE infml* 1 *vt* carry or drag (something heavy) 2 *vi* spend a lot of time and effort in getting from one place to another

schmaltz, schmalz /ʃmɔːlts, ʃmælts ‖ ʃmɔːlts, ʃmɑːlts/ *n* [U] *infml* art or esp. music which brings out feelings in a too easy, not serious or delicate, way **~y** *adj*

schmuck /ʃmʌk/ *n AmE taboo* fool

schnapps /ʃnæps/ *n* [U] strong alcoholic drink made from potatoes

schol·ar /'skɒlə ‖ 'skɑːlər/ *n* 1 person with great knowledge of a (non-science) subject 2 holder of a SCHOLARSHIP (1) ~ly *adj* 1 concerned with serious detailed study 2 of or like a SCHOLAR (1)

schol·ar·ship /'skɒləʃɪp‖'skɑːlər-/ *n* 1 [C] payment so that someone can attend a college 2 [U] exact and serious study

scho·las·tic /skə'læstɪk/ *adj* of schools and teaching

school¹ /skuːl/ *n* 1 [C;U] (attendance or work at) a place of education for children 2 [C] body of students (and teachers) at such a place: *She was liked by the whole school.* 3 [C;U] teaching establishment: *a driving school* 4 [C;U] (in some universities) department concerned with one subject: *the School of Law* 5 [C;U] *AmE* UNIVERSITY 6 [C] group of people with the same methods, style, etc: *Rembrandt and his school* ♦ *vt fml* teach, train, or bring under control ~ing *n* [U] school education

school² *n* large group of fish swimming together

school of thought /ˌ· · '·/ *n* group with the same way of thinking, opinion, etc.

schoo·ner /'skuːnə‖-ər/ *n* 1 large fast sailing ship 2 tall drinking glass esp. for SHERRY or BEER

schwa /ʃwɑː/ *n* vowel sound shown in this dictionary as /ə/ or /ɔ/

sci·at·i·ca /saɪ'ætɪkə/ *n* [U] pain in the lower back

sci·ence /'saɪəns/ *n* 1 [U] (study of) knowledge which depends on testing facts and stating general natural laws 2 [C] a branch of such knowledge, such as PHYSICS, chemistry, or BIOLOGY b anything which may be studied exactly

science fic·tion /ˌ· '··/ *n* [U] stories about imaginary future (scientific) developments

science park /'·· ·/ *n* an area where there are a lot of companies concerned esp. with new TECHNOLOGY and scientific study

sci·en·tif·ic /ˌsaɪən'tɪfɪk◄/ *adj* 1 of science 2 needing or showing exact knowledge or use of a system ~ally /-kli/ *adv*

sci·en·tist /'saɪəntɪst/ *n* person who works in a science

sci-fi /ˌsaɪ'faɪ/ *n* [U] *infml* SCIENCE FICTION

scim·i·tar /'sɪmɪtə‖-ər/ *n* curved sword

scin·til·lat·ing /'sɪntⱥleɪtɪŋ/ *adj* very interesting

scis·sors /'sɪzəz‖-ərz/ *n* [P] cutting tool with two joined blades

scle·ro·sis /sklⱥ'rəʊsⱥs‖-'roʊ-/ *n* [U] *med* hardening of some usu. soft bodily organ —see also MULTIPLE SCLEROSIS

scoff¹ /skɒf‖skɒːf, skɑːf/ *vi* speak laughingly and disrespectfully

scoff² *vt infml* eat eagerly and fast

scold /skəʊld‖skoʊld/ *vt* speak angrily and complainingly to (a wrong-doer)

scone /skɒn, skəʊn‖skoʊn, skɑːn/ *n* small round breadline cake

scoop /skuːp/ *n* 1 sort of deep spoon for lifting and moving liquids or loose material 2 news report printed, broadcast, etc. before one's competitors can do so ♦ *vt* take up or out (as if) with a SCOOP (1)

scoot /skuːt/ *vi* go quickly and suddenly

scoot·er /'skuːtə‖-ər/ *n* 1 child's two-wheeled vehicle pushed along by one foot 2 low vehicle with two small wheels, an enclosed engine, and usu. a wide curved part at the front to protect the legs

scope /skəʊp‖skoʊp/ *n* [U] 1 area within the limits of a question, subject, etc. 2 space or chance for action or thought

scorch /skɔːtʃ‖skɔːrtʃ/ *v* 1 *vt* burn the surface of (something) without destroying completely 2 *vt infml* travel very fast ♦ *n* scorched place ~er *n infml* 1 very hot day 2 something very exciting, angry, fast, etc. ~ing *adj* (of weather) very hot

scorched earth po·li·cy /ˌ· '· ˌ··/ *n* destruction by an army of all useful things, esp. crops, in an area before leaving it to an advancing army

score¹ /skɔː‖skɔːr/ *n* 1 number of points won in a game, examination, etc. 2 a written copy of a piece of music b music for a film or play 3 reason: *Don't worry on that score.* 4 old disagreement or hurt kept in the mind: *to have a score to settle with someone* 5 know the score understand the true and usu. unfavourable facts of a situation

score² *v* 1 *vi/t* make (a point) in a game 2 *vi* record the points made in a game 3 *vt* gain (a success, victory, etc.) 4 *vi/t* make (a clever point) esp. in an argument: *She always tries to score (points) off other people in a conversation.* 5 *vt* arrange (music) for a particular combination of instruments 6 *vt* cut one or more lines on 7 *sl* (usu. of a man) have sex with someone **8** *sl* obtain and use unlawful drugs **scorer** *n* person who SCORES² (1, 2)

score³ *determiner, n* score or scores *esp. lit* **20 scores** *n* [P] a lot

score·board /'skɔːbɔːd ‖ 'skɔːrbɔːrd/ *n* board on which a SCORE¹ (1) is recorded

scorn /skɔːn ‖ skɔːrn/ *n* [U] strong (angry) disrespect ♦ *vt* refuse to accept or consider because of scorn or pride **~ful** *adj* **~fully** *adv*

scor·pi·on /'skɔːpiən ‖ -ɔːr-/ *n* small animal with a long poisonous stinging tail

scotch /skɒtʃ ‖ skɑːtʃ/ *vt fml* put an end to

Scotch *adj* Scottish ♦ *n* [U] WHISKY made in Scotland

scot-free /ˌskɒt ˈfriː◄ ‖ ˌskɑːt-/ *adj* without harm or esp. punishment

Scots /skɒts ‖ skɑːts/ *adj* Scottish

Scot·tish /'skɒtɪʃ ‖ 'skɑːtɪʃ/ *adj* of Scotland

scoun·drel /'skaʊndrəl/ *n* wicked, selfish, or dishonest man

scour¹ /skaʊə ‖ skaʊr/ *vt* search (an area) thoroughly

scour² *vt* clean by hard rubbing with a rough material **~er** *n* pad of rough nylon for cleaning pots and pans

scourge /skɜːdʒ ‖ skɜːrdʒ/ *n* cause of great harm or suffering ♦ *vt* cause great harm or suffering to

scout /skaʊt/ *n* **1** member of an association (**the scouts**) for training boys in character and self-help **2** soldier sent ahead of an army to find out about the enemy **3** person who seeks out good young sportspeople, actors, etc. for new teams, shows, etc.: *a talent scout* ♦ *vi* go looking for something

scowl /skaʊl/ *n* angry FROWN ♦ *vi* make a scowl

scrab·ble /'skræbəl/ *vi* SCRAMBLE (1, 2)

scrag·gy /'skrægi/ *adj* thin and bony

scram /skræm/ *vi* **-mm-** [*often imperative*] *infml* get away fast

scram·ble /'skræmbəl/ *v* **1** *vi* move or climb quickly and untidily **2** *vi* struggle or compete eagerly or against difficulty **3** *vt* cook (an egg) while mixing the white and yellow parts together **4** *vt* mix up (a radio or telephone message) so that it cannot be understood ♦ *n* **1** [S] act of scrambling

(SCRAMBLE (1)) **2** [C] motorcycle race over rough ground

scrap¹ /skræp/ *n* **1** [C] small piece **2** [U] unwanted material (to be) thrown away: *She sold the car for scrap.* (=as metal to be used again) ♦ *vt* **-pp-** get rid of **~py** *adj* not well arranged or planned

scrap² *n* sudden short fight or quarrel ♦ *vi* **-pp-** fight or quarrel

scrap·book /'skræpbʊk/ *n* book of empty pages on which cut-out pictures, etc. are stuck

scrape /skreɪp/ *v* **1** *vi/t* (cause to) rub roughly against a surface **2** *vt* remove or clean by pulling or pushing an edge repeatedly across a surface **3** *vi* live, keep a business, etc. with no more than the necessary money **4** *vi* succeed by doing work of the lowest acceptable quality: *She scraped through the exam.* **5** **scrape a living** get just enough food or money to stay alive **6** **scrape the bottom of the barrel** take, use, suggest, etc. something of the lowest quality ♦ *n* **1** act or sound of scraping **2** mark or wound made by scraping **3** difficult situation

scrape up/together *phr vt* gather (enough money) with difficulty

scrap·heap /'skræphiːp/ *n* **1** pile of waste material, esp. metal **2** imaginary place, unwanted things, people, or ideas

scrap pa·per /'· ˌ·-/ *esp. BrE* ‖ usu. **scratch paper** *AmE* — *n* [U] used paper for making notes, shopping lists, etc.

scratch /skrætʃ/ *vi/t* **1** rub and tear or mark with something pointed or rough **2** rub (a part of the body) lightly and repeatedly **3** remove (oneself, a horse, etc.) from a race or competition **4** **scratch a living** get just enough food or money to stay alive **5** **scratch the surface** deal with only the beginning of a matter or only a few of many cases ♦ *n* **1** [C] mark or sound made by scratching **2** [S] act of SCRATCHing (2) **3** **from scratch** (starting) from the beginning **4** **up to scratch** at/to an acceptable standard **5** **without a scratch** without even the smallest amount of hurt or damage **~y** *adj* **1** (of a record, etc.) spoiled by scratches **2** (of clothes) hot, rough, and uncomfortable

scrawl /skrɔːl ‖ skrɒːl/ *vt* write carelessly or awkwardly ♦ *n* (piece of) careless or irregular writing

scraw·ny /ˈskrɔːni ‖ ˈskrɒː-/ adj unpleasantly thin

scream /skriːm/ vi/t 1 cry out in a loud high voice: (fig.) The wind screamed around the house. 2 draw attention, as if by such a cry ♦ 1 [C] sudden loud cry 2 [S] infml very funny person, thing, joke, etc.

scree /skriː/ n [U] small loose stones on a mountainside

screech /skriːtʃ/ vi 1 make an unpleasant high sharp sound, esp. in terror or pain 2 (of machines, brakes, etc.) make such a noise 3 **screech to a halt/standstill** stop very suddenly (as if) making this noise ♦ n very high unpleasant noise

screen /skriːn/ n 1 something, esp. a movable upright frame, that protects, shelters, or hides 2 surface on which a cinema film is shown 3 the cinema industry: star of stage, screen, and radio | screen test (=test of one's ability to act in a film) | She first appeared on the screen (=acted in her first film) last year. 4 front glass surface of an electrical instrument, esp. a television, on which pictures or information appear ♦ vt 1 shelter, protect, or hide (as if) with a screen 2 test so as to remove those that do not reach the proper standard 3 show or broadcast (a film or television show) —see also SMALL SCREEN ~ing n 1 [C;U] (a) showing of a film 2 [U] process of SCREENING (SCREEN (2))

screen·play /ˈskriːnpleɪ/ n story written for a film

screw /skruː/ n 1 metal pin having a head with a cut across it, a point at the other end, and a raised edge winding round it so that when twisted into the material it holds firmly 2 act of turning one of these 3 PROPELLER, esp. on a ship 4 taboo sl a act of having sex b someone considered as a person to have sex with 5 **have a screw loose** humor be slightly mad 6 **put the screws on someone** infml to force someone to do as one wishes, esp. by threatening ♦ v 1 vt fasten with one or more screws 2 vi/t tighten or fasten by turning 3 vi/t taboo sl have sex (with) 4 sl cheat: We really got screwed by that salesman.

screw up phr vt 1 twist (a part of the face) to express disapproval or uncertainty:

She screwed up her eyes to read the sign. 2 carelessly twist (paper, etc.) or so as to make a ball 3 sl a ruin b deal badly with: He really screwed up on that job. 4 **screw up one's courage** stop oneself from being afraid 5 **screwed up** infml very worried and confused

screw·ball /ˈskruːbɔːl ‖ -bɒːl/ adj, n very strange or slightly mad (person)

screw·driv·er /ˈskruːˌdraɪvə ‖ -ər/ n tool with a blade that fits into the top of a screw, for turning it

scrib·ble /ˈskrɪbəl/ v 1 vi write (meaningless marks) 2 vt write carelessly or hastily ♦ n [S;U] meaningless or careless writing

scrimp /skrɪmp/ vi scrimp and save save money slowly and with great difficulty

script /skrɪpt/ n 1 [C] written form of a play, film, or broadcast 2 [C;U] particular alphabet: Arabic script 3 [S;U] fml handwriting ~ed adj having a SCRIPT (1) ~writer n writer of SCRIPTS (1)

scrip·ture /ˈskrɪptʃə ‖ -ər/ also scriptures pl. — n [U] 1 the Bible 2 holy book(s) of the stated religion –tural adj

scroll¹ /skrəʊl ‖ skroʊl/ n 1 rolled-up piece of paper, esp. containing official writing 2 decoration or shape like this in stone or wood

scroll² vi scroll up/down phr vi move up/down text on a computer screen

scrooge /skruːdʒ/ n extremely ungenerous person

scro·tum /ˈskrəʊtəm ‖ ˈskroʊ-/ n -ta /-tə/ or -tums bag of flesh holding the TESTICLES

scrounge /skraʊndʒ/ vi/t get (something) without work or payment or by persuading others scrounger n

scrub /skrʌb/ v -bb- 1 vi/t clean or remove by hard rubbing 2 vt no longer do or have; CANCEL ♦ n [S] act of scrubbing

scrub² n [U] low-growing plants covering the ground thickly

scruff¹ /skrʌf/ n flesh at the back (of the neck)

scruff² n BrE infml dirty and untidy person

scruf·fy /ˈskrʌfi/ adj dirty and untidy

scrum /skrʌm/ n 1 group of players trying to get the ball in RUGBY 2 disorderly struggling crowd

scrump·tious /ˈskrʌmpʃəs/ adj infml (of

food) extremely good

scrunch /skrʌntʃ/ vt

    scrunch up phr vt twist or crush into a small shape

scrun·chy /ˈskrʌntʃi/ n small piece of gathered material, used to hold hair in place

scru·ple /ˈskruːpəl/ n **1** [C] moral principle which keeps one from doing something **2** [U] conscience

scru·pu·lous /ˈskruːpjʊləs/ adj **1** fml very exact **2** exactly honest ~**ly** adv

scru·ti·ny /ˈskruːtɪni/ n [U] careful and thorough examination –**nize**, ~**ise** vt examine closely

scu·ba div·ing /ˈskuːbə ˌdaɪvɪŋ/ n [U] swimming under water with a container of air on the back

scud /skʌd/ vi -dd- (esp. of clouds and ships) move along quickly

scuff /skʌf/ vt make rough marks on the smooth surface of (shoes, a floor, etc.) ♦ n mark made by scuffing

scuf·fle /ˈskʌfəl/ n disorderly fight among a few people **scuffle** vi

scull /skʌl/ vi/t row (a small light boat) ~**er** n

sculp·tor /ˈskʌlptə‖-ər/ n artist who makes sculptures

sculp·ture /ˈskʌlptʃə‖-ər/ n **1** [U] art of shaping solid representations **2** [C;U] (piece of) work produced by this ♦ vt make by shaping

scum /skʌm/ n **1** [S;U] (unpleasant) material formed on the surface of liquid **2** [P] often taboo worthless immoral people: the scum of the earth

scup·per /ˈskʌpə‖-ər/ vt BrE **1** sink (one's own ship) intentionally **2** wreck or ruin (a plan)

scur·ri·lous /ˈskʌrɪləs‖ˈskɜːr-/ adj fml containing very rude, improper, and usu. untrue statements ~**ly** adv ~**ness** n [U]

scur·ry /ˈskʌri‖ˈskɜːri/ vi hurry, esp. with short quick steps ♦ n [U] movement or sound of scurrying

scur·vy /ˈskɜːvi‖-ɜːr-/ n [U] disease caused by lack of VITAMIN C

scut·tle[1] /ˈskʌtl/ n sort of bucket for holding and carrying coal

scuttle[2] vi rush with short quick steps

scuttle[3] vt sink (a ship) by making holes in the bottom

scythe /saɪð/ n grass-cutting tool with a long curving blade fixed to a handle ♦ vt cut (as if) with a scythe

sea /siː/ n **1** [U] great body of salty water that covers much of the Earth's surface **2** [C] a particular (named) part of this: the Caribbean Sea **b** body of water (mostly) enclosed by land: the Mediterranean Sea **3** [C] any of a number of broad plains on the Moon: the Sea of Tranquillity **4** [C] large quantity spread out in front of one: a sea of faces **5 at sea** : **a** on a voyage **b** infml not understanding **6 by sea** on a ship **7 go to sea** become a sailor **8 put to sea** start a voyage

sea a·nem·o·ne /ˈ··ˌ···/ n simple flower-like sea animal

sea·board /ˈsiːbɔːd‖-bɔːrd/ n the part of a country along a seacoast

sea change /ˈ··/ n lit a complete but usu. gradual change

sea·far·ing /ˈsiːˌfeərɪŋ‖-ˌfer-/ adj connected with the sea and sailing

sea·food /ˈsiːfuːd/ n [U] fish and fishlike animals from the sea which can be eaten, esp. SHELLFISH

sea·front /ˈsiːfrʌnt/ n part of a coastal (holiday) town on the edge of the sea, often with a broad path along it

sea·gull /ˈsiːɡʌl/ n GULL

sea·horse /ˈsiːhɔːs‖-hɔːrs/ n small fish with a head and neck like those of a horse

seal[1] /siːl/ n **1** official mark put on an official paper, often by pressing a pattern into red wax **2** something fastened across an opening to protect it **3** tight connection to keep gas or liquid in or out **4 set the seal on** bring to an end in a suitable way ♦ vt **1** fix a SEAL (1) onto **2** fasten or close (as if) with a SEAL (2, 3): (fig.) My lips are sealed. **3** make (more) certain, formal, or solemn **4 seal someone's doom/fate** fml make someone's death or punishment certain

    seal off phr vt close tightly so as not to allow entrance or escape

seal[2] n large smooth-bodied sea animal with broad flat limbs for swimming

sea legs /ˈ··/ n [P] ability to walk comfortably on a moving ship

sea lev·el /ˈ··ˌ··/ n the average height of the sea, used as a standard for measuring heights on land

sealing wax /ˈ···/ n hard easily melted

substance used for SEALs (1)

sea li·on /'· ˌ·/ n large SEAL[2] of the Pacific Ocean

seam /siːm/ n 1 line of stitches joining two pieces of cloth, etc. 2 narrow band of coal between other rocks 3 **burst at the seams** infml be very full ~**less** adj 1 without SEAMS (1) 2 appearing to continue without joins or spaces

sea·man /'siːmən/ n -**men** /-mən/ 1 sailor, esp. of low rank 2 man skilled in handling ships at sea ~**ship** n [U] skill in handling a ship and directing its course

seam·y /'siːmi/ adj rough and immoral -**iness** n [U]

sé·ance /'seɪɑːns, -ɒns‖'seɪɑːns/ n meeting where people try to talk to the spirits of the dead

sear /sɪə‖sɪr/ vt burn with sudden powerful heat ~**ing** adj 1 burning 2 causing or describing very strong feelings, esp. of a sexual kind

search /sɜːtʃ‖sɜːrtʃ/ vi/t 1 look through or examine (a place or person) carefully and thoroughly to try to find something 2 **search me!** infml I don't know! ♦ n 1 act of searching 2 **in search of** searching for ~**ing** adj sharp and thorough: a searching look ~**er** n

search·light /'sɜːtʃlaɪt‖-ɜːr-/ n large powerful light that can be turned in any direction

search par·ty /'· ˌ·/ n group of searchers, esp. for a lost person

search war·rant /'· ˌ·/ n official written order allowing the police to search a place

sea·shore /'siːʃɔː‖-ʃɔːr/ n [U] land along the edge of the sea

sea·sick /'siː ˌsɪk/ adj sick because of a ship's movement ~**ness** n [U]

sea·side /'siːsaɪd/ n [the+S] esp. BrE coast, esp. as a holiday place

sea·son /'siːzən/ n 1 spring, summer, autumn, or winter 2 period of the year marked by a particular thing: the rainy/holiday/cricket season 3 **in/out of season** (of food) at/not at the best time of year for eating 4 **Season's Greetings!** (a greeting on a Christmas card) —see also SILLY SEASON ♦ vt 1 give a special taste to (a food) by adding salt, pepper, a SPICE, etc. 2 dry (wood) gradually for use ~**able** adj fml suitable or useful for the time of year

~**al** adj happening or active only at a particular season ~**ed** adj having much experience ~**ing** n [C;U] something that seasons food

season tick·et /'·· ˌ··‖ˌ·· ˈ·/ n ticket usable for a number of journeys, performances, etc. during a fixed period of time

seat /siːt/ n 1 place for sitting 2 the part on which one sits 3 place as a member of an official body: to lose one's seat in Parliament 4 place where a particular activity happens 5 **in the driver's seat** infml in control 6 **take a back seat (to someone)** infml allow someone else to take control or have the more important job 7 **take/have a seat** please sit down ♦ vt 1 cause or help to sit: be seated (=please sit down) 2 have room for seats for ~**ing** n [U] seats

seat belt /'· ˌ·/ n protective belt round a seated person in a car, plane, etc.

sea ur·chin /'· ˌ··/ n small ball-shaped sea animal with a prickly shell

sea·weed /'siːwiːd/ n [U] plant that grows in the sea

sea·wor·thy /'siːwɜːði‖-ɜːr-/ adj (of a ship) fit for a sea voyage

sec·a·teurs /'sekətɜːz‖ˌsekəˈtɜːrz/ n [P] BrE strong garden scissors

se·cede /sɪ'siːd/ vt formally leave an official group or organization **secession** /sɪ'seʃən/ n [U]

se·clude /sɪ'kluːd/ vt fml keep (esp. oneself) away from other people **secluded** adj very quiet and private **seclusion** /sɪ'kluːʒən/ n [U]

sec·ond[1] /'sekənd/ determiner, adv, pron 2nd

second[2] n 1 length of time equal to ¹⁄₆₀ of a minute 2 infml moment

second[3] n 1 [C] helper of a fighter in a boxing match (BOX[2]) or DUEL 2 [C] imperfect article sold cheaper 3 [C] British university examination result of middle to good quality 4 **second to none** infml the best **seconds** [P] infml second servings of food at a meal

second[4] vt support formally (a formal suggestion at a meeting) ~**er** n

se·cond[5] /sɪ'kɒnd‖sɪ'kɑːnd/ vt BrE fml move from usual duties to a special duty ~**ment** n [C;U]

sec·ond·a·ry /'sekəndəri‖-deri/ adj

1 (of education or a school) for children over 11 **2** not main: *of secondary importance* **3** developing from something earlier: *a secondary infection* –**rily** adv

second best /ˌ·· ˈ·◂/ adj not as good as the best

second-class /ˌ·· ˈ·◂/ adj (considered as) less valuable, important, etc: *They were treated as second-class citizens/a second-class education*

second-guess /ˌ·· ˈ·/ vt AmE infml **1** make a judgment about (someone or something) only after an event has taken place **2** try to say in advance what (someone) will do, how (something) will happen, etc.

second-hand /ˌ·· ˈ·◂/ adj, adv **1** owned or used by someone else before; new **2** (of information) not directly from its origin

second na·ture /ˌ·· ˈ··/ n [U] very firmly fixed habit

second-rate /ˌ·· ˈ·◂/ adj of low quality

second thoughts /ˌ·· ˈ·/ n [P] idea that a past decision or opinion may not be right: *On second thoughts I think I will have a beer.*

second wind /ˌ·· ˈ·/ n [S] return of one's strength during hard physical activity, when it seemed one had become too tired to continue

se·cre·cy /ˈsiːkrəsi/ n [U] **1** keeping secrets **2** being secret

se·cret /ˈsiːkrət/ adj **1** that no one else knows or must know about **2** undeclared ♦ n **1** matter kept hidden or known only to a few **2** special way of doing something well: *the secret of baking perfect bread* **3** mystery **4** **in secret** in a private way or place ~**ly** adv

secret a·gent /ˌ·· ˈ··/ n person gathering information secretly esp. for a foreign government

sec·re·tar·i·at /ˌsekrəˈteəriət ‖ -ˈter-/ n official office or department concerned with the running of a large organization

sec·re·ta·ry /ˈsekrətəri ‖ -teri/ n **1** person who prepares letters, keeps records, arranges meetings, etc. for another **2** government minister or high non-elected official: *the Secretary of State for Trade* **3** officer of an organization who keeps records, writes official letters, etc. –**rial** /ˌsekrəˈteəriəl ‖ -ˈter-/ adj

se·crete¹ /sɪˈkriːt/ vt (esp. of an animal or plant organ) produce (a usu. liquid substance) **secretion** /sɪˈkriːʃən/ n [C;U] (production of) a usu. liquid substance

secrete² vt fml hide **secretion** /sɪˈkriːʃən/ n [U]

se·cre·tive /ˈsiːkrətɪv, sɪˈkriːtɪv/ adj hiding one's thoughts or plans ~**ly** adv ~**ness** n [U]

secret ser·vice /ˌ·· ˈ··/ n government department dealing with special police work, esp. SECURITY (1)

sect /sekt/ n small group within or separated from a larger (esp. religious) group

sec·tar·i·an /sekˈteəriən ‖ -ˈter-/ adj of or between sects, esp. as shown in great strength and narrowness of beliefs ~**ism** n [U]

sec·tion /ˈsekʃən/ n **1** [C] separate part of a larger object, place, group, etc. **2** [C;U] representation of something cut through from top to bottom ~**al** adj **1** in sections (to be) put together **2** limited to one particular group or area

sec·tor /ˈsektə ‖ -ər/ n **1** part of a field of activity, esp. in business or trade —see also PRIVATE SECTOR, PUBLIC SECTOR **2** area of military control

sec·u·lar /ˈsekjələ ‖ -ər/ adj not connected with or controlled by a church

se·cure /sɪˈkjʊə ‖ -ˈkjʊr/ adj **1** protected against danger or risk **2** fastened firmly **3** certain: *a secure job* **4** having no anxiety ♦ vt **1** close tightly **2** make safe **3** fml get ~**ly** adv

se·cu·ri·ty /sɪˈkjʊərəti ‖ -ˈkjʊr-/ n **1** [U] state of being secure **2** [U] (department concerned with) protection, esp. against lawbreaking, violence, enemy acts, escape from prison, etc.: *strict security measures* | *a maximum security prison* **3** [U] property of value promised to a lender in case repayment is not made **4** [C] document giving the owner the right to some property: *government securities*

se·dan /sɪˈdæn/ n AmE for SALOON (1)

sedan chair /·ˌ· ˈ·/ n seat carried through the streets on poles in former times

se·date /sɪˈdeɪt/ adj calm or quiet ♦ vt make sleepy or calm, esp. with a drug **sedation** /sɪˈdeɪʃən/ n [U]

sed·a·tive /ˈsedətɪv/ n drug that makes

one calm, esp. by causing sleep

sed·en·ta·ry /'sedəntəri ‖ -teri/ adj fml used to or needing long periods of sitting and only slight activity

sed·i·ment /'sedɪmənt/ n [S;U] solid material that settles to the bottom of a liquid ~**ary** /ˌsedɪ'mentəri◂/ adj

se·di·tion /sɪ'dɪʃən/ n [U] speaking, actions, etc., encouraging people to disobey the government ~**tious** adj

se·duce /sɪ'djuːs ‖ -'duːs/ vt 1 persuade to have sex with one 2 persuade to do esp. something bad by making it seem attractive **seducer** n **seduction** /sɪ'dʌkʃən/ n [C;U] **seductive** /sɪ'dʌktɪv/ adj very desirable or attractive

see¹ /siː/ v saw /sɔː ‖ sɒː/, seen /siːn/ 1 vi have or use the power of sight 2 vt notice, recognize, or examine by looking 3 vi/t come to know or understand: I can't see why you don't like it. 4 vt form an opinion or picture in the mind: I see little hope of any improvement. 5 vt visit, meet, or receive as a visitor 6 vi/t (try to) find out: I'll see if he's there. 7 vt make sure; take care: See you're ready at 8 o'clock. 8 vt go with: I'll see you home. 9 vt be the occasion of (an event or course in history 10 vt have experience of: We've seen some good times together. | That sofa has seen better days. 11 (I'll) see you/be seeing you (soon/later/next week, etc.) (used when leaving a friend) 12 let me see (used for expressing a pause for thought) 13 see fit decide to 14 seeing is believing: a I'll believe it when I see it, but not before b Now I've seen it, so I believe it 15 see one's way (clear) to feel able or willing to 16 see red become very angry 17 see the back/last of someone have no more to do with 18 see the light: a understand or accept an idea b have a religious experience which changes one's belief c come into existence 19 see things think one sees something that is not there 20 so I see what you say is already clear 21 (you) see (used in explanations)

see about phr vt 1 deal with 2 consider further 3 We'll see about that! infml I will prevent that happening or continuing!

see in phr vt find attractive in: I can't think what she sees in him.

see off phr vt 1 go to the airport, station, etc. with (someone who is starting a trip) 2 chase away 3 remain firm until (something dangerous) stops

see out phr vt 1 last until the end of 2 go to the door with (someone who is leaving)

see through phr vt 1 not be deceived by 2 provide for, support, or help until the end of (esp. a difficult time)

see to phr vt attend to; take care of **see²** n area governed by a BISHOP

seed /siːd/ n [C;U] 1 usu. small hard plant part that can grow into a new plant 2 [U] something from which growth begins: seeds of future trouble 3 [U] lit SEMEN 4 [C] SEEDed (3) player 5 go/run to seed: a (of a plant) produce seed after flowers have been produced b (of a person) lose one's freshness, esp. by becoming lazy, careless, old, etc. ♦ vt 1 (of a plant) grow and produce seed 2 plant seeds in (a piece of ground) 3 place (esp. tennis players at the start of a competition) in order of likelihood to win ~**less** adj

seed·ling /'siːdlɪŋ/ n young plant grown from a seed

seed·y /'siːdi/ adj 1 looking poor, dirty, and uncared for 2 infml slightly unwell and/or in low spirits ~**iness** n [U]

see·ing /'siːɪŋ/ also seeing that — conj as it is true; since

seek /siːk/ v sought /sɔːt ‖ sɒːt/ fml or lit 1 vi/t search (for) 2 vt ask for 3 vt try

seem /siːm/ v give the idea or effect of being; appear: She seems happy. ~**ing** adj that seems to be, but perhaps is not real: his seeming calmness ~**ingly** adv according to what seems to be so (but perhaps is not)

seem·ly /'siːmli/ adj fml (socially) suitable ~**liness** n [U]

seen /siːn/ v past p. of SEE

seep /siːp/ vi (of liquid) flow slowly through small openings in a material ~**age** n [S;U] slow seeping flow

seer /sɪə ‖ sɪr/ n lit someone who knows about the future

see·saw /'siːsɔː ‖ -sɒː/ n 1 board balanced in the middle for people to sit on at opposite ends so that when one end goes up the other goes down 2 up and down movement ♦ vi move up and down esp. between opponents or opposite sides: seesawing prices

seethe /siːð/ vi 1 be in a state of anger or

unrest **2** (of a liquid) move about as if boiling

see-through /'· ·/ adj (esp. of a garment) that can be (partly) seen through

seg·ment /'segmənt/ n any of the parts into which something may be cut up or divided ♦ vt /seg'ment/ divide into segments ~**ation** /ˌsegmən'teɪʃən/ n [U]

seg·re·gate /'segrɪgeɪt/ vt separate or set apart, esp. from a different social or racial group –**gation** /ˌsegrɪ'geɪʃən/ n [U]

seis·mic /'saɪzmɪk/ adj of or caused by EARTHQUAKES

seis·mo·graph /'saɪzməgrɑːf/ –græf/ n instrument for measuring the force of EARTHQUAKES

seize /siːz/ vt **1** take possession of by force or official order: (fig.) *She was seized by a sudden idea.* **2** take hold of eagerly, quickly, or forcefully **seizure** /'siːʒə/ –ər/ n **1** [U] act of seizing **2** [C] sudden attack of illness

seize up phr vt BrE (of part of a machine) become stuck and stop working

sel·dom /'seldəm/ adv not often; rarely

se·lect /sɪ'lekt/ vt choose as best, most suitable, etc. from a group ♦ adj **1** limited to members of the best quality or class **2** of high quality ~**or** n –**ion** /–'lekʃən/ n **1** [U] act of selecting or fact of being selected **2** [C] something or someone selected **3** [C] collection of things to choose from —see also NATURAL SELECTION

se·lec·tive /sɪ'lektɪv/ adj **1** careful in choosing **2** having an effect only on certain things ~**ly** adv –**tivity** /sɪˌlek'tɪvəti/ ~**ness** /sɪ'lektɪvnəs/ n [U]

self /self/ n selves /selvz/ [C;U] whole being of a person, including their nature, character, abilities, etc.

self-ab·sorbed /ˌ· ·'·◂/ adj paying all one's attention to oneself and one's own affairs

self-ap·point·ed /ˌ· ·'··◂/ adj chosen by oneself to do something, unasked and usu. unwanted

self-as·sured /ˌ· ·'·◂/ adj confident –**surance** n [U]

self-ca·ter·ing /ˌ· '···/ adj providing one's own meals: *We're staying in self-catering accommodation.*

self-cen·tred /ˌ· '··◂/ adj interested only in oneself ~**ness** n [U]

self-con·fessed /ˌ· ·'·◂/ adj admitting to

the fault stated: *a self-confessed liar*

self-con·fi·dent /ˌ· '···◂/ adj sure of one's own power to succeed ~**ly** adv –**dence** n [U]

self-con·scious /ˌ· '··◂/ adj nervous and uncomfortable about oneself as seen by others ~**ly** adv ~**ness** n [U]

self-con·tained /ˌ·· ·'·◂/ adj **1** complete in itself; independent **2** not showing feelings or depending on others' friendship

self-con·trol /ˌ· ·'·/ n [U] control over one's feelings –**trolled** adj

self-de·fence /ˌ· ·'·/ n [U] act or skill of defending oneself: *He shot the man in self-defence.* (=only to protect himself)

self-de·ter·mi·na·tion /ˌ· ···'··/ n [U] country's right to govern itself

self-em·ployed /ˌ· ·'·◂/ adj earning money from one's own business, rather than being paid by an employer

self-es·teem /ˌ· ·'·/ n [U] one's good opinion of one's own worth

self-ev·i·dent /ˌ· '···/ adj plainly true without need of proof ~**ly** adv

self-ex·plan·a·to·ry /ˌ· ·'····/ adj easily understood

self-help /ˌ· '·/ adj intended to help one solve one's problems without official help: *a self-help group for sufferers*

self-im·age /ˌ· '··/ n [S] opinion of one's own character, appearance, etc.

self-im·port·ant /ˌ· ·'··◂/ adj having too high an opinion of one's own importance –**ance** n [U]

self-in·dul·gent /ˌ· ·'··◂/ adj too easily allowing oneself pleasure or comfort –**gence** n [U]

self-in·terest /ˌ· '··/ n [U] concern for what is best for oneself ~**ed** adj

self·ish /'selfɪʃ/ adj concerned with one's own advantage without care for others ~**ly** adv ~**ness** n [U]

self·less /'selfləs/ adj concerned with others' advantage without care for oneself ~**ly** adv ~**ness** n [U]

self-made /ˌ· '·◂/ adj having gained success and wealth by one's own efforts alone

self-pos·sessed /ˌ· ·'·◂/ adj calm and confident –**session** n [U]

self-re·li·ant /ˌ· ·'··/ adj not depending on others' help –**ance** n [U]

self-re·spect /ˌ· ·'·/ n [U] proper pride in oneself ~**ing** adj

self·right·eous /ˌ·ˈ·/ *adj* (too) proudly sure of one's own rightness or goodness ~**ly** *adv* ~**ness** *n* [U]

self·sac·ri·fice /ˌ·ˈ·ˌ·/ *n* [U] the giving up of things that one cares deeply about, esp. in order to help others

self·same /ˈselfseɪm/ *adj* exactly the same

self·sat·is·fied /ˌ·ˈ·ˌ·/ *adj* too pleased with oneself

self·seek·ing /ˌ·ˈ·ˌ·/ *n, adj* [U] (someone) working only for their own advantage

self·serv·ice /ˌ·ˈ·ˌ/ *adj, n* [U] (working by) the system in which buyers collect what they want and pay at a special desk

self·start·er /ˌ·ˈ·ˌ/ *n* **1** a usu. electrical apparatus for starting a car engine **2** a person able to work alone on their own ideas

self·styled /ˈ··ˌ/ *adj* given the stated title by oneself, usu. without any right to it

self·suf·fi·cient /ˌ·ˈ·ˈ·ˌ/ *adj* able to provide everything one needs without outside help –**ciency** *n* [U]

self·will /ˌ·ˈ·/ *n* [U] strong unreasonable determination to follow one's own wishes ~**ed** *adj*

sell /sel/ *v* **sold** /sould ‖ sould/ **1** *vi/t* give (property or goods) to someone in exchange for money **2** *vt* help or cause (something) to be bought: *Bad news sells newspapers.* **3** *vt* offer (goods) for sale **4** *vi* be bought: *The magazine sells at $5.* **5** *vt* make acceptable or desirable by persuading **6 sell oneself: a** make oneself or one's ideas seem attractive to others **b** give up one's principles for money or gain **7 sell one's soul (to the devil)** act dishonourably in exchange for money, power, etc. **8 sell someone down the river** put someone in great trouble by being disloyal to them **9 sell something/someone short** value something or someone too low ~**er** *n* **1** person or company that sells **2 a big/good seller** product that people buy a lot of

sell off *phr vt* get rid of by selling, usu. cheaply

sell out *phr v* **1** *vi/t* (cause to) sell all of (what was for sale): *The tickets are sold out; there are none left.* **2** *vi* be disloyal or unfaithful, esp. for payment **sell-out** /ˈ··ˈ/ *n* **1** performance, match, etc. for which all tickets have been sold **2** act of disloyalty or unfaithfulness

sell up *phr vi* sell something (esp. a business) completely

sell-by date /ˈ··ˌ·/ *n BrE* **1** date printed on food, after which it should not be sold **2 past their sell-by date** no longer young, useful, etc.

sel·lo·tape /ˈseləteɪp, ˈseləu- ‖ -lə-, -lou-/ *n* [U] *tdmk, BrE* band of thin clear sticky material ♦ *vt* put together or mend with sellotape

selves /selvz/ *pl. of* SELF

se·man·tic /sɪˈmæntɪk/ *adj* of meaning in language ~**ally** /-kli/ *adv* –**tics** *n* [U] study of meaning

sem·a·phore /ˈseməfɔː ‖ -fɔːr/ *n* [U] system of sending messages with flags

sem·blance /ˈsembləns/ *n* [S] appearance; outward form or seeming likeness: *a semblance of order*

se·men /ˈsiːmən/ *n* [U] SPERM-carrying liquid, passed into the female during the sexual act

se·mes·ter /sɪˈmestə ‖ -ər/ *n* either of the two teaching periods in the year at US colleges

sem·i·cir·cle /ˈsemɪˌsɜːkəl ‖ -ɜːr-/ *n* half a circle

sem·i·co·lon /ˌsemɪˈkəulən ‖ ˈsemɪˌkoulən/ *n* mark (;) used to separate independent parts of a sentence

sem·i·con·duc·tor /ˌsemɪkənˈdʌktə ‖ -ər/ *n* substance which allows the passing of an electric current more easily at high temperatures

sem·i·de·tached /ˌsemɪdɪˈtætʃt◂/ *adj, n* (being) one of a pair of joined houses

sem·i·fi·nal /ˌsemɪˈfaɪnl◂ ‖ ˈsemɪˌfaɪnl/ *n* either of two matches whose winners play in a FINAL

sem·i·nal /ˈsemɪnəl/ *adj* **1** *fml* influencing future development in a new way **2** containing or producing SEMEN

sem·i·nar /ˈsemɪnɑː ‖ -ɑːr/ *n* small study group

sem·i·na·ry /ˈsemɪnəri ‖ -neri/ *n* college for training esp. Roman Catholic priests

semi-skimmed milk /ˌ··· ·ˈ·/ *n* [U] milk that has had about half of the fat removed

Se·mit·ic /sɪˈmɪtɪk/ *adj* of a race of people including Jews and Arabs

sem·o·li·na /ˌseməˈliːnə/ *n* [U] crushed wheat used esp. for PASTA and cooked milky dishes

sen·ate /'senɪt/ n (usu. cap.) 1 higher of the two parts of the law-making body in the US, France, etc. 2 highest council of state in ancient Rome 3 governing council in some universities –**ator** n member of a senate –**atorial** /ˌsenəˈtɔːriəl◂/ adj

send /send/ sent /sent/ 1 vt cause to go or be taken, without going oneself: He sent her a birthday card. 2 vt cause to become: It sent him mad. 3 **send word** send a message ~**er** n

send away phr vi 1 send to another place 2 order goods to be sent by post

send down phr vt 1 cause to go down 2 BrE (of a student) to dismiss from a university for bad behaviour 3 BrE infml send (someone) to prison

send for phr vt ask or order to come: Send for a doctor!

send off phr vt 1 post (a letter, parcel, etc.) 2 BrE (in sport) order (a player) to leave the field because of a serious breaking of the rules 3 SEND away send-off /'· · ·/ n show of good wishes at the start of a journey, new business, etc.

send on phr vt 1 send (a letter) to the receiver's next address 2 send (belongings) in advance to a point on a journey

send out phr vt 1 send from a central point 2 (of a natural object) produce: The sun sends out light. 3 obtain something from somewhere else: We can send out for coffee later.

send up phr vt 1 cause to go up 2 BrE make fun of by copying 3 AmE infml SEND down (3) send-up /'· · ·/ n BrE something which makes fun of someone or something

se·nile /'siːnaɪl/ adj of or showing old age, esp. in weakness of mind **senility** /sɪˈnɪlɪti/ n [U]

se·ni·or /'siːniə ‖ –ər/ n, adj 1 (someone) older (someone) of high or higher rank ~**ity** /ˌsiːniˈɒrɪti ‖ –ˈɔːr-, –ˈɑːr-/ n [U]

senior cit·i·zen /ˌ··· '···/ n old person

Senior adj esp. AmE the older, esp. of two men in the same family who have the same name

sen·sa·tion /senˈseɪʃən/ n 1 [C;U] feeling, such as of heat or pain, coming from the senses 2 [C] general feeling in the mind or body 3 [C] (cause of) excited interest ~**al** adj 1 wonderful 2 causing

excited interest or shock ~**ally** adv

sen·sa·tion·al·ism /senˈseɪʃənəlɪzəm/ n [U] the intentional producing of excitement or shock, esp. by books, magazines, etc. of low quality

sense /sens/ n 1 [C] intended meaning 2 [U] good and esp. practical understanding and judgment 3 [C] any of the five natural powers of sight, hearing, feeling, tasting, and smelling —see also SIXTH SENSE 4 [C;U] power to understand and judge a particular thing: a poor sense of direction 5 [S] feeling, esp. one that is hard to describe 6 **in a sense** partly; in one way of speaking 7 **make sense a** have a clear meaning **b** be a wise course of action 8 **make sense (out) of** understand 9 **(there's) no sense (in)** no good reason for ♦ vt feel in the mind: I could sense danger. **senses** n [P] powers of (reasonable) thinking: He must have taken leave of his senses. (=gone mad) ~**less** adj 1 showing a lack of meaning, thought, or purpose 2 unconscious

sense of hu·mour BrE ‖ humor AmE /ˌ· · ' ·◂/ n [U] ability to understand and enjoy things that are funny

sen·si·bil·i·ty /ˌsensɪˈbɪlɪti/ also **sensibilities** pl. — n [U] delicate feeling about style or what is correct, esp. in art or behaviour

sen·si·ble /'sensɪbəl/ adj 1 having or showing good sense; reasonable 2 **sensible of** fml recognizing; conscious of –**bly** adv

sen·si·tive /'sensɪtɪv/ adj 1 quick to feel or show the effect of: sensitive to light 2 easily offended 3 showing delicate feelings or judgment: a sensitive performance 4 knowing or being conscious of the feelings and opinions of others 5 (of an apparatus) measuring exactly 6 needing to be dealt with carefully so as not to cause trouble or offence: a sensitive issue ~ **ly** adv –**tivity** /ˌsensɪˈtɪvɪti/ n [U]

sen·si·tize, -**tise** /'sensɪtaɪz/ vt make sensitive

sen·sor /'sensə ‖ –ər/ n apparatus for discovering the presence of something, such as heat or sound

sen·so·ry /'sensəri/ adj fml of or by the bodily senses

sen·su·al /'senʃuəl/ adj 1 of bodily feelings 2 interested in or suggesting physical, esp. sexual pleasure ~**ity**

/ˌsenʃuˈælɪti/ n [U]

sen·su·ous /ˈsenʃuəs/ adj 1 giving pleasure to the senses 2 SENSUAL (2) ~ly adv ~ness n [U]

sent /sent/ v past t. and p. of SEND

sen·tence /ˈsentəns/ n 1 group of words forming complete statement, command, question, etc. 2 (order given by a judge which fixes) a punishment for a criminal found guilty in court 3 give/pass/pronounce sentence (of a judge) say the order for a punishment 4 under sentence of death having received a death sentence ♦ vt (of a judge) give a punishment to

sen·ti·ment /ˈsentɪmənt/ n 1 [U] tender feelings of pity, love, sadness, etc. or imaginative remembrance of the past 2 [C] fml thought or judgment caused by a feeling ~al /ˌsentɪˈmentl◄/ adj 1 caused by sentiment 2 showing too much sentiment, esp. of a weak or unreal kind ~ally adv ~ality /ˌsentɪmenˈtælɪti/ n [U] sentiments /ˈsentɪmənts/ n [P] opinion

sen·ti·nel /ˈsentɪnəl/ n lit guard; sentry

sen·try /ˈsentri/ n soldier guarding a building, entrance, etc.

sep·a·ra·ble /ˈsepərəbəl/ adj fml that can be separated –bly adv

sep·a·rate[1] /ˈsepəreɪt/ v 1 vi/t move, set, keep, or break apart 2 vi stop living together as husband and wife –ration /ˌsepəˈreɪʃən/ n 1 [C;U] the act of separating or the fact of being separated 2 [C;U] (a time of) being or living apart 3 [U] law a formal agreement by a husband and wife to live apart

sep·a·rate[2] /ˈsepərɪt/ adj 1 different: a word with 3 separate meanings 2 not shared: We have separate rooms. 3 apart ~ly adv

sep·a·rat·is·m /ˈsepərətɪzəm/ n [U] belief that a particular political or religious group should be separate, not part of a larger whole –ist n

se·pi·a /ˈsiːpiə/ n [U] reddish-brown colour

Sep·tem·ber /sepˈtembə ‖ -ər/ n the ninth month of the year

sep·tic /ˈseptɪk/ adj infected with bacteria

sep·ti·cae·mi·a /ˌseptɪˈsiːmiə/ esp. BrE ‖ -cemia AmE — n [U] dangerous infection spread through the body in the blood

septic tank /ˈ·· ·/ n large container in which body waste matter is broken up and changed by bacteria

sep·ul·chre BrE ‖ -cher AmE /ˈsepəlkə ‖ -ər/ n lit burial place –chral /sɪˈpʌlkrəl/ adj fml or lit like or suitable for a grave

se·quel /ˈsiːkwəl/ n 1 something that follows, esp. as a result 2 film etc. which continues where an earlier one ended

se·quence /ˈsiːkwəns/ n 1 [C] group following each other in order 2 [U] order in which things follow each other 3 [C] scene in a film –quential /sɪˈkwenʃəl/ adj happening in sequence (2)

se·ques·tered /sɪˈkwestəd ‖ -ərd/ adj lit quiet and hidden

se·ques·trate /sɪˈkwestreɪt, ˈsiːkwɪs-/ vt seize (property) by legal order until claims on it are settled –tration /ˌsiːkwɪˈstreɪʃən/ n [U]

se·quin /ˈsiːkwɪn/ n small round shiny piece sewn on a garment for decoration

se·raph·ic /sɪˈræfɪk/ adj like an ANGEL, esp. in beauty or purity ~ally /-kli/ adv

ser·e·nade /ˌserɪˈneɪd/ n piece of music played or sung to a woman by a lover ♦ vt sing or play a serenade to

ser·en·dip·i·ty /ˌserənˈdɪpɪti/ n [U] ability to make useful discoveries by chance

se·rene /sɪˈriːn/ adj completely calm and peaceful ~ly adv serenity /sɪˈrenɪti/ n [U]

serf /sɜːf ‖ sɜːrf/ n slave-like farm worker in former times –dom /ˈsɜːfdəm ‖ ˈsɜːrf-/ n [U] state or fact of being a serf

ser·geant /ˈsɑːdʒənt ‖ ˈsɑːr-/ n 1 soldier in charge of others, but below the officers 2 policeman of middle rank

sergeant ma·jor /ˌ·· ˈ··◄/ n soldier just above a sergeant in rank

se·ri·al[1] /ˈsɪəriəl ‖ ˈsɪr-/ adj of, happening or arranged in a SERIES

serial[2] n written or broadcast story appearing in parts at fixed times ~ize, –ise vt print or broadcast as a serial

serial kil·ler /ˈ··· ˌ·/ n person who has murdered several people over a period of time

serial num·ber /ˈ··· ˌ·/ n number marked on something to show which one it is in a series

se·ries /'sɪəri:z‖'sɪr-/ *n* series group of the same or similar things coming one after another or in order

se·ri·ous /'sɪəriəs‖'sɪr-/ *adj* **1** causing worry and needing attention **2** not cheerful or funny **3** needing or having great skill or thought ~**ly** *adv* ~**ness** *n* [U]

ser·mon /'sɜːmən‖'sɜːr-/ *n* talk given by a priest as part of a church service

ser·pent /'sɜːpənt‖'sɜːr-/ *n lit* snake

ser·rat·ed /sə'reɪtᵻd, se-/ *adj* having (an edge with) a row of V-shapes like teeth

ser·ried /'serid/ *adj* serried ranks *lit* large numbers of people, etc. close together

se·rum /'sɪərəm‖'sɪr-/ *n* serums *or* sera /-rə/ [C;U] liquid containing disease-fighting substances, put into a sick person's blood

ser·vant /'sɜːvənt‖'sɜːr-/ *n* person paid to do personal services for someone, esp. in their home

serve /sɜːv‖sɜːrv/ *v* **1** *vi/t* do work (for); give service (to): *to serve in the army* **2** *vt* provide with something necessary or useful: *The pipeline serves the whole town.* **3** *vt* offer (food, a meal, etc.) for eating **4** *vt* attend to (a customer in a shop) **5** *vt* spend (a period of time): *She served (two years) in prison.* **6** *vi/t fml* be good enough or suitable for (a purpose) **7** *vi/t* (esp. in tennis) begin play by hitting (the ball) to one's opponent **8** *vt law* deliver (an official order to appear in court) **9** **if my memory serves me (right)** if I remember correctly **10** **serve someone right** be suitable punishment ♦ *n* act or manner of serving (SERVE (7))

serv·er /'sɜːvə‖'sɜːrvər/ *n* main computer on a NETWORK¹ that controls all the others

ser·vice /'sɜːvᵻs‖'sɜːr-/ *n* **1** [C;U] act or work done for someone **2** [U] attention to guests in a hotel, restaurant, etc. or to customers in a shop **3** [C;U] (operation of) an organization doing useful work: *a bus service* | *the postal service* **4** [C;U] (duty in) the army, navy, etc. **5** [C] religious ceremony **6** [C;U] examination of a machine to keep it in good condition **7** [C] SERVE **8** [C] set of dishes, etc.: *a dinner service* **9** **at your service** *fml* willing to help **10** **of service** *fml* useful; helpful ♦ *vt* repair or put in good condition ♦ *adj* something for the use of people working in a place, rather than the public: *service stairs*

ser·vice·a·ble /'sɜːvᵻsəbəl‖'sɜːr-/ *adj* fit for (long or hard) use; useful

service charge /'·· ·/ *n* amount added to a bill to pay for a particular service

ser·vice·man /'sɜːvᵻsmən‖'sɜːr-/ -**woman** /-,wʊmən/ *fem.* — *n* -**men** /-mən/ member of the army, navy, etc.

service sta·tion /'·· ,··/ *n* GARAGE (2)

ser·vi·ette /,sɜːvi'et‖,sɜːr-/ *n* NAPKIN

ser·vile /'sɜːvaɪl‖'sɜːrvəl, -vaɪl/ *adj* behaving like a slave –**vility** /sɜː'vɪlᵻti‖ sɜːr-/ *n* [U]

serv·ing /'sɜːvɪŋ‖'sɜːr-/ *n* amount of food for one person

ser·vi·tude /'sɜːvᵻtjuːd‖'sɜːrvᵻtuːd/ *n* [U] *lit* state of being a slave or one who is forced to obey another

ses·sion /'seʃən/ *n* **1** formal meeting or group of meetings of esp. a parliament or court **2** period of time used for a particular purpose: *a recording/drinking session*

set¹ /set/ *v* set, *pres. p.* -**tt**- **1** *vt* put (to stay) in the stated place: *to set a ladder against a wall* **2** *vt* fix; establish: *set a date for the wedding* **3** *vt* put into the correct condition for use: *set the clock/the table* **4** *vt* cause to be: *set a prisoner free* | *Her words set me thinking.* **5** *vt* put: *set a load down* **6** *vt* give (a piece of work) for someone to do **7** *vt* put the action of (a film, story, etc.) in the stated place and time **8** *vi/t* (cause to) become solid: *The jelly has set.* **9** *vi* (of the sun, moon, etc.) go below the horizon **10** *vt* write or provide music for (a poem or other words to be sung) **11** *vt* fix (a precious stone) into (a piece of jewellery) **12** *vt* put (a broken bone) into a fixed position to mend **13** *vt* arrange (hair) when wet to be in a particular style when dry **14** *vt* arrange for printing **15 set an example** offer a standard for other people to follow **16 set eyes on** see **17 set light/fire to** cause (something) to burn **18 set one's face against** oppose **19 set one's heart/hopes on** want very much **20 set one's mind to** decide firmly on

set about *phr vt* **1** begin **2** attack

set back *phr vt* **1** place at resp. the stated distance behind something: *The house is set back 15 feet from the road.* **2** delay **3** cost (a large amount)

set in *phr vi* (of bad weather, disease, etc.) begin (and continue)

set off phr v 1 vi begin a journey 2 vt cause to explode 3 vt cause (sudden activity) 4 vt make (one thing) look better by putting it near something different: A white belt set off her blue dress.

set on phr v 1 attack 2 cause to attack: I'll set the dogs on you.

set out phr v 1 vt arrange or spread out in order 2 vi begin a journey 3 vt begin with a purpose

set to phr vi begin eagerly or determinedly

set up phr vt 1 put into position 2 prepare (a machine, instrument, etc.) for use 3 establish or arrange (an organization, plan, etc.) 4 provide with what is necessary or useful

set² adj 1 given or fixed for study: set books 2 determined: He's very set on going. 3 fixed; PRESCRIBED: set hours 4 unmoving: a set smile 5 at a fixed price: a set dinner 6 infml ready: I'm all set, so we can go.

set³ n 1 group forming a whole: a set of gardening tools 2 television or radio receiving apparatus 3 a scenery, etc. representing the place of action in a stage play b place where a film is acted 4 group of games in a tennis match 5 group of people of a particular social type: the smart set 6 act of setting (SET¹ (13)) one's hair

set·back /'setbæk/ n something that delays or prevents successful progress

set piece /ˌ· '·◄/ n something carried out using a well-known formal pattern or plan

set·square /'setskweə ‖ -skwer/ n three-sided right-angled plate for drawing or testing angles

set·tee /se'tiː/ n long soft seat with a back, for more than one person

set·ter /'setə ‖ -ər/ n long-haired dog used by hunters

set·ting /'setɪŋ/ n 1 the going down (of the moon, sun, etc.) 2 way or position in which an instrument is prepared for use 3 a set of surroundings b time and place where the action of a book, film, etc. happens 4 set of articles (dishes, knives, forks, etc.) arranged at one place on a table for eating: a place setting

set·tle /'setl/ v 1 vi start to live in a place 2 vi/t (place so as to) stay or be comfortable 3 vi/t come or bring to rest, esp. from above: Dust had settled on the furniture. 4 vi/t

make or become quiet, calm, etc.: Settle down, children! 5 vt decide on firmly; fix: That settles it! (=That has decided the matter.) 6 vt provide people to live in (a place) 7 vi/t bring (a matter) to an agreement 8 vt pay (a bill) **settled** adj **settler** n member of a new population

settle down phr vi 1 (cause to) sit comfortably 2 give one's serious attention (to a job, etc.): I must settle down to some work today. 3 establish a home and live a quiet life 4 become used to a way of life, job, etc.

settle for phr vt accept (something less than hoped for)

settle in phr vi/t (help to) get used to a new home, job, etc.

settle on phr vt decide or agree on; choose

settle up phr vi pay what is owed

set·tle·ment /'setlmənt/ n 1 [U] movement of a new population into a new place to live there 2 [C] newly built small village in an area with few people 3 [C;U] agreement or decision ending an argument 4 [C;U] payment of money claimed 5 [C] a formal gift or giving of money: He made a settlement on his daughter when she married.

set-to /'· ·/ n [S] short fight or quarrel

set-up /'· ·/ n arrangement; organization

sev·en /'sevən/ determiner, n, pron 7 ~th determiner, adv, n, pron 7th

sev·en·teen /ˌsevən'tiːn◄/ determiner, n, pron 17 ~th determiner, adv, n, pron 17th

seventh heav·en /ˌ·· '··/ n complete happiness

sev·en·ty /'sevənti/ determiner, n, pron 70 –tieth determiner, adv, n, pron 70th

seven-year itch /ˌ·· '·/ n dissatisfaction after seven years of marriage

sev·er /'sevə ‖ -ər/ vt fml divide in two, esp. by cutting: (fig.) sever diplomatic relations ~ance n [U]

sev·er·al /'sevərəl/ determiner, pron more than a few but not very many; some adj fml separate: They went their several ways.

severance pay /'··· ·/ n [U] money paid by a company to a worker losing his job through no fault of his own

se·vere /sə'vɪə ‖ -'vɪr/ adj 1 causing serious harm, pain, or worry 2 not kind or gentle 3 completely plain and without decoration ~**ly** *adv* severity /sɔ́ːverɪ̀ti/ *n* [U]

sew /səʊ ‖ soʊ/ *vi/t* sewed, sewn /səʊn ‖ soʊn/ fasten (esp. cloth) with thread

sew up *phr vt* **1** close or repair by sewing **2** settle satisfactorily

sew·age /ˈsjuːɪdʒ, ˈsuː- ‖ ˈsuː-/ *n* [U] waste material and water carried in sewers

sew·er /ˈsjuːə, ˈsuːə ‖ ˈsuːər/ *n* large underground pipe for carrying away sewage and water, esp. in a city

sew·er·age /ˈsjuːərɪdʒ, ˈsuː- ‖ ˈsuː-/ *n* [U] system of removing waste material through sewers

sex /seks/ *n* **1** [U] condition of being male or female **2** [C] set of all male or female people **3** [U] (activity connected with) SEXUAL INTERCOURSE: *to have sex (with someone)* ♦ *vt* find out whether (an animal) is male or female

sex ap·peal /ˈ· ·ˌ·/ *n* [U] power of being sexually exciting to other people

sex·is·m /ˈseksɪzəm/ *n* [U] (unfair treatment coming from) the belief that one sex is better, cleverer, etc. than the other –**ist** *adj, n*

sex or·gan /ˈ· ˌ·/ *n* part of the body used in producing children

sex·tant /ˈsekstənt/ *n* instrument for measuring angles between stars, to find out where one is

sex·tet /seksˈtet/ *n* (music for) six musicians

sex·ton /ˈsekstən/ *n* someone who takes care of a church building

sex·tu·plet /sekˈstjuːplɪt ‖ -ˈstʌ-/ *n* any of six children born together

sex·u·al /ˈseksʃuəl/ *adj* of or connected with sex ~**ly** *adv*: *sexually active* –**ity** /ˌsekʃuˈælɪti/ *n* [U] someone's sexual activities and feelings

sexual har·ass·ment /ˌ··· ˈ···, ˌ··· ·ˈ··/ *n* [U] (continued) unwanted behaviour or remarks of a sexual nature

sexual in·ter·course /ˌ··· ˈ··· ·/ *n* [U] bodily act between two people in which the sex organs are brought together

sex·y /ˈseksi/ *adj* sexually exciting –**ily** *adv* –**iness** *n* [U]

sh, shh /ʃ/ *interj* (used for demanding silence)

shab·by /ˈʃæbi/ *adj* **1** untidy, uncared-for,
and worn-out **2** unfair and ungenerous –**bily** *adv* –**biness** *n* [U]

shack¹ /ʃæk/ *n* small roughly built house or hut

shack² *v* **shack up** *phr vi infml* (of a person, or persons) live together without being married

shack·le /ˈʃækəl/ *n* metal band for fastening the arms or legs: (fig.) *the shackles of slavery* ♦ *vt* fasten (as if) with shackles

shade /ʃeɪd/ *n* **1** [U] slight darkness, made esp. by blocking of direct sunlight **2** [C] something which provides shade or reduces light: *a lampshade* **3** [C] degree or variety of colour: *shades of blue* **4** [C] slight difference: *shades of meaning* **5** [S] slightly: *a shade too loud* **6** [C] *lit* GHOST **7 put someone/something in the shade** make someone/something seem much less important by comparison ♦ *v* **1** *vt* shelter from direct light **2** *vt* represent shadow on (an object in a picture) **3** *vi* change gradually **shady** *adj* **1** in or producing shade **2** probably dishonest

shades /ʃeɪdz/ *n* [P] **1** *infml* SUNGLASSES **2 shades of** this reminds me of

shad·ow /ˈʃædəʊ- ‖ -doʊ/ *n* **1** [U] SHADE (1): *Most of the room was in shadow.* **2** [C] dark shape made on a surface by something between it and direct light: *The tree cast a long shadow across the lawn.* **3** [C] dark area: *shadows under her eyes* **4** [S] slightest bit: *not a shadow of a doubt* **5** [C] a form from which the real substance has gone: *After his illness he was only a shadow of his former self.* **6 be afraid of one's own shadow** be habitually afraid or nervous ♦ *adj* (in Britain) of the party opposing the government in parliament: *the shadow cabinet* ♦ *vt* **1** make a shadow on **2** follow and watch closely, esp. secretly ~**y** *adj* **1** hard to see or know about clearly **2** full of shade

shadow-box /ˈʃædəʊbɒks ‖ -doʊbɑːks/ *vi* fight with an imaginary opponent ~**ing** *n* [U]

shaft¹ /ʃɑːft ‖ ʃæft/ *n* **1** thin rod forming the body of a weapon or tool, such as a spear or axe **2** bar which turns to pass power through a machine: *a propeller shaft* **3** long passage going down: *a mine shaft* **4** either of two poles that an animal is fastened between to pull a vehicle **5** beam (of light) **6** *lit* something shot like an arrow: *shafts of wit*

shaft² *vt AmE sl* treat unfairly and very severely

shag¹ /ʃæg/ *n* [U] rough strong tobacco

shag² *vt* -**gg**- *BrE taboo sl* have sex with

shagged out /ˌ· ˈ·/ *adj BrE sl* very tired

shag·gy /ˈʃægi/ *adj* being or covered with long uneven untidy hair –**giness** *n* [U]

shake /ʃeɪk/ *v* **shook** /ʃʊk/, **shaken** /ˈʃeɪkən/ **1** *vi/t* move up and down and from side to side with quick short movements **2** *vi/t* hold (someone's right hand) and move it up and down, to show esp. greeting or agreement **3** *vt* trouble; upset **4** *vi* (of a voice) tremble **5** **shake one's head** move one's head from side to side to answer 'no' ♦ *n* **1** [C] act of shaking **2** [C] *infml* moment **3** [C] *AmE infml* MILK SHAKE **4** [S] *AmE infml* treatment of the stated type —see also SHAKES **shaky** *adj* shaking; unsteady **shakily** *adv*

shake off *phr vt* get rid of; escape from

shake up *phr vt* **1** make big changes in (an organization), esp. to improve it **2** mix by shaking **shake-up** /ˈ· ·/ *n* rearrangement of an organization

shake·down /ˈʃeɪkdaʊn/ *n AmE infml* act of getting money by threats

shakes /ʃeɪks/ *n infml* **1** [*the*+P] nervous shaking of the body from disease, fear, etc. **2** **no great shakes** not very good

shale /ʃeɪl/ *n* [U] soft rock which splits naturally

shall /ʃəl· *strong* ʃæl/ *v aux neg. short form* **shan't** (used with **I** and **we**) **1** (expresses the future tense) **2** (used in questions or offers): *Shall I* (=would you like me to) *go?*

shal·low /ˈʃæləʊ ǁ -loʊ/ *adj* **1** not deep **2** lacking deep or serious thinking **shallows** *n* [P] shallow area in a river, lake, etc.

sham /ʃæm/ *n* **1** [C] something that is not what it appears or is said to be **2** [U] falseness: PRETENCE ♦ *adj* not real ♦ *vi/t* -**mm**- put on a false appearance

sham·ble /ˈʃæmbəl/ *vi* walk awkwardly, dragging the feet

sham·bles /ˈʃæmbəlz/ *n* [P] (place or scene of) great disorder

sham·bol·ic /ʃæmˈbɒlɪk ǁ -ˈbɑː-/ *adj BrE infml* completely disordered or confused

shame /ʃeɪm/ *n* **1** [U] painful feeling caused by knowledge of guilt, inability, or failure **2** [U] ability to feel this **3** [U] loss of honour **4** [S] something one is sorry about: *It's a shame you can't come.* **5** **put someone/something to shame** show someone/something to be less good by comparison ♦ *vt* **1** bring dishonour to **2** cause to feel shame ~**ful** *adj* which one ought to feel ashamed of ~**fully** *adv* ~**fulness** *n* [U] ~**less** *adj* **1** not feeling suitably ashamed: *a shameless liar* **2** done without shame ~**lessly** *adv* ~**lessness** *n* [U]

shame·faced /ˌʃeɪmˈfeɪst◀/ *adj* showing suitable shame ~**ly** /-ˈfeɪsɪdli/ *adv*

sham·poo /ʃæmˈpuː/ *n* -**poos** [C;U] liquid soap for washing the hair ♦ *vt* -**pooed**, *present p.* -**pooing** wash with shampoo

sham·rock /ˈʃæmrɒk ǁ -rɑːk/ *n* [U] plant with three leaves on each stem that is the national sign of Ireland

shan·dy /ˈʃændi/ *n* [U] beer mixed with esp. LEMONADE

shang·hai /ʃæŋˈhaɪ/ *vt* trick or force into doing something unwilling

Shan·gri-La /ˌʃæŋgri ˈlɑː/ *n* distant beautiful imaginary place where everything is pleasant

shank /ʃæŋk/ *n* smooth end of a SCREW (1) or DRILL

shan't /ʃɑːnt ǁ ʃænt/ *v short for:* shall not

shan·ty¹ /ˈʃænti/ *n* small roughly built house

shan·ty² *n* song sung by working sailors

shan·ty·town /ˈʃænti,taʊn/ *n* (part of) a town where poor people live in shanties

shape /ʃeɪp/ *n* **1** [C;U] outer form of something: *a cake in the shape of a heart* **2** [U] general character or nature of something **3** [U] (proper) condition, health, etc. **4** **get/put something into shape** arrange or plan something properly **5** **in any shape or form** of any kind; at all **6** **take shape** begin to be or look like the finished form ♦ *v* **1** *vt* give a particular shape to: *the influences that shape one's character* **2** *vi* develop in the stated way ~**less** *adj* ~**ly** *adj* (of a person) having an attractive shape

shape up *phr vi* **1** develop well or in the stated way **2** (usu. used threateningly or angrily) begin to perform more effectively, behave better, etc.

shard /ʃɑːd ǁ ʃɑːrd/ *n* broken piece of a

bowl, cup, etc.

share /ʃeə‖ʃer/ n **1** part belonging to, owed to, or done by a particular person **2** part of the ownership of a business company, offered for sale to the public **3 go shares** BrE divide cost, ownership, etc. among two or more people ♦ v **1** vi/t have, use, pay, etc. with others or among a group **2** vt divide and give out in shares **3 share and share alike** have an equal share in everything

share·hold·er /ˈʃeəˌhəʊldə‖ˈʃerˌhouldər/ n owner of SHARES (2)

share-out /ˈ· ·/ n [S] act of giving out shares of something

shark /ʃɑːk‖ʃɑːrk/ n **1 shark** or **sharks** large dangerous fish with sharp teeth **2** infml a person clever at getting money from others in dishonest ways

sharp /ʃɑːp‖ʃɑːrp/ adj **1** having or being a thin cutting edge or fine point: a sharp knife **2** not rounded: a sharp nose **3** causing a sensation like that of cutting, pricking, biting, or stinging: a sharp wind | the sharp taste of lemon juice **4** quick and strong: a sharp pain | a sharp blow to the head **5** sudden: a sharp turn **6** clear in shape or detail: a sharp photo **7** quick and sensitive in thinking, seeing, etc. **8** angry **9** (in music) above the right note **10** infml smart-looking ♦ adv **1** exactly at the stated time **2** suddenly: Turn sharp right. **3** above the right note **4 Look sharp!**: **a** be careful **b** hurry up ♦ n (in music) sharp note —**ly** adv ~**en** vi/t become or make sharp or sharper ~**ener** n: a pencil sharpener ~**ness** n [U]

sharp end /ˈ· ·/ n [the+S] infml part of a job, organization, etc. where the most severe problems are experienced

sharp prac·tice /ˌ· ˈ··/ n [U] dishonest but not quite illegal activity

sharp·shoot·er /ˈʃɑːpˌʃuːtə‖ˈʃɑːrpˌʃuːtər/ n person skilled in shooting

shat·ter /ˈʃætə‖-ər/ v **1** vi/t break suddenly into very small pieces **2** vt shock very much **3** vt infml tire very much

shave /ʃeɪv/ v **1** vi/t cut off (a beard or face hair) with a RAZOR or shaver **2** vt cut hair from (a part of the body) **3** vt cut off (very thin pieces) from (a surface) **4** vt come close to or touch in passing ♦ n act of shaving —see also CLOSE SHAVE **shaver** n electric shaving tool **shaving** n very thin

piece cut off from a surface

shav·en /ˈʃeɪvən/ adj having been SHAVEd

shawl /ʃɔːl‖ʃɒːl/ n large piece of cloth worn over a woman's head or shoulders or wrapped round the body

she /ʃi; strong ʃiː/ pron (used for the female subject of a sentence) ♦ n a female: a she-goat

sheaf /ʃiːf/ n **sheaves** /ʃiːvz/ **1** bunch of grain plants tied together **2** many things held or tied together: a sheaf of notes

shear /ʃɪə‖ʃɪr/ v **sheared**, **sheared** or **shorn** /ʃɔːn‖ʃɔːrn/ **1** vt cut off wool from (a sheep) **2** vi/t break under a sideways or twisting force **3 be shorn of** have (something) completely removed from one **shears** n [P] large cutting tool like scissors

sheath /ʃiːθ/ n **sheaths** /ʃiːðz/ **1** closefitting case for a blade **2** CONDOM

sheathe /ʃiːð/ vt put away in a SHEATH (1)

she·bang /ʃ·ˈbæn/ n **the whole shebang** infml everything

shed¹ /ʃed/ n lightly built single-floored (wooden) building

shed² vt shed; pres. p. **-dd- 1** cause to flow out: shedding tears (=crying) **2** get rid of (outer skin, leaves, hair, etc.) naturally **3** get rid of (something not wanted or needed) **4** (of a vehicle) drop (a load of goods) by accident **5 shed blood** cause wounding or esp. killing **6 shed light on** help to explain

she'd /ʃid; strong ʃiːd/ short for: **1** she would **2** she had

sheen /ʃiːn/ n [S;U] shiny surface

sheep /ʃiːp/ n **sheep 1** grass-eating animal farmed for its wool and meat **2 make/cast sheep's eyes at someone** behave fondly towards someone, esp. in an awkward or silly way **3 the sheep and the goats** those who are good, able, successful, etc. and those who are not —see also BLACK SHEEP ~**ish** adj uncomfortable because one knows one has done something wrong or foolish ~**ishly** adv ~**ishness** n [U]

sheep·dog /ˈʃiːpdɒg‖-dɒːg/ n dog trained to control sheep

sheer¹ /ʃɪə‖ʃɪr/ adj **1** pure; nothing but: He won by sheer luck. **2** very steep **3** (of cloth) very thin ♦ adv straight up or down

sheer² vi change direction quickly

sheet /ʃiːt/ n **1** large four-sided piece of cloth used on a bed **2** broad regularly shaped piece of a thin or flat material: a *sheet of glass/paper* **3 a** broad stretch of something: *a sheet of ice* **4** moving or powerful wide mass: *The rain came down in sheets.*

sheet mu·sic /'· ,··, ' ,·'·/ *n* [U] music printed on single sheets

sheikh /ʃeɪk ‖ ʃiːk/ *n* Arab chief or prince ~**dom** *n*

shek·els /'ʃekəlz/ *n* [P] *sl* money

shelf /ʃelf/ *n* **shelves** /ʃelvz/ **1** flat (narrow) board fixed against a wall or in a frame, for putting things on **2** narrow surface of rock underwater **3 on the shelf** (of a person) not likely to marry, esp. because one is too old

shelf life /'· ·/ *n* [S] length of time food, medicine, etc. can be kept before being used

shell[1] /ʃel/ *n* **1** [C;U] hard outer covering of a nut, egg, fruit, or certain types of animal: *a snail shell* **2** [C] outer surface or frame of something: (fig.) *He's only a shell of a man.* **3** [C] explosive for firing from a large gun **4 come out of one's shell** begin to be friendly or interested in others

shell[2] *vt* **1** remove from a SHELL[1] (1) or POD **2** fire SHELLS[1] (3) at

shell out *phr vt infml* pay

she'll /ʃil; *strong* ʃiːl/ *short for:* **1** she will **2** she shall

shel·lack·ing /ʃə'lækɪŋ/ *n AmE infml* severe defeat

shell·fish /'ʃel,fɪʃ/ *n* -**fish 1** [C] soft-bodied water animal with a shell: *Oysters and lobsters are shellfish.* **2** [U] such animals as food

shell·shock /'ʃelʃɒk ‖ -ʃɑːk/ *n* [U] illness of the mind, esp. in soldiers caused by the experience of war -**shocked** *adj*

shel·ter /'ʃeltə‖ -ər/ *n* **1** [C] building or enclosure giving protection **2** [U] protection, esp. from bad weather ♦ *v* **1** *vt* give shelter to **2** *vi* take shelter

shelve /ʃelv/ *v* **1** *vt* put aside until a later time **2** *vi* slope gradually

shelves /ʃelvz/ *pl. of* SHELF

she·nan·i·gans /ʃɪ'nænɪgənz/ *n* [P] *infml* **1** rather dishonest practices **2** MISCHIEF

shep·herd /'ʃepəd‖ -ərd/ **shepherdess** /'ʃepədes ‖ -ərdↄs/ *fem.* — *n* person who takes care of sheep ♦ *vt* lead or guide like sheep

shepherd's pie /,·· '·/ *n* [U] dish of finely

cut-up meat with a topping of potato

sher·bet /'ʃɜːbət ‖ 'ʃɜːr-/ *n* [U] sweet powder, often added to water

sher·iff /'ʃerↄf/ *n* **1** elected law officer in a local area in the US **2** royally appointed chief officer in an English COUNTY

sher·ry /'ʃeri/ *n* [U] pale or dark brown strong wine (originally) from Spain

she's /ʃiz; *strong* ʃiːz/ *short for:* **1** she is **2** she has

shib·bo·leth /'ʃɪbələθ ‖ -lↄθ/ *n* **1** word used to test to which party, class, etc. a person belongs **2** once-important custom or phrase which no longer has much meaning

shield /ʃiːld/ *n* **1** something carried as a protection from being hit **2** representation of this, used for a COAT OF ARMS, BADGE, etc. **3** protective cover ♦ *vt* protect

shift /ʃɪft/ *v* **1** *vi/t* move from one place to another **2** *vt* get rid of; remove **3 shift for oneself** take care of oneself ♦ *n* **1** change in position or direction **2** (period worked by) a group of workers which takes turns with others: *the night shift* **3** loose fitting simple dress ~**less** *adj* lazy and lacking in purpose ~**y** *adj* looking dishonest; not to be trusted ~**ily** *adv* ~**iness** *n* [U]

shift key /'· ·/ *n* KEY on a KEYBOARD, pressed to print a capital letter

shift stick /'· ·/ *AmE for* GEAR LEVER

shil·ling /'ʃɪlɪŋ/ *n* former British coin worth 12 old pence (1/20 of £1)

shil·ly-shal·ly /'ʃɪli ,ʃæli/ *vi* waste time instead of taking action

shim·mer /'ʃɪmə ‖ -ər/ *vi* shine with a soft trembling light

shin /ʃɪn/ *n* the part of the leg below the knee ♦ *vi* -**nn-** climb using the hands and legs, esp. quickly and easily

shine /ʃaɪn/ *v* **shone** /ʃɒn ‖ ʃoʊn/ **1** *vi/t* (cause to) give off light **2** *vt* (*past t. and p.* **shined**) polish **3** *vi* be clearly excellent ♦ *n* [S] **1** brightness **2** act of polishing **3** (**come**) **rain or shine** whatever happens **4 take a shine to** start to like **shiny** *adj* bright

shin·gle /'ʃɪŋɡəl/ *n* [U] stones on a seashore -**gly** *adj*

shin·gles /'ʃɪŋɡəlz/ *n* [U] disease producing painful red spots, esp. round the waist

shin·ny /'ʃɪni/ *vi AmE for* SHIN

ship /ʃɪp/ *n* **1** large boat **2** large aircraft or space vehicle **3 when one's ship comes in/home** when one becomes rich ♦ *vt* -**pp-**

1 send by ship **2** send over a large distance by road, air, etc. ~**per** *n* dealer who ships goods ~**ping** *n* [U] ships as a group

ship·board /'ʃɪpbɔːd ‖ -bɔːrd/ *n* **on shipboard** on a ship

ship·mate /'ʃɪpmeɪt/ *n* fellow sailor on the same ship

ship·ment /'ʃɪpmənt/ *n* **1** [C] load of goods sent by sea, road, or air **2** [C;U] sending, carrying, and delivering goods

ship·shape /'ʃɪpʃeɪp/ *adj* clean and neat

ship·wreck /'ʃɪp-rek/ *n* [C;U] destruction of a ship, as if by hitting rocks or by sinking ◆ *vt* **1** cause to suffer shipwreck **2** ruin

ship·yard /'ʃɪp-jɑːd ‖ -jɑːrd/ *n* place where ships are built or repaired

shirk /ʃɜːk ‖ ʃɜːrk/ *vi/t* avoid (unpleasant work) because of laziness, lack of determination, etc. ~**er** *n*

shirt /ʃɜːt ‖ ʃɜːrt/ *n* **1** cloth garment for the upper body with SLEEVES and usu. a collar **2 lose one's shirt** to lose all one has **3 put one's shirt on** risk all one's money on

shirt·sleeves /'ʃɜːtsliːvz ‖ 'ʃɜːrt-/ *n* **in (one's) shirtsleeves** wearing nothing over one's shirt

shirt·y /'ʃɜːti ‖ 'ʃɜːr-/ *adj infml* angry

shit /ʃɪt/ *n* [U] *taboo* **1** solid waste from the bowels **2** something of no value: *I don't give a shit.* (=I don't care) **3** worthless or unpleasant person ◆ *v* -**tt-** *taboo* pass solid waste from the bowels ◆ *interj taboo* (expressing anger or annoyance) ~**ty** *adj taboo sl* unpleasant

shiv·er /'ʃɪvə ‖ -ər/ *vi* shake, esp. from cold or fear ◆ *n* feeling of shivering ~**y** *adj*

shoal[1] /ʃəʊl ‖ ʃoʊl/ *n* dangerous bank of sand near the surface of water

shoal[2] *n* large group of fish swimming together

shock[1] /ʃɒk ‖ ʃɑːk/ *n* [C;U] **1** (state or feeling caused by) an unexpected and usu. very unpleasant event **2** violent force from a hard blow, crash, explosion, etc. or from electricity ◆ *vt* cause unpleasant or angry surprise to ◆ *adj* very surprising: *shock tactics* ~**ing** *adj* **1** very offensive, wrong, or upsetting **2** very bad: *I've got a shocking cold.*

shock[2] *n* thick mass (of hair)

shock ab·sorb·er /'· ·,··/ *n* apparatus

fitted to a vehicle to lessen the effect of violent movement

shod /ʃɒd ‖ ʃɑːd/ *past t. and p. of* SHOE

shod·dy /'ʃɒdi ‖ 'ʃɑːdi/ *adj* **1** cheaply and badly done **2** ungenerous; dishonourable -**dily** *adv* -**diness** *n* [U]

shoe /ʃuː/ *n* **1** covering worn on the foot **2 fill someone's shoes** take the place and do the job of someone **3 in someone's shoes** in someone's position: *I'd hate to be in your shoes.* ◆ *vt* **shod** /ʃɒd ‖ ʃɑːd/ fix a HORSESHOE to

shoe·horn /'ʃuːhɔːn ‖ -hɔːrn/ *n* small object used to help put shoes on ◆ *vt* put or force into a small space

shoe·lace /'ʃuːleɪs/ *n* thin cord for fastening a shoe

shoe·string /'ʃuːˌstrɪŋ/ *n* **on a shoestring** with a very small amount of money

shone /ʃɒn ‖ ʃoʊn/ *past t. and p. of* SHINE

shoo /ʃuː/ *interj* (used for driving away esp. birds and animals) ◆ *vt* drive away (as if) by saying 'shoo'

shook /ʃʊk/ *v past t. of* SHAKE

shoot /ʃuːt/ *v* **shot** /ʃɒt ‖ ʃɑːt/ **1** *vi* fire a weapon **2** *vt* (of a person or weapon) send out (bullets, etc.) with force: (fig.) *She shot him an angry glance.* **3** *vt* hit, wound, or kill with a bullet, etc. **4** *vi* move very quickly or suddenly: *The car shot past us.* | *Pain shot up my arm.* | (fig.) *Prices have shot up.* **5** *vi/t* make (a photograph or film) (of) **6** *vi* kick, throw, etc. a ball to make a point in a game **7** *vt AmE* play (a game of BILLIARDS, POOL, etc.) **8 shoot one's mouth off** talk foolishly about what one does not know about or should not talk about **9 shoot the bull/the breeze** *AmE infml* have an informal not very serious conversation ◆ *n* **1** new growth from a plant **2** occasion for shooting, esp. of animals ~**ing** *n* **1** [C] situation in which someone is shot **2** [U] sport of shooting animals

shoot down *phr vt* **1** bring down (a flying aircraft) by shooting **2** REJECT (an idea)

shoot up *phr v* **1** *vi* go upwards, increase, or grow quickly **2** *vt infml* damage or wound by shooting **3** *vi/t sl* take (a drug) directly into the blood using a needle

shooting star /'·· ·/ *n* METEOR

shoot-out /'· ·/ *n* battle between gunfighters, usu. to decide a quarrel

shop¹ /ʃɒp ‖ ʃɑːp/ n 1 [C] BrE building or room where goods are sold 2 [U] subjects connected with one's work: *Let's not talk shop.*

shop² v -pp- 1 vi visit shops to buy things 2 vt BrE infml tell the police about (a criminal) ~**per** n ~**ping** n [U] goods bought when visiting shops

shop around phr vt compare prices or values in different shops before buying: (fig.) *Shop around before deciding which club to join.*

shop assis·tant /'· ·,·/ n BrE person who serves customers in a shop

shop floor /,· '·◄/ n area, esp. in a factory, where the ordinary workers work

shop·keep·er /'ʃɒp,kiːpə ‖ 'ʃɑːp,kiːpər/ n esp. BrE person in charge of a small shop

shop·lift /'ʃɒp,lɪft ‖ 'ʃɑːp-/ vi steal from a shop ~**er** n

shopping cen·tre BrE ‖ **-center** AmE /'·· ,·/ n group of stores built together in one area

shop·soiled /'ʃɒpsɔɪld ‖ 'ʃɑːp-/ adj slightly damaged or dirty from being kept in a shop for a long time

shop stew·ard /,· '·◄/ n trade union officer representing members in a place of work

shore¹ /ʃɔː ‖ ʃɔːr/ n [C;U] 1 land along the edge of a sea, lake, etc. 2 **on shore** on land; away from one's ship

shore² v **shore up** phr vt support (something in danger of falling), esp. with wood

shorn /ʃɔːn ‖ ʃɔːrn/ past p. of SHEAR

short¹ /ʃɔːt ‖ ʃɔːrt/ adj 1 measuring a small or smaller than average amount in distance, length, or height 2 lasting only a little time, or less time than usual or expected 3 a shorter (and often more usual) way of saying: *The word 'pub' is short for 'public house'.* 4 not having or providing what is needed: *I'm short of money.* 5 rudely impatient 6 **little/nothing short of** fml nothing less than 7 **make short work of** deal with or defeat quickly 8 **short and sweet** short and direct in expression 9 **short of**: a not quite reaching b except for 10 **short on** without very much or enough (of): *He's a nice fellow but short on brains.*

short² adv 1 suddenly: *He stopped short.* 2 **fall short (of)** be less than (good) enough (for) 3 **go short (of)** be without enough (of)

4 **run short (of):** a not have enough left b become less than enough

short³ n 1 drink of strong alcohol, such as WHISKY 2 short film shown before the main film at a cinema 3 SHORT CIRCUIT 4 **for short** as a shorter way of saying it 5 **in short** all I mean is; to put it into as few words as possible —see also SHORTS

short·age /'ʃɔːtɪdʒ ‖ 'ʃɔːr-/ n [C;U] amount lacking; not enough

short·bread /'ʃɔːtbred ‖ 'ʃɔːrt-/ n [U] sweet buttery BISCUIT

short-change /,· '·/ vt 1 give back less than enough money to a buyer 2 fail to reward fairly

short cir·cuit /,· '·◄/ n faulty electrical connection where the current flows the wrong way and usu. puts the power supply out of operation **short-circuit** vi/t

short·com·ing /'ʃɔːt,kʌmɪŋ ‖ 'ʃɔːrt-/ n fault; failing

short cut /,· '·, '· ‖ '·· '·/ n quicker more direct way

short·en /'ʃɔːtn ‖ 'ʃɔːrtn/ vi/t make or become shorter

short·fall /'ʃɔːtfɔːl ‖ 'ʃɔːrtfɔːl/ n amount by which something fails to reach the expected total

short·hand /'ʃɔːthænd ‖ 'ʃɔːrt-/ n [U] system of special signs for fast writing

short-list /'· ·/ n BrE list of the best ones chosen from an original long list **short-list** vt BrE put on a short list

short-lived /,· '·◄/ adj lasting only a short time

short·ly /'ʃɔːtli ‖ 'ʃɔːrt-/ adv 1 soon 2 impatiently 3 in a few words

shorts /ʃɔːts ‖ ʃɔːrts/ n [P] 1 short trousers 2 esp. AmE short UNDERPANTS

short shrift /,ʃɔːt 'ʃrɪft ‖ ,ʃɔːrt-/ n [U] (unfairly) quick or unsympathetic treatment

short·sight·ed /,ʃɔːt'saɪtd◄ ‖ ,ʃɔːrt-/ adj 1 unable to see distant things clearly 2 not considering what may happen in the future ~**ly** adv ~**ness** n [U]

short-staffed /,· '·◄/ adj without enough workers or helpers

short-term, short term /,· '·◄/ adj, n (concerning) a short period of time; (in or for) the near future: *short-term planning*

short wave /,· '·◄/ n [U] radio broadcasting on waves of less than 60 metres

shot¹ /ʃɒt ‖ ʃɑːt/ v 1 *past t. and p. of* SHOOT 2 be/get shot of *sl* get rid of

shot² n 1 [C] (sound of) shooting a weapon 2 [C] hit, kick, etc. of a ball in sport 3 [C] person who shoots with the stated skill 4 [C] attempt: *I'll have a shot at it.* 5 [U] metal balls for shooting from shotguns or CANNONS 6 [C] a photograph b single part of a film made by one camera without interruption 7 [C] INJECTION: *a shot of penicillin* 8 [C] sending up of a spacecraft or ROCKET: *a moon shot* 9 [C] a small drink (esp. of WHISKY) all swallowed at once 10 **a shot in the arm** something which acts to bring back a better, more active condition 11 **a shot in the dark** a wild guess unsupported by arguments 12 **like a shot** quickly and eagerly —see also BIG SHOT

shot·gun /ˈʃɒtɡʌn ‖ ˈʃɑːt-/ n gun fired from the shoulder, usu. having two barrels, used esp. to kill birds

shot put /ˈ· ·/ n [U] sport of throwing a heavy metal ball as far as possible

should /ʃəd; *strong* ʃʊd/ v aux 1 a ought to b will probably 2 (used after **than** in certain expressions of feeling): *It's odd that you should mention him.* (=the fact that you have mentioned him is odd) 3 *fml* (used instead of **shall** in conditional sentences with **I** and **we** as the subject and a past tense verb): *I should be surprised if he came.* 4 (to express humour or surprise): *As I left the house, who should I meet but my old friend Sam.* 5 **I should** (when giving advice) you ought to: *I should go (if I were you).* 6 **I should have thought** esp. *BrE* (shows surprise): *I should have thought you'd know the answer.* 7 **I should like** *fml* I want 8 **I should think** I believe 9 **I should think so!/not!** of course!/of course not!

shoul·der /ˈʃəʊldə ‖ ˈʃoʊldər/ n 1 a the part of the body at each side of the neck where the arms are connected b part of a garment which covers this part of the body 2 part where something widens slopingly: *the shoulder of a bottle* 3 **head and shoulders above** very much better than 4 **put one's shoulder to the wheel** start work 5 **rub shoulders with** meet socially 6 **shoulder to shoulder: a** side by side b together: with the same intentions ♦ vt

accept (a heavy responsibility, duty, etc.)

shoulder blade /ˈ·· ·/ n either of two flat bones in the upper back

should·n't /ˈʃʊdnt/ v *short for:* should not

shout /ʃaʊt/ vi/t speak or say very loudly ♦ n loud cry or call

shout down *phr vt* prevent a speaker being heard by shouting

shout·ing /ˈʃaʊtɪŋ/ n 1 [U] shouts 2 **all over but the shouting** the important or interesting part (of a struggle, competition, etc.) has now been (successfully) completed and the result is no longer in doubt

shove /ʃʌv/ vi/t 1 push, esp. roughly or carelessly 2 *infml* move oneself: *Shove over and let me sit down.* ♦ n strong push

shov·el /ˈʃʌvəl/ n long-handled tool with a broad blade for lifting loose material ♦ vi/t -ll- *BrE* ‖ -l- *AmE* move or work (as if) with a shovel

show¹ /ʃəʊ ‖ ʃoʊ/ v showed, shown /ʃəʊn ‖ ʃoʊn/ 1 vt allow or cause to be seen: *Show me your ticket.* 2 vi be able to be seen: *The stain won't show.* 3 vt go with and guide or direct: *May I show you to your seat?* 4 vt explain, esp. by actions: *Show me how to do it.* 5 vt make clear; prove: *This piece of work shows what you can do when you try.* 6 vt cause to be felt in one's actions: *They showed their enemies no mercy.* 7 vi *sl for* SHOW up (2) 8 **it goes to show** it proves the point 9 **to show for** as a profit or reward from

show off *phr v* 1 vi *derog* behave so as to try to get attention and admiration 2 vt show proudly or to the best effect

show up *phr v* 1 vt make clear the (esp. unpleasant) truth about 2 vi arrive; be present

show² n 1 [C] performance, esp. in a theatre or on television or radio 2 [C] collection of things for the public to look at: *a flower show* 3 [S] showing of some quality; DISPLAY: *a show of temper* 4 [S] outward appearance: *a show of interest* 5 [U] splendid(-seeming) appearance or ceremony 6 [S] effort; act of trying: *They've put up a very good/poor show this year.* 7 **get this show on the road** *infml* start to work 8 **on show** being shown to the public —see also **steal the show** (STEAL) ~y adj (too) colourful, bright, attention-getting, etc.

show busi·ness /ˈ· ,··/ n [U] job of people

who work in television, films, the theatre, etc.

show·case /'ʃəʊkeɪs ‖ 'ʃoʊ-/ n a set of shelves enclosed in glass on which objects are placed for looking at in a shop, etc.: *a jewellery showcase* | (fig.) *The factory is a showcase for British industry.*

show·down /'ʃəʊdaʊn ‖ 'ʃoʊ-/ n settlement of a quarrel in an open direct way

show·er /'ʃaʊə ‖ -ər/ n 1 short-lasting fall of rain (or snow) 2 fall or sudden rush of many small things: *a shower of sparks* 3 (apparatus for) washing the body by standing under running water ♦ v 1 vi fall in showers 2 vt scatter or cover in showers 3 vi take a SHOWER (3) **~y** adj with showers of rain

show·ing /'ʃəʊɪŋ ‖ 'ʃoʊ-/ n 1 [S] performance: *a poor showing* 2 [C] act of putting on view

show jump·ing /'· ,··/ n [U] competition for riding horses over fences

show·man /'ʃəʊmən ‖ 'ʃoʊ-/ n **-men** /-mən/ 1 person whose business is producing public entertainments, etc. 2 person who is good at gaining public attention **~ship** n [U]

shown /ʃəʊn ‖ ʃoʊn/ *past p. of* SHOW

show-off /'· ·/ n person who SHOWS off (1)

show·piece /'ʃəʊpiːs ‖ 'ʃoʊ-/ n fine example fit to be admired

show·room /'ʃəʊrʊm, -ruːm ‖ 'ʃoʊ-/ n large shop where furniture, electrical goods, or cars are sold

shrank /ʃræŋk/ *past t. of* SHRINK

shrap·nel /'ʃræpnəl/ n [U] metal scattered from an exploding bomb

shred /ʃred/ n 1 small narrow piece torn or roughly cut off 2 slightest bit: *not a shred of evidence* ♦ vt **-dd-** cut or tear into shreds **~er** n

shrew /ʃruː/ n 1 very small mouselike animal 2 bad-tempered scolding woman **~ish** adj

shrewd /ʃruːd/ adj 1 showing good practical judgment 2 likely to be right: *a shrewd estimate* **~ly** adv

shriek /ʃriːk/ vi/t, n (cry out with) a wild high cry

shrift /ʃrɪft/ n —see SHORT SHRIFT

shrill /ʃrɪl/ adj (of a sound) high and (painfully) sharp **shrilly** /'ʃrɪl-li, 'ʃrɪli/ adv **~ness** n [U]

shrimp /ʃrɪmp/ n small ten-legged sea creature

shrine /ʃraɪn/ n 1 holy place, where one worships 2 box containing the remains of a holy person's body

shrink¹ /ʃrɪŋk/ v **shrank** /ʃræŋk/, **shrunk** /ʃrʌŋk/ 1 vi/t (cause to) become smaller 2 vi move back and away **~age** n [U] loss in size

shrink from phr vt avoid, esp. from fear

shrink² n infml PSYCHOANALYST or PSYCHIATRIST

shrinking vi·o·let /,·· '···/ n shy person

shrink-wrapped /'· ·/ adj in a tight plastic cover: *The book was shrink-wrapped.*

shriv·el /'ʃrɪvəl/ vi/t **-ll-** BrE‖ **-l-** AmE (cause to) become smaller by drying and twisting into small folds

shroud /ʃraʊd/ n 1 cloth for covering a dead body 2 something that covers and hides ♦ vt cover and hide

shrub /ʃrʌb/ n low bush

shrub·be·ry /'ʃrʌbəri/ n [C;U] mass or group of shrubs

shrug /ʃrʌg/ vi/t **-gg-** raise (one's shoulders), to express doubt or lack of interest ♦ n act of shrugging

shrug off phr vt treat as unimportant or easily dealt with

shrunk /ʃrʌŋk/ *past p. of* SHRINK

shrunk·en /'ʃrʌŋkən/ adj having been shrunk

shud·der /'ʃʌdə ‖ -ər/ vi shake uncontrollably for a moment ♦ n act of shuddering

shuf·fle /'ʃʌfəl/ v 1 vi/t mix up (playing cards) so as to produce a chance order 2 vi walk by dragging one's feet slowly along ♦ n 1 [C] act of shuffling cards 2 [S] slow dragging walk

shun /ʃʌn/ vt **-nn-** avoid with determination

shunt /ʃʌnt/ vt 1 esp. BrE move (a train) from one track to another 2 move around or away: *Smith has been shunted to a smaller office.*

shush /ʃʊʃ/ interj (used for demanding silence)

shut /ʃʌt/ v **shut**, pres. p. **-tt-** 1 vi/t close: *Shut the door.* 2 vt keep or hold by closing a door, window, etc.: *He shut himself in his room.* 3 vi/t stop operating: *The shops shut* *at 5.30.*

shut down *phr vi/t* (cause to) stop operation, esp. for a long time or forever
shutdown /'ʃʌtdaʊn/ *n*

shut off *phr vi/t* **1** stop in flow or operation, esp. by turning a handle or pressing a button **2** keep separate or away

shut up *phr v* **1** *vi/t* (cause to) stop talking **2** *vt* keep enclosed in **3 shut up shop** close a business at the end of a day or forever

shut·ter /'ʃʌtə‖-ər/ *n* **1** part of a camera which opens to let light fall on the film **2** movable cover for a window **3 put up the shutters** *infml* close a business at the end of the day or forever ♦ *vt* close (as if) with SHUTTERS (2)

shut·tle /'ʃʌtl/ *n* **1** (vehicle used on) a regular short journey: *a shuttle service between the town centre and the station* | *the London to Paris air shuttle* **2** reusable spacecraft **3** thread-carrier in weaving ♦ *vt* move by a SHUTTLE (1)

shut·tle·cock /'ʃʌtlkɒk‖-kɑːk/ *n* light feathered object struck in BADMINTON

shuttle di·plo·ma·cy /'·· ·,···/ *n* [U] international talks carried out by someone who travels between the countries concerned taking messages and suggesting answers to problems

shy¹ /ʃaɪ/ *adj* **1** nervous in the company of others **2** (of animals) unwilling to come near people **3 fight shy of** try to avoid **4 once bitten, twice shy** a person who has been tricked will be more careful in the future ~**ly** *adv* ~**ness** *n* [U]

shy² *vi* (esp. of a horse) make a sudden (frightened) movement

shy away from *phr vt* avoid something unpleasant

shys·ter /'ʃaɪstə‖-ər/ *n AmE infml* dishonest person, esp. a lawyer

Siamese twin /,saɪəmiːz 'twɪn/ *n* either of two people with their bodies joined from birth

sib·i·lant /'sɪbɪlənt/ *adj, n fml* (making or being) a sound like *s* or *sh*

sib·ling /'sɪblɪŋ/ *n* fml brother or sister

sic /sɪk/ *adv written* (used to show that a word used by someone else was used or spelled wrongly by them)

sick /sɪk/ *adj* **1** ill **2** throwing or about to throw food up out of the stomach: *The cat's*

been sick on the carpet. | *We felt sick as soon as the ship began to move.* **3** feeling annoyance, dislike, and loss of patience: *I'm sick of your complaints.* | *His hypocrisy makes me sick!* **4** unnaturally or unhealthily cruel: *a sick joke* **5 worried sick** very worried ~**ness** *n* **1** [C;U] illness **2** [U] feeling SICK (2)

sick·bay /'·/ *n* room in a school, etc. with beds for sick people

sick·en /'sɪkən/ *v* **1** *vt* cause to feel SICK (3) **2** *vi* become ill ~**ing** *adj* extremely displeasing or unpleasant

sick·le /'sɪkəl/ *n* small tool with a curved blade for cutting long grass

sick·ly /'sɪkli/ *adj* **1** weak and unhealthy **2** unhealthily pale **3** causing a sick feeling

side¹ /saɪd/ *n* **1** surface that is not the top, bottom, front, or back **2** edge; border: *A square has four sides.* **3** either of the two surfaces of a thin flat object **4** part in relation to a central line: *I live on the other side of town.* **5** place or area next to something: *On one side of the window was a mirror, and on the other a painting.* | *He never leaves his mother's side.* **6** part or quality to be considered: *Try to look at both sides of the question.* **7** (group holding) a position in a quarrel, war, etc.: *I'm on your side.* | *I never take sides.* (=support one side against the other) **8** sports team **9** part of a line of a family that is related to a particular person **10 get on the right/wrong side of someone** *infml* win/lose someone's favour **11 on the right/wrong side of** younger/older than (a stated age) **12 on the side** as a (sometimes dishonest) additional activity: *She does some teaching on the side.* **13 on the big/small/etc. side** rather; too big/small/etc. **14 on/to one side: a** out of consideration or use for the present **b** away from other people for a private talk **15 side by side** next to (one) another **16 -sided** having the stated number or kind of sides

side² *vi* support the stated SIDE¹ (7): *She sided with me.*

side·board /'saɪdbɔːd‖-bɔːrd/ *n* long table-like cupboard for dishes, glasses, etc.

side·boards /'saɪdbɔːdz‖-bɔːrdz/ *BrE* ‖ **side·burns** /'saɪdbɜːnz‖-bɜːrnz/ *AmE* —*n* [P] hair on the sides of a man's face

side·car /'saɪdkɑː‖-kɑːr/ *n* small

wheeled seat fastened to the side of a motorcycle

side dish /'· ·/ n separate dish served with the main food at a meal

side ef·fect /'· ·,·/ n effect in addition to the intended one

side is·sue /'· ,·/ n question or subject apart from the main one

side·kick /'saɪd,kɪk/ n infml a (less important) helper or companion

side·light /'saɪdlaɪt/ n small lamp at the side of a vehicle

side·line¹ /'saɪdlaɪn/ n 1 activity in addition to one's regular job 2 line marking the limit of a sports field

side·line² vt not include, esp. in a sports game

side·long /'saɪdlɒŋ ‖ -lɔːŋ/ adj directed sideways: a sidelong glance

side·show /'saɪdʃəʊ ‖ -ʃoʊ/ n separate small show at a fair or CIRCUS

side·step /'saɪdstep/ vi/t -pp- 1 step aside to avoid (esp. a blow) 2 avoid (an unwelcome question, problem, etc.)

side·track /'saɪdtræk/ vt cause to leave one subject or activity and follow another (less important) one

side·walk /'saɪdwɔːk ‖ -wɒːk/ n AmE for PAVEMENT

side·ways /'saɪdweɪz/ adv 1 with one side (not the back or front) forward or up 2 towards one side

sid·ing /'saɪdɪŋ/ n piece of railway track where carriages are parked

si·dle /'saɪdl/ v **sidle up** phr vi walk secretively or nervously up (to someone)

siege /siːdʒ/ n operation by an army surrounding a city, etc., to force the people inside to accept defeat

si·es·ta /si'estə/ n short sleep after the midday meal

sieve /sɪv/ n 1 tool with a net or holes for letting liquid or small objects through 2 **head/memory like a sieve** a mind that forgets quickly ♦ vt put through or separate with a sieve

sift /sɪft/ v 1 vt put (something non-liquid) through a sieve 2 vi/t examine (things in a mass or group) closely: sifting the evidence

sigh /saɪ/ vi let out a deep breath slowly and with a sound, usu. expressing sadness, satisfaction, or tiredness: (fig.) The wind sighed in the trees. (=made a sound like sighing) ♦ n act or sound of sighing

sight /saɪt/ n 1 [U] power of seeing 2 [S;U] the seeing of something: I caught sight of her (=noticed her) in the crowd. 3 [C] something seen 4 [U] range of what can be seen: The train came into sight. 5 [C] something worth seeing: the sights of London 6 [C] part of an instrument or weapon which guides the eye in aiming 7 [S] something which looks very bad or laughable 8 [S] infml a lot: She earns a sight more than I do. 9 **a sight for sore eyes** a person or thing that one is glad to see 10 **at first sight** at the first time of seeing or considering 11 **at/on sight** as soon as seen or shown 12 **in sight: a** in view **b** near 13 **know someone by sight** recognize someone without knowing them personally or without knowing their name 14 **set one's sights on** direct one's efforts (towards) —see also SECOND SIGHT ♦ vt see for the first time ~ed adj able to see ~ing n: case of someone or something being sighted: several sightings of rare birds ~less adj blind

sight·see·ing /'saɪt,siːɪŋ/ n [U] visiting places of interest -seer n

sign /saɪn/ n 1 mark which represents a known meaning: + is the plus sign. 2 movement of the body intended to express a meaning 3 notice giving information, a warning, etc. 4 something that shows the presence or coming of something else: There are signs that the economy may be improving. 5 also **star sign** — any of the 12 divisions of the year represented by groups of stars (Leo, Taurus, etc.) 6 **a sign of the times** something that is typical of the way things are just now ♦ vi/t 1 write (one's name) on (a written paper), esp. officially or to show that one is the writer 2 SIGNAL (1) 3 SIGN **up** ~er n

sign away phr vt give up (ownership, etc.) formally by signing a paper

sign on phr vi/t 1 (cause to) join a working force by signing a paper 2 state officially that one is unemployed

sign up phr vi/t (cause to) sign an agreement to take part in something or take a job

sig·nal /'sɪɡnəl/ n 1 sound or action which warns, commands, or gives a message: a *danger signal* **2** action which causes another to happen **3** apparatus by a railway track to direct train drivers ◆ message sent by radio or television waves ◆ *vi* -**ll**- *BrE* ‖ -**l**- *AmE* give a signal

signal box /'··· ·/ *n* small building near a railway from which signals and POINTS are controlled

sig·nal·man /'sɪɡnəlmən/ *n* -**men** /-mən/ someone who works railway signals

sig·na·to·ry /'sɪɡnətəri ‖ -tɔːri/ *n fml* signer of an agreement, esp. among nations

sig·na·ture /'sɪɡnətʃə ‖ -ər/ *n* person's name written by himself or herself —see also TIME SIGNATURE

signature tune /'··· ·/ *n* short piece of music used regularly to begin and end a particular radio or TV programme

sig·nif·i·cant /sɪɡ'nɪfɪkənt/ *adj* **1** of noticeable importance or effect **2** having a special meaning, indirectly expressed ~**ly** *adv* -**cance** *n* [S;U]

sig·ni·fy /'sɪɡnɪfaɪ/ *v fml* **1** *vt* mean **2** *vi/t* make known (esp. an opinion) by an action **3** *vi* matter

sign lan·guage /'· ,··/ *n* [U] language that uses hand movements, used by people who cannot hear

sign·post /'saɪnpəʊst ‖ -poʊst/ *n* sign showing directions and distances ◆ *vt esp. BrE* provide with signposts to guide the driver

Sikh /siːk/ *n* person whose religion is Sikhism ◆ *adj*

Sikh·ism /'siːkɪzəm/ *n* [U] Indian religion that developed from HINDUISM, whose followers believe that there is only one god

si·lage /'saɪlɪdʒ/ *n* [U] plants preserved as winter cattle food

si·lence /'saɪləns/ *n* **1** [C;U] (period of) absence of sound **2** [U] not speaking or making a noise **3** [U] failure to mention a particular thing ◆ *vt* cause or force to be silent **silencer** *n* apparatus for reducing noise

si·lent /'saɪlənt/ *adj* **1** free from noise **2** not speaking **3** failing or refusing to express an opinion, etc. **4** (of a letter) not pronounced ~**ly** *adv*

sil·hou·ette /ˌsɪluˈet/ *n* dark shape seen against a light background ◆ *vt* cause to appear as a silhouette

sil·i·con /'sɪlɪkən/ *n* [U] simple nonmetallic substance found commonly in natural compounds

silicon chip /ˌ··· '·/ *n* a CHIP¹ (4) in a computer or other ELECTRONIC machinery

si·li·cone /'sɪlɪkəʊn ‖ -koʊn/ *n* [U] strong substance made from SILICON, used to make RESIN (2), rubber (2) etc.: *silicone implants*

silk /sɪlk/ *n* [U] (smooth cloth from) fine thread produced by silkworms ~**en** *adj* **1** silky **2** made of silk ~**y** *adj* soft, smooth, and/or shiny

silk·worm /'sɪlkwɜːm ‖ -wɜːrm/ *n* CATER-PILLAR which produces silk

sill /sɪl/ *n* shelflike part at the bottom of a window

sil·ly /'sɪli/ *adj* not serious or sensible; foolish –**liness** *n* [U]

silly sea·son /'·· ,··/ *n* [*the*+S] *infml* period in the summer when there is not much news so newspapers print silly stories about unimportant things

si·lo /'saɪləʊ ‖ -loʊ/ *n* **1** round tower-like enclosure for storing SILAGE **2** underground MISSILE-firing base

silt /sɪlt/ *n* [U] loose mud brought by a river or current ◆ *v* **silt up** *phr vi/t* fill or become filled with silt

sil·ver /'sɪlvə ‖ -ər/ *n* **1** [U] soft whitish precious metal **2** [U] spoons, forks, dishes, etc. made of silver **3** [U] silver(-coloured) coins **4** [C] silver MEDAL ◆ *adj* **1** made of silver **2** of the colour of silver ~**y** *adj* **1** like silver in shine and colour **2** having a pleasant metallic sound

sil·ver·smith /'sɪlvəˌsmɪθ ‖ -ər-/ *n* maker of jewellery, etc. in silver

silver wed·ding /ˌ·· '··/ *n* the date that is exactly 25 years after the date of a wedding

sim·i·lar /'sɪmələ, 'sɪmɪlə ‖ -ər/ *adj* almost but not exactly the same; alike ~**ly** *adv* ~**ity** /ˌsɪmɪ'lærɪti/ *n* **1** [U] quality of being similar **2** [C] way in which things are similar

sim·i·le /'sɪmɪli/ *n* expression which describes one thing by comparing it with another (as in *as white as snow*)

sim·mer /'sɪmə ‖ -ər/ *vi/t* cook gently in (nearly) boiling liquid: (fig.) *simmering with anger/excitement*

sim·per /'sɪmpə ‖ -ər/ *vi* smile in a silly unnatural way

sim·ple /'sɪmpəl/ *adj* **1** without decoration; plain **2** easy **3** consisting of only one thing or part **4** (of something non-physical) pure: *the simple truth* **5** easily tricked; foolish –**ply** *adv* **1** in a simple way **2** just; only: *I simply don't know.* **3** really; absolutely: *a simply gorgeous day*

simple-mind·ed /ˌ·· '··◄/ *adj* **1** foolish **2** simple and unthinking in mind

sim·ple·ton /'sɪmpəltən/ *n* weak-minded trusting person

sim·plic·i·ty /sɪm'plɪs‹ti/ *n* [U] **1** quality of being simple **2** **simplicity itself** very easy

sim·pli·fy /'sɪmpl‹faɪ/ *vt* make simpler –**fication** /ˌsɪmpl‹f‹'keɪʃən/ *n* [C;U]

sim·plis·tic /sɪm'plɪstɪk/ *adj derog* treating difficult matters as if they were simple ~**ally** /-kli/ *adv*

sim·u·late /'sɪmj‹leɪt/ *vt* give the appearance or effect of –**lation** /ˌsɪmj‹-'leɪʃən/ *n* [U] –**ator** *n*

sim·ul·ta·ne·ous /ˌsɪməl'teɪniəs ‖ ˌsaɪ-/ *adj* happening or done at the same moment ~**ly** *adv*

sin /sɪn/ *n* [C;U] **1** offence against God or a religious law **2** *infml* something that should not be done: *He thinks it's a sin to stay in bed after 8 o'clock.* **3** **live in sin** *old-fashioned or humor* (of two unmarried people) live together as if married ♦ *vi* -**nn**- do wrong ~**ful** *adj* wicked ~**ner** *n*

since /sɪns/ *adv* **1** at a time between then and now: *She left in 1979, and I haven't seen her since.* **2** from then until now: *He came here two years ago and has lived here ever since.* **3** ago: *I've long since forgotten his name.* ♦ *prep* from (a point in past time) until now: *I haven't seen her since 1979.* ♦ *conj* **1 a** after the past time when: *I haven't seen her since she left.* **b** continuously from the time when: *We've been friends since we met at school.* **2** as: *Since you can't answer, I'll ask someone else.*

sin·cere /sɪn'sɪə ‖ -'sɪr/ *adj* free from deceit or falseness; honest and true ~**ly** *adv* –**cerity** /sɪn'ser‹ti/ *n* [U]

sin·ew /'sɪnjuː/ *n* [C;U] strong cord connecting a muscle to a bone ~**y** *adj*

sing /sɪŋ/ *v* **sang** /sæŋ/, **sung** /sʌŋ/ **1** *vi/t* produce (music, songs, etc.) with the voice **2** *vi* make or be filled with a ringing sound: *It made my ears sing.* ~**er** *n*

singe /sɪndʒ/ *vt* burn slightly

sin·gle¹ /'sɪŋgəl/ *adj* **1** being (the) only one: *a single sheet of paper* **2** considered by itself; separate: *He understands every single word I say.* **3** unmarried **4** for the use of only one person: *a single bed* **5** *BrE* (of a ticket) for a journey to a place but not back ♦ *n* **1** *BrE* a SINGLE¹ (5) ticket **2** record with only one short song on each side —see also SINGLES –**gly** *adv* one by one; not in a group

single² *v* **single out** *phr vt* choose from a group for special attention

single file /ˌ·· '·/ *adv, n* (in) a line of people, vehicles, etc. one behind another

single-hand·ed /ˌ·· '··◄/ *adj* without help from others

single-mind·ed /ˌ·· '··◄/ *adj* having one clear aim or purpose

single pa·rent /ˌ·· '··/ *n* parent who looks after her/his children alone

sin·gles /'sɪŋgəlz/ *n* **singles** *n* (tennis) match between two players

sing·song /'sɪŋsɒŋ ‖ -sɔːŋ/ *n* **1** [S] repeated rising and falling of the voice in speaking **2** [C] *BrE* informal gathering for singing songs

sin·gu·lar /'sɪŋgj‹lə ‖ -ər/ *adj* **1** (of a word) representing only one thing **2** *fml* unusually great ♦ *n* SINGULAR (1) word or form ~**ly** *adv fml* particularly

sin·is·ter /'sɪn‹stə ‖ -ər/ *adj* threatening or leading to evil

sink¹ /sɪŋk/ *v* **sank** /sæŋk/, **sunk** /sʌŋk/ **1** *vi/t* (cause to) go down below a surface, out of sight, or to the bottom (of water) **2** *vi* get smaller **3** *vi* fall from lack of strength: *He sank into a chair.* **4** *vi* lose confidence or hope: *My heart sank.* **5** *vt* make by digging: *sink a well* **6** *vt* put (money, labour, etc.) into

   sink in *phr vi* become fully and properly understood

sink² *n* large kitchen basin for washing pans, vegetables, etc.

sin·u·ous /'sɪnjuəs/ *adj* full of curves; winding ~**ly** *adv*

si·nus /'saɪnəs/ *n* any of the air-filled spaces in the bones including the nose

sip /sɪp/ *vi/t* -**pp**- drink with very small mouthfuls ♦ *n* very small amount drunk

si·phon /'saɪfən/ *n* **1** tube for removing liquid by natural pressure **2** bottle for holding and forcing out a gas-filled drink ♦ *vt* remove with a siphon: (fig:) *The new road will siphon off traffic from the town centre.*

sir /sə; *strong* sɜː ‖ sər; *strong* sɜːr/ *n*

1 (used respectfully when speaking to an older man or one of higher rank) **2** (used at the beginning of a formal letter): **Dear Sir, ... 3** (*cap.*) British rank of honour for a man

sire /saɪə‖ saɪr/ *n* **1** horse's male parent **2** *lit* (used when speaking to a king) ♦ *vt* (esp. of a horse) be the father of

si·ren /'saɪərən‖ 'saɪr-/ *n* **1** apparatus for making a loud long warning sound: *a police/air-raid siren* **2** dangerous beautiful woman

sir·loin /'sɜːlɔɪn‖ 'sɜːr-/ *n* [U] BEEF cut from the best part of the lower back

sis·sy ‖ also **cissy** *BrE* /'sɪsi/ *n* girlish or cowardly boy ♦ *adj* like a sissy

sis·ter /'sɪstə‖ -ər/ *n* **1** female relative with the same parents **2** *BrE* nurse in charge of a hospital WARD **3** female member of a religious group **4** female member of the same group (used esp. by supporters of the WOMEN'S MOVEMENT) ♦ *adj* belonging to the same group: *our sister organization* ~**hood** *n* **1** [U] being (like) sisters **2** [C] society of women leading a religious life ~**ly** *adj* like a sister

sister-in-law /'·· · ‚·/ *n* sisters-in-law sister of one's husband or wife; one's brother's wife

sit /sɪt/ *v* sat /sæt/, present p. -tt- **1** *vi* rest on a seat or on the ground with the upper body upright **2** *vi/t* (cause to) take a seat **3** *vi* (of an official body) have one or more meetings **4** *vt BrE* take (a written examination) **5** *vi* (take up a position to) be painted or photographed **6 be sitting pretty** be in a very good position **7 sit tight** keep in the same position; not move

  sit about/around *phr vt* do nothing, esp. while waiting or while others act

  sit back *phr vi* rest and take no active part

  sit down *phr vi* sit SIT (2)

  sit in *phr vi* take another's regular place, e.g. in a meeting

  sit in on *phr vi* attend without taking an active part

  sit on *phr vt* **1** be a member of (a committee, etc.) **2** delay taking action on

  sit up *phr v* **1** *vi/t* (cause or help to) rise to a sitting position from a lying one **2** *vi* sit properly upright in a chair **3** *vi* stay up late; not go to bed **4** *vi* show sudden interest, surprise, or fear: *Her speech really made*

them sit up (and take notice).

sit·com /'sɪtkɒm‖ -kɑːm/ *n* [C;U] situation comedy; amusing television or radio show that has the same characters every week in a different story

site /saɪt/ *n* place where a particular thing happened or is done ♦ *vt* put or esp. build in a particular position

sit-in /'· ·/ *n* method of expressing dissatisfaction and anger in which a group of people enter a public place, stop its usual services, and refuse to leave

sit·ter /'sɪtə‖ -ər/ *n* BABYSITTER

sit·ting /'sɪtɪŋ/ *n* **1** serving of a meal for a number of people at one time **2** act of having one's picture made **3** meeting of an official body

sitting duck /‚·· '·/ *n* person who is easy to attack or cheat

sitting room /'·· ·/ *n* esp. *BrE* for LIVING ROOM

sit·u·at·ed /'sɪtʃueɪtɪd/ *adj* **1** in the stated place or position **2** in the stated situation: *How are you situated for money?* (=have you got enough?)

sit·u·a·tion /‚sɪtʃu'eɪʃən/ *n* **1** set of conditions, facts, and/or events **2** *fml* position with regard to surroundings **3** *fml* job

six /sɪks/ *determiner, n, pron* **1** 6 **2 at sixes and sevens** in disorder ~**th** *determiner, adv, n, pron* 6th

six·teen /‚sɪk'stiːn◄/ *determiner, n, pron* 16 ~**th** *determiner, adv, n, pron* 16th

sixth sense /‚· '·/ *n* ability to know things without using any of the five ordinary senses

six·ty /'sɪksti/ *determiner, n, pron* 60 ~**tieth** *determiner, n, pron* 60th

size¹ /saɪz/ *n* **1** [C;U] (degree of) bigness or smallness **2** bigness: *A town of some size.* **3** [C] standard measurement: *These shoes are size 9.* **4** -**sized** of the stated size **5 cut someone down to size** show someone to be really less good, important, etc. **6 that's about the size of it** that's a fair statement of the matter

size² *v* **size up** *phr vt* form an opinion or judgment about

size·a·ble, **sizable**/'saɪzəbəl/ *adj* quite large

siz·zle /'sɪzəl/ *vi* make a sound like food cooking in hot fat

skate¹ /skeɪt/ n 1 blade fixed to a shoe for moving along on ice 2 ROLLER SKATE 3 **get/put one's skates on** infml move, act, or work quickly; hurry

skate² vi 1 move on skates 2 **(skate) on thin ice** infml (to be) doing something risky **skater** n

skate over/around phr vt avoid treating seriously

skate·board /'skeɪtbɔːd ‖ -bɔːrd/ n short board with two small wheels at each end for standing on and riding

skel·e·ton /'skelɪtən/ n 1 structure consisting of all the bones in the body 2 structure on which more is built or added 3 **skeleton in the cupboard** BrE ‖ AmE **closet** — a secret of which a person or family is ashamed ♦ adj enough simply to keep an operation going: a skeleton staff —**tal** adj

skeleton key /'··· ·/ n key that opens many different locks

skep·tic /'skeptɪk/ n AmE for SCEPTIC

sketch /sketʃ/ n 1 simple quickly made drawing 2 short description 3 short humorous scene ♦ vi/t draw a sketch (of) ~y adj not thorough or complete

skew /skjuː/ vt cause to be not straight or exact: DISTORT

skew·er /'skjuːə ‖ -ər/ n long pin put through meat for cooking

ski /skiː/ n skis long thin piece of wood, plastic, etc. fixed to boots for travelling on snow ♦ vi skied, present p. skiing travel on skis ~er n

skid /skɪd/ vi -dd- (of a vehicle or wheel) slip sideways out of control ♦ n act of skidding

skil·ful usu. skillful AmE /'skɪlfəl/ adj having or showing skill ~ly adv

skill /skɪl/ n [C;U] special ability to do something well ~ed adj having or needing skill: a skilled job

skim /skɪm/ v -mm- 1 vt remove from the surface of a liquid 2 vi/t read quickly to get the main ideas 3 vi/t (cause to) move quickly (nearly) touching (a surface)

skimmed milk /· ·ˈ·/ BrE ‖ **skim milk** AmE /'· ·/ n [U] milk that has had most of the fat removed

skimp /skɪmp/ vi/t spend, provide, or use less (of) than is needed ~y adj not enough

skin /skɪn/ n 1 [U] natural outer covering of the body 2 [C] skin of an animal for use as leather, etc. 3 [C] natural outer covering of some fruits and vegetables: banana skins 4 [C;U] the solid surface that forms over some liquids 5 **by the skin of one's teeth** only just 6 **get under someone's skin** annoy or excite someone deeply 7 **no skin off someone's nose** infml not something that upsets or causes disadvantage to someone 8 **save one's skin** save oneself, esp. in a cowardly way, from death, etc. 9 **skin and bone(s)** very thin ♦ vt -nn- remove the skin from ~ny adj very thin

skin-deep /ˌ· ˈ·◄/ adj on the surface only

skin-dive /'· ·/ vi swim underwater without heavy breathing apparatus **skin diver** n

skin·flint /'skɪnˌflɪnt/ n someone who dislikes giving or spending money

skin·head /'skɪnhed/ n (esp. in Britain) young person with very short hair, esp. one of a group who behaves violently

skin-tight /ˌ· ˈ·◄/ adj (of clothes) fitting tightly against the skin

skint /skɪnt/ adj BrE infml having no money

skip¹ /skɪp/ v -pp- 1 vi move in a light dancing way 2 vi/t leave out (something in order); not deal with (the next thing) 3 vi move in no fixed order 4 vi jump over a rope passed repeatedly beneath one's feet 5 vi/t leave hastily and secretly: The thieves have skipped the country. 6 vt fail to attend or take part in (an activity) ♦ n light quick stepping and jumping movement

skip² n BrE large metal container for carrying away unwanted things

skip·per /'skɪpə ‖ -ər/ n captain of a ship or sports team ♦ vt act as captain; lead

skir·mish /'skɜːmɪʃ ‖ -ɜːr-/ n short military fight, not as big as a battle

skirt¹ /skɜːt/ n woman's outer garment that hangs from the waist

skirt² vi/t 1 be or go round the outside (of) 2 avoid (a difficult subject)

skirting board /'·· ·/ n board fixed along the base of an inside wall

skit /skɪt/ n short acted scene making fun of something

skit·tish /'skɪtɪʃ/ adj (esp. of a horse) easily excited and frightened

skit·tle /'skɪtl/ n bottle-shaped object used in a game (**skittles**) where a player tries to knock down a set of them with a ball

skive /skaɪv/ *vi* also **skive off** *phr vi/t BrE infml* not go to school, work, etc. when one should be there **skiver** *n*

skulk /skʌlk/ *vi* hide or move about slowly and secretly, through fear or shame or for some evil purpose

skull /skʌl/ *n* head bone, enclosing the brain

skull·cap /'skʌlkæp/ *n* man's small hat, worn by followers of some religions

skunk /skʌŋk/ *n* **1** small N American animal which gives out a bad-smelling liquid when attacked **2** *infml* person who is bad, unfair, etc.

sky /skaɪ/ *n* **1** space above the Earth, where clouds and the sun, moon, and stars appear **2 the sky's the limit** there is no upper limit, esp. to the amount of money that can be spent

sky·div·ing /'skaɪˌdaɪvɪŋ/ *n* [U] sport of falling by PARACHUTE

sky-high /ˌ· '·◂/ *adj, adv* at or to a very high level

sky·jack /'skaɪdʒæk/ *vt* HIJACK (an aircraft)

sky·light /'skaɪlaɪt/ *n* window in a roof

sky·line /'skaɪlaɪn/ *n* shape or view of esp. city buildings against the sky

sky·rock·et /'skaɪˌrɒkət ‖ -ˌrɑː-/ *vi* increase suddenly and steeply

sky·scrap·er /'skaɪˌskreɪpə ‖ -ər/ *n* very tall city building

slab /slæb/ *n* thick flat usu. four-sided piece: *a stone slab*

slack /slæk/ *adj* **1** (of a rope, etc.) not pulled tight **2** not careful or quick **3** not firm; weak: *slack discipline* **4** not busy ♦ *n* **take up the slack** tighten a rope, etc. ♦ *vi* **1** be lazy **2** reduce in speed, effort, etc. make or become slack **~ness** *n* [U]

slacks *n* [P] informal trousers **~en** *vi/t*

slag¹ /slæg/ *n* **1** [U] waste material left when metal is separated from its rock **2** [C] *BrE sl* worthless or immoral woman

slag² *v* **-gg- slag off** *phr vt BrE sl* make extremely unfavourable remarks about

slain /sleɪn/ *past p. of* SLAY

slake /sleɪk/ *vt lit* satisfy (thirst) with a drink

sla·lom /'slɑːləm/ *n* SKI race down a very winding course

slam /slæm/ *v* **-mm-** **1** *vi/t* shut loudly and

forcefully **2** *vt* push or put hurriedly and forcefully: *She slammed on the brakes.* **3** *vt* attack with words ♦ *n* noise of a door being slammed —see also GRAND SLAM

slan·der /'slɑːndə ‖ 'slændər/ *n* [C;U] (act of) saying something false and damaging about someone ♦ *vt* harm by making a false statement **~ous** *adj*

slang /slæŋ/ *n* [U] very informal language that includes new and sometimes not polite words and meanings and is often used among particular groups of people, and not usu. in serious speech or writing

slanging match /'·· ˌ·/ *n* quarrel in which people are very rude to one another

slant /slɑːnt ‖ slænt/ *v* **1** *vi/t* (cause to) be at an angle **2** *vt usu. derog* express in a way favourable to a particular opinion ♦ *n* **1** [S] slanting direction or position **2** [C] particular way of looking at or expressing facts or a situation

slap /slæp/ *n* **1** hit with the flat hand **2 slap in the face** an action (seeming to be) aimed directly against someone else ♦ *vt* **-pp- 1** give a slap to **2** place quickly, roughly, or carelessly ♦ *adv* also **slap-bang** /ˌ· '·/ directly; right: *slap in the middle of lunch*

slap·dash /'slæpdæʃ/ *adj* careless

slap·stick /'slæpˌstɪk/ *n* [U] humorous acting with fast violent action and simple jokes

slap-up /'· ·/ *adj BrE* excellent and in large quantities: *a slap-up meal*

slash /slæʃ/ *v* **1** *vi/t* cut with long sweeping violent strokes: (fig.) *a slashing attack on the government* **2** *vt* reduce very greatly ♦ *n* **1** long sweeping cut or blow **2** straight cut making an opening in a garment

slat /slæt/ *n* thin narrow flat piece of wood, plastic, etc. **~ted** *adj*

slate¹ /sleɪt/ *n* **1** [U] dark grey easily splittable rock **2** [C] piece of this used in rows for covering roofs **3** [C] small board of this, used for writing on with chalk **4** [C] imaginary record of (mistakes of) the past: *a clean slate*

slate² *vt BrE* attack in words

slaugh·ter /'slɔːtə ‖ 'slɔːtər/ *vt* **1** kill (many people) cruelly or wrongly **2** kill (an animal) for food **3** *infml* defeat severely in a game ♦ *n* [U] slaughtering

slaugh·ter·house /'slɔːtəhaʊs ‖ 'slɔː-**

tər-/ *n* building where animals are killed for food

slave /sleɪv/ *n* 1 person who is owned by (and works for) another 2 person completely in the control of: *a slave to drink* ◆ *vi* work hard with little rest

slave driv·er /'·· ,··/ *n* person who makes you work very hard

slav·er /'slævə‖-ər/ *vi* 1 let SALIVA run out of the mouth 2 be unpleasantly eager or excited

slav·e·ry /'sleɪvəri/ *n* [U] 1 system of having slaves 2 condition of being a slave

slav·ish /'sleɪvɪʃ/ *adj* 1 showing complete obedience to and willingness to work for others 2 copied too exactly, without originality ~ly *adv*

slay /sleɪ/ *vt esp. lit* slew /sluː/, slain /sleɪn/ kill

sleaze /sliːz/ *n* [U] dishonest or immoral activities, esp. by politicians or JOURNALISTS

slea·zy /'sliːzi/ *adj* dirty, poor-looking, and suggesting immorality

sled /sled/ *vi, n* -dd- sledge

sledge /sledʒ/ *vi, n* (travel on) a vehicle for sliding along snow on two metal blades

sledge·ham·mer /'sledʒ,hæmə‖-ər/ *n* heavy long-handled hammer

sleek /sliːk/ *adj* 1 (of hair or fur) smooth and shining 2 stylish and without unnecessary decoration ~ly *adv*

sleep /sliːp/ *n* 1 [U] natural unconscious resting state 2 [S] act or period of sleeping 3 **get to sleep** succeed in sleeping 4 **go to sleep: a** begin to sleep **b** (of an arm, leg, etc.) become unable to feel, or feel PINS AND NEEDLES 5 **put to sleep** kill (a suffering animal) mercifully ◆ *vi* slept /slept/ 1 rest in sleep 2 provide beds or places for sleep (for a number of people): *The house sleeps six.* ~er *n* 1 sleeping person 2 *esp. BrE* heavy piece of wood, metal, etc. supporting a railway track 3 train with beds 4 *esp. AmE* book, play, record, etc. that has a delayed or unexpected success ~y *adj* 1 tired 2 inactive or slow-moving ~ily *adv*

 sleep around *phr vi derog* have sex with a lot of different people

 sleep in *phr vi* sleep late in the morning

 sleep off *phr vt* get rid of (a feeling or effect) by sleeping: *Sleep it off.* (=sleep until one is no longer drunk)

 sleep on *phr vt* delay deciding on (a matter) until next day

 sleep through *phr vt* fail to be woken by

 sleep together *phr vi* (of two people) have sex

 sleep with *phr vt* have sex with

sleeping bag /'·· ·/ *n* large cloth bag for sleeping in

sleeping car /'·· ·/ *n* railway carriage with beds for passengers

sleeping part·ner /,·· '··/ *n* business partner who does no active work in the business

sleeping pill /'·· ·/ *n* PILL which helps a person to sleep

sleeping sick·ness /'·· ,··/ *n* [U] serious African disease which causes great tiredness

sleep·less /'sliːpləs/ *adj* 1 not providing sleep: *a sleepless night* 2 unable to sleep ~ly *adv* ~ness *n* [U]

sleep·walk·er /'sliːp,wɔːkə‖-,wɔːkər/ *n* person who walks about while asleep sleepwalk *vi* -ing *n* [U]

sleet /sliːt/ *n* [U] partly frozen rain ◆ *vi* (of sleet) fall

sleeve /sliːv/ *n* 1 part of a garment for covering (part of) an arm 2 *esp. BrE* stiff envelope for keeping a record in 3 **have/keep something up one's sleeve** keep something secret for use at the right time in the future

sleigh /sleɪ/ *n* large (horse-drawn) SLEDGE

sleight of hand /,slaɪt əv 'hænd/ *n* [U] 1 skill and quickness of the hands in doing tricks 2 clever deception

slen·der /'slendə‖-ər/ *adj* 1 gracefully or pleasingly thin 2 small and hardly enough: *slender resources*

slept /slept/ *v past t. and p. of* SLEEP

sleuth /sluːθ/ *n* DETECTIVE

slew¹ /sluː/ *v past t. of* SLAY

slew² *vi/t* turn or swing violently

slice /slaɪs/ *n* 1 thin flat piece cut off: *a slice of bread* | (fig.) *a slice of the profits* 2 kitchen tool with a broad blade for serving food 3 **a slice of life** a representation of life as it really is ◆ *v* 1 *vt* cut into slices 2 *vi/t* hit (a ball) so that it moves away from a straight course

slick¹ /slɪk/ *adj* 1 smooth and slippery 2 skilful and effective, so as to seem easy 3 clever and able to persuade, but perhaps not honest ~ly *adv*

slick² *n* area of oil floating on esp. the sea

slick·er /ˈslɪkəl -ər/ *n* 1 *infml* a well-dressed, self-confident, but probably untrustworthy person: *a city slicker* 2 *AmE* coat made to keep out the rain

slide /slaɪd/ *v* slid /slɪd/ 1 *vi/t* go or send smoothly across a surface 2 *vi* move quietly and unnoticed 3 **let something slide** let a situation or condition continue, esp. getting worse, without taking action, usu. because of laziness *n* 1slipping movement 2 fall: *a slide in living standards* 3 apparatus for sliding down 4 piece of film through which light is passed to show a picture on a surface 5 small piece of thin glass to put an object on for seeing under a microscope

slide rule /ˈ··/ *n* ruler with a middle part that slides along, for calculating numbers

sliding scale /ˌ·· ˈ·/ *n* system of pay, taxes, etc. calculated by rates which may vary according to changing conditions

slight¹ /slaɪt/ *adj* 1 small in degree: *a slight improvement* 2 thin and delicate 3 **in the slightest** at all ~ly *adv* 1 a little: *slightly better* 2 in a SLIGHT (2) way: *He's very slightly built.*

slight² *vt* treat disrespectfully or rudely ♦ *n* INSULT

slim /slɪm/ *adj* -mm- 1 attractively thin 2 (of probability, hope, etc.) very small ♦ *vi* -mm- try to make oneself thinner ~ly *adv* ~mer *n*

slime /slaɪm/ *n* unpleasant thick sticky liquid **slimy** *adj* 1 unpleasantly slippery 2 *derog* trying to please in order to gain advantage for oneself

sling /slɪŋ/ *vt* slung /slʌŋ/ 1 throw roughly or with effort 2 hang 3 **sling one's hook** *BrE sl* go away 4 **sling mud** at say unfair and damaging things about (esp. a political opponent) ♦ *n* piece of cloth hanging from the neck to support a damaged arm

slink /slɪŋk/ *vi* slunk /slʌŋk/ move quietly and slowly, as if in fear or shame

slip¹ /slɪp/ *v* -pp- 1 *vi* slide out of place unexpectedly or by accident 2 *vi/t* move or put smoothly and unnoticed 3 *vi/t* put on or take off (a garment) quickly 4 *vi* get worse or lower: *slipping standards* 5 *vi* make a mistake 6 *vt* fail to be remembered by: *It slipped my mind.* (=I forgot) 7 give secretly:

I slipped the waiter some money. 8 **let slip: a** fail to take (a chance) **b** make known accidentally ♦ *n* 1 small mistake 2 woman's undergarment like a skirt or loose dress 3 young, slender person: *a slip of a girl* 4 SLIPWAY 5 **give someone the slip** escape from someone

slip² *n* small or narrow piece of paper

slip·page /ˈslɪpɪdʒ/ *n* [C;U] (amount of) slipping

slipped disc /ˌ· ˈ·/ *n* painful displacement of one of the connecting parts between the bones of the backbone

slip·per /ˈslɪpəl -ər/ *n* light soft shoe worn indoors

slip·per·y /ˈslɪpəri/ *adj* 1 very smooth or wet, so one cannot easily hold or move on it 2 not to be trusted 3 **a/the slippery slope** a course of action that cannot be stopped and leads to ruin

slip road /ˈ· ·/ *n BrE* road for driving onto or off a MOTORWAY

slip·shod /ˈslɪpʃɒd‖ -ʃɑːd/ *adj* carelessly done

slip·stream /ˈslɪpstriːm/ *n* 1 area of low air pressure behind a fast-moving vehicle 2 stream of air driven backwards by an aircraft engine

slip-up /ˈ· ·/ *n* usu. slight mistake

slip·way /ˈslɪpweɪ/ *n* sloping track for moving ships into or out of water

slit /slɪt/ *n* long narrow cut or opening ♦ *vt* slit; *present p.* -tt- make a slit in

slith·er /ˈslɪðəl -ər/ *vi* 1 move smoothly and twistingly 2 slide unsteadily

sliv·er /ˈslɪvəl -ər/ *n* small thin piece cut or broken off

slob /slɒbl slɑːb/ *n* rude, dirty, lazy, or carelessly dressed person

slob·ber /ˈslɒbəl -ər/ *vi infml* DRIBBLE (1) ~y *adj*

slog /slɒgl slɑːg/ *vi* -gg- *BrE* move or work with much effort ♦ *n* something needing much effort

slo·gan /ˈsləʊgənl ˈsloʊ-/ *n* short phrase expressing a political or advertising message

sloop /sluːp/ *n* small sailing ship

slop¹ /slɒpl slɑːp/ *vi/t* -pp- go or cause (a liquid) to go over the side of a container: *You're slopping paint everywhere!*

  slop about/around *phr vi infml* 1 move about in a lazy purposeless way

2 play in or move about in anything wet or dirty

slop² *n* [U] 1 [*usu.* P] food waste, esp. for feeding animals 2 *derog* tasteless liquid food

slope /sləʊp ‖ sloʊp/ *vi* lie neither completely upright nor completely flat ◆ *n* 1 piece of sloping ground 2 degree of sloping

slope off *phr vt BrE* go away secretly esp. to avoid work

slop·py /'slɒpi ‖ 'slɑːpi/ *adj* 1 (of clothes) loose, informal, and careless 2 not careful or thorough enough 3 silly in showing feelings –**pily** *adv* –**piness** *n* [U]

slosh /slɒʃ ‖ slɑːʃ/ *v* 1 *vi/t* move or cause (liquid) to move about roughly and noisily, making waves 2 *vt BrE infml* hit –**ed** *adj infml* drunk

slot /slɒt ‖ slɑːt/ *n* 1 long straight narrow hole 2 place or position in a list, system, organization, etc. ◆ *vi/t* -**tt**- 1 (be) put into a SLOT (1) 2 fit into a SLOT (2)

sloth /sləʊθ ‖ sloʊθ/ *n* 1 [U] *esp. lit* laziness 2 [C] slow-moving animal of S America ~**ful** *adj* lazy

slot ma·chine /'· ·,·/ *n* 1 *BrE* VENDING MACHINE 2 *AmE for* ONE-ARMED BANDIT

slouch /slaʊtʃ/ *vi* walk, stand, or sit in a tired-looking round-shouldered way ◆ *n* lazy, useless person: *She's no slouch when it comes to tennis.* (=she's very good)

slough /slʌf/ *v* **slough off** *phr vt* 1 (esp. of a snake) throw off (dead outer skin) 2 *esp. lit* get rid of as something worn out or unwanted

slov·en·ly /'slʌvənli/ *adj* 1 untidy 2 very carelessly done –**liness** *n* [U]

slow /sləʊ ‖ sloʊ/ *adj* 1 having less than a usual speed; not fast 2 taking a long time: *a slow job* 3 (of a clock) showing a time that is earlier than the right time 4 not quick in understanding 5 not active: *Business is slow.* ◆ *vi/t* make or become slower ◆ *adv* slowly: *slow-moving traffic* –**ly** *adv* ~**ness** *n* [U]

slow·coach /'sləʊkəʊtʃ ‖ 'sloʊkoʊtʃ/ *n BrE infml* slow-acting person

slow·down /'sləʊdaʊn ‖ 'sloʊ-/ *n* 1 lessening of speed or activity 2 *AmE for* GO-SLOW

slow mo·tion /,· '··/ *n* [U] movement (in a film, etc.) that is much slower than in

reality: *They showed it in slow motion.*

sludge /slʌdʒ/ *n* [U] thick soft mud

slug¹ /slʌg/ *n* small soft limbless creature, like a SNAIL with no shell

slug² *vt* -**gg**- *esp. AmE* hit hard

slug³ *n esp. AmE* 1 bullet 2 *infml* amount of strong alcoholic drink taken at one swallow

slug·gish /'slʌgɪʃ/ *adj* not very active or quick ~**ly** *adv* ~**ness** *n* [U]

sluice /sluːs/ *n* passage for controlling the flow of water ◆ *vt* wash with a large flow of water

slum /slʌm/ *n* city area of bad living conditions and old unrepaired buildings ◆ *vi* 1 amuse oneself by visiting a place on a much lower social level: *go slumming* 2 **slum it** live very cheaply ~**my** *adj*

slum·ber /'slʌmbə ‖ -ər/ *vi, n lit* sleep

slump /slʌmp/ *vi* 1 drop down suddenly and heavily 2 decrease suddenly ◆ *n* 1 sudden decrease, esp. in business 2 time of seriously bad business conditions and high unemployment

slung /slʌŋ/ *past t. and p. of* SLING

slunk /slʌŋk/ *past t. and p. of* SLINK

slur¹ /slɜː ‖ slɜːr/ *vt* -**rr**- pronounce unclearly

slur² *vt* -**rr**- make unfair damaging remarks about ◆ *n: a slur on my reputation*

slurp /slɜːp ‖ slɜːrp/ *vt* drink noisily **slurp** *n*

slush /slʌʃ/ *n* [U] 1 partly melted snow 2 books, films, etc. full of silly love stories ~**y** *adj*

slush fund /'· ·/ *n* money secretly kept for dishonest payments

slut /slʌt/ *n* 1 sexually immoral woman 2 untidy, lazy woman ~**tish** *adj*

sly /slaɪ/ *adj* 1 secretly deceitful or tricky 2 playfully unkind: *a sly joke* 3 **on the sly** secretly ~**ly** *adv* ~**ness** *n* [U]

smack¹ /smæk/ *vt* 1 hit with the flat hand 2 open and close (one's lips) noisily in eagerness to eat ◆ *n* blow with the open hand ◆ *adv* exactly; right: *smack in the middle*

smack² *v* **smack of** *phr vt* have a taste or suggestion of

small /smɔːl ‖ smɒːl/ *adj* 1 of less than usual size, amount, importance, etc. 2 young: *small children* 3 doing only a limited amount of business: *small* *shopkeepers* **4** slight: *small hope of success* **5 feel small** feel ashamed or humble ♦ *n* [*the*+S] narrow middle part (of the back) ~**ness** *n* [U]

small beer /ˈ· ˌ·/ *n* [U] *infml* person or thing of little importance

small for·tune /ˌ· ˈ··/ *n* [S] very large amount of money

small fry /ˈ· ·/ *n* young or unimportant person

small·hold·ing /ˈsmɔːlˌhəʊldɪŋ ‖ ˈsmɔːl-ˌhoʊ-/ *n BrE* small farm

small hours /ˈ· ·/ *n* [P] after midnight

small-mind·ed /ˌ· ˈ··◂/ *adj* having narrow or ungenerous views

small·pox /ˈsmɔːlpɒks ‖ ˈsmɔːlpɑːks/ *n* [U] serious infectious disease which leaves marks on the skin

small print /ˈ· ˌ·/ *n* [*the*+U] something that is purposely made difficult to understand or is easy not to notice, such as part of an agreement or CONTRACT

small screen /ˈ· ˌ·/ *n* [*the*+S] television

small talk /ˈ· ·/ *n* [U] light conversation on non-serious subjects

small-time /ˌ· ˈ·◂/ *adj* limited in activity, ability, profits, etc.

smarm·y /ˈsmɑːmi ‖ -ɑːr-/ *adj BrE* unpleasantly and falsely polite

smart[1] /smɑːt ‖ smɑːrt/ *adj* **1** quick or forceful: *a smart blow on the head* **2** *esp. BrE* neat and stylish **3** *esp. AmE* clever **4** fashionable ~**ly** *adv* ~**ness** *n* [U]

smart[2] *vi, n* (cause or feel) a stinging pain: (fig.) *She was still smarting over his unkind words.*

smart al·eck /ˈsmɑːt ˌælɪk ‖ -ɑːr-/ *n* annoying person who pretends to know everything

smart card /ˈ··/ *n* small plastic card used, e.g. as a key, bank card, or IDENTIFICATION

smart·en /ˈsmɑːtn ‖ -ɑːr-/ *v* **smarten up** *phr v/t* improve in appearance

smash /smæʃ/ *v* **1** *vi/t* break into pieces violently **2** *vi/t* go, drive, hit forcefully: *The car smashed into a lamppost.* **3** *vt* put an end to: *The police have smashed the drugs ring.* **4** *vt* hit (the ball) with a SMASH (2) ♦ *n* **1** (sound of) a violent breaking **2** hard downward, attacking shot, as in tennis **3** very successful new play, film, etc.: *a smash hit* **4** SMASH-UP ~**ing** *adj esp. BrE* very fine: wonderful

smash-up /ˈ· ·/ *n* serious road or railway accident

smat·ter·ing /ˈsmætərɪŋ/ *n* limited knowledge: *a smattering of German*

smear /smɪə ‖ smɪr/ *vt* **1** spread (a sticky or oily substance) untidily across (a surface) **2** make unproved charges against (someone) in order to produce unfavourable public opinion ♦ *n* **1** mark made by smearing **2** unfair unproved charge against someone: *a smear campaign*

smear test /ˈ· ·/ *n* medical test on material from inside the body, esp. for discovering CANCER

smell /smel/ *v* **smelled** *or* **smelt** /smelt/ **1** *vi* have or use the sense of the nose **2** *vt* notice, examine, etc. (as if) by this sense: *I think I smell gas!* | *I could smell trouble coming.* **3** *vi* have a particular smell: *The bread smells stale.* **4** *vi* have a bad smell **5 smell a rat** guess that something wrong or dishonest is happening ♦ *n* **1** [U] power of using the nose to discover the presence of gases in the air **2** [C] quality that has an effect on the nose: *a flower with a sweet smell* **3** [C] bad smell ~**y** *adj* bad-smelling

smelt /smelt/ *vt* melt (ORE) for removing the metal

smid·gin /ˈsmɪdʒɪn/ *n* [S] *infml* small amount

smile /smaɪl/ *n* pleased or amused expression in which the mouth is turned up at the ends ♦ *vi* make a smile **smilingly** *adv*

smirk /smɜːk ‖ smɜːrk/ *vi, n* (make) a silly self-satisfied smile

smite /smaɪt/ *vt* **smote** /sməʊt ‖ smoʊt/, **smitten** /ˈsmɪtn/ *lit* strike hard

smith /smɪθ/ *n* maker of metal things: *a silversmith*

smith·e·reens /ˌsmɪðəˈriːnz/ *n* **(in)to smithereens** into extremely small bits

smit·ten /ˈsmɪtn/ *v past p. of* SMITE ♦ *adj* suddenly in love

smock /smɒk ‖ smɑːk/ *n* long loose shirtlike garment

smog /smɒg ‖ smɑːg, smɔːg/ *n* [U] thick dark unpleasant mist in cities

smoke /sməʊk ‖ smoʊk/ *n* **1** [U] usu. white, grey, or black gas produced by burning **2** [S] act of smoking tobacco **3 go up in smoke** end or fail without results, esp. suddenly ♦ *v* **1** *vi/t* suck in smoke from (a cigarette, pipe, etc.) **2** *vi* give off smoke: *smoking chimneys* **3** *vt* preserve (fish, meat, etc.) with smoke **smoker** *n* person who smokes **smoky** *adj* **1** filled with smoke **2** tasting of or looking like smoke **smoking** *n* [U] practice or habit of smoking cigarettes, etc.

smoke out *phr vt* fill a place with smoke to force (a person, animal, etc.) to come out from hiding

smoke·screen /'sməʊkskriːn ‖ 'smoʊk-/ *n* **1** cloud of smoke produced to hide something **2** something that hides one's real intentions

smoke·stack /'sməʊkstæk ‖ 'smoʊk-/ *n* **1** tall chimney of a factory or ship **2** *AmE for* FUNNEL (2)

smol·der /'sməʊldə ‖ 'smoʊldər/ *v AmE for* SMOULDER

smooch /smuːtʃ/ *vi* kiss and hold lovingly

smooth[1] /smuːð/ *adj* **1** having an even surface; not rough **2** (of a liquid mixture) without lumps **3** even in movement, without sudden changes: *a smooth flight* **4** (too) pleasant or polite ~**ly** *adv* ~**ness** *n* [U]

smooth[2] *vt* make smooth(er)

smooth over *phr vt* make (difficulties) seem small or unimportant

smote /sməʊt ‖ smoʊt/ *v past t. of* SMITE

smoth·er /'smʌðə ‖ -ər/ *vt* **1** cover thickly or in large numbers: *a face smothered in/with spots* **2** die or kill from lack of air **3** keep from developing or happening: *smother a yawn*

smoul·der /'sməʊldə ‖ 'smoʊldər/ *vi* **1** burn slowly with (almost) no flame **2** have or be violent without showing feelings

smudge /smʌdʒ/ *n* dirty mark with unclear edges ♦ *vi/t* make or become dirty with a smudge

smug /smʌg/ *adj* -gg- too pleased with oneself ~**ly** *adv* ~**ness** *n* [U]

smug·gle /'smʌgəl/ *vt* take in or out secretly or illegally ~**gler** *n* –**gling** [U] taking goods to another country without paying the necessary tax

smut /smʌt/ *n* **1** [C] small piece of dirt **2** [U] morally offensive talk, stories, etc. ~**ty** *adj* rude

snack /snæk/ *n* amount of food smaller than a meal ♦ *vi AmE* eat a snack

snag /snæg/ *n* **1** hidden or unexpected difficulty **2** rough or sharp part of something that may catch and hold things passing it ♦ *vt* -gg- catch on a SNAG (2)

snail /sneɪl/ *n* small slow-moving soft-bodied limbless creature with a shell on its back

snake /sneɪk/ *n* **1** long thin limbless creature, often with a poisonous bite **2** deceitful person **3 a snake in the grass** a false friend ♦ *vi* move twistingly

snake charm·er /'· ,·/ *n* person who controls snakes by playing music

snap /snæp/ *v* -pp- **1** *vi/t* close the jaws quickly (on): *The dog snapped at my ankles.* **2** *vi/t* break suddenly and sharply **3** *vi/t* move with a sharp sound: *The lid snapped shut.* **4** *vi* speak quickly and angrily **5** *vt infml* to photograph **6 snap one's fingers** make a noise by moving the second finger quickly along the thumb **7 snap out of it** free oneself quickly from a bad state of mind **8 snap someone's head off** answer someone in a short rude way ♦ *n* **1** act or sound of snapping **2** informal photograph ♦ *adj* done without warning or long consideration: *snap judgments* ~**py** *adj* **1** stylish; fashionable **2** hasty; quick: *Make it snappy!* (=Hurry up!)

snap up *phr vt* take or buy quickly and eagerly

snap·shot /'snæpʃɒt ‖ -ʃɑːt/ *n* **1** a SNAP (2) **2** fixed idea of what something is like

snare /sneə ‖ sner/ *n* **1** trap for small animals **2** deceiving situation ♦ *vt* catch in a snare

snarl[1] /snɑːl ‖ snɑːrl/ *vi* **1** (of an animal) make a low angry sound **2** speak angrily ♦ *n* act or sound of snarling

snarl[2] *v* **snarl up** *phr vt* mix together so as to make movement difficult: *The traffic had got snarled up.* **snarl-up** /'· ·/ *n* confused state, esp. of traffic

snatch /snætʃ/ *vi/t* take (something) quickly and often violently or wrongingly ♦ *n* **1** act of snatching **2** short incomplete part: *overhearing snatches of conversation*

snaz·zy /'snæzi/ *adj infml* stylishly good-looking or attractive ~**zily** *adv*

sneak /sniːk/ *vi/t* snuck /snʌk/ *AmE* go or take quietly and secretly ♦ *n BrE derog sl* schoolchild who gives information about the wrongdoings of others ~**er** *n AmE for*

PLIMSOLL ~**ing** *adj* **1** secret: *a sneaking admiration* **2** not proved but probably right: *a sneaking suspicion* ~**y** *adj* acting or done secretly or deceitfully

sneak pre·view /ˌ· '·-/ *n* a chance to see something new, esp. a film, before anyone else has done so

sneer /snɪə ‖ snɪr/ *vi* express proud dislike and disrespect, esp. with an unpleasant curling smile ♦ *n* sneering look or remark

sneeze /sniːz/ *vi, n* (have) a sudden uncontrolled burst of air from the nose

snide /snaɪd/ *adj* indirectly but unpleasantly expressing a low opinion ~**ly** *adv*

sniff /snɪf/ *v* **1** *vi* breathe in loudly, esp. in short repeated actions **2** *vi/t* do this to discover a smell (in or on) **3** *vt* take (a harmful drug) through the nose ♦ *n* act or sound of sniffing ~**er** *n* ~**y** *infml* unfriendly or showing negative feelings

sniff at *phr vt* dislike or refuse proudly

sniff out *phr vt* discover or find out (as if) by smelling

snif·fle /'snɪfəl/ *vi* sniff a lot, esp. when crying or ill

snig·ger /'snɪgə ‖ -ər/ *vi* laugh quietly or secretly in a disrespectful way **snigger** *n*

snip /snɪp/ *vt* **-pp-** cut with quick short strokes, esp. with scissors ♦ *n* **1** act of snipping **2** *BrE* thing cheaply bought

snipe /snaɪp/ *vi* **1** shoot from a hidden position **2** make an unpleasant indirect attack in words **sniper** *n* person shooting from a hidden position

snip·pet /'snɪpɪt/ *n* small bit: *a snippet of information*

sniv·el /'snɪvəl/ *vi* **-ll-** *BrE* ‖ **-l-** *AmE* act or speak in a weak complaining crying way

snob /snɒb ‖ snɑːb/ *n* person who pays too much attention to social class, and dislikes people of a lower class ~**bery** *n* [U] behaviour of snobs ~**bish** *adj*

snog /snɒg ‖ snɑːg/ *vi* **-gg-** *BrE infml* hold and kiss each other for a long time

snook /snuːk ‖ snʊk, snuːk/ *n* —see **cock a snook** (COCK)

snoo·ker /'snuːkə ‖ 'snʊkər/ *n* [U] game in which a player hits balls into holes round a table ♦ *vt infml* defeat (someone, a plan, etc.)

snoop /snuːp/ *vi* search about or concern oneself with other people's affairs without permission ~**er** *n*

snoot·y /'snuːti/ *adj infml* proudly rude ~**ily** *adv* -**iness** *n* [U]

snooze /snuːz/ *vi, n* (have) a short sleep

snore /snɔː ‖ snɔːr/ *vi* breathe noisily while asleep ♦ *n* act or sound of snoring

snor·kel /'snɔːkəl ‖ -ɔːr-/ *n* breathing tube for underwater swimmers ♦ *vi* go snorkeling

snort /snɔːt ‖ snɔːrt/ **1** *vi* make a rough noise by forcing air down the nose, often in impatience or anger **2** *vt* SNIFF (3) ♦ *n* act or sound of snorting

snot /snɒt ‖ snɑːt/ *n* [U] *infml* thick liquid from the nose

snot·ty /'snɒti ‖ 'snɑː-/ *adj infml* **1** covered in SNOT **2** showing that one thinks one is better than other people

snout /snaʊt/ *n* animal's long nose: *a pig's snout*

snow¹ /snəʊ ‖ snoʊ/ *n* frozen rain that falls in white pieces (FLAKES) and often forms a soft covering on the ground ~**y** *adj*

snow² *vi* (of snow) fall

snow in/up *phr vt* prevent from travelling by a heavy fall of snow

snow under *phr vt* cause to have more of something than one can deal with: *snowed under with work*

snow·ball /'snəʊbɔːl ‖ 'snoʊbɔːl/ *n* ball of pressed snow, as thrown by children ♦ *vi* increase faster and faster

snow·board·ing /'snəʊbɔːdɪŋ ‖ 'snoʊbɔːr-/ *n* [U] sport of moving down snow-covered surfaces on a wide board (**snowboard**) -**der** *n*

snow·drift /'snəʊˌdrɪft ‖ 'snoʊ-/ *n* deep mass of snow piled up by the wind

snow·drop /'snəʊdrɒp ‖ 'snoʊdrɑːp/ *n* plant of early spring with a small white flower

snow·man /'snəʊmæn ‖ 'snoʊ-/ *n* -**men** /-men/ figure of a person made out of snow

snow·plough *BrE* ‖ -**plow** *AmE* /'snəʊplaʊ ‖ 'snoʊ-/ *n* apparatus or vehicle for clearing away snow

snow·storm /'snəʊstɔːm ‖ 'snoʊstɔːrm/ *n* very heavy fall of snow

Snr *BrE written abbrev. for:* SENIOR

snub¹ /snʌb/ *vt* **-bb-** treat (someone) rudely, esp. by paying no attention to them ♦ *n* act of snubbing

snub² *adj* (of a nose) short and flat

snuck /snʌk/ *AmE past t. and p. of* SNEAK

snuff¹ /snʌf/ *n* [U] powdery tobacco for breathing into the nose

snuff² *vt* put out (a candle) by pressing the burning part

snuff out *phr vt* put a sudden end to

snuf·fle /ˈsnʌfəl/ *vi* breathe noisily through the nose

snug /snʌg/ *adj* **-gg-** **1** giving warmth, comfort, protection, etc. **2** (of clothes) fitting closely and comfortably

snug·gle /ˈsnʌgəl/ *vi* settle into a warm comfortable position

so¹ /səʊ‖soʊ/ *adv* **1** to such a (great) degree: *It was so dark I couldn't see.* **2** (used instead of repeating something): *He hopes he'll win and I hope so too.* **3** also: *He hopes he'll win and so do I.* **4** very: *We're so glad you could come!* **5** in this way **6** yes; it is true: *'There's a fly in your soup.' 'So there is!'* **7** *fml* therefore **8 and so on/forth** and other things of that kind **9 or so** more or less: *It'll only cost 15p or so.* **10 so as to: a** in order to **b** in such a way as to **11 so long!** *infml* goodbye **12 so many/much: a** a certain number/amount: *a charge of so much a day* **b** an amount equal to: *These books are just so much waste paper!*

so² *conj* **1** with the result that: *It was dark, so I couldn't see.* **2** therefore: *He had a headache, so he went to bed.* **3** with the purpose (that): *I gave him an apple so (that) he wouldn't go hungry.* **4** (used at the beginning of a sentence) **a** (with weak meaning): *So here we are again.* **b** (to express discovery): *So that's how they did it!* **5 so what?** Why is that important?; Why should I care?

so³ *adj* **1** true: *Is that really so?* **2 just so** arranged exactly and tidily

soak /səʊk‖soʊk/ *vi/t* **1** (cause to) remain in liquid, becoming completely wet **2** (of liquid) enter (a solid) through the surface ♦ *n* [C;U] (act of) soaking **~ed** *adj* thoroughly wet, esp. from rain **~ing** *adv, adj* (wet) (wet)

soak up *phr vt* draw in (a liquid) through a surface: (fig.) *to soak up the sun* ‖ *to soak up information*

so-and-so /ˈ· · ·/ *n* **1** one not named **2** unpleasant or annoying person

soap /səʊp‖soʊp/ *n* **1** [U] usu. solid substance used with water for cleaning esp. the body **2** [C] *infml* SOAP OPERA —see also

SOFT SOAP **~y** *adj*

soap·box /ˈsəʊpbɒks‖ˈsoʊpbɑːks/ *n* **on one's soapbox** stating one's opinions loudly and forcefully

soap op·e·ra /ˈ· ‚···/ *n* continuing television or radio story about the daily life and troubles of the same set of characters

soar /sɔː‖sɔːr/ *vi* **1** (of a bird) fly high without moving the wings **2** rise steeply: *Prices soared.*

sob /sɒb‖sɑːb/ *vi* **-bb-** cry while making short bursts of sound breathing in ♦ *n* act or sound of sobbing

so·ber /ˈsəʊbə‖ˈsoʊbər/ *adj* **1** not drunk **2** *fml* thoughtful, serious, or solemn; not silly ♦ *vi/t* make or become SOBER (2): *a sobering thought* **~ly** *adv*

sober up *phr vi/t* make or become SOBER (1)

so·bri·e·ty /səˈbraɪəti/ *n fml* being sober

so·bri·quet /ˈsəʊbrɪkeɪ‖ˈsoʊ-/ *n fml for* NICKNAME

sob sto·ry /ˈ· ‚··/ *n* story intended to make the hearer or reader cry, feel pity, or feel sorry

so-called /ˌ· ˈ·◂/ *adj* (undeservedly but) commonly described in the stated way

soc·cer /ˈsɒkə‖ˈsɑːkər/ *n* [U] *BrE* game played with a round ball between two teams of 11 players; football *BrE*

so·cia·ble /ˈsəʊʃəbəl‖ˈsoʊ-/ *adj* fond of being with others; friendly **–bly** *adv* **–bility** /ˌsəʊʃəˈbɪləti‖ˌsoʊ-/ *n* [U]

so·cial /ˈsəʊʃəl‖ˈsoʊ-/ *adj* **1** of human society or its organization **2** living together by nature **3** based on rank in society: *social class* **4** for or spent in time or activities with friends (rather than work): *an active social life* ‖ *a social club* **~ly** *adv*

social climb·er /ˌ·· ˈ··/ *n derog* person who tries to get accepted into a higher social class

so·cial·is·m /ˈsəʊʃəl‚ɪzəm‖ˈsoʊ-/ *n* [U] political system aiming at establishing a society in which everyone is equal **–ist** *adj, n*

so·cia·lite /ˈsəʊʃəl‚aɪt‖ˈsoʊ-/ *n* person who goes to many fashionable parties

so·cial·ize also **-ise** *BrE* /ˈsəʊʃəl‚aɪz‖ˈsoʊ-/ *vi* spend time with others in a friendly way

social sci·ence /ˌ·· ˈ··‖ ‚·· ˌ··/ *n* [C;U] study of people in society, including

SOCIOLOGY, ECONOMICS, etc.

social se·cu·ri·ty /ˌ·· ·'···/ n [U] government money paid to the unemployed, old, sick, etc.

social serv·i·ces /ˌ·· '···/ n [P] esp. BrE (local) government services to help people, such as education, health care, etc.

social work /'·· ·/ n [U] work done to help the old, sick, unemployed, etc. **~er** n

so·ci·e·ty /sə'saɪəti/ n 1 [U] everyone considered as a whole: Society has a right to expect obedience to the law. 2 [C;U] group of people who share laws, organization, etc.: modern Western society 3 [C] organization of people with similar aims or interests: She joined the university film society. 4 [U] fashionable people 5 [U] fml being with other people —see also BUILDING SOCIETY **–tal** adj of society

so·ci·o·ec·o·nom·ic /ˌsəʊsiəʊekə-'nɒmɪk, ˌsəʊʃiəʊ-, -iːkə-‖ˌsoʊsiou-ekə'nɑːɪ-, ˌsoʊʃiou-, -iːkə-/ adj based on a combination of social and money conditions

so·ci·ol·o·gy /ˌsəʊsi'ɒlədʒi, ˌsəʊʃi-‖ ˌsoʊsi'ɑːlə-, ˌsoʊʃi-/ n [U] study of society and group behaviour **–ogical** /ˌsəʊsiə-'lɒdʒɪkəl, ˌsəʊʃiə-‖ ˌsoʊsiə'lɑː-, ˌsoʊʃi-/ adj **–ogist** /ˌsəʊsi'ɒlədʒɪst, ˌsəʊʃi-‖ ˌsoʊsi'ɑːl-, ˌsoʊʃi-/ n

sock¹ /sɒk‖saːk/ n 1 cloth covering for the foot 2 **pull one's socks up** BrE try to improve

sock² vt sl strike hard ♦ n forceful blow

sock·et /'sɒkɪt‖'saː-/ n hole into which something fits

sod¹ /sɒd‖saːd/ n [C;U] (piece of) earth with grass and roots growing in it

sod² n BrE sl person or thing that causes a lot of trouble and difficulty

so·da /'səʊdə‖'soʊ-/ n [U] 1 SODA WATER: a whisky and soda 2 sodium

soda foun·tain /'·· ˌ·/ n AmE place in a shop at which fruit drinks, ice cream, etc. are served

soda wa·ter /'·· ˌ·/ n gas-filled water esp. for mixing with other drinks

sod·den /'sɒdn‖'saːdn/ adj very wet

so·di·um /'səʊdiəm‖'soʊ-/ n [U] silver-white metal found naturally only in compounds

sod·o·my /'sɒdəmi‖'saː-/ n [U] fml or law any of various sexual acts, esp. ANAL sex between males

sod's law /ˌ· '·/ n [U] sl (often cap. S) natural tendency for things to go wrong

so·fa /'səʊfə‖'soʊ-/ n comfortable seat for two or three people

soft /sɒft‖sɔːft/ adj 1 not hard or stiff 2 smooth to the touch: soft skin 3 quiet 4 restful and pleasant: soft colours 5 with little force; gentle: a soft breeze 6 easy: a soft job 7 too kind 8 not in good physical condition 9 dealing with ideas not facts: one of the soft sciences like PSYCHOLOGY 10 not of the worst or most harmful kind: Cannabis is a soft drug. 11 (of a drink) containing no alcohol and usu. sweet and served cold 12 (in English pronunciation) **a** (of the letter c) having the sound /s/ and not /k/ **b** (of the letter g) having the sound /dʒ/ and not /g/ 13 (of water) free from minerals that stop soap forming LATHER easily 14 infml foolish: He's soft in the head. **~ly** adv **~ness** n [U]

soft-boiled /ˌ· '·◄/ adj (of an egg) boiled not long enough for the YOLK to become solid

soft drink /ˌ· '·◄/ n cold drink that does not contain alcohol

soft·en /'sɒfən‖'sɔː-/ vi/t (cause to) become soft(er) or more gentle **~er** n: a water softener

soften up phr vt break down opposition of (someone)

soft-heart·ed /ˌsɒft'hɑːtɪd◄‖ˌsɔːft-'hɑːr-/ adj easily made to act kindly or feel sorry for someone

soft op·tion /ˌ· '··/ n course of action which will give one less trouble

soft-ped·al /ˌ· '··‖ ˌ·, ·'·/ vt make (a subject, fact, etc.) seem unimportant

soft sell /ˌ· '·◄/ n [U] selling by gentle persuading

soft soap /ˌ· '·/ n [U] saying nice things about people, esp. as a means of persuading

soft-soap /'·· ·/ vt use soft soap on

soft spot /'· ·/ n fondness

soft touch /ˌ· '·/ n infml someone from whom it is easy to get what one wants because they are kind, easily deceived, etc.

soft·ware /'sɒftweə‖'sɔːftwer/ n [U] set of PROGRAMs that control a computer

soft·wood /'sɒftwʊd‖'sɔːft-/ n [U] cheap easily-cut wood from trees such as PINE and FIR

sog·gy /'sɒgi ‖ 'sɑːgi/ adj completely (and unpleasantly) wet -**giness** n [U]

soil¹ /sɔɪl/ n [U] top covering of the earth in which plants grow; ground

soil² vt fml make dirty

soi·ree /'swɑːreɪ ‖ swɑː'reɪ/ n evening party, often including an artistic performance

sol·ace /'sɒləs ‖ 'sɑː-/ n [C;U] (something that gives) comfort for someone full of grief or anxiety

so·lar /'səʊlə ‖ 'soʊlər/ adj of or from the sun

solar cell /'·· '·/ n apparatus for producing electric power from sunlight

so·lar·i·um /səʊ'leəriəm ‖ soʊ'ler-/ n -ia /-riə/ or -iums glass-walled room for sitting in the sunshine

solar pan·el /'·· '·/ n number of SOLAR CELLS working together

solar plex·us /ˌsəʊlə 'pleksəs ‖ ˌsoʊlər-/ n 1 system of nerves between the stomach and the BACKBONE 2 infml stomach

solar sys·tem /'·· ˌ·/ n sun and the PLANETs going round it

sold /səʊld ‖ soʊld/ past t. and p. of SELL

sol·der /'sɒldə, 'səʊl- ‖ 'sɑːdər/ n [U] easily meltable metal used for joining metal surfaces ♦ vt join with solder

sol·dier¹ /'səʊldʒə ‖ 'soʊldʒər/ n member of an army

soldier² v soldier on phr vi continue working steadily in spite of difficulties

sole¹ /səʊl ‖ soʊl/ n bottom surface of the foot or of a shoe

sole² n flat fish often used for food

sole³ adj 1 only 2 unshared: sole responsibility ~ly adv only

sol·emn /'sɒləm ‖ 'sɑː-/ adj 1 without humour or lightness; serious 2 (of a promise) made sincerely and meant to be kept 3 of the grandest most formal kind ~ly adv ~ness n [U] ~ity /sə'lemnɪti/ n 1 [U] solemnness 2 [C] formal act proper to a grand event

so·lic·it /sə'lɪsɪt/ v 1 vt fml ask for 2 vi esp. law advertise oneself as a PROSTITUTE

so·lic·i·tor /sə'lɪsɪtə ‖ -ər/ n (esp. in England) lawyer who advises people, prepares contracts, etc.

sol·id /'sɒlɪd ‖ 'sɑː-/ adj 1 not liquid or gas 2 not hollow 3 firm and well made 4 that may be depended on 5 in or showing complete agreement: The strike was 100 per cent solid. 6 not mixed with any other (metal): a watch of solid gold 7 infml continuous: waiting for four solid hours 8 having length, width, and height ♦ n solid object or substance ~ly adv -ity /sə'lɪdɪti/ n [U] quality or state of being solid

sol·i·dar·i·ty /ˌsɒlɪ'dærɪti ‖ ˌsɑː-/ n [U] loyalty within a group

so·lid·i·fy /sə'lɪdɪfaɪ/ vi/t (cause to) become solid or hard

solid-state /ˌ·· '·◂/ adj having electrical parts, esp. TRANSISTORS that run without heating or moving parts

so·lil·o·quy /sə'lɪləkwi/ n speech made by an actor alone on stage

sol·i·taire /ˌsɒlɪ'teə ‖ ˌsɑːlɪ'ter/ n 1 AmE for PATIENCE (2) 2 (piece of jewellery having) a single jewel, esp. a diamond

sol·i·ta·ry /'sɒlɪtəri ‖ 'sɑːlɪteri/ adj 1 (fond of being) alone 2 in a lonely place 3 single

sol·i·tude /'sɒlɪtjuːd ‖ 'sɑːlɪtuːd/ n [U] fml state of being alone

so·lo /'səʊləʊ ‖ 'soʊloʊ/ n solos something done by one person alone, esp. a piece of music for one performer ♦ adj, adv 1 without a companion or esp. instructor 2 as or being a musical solo ~ist n performer of a musical solo

sol·stice /'sɒlstɪs ‖ 'sɑːl-/ n time of the longest and shortest days of the year

sol·u·ble /'sɒljʊbəl ‖ 'sɑː-/ adj 1 that can be dissolved (DISSOLVE) 2 fml solvable -**bility** /ˌsɒljʊ'bɪlɪti ‖ ˌsɑː-/ n [U]

so·lu·tion /sə'luːʃən/ n 1 [C] answer to a problem or question 2 [C;U] liquid with a solid mixed into it

solve /sɒlv ‖ sɑːlv, sɒːlv/ vt find an answer to or explanation of **solvable** adj

sol·vent¹ /'sɒlvənt ‖ 'sɑːl-,'sɒːl-/ adj not in debt -**vency** n [U]

solvent² n [C;U] liquid that can turn solids into liquids

solvent a·buse /'·· ·,·/ n [U] illegal activity of breathing in dangerous gases from glue, AEROSOLS, etc.

som·bre BrE ‖ -**ber** AmE /'sɒmbə ‖ 'sɑːmbər/ adj sadly serious or dark ~ly adv ~ness n [U]

some /səm; strong sʌm/ determiner 1 a certain number or amount of: I bought some bread. | *Some people like tea, others prefer coffee.* **2** an unknown or unstated: *She went to work for some computer firm (or other).* **3** quite a large number or amount of: *The fire lasted for some time.* **4** *infml* no kind of: *Some friend you are!* **5** a fine or important: *That was some speech you made!* **6 some ... or (an)other** one or several which the speaker cannot or does not care to state exactly: *He's staying with some friend or other.* ♦ *pron* **1** an amount or number of the stated thing(s) **2** certain ones but not all ♦ *adv* **1** about (the stated number): *Some 50 people came.* **2** *AmE* rather; a little: *'Are you feeling better?' 'Some, I guess.'* **some more** an additional amount (of)

some·bod·y /ˈsʌmbɒdi, -bədi ‖ -bɑːdi/ *pron* someone ♦ *n* [U] a person of some importance: *He thinks he's really somebody.*

some·day /ˈsʌmdeɪ/ *adv* at an unknown time in the future: *Someday I'll be rich.*

some·how /ˈsʌmhaʊ/ *adv* **1** in some way not yet known or stated **2** for some reason: *Somehow I don't believe her.*

some·one /ˈsʌmwʌn/ *pron* **1** a person (but not a particular or known one) **2 or someone** or a person like that: *We need a builder or someone.*

some·place /ˈsʌmpleɪs/ *adv AmE* for SOMEWHERE

som·er·sault /ˈsʌməsɔːlt ‖ -ərsɔːlt/ *n* rolling jump in which the feet go over the head and then land on the ground **somersault** *vi*

some·thing /ˈsʌmθɪŋ/ *pron* **1** some unstated or unknown thing **2** better than nothing: *At least we've got the car, that's something.* **3 make something of oneself/one's life** be successful **4 or something** (to show that the speaker is not sure): *He's a director or something.* **5 something of a(n)** rather a(n); a fairly good **6 something like: a** rather like **b** *infml* about: *There were something like 1000 people there.* **7 something over/under** rather more/less than **8 something to do with** (having) a connection with

some·time /ˈsʌmtaɪm/ *adv* at some uncertain or unstated time ♦ *adj fml* former

some·times /ˈsʌmtaɪmz/ *adv* on some occasions but not all

some·what /ˈsʌmwɒt ‖ -wɑːt/ *adv* a little; rather

some·where /ˈsʌmweə ‖ -wer/ *adv* **1** (at or to) some place **2 get somewhere** begin to succeed

son /sʌn/ *n* **1** someone's male child **2** (used by an older man to a much younger man or boy): *What's your name, son?*

so·nar /ˈsəʊnɑː, -nə ‖ ˈsəʊnɑːr, -nər/ *n* apparatus for finding underwater objects with sound waves

so·na·ta /səˈnɑːtə/ *n* usu. three- or four-part piece of music for one or two instruments

song /sɒŋ ‖ sɒːŋ/ *n* **1** [C] short piece of music with words for singing **2** [U] act or art of singing **3** [C;U] music-like sound of birds **4 for a song** very cheaply

song and dance /ˌ· · ˈ·/ *n* [S;U] *infml* an unnecessary or unwelcome expression of excitement, anger, etc.

son·ic /ˈsɒnɪk ‖ ˈsɑː-/ *adj* of or concerning the speed of sound or sound

son-in-law /ˈ· · ˌ·/ *n* **sons-in-law** daughter's husband

son·net /ˈsɒnət ‖ ˈsɑː-/ *n* 14-line poem

son·ny /ˈsʌni/ *n* (used in speaking to a young boy)

son-of-a-bitch /ˌ· · · ˈ·/ *n* **sons-of-bitches, son-of-a-bitches** *taboo* someone strongly disliked

so·nor·ous /ˈsɒnərəs, səˈnɔːrəs ‖ səˈnɔːrəs, ˈsɑːnərəs/ *adj* having a pleasantly full loud sound **–ly** *adv* **–ity** /səˈnɒrəti ‖ səˈnɔː-/ *n* [U]

soon /suːn/ *adv* **1** within a short time **2** quickly; early: *How soon can you finish it?* **3** willingly: *I'd sooner stay here.* **4 as soon as** at once after; when **5 no sooner ... than** when ... at once: *No sooner had she arrived than it was time to go.* **6 sooner or later** certainly, although one cannot be sure when

soot /sʊt/ *n* [U] black powder produced by burning **~y** *adj* **~iness** *n* [U]

soothe /suːð/ *vt* **1** make less angry or excited **2** make less painful **soothingly** *adv*

sooth·say·er /ˈsuːθˌseɪə ‖ -ər/ *n lit* person who tells the future

sop¹ /sɒp ‖ sɑːp/ *n* something offered to gain someone's favour or stop them complaining

sop² *v* **-pp- sop up** *phr vt* take up (liquid) into something solid

soph·is·m /'sɒfɪzəm‖'saː-/ n fml 1 [U] SOPHISTRY 2 [C] correct-sounding but false argument

so·phis·ti·cat·ed /sə'fɪstɪ̣keɪtɪ̣d/ adj 1 experienced in and understanding the ways of society 2 highly developed and including the best or most modern systems –**ion** /sə,fɪstɪ̣'keɪʃən/ n [U]

soph·o·more /'sɒfəmɔː‖'saːfəmɔːr/ n student in the second year of a US college course

sop·o·rif·ic /,sɒpə'rɪfɪk◀‖,saː-/ adj causing sleep

sop·ping /'sɒpɪŋ‖'saː-/ adv, adj very (wet)

sop·py /'sɒpi‖'saːpi/ adj BrE 1 foolish 2 too full of expressions of tender feelings

so·pra·no /sə'prɑːnəʊ‖-'prænoʊ/ n -**nos** 1 (someone, esp. a woman, with) the highest human singing voice 2 instrument which plays notes in the highest range

sor·bet /'sɔːbɪ̣t, 'sɔːbeɪ‖'sɔːrbɪ̣t/ n [C;U] dish of ice with a usu. fruit taste

sor·cer·y /'sɔːsəri‖'sɔːr-/ n [U] doing of magic with the help of evil spirits **sorcerer**, **sorceress** fem. — n

sor·did /'sɔːdɪ̣d‖'sɔːr-/ adj 1 completely lacking fine or noble qualities; low 2 dirty and badly cared for ~**ly** adv ~**ness** n [U]

sore /sɔː‖sɔːr/ adj 1 painful, esp. from a wound or hard use 2 likely to cause offence: *Don't joke about his weight: it's a sore point with him.* 3 AmE angry ♦ n painful usu. infected place on the body ♦ adv lit sorely ~**ly** adv fml very much –**ness** n [U]

sor·row /'sɒrəʊ‖'saːroʊ, 'sɔː-/ n [C;U] sadness; grief ♦ vi grieve ~**ful** adj ~**fully** adv ~**fulness** n [U]

sor·ry /'sɒri‖'saːri, 'sɔːri/ adj 1 feeling sadness, pity, or sympathy 2 ashamed of or unhappy about an action and wishing one had not done it 3 causing pity mixed with disapproval: *You look a sorry sight.* ♦ interj 1 (used for excusing oneself or expressing polite refusal, disagreement, etc.) 2 (used for asking someone to repeat something one has not heard)

sort¹ /sɔːt‖sɔːrt/ n 1 group of people, things, etc. all sharing certain qualities; kind 2 person: *She's not such a bad sort.* 3 **of sorts** of a poor or doubtful kind 4 **out of sorts** feeling unwell or annoyed 5 **sort of** infml rather

sort² vi/t put (things) in order

   sort out phr vt 1 separate from a mass or group 2 BrE deal with

sor·tie /'sɔːti‖'sɔːrti/ n 1 short trip into an unfamiliar place 2 short attack by an army

SOS /,es əʊ 'es‖-oʊ-/ n urgent message for help

so-so /'· ·/ adj, adv neither very bad(ly) nor very good/well

souf·flé /'suːfleɪ‖suː'fleɪ/ n [C;U] light airy baked dish of eggs and flour

sought /sɔːt‖sɔːt/ past t. and p. of SEEK

sought-af·ter /'· ,··/ adj esp. BrE wanted because of rarity or high quality

soul /səʊl‖soʊl/ n 1 part of a person that is not the body and is thought not to die 2 person: *Not a soul* (=no one) *was there.* 3 perfect example: *Your secret is safe with him; he's the soul of discretion.* 4 most active part or influence: *She's the life and soul of any party.* 5 attractive quality of sincerity: *The performance lacks soul.* 6 SOUL MUSIC 7 **heart and soul** (with) all one's power and feeling 8 **keep body and soul together** have enough money, etc. to live ~**ful** adj expressing deep feeling ~**fully** adv ~**less** adj having no attractive or tender human qualities ~**ly** adv

soul-des·troy·ing /'· ·,··/ adj (esp. of a job) very uninteresting

soul mu·sic /'· ,··/ n [U] type of popular music usu. performed by black singers

soul-search·ing /'· ,··/ n deep examination of one's mind and conscience

sound¹ /saʊnd/ n 1 [C;U] what is or may be heard 2 [S] idea produced by something read or heard: *From the sound of it, I'd say the matter was serious.* ♦ v 1 vi seem when heard: *His explanation sounded suspicious.* 2 vi/t (cause to) make a sound: *Sound the trumpets.* 3 vt signal by making sounds: *Sound the alarm.* 4 vt pronounce 5 vt measure the depth of (water, etc.) using a weighted line

   sound off phr vi express an opinion freely and forcefully

   sound out phr vt try to find out the opinion or intention of

sound² adj 1 not damaged or diseased 2 showing good sense or judgment: *sound advice* 3 thorough 4 (of sleep) deep and untroubled 5 **as sound as a bell** in perfect condition ~**ly** adv ~**ness** n [U]

sound³ adv **sound asleep** deeply asleep

sound bar·ri·er /'·· ,···/ n point at which an aircraft, etc. reaches the speed of sound

sound·bite /'saundbaɪt/ n short (part of a) statement, included in a news report

sound ef·fects /'· ·,·/ n [P] sounds produced to give the effect of natural sounds in a radio or TV broadcast or film

sounding board /'·· ·/ n means used for testing thoughts, opinions, etc.

sound·ings /'saundɪŋz/ n [P] 1 measurements made by sounding (SOUND¹ (5)) water 2 carefully quiet or secret enquiries

sound·proof /'saundpruːf/ adj that sound cannot get through or into ♦ vt make soundproof

sound·track /'saundtræk/ n recorded music from a film

soup /suːp/ n [U] 1 liquid cooked food often containing pieces of meat or vegetables 2 **in the soup** in trouble

sour /sauə‖saur/ adj 1 acid-tasting: sour green apples 2 tasting bad because of chemical action by bacteria: sour milk 3 bad-tempered; unfriendly 4 **go/turn sour** go wrong ♦ vi/t (cause to) become sour ~**ly** adv ~**ness** n [U]

source /sɔːs‖sɔːrs/ n where something comes from; cause

sour grapes /,· '·/ n [U] pretending to dislike what one really desires, because it is unobtainable

sour·puss /'sauəpus‖-ər-/ n complaining humourless person

south /sauθ/ n (often cap.) 1 the direction which is on the right of a person facing the rising sun 2 [the+S] **a** a part of a country which is further south than the rest **b** the southeastern states of the US ♦ adj 1 in the south 2 (of wind) from the south ♦ adv towards the south ~**ward** adj, adv

south·east /,sauθ'iːst◄/ n, adj, adv (direction) halfway between south and east ~**ern** /-'iːstən‖-ərn/ adj

south·er·ly /'sʌðəli‖-ər-/ adj

south·ern /'sʌðən‖-ərn/ adj of the south part of the world or of a country ~**er** n (often cap.) person who lives in or comes from the southern part of a country

south·west /,sauθ'west◄/ n, adj, adv (direction) halfway between south and west ~**ern** /-'westən‖-ərn/ adj

sou·ve·nir /,suːvə'nɪə, 'suːvənɪə‖-nɪr/ n object kept as a reminder of an event, journey, place, etc.

sou'west·er /sau'westə‖-ər/ n hat of shiny material to keep off the rain, worn esp. by sailors

sove·reign /'sɒvrɪn‖'saː-/ n 1 fml king, queen, etc. 2 former British gold coin worth £1 ♦ adj (of a country) independent and self-governing ~**ty** n [U] 1 complete freedom and power to act or govern 2 quality of being a sovereign state

So·vi·et /'səuviət, 'sɒ-‖'sou-, 'saː-/ adj of the former USSR or its people

sow¹ /səu‖sou/ vi/t **sowed**, **sown** /səun‖soun/ or **sowed** plant (seeds) on (a piece of ground) ~**er** n

sow² /sau/ n female pig

soy·a bean /'sɔɪə biːn/ n bean of an Asian plant which produces oil and is made into a special dark liquid used in Chinese cooking

spa /spaː/ n place with a spring of mineral water where people come to be cured

space /speɪs/ n 1 [U] something measurable in length, width, or depth; room: There's not enough space in the cupboard for all my clothes. 2 [C;U] quantity or bit of this: looking for a parking space 3 [U] what is outside the Earth's air; where the stars and PLANETs are 4 [U] what surrounds all objects and continues outwards in all directions: staring into space 5 [C;U] period of time: within the space of a few years ♦ vt place apart; arrange with spaces between

space·craft /'speɪs-kraːft‖-kræft/ n vehicle able to travel in SPACE (3)

space sta·tion /'· ,··/ n large spacecraft intended to stay above the Earth and act as a base for scientific tests, etc.

space·suit /'speɪs-suːt, -sjuːt‖-suːt/ n special garment worn in SPACE (3), covering the whole body

spa·cious /'speɪʃəs/ adj having a lot of room: a spacious office ~**ness** n [U]

spade¹ /speɪd/ n 1 broad-bladed tool for digging 2 **call a spade a spade** speak the plain truth without being delicate or sensitive

spade² n playing card with one or more figures shaped like black printed leaves on it

spa·ghet·ti /spəˈɡeti/ n [U] stringlike PASTA

spam /spæm/ -mm- vi/t, n (send) an unfriendly E-MAIL message (to a lot of people)

span¹ /spæn/ past t. of SPIN

span² n 1 length between two limits, esp. of time: over a span of three years 2 length of time over which something continues: concentration span 3 (part of) a bridge, arch, etc. between supports 4 distance from the end of the thumb to the little finger in a spread hand ♦ vt -nn- 1 form an arch or bridge over 2 include in space or time

span·gle /ˈspæŋɡəl/ n small shiny piece sewn on for decoration ♦ vt decorate with spangles

Span·iard /ˈspænjəd‖-ərd/ n Spanish person

span·iel /ˈspænjəl/ n dog with long ears and long wavy hair

Span·ish /ˈspænɪʃ/ adj of Spain or its language

spank /spæŋk/ vt hit (esp. a child) with the open hand for punishment, esp. on the BUTTOCKS **spank** n

span·ner /ˈspænə‖-ər/ n BrE 1 metal tool with jaws or a hollow end, for twisting NUTS (2) 2 **a spanner in the works** a cause of confusion to a plan or operation

spar¹ /spɑː‖spɑːr/ vi -rr- 1 practise boxing (BOX²) 2 fight with words

spar² n pole supporting a ship's ropes or sails

spare /speə‖sper/ vt 1 give up (something that is not needed): We have no money to spare. (=we have only just enough) 2 keep from using, spending, etc.: No expense was spared. (=a lot of money was spent) 3 not give (something unpleasant): Spare me the gory details. 4 esp. lit not punish or harm 5 **spare a thought** stop and consider 6 **spare someone's blushes** infml avoid making someone feel awkward, esp. by praising them too much ♦ adj 1 kept for use if needed: a spare tyre 2 free: spare time 3 rather thin ♦ n BrE for SPARE PART

spare part /ˌ· ˈ·/ n machine part to take the place of one that is damaged

spare·ribs /ˈspeəˌrɪbz‖ˈsper-/ n [P] (dish of) pig's RIBS with their meat

spar·ing /ˈspeərɪŋ‖ˈsper-/ adj using only

a small amount of something: You've been a bit sparing with the salt. **-ly** adv

spark /spɑːk‖spɑːrk/ n 1 small bit of burning material flying through the air: (fig.) His murder was the spark that set off the war. 2 electric flash passing across a space 3 very small but important bit: not a spark of humour —see also BRIGHT SPARK ♦ vi 1 produce a spark 2 lead to (esp. something unpleasant) 3 esp. AmE encourage

spark off phr vt cause (esp. something violent or unpleasant)

spar·kle /ˈspɑːkəl‖ˈspɑːr-/ vi shine in small flashes: (fig.) Her conversation sparkled with wit. (=was bright and interesting) ♦ n [C;U] act or quality of sparkling **-kler** n type of small FIREWORK held in the hand **-kling** adj 1 full of life and brightness 2 (of wine) giving off gas in small BUBBLES

spark plug /ˈ· ·/ also **sparking plug** /ˈ·· ·/ BrE — n part inside an engine that makes a SPARK (2) to light the petrol and start the engine

spar·row /ˈspærəʊ‖-roʊ/ n very common small brownish bird

sparse /spɑːs‖spɑːrs/ adj scattered; not crowded **-ly** adv **~ness** n [U]

spar·tan /ˈspɑːtn‖-ɑːr-/ adj simple, severe, and without attention to comfort

spas·m /ˈspæzəm/ n 1 sudden uncontrolled tightening of muscles 2 sudden short period of uncontrolled activity: spasms of coughing

spas·mod·ic /spæzˈmɒdɪk‖-ˈmɑː-/ adj happening irregularly or non-continuously: spasmodic interest **~ally** /-kli/ adv

spat /spæt/ past t. and p. of SPIT

spate /speɪt/ n [S] esp. BrE large number or amount coming together at the same time

spa·tial /ˈspeɪʃəl/ adj fml of or in SPACE (1) **-ly** adv

spat·ter /ˈspætə‖-ər/ vi/t scatter (drops of liquid) or be scattered on (a surface)

spat·u·la /ˈspætjʊlə‖-tʃələ/ n (kitchen) tool with a wide flat blade for spreading, mixing, etc.

spawn /spɔːn‖spɑːn/ n [U] eggs of water animals like fishes and FROGS ♦ vi 1 produce spawn 2 produce esp. in large numbers

speak /spiːk/ *v* **spoke** /spəʊk ‖ spoʊk/, **spoken** /'spəʊkən ‖ 'spoʊ-/ **1** *vi* say things; talk **2** *vi* express thoughts, ideas, etc. in some other way than this: *Actions speak louder than words.* **3** *vt* say; express: *Is he speaking the truth?* **4** *vt* be able to talk in (a language) **5** *vi* make a speech **6** *vi* mean in the stated way what is said: *generally/ personally speaking, I agree* **7 on speaking terms** willing to talk and be polite to another **8 so to speak** as one might say **9 speak one's mind** express one's thoughts (too) directly **10 to speak of** worth mentioning ~**er** *n* **1** person making a speech **2** person who speaks a language **3** part of a radio, CD PLAYER, etc. where the sound comes out

    speak for *phr vt* express the thoughts, opinions, etc. of

    speak out *phr vi* speak boldly, freely, and plainly

    speak up *phr vi* **1** speak more loudly **2** SPEAK out

spear /spɪə ‖ spɪr/ *n* weapon consisting of a sharp-pointed pole ♦ *vt* push or throw a spear into

spear·head /'spɪəhed ‖ 'spɪr-/ *n* forceful beginner and/or leader of an attack or course of action ♦ *vt* lead forcefully

spec /spek/ *n* **on spec** *BrE* as a risk

spe·cial /'speʃəl/ *adj* **1** of a particular kind; not ordinary **2** particularly great or fine: *a special occasion* ♦ *n* **1** something not of the regular kind **2** *AmE infml* an advertised reduced price in a shop ~**ly** *adv* **1** for one particular purpose **2** unusually

special ef·fects /ˌ·· ·'·/ *n* [P] unusual parts in a film or television programme that appear real but are produced by computers, special photography, etc.

spe·cial·ist /'speʃəlɪst/ *n* person with skill or interest in a particular subject: *a heart specialist*

spe·ci·al·i·ty /ˌspeʃi'æləti/ usu. **spe·cia·l·ty** /'speʃəlti/ *AmE* — *n* **1** person's particular field of work or study **2** finest product

spe·cial·ize also **-ise** *BrE* /'speʃəlaɪz/ *vi* limit one's study, business, etc. to one particular area **-ization** /ˌspeʃəlaɪ'zeɪʃən ‖ -lə-/ *n* [C;U]

spe·cies /'spiːʃiːz/ *n* **-cies** group of similar types of animal or plant

spe·cif·ic /spə'sɪfɪk/ *adj* **1** detailed and exact: *specific instructions* **2** particular; fixed or named: *a specific tool for each job* ~**ally** /-kli/ *adv*

spe·ci·fi·ca·tion /ˌspesəfə'keɪʃən/ *n* **1** [C] detailed plan or set of descriptions or directions **2** [U] act of specifying

spe·ci·fy /'spesəfaɪ/ *vt* state exactly

spe·ci·men /'spesəmən/ *n* **1** single typical thing or example **2** piece or amount of something to be shown, tested, etc.: *The doctor needs a specimen of your blood.*

speck /spek/ *n* very small piece or spot: *a speck of dust*

speck·le /'spekəl/ *n* any of a number of small irregular marks **-led** *adj*

spec·ta·cle /'spektəkəl/ *n* **1** something unusual that one sees, esp. something grand and fine **2** object of laughing, disrespect, or pity **spectacles** *n* [P] GLASSES

spec·tac·u·lar /spek'tækjʊlə ‖ -ər/ *adj* unusually interesting and grand ♦ *n* spectacular entertainment ~**ly** *adv*

spec·ta·tor /spek'teɪtə ‖ 'spekteɪtər/ *n* person watching an event or show

spec·tre *BrE* ‖ **-ter** *AmE* /'spektə ‖ -ər/ *n fml or lit for* GHOST **-tral** *adj*

spec·trum /'spektrəm/ *n* **-tra** /-trə/ **1** set of bands of different colours into which light may be separated by a PRISM **2** broad and continuous range: *both ends of the political spectrum*

spec·u·late /'spekjʊleɪt/ *vi* **1** make guesses **2** buy things to sell later in the hope of profit **-lator** *n* **-lative** /-lətɪv/ *adj* **-lation** /ˌspekjʊ'leɪʃən/ *n* [C;U]

sped /sped/ *past t. and p. of* SPEED

speech /spiːtʃ/ *n* **1** [U] act, power, or way of speaking **2** [C] set of words spoken formally to a group of listeners —see also FREE SPEECH ~**less** *adj* unable to speak because of strong feeling, shock, etc.

speed /spiːd/ *n* **1** [C] rate of movement: *a speed of 2000 kilometres an hour* **2** [U] quickness of movement or action: *travelling at speed* (=fast) **3** [U] *sl for* AMPHETAMINE ♦ *v* **speeded** *or* **sped** /sped/ **1** *vi/t* go or take quickly **2** *vi* drive illegally fast ~**y** *adj* fast

    speed up *phr vi/t* (cause to) go faster

speed·om·e·ter /spɪ'dɒmətə, spiː- ‖ -'dɑːmətər/ *n* instrument showing how fast a vehicle is going

speed·way /'spiːdweɪ/ *n* [U] sport of

racing motorcycles on a closed track

spell¹ /spel/ v spelt /spelt/ esp. BrE ‖ spelled esp. AmE 1 vi form words (correctly) from letters 2 vt name in order the letters of (a word) 3 vt (of letters) form (a word): B-O-O-K spells 'book'. 4 vt have as an effect: His disapproval spells defeat for our plan. ~er n ~ing n way a word is spelt

spell out phr vt explain in the clearest possible way

spell² n 1 unbroken period of time: spells of sunshine 2 quickly passing attack of illness: a dizzy spell

spell³ n (words producing) a condition produced by magical power: (fig.) The first time we saw Venice, we fell under its spell.

spell·bound /'spelbaʊnd/ adj, adv extremely interested in what one is listening to

spend /spend/ vt spent /spent/ 1 pay (money) for goods or services 2 pass or use (time): He spent three years in prison. ~er n spent adj 1 already used; no longer for use 2 worn out

spend·thrift /'spend,θrɪft/ n person who wastes money

sperm /spɜːm ‖ spɜːrm/ n male sex cell which unites with the female egg to produce new life

spew /spjuː/ vi/t (cause to) come out in a rush or flood

sphere /sfɪə ‖ sfɪr/ n 1 ball-shaped mass 2 area or range of existence, meaning, action, etc.: this country's sphere of influence **spherical** /'sferɪkəl/ adj ball-shaped

sphinx /sfɪŋks/ n 1 ancient Egyptian image of a lion with a human head 2 person who behaves or speaks in a mysterious way

spice /spaɪs/ n 1 [C;U] vegetable product used for giving taste to food 2 [S;U] (additional) interest or excitement ♦ vt add spice to **spicy** adj containing (much) spice

spick-and-span /ˌspɪk ən 'spæn/ adj completely clean and tidy

spi·der /'spaɪdə ‖ -ər/ n small eight-legged creature, of which many types make WEBS to catch insects ~**y** adj long and thin like a spider's legs

spiel /ʃpiːl, spiːl/ n infml long explanation, often intended to persuade someone to do something

spike /spaɪk/ n 1 pointed piece, esp. of

metal 2 metal point fixed to the bottom of a (sports) shoe ♦ vt 1 drive a spike into 2 add a strong alcoholic drink to (a weak or non-alcoholic one) **spiky** adj

spill /spɪl/ vi/t spilt /spɪlt/ esp. BrE ‖ spilled esp. AmE 1 pour out accidentally and be lost: I've spilt some coffee on the carpet. | (fig.) The crowd spilt into the streets. 2 **spill the beans** infml tell a secret too soon or to the wrong person ♦ n act of spilling something, or the amount spilled ~**age** n spill

spin /spɪn/ v span /spæn/ or spun /spʌn/, spun; pres. p. -nn- 1 vi/t turn round and round fast 2 vi/t make (thread) by twisting (cotton, wool, etc.): (fig.) spin a yarn (=tell a story) 3 vt produce in threadlike form: a spider spinning a web ♦ n 1 [C] act of spinning 2 [S;U] fast turning movement 3 [C] short trip for pleasure 4 [S] a steep drop: The news sent prices into a spin. 5 infml [S;U] way of giving information, esp. to make a situation, political party, etc. seem good **spin** phr vt cause to last long enough or too long

spin·ach /'spɪnɪdʒ, -ɪtʃ ‖ -ɪtʃ/ n [U] vegetable with large soft leaves

spin·al cord /ˌ· '·/ n thick cord of important nerves enclosed in the SPINE (1)

spin·dle /'spɪndl/ n 1 machine part round which something turns 2 pointed rod onto which thread is twisted –**dly** adj long, thin, and weak-looking

spin doc·tor /'· ˌ·/ n infml person who gives information to the public in a way that makes a situation, political party, etc. seem good

spine /spaɪn/ n 1 row of bones down the centre of the back 2 prickly animal or plant part 3 side of a book along which the pages are fastened ~**less** adj weak and cowardly **spiny** adj prickly

spine-chil·ling /'· ˌ·/ adj very frightening

spinning wheel /'·· ·/ n machine for SPINning wool, etc.

spin-off /'· ·/ n (useful) indirect product of a process

spin·ster /'spɪnstə ‖ -ər/ n derog unmarried woman

spi·ral /'spaɪərəl ‖ 'spaɪr-/ n, adj 1 (curve) winding round and round a central line or away from a central point 2 process of continuous upward or downward change ♦ *vi* -ll- *BrE* ‖ -l- *AmE* move in a spiral

spire /spaɪə ‖ spaɪr/ *n* tall thin pointed roof of a church tower

spir·it /'spɪrɪt/ *n* 1 [C] person's mind or soul 2 [C] a being without a body, such as a GHOST 3 [U] quality of lively determination or brave effort: *a woman with spirit* | *team spirit* 4 [C] person of the stated kind of temper: *a free spirit* 5 [C] central quality or force: *the spirit of the law* (=its real intention) 6 [S;U] feeling in the mind towards something; ATTITUDE: *Please take my remarks in the spirit in which they were intended, and don't be offended.* 7 [C] strong alcoholic drink 8 **in spirit** in one's thoughts 9 **-spirited** having the stated feelings or spirits: *high-spirited* ♦ *vt* take secretly or mysteriously **spirits** *n* [P] state of one's mind: *in high spirits* (=cheerful) ~**ed** *adj* full of SPIRIT (3) ~**edly** *adv* ~**less** *adj* without SPIRIT (3) ~**lessness** *n* [U]

spir·i·tu·al /'spɪrɪtʃuəl/ *adj* 1 of the spirit rather than the body 2 religious ♦ *n* religious song originally sung by US blacks ~**ly** *adv*

spit[1] /spɪt/ *v* **spat** /spæt/, *pres. p.* **-tt-** 1 *vi/t* throw out (liquid or other contents) from the mouth with force 2 *vt* say with effort or anger 3 *vi* rain very lightly ♦ *n* [U] SALIVA

spit[2] *n* 1 thin rod on which meat is cooked over a fire 2 small usu. sandy point of land running out into a stretch of water

spit and pol·ish /ˌ· · '··/ *n* [U] great military attention to a clean and shiny appearance

spite /spaɪt/ *n* [U] 1 desire to annoy or harm 2 **in spite of** taking no notice of: *They continued, in spite of my warning.* ♦ *vt* annoy or harm intentionally ~**ful** *adj*

spitting im·age /ˌ·· '··/ *n* exact likeness

spit·tle /'spɪtl/ *n* [U] SALIVA

splash /splæʃ/ *v* 1 *vi/t* **a** (cause to) fall or move about in drops or waves, esp. wildly or noisily: *Rain splashed against the window.* **b** throw a liquid against (something): *He splashed his face with cold water.* 2 *vt* report as if very important, esp. in a newspaper 3 *vi/t* *BrE* spend freely: *I splashed out and bought a new dress.* ♦ *n* 1 (sound or mark made by) splashing 2 forceful effect: *make a splash in society*

splash down *phr vi* (esp. of a spacecraft) land in the sea **splashdown** /'splæʃdaʊn/ *n* [C;U]

splash·y /'splæʃi/ *adj esp. AmE* big, bright, and very noticeable

splat·ter /'splætə ‖ -ər/ *vi/t* (of a liquid) hit a surface and spread out over it

splay /spleɪ/ *vi/t* spread out or become larger at one end

spleen /spliːn/ *n* 1 organ that controls the quality of the body's blood supply 2 **vent one's spleen** express one's annoyance

splen·did /'splendɪd/ *adj* 1 grand in appearance or style 2 very fine; excellent ~**ly** *adv*

splen·dour *BrE* ‖ **-dor** *AmE* /'splendə ‖ -ər/ *n* [U] excellent or grand beauty

splice /splaɪs/ *vt* fasten end to end to make one continuous length

splint /splɪnt/ *n* flat piece for keeping a broken bone in place

splin·ter /'splɪntə ‖ -ər/ *n* small sharp piece, esp. of wood, broken off ♦ *vi/t* break into splinters

splinter group /'·· ˌ·/ *n* group of people that has separated from a larger body

split /splɪt/ *v* **split**; *pres. p.* **-tt-** 1 *vi/t* divide along a length, esp. by a blow or tear 2 *vi/t* divide into separate parts 3 *vt* share 4 *vi/t* separate into opposing groups or parties: *Did you two John and Mary had split up?* (=their marriage had ended) 5 **split hairs** concern oneself with small unimportant differences ♦ *n* 1 cut, break, or division made by splitting —see also SPLITS ~**ting** *adj* (of a headache) very bad

split per·son·al·i·ty /ˌ· ··'···/ *n* set of two very different ways of behaving, present in one person

splits /splɪts/ *n* [*the*+P] movement in which a person's legs are spread wide and touch the floor along their whole length

split sec·ond /ˌ· '··◂/ *n* very short moment

splurge /splɜːdʒ ‖ splɜːrdʒ/ *vi/t* spend more than one can usu. afford

splut·ter /'splʌtə ‖ -ər/ *vi* 1 talk quickly, as if confused 2 make a wet spitting (SPIT) noise **splutter** *n*

spoil /spɔɪl/ *v* **spoiled** *or* **spoilt** /spɔɪlt/ 1 *vt* destroy the value, worth, or pleasure of; ruin 2 *vt* treat very or too well: *Go on, spoil yourself, have another cake.* 3 *vi* decay **spoils** *n* [P] *fml or lit* things taken without payment

spoil for *phr vt* **1** be very eager to **2** cause to be unsatisfied with: *Fine French wine spoils you for cheaper kinds.* **3 be spoilt for choice** find it difficult to decide or choose

spoil·sport /'spɔɪlspɔːt ‖ -ɔːrt/ *n* person who ruins others' fun

spoke[1] /spəʊk ‖ spoʊk/ *v past t. of* SPEAK

spoke[2] *n* any of the bars connecting the outer ring of a wheel to the centre

spok·en /'spəʊkən ‖ 'spoʊ-/ *v past p. of* SPEAK

spoken for /'·· ·/ *adj infml* closely connected with a person of the opposite sex

spokes·per·son /'spəʊks,pɜːsən ‖ 'spoʊks,pɜːr-/ **spokes·man** /-mən/ *masc.*, **spokes·wom·an** /-,wʊmən/ *fem.* — *n* person chosen to speak officially for a group

sponge /spʌndʒ/ *n* **1** [C] simple sea creature with a rubber-like body **2** [C;U] piece of this or plastic like it, which can suck up water and is used for washing **3 throw in the sponge** accept defeat ♦ *v* **1** *vt* clean with a sponge **2** *vi derog* get things from people free by taking advantage of their generosity **sponger** *n* person who SPONGES (2) **spongy** *adj* not firm

sponge cake /'· ·/ *n* [U;C] light cake made from eggs, sugar, and flour

spon·sor /'spɒnsə ‖ 'spɑːnsər/ *n* **1** company or person giving money to help others to do something **2** person who takes responsibility for a person or thing ♦ *vt* act as a sponsor for: *a concert sponsored by American Express* ~**ship** *n* [U]

spon·ta·ne·ous /spɒn'teɪnɪəs ‖ spɑːn-/ *adj* happening naturally, without planning or another's suggestion ~**ly** *adv* **-taneity** /,spɒntə'niːɪti, -'neɪɪti ‖ ,spɑːn-/ *n* [U]

spoof /spuːf/ *n* funny untrue copy or description

spook /spuːk/ *vt esp. AmE* cause (esp. an animal) to be suddenly afraid ♦ *n infml for* GHOST

spook·y /'spuːki/ *adj* causing fear in a strange way **-ily** *adv*

spool /spuːl/ *n* wheel-like object onto which things are wound

spoon /spuːn/ *n* kitchen tool consisting of a small bowl with a handle, used esp. for eating —see also WOODEN SPOON ♦ *vt* take up

with a spoon

spoon-feed /'· ·/ *vt* **1** feed with a spoon **2** teach (people) in very easy lessons

spoon·ful /'spuːnfʊl/ *n* amount that a spoon can hold

spo·rad·ic /spə'rædɪk/ *adj* happening irregularly ~**ally** /-kli/ *adv*

spore /spɔː ‖ spɔːr/ *n* very small cell that acts like a seed: *a mushroom's spores*

sport /spɔːt ‖ spɔːrt/ *n* **1** [C;U] activity needing physical effort and skill and usu. done as a competition according to rules **2** [C] friendly or kind person ♦ *vt* wear or show publicly: *sporting a brand new coat* **sports** *n* [P] *BrE* ATHLETICS competition ~**ing** *adj* **1** fair and generous **2** (fond) of outdoor sports ~**y** *BrE infml* good at and/or fond of sport

sports car /'· ·/ *n* low fast car

sports·man /'spɔːtsmən ‖ 'spɔːr-/ **sports·wom·an** /-,wʊmən/ *fem.* — *n* **-men** /-mən/ person who plays sport(s) ~**ship** *n* [U] fairness to one's opponent, esp. in sport

spot /spɒt ‖ spɑːt/ *n* **1** usu. round part different from the main surface: *a blue dress with white spots* | *You've got ink spots on your trousers.* **2** small diseased mark on the skin **3** place: *a beautiful spot for a picnic* **4** small or limited part of something: *one of the brighter spots in the news* **5** *BrE* small amount: *a spot of bother* **6** *infml* difficult situation **7** SPOTLIGHT **8** place in a broadcast: *a guest spot on TV* **9 change one's spots** change one's qualities or way of life **10 knock spots off** be very much better than **11 on the spot: a** at once **b** at the place of the action **c** in a position of having to make the right action or answer: *The question really put me on the spot.* —see also BLACK SPOT, HIGH SPOT, SOFT SPOT ♦ *vt* **-tt-** **1** see; recognize **2** mark with spots **3** *AmE* allow as an advantage in a game ~**less** *adj* completely clean ~**ter** *n* person who looks for the stated thing: *a train spotter* ~**ty** *adj* **1** having spots on the face **2** *AmE* with some parts less good than others

spot check /,· '·‖'· ,·/ *n* examination of a few chosen by chance to represent all **spot-check** *vt*

spot·light /'spɒtlaɪt ‖ 'spɑːt-/ *n* **1** (light from) a large lamp with a directable beam **2** public attention ♦ *vt* direct attention to

spot on /,· '·/ *adj BrE* exactly right: *Your*

calculations were spot on.

spot·ted /'spɒtɪd‖'spɑ:-/ *adj* having a pattern of spots

spouse /spaʊs, spaʊz/ *n fml or law* husband or wife

spout /spaʊt/ *n* 1 opening from which liquid comes out: *the spout of a teapot* 2 forceful (rising) stream of liquid ◆ *v* 1 *vi/t* come or throw out in a forceful stream 2 *vt derog* pour out in a stream of words

sprain /spreɪn/ *vt* damage (a joint in the body) by sudden twisting **sprain** *n*

sprang /spræŋ/ *past t. of* SPRING

sprawl /sprɔ:l‖sprɒ:l/ *vi/t* spread out awkwardly or ungracefully ◆ *n* sprawling position or area

spray /spreɪ/ *vi/t* send or come out in a stream of small drops (onto) ◆ *n* 1 [U] water blown in very small drops 2 [C;U] liquid to be sprayed out from a container under pressure: *hair spray* (=to keep hair in place) 3 [C] small branch with its leaves and flowers

spread /spred/ *v* **spread** 1 *vi/t* (cause to) become longer, broader, wider, etc. 2 *vi/t* (cause to) have an effect or influence or become known over a wider area: *The fire/news soon spread.* 3 *vi* cover a large area or period 4 *vt* put over (a surface): *Spread butter on the bread.* ◆ *n* 1 [U] act or action of spreading 2 [U] soft food for spreading on bread: *cheese spread* 3 [C] large or grand meal —see also MIDDLE AGED SPREAD

spread-ea·gle /ˌ· '··‖'·· ˌ··/ *vt* put into a position with arms and legs spread wide

spread·sheet /'spredʃi:t/ *n* type of computer PROGRAM that shows and calculates financial information

spree /spri:/ *n* period of much wild fun, spending, drinking, etc.

sprig /sprɪg/ *n* small end of a stem with leaves

spright·ly /'spraɪtli/ *adj* cheerful and active –**liness** *n* [U]

spring¹ /sprɪŋ/ *v* **sprang** /spræŋ/, **sprung** /sprʌŋ/ 1 *vi* move quickly and suddenly as if by jumping: *The soldiers sprang to attention.* | (fig.) *The engine sprang into life.* 2 *vi/t* open or close with a SPRING (2): *The box sprang open.* (=opened suddenly) | *to spring a trap* 3 *vt* produce

(as) (a surprise): *She sprang the news on us.* 4 **spring a leak** (of a ship, container, etc.) begin to let liquid through a hole, etc.

spring from *phr vt* have as its origin

spring up *phr vi* come into existence suddenly

spring² *n* 1 [C;U] season between winter and summer 2 [C] length of wound metal that comes up again after being pressed down 3 [C] place where water comes naturally from the ground 4 [U] elastic quality 5 [C] act of springing –**y** *adj* elastic

spring·board /'sprɪŋbɔ:d‖-bɔ:rd/ *n* 1 bendable board off which people who DIVE jump 2 strong starting point

spring-clean /ˌ· '·◁/ *vi/t* clean (a house, etc.) thoroughly **spring-clean** /'· ·/*n*

sprin·kle /'sprɪŋkəl/ *vt* scatter (small drops or bits) on or over (a surface) –**kler** *n* apparatus for sprinkling drops of water

sprint /sprɪnt/ *vi* run very fast **sprint** *n* ~**er** *n*

sprout /spraʊt/ *vi/t* send or come out as new growth ◆ *n* 1 new growth on a plant 2 BRUSSELS SPROUT

spruce¹ /spru:s/ *adj* neat and clean ◆ **spruce up** *phr vt* make (esp. oneself) spruce

spruce² *n* tree of northern countries with short needle-shaped leaves

sprung /sprʌŋ/ *past p. of* SPRING

spry /spraɪ/ *adj* (esp. of older people) active

spud /spʌd/ *n infml* potato

spun /spʌn/ *past t. and p. of* SPIN

spur /spɜ:‖spɜ:r/ *n* 1 sharp object fitted to a rider's boot, used to make a horse go faster 2 event or influence leading to action 3 length of high ground coming out from a mountain range 4 **on the spur of the moment** without preparation or planning ◆ *vt* -**rr**- urge or encourage forcefully

spu·ri·ous /'spjʊəriəs‖'spjʊr-/ *adj* 1 based on incorrect reasoning or pretended; false ~**ly** *adv* ~**ness** *n* [U]

spurn /spɜ:n‖spɜ:rn/ *vt* refuse or send away with angry pride

spurt /spɜ:t‖spɜ:rt/ *vi/t* 1 make a SPURT (1) 2 (cause to) flow out suddenly or violently ◆ *n* 1 sudden short increase of effort or speed 2 spurting of liquid or gas

sput·ter /'spʌtə‖-ər/ *vi* make repeated soft explosive sounds

spu·tum /'spju:təm/ *n* [U] liquid coughed

up

spy /spaɪ/ n 1 person employed to find out secret information 2 person who watches secretly ♦ v 1 vi watch or search secretly 2 vt catch sight of

sq written abbrev. for: square

squab·ble /'skwɒbəl ‖ 'skwɑ:-/ vi, n (have) a quarrel about unimportant things

squad /skwɒd ‖ skwɑ:d/ n group of people working as a team —see also FLYING SQUAD

squad car /'· ·/ n police car

squad·ron /'skwɒdrən ‖ 'skwɑ:-/ n large group of soldiers with TANKS (2), of warships, or of aircraft in the airforce

squal·id /'skwɒlɪd ‖ 'skwɑ:-/ adj 1 very dirty and unpleasant 2 of low moral standards ~ly adv

squall /skwɔːl ‖ skwɒːl/ n sudden strong wind ~y adj

squal·or /'skwɒlə ‖ 'skwɑːlər/ n [U] SQUALID (1) conditions

squan·der /'skwɒndə ‖ 'skwɑːndər/ vt spend foolishly and wastefully

square¹ /skweə ‖ skwer/ n 1 shape with four straight equal sides forming four right angles 2 broad open area with buildings round it in a town 3 result of multiplying a number by itself ♦ adj 1 being a SQUARE (1) 2 of an area equal to a square with sides of the stated length: one square metre 3 forming (nearly) a right angle: a square jaw 4 fair; honest: a square deal 5 equal in points: The teams are all square. 6 having paid and settled what is owed

square² v 1 vt put into a square shape 2 vt divide into squares 3 vt multiply by itself: 2 squared is 4. 4 vi/t (cause to) fit a particular explanation or standard 5 vt cause (totals of points or games won) to be equal 6 vt pay or pay for 7 vt pay or settle dishonestly: There are government officers who will have to be squared. ♦ adv squarely ~ly adv directly: He looked her squarely in the eye.

square up phr vi settle a bill

square meal /ˌ· '·/ n infml good satisfying meal

square one /ˌ· '·/ n back to square one back to the situation in which one started

square root /ˌ· '·/ n number which when squared (SQUARE²) equals a particular number: 2 is the square root of 4.

squash /skwɒʃ ‖ skwɑː ʃ, skwɔːʃ/ v 1 vt flatten; crush 2 vi/t push or fit into a small space 3 vt force into silence or inactivity ♦ n 1 [S] act or sound of squashing 2 [U] game played in a four-walled court with RACKETS and a small ball 3 [U] BrE sweet fruit drink 4 [C;U] esp. AmE any of a group of vegetables with hard skins, including MARROWS and PUMPKINS ~y adj soft and easy to squash

squat /skwɒt ‖ skwɑːt/ vi -tt- 1 sit with the legs drawn up under the body 2 live in an empty building without permission ♦ adj ungracefully short or low and thick ~ter n person who SQUATS (2)

squawk /skwɔːk ‖ skwɒːk/ vi 1 (of a bird) make a loud rough cry 2 complain loudly squawk n

squeak /skwiːk/ vi, n (make) a short very high quiet sound —see also NARROW SQUEAK ~y adj: a squeaky door

squeal /skwiːl/ n a long very high cry ♦ vi 1 make a squeal 2 sl give secret information about one's criminal friends to the police ~er n

squeam·ish /'skwiːmɪʃ/ adj easily shocked or upset by unpleasant things ~ly adv ~ness n [U]

squeeze /skwiːz/ v 1 vt press firmly (together), esp. from opposite sides 2 vt get or force out (as if) by pressure: squeeze the juice from an orange 3 vi/t fit or go by crowding: She squeezed through the narrow opening. 4 vt cause many difficulties to: Higher lending rates are squeezing small businesses. ♦ n 1 act of squeezing 2 difficult situation caused by high costs or not enough supplies

squelch /skweltʃ/ vi, n (make) the sound of soft mud being pressed ~y adj

squib /skwɪb/ n small toy explosive —see also DAMP SQUIB

squid /skwɪd/ n squid or squids sea creature with ten arms at the end of its long body

squidg·y /'skwɪdʒi/ adj BrE infml pastelike; soft and wet

squig·gle /'skwɪɡəl/ n short wavy or twisting line

squint /skwɪnt/ vi 1 look with almost closed eyes 2 have a SQUINT (1) ♦ n 1 condition in which the eyes look in different directions 2 act of SQUINTing (1)

squire /skwaɪə ‖ skwaɪr/ n main

landowner in an English village or country area

squirm /skwɜːm ‖ skwɜːrm/ *vi* twist the body about, esp. from discomfort, shame, or nervousness

squir·rel /'skwɪrəl ‖ 'skwɜːrəl/ *n* small furry tree-climbing animal

squirt /skwɜːt ‖ skwɜːrt/ *vi/t, n* (force to be forced out in) a thin stream

Sr *written abbrev. for:* SENIOR

SS /'es es/ *abbrev. for:* STEAMSHIP

ssh /ʃ/ *interj* (used for asking for less noise)

St *written abbrev. for:* 1 Street 2 SAINT

stab /stæb/ *vi/t* -bb- strike forcefully (into) with a pointed weapon ♦ *n* 1 act of stabbing 2 try: *I'll have a stab at it.* 3 **a stab in the back** an attack from someone supposed to be a friend ~**bing** *adj* (of pain) sharp and sudden ~**bing** *n* [C;U]: *a big increase in the number of stabbings at football matches*

sta·ble¹ /'steɪbəl/ *adj* not easily moved, upset, or changed –**bilize**, –**bilise** *vi/t* –**bilizer**, –**biliser** *n* –**bility** /stə'bɪləti/ *n* [U]

stable² *n* 1 building where horses are kept 2 group of things with one owner ♦ *vt* keep in a stable

stac·ca·to /stə'kɑːtəʊ ‖ -toʊ/ *adj, adv* played, sung or said with very short notes or sounds

stack /stæk/ *n* 1 neat pile: *a stack of dishes* 2 large pile of dried grass stored outdoors 3 also **stacks** *pl.* — large amount ♦ *vt* make into a neat pile (on)

sta·di·um /'steɪdiəm/ *n* -**diums** *or* -**dia** /-diə/ large building containing a sports field and seats for SPECTATORS

staff /stɑːf ‖ stæf/ *n* 1 the workers in a place 2 long thick stick or pole ♦ *vt* provide workers for

stag /stæg/ *n* 1 fully grown male deer 2 for men only: *a stag night/party* 3 *BrE* person who buys shares in a new company hoping to sell them quickly at a profit

stage /steɪdʒ/ *n* 1 raised floor on which plays are performed: *He wants to go on the stage.* (=become an actor) 2 a centre of action or attention: *on the centre of the political stage* 3 state reached at a particular time in a course of events: *The project was cancelled at an early stage.* 4 part of a journey or long race 5 any of the

separate driving parts of a ROCKET ♦ *vt* 1 perform or arrange for public show 2 cause to happen, esp. for public effect

stage·coach /'steɪdʒkəʊtʃ ‖ -koʊtʃ/ *n* (in former times) horse-drawn carriage providing a regular passenger service

stage-man·age /'· ,··/ *vt* arrange for public effect, so that a desired result will happen as if naturally

stage man·ag·er /'· ,···/ *n* person in charge of a theatre stage

stage·struck /'steɪdʒstrʌk/ *adj* in love with the theatre and stage, wishing to be an actor

stage whis·per /,· '··/ *n* loud whisper intended to be heard by everyone

stag·ger /'stægə ‖ -ər/ *v* 1 *vi/t* walk unsteadily, almost falling 2 *vt* shock greatly 3 *vt* arrange so as to happen at different times ♦ *n* unsteady movement, as if about to fall

stag·ing post /'·· /*n* place where regular stops are made on long journeys

stag·nant /'stægnənt/ *adj* 1 (esp. of water) not flowing or moving, and often bad-smelling 2 not developing or growing –**nate** /stæg'neɪt ‖ 'stægneɪt/ *vi* become STAGNANT (2) –**nation** /stæg'neɪʃən/ *n* [U]

staid /steɪd/ *adj* serious and dull by habit ~**ness** *n* [U]

stain /steɪn/ *vi/t* discolour in a way that is hard to repair ♦ *n* 1 stained place or spot 2 mark of guilt or shame

stained glass /,· '·◄/ *n* [U] coloured glass for making patterns in windows

stain·less steel /,·· '·◄/ *n* [U] steel that does not RUST

stair /steə ‖ ster/ *n* step in a set of stairs **stairs** *n* [P] number of steps for going up or down, esp. indoors: *a flight of stairs*

stair·case /'steəkeɪs ‖ 'ster-/ *n* set of stairs with its supports and side parts

stake /steɪk/ *n* 1 pointed post for driving into the ground 2 share in something so that one is interested in whether it succeeds or fails 3 money risked on the result of something 4 post to which a person was tied for being killed, esp. by burning 5 **at stake** at risk ♦ *vt* 1 risk the loss of (something) on a result 2 **stake a claim** state that something should belong to one

stal·ac·tite /'stæləktaɪt ‖ stə'læktaɪt/ *n* sharp point of rock hanging from a cave roof

stal·ag·mite /'stæləgmaɪt ‖ stə'læg-maɪt/ n sharp point of rock standing on a cave floor

stale /steɪl/ adj 1 no longer fresh: stale bread/(fig.) news 2 no longer interesting or new ~**ness** n [U]

stale·mate /'steɪlmeɪt/ n 1 (in CHESS) position in which neither player can win 2 situation in which neither side in a quarrel can get an advantage

stalk¹ /stɔːk ‖ stɔːk/ n thin plant part with one or more leaves, fruits, or flowers on it

stalk² v 1 vt hunt by following closely and secretly 2 vi walk stiffly or proudly ~**er** n person who STALKS another person

stall¹ /stɔːl ‖ stɔːl/ n 1 BrE small open-fronted shop or other selling place in a market 2 indoor enclosure for an animal **stalls** n [P] BrE seats on the main level of a theatre or cinema

stall² vi/t 1 (cause to) stop because there is not enough speed or engine power 2 delay ♦ n act of stalling

stal·lion /'stæljən/ n male horse kept for breeding

stal·wart /'stɔːlwət ‖ -ərt/ adj, n strong and dependable (person)

sta·men /'steɪmən/ n male POLLEN-producing part of a flower

stam·i·na /'stæmɪnə/ n [U] strength to keep going

stam·mer /'stæmə ‖ -ər/ vi/t speak or say with pauses and repeated sounds ♦ n habit of stammering

stamp /stæmp/ v 1 vi/t put (the feet) down hard 2 vt mark by pressing: The title was stamped in gold on the book. | (fig.) His manners stamped him as a military man. 3 vt stick a stamp onto ♦ n 1 small piece of paper for sticking onto a letter, parcel, etc. to be posted 2 tool for pressing or printing onto a surface: a date-stamp 3 mark made by this: (fig.) a remark which bears the stamp of truth 4 act of stamping the foot

stamp out phr vt put an end to

stam·pede /stæm'piːd/ n 1 sudden rush of frightened animals 2 sudden mass movement ♦ vi/t (cause to) go in a stampede or unreasonable rush

stamping ground /'·· ·/ n a favourite very familiar place

stance /stɑːns ‖ stæns/ n 1 way of standing 2 way of thinking; ATTITUDE

stan·chion /'stɑːntʃən ‖ 'stæn-/ n strong upright supporting bar

stand¹ /stænd/ v stood /stʊd/ 1 vi support oneself on one's feet in an upright position 2 vi rise to a position of doing this: They stood (up) when he came in. 3 vi be in height: He stands 5 feet 10 inches. 4 vi/t (cause to) rest in a position, esp. upright or on a base: The clock stood on the shelf. 5 vi be in a particular state of affairs: How do things stand at the moment? 6 vi be in a position (to gain or lose): He stands to win a fortune if he comes top. 7 vt like; bear: I can't stand (=don't like) whisky. 8 vi remain true or in force: My offer still stands. 9 vt pay the cost of (something) for (someone else): He stood them a wonderful meal. 10 vi BrE compete for an office in an election: standing for Parliament 11 **know how/where one stands (with someone)** know how someone feels about one 12 **stand a chance/hope** have a chance/hope 13 **standing on one's head** with great ease: I could do the job standing on my head. 14 **stand on one's hands/head** support oneself on the hands/head and hands, with the feet in the air 15 **stand on one's own two feet** be able to do without help from others 16 **stand something on its head** change or upset violently 17 **stand to reason** be clear to all sensible people

stand by phr v 1 vt remain loyal to 2 vt keep (a promise, agreement, etc.) 3 vi be present or near 4 vi remain inactive when action is needed 5 vi wait in readiness

stand down phr vi 1 yield one's position or chance of election 2 leave the witness box in court

stand for phr vt 1 represent; mean: The B in his name stands for Brian. 2 have as a principle 3 accept without complaining

stand in phr vi take the place of the usual person for a time

stand out phr vi 1 have an easily seen shape, colour, etc. 2 be clearly the best

stand up phr vt 1 remain in good condition in spite of: Will it stand up to continuous use? 2 be accepted as true: The charges will never stand up in court. 3 fail to meet (someone, esp. of the opposite sex) as arranged

stand up for *phr vt* defend; support

stand² *n* **1** place for selling or showing things **2** piece of furniture for putting things on: *a hatstand* **3** open-fronted building for watchers at a sports ground **4** raised stage: *the judge's stand* **5** strong defensive effort **6** *AmE for* WITNESS BOX —see also ONE-NIGHT STAND

stan·dard /'stændəd‖-ərd/ *n* **1** level of quality that is considered proper or acceptable **2** something fixed as a rule for measuring weight, value, etc. **3** ceremonial flag ♦ *adj* of the usual kind; ordinary ~**ize**, **-ise** *vt* make all the same in accordance with a single STANDARD (2) **-ization**, **-isation** /ˌstændədəˈzeɪʃən‖-dərdə-/ *n* [U]

standard lamp /'·· ‖·/ *n BrE* lamp on a tall base which stands on the floor

standard of liv·ing /ˌ·· · '··/ *n* degree of wealth and comfort in everyday life that a person, country, etc. has

stand·by /'stændbaɪ/ *n* **1** one kept ready for use **2 on standby: a** ready for action **b** able to travel, esp. in a plane, only if there is a seat no one else wants

stand-in /'· ·/ *n* person who takes the place or job of someone else for a time

stand·ing /'stændɪŋ/ *n* [U] **1** rank, esp. based on experience or respect **2** continuance: *a friend of long standing* (=who has been a friend for a long time) ♦ *adj* continuing in use or force: *a standing invitation*

standing or·der /ˌ·· '··/ *n BrE* order to a bank to pay a fixed amount to someone at fixed periods

stand-off /'· ·/ *n* situation in which neither person or group in a fight, etc. can get an advantage, so neither does anything

stand-off·ish /ˌstænd'ɒfɪʃ‖-'ɔːfɪʃ/ *adj* rather unfriendly ~**ly** *adv* ~**ness** *n* [U]

stand·point /'stændpɔɪnt/ *n* POINT OF VIEW

stand·still /'stænd,stɪl/ *n* [S] condition of no movement; stop

stank /stæŋk/ *past t. of* STINK

stan·za /'stænzə/ *n* division of a poem

sta·ple¹ /'steɪpəl/ *n* piece of wire put through sheets of paper and bent to fasten them together ♦ *vt* fasten with staples **stapler** *n*

staple² *adj* **1** used all the time; usual; ordinary **2** main product: *a staple among British products*

star /stɑː‖stɑːr/ *n* **1** very large mass of burning gas in space, seen as a small bright spot in the night sky **2** figure with four or more points, used as a sign of something: *a five-star hotel* (=a very good hotel) **3** heavenly body regarded as determining one's fate: *born under an unlucky star* **4** famous performer: *a film star* **5 stars in one's eyes** an unthinking feeling that some wonderful thing is really possible **6 see stars** see flashes of light, esp. as a result of being hit on the head ♦ *v* -rr- **1** *vi/t* appear or have as a main performer: *a film starring Charlie Chaplin* **2** *vt* mark with STARS (2) ~**ry** *adj* filled with stars

star·board /'stɑːbəd‖'stɑːrbərd/ *n* [U] right side of a ship or aircraft

starch /stɑːtʃ‖stɑːrtʃ/ *n* [U] **1** white tasteless substance that is an important part of foods such as grain and potatoes **2** cloth-stiffening substance *vt* stiffen with STARCH (2) ~**y** *adj* **1** full of, or like, STARCH **2** stiffly correct and formal **-ily** *adv*

star·dom /'stɑːdəm‖'stɑːr-/ *n* [U] state of being a famous performer

stare /steə‖ster/ *vi* look for a long time with great attention ♦ *n* long steady look

star·fish /'stɑː,fɪʃ‖'stɑːr-/ *n* flat sea animal with five arms forming a star shape

stark /stɑːk‖stɑːrk/ *adj* **1** hard, bare, or severe in appearance **2** complete: *stark terror* ♦ *adv* completely: *stark naked* | *stark staring mad* (=completely mad)

star·let /'stɑːlɪt‖'stɑːr-/ *n* young actress hoping to become famous

star·ling /'stɑːlɪŋ‖'stɑːr-/ *n* common greenish-black European bird

starry-eyed /ˌ·· '·◄/ *adj* full of unreasonable hopes

stars and stripes /ˌ·· · '·/ *n* [the+S] the flag of the US

star-stud·ded /'· ˌ··/ *adj* filled with famous performers

start¹ /stɑːt‖stɑːrt/ *v* **1** *vi/t* begin **2** *vi/t* (cause to) come into existence: *How did the trouble start?* **3** *vi/t* (cause to) begin operation: *The car won't start.* **4** *vi* begin a journey **5** *vi* make a sudden sharp movement, esp. from surprise ~**er** *n* **1** person, etc. in a race or match at the start

2 person who gives the signal for a race to begin 3 instrument for starting a machine 4 first part of a meal 5 **for starters** first of all

start² n 1 [C] beginning of activity 2 [*the*+S] first part or moments 3 [C] place of starting 4 [C;U] amount by which one is ahead of another 5 [C] sudden sharp movement —see also FLYING START

start·le /'stɑːtl ‖ 'stɑːrtl/ vt give a sudden slight shock to

starve /stɑːv ‖ stɑːrv/ vi/t 1 (cause to) suffer from great hunger 2 (cause to) not have enough: *starved of affection/funds* **starvation** /stɑːˈveɪʃən ‖ stɑːr-/ n [U]

stash /stæʃ/ vt infml store secretly; hide ♦ **stash** n

state¹ /steɪt/ n 1 [C] particular way of being; condition: *the current state of our economy* 2 [C] infml esp. BrE a very nervous, anxious condition: *Don't get in(to) such a state.* 3 [C;U] government or political organization of a country: *industry controlled by the state | state secrets* 4 [C] nation; country 5 [C] self-governing area within a nation: *the states of the US* 6 [U] official grandness and ceremony ~**less** adj belonging to no country ~**lessness** n [U] ~**ly** adj 1 formal; ceremonious 2 grand in style or size ~**liness** n [U]

state² vt say or mention, esp. formally or in advance

State De·part·ment /'· ·,··/ n [*the*] the American government department which deals with foreign affairs

state·ly home /,·· '·/ n large country house of historical interest, esp. one which people pay to visit

state·ment /'steɪtmənt/ n 1 (formal) written or spoken declaration 2 list showing money paid, received, etc.

state-of-the-art /,· · · '·◂/ adj using the most modern methods or materials

state·room /'steɪtrʊm, -ruːm/ n passenger's private room on a ship

States /steɪts/ [*the*] infml the US

state school /'· ,·/ n BrE school paid for by the government

states·man /'steɪtsmən/ n -men /-mən/ respected political or government leader —see also ELDER STATESMAN ~**ship** n [U]

stat·ic /'stætɪk/ adj 1 not moving or changing 2 of or being electricity that

collects on the surface of objects ♦ n [U] electrical noise spoiling radio or television signals

sta·tion /'steɪʃən/ n 1 **a** (building at) a place where the stated public vehicles regularly stop: *a bus station* **b** esp. BrE place like this where trains regularly stop 2 building for the stated service or activity: *a polling station* (=where people vote) 3 broadcasting company or apparatus 4 one's position in life; social rank: *She married beneath her station.* —see also SPACE STATION ♦ vt put (esp. a person) into a certain place for esp. military duty

sta·tion·a·ry /'steɪʃənəri ‖ -neri/ adj not moving

sta·tion·er /'steɪʃənə ‖ -ər/ n seller of stationery

sta·tion·er·y /'steɪʃənəri ‖ -neri/ n [U] paper, pens, pencils, envelopes, etc.

sta·tion·mas·ter /'steɪʃən,mɑːstə ‖ -,mæstər/ n person in charge of a railway station

sta·tis·tics /stəˈtɪstɪks/ n 1 [P] numbers which represent facts or measurements 2 [U] science that deals with and explains these —**tical** adj —**tically** /-kli/ adv **statistician** /,stætɪˈstɪʃən/ n person who works with statistics

stat·ue /'stætʃuː/ n (large) stone or metal likeness of a person, animal, etc.

stat·u·esque /,stætʃuˈesk◂/ adj like a statue in formal still beauty

stat·u·ette /,stætʃuˈet/ n small statue that goes on a table or shelf

stat·ure /'stætʃə ‖ -ər/ n [C;U] fml 1 degree to which someone is regarded as important or admirable 2 person's height

sta·tus /'steɪtəs/ n 1 [C;U] rank or condition in relation to others 2 [U] high social position 3 [C] state of affairs at a particular time

status quo /,steɪtəs ˈkwəʊ ‖ -ˈkwoʊ/ n existing state of affairs

stat·ute /'stætʃuːt/ n fml law

stat·u·to·ry /'stætʃʊtəri ‖ -tʃətɔːri/ adj fixed or controlled by law

staunch¹ /stɔːntʃ ‖ stɒːntʃ, stɑːntʃ/ adj dependably loyal; firm ~**ly** adv ~**ness** n [U]

staunch² vt stop the flow of (blood)

stave /steɪv/ v **stave off** phr vt keep away: *just enough food to stave off hunger*

stay /steɪ/ vi 1 remain in a place rather

than leave **2** continue to be; remain: *trying to stay healthy* **3** live in a place for a while: *staying at a hotel* **4 stay put** not move **5 stay the course** last or continue for the whole length of ♦ *n* **1** period of living in a place **2** *law* stopping or delay: *a stay of execution* (=not carrying out a punishment)

stay on *phr vt* remain after the usual leaving time

staying pow·er /'·· ,··/ *n* [U] STAMINA

St Ber·nard /sənt 'bɜːnəd ‖ ,seɪnt bərˈnɑːrd/ *n* large strong Swiss dog used in mountain rescue

stead /sted/ *n* **in someone's stead** *fml* instead of someone

stead·fast /'stedfɑːst ‖ -fæst/ *adj fml or lit* **1** firmly loyal **2** not moving or movable ~**ly** *adv* ~**ness** *n* [U]

stead·y /'stedi/ *adj* **1** firm; not shaking: *a steady hand* **2** not varying wildly; regular: *a steady speed* **3** not likely to change: *a steady job* **4** dependable ♦ *vi/t* make or become steady ~**ily** *adv* ~**iness** *n* [U]

steak /steɪk/ *n* [C;U] flat piece of meat, esp. BEEF or fish

steal /stiːl/ *v* **stole** /stəʊl ‖ stoʊl/, **stolen** /'stəʊlən ‖ stoʊ-/ **1** *vi/t* take (what belongs to someone else) without permission **2** *vi* move secretly or quietly **3** *vt* take secretly or improperly: *stealing a look at someone* **4 steal the show** get all the attention and praise expected by someone else, at a show or other event ♦ *n* [S] *infml, esp. AmE* something for sale very cheaply

stealth /stelθ/ *n* [U] acting quietly and secretly or unseen ~**y** *adj*

steam /stiːm/ *n* [U] **1** water gas produced by boiling **2** power produced by steam under pressure: *The ship sailed full steam ahead.* (=at its fastest speed) **3 let off steam** get rid of anger or unwanted ENERGY **4 under one's/its own steam** by one's/its own power or effort ♦ *v* **1** *vi* give off steam **2** *vi vt* cook with steam **3** *vt* use steam on: *He steamed the letter open.* ~**er** *n* **1** ship driven by steam power **2** container for cooking food with steam ~**y** *adj* **1** of or containing steam **2** *infml* sexually exciting

steam up *phr vi/t* **1** cover or become covered with a mist of cooling water **2** *infml* make angry or excited **steamed-up** *adj infml* excited and angry

steam·roll·er /'stiːm,rəʊlə ‖ -,roʊlər/ *n* vehicle with heavy metal wheels for flattening new road surfaces ♦ *vt* force in spite of all opposition: *He was steamrollered into signing the agreement.*

steam·ship /'stiːm,ʃɪp/ *n* a large non-naval ship driven by steam power

steed /stiːd/ *n lit*

steel /stiːl/ *n* [U] hard strong metal made from iron ♦ *vt* make (esp. oneself) unfeeling or determined ~**y** *adj* like steel in colour or hardness

steel band /'· ·/ *n* West Indian band playing drums cut from metal oil barrels

steep[1] /stiːp/ *adj* **1** rising or falling at a large angle **2** (esp. of a price) too high ~**ly** *adv* ~**ness** *n* [U]

steep[2] *vt* **1** keep in liquid **2 steeped in** thoroughly familiar or familiar with

stee·ple /'stiːpəl/ *n* high pointed church tower

stee·ple·chase /'stiːpəl,tʃeɪs/ *n* long race with fences to jump over

stee·ple·jack /'stiːpəl,dʒæk/ *n* person who repairs towers, tall chimneys, etc.

steer[1] /stɪə ‖ stɪr/ *vt* **1** direct the course of (esp. a boat or road vehicle) **2 steer clear (of)** keep away (from); avoid

steer[2] *n* young male animal of the cattle family with its sex organs removed

steering wheel /'·· ·/ *n* wheel turned to make a vehicle go left or right

stel·lar /'stelə ‖ -ər/ *adj fml* of the stars

stem[1] /stem/ *n* **1** part of a plant on which leaves or smaller branches grow **2** narrow upright support: *the stem of a wineglass*

stem[2] *vt* -**mm**- stop (the flow of)

stem from *phr vt* result from

stench /stentʃ/ *n* very strong bad smell

sten·cil /'stensəl/ *n* **1** card, etc. with patterns or letters cut in it **2** mark made by putting paint, etc. through the holes in this onto paper, etc. ♦ *vt* -**ll**- *BrE* -**l**- *AmE* make (a copy of) with a stencil

sten·to·ri·an /sten'tɔːriən/ *adj fml* (of the voice) very loud

step[1] /step/ *n* **1** act of moving by raising one foot and bringing it down somewhere else **2** the sound this makes **3** short distance: *It's just a step away from here.* **4** flat edge, esp. in a set one above the other, on which the foot is placed for going up or down **5** act, esp. in a set of actions, which should produce a certain result: *We must*

take steps (=take action) *to improve matters.*
6 movement of the feet in dancing **7 in/out
of step: a** moving/not moving the feet at
the same time as others in marching
b in/not in accordance or agreement with
others **8 step by step** gradually **9 watch
one's step** behave or act carefully

step² *vi* -pp- **1** go by putting one foot usu.
in front of the other **2** bring the foot down;
TREAD **3 step on it!** go faster **4 step out of
line** act differently from others or from
what is expected

  step down/aside *phr vi* leave one's
job, position, etc.

  step in *phr vi* INTERVENE

  step up *phr vt* increase

step·lad·der /'step,lædə ‖ -ər/ *n* folding
two-part ladder joined at the top

steppes /steps/ *n* [P] large treeless area
in Russia and parts of Asia

stepping-stone /'·· ·/ *n* **1** any of a row of
large stones for walking across a stream on
2 way of improvement or getting ahead

ster·e·o /'steriəu, 'stiər- ‖ 'steriou,
'stɪr-/ *adj* using a system of sound
recording in which the sound comes from
two different places ♦ *n* **-os 1** [C] stereo
equipment for playing CDs, etc. [U] stereo
sound —see also PERSONAL STEREO

ster·e·o·type /'steriətaɪp/ *n usu. derog*
fixed set of ideas about what a particular
type of person or thing is like ♦ *vt derog*
treat as an example of a fixed general type
-**typical** /,steriə'tɪpɪkəl◂/ *adj*

ster·ile /'sterail ‖ -rəl/ *adj* **1** which cannot
produce young **2** free from all (harmful)
bacteria, etc. **3** lacking new thought,
imagination, etc. **4** (of land) not producing
crops -**ility** /stə'rɪləti/ *n* [U] -**ilize, -ilise**
/'sterəlaɪz/ *vt* make STERILE (1, 2) -**ilization,
-ilisation** /,sterəlaɪ'zeɪʃən ‖ -lə-/ *n* [U]

ster·ling /'stɜːlɪŋ ‖ -ɜːr-/ *n* [U] British
money ♦ *adj* **1** (esp. of silver) of standard
value **2** of the highest standard, esp. in
being loyal and brave

stern¹ /stɜːn ‖ stɜːrn/ *n* severe and
serious: *a stern look/reprimand* ~**ly** *adv*
~**ness** *n* [U]

stern² *n* back part of a ship

ste·roid /'stɪərɔɪd,'ste- ‖ 'stɪr-/ *n* drug
used in medicine, sometimes used illegally
to improve sports performance

steth·o·scope /'steθəskəup ‖ -skoup/ *n*

tube with which doctors can listen to
people's heartbeats

stet·son /'stetsən/ *n* hat with a wide BRIM
worn by US COWBOYS

ste·ve·dore /'stiːvɪdɔː ‖ -dɔːr/ *n* person
who loads and unloads ships

stew /stjuː ‖ stuː/ *vi/t* cook slowly and
gently in liquid ♦ *n* **1** [C;U] dish of stewed
meat and vegetables **2** [S] confused anxious
state of mind

stew·ard /'stjuːəd ‖ 'stuːərd/ *n*
1 stewardess /-dəs/ *fem.* — person who
serves passengers on a ship, plane, etc.
2 person in charge of a public meeting,
horse race, etc. —see also SHOP STEWARD

stick¹ /stɪk/ *n* **1** small thin piece of wood
2 thin wooden or metal rod used for support
while walking, for hitting things, etc. **3** thin
rod of any material: *a stick of chalk/celery*
4 get the wrong end of the stick *infml*
misunderstand —see also STICKS

stick² *v* stuck /stʌk/ **1** *vt* push: *She stuck
her fork into the meat.* **2** *vi/t* fasten or be
fastened with glue or a similar substance
3 *vi/t* (cause to) become fixed in position:
He got his finger stuck in the hole. **4** *vt infml*
put: *Stick your coat down over there.* **5** *vt esp.
BrE* like; bear **6** *vt BrE sl* keep (something
unwanted) ~**er** *n* **1** LABEL with a message or
picture, which can be stuck to things
2 *infml* determined person

  stick around *phr vi* not go away

  stick at *phr vt* continue to work hard at

  stick by *phr vt* continue to support

  stick out *phr v* **1** *vi/t* (cause to) come
out beyond a surface: *Her ears stick out.* **2** *vt*
continue to the end of (something difficult)
3 stick one's neck out *infml* take a risk

  stick out for *phr vt* **1** refuse to accept
less than

  stick to *phr vt* **1** refuse to leave or
change: *stick to one's decision* **2 stick to
one's guns** *infml* continue to express one's
beliefs or carry on a course of action in
spite of attacks

  stick together *phr vi* (of two or more
people) stay loyal to each other

  stick up for *phr vt* defend (someone) by
words or actions

  stick with *phr vt* **1** stay close to **2 stick
with it** *infml* continue in spite of
difficulties

stick-in-the-mud /'· ··· ,·/ *n* person who

will not change or accept new things

stick·ler /'stɪklə‖-ər/ n person who demands the stated quality: *a stickler for punctuality*

sticks /stɪks/ n [the+P] *infml* a country area far from modern life

stick-up /'· ·/ n *infml* robbery carried out by threatening with a gun

stick·y /'stɪki/ adj 1 like or covered with glue or a similar substance 2 difficult; awkward: *a sticky situation* 3 **come to/meet a sticky end** (suffer) ruin, death, etc. –**iness** n [U]

stiff /stɪf/ adj 1 not easily bent or changed in shape 2 formal; not friendly 3 strong, esp. in alcohol 4 difficult; severe: *stiff competition* ♦ adv extremely: *I was scared stiff.* ♦ n *sl* dead body ~**ly** adv ~**en** vi/t make or become stiff ~**ness** n [U]

stiff-necked /,· '·◂/ adj proudly OBSTINATE

stiff upper lip /,· ·· '·/ n [S] ability to accept bad luck or unpleasant events without appearing upset

sti·fle /'staɪfəl/ v 1 vi/t (cause) to be unable to breathe properly 2 vt keep from happening: *stifling a yawn*

stig·ma /'stɪgmə/ n feeling of shame ~**tize**, **-tise** vt describe very disapprovingly

stile /staɪl/ n arrangement of steps for climbing over a fence or wall

sti·let·to /stɪ'letəʊ‖-toʊ/ n **-tos** 1 small thin DAGGER 2 *BrE* (woman's shoe with) a very high pointed heel

still¹ /stɪl/ adv 1 (even) up to this/that moment: *He's still here.* 2 in spite of that: *It's raining. Still, we must go out.* 3 even: *a still greater problem* 4 yet: *He gave still another reason.*

still² adj 1 not moving 2 without wind 3 silent; calm 4 (of a drink) not containing gas –**ness** n [U]

still³ n photograph of a scene from a (cinema) film

still⁴ n apparatus for making alcohol

still·birth /'stɪlbɜːθ, ˌstɪl'bɜːθ‖-ɜːrθ/ n child born dead

still·born /'stɪlbɔːn, ˌstɪl'bɔːn‖-ɔːrn/ adj born dead

still life /,· '·◂/ n still lifes [C;U] painting of objects, esp. flowers and fruit

stilt /stɪlt/ n either of a pair of poles for walking around on high above the ground

stilt·ed /'stɪltɪd/ adj very formal and unnatural

stim·u·late /'stɪmjʊleɪt/ vt 1 cause to become more active, grow faster, etc. 2 *fml* excite (the body or mind) –**lant** n 1 drug which gives one more power to be active 2 stimulus –**lation** /ˌstɪmjʊ'leɪʃən/ n [U]

stim·u·lus /'stɪmjʊləs/ n **-li** /-laɪ/ something that causes activity

sting /stɪŋ/ vi/t stung /stʌŋ/ 1 have, use, or prick with a STING (1) 2 (cause to) feel sharp pain: (fig.) *stinging criticism* ♦ n 1 pain-producing organ used by certain insects and plants for attack or protection 2 wound caused by this 3 sharp pain

stin·gy /'stɪndʒi/ adj *infml* ungenerous; mean –**gily** adv

stink /stɪŋk/ vi stank /stæŋk/, stunk /stʌŋk/ 1 give off a strong bad smell 2 *infml* be very unpleasant or bad: *Your plan stinks.* ♦ n strong bad smell

stink out phr vt fill with a stink

stint /stɪnt/ n limited or fixed amount, esp. of shared work ♦ vt give too small an amount (of)

sti·pend /'staɪpend/ n priest's wages

sti·pen·di·a·ry /staɪ'pendiəri‖-dieri/ adj receiving regular payment for professional services

stip·ple /'stɪpəl/ vt draw or paint (on) with dots instead of lines –**pling** n [U]

stip·u·late /'stɪpjʊleɪt/ vt state as a necessary condition –**lation** /ˌstɪpjʊ'leɪʃən/ n [C;U] statement of conditions

stir /stɜː‖stɜːr/ v **-rr-** 1 vt move around and mix (esp. liquid) with a spoon, etc. 2 vi/t make or cause a slight movement (in): *She stirred in her sleep.* 3 vt excite: *a stirring tale of adventure* 4 vi *infml* cause trouble between others ♦ n 1 [C] act of stirring 2 [S] (public) excitement

stir up phr vt cause (trouble)

stir-fry /'· ·/ vt cook quickly in a very small amount of hot oil ♦ n

stir·rup /'stɪrəp‖'stʌ-/ n D-shaped metal piece for a horse-rider's foot to go in

stitch /stɪtʃ/ n 1 [C] amount of thread put with a needle through cloth or through skin to close a wound 2 [C] single turn of the wool round the needle in knitting (KNIT) 3 [S] sharp pain in the side caused by running 4 [S] *infml* clothes: *He hadn't got a stitch on.* (=was completely NAKED) 5 **in stitches** laughing helplessly ♦ vi/t sew

stoat /stəʊt ‖ stoʊt/ n small brown furry European animal

stock /stɒk ‖ staːk/ n 1 [C] supply: *a large stock of food* 2 [C;U] (supply of) goods for sale: *Have you any blue shirts in stock?* 3 [C;U] money lent to a government or company: *stocks and shares* 4 [U] liquid made from meat, bones, etc. used in cooking 5 [U] farm animals, esp. cattle 6 [C;U] a family line, of the stated sort: *She comes from farming/good stock.* 7 **take stock (of)** consider a situation carefully so as to make a decision —see also STOCKS ♦ *vt* keep supplies of ♦ *adj* commonly used, esp. without much meaning: *stock excuses*

stock up *phr vi* provide oneself with a full store of goods

stock·ade /stɒˈkeɪd ‖ staː-/ n strong defensive fence

stock·brok·er /ˈstɒkˌbrəʊkə ‖ ˈstaːkˌbroʊkər/ n someone who buys and sells STOCKS (3) and SHARES (2) for others

stock ex·change /ˈ· ·ˌ·/ n place where STOCKS (3) and SHARES (2) are bought and sold

stock·ing /ˈstɒkɪŋ ‖ ˈstaː-/ n close-fitting garment for a woman's foot and leg

stock-in-trade /ˌ· · ˈ·/ n [U] things habitually used: *A pleasant manner is part of a politician's stock-in-trade.*

stock·ist /ˈstɒkɪst ‖ ˈstaː-/ n *BrE* one who keeps particular goods for sale

stock·man /ˈstɒkmən ‖ ˈstaːk-/ n -men /-mən/ man who looks after farm animals

stock mar·ket /ˈ· ˌ··/ n STOCK EXCHANGE

stock·pile /ˈstɒkpaɪl ‖ ˈstaːk-/ n large store for future use ♦ *vt* make a stockpile of

stocks /stɒks ‖ staːks/ n [P] wooden frame in which criminals were fastened in former times

stock-still /ˌ· ˈ·◄/ adv not moving at all

stock·tak·ing /ˈstɒkˌteɪkɪŋ ‖ ˈstaːk-/ n [U] making a list of goods held in a business

stock·y /ˈstɒki ‖ ˈstaː-/ adj thick, short, and strong **-ily** adv **-iness** n [U]

stodge /stɒdʒ ‖ staːdʒ/ n [U] unpleasantly heavy and uninteresting food **stodgy** adj 1 like stodge 2 uninteresting and difficult

sto·ic /ˈstəʊɪk ‖ ˈstoʊ-/ n person who remains calm and uncomplaining **~al** adj patient when suffering, like a stoic **~ally** /-kli/ adv **~ism** /-ˌsɪzəm/ n [U] stoical behaviour

stoke /stəʊk ‖ stoʊk/ vt fill (an enclosed fire) with FUEL **~stoker** n

stole¹ /stəʊl ‖ stoʊl/ past t. of STEAL

stole² n long piece of material worn over the shoulders

sto·len /ˈstəʊlən ‖ ˈstoʊ-/ past p. of STEAL

stol·id /ˈstɒlɪd ‖ ˈstaː-/ adj showing no excitement when strong feelings might be expected

stom·ach /ˈstʌmək/ n 1 [C] baglike organ in the body where food is digested (DIGEST¹) 2 [C] front part of the body below the chest 3 [S;U] desire; liking: *He's got no stomach for a fight.* ♦ *vt* accept without displeasure; bear

stomach pump /ˈ·· ·/ n apparatus for drawing the contents out of the stomach

stomp /stɒmp ‖ staːmp, stɔːmp/ vi walk heavily

stone /stəʊn ‖ stoʊn/ n 1 [C] fairly large piece of rock 2 [U] rock 3 [C] (*pl.* **stone** or **stones**) a measure of weight equal to 14 pounds or 6.35 kilograms 4 [C] single hard seed of certain fruits 5 [C] piece of hard material formed in an organ of the body ♦ *vt* 1 throw stones at 2 take the STONE (4) out of **stoned** adj *infml* 1 under the influence of drugs 2 very drunk **stony** adj 1 containing or covered with stones 2 cruel

stone- —see WORD-BEGINNINGS

Stone Age /ˈ· ·/ n earliest known time in human history, when stone tools were used

stone·ma·son /ˈstəʊnˌmeɪsən ‖ ˈstoʊn-/ n person who cuts stone for building

stone's throw /ˈ· ·/ n [S] short distance

stone·work /ˈstəʊnwɜːk ‖ ˈstoʊnwɜːrk/ n [U] parts of a building made of stone

stony broke /ˌ·· ˈ·/ adj *BrE infml* having no money at all

stood /stʊd/ past t. and p. of STAND

stooge /stuːdʒ/ n person who habitually does what another wants

stool /stuːl/ n seat without back or arm supports

stoop /stuːp/ vt 1 bend the upper body forwards and down 2 stand like this habitually ♦ *n* [S] habitual stooping position

stoop to *phr vt* fall to a low standard of behaviour by allowing oneself to do (something)

stop¹ /stɒp ‖ staːp/ v -pp- 1 vi/t (cause to)

no longer be moving or operating **2** *vi/t* (cause to) end: *The rain has stopped.* **3** *vt* prevent **4** *vi* pause **5** *vi esp. BrE* remain; stay: *stopping at a fine hotel* **6** *vt* block: *The pipe's stopped up.* **7** *vt* stop from being given or paid: *stop a cheque* **~per** *n* object for closing a bottle

stop off *phr vi* make a short visit to a place while making a journey elsewhere

stop over *phr vi* make a short stay before continuing a journey

stop² *n* **1** act of stopping or the state of being stopped **2** BUS STOP **3 pull all the stops out** do everything possible to complete an action **4 put a stop to** stop (esp. an undesirable activity)

stop·cock /'stɒpkɒk ‖ 'staːpkaːk/ *n* turnable apparatus for controlling the flow of water in a pipe

stop·gap /'stɒpgæp ‖ 'staːp-/ *n* something that fills a need for a time

stop·o·ver /'stɒp,əʊvə ‖ 'staːp,oʊvər/ *n* short stay between parts of a journey

stop·page /'stɒpɪdʒ ‖ 'staː-/ *n* **1** [C] stopping, esp. of work **2** [C;U] amount taken away from one's pay **3** [C;U] blocked state

stop press /ˌ· '·◄/ *n [the-S]* late news put into a paper

stop·watch /'stɒpwɒtʃ ‖ 'staːpwaːtʃ, -wɒːtʃ/ *n* watch that can be started and stopped to measure periods exactly

stor·age /'stɔːrɪdʒ/ *n* [U] (price paid for) storing

store /stɔː ‖ stɔːr/ *vt* **1** make and keep a supply of for future use **2** keep in a special place while not in use ♦ *n* **1** supply for future use **2** place for keeping things **3** large shop **4** *esp. AmE* SHOP (1) **5 in store:** **a** being stored **b** about to happen: *There's trouble in store.* **6 set ... store by** feel to be of (the stated amount of) importance **stores** *n* [S;P] (building or room containing) military or naval goods and food

sto·rey *BrE* ‖ **-ry** *AmE* /'stɔːri/ *n* floor or level in a building

stork /stɔːk ‖ stɔːrk/ *n* large bird with a long beak, neck, and legs

storm /stɔːm ‖ stɔːrm/ *n* **1** rough weather condition with rain and strong wind **2** sudden violent show of feeling: *a storm of protest* **3 take by storm: a** conquer by a sudden violent attack **b** win great approval from (those who watch a performance) ♦ *v*

1 *vt* attack (a place) with sudden violence **2** *vi* go angrily **~y** *adj*

sto·ry /'stɔːri/ *n* **1** account of events, real or imagined **2** news article **3** lie: *Have you been telling stories again?* **4** *AmE for* STOREY **5 the same old story** the usual excuse or difficulty —see also TALL STORY

sto·ry·book /'stɔːribʊk/ *adj* as perfectly happy as in a fairy story for children

story line /'·· ·/ *n* events in a film, book, or play

stout /staʊt/ *adj* **1** rather fat **2** brave and determined **3** strong and thick ♦ *n* [U] strong dark beer **~ly** *adv* **~ness** *n* [U]

stove /stəʊv ‖ stoʊv/ *n* enclosed apparatus that can be heated for cooking or to provide warmth

stow /stəʊ ‖ stoʊ/ *vt* put away or store, esp. on a ship

stow away *phr vi* hide on a ship or plane in order to make a free journey

stow·a·way /'stəʊəweɪ ‖ 'stoʊ-/ *n* person who stows away

strad·dle /'strædl/ *vt* **1** have one's legs on either side of **2** be, land, etc. on either side of (something), rather than in the middle

strag·gle /'strægəl/ *vi* move, grow, or spread untidily **–gler** *n* one who is behind a main group **–gly** *adj* growing or lying untidily

straight¹ /streɪt/ *adj* **1** not bent or curved **2** level or upright **3** neat; tidy **4** honest, open, and truthful **5** (of the face) with a serious expression **6** (of alcohol) without added water **7** correct: *set the record straight* **8** *sl* HETEROSEXUAL ♦ *n* straight part, esp. on a race track **~ness** *n* [U]

straight² *adv* **1** in a straight line **2** directly (and without delay): *Get straight to the point.* **3** clearly: *I can't think straight.* **4 go straight** leave a life of crime

straight and nar·row /ˌ· · '··/ *n* [U] honest life

straight·a·way /ˌstreɪtə'weɪ/ *adv* at once

straight·en /'streɪtn/ *vt* (cause to) become straight, level, or tidy

straighten out *phr vt* remove (the confusions or difficulties) in: *straighten out one's business affairs*

straighten up *phr vi* get up from a bent position

straight·for·ward /ˌstreɪt'fɔːwəd◄/

-'fɔːwərd◂/ *adj* 1 honest and open, without hidden meanings 2 simple ~**ly** *adv* ~**ness** *n* [U]

strain¹ /streɪn/ *v* 1 *vt* damage (a body part) through too much effort or pressure 2 *vi* make (too) great efforts 3 *vt* separate (a liquid and solid) by pouring through esp. a strainer 4 *vt* force beyond acceptable or believable limits: *straining the truth* ♦ *n* [C;U] 1 (force causing) the condition of being tightly stretched 2 troubling influence 3 damage caused by straining a body part ~**ed** *adj* not natural in behaviour; unfriendly 2 tired or nervous ~**er** *n* instrument with a net for STRAINing (3) things

strain² *n* 1 breed or type of plant or animal 2 *lit* tune

strait /streɪt/ also **straits** *pl.* — *n* narrow water passage between two areas of land

straits *n* [P] difficult situation: *in dire straits*

strait·ened /'streɪtnd/ *adj fml* difficult because lacking money

strait·jack·et /'streɪt͵dʒækɪt/ *n* 1 garment for a violently mad person that prevents arm movement 2 something preventing free development

strait·laced /͵streɪt'leɪst◂/ *adj* having severe, rather old-fashioned ideas about morals

strand /strænd/ *n* single thin thread, wire, etc.

strand·ed /'strændɪd/ *adj* in a helpless position, unable to get away

strange /streɪndʒ/ *adj* 1 unusual; surprising 2 unfamiliar ~**ly** *adv* ~**ness** *n* [U]

strang·er /'streɪndʒə ‖ -ər/ *n* 1 unfamiliar person 2 person in an unfamiliar place

stran·gle /'stræŋgəl/ *vt* 1 kill by pressing the throat to stop breathing 2 stop the proper development of –**gler** *n* –**gulation** /͵stræŋgjʊ'leɪʃən/ *n* [U]

stran·gle·hold /'stræŋgəl͵həʊld ‖ -͵hoʊld/ *n* strong control which prevents action

strap /stræp/ *n* strong narrow band used as a fastening or support: *a leather watchstrap* ♦ *vt* -**pp**- fasten with straps

strap·ping /'stræpɪŋ/ *adj* big and strong

stra·ta /'strɑːtə ‖ 'streɪtə/ *pl. of* STRATUM

strat·a·gem /'strætədʒəm/ *n* trick or plan for deceiving or gaining an advantage

stra·te·gic /strə'tiːdʒɪk/ *adj* 1 part of a plan, esp. in war 2 right for a purpose ~**ally** /-kli/ *adv*

strat·e·gist /'strætɪdʒɪst/ *n* person skilled in (military) planning

strat·e·gy /'strætɪdʒi/ *n* 1 [U] skilful (military) planning 2 [C] particular plan for winning success

strat·i·fy /'strætɪfaɪ/ *vt* arrange in separate levels or strata –**fication** /͵strætɪfɪ'keɪʃən/ *n* [C;U]

strat·os·phere /'strætəsfɪə ‖ -sfɪr/ *n* outer air surrounding the Earth, starting at about 10 kilometres above the Earth

stra·tum /'strɑːtəm ‖ 'streɪ-/ *n* -**ta** /-tə/ 1 band of a particular rock 2 part of something thought of as divided into different levels

straw /strɔː ‖ strɑː/ *n* 1 [U] dried stems of grain plants, such as wheat 2 [C] single such stem 3 [C] thin tube for sucking up liquid —see also LAST STRAW, MAN OF STRAW

straw·ber·ry /'strɔːbəri ‖ 'strɔːbȇri, -bəri/ *n* (plant with) a small red juicy fruit

straw poll /ˌ· '·/ *n* unofficial examination of opinions before an election, to see what the result is likely to be

stray /streɪ/ *vi* wander away ♦ *n* animal lost from its home ♦ *adj* 1 wandering; lost 2 single; not in a group

streak /striːk/ *n* 1 thin line or band, different from what surrounds it 2 bad quality of character: *a stubborn streak* 3 period marked by a particular quality: *a lucky streak* 4 like a streak (of lightning) very quickly ♦ *v* 1 *vi* move very fast 2 *vt* cover with streaks ~**y** *adj* marked with streaks

stream /striːm/ *n* 1 small river 2 something flowing: *a stream of traffic* | (fig.) *a stream of abuse* 3 group of pupils of similar ability 4 **go with/against the stream** agree/not agree with a general way of thinking, etc. in society 5 **on stream** in(to) production ♦ *v* 1 *vi* flow strongly 2 *vi* move in a continuous flowing mass 3 *vi* float in the air 4 *vt* esp. BrE group in STREAMS (3) ~**er** *n* long narrow piece of paper for throwing

stream·line /'striːmlaɪn/ *vt* 1 give a smooth shape which moves easily through water or air **2** make more simple and effective –**lined** *adj*

street /striːt/ *n* **1** road in a town **2 streets ahead** much better **3 up/down one's street** in one's area of interest —see also HIGH STREET

street-cred /ˈstriːt kred/ also **street-cred·i·bil·i·ty** /ˌ··ˈ···/ *infml* — *n* [U] popular acceptance among young people

street·wise /ˈstriːtwaɪz/ *adj infml* clever enough to succeed and live well in the hard world of the city streets

strength /streŋθ, streŋθ/ *n* **1** [U] (degree of) being strong **2** [C] way in which something is good or effective: *the strengths and weaknesses of the plan* **3** [U] force measured in numbers: *The police are at full strength.* **4 on the strength of** persuaded or influenced by –**en** *vi/t* become or make strong or stronger

stren·u·ous /ˈstrenjuəs/ *adj* **1** needing great effort **2** showing great activity: *a strenuous denial* ~**ly** *adv* ~**ness** *n* [U]

stress /stres/ *n* [C;U] **1** (worry resulting from) pressure caused by difficulties **2** force of weight caused by pressure **3** sense of special importance **4** degree of force put on a part of a word when spoken, or on a note in music: *In 'under' the main stress is on 'un'.* ♦ *vt* **1** mention strongly **2** put STRESS (1, 4) on ~**ed** also **stressed out** *adj* suffering from STRESS (1) ~**ful** *adj* causing STRESS (1)

stretch /stretʃ/ *v* **1** *vi/t* (cause to) become wider or longer **2** *vi* spread out: *The forest stretched for miles.* **3** *vi* be elastic **4** *vi* straighten one's limbs to full length: *stretch out your arms* **5** *vt* allow to go beyond exact limits: *stretch a rule* **6 stretch one's legs** have a walk esp. after sitting for a long time ♦ *n* **1** [C] act of stretching **2** [U] elasticity **3** [C] long area of land or water **4** [C] continuous period: *14 hours at a stretch* (=without stopping) **5 at full stretch** using all one's powers –**y** *adj* elastic

stretch·er /ˈstretʃə‖-ər/ *n* covered frame for carrying a sick person

strew /struː/ *vt* **strewed, strewn** /struːn/ or **strewed** *esp. lit* **1** scatter **2** lie scattered over

strick·en /ˈstrɪkən/ *adj* showing the effect of trouble, illness, etc.: *grief-stricken*

strict /strɪkt/ *adj* **1** severe in making

people behave properly **2 a** exact: *strict instructions* **b** complete: *in strict secrecy* ~**ly** *adv* ~**ness** *n* [U]

stride /straɪd/ *vi* **strode** /strəʊd‖ strəʊd/, **stridden** /ˈstrɪdn/ walk with long steps ♦ *n* **1** long step **2 make strides** improve or do well **3 take something in one's stride** deal with a difficult situation easily and without complaint

stri·dent /ˈstraɪdənt/ *adj* with a hard sharp sound or voice ~**ly** *adv* –**dency** *n* [U]

strife /straɪf/ *n* [U] trouble and quarrelling between people

strike¹ /straɪk/ *v* **struck** /strʌk/ **1** *vt* hit sharply **2** *vt* make a (sudden) attack **3** *vt* harm suddenly: *They were struck down with illness.* **4** *vt* light (a match) **5** *vi/t* **a** make known (the time), esp. by the hitting of a bell **b** (of time) be made known in this way **6** *vi* stop working because of disagreement **7** *vt* find; meet: *strike oil/difficulties* **8** *vt* have a particular effect on: *Her behaviour struck me as odd.* | *struck down with fear* **9** *vt* come suddenly to mind **10** *vt* produce (a coin or similar object) **11** *vt* make (an agreement): *strike a bargain/balance* **12 strike a chord** remind someone of something **13 strike a note of** express (a need for): *The book strikes a warning note.* **14 strike camp** take down tents when leaving a camping place **15 strike it rich** find sudden wealth

strike off *phr vt* remove (someone or their name) from (an official list)

strike out *phr vi* **1** go purposefully in the stated direction **2 strike out on one's own** take up an independent life **3** CROSS OUT

strike up *phr vt* **1** begin playing or singing **2** start to make (a friendship)

strike² *n* **1** act or time of striking (STRIKE¹ (6)): *The workers are on strike.* **2** attack, esp. by aircraft **3** success in finding esp. a mineral in the earth: *an oil strike* —see also FIRST STRIKE, GENERAL STRIKE

strik·er /ˈstraɪkə‖-ər/ *n* **1** person on STRIKE² (1) **2** attacking player in football

strik·ing /ˈstraɪkɪŋ/ *adj* very noticeable, esp. because beautiful or unusual ~**ly** *adv*

striking dis·tance /ˈ·· ˌ·/ *n* within striking distance very close (to)

string¹ /strɪŋ/ *n* **1** [C;U] thin cord **2** [C] thin cord or wire stretched across a musical instrument to give sound **3** [C] set of objects on a thread: *a string of pearls* **4** [C] set of things, events, etc. following each other closely: *a whole string of complaints* **5 no strings attached** (esp. of an agreement) with no limiting conditions **6 pull strings** use secret influence **7 two strings to one's bow** an additional interest, ability, etc. which can be used as well as the main one **strings** *n* [P] all the (players of) VIOLINS, CELLOS, etc. in an ORCHESTRA ~**y** *adj* **1** (of food) full of unwanted threadlike parts **2** unpleasantly thin

string² *vt* **strung** /strʌŋ/ **1** put STRINGS¹ (2) on (a musical instrument or RACKET¹) **2** put with others onto a thread **3 highly strung** (of a person) very sensitive and easily excited **4 strung up** very excited, nervous, or worried

string along *phr v* **1** *vt* encourage the hopes of deceitfully **2** *vi* go (with someone else) for a time, esp. for convenience

string out *phr vt* spread out in a line

string up *phr vt* **1** hang high **2** kill by hanging

stringed in·stru·ment /ˌ ˈ···/ *n* musical instrument with strings

strin·gent /ˈstrɪndʒənt/ *adj* (esp. of rules, limits, etc.) severe ~**ly** *adv*

strip /strɪp/ *v* -**pp**- **1** *vt* remove (the covering or parts of) **2** *vi/t* undress, usu. completely **3** *vt* remove the parts of (esp. an engine) ♦ *n* **1** narrow piece: *a strip of paper/land* **2** clothes of a particular colour worn by a team in SOCCER ~**per** *n* **1** [C] striptease performer **2** [C;U] tool or liquid for removing things: *paint stripper*

strip of *phr vt* take away (something of value) from

stripe /straɪp/ *n* **1** different-coloured band **2** usu. V-shaped sign worn on a uniform to show rank ~**striped** *adj* **stripy** *adj*

strip light·ing /ˈ· ˌ··, ˌ· ˈ··/ [U] long tube-shaped lamps

strip·tease /ˈstrɪptiːz, ˌstrɪpˈtiːz/ *n* [U] removal of clothes by a person, performed as a show

strive /straɪv/ *vi* **strove** /strəʊv ‖ stroʊv/ *or* **strived**, **striven** /ˈstrɪvən/ *or* **strived** *fml or lit* make a great effort

strobe /strəʊb ‖ stroʊb/ *also* **strobe light** /ˈ· ·/ *n* light that flashes very quickly, used esp. where people are dancing

strode /strəʊd ‖ stroʊd/ *past t. of* STRIDE

stroke¹ /strəʊk ‖ stroʊk/ *vt* pass the hand over gently

stroke² *n* **1** hit, esp. with a weapon **2** act of stroking **3** line made by a single movement of a pen or brush **4** act of hitting a ball **5** (single movement or set of movements that is repeated in) a method of swimming **6** sudden bursting of a blood tube in the brain **7** unexpected piece (of luck) **8** sound of a clock striking: *on the stroke of* (=exactly at) *6 o'clock* **9 at a stroke** with one direct action

stroll /strəʊl ‖ stroʊl/ *vi, n* (take) a slow walk for pleasure ~**er** *n* **1** person who strolls or is strolling **2 a** *BrE* light foldable PUSHCHAIR **b** *AmE for* PUSHCHAIR

strong /strɒŋ ‖ strɔːŋ/ *adj* **1** having great power **2** not easily becoming broken, changed, or ill **3** having a powerful effect on the mind or senses: *a strong smell* **4** (of a drink, drug, etc.) having a lot of the substance which gives taste, produces effect, etcs.: *This coffee's too strong.* **5** having the stated number of members: *a club 50 strong* **6 (still) going strong** continuing with energy, good health, etc. **7 strong on: a** good at doing **b** eager and active in dealing with ~**ly** *adv*

strong-box /ˈstrɒŋbɒks ‖ ˈstrɔːŋbɑːks/ *n* firm lockable box for keeping valuable things in

strong·hold /ˈstrɒŋhəʊld ‖ ˈstrɔːŋhoʊld/ *n* **1** fort **2** place where a particular activity is common

strong lan·guage /ˌ· ˈ··/ *n* [U] swearing; curses

strong point /ˈ· ·/ *n* something one is good at

strong room /ˈ· ·/ *n* special lockable room in a bank, etc. where valuable things are kept

stron·ti·um /ˈstrɒntiəm ‖ ˈstrɑːntʃiəm, -tiəm/ *n* [U] soft metal, of which a harmful form (**strontium 90**) is given off by atomic explosions

strop·py /ˈstrɒpi ‖ ˈstrɑːpi/ *adj BrE infml* tending to quarrel or disobey —**pily** *adv*

strove /strəʊv ‖ stroʊv/ *past t. of* STRIVE

struck /strʌk/ *past t. and p. of* STRIKE

struc·ture /ˈstrʌktʃə ‖ -ər/ *n* **1** [C;U] way in which parts are formed into a whole **2** [C] large thing built ♦ *vt* arrange so that each

part is properly related to others –**tural** *adj*
–**turally** *adv*

strug·gle /'strʌɡəl/ *vi* **1** make violent
movements, esp. in fighting **2** make a great
effort ♦ *n* hard fight or effort

strum /strʌm/ *vi/t* -**mm**- play carelessly or
informally on (esp. a GUITAR, BANJO, or
piano)

strung /strʌŋ/ *past t. and p. of* STRING

strut¹ /strʌt/ *n* supporting rod in a
structure

strut² *vi* -**tt**- walk proudly

strych·nine /'strɪkniːn ‖ -naɪn, -niːn/ *n*
[U] poisonous drug

stub /stʌb/ *n* **1** short left-over part of esp.
a cigarette or pencil **2** small piece left in a
book of cheques or tickets after tearing out
a cheque or ticket ♦ *vt* -**bb**- hit (one's toe)
against something –**by** *adj* short and thick:
stubby fingers

 stub out *phr vt* put out (a cigarette) by
pressing

stub·ble /'stʌbəl/ *n* [U] **1** short growth of
beard **2** remains of cut wheat –**bly** *adj*

stub·born /'stʌbən ‖ -ərn/ *adj* **1** having a
strong will; (unreasonably) determined
2 difficult to use, move, change, etc. –**ly** *adv*
–**ness** *n* [U]

stuc·co /'stʌkəʊ ‖ -koʊ/ *n* [U] PLASTER
stuck (decoratively) onto walls

stuck¹ /stʌk/ *v past t. and p. of* STICK

stuck² *adj* **1** unable to go further because
of difficulties **2 stuck in** having to do or
have, esp. unwillingly **3 get stuck in** *infml*
begin forcefully

stuck-up /ˌ· '·◂/ *adj infml* too proud in
manner

stud¹ /stʌd/ *n* **1** removable button-like
fastener, esp. for collars **2** large-headed nail
♦ *vt* -**dd**- cover (as if) with STUDS¹ (2)

stud² *n* **1** number of horses kept for
breeding **2** *derog or humor* man who has
sex a lot and thinks he is very good at it

stu·dent /'stjuːdənt ‖ 'stuː-/ *n* **1** person
studying at a college or university **2** person
with a stated interest: *a student of life*

stu·di·o /'stjuːdiəʊ ‖ 'stuːdioʊ/ *n* **1** place
where films, recordings, or broadcasts are
made **2** workroom for a painter,
photographer, etc.

stu·di·ous /'stjuːdiəs ‖ 'stuː-/ *adj* **1** fond
of studying **2** careful –**ly** *adv* –**ness** *n* [U]

stud·y /'stʌdi/ *n* **1** [U] also **studies** *pl.* —

act of studying **2** [C] thorough enquiry into
a particular subject, esp. including a piece
of writing on it **3** [C] workroom; office **4** [C]
drawing or painting of a detail: *a study of a
flower* **5** [C] piece of music for practice ♦ *v*
1 *vi/t* spend time in learning **2** *vt* examine
carefully **studied** *adj* carefully thought
about or considered, esp. before being
expressed: *a studied remark*

stuff¹ /stʌf/ *n* [U] **1** matter; material
2 one's possessions or the things needed to
do something **3 do one's stuff** show one's
ability as expected **4 know one's stuff** be
good at what one is concerned with
5 That's the stuff! *infml* That's the right
thing to do/say

stuff² *vt* **1** fill **2** push so as to be inside
3 put STUFFING (2) inside **4** fill the skin of (a
dead animal) to make it look real **5** cause
(oneself) to eat as much as possible **6 get
stuffed!** *sl* (an expression of dislike, esp. for
what someone has said) ~**ing** *n* [U] **1** filling
material **2** cut-up food put inside a chicken,
etc. before cooking

 stuff up *phr vt* block

stuffed shirt /ˌ· '·, '· '·/ *n* dull person who
thinks himself important

stuff·y /'stʌfi/ *adj* **1** (having air) that is
not fresh **2** *derog* formal and old-fashioned
–**ily** *adv* –**iness** *n* [U]

stul·ti·fy /'stʌltɪfaɪ/ *vt fml* make
(someone's) mind dull –**fication**
/ˌstʌltɪfɪˈkeɪʃən/ *n*

stum·ble /'stʌmbəl/ *vi* **1** catch one's foot
on something and start to fall **2** stop and/or
make mistakes in speaking

 stumble across/on/upon *phr vt*
meet or find by chance

stumbling block /'·· ·/ *n* something
preventing action or development

stump¹ /stʌmp/ *n* **1** base of a cut-down
tree **2** useless end of something long that
has been worn down, cut off, etc. **3** any of
the three sticks at which the ball is aimed in
cricket ~**y** *adj* short and thick in body

stump² *v* **1** *vt* leave (someone) unable to
reply **2** *vi* walk heavily or awkwardly

stun /stʌn/ *vt* -**nn**- **1** make unconscious
2 shock greatly **3** delight ~**ning** *adj* very
attractive

stung /stʌŋ/ *past t. and p. of* STING

stunk /stʌŋk/ *past p. of* STINK

stunt¹ /stʌnt/ *n* **1** dangerous act of skill

2 attention-getting action: *publicity stunts*
3 pull a stunt do a trick, sometimes silly
stunt² *vt* prevent full growth (of)
stunt man /'·␣·/ **stunt wo·man** /'·␣␣·/ *fem.*
— *n* person who does STUNTS¹ (1) in films, etc.

stu·pe·fy /'stjuːpˀfaɪ ‖ 'stuː-/ *vt fml*
1 surprise (and annoy) extremely **2** make unable to think —**faction** /ˌstjuːpˀ'fækʃən ‖ ˌstuː-/ *n* [U]

stu·pen·dous /stjuː'pendəs ‖ stuː-/ *adj* surprisingly great or good

stu·pid /'stjuːpˀd ‖ 'stuː-/ *adj* foolish ~**ly** *adv* ~**ity** /stjuː'pɪdˀti ‖ stuː-/ *n* [U]

stu·por /'stjuːpə ‖ 'stuːpər/ *n* [C;U] nearly unconscious unthinking state

stur·dy /'stɜːdi ‖ -ɜːr-/ *adj* **1** strong and firm **2** determined —**dily** *adv* —**diness** *n* [U]

stut·ter /'stʌtə ‖ -ər/ *vi/t* speak or say with difficulty in pronouncing esp. the first consonant of words ♦ *n* habit of stuttering

sty¹, **stye** /staɪ/ *n* infected place on the eyelid

sty² *n* PIGSTY

style /staɪl/ *n* [C;U] (typical) manner of doing something: *the modern style of architecture* | *written in a formal style* **2** [C] fashion, esp. in clothes **3** [U] high quality of social behaviour or appearance **4** [C] type or sort **5 in style** in a grand way ♦ *vt* **1** DESIGN **2** give (a title) to: *He styles himself 'Lord'.* **stylish** *adj* fashionable and good-looking **stylist** *n* **1** person who invents styles or fashions **2** person with a (good) style of writing **stylize**, **-ise** *vt* present in a simplified style rather than naturally **stylistic** /staɪˈlɪstɪk/ *adj* of STYLE (1)

suave /swɑːv/ *adj* with smooth (but perhaps insincere) good manners ~**ly** *adv* ~**ness** *n* [U]

sub /sʌb/ *n infml* **1** SUBMARINE **2** SUBSTITUTE **3** *BrE* amount of money paid to someone from their wages before the usual day of payment ♦ *vt* **-bb-** SUBEDIT

sub·con·scious /ˌsʌbˈkɒnʃəs ‖ -ˈkɑːn-/ *adj*, *n* (present at) a hidden level of the mind, not consciously known about ~**ly** *adv*

sub·con·ti·nent /ˌsʌbˈkɒntˀnənt ‖ -ˈkɑːn-/ *n* large mass of land smaller than a CONTINENT, esp. India

sub·con·tract /ˌsʌbkənˈtrækt ‖ -ˈkɑːn-trækt/ *vt* hire someone else to do (work which someone has agreed to do) ~**or** *n* person or

firm that has had work subcontracted to it

sub·cul·ture /'sʌbˌkʌltʃə ‖ -ər/ *n* the ideas, behaviour, etc. of a particular group within society

sub·cu·ta·ne·ous /ˌsʌbkjuːˈteɪniəs◂/ *adj med* beneath the skin

sub·di·vide /ˌsʌbdˀˈvaɪd/ *vt* divide into even smaller parts —**division** /-ˈvɪʒən/ *n* [C;U]

sub·due /səbˈdjuː ‖ -ˈduː/ *vt* **1** gain control of **2** make gentler —**dued** *adj* **1** of low brightness or sound **2** unusually quiet in behaviour

sub·ed·it /ˌsʌbˈedˀt/ *vt* look at and put right (material to be printed in a newspaper, etc.) ~**or** *n*

sub·ject¹ /'sʌbdʒɪkt/ *n* **1** thing being dealt with, represented, or considered: *the subject of the painting* / *of the conversation* **2** branch of knowledge being studied **3** word that comes before a main verb and represents the person or thing that performs the action of the verb or about which something is stated **4** member of a state: *British subjects* ♦ *adj* **1** tending; likely: *He's subject to ill health.* **2** not independent: *a subject race* **3 subject to** depending on: *subject to your approval* (=if you approve)

sub·ject² /səbˈdʒekt/ *vt fml* defeat and control —**ion** /-ˈdʒekʃən/ *n* [U] **1** act of subjecting **2** state of being severely controlled by others

   subject to *phr vt* cause to experience or suffer

sub·jec·tive /səbˈdʒektɪv/ *adj* **1** influenced by personal feelings (and perhaps unfair) **2** existing only inside the mind; not real ~**ly** *adv* —**tivity** /ˌsʌbdʒekˈtɪvˀti/ *n* [U]

sub ju·di·ce /ˌsʌb ˈdʒuːdɪsi ‖ ˌsʊb ˈjuːdɪkeɪ/ *adj* now being considered in a court of law, and therefore not allowed to be publicly mentioned

sub·ju·gate /'sʌbdʒˀgeɪt/ *vt* defeat and make obedient —**gation** /ˌsʌbdʒˀ'geɪʃən/ *n* [U]

sub·junc·tive /səbˈdʒʌŋktɪv/ *adj*, *n* (of) a verb form expressing doubt, wishes, unreality, etc.: *In 'if I were you' the verb 'were' is in the subjunctive.*

sub·let /ˌsʌbˈlet/ *vt* **-let**, *pres. p.* **-tt-** rent (property rented from someone) to someone else

sub·li·mate /'sʌblɪmeɪt/ vt fml replace (natural urges, esp. sexual) with socially acceptable activities –**mation** /ˌsʌblɪ-'meɪʃən/ n [U]

sub·lime /sə'blaɪm/ adj 1 very noble or wonderful 2 infml complete and usu. careless or unknowing ~**ly** adv

sub·lim·i·nal /ˌsʌb'lɪmɪnəl/ adj at a level which the ordinary senses are not conscious of

sub·ma·chine gun /ˌsʌbmə'ʃiːn gʌn/ n light MACHINEGUN

sub·ma·rine /ˌsʌbməriːn, ˌsʌbmə'riːn/ n (war)ship which can stay under water ♦ adj under or in the sea

sub·merge /səb'mɜːdʒ ‖ -ɜːr-/ vi/t 1 (cause to) go under the surface of water 2 cover or competely hide –**mersion** /-'mɜːʃən ‖ -'mɜːrʒən/ n [U] act of submerging or state of being submerged

sub·mit /səb'mɪt/ v -**tt**- 1 vi admit defeat 2 vt offer for consideration 3 vt esp. law suggest –**mission** /-'mɪʃən/ n 1 [C;U] submitting 2 [U] fml opinion 3 [U] fml obedience 4 [C] law request; suggestion –**missive** /-'mɪsɪv/ adj too obedient

sub·or·di·nate[1] /sə'bɔːdɪnət ‖ -ɔːr- / adj less important ♦ n someone of lower rank

sub·or·di·nate[2] /sə'bɔːdɪneɪt ‖ -ɔːr-/ vt put in a subordinate position –**ation** /sə,bɔːdɪ'neɪʃən ‖ -ɔːr-/ n [U]

sub·poe·na /sə'piːnə, səb-/ n written order to attend a court of law **subpoena** vt

sub·scribe /səb'skraɪb/ vi pay regularly, esp. to receive a magazine –**scriber** n

    subscribe to phr vt agree with; approve of

sub·scrip·tion /səb'skrɪpʃən/ n 1 act of subscribing (to) 2 amount paid regularly, esp. to belong to a society, receive a magazine, etc.

sub·se·quent /'sʌbsɪkwənt/ adj coming afterwards or next ~**ly** adv

sub·ser·vi·ent /səb'sɜːviənt ‖ -ɜːr-/ adj too willing to obey ~**ly** adv –**ence** n [U]

sub·side /səb'saɪd/ vi 1 return to its usual level; become less: The flood waters/The wind/His anger subsided. 2 (of land or a building) sink down **subsidence** /səb'saɪdəns, 'sʌbsɪdəns/ n

sub·sid·i·a·ry /səb'sɪdiəri ‖ -dieri/ adj connected with but less important than the main one ♦ n subsidiary company

sub·si·dy /'sʌbsɪdi/ n paid, esp. by government, to make prices lower, etc. –**dize**, –**dise** vt give a subsidy to (someone) for (something): subsidized school meals

sub·sist /səb'sɪst/ vi fml remain alive ~**ence** [U] 1 ability to live, esp. on little money or food 2 state of living with little money or food

sub·stance /'sʌbstəns/ n 1 [C] material; type of matter: a sticky substance 2 [U] fml truth: There is no substance in these rumours. 3 [U] fml real meaning, without the unimportant details 4 [U] fml wealth 5 [U] importance, esp. in relation to real life: There was no real substance in the speech.

sub·stan·tial /səb'stænʃəl/ adj 1 solid; strongly made 2 satisfactorily large: a substantial meal 3 noticeably large (and important): substantial changes 4 concerning the main part 5 wealthy ~**ly** adv 1 in all important ways: They are substantially the same. 2 quite a lot

sub·stan·ti·ate /səb'stænʃieɪt/ vt fml prove the truth of –**ation** /səb,stæn-ʃi'eɪʃən/ n [U]

sub·stan·tive /'sʌbstəntɪv/ adj fml having reality, actuality, or importance

sub·sti·tute /'sʌbstɪtjuːt ‖ -tuːt/ n one taking the place of another ♦ v 1 vt put in place of another 2 vi act or be used instead –**tution** /ˌsʌbstɪ'tjuːʃən ‖ -'tuː-/ n [C;U]

sub·ter·fuge /'sʌbtəfjuːdʒ ‖ -ər-/ n [C;U] deceiving or slightly dishonest trick(s)

sub·ter·ra·ne·an /ˌsʌbtə'reɪniən◂/ adj underground

sub·ti·tles /'sʌb,taɪtlz/ n [P] translation printed over a foreign film

sub·tle /'sʌtl/ adj 1 hardly noticeable: subtle differences 2 clever in arrangement: a subtle plan 3 very clever in noticing and understanding –**tly** adv –**tlety** n [C;U]

sub·tract /səb'trækt/ vt take (a number or amount) from a larger one ~**ion** /-'trækʃən/ n [C;U]

sub·urb /'sʌbɜːb ‖ -ɜːrb/ n outer area of a town, where people live ~**an** /sə'bɜːbən ‖ -ɜːr-/ adj

sub·ur·bi·a /sə'bɜːbiə ‖ -ɜːr-/ n [U] (life and ways of people who live in) suburbs

sub·vert /səb'vɜːt ‖ -ɜːrt/ vt try to

destroy the power and influence of -**versive** *adj* trying to destroy established ideas or defeat those in power -**version** /-ˈvɜːʃən‖-ˈvɜːrʒən/ *n* [U]

sub·way /ˈsʌbweɪ/ *n* 1 path under a road or railway 2 *AmE* underground railway

suc·ceed /səkˈsiːd/ *v* 1 *vi* do what one has been trying to do 2 *vi* do well, esp. in gaining position or popularity 3 *vt* follow after 4 *vi/t* be the next to take a rank or position (after): *Hammond succeeded Jones as champion.*

suc·cess /səkˈses/ *n* 1 [U] degree of succeeding; good result 2 [C] person or thing that succeeds -**ful** -**fully** *adv*

suc·ces·sion /səkˈseʃən/ *n* 1 [U] following one after the other: *in quick succession* 2 [S] many following each other closely: *a succession of visitors* 3 [U] SUCCEEDing (4)

suc·ces·sive /səkˈsesɪv/ *adj* following each other closely in time -**ly** *adv*

suc·ces·sor /səkˈsesə‖-ər/ *n* person who takes an office or position formerly held by another

suc·cinct /səkˈsɪŋkt/ *adj* clearly expressed in few words -**ly** *adv*

suc·cour *BrE‖* -**cor** *AmE* /ˈsʌkə‖-ər/ *vt, n* [U] *lit* help

suc·cu·lent /ˈsʌkjˑlənt/ *adj* juicy and tasty -**lence** *n* [U]

suc·cumb /səˈkʌm/ *vi fml* stop opposing

such /sʌtʃ/ *predeterminer, determiner* 1 of that kind: *I dislike such people.* | *some flowers, such as* (=for example) *roses* 2 to so great a degree: *He's such a kind man.* 3 so great; so good, bad, or unusual: *He wrote to her every day, such was his love for her.* ♦ *pron* 1 any/no/some **such** any/no/some (person or thing) like that: *No such person exists.* 2 **as such** properly so named

such and such /ˈ· · ‚·/ *predeterminer infml* a certain (time, amount, etc.) not named

such·like /ˈsʌtʃlaɪk/ *adj, pron* (things) of that kind

suck /sʌk/ *v* 1 *vi/t* draw (liquid) in with the muscles of the mouth 2 *vt* hold (something) in one's mouth and move one's tongue against it: *sucking one's thumb* 3 *vt* draw powerfully: *The current sucked them under.* **suck** *n*

suck·er /ˈsʌkə‖-ər/ *n* 1 person or thing

that sucks 2 flat piece which sticks to a surface by suction 3 **a** easily cheated person **b** someone who likes the stated thing very much: *a sucker for ice cream*

suck·le /ˈsʌkəl/ *vi/t* feed with milk from the breast

suc·tion /ˈsʌkʃən/ *n* [U] drawing away air or liquid, esp. to lower the air pressure between two objects and make them stick to each other

sud·den /ˈsʌdn/ *adj* happening unexpectedly and quickly -**ly** *adv* ~**ness** *n* [U]

suds /sʌdz/ *n* [P] mass of soapy BUBBLES

sue /sjuː‖suː/ *vi/t* bring a legal claim (against)

suede /sweɪd/ *n* [U] soft leather with a rough surface

su·et /ˈsuːɪt, ˈsjuːɪt‖ˈsuː-/ *n* [U] hard fat used in cooking

suf·fer /ˈsʌfə‖-ər/ *v* 1 *vi* experience pain or difficulty 2 *vt* experience (something unpleasant) 3 *vt* accept without dislike: *He doesn't suffer fools gladly.* 4 *vi* grow worse: *His work has suffered since his illness.* ~**ing** *n* [U;C]

suf·fer·ance /ˈsʌfərəns/ *n* **on sufferance** with permission, though not welcomed

suf·fice /səˈfaɪs/ *vi/t fml* 1 be enough (for) 2 **suffice (it) to say that ...** I will say only that ...

suf·fi·cient /səˈfɪʃənt/ *adj* enough -**ly** *adv* -**ciency** *n* [S;U] *fml*

suf·fix /ˈsʌfɪks/ *n* group of letters or sounds added at the end of a word (as in kind**ness**, quick**ly**)

suf·fo·cate /ˈsʌfəkeɪt/ *vi/t* (cause to) die because of lack of air -**cation** /ˌsʌfəˈkeɪʃən/ *n* [U]

suf·frage /ˈsʌfrɪdʒ/ *n* [U] right to vote in national elections

suf·fuse /səˈfjuːz/ *vt* spread all through -**fusion** /-ˈfjuːʒən/ *n* [U]

sug·ar /ˈʃʊɡə‖-ər/ *n* [U] sweet white or brown plant substance used in food and drinks ♦ *vt* put sugar in ~**y** *adj* 1 containing or tasting of sugar 2 too sweet, nice, kind, etc. in an insincere way

sug·ar·cane /ˈʃʊɡəkeɪn‖-ər-/ *n* [U] tall tropical plant from whose stems sugar is obtained

sugar dad·dy /ˈ·· ‚·/ *n infml* older man

who provides a young woman with money and presents in return for sex and companionship

sug·gest /sə'dʒest‖səg'dʒest/ vt **1** state as an idea for consideration: *I suggest we do it this way.* **2** give signs (of): *The latest figures suggest that business is improving.* **~ive** adj **1** (perhaps) showing thoughts of sex **2** fml which leads the mind into a particular way of thinking **~ion** /sə'dʒest-ʃən‖səg-/ n [C;U] act of suggesting or something suggested

su·i·cide /'suːɪˌsaɪd, 'sjuː-‖'suː-/ n **1** [C;U] killing oneself **2** [C] person who does this **3** [U] action that destroys one's position **–cidal** /ˌsuːɪˈsaɪd◂, ˌsjuː-‖ˌsuː-/ adj **1** likely or wishing to kill oneself **2** likely to lead to death or destruction

suit¹ /suːt, sjuːt‖suːt/ n **1** short coat with trousers or skirt of the same material **2** garment for a special purpose: *a bathing suit* | *a suit of armour* **3** any of the four sets of playing cards **4 follow suit** do the same as everyone else

suit² vt **1** be convenient for; satisfy **2** match or look good on (someone): *That hairstyle doesn't suit you.* **3** be suited (to/for) be suitable **4 suit oneself** do what one likes

sui·ta·ble /'suːtəbəl, 'sjuː-‖'suː-/ adj fit or right for a purpose **–bly** adv **–bility** /ˌsuːtəˈbɪləti, ˌsjuː-‖ˌsuː-/ n [U]

suit·case /'suːtkeɪs, 'sjuːt-‖'suːt-/ n case for carrying clothes and possessions when travelling

suite /swiːt/ n **1** set of matching furniture **2** set of hotel rooms **3** piece of music made up of several parts

sui·tor /'suːtə, 'sjuː-‖'suːtər/ n lit man wishing to marry a particular woman

sulk /sʌlk/ vi be silently bad-tempered **~y** adj **–ily** adv **~iness** n [U]

sul·len /'sʌlən/ adj showing silent dislike, bad temper, lack of interest, etc. **–ly** adv **–ness** n [U]

sul·ly /'sʌli/ vt lit spoil

sul·phur BrE ‖ **-fur** AmE /'sʌlfə‖-ər/ n [U] substance found esp. as a light yellow powder

sul·phu·ric ac·id /ˌsʌlˌfjʊərɪk 'æsɪd‖-ˌfjʊr-/ n [U] powerful acid

sul·tan /'sʌltən/ n (often cap.) Muslim ruler

sul·ta·na /sʌl'tɑːnə‖-'tænə/ n **1** small dried GRAPE used in cakes, etc. **2** (often cap.) wife, mother, or daughter of a sultan

sul·try /'sʌltri/ adj **1** (of weather) hot, airless, and uncomfortable **2** causing or showing strong sexual desire

sum¹ /sʌm/ n **1** total produced when numbers are added together **2** amount (of money) **3** simple calculation

sum² v **-mm- sum up** phr v **1** vi/t SUMMARIZE **2** vt consider and form a judgment of

sum·ma·ry /'sʌməri/ n short account giving the main points. ♦ adj **1** short **2** done at once without attention to formalities: *summary dismissal* **–rize, –rise** vt make a summary of

sum·mer /'sʌmə‖-ər/ n [C;U] hot season between spring and autumn **~y** adj like or suitable for summer

sum·mit /'sʌmɪt/ n **1** highest point **2** top of a mountain **3** meeting between heads of government

sum·mon /'sʌmən/ vt order officially to come

summon up phr vt get (a quality in oneself) ready for use

sum·mons /'sʌmənz/ n, vt order to appear in a court of law

sump /sʌmp/ n part of an engine holding the oil supply

sump·tu·ous /'sʌmptʃuəs/ adj expensive and grand **~ly** adv

sum to·tal /ˌ· '··/ n [the+S] the whole, esp. when less than expected or needed

sun /sʌn/ n **1** [the+S] star round which the Earth moves **2** [the+S;U] sun's light and heat: *sitting in the sun* **3** [C] star round which PLANETs may turn **4 under the sun** at all ♦ vt **-nn-** place (oneself) in sunlight **~ny** adj **1** having bright sunlight **2** cheerful

sun·bathe /'sʌnbeɪð/ vi sit or lie in strong sunlight **–bather** n

sun·beam /'sʌnbiːm/ n a beam of sunlight

sun·belt /'sʌnbelt/ n [the+S] southern and southwestern parts of the US

sun·burn /'sʌnbɜːn‖-ɜːrn/ n [U] sore skin caused by too much strong sunlight **–burnt, ~ed** adj

sun·dae /'sʌndeɪ‖-di/ n ice cream dish with fruit, nuts, etc.

sun cream /'· ·/ n [U] SUNSCREEN

Sun·day /'sʌndi/ n the seventh day of the week, between Saturday and Monday

sun·der /'sʌndə ‖ -ər/ vt lit separate

sun·dial /'sʌndaɪəl/ n apparatus producing a shadow which shows the time

sun·down /'sʌndaʊn/ n [U] sunset

sun·dry /'sʌndri/ adj 1 various 2 **all and sundry** all types of people; everybody

sun·flow·er /'sʌn,flaʊə ‖ -,flaʊr/ n tall plant with large yellow flowers and seeds that are eaten or used for oil

sung /sʌŋ/ past p. of SING

sun·glass·es /'sʌn,ɡlɑːsɪz ‖ -,ɡlæ-/ n [P] glasses with dark glass for protection from sunlight

sunk /sʌŋk/ past p. of SINK

sunk·en /'sʌŋkən/ adj 1 that has (been) sunk 2 below the surrounding level: *sunken eyes* | *a sunken garden*

sun·lamp /'sʌnlæmp/ n ULTRAVIOLET lamp for browning the skin

sun·light /'sʌnlaɪt/ n [U] light from the sun

sun·lit /'sʌn,lɪt/ adj brightly lit by the sun

sun·rise /'sʌnraɪz/ n [U] time when the sun appears after the night

sun·roof /'sʌnruːf/ n opening in the roof of a car

sun·screen /'sʌnskriːn/ n [U] cream to stop the sun burning the skin

sun·set /'sʌnset/ n [C;U] time when the sun disappears as night begins

sun·shade /'sʌnʃeɪd/ n sort of UMBRELLA for protection from sunshine

sun·shine /'sʌnʃaɪn/ n [U] strong sunlight

sun·spot /'sʌnspɒt ‖ -spɑːt/ n dark cooler area on the sun's surface

sun·stroke /'sʌnstrəʊk ‖ -strouk/ n [U] illness caused by too much strong sunlight

sun·tan /'sʌntæn/ n brownness of the skin caused by being in strong sunlight

su·per /'suːpə, 'sjuː- ‖ 'suːpər/ adj wonderful; extremely good

su·per·an·nu·at·ed /,suːpər'ænjueɪtɪd, ,sjuː- ‖ ,suː-/ adj fml 1 too old for work 2 old-fashioned **–ion** /,suːpərænju'eɪʃən, ,sjuː- ‖ ,suː-/ n [U] fml for PENSION

su·perb /suː'pɜːb, sjuː- ‖ suː'pɜːrb/ adj excellent; wonderful **~ly** adv

su·per·cil·i·ous /,suːpə'sɪliəs◂, ,sjuː- ‖ ,suːpər-/ adj fml derog (as if) thinking that others are of little importance **~ly** adv

~ness n [U]

su·per·con·duc·tor /,suːpəkən'dʌktə, ,sjuː- ‖ ,suːpərkən'dʌktər/ n substance which at very low temperatures allows electricity to pass freely

su·per·fi·cial /,suːpə'fɪʃəl◂, ,sjuː- ‖ ,suːpər-/ adj 1 on the surface; not deep 2 not thorough or complete **~ly** adv **~ity** /,suːpəfɪʃi'ælɪti,,sjuː- ‖ ,suːpər-/ n [U]

su·per·flu·ous /suː'pɜːfluəs, sjuː- ‖ suː'pɜːr-/ adj more than is necessary; not needed **~ly** adv

su·per·grass /'suːpəɡrɑːs, 'sjuː- ‖ 'suːpərɡræs/ n BrE person, esp. a criminal, who supplies the police with a lot of information about the activities of criminals

super·hu·man /,suːpə'hjuːmən◂, ,sjuː- ‖ ,suːpər'hjuː-, -'juː-/ adj (as if) beyond or better than human powers

su·per·im·pose /,suːpərɪm'pəʊz, ,sjuː- ‖ ,suːpərɪm'poʊz/ vt put (something) over something else, esp. so that both can be (partly) seen

su·per·in·ten·dent /,suːpərɪn'tendənt, ,sjuː- ‖ ,suː-/ n 1 person in charge 2 British police officer of middle rank

su·pe·ri·or /suː'pɪəriə, sjuː- ‖ suː'pɪriər/ adj 1 of higher rank 2 better 3 of high quality 4 derog (as if) thinking oneself better than others ♦ n person of higher rank **~ity** /suː,pɪəri'ɒrɪti, sjuː- ‖ suː,pɪri'ɔː-, -'ɑː-/ n [U]

su·per·la·tive /suː'pɜːlətɪv, sjuː- ‖ suː'pɜːr-/ adj 1 gram expressing 'most' 2 extremely good ♦ n gram superlative form of an adjective or adverb

su·per·mar·ket /'suːpə,mɑːkɪt, 'sjuː- ‖ 'suːpər,mɑːr-/ n large food shop where one serves oneself

su·per·mo·del /'suːpə,mɒdl, 'sjuː- ‖ 'suːpər,mɑː-/ n very famous fashion model

su·per·nat·u·ral /,suːpə'nætʃərəl◂, ,sjuː- ‖ ,suːpər-/ adj of or caused by the power of spirits, gods, or magic **~ly** adv

su·per·pow·er /'suːpə,paʊə, 'sjuː- ‖ 'suːpər,paʊr/ n very powerful nation

su·per·sede /,suːpə'siːd, ,sjuː- ‖ ,suːpər-/ vt take the place of

su·per·son·ic /,suːpə'sɒnɪk◂, ,sjuː- ‖ ,suːpər'sɑː-/ adj (flying) faster than the speed of sound

su·per·star /'suːpəstɑː, 'sjuː- ‖ 'suːpər-

,stɑːr/ n very famous performer

su·per·sti·tion /ˌsuːpəˈstɪʃən, ˌsjuː-ǁ ˌsuːpər-/ n [C;U] (unreasonable) belief based on old ideas about luck, magic, etc. **-tious** adj

su·per·store /ˈsuːpəstɔː, ˈsjuː-ǁ ˈsuːpərˌstɔːr/ n BrE very large store, usu. just outside a town

su·per·struc·ture /ˈsuːpəˌstrʌktʃə, ˈsjuː-ǁ ˈsuːpərˌstrʌktʃər/ n upper structure built on a base

su·per·vise /ˈsuːpəvaɪz, ˈsjuː-ǁ ˈsuːpər-/ vt watch (people or work) to make sure things are done properly **-visor** n **-visory** /ˌsuːpəˈvaɪzəri◂, ˌsjuː-ǁ adj **-vision** /ˌsuːpəˈvɪʒən, ˌsjuː-ǁ ˌsuːpər-/ n [U]

sup·per /ˈsʌpə ǁ -ər/ n [C;U] evening meal

sup·plant /səˈplɑːnt ǁ səˈplænt/ vt take the place of

sup·ple /ˈsʌpəl/ adj bending easily and gracefully **-ness** n [U]

sup·ple·ment /ˈsʌpləmənt/ n 1 additional amount to supply what is needed 2 additional separate part of a newspaper, magazine, etc. —see also COLOUR SUPPLEMENT ♦ vt /-ment/ make additions to **-ary** /ˌsʌpləˈmentəri◂/ adj additional

sup·ply /səˈplaɪ/ vt 1 provide (something) 2 provide things to (someone) for use ♦ n 1 amount for use: a supply of food 2 (system for) supplying: the supply of electricity 3 **in short supply** scarce —see also MONEY SUPPLY **-plier** n **supplies** n [P] things necessary for daily life, esp. food

supply and de·mand /ˌ· · ·ˈ·/ n [U] balance between the amount of goods for sale and the amount that people actually want to buy

sup·port /səˈpɔːt ǁ -ɔːrt/ vt 1 bear the weight of, esp. so as to prevent from falling 2 approve of and encourage 3 be loyal to: supporting the local football team 4 provide money for (someone) to live on 5 strengthen (an idea, opinion, etc.) ♦ n 1 [U] state of being supported 2 [C] something that supports 3 [U] active approval and encouragement 4 [U] money to live on **-er** n person who supports a particular activity or team, defends a particular principle, etc. **-ive** adj providing encouragement, help, etc.

sup·port·ing /səˈpɔːtɪŋ ǁ -ɔːr-/ adj playing or being a part in a play or film

which is not the main one: the award for best supporting actor

sup·pose /səˈpəʊz ǁ -ˈpoʊz/ vt 1 consider to be probable: As she's not here, I suppose she must have gone home. 2 **be supposed to:** a ought to; should **b** be generally considered to be ♦ conj 1 (used for making a suggestion): Suppose we wait a while. 2 what would/will happen if? **~dly** /-zɪdli/ adv as is believed; as it appears **-posing** conj suppose

sup·po·si·tion /ˌsʌpəˈzɪʃən/ n 1 [U] act of supposing or guessing 2 [C] guess

sup·pos·i·to·ry /səˈpɒzɪtəri ǁ səˈpɑːzɪtɔːri/ n piece of meltable medicine placed in the RECTUM or VAGINA

sup·press /səˈpres/ vt 1 bring to an end by force 2 prevent from being shown or made public: suppressing her anger/the truth **-ion** /-ˈpreʃən/ n [U]

su·preme /suːˈpriːm, sjuː-, sə-ǁ suː-, suː-/ adj 1 highest in degree: supreme happiness | the supreme sacrifice (=giving one's life) 2 most powerful **-ly** adv extremely **supremacy** /suːˈpreməsi/ n [U]

sur·charge /ˈsɜːtʃɑːdʒ ǁ ˈsɜːrtʃɑːrdʒ/ n (demand for) an additional payment ♦ vt make (someone) pay a surcharge

sure /ʃʊə ǁ ʃʊr/ adj 1 having no doubt 2 certain (to happen): You're sure to happen): b take certain (=certainly will) like it. 3 confident of having: I've never felt surer of success. 4 **be sure to** don't forget to 5 **make sure: a** find out (if something is really true) **b** take action (so that something will certainly 6 **sure of oneself** certain that one's actions are right ♦ adv 1 certainly 2 **for sure** certainly so 3 **sure enough** as was expected **-ly** adv 1 I believe, hope, or expect: Surely you haven't forgotten? 2 safely

sure-fire /ˈʃʊəfaɪə ǁ ˈʃʊrfaɪr/ adj certain to succeed

sure·foot·ed /ˌʃʊəˈfʊtɪd◂ ǁ ˌʃʊr-/ adj able to walk, climb, etc. in difficult places without falling

sure·ty /ˈʃʊəʃti ǁ ˈʃʊr-/ n [C;U] 1 person who takes responsibility for the behaviour of another 2 money given to make sure that a person will appear in court

surf /sɜːf ǁ sɜːrf/ n [U] white air-filled waves breaking on a shore ♦ v 1 vi ride as a sport over breaking waves near the shore.

on a SURFBOARD **2** *vt* **surf the net** look for information on the INTERNET ~**ing** *n* [U] sport of surfing ~**er** *n* person who goes surfing

sur·face /'sɜːfɪs‖'sɜːr-/ *n* **1** outer part of an object **2** top of liquid **3** what is easily seen, not the main (hidden) part ♦ *adj* **1** not deep; SUPERFICIAL: *surface friendliness* ♦ *vi* come up to the surface of water: (fig.) *He doesn't usually surface* (=get out of bed) *until midday.*

surface mail /'·· ·/ *n* [U] post carried by land or sea

surface-to-air /,·· ·'·◄/ *adj* (of a weapon) fired from the earth towards aircraft

surf·board /'sɜːfbɔːd‖'sɜːrfbɔːrd/ *n* board for riding on surf

sur·feit /'sɜːfɪt‖'sɜːr-/ *n* [S] too large an amount

surge /sɜːdʒ‖sɜːrdʒ/ *n* **1** sudden powerful forward movement **2** sudden increase of strong feeling ♦ *vi* **1** move forwards like powerful waves **2** (of a feeling) arise powerfully

sur·geon /'sɜːdʒən‖'sɜːr-/ *n* doctor who does SURGERY (1)

sur·ge·ry /'sɜːdʒəri‖'sɜːr-/ *n* **1** [U] performing of medical operations **2** [C;U] *BrE* place where or time when a doctor or DENTIST treats patients **3** [C] *BrE* period of time when people can come and see a member of parliament, lawyer, etc. to ask advice

sur·gi·cal /'sɜːdʒɪkəl‖'sɜːr-/ *adj* **1** of or used for surgery **2** (of a garment) worn as treatment for a particular physical condition ~**ly** /-kli/ *adv*

sur·ly /'sɜːli‖'sɜːrli/ *adj* bad-tempered and bad-mannered **surliness** *n* [U]

sur·mise /sə'maɪz‖sər-/ *vt fml* suppose; guess

sur·mount /sə'maʊnt‖sər-/ *vt* **1** succeed in dealing with (a difficulty) **2** be on top of

sur·name /'sɜːneɪm‖'sɜːr-/ *n* person's family name

sur·pass /sə'pɑːs‖sər'pæs/ *vt fml* go beyond, esp. be better than

sur·plus /'sɜːpləs‖'sɜːr-/ *n, adj* (amount) additional to what is needed or used

sur·prise /sə'praɪz‖sər-/ *n* [C;U] **1** (feeling caused by) an unexpected event **2 take by surprise** come on (someone) unprepared ♦ *vt* **1** cause surprise to **2** find,

catch, or attack when unprepared

sur·pris·ing /sə'praɪzɪŋ‖sər-/ *adj* unusual; causing surprise ~**ly** *adv*

sur·real /sə'rɪəl/ *adj* having a strange dreamlike unreal quality ~**ism** *n* [U] modern art or literature that treats subjects in a surreal way ~**ist** *n* (artist or writer) concerned with surrealism

sur·ren·der /sə'rendə‖-ər/ *v* **1** *vi/t* give up or give in to the power (esp. of an enemy); admit defeat **2** *vt fml* give up possession of ♦ *n* [C;U] act of surrendering

sur·rep·ti·tious /,sʌrəp'tɪʃəs◄/ *adj* done secretly, esp. for dishonest reasons ~**ly** *adv*

sur·ro·gate /'sʌrəgət, -gāt‖'sɜːr-/ *n, adj* (person or thing) acting or used in place of another: *a* **surrogate mother** (=a woman who has a baby for another woman who cannot have children) -**cy** *n* [U]

sur·round /sə'raʊnd/ *vt* be or go all around on every side ♦ *n* (decorative) edge or border ~**ing** *adj* around and nearby ~**ings** *n* [P] place and conditions of life

sur·veil·lance /sɜː'veɪləns‖sɜːr-/ *n* [U] close watch kept on someone or something

sur·vey¹ /sə'veɪ‖sər-/ *vt* **1** look at or examine as a whole **2** examine the condition of (a building) **3** measure (land) ~**or** *n* person whose job is to SURVEY¹ (2, 3)

sur·vey² /'sɜːveɪ‖'sɜːr-/ *n* **1** act of surveying: *a survey of public opinion/of a house* **2** general description

sur·vive /sə'vaɪv‖sər-/ *vi/t* continue to live or exist (after), esp. after coming close to death: *She survived the accident.* -**vival** *n* **1** [U] act of surviving **2** [C] something which has survived from an earlier time -**vivor** *n*

sus·cep·ti·ble /sə'septəbəl/ *adj* **1** easily influenced (by) **2** likely to suffer (from) -**bility** /sə,septə'bɪlɪti/ *n*

sus·pect /sə'spekt/ *vt* **1** believe to be so; think likely: *I suspected he was ill but didn't like to ask him.* **2** believe to be guilty ♦ *n* /'sʌspekt/ person suspected of guilt ♦ *adj* of uncertain truth, quality, legality, etc.

sus·pend /sə'spend/ *vt* **1** *fml* hang from above **2** hold still in liquid or air **3** make inactive for a time: *The meeting was suspended while the lights were repaired.* **4** prevent from taking part for a time, esp. for breaking rules ~**er** *n* fastener for holding up a woman's stockings ~**ers** *n* [P]

AmE for BRACES for trousers

sus·pense /sə'spens/ *n* [U] state of uncertainty causing anxiety or pleasant excitement

sus·pen·sion /sə'spenʃən/ *n* **1** [U] act of suspending or fact of being suspended **2** [C] apparatus fixed to a vehicle's wheels to lessen the effect of rough roads

suspension bridge /·'·· ·/ *n* bridge hung from strong steel ropes fixed to towers

sus·pi·cion /sə'spiʃən/ *n* **1** [U] **a** a case of suspecting or being suspected (SUSPECT (2)): *under suspicion of murder* **b** lack of trust: *treat someone with suspicion* **2 a** a feeling of SUSPECTing: *I have a suspicion you're right.* **b** belief about someone's guilt: *They have their suspicions.* **3** [S] slight amount **–cious** *adj* **1** suspecting guilt or wrongdoing **2** making one suspicious: *suspicious behaviour* **–ciously** *adv*

suss /sʌs/ *vt BrE sl* **suss out** *phr vt* find out details about

sus·tain /sə'stein/ *vt* **1** keep strong **2** keep in existence over a long period **3** *fml* suffer: *The car sustained severe damage.* **~able** *adj*: *wood from sustainable sources*

sus·te·nance /'sʌstənəns/ *n* [U] *fml* food or its ability to keep people strong and healthy

svelte /svelt/ *adj* thin and graceful

swab /swɒb ‖ swɑːb/ *n* piece of material that can take up liquid, esp. used medically ♦ *vt* **-bb-** clean (a wound) with a swab

swag /swæg/ *n* material hung loosely across the top of a window

swag·ger /'swægə ‖ -ər/ *vi* walk or behave (too) confidently or proudly swagger *n* [S;U]

swal·low¹ /'swɒləʊ ‖ 'swɑːloʊ/ *v* **1** *vi/t* move (the contents of the mouth) down the throat **2** *vt* accept patiently or with too easy belief: *It was an obvious lie, but he swallowed it.* **3** *vt* hold back (uncomfortable feelings); not show or express: *swallow one's pride* ♦ *n* act of swallowing or amount swallowed

swallow up *phr vt* take in and cause to disappear

swal·low² *n* small bird with a double-pointed tail

swam /swæm/ *past t. of* SWIM

swamp /swɒmp ‖ swɑːmp, swɒːmp/ *n* [C;U] (area of) soft wet land ♦ *vt* cause to

have (too) much to deal with **–y** *adj* wet like a swamp

swan¹ /swɒn ‖ swɑːn/ *n* large white long-necked water bird

swan² *vi* **-nn-** *infml* go or travel purposelessly or irresponsibly: *She just swanned off to Italy for the summer.*

swank /swæŋk/ *vi, n* [U] *infml* (act or speak too proudly, making) false or too great claims **–y** *adj infml* very fashionable or expensive

swan·song /'swɒnsɒŋ ‖ 'swɑːnsɔːŋ/ *n* one's last performance or piece of artistic work

swap /swɒp ‖ swɑːp/ *vi/t* **-pp-** exchange (goods or positions) so that each person gets what they want ♦ *n* **1** exchange **2** something to be exchanged

swarm /swɔːm ‖ swɔːrm/ *n* large moving mass of insects: (fig.) *swarms of tourists* ♦ *vi* move in a crowd or mass

swarm with *phr vt* be full of (a moving crowd)

swar·thy /'swɔːði ‖ -ɔːr-/ *adj* having fairly dark skin

swash·buck·ling /'swɒʃ,bʌkəliŋ ‖ 'swɑːʃ-, 'swɒːʃ-/ *adj* full of showy adventures, sword fighting, etc.

swat /swɒt ‖ swɑːt/ *vt* **-tt-** hit (an insect), esp. so as to kill it

swathe /sweið ‖ swɑːð, swɒːð, sweið/ *v* **swathe in** *phr vt* wrap round in (cloth): (fig.) *hills swathed in mist*

sway /swei/ *v* **1** *vi/t* swing from side to side **2** *vt* influence, esp. so as to change opinion ♦ *n* [U] **1** swaying movement **2** *lit* influence

swear /sweə ‖ swer/ *v* swore /swɔː ‖ swɔːr/, sworn /swɔːn ‖ swɔːrn/ *v* **1** curse **2** *vi/t* make a solemn promise or statement, esp. by taking an OATH (1): *She swore to tell the truth/swore that she had been there.* **3** cause to take an OATH

swear by *phr vt* have confidence in (something)

swear in *phr vt* **1** cause (a witness) to take the OATH (1) in court **2** cause to make a promise of responsible action, etc.: *The elected President was sworn in.*

swear word /'· ·/ *n* word considered rude by most people

sweat /swet/ *n* **1** [U] body liquid that comes out through the skin **2** [S] anxious state 3 [S] *infml* hard work 4 **no sweat** *infml* (used for saying that something will not cause any difficulty) ♦ *vi* 1 produce sweat 2 be very anxious or nervously impatient 3 **sweat blood** *infml* work unusually hard ~**y** *adj* 1 covered in or smelly with sweat 2 unpleasantly hot

sweat·er /'swetə‖-ər/ *n* (woollen) garment for the upper body with fastenings

sweat·shirt /'swet-ʃɜːt‖-ʃɜːrt/ *n* loose cotton garment for the upper body

sweat·shop /'swetʃɒp‖-ʃɑːp/ *n* factory where people work in bad conditions for little money

swede /swiːd/ *n* large round yellow root vegetable

sweep¹ /swiːp/ *v* swept /swept/ 1 *vt* clean or remove by brushing 2 *vi/t* move (over) or carry quickly and powerfully: *A wave of panic swept over her.* | *We were swept along by the crowd.* 3 *vi* lie in a curve across land 4 *vt* win completely and easily, as in elections 5 *vi* (of a person) move in a proud, firm manner 6 **sweep someone off their feet** fill someone with sudden love or excitement 7 **sweep something under the carpet** *BrE* ‖ **under the rug** *AmE* keep (something bad or shocking) secret ~**er** *n* ~**ing** *adj* 1 including many or most things: *sweeping changes* 2 too general: *a sweeping statement*

sweep aside *phr vt* refuse to pay any attention to

sweep² *n* 1 act of sweeping 2 long curved line or area of country: (fig.) *the broad sweep of her narrative* (=covering all parts of the subject) 3 person who cleans chimneys 4 sweepstake

sweep·stake /'swiːpsteɪk/ *n* form of risking money, esp. on a horserace, in which the winner gets all the losers' money

sweet /swiːt/ *adj* 1 tasting like sugar 2 pleasing to the senses: *sweet music* 3 charming; lovable: *What a sweet little boy!* —see also **short and sweet** (SHORT¹) ♦ *n BrE* 1 [C] small piece of food made of sugar, chocolate, etc. 2 [C;U] (dish of) sweet food at the end of a meal ~**en** *vt* 1 make sweeter 2 *infml* give money or presents in order to persuade ~**ly** *adv* ~**ness** *n* [U]

sweet·bread /'swiːtbred/ *n* sheep's or cow's PANCREAS used as food

sweet·corn /'swiːtkɔːn‖-kɔːrn/ *n* [U] *BrE* yellow MAIZE seeds cooked as a vegetable

sweet·en·er /'swiːtnə‖-ər/ *n* 1 substance used instead of sugar to make food or drink taste sweet 2 *infml* money, a present, etc. given in order to persuade someone

sweet·heart /'swiːthɑːt‖-hɑːrt/ *n* (used to address a person one loves)

sweet talk /'· ·/ *n* [U] *infml* insincere talk intended to please or persuade **sweet-talk** /'·· ·/ *vt*

sweet tooth /· '·, '· ·/ *n* [S] liking for sweet and sugary things

swell /swel/ *vi/t* swelled, swollen /'swəʊlən‖'swoʊ-/ *or* swelled 1 increase gradually to beyond the usual or original size 2 fill or be filled, giving a full round shape ♦ *n* [S] rolling up-and-down movement of the surface of the sea ♦ *adj AmE* excellent ~**ing** *n* 1 act of swelling 2 swollen place on the body

swel·ter /'sweltə‖-ər/ *vi* experience the effects of unpleasantly great heat

swept /swept/ *past t. and p. of* SWEEP

swerve /swɜːv‖swɜːrv/ *vi, n* (make) a sudden change of direction

swift¹ /swɪft/ *adj* quick ~**ly** *adv* ~**ness** *n* [U]

swift² *n* small brown fast-flying bird like a SWALLOW²

swig /swɪg/ *vt* -gg- *infml* drink, esp. in large mouthfuls **swig** *n*

swill /swɪl/ *vt* 1 wash with large streams of water 2 *infml* drink, esp. in large amounts ♦ *n* [U] partly liquid pig food

swim /swɪm/ *v* swam /swæm/, swum /swʌm/· *present p.* -mm- 1 *vi* move through water using the limbs, FINS, etc. 2 *vt* cross by doing this 3 *vi* be full of or surrounded with liquid 4 *vi* seem to spin round and round: *My head was swimming.* 5 **swim with the tide** follow the behaviour of other people around one ♦ *n* 1 [S] act of swimming 2 **in the swim** knowing about and concerned in what is going on in modern life ~**mer** *n*

swimming cos·tume /'·· ,··/ *n BrE* SWIMSUIT

swimming pool /'·· ·/ *n* large usu. outdoor container filled with water and used for swimming

swim·suit /'swɪmsuːt, -sjuːt‖-suːt/ *n*

piece of clothing worn by girls and women for swimming

swin·dle /'swɪndl/ vt cheat, esp. so as to get money ♦ n act of swindling **swindler** n

swine /swaɪn/ n swine 1 fml or lit pig 2 sl unpleasant person

swing /swɪŋ/ swung /swʌŋ/ 1 vi/t move backwards and forwards or round and round from a fixed point: Soldiers swing their arms as they march. 2 vi/t move in a smooth curve: The door swung shut. 3 vi turn quickly ♦ vi start smoothly and rapidly: We're ready to swing into action. 5 vi infml be hanged to death, as a punishment 6 **not enough room to swing a cat** infml very little space ♦ n 1 [C] act of swinging 2 [C] children's swinging seat fixed from above by ropes or chains 3 [C] noticeable change: a big swing in public opinion 4 [S] JAZZ music of the 1930s and 1940s with a strong regular active beat 5 **go with a swing** happen successfully 6 **in full swing** having reached a very active stage 7 **what you lose on the swings you gain on the roundabouts** (often shortened to **swings and roundabouts**) infml, esp. BrE the disadvantages of a particular situation or course of action are balanced by the advantages

swinge·ing /'swɪndʒɪŋ/ adj esp. BrE very severe

swipe /swaɪp/ vt 1 hit hard 2 move (a CREDIT CARD, etc.) quickly through a machine that reads information from it 3 infml steal ♦ n sweeping blow

swipe card /'· ·/ n small plastic card that operates electronic equipment

swirl /swɜːl‖swɜːrl/ vi/t move with twisting turns ♦ n twisting mass

swish¹ /swɪʃ/ vi/t move through the air with a sharp whistling noise ♦ n act of swishing

swish² adj infml fashionable and expensive

Swiss /swɪs/ adj of Switzerland

switch /swɪtʃ/ n 1 apparatus for stopping or starting an electric current 2 sudden complete change ♦ vi/t change or exchange: They switched jobs. | The lights have switched to green.

switch off/on phr vt turn (an electric light or apparatus) off/on with a switch

switch over phr vi 1 change

completely 2 change from one radio or television CHANNEL (3) to another

switch·board /'swɪtʃbɔːd‖-bɔːrd/ n place where telephone lines in a large building are connected

swiv·el /'swɪvəl/ vi/t -ll- BrE‖-l- AmE turn round (as if) on a central point

swiz, **swizz** /swɪz/ n [S] BrE infml something that makes one feel cheated or disappointed

swiz·zle stick /'swɪzəl ˌstɪk/ n rod for mixing drinks

swol·len /'swəʊlən‖'swoʊ-/ past. p. of SWELL

swoon /swuːn/ vi lit 1 experience deep joy, desire, etc. 2 FAINT

swoop /swuːp/ vi come down sharply, esp. to attack **swoop** n 1 swooping action 2 **at one fell swoop** all at once

swop /swɒp‖swɑːp/ v, n SWAP

sword /sɔːd‖sɔːrd/ n 1 weapon with a long sharp metal blade and a handle 2 **cross swords (with)** be opposed (to), esp. in argument

swords·man /'sɔːdzmən‖-ɔːr-/ n -men /-mən/ (skilled) fighter with a sword ~**ship** n [U]

swore /swɔː‖swɔːr/ past t. of SWEAR

sworn /swɔːn‖swɔːrn/ past p. of SWEAR

swot /swɒt‖swɑːt/ vi -tt- BrE infml study hard, esp. to get good examination results ♦ n derog person who swots

swum /swʌm/ past p. of SWIM

swung /swʌŋ/ past t. and p. of SWING

sy·ca·more /'sɪkəmɔː‖-mɔːr/ n [C;U] broad-leaved tree whose seed cases spin down on two wings

syc·o·phant /'sɪkəfənt/ n person who praises people insincerely to gain personal advantage ~**ic** /ˌsɪkəˈfæntɪk◂/ adj ~**ically** /-kli/ adv ~**phancy** /'sɪkəfənsi/ n [U]

syl·la·ble /'sɪləbəl/ n part of a word containing a single vowel sound: There are two syllables in 'window': 'win-' and '-dow'. ~**labic** /sɪˈlæbɪk/ adj

syl·la·bus /'sɪləbəs/ n arrangement of subjects for study over a period of time

sylph·like /'sɪlf-laɪk/ adj (of a woman) gracefully thin

syl·van /'sɪlvən/ adj lit of or in the woods

sym·bi·o·sis /ˌsɪmbiˈəʊsɪs‖-baɪˈoʊ-, -bi-/ n [U] condition in which one living thing depends on another for existence

symbol

-otic /-ˈɒtɪk ‖ -ˈɑːtɪk/ adj

sym·bol /ˈsɪmbəl/ n something that represents something else: *The dove is the symbol of peace.* ~ism n [U] use of symbols ~ize, ~ise vt represent by or as a symbol ~ic /sɪmˈbɒlɪk ‖ -ˈbɑː-/ adj representing: *The snake is symbolic of evil.* ~ically /-kli/ adv

sym·me·try /ˈsɪmɪtri/ n [U] 1 exact likeness in size, shape, etc. between opposite sides 2 effect of pleasing balance **symmetrical** /sɪˈmetrɪkəl/ adj

sym·pa·thy /ˈsɪmpəθi/ n [U] 1 sensitivity to and pity for others' suffering 2 agreement and/or understanding: *I am in sympathy with their aims.* 3 **come out in sympathy** support workers who have gone on STRIKE² (1) by stopping work oneself ~thize, ~thise vt feel or show sympathy ~thizer, ~thiser n person who supports an idea, political party, etc. **sympathies** n [P] feelings of support or loyalty ~thetic /ˌsɪmpəˈθetɪk◂/ adj feeling or showing sympathy ~thetically /-kli/ adv

sym·pho·ny /ˈsɪmfəni/ n usu. four-part piece of music for an ORCHESTRA

sym·po·si·um /sɪmˈpəʊziəm ‖ -ˈpoʊ-/ n -ums or -a /-ziə/ meeting to talk about a subject of study

symp·tom /ˈsɪmptəm/ n 1 outward sign of a disease 2 outward sign of inner change, new feelings; etc. ~atic /ˌsɪmptəˈmætɪk◂/ adj being a symptom

syn·a·gogue /ˈsɪnəgɒg ‖ -gɑːg/ n building where Jews worship

sync /sɪŋk/ infml 1 **in sync** acting (well together) at the same time 2 **out of sync** not in sync

syn·chro·nize also -nise BrE /ˈsɪŋkrənaɪz/ vt 1 cause to happen at the same time or speed 2 cause (watches, etc.) to show the same time ~nization, ~nisation /ˌsɪŋkrənaɪˈzeɪʃən ‖ -krənə-/ n [U]

syn·co·pate /ˈsɪŋkəpeɪt/ vt change (the beat of music) by giving force to the beats that are usu. less forceful ~pation /ˌsɪŋkəˈpeɪʃən/ n [U]

syn·di·cate¹ /ˈsɪndɪkət/ n group of people or companies combined for usu. business purposes

syn·di·cate² /ˈsɪndɪkeɪt/ vt sell (written work, pictures, etc.) to many different newspapers or magazines

syn·drome /ˈsɪndrəʊm ‖ -droʊm/ n 1 set

of medical SYMPTOMs which represent an illness 2 any pattern of qualities, happenings, etc. typical of a general condition

syn·o·nym /ˈsɪnənɪm/ n word with the same meaning as another ~ous /sɪˈnɒnɪməs ‖ -ˈnɑː-/ adj

sy·nop·sis /sɪˈnɒpsɪs ‖ -ˈnɑːp-/ n short account of something longer

syn·tax /ˈsɪntæks/ n [U] way in which words are ordered and connected in sentences ~tactic /sɪnˈtæktɪk/ adj

syn·the·sis /ˈsɪnθəsɪs/ n -ses /-siːz/ 1 [U] combining of separate things, ideas, etc. into a complete whole 2 [C] something made by synthesis ~size, ~sise vt make by synthesis, esp. make (something similar to a natural product) by combining chemicals ~sizer, ~siser n electrical instrument, like a piano, that can produce many sorts of different sounds, used esp. in popular music

syn·thet·ic /sɪnˈθetɪk/ adj artificial ~ally /-kli/ adv

syph·i·lis /ˈsɪfəlɪs/ n [U] very serious VENEREAL DISEASE

sy·phon /ˈsaɪfən/ n, v SIPHON

sy·ringe /sɪˈrɪndʒ/ n (medical) instrument with a hollow tube for sucking in and pushing out liquid, esp. through a needle ♦ vt clean with a syringe

syr·up /ˈsɪrəp ‖ ˈsɜː-, ˈsɪ-/ n [U] sweet liquid, esp. sugar and water

sys·tem /ˈsɪstəm/ n 1 [C] group of related parts which work together forming a whole: *the postal system | the digestive system* 2 [C] ordered set of ideas, methods, or ways of working: *the American system of government* 3 [C] the body, thought of as a set of working parts: *Travelling always upsets my system.* 4 [U] orderly methods 5 [the+S] society seen as something which uses and limits individuals: *to fight the system* —see also EXPERT SYSTEM, OPERATING SYSTEM ~atic /ˌsɪstəˈmætɪk◂/ adj based on orderly methods and careful organization; thorough ~atically /-kli/ adv ~atize, ~atise /ˈsɪstəmətaɪz/ vt

systems an·a·lyst /ˈ·· ˌ·/ n someone who studies (esp. business) activities and uses computers to plan ways of carrying them out, etc.

T

T, t /tiː/ the 20th letter of the English alphabet

ta /tɑː/ interj BrE sl thank you

tab /tæb/ n 1 small piece of paper, cloth, metal, etc. fixed to something to hold it by, open it with, etc. 2 **keep tabs on** watch closely

tab·by /'tæbi/ n cat with dark and light bands of fur

tab·er·nac·le /'tæbənækəl ‖ -ər-/ n container for religious objects

ta·ble /'teɪbl/ n 1 piece of furniture with a flat top on upright legs 2 set of figures arranged in rows across and down a page 3 **turn the tables on** gain an advantage over (someone who had an advantage over you) see also WATER TABLE ♦ vt 1 BrE put forward for consideration by a committee, etc. 2 AmE leave until a later date for consideration

tab·leau /'tæbləʊ ‖ 'tæbloʊ, tæˈbloʊ/ n scene on stage shown by a group of people who do not move or speak

ta·ble d'hôte /ˌtɑːbəl 'dəʊt ‖ -'doʊt/ n complete meal at a fixed price

ta·ble·spoon /'teɪbəlspuːn/ n large spoon for serving food

tab·let /'tæblət/ n 1 small solid piece of medicine 2 small block (of soap) 3 flat piece of stone or metal with words on it

table ten·nis /'·· ,··/ n [U] indoor game in which a small ball is hit across a net on a table

tab·loid /'tæblɔɪd/ n newspaper with small pages and many pictures

ta·boo /təˈbuː, tæˈbuː/ n -boos [C;U] strong social or religious custom forbidding something ♦ adj strongly forbidden by social custom: taboo words

tab·u·late /'tæbjəleɪt/ vt arrange as a TABLE (2) -lar adj -lation /ˌtæbjəˈleɪʃən/ n [U]

ta·cit /'tæsɪt/ adj accepted or understood without being openly expressed: tacit approval ~ly adv

ta·ci·turn /'tæsɪtɜːn ‖ -ɜːrn/ adj tending to speak very little

tack /tæk/ n 1 small nail 2 sailing ship's direction: (fig.) He switched the conversation onto a new tack. 3 long loose stitch ♦ v 1 vt fasten with tacks 2 vi change the course of a sailing ship

tack·le /'tækəl/ n 1 [C] act of stopping or taking the ball away from an opponent in sport 2 [U] apparatus used in certain sports: fishing tackle 3 [C;U] (system of) ropes and wheels for heavy pulling and lifting ♦ v 1 vt take action in order to deal with 2 vt speak to fearlessly so as to deal with a problem 3 vi/t stop or rob with a TACKLE (1)

tack·y /'tæki/ adj 1 sticky 2 of low quality: a tacky hotel/remark (=in bad TASTE (3)) –iness n [U]

tact /tækt/ n [U] skill of speaking or acting without offending people ~ful adj ~fully adv ~less adj ~lessly adv

tac·tic /'tæktɪk/ n plan or method for gaining a desired result **tactics** n [U] art of arranging and moving military forces in battle **tactical** adj 1 of tactics 2 done to get a desired result in the end: a tactical retreat **tactician** /tækˈtɪʃən/ n person skilled in tactics

tac·tile /'tæktaɪl ‖ 'tæktl/ adj of or able to be felt by the sense of touch

tad·pole /'tædpəʊl ‖ -poʊl/ n small creature that grows into a FROG or TOAD

taf·fe·ta /'tæfɪtə/ n [U] shiny stiff cloth made from silk or NYLON

tag /tæg/ n 1 [C] small piece of paper or material fixed to something to show who owns it, its cost, etc. 2 [U] game in which one child chases the others until he/she touches one of them ♦ vt -gg- 1 fasten a tag to 2 provide with a name or NICKNAME

tag along phr vi go with someone by following closely behind

tag on phr vt add

tail¹ /teɪl/ n 1 long movable growth at the back of a creature's body 2 last or back part (of something long): the tail of an aircraft/a queue 3 person employed to follow someone 4 **turn tail** turn round ready to run away **tails** n [P] 1 side of a coin without a ruler's head on it 2 tailcoat

tail² vt follow (someone) closely, esp. without their knowledge

tail away/off phr vi lessen gradually

tail·back /'teɪlbæk/ n line of traffic

stretching back from where its flow has been halted

tail·coat /'teɪl'kəʊt, 'teɪlkəʊt ‖ -kout/ n man's coat with a long back divided into two below the waist

tail·gate /'teɪlgeɪt/ vi/t drive too close to (another vehicle)

tai·lor /'teɪlə ‖ -ər/ n person who makes outer garments for men ♦ vt fit to a particular need ~**made** /ˌ·· '·◄/ adj exactly right for a particular need, person, etc.

tail-light, **tail light** /'·· ·/ n one of two red lights at the back of a car, etc.

tail·wind /'teɪl,wɪnd/ n wind coming from behind

taint /teɪnt/ vt, n [S] (spoil with) a small amount of decay, infection, or bad influence

take¹ /teɪk/ v took /tʊk/, taken /'teɪkən/ 1 vt move from one place to another: *Take the chair into the garden.* | *Take the children with you.* | *I had a tooth taken out.* 2 vt remove without permission: *Someone's taken my pen.* 3 vt subtract: *What you get if you take 5 from 12?* 4 vt get possession of, seize: *Rebels have taken the airport.* 5 vt get by performing an action: *Take his temperature.* | *He took notes.* | *Take a seat.* 6 vt start to hold: *She took my arm.* 7 vt use for travel: *I take the train to work.* 8 vt be willing to accept: *Will you take a cheque?* 9 vt accept as true or worthy of attention: *Take my advice.* | *I took his suggestion seriously.* 10 vt be able to contain: *The bus takes 55 passengers.* 11 vt be able to accept; bear: *I can't take his rudeness.* 12 vt need: *The journey takes (=lasts) two hours.* | *It took ten men to pull down the wall.* 13 vt do; perform: *He took a walk/a bath.* 14 vt put into the body: *take some medicine/a deep breath* 15 vt make by photography 16 vt have (a feeling): *take offence/pity* 17 vi have the intended effect; work: *Did the vaccination take?* 18 vt attract; delight: *The little house took my fancy.* 19 vt understand: *I take it you know each other.* 20 **be taken ill** become (suddenly) ill 21 **take it easy** infml RELAX 22 **take one's time**: a use as much time as is necessary b use too much time 23 **take something as read** agree on something without needing to talk about it

take aback phr vt surprise and confuse

take after phr vt look or behave like (an older relative)

take apart phr vt 1 separate into pieces 2 sl harm a place or person

take back phr vt 1 admit that (what one said) was wrong 2 cause to remember a former period in one's life: *That takes me back!*

take in phr vt 1 reduce the size of (a garment) 2 provide lodgings for 3 include 4 understand fully 5 deceive

take off phr v 1 vt remove (a garment) 2 vi (of a plane, etc.) rise into the air to begin a flight 3 vi infml leave without warning: *One day he just took off.* 4 vt copy the speech or manners of; MIMIC 5 vt have as a holiday from work: *I took Tuesday off.*

take on phr vt 1 start to employ 2 begin to have (a quality or appearance) 3 start to quarrel or fight with 4 accept (work, responsibility, etc.)

take out phr vt 1 go somewhere with (someone) as a social activity 2 obtain officially: *take out insurance* 3 **take someone out of himself** amuse or interest someone so that their worries are forgotten 4 **take it out of someone** use all the strength of someone

take out on phr vt express (one's feelings) by making (someone) suffer: *He tends to take things out on his wife.*

take over phr vi/t gain control of and responsibility for (something)

take to phr vt 1 like, esp. at once 2 begin as a practice or habit: *He took to drink.* 3 go to (one's bed, etc.) for rest, escape, etc.

take up phr vt 1 begin to interest oneself in: *I've taken up the guitar.* 2 complain, ask, or take further action about: *I'll take the matter up with my lawyer.* 3 fill or use (space or time), esp. undesirably 4 accept (someone's) offer: *I'll take you up on that.* 5 continue (a story, etc.)

take up with phr vt 1 become friendly with 2 be very interested in: *She's very taken up with her work.*

take² n 1 [C] filming of a scene 2 [C] takings 3 [S] infml way of thinking about something: *a new take on the situation*

take·a·way /'teɪkəweɪ/ n BrE (meal from) a restaurant that sells food to eat elsewhere

take·off /'teɪk-ɒf ‖ -ɒːf/ n 1 [C;U] rising of a plane, etc. from the ground 2 amusing copy of someone's typical behaviour

take·o·ver /'teɪk,əʊvə‖-,oʊvər/ n act of gaining control of esp. a business company

ta·ker /'teɪkə‖-ər/ n [usu. pl.] infml person willing to accept an offer

tak·ings /'teɪkɪŋz/ n [P] money received, esp. by a shop

tal·cum pow·der /'tælkəm ,paʊdə‖ -dər/ also talc /tælk/ infml — n [U] crushed mineral put on the body to dry it or make it smell nice

tale /teɪl/ n 1 story 2 false story; lie

tal·ent /'tælənt/ n [S;U] special natural ability or skill ~ed adj

tal·is·man /'tælɪzmən/ n -s object with magic protective powers

talk /tɔːk‖ tɔːk/ v 1 vi speak: Can the baby talk yet? | Is there somewhere quiet where we can talk? 2 vi give information by speaking, usu. unwillingly: We have ways of making you talk. 3 vi speak about others' affairs; GOSSIP 4 vt speak about: It's time to talk business. ♦ n 1 [S] conversation 2 [C] informal LECTURE 3 [U] way of talking: baby talk 4 [the+S] subject much talked about: Her sudden marriage is the talk of the street. 5 [U] empty or meaningless speech —see also SMALL TALK, SWEET TALK **talks** n [P] formal exchange of opinions ~er n

talk down to phr vt speak to (someone) as if one were more important, clever, etc.

talk into/out of phr vt persuade (someone) to do/not to do (something)

talk over phr vt speak about thoroughly and seriously

talk round phr vt persuade (someone) to change their mind

talk·a·tive /'tɔːkətɪv‖ 'tɔːk-/ adj liking to talk a lot

talking point /'·· ·/ n subject of conversation or argument

talking-to /'·· ·/ n angry talk in order to blame or CRITICIZE

tall /tɔːl‖ tɔːl/ adj 1 of greater than average height 2 of the stated height from top to bottom: He is 6 feet tall.

tall or·der /,· '·/ n [S] something unreasonably difficult to do

tal·low /'tæləʊ‖-loʊ/ n [U] hard animal fat used for candles

tall sto·ry /,· '··/ n story that is difficult to believe

tal·ly /'tæli/ n recorded total of money spent, points made in a game, etc. ♦ vi be exactly equal; match

tal·on /'tælən/ n sharp powerful curved nail on a hunting bird's foot

tam·bou·rine /,tæmbə'riːn/ n drumlike musical instrument with small metal plates round the edge

tame /teɪm/ adj 1 not fierce or wild 2 dull; unexciting ♦ vt make (an animal) tame ~ly adv ~ness n [U] tamer n

tam·per /'tæmpə‖-ər/ v **tamper with** phr vt touch or change without permission, esp. causing damage

tam·pon /'tæmpɒn‖-pɑːn/ n mass of cotton put into a woman's body to take up the monthly bleeding

tan /tæn/ v -nn- 1 vt change (animal skin) into leather by treating with TANNIN 2 vi/t turn brown, esp. by sunlight ♦ n 1 [C] brown skin colour from sunlight 2 [U] yellowish brown colour

tan·dem /'tændəm/ n 1 bicycle for two riders 2 **in tandem** with both working closely together

tan·doo·ri /tæn'dʊəri‖-'dʊri/ n [C;U] (meat cooked by) an Indian method of cooking in a big clay pot

tang /tæŋ/ n strong sharp taste or smell ~y adj

tan·gent /'tændʒənt/ n 1 straight line touching the edge of a curve 2 **go/fly off at a tangent** change suddenly to a different course of action or thought

tan·ge·rine /,tændʒə'riːn‖ 'tændʒəriːn/ n sort of small orange

tan·gi·ble /'tændʒəbəl/ adj 1 clear and certain; real: tangible proof 2 touchable –bly adv

tan·gle /'tæŋgəl/ vi/t (cause to) become a confused mass of twisted threads ♦ n confused mass or state

tan·go /'tæŋgəʊ‖-goʊ/ n -gos American dance

tank /tæŋk/ n 1 large liquid or gas container 2 enclosed armoured military vehicle

tan·kard /'tæŋkəd‖-ərd/ n large usu. metal cup for beer, etc.

tank·er /'tæŋkə‖-ər/ n ship, road vehicle, etc. carrying large quantities of liquid or gas

tan·nin /'tænɪn/ n [U] reddish acid found in certain plants, including tea

Tan·noy /'tænɔɪ/ *n tdmk, esp. BrE* system of LOUDSPEAKERS for public information

tan·ta·lize also **-lise** *BrE* /'tæntəl-aɪz/ *vt* cause to desire something even more strongly by keeping it just out of reach

tan·ta·mount /'tæntəmaʊnt/ *adj* having the same effect (as): *Her answer is tantamount to a refusal.*

tan·trum /'tæntrəm/ *n* sudden uncontrolled attack of angry bad temper

tap¹ /tæp/ **1** turnable apparatus for controlling the flow of water, etc. from a pipe, barrel, etc. **2 on tap** ready for use when needed

tap² *vt* **-pp- 1** use or draw from: *tapping our reserves of oil* **2** listen secretly by making an illegal connection to (a telephone)

tap³ *vt/i, n* **-pp-** (strike with) a light short blow: *She tapped her fingers on the table/tapped me on the shoulder.*

tap dance /'· ·/ *n* dance in which one makes loud sounds on the floor with special shoes

tape /teɪp/ *n* [C;U] **1** (long piece of) narrow material: *fastening a parcel with sticky tape* **2** (long piece of) narrow plastic MAGNETIC material on which sounds or pictures are recorded ♦ *vt* **1** record on TAPE (2) **2** fasten or tie with TAPE (1) **3 have something taped** *infml* understand something thoroughly or have learnt how to deal with it

tape deck /'· ·/ *n* part of a STEREO for TAPES (2)

tape mea·sure /'· ,··/ *n* narrow band of cloth or bendable metal used for measuring

ta·per /'teɪpə‖-ər/ *vi/t* make or become gradually narrower towards one end ♦ *n* thin candle

tape re·cord·er /'· ·,··/ *n* electrical apparatus for recording and playing sound with TAPE (2)

tap·es·try /'tæpɪstri/ *n* [C;U] (piece of) cloth with pictures or patterns woven into it

tar /tɑː‖tɑːr/ *n* [U] black meltable substance used for making roads, preserving wood, etc. ♦ *vt* **-rr- 1** cover with tar **2 tarred with the same brush** (thought of as) having the same faults

ta·ran·tu·la /tə'ræntjʊlə‖-tʃələ/ *n* large poisonous SPIDER

tar·dy /'tɑːdi‖'tɑːrdi/ *adj fml or lit* **1** slow in acting or happening **2** *AmE* late **–dily** *adv* **–diness** *n* [U]

tar·get /'tɑːgɪt‖'tɑːr-/ *n* **1** object aimed at in shooting practice **2** place, thing, or person at which an attack is directed **3** total or object which one tries to reach: *a production target of 500 cars a week* ♦ *vt* cause to be a target

tar·iff /'tærɪf/ *n* **1** tax on goods coming into a country **2** *fml* list of prices in a hotel, restaurant, etc.

tar·mac /'tɑːmæk‖'tɑːr-/ *n* [U] **1** tar and small stones for making road surfaces **2** area where aircraft take off and land

tar·nish /'tɑːnɪʃ‖'tɑːr-/ *vi/t* make or become discoloured or less bright: *tarnished silver/(fig.) reputations*

tar·ot /'tærəʊ‖-roʊ/ *n* set of 78 special cards used for telling the future

tar·pau·lin /tɑː'pɔːlɪn‖'tɑːrpɒː-/ *n* [C;U] (sheet or cover of) heavy WATERPROOF cloth

tar·ry /'tæri/ *vi lit* stay in a place for a while

tart¹ /tɑːt‖tɑːrt/ *v* **tart up** *phr vt infml derog* decorate or dress someone or something in a cheap colourful way

tart² *adj* bitter ♦ **–ness** *n* [U]

tart³ *n* sexually immoral woman

tart⁴ *n BrE* pastry container holding fruit or JAM

tar·tan /'tɑːtn‖'tɑːrtn/ *n* [C;U] (woollen cloth with) a pattern of bands crossing each other, esp. representing a particular Scottish CLAN

tar·tar /'tɑːtə‖'tɑːrtər/ *n* [U] chalklike substance that forms on teeth

task /tɑːsk‖tæsk/ *n* **1** piece of (hard) work (to be) done **2 take someone to task** speak severely to someone for a fault or failure

task force /'· ·/ *n* military or police group set up for a special purpose

task·mas·ter /'tɑːsk,mɑːstə‖'tæsk-,mæstər/ , **-mistress** /-,mɪstrɪs/ *fem. —n* someone who makes people work very hard

tas·sel /'tæsəl/ *n* tied bunch of threads hung decoratively

taste /teɪst/ *n* **1** [C;U] quality by which a food or drink is recognized in the mouth: *Sugar has a sweet taste.* **2** [U] sense which recognizes food or drink as sweet, salty, etc. **3** [U] ability to make (good) judgments about beauty, style, fashion, etc. **4** [C;U] personal liking: *She has expensive tastes in clothes.* ♦ *v* **1** *vt* experience or test the taste of **2** *vi* have a particular taste: *These oranges taste nice.* **3** *vt lit* experience: *having tasted freedom* **~ful** *adj* showing good TASTE (3) **~less** *adj* **1** not tasting of anything **2** showing bad TASTE (3) **tasty** *adj* pleasant-tasting

taste bud /'· ·/ *n* group of cells on the tongue used in tasting

ta·ta /tæˈtɑː/ *interj esp. BrE* goodbye

tat·ters /'tætəz‖-ərz/ *n* **in tatters: a** (of clothes) old and torn **b** ruined **~tered** *adj* (dressed in clothes that are) in tatters

tat·too¹ /təˈtuː, tæˈtuː/ *n* **-toos** pattern made by tattooing ♦ *vt* make (a pattern) on the skin (of) by pricking with a needle and then pouring coloured DYES in **~ist** *n*

tat·too² *n* **-toos 1** outdoor military show with music **2** fast beating of drums

tat·ty /'tæti/ *adj sl, esp. BrE* untidy or in bad condition

taught /tɔːt‖tɔːt/ *past t. and p. of* TEACH

taunt /tɔːnt‖tɔːnt/ *vt* try to upset with unkind remarks or by laughing at faults or failures ♦ *n* taunting remark

taut /tɔːt‖tɔːt/ *adj* stretched tight **~en** *vi/t* make taut **~ly** *adv* **~ness** *n* [U]

tau·tol·o·gy /tɔːˈtɒlədʒi‖tɔːˈtɑː-/ *n* [C;U] unnecessary repeating of the same idea in different words **~gical** /ˌtɔːtə-ˈlɒdʒɪkəl◄‖ˌtɔːtəˈlɑː-/ *adj*

tav·ern /'tævən‖-ərn/ *n lit* pub

taw·dry /'tɔːdri‖'tɔː-/ *adj* cheaply showy; showing bad TASTE (3) **~driness** *n* [U]

taw·ny /'tɔːni‖'tɔː-/ *adj* brownish yellow

tax /tæks/ *n* [C;U] money which must be paid to the government ♦ *vt* **1** make (someone) pay a tax **2** charge a tax on: *Cigarettes are heavily taxed.* **3** push to the limits of what one can bear: *Such stupid questions tax my patience.* **~able** *adj* that can be TAXed (2) **~ation** /tækˈseɪʃən/ *n* [U] (money raised by) taxing **~ing** *adj* needing great effort

tax-deductible /ˌ· ·'···/ *adj* that may legally be subtracted from one's total income before it is taxed

tax-free /ˌ· '·◄/ *adj* on which no tax has to be paid

tax·i¹ /'tæksi/ *n* car with a driver which can be hired

tax·i² *vi* (of an aircraft) move along the ground before taking off or after landing

tax·i·der·my /'tæksɪˌdɜːmi‖-ˌdɜːr-/ *n* [U] filling the skins of dead animals so that they look real **~mist** *n*

taxi rank /'·· ·/ *n* place where taxis wait to be hired

TB /ˌtiː 'biː/ *n* [U] TUBERCULOSIS

tea /tiː/ *n* [C;U] **1** (drink made by pouring boiling water onto) the dried cut-up leaves of an Asian bush **2** drink made like tea from the stated leaves: *mint tea* **3** (esp. in Britain) small afternoon meal —see also HIGH TEA **4** **one's cup of tea** the sort of thing one likes: *Running isn't my cup of tea.*

tea·bag /'tiːbæg/ *n* small paper bag full of tea leaves

teach /tiːtʃ/ *v* **taught** /tɔːt‖tɔːt/ **1** *vi/t* give knowledge or skill of (something) to (someone): *He taught me French.* **2** *vt* show (someone) the bad results of doing something: *I'll teach you to be rude to me!* (=a threat) **~er** *n* person who teaches, esp. as a job **~ing** *n* [U] **1** job of a teacher **2** also **teachings** *pl.* — moral beliefs taught by someone of historical importance: *the teachings of Christ*

teak /tiːk/ *n* [U] hard yellowish brown wood from Asia, used for furniture

team¹ /tiːm/ *n* **1** group of people who work or esp. play together: *a football team* **2** two or more animals pulling the same vehicle

team² *v* **team up** *phr vi* work together for a shared purpose

team·ster /'tiːmstə‖-ər/ *n AmE* TRUCK driver

team·work /'tiːmwɜːk‖-wɜːrk/ *n* [U] (effective) combined effort

tea·pot /'tiːpɒt‖'tiːpɑːt/ *n* container in which tea is made and served

tear¹ /teə‖ter/ *v* **tore** /tɔː‖tɔːr/, **torn** /tɔːn‖tɔːrn/ **1** *vt* pull apart by force, esp. so as to leave irregular edges **2** *vi* become torn **3** *vt* remove with sudden force: *He tore off his clothes.* **4** *vi* rush excitedly **5** **be torn between** be unable to decide between ♦ *n* hole made by tearing

tear down *phr vt* pull down; destroy

tear up *phr vt* destroy completely by tearing

tear² /tɪə‖tɪr/ *n* **1** drop of salty liquid that

flows from the eye, esp. because of sadness
2 **in tears** crying ~**ful** *adj* ~**fully** *adv*

tear·a·way /'teərəweɪ ‖ 'ter-/ *n BrE* noisy, sometimes violent young person

tear gas /'tɪə gæs ‖ 'tɪr-/ *n* [U] gas that stings the eyes

tear·jerk·er /'tɪə,dʒɜːkə ‖ 'tɪr,dʒɜːrkər/ *n* very sad book, film, etc.

tease /tiːz/ *v* 1 *vi/t* make jokes (about) or laugh (at) unkindly or playfully 2 *vt* annoy on purpose 3 *vt* separate the threads in (wool, etc.) ♦ *n* someone fond of teasing

teaser *n* difficult question

tea·spoon /'tiːspuːn/ *n* small spoon

teat /tiːt/ *n* 1 rubber object through which a baby sucks milk, etc. from a bottle 2 animal's NIPPLE

tea tow·el /'· ‚·/ *n* cloth for drying washed cups, plates, etc.

tech /tek/ *n* TECHNICAL COLLEGE —see also HIGH TECH

tech·ni·cal /'teknɪkəl/ *adj* 1 concerned with scientific or industrial subjects or skills 2 needing special knowledge in order to be understood: *His arguments are rather too technical for me.* 3 according to an (unreasonably) exact acceptance of the rules ~**ly** -kli/ *adv*

tech·ni·cal·i·ty /,teknɪ'kælɪti/ *n* small (esp. unimportant) detail or rule

technical col·lege /'·· ‚·/ *n* (esp. in Britain) college teaching practical subjects

tech·ni·cian /tek'nɪʃən/ *n* highly skilled scientific or industrial worker

tech·nique /tek'niːk/ *n* method of doing an activity that needs skill

tech·no·crat /'teknəkræt/ *n often derog* scientist or technician in charge of an organization

tech·nol·o·gy /tek'nɒlədʒi ‖ -'nɑː-/ *n* practical science, esp. as used in industrial production –**gist** *n* –**gical** /,teknə'lɒdʒɪkəl◄ ‖ -'lɑː-/ *adj*

ted·dy bear /'tedi beə ‖ -ber/ also **teddy** *infml* — *n* toy bear

te·di·ous /'tiːdiəs/ *adj* long and uninteresting ~**ly** *adv* ~**ness** *n* [U]

te·di·um /'tiːdiəm/ *n* [U] state of being tedious

tee /tiː/ *n* small object on which a GOLF ball is placed to be hit ♦ *v*

tee off *phr vi* drive the ball from a tee

tee up *phr vi/t* place (the ball) on a tee

teem /tiːm/ *vi BrE* (of rain) fall very heavily

teem with *phr vt* have (a type of creature) present in great numbers

teen·ag·er /'tiːneɪdʒə ‖ -ər/ *n* person of between 13 and 19 years old **teenage** *adj*

teens /tiːnz/ *n* [P] period of being a teenager

tee·ny wee·ny /,tiːni 'wiːni◄/ *adj infml* extremely small

tee shirt /'· ·/ *n* T-SHIRT

tee·ter /'tiːtə ‖ -ər/ *vi* stand or move unsteadily

teeter-tot·ter /'·· ‚·/ *n AmE for* SEESAW (1)

teeth /tiːθ/ *pl. of* TOOTH

teethe /tiːð/ *vi* (of a baby) grow teeth

teething troub·les /'·· ‚·/ *n* [P] problems in the early stages of using something

tee·to·tal /,tiː'təʊtl◄ ‖ -'toʊtl◄/ *adj* drinking no alcohol ~**ler** *n*

Tef·lon /'teflɒn ‖ -lɑːn/ *n tdmk* [U] artificial substance to which things will not stick, used on kitchen pans, etc.

tel·e·com·mu·ni·ca·tions /,telɪkə-mjuːnɪ'keɪʃənz/ *n* [P] sending and receiving of messages by means of radio, telephone, SATELLITE, etc.

tel·e·gram /'telɪgræm/ *n* message sent by telegraph

tel·e·graph /'telɪgrɑːf ‖ -græf/ *n* [U] method of sending messages along wire by electric signals ♦ *vt* send a telegraph ~**ic** /,telɪ'græfɪk◄/ *adj*

telegraph pole /'··· ‚·/ *n* pole for supporting telephone wires

te·lep·a·thy /tɪ'lepəθi/ *n* [U] sending of messages directly from one mind to another –**thic** /,telɪ'pæθɪk◄/ *adj*

tel·e·phone /'telɪfəʊn ‖ -foʊn/ *n* [C;U] (apparatus for) the sending and receiving of sounds over long distances by electric means ♦ *vi/t* (try to) speak (to) by telephone

te·le·pho·to lens /,telɪfəʊtəʊ 'lenz ‖ -foʊtoʊ-/ *n* special LENS used for photographing very distant objects

tel·e·scope /'telɪskəʊp ‖ -skoʊp/ *n* tube with a special piece of glass in it for looking at very distant objects ♦ *vi/t* shorten, esp. **a** by one part sliding over another **b** by crushing –**scopic** /,telɪ'skɒpɪk◄ ‖ -'skɑː-/ *adj* 1 of or related to a telescope 2 that telescopes

tel·e·text /'telitekst/ *n* [U] system of broadcasting written information (e.g. news) on television

tel·e·vise /'teləvaɪz/ *vt* broadcast on television

tel·e·vi·sion /'telɪˌvɪʒən, ˌtelə'vɪʒən/ *n* [C;U] (apparatus for receiving) the broadcasting of pictures and sounds by electric waves

tel·ex /'teleks/ *n* 1 [U] method of sending written messages round the world by telephone wires, SATELLITES, etc. 2 [C] message sent by telex ♦ *vt* send by telex

tell /tel/ *v* told /təʊld/ toʊld/ 1 *vt* make (something) known to (someone) in words: *Are you telling me the truth? | Tell me how to do it.* 2 *vt* warn; advise: *I told you it wouldn't work.* 3 *vt* order: *I told him to do it.* 4 *vi/t* find out; know: *How can you tell which button to press? | It was so dark that I couldn't tell if it was you.* 5 **all told** when all have been counted 6 **tell the time** read the time from a watch or clock 7 **there's no telling** it is impossible to know 8 **you're telling me** (used as a strong way of saying) I know this already

tell against *phr vt* count in judgment against

tell off *phr vt* speak severely to (someone who has done something wrong)

tell on *phr vt* 1 have a bad effect on 2 *infml* (used esp. by children) inform against (someone)

tell·er /'telə‖-ər/ *n* 1 bank clerk 2 person who counts votes

tell·ing /'telɪŋ/ *adj* sharply effective: *a telling argument*

tell·tale /'telteɪl/ *adj* being a small sign that shows something: *a few telltale hairs on the murderer's sleeve*

tel·ly /'teli/ *n BrE infml* (a) television

te·mer·i·ty /tɪ'merɪti/ *n* [U] *fml* foolish confidence; rashness

temp /temp/ *n infml* secretary employed for a short time ♦ *vi infml, esp. BrE* work as a temp

tem·per /'tempə‖-ər/ *n* 1 [C] state of mind; MOOD: *He's in a good/bad temper.* 2 [C;U] angry or impatient state of mind 3 **keep one's temper** stay calm 4 **lose one's temper** become angry ♦ *vt* 1 harden (esp. metal) by special treatment 2 make

less severe: *justice tempered with mercy*

tem·pe·ra·ment /'tempərəmənt/ *n* person's character with regard to being calm, easily excited, etc. **~al** /ˌtempərə'mentl◄/ *adj* 1 having or showing frequent changes of temper 2 caused by temperament **~ally** *adv*

tem·pe·rance /'tempərəns/ *n* [U] 1 *fml* being TEMPERATE (2) 2 complete avoiding of alcohol

tem·pe·rate /'tempərət/ *adj* 1 (of an area's weather) neither very hot nor very cold 2 *fml* avoiding too much of anything

tem·pe·ra·ture /'tempərətʃə‖-ər/ *n* 1 [C;U] degree of heat or coldness: *the average temperature* 2 [S] bodily temperature higher than the correct one; fever

tem·pest /'tempɪst/ *n lit* violent storm

tem·pes·tu·ous /tem'pestʃuəs/ *adj* full of wildness or anger

tem·plate /'templeɪt, -plɪt/ *n* shape used as a guide for cutting metal, wood, etc.

tem·ple¹ /'tempəl/ *n* building where people worship a god or gods, esp. in the Hindu and Buddhist religions

tem·ple² *n* flattish area on each side of the forehead

tem·po /'tempəʊ‖-poʊ/ *n* **-pos** 1 rate of movement or activity 2 speed of music

tem·po·ral /'tempərəl/ *adj fml* 1 of practical rather than religious affairs 2 of time

tem·po·ra·ry /'tempəri, -pəreri‖ -pəreri/ *adj* lasting for only a limited time **-rily** /'tempərəli‖ ,tempə'rerəli/ *adv*

tempt /tempt/ *vt* (try to) persuade (someone) to do something wrong **~ation** /temp'teɪʃən/ *n* 1 [U] act of tempting 2 [C] something that tempts, esp. by being very attractive **~ing** *adj* very attractive

ten /ten/ *determiner, n, pron* 10

ten·a·ble /'tenəbəl/ *adj* 1 (of a point of view, etc.) that can be reasonably supported or held 2 (of a job) that can be held for the stated period

te·na·cious /tɪ'neɪʃəs/ *adj* bravely firm **~ly** *adv* **-city** /tɪ'næsɪti/ *n* [U]

ten·ant /'tenənt/ *n* person who pays rent for the use of a building, land, etc. **-ancy** *n* 1 [C] length of time a person is a tenant 2 [U] use of land, etc. as a tenant

tend¹ /tend/ *vt* be likely: *She tends to lose* (=often loses) *her temper if you disagree* *with her.*

tend² *vt* take care of

ten·den·cy /'tendənsi/ *n* **1** likelihood of often happening or behaving in a particular way **2** special liking and natural skill: *She has artistic tendencies.*

ten·der¹ /'tendə‖-ər/ *adj* **1** not difficult to bite through **2** needing careful handling; delicate **3** sore **4** gentle, kind, and loving ~**ly** *adv* ~**ness** *n* [U]

tender² *v fml* **1** *vt* present for acceptance: *She tendered her resignation.* **2** *vt* offer in payment of debt **3** *vi* make a tender ♦ *n* statement of the price one would charge

tender³ *n* coal- or water-carrying railway vehicle —see also LEGAL TENDER

ten·don /'tendən/ *n* strong cord connecting a muscle to a bone

ten·dril /'tendrəl/ *n* thin curling stem by which a plant holds on to things

ten·e·ment /'tenəmənt/ *n* large building divided into flats, esp. in a poor city area

ten·et /'tenət/ *n fml* principle; belief

ten·ner /'tenə‖-ər/ *n BrE infml* £10

ten·nis /'tenəs/ *n* [U] game played by hitting a ball over a net with a RACKET

ten·or /'tenə‖-ər/ *n* **1** (man with) the highest man's singing voice **2** instrument with the same range of notes as this: *a tenor saxophone* **3** *fml* general meaning (of something written or spoken)

ten·pin /'ten,pɪn/ *n* any of the ten bottle-shaped objects to be knocked down by a ball in **tenpin bowling**

tense¹ /tens/ *adj* **1** stretched tight **2** nervously anxious ♦ *vi/t* (cause to) become tense ~**ly** *adv* ~**ness** *n* [U]

tense² *n* form of a verb showing time and continuity of action: *the future tense*

ten·sile /'tensaɪl‖'tensəl/ *adj* of TENSION (1)

ten·sion /'tenʃən/ *n* **1** [C;U] degree to which something is (able to be) stretched **2** [U] nervous anxiety caused by problems, uncertain waiting, etc. **3** [C;U] anxious, untrusting, and possibly dangerous relationship: *racial tensions in the inner city* **4** [U] *tech* electric power: *high-tension cables*

tent /tent/ *n* cloth shelter supported usu. by poles and ropes, used esp. by campers

ten·ta·cle /'tentəkəl/ *n* long snakelike boneless limb of certain creatures: *the tentacles of an octopus*

ten·ta·tive /'tentətɪv/ *adj* **1** not firmly arranged or fixed: *a tentative agreement* **2** not firm in making statements or decisions ~**ly** *adv*

ten·ter·hooks /'tentəhʊks‖-ər-/ *n* **on tenterhooks** anxiously waiting

tenth /tenθ/ *determiner, adv, n, pron* 10th

ten·u·ous /'tenjuəs/ *adj* slight: *a tenuous connection* ~**ly** *adv* ~**ness** *n* [U]

ten·ure /'tenjə, -jʊə‖-jər/ *n* [U] **1** act, right, or period of holding a job or land **2** right to keep one's job, esp. as a university teacher

te·pee /'tiːpiː/ *n* round tent used by some Native Americans

tep·id /'tepɪd/ *adj* only slightly warm: *tepid water!* (fig.) *enthusiasm*

term /tɜːm‖tɜːrm/ *n* **1** division of the school or university year: *the summer term* **2** fixed period: *a four-year term as president* **3** word or expression, esp. as used in a particular activity: *'Tort' is a legal term.* **4** **in the long/short term** over a long/short period —see also TERMS ♦ *vt* name; call; describe as

ter·mi·nal /'tɜːmɪnəl‖'tɜːr-/ *adj* of or being an illness that will cause death ♦ *n* **1** main building for passengers or goods at an airport, port, etc. **2** KEYBOARD and screen connected to a computer **3** place for electrical connections: *the terminals of a battery* ~**ly** *adv*

ter·mi·nate /'tɜːmɪneɪt‖'tɜːr-/ *vi/t fml* (cause to) come to an end **-nation** /,tɜːmɪ'neɪʃən‖,tɜːr-/ *n* [U]: *the termination of a pregnancy*

ter·mi·nol·o·gy /,tɜːmɪ'nɒlədʒi‖,tɜːr-mɪ'nɑː-/ *n* [U] (use of) particular TERMS (3): *legal terminology* **-logical** /,tɜːmɪnə-'lɒdʒɪkəl◂‖,tɜːrmɪnə'lɑː-/ *adj*

ter·mi·nus /'tɜːmɪnəs‖'tɜːr-/ *n* **-ni** /naɪ/ *or* **-nuses** stop or station at the end of a bus or railway line

ter·mite /'tɜːmaɪt‖'tɜːr-/ *n* antlike insect

terms /tɜːmz‖tɜːrmz/ *n* [P] **1** conditions of an agreement or contract **2** conditions of sale **3** **come to terms** reach an agreement **4** **come to terms with** accept (something unwelcome) **5** **on good/bad/friendly terms** having a good, bad, etc. relationship

ter·race /'terəs/ *n* **1** level area cut from a slope **2** flat area next to a building **3** steps on which watchers stand in football grounds 4 row of joined houses ♦ vt form into TERRACES (1)

ter·raced house /ˌ·· ˈ·/ n BrE house which is part of a TERRACE (4)

ter·ra·cot·ta /ˌterəˈkɒtəˈ‖-ˈkɑː-/ n [U] (articles of) reddish brown baked clay

ter·rain /teˈreɪn, tə-/ n [C;U] (area of) land of the stated sort: rocky terrain

ter·res·tri·al /tɪˈrestriəl/ adj fml of the Earth or land, as opposed to space or the sea

ter·ri·ble /ˈterəbəl/ adj 1 extremely severe: a terrible accident 2 extremely bad or unpleasant: a terrible meal –**bly** adv 1 extremely severely or badly 2 extremely: terribly sorry

ter·ri·er /ˈteriə‖-ər/ n type of small active dog

ter·rif·ic /təˈrɪfɪk/ adj 1 excellent 2 very great ~**ally** /-kli/ adv extremely

ter·ri·fy /ˈterəfaɪ/ vt frighten extremely: a terrified horse

ter·ri·to·ry /ˈterətəri‖-tɔːri/ n [C;U] 1 (area of) land, esp. as ruled by one government: This island is French territory. 2 area belonging to (and defended by) a particular person, animal, or group 3 area for which one person or group is responsible –**rial** /ˌterəˈtɔːriəl◂/ adj 1 of or being land or territory 2 (of animals, birds, etc.) showing a tendency to guard one's own TERRITORY (2)

ter·ror /ˈterə‖-ər/ n [U] extreme fear

ter·ror·is·m /ˈterərɪzəm/ n [U] use of violence for political purposes –**ist** n

ter·ror·ize also –**ise** BrE /ˈterəraɪz/ vt fill with terror by threats or acts of violence

terse /tɜːs‖tɜːrs/ adj using few words, often to show anger –**ly** adv –**ness** n [U]

ter·tia·ry /ˈtɜːʃəri‖ˈtɜːrʃieri, -ʃəri/ adj fml third in order

TESOL /ˈtesɒl‖-sɑːl/ n [U] Teaching English to Speakers of Other Languages

test /test/ n 1 set of questions or jobs to measure someone's knowledge or skill: a history/driving test 2 short medical examination: an eye test 3 use of something to see how well it works: nuclear weapon tests 4 **put to the test** find out the qualities of (something) by use ♦ vt 1 study or examine with a test 2 provide difficult conditions for: a testing time (=a difficult period) for the country 3 search by means of

tests: The company is testing for oil.

tes·ta·ment /ˈtestəmənt/ n 1 fml for WILL² (5) 2 (cap.) either of the two main parts of the Bible: the Old Testament

tes·ti·cle /ˈtestɪkəl/ n either of the two round SPERM-producing organs in male animals

tes·ti·fy /ˈtestəfaɪ/ vi/t 1 make a solemn statement of truth 2 show (something) clearly; prove

tes·ti·mo·ni·al /ˌtestəˈməʊniəl‖-ˈmoʊ-/ n 1 formal written statement of someone's character and ability 2 something given or done to show respect, thanks, etc.

tes·ti·mo·ny /ˈtestəməni‖-moʊni/ n formal statement of facts, esp. in a court of law

test match /ˈ· ·/ n international cricket or RUGBY match

test tube /ˈ· ·/ n small glass tube, closed at one end, used in scientific tests

tes·ty /ˈtesti/ adj fml bad-tempered –**tily** adv

tet·a·nus /ˈtetənəs/ n [U] serious disease, caused by infection of a cut, which causes the muscles to stiffen

tetch·y /ˈtetʃi/ adj sensitive in a bad-tempered way –**ily** adv –**iness** n [U]

tête-à-tête /ˌteɪt ɑː ˈteɪt, ˌteɪt ə ˈteɪt/ n private conversation between two people

teth·er /ˈteðə‖-ər/ n 1 rope, etc. to which an animal is tied 2 **at the end of one's tether** unable to bear any more difficulties, annoyances, etc. ♦ vt fasten with a tether

text /tekst/ n 1 [C;U] main body of printed words in a book 2 [C;U] exact original words of a speech, etc. 3 [C] textbook: a set text 4 [C] sentence from the Bible used by a priest in a SERMON –**ual** adj

text·book /ˈtekstbʊk/ n standard book used for studying a particular subject, esp. in schools ♦ adj 1 as it ought to be; IDEAL: textbook journalism 2 typical

tex·tile /ˈtekstaɪl/ n woven material

tex·ture /ˈtekstʃə‖-ər/ n [C;U] quality of roughness or smoothness, coarseness or fineness, of a surface or substance

tha·lid·o·mide /θəˈlɪdəmaɪd/ n [U] drug no longer used because it caused unborn babies to develop wrongly

than /ðən; strong ðæn/ conj, prep 1 (used in comparing things): This is bigger than that. 2 when; as soon as: No sooner had we *started to eat than the doorbell rang.*

thank /θæŋk/ *vt* express one's gratefulness to **thanks** *n* [P] 1 (words expressing) gratefulness 2 **thanks to** because of ~**ful** *adj* 1 glad 2 grateful ~**fully** *adv* ~**less** *adj* not likely to be rewarded with thanks or success

thanks /θæŋks/ *interj* thank you

thanks·giv·ing /ˌθæŋks'ɡɪvɪŋ◂/ *n* [C;U] 1 (an) expression of gratefulness, esp. to God 2 (*cap.*) holiday in the US

thank you /'· ·/ *interj* 1 (used for politely expressing thanks or acceptance) 2 **no, thank you** (used for politely refusing an offer)

that[1] /ðæt/ *determiner, pron* those /ðəʊz ‖ ðoʊz/ 1 (being) the person, thing, or idea which is understood or has just been mentioned or shown: *Look at that man over there.* | *Who told you that?* | *I'd like these apples, not those.* 2 **that's that** that is the end of the matter

that[2] /ðət ‖ *strong* ðæt/ *conj* 1 (used for introducing CLAUSES): *She said that she couldn't come.* 2 (used as a RELATIVE PRONOUN) which/ who(m): *This is the book that I bought.*

that[3] /ðæt/ *adv* to such a degree; so: *It wasn't that difficult.*

thatch /θæt∫/ *vt, n* [U] (make or cover with) a roof covering of STRAW: *a thatched roof/cottage*

thaw /θɔː ‖ θɒː/ *v* 1 *vi/t* change from a solid frozen state to being liquid or soft 2 *vi* become friendlier, less formal, etc. ♦ *n* 1 period when ice and snow melt 2 increase in friendliness

the /ðə, ði; *strong* ðiː/ *definite article, determiner* 1 (used for referring to a particular thing): *the sky* | *Close the door.* 2 (used with some geographical names): *the Rhine* | *the Pacific* 3 (used before a singular noun to make it general): *The lion is a wild animal.* 4 (used for making an adjective into a noun): *I like the French.* (=French people) | *To do the impossible.* 5 (used with measures) each: *paid by the hour* | *sold by the metre* 6 (used before names of musical instruments): *She plays the piano.* 7 (used before the plural of 20, 30, etc. to show a period of ten years): *music of the 60s* ♦ *adv* 1 (used in comparisons, to show that two things happen together): *The more he eats,*

the fatter he gets. 2 (in comparisons to show that someone or something is better, worse, etc. than before): *She looks (all) the better for two weeks' holiday in Spain.* 3 (to show that someone or something is more than any other): *She's the cleverest/the most sensible of them all.*

thea·tre usu. *-er AmE* /'θɪətə ‖ -'ər/ *n* 1 building where plays are performed 2 the work of people involved with plays: *He's in the theatre.* 3 large room where public talks are given 4 room where medical operations are done 5 area of activity in a war **–atrical** /θi'ætrɪkəl/ *adj* 1 of the theatre 2 too showy; not natural

thea·tre·go·er /'θɪətəˌɡəʊə ‖ -tərˌɡoʊər/ *n* person who goes (regularly) to the THEATRE (1)

thee /ðiː/ *pron lit* (*object form of* **thou**) you

theft /θeft/ *n* [C;U] stealing

their /ðeə ‖ ðər/ *strong* ðer/ *determiner* of them: *their house*

theirs /ðeəz ‖ ðerz/ *pron* of them; their one(s): *It's theirs.*

them /ðəm; *strong* ðem/ *pron* (*object form of* **they**): *I want those books; give them to me.*

theme /θiːm/ *n* 1 subject of a talk, piece of writing, etc. 2 repeated idea, image, or tune in writing, music, etc. 3 **theme music/song/tune** music played with a particular film, television programme, etc.

theme park /'· ·/ *n* AMUSEMENT PARK (AMUSE) based on a single subject

them·selves /ðəm'selvz/ *pron* 1 (*reflexive form of* **they**): *They saw themselves on television.* 2 (*strong form of* **they**): *They built it themselves.* 3 (**all**) **by themselves: a** alone **b** without help 4 **to themselves** not shared

then /ðen/ *adv* 1 at that time: *...I was happier then.* 2 next; afterwards: *...and then we went home.* 3 in that case; as a result: *Have you done your homework? Then you can watch television.* 4 besides; also

thence /ðens/ *adv fml* from that place

the·ol·o·gy /θi'ɒlədʒi ‖ θi'ɑː-/ *n* [U] study of religious ideas and beliefs **–ologian** /ˌθiːə'ləʊdʒən ‖ -'loʊ-/ *n* **–ological** /ˌθiːə-'lɒdʒɪkəl◂ ‖ -'lɑː-/ *adj*

theo·rem /'θɪərəm ‖ 'θiːə-/ *n* MATHEMATICAL statement that can be proved by reasoning

the·o·ry /'θɪəri ‖ 'θiːə-/ *n* 1 [C] statement

intended to explain a fact or event **2** [U] general principles and methods as opposed to practice **–retical** /ˌθiːəˈretɪkəl◀/ adj existing in or based on theory, not practice or fact **–rize, –rise** /ˈθɪəraɪz ‖ ˈθiːə–/ vi form a theory

ther·a·peu·tic /ˌθerəˈpjuːtɪk◀/ adj **1** for the treating or curing of disease **2** having a good effect on one's health or state of mind: *I find swimming/knitting very therapeutic.*

ther·a·py /ˈθerəpi/ n [C;U] treatment of illnesses of the body or mind **–pist** n

there¹ /ðeə ‖ ðer/ adv **1** at or to that place: *He lives over there.* **2** (used for drawing attention to someone or something): *There goes John.* **3 all there** healthy in mind **4 there and then** at that exact place and time **5 there you are: a** here is what you wanted **b** I told you so ♦ interj (used for comforting someone or expressing victory, satisfaction, etc.): *There, there. Stop crying. | There, I knew I was right.*

there² pron (used for showing that something or someone exists or happens, usu. as the subject of *be, seem,* or *appear*): *There's someone at the door to see you.*

there·a·bouts /ˌðeərəˈbaʊts ‖ ˌðer–/ adv near that place, time, number, etc.

there·af·ter /ðeərˈɑːftə ‖ ðerˈæftər/ adv fml after that

there·by /ðeəˈbaɪ, ˈðeəbaɪ, ðer–/ adv fml by doing or saying that

there·fore /ˈðeəfɔː ‖ ˈðerfɔːr/ adv for that reason; as a result

there·up·on /ˌðeərəˈpɒn, ˈðeərəpɒn ‖ ˌðerəˈpɔːn, ˈðerə–/ adv fml **1** about that matter **2** without delay

ther·mal /ˈθɜːməl ‖ ˈθɜːr–/ adj of, using, producing, or caused by heat ♦ n rising current of warm air

ther·mo·dy·nam·ics /ˌθɜːməʊdaɪˈnæmɪks ‖ ˌθɜːrmoʊ–/ n [U] scientific study of heat and its power in driving machines

ther·mom·e·ter /θəˈmɒmɪtə ‖ θərˈmɑːmɪtər/ n instrument for measuring temperature

ther·mo·nu·cle·ar /ˌθɜːməʊˈnjuːkliə◀ ‖ ˌθɜːrmoʊˈnuːkliər◀/ adj relating to a NUCLEAR reaction involving extremely high temperatures

ther·mos /ˈθɜːmɒs ‖ ˈθɜːr–/ n tdmk for FLASK (3)

ther·mo·stat /ˈθɜːməstæt ‖ ˈθɜːr–/ n

apparatus for keeping a machine, room, etc. at an even temperature

the·sau·rus /θɪˈsɔːrəs/ n dictionary with words grouped according to similarities in meaning

these /ðiːz/ pl. of THIS

the·sis /ˈθiːsɪs/ n **-ses** /-siːz/ **1** long piece of writing on a particular subject, done to gain a higher university degree **2** opinion or statement supported by reasoned arguments

they /ðeɪ/ pron (used as the subject of a sentence) **1** those people, animals, or things **2** people in general: *They say prices are going to rise.* **3** (used to avoid saying he or she): *If anyone knows, they should tell me.*

they'd /ðeɪd/ short for: **1** they had **2** they would

they'll /ðeɪl/ short for: they will

they're / ðeə ‖ ðər; strong ðer/ short for: they are

they've /ðeɪv/ short for: they have

thick /θɪk/ adj **1** having a large or the stated distance between opposite surfaces: *thick walls | walls 2 metres thick* **2** (of liquid) not flowing easily **3** difficult to see through: *thick mist* **4** full of; covered with: *furniture thick with dust* **5** with many objects set close together: *a thick forest* **6** *BrE sl* stupid ♦ adv **1** thickly **2 thick and fast** quickly and in large numbers ♦ n **1** [the+S] part, place, etc. of greatest activity **2 through thick and thin** through both good and bad times **~ly** adv **~en** vi/t make or become thicker **~ness** n **1** [C;U] being thick **2** [C] LAYER

thick·et /ˈθɪkɪt/ n thick growth of bushes and small trees

thick·set /ˌθɪkˈset◀/ adj having a broad strong body

thick-skinned /ˌ· ˈ·◀/ adj not easily offended

thief /θiːf/ n **thieves** /θiːvz/ person who steals

thieve /θiːv/ vi steal

thigh /θaɪ/ n top part of the human leg

thim·ble /ˈθɪmbəl/ n small cap put over the end of the finger when sewing

thin /θɪn/ adj **-nn- 1** having a small distance between opposite surfaces **2** not fat **3** (of a liquid) flowing (too) easily; weak **4** with few objects widely separated: *a thin audience* **5** easy to see through: *thin mist*

6 lacking force or strength: *a thin excuse*
7 thin end of the wedge something which seems unimportant but will open the way for more serious things of a similar kind ♦ *adv* thinly ♦ *vi/t* make or become thinner ~ly *adv* ~ness *n* [U]

thin air /· '·/ *n* [U] *infml* state of not being seen or not existing

thine /ðaɪn/ *determiner* THY ♦ *pron lit* (*possessive form of* **thou**) yours

thing /θɪŋ/ *n* **1** [C] unnamed or unnameable object: *What do you use this thing for?* **2** [C] remark, idea, or subject: *What a nasty thing to say!* **3** [C] act; activity: *the first thing we have to do* **4** [C] event: *A funny thing happened today.* **5** [S] that which is necessary or desirable: *Cold beer's just the thing on a hot day.* **6** [S] the fashion or custom: *the latest thing in shoes* **7** [S] *sl* activity satisfying to one personally: *Tennis isn't really my thing.* **8 first thing** early in the morning **9 for one thing** (used for introducing a reason) **10 have a thing about** have a strong like or dislike for **11 a good/bad thing** it's sensible/not sensible: *It's a good thing we found you.* (=it's lucky) **12 make a thing of** give too much importance to **13 a close/near thing** a situation in which something unpleasant is only just avoided **14 the thing is** what we must consider is —see also NEAR THING

things *n* [P] **1** general state of affairs; situation **2** one's personal possessions: *Pack your things.*

think /θɪŋk/ *v* thought /θɔːt ‖ θɒːt/ **1** *vi* use the mind to make judgments **2** *vt* have as an opinion; believe: *Do you think it will rain?* **3** *vt* understand; imagine: *I can't think why you did it.* **4** *vt* have as a plan: *I think I'll go swimming tomorrow.* **5 think aloud** to speak one's thoughts as they come ♦ *n* [S] act of thinking ~er *n*

think about *phr vt* consider seriously before making a decision

think of *phr vt* **1** form a possible plan for **2** have as an opinion about: *what do you think of that?* **3** take into account: *But think of the cost!* **4** remember **5 not think much of** have a low opinion of **6 think better of** decide against **7 think highly/well/little of** have a good/bad, etc. opinion of someone or something **8 think nothing of** regard as usual or easy

think out/through *phr vt* consider carefully and in detail

think over *phr vt* consider seriously

think up *phr vt* invent (esp. an idea)

think·ing /'θɪŋkɪŋ/ *n* [U] opinion: *What's the government's thinking on this?* ♦ *adj* thoughtful; able to think clearly

thin-skinned /ˌ· '·◀/ *adj* easily offended

third /θɜːd ‖ θɜːrd/ *determiner, adv, n, pron* 3rd

third de·gree /ˌ· ·'·◀/ *n* [*the*+S] hard questioning and rough treatment

third par·ty /ˌ· '··◀/ *n* **1** person other than the two main people concerned **2** person other than the holder protected by an insurance agreement

third-rate /ˌ· '·◀/ *adj* of very low quality

Third World /ˌ· '·◀/ *n* often derog [*the*+S] the countries of the world which are industrially less well-developed

thirst /θɜːst ‖ θɜːrst/ *n* **1** [S;U] desire for drink **2** [U] lack of drink: *I'm dying of thirst* **3** [S] strong desire: *the thirst for knowledge* ~y *adj* feeling or causing thirst

thir·teen /ˌθɜːˈtiːn◀ ‖ ˌθɜːr-/ *determiner, n, pron* 13 ~**th** *determiner, adv, n, pron* 13th

thir·ty /'θɜːti ‖ 'θɜːrti/ *determiner, n, pron* 30 ~**tieth** *determiner, adv, n, pron* 30th

this /ðɪs/ *determiner, pron* **these** /ðiːz/ **1** (one) going to be mentioned, to happen: *I'll come this morning.* | *Do it like this.* (=in the way about to be shown) **2** (one) near or nearer in place, time, thought, etc.: *Give me these, not those.* **3** *infml* a certain: *There were these two men standing there…* ♦ *adv* to this degree: *It was this big.*

this·tle /'θɪsəl/ *n* plant with prickly leaves and usu. purple flowers

thong /θɒŋ ‖ θɔːŋ/ *n* narrow length of leather used esp. for fastening

tho·rax /'θɔːræks/ *n med* part of the body between the neck and the ABDOMEN

thorn /θɔːn ‖ θɔːrn/ *n* **1** sharp growth on a plant **2 thorn in one's flesh/side** continual cause of annoyance ~y *adj* **1** prickly **2** difficult to deal with

thor·ough /'θʌrə ‖ 'θʌroʊ, 'θʌrə/ *adj* **1** complete in every way: *a thorough search* **2** careful about details ~ly *adv* ~ness *n* [U]

thor·ough·bred /'θʌrəbred ‖ 'θʌroʊ-, 'θʌrə-/ *n, adj* (animal, esp. a horse) born from parents of one very good breed

thor·ough·fare /'θʌrəfeə ‖ 'θʌroʊfer,

'θʌrə-/ n fml large public road

those /ðəʊz ‖ ðoʊz/ pl. of THAT

thou /ðaʊ/ pron lit (used of a single person) you

though /ðəʊ ‖ ðoʊ/ conj, adv 1 in spite of the fact (that): Though it's hard work, I enjoy it. 2 but: I'll try, though I don't think I can. 3 **as though** as if

thought¹ /θɔːt ‖ θɒːt/ n 1 [C] something thought; idea, etc. 2 [U] thinking 3 [U] serious consideration 4 [U] intention: I had no thought of causing any trouble. 5 [C;U] attention; regard: acting with no thought to her own safety —see also SECOND THOUGHT ~**ful** adj 1 thinking deeply 2 paying attention to the wishes, needs, etc. of others ~**fully** adv ~**less** adj showing a selfish or careless lack of thought ~**lessly** adv

thought² past t. and p. of THINK

thou·sand /ˈθaʊzənd/ determiner, n, pron thousand or thousands 1000 ~**th** determiner, adv, n, pron 1000th

thrash /θræʃ/ v 1 vt beat (as if) with a whip or stick 2 vt defeat thoroughly 3 vi move wildly or violently

  thrash out phr vt find an answer (to) by much talk and consideration

thread /θred/ n 1 [C;U] very fine cord made by spinning cotton, silk etc. 2 [C] line of reasoning connecting the parts of an argument or story 3 [C] raised line that winds round the outside of a screw 4 **hang by a thread** be in a very dangerous position ♦ vt 1 put thread through the hole in (a needle) 2 put (a film or TAPE) in place on an apparatus 3 put (things) together on a thread 4 **thread one's way through** go carefully through (crowds, etc.)

thread·bare /ˈθredbeə ‖ -ber/ adj (of cloth) very worn: (fig.) a threadbare (=too often used) excuse

threat /θret/ n 1 [C;U] expression of an intention to harm or punish someone 2 [C] something or someone regarded as a possible danger

threat·en /ˈθretn/ v 1 vt make a threat (against): They threatened to blow up the plane. 2 vt give warning of (something bad): The sky threatened rain. 3 vi (of something bad) seem likely: Danger threatens.

three /θriː/ determiner, n, pron 3

three-D /ˌθriː ˈdiː◂/ n adj [U] (having) a three-dimensional form or appearance

three-di·men·sion·al /ˌ· ·ˈ···◂/ adj having length, depth, and height

three R's /ˌθriː ˈɑːz ‖ -ˈɑːrz/ n [the+P] reading, writing, and ARITHMETIC. considered as forming the basis of children's education

thresh /θreʃ/ vt separate the grain from (corn, rice) by beating

thresh·old /ˈθreʃhəʊld, -ʃəʊld ‖ -oʊld/ n 1 point of beginning: scientists on the threshold of (=about to make) a research breakthrough 2 piece of stone or wood across the bottom of a doorway

threw /θruː/ past t. of THROW

thrice /θraɪs/ adv lit three times

thrift /θrɪft/ n [U] not spending too much money ~**y** adj

thrill /θrɪl/ n (something producing) a sudden strong feeling of excitement, fear, etc. ♦ vt (cause to) feel a thrill ~**er** n book, film, etc. telling a very exciting (crime) story

thrive /θraɪv/ vi **thrived** or **throve** /θrəʊv ‖ θroʊv/, **thrived** develop well and be healthy, strong, or successful

throat /θrəʊt ‖ θroʊt/ n 1 passage from the mouth down inside the body 2 front of the neck ~**y** adj making a low rough sound when speaking or singing

throb /θrɒb ‖ θrɑːb/ vi -**bb**- (of a machine, the action of the heart, etc.) beat heavily and regularly ♦ n throbbing

throes /θrəʊz ‖ θroʊz/ n [P] 1 lit sudden violent pains, esp. caused by dying 2 **in the throes of** struggling with (some difficulty)

throm·bo·sis /θrɒmˈbəʊsɪs ‖ θrɑːm-ˈboʊ-/ n -**ses** /-siːz/ having a thickened mass of blood in a blood tube or the heart

throne /θrəʊn ‖ θroʊn/ n ceremonial seat of a king, queen, etc.: (fig.) He ascended the throne. (=became king)

throng /θrɒŋ ‖ θrɒːŋ/ n large crowd ♦ vi/t go as or fill with a crowd

throt·tle /ˈθrɒtl ‖ ˈθrɑːtl/ vt seize (someone) by the throat to stop them breathing ♦ n VALVE controlling the flow of petrol, etc. into an engine

through /θruː/ prep, adv 1 in at one side (of) and out at the other: Water flows through this pipe. I opened the door and went through. 2 from beginning to end (of): I read through the letter. 3 so as to finish successfully: *Did you get through your exam?* **4** past: *He drove through a red light.* ♦ *prep* **1** by means of; because of: *The war was lost through bad organization.* **2** *AmE* up to and including: *Wednesday through Saturday* ♦ *adv* **1** so as to be connected by telephone **2 through and through** completely ♦ *adj* **1** finished; done: *Are you through yet?* **2** having no further relationship: *I'm through with him!* **3** allowing a continuous journey: *a through train*

through·out /θruːˈaʊt/ *prep, adv* in, to, through, or during every part (of)

through·put /ˈθruːpʊt/ *n* amount of work, materials, etc. dealt with in a particular time

throw /θrəʊ‖θroʊ/ *v* **threw** /θruː/, **thrown** /θrəʊn‖θroʊn/ **1** *vi/t* send (something) through the air with a sudden movement of the arm **2** *vt* move or put forcefully or quickly: *The two fighters threw themselves at each other.* | *I'll just throw on some clothes.* **3** *vt* cause to fall to the ground: *Her horse threw her.* **4** *vt* direct: *I think I can throw some light on the mystery.* **5** *vt* operate (a SWITCH) **6** *vt* shape from wet clay when making POTTERY **7** *vt* make one's voice appear to come from somewhere other than one's mouth **8** *vt infml* arrange (a party) **9** *vt* confuse; shock: *Her reply really threw me.* **10 throw a fit** have a sudden uncontrolled attack of anger **11 throw oneself into** to start to work very busily at **12 throw oneself on/upon** put complete trust in **13 throw one's weight about** give orders to others, because one thinks one is important **14 throw oneself at** *phr vt* **a** rush violently towards someone **b** attempt forcefully to win someone's love ♦ *n* **1** act of throwing **2** distance thrown ~**er** *n*

throw away *phr vt* **1** get rid of **2** waste (an opportunity, chance, etc.)

throw in *phr vt* **1** supply additionally without increasing the price **2 throw in the sponge/towel** admit defeat

throw off *phr vt* **1** recover from **2** escape from

throw open *phr vt* **1** allow people to enter

throw out *phr vt* **1** get rid of **2** refuse to accept

throw over *phr vt* end a relationship with

throw together *phr vt* build or make hastily

throw up *phr v* **1** *vt* stop doing (esp. a job) **2** *vt* bring to notice: *The investigation has thrown up some interesting facts.* **3** *vi infml for* VOMIT

throw·back /ˈθrəʊbæk‖ˈθroʊ-/ *n* something as if from an earlier period

thrush[1] /θrʌʃ/ *n* common singing bird with a spotted breast

thrush[2] *n* [U] infectious disease of the mouth, throat, and VAGINA

thrust /θrʌst/ *vi/t* **thrust** push forcefully and suddenly ♦ *n* **1** [C] act of thrusting **2** [U] forward-moving power of an engine **3** [U] (main) meaning —see also CUT AND THRUST

thud /θʌd/ *vi, n* **-dd-** (make) the dull sound of something heavy falling

thug /θʌg/ *n* violent criminal

thumb[1] /θʌm/ *n* **1** short thick finger set apart from the other four **2 all thumbs** *infml* very awkward with the hands **3 stick out like a sore thumb** *infml* seem out of place **4 thumb one's nose at** *infml* make fun of **5 thumbs up/down** *infml* an expression of approval/disapproval **6 under someone's thumb** *infml* under the control of someone —see also RULE OF THUMB

thumb[2] *v* **thumb a lift** ask passing motorists for a ride by signalling with one's thumb

thumb through *phr vi/t* look through (a book) quickly

thumb·nail /ˈθʌmneɪl/ *n* nail of the thumb ♦ *adj* small or short: *a thumbnail description/sketch*

thumb·screw /ˈθʌmskruː/ *n* **1** instrument for crushing the thumbs to cause great pain **2 put the thumb screws on** put great pressure on, so that someone will do something

thump /θʌmp/ *v* **1** *vt* hit hard **2** *vi* make a repeated dull sound: *My heart thumped.* ♦ *n* (sound of) a heavy blow

thun·der /ˈθʌndə‖-ər/ *n* [U] **1** loud explosive noise that follows lightning: (fig.) *the thunder of distant guns* **2 steal someone's thunder** spoil effect of someone's action by doing it first ♦ *v* **1** *vi* produce thunder **2** *vi* produce or go with a loud noise 3 *vt* shout loudly ~**ous** *adj* very loud: *thunderous applause* ~**y** *adj* with a lot of thunder

thun·der·bolt /'θʌndəbəʊlt ‖ -dərbɔʊlt/ *n* 1 thunder and lightning together 2 event causing great shock

thun·der·clap /'θʌndəklæp ‖ -ər-/ *n* a single loud crash of thunder

thun·der·struck /'θʌndəstrʌk ‖ -ər-/ *adj* shocked

Thurs·day /'θɜːzdi ‖ 'θɜːr-/ *n* the fourth day of the week, between Wednesday and Friday

thus /ðʌs/ *adv fml* 1 in this way 2 with this result 3 **thus far** up until now

thwack /θwæk/ *n*, *v* WHACK

thwart /θwɔːt ‖ θwɔːrt/ *vt* prevent from happening or succeeding

thy /ðaɪ/ *determiner lit* (*possessive form of* thou) your

thyme /taɪm/ *n* [U] HERB used in cooking

thy·roid /'θaɪrɔɪd/ *n* organ in the neck that controls growth and activity

ti·a·ra /ti'ɑːrə/ *n* piece of jewellery like a small crown

tic /tɪk/ *n* sudden unconscious movement of the muscles

tick¹ /tɪk/ *n* 1 short repeated sound of a watch or clock 2 mark (✔) showing esp. correctness 3 *infml*, *esp. BrE* moment

tick² *v* 1 *vi* make a TICK¹ (1) 2 *vt* mark with a TICK¹ (2) 3 **make someone/something tick** *infml* provide a person/thing with reasons for behaving, working, etc. in a particular way

tick off *phr vt infml* speak sharply to, expressing disapproval or annoyance

tick over *phr vi* continue working at slow steady rate

tick³ *n* small blood-sucking insect

tick⁴ on tick *infml* on CREDIT¹ (1)

tick·et /'tɪkɪt/ *n* 1 piece of paper or card showing that payment for a service has been made: *a bus/cinema ticket* 2 piece of card showing the price, size, etc. of goods 3 printed notice of an offence against the traffic laws 4 *infml* exactly the thing needed: *This hammer is just the ticket.*

tick·le /'tɪkəl/ *v* 1 *vt* touch (someone's body) lightly to produce laughter, a feeling of nervous excitement, etc.: *Stop tickling my toes!* 2 *vi* give or feel a prickly sensation 3 *vt* delight or amuse ♦ *n* [C;U] (act or feel of) tickling –**lish** *adj* 1 sensitive to being tickled 2 (of a problem or situation) rather difficult

tid·al wave /'taɪdl weɪv/ *n* very large dangerous ocean wave: (fig.) *a tidal wave of public disapproval*

tid·dler /'tɪdlə ‖ -ər/ *n BrE* very small fish

tide¹ /taɪd/ *n* 1 regular rise and fall of the sea: *The tide's out.* (=has fallen to its lowest point) 2 current caused by this: *strong tides* 3 feeling or tendency that moves or changes like the tide: *the tide of public opinion* **tidal** *adj*

tide² *v* **tide over** *phr vt* help (someone) through (a difficult period)

tide·mark /'taɪdmɑːk ‖ -mɑːrk/ *infml* mark round the inside of an empty bath showing the level to which it was filled

tid·ings /'taɪdɪŋz/ *n* [P] *lit* news

ti·dy /'taɪdi/ *adj* 1 neat 2 *infml* fairly large: *a tidy income* ♦ *vi/t* make (things) tidy **tidily** *adv* **tidiness** *n* [U]

tie¹ /taɪ/ *n* 1 band of cloth worn round the neck 2 a cord, string, etc. used for fastening something 3 something that unites: *the ties of friendship* 4 something that limits one's freedom 5 result in which each competitor gains an equal number of points, votes, etc.

tie² *v* **tied**; *pres. p.* **tying** 1 *vt* fasten by knotting: *tie a parcel/one's shoe laces* 2 *vt* make (a knot or BOW²) (3) 3 *vi/t* finish (a match or competition) with a TIE¹ (5)

tie down *phr vt* 1 limit the freedom of 2 force to be exact

tie in *phr vi* have a close connection

tie up *phr vt* 1 limit free use of (money, property, etc.) 2 connect 3 **tied up** very busy

tie-breaker /'· ‚··/ also **tie·break** /'taɪbreɪk/ — *n* number of quickly played points to decide the winner of a tennis SET³ (4)

tie-in /'· ·/ *n* product that is connected in some way with a new film, TV show, etc.

tie·pin /'taɪ‚pɪn/ *n* decorative CLIP for holding a TIE¹ (1) in place

tier /tɪə ‖ tɪr/ *n* 1 any of a number of rising rows of esp. seats 2 level of organization

tiff /tɪf/ *n* slight quarrel

ti·ger /'taɪgə ‖ -ər/ — *n* 1 large Asian wild cat that has yellowish fur with black bands 2 fierce or brave person

tight /taɪt/ *adj* 1 firmly fixed in place;

closely fastened: *The cases were packed tight in the back.* | *Is the roof watertight?* **2** fully stretched **3** fitting (too) closely; leaving no free room or time: *tight shoes* | *a tight schedule* **4** difficult to obtain: *Money is tight just now.* **5** marked by close competition: *a tight game/finish* **6** *sl* ungenerous with money **7** *sl* drunk **8 in a tight corner/spot** in a difficult position ♦ *adv* tightly ~**ly** *adv* ~**en** *vi/t* make or become tighter ~**ness** *n* [U] **tights** *n* [P] very close fitting garment covering the legs and lower body

tight-fisted /ˌtaɪt ˈfɪstɪd◄/ *adj infml* very ungenerous with money ~**ness** *n* [U]

tight-lipped /ˌ· ˈ·◄/ *adj* **1** having the lips pressed together **2** not saying anything

tight·rope /ˈtaɪt-rəʊp ‖ -roʊp/ *n* rope tightly stretched high above the ground, on which someone walks

tile /taɪl/ *n* **1** thin shaped piece of baked clay, etc. used for covering roofs, walls, floors, etc. **2 (out) on the tiles** enjoying oneself wildly ♦ *vt* cover with tiles

till¹ /tɪl, tl/ *prep, conj* until

till² /tɪl/ *n* drawer where money is kept in a shop

till³ *vt lit* cultivate (the ground)

til·ler /ˈtɪlə ‖ -ər/ *n* long handle for turning a boat's RUDDER

tilt /tɪlt/ *vi/t* slope (as if by raising one end ♦ *n* [C;U] **1** slope **2 (at) full tilt** at full speed

tim·ber /ˈtɪmbə ‖ -ər/ *n* **1** [U] wood for building **2** [U] growing trees **3** [C] wooden beam, esp. in a ship

time /taɪm/ *n* **1** [U] continuous measurable quantity from the past, through the present, and into the future **2** [S;U] period: *It happened a long time ago.* | *I haven't got (the) time to do it.* (=I am too busy doing other things) **3** period in which an action is completed, esp. in a race: *Her time was just under 4 minutes.* **4** [U] particular point stated in hours, minutes, seconds, etc.: *The time is 4 o'clock.* **5** [C;U] particular point in the year, day, etc.: *We both arrived at the same time.* | *in summertime* | *It's time we were leaving.* **6** [C] occasion: *I've been here several times.* **7** [C] experience connected with a period or occasion: *We had a great time at the party.* **8** [C] period in history: *in ancient times* **9** [U] point when something should happen: *The plane arrived on time.*

(=not early or late) **10** [U] rate of speed of a piece of music **11 ahead of one's time** with ideas not accepted in the period in which one lives **12 all the time** continuously **13 at a time** singly/in groups of two/three, etc.: *We went into her office two at a time.* **14 at all times** always **15 at one time** formerly **16 at the same time: a** together **b** however; nevertheless **17 at times** sometimes **18 behind the times** old-fashioned **19 buy time** *infml* delay an action or decision in order to give oneself more time **20** *sl* **do time** go to prison **21 for a time** for a short period **22 for the time being** for a limited period at present **23 from time to time** sometimes **24 have no time for someone** dislike someone **25 in no time** very quickly **26 in time: a** after a certain amount of time has passed **b** early or soon enough **27 take one's time** not hurry **28 the time of one's life** have a very enjoyable experience **29 time and (time) again/time after time** repeatedly —see also TIMES ♦ *vt* **1** arrange the time at which (something) happens **2** measure the time taken by or for **3** (in sport) make (a shot) at exactly the right moment ~**less** *adj* **1** unending **2** not changed by time ~**ly** *adj fml* happening at just the right time: *a timely warning* **timer** *n* person or machine that measures or records time —see also OLD TIMER

time bomb /ˈ· ·/ *n* **1** bomb set to explode at a particular time **2** situation likely to become very dangerous

time im·me·mo·ri·al /ˌ· ··ˈ···/ *n* [U] *lit* long ago in the past

time lim·it /ˈ· ˌ··/ *n* period of time in which something must be done

times /taɪmz/ *n* (used to show an amount that is calculated by multiplying together the stated number of times): *Their house is at least three times the size of ours.* ♦ *prep* multiplied by: *3 times 3 is 9.*

time·serv·er /ˈtaɪmˌsɜːvə ‖ -ˌsɜːrvər/ *n derog* person who acts so as to please those in power at the time —**ing** *adj, n* [U]

time-shar·ing /ˈ· ˌ··/ *n* [U] several people buying or renting an apartment, etc. (esp. for holidays), each using it for short periods each year **timeshare** *n* apartment, etc. rented

time sig·na·ture /ˈ· ˌ··/ *n* mark, esp. two

time·ta·ble /ˈtaɪmˌteɪbəl/ n 1 list of the travelling times of buses, trains, etc. 2 (list of) the times of classes in a school, etc. ♦ vt 1 to plan for a future time: *The meeting was timetabled for tomorrow.* 2 arrange according to a TIMETABLE (2)

tim·id /ˈtɪmɪd/ adj fearful; lacking courage ~ly adv ~ity /tɪˈmɪdəti/ n [U]

tim·o·rous /ˈtɪmərəs/ adj fml fearful ~ly adv ~ness n [U]

tin /tɪn/ n 1 [U] soft whitish metal 2 [C] BrE small closed tin container in which food is sold ♦ vt -nn- pack (food) in tins ~ny adj 1 of or like tin 2 having a thin metallic sound

tinc·ture /ˈtɪŋktʃə‖-ər/ n [C;U] medical substance mixed with alcohol

tin·der /ˈtɪndə‖-ər/ n [U] material that burns easily, used esp. for lighting fires

tin·foil /ˈtɪnfɔɪl/ n [U] very thin bendable sheet of shiny metal

tinge /tɪndʒ/ vt give a small amount of colour to: *black hair tinged with grey* | (fig.) *admiration tinged with jealousy* ♦ n [S] small amount

tin·gle /ˈtɪŋɡəl/ vi, n [S] (feel) a slight, not unpleasant, stinging sensation

tin·ker /ˈtɪŋkə‖-ər/ vi work without a definite idea or useful results, making small changes, esp. when trying to repair or improve something ♦ n 1 [S] act of tinkering 2 [C] travelling mender of pots and pans

tin·kle /ˈtɪŋkəl/ vi make light metallic sounds ♦ n 1 tinkling sound 2 BrE sl telephone call

tin o·pen·er /ˈ· ˌ···/ n BrE tool for opening tins

tin-pot /ˈ··/ adj worthless and unimportant, but perhaps thinking oneself to be important

tin·sel /ˈtɪnsəl/ n [U] 1 threads of shiny material used for (Christmas) decorations 2 something showy that is really cheap and worthless

tint /tɪnt/ n pale or delicate shade of a colour ♦ vt give a tint to

ti·ny /ˈtaɪni/ adj extremely small

tip¹ /tɪp/ n 1 (pointed) end of something: *the tips of one's fingers* 2 part stuck on the end: *cigarettes with tips* 3 **on the tip of one's tongue** not quite able to be remembered ♦ vt -pp- put a tip on: *tipped cigarettes*

tip² v -pp- 1 vt BrE pour 2 vi/t (cause to) fall over 3 vi/t (cause to) lean at an angle ♦ n esp. BrE 1 place where unwanted waste is left 2 infml extremely untidy dirty place: *His room is an absolute tip.*

tip³ n small amount of money given to someone who does a service ♦ vi/t -pp- give a tip (to)

tip⁴ n helpful piece of advice ♦ vt -pp- suggest as likely to succeed

tip off phr vt give a piece of secret information to **tip-off** /ˈ··/ n

tip·ple /ˈtɪpəl/ n infml alcoholic drink

tip·ster /ˈtɪpstə‖-ər/ n person who gives advice about the likely winner of horse and dog races

tip·sy /ˈtɪpsi/ adj infml slightly drunk

tip·toe /ˈtɪptəʊ‖-toʊ/ n **on tiptoe** on one's toes with the rest of the foot raised ♦ vi walk on tiptoe

tip-top /ˌ· ˈ·◄/ adj infml excellent

ti·rade /taɪˈreɪd, tɪ-‖ˈtaɪreɪd, tɪˈreɪd/ n long, angry speech

tire¹ /taɪə/ vi/t (cause to) become tired ~less adj never getting tired ~some adj 1 annoying 2 uninteresting

tire² n AmE for TYRE

tired /taɪəd‖taɪrd/ adj 1 needing rest or sleep 2 no longer interested: *I'm tired of doing this; let's go for a walk.* 3 showing lack of imagination or new thought: *tired ideas* ~ness n [U]

tis·sue /ˈtɪʃuː, -sjuː‖-ʃuː/ n 1 [C;U] the material animals and plants are made of; cells: *lung tissue* 2 [U] thin light paper, esp. for wrapping 3 [C] paper handkerchief 4 [C] fml something formed as if by weaving threads together: *a tissue of lies*

tit¹ /tɪt/ n small bird of various sorts

tit² n sl, not polite woman's breast

ti·tan·ic /taɪˈtænɪk/ adj very great in degree: *a titanic struggle*

ti·ta·ni·um /taɪˈteɪniəm/ n [U] light strong metal used in compounds

tit·bit /ˈtɪtˌbɪt/ n small piece of particularly nice food: (fig.) *a few titbits of information*

tit for tat /ˌ·· ·ˈ·/ n [U] something unpleasant given in return for something unpleasant one has suffered

tithe /taɪð/ n tax paid to the church in former times

tit·il·late /ˈtɪtᵻleɪt/ vt excite, esp. sexually –**lation** /ˌtɪtᵻˈleɪʃən/ n [U]

ti·tle /ˈtaɪtl/ n 1 [C] name of a book, play, painting, etc. 2 [C] word such as 'Lord', 'President', or 'Doctor' used before someone's name to show rank, office, or profession 3 [S;U] legal right to ownership 4 [C] position of unbeaten winner: *the world heavyweight boxing title* **titled** *adj* having a noble title, such as 'Lord'

tit·ter /ˈtɪtəʳ/ vi laugh quietly in a nervous or silly way **titter** n

tit·tle-tat·tle /ˈtɪtl ˌtætl/ n [U] GOSSIP

tit·u·lar /ˈtɪtʃᵻlə ‖ -əʳ/ adj holding a title but not having any real power: *a titular head of state*

T-junc·tion /ˈtiː ˌdʒʌŋkʃən/ n place where two roads meet in the shape of a T

TNT /ˌtiː en ˈtiː/ n [U] powerful explosive

to /tə, tʊ; *strong* tuː/ prep 1 in a direction towards: *the road to London* 2 **a** (used before a verb to show it is the INFINITIVE): *I want to go.* **b** used in place of an infinitive: *We didn't want to come but we had to.* 3 in order to: *I came by car to save time.* 4 so as to be in: *I was sent to prison.* 5 touching: *Stick the paper to the wall.* 6 as far as: *from beginning to end* 7 for the attention or possession of: *I told/gave it to her.* 8 in connection with: *the answer to a question* 9 in relation or comparison with: *That's nothing to what it could have been.* | *We won by 6 points to 3.* 10 (of time) before: *It's ten to four.* 11 per: *This car does 30 miles to the gallon.* ♦ *adv* 1 so as to be shut: *Pull the door to.* 2 into consciousness: *She came to.* 3 close/near to from really close: *He doesn't look so young when you see him close to.*

toad /təʊd ‖ toʊd/ n animal like a large FROG

toad·stool /ˈtəʊdstuːl ‖ ˈtoʊd-/ n (uneatable) FUNGUS

to and fro /ˌtuː ənd ˈfrəʊ ‖ -ˈfroʊ/ adv forwards and backwards or from side to side: *The door swung to and fro in the breeze.*

toast /təʊst ‖ toʊst/ n 1 [U] bread made brown by heating 2 [C] act of ceremonial drinking to show respect or express good

wishes: *They drank a toast to their guest.* ♦ *vt* 1 make brown by heating 2 warm thoroughly 3 drink a TOAST (2) to ~**er** n electrical apparatus for making TOAST (1)

toast·mas·ter /ˈtəʊstˌmɑːstə ‖ ˈtoʊst-ˌmæstəʳ/ n person who introduces TOASTS (2) and speakers at a formal dinner

to·bac·co /təˈbækəʊ ‖ -koʊ/ n [U] dried leaves of a certain plant prepared esp. for smoking in cigarettes, pipes, etc. ~**nist** /təˈbækənᵻst/ n seller of tobacco, cigarettes, etc.

to·bog·gan /təˈbɒgən ‖ -ˈbɑː-/ n long board for carrying people over snow **toboggan** vi

to·day /təˈdeɪ/ adv, n [U] 1 (on) this day 2 (at) this present time

tod·dle /ˈtɒdl ‖ ˈtɑːdl/ vi 1 walk, esp. with short unsteady steps 2 *infml* walk; go –**dler** n child who has just learnt to walk

to-do /tə ˈduː/ n *infml* **to-dos** state of excited confusion or annoyance

toe¹ /təʊ ‖ toʊ/ n 1 any of the five small movable parts at the end of the foot 2 part of a shoe or sock covering these 3 **on one's toes** fully ready for action

toe² v **toe the line** act obediently

toe cap /ˈ· ·/ n strengthened toe of a shoe

toe·hold /ˈtəʊhəʊld ‖ ˈtoʊhoʊld/ n place for putting the end of the foot when climbing: (fig.) *We need to get a toehold in the Japanese market*

tof·fee /ˈtɒfi ‖ ˈtɑːfi/ n [C;U] (piece of) a hard brown substance made from sugar and butter

toffee-nosed /ˈ·· ·/ adj BrE *infml* for SNOBBISH

to·geth·er¹ /təˈgeðə ‖ -əʳ/ adv 1 in or into a single group, body, or place 2 with each other 3 at the same time 4 in agreement; combined 5 **together with** in addition to ~**ness** n [U] friendliness

together² adj *infml* 1 (of a person) very much in control of life, actions, etc. 2 **get it together** have things under control

tog·gle /ˈtɒgəl ‖ ˈtɑː-/ n bar-shaped wooden button

togs /tɒgz ‖ tɑːgz, tɔːgz/ n [P] *infml* clothes

toil /tɔɪl/ n [U] *lit* hard work ♦ *vi lit* work or move with great effort

toi·let /ˈtɔɪlᵻt/ n 1 [C] (room containing) a seatlike apparatus for receiving and taking away the body's waste matter **2** [U] *fml* act of washing, dressing oneself, etc.

toilet pa·per /'·· ,·-/ *n* [U] paper for cleaning oneself after passing waste matter from the body

toi·let·ries /'tɔɪlɪtriz/ *n* [P] things used in washing, making oneself tidy, etc.

toilet roll /'·· ·/ *n* rolled-up length of TOILET PAPER

to·ken /'təʊkən‖'toʊ-/ *n* **1** outward sign: *They wore black as a token of mourning.* **2** card which can be exchanged for goods: *a book token* —see also **by the same token** (SAME ♦ *adj* **1** being a small part representing something greater **2** *derog* done so as to seem acceptable: *a token effort*

told /təʊld‖toʊld/ *past t. and p. of* TELL

tol·e·rate /'tɒləreɪt‖'tɑ:-/ *vt* **1** permit (something one disagrees with) **2** suffer (someone or something) without complaining –**rable** *adj* fairly good; not too bad –**rably** *adv fml* fairly –**rance** *n* **1** [C;U] ability to suffer pain, hardship, etc. without being harmed or damaged: *a low tolerance to cold* **2** [U] allowing people to behave in a way one disagrees with, without getting annoyed **3** [U] TOLERATION (1) –**rant** *adj* showing toleration –**ration** /,tɒlə'reɪʃən‖,tɑ:-/ *n* [U] **1** allowing opinions, customs, etc. different from one's own to be freely held or practised **2** TOLERANCE (2)

toll[1] /təʊl‖toʊl/ *n* **1** tax paid for using a road, bridge, etc. **2** bad effect of illness, misfortune, etc.: *The death toll in the accident was nine.*

toll[2] *vi/t* ring (a bell) or be rung slowly and repeatedly

tom·a·hawk /'tɒməhɔːk‖'tɑːməhɔːk/ *n* Native American axe

to·ma·to /tə'mɑːtəʊ‖-'meɪtoʊ/ *n* **-toes** soft red fruit eaten raw or cooked as a vegetable

tomb /tuːm/ *n* (large decorative cover for) a grave

tom·boy /'tɒmbɔɪ‖'tɑːm-/ *n* spirited young girl who enjoys rough and noisy activities

tom·cat /'tɒmkæt‖'tɑːm-/ *n* male cat

tome /təʊm‖toʊm/ *n lit or humor* large heavy book

tom·fool·e·ry /tɒm'fuːləri‖tɑːm-/ *n* [U] *fml* foolish behaviour

to·mor·row /tə'mɒrəʊ‖-'mɔːroʊ,

-'mɑː-/ *adv* on the day following today ♦ *n* **1** [U] day after today **2** [S;U] future

tom-tom /'tɒm tɒm‖'tɑːm tɑːm/ *n* long narrow drum played with the hands

ton /tʌn/ *n* **1** a measure of weight equal to 1.016 TONNES **2** also **tons** *pl.* — a very large amount **3** **come down on someone like a ton of bricks** *infml* turn the full force of one's anger against someone, usu. as a punishment **tons** *adv infml* very much

tone[1] /təʊn‖toʊn/ *n* **1** [C] quality of sound, esp. of a musical instrument or the voice **2** [C] variety or shade of a colour **3** [U] general quality or nature **4** [U] proper firmness of bodily organs and muscles **tonal** *adj*

tone[2] *v*

tone down *phr vt* reduce in force

tone in *phr vi/t* (cause to) match

tone up *phr vt* make stronger, brighter, more effective or healthy, etc.

tone-deaf /,· '·◄/ *adj* unable to tell the difference between musical notes

to·ner /'təʊnə‖'toʊnər/ *n* [C;U] ink used in printers, PHOTOCOPIERS, etc.

tongs /tɒŋz‖tɑːŋz, tɔːŋz/ *n* [P] two movable arms joined at one end, for holding and lifting things

tongue /tʌŋ/ *n* **1** movable organ in the mouth in talking, tasting, licking, etc.: (fig.) *She has a sharp tongue.* (=a severe or unkind way of speaking) **2** object like this in shape or purpose: *tongues of flame* **3** *fml* language **4** **hold one's tongue** remain silent **5** **(with) tongue in cheek** saying or doing something one does not seriously mean

tongue-tied /'·· ·/ *adj* unable to speak freely, esp. because of nervousness

tongue twist·er /'· ,·-/ *n* word or phrase difficult to say

ton·ic /'tɒnɪk‖'tɑː-/ *n* **1** [C] something, esp. a medicine, that increases health or strength **2** [U] tonic water: *a gin and tonic*

tonic wa·ter /'·· ,·-/ *n* [U] sort of gassy water usu. mixed with strong alcoholic drink

to·night /tə'naɪt/ *adv, n* (during) the night of today

ton·nage /'tʌnɪdʒ/ *n* [C;U] **1** amount of goods a ship can carry, expressed in TONS **2** ships, esp. those that carry goods

tonne /tʌn/ *n* a measure of weight equal

to 1000 kilograms

ton·sil /ˈtɒnsəl ‖ ˈtɑːn-/ n either of two small organs at the back of the throat

ton·sil·li·tis /ˌtɒnsəˈlaɪtɪs ‖ ˌtɑːn-/ n [U] painful soreness of the tonsils

too /tuː/ adv 1 to a greater degree than is necessary or good: *You're driving too fast.* 2 also: *I've been to Australia, and to New Zealand too.* 3 only too very

took /tʊk/ past t. of TAKE

tool /tuːl/ n 1 hand-held instrument, such as an axe, hammer, etc. 2 down tools *infml* to stop working

toot /tuːt/ vt make a short warning sound with (a horn) **toot** n

tooth /tuːθ/ n **teeth** /tiːθ/ 1 small bony object growing in the mouth, used for biting 2 any of the pointed parts standing out from a comb, SAW, COG, etc. 3 ability to produce an effect: *The present law has no teeth.* 4 armed to the teeth very heavily armed 5 fight tooth and nail very violently 6 get one's teeth into do a job very actively and purposefully 7 in the teeth of against and in spite of: *in the teeth of fierce opposition* 8 lie in/through one's teeth lie shamelessly 9 long in the tooth *infml* old 10 set someone's teeth on edge give someone an unpleasant sensation caused by certain acid tastes or high sounds —see also SWEET TOOTH **-less** adj ~y adj

tooth·brush /ˈtuːθbrʌʃ/ n small brush for cleaning one's teeth

tooth·paste /ˈtuːθpeɪst/ n [U] paste for cleaning one's teeth

tooth·pick /ˈtuːθˌpɪk/ n short thin pointed stick for removing food from the teeth

top¹ /tɒp ‖ tɑːp/ n 1 the highest or upper part: *the top of a tree* 2 the best or most important part or place: *at the top of the class* 3 cover: *bottle tops* 4 at the top of (one's) voice as loudly as possible 5 from top to bottom all through; completely 6 from top to toe (of a person) completely 7 get on top of *infml* be too much for: *This work is getting on top of me.* 8 on top of: a able to deal with b in addition to 9 on top of the world *infml* very happy 10 over the top *infml, esp. BrE* more than is reasonable, sensible, or proper —see also blow one's top (BLOW¹) **-less** adj leaving the breasts bare ♦ adj highest, best, etc.: *at top speed*

(=very fast)

top² vt **-pp-** 1 be higher, better, or more than: *Our profits have topped £1 million.* 2 form a top for: *a cake topped with cream* 3 top the bill be chief actor or actress in a play

top off phr vt *esp. AmE* complete successfully by a last action

top up phr vt fill (a partly empty container) with liquid

top³ n 1 child's toy that spins round 2 sleep like a top sleep deeply and well

to·paz /ˈtəʊpæz ‖ ˈtoʊ-/ n [C;U] (precious stone cut from) a yellowish mineral

top brass /ˌ· ˈ·/ n [U;P] *infml* officers of high rank in the armed forces

top dog /ˌ· ˈ·/ n person in the most advantageous or powerful position

top hat /ˌ· ˈ·/ n man's formal tall usu. black or grey hat

top-heav·y /ˌ· ˈ·◄/ adj too heavy at the top

top·ic /ˈtɒpɪk ‖ ˈtɑː-/ n subject for conversation, writing, etc.

top·ic·al /ˈtɒpɪkəl ‖ ˈtɑː-/ adj of or being a subject of present interest ~ly /-kli/ adv

top-notch /ˌ· ˈ·◄/ adj being one of the best

to·pog·ra·phy /təˈpɒɡrəfi ‖ -ˈpɑː-/ n [U] (science of describing) the shape and height of land **-phical** /ˌtɒpəˈɡræfɪkəl◄ ‖ ˌtɑː-, ˌtoʊ-/ adj

top·ple /ˈtɒpəl ‖ ˈtɑː-/ vi/t (cause to) become unsteady and fall down: (fig.) *The scandal toppled the government.*

top-se·cret /ˌ· ˈ··◄/ adj that must be kept extremely secret

top·sy-tur·vy /ˌtɒpsi ˈtɜːvi◄ ‖ ˌtɑːpsi ˈtɜːrvi/ adj, adv in complete disorder and confusion

torch /tɔːtʃ ‖ tɔːrtʃ/ n 1 *BrE* small electric light carried in the hand 2 mass of burning material carried by hand to give light 3 *AmE* for BLOWLAMP

tore /tɔː ‖ tɔːr/ past t. of TEAR¹

tor·ment¹ /ˈtɔːment ‖ ˈtɔːr-/ n [C;U] very great suffering

tor·ment² /tɔːˈment ‖ tɔːr-/ vt cause torment to ~or n

torn /tɔːn ‖ tɔːrn/ past p. of TEAR

tor·na·do /tɔːˈneɪdəʊ ‖ tɔːrˈneɪdoʊ/ n **-does** or **-dos** very violent wind that spins at great speed

tor·pe·do /tɔːˈpiːdəʊ ‖ tɔːrˈpiːdoʊ/ n **-does** long narrow motor-driven explosive apparatus fired through the sea to destroy ships ♦ *vt* attack or destroy (as if) with a torpedo

tor·pid /'tɔːpɪd ‖ 'tɔːr-/ *adj fml derog* inactive; slow

tor·por /'tɔːpə ‖ 'tɔːrpər/ *n* [U] *fml derog* inactivity

tor·rent /'tɒrənt ‖ 'tɔː-, 'tɑː-/ *n* violently rushing stream of water: (fig.) *torrents of abuse* **–rential** /tə'renʃəl ‖ tɔː-/ *adj*: *torrential rain*

tor·rid /'tɒrɪd ‖ 'tɔː-, 'tɑː-/ *adj* **1** (esp. of weather) very hot **2** full of strong feelings and uncontrolled activity, esp. sexual: *a torrid love affair*

tor·so /'tɔːsəʊ ‖ 'tɔːrsoʊ/ *n* **-sos** human body without the head and limbs

tort /tɔːt ‖ tɔːrt/ *n law* wrongful but not criminal act

tor·toise /'tɔːtəs ‖ 'tɔːr-/ *n* slow-moving land animal with a hard shell

tor·toise·shell /'tɔːtəsʃel, 'tɔːtəʃel ‖ 'tɔːr-/ *n* [U] material from a tortoise's or TURTLE's shell, brown with yellowish marks

tor·tu·ous /'tɔːtʃuəs ‖ 'tɔːr-/ *adj* **1** twisted; winding **2** not direct in speech, thought or action **~ly** *adv*

tor·ture /'tɔːtʃə ‖ 'tɔːrtʃər/ *vt* cause great pain or suffering to out of cruelty, as a punishment, etc. ♦ *n* **1** [U] act of torturing **2** [C;U] severe pain or suffering **–turer** *n*

To·ry /'tɔːri/ *n*, *adj* (member) of the CONSERVATIVE PARTY **~ism** *n* [U]

toss /tɒs ‖ tɔːs/ *v* **1** *vt* throw **2** *vi/t* (cause to) move about rapidly and pointlessly: *He tossed and turned all night, unable to sleep.* **3** *vt* move or lift (part of the body) rapidly: *She tossed her head.* **4** *vt* mix lightly: *toss a salad* **5** *vi/t* throw (a coin) to decide something according to which side lands upwards: *There's only one cake left – let's toss for it.* ♦ *n* **1** [C] act of tossing **2** [S] *BrE sl* the least amount: *I couldn't give a toss* (=I don't care at all) *what he thinks.*

toss-up /'··/ *n* [S] even chance; uncertainty

tot¹ /tɒt ‖ tɑːt/ *n* **1** very small child **2** small amount of a strong alcoholic drink

tot² *v* **-tt- tot up** *phr vt* add up

to·tal /'təʊtl ‖ 'toʊ-/ *adj* complete; whole ♦ *n* **1** complete —see also GRAND TOTAL, SUM TOTAL **2 in total** when all have been added up ♦ *vt* **-ll-** *BrE* ‖ **-l-** *AmE* be when added up: *His debts totalled £9000.* **~ly** *adv*: *totally*

different ~**ity** /təʊ'tælɪti ‖ toʊ-/ *n* [U] *fml* completeness

to·tal·i·tar·i·an /ˌtəʊˌtælɪ'teəriən ‖ toʊˌtælə'ter-/ *adj* of or based on a centrally controlled system of government that does not allow any political opposition **~ism** *n* [U]

tote /təʊt ‖ toʊt/ *vt infml*, *esp. AmE* carry, esp. with difficulty

to·tem /'təʊtəm ‖ 'toʊ-/ *n* person or thing used as sign or SYMBOL of an organization, society, etc.

tot·ter /'tɒtə ‖ 'tɑːtər/ *vi* move or walk unsteadily, as if about to fall: (fig.) *their tottering economy*

touch¹ /tʌtʃ/ *v* **1** *vi/t* be separated (from) by no space at all: *Their hands touched.* **2** *vi/t* feel or make connection (with), esp. with the hands: *The model is fragile, don't touch (it).* **3** *vt* eat or drink: *You haven't touched your food.* | *I never touch alcohol.* **4** *vt* compare with: *Nothing can touch a cold drink on a hot day!* **5** *vt* cause to feel pity, sympathy, etc.: *a touching story* **6 touch wood** touch something made of wood to keep away bad luck **~ed** *adj* **1** grateful **2** slightly mad **~y** *adj* easily offended or annoyed **~ily** *adv* **~iness** *n* [U]

touch down *phr vi* (of a plane or spacecraft) land

touch off *phr vt* cause (a violent event) to start

touch on/upon *phr vt* talk about shortly

touch up *phr vt* **1** improve with small additions **2** *sl* touch a person in a sexually improper way

touch² *n* **1** [U] sense of feeling **2** [C] way something feels: *the silky touch of her skin* **3** [C] act of touching **4** [U] connection, esp. so as to receive information: *He's gone to Australia, but we keep in touch by letter.* **5** [S] particular way of doing things: *a woman's touch* **6** [C] small details: *putting the finishing touches to the plan* **7** [S] special ability: *I'm losing my touch.* **8** [S] slight attack of an illness: *a touch of flu* **9** [S] slight amount: *It needs a touch more salt.* **10** [U] (in football) area outside the field of play **11 lose touch** lose contact —see also SOFT TOUCH

touch-and-go /ˌ· · '·◂/ *adj* of uncertain result; risky

touch·down /'tʌtʃdaʊn/ n landing of a plane or spacecraft

touch·line /'tʌtʃlaɪn/ n line along each of the longer sides of a football field

touch·stone /'tʌtʃstəʊn ‖ -stoʊn/ n lit something used as a test or standard

tough /tʌf/ adj 1 not easily weakened or broken 2 difficult to cut or eat: tough meat 3 difficult: a tough job/problem 4 not kind, severe: a tough new law against drunken driving 5 unfortunate: tough luck ~ly adv ~en vi/t make or become tougher ~ness n [U]

tou·pee /'tu:peɪ ‖ tu:'peɪ/ n small WIG worn by a man

tour /tʊə ‖ tʊr/ n 1 act of travelling round a country, walking round a building, etc. looking at interesting things 2 period of duty in a job, esp. abroad 3 journey to take part in performances, sports matches, etc. ♦ vi/t visit as a tourist ~ism n [U] 1 travelling for pleasure, esp. on one's holidays 2 the business of providing holidays for tourists ~ist n [C] 1 person travelling for pleasure 2 sportsman on TOUR (3)

tour de force /ˌtʊə də 'fɔːs ‖ ˌtʊr də 'fɔːrs/ n [S] show of great skill

tour·na·ment /'tʊənəmənt, 'tɔː- ‖ 'tɜːr-, 'tʊr-/ n 1 competition: a chess/tennis tournament 2 (in former times) competition of fighting skill

tour·ni·quet /'tʊənɪkeɪ, 'tɔː- ‖ 'tɜːr-nɪkət, 'tʊr-/ n something twisted tightly round a limb to stop bleeding

tou·sle /'taʊzəl/ vt make (hair) untidy

tout /taʊt/ vt derog try to persuade people to buy (one's goods or services) ♦ n BrE derog person who offers tickets for the theatre, etc. at very high prices

tow /təʊ ‖ toʊ/ vt pull (esp. a vehicle) with a rope or chain ♦ n 1 act of towing 2 **in tow** following closely behind 3 **on tow** being towed

to·wards /tə'wɔːdz ‖ tɔːrdz/ esp. BrE ‖ **toward** /tə'wɔːd ‖ tɔːrd/ esp. AmE — prep 1 in the direction of: He walked towards me. ‖ She had her back towards me. 2 just before in time: We arrived towards noon. 3 in relation to: What are their feelings towards us? 4 for the purpose of: Each week we save £5 towards our holiday.

tow·el /'taʊəl/ n piece of cloth or paper for drying things ♦ vt -ll- BrE ‖ -l- AmE rub or dry with a towel

tow·el·ling BrE ‖ **toweling** AmE /'taʊəlɪŋ/ n [U] thickish cloth, used for making esp. towels

tow·er /'taʊə ‖ -ər/ n 1 tall (part of a) building: a church tower 2 tall metal framework for signalling or broadcasting ♦ vi be very tall: (fig.) Intellectually he towers above (=is much better than) them all. ~ing adj very great: a towering rage

tower block /'·· ·/ n esp. BrE tall block of flats or offices

tower of strength /ˌ·· · '·/ n person who can be depended on for help or support

town /taʊn/ n 1 [C] large group of houses and other buildings where people live and work 2 [C] all the people who live in such a place 3 [U] the business or shopping centre of a town 4 [U] the chief city in an area 5 [S] (life in) towns and cities in general 6 **go to town** act or behave freely or wildly 7 **(out) on the town** enjoying oneself, esp. at night 8 **paint the town red** have a very enjoyable time, esp. in wild or noisy manner

town hall /ˌ· '·/ n public building for a town's local government

town·ship /'taʊnʃɪp/ n (in South Africa) a place where black citizens live

tow·path /'təʊpɑːθ ‖ 'toʊpæθ/ n path along the bank of a CANAL or river

tox·ic /'tɒksɪk ‖ 'tɑːk-/ adj poisonous: toxic waste (=harmful waste products from industry) ~ity /tɒk'sɪsəti ‖ tɑːk-/ n [U]

tox·in /'tɒksən ‖ 'tɑːk-/ n poison produced in plants and animals

toy[1] /tɔɪ/ n 1 object for children to play with 2 small breed of dog

toy[2] v toy with phr vt 1 consider (an idea) not very seriously 2 play with or handle purposelessly

trace[1] /treɪs/ vt 1 find, esp. by following a course 2 copy lines or the shape of something using transparent paper ♦ n 1 [C;U] mark or sign showing the former presence of someone or something: She had vanished without trace. (=completely) 2 [C] small amount of something: traces of poison in his blood

trace[2] n rope, chain, etc. fastening a cart or carriage to the animal pulling it

track[1] /træk/ n 1 marks left by a person,

animal, or vehicle that has passed before **2** narrow (rough) path or road **3** railway line **4** course for racing **5** piece of music on a record or TAPE (2) **6 cover one's tracks** keep one's movements, activities, etc. secret **7 in one's tracks** *infml* where one is; suddenly **8 keep/lose track of** keep/fail to keep oneself informed about a person, situation, etc. **9 make tracks** leave, esp. in a hurry **10 off the beaten track** not well-known or often visited **11 on the right/wrong track** thinking or working correctly/incorrectly **12 a one-track mind** *infml* a tendency to think only of one thing or subject

track² *vt* follow the TRACK¹ (1) of ~**er** *n*

track down *phr vt* find by hunting or searching

track rec·ord /'· ,··/ *n* degree to which someone or something has performed well or badly up to now

track·suit /'træksuːt, -sjuːt ‖ -suːt/ *n* loose-fitting suit worn by people when training for sport

tract¹ /trækt/ *n* **1** wide stretch of land **2** system of related organs in an animal: *the digestive tract*

tract² *n fml* short article on a religious or moral subject

trac·tion /'trækʃən/ *n* [U] **1** type of pulling power: *steam traction* **2** force that prevents a wheel from slipping **3** medical treatment with a pulling apparatus used to cure a broken bone or similar INJURY

trac·tor /'træktə ‖ -ər/ *n* motor vehicle for pulling farm machinery

trade¹ /treɪd/ *n* **1** [U] business of buying, selling, or exchanging goods, esp. between countries **2** [C] particular business: *the wine trade* **3** [C] job, esp. needing skill with the hands: *the printer's trade* **4** [S] stated amount of business: *doing a good trade* —see also FREE TRADE

trade² *v* **1** *vi* buy and sell goods **2** *vt* exchange: *I traded my radio for a type writer.* | (fig.) *trading insults* –**der** *n* person whose job is buying and selling esp. STOCKS and SHARES

trade in *phr vt* give in part payment for something new: *I traded my old car in.*

trade off *phr vt* balance (one situation or quality) against another, with the aim of producing an acceptable or desirable result

trade on *phr vt* take unfair advantage of

trade·mark /'treɪdmɑːk ‖ -mɑːrk/ *n* **1** sign or word put on a product to show who made it **2** thing by which a person or thing may habitually be recognized

trade name /'· ·/ *n* name given by a producer to a particular product

trade off /'· ·/ *n* balance between two (opposing) situations or qualities

trades·man /'treɪdzmən/ *n* -**men** /-mən/ **1** shopkeeper **2** worker or seller who comes to people's homes

trade u·nion /,· '··◂/ *n* workers' organization to represent their interests and deal with employers –**ist** *n*

trade wind /'· ·/ *n* wind blowing almost continually towards the EQUATOR

tra·di·tion /trə'dɪʃən/ *n* **1** [C] opinion, custom, principle, etc. passed down from the past to the present **2** [U] (passing down of) such customs, etc.: *By tradition, brides in the West wear white.* ~**al** *adj* ~**ally** *adv*

traf·fic /'træfɪk/ *n* [U] **1** (movement of) vehicles on the road, planes in the sky, etc. **2** trade, esp. in illegal things: **3** business done in carrying passengers or goods ♦ *v* -**ck**- **traffic in** *phr vt* trade in (esp. illegal things) ~**ker** *n*: *drug traffickers* ~**king** *n* [U]

traffic lights /'·· ·/ *n* [P] set of coloured lights for controlling road traffic

traffic war·den /'·· ,··/ *n BrE* official who controls the parking of vehicles on streets

tra·ge·dy /'trædʒɪdi/ *n* [C;U] **1** serious play that ends sadly **2** [U] these plays considered as a group **3** terrible, unhappy, or unfortunate event

tra·gic /'trædʒɪk/ *adj* **1** of or related to TRAGEDY (2) **2** very sad, unfortunate, etc. ~**ally** /-kli/ *adv*

trail /treɪl/ *n* **1** track or smell followed by a hunter: *We're on their trail.* (=following them closely) **2** path across rough country **3** stream of dust, smoke, people, etc. behind something moving ♦ *v* **1** *vi/t* drag or be dragged along behind **2** *vt* TRACK **3** *vi* (of a plant) grow along a surface ~**er** *n* **1** vehicle pulled by another **2** small pieces of a new film shown to advertise it

train¹ /treɪn/ *n* **1** line of railway carriages pulled by an engine **2** set of related things one after another: *It interrupted my train of thought.* **3** part of a long garment that

spreads over the ground behind the wearer
4 long line of moving people, animals, or
vehicles

train /treɪn/ v 1 vi/t give or be given instruction,
practice, or exercise: *training a dog to jump
over a fence* 2 vt aim (a gun, etc.) 3 vt direct
the growth of (a plant) **~ee** n person being
trained **~er** n 1 person who trains other
people 2 sports shoe **~ing** n [S;U] 1 practical instruction 2 **in/out of training**
in/not in a healthy condition for a sport,
test of skill, etc.

traipse /treɪps/ vi walk tiredly

trait /treɪ, treɪt ‖ treɪt/ n fml particular
quality of someone or something

trai·tor /'treɪtə ‖ -ər/ n someone disloyal,
esp. to their country

tra·jec·to·ry /trə'dʒektəri/ n fml curved
path of an object fired or thrown through
the air

tram /træm/ n usu. electric bus that runs
on metal lines set in the road

tramp /træmp/ vi 1 walk heavily 2 sound
of heavy walking 3 walk steadily, esp. over
a long distance ♦ n 1 esp. BrE wandering
person with no home or job who begs for
food or money 2 long walk

tram·ple /'træmpəl/ vi/t step (on)
heavily; crush under the feet

tram·po·line /'træmpəli:n ‖, træm-
pə'li:n/ n frame with springy material
on which people jump up and down

trance /trɑːns ‖ træns/ n sleeplike condition
of the mind

tran·quil /'træŋkwəl/ adj pleasantly calm,
quiet, or free from worry **~lity** BrE ‖ ˜ity
AmE /træŋ'kwɪləti/ n [U] calmness **~lize**,
-lise BrE ‖ ˜ize AmE /'træŋkwəlaɪz/ vt
make calm (esp. with tranquillizers) **~lizer**,
-iser BrE ‖ ˜izer AmE — n drug for
reducing anxiety and making people calm

trans·act /træn'zækt/ vt fml do and
complete (a piece of business) **~ion** n 1 [U]
act of transacting 2 [C] piece of business
transactions /-'zæk∫ən/ n [P] records of
meetings of a society

trans·at·lan·tic /,trænzət'læntɪk◄/ adj
connecting or concerning countries on both
sides of the Atlantic ocean

tran·scend /træn'send/ vt fml or lit go
beyond (a limit or something within limits)
~ent adj going far beyond ordinary limits

tran·scribe /træn'skraɪb/ vt 1 write an

exact copy of 2 write down (something
said) 3 arrange (a piece of music) for
instrument or voice other than the original

tran·script /'trænskrɪpt/ n exact written
or printed copy **~ion** /træn'skrɪp∫ən/ n
1 [U] act or process of transcribing 2 [C]
transcript

trans·fer¹ /træns'fɜː ‖ -'fɜːr/ v -rr- 1 vi/t
move from one place, job, etc. to another
2 vt give ownership of property to another
person 3 vi move from one vehicle to
another **~able** adj

trans·fer² /'trænsfɜː ‖ -fɜːr/ n 1 [C;U] act
or process of transferring 2 [C] something
transferred 3 [C] esp. BrE picture for
sticking or printing onto a surface **~ence** n
[U]

trans·fig·ure /træns'fɪgə ‖ -ɡjər/ vt fml
or lit change so as to be more glorious

trans·fix /træns'fɪks/ vt fml make unable
to move or think because of terror, shock,
etc.

trans·form /træns'fɔːm ‖ -'fɔːrm/ vt
change completely **~ation** /,trænsfə-
'meɪ∫ən ‖ -fər-/ n [C;U]: *the transformation
of heat into power* **~er** /træns'fɔːmə ‖
-'fɔːrmər/ n apparatus for changing
electrical force, esp. to a different VOLTAGE

trans·fu·sion /træns'fjuːʒən/ n [C;U] act
of putting one person's blood into another's
body

trans·gress /trænz'gres ‖ træns-/ v fml
1 vt go beyond (a proper or legal limit) 2 vi
do wrong **~ion** /-'gre∫ən/ n [C;U] **~or**
/-'gresə ‖ -ər/ n

tran·si·ent /'trænziənt ‖ 'trænʃənt/ adj
fml lasting or staying for only a short time
~ence n [U]

tran·sis·tor /træn'zɪstə, -'sɪstə ‖ -ər/ n
1 small apparatus for controlling the flow of
electric current 2 small radio with
TRANSISTORS **~ize**, **-ise** vt provide with
transistors (1)

tran·sit /'trænsɪt, -zɪt/ n [U] going or
moving of people or goods from one place to
another: *The parcel was lost in transit.*

tran·si·tion /træn'zɪ∫ən, -'sɪ-/ n [C;U]
(act of) changing from one state to another
~al adj

tran·si·tive /'trænsɪtɪv, -zɪ-/ adj (of a
verb) that must have an object or a phrase
acting like an object

tran·si·to·ry /'trænzɪtəri ‖ -tɔːri/ adj

TRANSIENT

trans·late /træns'leɪt, trænz-/ *vi/t*
change (speech or writing) into a different
language –**lation** /-'leɪʃən/ *n* [C;U] –**lator**
/-'leɪtə‖-ər/ *n*

trans·lu·cent /trænz'luːsənt‖ træns-/
adj allowing light to pass through (although
not transparent)

trans·mit /trænz'mɪt‖ træns-/ *v* -**tt**-
1 *vi/t* broadcast: *transmit a radio distress
signal* 2 *vt* pass to another person: *transmit
a disease* 3 *vt* allow to pass through itself:
Water transmits sound. –**mission** /-'mɪʃən/
n 1 [U] act of transmitting 2 [C] television
or radio broadcast 3 [C] parts of a vehicle
that carry power to the wheels –**ter** /-'mɪtə
‖-ər/ *n* broadcasting apparatus

trans·par·ent /træn'spærənt, -'speər-‖
-'spær-, -'sper-/ *adj* 1 that can be seen
through 2 *fml* easily understood 3 *fml* clear
and certain: *a transparent lie* –**ency** *n* 1 [U]
quality of being transparent 2 [C] SLIDE (4)

trans·plant /træns'plɑːnt‖-'plænt/ *vt*
1 move (a plant) from one place and plant it
in another 2 move (an organ, piece of skin,
hair, etc.) from one part of the body to
another, or from one person to another ♦
/'trænsplɑːnt‖-plænt/ *n* 1 something
transplanted 2 act or operation of
transplanting an organ: *a heart transplant*

trans·port /'trænspɔːt‖-ɔːrt/ *vt* carry
(goods, people, etc.) from one place to
another ♦ *n* 1 [U] also **transportation**
/,trænspɔː'teɪʃən‖-spər-/ *esp. AmE* —
(means or system of) transporting:
*London's public transport includes buses
and trains.* 2 **in a transport/in
transports of** *lit* filled with (joy, delight,
etc.) –**er** /træn'spɔːtə‖-ɔːrtər/ *n* long
vehicle on which several cars can be
carried

trans·pose /træn'spəʊz‖-'spoʊz/ *vt* fml
1 change the order or position of (two or
more things) 2 to change the KEY of a piece
of music –**position** /,trænspə'zɪʃən/ *n*
[C;U]

trans·put·er /trænz'pjuːtə‖ træns
'pjuːtər/ *n* extremely powerful computer
MICROCHIP

trans·verse /,trænz'vɜːs◄‖,træns'vɜːrs◄/
adj fml lying or placed across: *a transverse
beam* –**ly** *adv*

trans·ves·tite /trænz'vestaɪt‖ træns-/

n person who likes to wear the clothes of
the opposite sex –**tism** *n* [U]

trap /træp/ *n* 1 apparatus for catching and
holding an animal: *a mousetrap* 2 plan for
deceiving (and catching) a person: *The
police set a trap to catch the thief.* 3 two-
wheeled horse-drawn vehicle 4 *sl* mouth:
Keep your trap shut! 5 *AmE for* BUNKER (3) ♦
vt -**pp**- 1 place or hold firmly with no hope
of escape: *The miners were trapped
underground.* 2 trick; deceive 3 catch (an
animal) in a trap –**per** *n*

trap·door /'træpdɔː‖-dɔːr/ *n* small door
in a roof or floor

tra·peze /trə'piːz/ *n* short bar hung high
above the ground used by ACROBATS to swing
on

trap·pings /'træpɪŋz/ *n* [P] articles of
dress or decoration, esp. as an outward sign
of rank

trash /træʃ/ *n* [U] 1 something of
extremely low quality or value 2 *AmE for*
RUBBISH (1) –**y** *adj*

trash·can /'træʃkæn/ *n AmE for* DUSTBIN

trau·ma /'trɔːmə, 'traʊmə‖'traʊmə,
'trɔː-/ *n* damage to the mind caused by a
shock or terrible experience –**tic**
/trɔː'mætɪk‖ trɑː-/ *adj* deeply and
unforgettably shocking –**tize**, –**tise**
/'trɔːmətaɪz‖'trɑː-/ *vt* cause to suffer
trauma

trav·el¹ /'trævəl/ *v* -**ll**- *BrE‖* -**l**- *AmE*
1 *vi/t* make a journey (through) 2 *vt* cover
(the stated distance) on a journey 3 *vi* go,
pass, move, etc.: *At what speed does light
travel?* 4 **travel light** travel without much
luggage ♦ *n* [U] travelling: *foreign travel*
–**led** *BrE‖* ¯**ed** *AmE adj* experienced in
travel: *a much travelled writer* –**ler** *BrE‖*
¯**er** *AmE* 1 person on a journey 2 travelling
SALESMAN **travels** *n* [P] journeys, esp.
abroad

travel a·gent /'·· ,··/ *n* someone who
makes people's travel arrangements

traveller's cheque /,··· '·/ *n* cheque that
can be exchanged abroad for foreign money

trav·el·ogue also -**og** *AmE* /'trævəlɒg
-lɔːg, -lɑːg/ *n* film or talk describing
foreign travel

tra·verse /'trævɜːs‖ trə'vɜːrs/ *vt* fml
pass across, over, or through

trav·es·ty /'trævəsti/ *n* something that
completely misrepresents the nature of the

real thing: *The trial was a travesty of justice.* (=was very unjust)

trawl /trɔːl ‖ trɒːl/ *vi/t, n* (fish with) a large net drawn along the sea bottom ~**er** *n* boat that uses a trawl

tray /treɪ/ *n* flat piece of plastic, metal, etc. for carrying things, esp. food

treach·e·ry /'tretʃəri/ *n* 1 [U] disloyalty or deceit 2 [C] disloyal or deceitful act ~**rous** *adj* 1 very disloyal or deceitful 2 full of hidden dangers: *treacherous currents* ~**rously** *adv*

trea·cle /'triːkəl/ *n* [U] *BrE* thick dark liquid made from sugar

tread /tred/ *v* **trod** /trɒd ‖ trɑːd/, **trodden** /'trɒdn ‖ 'trɑː-/ 1 *vi* put one's foot when walking; step: *Don't tread on the flowers!* 2 *vt fml* walk along: *tread a path* 3 *vt* press firmly with the feet 4 **tread on someone's toes** offend someone 5 **tread water** keep upright in water by moving the legs ♦ *n* 1 [S] act, way, or sound of walking 2 [C;U] pattern of raised lines on a tyre 3 [C] part of a stair on which the foot is placed

trea·dle /'tredl/ *n* apparatus worked by the feet to drive a machine

tread·mill /'tred,mɪl/ *n* something providing repeated uninteresting work

trea·son /'triːzən/ *n* [U] disloyalty to one's country, esp. by helping its enemies ~**able** *adj law* of or being treason

trea·sure /'treʒə ‖ -ər/ *n* 1 [U] wealth in gold, jewels, etc. 2 [C] very valuable object or person ♦ *vt* keep or regard as precious: *treasured memories*

trea·sur·er /'treʒərə ‖ -ər/ *n* person in charge of an organization's money

treasure trove /'treʒə trəʊv ‖ -ʒər troʊv/ *n* [U] something valuable found in the ground and claimed by no one

trea·su·ry /'treʒəri/ *n* government department that controls and spends public money

treat /triːt/ *vt* 1 act or behave towards: *He treated his horses very cruelly.* 2 deal with or handle: *Treat the glass carefully.* | *He treated my request as a joke.* 3 try to cure medically 4 put through a chemical or industrial action: *metal treated against rust* 5 pay for (someone's) food, drink, amusement, etc. ♦ *n* 1 something that gives great pleasure, esp. when unexpected: *What a treat to have real champagne!* 2 act of

treating (TREAT (5)) someone: *The meal's my treat, so put away your money.* ~**ment** *n* 1 [U] act or way of treating someone or something 2 [C] substance or method for treating someone or something

trea·tise /'triːtɪs, -tɪz/ *n* serious book on a particular subject

treat·y /'triːti/ *n* formally signed agreement between countries

treb·le¹ /'trebəl/ *predeterminer* three times as much or as many as ♦ *vi/t* make or become three times as much

treble² *n* 1 [C] boy with a high singing voice 2 [U] upper half of the whole range of musical notes

tree /triː/ *n* 1 tall long-living plant with a wooden trunk or stem 2 treelike bush: *a rose tree* ~**less** *adj*

trek /trek/ *vi, n* -**kk**- (make) a long hard journey, esp. on foot

trel·lis /'trelɪs/ *n* light upright wooden framework on which plants are grown

trem·ble /'trembəl/ *vi* 1 shake uncontrollably 2 be very worried: *I tremble to think what may happen.* **tremble** *n* [S]

tre·men·dous /trɪ'mendəs/ *adj* 1 very great in amount or degree 2 wonderful: *What a tremendous party!* ~**ly** *adv*

trem·or /'tremə ‖ -ər/ *n* shaking movement: *an earth tremor* (=a small EARTHQUAKE) | *a tremor in his voice*

trem·u·lous /'tremjʊləs/ *adj* slightly shaking ~**ly** *adv*

trench /trentʃ/ *n* long narrow hole cut in the ground, esp. as a protection for soldiers

tren·chant /'trentʃənt/ *adj* (of language) forceful and effective

trench coat /'· ·/ *n* long coat (in a military style)

trend /trend/ *n* 1 general direction or course of development: *a rising trend of violent crime* 2 **set a/the trend** start or popularize a fashion ~**y** *adj infml* very fashionable

trend·set·ter /'trend,setə ‖ -ər/ *n* person who starts or popularizes the latest fashion ~**ting** *adj*

trep·i·da·tion /,trepɪ'deɪʃən/ *n* [U] *fml* anxiety

tres·pass /'trespəs, -pæs/ *vi* go onto privately owned land without permission ♦ *n* 1 [C] *lit for* SIN 2 [C;U] (act of) trespassing ~**er** *n*

trespass on *phr vt fml* use too much

tress·es /'tresɪz/ *n* [P] *lit* woman's long hair

tres·tle /'tresəl/ *n* wooden beam with a pair of spreading legs, used esp. for supporting a table (**trestle table**)

tri·al /'traɪəl/ *n* **1** [C;U] (act of) hearing and judging a person or case in a court of law: *He's on trial for murder.* **2** [C;U] (act of) testing to find out if something is good: *We gave her the job for a trial period.* **3** [C] cause of worry or trouble **4 stand trial** be tried in court **5 trial and error** trying several methods and learning from one's mistakes

trial run /ˌ·· '·/ *n* testing of something new to see if it works properly

tri·an·gle /'traɪæŋgəl/ *n* figure or shape with three straight sides and three angles —see also ETERNAL TRIANGLE –**gular** /traɪˈæŋgjɐ̃lə‖ -ər/ *adj*

tribe /traɪb/ *n* people of the same race, beliefs, language, etc. living together under the leadership of a chief **tribal** *adj*

trib·u·la·tion /ˌtrɪbjɐ̃ˈleɪʃən/ *n* TRIAL (3)

tri·bu·nal /traɪˈbjuːnl/ *n* sort of court that deals with particular matters: *an industrial relations tribunal*

trib·u·ta·ry /'trɪbjɐ̃təri‖-teri/ *n* river that flows into a larger river

trib·ute /'trɪbjuːt/ *n* [C;U] something said or given to show respect or admiration: *The chairman paid tribute to* (=praised) *their hard work.*

trice /traɪs/ *n* **in a trice** very quickly

trick /trɪk/ *n* **1** clever act or plan to deceive or cheat someone **2** something done to make someone look stupid: *children playing tricks on their teacher* **3** amusing or confusing skilful act: *magic/card tricks* **4** quick or clever way to do something **5** cards played or won in a single part of a card game **6 do the trick** fulfil one's purpose ♦ *vt* deceive ♦ *adj* full of hidden difficulties: *a trick question* ~**ery** *n* [U] use of deceiving tricks ~**y** *adj* **1** difficult to deal with: *a tricky problem* **2** (of a person or actions) clever and deceitful

trick·le /'trɪkəl/ *vi* flow in drops or a thin stream ♦ *n* [S] thin slow flow: (fig.) *a trickle of enquiries*

trick-or-treat /ˌ· · '·/ *vi* (of children) go to people's houses on HALLOWE'EN and ask for

TREATS (1) under threat of playing tricks on people who refuse

trick·ster /'trɪkstə‖ -ər/ *n* deceiver: cheater

tri·col·our *BrE* ‖ **-or** *AmE* /'trɪkələ‖ 'traɪˌkʌlər/ *n* three-coloured flag, esp. the national flag of France

tri·cy·cle /'traɪsɪkəl/ *n* three-wheeled bicycle

tri·dent /'traɪdənt/ *n* forklike weapon with three points

tried /traɪd/ *past t. and p. of* TRY

tri·er /'traɪə‖ -ər/ *n* person who always tries hard

tri·fle¹ /'traɪfəl/ *n* **1** [C;U] (esp. in Britain) sweet dish made of cake set in fruit, jelly, cream, etc. **2** [C] *fml* something of little value or importance **3 a trifle** *fml* rather: *You were a trifle rude* –**fling** *adj fml* of little value or importance

trifle² *v* **trifle with** *phr vt* treat without seriousness or respect

trig·ger /'trɪgə‖ -ər/ *n* piece pulled with the finger to fire a gun ♦ *vt* start (esp. a number of things that happen one after the other)

trigger-hap·py /'·· ˌ·/ *adj* too eager to use violent methods

trig·o·nom·e·try /ˌtrɪgəˈnɒmɐ̃tri‖ -'nɑː-/ *n* [U] MATHEMATICS dealing with the relationship between the sides and angles of TRIANGLES

tril·by /'trɪlbi/ *n* esp. *BrE* man's soft hat with a BRIM

trill /trɪl/ *vi/t, n* (sing, play, or pronounce with) a rapidly repeated sound

tril·o·gy /'trɪlədʒi/ *n* group of three related books, plays, etc.

trim /trɪm/ *vt* -**mm**- **1** make neat by cutting **2** decorate, esp. round the edges **3** move (sails) into the correct position for sailing well ♦ *n* **1** [S] act of cutting **2 in (good) trim** [U] proper condition ♦ *adj* -**mm**- pleasingly neat ~**ming** *n* decoration or useful addition: *roast duck with all the trimmings* (=vegetables, potatoes, SAUCE, etc.)

Trin·i·ty /'trɪnɐ̃ti/ *n* [*the*] (in the Christian religion) the union of the three forms of God (the Father, Son, and Holy Spirit) as one God

trin·ket /'trɪŋkɐ̃t/ *n* small decorative object of low value

tri·o /'triːəʊ ‖ -oʊ/ *n* **-os 1** group of three **2** piece of music for three performers

trip /trɪp/ *v* **-pp- 1** *vi/t* (cause to) catch the foot and lose balance: *I tripped over a stone and fell down.* **2** *vi/t* (cause to) make a mistake: *He tried to trip me up with awkward questions.* **3** *vi lit* move or dance with quick light steps ♦ *n* **1** short journey, esp. for pleasure **2** act of tripping (TRIP (1)) **3** *sl* period under the influence of a mind-changing drug ~**per** *n esp. BrE* person on a pleasure TRIP (1)

tripe /traɪp/ *n* [U] **1** wall of a cow's stomach used as food **2** *sl* worthless talk or writing

trip·le /'trɪpəl/ *adj* having three parts or members ♦ *vi/t* increase to three times the amount or number

trip·let /'trɪplɪt/ *n* any of three children born together

trip·li·cate /'trɪplɪkət/ *n* **in triplicate** in three copies, one of which is the original

tri·pod /'traɪpɒd ‖ -pɑːd/ *n* three-legged support, esp. for a camera

trip·wire /'trɪp,waɪə ‖ -,waɪr/ *n* stretched wire that sets off a trap, explosive, etc. if touched

trite /traɪt/ *adj* (of a remark) common and uninteresting

tri·umph /'traɪəmf/ *n* [C;U] (joy or satisfaction caused by) a complete victory or success ♦ *vi* be victorious ~**al** /traɪ'ʌmfəl/ *adj* of or marking a triumph ~**ant** *adj* (joyful because one is) victorious ~**antly** *adv*

triv·i·a /'trɪvɪə/ *n* [P] trivial things

triv·i·al /'trɪvɪəl/ *adj* **1** of little worth or importance **2** ordinary ~**ality** /,trɪvɪ'ælɪti/ *n* [C;U] ~**ize**, **-ise** /'trɪvɪəlaɪz/ *vt*

trod /trɒd ‖ trɑːd/ *past t. of* TREAD

trod·den /'trɒdn ‖ 'trɑːdn/ *past p. of* TREAD

trog·lo·dyte /'trɒɡlədaɪt ‖ 'trɑːɡ-/ *n* person who lives in a CAVE

Tro·jan horse /,trəʊdʒən 'hɔːs ‖ ,troʊdʒən 'hɔːrs/ *n* something or someone that attacks or weakens something secretly from within

trol·ley /'trɒli ‖ 'trɑːli/ *n* **1** small cart, esp. pushed by hand **2** *esp. BrE* small table on wheels, for serving food and drink **3** trolleybus

trol·ley·bus /'trɒlibʌs ‖ 'trɑː-/ *n* bus driven by electricity from wires above it

trom·bone /trɒm'bəʊn ‖ trɑːm'boʊn/ *n* brass musical instrument with a long sliding tube

troop /truːp/ *n* **1** (moving) group of people or animals **2** group of soldiers esp. on horses ♦ *vi* move in a group **troops** *n* [P] soldiers

tro·phy /'trəʊfi ‖ 'troʊ-/ *n* **1** prize for winning a competition or test of skill **2** something kept as a reminder of success

trop·ic /'trɒpɪk ‖ 'trɑː-/ *n* line round the world at 23½° north (**the tropic of Cancer**) and south (**the tropic of Capricorn**) of the EQUATOR **tropics** *n* [P] hot area between these lines ~**al 1** *adj* of the tropics **2** very hot: *tropical weather*

trot¹ /trɒt ‖ trɑːt/ *n* [S] **1** horse's movement, slower than a CANTER **2** slow run **3 on the trot: a** one after another: *She won three races on the trot.* **b** continuously active

trot² *vi* **-tt-** move at the speed of a trot

trot out *phr vt* repeat in an uninteresting unchanged way: *trotting out the same old excuses*

trou·ba·dour /'truːbədɔː, -dʊə ‖ -dɔːr, -dʊr/ *n* travelling singer and poet of former times

trou·ble /'trʌbəl/ *n* **1** [C;U] (cause of) difficulty, worry, annoyance, etc.: *I didn't have any trouble doing it; it was easy.* **2** [U] state of being blamed: *He's always getting into trouble with the police.* **3** [S;U] inconvenience or more than usual work or effort: *I took a lot of trouble to get it right.* **4** [C;U] political or social disorder **5** [U] failure to work properly: *engine/heart trouble* **6 ask/look for trouble** behave so as to cause difficulty or danger for oneself **7 get a girl into trouble** *infml* make pregnant ♦ *v* **1** *vi/t* worry **2** *vt* cause inconvenience to **3** *vi* make an effort; BOTHER ~**some** *adj* annoying

trou·ble·shoot·er /'trʌbəl,ʃuːtə ‖ -ər/ *n* person who finds and removes causes of trouble in machines, organizations, etc.

trough /trɒf ‖ trɔːf/ *n* **1** long container for animal's food **2** long hollow area between waves **3** area of low air pressure

trounce /traʊns/ *vt* defeat completely

troupe /truːp/ *n* company of entertainers

trou·sers /'traʊzəz ‖ -ərz/ *n* [P] two-legged outer garment covering the body from the waist downwards **trouser** *adj: a trouser leg*

trout /traʊt/ *n* **trout** or **trouts** river (or sea) fish used for food

trove *n* —see TREASURE TROVE

trow·el /ˈtraʊəl/ *n* 1 flat-bladed tool for spreading cement, etc. 2 garden tool like a small spade

tru·ant /ˈtruːənt/ *n* 1 pupil who stays away from school without permission 2 **play truant** be a truant **-ancy** *n* [U]

truce /truːs/ *n* [C;U] agreement for the stopping of fighting

truck[1] /trʌk/ *n* 1 large motor vehicle for carrying goods 2 *BrE* open railway goods vehicle ♦ *vt AmE* carry by truck **-er** *n AmE* truck driver

truck[2] *n* **have no truck with** *fml* avoid any connection with

truck farm /ˈ· ·/ *n AmE for* MARKET GARDEN

truc·u·lent /ˈtrʌkjʊlənt/ *adj* willing or eager to quarrel or fight **-ly** *adv* **-lence** *n* [U]

trudge /trʌdʒ/ *vi* walk slowly and with effort ♦ *n* long tiring walk

true /truː/ *adj* 1 in accordance with fact or reality 2 real: *true love* 3 faithful; loyal 4 exact: *a true likeness* 5 **come true** happen as was wished, expected, or dreamt **truly** *adv* 1 in accordance with the truth 2 really: *a truly wonderful experience* 3 sincerely: *truly sorry* ♦ *n* **out of true** not having correct shape or balance

true-blue /ˌ· ˈ·◁/ *adj* completely loyal

truf·fle /ˈtrʌfəl/ *n* 1 piece of soft sweet food made with chocolate 2 underground FUNGUS highly regarded as food

tru·is·m /ˈtruːɪzəm/ *n* statement that is clearly true

trump[1] /trʌmp/ *n* 1 card of a sort (SUIT[1] (3)) chosen to be of higher rank than other suits in a game 2 **turn/come up trumps** do the right or needed thing, esp. unexpectedly at the last moment

trump[2] *vt* beat by playing a trump

trump up *phr vt* invent (a false charge or reason)

trump card /ˈ· ·/ *n* something that gives a clear and unquestionable advantage

trum·pet /ˈtrʌmpɪt/ *n* 1 high-sounding brass musical instrument consisting of a long usu. winding tube 2 **blow one's own trumpet** praise oneself ♦ *v* 1 *vi* (of an elephant) make a loud sound 2 *vt* declare or shout loudly **-er** *n* trumpet player

trun·cate /trʌŋˈkeɪt ‖ ˈtrʌŋkeɪt/ *vt* shorten (as if) by cutting off the top or end

trun·cheon /ˈtrʌnʃən/ *n* short thick stick used as a weapon by a policeman

trun·dle /ˈtrʌndl/ *vi/t* move heavily or awkwardly on wheels

trunk /trʌŋk/ *n* 1 main stem of a tree 2 large box in which things are packed for travelling 3 elephant's long nose 4 body without the head or limbs 5 *AmE for* BOOT[1] (2) **trunks** *n* [P] men's SHORTS for swimming

trunk call /ˈ· ·/ *n BrE* a telephone call made over a long distance

trunk road /ˈ· ·/ *n* main road for long-distance travel

truss /trʌs/ *vt* 1 tie up firmly and roughly 2 tie (a bird's) wings and legs in place for cooking ♦ *n* 1 medical supporting belt worn by someone with a HERNIA 2 framework of beams built to support a roof, bridge, etc.

trust[1] /trʌst/ *n* 1 [U] firm belief in the honesty, goodness, worth, etc. of someone or something 2 [C;U] (arrangement for) the holding and controlling of money for someone else: *a charitable trust* 3 [U] *fml* responsibility: *employed in a position of trust* 4 **take on trust** accept without proof

trust[2] *vt* 1 believe in the honesty and worth of, esp. without proof 2 allow someone to do or have something: *Can he be trusted with a gun?* 3 depend on 4 *fml* hope, esp. confidently: *I trust you enjoyed yourself.* **~ful**; also **~ing** *adj* (too) ready to trust others **~fully**, **~ingly** *adv* **~y** *adj lit* dependable

trust in *phr vt fml* have faith in

trust·ee /trʌsˈtiː/ *n* 1 person in charge of a TRUST[1] (2) 2 member of a group controlling the affairs of a company, college, etc.

trust·wor·thy /ˈtrʌstˌwɜːði ‖ -ɜːr-/ *adj* dependable

truth /truːθ/ *n* **truths** /truːðz, truːθs/ 1 [U] that which is true: *Are you telling the truth?* 2 [U] quality of being true: *I doubted the truth of what he said.* 3 [C] true fact —see also HOME TRUTH, MOMENT OF TRUTH **~ful** *adj* 1 (of a statement) true 2 habitually telling the truth **~fully** *adv* **~fulness** *n* [U]

try /traɪ/ *v* 1 *vi/t* make an attempt: *I tried to*

persuade him, but failed. **2** *vt* test by use and experience: *Have you tried this new soap?* | *We need to try the idea out in practice.* **3** *vt* examine in a court of law: *He was tried for murder.* **4** *vt* cause to suffer, esp. with small annoyances: *Her constant questions try my patience.* | *I've had a very trying day.* **5** *vt* attempt to open (a door, window, etc.) ♦ *n* **1** attempt **2** winning of points in RUGBY by pressing the ball to the ground behind the opponents' line **tried** *adj* known to be good from experience

try on *phr vt* **1** put on (a garment, etc.) to see if it fits or looks well **2** *infml* behave badly to see if it will be tolerated: *Take no notice, he's just trying it on.*

try out *phr vt* test by use or experience

tsar, tzar /zɑː, tsɑː‖zɑːr, tsɑːr/ *n* (until 1917) male ruler of Russia

tsa·ri·na, tzarina /zɑːˈriːnə, tsɑː-/ *n* (until 1917) **1** female ruler of Russia **2** wife of the tsar

tset·se fly /ˈtetsi flaɪ, ˈtsetsi-, ˈsetsi-/ *n* African fly that causes SLEEPING SICKNESS

T-shirt /ˈtiː ʃɜːt‖-ʃɜːrt/ *n* light informal collarless garment for the upper body

tub /tʌb/ *n* **1** round container for washing, packing, storing, etc. **2** bath

tu·ba /ˈtjuːbə‖ˈtuːbə/ *n* large brass musical instrument that produces low notes

tub·by /ˈtʌbi/ *adj infml* rather fat

tube /tjuːb‖tuːb/ *n* **1** hollow round pipe **2** small soft metal or plastic container for paint, paste, etc. which you get out by pressing: *a tube of toothpaste* **3** pipe in the body: *the bronchial tubes* **4** *BrE for* the UNDERGROUND **tubing** *n* [U] tubes **tubular** /ˈtjuːbj̊lə‖ˈtuːbj̊lər/ *adj* in the form of tubes

tu·ber /ˈtjuːbə‖ˈtuːbər/ *n* fleshy underground stem, such as a potato

tu·ber·cu·lo·sis /tjuːˌbɜːkj̊ˈləʊsɨs‖ tuːˌbɜːrkj̊ˈloʊ-/ *n* [U] serious infectious disease that attacks esp. the lungs **tubercular** /tjuːˈbɜːkj̊lə‖tuːˈbɜːrkj̊lər/ *adj*

TUC /ˌtiː juː ˈsiː/ *n* [*the*] Trades Union Congress; the association of British trade unions

tuck /tʌk/ *vt* **1** put (the edge of) into a tight place for neatness, protection, etc.: *Tuck your shirt in.* | *She tucked the newspaper*

under her arm. **2** put into a private or almost hidden place: *a house tucked away among the trees* ♦ *n* **1** narrow flat fold of material sewn into a garment **2** [U] *BrE* sweets, cakes, etc. as eaten by schoolchildren: *a tuck shop*

tuck in *phr vi* eat eagerly

tuck up *phr vt* make (esp. a child) comfortable in bed by pulling the sheets tight

Tues·day /ˈtjuːzdi‖ˈtuːz-/ *n* the second day of the week

tuft /tʌft/ *n* small bunch (of hair, grass, etc.)

tug /tʌg/ *vi/t* **-gg-** pull hard ♦ *n* **1** sudden strong pull **2** *also* **tug·boat** /ˈtʌgbəʊt/ — small boat used for pulling and guiding ships in narrow places

tug-of-love /ˌ· · ·ˈ◂/ *n BrE infml* situation in which a child's parents try to get the child back from someone else, such as the child's other parent

tug-of-war /ˌ· · ·ˈ·/ *n* [C;U] sport in which two teams pull against each other on a rope

tu·i·tion /tjuːˈɪʃən‖tuː-/ *n* [U] *fml* teaching; instruction

tu·lip /ˈtjuːlɨp‖ˈtuː-/ *n* garden plant with large colourful cup-shaped flowers

tum·ble /ˈtʌmbəl/ *vi* fall suddenly and helplessly, esp. rolling over ♦ *n* fall

tumble down *phr vi* fall to pieces; COLLAPSE

tum·ble·down /ˈtʌmbəldaʊn/ *adj* nearly in ruins

tum·bler /ˈtʌmblə‖-ər/ *n* straight-sided drinking glass

tum·my /ˈtʌmi/ *n infml* stomach

tu·mour *BrE* ‖ **-mor** *AmE* /ˈtjuːmə‖ ˈtuːmər/ *n* mass of quickly growing diseased cells in the body

tu·mult /ˈtjuːmʌlt‖ˈtuː-/ *n* [S;U] confused noise and excitement **~uous** /tjuːˈmʌltʃuəs‖tuː-/ *adj* noisy

tu·na /ˈtjuːnə‖ˈtuːnə/ *n* **tuna** *or* **tunas** [C;U] large sea fish used for food

tune /tjuːn‖tuːn/ *n* **1** (pleasing) pattern of musical notes **2 call the tune** be in a position to give orders **3 change one's tune** change one's opinion, behaviour, etc. **4 in/out of tune a** at/not at the correct musical level **b** in/not in agreement or sympathy **5 to the tune of** to the amount of ♦ *vt* **1** set (a musical instrument) to the correct musical level **2** put (an engine) in good working order **~ful** *adj* having a pleasant tune **tuner** *n* person who tunes musical instruments

tune in *phr vi* turn on a radio, esp. so as to listen to a particular radio station

tung·sten /'tʌŋstən/ *n* hard metal used esp. in making steel

tu·nic /'tjuːnɪk‖'tuː-/ *n* **1** loose usu. belted garment which reaches to the knees **2** short coat forming part of a uniform

tun·nel /'tʌnl/ *n* usu. man-made underground passage for road, railway, etc. ♦ *vi/t* **-ll-** *BrE*‖ **-l-** *AmE* make a tunnel (under or through)

tunnel vi·sion /'··ˌ··/ *n* [U] tendency to consider only one part of a question, without even trying to examine others

tur·ban /'tɜːbən‖'tɜːr-/ *n* **1** Asian head covering made by winding cloth round the head **2** woman's small high-fitting hat

tur·bid /'tɜːbɪd‖'tɜːr-/ *adj* **1** (of a liquid) not clear; muddy **2** confused

tur·bine /'tɜːbaɪn‖'tɜːrbɪn, -baɪn/ *n* motor in which liquid or gas drives a wheel to produce circular movement

tur·bo·jet /'tɜːbəʊdʒet‖'tɜːrboʊ-/ *n* (aircraft) engine that forces out a stream of gases behind itself

tur·bu·lent /'tɜːbjʊlənt‖'tɜːr-/ *adj* violent and disorderly or irregular **-lence** *n* [U] **1** being turbulent **2** turbulent air movements

turd /tɜːd‖tɜːrd/ *n taboo* **1** piece of solid waste passed from the body **2** *sl* offensive person

tu·reen /tjʊ'riːn‖tə'riːn/ *n* large deep dish for serving soup from

turf¹ /tɜːf‖tɜːrf/ *n* **1** [U] grass surface **2** [C] piece of this **3** [*the*+S] horseracing

turf² *vt* cover with turf

turf out *phr vt sl, esp. BrE* throw out; get rid of

tur·gid /'tɜːdʒɪd‖'tɜːr-/ *adj fml* (of language or style) too solemn and self-important

tur·key /'tɜːki‖'tɜːrki/ *n* **1** [C;U] bird rather like a large chicken, used for food **2** *AmE sl* play in theatre which does not succeed **3** *sl, esp. AmE* stupid person **4** **talk turkey** *infml, esp. AmE* speak seriously and plainly esp. about business —see also COLD TURKEY

Tur·kish bath /ˌtɜːkɪʃ 'bɑːθ‖ˌtɜːrkɪʃ 'bæθ/ *n* health treatment in which one sits in a very hot steamy room

tur·moil /'tɜːmɔɪl‖'tɜːr-/ *n* [S;U] state of confusion and trouble

turn¹ /tɜːn‖tɜːrn/ *v* **1** *vi/t* move round a central point: *The wheels turned.* **2** *vi/t* move so that a different side faces upwards or outwards: *She turned the pages.* **3** *vi* change direction: *Turn right at the end of the road.* | *He turned to crime.* (=became a criminal) **4** *vt* go round: *The car turned the corner.* **5** *vi* look round: *She turned to wave.* **6** *vt* aim; point: *They turned their hoses on the burning building.* | *I turned my thoughts to home.* **7** *vi/t* (cause to) become: *His hair has turned grey.* | *The witch turned the prince into a frog.* **8** *vi* go sour: *The milk's turned.* **9** *vt* pass: *It's just turned 3 o'clock.* | *She's turned 40.* **10** **turn a phrase** *fml* say a clever thing neatly **11** **turn one's hand to** begin to practise (a skill) **12** **turn one's head** make one too proud **13** **turn one's stomach** make one feel sick

turn against *phr vt* (cause to) become opposed to

turn away *phr vt* **1** refuse to let in **2** refuse to help

turn down *phr vt* **1** refuse **2** reduce the force, speed, loudness, etc. of (something) by using controls: *Can you turn that radio down?*

turn in *phr v* **1** *vt* no longer continue **2** *vi* go to bed **3** *vt* deliver to the police **4** *vt* give back; return **5** *esp. AmE* hand in; deliver: *He's turned in some very poor work lately.*

turn off *phr vt* **1** stop the flow or operation of: *turn off the tap/television* **2** *sl* cause to lose interest, often sexually

turn on *phr vt* **1** cause to flow or operate: *turn on the tap/television* **2** depend on **3** attack suddenly and without warning **4** *infml* excite or interest strongly, often sexually **5** *sl* (cause to) take an illegal drug, esp. for the first time

turn out *phr v* **1** *vt* stop the operation of (a light) **2** *vt* drive out; send away **3** *vi* come out or gather (as if) for a meeting or public event **4** *vt* produce: *The factory turns out 100 cars a day.* **5** *vt* empty (a cupboard, pocket, etc.) **6** happen to be in the end: *The party turned out a success.* **7** *vt* dress: *an elegantly* *turned-out woman*

turn over *phr vt* 1 think about; consider 2 deliver to the place 3 (of an engine) to run at the lowest speed 4 do business

turn over to *phr vt* give control of (something) to

turn to *phr vt* go to for sympathy, help, advice, etc.

turn up *phr v* 1 *vi* be found 2 *vi* arrive 3 *vt* find 4 *vt* shorten (a garment) by folding up the bottom 5 *vi* happen 6 **turn up one's nose (at something or someone)** suggest by one's behaviour that (something or someone) is not good enough for one

turn² *n* 1 act of turning (something) 2 change of direction 3 rightful chance or duty to do something: *It's my turn to speak.* | *We took it in turns to do it.* (=did it one after the other) 4 development: *She's taken a turn for the worse.* (=has become more ill) 5 point of change in time: *at the turn of the century* 6 attack of illness: *He had one of his funny turns.* 7 shock: *You did give me a turn, appearing like that suddenly!* 8 short stage performance 9 **a good turn** a useful or helpful action 10 **at every turn** in every place; at every moment 11 **on the turn: a** about to turn or change **b** *infml* about to go sour 12 **out of turn** unsuitably: *I hope I haven't spoken out of turn.* 13 **to a turn** (of food) cooked perfectly 14 **turn and turn about** one after another ~**ing** *n* place where one road branches off from another

turn·coat /'tɜːnkəʊt ‖ 'tɜːrnkoʊt/ *n* disloyal person

turn·ing point /'·· ·/ *n* point at which a very important change happens

tur·nip /'tɜːnɪp ‖ 'tɜːr-/ *n* [C;U] plant with a large round yellowish root used as a vegetable

turn-off /'· ·/ *n* 1 smaller road branching off from a main road 2 *infml* something that causes one to feel dislike or lose interest, esp. sexually

turn-on /'· ·/ *n infml* something that excites or interests one strongly, esp. sexually

turn-out /'tɜːnaʊt ‖ 'tɜːrn-/ *n* 1 number of people who attend 2 occasion on which one empties all unwanted things from drawers, rooms, etc. 3 *AmE* wide place in a narrow road

turn·o·ver /'tɜːn‚əʊvə ‖ 'tɜːrn‚oʊvər/ *n* [S] 1 rate at which a particular kind of goods is sold 2 amount of business done 3 number of workers hired to fill the places of those who leave 4 small pie: *apple turnover*

turn·stile /'tɜːnstaɪl ‖ 'tɜːrn-/ *n* small gate that turns round, set in an entrance to admit people one at a time

turn·ta·ble /'tɜːn‚teɪbəl ‖ 'tɜːrn-/ *n* 1 round spinning surface on which a record is placed to be played 2 machine including such a round surface

turn-up /'· ·/ *n* 1 [C] *BrE* turned-up bottom of a trouser leg 2 [S] also **turn-up for the book(s)** — unexpected and surprising event

tur·pen·tine /'tɜːpəntaɪn ‖ 'tɜːr-/ *n* [U] thin oil used esp. for cleaning off unwanted paint

tur·quoise /'tɜːkwɔɪz, -kwɑːz ‖ 'tɜːr-kwɔɪz/ *n* [C;U] (piece of) a precious green-ish-blue mineral ♦ *adj* turquoise-coloured

tur·ret /'tʌrɪt ‖ 'tɜːr-/ *n* 1 small tower at the corner of a building 2 turning structure on a warship, plane, etc. that contains a gun

tur·tle /'tɜːtl ‖ 'tɜːrtl/ *n* 1 four-legged (sea) animal with a hard horny shell 2 **turn turtle** (of a ship) turn over

tur·tle·neck /'tɜːtlnek ‖ 'tɜːr-/ *n esp. AmE* (garment with) a POLO NECK

tusk /tʌsk/ *n* very long pointed tooth, usu. one of a pair: *an elephant's tusks*

tus·sle /'tʌsəl/ *vi infml* fight roughly without weapons ♦ *n* rough struggle or fight

tut /tʌt/ *interj* (shows annoyance or disapproval)

tu·tor /'tjuːtə ‖ 'tuːtər/ *n* 1 private teacher 2 (in British colleges) teacher who guides a student's studies ♦ *vt* teach —**ial** /tjuːˈtɔːriəl ‖ tuː-/ *n* short period of instruction given by a TUTOR (2)

tu·tu /'tuːtuː/ *n* short stiff skirt worn by women BALLET dancers

tux·e·do /tʌkˈsiːdəʊ ‖ -doʊ/ also **tux** /tʌks/ *infml* — *n* **-dos** *AmE* for DINNER JACKET

TV /‚tiː ˈviː ◂/ *n* [C;U] *abbrev. for:* television

TV din·ner /‚tiː viː ˈdɪnə ‖ -ər/ *n* meal eaten at home whilst watching TV

twad·dle /'twɒdl ‖ 'twɑː-/ *n* [U] *infml*

nonsense

twang /twæŋ/ n **1** quick ringing sound **2** sound of human speech (as if) produced partly through the nose ♦ vi/t (cause to) make a TWANG (1)

tweak /twiːk/ vt seize, pull, and twist: *He tweaked her ear.* **tweak** n

twee /twiː/ adj infml BrE looking too pretty, CUTE, etc., esp. in a tasteless way

tweed /twiːd/ n [U] coarse woollen cloth **tweeds** n [P] (suit of) tweed clothes

tweet /twiːt/ vi, n (make) the short weak high noise of a small bird

tweet·er /ˈtwiːtə‖-ər/ n a LOUDSPEAKER that gives out high sounds

twee·zers /ˈtwiːzəz‖-ərz/ n [P] small two-part jointed tool for picking up and pulling out very small objects

twelfth /twelfθ/ determiner, adv, n, pron 12th

twelve /twelv/ determiner, n, pron 12

twen·ty /ˈtwenti/ determiner, n, pron 20 –tieth determiner, adv, n, pron 20th

twice /twaɪs/ predeterminer, adv **1** two times **2** think twice (about something) consider (something) carefully

twid·dle /ˈtwɪdl/ vi/t turn (something) round with one's fingers, usu. purposelessly

twig[1] /twɪg/ n small thin stem on a tree or bush

twig[2] vi -gg- BrE infml understand

twi·light /ˈtwaɪlaɪt/ n [U] **1** (faint darkish light at) the time when day is about to become night **2** period when something is ending, becoming weaker, etc.: *in the twilight of his life*

twill /twɪl/ n [U] strong woven cotton cloth

twin /twɪn/ n either of two people born to the same mother at the same time —see also SIAMESE TWIN

twin bed /ˌ· ˈ·/ n either of two single beds in a room for two people

twine /twaɪn/ n [U] strong string ♦ vi/t twist; wind

twinge /twɪndʒ/ n sudden sharp pain: (fig.) *a twinge of conscience*

twin·kle /ˈtwɪŋkəl/ vi **1** shine with an unsteady light: *The stars twinkled.* **2** (of the eyes) be bright with cheerfulness, amusement, etc. ♦ n [S] **1** twinkling light **2** brightness in the eye

twirl /twɜːl‖twɜːrl/ vi/t **1** spin **2** curl ♦ n

sudden quick spin or circular movement

twist /twɪst/ v **1** vi/t bend, turn, etc. so as to change shape: *She twisted the wire into the shape of a star.* **2** vt wind: *Twist the wires together.* **3** vi move windingly **4** vt turn: *She twisted her head round.* **5** vt hurt (a joint or limb) by turning it sharply **6** vt derog change the true meaning of **7** twist someone's arm persuade someone forcefully or threateningly **8** twist someone round one's little finger be able to get someone to do what one wants ♦ n **1** act of twisting **2** bend **3** unexpected development: *a strange twist of fate* –er n **1** dishonest cheating person **2** AmE infml TORNADO ~y adj: *a twisty road*

twit /twɪt/ n BrE infml fool

twitch /twɪtʃ/ vi/t move with a twitch: *His eyelid twitched.* ♦ n repeated short sudden unconscious muscle movement ~y adj nervous; anxious

twit·ter /ˈtwɪtə‖-ər/ vi, n [U] (of a bird) (make) short high rapid sounds

two /tuː/ determiner, n, pron **1** (the number) 2 **2** in two in two parts **3** one or two a few **4** put two and two together calculate the meaning of what one sees or hears **5** two can play at that game (used as a threat to someone who has been unfair, unkind, etc. to oneself)

two-di·men·sion·al /ˌtuː daɪˈmenʃənəl◂/ adj **1** appearing as a flat picture, not as a solid object **2** (of a character/ performance) too simple and difficult to believe in

two-faced /ˌtuːˈfeɪst◂/ adj deceitful; insincere

two·some /ˈtuːsəm/ n group of two people or things

two-time /ˈ· ·/ vt be unfaithful to (a girlfriend or boyfriend)

two-way /ˌ· ˈ·◂/ adj moving or allowing movement in both directions

ty·coon /taɪˈkuːn/ n rich powerful businessman

ty·ing /ˈtaɪ-ɪŋ/ pres. p. of TIE

type /taɪp/ n **1** [C] sort; kind; example of a group or class: *She's just that type of person.* **2** [U] small blocks with raised letters on them, used in printing **3** [U] printed letters: *italic type* **4** true to type behaving or acting (esp. badly) just as one would expect ♦ vi/t write with a typewriter or WORD PROCESSOR

type·cast /'taɪpkɑːst ‖ -kæst/ vt –cast repeatedly give (an actor) the same kind of part

type·face /'taɪpfeɪs/ n size and style of printed letters

type·script /'taɪpˌskrɪpt/ n typewritten copy of something

type·writ·er /'taɪpˌraɪtə ‖ -ər/ n machine that prints letters by means of finger-operated keys

ty·phoid /'taɪfɔɪd/ n [U] infectious disease causing fever and often death, produced by bacteria in food or drink

ty·phoon /taɪ'fuːn/ n very violent tropical storm

ty·phus /'taɪfəs/ n [U] serious disease that causes fever, severe headaches, and red spots on the body

typ·i·cal /'tɪpɪkəl/ adj showing the usual or main qualities of a particular sort of thing: a typical British summer, with lots of rain ~ly /-kli/ adv

typ·i·fy /'tɪpɪfaɪ/ vt be a typical mark, sign, or example of

typ·ist /'taɪpɪst/ n secretary employed mainly for typing letters

tyr·an·nize also **-nise** BrE /'tɪrənaɪz/ vt use power over (a person, country, etc.) with unjust cruelty

tyr·an·ny /'tɪrəni/ n [U] use of cruel or unjust ruling power –**ical** /tɪˈrænɪkəl/ adj

ty·rant /'taɪərənt ‖ 'taɪr-/ n cruel unjust ruler

tyre /taɪə ‖ taɪr/ n BrE thick band of rubber round the outside edge of a wheel

tzar /zɑː, tsɑː ‖ zɑːr, tsɑːr/ n TSAR

tza·ri·na /zɑːˈriːnə, tsɑː-/ n TSARINA

U

U, u /juː/ the 21st letter of the English alphabet

u·biq·ui·tous /juːˈbɪkwɪtəs/ adj fml happening or existing everywhere

U-boat /'juː bəʊt ‖ -boʊt/ n German SUBMARINE of the Second World War

ud·der /'ʌdə ‖ -ər/ n milk-producing organ of a cow, female goat, etc.

UFO /ˌjuː ef 'əʊ ‖ -'oʊ/ n UFO's or UFOs strange object in the sky, thought of as a spacecraft from other worlds

ugh /ʌx, ʌg/ interj (expresses extreme dislike)

ug·ly /'ʌgli/ adj 1 unpleasant to see 2 very unpleasant or threatening: in an ugly mood **ugliness** n [U]

ugly duck·ling /ˌ·· '··/ n person less attractive than others in early life but becoming attractive later

UK /ˌjuː 'keɪ/ n [the] the United Kingdom (of GREAT BRITAIN and Northern Ireland)

u·ku·le·le /ˌjuːkəˈleɪli/ n sort of small GUITAR

ul·cer /'ʌlsə ‖ -ər/ n sore place where the skin is broken ~**ate** vi turn into or become covered with ulcers ~**ous** adj

ul·te·ri·or /ʌlˈtɪəriə ‖ -ˈtɪriər/ adj kept secret, esp. because bad: an ulterior motive

ul·ti·mate /'ʌltəmɪt/ adj being or happening after all others: our ultimate destination ~**ly** adv in the end

ul·ti·ma·tum /ˌʌltəˈmeɪtəm/ n -**tums** or -**ta** /-tə/ statement of conditions to be met, not open to argument

ul·tra·ma·rine /ˌʌltrəməˈriːn◄/ adj very bright blue

ul·tra·son·ic /ˌʌltrəˈsɒnɪk◄ ‖ -'sɑː-/ adj (of a sound wave) beyond the range of human hearing

ul·tra·vi·o·let /ˌʌltrəˈvaɪələt◄/ adj (of light) beyond the purple end of the range of colours that can be seen by humans

um·bil·i·cal cord /ʌmˌbɪlɪkəl 'kɔːd ‖ -'kɔːrd/ n tube of flesh which joins an unborn creature to its mother

um·brage /'ʌmbrɪdʒ/ n take umbrage be offended

um·brel·la /ʌmˈbrelə/ n 1 folding cloth-covered frame for keeping rain off the head 2 protecting power or influence 3 anything which covers or includes a wide range of different parts

um·laut /'ʊmlaʊt/ n sign placed over German vowels (¨) for pronunciation

um·pire /'ʌmpaɪə ‖ -paɪr/ n judge in charge of certain games, such as cricket and tennis ♦ vi/t act as an umpire (for)

ump·teen /ˌʌmpˈtiːn◂/ determiner, pron infml a large number (of) ~**th** n, determiner

UN /ˌjuːˈen◂/ n [the+S] United Nations

un·a·ble /ʌnˈeɪbəl/ adj not able

un·ac·count·a·ble /ˌʌnəˈkaʊntəbəl◂/ adj fml hard to explain; surprising –**bly** adv

un·ac·cus·tomed /ˌʌnəˈkʌstəmd◂/ adj 1 not used (to) 2 unusual

u·nan·i·mous /juːˈnænɪməs/ adj with everyone agreeing: a unanimous decision ~**ly** adv –**nimity** /ˌjuːnəˈnɪmɪti/ n [U]

un·an·swer·a·ble /ʌnˈɑːnsərəbəl ‖ ʌnˈæn-/ adj that cannot be answered or argued against

un·as·sum·ing /ˌʌnəˈsjuːmɪŋ◂, -ˈsuː- ‖ -ˈsuː-/ adj quiet and unwilling to make claims about one's good qualities

un·at·tached /ˌʌnəˈtætʃt◂/ adj 1 not connected 2 not married or ENGAGED (1)

un·at·tend·ed /ˌʌnəˈtendɪd◂/ adj alone, with no one present or in charge

un·a·wares /ˌʌnəˈweəz ‖ -ˈwerz/ adv unexpectedly or without warning: I took/caught her unawares. (=surprised her by my presence)

un·bal·ance /ʌnˈbæləns/ vt make slightly mad: an unbalanced mind

un·be·known /ˌʌnbɪˈnəʊn ‖ -ˈnoʊn/ adv without the stated person knowing: Unbeknown to me, he had left.

un·bend /ʌnˈbend/ v -bent /-ˈbent/ 1 vi/t straighten 2 vi behave more informally

un·born /ˌʌnˈbɔːn◂ ‖ -ˈbɔːrn◂/ adj not yet born

un·bowed /ˌʌnˈbaʊd◂/ adj esp. lit not defeated

un·bri·dled /ʌnˈbraɪdld/ adj not controlled, and esp. too active or violent

un·bur·den /ʌnˈbɜːdn ‖ -ɜːr-/ vt fml free (oneself, one's mind, etc.) by talking about a secret trouble

un·called-for /ʌnˈkɔːld ˌfɔː ‖ -ˈkɔːld fɔːr/ adj not deserved, necessary, or right: uncalled-for rudeness

un·can·ny /ʌnˈkæni/ adj not natural or usual; mysterious –**nily** adv

un·ce·re·mo·ni·ous /ˌʌnserəˈməʊniəs◂ ‖ -ˈmoʊ-/ adj 1 informal 2 rude without the usual polite ~**ly** adv: He was thrown out unceremoniously into the street.

un·cer·tain /ʌnˈsɜːtn ‖ -ɜːr-/ adj 1 doubtful 2 undecided or unable to decide 3 likely to change: uncertain weather ~**ly**

adv ~**ty** n [C;U]

un·chart·ed /ʌnˈtʃɑːtɪd ‖ -ɑːr-/ adj esp. lit (of a place) not well known enough for maps to be made

un·cle /ˈʌŋkəl/ n brother of one's father or mother, or husband of one's aunt

un·clean /ʌnˈkliːn◂/ adj not (religiously) pure

Uncle Sam /ˌʌŋkəl ˈsæm/ n infml lit the US

un·com·fort·a·ble /ʌnˈkʌmftəbəl, -ˈkʌmfət- ‖ ʌnˈkʌmfort-, -ˈkʌmft-/ adj 1 not comfortable 2 EMBARRASSed –**bly** adv

un·com·mon·ly /ʌnˈkɒmənli ‖ -ˈkɑː-/ adv/real very

un·com·pro·mis·ing /ʌnˈkɒmprə-maɪzɪŋ ‖ -ˈkɑːm-/ adj (bravely) unchangeable in one's opinions, actions, etc.

un·con·scion·a·ble /ʌnˈkɒnʃənəbəl ‖ -ˈkɑːn-/ adj fml unreasonable in degree or amount –**bly** adv

un·con·scious /ʌnˈkɒnʃəs ‖ -ˈkɑːn-/ adj 1 having lost consciousness 2 intentional

un·count·a·ble /ʌnˈkaʊntəbəl/ adj that cannot be counted: 'Furniture' is an uncountable noun – you can't say 'two furnitures'.

un·couth /ʌnˈkuːθ◂/ adj fml rough and bad-mannered

un·cov·er /ʌnˈkʌvə ‖ -ər/ vt 1 remove a covering from 2 find out (something unknown or kept secret)

unc·tu·ous /ˈʌŋktʃuəs/ adj fml full of unpleasantly insincere kindness, interest, etc.

un·daunt·ed /ʌnˈdɔːntɪd ‖ -ˈdɔːn-/ adj not at all discouraged or frightened

un·de·cid·ed /ˌʌndɪˈsaɪdɪd◂/ adj not yet having (been) decided; in doubt

un·de·ni·a·ble /ˌʌndɪˈnaɪəbəl◂/ adj clear and certain –**bly** adv

un·der /ˈʌndə ‖ -ər/ prep 1 below; covered by: The ball rolled under the table. | (fig.) She wrote under the name of George Eliot. 2 less than: under £5 3 working for; controlled by: She has three secretaries under her. | Spain under Franco. 4 (expresses various states or relationships): He was under threat of (=threatened with) dismissal. | I was under the impression (=thought) that you'd gone. 5 in the state or act of: under *discussion/contract* **6 under age** too young in law, esp. for drinking alcohol, driving a car, etc. **7 under cover (of)** hidden (by): *They escaped under cover of darkness.* ♦ *adv* **1** in or to a lower place **2** less: *children of 9 or under*

un·der·arm /'ʌndərɑːm‖-ɑːrm/ *adj, adv* (in sport) with the hand below the shoulder

un·der·bel·ly /'ʌndə‚beli‖-ər-/ *n esp. lit* weak or undefended part of a place, plan, etc.

un·der·car·riage /'ʌndə‚kærɪdʒ‖-ər-/ *n* aircraft's wheels and wheel supports

und·er·charge /‚ʌndə'tʃɑːdʒ‖-dər-'tʃɑːrdʒ/ *vi/t* take too small an amount of money from (someone)

un·der·clothes /'ʌndəkləʊðz, -kləʊz‖-dərkloʊðz, -kloʊz/ *n* [P] UNDERWEAR

un·der·coat /'ʌndəkəʊt‖-dərkoʊt/ *n* covering of paint that goes under the main covering

un·der·cov·er /‚ʌndə'kʌvə◂‖-dər-'kʌvər◂/ *adj* acting or done secretly, esp. as a SPY

un·der·cur·rent /'ʌndə‚kʌrənt‖-dər-‚kɜːr-/ *n* **1** hidden current of water beneath the surface **2** hidden tendency: *an undercurrent of discontent*

un·der·cut /‚ʌndə'kʌt‖-ər-/ *vt* **-cut; pres. p. -tt-** sell things more cheaply than (a competitor)

un·der·dog /'ʌndədɒg‖-dərdɔːg/ *n* one always treated badly by others or expected to lose in a competition

un·der·done /‚ʌndə'dʌn◂‖-ər-/ *adj* not completely cooked

un·der·es·ti·mate /‚ʌndər'estɪmeɪt/ *v* **1** *vi/t* guess, too low a value (for) **2** *vt* have too low an opinion of ♦ *n* /-stɪmət/ ESTIMATE which is too small

un·der·fed /‚ʌndə'fed◂‖-ər-/ *adj* having not enough food

un·der·foot /‚ʌndə'fʊt‖-ər-/ *adv* beneath the feet: *The path was stony underfoot.*

un·der·go /‚ʌndə'gəʊ‖-dərgoʊ/ *vt* **-went** /-'went/, **-gone** /-'gɒn‖-'gɔːn/ experience (esp. something unpleasant or difficult)

un·der·grad·u·ate /‚ʌndə'grædʒuɪt‖-ər-/ *n* person doing a university course for a first degree

un·der·ground /'ʌndəgraʊnd‖-ər-/ *adj* **1** below the Earth's surface **2** secret; representing a political view not acceptable to the government ♦ *n* **1** (*often cap.*) underground railway system **2** secret group fighting or opposing the rulers of a country ♦ *adv* /‚ʌndə'graʊnd‖-ər-/ **go underground** hide from political view for a time

un·der·growth /'ʌndəgrəʊθ‖-dərgroʊθ/ *n* [U] bushes and low plants growing around trees

un·der·hand¹ /‚ʌndə'hænd◂‖-ər-/ also **un·der·hand·ed** /-'hændɪd◂/ — *adj* (secretly) dishonest

underhand² *adj, adv* UNDERARM

un·der·lie /‚ʌndə'laɪ‖-ər-/ *vt* **-lay** /-'leɪ/, **-lain** /-'leɪn/ be a hidden cause or meaning of

un·der·line /‚ʌndə'laɪn‖-ər-/ *vt* **1** draw a line under **2** give additional force to, so as to show importance

un·der·ling /'ʌndəlɪŋ‖-ər-/ *n* person of low rank

un·der·manned /‚ʌndə'mænd◂‖-ər-/ *adj* (of a factory, etc.) having too few workers

un·der·mine /‚ʌndə'maɪn‖-ər-/ *vt* **1** weaken or destroy gradually: *Criticism undermines his confidence.* **2** wear away the earth beneath

un·der·neath /‚ʌndə'niːθ‖-ər-/ *prep, adv* under; below

un·der·pants /'ʌndəpænts‖-ər-/ *n* [P] underclothes for the lower part of the body

un·der·pass /'ʌndəpɑːs‖-dərpæs/ *n* path or road under another road, railway, etc.

un·der·pin /‚ʌndə'pɪn‖-ər-/ *vt* **-nn-** strengthen or support (an argument)

un·der·priv·i·leged /‚ʌndə'prɪvɪlɪdʒd◂‖-dər-/ *adj* poor and living in bad social conditions

un·der·rate /‚ʌndə'reɪt/ *vt* give too low an opinion of

un·der·sec·re·ta·ry /‚ʌndə'sekrətəri‖-dər'sekrəteri/ *n* (in Britain) high-ranking government official who advises ministers

un·der·side /'ʌndəsaɪd‖-ər-/ *n* lower side or surface

un·der·signed /'ʌndəsaɪnd‖-ər-/ *n* whose signature is/are beneath the writing: *We, the undersigned…*

un·der·stand /‚ʌndə'stænd‖-ər-/ *v* **-stood** /-'stʊd/ **1** *vi/t* know or find the meaning (of): *She spoke in Russian, and I didn't understand.* **2** *vt* know or feel closely the nature of (a person, feelings, etc.) **3** *vt* take or judge (as the meaning) **4** *vt fml* have been informed: *I understand you wish to join.* **5** *vt* add (something unexpressed) in the mind to make a meaning complete **6 make oneself understood** make one's meaning clear to others, esp. in speech **~able** *adj* **1** that can be understood **2** reasonable **~ably** *adv* **~ing** *n* **1** [U] brain power; ability to understand **2** [C] private informal agreement **3** [U] sympathy ♦ *adj* sympathetic

un·der·state /ˌʌndəˈsteɪt ‖ -ər-/ *vt* express less strongly than one could or should **~ment** *n* [C;U]

un·der·stud·y /ˈʌndəˌstʌdi ‖ -ər-/ *n* actor able to take over from another in a particular part if necessary ♦ *vt* be an understudy for

un·der·take /ˌʌndəˈteɪk ‖ -ər-/ *vt* **-took** /-ˈtʊk/, **-taken** /-ˈteɪkən/ *fml* **1** take up or accept (a position, work, etc.) **2** promise **-taking** /ˌʌndəˈteɪkɪŋ ‖ ˈʌndərteɪ-/ *n* **1** piece of work; job **2** *fml* promise

un·der·tak·er /ˈʌndəteɪkə ‖ -dərteɪkər/ *n* funeral arranger **-ing** *n* [U]

un·der·tone /ˈʌndətəʊn ‖ -dərtoʊn/ *n* **1** low voice **2** hidden meaning or feeling

un·der·wear /ˈʌndəweə ‖ -dərwer/ *n* [U] clothes worn next to the body under other clothes

un·der·went /ˌʌndəˈwent ‖ -ər-/ *past t. of* UNDERGO

un·der·world /ˈʌndəwɜːld ‖ -dərwɜːrld/ *n* **1** criminals considered as a social group **2** home of the dead in ancient Greek stories

un·der·write /ˌʌndəˈraɪt ‖ -ər-/ *vt* **-wrote** /-ˈrəʊt ‖ -ˈroʊt/, **-written** /-ˈrɪtn/ *fml* support, esp. with money **-writer** /ˈʌndəraɪtə ‖ -dəraɪtər/ *n* person who makes insurance contracts

un·de·si·ra·ble /ˌʌndɪˈzaɪərəbəl ‖ -ˈzaɪr-/ *adj fml* not wanted; unpleasant ♦ *n* someone regarded as immoral, criminal, or socially unacceptable **-bility** /ˌʌndɪzaɪərəˈbɪləti ‖ -zaɪr-/ *n* [U]

un·de·vel·oped /ˌʌndɪˈveləpt◀/ *adj* (usu. of a place) not having industry, mining, building, etc.

un·dies /ˈʌndiːz/ *n* [P] *infml* (women's) underwear

un·di·vid·ed /ˌʌndɪˈvaɪdɪd◀/ *adj* complete

un·do /ʌnˈduː/ *vt* **-did** /-ˈdɪd/, **-done** /-ˈdʌn/ **1** unfasten (something tied or wrapped) **2** remove the effects of: *The fire undid months of hard work.* **~ing** *n* [S] cause of someone's ruin, failure, etc.

un·doubt·ed /ʌnˈdaʊtɪd/ *adj* known for certain to be (so) **~ly** *adv*

un·dress /ʌnˈdres/ *v* **1** *vi* take one's clothes off **2** *vt* take (someone's) clothes off ♦ *n fml* lack of clothes **~ed** *adj* wearing no clothes

un·due /ˌʌnˈdjuː◀ ‖ -ˈduː◀/ *adj* too much; unsuitable **unduly** *adv: not unduly worried*

un·du·late /ˈʌndjʊleɪt ‖ -dʒə-/ *vi* rise and fall like waves **-lation** /ˌʌndjʊˈleɪʃən ‖ -dʒə-/ *n* [C;U]

un·dy·ing /ʌnˈdaɪ-ɪŋ/ *adj lit* which will never end

un·earth /ʌnˈɜːθ ‖ -ˈɜːrθ/ *vt* **1** dig up **2** discover

un·earth·ly /ʌnˈɜːθli ‖ -ˈɜːr-/ *adj* **1** very strange and unnatural **2** *infml* (of time) very inconvenient

un·eas·y /ʌnˈiːzi/ *adj* worried; anxious **-ily** *adv* **-iness** *n* [U]

un·ec·o·no·mic /ˌʌniːkəˈnɒmɪk◀, ˌʌnekə- ‖ -ˈnɑː-/ *also* **un·e·co·nom·i·cal** /-mɪkəl/ — *adj* not producing profit; wasteful

un·ed·i·fy·ing /ʌnˈedɪfaɪ-ɪŋ/ *adj* unpleasant or offensive to the moral sense

un·em·ployed /ˌʌnɪmˈplɔɪd◀/ *adj* not having a job ♦ *n* [*the*+S] people without jobs

un·em·ploy·ment /ˌʌnɪmˈplɔɪmənt/ *n* [U] **1** condition of lacking a job **2** lack of jobs for numbers of people in society

un·en·vi·a·ble /ʌnˈenviəbəl/ *adj* not to be wished for, esp. because of difficulty

un·e·qualled *BrE* || **-qualed** *AmE* /ʌnˈiːkwəld/ *adj* the greatest possible

un·e·quiv·o·cal /ˌʌnɪˈkwɪvəkəl◀/ *adj* totally clear in meaning

un·er·ring /ʌnˈɜːrɪŋ/ *adj* without making a mistake

un·eth·i·cal /ʌnˈeθɪkəl/ *adj* morally wrong **~ly** *adv*

un·e·ven /ʌnˈiːvən/ *adj* **1** not smooth, straight, or regular **2** ODD (2) **3** varying in quality: *uneven work* (=often rather bad) **~ly** *adv* **-ness** *n* [U]

un·fail·ing /ʌnˈfeɪlɪŋ/ *adj* continuous **~ly**

adv

un·faith·ful /ʌnˈfeɪθfəl/ *adj* having sex with someone other than one's regular partner

un·fee·ling /ʌnˈfiːlɪŋ/ *adj* showing no sympathy for others .

un·fath·om·a·ble /ʌnˈfæðəməbəl/ *adj* that one cannot understand; mysterious

un·flap·pa·ble /ʌnˈflæpəbəl/ *adj* always calm, esp. in difficult situations

un·fold /ʌnˈfəʊld ‖ -ˈfoʊld/ *v* **1** *vt* open from a folded position **2** *vi/t* (cause to) become clear, more fully known, etc.: *as the story unfolded*

un·fore·seen /ˌʌnfɔːˈsiːn◂ ‖ -fər-/ *adj* not expected: *unforeseen problems*

un·for·get·ta·ble /ˌʌnfəˈgetəbəl◂ ‖ -fər-/ *adj* too strong in effect to be forgotten –**bly** *adv*

un·for·giv·a·ble /ˌʌnfəˈgɪvəbəl ‖ -fər-/ *adj* too bad to be forgiven

un·for·tu·nate /ʌnˈfɔːtʃənət ‖ -ˈfɔːr-/ *adj* **1** that makes one sorry **2** unlucky **3** slightly rude –**ly** *adv*

un·found·ed /ʌnˈfaʊndɪd/ *adj* not supported by facts

un·furl /ʌnˈfɜːl ‖ -ɜːrl/ *vt* unroll and open (a flag, sail, etc.)

un·gain·ly /ʌnˈgeɪnli/ *adj* not graceful; awkward

un·god·ly /ʌnˈgɒdli ‖ -ˈgɑː-/ *adj* **1** not religious **2** *infml* UNEARTHLY (2)

un·grate·ful /ʌnˈgreɪtfəl/ *adj* **1** not grateful **2** *lit* (of work) giving no reward or result

un·guard·ed /ʌnˈgɑːdɪd ‖ -ɑːr-/ *adj* unwisely careless, esp. in speech

un·hand /ʌnˈhænd/ *vt* *lit* stop holding or touching: *Unhand me, sir!*

un·heard-of /ʌnˈhɜːd ɒv ‖ -ˈhɜːrd ɑːv/ *adj* very unusual

un·hinge /ʌnˈhɪndʒ/ *vt* make mad

un·ho·ly /ʌnˈhəʊli ‖ -ˈhoʊ-/ *adj* terrible; unreasonable: *an unholy row*

unholy al·li·ance /ˌ·· ·ˈ··/ *n* grouping of people or esp. organizations that are usu. separate or opposed but have come together for a bad purpose

u·ni·corn /ˈjuːnɪkɔːn ‖ -kɔːrn/ *n* imaginary horselike animal with a single horn

un·i·dent·i·fied /ˌʌnaɪˈdentɪfaɪd◂/ *adj* not known or recognized

u·ni·form /ˈjuːnɪfɔːm ‖ -ɔːrm/ *n* sort of clothes worn by all members of a group: *school/army uniform* ♦ *adj* the same all over; regular ~**ly** *adv* ~**ed** *adj*: *uniformed soldiers* ~**ity** /ˌjuːnɪˈfɔːməti ‖ -ɔːr-/ *n* [U]

u·ni·fy /ˈjuːnɪfaɪ/ *vt* bring together so as to be a single whole or all the same –**fication** /ˌjuːnɪfɪˈkeɪʃən/ *n* [U]

u·ni·lat·e·ral /ˌjuːnɪˈlætərəl◂/ *adj* done by only one group: *unilateral disarmament*

un·i·ni·ti·at·ed /ˌʌnɪˈnɪʃieɪtɪd/ *n* [the+P] *fml* people who are not among those who have special knowledge or experience

un·in·terest·ed /ʌnˈɪntrəstɪd/ *adj* not interested

u·nion /ˈjuːnjən/ *n* **1** [C] club or society, esp. a TRADE UNION **2** [C] group of states: *the Soviet Union* **3** [U] *fml* joining **4** [C;U] *lit* (unity in) marriage

Union Jack /ˌ·· ˈ·/ *n* [the] British flag

u·nique /juːˈniːk/ *adj* **1** being the only one of its type **2** unusual **3** better than any other ~**ly** *adv*

u·ni·sex /ˈjuːnɪseks/ *adj* of one type for both male and female

u·ni·son /ˈjuːnɪsən, -zən/ *n* [U] **1** being together in taking action **2** everyone singing or playing the same note

u·nit /ˈjuːnɪt/ *n* **1** group within a larger organization: *the hospital's X-ray unit* **2** amount forming a standard of measurement: *The pound is a unit of currency.* **3** whole number less than ten **4** piece of furniture, etc. which can be fitted with others of the same type

u·nite /juːˈnaɪt/ *v* **1** *vt* join **2** *vi* become one **3** *vi* act together for a purpose

United King·dom /ˌ·· ˈ··/ *n* [the] England, Scotland, Wales, and Northern Ireland

United Na·tions /ˌ·· ˈ··/ *n* [the+S] international organization of countries, which tries to find peaceful solutions to world problems

unit trust /ˌ·· ·ˈ·/ *n* company through which one can buy SHARES in various companies

u·ni·ty /ˈjuːnɪti/ *n* [U] being united or in agreement

u·ni·verse /ˈjuːnɪvɜːs ‖ -ɜːrs/ *n* [the+S] everything which exists in all space –**versal** /ˌjuːnɪˈvɜːsəl◂ ‖ -ɜːr-/ *adj* among or for everyone or in every place: *universal* *agreement* –**versally** *adv*

u·ni·ver·si·ty /ˌjuːnɨˈvɜːsɨti◄‖-ɜːr-/ *n* 1 place of education at the highest level, where degrees are given 2 members of this place

un·kempt /ˌʌnˈkempt◄/ *adj* (esp. of hair) untidy

un·kind /ˌʌnˈkaɪnd◄/ *adj* not kind; cruel or thoughtless

un·known quan·ti·ty /ˌʌn·noʊn ˈkwɒntɨti‖-noʊn ˈkwɑːn-/ *n* 1 person or thing whose qualities and abilities are not yet known 2 (in MATHEMATICS) a number represented by the letter *x*

un·leash /ʌnˈliːʃ/ *vt* allow (feelings, forces, etc.) to act with full force

un·less /ʌnˈles, ən-/ *conj* except if: *Don't come unless I ask you to.*

un·like /ˌʌnˈlaɪk◄/ *prep* 1 completely different from: *Unlike me, she's very quiet.* 2 not behaving typically: *It's unlike her to be late.*

un·like·ly /ʌnˈlaɪkli/ *adj* 1 not expected; improbable 2 not likely to happen or be true

un·load /ʌnˈloʊd‖-ˈloʊd/ *v* 1 *vt* remove (a load) from (something) 2 *vi/t* remove bullets from (a gun) or film from (a camera) 3 *vt* get rid of

un·loose /ʌnˈluːs/ *vt* set free

un·loos·en /ʌnˈluːsən/ *vt* loosen

un·marked /ˌʌnˈmɑːkt◄‖-ˈmɑːrkt◄/ *adj* having no marks, signs, etc. to show what it is: *an unmarked police car*

un·mask /ʌnˈmɑːsk‖-ˈmæsk/ *vt* show the hidden truth about

un·men·tion·a·ble /ʌnˈmenʃənəbəl/ *adj* too shocking to be spoken about

un·mis·tak·a·ble /ˌʌnmɨˈsteɪkəbəl◄/ *adj* very easily recognized: *the unmistakable sound of her voice*

un·mit·i·gat·ed /ʌnˈmɪtɨɡeɪtɨd/ *adj* in every way (bad): *an unmitigated disaster*

un·nat·u·ral /ʌnˈnætʃərəl/ *adj* 1 unusual 2 against ordinary good ways of behaving: *unnatural sexual practices*

un·nerve /ˌʌnˈnɜːv‖-ɜːrv/ *vt* take away (someone's) confidence or courage

un·ob·tru·sive /ˌʌnəbˈtruːsɪv◄/ *adj* not (too) noticeable ~**ly** *adv*

un·pack /ʌnˈpæk/ *vi/t* remove (possessions) from (a container)

un·pal·at·a·ble /ʌnˈpælətəbəl/ *adj fml* unpleasant and difficult for the mind to accept

un·par·al·leled /ʌnˈpærəleld/ *adj fml* better than anything/anyone else

un·pick /ʌnˈpɪk/ *vt* take out (the stitches) from (something)

un·pleas·ant /ʌnˈplezənt/ *adj* 1 not enjoyable 2 unkind

un·pre·ce·dent·ed /ʌnˈpresɨdentɨd/ *adj* never having happened before

un·pre·ten·tious /ˌʌnprɨˈtenʃəs◄/ *adj* not showing too great signs of wealth, importance, etc.; simple

un·print·a·ble /ʌnˈprɪntəbəl/ *adj* too offensive to express

un·qual·i·fied /ʌnˈkwɒlɨfaɪd‖-ˈkwɑː-/ *adj* 1 not limited 2 not having suitable knowledge or experience

un·ques·tion·a·ble /ʌnˈkwestʃənəbəl/ *adj* which cannot be doubted; certain –**bly** *adv*

un·rav·el /ʌnˈrævəl/ *vt* -**ll**- *BrE* ‖ -**l**- *AmE* 1 *vi/t* become or cause (threads, cloth, etc.) to become separated or unwoven 2 *vt* make clear (a mystery)

un·real /ˌʌnˈrɪəl◄/ *adj* seeming imaginary or unlike reality –**ity** /ˌʌnriˈælɨti/ *n* [U]

un·re·mit·ting /ˌʌnrɨˈmɪtɪŋ◄/ *adj fml* (of something difficult) never stopping

un·re·quit·ed /ˌʌnrɨˈkwaɪtɨd◄/ *adj fml* not given in return

un·rest /ʌnˈrest/ *n* [U] troubled or dissatisfied confusion, often with fighting

un·ri·valled *BrE* ‖ -**valed** *AmE* /ʌnˈraɪvəld/ *adj* better than any other

un·roll /ʌnˈroʊl‖-ˈroʊl/ *vi/t* open from a rolled condition

un·ruf·fled /ʌnˈrʌfəld/ *adj* not upset; calm

un·ru·ly /ʌnˈruːli/ *adj* 1 behaving wildly; *unruly children* 2 hard to keep in place: *unruly hair*

un·sa·vour·y *BrE* ‖ -**vory** *AmE* /ʌn-ˈseɪvəri/ *adj* unpleasant or unacceptable in moral values

un·scathed /ʌnˈskeɪðd/ *adj* not harmed

un·scru·pu·lous /ʌnˈskruːpjɨləs/ *adj* not caring about honesty and fairness

un·sea·son·a·ble /ʌnˈsiːzənəbəl/ *adj* unusual for the time of year, esp. bad –**bly** *adv*

un·seat /ʌnˈsiːt/ *vt* 1 remove from a position of power 2 (of a horse) throw off (a rider)

un·seem·ly /ʌnˈsiːmli/ *adj* not proper or suitable (in behaviour)

un·set·tle /ʌnˈsetl/ *vt* make more anxious, dissatisfied, etc. **–tled** *adj* (of weather, a political situation, etc.) likely to get worse

un·sha·ven /ʌnˈʃeɪvən/ *adj* having not SHAVEd

un·sight·ly /ʌnˈsaɪtli/ *adj* ugly

un·so·cial /ˌʌnˈsəʊʃəl◁ ‖ -ˈsoʊ-/ *adj* unsuitable for combining with family and social life: *working unsocial hours*

un·so·li·ci·ted /ˌʌnsəˈlɪsɪtɪd◁/ *adj fml* given without being asked for

un·sound /ˌʌnˈsaʊnd◁/ *adj* **1** based on ideas, etc. that are wrong **2** in bad condition; not safe

un·speak·a·ble /ʌnˈspiːkəbəl/ *adj* terrible **–bly** *adv*

un·stint·ing /ʌnˈstɪntɪŋ/ *adj fml* very generous

un·stuck /ʌnˈstʌk/ *adj* **1** not fastened **2 come unstuck** go wrong; be unsuccessful

un·sung /ˌʌnˈsʌŋ◁/ *adj lit* not famous (though deserving to be)

un·swerv·ing /ʌnˈswɜːvɪŋ ‖ -ɜːr-/ *adj* firm: *unswerving loyalty*

un·tapped /ˌʌnˈtæpt◁/ *adj* (of a supply) unused: *untapped oil reserves*

un·think·a·ble /ʌnˈθɪŋkəbəl/ *adj* that cannot be considered or accepted; impossible

un·til /ʌnˈtɪl, ən-/ *prep, conj* **1** up to (the time that): *Don't start until he arrives.* **2** as far as: *We stayed on the train until London.*

un·time·ly /ʌnˈtaɪmli/ *adj* happening too soon: *her untimely death*

un·to /ˈʌntu/ *prep lit* to

un·told /ˌʌnˈtəʊld◁ ‖ -ˈtoʊld◁/ *adj* very great: *untold damage*

un·to·ward /ˌʌntəˈwɔːd◁ ‖ ˌʌnˈtɔːrd◁/ *adj fml* unexpected and undesirable

un·truth /ʌnˈtruːθ, ˈʌntruːθ/ *n fml* lie

un·u·su·al /ʌnˈjuːʒuəl, -ʒəl/ *adj fml* **1** not common **2** interesting because different from others **~ly** *adv* **1** very **2** in an unusual way

un·ut·ter·a·ble /ʌnˈʌtərəbəl/ *adj fml* **1** terrible **2** complete: *an unutterable fool* **~bly** *adv*

un·var·nished /ʌnˈvɑːnɪʃt ‖ -ɑːr-/ *adj* without additional description

un·veil /ˌʌnˈveɪl/ *vt* **1** remove a covering

from **2** show publicly for the first time

un·war·rant·ed /ʌnˈwɒrəntɪd ‖ -ˈwɔː-, -ˈwɑː-/ *adj* (done) without good reason

un·well /ʌnˈwel/ *adj* (slightly) ill

un·wiel·dy /ʌnˈwiːldi/ *adj* awkward to move, handle, or use

un·wind /ʌnˈwaɪnd/ *v* **-wound** /-ˈwaʊnd/ **1** *vi/t* undo (something wound) or become undone: *unwinding a ball of wool* **2** *vi* become calmer and free of care

un·wit·ting /ˌʌnˈwɪtɪŋ/ *adj* not knowing or intended: *their unwitting accomplice*

un·writ·ten rule /ˌʌnrɪtn ˈruːl/ *n* usual custom (not officially stated)

up /ʌp/ *adv* **1** to or at a higher level: *She climbed up onto the roof.* | *He turned up his collar.* **2** (shows increase): *Profits are up.* | *Turn the radio up.* **3** (=louder) **3** to the north: *driving up to Scotland* **4** out of bed: *We stayed up late.* **5** so as to be completely finished: *Eat up your vegetables.* **6** into small pieces: *She tore it up.* **7** firmly; tightly: *He tied up the parcel.* **8** together: *Add up the figures.* **9** more loudly: *Sing up!* **10** on top: *right side up* **11 up against** having to face (something difficult) **12 up and down: a** higher and lower: *jumping up and down* **b** backwards and forwards: *walking up and down* **13 up to: a** towards and as far as: *He walked up to me and asked my name.* **b** until: *up to now* **c** good, well, or clever enough for: *He's not up to the job.* **d** the duty or responsibility of: *I'll leave it up to you.* (=you must decide) **e** doing (something bad): *What are you up to?* **14 Up (with)** We want or approve of: *Up the workers!* ♦ *prep* **1** to or at a higher level on: *walking up the stairs* **2** to or at the top or far end of: *They live just up the road.* ♦ *adj* **1** directed up: *the up escalator* **2** (of a road) being repaired **3 be up** be happening; be the matter **4 be well up in/on** know a lot about **5 up and about** out of bed (again) and able to walk **6 up for: a** intended or being considered for **b** on trial for ♦ *vt* **-pp-** increase

up-and-com·ing /ˌ· · ˈ··◁/ *adj* active and likely to succeed

up-and-up /ˌ· · ˈ·/ *n* **on the up-and-up** improving; succeeding

up·bring·ing /ˈʌpbrɪŋɪŋ/ *n* [S] (way of) training and caring for a child

up·com·ing /ˈʌpˌkʌmɪŋ/ *adj* about to happen

up·date /ˌʌpˈdeɪt/ vt 1 make more modern 2 supply with the latest information

up·end /ʌpˈend/ vt stand on a part that does not usually stand on the floor

up·front /ˌʌpˈfrʌnt/ adj very direct and making no attempt to hide one's meaning

up·grade /ˌʌpˈɡreɪd/ vt give a more important position to

up·heav·al /ʌpˈhiːvəl/ n [C;U] great change and confusion, with much activity

up·held /ʌpˈheld/ past t. and p. of UPHOLD

up·hill /ˌʌpˈhɪl◄/ adj, adv 1 up a slope 2 difficult: an uphill task

up·hold /ʌpˈhəʊld/ -ˈhoʊld/ vt -held /-ˈheld/ 1 prevent from being weakened or taken away 2 declare (a decision) to be right ~er n

up·hol·ster /ʌpˈhəʊlstə ‖ -ˈhoʊlstər/ vt cover and fill (a seat) ~er n ~y n [U] material covering and filling a seat

up·keep /ˈʌpkiːp/ n [U] (cost of) keeping something repaired and in order

up·lift·ing /ʌpˈlɪftɪŋ/ adj causing cheerful and happy feelings

up·mar·ket /ˌ· ˈ·◄/ adj being or using goods produced to meet the demand of the higher social groups

up·on /əˈpɒn ‖ əˈpɑːn/ prep fml for ON¹ (1,3,4,6,7)

up·per /ˈʌpə ‖ -ər/ adj at or nearer the top: the upper arm ♦ n 1 top part of a shoe 2 on one's uppers infml very poor

upper class /ˌ·· ˈ·◄/ n highest social class, esp. with noble titles **upper-class** adj

upper hand /ˌ·· ˈ· the+S/ control

up·per·most /ˈʌpəməʊst ‖ -pərmoʊst/ adv in the highest or strongest position

up·right /ˈʌp-raɪt/ adj 1 exactly straight up; not bent or leaning 2 completely honest ♦ n upright supporting beam

up·ris·ing /ˈʌpˌraɪzɪŋ/ n act of the ordinary people suddenly and violently opposing the current of a river

up·roar /ˈʌpˈrɔː ‖ -rɔːr/ n [S;U] confused noisy activity, esp. shouting ~ious /ʌpˈrɔːriəs/ adj very noisy, esp. with laughter

up·root /ʌpˈruːt/ vt 1 tear (a plant) from the earth 2 remove from a home, settled habits, etc.

ups and downs /ˌ· · ˈ·/ n [P] good and bad periods

up·set /ʌpˈset/ vt -set; pres. p. -tt- 1 turn over, esp. accidentally, causing confusion or scattering 2 cause to be worried, sad, angry, etc. 3 make slightly ill ♦ n /ˈʌpset/ 1 slight illness: a stomach upset 2 unexpected result

up·shot /ˈʌpʃɒt ‖ ˈʌpʃɑːt/ n result in the end

up·side down /ˌʌpsaɪd ˈdaʊn◄/ adj 1 with the top turned to the bottom 2 in disorder

up·stage /ˌʌpˈsteɪdʒ/ vt take attention away from (someone) for oneself

up·stairs /ˌʌpˈsteəz◄ ‖ -ˈsterz/ adv, adj on or to a higher floor

up·stand·ing /ˌʌpˈstændɪŋ/ adj 1 tall and strong 2 honest

up·start /ˈʌpstɑːt ‖ -ɑːrt/ n someone who has risen too suddenly or unexpectedly to a high position

up·stream /ˌʌpˈstriːm◄/ adv, adj moving against the current of a river

up·take /ˈʌpteɪk/ n [U] ability to understand: He's rather slow on the uptake.

up·tight /ˈʌptaɪt, ˌʌpˈtaɪt/ adj infml anxious and nervous

up-to-date /ˌ· · ˈ·◄/ adj 1 modern 2 including or having all the latest information

up·turn /ˈʌptɜːn ‖ -ɜːrn/ n a favourable change

up·ward /ˈʌpwəd ‖ -ərd/ adj going up **upwards** adv more than

upwardly-mo·bile /ˌ··· ˈ·◄/ adj able or wishing to move into a higher social class and become more wealthy

u·ra·ni·um /juˈreɪniəm/ n [U] RADIOACTIVE metal used in producing atomic power

U·ra·nus /juˈreɪnəs/ n the PLANET seventh in order from the sun

ur·ban /ˈɜːbən ‖ ˈɜːr-/ adj of towns

ur·bane /ɜːˈbeɪn ‖ ɜːr-/ adj smoothly polite ~ity adv –banity /juˈræn- ‖ ˈbænɪti/ n [U]

ur·chin /ˈɜːtʃɪn ‖ ˈɜːr-/ n small dirty untidy child —see also SEA URCHIN

urge /ɜːdʒ ‖ ɜːrdʒ/ vt 1 try strongly to persuade: He urged me to reconsider. 2 drive forwards: He urged the horses onwards with a whip. ♦ n strong desire or need

ur·gent /ˈɜːdʒənt ‖ ˈɜːr-/ adj that must be dealt with at once ~ly adv urgency n [U]

u·ri·nal /juəˈraɪnəl, juˈraɪ- ‖ ˈjurəl-/ n container or building for (men) urinating

u·rine /ˈjʊərɪn ‖ ˈjur-/ n [U] liquid waste

passed from the body **urinary** adj **urinate**
vi pass urine from the body **urination**
/ˌjʊərɪ'neɪʃən ‖ ˌjʊr-/ n [U]

urn /ɜːn ‖ ɜːrn/ n 1 large metal container
for serving tea or coffee 2 container for the
ashes of a burnt dead body

us /əs, s; strong ʌs/ pron (object form of
we)

US /ˌjuː 'es◂/ abbrev. for: 1 also **USA** /ˌjuː
es 'eɪ/ — the United States (of America)
2 of the United States: the US navy

us·age /'juːzɪdʒ, 'juːsɪdʒ/ n 1 [C;U] way
of using a language: a book on English
usage 2 fml (type or degree of) use

use¹ /juːs/ n 1 [U] using or being used
2 [U] ability or right to use something: He
lost the use of his legs. 3 [C;U] purpose: A
machine with many uses. 4 [U] advantage;
usefulness: It's no use complaining.
(=complaining will have no effect) 5 in use
being used 6 make use of use 7 of use
useful ~ful adj that fulfils a need well
~fully adv ~fulness n [U] ~less adj 1 not
useful 2 unable to do anything properly
~lessly adv

use² /juːz/ vt 1 employ for a purpose; put
to use: Oil can be used as a fuel. 2 finish;
CONSUME (2) 3 take unfair advantage of;
EXPLOIT **usable** adj **used** adj that has
already had an owner: used cars **user** n

   use up phr vt finish completely

use³ /juːs/ vi (used in the past tense for
showing what always or regularly
happened): I used to go there every week, but
I no longer do.

used to /'juːst tʊ,-tə/ adj no longer
finding (something) strange or annoying
because it has become familiar: I'm used to
the noise.

user-friend·ly /ˌ·· '··◂/ adj easy to use or
understand

ush·er /'ʌʃə ‖ -ər/ n someone who shows
people to their seats in a public place ♦ vt
fml bring by showing the way: (fig.) The
bombing of Hiroshima ushered in the
nuclear age.

ush·er·ette /ˌʌʃə'ret/ n female usher in a
cinema

USSR /ˌjuː es es 'ɑː ‖ -'ɑːr/ abbrev. for:
Union of Soviet Socialist Republics; the
former Soviet Union

u·su·al /'juːʒʊəl, 'juːʒəl/ adj in accordance
with what happens most of the time: He

lacked his usual cheerfulness. ~ly adv in
most cases; generally

u·surp /juː'zɜːp ‖ -ɜːrp/ vt fml steal
(someone else's power or position) ~er n

u·ten·sil /juː'tensəl/ n fml object with a
particular use, esp. a tool or container

u·te·rus /'juːtərəs/ n med for WOMB

u·til·i·tar·i·an /juːˌtɪlɪ'teəriən ‖ -'ter-/
adj fml, sometimes derog made to be useful
rather than decorative

u·til·i·ty /juː'tɪlɪti/ n 1 [U] fml degree of
usefulness 2 [C] public service, such as
water supplies, a bus service, etc.

u·til·ize also **-ise** BrE /'juːtɪlaɪz/ vt fml for
USE² (1) **-ization, -isation** /ˌjuːtɪlaɪ'zeɪʃən
‖ -lə-/ n [U]

ut·most /'ʌtməʊst ‖ -moʊst/ adj fml very
great: done with (the) utmost care ♦ n [U]
the most that can be done: I did my utmost to
prevent it.

u·to·pi·a /juː'təʊpiə ‖ -'toʊ-/ n [C;U]
perfect society **-pian** adj impractically
trying to bring social perfection

ut·ter¹ /'ʌtə ‖ -ər/ adj (esp. of something
bad) complete: utter nonsense ~ly adv

utter² vt fml make (a sound) or produce
(words) **~ance** n fml 1 [U] speaking 2 [C]
something said

U-turn /'juː tɜːn ‖ -tɜːrn/ n 1 turning
movement in a vehicle which takes one
back in the direction one came from
2 complete change, resulting in the
opposite of what has gone before

V

V, v /viː/ the 22nd letter of the English
alphabet

v abbrev. for: 1 verb 2 VERSUS 3 very

va·can·cy /'veɪkənsi/ n unfilled place,
such as a job or hotel room

va·cant /'veɪkənt/ adj 1 empty 2 (of a job)
having no worker to do it 3 showing lack of
interest or serious thought ~ly adv

va·cate /vəˈkeɪt, veɪ-‖ˈveɪkeɪt/ vt fml cease to use or live in: *Kindly vacate your seats.*

va·ca·tion /vəˈkeɪʃən‖veɪˈkeɪ-/ n 1 [C] a esp. AmE holiday b esp. BrE time when universities are closed 2 [U] fml vacating ♦ vi esp. AmE have a holiday

vac·cine /ˈvæksiːn‖vækˈsiːn/ n [C;U] substance put into the body to protect it against disease –**cinate** /ˈvæksɔneɪt/ vt put vaccine into –**cination** /ˌvæksɔˈneɪʃən/ n [C;U]

vac·u·ous /ˈvækjuəs/ adj fml 1 showing foolishness: *a vacuous grin* 2 with no purpose or meaning –**ly** adv –**uity** /vəˈkjuːɨti, væ-‖væ-/ n [U]

vac·u·um /ˈvækjuəm, -kjum/ n space completely without air or other gas: (fig.) *Her death left a vacuum* (=emptiness) *in our lives.* ♦ vt clean with a vacuum cleaner

vacuum clean·er /ˈ··· ,··/ n electric apparatus for sucking up dirt from floors, etc.

vacuum flask /ˈ··· ·/ n FLASK (3)

vacuum-packed /ˌ··· ·‖ˌ··· ˈ·/ adj wrapped in plastic with all air removed

vag·a·bond /ˈvæɡəbɒnd‖-bɑːnd/ n lit person who lives a wandering life

va·ga·ry /ˈveɪɡəri/ n chance event that has an effect on one

va·gi·na /vəˈdʒaɪnə/ n passage from the outer female sex organs to the WOMB

va·grant /ˈveɪɡrənt/ n fml or law person with no home who wanders around and usu. begs **vagrancy** n [U] being a vagrant

vague /veɪɡ/ adj 1 not clearly seen, described, understood, etc. 2 unable to express oneself clearly –**ly** adv –**ness** n [U]

vain /veɪn/ adj 1 admiring oneself too much 2 unsuccessful; unimportant: *a vain attempt* 3 **in vain** unsuccessfully 4 **take someone's name in vain** talk disrespectfully about someone –**ly** adv

vale /veɪl/ n (in poetry and place-names) broad low valley

va·len·cy /ˈveɪlənsi/ n measure of the power of atoms to form compounds

val·en·tine /ˈvæləntaɪn/ n (card sent to) a lover chosen on **Saint Valentine's Day** (February 14th)

val·et /ˈvælɪt, ˈvæleɪ/ n 1 man's personal male servant 2 AmE person who parks customers' cars at a hotel or restaurant

val·i·ant /ˈvæliənt/ adj esp. fml or lit very brave –**ly** adv 1 very bravely 2 very hard: *He tried valiantly (but without success) to pass the exam.*

val·id /ˈvælɪd/ adj 1 (of a reason, argument, etc.) firmly based and acceptable 2 that can legally be used: *a ticket valid for 3 months* –**ly** adv –**ate** vt fml make valid **validity** /vəˈlɪdɨti/ n [U]

val·ley /ˈvæli/ n land between two lines of hills or mountains

val·our BrE ‖ -**or** AmE /ˈvælə‖-ər/ n [U] esp. fml or lit great bravery –**orous** adj

val·u·a·ble /ˈvæljuəbəl, -jɐbəl‖ˈvæljɐbəl/ adj 1 worth a lot of money 2 very useful ♦ n something VALUABLE (1)

val·u·a·tion /ˌvæljuˈeɪʃən/ n 1 [C;U] calculating how much something is worth 2 [C] value decided on

val·ue /ˈvæljuː/ n 1 [S;U] usefulness or importance, esp. compared with other things: *The map was of great value in finding the way.* 2 [C;U] worth in esp. money: *goods to the value of £500* 3 [U] worth compared with the amount paid: *a restaurant offering the best value in town* ♦ vt 1 calculate the value of 2 consider to be of great worth **values** n [P] standards or principles; people's ideas about the worth of certain qualities: *moral values* –**less** adj –**uer** n

value-ad·ded tax /ˌ··· ·ˈ·/ n [U] VAT

value judg·ment /ˈ·· ,··/ n judgment about the quality of something, based on opinion rather than facts

valve /vælv/ n 1 part inside a pipe which opens and shuts to control the flow of liquid or gas through it 2 closed airless glass tube for controlling a flow of electricity

vam·pire /ˈvæmpaɪə‖-paɪr/ n imaginary evil creature that sucks people's blood

van¹ /væn/ n covered road vehicle or railway carriage for carrying esp. goods

van² n **in the van** fml or lit taking a leading part

van·dal /ˈvændl/ n person who destroys beautiful or useful things –**ism** n [U] needless damage to esp. public buildings –**ize**, -**ise** vt destroy or damage intentionally

vane /veɪn/ n bladelike turning part of a machine —see also WEATHER VANE

van·guard /ˈvænɡɑːd‖-ɡɑːrd/ n

1 leading part of some kind of advancement in human affairs: *scientists in the vanguard of medical research* 2 front of a marching army

va·nil·la /vəˈnɪlə/ n [U] strong-smelling plant substance used in food

van·ish /ˈvænɪʃ/ vi 1 disappear 2 cease to exist

van·i·ty /ˈvænɪti/ n [U] 1 being too proud of oneself 2 quality of being without lasting value

van·quish /ˈvæŋkwɪʃ/ vt esp. lit defeat completely

van·tage point /ˈ·· ·/ n 1 good position from which to see 2 point of view

va·pour BrE ‖ **-por** AmE /ˈveɪpə ‖ -ər/ n [U] gaslike form of a liquid, such as mist or steam **vaporize, -ise** vi/t change into vapour **vaporous** adj

var·i·a·ble /ˈveəriəbəl ‖ ˈver-/ adj that changes or can be changed; not fixed or steady ♦ n variable amount **-bly** adv

var·i·ance /ˈveəriəns ‖ ˈver-/ n at variance (with) not in agreement (with)

var·i·ant /ˈveəriənt ‖ ˈver-/ n, adj (form, etc.) that is different and can be used instead: *variant spellings*

var·i·a·tion /ˌveəriˈeɪʃən ‖ ˌver-/ n 1 [C;U] (example or degree of) varying: *price variations* 2 [C] any of a set of pieces of music based on a single tune

var·i·cose veins /ˌværɪkəʊs ˈveɪnz ‖ -koʊs-/ n [P] swollen blood tubes, esp. in the legs

var·ied /ˈveərid ‖ ˈver-/ adj 1 VARIOUS (1) 2 (always) changing: *a varied life*

var·ie·gat·ed /ˈveərɪgeɪtɪd ‖ ˈver-/ adj marked irregularly with different colours **-gation** /ˌveərɪˈgeɪʃən ‖ ˌver-/ n [U]

va·ri·e·ty /vəˈraɪəti/ n 1 [U] not being always the same: *a job lacking variety* 2 [S] group containing different sorts of the same thing: *a wide variety of colours* 3 [C] sort: *a new variety of wheat* 4 [U] entertainment with many short performances of singing, dancing, telling jokes, etc.

var·i·ous /ˈveəriəs ‖ ˈver-/ adj 1 different from each other: *There are various ways of doing it.* 2 several **~ly** adv

var·nish /ˈvɑːnɪʃ ‖ ˈvɑːr-/ n [C;U] liquid that gives a hard shiny surface to esp. wooden articles ♦ vt cover with varnish

var·y /ˈveəri ‖ ˈveri/ v 1 vi be different

(from each other): *Houses vary in size.* 2 vi/t change, esp. continually: *varying one's work methods*

vas·cu·lar /ˈvæskj ̊lə ‖ -ər/ adj of or containing VEINS

vase /vɑːz ‖ veɪs, veɪz/ n deep decorative pot for esp. flowers

va·sec·to·my /vəˈsektəmi/ n operation for cutting the SPERM-carrying tubes in a man, to prevent him from becoming a father

vas·sal /ˈvæsəl/ n person of low social rank in the Middle Ages

vast /vɑːst ‖ væst/ adj extremely large: *a vast desert/improvement* **~ly** adv

vat /væt/ n large liquid container for industrial use: *a whisky vat*

VAT /ˌvi: eɪ ˈti:, væt/ n [U] tax added to the price of an article

Vat·i·can /ˈvætɪkən/ n (palace in Rome which is) the centre of government of the Roman Catholic Church

vau·de·ville /ˈvɔːdəvɪl, ˈvəʊ- ‖ ˈvɒː-, ˈvoʊ-/ n [U] AmE for VARIETY (4)

vault¹ /vɔːlt ‖ vɒːlt/ n 1 thick-walled room for storing valuable things 2 underground room, esp. for storage or for dead bodies 3 arched roof

vault² vi jump using the hands or a pole to gain more height ♦ n act of vaulting **~er** n

vaunt /vɔːnt ‖ vɒːnt/ vt esp. lit BOAST about

VCR /ˌvi: si: ˈɑː ‖ -ˈɑːr/ n abbrev. for: Video Cassette Recorder; VIDEO (2)

VD /ˌvi: ˈdi:/ n [U] abbrev. for: VENEREAL DISEASE

VDU /ˌvi: di: ˈjuː/ n abbrev. for: Visual Display Unit; apparatus with a SCREEN which shows information from a computer

veal /viːl/ n [U] meat from a young cow

veer /vɪə ‖ vɪr/ vi change direction

veg¹ /vedʒ/ n [U] BrE infml vegetables

veg² v infml

veg out phr vi infml relax and do nothing

ve·gan /ˈviːgən ‖ ˈveɪgən, ˈviː-/ n person who eats no meat, eggs, or milk products ♦ adj

vege·ta·ble /ˈvedʒtəbəl/ n 1 plant grown for food to be eaten with the main part of a meal, rather than with sweet things: *Potatoes and carrots are vegetables.* 2 human being who exists but has little or no power of thought

veg·e·tar·i·an /ˌvedʒɪ'teəriən◄‖-'ter-/ n person who eats no meat ♦ adj 1 of or related to vegetarians 2 made up only of vegetables

veg·e·tate /'vedʒɪteɪt/ vi lead a dull inactive life

veg·e·ta·tion /ˌvedʒɪ'teɪʃən/ n [U] plants

vehe·ment /'viːəmənt/ adj fml forceful ~ly adv —mence n [U]

ve·hi·cle /'viːɪkəl/ n 1 something in or on which people or goods are carried, such as a car, bicycle, etc. 2 means of expressing or showing something: He bought the newspaper company as a vehicle for his own political views.

veil /veɪl/ n 1 covering for a woman's face 2 something that covers and hides: a veil of mist 3 take the veil (of a woman) become a NUN ♦ vt cover (as if) with a veil: veiled in secrecy ~ed adj expressed indirectly: veiled threats

vein /veɪn/ n 1 tube carrying blood back to the heart 2 thin line running through a leaf or insect's wing 3 metal-containing crack in rock 4 small but noticeable amount: a vein of cruelty 5 state of mind: in a sad vein

Vel·cro /'velkrəʊ‖-roʊ/ tdmk n [U] material for fastening shoes, clothes, etc. consisting of two pieces of cloth that stick together

veldt, veld /velt/ n high flat grassland of southern Africa

ve·loc·i·ty /vɪ'lɒsɪti‖vɪ'lɑː-/ n [U] fml speed

ve·lour /və'lʊə‖-'lʊr/ n [U] soft VELVET-like cloth

vel·vet /'velvɪt/ n [U] cloth with a soft furry surface on one side only —y adj soft like velvet

ven·det·ta /ven'detə/ n long-lasting situation in which one person repeatedly tries to harm another

vending ma·chine /'vendɪŋ məˌʃiːn/ n machine into which one puts money to obtain small articles

vend·or /'vendə‖-ər/ n fml seller, esp. of a house, land, etc.

ve·neer /vɪ'nɪə‖-'nɪr/ n 1 thin covering of wood on an article 2 false outer appearance: a veneer of respectability ♦ vt cover with a veneer

ven·e·ra·ble /'venərəbəl/ adj fml deserving respect or honour because of great age

ven·e·rate /'venəreɪt/ vt fml treat (someone or something old) with great respect or honour –ration /ˌvenə'reɪʃən/ n [U]

ve·ne·re·al dis·ease /vɪˈnɪəriəl dɪˌziːz ‖-'nɪr-/ n [C;U] disease passed on by sexual activity

ve·ne·tian blind /vɪˌniːʃən 'blaɪnd/ n window covering with long flat bars that can be turned to let in or shut out light

ven·geance /'vendʒəns/ n 1 [U] harm done in return for harm done to oneself: He took vengeance on his tormentors. 2 with a vengeance infml very greatly

venge·ful /'vendʒfəl/ adj esp. lit fiercely wishing to take vengeance —ly adv

ven·i·son /'venɪzən, -sən/ n [U] deer meat

ven·om /'venəm/ n 1 liquid poison produced by certain animals 2 great anger or hatred ~ous adj: a venomous snake/look

vent¹ /vent/ n 1 opening or pipe by which gas, smoke, etc. escape 2 give vent to express freely: giving vent to his anger

vent² v vent on phr vt express by making (someone or something) suffer: venting her fury on the cat

ven·ti·late /'ventɪleɪt‖-tl-eɪt/ vt let or bring fresh air into (a room, building, etc.) –lator n 1 apparatus for ventilating 2 apparatus for pumping air into and out of the lungs of someone who cannot breathe properly –lation /ˌventɪ'leɪʃən‖-tl'eɪ-/ n [U]

ven·tri·cle /'ventrɪkəl/ n space in the bottom of the heart that pushes blood out into the body

ven·tril·o·quist /ven'trɪləkwɪst/ n someone who can make their voice seem to come from someone or somewhere else –quism n [U]

ven·ture /'ventʃə‖-ər/ v 1 vi risk going: She ventured too near the cliff edge, and fell over. 2 vt fml dare to say ♦ n (new and risky) course of action: her latest commercial venture

venture cap·i·tal /'··ˌ···/ n [U] money lent to start up a new business company, esp. a risky one

ven·ture·some /'ventʃəsəm‖-tʃər-/ adj lit or AmE ready to take risks

ven·ue /'venjuː/ n place arranged for something to happen

Ve·nus /'viːnəs/ n the PLANET second in order from the sun

ve·rac·i·ty /və'ræsɨti/ n [U] fml truthfulness

ve·ran·da, -dah /və'rændə/ n open area with a floor and roof beside a house

verb /vɜːb‖vɜːrb/ n word or group of words that is used in describing an action, experience, or state, such as wrote in She wrote a letter, was in He put on his coat

verb·al /'vɜːbəl‖'vɜːr-/ adj 1 spoken, not written 2 of words and their use 3 of a verb ~ly adv in spoken words

verb·al·ize also -ise BrE /'vɜːbəlaɪz‖ 'vɜːr-/ vi/t express (something) in words

verbal noun /ˌ·· '·/ n noun describing an action, formed by adding -ing to the verb: In the sentence 'The building of the bridge was slow work', 'building' is a verbal noun.

ver·ba·tim /vɜː'beɪtɨm‖vɜːr-/ adv, adj repeating the actual words exactly

ver·bi·age /'vɜːbi-ɪdʒ‖'vɜːr-/ n [U] fml too many unnecessary words

ver·bose /vɜː'bəʊs‖vɜːr'boʊs/ adj fml using too many words –bosity /-'bɒsɨti‖ -'bɑː-/ n [U]

ver·dant /'vɜːdənt‖'vɜːr-/ adj lit green with growing plants

ver·dict /'vɜːdɪkt‖'vɜːr-/ n 1 decision made by a JURY at the end of a trial about whether the prisoner is guilty 2 judgment; opinion

verge¹ /vɜːdʒ‖vɜːrdʒ/ n 1 edge, esp. of a path or road 2 **on the verge of** nearly; about to

verge² v verge on phr vt be near to: dark grey, verging on black

ver·ger /'vɜːdʒə‖'vɜːrdʒər/ n person who looks after the inside of a church

ver·i·fy /'verɨfaɪ/ vt make certain that (something) is true –fiable adj –fication /ˌverɨfɨ'keɪʃən/ n [U]

ver·i·ta·ble /'verɨtəbəl/ adj fml (used to give force to an expression) real: a veritable feast –bly adv

ver·min /'vɜːmɨn‖'vɜːr-/ n [P] 1 insects and small animals that do damage 2 people who are a trouble to society

ver·mouth /'vɜːməθ‖vər'muːθ/ n [U] drink made from wine with strong-tasting substances added

ver·nac·u·lar /və'nækjɨlə‖vər'nækjɨlər/ adj, n (in or being) the language spoken in a particular place

ver·sa·tile /'vɜːsətaɪl‖'vɜːrsɨtl/ adj that can do many different things or has many uses –tility /ˌvɜːsə'tɪlɨti‖ˌvɜːr-/ n [U]

verse /vɜːs‖vɜːrs/ n 1 [U] writing in the form of poetry, esp. with RHYMES —see also BLANK VERSE, FREE VERSE 2 [C] single division of a poem 3 [C] short numbered group of sentences in the Bible or other holy book

versed /vɜːst‖vɜːrst/ adj fml experienced; skilled: thoroughly versed in the arts of diplomacy

ver·sion /'vɜːʃən‖'vɜːrʒən/ n 1 form of something that is slightly different from others of the same sort: This dress is a cheaper version of the one we saw in the other shop. 2 one person's account of an event: The two eyewitnesses gave different versions of the accident.

ver·sus /'vɜːsəs‖'vɜːr-/ prep in competition with; against

ver·te·bra /'vɜːtɨbrə‖'vɜːr-/ n -brae /-briː, -breɪ/ small bone in the BACKBONE

ver·te·brate /'vɜːtɨbrɨt, -breɪt‖'vɜːr-/ n animal with a BACKBONE

ver·ti·cal /'vɜːtɪkəl‖'vɜːr-/ adj forming a 90° angle with the ground or bottom; upright ~ly /-kli/ adv

ver·ti·go /'vɜːtɪgəʊ‖'vɜːrtɪgoʊ/ n [U] unpleasant feeling of unsteadiness at great heights

verve /vɜːv‖vɜːrv/ n [U] forcefulness and eager enjoyment

ve·ry /'veri/ adv 1 to a great degree: a very exciting book 2 in the greatest possible degree: I did my very best to help. 3 **very good** (used as a respectful form of agreement) of course 4 **very well** (used as a (form of agreement, often with some degree of unwillingness) ♦ adj 1 (used for giving force to an expression): actual: He died in that very bed. 2 **the very idea!** (used for expressing surprise at something said by someone else)

ves·pers /'vespəz‖-ərz/ n [P;U] church service in the evening

ves·sel /'vesəl/ n 1 ship or large boat 2 (round) container, esp. for liquids 3 tube that carries liquid through a body or plant

vest¹ /vest/ n 1 BrE undergarment for the

upper body **2** *AmE for* WAISTCOAT

vest² /vest/ v vest in/with *phr vt fml* give the legal right to possess or use (power, property, etc.) to (someone)

vested in·terest /ˌ·· ˈ··/ n a personal reason for doing something, because one gains advantage from it

ves·ti·bule /ˈvestɨbjuːl/ n *fml* **1** room or passage through which larger rooms are reached **2** *AmE* enclosed passage at each end of a railway carriage which connects it with the next carriage

ves·tige /ˈvestɪdʒ/ n **1** (small) remaining part: *the last vestiges of royal power* **2** slightest bit: *not a vestige of truth*

vest·ment /ˈvestmənt/ n (priest's) ceremonial garment

ves·try /ˈvestri/ n room in a church for esp. changing into vestments

vet /vet/ n animal doctor ♦ vt **-tt-** examine carefully for correctness, past record, etc.

vet·er·an /ˈvetərən/ n, adj **1** (person) with long service or (former) experience, esp. as a soldier **2** (thing) that has grown old with long use: *a veteran car* (=one built before 1905)

vet·er·i·na·ry /ˈvetərɨnəri ‖ -neri/ adj of the medical care of animals: *veterinary surgeon*

ve·to /ˈviːtəʊ ‖ -toʊ/ vt **-toed;** *pres. p.* **-toing** officially refuse to allow ♦ n vetoes [C;U] (act of) vetoing

vex /veks/ vt *fml* displease; trouble ~**ation** /vekˈseɪʃən/ n [C;U]

vexed ques·tion /ˌ· ˈ··/ n matter that causes fierce argument and is difficult to decide

vi·a /vaɪə ‖ ˈviːə/ prep travelling through

vi·a·ble /ˈvaɪəbəl/ adj able to succeed in actual use: *an economically viable plan* **-bility** /ˌvaɪəˈbɪlɨti/ n [U]

vi·a·duct /ˈvaɪədʌkt/ n high bridge across a valley

Vi·a·gra /vaɪˈægrə/ *tdmk* n [U] drug used to treat men who cannot have sex

vi·al /ˈvaɪəl/ n PHIAL

vi·brant /ˈvaɪbrənt/ adj **1** powerful and exciting **2** (of colour or light) bright and strong ~**ly** adv **vibrancy** n [U]

vi·brate /vaɪˈbreɪt ‖ ˈvaɪbreɪt/ vi/t (cause to) move with a short continuous shake **vibration** /vaɪˈbreɪʃən/ n [C;U]

vic·ar /ˈvɪkə ‖ -ər/ n priest in charge of an

area (PARISH)

vic·ar·age /ˈvɪkərɪdʒ/ n vicar's house

vi·car·i·ous /vɪˈkeəriəs ‖ vaɪˈker-/ adj experienced indirectly, by watching, reading, etc.: *vicarious pleasure* ~**ly** adv

vice¹ /vaɪs/ n [C;U] **1** (kind of) evil behaviour or living: *She was arrested by the vice squad for prostitution.* **2 a** fault of character: *Laziness is his one vice.* **b** bad habit: *Smoking is my only vice.*

vice² *BrE* n tool with metal jaws for holding things firmly

vice-chan·cel·lor /ˌ· ˈ··/ n (in Britain) head of a university

vice·roy /ˈvaɪsrɔɪ/ n person ruling as a representative of a king or queen

vice ver·sa /ˌvaɪs ˈvɜːsə, ˌvaɪsɪ- ‖ -ɜːr-/ adv the opposite way around

vi·cin·i·ty /vɨˈsɪnɨti/ n [U] area nearby

vi·cious /ˈvɪʃəs/ adj **1** showing an unpleasant desire to hurt: *a vicious kick* **2** dangerous: *a vicious-looking knife* ~**ly** adv

vicious cir·cle /ˌ·· ˈ··/ n situation in which unpleasant causes and effects lead back to the original starting point

vic·tim /ˈvɪktɨm/ n one who suffers as the result of something: *the murderer's victim* (=the person he killed) ‖ *the victims of the plane crash* **-ize, -ise** vt cause to suffer unfairly **-ization, -isation** /ˌvɪktɨmaɪˈzeɪʃən ‖ -mə-/ n [U]

vic·tor /ˈvɪktə ‖ -ər/ n *fml or lit* winner

Vic·to·ri·an /vɪkˈtɔːriən/ adj **1** of the time when Queen Victoria ruled Britain (1837–1901) **2** very respectable (esp. in matters of sex)

vic·to·ry /ˈvɪktəri/ n [C;U] winning: *her victory in the election/golf tournament* **-torious** /vɪkˈtɔːriəs/ adj **1** that has won: *the victorious team* **2** showing victory: *a victorious shout*

vid·e·o /ˈvɪdiəʊ ‖ -dioʊ/ adj for (recording and) showing pictures on television ♦ n **-os 1** [C;U] videotape recording **2** [C] machine for making and showing these ♦ vt **-oed;** *pres. p.* **-oing** videotape

video game /ˈ··· ˌ·/ n game in which images are moved on a screen using electronic controls

vid·e·o·re·cord·er /ˈvɪdiəʊrɪˌkɔːdə ‖ -dioʊrɪˌkɔːrdər/ n VIDEO (2)

vid·e·o·tape /ˈvɪdiəʊteɪp ‖ -dioʊ-/ n [C;U] band of MAGNETIC material on which moving pictures are recorded ♦ *vt* record on videotape

vie /vai/ *vi* vied; *pres. p.* **vying** compete

view /vjuː/ *n* **1** [C;U] what one can see: *The train came into view round the corner.* | *You get a beautiful view of the sea from this window.* **2** [C] opinion: *In my view, he's a fool.* **3 in view of** taking into consideration: *In view of the unusual circumstances, we'll cancel it.* **4 on view** being shown to the public **5 with a view to** with the intention of ♦ *vt* **1** consider; regard: *I view the matter very seriously.* **2** examine by looking **3** watch television ~**er** *n* person watching television

view·find·er /'vjuː,faɪndə‖-ər/ *n* apparatus on a camera showing a small picture of what is to be photographed

view·point /'vjuːpɔɪnt/ *n* POINT OF VIEW

vig·il /'vɪdʒɪl/ *n* act of staying (awake and) watchful for some purpose

vig·i·lance /'vɪdʒɪləns/ *n* [U] watchful care –**lant** *adj fml* always prepared for possible danger –**lantly** *adv*

vigilance com·mit·tee /'·· ·,··/ *n AmE* group of vigilantes

vig·i·lan·te /,vɪdʒɪ'lænti/ *n sometimes derog* person who tries by unofficial means to punish crime: *vigilantes on the New York subway*

vig·our *BrE* ‖ **-or** *AmE* /'vɪgə‖-ər/ *n* [U] active strength or force –**orous** *adj* –**orously** *adv*

Vi·king /'vaɪkɪŋ/ *n* Scandinavian attacker (and settler) in northern and western Europe from the 8th to the 10th centuries

vile /vaɪl/ *adj* **1** *fml* low, shameful, and worthless: *a vile slander* **2** extremely unpleasant: *vile food* ~**ly** /'vaɪl-li/ *adv*

vil·i·fy /'vɪlɪfaɪ/ *vt fml* say unfairly bad things about –**fication** /,vɪlɪfɪ'keɪʃən/ *n* [C;U]

vil·la /'vɪlə/ *n* **1** house in a holiday area, esp. which one can hire **2** large ancient Roman country house

vil·lage /'vɪlɪdʒ/ *n* collection of houses, shops, etc. in a country area, smaller than a town –**lager** *n* person who lives in a village

vil·lain /'vɪlən/ *n* **1** (esp. in stories) bad person **2** *BrE infml* criminal **3 the villain of the piece** *infml* person or thing to be blamed –**ous** *adj* causing great harm; evil

vin·ai·grette /,vɪnɪ'gret, ,vɪneɪ-/ *n* [U] mixture of oil, VINEGAR, etc. put on SALADs

vin·di·cate /'vɪndɪkeɪt/ *vt* **1** free from blame **2** prove (something that was in doubt) to be right –**cation** /,vɪndɪ'keɪʃən/ *n* [S;U]

vin·dic·tive /vɪn'dɪktɪv/ *adj* wishing to harm someone who has harmed you ~**ly** *adv* ~**ness** *n* [U]

vine /vaɪn/ *n* climbing plant, esp. one that produces GRAPEs

vin·e·gar /'vɪnɪgə‖-ər/ *n* [U] acid-tasting liquid used in preparing food ~**y** *adj*

vine·yard /'vɪnjəd‖-jərd/ *n* piece of land with vines for making wine

vin·tage /'vɪntɪdʒ/ *n* particular year in which a wine is made ♦ *adj* **1** of the best quality **2** *BrE* (of a car) made between 1919 and 1930

vi·nyl /'vaɪnɪl/ *n* [U] firm bendable plastic

vi·o·la /vi'əʊlə‖-'oʊlə/ *n* musical instrument like a large VIOLIN

vi·o·late /'vaɪəleɪt/ *vt* **1** act against (something solemnly promised or officially agreed): *violate a treaty* **2** *fml* come violently into (and spoil) **3** have sex (with a woman) by force –**lation** /,vaɪə'leɪʃən/ *n* [C;U]

vi·o·lent /'vaɪələnt/ *adj* using, showing, or produced by great damaging force: *He became violent and began to hit her.* | *a violent storm* | *a violent death* ~**ly** *adv* –**lence** *n* [U] **1** extreme (and damaging) force **2** use of force to hurt people

vi·o·let /'vaɪələt/ *n* small plant with sweet-smelling purple flowers —see also SHRINKING VIOLET

vi·o·lin /,vaɪə'lɪn/ *n* small four-stringed wooden musical instrument played by drawing a BOW² (2) across the strings —**ist** *n*

VIP /,viː aɪ 'piː/ *n* person of great influence or fame

vi·per /'vaɪpə‖-ər/ *n* small poisonous snake

vir·gin /'vɜːdʒɪn‖'vɜːr-/ *n* person who has not had sex ♦ *adj* unused; unspoiled ~**al** *adj* VIRGINlike ~**ity** /vɜː'dʒɪnəti‖vɜːr-/ *n* [U] state of being a VIRGIN

vir·ile /'vɪraɪl‖'vɪrəl/ *adj* having the strong and forceful qualities expected of a man, esp. in matters of sex –**ility** /və'rɪləti/ *n* [U]

vir·tu·al /'vɜːtʃuəl‖'vɜːr-/ *adj* **1** almost

or unofficially the stated thing: *Though her husband was king, she was the virtual ruler of the country.* 2 using VIRTUAL REALITY ~ly *adv* almost; very nearly

virtual re·al·i·ty /,⋯ ⋅⋯/ *n* [U] environment produced by a computer, which surrounds the person looking at it and seems almost real

vir·tue /'vɜːtʃuː‖'vɜːr-/ *n* 1 [U] *fml* condition of being morally good 2 [C] morally good quality, such as truthfulness or loyalty 3 [C;U] advantage: *The plan's great virtue is its simplicity.* 4 **by virtue of** as a result of; by means of –**tuous** *adj* morally good

vir·tu·o·so /,vɜːtʃu'əʊzəʊ‖,vɜːrtʃu 'oʊsoʊ/ *n* -si extremely skilled (musical) performer –**osity** /-'ɒsəti‖-'ɑːs-/ *n* [U] virtuoso's skill

vir·u·lent /'vɪrʊlənt/ *adj* 1 (of a poison, disease, etc.) very powerful and dangerous 2 *fml* full of bitter hatred: *virulent abuse* ~ly *adv* –**lence** *n* [U]

vi·rus /'vaɪərəs‖'vaɪr-/ *n* 1 extremely small living thing that causes infectious disease: *the flu virus* 2 instructions secretly put into a computer to destroy information stored in it **viral** *adj*

vi·sa /'viːzə/ *n* official mark put on a PASSPORT to allow someone to enter or leave a particular country

vis·age /'vɪzɪdʒ/ *n lit* face

vis-à-vis /,viːz ɑː 'viː, ,viːz ə 'viː/ *prep fml* with regard to

vis·count /'vaɪkaʊnt/ *n* British nobleman between an EARL and a BARON in rank

vis·count·ess /'vaɪkaʊntɪs/ *n* the wife of a viscount, or a woman of the rank of viscount in her own right

vis·cous /'vɪskəs/ *adj* (of a liquid) thick and sticky –**cosity** /vɪs'kɒsəti‖-'kɑː-/ *n* [U]

vise /vaɪs/ *n AmE for* VICE²

vis·i·ble /'vɪzəbəl/ *adj* 1 that can be seen 2 noticeable –**bly** *adv* noticeably: *He was visibly shaken by the unpleasant experience.* –**bility** /,vɪzə'bɪləti/ *n* [U] 1 clearness with which things can be seen over a particular distance 2 ability to give a clear view

vi·sion /'vɪʒən/ *n* 1 [U] ability to see 2 [U] wise understanding of the future 3 [C] picture in the mind: *I had visions of missing* (=thought I might miss) *my plane.* 4 [C] something supposedly seen when in a

sleeplike state or as a religious experience

vi·sion·a·ry /'vɪʒənəri‖-neri/ *adj* 1 having VISION (2) 2 grand but impractical ♦ *n* visionary person

vis·it /'vɪzət/ *v* 1 *vi/t* go to and spend time in (a place) or with (a person): *We visited my sick uncle in hospital.* 2 *vt* go to (a place) to make an official examination 3 *vi AmE* stay ♦ *n* act or time of visiting: *We paid him a visit.* (=visited him) ~**or** *n*

visit on *phr vt* direct (anger, etc.) against

visit with *phr vt AmE* talk socially with

vi·sor /'vaɪzə‖-ər/ *n* face or eye protector on a hat or HELMET

vis·ta /'vɪstə/ *n* view stretching away into the distance

vi·su·al /'vɪʒuəl/ *adj* 1 of or done by seeing 2 having an effect on the sense of sight: *the visual arts* ~ly *adv* –**ize**, –**ise** *vt* imagine, esp. as if by seeing

vi·tal /'vaɪtl/ *adj* 1 extremely necessary or important 2 necessary to stay alive 3 full of life and force ~ly *adv* in the highest possible degree

vi·tal·i·ty /vaɪ'tæləti/ *n* [U] 1 cheerful forceful quality 2 ability to remain alive or effective

vital sta·tis·tics /,⋯ ⋅'⋯/ *n* [P] measurements round a woman's chest, waist, and HIPS

vit·a·min /'vɪtəmɪn, 'vaɪ-‖'vaɪ-/ *n* chemical substance found in certain foods and important for growth and good health: *Oranges contain vitamin C.*

vit·ri·ol /'vɪtriəl/ *n* [U] 1 extremely powerful acid 2 cruel wounding quality of speech and writing ~**ic** /,vɪtri'ɒlɪk◂‖-'ɑːl-/ *adj fml* fiercely cruel in speech or judgment

vi·tro /'viːtrəʊ‖-troʊ/ —see IN VITRO

vi·tu·pe·ra·tive /vɪ'tjuːpərətɪv‖vaɪ-'tuː-/ *adj fml* full of angry disapproval

vi·va·cious /və'veɪʃəs/ *adj* (esp. of a woman) full of life and fun ~ly *adv* –**city** /və'væsəti/ *n* [U]

viv·id /'vɪvəd/ *adj* 1 (of light or colour) bright and strong 2 producing sharp clear pictures in the mind: *a vivid description* ~ly *adv*

viv·i·sec·tion /,vɪvə'sekʃən/ *n* [U] performing of operations on animals to test medical treatments, new products, etc.

vix·en /'vɪksən/ *n* female fox

V-neck /'vi: nek/ n V-shaped neck opening of a dress, shirt, etc.

vo·cab·u·la·ry /və'kæbjŝləri, vəʊ- ‖ -leri, -voʊ-/ n 1 [C;U] words known, learnt, used, etc.: *a child's limited vocabulary* 2 [C] short list of words with their meanings

vo·cal /'vəʊkəl ‖ 'voʊ-/ adj 1 of or produced by the voice: *vocal music* 2 expressing one's opinion loudly ~**ly** adv ~**ist** n singer

vocal cords /'·· ·, ·· '·/ n [P] muscles in the throat that produce sounds when air passes through them

vo·ca·tion /vəʊ'keɪʃən ‖ voʊ-/ n 1 [S] particular fitness or ability for a certain worthy kind of work, such as being a nurse 2 [C] job, esp. one which you do because you have a vocation ~**al** adj of or for a job: *vocational training*

vo·cif·er·ous /və'sɪfərəs, vəʊ- ‖ voʊ-/ adj fml expressing oneself forcefully or noisily ~**ly** adv

vod·ka /'vɒdkə ‖ 'vɑːdkə/ n [U] strong colourless Russian alcoholic drink

vogue /vəʊg ‖ voʊg/ n [C;U] popular fashion: *Short skirts were in vogue then.* ♦ adj popular at present: *vogue words*

voice /vɔɪs/ n 1 [C;U] sound(s) produced in speaking or singing: *a loud/kind voice* | *She shouted at the top of her voice.* (=very loudly) 2 [C] ability to produce such sounds: *She's lost her voice.* 3 [S;U] right to express oneself: *I have no voice in* (=influence over) *the decision.* ♦ vt express in words, esp. forcefully: *voicing their opinions*

voice·mail /'vɔɪsmeɪl/ n [U] system that records telephone messages

voice-o·ver /'· ··/ n voice of an unseen person on a film or television show

void /vɔɪd/ n empty space ♦ adj law having no value or effect ♦ vt make void

vol·a·tile /'vɒlətaɪl ‖ 'vɑːlətl̩/ adj 1 quickly changing, esp. easily becoming angry or dangerous 2 (of a liquid) easily changing into gas –**tility** /,vɒlə'tɪlŝti ‖ ,vɑː-/ n [U]

vol-au-vent /,vɒl əʊ 'vɒn ‖ ,vɒl oʊ 'vɑːn/ n small pastry case filled with meat, vegetables, etc.

vol·ca·no /vɒl'keɪnəʊ ‖ vɑːl'keɪnoʊ/ n -noes or -nos mountain which sometimes throws out hot gases and melted rock

–**canic** /-'kænɪk/ adj 1 of a volcano 2 violently forceful

vole /vəʊl ‖ voʊl/ n small mouselike animal

vo·li·tion /və'lɪʃən ‖ voʊ-, və-/ n of one's own volition fml because one wishes, not because told to by someone else

vol·ley /'vɒli ‖ 'vɑːli/ n 1 many shots fired together: (fig.) *a volley of blows/curses* 2 kicking or hitting of a ball before it has hit the ground ♦ v 1 vi (of guns) be fired together 2 vi/t hit or kick (as) a VOLLEY (2)

vol·ley·ball /'vɒlibɔːl ‖ 'vɑːlibɔːl/ n [U] team game played by hitting a large ball across a net with the hands

volt /vəʊlt ‖ voʊlt/ n unit of electrical force ~**age** n [C;U] electrical force measured in volts

vol·u·ble /'vɒljŝbəl ‖ 'vɑː-/ adj fml talking a lot –**bly** adv –**bility** /,vɒljŝ'bɪlŝti ‖ ,vɑː-/ n [U]

vol·ume /'vɒljuːm ‖ 'vɑːljəm/ n 1 [U] (degree of) loudness of sound: *Turn down the volume on the TV.* 2 [U] size of something measured by multiplying its length by its height by its width 3 [C] any of a set of books: *volume 9 of the encyclopedia* 4 [C;U] amount: *the increasing volume of passenger traffic* 5 speak volumes (for something) show or express (something) very clearly or fully

vo·lu·mi·nous /və'luːmŝnəs, və'ljuː- ‖ və'luː-/ adj fml 1 filling or containing a lot of space: *a voluminous skirt/suitcase* 2 producing or containing (too) much writing

vol·un·ta·ry /'vɒləntəri ‖ 'vɑːlənteri/ adj acting or done willingly, without being forced –**arily** adv

vol·un·teer /,vɒlən'tɪə ‖ ,vɑːlən'tɪr/ n person who has volunteered ♦ v 1 vi/t offer to do something without payment or reward, or without being forced: *Jenny volunteered to clear up afterwards.* 2 vt tell without being asked: *He volunteered a statement to the police.*

vo·lup·tu·ous /və'lʌptʃuəs/ adj 1 suggesting or expressing sexual pleasure 2 giving a fine delight to the senses

vom·it /'vɒmŝt ‖ 'vɑː-/ vi throw up (the contents of the stomach) through the mouth ♦ n [U] swallowed food thrown back up through the mouth

voo·doo /'vu:du:/ n [U] set of magical religious practices in esp. Haiti

vo·ra·cious /və'reɪʃəs, vɒ-‖ vɔ:-, və-/ adj eating or wanting a lot of food: (fig.) a voracious reader (=who reads a lot) ~ly adv ~city /və'ræsɪti/ n [U]

vor·tex /'vɔ:teks‖ 'vɔ:r-/ n -texes or -tices /-tɪsi:z/ 1 powerful circular moving mass of water or wind 2 lit situation that makes one powerless: sucked into the vortex of war

vote /vəʊt‖ voʊt/ v 1 vi express one's choice officially, esp. by marking a piece of paper or raising one's hand: Which candidate will you vote for at the election? | As we can't reach an agreement, let's vote on it. 2 vt agree, by a vote, to provide (something) 3 vt infml agree as the general opinion: I vote we leave now. ♦ n 1 [C;U] (choice or decision made by) voting: I shall cast my vote for Tom Smith. | Let's put the matter to a vote. 2 [U] number of such choices made by or for a particular person or group: an increase in the Liberal vote 3 [U] right to vote in political elections voter n

vouch /vaʊtʃ/ v **vouch for** phr vt state one's firm belief in the good qualities of, based on experience

vouch·er /'vaʊtʃə‖ -ər/ n 1 BrE ticket usable instead of money 2 official paper given to prove that money has been paid

vouch·safe /vaʊtʃ'seɪf/ vt lit give, say, or do as a favour

vow /vaʊ/ vt, n (make) a solemn promise or declaration of intention: He vowed he would never steal again.

vow·el /'vaʊəl/ n speech sound made without closing the air passage in the mouth or throat: In English, vowels are represented by the letters a, e, i, o, u.

voy·age /'vɔɪ-ɪdʒ/ n long journey by ship ♦ vi lit make a voyage ~ager n

voy·eur /vwɑː'jɜː‖ -'jɜːr/ n person who gets sexual excitement by (secretly) watching others have sex ~ism n [U]

vs abbrev. for: VERSUS

vul·can·ize, -ise /'vʌlkənaɪz/ vt strengthen (rubber) by chemical treatment

vul·gar /'vʌlgə‖ -ər/ adj 1 very rude or bad-mannered 2 showing bad judgment in matters of beauty, style, etc. ~ly adv ~ity /vʌl'gærɪti/ n [U]

vul·ne·ra·ble /'vʌlnərəbəl/ adj 1 easy to attack 2 (of a person) easily harmed: sensitive ~bility /ˌvʌlnərə'bɪlɪti/ n [U]

vul·ture /'vʌltʃə‖ -ər/ n 1 large tropical bird which feeds on dead animals 2 person who has no mercy and who uses people

vy·ing /'vaɪ-ɪŋ/ pres. p. of VIE

W

W, w /'dʌbəlju:/ the 23rd letter of the English alphabet

W written abbrev. for: 1 west(ern) 2 WATT

wack·y /'wæki/ adj silly -iness n [U]

wad /wɒd‖ wɑːd/ n 1 many thin things pressed or folded thickly together: a wad of bank notes 2 small thick soft mass: a wad of cotton wool

wad·ding /'wɒdɪŋ‖ 'wɑː-/ n [U] soft material used esp. for packing or in medicine

wad·dle /'wɒdl‖ 'wɑːdl/ vi walk like a duck

wade /weɪd/ vi/t walk through (water) **wader** n 1 bird that wades to find its food 2 either of a pair of high rubber boots to protect the legs while wading

wade into phr vt begin (to attack) forcefully and with determination

wade through phr vt do or complete (something long or dull) with an effort

wadge /wɒdʒ‖ wɑːdʒ/ n BrE infml for WAD (1)

wa·fer /'weɪfə‖ -ər/ n 1 thin BISCUIT 2 thin round piece of special bread used in the Christian ceremony of COMMUNION

wafer-thin /ˌ·· '·◂/ adj extremely thin

waf·fle¹ /'wɒfəl‖ 'wɑː-/ n light sweet cake marked with raised squares

waffle² vi BrE infml talk or write meaninglessly and at great length **waffle** n [U]

waft /wɑːft, wɒft‖ wɑːft, wæft/ vi/t move lightly (as if) on wind or waves

wag[1] /wæg/ *vi/t* **-gg-** shake (esp. a body part) or be shaken from side to side: *The dog wagged its tail.* **wag** *n*

wag[2] *n infml* amusing man

wage /weidʒ/ *vt* carry on (a war)

wage freeze /ˈ· ·/ *n* attempt, esp. by government, to keep pay from rising

wa·ger /ˈweidʒə‖-ər/ *n, vi fml for* BET

wag·es /ˈweidʒiz/ *n* [P] *also* **wage** [S] — payment for work done: *He gets his wages every Friday.* | *a wage rise*

wag·gle /ˈwægəl/ *vi/t* move quickly from side to side

wag·on *also* **waggon** *BrE* /ˈwægən/ *n* 1 strong usu. horse-drawn goods vehicle 2 *BrE* railway goods vehicle 3 *esp. AmE* TROLLEY: *a drinks wagon* 4 **on the wagon** no longer willing to drink alcohol

waif /weif/ *n esp. lit* uncared-for or homeless child or animal

wail /weil/ *vi, n* (make) a long cry (as if) in grief or pain

wain·scot /ˈweinskət, -skɒt‖-skət, -skɑːt/ *n* SKIRTING BOARD

waist /weist/ *n* 1 narrow part of the human body below the chest 2 narrow part of a garment or apparatus

waist·band /ˈweistbænd/ *n* strengthened part of trousers, a skirt, etc. that fastens round the waist

waist·coat /ˈweiskəut, ˈweskət‖ˈweskət/ *n esp. BrE* garment without arms worn under a JACKET

waist·line /ˈweistlain/ *n* (length or height of) an imaginary line round the waist: (fig.) *No sugar for me – I'm watching my waistline.* (=trying not to become fatter)

wait /weit/ *v* 1 *vi* do nothing in the expectation of something happening: *I had to wait two hours for the bus!* | *Are you waiting to use the phone?* 2 *vt* not act until: *You'll have to wait your turn.* 3 *vi* remain unspoken, unheard, etc.: *My news can wait till later.* 4 **wait and see** delay an action or decision until the future becomes clearer 5 **wait at table** serve meals, esp. as a regular job ♦ *n* [S] act or period of waiting **-er, ~ress** /-trɪs/ *fem.* — *n* someone who serves food to people

wait on *phr vt* 1 serve food, esp. in a restaurant 2 **wait on someone hand and foot** serve someone very humbly

waiting list /ˈ·· ·/ *n* list of people who will be dealt with later

waiting room /ˈ·· ·/ *n* room at a station, doctor's office, etc. where people wait

waive /weiv/ *vt fml* state that (a rule, claim, etc.) is no longer in effect **waiver** *n* written statement waiving a right, etc.

wake[1] /weik/ *vi/t* **woke** /wəuk‖wouk/ *or* **waked, woken** /ˈwəukən‖ˈwou-/ *or* **waked** (cause) to stop sleeping: *I woke up late.* **~ful** *adj* sleepless **waking** *adj* of the time when one is awake: *all my waking hours*

wake[2] *n* 1 track left by a ship: (fig.) *The car left clouds of dust in its wake.* 2 **in the wake of** as a result of: *war, with hunger and disease in its wake*

wake[3] *n* gathering to grieve over a dead person

wak·en /ˈweikən/ *vi/t fml* wake

walk /wɔːk‖wɔːk/ *v* 1 *vi* move slowly on foot so that at least one foot is always touching the ground 2 *vt* walk along: *He'd walked the streets looking for work.* 3 *vt* go with on foot: *I'll walk you to the bus stop.* 4 *vt* take (an animal) for a walk ♦ *n* 1 [C] (short) journey on foot: *Let's go for a walk.* | *The station's just a 5-minute walk from here.* 2 [S] way of walking 3 [C] place, path, or course for walking **-er** *n*

walk into *phr vt* 1 get caught by (something) through carelessness 2 get (a job) very easily

walk off/away with *phr vt* 1 steal and take away 2 win easily

walk out *phr vi* 1 leave suddenly and disapprovingly 2 go on STRIKE[2] (1)

walk out on *phr vt* leave suddenly

walk over *phr vt* treat badly

walk·ie-talk·ie /ˌwɔːki ˈtɔːki‖ˌwɔːki ˈtɔːki/ *n* radio for talking as well as listening, that can be carried

walking stick /ˈ·· ·/ *n* stick for support while walking

walk·man /ˈwɔːkmən‖ˈwɒk-/ *n tdmk for* PERSONAL STEREO

walk of life /ˌ· · ˈ·/ *n* position in society, esp. one's job

walk-on /ˈ· ·/ *n, adj* small usu. non-speaking (part in a play)

walk·out /ˈwɔːk-aut‖ˈwɒk-/ *n* 1 action of disapprovingly leaving a meeting, organization, etc. 2 STRIKE[2] (1)

walk·o·ver /ˈwɔːkˌəuvə‖ˈwɔːkˌouvər/

n easy victory

wall /wɔːl ‖ wɒːl/ *n* 1 upright surface, esp. of brick or stone, for enclosing something: *the garden wall* ‖ (fig.) *a wall of flames* 2 side of a room or building: *pictures hanging on the wall* 3 enclosing or inside surface: *the walls of a blood vessel* 4 **bang one's head against a (brick) wall** *infml* try to do the impossible 5 **go to the wall** (esp. in business) be ruined 6 **go up the wall** *infml* get very angry ~**ed** *adj* surrounded with a wall

wall off *phr vt* separate with a wall

wall up *phr vt* close or enclose with a wall

wal·la·by /'wɒləbi ‖ 'wɑː-/ *n* small KANGAROOlike animal

wal·let /'wɒlɪt ‖ 'wɑː-/ *n* small flat case for papers and paper money

wall·flow·er /'wɔːlˌflaʊə ‖ 'wɒːlˌflaʊr/ *n* 1 garden plant with sweet-smelling flowers 2 person who gets left out of social activity

wal·lop /'wɒləp ‖ 'wɑː-/ *vt, n infml* (hit with) a powerful blow

wal·low /'wɒləʊ ‖ 'wɑːloʊ/ *vi* move, roll, or lie about happily in deep mud, water, etc.: *wallowing in a hot bath* ‖ (fig.) *in self-pity*

wall·pa·per /'wɔːlˌpeɪpə ‖ 'wɒːlˌpeɪpɔr/ *n* [U] decorative paper (for) covering the walls of a room ♦ *vt* cover the walls of (a room) with wallpaper

Wall Street /'· ·/ *n* centre of the American business and money world, in New York

wall-to-wall /ˌ· · '·◄/ *adj* covering the whole floor: (fig.) *wall-to-wall advertising*

wal·nut /'wɔːlnʌt ‖ 'wɒːl-/ *n* 1 [C] eatable brain-shaped nut 2 [U] wood from its tree, used for furniture

wal·rus /'wɔːlrəs ‖ 'wɒːl-, 'wɑːl-/ *n* -ruses *or* -rus large sea animal with two very long downward-pointing teeth

waltz /wɔːls ‖ wɒːlts/ *vi, n* (do) a rather slow dance for a man and a woman

wan /wɒn ‖ wɑːn/ *adj esp. lit* weak and tired

wand /wɒnd ‖ wɑːnd/ *n* stick used by someone doing magic tricks

wan·der /'wɒndə ‖ 'wɑːndər/ *v* 1 *vi/t* move about without a fixed course or purpose: *the wandering tribes of the Sahara.* ‖ (fig.) *The discussion seems to have wandered from its main point.* 2 *vi* be or become confused and unable to make or

follow ordinary conversation ~**er** *n* ~**ings** *n* [P] long travels

wan·der·lust /'wɒndəlʌst ‖ 'wɑːndər-/ *n* [S;U] strong desire to travel to faraway places

wane /weɪn/ *vi* get gradually smaller ♦ *n* **on the wane** becoming smaller or weaker

wan·gle /'wæŋgəl/ *vt infml* get by a trick

wank /wæŋk/ *vi BrE taboo sl for* MASTURBATE ~**er** *n* fool

wan·na·be /'wɒnəbi ‖ 'wɑː-/ *n infml* someone who wants to be (like) a particular person

want /wɒnt ‖ wɒːnt, wɑːnt/ *vi* 1 have a strong desire for: *I don't want to go.* 2 wish the presence of: *Your mother wants you.* 3 wish to find; hunt: *He's wanted by the police for murder.* 4 *infml* need: *The house wants painting.* 5 *fml* lack: *to be found wanting* (=not considered good, strong, etc. enough) ♦ *n* 1 [C;U] lack: *The plants died for/from want of water.* 2 [U] severe lack of things necessary for life ~**ing** *adj fml* 1 lacking 2 not good enough

want for *phr vt fml* lack: *The children want for nothing.*

wan·ton /'wɒntən ‖ 'wɒn-, 'wɑːn-/ *adj fml* 1 (of something bad) having no just cause: *wanton disregard of the rules* 2 (esp. of a woman) sexually improper

war /wɔː ‖ wɔːr/ *n* [C;U] 1 (example or period of) armed fighting between nations: *The two countries are at war.* ‖ *The Second World War* ‖ (fig.) *waging a war against poverty and ignorance* 2 **in the wars** *infml* having been hurt or damaged ~**ring** *adj* fighting (each other)

war·ble /'wɔːbəl ‖ 'wɔːr-/ *vi* (esp. of a bird) sing with a continuous varied note ~**bler** *n* any of various songbirds

war clouds /'· ·/ *n lit* [P] signs that a war is getting likelier

war crime /'· ·/ *n* illegal act done while fighting a war

ward¹ /wɔːd ‖ wɔːrd/ *n* 1 large room in a hospital 2 political division of a city 3 person legally protected by another: *The children were made wards of court.*

ward² *v* **ward off** *phr vt* keep away (something bad)

war·den /'wɔːdn ‖ 'wɔːrdn/ *n* person in charge of a place or people

ward·er /'wɔːdə ‖ 'wɔːrdər/ *n BrE* prison

guard

war·drobe /'wɔːdrəʊb ‖ 'wɔːrdroʊb/ *n*
1 large cupboard for clothes 2 person's
collection of clothes

ware·house /'weəhaʊs ‖ 'wer-/ *n* large
building for storing things

wares /weəz ‖ werz/ *n* [P] *esp. lit* things
for sale

war·fare /'wɔːfeə ‖ 'wɔːrfer/ *n* [U] war

war game /'· ‚·/ *n* pretended battle to test
military plans

war·head /'wɔːhed ‖ 'wɔːr-/ *n* explosive
front end of a MISSILE

war·like /'wɔːlaɪk ‖ 'wɔːr-/ *adj* fierce;
liking to fight

war·lock /'wɔːlɒk ‖ 'wɔːrlɑːk/ *n* male
WITCH

warm¹ /wɔːm ‖ wɔːrm/ *adj* 1 having
enough heat or pleasant heat: *a warm bath*
2 able to keep one warm: *warm clothes*
3 showing strong good feelings: *a warm
welcome* 4 seeming cheerful or friendly:
warm colours

warm² *vi/t* make or become warm ~**ly** *adv*

warm to *phr vt* 1 begin to like 2 become
interested in

warm up *phr vi/t* prepare for action or
performance by exercise or operation in
advance **warm-up** *n*

war·mon·ger /'wɔː‚mʌŋgə ‖ 'wɔːr-
‚mɑːŋgər, -‚mʌŋ-/ *n derog* person who
wants war

warmth /wɔːmθ ‖ wɔːrmθ/ *n* [U] being
warm

warn /wɔːn ‖ wɔːrn/ *v* 1 *vi/t* tell of
something bad that may happen, or of how
to prevent it 2 *vt* give knowledge of some
future need or action: *We warned them we'd
be away.* ~**ing** *n* [C;U] 1 telling in advance:
They attacked without warning. 2 something that warns: *That's the second warning
we've had.* —see also EARLY WARNING SYSTEM

warp /wɔːp ‖ wɔːrp/ *vi/t* turn or twist out
of shape: *a warped plank*/(fig.) *mind* ♦ *n*
1 warped place 2 threads running along the
length of cloth

war·path /'wɔːpɑːθ ‖ 'wɔːrpæθ/ *n* **on the
warpath** angry and looking for someone to
fight or punish

war·rant /'wɒrənt ‖ 'wɔː-, 'wɑː-/ *n* 1 [C]
official paper allowing something: *The
police have a warrant for her arrest.* 2 [U]
fml proper reason for action ♦ *vt* 1 cause to

seem right or reasonable 2 promise (that
something is so)

warrant of·fic·er /'·· ‚·‚·/ *n* one just
below an officer in rank

war·ran·ty /'wɒrənti ‖ 'wɔː-, 'wɑː-/ *n*
written GUARANTEE

war·ren /'wɒrən ‖ 'wɔː-, 'wɑː-/ *n* 1 area
where rabbits live 2 **rabbit warren** place
where one can easily get lost

war·ri·or /'wɒriə ‖ 'wɔːriər, 'wɑː-/ *n lit*
soldier

war·ship /'wɔː‚ʃɪp ‖ 'wɔːr-/ *n* naval ship
used for war

wart /wɔːt ‖ wɔːrt/ *n* small hard swelling
on the skin

wart·hog /'wɔːthɒg ‖ 'wɔːrthɔːg, -hɑːg/
n African wild pig

war·time /'wɔːtaɪm ‖ 'wɔːr-/ *n* [U] period
during which a war is going on

war-torn /'wɔːtɔːn ‖ 'wɔːrtɔːrn/ *adj*
badly affected by a war

war·y /'weəri ‖ 'weri/ *adj* careful; looking
out for danger –**ily** *adv*

was /wəz; *strong* wɒz ‖ wəz; *strong* wɑːz/
v 1st and 3rd person sing. past t. of BE

wash /wɒʃ ‖ wɒːʃ, wɑːʃ/ *v* 1 *vt* clean with
liquid 2 *vi* be able to be cleaned with liquid
without damage: *This shirt doesn't wash
well.* 3 *vi* wash oneself 4 *vt* carry by the
force of moving water: *crops washed away
by the floods* 5 *vi/t esp. lit* flow (against or
over) continually 6 *vi* be (easily) believed:
His story won't wash. 7 **wash one's dirty
linen (in public)** make public unpleasant
subjects which ought to be kept private
8 **wash one's hands of** refuse to have
anything more to do with or to accept
responsibility for ♦ *n* 1 [S] act of washing
2 [U] things to be washed 3 [S;U] movement
of water caused by a passing boat 4 **come
out in the wash** *infml* a (of something
shameful) become known b turn out all
right in the end 5 **in the wash** being
washed ~**able** *adj* ~**ing** [U] clothes that are
to be washed or have just been washed

wash down *phr vt* 1 clean with a lot of
water 2 swallow with the help of liquid

wash out *phr vt* 1 cause to wash free of
an unwanted substance 2 destroy or
prevent by the action of water, esp. rain

wash up *phr v* 1 *vi BrE* wash dishes.
knives. etc. after a meal 2 *vt* (of the sea)
bring in to the shore 3 *vi AmE for* WASH (3)

wash·ba·sin /'wɒʃˌbeɪsən ‖ 'wɔː ʃ-, 'wɑː ʃ-/ *BrE* ‖ **wash·bowl** /-ˌbəʊl ‖ -ˌboʊl/ *AmE* — n fixed basin for washing hands and face

washed-out /ˌ· '·◂/ adj 1 faded 2 very tired 3 prevented because of rain: *The match was washed-out.*

washed-up /ˌ· '·◂/ adj *infml* with no further possibilities of success

wash·er /'wɒʃə ‖ 'wɔː ʃər, 'wɑː-/ n ring of metal, plastic, etc. for making a joint tight under a screw, between two pipes, etc.

washing ma·chine /'···ˌ·/ n machine for washing clothes

washing-up /ˌ· '·/ n [U] *BrE* dishes, knives, etc. (to be) washed after a meal

wash·out /'wɒʃ-aʊt ‖ 'wɔː ʃ-, 'wɑː ʃ-/ n failure

wash·room /'wɒʃrʊm, -ruːm ‖ 'wɔː ʃ-, 'wɑː ʃ-/ n *AmE for* TOILET (1)

wasn't /'wɒzənt ‖ 'wɑː-/ *short for:* was not

wasp /wɒsp ‖ wɑːsp, wɔːsp/ n black and yellow beelike insect ~**ish** adj sharply bad-tempered and cruel ~**ishness** n [U]

WASP *also* **Wasp** /wɒsp ‖ wɑːsp, wɔːsp/ n *esp. AmE abbrev. for:* White Anglo-Saxon Protestant; a white American, esp. considered as a member of the social class with money and power

wast·age /'weɪstɪdʒ/ n [S;U] 1 wasteful loss 2 reduction in numbers

waste[1] /weɪst/ n 1 [S;U] loss through wrong use or less than full use: *a waste of time* | *Don't let it go to waste.* (=be wasted) 2 [U] used or unwanted matter: *industrial/bodily waste* 3 [U] wide empty lonely stretch of water or land ♦ adj 1 (of ground) empty and unused 2 got rid of as used or useless: *waste paper/products* ~**ful** adj tending to waste things ~**fully** adv

waste[2] vt use wrongly or not at all: *wasting his money on silly things*

waste away phr vi become weaker and thinner, usu. because of illness

waste·pa·per bas·ket /ˌweɪst'peɪpə ˌbɑːskɪt, 'weɪstˌpeɪpə- ‖ 'weɪstˌpeɪpər ˌbæ-/ ‖ *also* **waste·bas·ket** /'weɪstˌbɑːskɪt ‖ -ˌbæ-/ *esp. AmE* — n small container for throwing away unwanted paper, etc.

watch /wɒtʃ ‖ wɑːtʃ, wɔːtʃ/ v 1 *vi/t* look (at) attentively: *Watch me and you'll see how it's done.* 2 vt be careful about: *Watch what you're doing with that knife!* 3 **watch it!** be careful 4 **watch one's step** act with great care 5 **watch the clock** be waiting for one's working day to end rather than thinking about one's work ♦ n 1 [C] small clock worn esp. on the wrist 2 [S;U] act of watching: *The police are keeping (a) watch on their activities.* 3 [C;U] period of duty on a ship ~**er** n ~**ful** adj careful to notice things

watch for phr vt look for; expect and wait for

watch out phr vi take care

watch out for phr vt 1 keep looking for 2 be careful of

watch over phr vt guard and protect; take care of

watch·dog /'wɒtʃdɒg ‖ 'wɑːtʃdɔːg, 'wɔːtʃ-/ n 1 dog kept to guard property 2 person or group that tries to prevent loss, waste, or undesirable practices

watch·word /'wɒtʃwɜːd ‖ 'wɑːtʃwɜːrd, 'wɔːtʃ-/ n word or phrase expressing a guiding principle

wa·ter /'wɔːtə ‖ 'wɔːtər, 'wɑː-/ n [U] 1 liquid found as rain, in the sea, etc. and commonly drunk 2 a mass of this: *She dived into the water.* | *After the flood the fields were under water.* | *The goods came by water.* (=by boat) 3 **above water** out of difficulty: *keep one's head above water* (=keep oneself out of difficulty) 4 **hold water** be true or reasonable: *Your story doesn't hold water.* 5 **like water** in great quantity: *The wine flowed like water* 6 **make/pass water** URINATE 7 **throw cold water on** point out difficulties in (a plan, idea, etc.)—see also HOT WATER ♦ v 1 vt pour water on (a plant or area) 2 vt supply (esp. animals) with water 3 vi (of the mouth or eyes) form or let out watery liquid **waters** n [P] 1 sea near or round a country: *in Icelandic waters* 2 water of the stated river, lake, etc. ~**y** adj 1 containing too much water 2 very pale

water down phr vt 1 weaken by adding water 2 reduce the force of: *a watered-down report*

water can·non /'·· ˌ·/ n apparatus for shooting out a powerful stream of water, esp. for controlling crowds

wa·ter·col·our /'wɔːtəˌkʌlə ‖ 'wɔːtər-ˌkʌlər, 'wɑː-/ n 1 [C;U] paint mixed with water rather than oil **2** [C] picture painted with this

wa·ter·cress /'wɔːtəkres ‖ 'wɒːtər-, 'wɑː-/ n [U] water plant with leaves used as food

wa·ter·fall /'wɔːtəfɔːl ‖ 'wɒːtərfɒːl, 'wɑː-/ n very steep fall of water in a river, etc.

wa·ter·front /'wɔːtəfrʌnt ‖ 'wɒːtər-, 'wɑː-/ n land along a stretch of water, esp. in a port

wa·ter·hole /'wɔːtəhəʊl ‖ 'wɒːtərhoʊl, 'wɑː-/ n pool where animals come to drink

watering can /'··· ·/ n container for pouring water onto garden plants

water lev·el /'·· ,··/ n height to which a mass of water has risen or sunk

wa·ter·line /'wɔːtəlaɪn ‖ 'wɒːtər-, 'wɑː-/ n level reached by water up the side of a ship

wa·ter·logged /'wɔːtəlɒgd ‖ 'wɒːtərlɒːgd, 'wɑː-, -lɑːgd/ adj **1** (of ground) very wet **2** (of a boat) full of water

Wa·ter·loo /ˌwɔːtəˈluː ‖ ,wɒːtər-, ,wɑː-/ n (deserved) defeat after a time of unusual success

wa·ter·mark /'wɔːtəmɑːk ‖ 'wɒːtərmɑːrk, 'wɑː-/ n **1** partly transparent mark in paper **2** mark that shows a level reached: *the high watermark of her success*

wa·ter·mel·on /'wɔːtəˌmelən ‖ 'wɒːtər-, 'wɑː-/ n large round green fruit with juicy red flesh

wa·ter·mill /'wɔːtəˌmɪl ‖ 'wɒːtər-, 'wɑː-/ n MILL¹ (1) driven by moving water

water po·lo /'·· ,··/ n [U] game played by two teams of swimmers with a ball

wa·ter·proof /'wɔːtəpruːf ‖ 'wɒːtər-, 'wɑː-/ adj, n (an outer garment) which does not allow water, esp. rain, through ♦ vt make waterproof

wa·ter·shed /'wɔːtəʃed ‖ 'wɒːtər-, 'wɑː-/ n point of very important change

wa·ter·side /'wɔːtəsaɪd ‖ 'wɒːtər-, 'wɑː-/ n [U] edge of a river, lake, etc.

water ski·ing /'·· ,··/ n [U] sport of being pulled across water on SKIS **-er** n

water ta·ble /'·· ,··/ n level below which water can be found in the ground

wa·ter·tight /'wɔːtətaɪt ‖ 'wɒːtər-, 'wɑː-/ adj **1** which water cannot pass through **2** allowing or having no mistakes or possibility of doubt: *a watertight plan*

wa·ter·way /'wɔːtəweɪ ‖ 'wɒːtər-, 'wɑː-/

n stretch of water which ships travel along

wa·ter·wheel /'wɔːtəwiːl ‖ 'wɒːtər-, 'wɑː-/ n wheel which is turned by moving water, esp. to give power to machines

wa·ter·works /'wɔːtəwɜːks ‖ 'wɒːtərwɜːrks, 'wɑː-/ n **1** place from which a public water supply is provided **2** infml body's system for removing water from the body **3 turn on the waterworks** start to cry, esp. to get attention, or what one wants

watt /wɒt ‖ wɑːt/ n measure of electrical power **~age** n [U] electrical power

wat·tle /'wɒtl ‖ 'wɑːtl/ n [U] thin sticks woven over poles to form a fence or wall

wave /weɪv/ v **1** move (one's hand or something in it) as a signal: *We waved as the train pulled out.* **2** vt direct with a movement of the hand: *The policeman waved the traffic on.* **3** vi move gently from side to side in the air: *The flags waved.* **4** vi/t (cause to) curve regularly: *waved hair* ♦ n **1** raised moving area of water, esp. on the sea **2** movement of the hand in waving **3** feeling, way of behaving, etc. that suddenly starts and increases: *a wave of nausea | a crime wave* **4** form in which light, sound, etc. move: *radio waves* **5** evenly curved part of the hair **wavy** adj having regular curves

wave aside phr vt push aside without giving attention to (esp. ideas, etc.)

wave·length /'weɪvleŋθ/ n **1** distance between two WAVES (4) **2** radio signal sent out on radio WAVES that are a particular distance apart: (fig.) *We're on completely different wavelengths.* (=are completely different, cannot understand each other, etc.)

wa·ver /'weɪvə ‖ -ər/ vi be uncertain or unsteady in direction or decision: *Her loyalty never wavered.*

wax¹ /wæks/ n [U] solid meltable fatty or oily substance, esp. as used in candles or polish ♦ vt **1** put wax on **2** remove hair from (legs, etc.), using wax **~y** adj

wax² vi **1** (esp. of the moon) get gradually larger **2** lit (of a person) become: *He waxed eloquent as he described his plans.*

wax·works /'wækswɜːks ‖ -wɜːrks/ n **-works** (place with) models of people made in wax

way /weɪ/ n **1** [C] road, path, etc. to follow in order to reach a place: *She asked me the* *way to the station.* | *We lost our way.* **2** [C] direction: *He went that way.* **3** [S] distance: *We're a long way from home.* **4** [C] method: *Do it this way.* **5** [C] manner: *the cruel way in which he treats his animals* **6** [C] single part of a whole; detail; point: *In many ways I agree with you, but I don't think you're completely right.* **7 by the way** (used to introduce a new subject in speech) **8 by way of: a** by going through **b** as a sort of: *a few sandwiches by way of lunch* **9 get one's own way** do or get what one wants in spite of others **10 go one's own way** do what one wants **11 go out of the/one's way (to do)** take the trouble (to do); make a special effort **12 have a way with one** have an attractive quality which persuades others **13 have it both ways** gain advantage from 2 opposing opinions or actions **14 out of/in the way** (not) blocking space for forward movement: *You're in the way; move!* **15 make one's way** go **16 make way for** leave so as to allow to develop freely **17 no way** *infml* no: *'Will you help me?' 'No way!'* **18 out of the way** unusual or not commonly known **19 see one's way (clear) to (doing)** feel able to do **20 under way** moving forwards —see also **give way** (GIVE¹), RIGHT OF WAY ♦ *adv far: That's way outside my area.* **ways** *n* [P] customs; habits: *mend one's ways* (=improve one's manners, etc.)

way·far·er /'weɪˌfeərə ‖ -ˌferər/ *n lit* traveller

way·lay /weɪˈleɪ/ *vt* **-laid** /-ˈleɪd/, **-laid** /-ˈleɪn/ *or* **-laid 1** attack (a traveller) **2** find or stop (someone) to speak to them

way-out /ˌ·ˈ·◄/ *adj infml* strange; unusual

way·side /'weɪsaɪd/ *n* side of the road or path

way·ward /'weɪwəd ‖ -wərd/ *adj* **1** difficult to guide or control **2** not well aimed

WC /ˌdʌbəljuː ˈsiː/ *n* TOILET (1)

we /wi; *strong* wiː/ *pron* (used as the subject of a sentence) **1** the people speaking; oneself and one or more others **2** *fml* (used by a king or queen) I

weak /wiːk/ *adj* **1** having little power: *weak muscles/eyes* **2** easily becoming broken, changed, destroyed, or ill: *a weak heart* **3** having little taste: *weak tea* **4** unable to control people: *a weak teacher* **5** not reaching a good standard: *His maths is*

rather weak. **~ly** *adv* **~en** *vi/t* (cause to) become weaker **~ness** *n* **1** [U] fact or state of being weak **2** [C] part that spoils the rest: *The plan's only weakness is its cost.* **3** [C] fault in character **4** [C] strong liking: *a weakness for chocolate*

weak-kneed /ˌ·ˈ·◄/ *adj* cowardly

weak·ling /'wiːk-lɪŋ/ *n derog* weak person

weal /wiːl/ *n* mark on the skin where one has been hit

wealth /welθ/ *n* **1** [U] (large amount of) money and possessions **2** [S] *fml* large number: *a wealth of examples* **~y** *adj* rich

wean /wiːn/ *vt* gradually give (a baby) solid food instead of milk

wean off *phr vt* gradually give to stop doing or using

weap·on /'wepən/ *n* something to fight with, such as a gun or sword **~ry** *n* [U] weapons

wear /weə ‖ wer/ *v* **wore** /wɔː ‖ wɔːr/, **worn** /wɔːn ‖ wɔːrn/ **1** *vt* have (esp. clothes) on the body **2** *vt* have (a particular expression) on the face **3** *vi/t* (cause to) show the effects of continued use, rubbing, etc.: *You've worn a hole in your sock.* | (fig.) *That excuse is wearing thin.* (=becoming unbelievable) **4** *vi* last in the stated condition: *an old person who has worn well* **5** *vt infml* find acceptable ♦ *n* [U] **1** clothes: *evening wear* | *men's wear* **2** act of wearing esp. clothes **3** damage from use: *signs of wear* **4** quality of lasting in use: *There's a lot of wear in these shoes.*

wear down *phr vt* weaken

wear off *phr vi* (of a feeling, effect, etc.) become gradually less

wear on *phr vi* pass slowly in time

wear out *phr v* **1** *vi/t* (cause to) be reduced to nothing or a useless state by use **2** *vt* tire greatly

wear and tear /ˌ·ˈ·/ *n* [U] damage from use; WEAR (3)

wear·i·some /'wɪərɪsəm ‖ 'wɪr-/ *adj* tiring and boring (BORE²) or annoying

wear·y /'wɪərɪ ‖ 'wɪrɪ/ *adj* very tired **v** (cause to) become weary **-ily** *adv* **-iness** *n*

wea·sel¹ /'wiːzəl/ *n* small fierce furry animal

weasel² *v* weasel out *phr vi AmE infml* escape a duty by clever dishonest means

weath·er /'weðə ‖ -ər/ *n* [U] **1** particular

condition of wind, sunshine, rain, snow, etc.: *a day of fine weather* **2 make heavy weather** of make (something) seem difficult for oneself **3 under the weather** slightly ill ♦ *v* **1** *vt* pass safely through (a storm or difficulty) **2** *vi/t* change from the effects of air, rain, etc.: *weathered stone*

weather-beat·en /'·· ˌ·ˈ/ *adj* marked or damaged by the wind, sun, etc.

weather fore·cast /'·· ˌ·ˈ/ *n* description of weather conditions as they are expected to be ~**er** *n*

weath·er·man /'weðəmæn ‖ -ər-/ *n* -men /-men/ **weather girl** *fem.* — person who describes likely future weather conditions on television or radio

weather sta·tion /'·· ˌ·ˈ/ *n* place for noting weather conditions

weather vane /'·· ·ˈ/ *n* small apparatus that is blown round to show the direction of the wind

weave /wiːv/ *v* **wove** /wəʊv ‖ woʊv/, **woven** /'wəʊvən ‖ 'woʊ-/ **1** *vi/t* form threads into (material) by drawing them singly under and over a set of longer threads **2** *vt* twist; wind: *a bird's nest woven from straws* **3** *vt* produce (a story) esp. from a suggestion **4** (*past t. and p.* **weaved**) *vi* move twistingly: *The cyclist weaved through the traffic.* ♦ *n* style or pattern of woven material: *a loose weave* **weaver** *n*

web /web/ *n* **1** [C] net of thin threads made by a SPIDER: (fig.) *a web of lies* **2 the Web** the World Wide Web; system that connects computers around the world, so that people can use the INTERNET

webbed /webd/ *adj* having skin between the toes

web·site /'websaɪt/ *n* place on the INTERNET with information about a person, company, etc.

web·bing /'webɪŋ/ *n* [U] strong woven bands used for belts, supports, etc.

wed /wed/ *vi/t* **wedded** or **wed** *esp. lit* marry

we'd /wid; *strong* wiːd/ *short for:* **1** we had **2** we would

wed·ding /'wedɪŋ/ *n* marriage ceremony

wedding ring /'·· ·ˈ/ *n* ring worn to show that one is married

wedge /wedʒ/ *n* **1** V-shaped piece of wood, etc. for keeping something in place or splitting something **2** V-shaped piece: *a*

wedge of cake **3** something shaped like this: *shoes with wedge heels* —see also **thin end of the wedge** (THIN) ♦ *vt* fix firmly (as if) with a wedge: *Wedge the door open.* | *I got wedged between two people on the bus.*

wed·lock /'wedlɒk ‖ -lɑːk/ *n* [U] *lit* **in/out of wedlock** of married/unmarried parents

Wednes·day /'wenzdi/ *n* the third day of the week

wee /wiː/ *adj* very small

weed¹ /wiːd/ *n* **1** unwanted wild plant **2** physically weak person ~**y** *adj* **1** thin and weak **2** full of weeds

weed² *vi/t* remove weeds from (a garden)

weed out *phr vt* get rid of (less good ones)

week /wiːk/ *n* **1** period of seven days, usu. thought of as starting on Monday and ending on Sunday, but sometimes measured from Sunday to Saturday **2** period worked during a week: *a 35-hour week* **3 week after week** also **week in, week out** — continuously

week·day /'wiːkdeɪ/ *n* day other than Saturday or Sunday

week·end /ˌwiːk'end, 'wiːkend ‖ 'wiːkend/ *n* Saturday and Sunday

week·ly /'wiːkli/ *adj, adv* (happening) every week or once a week ♦ *n* magazine or newspaper which appears once a week

weep /wiːp/ *vi* **wept** /wept/ *fml or lit* cry ~**ing** *adj* (of a tree) with branches hanging down

wee·vil /'wiːvəl/ *n* small insect which eats (and spoils) grain, seeds, etc.

weft /weft/ *n* threads running across cloth

weigh /weɪ/ *v* **1** *vt* find the weight of: *weigh oneself* **2** *vi* have the stated weight: *It weighs 6 kilos.* **3** *vt* consider or compare carefully **4** *vt* raise (an ANCHOR)

weigh down *phr vt* make heavy with a load: (fig.) *weighed down with grief*

weigh in *phr vi* join in a fight or argument

weigh on *phr vt* worry: *His responsibilities weighed on him.*

weigh up *phr vt* form an opinion about, esp. by balancing opposing arguments

weigh·bridge /'weɪˌbrɪdʒ/ *n* machine for weighing vehicles and their loads

weight /weɪt/ *n* **1** [C;U] (measured) heaviness of something: *The weight of the* *sack is 2 kilos.* **2** [C] something heavy: *lifting weights* **3** [C] piece of metal of known heaviness, used for weighing things **4** [U] system of standard measures of heaviness: *metric weight* **5** [U] value; importance: *I don't attach much weight to these rumours.* **6** [C] (something that causes) a feeling of anxiety: *a great weight off my mind* **7 pull one's weight** do one's full share of work **8 put on/lose weight** (of a person) become heavier/lighter **9 throw one's weight about** give orders to others ♦ *vt* **1** make heavy, esp. by fastening weights **2** include conditions in (something) that give a (dis)advantage: *a competition weighted against younger children* ~**less** *adj*: *a weightless flight in space* ~**y** *adj* **1** heavy **2** *fml* important and serious

weight lift·ing /ˈ· ˌ··/ also **weight training** — *n* [U] sport of lifting heavy weights -**er** *n*

weir /wɪə ‖ wɪr/ *n* wall-like structure across a river controlling its flow

weird /wɪəd ‖ wɪrd/ *adj* **1** strange; unusual: *a weird shriek* **2** unusual and not sensible or acceptable: *weird ideas* ~**ly** *adv* ~**ness** *n* [U]

weird·o /ˈwɪədəʊ ‖ ˈwɪrdoʊ/ *n* -**os** *sl* strange person

wel·come /ˈwelkəm/ *interj* (a greeting to someone who has arrived) ♦ *vt* **1** greet (someone newly arrived), esp. with friendliness **2** wish to have; like: *I'd welcome some help.* ♦ *adj* **1** acceptable and wanted: *A cool drink is always welcome on a hot day.* **2** allowed freely (to have): *I've plenty of cigarettes; you're welcome to one.* **3 You're welcome** (a polite expression when thanked for something) ♦ *n* greeting

weld /weld/ *vt* join (metal) by melting ~**er** *n*

wel·fare /ˈwelfeə ‖ -fer/ *n* [U] **1** comfort, health, and happiness: *I was concerned for her welfare.* (=thought she might be in trouble) **2** help with living conditions, social problems, etc.

welfare state /ˌ·· ˈ·‖ˈ·· ˌ·/ *n* (country with) a system of social help for poor, sick, etc. people

well[1] /wel/ *adv* better /ˈbetə ‖ -ər/, best /best/ **1** in a good way: *She sings well.* | *a well-dressed man* **2** thoroughly: *They were well beaten.* **3** much; quite: *She finished well*

within the time allowed. **4** suitably: properly: *I couldn't very well refuse.* **5 as well: a** also: *She came as well.* **b** with a good result: *We might just as well have stayed at home.* **6 as well as** in addition to **7 come off well** be lucky in the end **8 do well** succeed or improve **9 do well out of** gain profit from **10 do well to** act wisely to **11 just as well** it is fortunate (that); there's no harm done **12 may well** could suitably **13 pretty well** almost **14 well and truly** completely **15 well away: a** getting ahead **b** *infml* starting to be drunk **16 Well done!** (said when someone has been successful) **17 well in with** having a good relationship **18 well out of** lucky enough to be free from (an affair) ♦ *adj* better, best **1** in good health **2** in an acceptable state **3 It's all very well** (an expression of dissatisfaction when comparing what is practical to what is suggested): *It's all very well for you to laugh but what was I supposed to do?* ♦ *interj* **1** (expresses surprise) **2** (introduces an expression of surprise, doubt, etc.)

well[2] *n* **1** place where water can be taken from underground **2** OIL WELL **3** deep narrow space inside a building, for stairs or a LIFT[2] (2) ♦ *vi* flow

we'll /wil; *strong* wiːl/ *short for:* **1** we will **2** we shall

well-ad·jus·ted /ˌ· ·'··◄/ *adj* (of a person) fitting in well with society

well-ad·vised /ˌ· ·'·◄/ *adj* sensible

well-ba·lanced /ˌ· '··◄/ *adj* **1** (of a person) sensible **2** (of a meal) containing everything necessary for good health

well-be·ing /ˌwelˈbiːɪŋ◄ ‖ ˈwelˌbiːɪŋ/ *n* [U] personal and physical comfort, esp. good health and happiness

well-bred /ˌ· '·◄/ *adj* having or showing high social rank, with good manners

well-con·nect·ed /ˌ· ·'··◄/ *adj* knowing or esp. related to people of high social rank or influence

well-done /ˌ· '·◄/ *adj* thoroughly cooked

well-groomed /ˌ· '·◄/ *adj* neat and clean

well-heeled /ˌ· '·◄/ *adj* *infml* rich

well·ly /ˈweli/ *n* *BrE* WATERPROOF boot

well-in·formed /ˌ· ·'·◄/ *adj* knowing a lot about several subjects or parts of a particular subject

wel·ling·ton /ˈwelɪŋtən/ *n* *BrE* WELLY

well-in·ten·tioned /ˌ· ·'··◄/ *adj* acting in

the hope of good results, though often failing

well-known /ˌ· ˈ·◄/ adj known by many people; famous

well-mean·ing /ˌ· ˈ··◄/ adj well-intentioned

well-nigh /ˈ· ·/ adv almost: well-nigh impossible

well-off /ˌ· ˈ·◄/ adj 1 rich 2 lucky

well-pre·served /ˌ· ·ˈ·◄/ adj still in good condition

well-read /ˌ· ˈ·◄/ adj having read many books and got a lot of information

well-spok·en /ˌ· ˈ··◄/ adj having a socially acceptable way of speaking

well-timed /ˌ· ˈ·◄/ adj said or done at the most suitable time

well-to-do /ˌ· · ˈ·◄/ adj rich

well-wish·er /ˈ· ˌ··/ n person who wishes another to succeed, have good luck, etc.

well-worn /ˌ· ˈ·◄/ adj (of a phrase) overused

welsh /welʃ/ vi derog avoid payment

Welsh adj of Wales

wel·ter /ˈweltə ‖ -ər/ n [S] confused mixture: a welter of statistics

wel·ter·weight /ˈweltəweɪt ‖ -ər-/ n boxer (BOX²) of middle weight

wench /wentʃ/ n lit young woman

wend /wend/ v wend one's way: a travel (slowly) b leave

went /went/ past t. of GO

wept /wept/ past t. and p. of WEEP

were /wə; strong wɜː ‖ wər; strong wɜːr/ v past t. of BE

we're /wɪə ‖ wɪr/ short for: we are

were·wolf /ˈweəwolf, ˈwɪə- ‖ ˈwer-, ˈwɪr-/ n (in stories) person who sometimes turns into a WOLF (1)

west /west/ n 1 (often cap.) direction towards which the sun sets 2 [the+S] (cap.) western Europe and the US ♦ adj 1 in the west 2 (of wind) from the west ♦ adv 1 towards the west 2 go west: a to die b be damaged or broken ~ward adj, adv

West End /ˌ· ˈ·◄/ n [the] western part of central London, where shops, theatres, etc. are

west·er·ly /ˈwestəli ‖ -ərli/ adj west

west·ern /ˈwestən ‖ -ərn/ adj of the west part of the world or of a country ♦ n story about life in the middle of the US in the past, with COWBOYS and gunfights ~er n

someone who lives in or comes from the WEST (2)

west·ern·ize also -ise BrE /ˈwestənaɪz ‖ -ər-/ vt cause to have or copy the customs typical of the western world (that is, America and Europe)

wet /wet/ adj -tt- 1 covered with or being liquid: wet grass/paint 2 rainy: a wet day 3 BrE weak in character and unable to get things done 4 **wet through** completely covered in or with liquid ♦ n 1 [the+S] rainy weather 2 [C] BrE infml MODERATE¹ (2) person in the British Conservative Party ♦ vt wet or wetted; pres. p. -tt- make wet ~ness n [U]

wet blan·ket /ˌ· ˈ··‖ ˌ· ˌ·-/ n person who discourages others or prevents them from enjoying themselves

wet dream /ˌ· ˈ·/ n sexually exciting dream resulting in a male ORGASM

wet-nurse /ˈ· ·/ vt treat with too much care

wet suit /ˈ· ·/ n rubber garment for keeping the body warm in sea sports

we've /wiv; strong wiːv/ short for: we have

whack /wæk/ vt hit with a noisy blow ♦ n 1 (noise of) a hard blow 2 BrE infml (fair) share ~ed adj BrE infml very tired ~ing adj, adv infml very big

whale /weɪl/ n 1 extremely large fishlike animal 2 **a whale of a time** a very enjoyable time **whaler** n a person who hunts whales b ship from which whales are hunted **whaling** n [U] hunting whales

wham /wæm/ n (sound of) a hard blow

wharf /wɔːf ‖ wɔːrf/ n wharfs or wharves /wɔːvz ‖ wɔːrvz/ place where ships are tied up to unload and load goods

what /wɒt ‖ wɑːt, wʌt/ predeterminer, determiner, pron 1 (used in questions about an unknown thing or person): What are you doing? | What colour is it? 2 the thing(s) that: He told me what to do. 3 (shows surprise): What a strange hat! 4 **what for?** why? 5 **what if?** what will happen if? 6 **what's more** and this is more important 7 **what's what** the true state of things: to know what's what ♦ adv 1 (used esp. in questions when no answer is expected) in what way: What do you care? (=I don't think you care at all) 2 **what with** (used for introducing the cause of something, esp. something bad)

what·ev·er /wɒt'evə ‖ wɑːt'evər, wʌt-/ *determiner, pron* **1** no matter what: *Whatever I said, he'd disagree.* **2** anything: *They eat whatever they can find.* **3** (shows surprise) what: *Whatever is that peculiar thing?* ♦ *adj* at all: *I have no money whatever.*

what·not /'wɒtnɒt ‖ 'wɑːtnɑːt, ,wʌt-/ *n* [U] *infml* anything (else): *carrying his bags and whatnot*

wheat /wiːt/ *n* [U] (plant producing) grain from which flour is made

whee·dle /'wiːdl/ *vi/t* try to persuade (someone) by pleasant but insincere words

wheel /wiːl/ *n* **1** circular frame which turns to allow vehicles to move, to work machinery, etc. **2** movement by which a group of marching soldiers curve to the left or right **3** [*the+S*] the STEERING WHEEL of a car or ship **4 at the wheel: a** driving or guiding a car or ship **5 wheels within wheels** hidden influences having effects on surface behaviour ♦ *v* **1** *vt* move (a wheeled object) with the hands **2** *vi* turn round suddenly **3** *vi* (of birds) fly round and round in circles **4 wheel and deal** *vi infml* make deals, esp. in business or politics, in a skilful and perhaps dishonest way ~**ed** *adj* having wheels

wheel·bar·row /'wiːl,bærəʊ ‖ -roʊ/ *n* small one-wheeled cart pushed by hand

wheel·chair /'wiːltʃeə ‖ -tʃer/ *n* wheeled chair for someone who cannot walk

wheel·clamp /'wiːlklæmp/ *n BrE* equipment fixed to the wheel of an illegally parked car, so that it cannot be moved ♦ *vt*

wheeler-deal·er /,·· '·-/ *n* someone skilled at doing clever (but perhaps not always honest) deals, esp. in business or politics

wheel·ie /'wiːli/ *n* act of riding a bicycle on its back wheel

wheeze /wiːz/ *vi* make a noisy whistling sound in breathing ♦ *n* **1** wheezing sound **2** *infml* joke or clever trick **wheezy** *adj*

whelk /welk/ *n* sea animal that lives in a shell

whelp /welp/ *n* esp. *lit derog* young animal, esp. a dog

when /wen/ *adv, conj* **1** at what time; at the time that: *When will they come?* | *He looked up when she came in.* **2** considering that; although: *Why did you do it when I told you*

not to?

whence /wens/ *adv, conj lit* from where

when·ev·er /wen'evə ‖ -ər/ *adv, conj* **1** at whatever time **2** every time

where /weə ‖ wer/ *adv, conj* at or to what place; at or to the place that: *Where do you live?* | *Sit where you like.*

where·a·bouts /,weərə'baʊts◂ ‖ 'werə-baʊts/ *adv* where in general (not exactly): *Whereabouts did I leave my glasses?* ♦ *n* [U] place where a person or thing is

where·as /weər'æz ‖ wer-/ *conj* (shows an opposite) but: *They live in a house, whereas we have a flat.*

where·by /weə'baɪ ‖ wer-/ *adj fml* by means of which

where·fore /'weəfɔː ‖ 'werfɔːr/ *adv, conj lit* why

where·u·pon /,weərə'pɒn ‖ 'werəpɑːn, -pɔːn/ *conj* without delay after and because of which: *He stood up to speak, whereupon everyone cheered.*

wher·ev·er /weər'evə ‖ wer'evər/ *adv* **1** to or at whatever place **2** (shows surprise) where

where·with·al /'weəwɪðɔːl ‖ 'werwɪðɔːl/ *n* [U] enough money

whet /wet/ *vt* **-tt- whet someone's appetite** make someone wish for more

wheth·er /'weðə ‖ -ər/ *conj* if … or not: *I'm trying to decide whether to go.*

whey /weɪ/ *n* [U] watery part of milk

which /wɪtʃ/ *determiner, pron* **1** (used in questions, when a choice is to be made): *Which shoes shall I wear, the red ones or the brown?* **2** (shows what thing is meant): *This is the book which I told you about.* **3** (used to add more information about something): *The train, which only takes an hour, is quicker than the bus.* —see also EVERY WHICH WAY

which·ev·er /wɪtʃ'evə ‖ -ər/ *determiner, pron* **1** only (one) of the set that: *Take whichever seat you like.* **2** no matter which: *It has the same result, whichever way you do it.*

whiff /wɪf/ *n* [S] **1** short-lasting smell of something **2** a breath in: *A few whiffs of gas and she'll fall asleep.*

while¹ /waɪl/ *n* [S] **1** length of time: *He's been gone quite a while.* (=a fairly long time) **2 once in a while** sometimes, but not often **3 worth one's/someone's while** WORTH-

WHILE to one/someone: *We'll make it worth your while.* (=pay you) ♦ *conj* **1** during the time that: *They arrived while we were having dinner.* **2** although: *While I agree with your reasons, I can't allow it.* **3** WHEREAS **4** and what is more

while² *v* **while away** *phr vt* pass (time) in a pleasantly lazy way

whilst /waɪlst/ *conj* while

whim /wɪm/ *n* sudden (often unreasonable) idea or wish

whim·per /'wɪmpə‖-ər/ *vi* make small weak trembling cries **whimper** *n*

whim·sy /'wɪmzi/ *n* [U] strange humour –sical *adj* fanciful; with strange ideas

whine /waɪn/ *vi* **1** make a high sad sound **2** complain (too much) in an unnecessarily sad voice **whine** *n*: *the whine of the jet engines*

whinge /wɪndʒ/ *vi derog* complain, esp. of unfair treatment

whin·ny /'wɪni/ *vi* make a gentle sound which horses make

whip¹ /wɪp/ *n* **1** long piece of esp. rope or leather on a handle, used for striking sharp blows **2** *esp. BrE* (person who gives) an order to a member of Parliament to attend and vote

whip² *v* **-pp-** **1** *vt* hit with a whip **2** *vi/t* move quickly: *He whipped out his gun.* **3** *vt* beat (esp. cream or eggs) until stiff **4** *vt infml* defeat **5** *vt BrE infml* steal ~**ping** *n* beating as a punishment

    whip up *phr vt* **1** cause (feelings) to become stronger, etc. **2** make quickly

whip hand /'· ·/ *n* [U] control

whip·lash /'wɪp-læʃ/ *n* **1** blow from a whip **2** harm done by sudden violent movement of the head and neck, as in a car accident: *a whiplash injury*

whip·ping boy /'·· ·/ *n* person who (unfairly) gets the blame and/or punishment

whip-round /'· ·/ *n esp. BrE* collection of money within a group

whirl /wɜːl‖wɜːrl/ *vi/t* move round and round very fast ♦ *n* **1** [S] act or sensation of whirling: (fig.) *My head's in a whirl.* (=confused) **2** [C] very fast (confused) movement or activity **3** **give something a whirl** *infml* try something

whirl·pool /'wɜːlpuːl‖'wɜːrl-/ *n* fast circular current of water

whirl·wind /'wɜːl‖wɪnd‖'wɜːrl-/ *n* tall tube of air moving dangerously at high speed: (fig.) *a whirlwind romance* (=happening very quickly)

whirr /wɜː‖wɜːr/ *vi, n* (make) the regular sound of something turning and beating against the air

whisk /wɪsk/ *vt* **1** remove, either by quick light brushing or by taking suddenly: *She whisked my cup away before I'd finished.* **2** beat (esp. eggs), esp. with a whisk ♦ *n* small hand-held apparatus for beating eggs, cream, etc.

whis·ker /'wɪskə‖-ər/ *n* **1** long stiff hair near an animal's mouth **whiskers** *n* [P] hair on the sides of a man's face

whis·key /'wɪski/ *n* [U] Irish or US whisky

whis·ky /'wɪski/ *n* [U] strong alcoholic drink made from grain, esp. in Scotland

whis·per /'wɪspə‖-ər/ *v* **1** *vi/t* speak or say very quietly **2** *vt* suggest or pass (information) secretly: *It's whispered he may resign.* ♦ *n* **1** very quiet voice **2** RUMOUR

whist /wɪst/ *n* [U] card game for four players

whis·tle /'wɪsəl/ *n* **1** simple (musical) instrument played by blowing **2** high sound made by air blowing through a narrow opening ♦ *v* **1** *vi* make a WHISTLE (2), esp. by blowing through the lips: (fig.) *The wind whistled round us.* **2** *vt* produce (a tune) by doing this

white /waɪt/ *adj* **1** of the colour of snow and milk **2** pale **3** of a pale-skinned race **4** (of coffee) without milk or cream ♦ *n* **1** [U] white colour **2** [C] WHITE (3) person **3** [C] part of an egg surrounding the central yellow part **whiten** *vi/t* (cause to) become white(r)

white-col·lar /ˌ· '··◄/ *adj* of or being office workers, indoor workers, etc.

white el·e·phant /ˌ· '···/ *n* useless article

white flag /ˌ· '·/ *n* sign that one accepts defeat

White·hall /'waɪthɔːl, ˌwaɪt'hɔːl‖-hɔːl/ *n* [U] **1** (street in London containing many of the offices of the British government **2** the British Government

white heat /ˌ· '·/ *n* [U] temperature at which metal turns white

White House /'· ·/ *n* [the+S] official Washington home of the US president

white knight /ˌ· '·/ n person or organization that puts money into a business company to save it from being taken over by another company

white lie /ˌ· '·/ n harmless lie

white meat /ˌ· ·/ n [U] meat such as chicken that looks pale after it has been cooked

white pa·per /ˌ· '··/ n official British government report explaining what the government intends to do

white·wash /ˈwaɪtwɒʃ‖-wɒːʃ, -wɑːʃ/ n 1 [U] white liquid for covering walls 2 [C;U] derog attempt to hide something wrong 3 [C] complete defeat ♦ vt 1 cover with WHITEWASH (1) 2 make (what is bad) seem good

whith·er /ˈwɪðə‖-ər/ adv lit to which place

Whit·sun /ˈwɪtsən/ n (period around) the seventh Sunday after Easter

whit·tle /ˈwɪtl/ vt cut thin pieces off (wood): (fig.) We've whittled the list of candidates down (=reduced it) to five.

whizz, whiz /wɪz/ vi -zz- move very fast (and noisily) ♦ n 1 [S] whizzing sound 2 [C] infml someone who is very fast, clever, or skilled in the stated activity

whizz kid /ˈ· ·/ n person who makes successes in life

who /huː/ pron (used esp. as the subject of a sentence) 1 what person?: Who said that? 2 (shows what person is meant): the people who live in that house 3 (adds more information about a person): This is my father, who lives in Glasgow.

whoa /wəʊ, həʊ‖ woʊ, hoʊ/ interj (call to a horse to stop)

who·dun·it, whodunnit /ˌhuːˈdʌnɪt/ n story, film, etc. about a crime mystery

who·ev·er /huːˈevə‖-ər/ pron 1 anyone at all: I'll take whoever wants to go. 2 no matter who: Whoever it is, I don't want to see them. 3 (shows surprise) who: Whoever can that be at the door?

whole /həʊl‖ hoʊl/ adj 1 all; complete: I spent the whole day in bed. | She swallowed it whole. (=not divided up) 2 **swallow something whole** accept something without questioning it ♦ n 1 complete amount, thing, etc. 2 **on the whole** generally; mostly **wholly** /ˈhəʊl-li‖ ˈhoʊl-/ adv: not wholly to blame

whole·food /ˈhəʊlfuːd‖ ˈhoʊl-/ n [C;U] food in a simple natural form

whole-heart·ed /ˌ· '··◄/ adj with all one's ability, interest, etc.; full: whole-hearted support

whole·meal /ˈhəʊlmiːl‖ ˈhoʊl-/ adj (made from flour) without the grain-covering removed

whole·sale /ˈhəʊlseɪl‖ ˈhoʊl-/ adj, adv 1 sold in large quantities to shopkeepers (rather than directly to customers) 2 usu. derog very great or complete: wholesale slaughter –**saler** n seller of goods wholesale

whole·some /ˈhəʊlsəm‖ ˈhoʊl-/ adj 1 good for the body: wholesome food 2 having a good moral effect ~**ness** n [U]

whom /huːm/ pron fml (object form of who): We have 200 members, most of whom are men.

whoop /wuːp, huːp/ vi 1 make a loud cry, as of joy 2 **whoop it up** infml enjoy oneself a lot ♦ n a loud shout of joy

whoop·ing cough /ˈhuːpɪŋ kɒf‖-kɒːf/ n [U] (children's) disease with attacks of serious coughing and difficult breathing

whoops /wʊps/ interj (said when one has made a mistake)

whoosh /wʊʃ‖ wuːʃ/ vi, n (move quickly with) a rushing sound

whop·per /ˈwɒpə‖ ˈwɑːpər/ n infml 1 big thing 2 big lie –**ping** adj, adv very (big): a whopping (great) bonus

whore /hɔː‖ hɔːr/ n lit or derog for PROSTITUTE

whorl /wɜːl‖ wɔːrl/ n shape of a line curving outwards from a centre

whose /huːz/ determiner, pron of whom: Whose car is that? (=who does it belong to?) | That's the man whose house burnt down.

why /waɪ/ adv, conj 1 for what reason: Why did you do it? 2 the reason why: Is that why you did it? 3 **why not** (used in suggestions): Why not sell it? (=I suggest you sell it) ♦ n **the whys and wherefores (of)** reasons (for)

wick /wɪk/ n burning thread in a candle or lamp

wick·ed /ˈwɪkɪd/ adj 1 morally bad; evil 2 playfully bad: a wicked twinkle in his eye ~**ly** adv ~**ness** n [U]

wick·er·work /ˈwɪkəwɜːk‖ ˈwɪkər-wɜːrk/ n [U] (objects made from) woven

CANES, sticks, etc. *adj* also **wicker** /ˈwɪkə‖ -ər/ — made of wickerwork: *wicker baskets*

wicket /ˈwɪkɪt/ *n* 1 set of three sticks (STUMPS[1] (3)) at which the ball is aimed in cricket 2 stretch of grass on which cricket is played

wide /waɪd/ *adj* 1 large from side to side: *The car's too wide to go through the gate.* 2 covering a large range: *wide experience* ♦ *adv* 1 completely (open or awake) 2 (in sport) away from the correct or central point 3 **wide of the mark** not suitable, correct, etc. at all ~**ly** *adv* over a wide range: *It's widely believed* (=believed by many people) *that the government will lose the election.* **widen** *vi/t* make or become wider

wide boy /ˈ· ·/ *n BrE infml* cleverly dishonest person, esp. a businessman

wide-eyed /ˌ· ˈ·◄/ *adj* 1 with eyes very fully open 2 accepting or admiring things too easily

wide·screen /ˈwaɪdskriːn/ *adj* of or for the cinema: *the widescreen version of the film*

wide·spread /ˈwaɪdspred/ *adj* common

wid·ow /ˈwɪdəʊ‖-doʊ/ *n* woman whose husband has died

wi·dowed /ˈwɪdəʊd‖-doʊd/ *adj* whose wife or husband has died

wid·ow·er /ˈwɪdəʊə‖-doʊər/ *n* man whose wife has died

width /wɪdθ/ *n* [C;U] size from side to side

wield /wiːld/ *vt* have and/or use (power, influence, etc.)

wife /waɪf/ *n* **wives** /waɪvz/ woman to whom a man is married

wig /wɪg/ *n* covering of false hair for the head

wig·gle /ˈwɪgəl/ *vi/t* move with quick small movements: *He wiggled his toes.*

wig·wam /ˈwɪgwæm‖-wɑːm/ *n* Native American tent

wild /waɪld/ *adj* 1 **a** living in natural conditions, not changed by human beings: *wild animals* **b** (of people) not civilized 2 uncontrollably violent 3 showing very strong feelings, esp. of anger 4 showing lack of thought or control: *a wild guess/throw* 5 *infml* having a very eager liking: *He's wild about football.* 6 *infml* good ♦ *n* [U] natural areas full of animals and plants, with few people ♦ *adv* 1 **go wild** be

filled with feeling, esp. anger or joy 2 **run wild** behave as one likes, without control ~**ly** *adv*: *wildly* (=too greatly) *optimistic*

wil·de·beest /ˈwɪldəbiːst/ *n* large African animal with a hairy neck and curved horns

wil·der·ness /ˈwɪldənɪs‖-dər-/ *n* 1 unchanging stretch of land, etc. with no sign of human presence 2 **into the wilderness** (sent) out of political life, esp. for doing wrong

wild·fire /ˈwaɪldfaɪə‖-faɪr/ *n* **like wildfire** very quickly

wild·fowl /ˈwaɪldfaʊl/ *n* [P] (water) birds shot for sport

wild-goose chase /ˌ· ˈ· ·/ *n* useless search for something that cannot be found

wild·life /ˈwaɪldlaɪf/ *n* [U] animals living in natural conditions

wild oats /ˌ· ˈ·/ *n* **sow one's wild oats** behave wildly, esp. having many sexual partners while young

wiles /waɪlz/ *n* [P] tricks; deceitful persuading

wil·ful *BrE* ‖ **willful** *AmE* /ˈwɪlfəl/ *adj* 1 doing what one wants in spite of other people 2 (of something bad) done on purpose ~**ly** *adv* ~**ness** *n* [U]

will[1] /wɪl/ *v aux 3rd person sing.* **will**, *pres. t. negative short form* **won't** 1 (expresses the future tense): *Will it rain tomorrow?* 2 be willing to: *I won't go!* 3 (used in requests): *Shut the door, will you?* 4 (shows what always happens): *Oil will float on water.* 5 (used like **can** to show what is possible): *This car will hold five people.* 6 (used like **must** to show what is likely): *That will be the postman at the door now.*

will[2] *n* 1 [C;U] power of the mind to make decisions and act in accordance with them: *You need a strong will to give up smoking.* —see also FREE WILL 2 [U] what someone wishes or intends: *She was forced to sign a confession against her will.* 3 [U] stated feelings towards someone: *I bear you no ill will.* 4 [S] force and interest: *They set to work with a will.* 5 [C] official statement of the way someone wants their property to be shared out after they die 6 **at will** as one wishes 7 **of one's own free will** according to one's own will 8 **-willed** having a certain kind of WILL[2] (1) ♦ *vt* 1 make or intend to happen, esp. by the power of the mind

2 leave to someone in a WILL² (5)

will·ing /'wɪlɪŋ/ *adj* **1** ready: not refusing: *Are you willing to help?* **2** done or given gladly: *willing help* **3** eager: *a willing helper* ~**ly** *adv* ~**ness** *n* [U]

wil·low /'wɪləʊ ‖ -loʊ/ *n* tree which grows near water, with long thin branches ~**y** *adj* pleasantly thin and graceful

will·pow·er /'wɪl,paʊə ‖ -paʊr/ *n* [U] strength of WILL² (1)

wil·ly-nil·ly /,wɪli 'nɪli/ *adv* regardless of whether it is wanted or not

wilt /wɪlt/ *v* **1** *vi/t* become or cause (a plant) to become less fresh and start to die **2** *vi* (of a person) become tired and weaker

wil·y /'waɪli/ *adj* clever, esp. at getting what one wants **wiliness** *n* [U]

wimp /wɪmp/ *n* weak or useless person, esp. a man ~**ish**, ~**y** *adj*

win /wɪn/ *v* won /wʌn/, *pres. p.* -**nn**- **1** *vi/t* be first or best (in) beating one's opponent(s): *Who won the race?* **2** *vt* be given as the result of success: *I won £100 in the competition.* **3** *vt* gain: *trying to win his friendship* **4** *vi* be right in a guess or argument **5 win hands down** win easily ♦ *n* (esp. in sport) victory; success ~**ner** *n* ~**ning** *adj* very pleasing or attractive: *a winning smile* ~**nings** *n* [P] money won

win over *phr vt* gain the support of by persuading

wince /wɪns/ *vi* move back suddenly (as if) from something unpleasant, often twisting the face

winch /wɪntʃ/ *n* apparatus that turns to pull up heavy objects ♦ *vt* pull up with a winch

wind¹ /wɪnd/ *n* **1** [C;U] strongly moving air **2** [U] breath or breathing: —see also SECOND WIND **3** [U] *esp. BrE* (condition of having) gas in the stomach **4 get wind of** hear about, esp. accidentally or unofficially **5 it's an ill wind (that blows no good/no one any good)** even bad things may have good results **6 put/get the wind up** *infml* make/become afraid or anxious **7 see/find out which way the wind blows** find out what the situation is before taking action **8 (something) in the wind** (something, esp. that is secret or not generally known) about to happen/being done **9 take the wind out of someone's sails** *infml* take away someone's confidence or advantage,

esp. by saying or doing something unexpected ♦ *vt* make breathless ~**y** *adj* with a lot of wind: *a windy day*

wind² /waɪnd/ *v* **wound** /waʊnd/ **1** *vt* turn round and round: *wind a handle* **2** *vt* make into a twisted round shape: *winding wool* **3** *vi* go twistingly: *The path winds through the woods.* **4** *vt* tighten the working parts of by turning: *I wound the clock (up).* **5** *vt* move by turning a handle: *Wind down the car window.* **6** *vt* place around several times: *She wound a bandage round his arm.* **7 wind someone round one's little finger** make someone do what one wants

wind down *phr vi* **1** (of a clock or watch) work more slowly before at last stopping **2** (of a person) to rest until calmer, after work or excitement **3** cause to be no longer in operation, esp. gradually: *They're winding down their business in Hong Kong.*

wind up *phr v* **1** *vt* bring to an end **2** *vi* get into the stated unwanted situation in the end: *I wound up having to pay for it myself.* **3** *vt* annoy or deceive (someone) playfully

wind·break /'wɪndbreɪk/ *n* fence, wall, piece of material, etc. which gives protection from the wind

wind·chill /'wɪndtʃɪl/ *n* [U] combination of cold weather and strong winds, making the temperature seem lower: *the windchill factor*

wind·fall /'wɪndfɔːl ‖ -fɔːl/ *n* **1** fruit blown down off a tree **2** unexpected lucky gift

wind farm /'· ,·/ *n* group of WINDMILLS used to produce electricity

wind in·stru·ment /'wɪnd ,ɪnstrəmənt/ *n* musical instrument played by blowing air through it

wind·mill /'wɪnd,mɪl/ *n* building with large sails turned by the wind

win·dow /'wɪndəʊ ‖ -doʊ/ *n* (glass-filled) opening in the wall of a building, in a car, etc. to let in light and air —see also FRENCH WINDOWS

window box /'·· ·/ *n* box of earth for growing plants outside a window

window dress·ing /'·· ,··/ *n* **1** art of arranging goods in shop windows **2** *derog* something done to make a situation seem better, less unpleasant, etc. than it is

win·dow·pane /'wɪndəʊpeɪn ‖ -doʊ-/ *n*

one whole piece of glass in a window

window-shop /'·· ·/ *vi* **-pp-** look at goods in shop windows without necessarily intending to buy

wind·pipe /'wɪndpaɪp/ *n* air passage from the throat to the lungs

wind·screen /'wɪndskriːn/ *BrE* ‖

wind·shield /'wɪndʃiːld/ *AmE* — *n* piece of transparent material across the front of a vehicle, for the driver to look through

windscreen wip·er /'·· ‚·/ *n* movable arm which clears rain from the WINDSCREEN of a car

wind·surf·ing /'wɪnd‚sɜːfɪŋ ‖ -‚sɜːr-/ *n* [U] sport of sailing across water on a board with a sail **-er** *n*

wind·swept /'wɪndswept/ *adj* **1** open to continual strong wind: *a windswept moor* **2** as if blown into an untidy state: *a windswept appearance*

wind·ward /'wɪndwəd ‖ -wərd/ *n, adj, adv* [U] (direction) against or facing the wind

wine¹ /waɪn/ *n* [C;U] alcoholic drink made from GRAPES

wine² *vt* **wine and dine** give a very good meal to, esp. at a restaurant

wing /wɪŋ/ *n* **1** limb used by a bird, insect, etc. for flying **2** part standing out from a plane which supports it in flight **3** part standing out from the side: *the west wing of the palace* **4** *BrE* side part of a car that covers the wheels **5** (in sport) far left or right of the field **6** group with different opinions or purposes from the main organization: *the left wing of the Labour Party* **7 on the wing** (of a bird) flying **8 take wing** fly (away) **9 under someone's wing** being protected, helped, etc. by someone ♦ *v* **1** *vi* fly (as if) on wings **2** *vt* wound slightly **wings** *n* [P] **1** side of a stage, where an actor is hidden from view **2 in the wings** hidden and waiting for action **~ed** *adj* having wings **~er** *n* **1** player on the WINGS (5) **2** person on the stated WING (6)

winge /wɪndʒ/ *vi* WHINGE

wing·span /'wɪŋspæn/ *n* distance from the end of one wing to the end of the other

wink /wɪŋk/ *vi/t* **1** close and open (an eye) quickly **2** flash or cause (a light) to flash on and off ♦ *n* **1** [C] winking of the eye **2** [S] even a short period of sleep: *I didn't get a wink all night.* (=didn't sleep at all) **3 tip**

someone the wink give someone information or a sign about something —see also FORTY WINKS

wink at *phr vt* pretend not to notice (something bad)

win·kle¹ /'wɪŋkəl/ *n* small sea animal with a shell

winkle² *v* **winkle out** *phr vt* esp. *BrE* get or remove with difficulty

wi·no /'waɪnəʊ ‖ -noʊ/ *n infml derog* **-os** person who drinks too much alcohol and lives on the streets

win·some /'wɪnsəm/ *adj lit* attractive

win·ter /'wɪntə ‖ -ər/ *n* cold season between autumn and spring ♦ *vi* spend the winter **-try** /'wɪntri/ *adj*

winter sports /‚·· '·/ *n* [P] sports done on snow or ice

wipe /waɪp/ *vt* **1** rub (a surface or object) to remove (dirt, liquid, etc.): *Wipe your shoes on the mat.* | *She wiped the tears away.* **2 wipe the floor with a** severely defeat in an argument **b** speak very angrily to ♦ *n* act of wiping

wipe off *phr vt* get rid of on purpose: *to wipe off a debt*

wipe out *phr vt* **1** destroy or remove all of **2** *sl* knock down

wipe up *phr vt* remove with a cloth: *Wipe up that mess!*

wip·er /'waɪpə ‖ -ər/ *n* WINDSCREEN WIPER

wire /waɪə ‖ waɪr/ *n* **1** [C;U] (piece of) thin threadlike metal: *a wire fence* | *electric wires* **2** [C] *AmE* for TELEGRAM ♦ *vt* **1** connect up wires in (esp. an electrical system) **2** fasten with wire(s) **3** *AmE* send a TELEGRAM to **wiring** *n* [U] system of (electric) wires **wiry** *adj* rather thin, with strong muscles

wire·less /'waɪələs ‖ 'waɪr-/ *n old-fash* radio

wire-tap·ping /'·· ‚·/ *n* [U] listening secretly to other people's telephone conversations with an electrical connection

wis·dom /'wɪzdəm/ *n* [U] quality of being wise

wisdom tooth /'·· ·/ *n* large late-growing back tooth

wise¹ /waɪz/ *adj* **1** sensible **2** having long experience and much knowledge **3 none the wiser** knowing no more, after being told **4 -wise: a** in the manner of **b** in the direction of: *clockwise* **c** in connection with: *taxwise* **~ly** *adv*

wise² *v* **wise up** *phr vi/t AmE* (cause to) learn or become conscious of the true situation or true nature of someone or something

wise·crack /'waɪzkræk/ *vi, n* (make) a clever joke

wish /wɪʃ/1 *vt* want (something impossible): *I wish I hadn't agreed.* | *I wish I were a bird.* **2** *vi* want and try to cause something (as if) by magic: *If you wish hard enough you may get what you want.* **3** *vt* hope that (someone) will have (something), esp. expressed as a greeting: *We wished him a safe journey.* **4** *vt fml* want ♦ *n* **1** feeling of wanting something: *the wish for these peace talks to succeed* **2** thing wished for **3** attempt to make a wanted thing happen (as if) by magic

wish·bone /'wɪʃbəʊn ‖ -boʊn/ *n* V-shaped chicken bone pulled apart before making a wish

wishful think·ing /ˌ· '·· / *n* false belief that something is true or will happen simply because one wishes it

wish·y-wash·y /'wɪʃi ˌwɒʃi ‖ -ˌwɔːʃi, -ˌwɑːʃi/ *adj* without determination or clear aims and principles

wisp /wɪsp/ *n* small twisted bunch, piece (of something): *a wisp of hair/steam* **~y** *adj*

wist·ful /'wɪstfəl/ *adj* sad because of unfulfilled hopes or thoughts of the past **~ly** *adv* **~ness** *n* [U]

wit¹ /wɪt/ *n* **1** ability to say clever amusing things **2** [C] witty person **3** [U] also **wits** *pl.* — power of thought; cleverness: *He hadn't the wit to say no.* | (fig.) *It scared me out of my wits.* (=very much) **4 at one's wits end** too worried by difficulties to know what to do next **5 have/keep one's wits about one** be ready to act quickly and sensibly **~ty** *adj* having or showing wɪᴛ¹ (1) **~tily** *adv*

wit² *v* **to wit** *lit or law* that is (to say)

witch /wɪtʃ/ *n* woman with magic powers

witch·craft /'wɪtʃkrɑːft ‖ -kræft/ *n* [U] performing of magic

witch·doc·tor /'wɪtʃˌdɒktə ‖ -ˌdɑːktər/ *n* man who cures people by magic

witch-hunt /'·· ·/ *n* search for people with disliked political views, in order to remove them from power

with /wɪð, wɪθ/ *prep* **1** in the presence or company of: *I went to the cinema with Jim.*

2 having: *a book with a green cover* **3** by means of; using: *Cut it with scissors.* | *Fill it with sugar.* **4** in support of: *Are you with us or against us?* **5** against: *competing with foreign companies* **6** with regard to; in the case of: *Be careful with that glass.* | *He's in love with you.* **7** at the same time and rate as: *This wine improves with age.* **8** (used in comparisons): *The window is level with the street.* **9** in spite of: *With all his faults, I still like him.* **10** because of: *trembling with fear* **11 in with** a friend of (a person or group) **12 with it** giving proper attention to what is going on **13 with me/you** following my/your argument: *I'm not with you, what do you mean?* **14 with that** at once after that; then

with·draw /wɪð'drɔː, wɪθ-‖-'drɔː/ *v* **-drew** /-'druː/, **-drawn** /-'drɔːn‖-'drɔːn/ **1** *vt* take away or back: *She withdrew £50 from her bank account.* | *I withdraw that remark.* **2** *vi/t* move away or back: *I withdrew from* (=left) *the room.* **3** *vi/t* (cause to) not take part: *She withdrew from the election.* **~al** *n* [C;U] (act of) withdrawing **-drawn** *adj* quiet and not interested in other people

with·draw·al symp·toms /·'·· ˌ··/ *n* [P] painful or unpleasant effects which are the result of breaking or stopping a habit, esp. the taking of a drug

with·er /'wɪðə ‖ -ər/ *vi/t* (cause to) become dry, pale, and lifeless: *The heat had withered the plants.* **~ing** *adj* sharply severe: *withering scorn*

with·hold /wɪð'həʊld, wɪθ-‖-'hoʊld/ *vt* **-held** /-'held/ refuse to give: *withhold payment*

with·in /wɪð'ɪn ‖ wɪð'ɪn, wɪθ'ɪn/ *adv, prep* **1** not more than: *He'll arrive within an hour.* **2** inside: *within the castle walls*

with·out /wɪð'aʊt ‖ wɪð'aʊt, wɪθ-/ *prep, adv* **1** not having; lacking: *a pot without a lid* | *He went out without telling me.* **2 do/go without** continue as usual in spite of the lack (of)

with·stand /wɪð'stænd, wɪθ-‖ *vt* **-stood** /-'stʊd/ not be defeated or damaged by

wit·ness /'wɪtnᵻs/ *n* **1** person who saw something happen **2** person who gives information to a court of law **3** person who watches another sign an official paper, and then signs it as proof of having seen them

4 bear witness to show or prove (a quality) ♦ *vt* **1** be present at and see **2** watch or sign as a WITNESS (3) **3** be a sign or proof of

witness box /'·· ·/ *BrE* ‖ **witness stand** *AmE* — *n* enclosed area where witnesses stand in a court

wit·ti·cis·m /'wɪtɪˌsɪzəm/ *n* clever amusing remark

wives /waɪvz/ *pl. of* WIFE —see also OLD WIVES' TALE

wiz·ard /'wɪzəd ‖ -ərd/ *n* **1** (in stories) old man with magical powers **2** extremely skilful person: *a computer wizard* **~ry** *n* [U]

wiz·ened /'wɪzənd/ *adj* (as if) dried up, with lines on the skin

wob·ble /'wɒbəl ‖ 'wɑː-/ *vi/t* move unsteadily from side to side: *Don't wobble the table.* **wobble** *n* **-bly** *adj* wobbling: *wobbly jelly*

woe /wəʊ ‖ woʊ/ *n fml or lit* **1** [U] great sorrow **2** [C] trouble **~ful** *adj* **1** *esp. lit* very sad **2** (of something bad) very great: *woeful ignorance* **~fully** *adv*

wok /wɒk ‖ wɑːk/ *n* deep round Chinese cooking pan

woke /wəʊk ‖ woʊk/ *past t. of* WAKE

wok·en /'wəʊkən ‖ 'woʊ-/ *past p. of* WAKE

wolf /wʊlf/ *n* **wolves** /wʊlvz/ **1** fierce wild animal of the dog family **2** man who seeks woman for sex only **3 cry wolf** call for help unnecessarily **4 keep the wolf from the door** earn enough to eat and live **5 a wolf in sheep's clothing** person who seems harmless but is hiding evil intentions ♦ *vt* eat quickly in large amounts

wolf whis·tle /'· ˌ··/ *n* whistle of admiration

wom·an /'wʊmən/ *n* **women** /'wɪmɪn/ **1** adult female person **2** women in general **3** female nature or qualities **4 woman of the world** an experienced woman who knows how people behave **~hood** *n* [U] quality or time of being a woman **~ly** *adj* typical of a woman

wom·an·ize also **-ise** *BrE* /'wʊmənaɪz/ *vi* (of a man) habitually pay attention to many women for sexual purposes **-izer, -iser** *n*

womb /wuːm/ *n* organ inside female MAMMALS in which young develop

women's move·ment /'· ˌ··/ *n* [*the*+S] (all the women who join in making) a united effort to improve the social and political position of women

won /wʌn/ *past t. and p. of* WIN

won·der /'wʌndə ‖ -ər/ *n* **1** [U] feeling of strangeness, surprise, and usu. admiration **2** [C] wonderful or surprising thing —see also NINE DAYS' WONDER **3 do/work wonders** bring unexpectedly good results **4 (it's) no/little/small wonder** it is not surprising; naturally ♦ *vi/t* **1 express a** wish to know, in words or silently: *I wonder how you work this machine.* **2** be surprised: *It's not to be wondered at that she's angry.* ♦ *adj* unusually good or effective: *a wonder drug* **~ful** *adj* unusually good; causing pleasure or admiration **~fully** *adv* **~ment** *n* [U] WONDER (1)

won·drous /'wʌndrəs/ *adj lit* wonderful

won·ky /'wɒŋki ‖ 'wɑːŋki/ *adj BrE infml* **1** unsteady and likely to break or fail **2** not in a straight line

wont /wəʊnt ‖ wɒːnt/ *adj fml* likely (to) ♦ *n* [S] *fml* what the stated person usually does **~ed** *adj fml* customary

won't /wəʊnt ‖ woʊnt/ *short for:* will not

woo /wuː/ *vt* **1** *lit* try to make (a woman) love and marry one **2** try to gain the support of

wood /wʊd/ *n* **1** [U] substance of which trees are made **2** [C] also **woods** *pl.* — place where trees grow, smaller than a forest **3** [*the*+S] barrels **4 not see the wood for the trees** miss what is clear by looking too closely **5 out of the wood** *BrE* free from danger, difficulty, etc. **~ed** *adj* covered with trees **~en** *adj* **1** made of wood **2** stiff; unbending **~y** *adj* of or like wood

wood·en spoon /ˌ·· '·/ *n BrE* imaginary prize for finishing last in a competition

wood·land /'wʊdlənd, -lænd/ also **woodlands** *pl.* — *n* [U] wooded country

wood·peck·er /'wʊdˌpekə ‖ -ər/ *n* bird with a long beak that makes holes in trees

wood·wind /'wʊdˌwɪnd/ *n* [U;P] (players of) WIND INSTRUMENTS made of wood

wood·work /'wʊdwɜːk ‖ -wɜːrk/ *n* [U] **1** *esp. BrE* skill of making wooden objects **2** parts of a house that are made of wood

wood·worm /'wʊdwɜːm ‖ -wɜːrm/ *n* [U] damaged condition of wood caused by the young of certain BEETLES, which make holes

woof¹ /wʊf/ *n, interj* sound made by a dog

woof² /wuːf ‖ wʊf, wuːf/ *n* WEFT

woof·er /'wuːfə ‖ 'wʊfər/ *n* LOUDSPEAKER

that gives out deep sounds

wool /wul/ n [U] 1 soft thick hair of sheep 2 thick thread made from this 3 **pull the wool over someone's eyes** trick someone by hiding the facts ~**len** BrE ‖ ¯**en** AmE — adj made of wool ~**ly** adj 1 of or like wool 2 (of thoughts) not clear in the mind ♦ n woollen garment

woo·zy /ˈwuːzi/ adj infml having an unsteady feeling in the head –**iness** n [U]

word /wɜːd ‖ wɜːrd/ n 1 [C] (written representation of) 1 or more sounds which can be spoken to represent an idea, object, etc. 2 [S] shortest (type of) statement: *Don't say a word* (=anything) *about it to anyone.* 3 [S] short conversation: *I'd like a word with you.* 4 [U] message or piece of news: *He sent word that he wanted to see me.* 5 [S] promise: *I give you my word that I'll do it.* 6 [C] suggestion or RECOMMENDATION: *put in/say a good word for someone* 7 **by word of mouth** by speaking and not by writing 8 **eat one's words** admit to having said something wrong 9 **get a word in edgeways** infml get a chance to speak 10 **have a word with someone/in someone's ear** (speak to someone) secretly, esp. giving advice or asking a question 11 **(have) the last word (on)** (make) the remark which finishes an argument, etc. 12 **have words (with)** argue angrily (with) 13 **in other words** expressing the same thing in different words 14 **(not) in so many words** (not) directly expressed in those words but only suggested 15 **put words in(to) someone's mouth: a** tell someone what to say **b** claim falsely that someone has said a particular thing 16 **take someone's word for it** accept what someone says as correct 17 **the last word in** the most recent development in 18 **word for word** in exactly the same words ♦ vt express in words –**ing** n [U] words in which something is expressed ~**y** adj using or containing more words than necessary

word-per·fect /ˌ· ˈ··/ adj repeating or remembering every word correctly

word pro·cess·or /ˈ· ˌ···/ n small computer for esp. ordinary office work

wore /wɔː ‖ wɔːr/ past t. of WEAR

work¹ /wɜːk ‖ wɜːrk/ n 1 [U] activity done to produce something or gain a result

rather than for amusement 2 [U] job; business: *I go to work by train.* 3 [U] something produced by work, esp. of the hands: *This mat is my own work.* (=I made it) | (fig.) *The murder was the work of a madman.* 4 [C] object produced by painting, writing, etc.: *a work of art* | *the works of Shakespeare* 5 **all in a day's work** not unusual 6 **at work (on)** doing something. esp. work 7 **go/set to work (on)** start doing 8 **have one's work cut out** have something difficult to do, esp. in the time allowed 9 **in/out of work** having a job/ unemployed 10 **make short work of** finish quickly and easily —see also WORKS

work² v 1 vi do an activity which uses effort, esp. as one's job: *She works at the factory.* 2 vi (of a machine, plan, etc.) operate (properly): *It works by electricity.* | *Your scheme will never work.* 3 vt make (a person) do work: *They work us too hard.* 4 vt make (a machine) do work: *How do you work this lift?* 5 vt make (one's way) by work or effort 6 vi/t make or become by small movements: *This little screw has worked loose.* 7 vt produce (an effect): *This medicine works wonders.* 8 vt arrange, esp. unofficially: *We'll work it so that we can all go together.* 9 vi move or act for a certain result: *This will work against you in the future.* 10 **work to rule** obey the rules of one's work so exactly that one causes inconvenience to others, in order to support a claim for higher wages, etc. ~**able** adj which can be put into effect; usable: *a workable plan* ~**er** n 1 person who works: *an office worker* 2 member of the WORKING CLASS

work off phr vt get rid of by work or effort: *He worked off his anger by chopping wood.*

work out phr v 1 vt calculate (the answer to) 2 vi have a result; develop: *The plan worked out very well in practice.* 3 vt plan; decide: *We're trying to work out how to get there.* 4 vi reach the stated amount by being calculated: *The cost works out at £10 each.* 5 vi do physical exercises: *She works out twice a week.*

work up phr vt 1 excite the feelings of: *He gets very worked up* (=anxious and upset) *about exams.* 2 cause oneself to have: *I couldn't work up much enthusiasm for it.*

3 develop steadily: *She worked the firm up from nothing*.

work·a·day /ˈwɜːkədeɪ ‖ ˈwɜːr-/ *adj* ordinary and/or dull

work·a·hol·ic /ˌwɜːkəˈhɒlɪk ‖ ˌwɜːrkə-ˈhɒː-/ *n* person who likes to work too hard

work·bench /ˈwɜːkbentʃ ‖ ˈwɜːrk-/ *n* (a table with) a hard surface for working on with tools

work·book /ˈwɜːkbʊk ‖ ˈwɜːrk-/ *n* school book with questions and exercises

work coat /ˈ· ·/ *n AmE for* OVERALL (1)

work·force /ˈwɜːkfɔːs ‖ ˈwɜːrkfɔːrs/ *n* all the workers in a factory or in industry generally

work·horse /ˈwɜːkhɔːs ‖ ˈwɜːrkhɔːrs/ *n* 1 person who does most of the (dull) work 2 useful machine, vehicle, etc. for performing continuous jobs

work·house /ˈwɜːkhaʊs ‖ ˈwɜːrk-/ *n* (in former times) place where unemployed people lived

work·ing /ˈwɜːkɪŋ ‖ ˈwɜːr-/ *adj* 1 used for work: *working clothes* 2 (of time) spent in work 3 useful as a base for further development: *a working hypothesis*

working class /ˌ·· ˈ·◄/ *n* social class of people who work with their hands **working-class** *adj*

working knowl·edge /ˌ·· ˈ·◄/ *n* [S] enough practical knowledge to do something

working or·der /ˌ·· ˈ·◄/ *n* [U] state of working well, with no trouble

working par·ty /ˈ·· ˌ·◄/ *n* committee which examines and reports on a particular matter

work·ings /ˈwɜːkɪŋz ‖ ˈwɜːr-/ *n* [P] 1 way something works or acts: *the workings of an engine/of his mind* 2 parts of a mine which have been dug out

work·load /ˈwɜːkləʊd ‖ ˈwɜːrkloʊd/ *n* amount of work that a person or machine is expected to do in a particular period of time

work·man /ˈwɜːkmən ‖ ˈwɜːrk-/ *n* **-men** /-mən/ man who works with his hands, esp. in a particular skill or trade ~**like** *adj* showing the qualities of a good workman ~**ship** *n* [U] (signs of) skill in making things

work·out /ˈwɜːkaʊt ‖ ˈwɜːrk-/ *n* period of physical exercise

works /wɜːks ‖ wɜːrks/ *n* **works** 1 [P] moving parts of a machine 2 [C] factory: *a*

dye works 3 **give someone the works** *sl* a give someone everything: *They gave us supper, wine, chocolates, the works.* b attack violently

work·shop /ˈwɜːkʃɒp ‖ ˈwɜːrkʃɑːp/ *n* 1 room where heavy repairs and jobs on machines are done 2 period of group activity and study: *a drama workshop*

work-shy /ˈ· ·/ *adj* not liking work and trying to avoid it

work·sta·tion /ˈwɜːkˌsteɪʃən ‖ ˈwɜːrk-/ *n* area (of an office) where one works, with a desk, computer, etc.

work·top /ˈwɜːktɒp ‖ ˈwɜːrktɑːp/ *n* flat surface in a kitchen for preparing food, etc.

work-to-rule /ˌ· · ·/ *n* act of working to rule (WORK² (10))

world /wɜːld ‖ wɜːrld/ *n* 1 [*the*+S] a the Earth: *the richest man in the world* b particular part of it: *the Old World* 2 [*the*+S] the universe 3 [*the*+S] group of living things: *the animal world* 4 [*the*+S] a particular area of human activity: *the world of football* 5 [*the*+S] people generally: *We don't want the whole world* (=everyone) *to know about it.* 6 [*the*+S] human life and its affairs: *the ways of the world* 7 [C] PLANET: *life on other worlds* 8 [*the*+S] large number or amount: *This medicine did me the world of good.* 9 [*the*+S] *fml* material standards: *to give up the world to serve God* 10 **all the world to** very important to 11 **for all the world like/as if** exactly like/as if 12 **(have) the best of both worlds** (to have) the advantage which each choice offers, without having to choose between them 13 **in the world** (in a question expressing surprise): *Where in the world have you been?* 14 **not for the world** certainly not: *I wouldn't hurt her for the world.* 15 **on top of the world** very happy 16 **out of this world** unusually good; wonderful 17 **worlds apart** completely different ~**ly** *adj* 1 material: *all my worldly goods* (=everything I own) 2 too much concerned with human society, rather than religious things ~**liness** *n* [U]

world-class /ˌ· ˈ·◄/ *adj* among the best in the world

world-fam·ous /ˌ· ˈ··◄/ *adj* known all over the world

world pow·er /ˌ· ˈ·/ *n* nation with very great power and influence

world-wear·y /ˌ· ˈ-◄/ adj tired of life
world·wide /ˌwɜːldˈwaɪd◄ ‖ ˌwɜːrld-/ adj, adv in or over all the world
World Wide Web /ˌ· · ·ˈ·/ n [the+S] —see WEB (2)

worm /wɜːm ‖ wɜːrm/ n 1 small thin creature with no bones or limbs, like a tube of flesh 2 worthless, cowardly, etc. person ♦ vt move by twisting or effort: We wormed our way through the crack in the wall. | (fig.) He wormed his way into her affections.

worm out phr vt obtain gradually by questioning

worn /wɔːn ‖ wɔːrn/ past p. of WEAR
worn-out /ˌ· ˈ-◄/ adj 1 no longer usable 2 very tired

wor·ry /ˈwʌri ‖ ˈwɜːri/ v 1 vi/t (cause to) be anxious or uncomfortable: worrying about the exams | Heights don't worry me. 2 vt (esp. of a dog) chase and bite (an animal) ♦ n [C;U] 1 feeling of anxiety 2 (person or thing that causes) anxiety –ried adj anxious ~ing adj

worse /wɜːs ‖ wɜːrs/ adj 1 (comparative of BAD) of lower quality; more bad 2 more ill (than before) 3 none the worse (for) not harmed (by) 4 the worse for wear harmed by use over a period ♦ adv in a worse way or to a worse degree ♦ n [U] something worse **worsen** vi/t (cause to) become worse

wor·ship /ˈwɜːʃɪp ‖ ˈwɜːrʃɪp-/ n [U] (showing of) strong (religious) feelings of love, respect, and admiration ♦ vi/t -pp-BrE ‖ -p- AmE show worship (to): to worship God | She worships her brother. (=admires him (too) greatly) ~per BrE ‖ ~er AmE n

worst /wɜːst ‖ wɜːrst/ adj (superlative of BAD) of lowest quality; most bad ♦ n 1 worst worst thing or part: These ones are the worst. 2 at (the) worst if the worst happens 3 get the worst of suffer most from 4 if the worst comes to the worst if there is no better way ♦ adv (superlative of BADLY) most badly: the worst-dressed man in the office

wor·sted /ˈwʊstɪd/ n [U] wool cloth
worth /wɜːθ ‖ wɜːrθ/ prep 1 of the stated value: a painting worth £5000 2 deserving: That film isn't worth seeing. 3 for all one is worth with all possible effort 4 for what it's worth though I'm not sure it's of any value 5 worth it useful; worthwhile 6 worth one's salt worthy of respect or of

being so called 7 worth one's/someone's while worthwhile to one/someone ♦ n [U] value ~less adj 1 of no value 2 (of a person) of bad character

worth·while /ˌwɜːθˈwaɪl◄ ‖ ˌwɜːrθ-/ adj with a good enough result to deserve the trouble taken

wor·thy /ˈwɜːði ‖ ˈwɜːrði/ adj 1 deserving respect or serious attention 2 deserving: worthy of admiration 3 good but not very exciting or interesting –thily adv –thiness n [U]

would /wʊd/ v aux 1 (past of will): They said they would meet us at 10.30. 2 (shows what is likely or possible): What would you do if you won a million pounds? 3 (shows what always happened): We would meet for a drink after work. 4 (shows choice): I'd rather have tea. 5 (expressing a polite request): Would you lend me your pencil? 6 would better AmE had better (HAVE[1])

would-be /ˈ· ·/ adj which one wants or intends to be, but isn't: a would-be musician
wouldn't /ˈwʊdnt/ short for: would not
wound[1] /wuːnd/ n damaged place on the body, esp. caused by a weapon: a bullet wound ♦ vt cause a wound to: a wounded leg | (fig.) wounded pride

wound[2] /waʊnd/ past t. and p. of WIND[2]
wound-up /ˌwaʊnd ˈʌp◄/ adj anxiously excited

wove /wəʊv ‖ woʊv/ past t. of WEAVE
wov·en /ˈwəʊvən ‖ ˈwoʊ-/ past p. of WEAVE

wow /waʊ/ interj infml (expresses surprise and admiration) ♦ n [S] sl a great success ♦ vt sl cause surprise and admiration in someone

WPC /ˌdʌbəljuː piː ˈsiː◄/ n abbrev. for: Woman Police Constable
wran·gle /ˈræŋɡəl/ vi, n (take part in) an angry or noisy quarrel

wrap /ræp/ vt -pp- cover in material folded over: I wrapped the box in brown paper. | She had a bandage wrapped round her finger. ♦ n 1 esp. AmE garment for covering a woman's shoulders 2 under wraps secret ~per n loose paper cover ~ping n [C;U] material for folding round and covering something

wrap up phr vt 1 wear warm clothes 2 complete (a business arrangement, meeting, etc.) 3 wrapped up in giving

wrath /rɒθ ‖ ræθ/ *n* [U] *fml or lit* strong fierce anger ~**ful** *adj*

wreak /riːk/ *vt esp. lit* perform or bring about (something violent or unpleasant)

wreath /riːθ/ *n* usu. circular arrangement of flowers or leaves **a** given at a funeral **b** placed on the head as a sign of honour

wreathe /riːð/ *vt esp. lit* circle round and cover: *Mist wreathed the hilltops.*

wreck /rek/ *n* **1** [C] sunken or destroyed ship **2** [C] something in a very bad condition: *Have you seen the old wreck he drives around in!* **3** [U] *fml* ruin; destruction: *the wreck of our hopes* **4** [C] person whose health is destroyed ♦ *vt* destroy: *a ship wrecked on the rocks | The bad weather wrecked our plans.* ~**age** *n* [U] broken parts of a destroyed thing

wren /ren/ *n* very small brown European bird

wrench /rentʃ/ *vt* **1** pull hard with a twist **2** twist and damage (a joint of the body) ♦ *n* **1** act of or damage caused by wrenching **2** separation that causes suffering of the mind **3** SPANNER

wrest /rest/ *vt* **1** pull (away) violently **2** *esp. lit* obtain with difficulty

wres·tle /ˈresəl/ *vi/t* fight by trying to hold or throw one's opponent: (fig.) *wrestling with a difficult problem* ~**tler** *n* person who wrestles as a sport

wretch /retʃ/ *n* **1** unfortunate person **2** annoying person

wretch·ed /ˈretʃɪd/ *adj* **1** very unhappy **2** of a bad type which makes one unhappy: *a wretched headache* **3** annoying: *Why can't that wretched child behave himself!* ~**ly** *adv* ~**ness** *n* [U]

wrig·gle /ˈrɪɡəl/ *vi/t* move from side to side: *He wriggled uncomfortably on the hard seat.* ♦ *n* wriggling movement

wriggle out of *phr vt* escape (a difficulty) by clever tricks

wring /rɪŋ/ *vt* **wrung** /rʌŋ/ **1** twist or press (wet clothes) to remove (water) **2** twist (the neck) hard, causing death **3** press hard on, esp. hands: *wringing her hands in sorrow* **4** obtain by severe or cruel methods: *Her torturers wrung a confession out of her.* **5 wringing wet** very wet ~**er** *n* machine for wringing clothes

wrin·kle /ˈrɪŋkəl/ *n* **1** small line or fold, esp. on the skin owing to age **2** *infml* useful suggestion or trick ♦ *vi/t* (cause to) form wrinkles ~**kly** *adj*

wrist /rɪst/ *n* joint between the hand and the arm

wrist·watch /ˈrɪstwɒtʃ ‖ -wɑːtʃ, -wɔːtʃ/ *n* watch with a band for fastening round the wrist

writ /rɪt/ *n* official legal paper telling someone (not) to do a particular thing

write /raɪt/ *v* **wrote** /rəʊt ‖ rəʊt/, **written** /ˈrɪtn/ **1** *vi/t* make (marks representing letters or words) with a tool, esp. a pen or pencil **2** *vt* think of and record, esp. on paper: *He wrote a report on the match.* **3** *vt* complete by writing words: *write a cheque* **4** *vi/t* produce and send (a letter): *He writes to me every week.* **5** *vi* be a writer (of books, plays, etc.): *She writes for television.* **6 be written on/all over** clearly showing because of the expression on: *Guilt was written all over his face.* **7 writ large** *lit* on a larger or grander scale **writer** *n* **writing** *n* [U] **1** handwriting **2** written work or form: *Put it down in writing.* **3** activity of writing books, etc. **writings** *n* [P] written works

write away *phr vi* write to a far-off place, esp. to buy something

write down *phr vt* record (esp. what has been said) in writing

write off *phr vt* **1** accept as lost or useless or as a failure **2** remove (esp. a debt) from the record **3** WRITE away ♦ **write-off** /ˈ··/ *n* something completely ruined and unrepairable

write out *phr vt* write in full

write up *phr vt* write (again) in a complete and useful form **write-up** /ˈ· ·/ *n* written report giving a judgment

writhe /raɪð/ *vi* twist the body (as if) in great pain

writ·ten /ˈrɪtn/ *v past p. of* WRITE

wrong /rɒŋ ‖ rɔːŋ/ *adj* **1** not correct: *the wrong answer* **2** morally bad **3** not in a proper or healthy state: *There's something wrong with the engine.* **4** not suitable: *the wrong time to visit* ♦ *adv* **1** wrongly **2 go wrong: a** stop working properly **b** make a mistake **c** end badly ♦ *n* **1** [U] morally bad behaviour **2** [C] *fml* unjust or bad action **3 in the wrong** mistaken or deserving blame ♦ *vt* be unfair to or cause to suffer

~ful *adj* unjust or illegal: *wrongful arrest* **~fully** *adv*

wrong·do·ing /'rɒŋ,duːɪŋ ‖ ,rɔːɪŋ'duːɪŋ/ *n* [C;U] (example of) bad or illegal behaviour **wrongdoer** *n* [C]

wrote /rəʊt ‖ roʊt/ *past t. of* WRITE

wrought /rɔːt ‖ rɔːt/ *adj lit* made: *wrought of steel*

wrought i·ron /ˌ· '·◂/ *n* [U] iron shaped into a useful, pleasing form

wrung /rʌŋ/ *past t. and p. of* WRING

wry /raɪ/ *adj* showing a mixture of amusement and dislike, disappointment, etc.: *a wry smile* **~ly** *adv*

WWW /ˌdʌbəljuː ˌdʌbəlju: 'dʌbəlju:/ *abbrev. for:* World Wide Web; –see WEB (2)

X, x /eks/ the 24th letter of the English alphabet

xen·o·pho·bi·a /ˌzenəˈfəʊbɪə ‖ -ˈfoʊ-/ *n* [U] unreasonable fear and dislike of foreigners **–bic** *adj*

xe·rox /'zɪərɒks, 'ze- ‖ 'zɪrɑːks, 'zi:-/ *vt, n* (make) a photographic copy on a photocopier (PHOTOCOPY)

X·mas /'krɪsməs, 'eksməs/ *n infml* CHRISTMAS

X-ray /'eks reɪ/ *n* 1 powerful unseen beam which can pass through solid things, used esp. for photographing conditions inside the body 2 photograph taken with this 3 medical examination with this **x-ray** *vt* photograph, examine, or treat with X-rays

xy·lo·phone /'zaɪləfəʊn ‖ -foʊn/ *n* musical instrument with many small wooden bars hit with a hammer

Y, y /waɪ/ the 25th letter of the English alphabet

yacht /jɒt ‖ jɑːt/ *n* 1 light sailing boat used esp. for racing 2 large motor-driven pleasure boat **~ing** *n* [U] sailing in a yacht

yachts·man /'jɒtsmən ‖ 'jɑːts-/**yachts·woman** /-ˌwʊmən/ *fem.* — *n* -**men** /-mən/ sailor in a yacht

yak¹ /jæk/ *n* long-haired cow of central Asia

yak² *vi* -**kk-** *derog* talk continuously about unimportant things

yam /jæm/ *n* tropical plant with a root eaten as a vegetable

yank /jæŋk/ *vi/t* pull suddenly and sharply **yank** *n*

Yank *n BrE derog* American person

yap /jæp/ *vi* -**pp-** *derog* 1 (of a dog) BARK continuously 2 talk noisily about unimportant things

yard¹ /jɑːd ‖ jɑːrd/ *n* a measure of length equal to 3 feet or 0.9144 metres

yard² *n* 1 (partly) enclosed area next to a building 2 area enclosed for the stated activity or business: *a coalyard*

yard·stick /'jɑːd,stɪk ‖ 'jɑːrd-/ *n* standard of measurement or comparison

yarn /jɑːn ‖ jɑːrn/ *n* 1 [U] long continuous thread used esp. in making cloth 2 [C] story

yash·mak /'jæʃmæk/ *n* cloth worn across the face by Muslim women

yawn /jɔːn ‖ jɒːn/ *vi* 1 open the mouth wide and breathe deeply, esp. from tiredness 2 be(come) wide open: *a yawning chasm* ♦ *n* 1 act of yawning 2 *infml* something dull

yd *written abbrev. for:* YARD(s)¹

ye /jiː/ *pron lit* (used of more than one person) you

yea /jeɪ/ *adv lit* yes

yeah /jeə/ *adv infml* yes

year /jɪə, jɜː ‖ jɪr/ *n* 1 period of 365 (or 366) days, or 12 months, esp. as measured from January 1st to December 31st 2 period of about a year in the life of an organization: *the school year* 3 **all the year round** during the whole year 4 **year after year** continuously for many years 5 **year in,**

year out regularly each year ~**ly** *adj, adv* (happening) every year or once a year

year dot /ˌ· '·/ *n* [the+S] *BrE infml* a very long time ago

year·ling /'jɪəlɪŋ, 'jɜ:- ‖ 'jɪr-/ *n* animal between one and two years old

year·long /'jɪəlɒŋ, 'jɜ:- ‖ 'jɪrlɔ:ŋ/ *adj* lasting a whole year

yearn /jɜ:n ‖ jɜ:rn/ *vi esp. lit* have a strong (sad) desire: *I yearn for your return.* ~**ing** *n* [C;U] *esp. lit* strong desire

yeast /ji:st/ *n* [U] form of very small plant with a chemical action used for producing alcohol in making wine and beer and for making bread light and soft ~**y** *adj*

yell /jel/ *vi/t, n* shout

yel·low /'jeləʊ ‖ -loʊ/ *adj* **1** of the colour of gold **2** *infml* cowardly ♦ *vi/t* (cause to) become yellow ~**ish** *adj*

yellow fe·ver /ˌ·· '··/ *n* [U] serious tropical disease

Yellow Pag·es /ˌ·· '··/ *n* [P] book with telephone numbers of businesses

yelp /jelp/ *vi, n* (make) a sharp high cry, esp. of pain

yen¹ /jen/ *n* yen unit of Japanese money

yen² *n* strong desire

yes /jes/ *adv* **1** (used for accepting or agreeing) **2** (used for replying to a call)

yes-man /'· ·/ *n* -**men** /-men/ *derog* someone who always agrees with their leader or employer

yes·ter·day /'jestədi ‖ -ər-/ *adv, n* (on) the day before today

yes·ter·year /'jestəjɪə, -jɜ: ‖ 'jestərjɪr/ *n* [U] *esp. lit* the recent past

yet /jet/ *adv* **1** up until this time: *He hasn't arrived yet.* **2** in future, and in spite of how things seem now: *We may yet win.* **3** even: *a yet bigger problem* **4** still: *I have yet to be told.* (=I have still not been told) **5 as yet** YET (1) ♦ *conj* but even so: *strange yet true*

yet·i /'jeti/ *n* large hairy manlike animal said to live in the Himalaya mountains

yew /ju:/ *n* tree with small dark leaves and red berries

Y-fronts /'waɪ frʌnts/ *n* [P] *BrE* type of men's UNDERPANTS

yield /ji:ld/ *v* **1** *vt* produce: *a tree which yields a large crop* **2** *vt fml* give up control of: *yield a position of advantage* **3** *vi fml or lit* admit defeat ♦ *n* amount produced: *a high yield of fruit* ~**ing** *adj* **1** not stiff or fixed

2 (too) easily persuaded

yip·pee /jɪ'pi: ‖ 'jɪpi/ *interj* (shout of delight or success)

yob /jɒb ‖ jɑ:b/ *n BrE infml* rude or troublesome young man

yo·del /'jəʊdl ‖ 'joʊ-/ *vi/t* -**ll**- *BrE* ‖ -**l**- *AmE* sing with many changes between the natural voice and a very high voice

yo·ga /'jəʊɡə ‖ 'joʊ-/ *n* [U] Hindu system of control of the mind and body, often including special exercises

yog·hurt /'jɒɡət ‖ 'joʊɡərt/ *n* [U] milk that has thickened and turned slightly acid through the action of certain bacteria

yo·gi /'jəʊɡi ‖ 'joʊ-/ *n* person who practises (and teaches) yoga

yoke /jəʊk ‖ joʊk/ *n* **1** bar joining two animals for pulling a vehicle or heavy load **2** frame across someone's shoulders for carrying two equal loads **3** *lit* controlling power: *the hated yoke of their conquerors* **4** part of garment from which the rest hangs ♦ *vt* join (as if) with a yoke

yo·kel /'jəʊkəl ‖ 'joʊ-/ *n humor or derog* simple or foolish country person

yolk /jəʊk ‖ joʊk, jelk/ *n* [C;U] yellow part of an egg

yon·der /'jɒndə ‖ 'jɑ:ndər/ *adj, adv esp. lit* that; over there

yonks /jɒŋks ‖ jɑ:ŋks/ *n* [U] *BrE infml* very long time

yore /jɔ: ‖ jɔ:r/ *n* [U] *lit* very long time ago

York·shire pud·ding /ˌjɔ:kʃə 'pʊdɪŋ, ˌjɔ:rkʃər-/ *n* [U] food made from flour, eggs, and milk, eaten with BEEF

you /jə, jʊ; *strong* ju:/ *pron* (used as subject or object) **1** person or people being spoken to: *I love you.* **2** anyone; one: *You can't trust such people.* **3** (used for addressing someone, esp. angrily): *You fool!*

you'd /jəd, jʊd; *strong* ju:d/ *short for:* **1** you had **2** you would

you'll /jəl, jʊl; *strong* ju:l/ *short for:* **1** you will **2** you shall

young /jʌŋ/ *adj* **younger** /'jʌŋɡə ‖ -ər/, **youngest** /'jʌŋɡəst/ in an early stage of life or development ♦ *n* [P] **1** young people generally **2** young animals

young·ster /'jʌŋstə ‖ -ər/ *n* young person

your /jə; *strong* jɔ: ‖ jər; *strong* jʊr, jɔ:r/ *determiner of* you: *your house*

you're /jə; *strong* jɔ: ‖ jər; *strong* jʊr, jɔ:r/ *short for:* you are

yours /jɔːz ‖ jʊrz, jɔːrz/ *pron* **1** of you; your one(s) **2** (used at the end of a letter): *Yours sincerely, Janet Smith.* **3 yours truly: a** (polite phrase written at the end of a letter) **b** *infml* I; me; myself

your·self /jəˈself ‖ jər-/ *pron* -selves /-ˈselvz/ **1** (reflexive form of **you**): *Don't hurt yourself.* **2** (strong form of **you**): *Did you make it yourself?* **3 (all) by yourself: a** alone **b** without help **4 to yourself** not shared

youth /juːθ/ *n* youths /juːðz ‖ juːðz, juːθs/ **1** [U] period of being young **2** [C] *often derog* young person, esp. male **3** [U;P] young people as a group: *the youth of today* ~**ful** *adj* (seeming) young

youth hos·tel /'· ‚··/ *n* place for people to stay cheaply when travelling

you've /jəv; *strong* juːv/ *short for:* you have

yo-yo /'jəʊ jəʊ ‖ 'joʊ joʊ/ *n* toy that moves up and down on a string

yuc·ca /'jʌkə/ *n* desert plant with pointed leaves

yuck·y /'jʌki/ *adj infml* extremely unpleasant

yule /juːl/ *n* [U] *lit for* CHRISTMAS

yup·pie, yuppy /'jʌpi/ *n* young person in a professional job with a high income, esp. one with an expensive and fashionable way of life

Z

Z, z /zed ‖ ziː/ *n* the 26th and last letter of the English alphabet

za·ny /'zeɪni/ *adj* amusingly foolish

zap /zæp/ *v* -pp- *infml* **1** *vt* attack and/or destroy **2** *vi/t* move quickly and forcefully ~**py** *adj* full of life and force

zap·per /'zæpə ‖ -ər/ *n* *infml* television REMOTE CONTROL

zeal /ziːl/ *n* [U] *fml* eagerness ~**ous** /'zeləs/ *adj* eager; keen ~**ously** *adv*

zeal·ot /'zelət/ *n* someone who is (too) eager in their beliefs

ze·bra /'ziːbrə, 'ze- ‖ 'ziːbrə/ *n* -bra or -bras horselike African animal with broad black and white lines

zebra cross·ing /'·· ‚··/ *n* (in Britain) set of black and white lines across a road where people have a right to walk across

ze·nith /'zenɪθ ‖ 'ziː-/ *n* highest or greatest point of development, success, etc.

ze·ro¹ /'zɪərəʊ ‖ 'ziːroʊ/ *n* -ros or -roes **1** (sign representing) the number 0 **2** point between + and – on a scale: *The temperature was below zero.* (=below the freezing point of water) **3** nothing: *zero growth*

zero² *v* **zero in on** *phr vt* **1** aim a weapon directly at **2** aim one's attention directly towards

zest /zest/ *n* **1** [S;U] pleasantly exciting quality: *The danger adds zest to the affair.* **2** [S;U] eagerness: *a zest for life* **3** [U] outer skin of an orange or LEMON ~**ful** *adj*

zig-zag /'zɪgzæg/ *vi n* -gg- (go in) a line shaped like a row of z's: *The path zigzags up the hill.*

zil·lion /'zɪljən/ also **zillions** *pl.* — *determiner, n, pron infml* extremely large number

zinc /zɪŋk/ *n* [U] bluish-white metal

Zi·on·is·m /'zaɪənɪzəm/ *n* [U] political movement supporting (first the establishment and now the development of) the state of Israel -**ist** *adj, n*

zip /zɪp/ *n* **1** [C] fastener with two sets of teeth and a sliding piece that joins the edges of an opening by drawing the teeth together **2** [U] liveliness ♦ *v* -pp- **1** *vt* fasten with a ZIP (1) **2** *vi/t* move very quickly and forcefully ~**per** *n AmE for* ZIP (1)

zip code /'· ‚·/ *n AmE for* POSTCODE

zith·er /'zɪðə ‖ -ər/ *n* flat musical instrument played by pulling sharply at its strings

zits /zɪts/ *n* [P] *sl* spots on the skin

zo·di·ac /'zəʊdiæk ‖ 'zoʊ-/ *n* [the+S] imaginary belt in space along which the sun, moon, and nearest PLANETS seem to travel, divided into 12 equal parts used in ASTROLOGY

zom·bie /'zɒmbi ‖ 'zɑːm-/ *n* **1** *derog* someone who moves or acts very slowly or lifelessly **2** dead person made to move by magic

zone /zəʊn ‖ zoʊn/ n area marked off from others by particular qualities or activities: *a war/danger zone* ♦ vt give a particular purpose to (an area): *a part of town zoned for industrial development* **zonal** adj

zonked /zɒŋkt ‖ zɑːŋkt/ adj infml extremely tired

zoo /zuː/ n **zoos** park where many types of wild animal are kept for show

zo·ol·o·gy /zuːˈɒlədʒi, zəʊ- ‖ zuːˈɑːl-, zoʊ-/ n [U] scientific study of animals **-gist** n **zoological** /ˌzuːəˈlɒdʒɪkəl◄, ˌzəʊə- ‖ ˌzuːəˈlɑː-, ˌzoʊə-/ adj

zoom /zuːm/ vi **1** go quickly with a loud noise **2** (of a cinema camera) move quickly between a distant and a close view **3** increase suddenly and greatly

zoom lens /ˈ· ˌ·/ n curved piece of glass by which a camera can zoom in and out while keeping the picture clear

zuc·chi·ni /zʊˈkiːni/ n **-ni** or **-nis** AmE for COURGETTE

Word beginnings

Afro- /ˈæfrəʊ ‖ -roʊ/ **1** of Africa: *an Afro-American* **2** African and: *Afro-Asian peoples*

Anglo- /ˈæŋɡləʊ ‖ -gloʊ/ **1** of England or Britain: *an Anglophile* (someone who loves Britain) **2** English or British and: *an Anglo-American treaty*

ante- /ˈænti/ before: *antenatal care* –compare POST-

anti- /ˈænti/ against; not in favour of; trying to prevent or destroy: *an anticancer drug* | *an antitank gun* | *He's very anti-war.* -compare PRO-

arch- /ɑːtʃ ‖ ɑːrtʃ/ chief; main: *our archenemy*

astro- /ˈæstrəʊ ‖ -roʊ/ of or about the stars and space: *astrophysics*

audio- /ˈɔːdiəʊ ‖ ˈɒdioʊ/ of, for, or using sound, esp. recorded sound: *audiovisual teaching aids* –compare VIDEO-

Austro- /ˈɒstrəʊ ‖ ˈɒːstroʊ/ **1** Australian and: *Austro-Malayan* **2** Austrian and: *the Austro-Italian border*

be- /bɪ/ (makes verbs and adjectives cause to be or have: *a bewigged judge* (= wearing a wig) | *She befriended me.*

bi- /baɪ/ two; twice: *a biannual publication* (= coming out twice a year)

bio- /ˈbaɪəʊ ‖ -oʊ/ connected with (the study of) living things: *biochemistry*

centi- /ˈsentɪ/ hundredth part: *a centimetre* (= a hundredth of a metre)

co- /kəʊ ‖ koʊ/ with; together: *my co-author, who wrote the book with me*

counter- /ˈkaʊntə ‖ -tər/ in return or so as to have an opposite effect or make ineffective: *a counterattack* | *counter-espionage operations*

cross- /krɒs ‖ krɔːs/ going between the stated things: *cross-cultural influences*

de- /diː, dɪ/ **1** (showing an opposite): *a depopulated area* (= which all or most of the population has left) **2** to remove: *to dethrone a king* | *to debug a computer program* **3** to make less: *devalue the currency*

deca- /ˈdekə/ ten: *a decalitre* (= ten litres)

deci- /ˈdesɪ/ tenth part: *a decilitre* (= a tenth of a litre)

dis- /dɪs/ **1** not; the opposite of: *I disagree.* | *He is dishonest.* **2** removal: *nuclear disarmament*

em- /ɪm, em/ (*before* b, m, *or* p) EN-: *emboldened*

en- /ɪn, en/ (makes verbs) cause to be (more): *Enlarge the hole.*

equi- /ˈekwɪ/ equally: *two points equidistant from a third*

Euro- /ˈjʊərəʊ ‖ ˈjʊəroʊ/ of Europe, esp. the EEC: *the Europarliament*

ex- /eks/ former: *my ex-fiance*

extra- /ˈekstrə/ not (usu.) included; beyond: outside: *extracurricular lessons* | *extravehicular activity by astronauts*

fore- /fɔː ‖ fɔːr/ **1** before; in advance: *I was forewarned of their visit.* **2** in or at the front: *a boat's foresail*

foster- /ˈfɒstə ‖ ˈfɔːstər, fɑ-/ giving or receiving parental care although not of the same family: *my foster-parents*

Franco- /ˈfræŋkəʊ ‖ -koʊ/ **1** of France: *a Francophile* (= someone who loves France) **2** French and: *the Franco-Prussian war*

geo- /ˈdʒiːəʊ ‖ -oʊ/ connected with the study of the Earth or its surface: *geophysics*

hecto- /ˈhektəʊ ‖ -toʊ/ hundred: *a hectolitre* (= a hundred litres) -compare CENTI-

hydro- /ˈhaɪdrəʊ ‖ -droʊ/ concerning or using water: *hydroelectricity*

hyper- /ˈhaɪpə ‖ -pər/ very or too much: *hyperactive* | *hypercritical*

il- /ɪ/ (*before* l) not: *illiberal*

im- /ɪm/ (*before* b, m, *or* p) IN-: *impossible*

in- /ɪn/ **1** not: *indecisive* l *insane* **2** inwards: *a sudden inrush of water*

inter- /ˈɪntə ‖ -ər/ between or including both or all: *the intercity train service* | *an interdenominational marriage ceremony*

ir- /ɪ/ (*before* r) not: *irrational*

kilo- /ˈkɪlə/ thousand: *a kilogram* (= a thousand grams) -compare MILLI-

mal- /mæl/ bad(ly); wrong(ly): *a malformed body* l *maladministration*

maxi- /ˈmæksi/ unusually large or long -compare MINI-

mega- /ˈmegə/ **1** million: *a ten-megaton nuclear bomb* **2** sl very great: *a movie megastar*

micro- /ˈmaɪkrəʊ ‖ -kroʊ/ **1** (esp. with

scientific words) extremely small: *a microcomputer* **2** using a microscope: *microsurgery* **3** millionth part: *a microsecond* (= a millionth of a second)

mid- /mɪd/ middle; in the middle of: *midwinter* | *mid-Atlantic* | *She's in her mid-20s.* (= is about 25 years old)

milli- /mɪlɪ/ thousandth part: *a millilitre* (= a thousandth of a litre) -compare KILO-

mini- /mɪni/ unusually small or short: *a miniskirt* | *a TV miniseries*

mis- /mɪs/ **1** bad(ly); wrong(ly): *He mistreats his dog terribly.* | *I misheard what you said.* **2** lack of; opposite of: *mistrust* | *misfortune*

mono- /mɒnəʊ ‖ mɑ:noʊ/ one; single; UNI-: *monosyllabic* | *a monoplane* (with one wing on each side) -compare POLY-

multi- /mʌltɪ/ many: *a multipurpose tool* | *a multistorey carpark*

non- /nɒn‖nɑ:n/ not: *nonaddictive* | *non-profitmaking*

over- /əʊvə ‖ oʊvər/ **1** too much: *an overindulgent parent* | *an overcooked dish* -compare UNDER- **2** above; across: *We took the overland route.*

poly- /pɒlɪ ‖ pɑ:lɪ/ many: *polysyllabic* -compare MONO-

post- /pəʊst ‖ poʊst/ after; later than: *the postwar years* -compare PRE-

pre- /pri:/ before; earlier than: *the prewar years* | *a prelunch drink* -compare POST-

pro- /prəʊ ‖ proʊ/ in favour of; supporting: *She's pro-Conservative.* -compare ANTI-

pseudo- /sju:dəʊ‖su:doʊ/ only pretending to be; false: *pseudo-intellectuals*

psycho- /saɪkəʊ ‖ -koʊ/ connected with (illness of) the mind: *psychotherapy* | *psychosexual disorders*

quasi- /kwɑ:zi, kweɪzaɪ/ seeming to be; almost like: *a quasijudicial function*

re- /ri:/ again: *The body was dug up and then reburied.*

self- /self/ of or by oneself or itself: *a self-charging battery* | *self-deception* | *She's completely self-taught.*

semi- /semɪ/ **1** half: *a semicircle* **2** partly; incomplete(ly): *semipermanent* | *in the semidarkness*

step- /step/ related through a parent who has remarried

sub- /sʌb/ **1** under, below: *subsoil* | *subzero temperatures* **2** smaller part of: *a subcategory* **3** less than; worse than: *subhuman intelligence* **4** next in rank below: *a sublieutenant* -compare SUPER-

super- /su:pə ‖ -ər/ greater or more than: *superhuman strength* | *supertankers* (= very large ships) carrying oil -compare SUB-

trans- /træns, trænz/ across; on or to the other side of: *a transatlantic flight*

tri- /traɪ/ three: *trilingual* (= speaking three languages)

ultra- /ʌltrə/ very, esp. too: *ultramodern* | *ultracautious*

un- /ʌn/ **1** (makes adjectives and adverbs) not: *uncomfortable* | *unfairly* | *unwashed* **2** (makes verbs) make or do the opposite of: *She tied a knot, and then untied it.*

under- /ʌndə ‖ -ər/ **1** too little: *undercooked potatoes* | *underproduction* **2** below: *an undersea cable* -compare OVER-

vice- /vaɪs/ next in rank below: *the vice-chairman of the committee*

video- /vɪdiəʊ ‖ -oʊ/ of, for, or using recorded pictures, esp. as produced by a video (2): *a videocassette* -compare AUDIO-

Word endings

-able /əbəl/ also **-ible** (*in adjectives*) that can have the stated thing done to it: *a washable fabric*

-age /ɪdʒ/ (*in nouns*) **1** the action or result of doing the stated thing: *to allow for shrinkage* (= getting smaller) | *several breakages* (= things broken) **2** the cost of doing the stated thing: *Postage is extra.* **3** the state or rank of: *given a peerage*

-al /əl, əl/ **1** (*in adjectives*) of; connected with: *autumnal mists* | *a musical performance* **2** (*in nouns*) (an example of the) act of doing something: *the arrival of the bus* | *several rehearsals*

-an /ən, ən/ -IAN: *the Elizabethan Age*

-ance /əns, əns/ (*in nouns*) (an example of) the action, state or quality of doing or being the stated thing: *his sudden appearance* (= he appeared suddenly) | *her brilliance* (= she is brilliant)

-ant /ənt, ənt/ (*in adjectives and nouns*) (person or thing) that does the stated thing: *in the resultant confusion* | *a bottle of disinfectant*

-ar /ə ‖ ər, ɑːr/ **1** (*in adjectives*) of; connected with; being: *the Polar regions* **2** (*in nouns*) -ER²: *a liar*

-arian /eəriən ‖ er-/ (*in nouns*) person who supports and believes in: *a libertarian* (= person who supports freedom)

-ary /əri, əri‖eri/ (*in nouns*) being: *with his customary* (= usual) *caution* | *her legendary* (= very famous) *courage*

-ate /ɪt, eɪt/ (*in verbs*) (cause to) become or have: *a hyphenated word* **2** (*in adjectives*) having: *a fortunate* (= lucky) *woman*

-ation /eɪʃən/ (*in nouns*) (an) act or result of doing the stated thing: *the continuation of the story*

-ative /ətɪv/ (*in adjectives*) **1** liking or tending to have or do: *argumentative* | *talkative* **2** for the purpose of the stated thing: *a consultative meeting*

-bound /baʊnd/ (*in adjectives*) limited, kept in, or controlled in the stated way: *a fog-bound aircraft*

-cy /si/ (*makes nouns from adjectives ending in* /t/ *or* /tɪk/) -ITY: *several inaccuracies in the report*

-d /d, t/ (*after e*) -ED: *a wide-eyed stare*

-dom /dəm/ (*in nouns*) **1** condition of being the stated thing: *freedom* | *boredom* **2** country or area ruled by: *a kingdom* **3** people of the stated sort: *despite the opposition of officialdom*

-ean /iən/ -IAN

-ed /d, ɪd, t/ **1** (*makes regular past t. and p. of verbs*): *We landed safely.* **2** (*in adjectives*) having or wearing the stated thing; with: *a long-tailed dog* | *a bowler-hatted man*

-ee /iː/ (*in nouns*) **1** person to whom the stated thing is done: *an employee* | *a trainee* **2** person who is or does the stated thing: *an absentee*

-eer /ɪə ‖ ɪr/ (*in nouns*) person who does or is connected with the stated thing: *a mountaineer* | *The auctioneer asked for bids.*

-en /ən, ən/ **1** (*in adjectives*) made of: *a wooden box* **2** (*in verbs*) make or become (more): *unsweetened tea* | *The sky darkened.*

-ence /əns, əns/ (*in nouns*) -ANCE: *its existence* | *reference* | *occurrence*

-ent /ənt, ənt/ -ANT: *nonexistent*

-er¹ /ə ‖ ər/ (*in comparative of short adjectives and adverbs*) more: *faster* | *colder*

-er² /ə ‖ ər/ (*in nouns*) **1** person or thing that does the stated thing: *a singer* | *a footballer* (= person who plays football) | *an electric water heater* **2** person who comes from or lives in the stated place: *a Londoner*

-ery /əri, əri/ (*in nouns*) **1** the stated condition; -NESS: *bravery* **2** the stated art or practice; -ING (2): *cookery* **3** place where the stated thing is done: *a brewery*

-es /ɪz/ (*after* /s,z,ʃ,tʃ,dʒ/) -s: *bosses* | *matches*

-ese /iːz/ (*in nouns and adjectives*) (language) of the stated country: *Do you speak Japanese?* | *Portuguese food*

-esque /esk/ (*in adjectives*) in the manner or style of; like: *statuesque beauty* | *Kafkaesque*

-ess /ɪs, es/ (*in nouns*) female: *an actress* (= a female actor) | *a lioness*

-est /ɪst/ (*in superlative of short adjectives and adverbs*) most: *slowest* | *loveliest*

-eth /θ/ -TH: *the twentieth time*

-ette /ɪt/ (*in nouns*) small: *a kitchenette*

-ey /i/ (*esp. after* y) -Y: *clayey soil*

-fashion /fæʃən/ (*in adverbs*) in the way of: *They ate Indian-fashion, using their fingers.*

-fold /fəʊld ‖ foʊld/ (*in adjectives and adverbs*) multiplied by the stated number: *a fourfold increase*

-free /friː/ (*in adjectives*) -LESS (1): *a troublefree journey*

-friendly /frendli/ (*in adjectives*) not difficult for the stated people to use: *a user-friendly computer*

-ful /fəl/ 1 (*in adjectives*) having or giving: *a sinful man* | *a restful day* 2 /fʊl/ (*in nouns*) amount contained by: *a handful of coins* | *two spoonfuls of sugar*

-hood /hʊd/ (*in nouns*) condition or period of being the stated thing: *falsehood* | *during her childhood*

-ial /iəl, əl/ -AL (1): *a commercial transaction* | *the presidential car*

-ian /iən, ən/ 1 (*in adjectives and nouns*) of or connected with the stated place or person: *Parisian restaurants* | *a cassette Russian.* 2 (in nouns) person who studies the stated subject; EXPERT: *a historian* | *a theologian*

-ible /ɪbəl/ -ABLE: *deductible*

-ic /ɪk/ also **-ical** /ɪkəl/ (*in adjectives*) connected with; having or showing: *The design is completely symmetric/symmetrical.* | *an historic occasion* | *a historical novel*

-icide /ɪsaɪd/ (*in nouns*) killing of: *infanticide*

-ics /ɪks/ (*in nouns*) science or skill: *linguistics* | *aeronautics*

-ie /i/ -Y (2)

-ify /ɪfaɪ/ (*in verbs*) make or become: *purify* | *simplify*

-ine /aɪn/ 1 of or concerning: *equine* (= of horses) 2 made of; like: *crystalline*

-ing /ɪŋ/ 1 (*makes pres. p. of verbs*): *I'm coming.* | *a sleeping child* 2 (makes nouns from verbs): *Eating sweets makes you fat.* | *a fine painting*

-ise /aɪz/ *esp. BrE* for -IZE

-ish /ɪʃ/ 1 (*in nouns and adjectives*) (language) of the stated country: *I speak Swedish.* | *British customs* 2 (*in adjectives*) **a** typical of: *a foolish man* | *girlish giggles* **b** rather: *a reddish glow* **c** about the stated number: *He's fortyish.* | *Come at sixish.*

-ism /ɪzəm/ (*in nouns*) 1 set of beliefs: *Buddhism* | *socialism* 2 quality or way of behaving: *heroism* | *male chauvinism* 3 way of speaking: *Americanisms*

-ist /ɪst/ 1 (*in nouns*) person who works with or does the stated thing: *A violinist plays the violin.* | *A machinist works machines.* 2 (*in adjectives and nouns*) (follower) of a set of beliefs: *a Buddhist* 3 making unfair differences between people because of the stated thing: *racist* | *ageist*

-ite /aɪt/ -IST (2): *a Trotskyite*

-itude /ɪtjuːd ‖ ɪtuːd/ (*in nouns*) the state or degree of being: *exactitude* | *certitude* (= being certain)

-ity /ɪti/ (*in nouns*) the stated condition or quality; -NESS: *stupidity* | *sublimity*

-ive /ɪv/ (*in adjectives*) tending to do the stated thing: *a creative child* | *a supportive partner*

-ize /aɪz/ (*in verbs*) make or become: *popularizing a new brand of soap* | *to modernize our procedures*

-less /ləs/ (*in adjectives*) 1 without: *a windless day* | *We are powerless to act.* 2 that never does the stated thing: *a tireless worker*

-let /lɪt/ (*in nouns*) small: *I lived in a flatlet.*

-like /laɪk/ (*in adjectives*) typical of: *childlike innocence*

-ly /li/ 1 (*in adverbs*) in the stated way: *Drive carefully!* 2 (*in adjectives and adverbs*) every: *an hourly report* | *I see him daily.* 3 (*in adjectives*) typical of: *brotherly love* 4 (*in adverbs*) from the stated point of view: *Musically she's very gifted.*

-man /mən/ 1 man who comes from the stated place: *a Frenchman* 2 person with the stated job or skill: *a postman*

-manship /mənʃɪp/ (*in [U] nouns*) the art or skill of a person of the stated type: *seamanship* | *horsemanship*

-ment /mənt/ (*in nouns*) act or result of doing the stated thing; -ING (2): *enjoyment* | *encouragement*

-most /məʊst ‖ moʊst/ -EST: *the northernmost parts of the country*

-ness /nəs/ (*in nouns*) the stated condition or quality: *loudness* | *gentleness*

-nik /nɪk/ (*in nouns*) person who is connected with or keen on: *a peacenik*

-ology /ɒlədʒi ‖ ɑː-/ (*in nouns*) science or study of: *toxicology* (= the study of poisons)

| musicology

-or /ə ‖ -ər/ -ER²: *a sailor*

-ory¹ /əri ‖ ɔːri, əri/ (*in nouns*) place or thing used for doing the stated thing: *an observatory*

-ory² (*in adjectives*) that does the stated thing: *a congratulatory telegram*

-ous /əs/ (*in adjectives*) having; full of: *a dangerous place* | *a spacious room*

-phile /faɪl/ (*in nouns*) person who likes the stated thing or person very much: *an Anglophile* (= who likes England)

-phobe /fəʊb ‖ foʊb/ (*in nouns*) person who dislikes the stated thing or person very much: *an Anglophobe* (= who dislikes England)

-phobia /fəʊbiə ‖ foʊ-/ (*in nouns*) great dislike: *Anglophobia*

-proof /pruːf/ **1** (*in adjectives*) treated or made so as not to be harmed by the stated thing: *a bulletproof car* | *an ovenproof dish* **2** (*in verbs*) to treat or make in this way: *to soundproof a room*

-r /ə ‖ ər/ (*after e*) -ER

-ridden /rɪdn/ (*in adjectives*) **1** suffering from the effects of: *guiltridden* **2** too full of: *mosquito ridden*

-ry /ri/ (in nouns) -ERY: *sheer wizardry*

-s /z, s/ **1** (*makes the pl. of nouns*): *one cat and two dogs* **2** (*makes the 3rd person pres. sing. of verbs*): *She laughs too much.*

-'s **1** (*forms the possessive case of sing. nouns and of plural nouns that do not end in* -s): *my sister's husband* | *yesterday's lesson* | *the sheep's heads* **2** *BrE* the shop or home of: *I met him at Mary's.*

-s' (*forms the possessive case of plural nouns*): *the girls' dresses*

-scape /skeɪp/ (*in nouns*) a wide view of the stated area: *some old Dutch seascapes*

-ship /ʃɪp/ (*in nouns*) **1** condition of having or being the stated thing: *a business in partnership with his brother* | *kingship* **2** the stated skill: *her masterly musicianship*

-some /səm/ **1** (*in adjectives*) causing; producing: *a troublesome problem* **2** (*in nouns*) group of the stated number of people or things: *a twosome*

-speak /spiːk/ *often derog* (*in nouns*) the special language, esp. slang words, used in the stated business or activity: *computerspeak*

-st /st/ (*after e*) -EST

-th /θ/ (*makes adjectives from numbers, except those ending in 1, 2, or 3*): *the seventh day*

-tion /ʃən/ (*in nouns*) -ION

-tude /tjuːd ‖ tuːd/ (*in nouns*) -ITUDE: *disquietude*

-ty /ti/ -ITY: *cruelty*

-ure /jʊə, jə, ə ‖ jʊr, jər, ər/ (*in nouns*) act or result of doing the stated thing; -ING (2): *the closure of the factory*

-ward /wəd ‖ wərd/ also **-wards** /wədz ‖ wərdz/ (*in adjectives and adverbs*) in the stated direction: *the homeward journey* | *travelling northwards*

-ware /weə ‖ wer/ (*in nouns*) containers, tools, etc., made of the stated material or for the stated purpose: *pewterware* | *kitchenware* (= for cooking)

-ways /weɪz/ -WISE: *sideways*

-wise /waɪz/ (*in adverbs*) **1** in the stated way or direction: *walked crabwise* **2** with regard to: *very inexperienced businesswise*

-y /i/ **1** (*in adjectives*) of; like; having: *a lemony smell* | *a noisy room* **2** (*makes nouns more informal; used esp. when speaking to children*): *my granny* | *a nice little doggy* **3** (*in nouns*) -ITY: *jealousy*

Irregular verbs

verb	past tense	past participle
abide	abided, abode	abided
arise	arose	arisen
awake	awoke, awakened	awoken
baby-sit	baby-sat	baby-sat
be	*see dictionary entry*	
bear	bore	borne
beat	beat	beaten
become	became	become
befall	befell	befallen
beget	begot (*also* begat *bibl*)	begotten
begin	began	begun
behold	beheld	beheld
bend	bent	bent
beseech	besought, beseeched	besought, beseeched
beset	beset	beset
bet	bet, betted	bet, betted
bid	bade, bid	bade, bid
bind	bound	bound
bite	bit	bitten
bleed	bled	bled
bless	blessed, blest	blessed, blest
blow	blew	blown
break	broke	broken
breed	bred	bred
bring	brought	brought
broadcast	broadcast	broadcast
build	built	built
burn	burned, burnt	burned, burnt
burst	burst	burst
buy	bought	bought
cast	cast	cast
catch	caught	caught
chide	chided, chid	chid, chidden
choose	chose	chose
cleave	cleaved, cleft, clove	cleaved, cleft, clove
cling	clung	clung
come	came	come
cost	cost	cost
creep	crept	crept
cut	cut	cut
deal	dealt /delt/	dealt
dig	dug	dug
dive	dived, (*AmE*) dove	dived

verb	past tense	past participle
do	did	done
draw	drew	drawn
dream	dreamed, dreamt	dreamed, dreamt
drink	drank	drunk
drive	drove	driven
dwell	dwelt, dwelled	dwelt, dwelled
eat	ate	eaten
fall	fell	fallen
feed	fed	fed
feel	felt	felt
fight	fought	fought
find	found	found
flee	fled	fled
fling	flung	flung
fly	flew	flown
forbear	forbore	forborne
forbid	forbade, forbad	forbidden
forecast	forecast, forecasted	forecast, forecasted
foresee	foresaw	foreseen
foretell	foretold	foretold
forget	forgot	forgotten
forgive	forgave	forgiven
forgo	forwent	forgone
forsake	forsook	forsaken
freeze	froze	frozen
gainsay	gainsaid	gainsaid
get	got	got (*also* gotten *AmE*)
gird	girded, girt	girded, girt
give	gave	given
go	went	gone
grind	ground	ground
grow	grew	grown
hamstring	hamstringed, hamstrung	hamstringed, hamstrung
hang	hung, hanged	hung, hanged
have	had	had
hear	heard	heard
heave	heaved, hove	heaved, hove
hew	hewed	hewn, hewed
hide	hid	hidden
hit	hit	hit
hold	held	held
hurt	hurt	hurt
keep	kept	kept
kneel	knelt, (*esp. AmE*) kneeled	knelt, (*esp. AmE*) kneeled
knit	knitted, knit	knitted, knit

verb	past tense	past participle
know	knew	known
lay	laid	laid
lead	led	led
lean	leaned, (*esp. BrE*) leant	leaned, (*esp. BrE*) leant
leap	leapt, (*esp. AmE*) leaped	leapt, (*esp AmE*) leaped
learn	learned, (*esp. BrE*) learnt	learned, (*esp. BrE*) learnt
leave	left	left
lend	lent	lent
let	let	let
lie	lay	lay
light	lit, lighted	lit, lighted
lose	lost	lost
make	made	made
mean	meant	meant
meet	met	met
miscast	miscast	miscast
mislay	mislaid	mislaid
mislead	misled	misled
misspell	misspelt, misspelled	misspelt, misspelled
misspend	misspent	misspent
mistake	mistook	mistaken
misunderstand	misunderstood	misunderstood
mow	mowed	mown
outdo	outdid	outdone
outgrow	outgrew	outgrown
outshine	outshone	outshone
overcome	overcame	overcome
overdo	overdid	overdone
overhang	overhung	overhung
overload	overloaded	overladen
overrun	overran	overrun
oversee	oversaw	overseen
oversleep	overslept	overslept
overtake	overtook	overtaken
overthrow	overthrew	overthrown
partake	partook	partaken
pay	paid	paid
prove	proved	proven
put	put	put
read	read /red/	read /red/
rend	rent	rent
repay	repaid	repaid
rethink	rethought	rethought
rid	rid, ridded	rid, ridden
ride	rode	ridden

verb	past tense	past participle
ring	rang	rung
rise	rose	risen
run	ran	run
saw	sawed	sawn, sawed
say	said	said
see	saw	seen
seek	sought	sought
sell	sold	sold
send	sent	sent
set	set	set
sew	sewed	sewn, sewed
shake	shook	shaken
shear	sheared	shorn, sheared
shed	shed	shed
shine	shone, shined	shone, shined
shoe	shod	shod
shoot	shot	shot
show	showed	shown, showed
shrink	shrank, shrunk	shrunk
shut	shut	shut
sing	sang	sung
sink	sank, sunk	sunk
sit	sat	sat
slay	slew	slain
sleep	slept	slept
slide	slid	slid
sling	slung	slung
slink	slunk	slunk
slit	slit	slit
smell	(*esp. BrE*) smelt, (*esp. AmE*) smelled	(*esp. BrE*) smelt, (*esp. AmE*) smelled
smite	smote	smitten
sow	sowed	sown, sowed
speak	spoke	spoken
speed	sped, speeded	sped, speeded
spell	(*esp. BrE*) spelt, (*esp. AmE*) spelled	(*esp. BrE*) spelt, (*esp. AmE*) spelled
spend	spent	spent
spill	(*esp. BrE*) spilt, (*esp. AmE*) spilled	(*esp. BrE*) spilt, (*esp. AmE*) spilled
spin	spun, span	spun
spit	spat (*also* spit *AmE*)	spat (*also* spit *AmE*)
split	split	split
spoil	spoiled, spoilt	spoiled, spoilt
spread	spread	spread

verb	past tense	past participle
spring	sprang (*also* sprung *AmE*)	sprung
stand	stood	stood
steal	stole	stolen
stick	stuck	stuck
sting	stung	stung
stink	stank, stunk	stunk
strew	strewed	strewn, strewed
stride	strode	stridden
strike	struck	struck
string	strung	strung
strive	strove, strived	striven, strived
swear	swore	sworn
sweep	swept	swept
swell	swelled	swollen, swelled
swim	swam	swum
swing	swung	swung
take	took	taken
teach	taught	taught
tear	tore	torn
tell	told	told
think	thought	thought
thrive	thrived, throve	thrived
throw	threw	thrown
thrust	thrust	thrust
tread	trod	trodden, trod
unbend	unbent	unbent
undergo	underwent	undergone
understand	understood	understood
undertake	undertook	undertaken
undo	undid	undone
unwind	unwound	unwound
uphold	upheld	upheld
upset	upset	upset
wake	woke, waked	woken, waked
wear	wore	worn
weave	wove	woven
wed	wedded, wed	wedded, wed
weep	wept	wept
wet	wetted, wet	wetted, wet
win	won	won
wind /waɪnd/	wound	wound
withdraw	withdrew	withdrawn
withhold	withheld	withheld
withstand	withstood	withstood
wring	wrung	wrung
write	wrote	written

in my ha[nd]

This pill of blue ~~within my fis~~

seems to me

~~thought of it~~ as a magic wave

it
but I won't let the ~~superstition~~

take control

for there's no ~~foolish~~ hope

Thus no ritual shall ever

work.

Sore and sick the rose

~~sa~~ yearns to flee

but through this icy cage of time

It howls and waits to ~~freeze~~